Frommer's®
Mexico

My Mexico
by David Baird

THERE ARE MANY REASONS TO TRAVEL, BUT THE ONE THAT MOST often prompts me to leave home is a foreign culture's ability to jostle me from complacency. Mexico is good for this. It's vibrant and full of vivid sights and sensations. In the mountains, the contrast between strong sun and cool air makes me feel alive. There's a lifetime's worth of beaches to explore. But above all, I appreciate the Mexican people, who have a love of vigorous expression in just about every form of human endeavor. Witness the country's emphatically flavored food and drink, its over-the-top music and dance, its bold creations in art and architecture. After spending time in Mexico, I find other places to be dull and lackluster.

If this were all Mexico had to offer, it would be enough. But beneath the color lies a deep-seated complexity that makes the country fascinating. The national culture was born of two distinct civilizations: the Spanish and the Indian. The end result after centuries of synthesizing these contradictory forces is a rich symbolism that encapsulates multiple, often opposing, meanings. To get to know and understand Mexico in its entirety would be the work of several lifetimes. But to enjoy Mexico need take no more than an open mind and heart. These photos give you a taste of Mexico's complex allure.

Few experiences inspire as much awe as close contact with a whale in its natural habitat. Along Baja's Pacific coast, various protected bays and lagoons have become the preferred winter waters for migrating **GRAY WHALES (left)** as they journey south to mate and give birth to their calves. Naturally friendly and curious, these whales frequently come up to the sightseeing boats and stay close by. Baja's whale-watching season generally runs from January to March.

The megalithic **OLMEC HEADS (above)** are some of the most intriguing pre-Colombian artifacts. Seventeen have been discovered, and though they share a common style, the variations in their facial features suggest that they might depict something part human, part Jaguar god. Most of the heads are in out-of-the-way places such as Villahermosa and Xalapa. This modern reproduction can be found at the Chankanaab National Park, on the island of Cozumel.

OCT – 4 2005

The various regional cuisines of Mexico lend great variety to eating in Mexico, especially when you choose to eat in a local **FONDA (above)**, or food stall, like this one at Libertad Market in Guadalajara. I love the guisados (stews), such as the ones this woman has prepared here.

I always enjoy visiting **MARKETS (right)** like this one, Oaxaca's Abastos Market. You see a variety of produce in most of them that would put a supermarket to shame. They also serve as a place for friends and neighbors to meet, eat, and chat about local events and the latest scandals.

Mexicans have a genius for working with their hands. When given the opportunity many artisans really shine, but more often they produce the everyday goods that demand dictates. I seek out the less commonplace work that is created from the need for personal expression. Even if I have no success, the effort often bears other fruit. This **MAYA VENDOR IN SAN CRISTOBAL DE LAS CASAS** is selling nontraditional garments to tourists. She may have other, more interesting pieces, but the highland Maya are often difficult to engage in conversation.

One of my favorite pastimes in Puerto Vallarta is strolling along its waterfront boardwalk, known as the malecón. Here, you'll find a collection of majestic monumental sculptures, including these, part of the *FANTASY OF THE SEA COLLECTION* (above) by noted Mexican artist Alejandro Colunga. Especially at sunset, or on Sunday evenings, the malecón buzzes with activity: vendors selling balloons, street musicians, and romantics of all ages holding hands.

No trip to Acapulco is complete without witnessing the dramatic performance of the **CLIFF-DIVERS** (right) at La Quebrada. For just a moment, when the diver springs from his perch, he seems suspended, weightless in the still air high above the roiling sea. It's almost impossible to tear your eyes away as he plummets more than 40m (130 ft.) toward the rocks and surf below.

I don't know of a place more emblematic of travel to Mexico than the **RUINS OF TULUM (right)**. Facing the blue Caribbean from a rocky promontory is the elegant form of a Maya temple platform. I like it best in the early morning when the sun glimmers off the water.

In the early '70s, the Mexican government ran a computer analysis to determine the best place to build the country's premier beach resort. But given **CANCUN'S (below)** gorgeous white-sand beaches, large sheltered lagoon, and proximity to America's eastern seaboard, could the decision have been that difficult?

The 17th and 18th centuries, when a European art form known as baroque arrived, was a time of great artistic achievement in Mexico, especially in architecture. This church in Oaxaca City, **SANTO DOMINGO (above)**, is one of my favorite examples. Think of it as an expression of ecstatic religious feeling that rejects limitations of structure, proportion, and balance.

Mexicans have a direct, almost personal, relationship with their Catholic saints. You need go no further than Mexico City to see this dynamic unfold. Stalls selling **RELIGIOUS ICONS (right)** line the way to the Basilica of Our Lady of Guadalupe.

The towers of this parochial church are all that can be seen of **THE BURIED TOWN OF PARANGARICUTIRO** in the southwestern state of Michoacán. In the 1940s, this area was an unremarkable little corner of Mexico— then steam began spewing up from a cornfield. Fissures appeared and from them lava and ash rose to the surface. Just like that the Paracutín volcano was born, expanded for a few years, and then, as promptly as it had begun, it stopped.

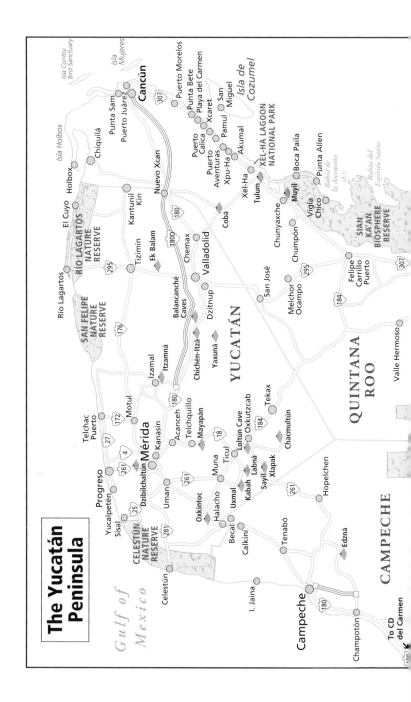

The Yucatán Peninsula

Gulf of Mexico

Isla Contoy Bird Sanctuary

Isla Mujeres

Cancún

Isla Holbox

Isla de Cozumel

Bahía de la Ascensión

Bahía del Espíritu Santo

Celestún

CELESTÚN NATURE RESERVE

Sisal

Yucalpetén

Progreso

Telchac Puerto

Mérida

Dzibilchaltún

SAN FELIPE NATURE RESERVE

Río Lagartos

El Cuyo

Holbox

RÍO LAGARTOS NATURE RESERVE

Kantunil Kin

Chiquilá

Punta Sam
Puerto Juárez

Nuevo Xcan

Puerto Morelos

Punta Bete
Playa del Carmen
Xcaret
San Miguel

Pamul
Akumal
Puerto Calica
Puerto Aventuras
Xpu-Ha
Xel-Ha

XEL-HA LAGOON NATIONAL PARK

Tulum

Boca Paila

Punta Allen

Muyil

Vigía Chico

SIAN KA'AN BIOSPHERE RESERVE

Chunyaxche

Chumpón

Tizimín

Ek Balam

Chemax

Valladolid

Balancanché Caves

Dzitnup

Cobá

San José

Melchor Ocampo

Felipe Carrillo Puerto

Chichén-Itzá

Yaxuná

YUCATÁN

Izamal

Itzamná

Motul

Telchac Puerto

Kanasín

Acanceh

Telchaquillo

Mayapán

Tekax

Loltún Cave
Oxkutzcab

Chacmultún

Muna

Ticul

Oxkintoc

Uman

Halachó

Uxmal

Kabah
Sayil
Xlapak

Labná

Hopelchén

QUINTANA ROO

Valle Hermoso

Becal

Calkiní

Tenabó

Edzná

I. Jaina

CAMPECHE

Campeche

Champotón

To CD del Carmen

295

307

307

180

800

180

295

184

184

261

18

261

261

4

27

72

180

25

281

176

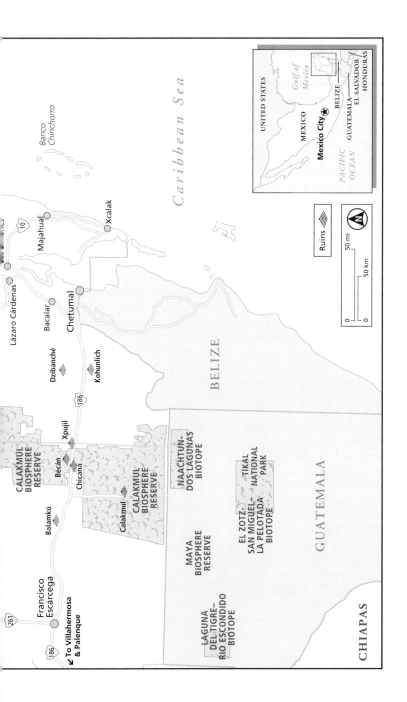

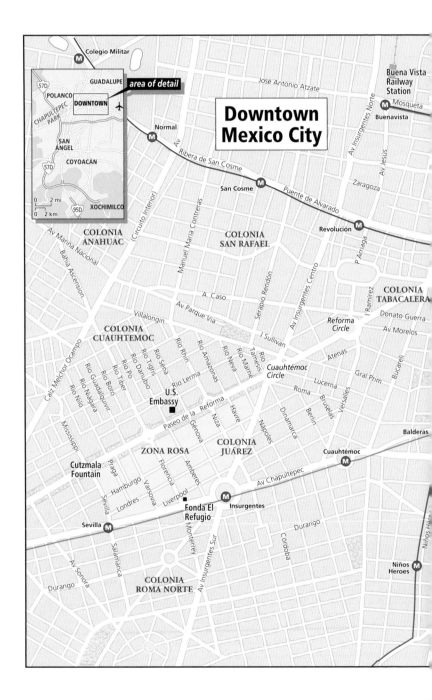

Downtown Mexico City

Colegio Militar Ⓜ

Buena Vista Railway Station

José Antonio Atzate

Ⓜ Mosqueta

Buenavista

Normal Ⓜ

Ribera de San Cosme

San Cosme Ⓜ

Puente de Alvarado

Zaragoza

Revolución Ⓜ

area of detail

57D

GUADALUPE

POLANCO

CHAPULTEPEC PARK

DOWNTOWN

SAN ÁNGEL

COYOACÁN

57D

95D

XOCHIMILCO

0   2 mi
0   2 km

Av Insurgentes Norte

Av Jesús

P Arriaga

COLONIA ANAHUAC

Av Marina Nacional

Bahía Ascensión

(Circuito Interior)

Manuel María Contreras

COLONIA SAN RAFAEL

Ramírez

COLONIA TABACALERA

A. Caso

Av Parque Via

Serapio Rendón

Av Insurgentes Centro

Reforma Circle

Donato Guerra

Av Morelos

Villalongin

COLONIA CUAUHTEMOC

J Sullivan

Atenas

Bucareli

Río Sena

Río Rhin

Río Amazonas

Río Neva

Río Marne

Río Tamesis

Río Lerma

Río Tigris

Río Danubio

Río Po

Río Tiber

Río Boro

Río Guadalquivir

Río Niágara

Río Nilo

Calz Melchor Ocampo

ZONA ROSA

COLONIA JUÁREZ

Cuauhtémoc Circle

Lucerna

Roma

Bruselas

Versalles

Berlín

Gral Prim

U.S. Embassy ■

Paseo de la Reforma

Genova

Niza

Havre

Nápoles

Dinamarca

Balderas

Cuauhtémoc Ⓜ

Mississippi

Cutzmala Fountain

Praga

Hamburgo

Varsovia

Londres

Florencia

Amberes

Liverpool

Av Chapultepec

Sevilla Ⓜ

Fonda El Refugio ■

Insurgentes Ⓜ

Sevilla

Salamanca

Monterrey

Av Insurgentes Sur

Durango

Córdoba

Niños Heroes

Ⓜ

Av Sonora

Durango

COLONIA ROMA NORTE

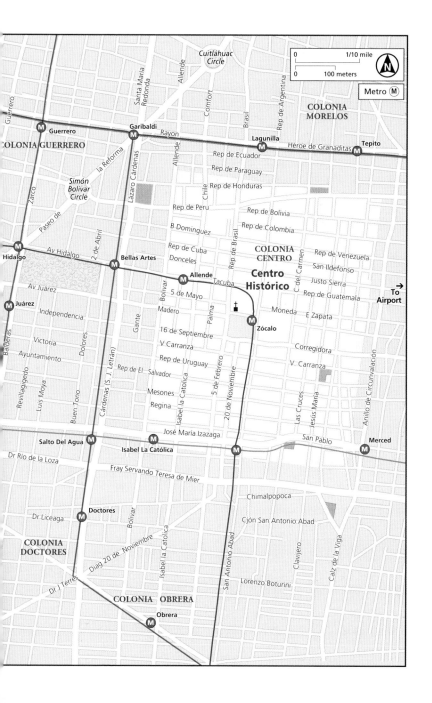

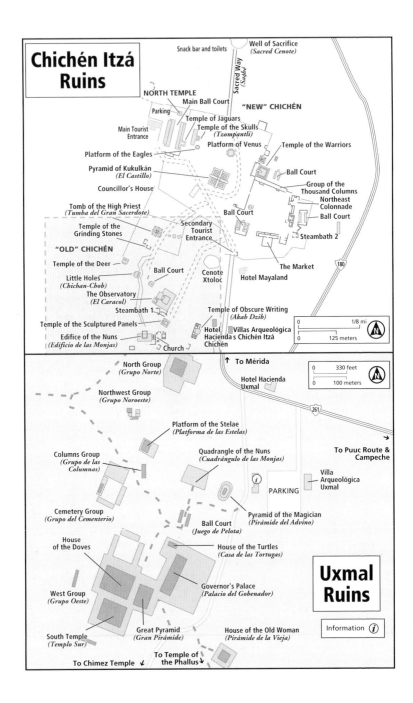

Chichén Itzá Ruins

Snack bar and toilets

Well of Sacrifice
(Sacred Cenote)

Sacred Way
(Sacbé)

NORTH TEMPLE

Main Ball Court

Parking

Temple of Jaguars

"NEW" CHICHÉN

Main Tourist
Entrance

Temple of the Skulls
(Tzompantli)

Platform of Venus

Temple of the Warriors

Platform of the Eagles

Pyramid of Kukulkán
(El Castillo)

Ball Court

Councillor's House

Group of the
Thousand Columns

Tomb of the High Priest
(Tumba del Gran Sacerdote)

Ball Court

Northeast
Colonnade

Ball Court

Temple of the
Grinding Stones

Secondary
Tourist
Entrance

Steambath 2

"OLD" CHICHÉN

Temple of the Deer

Ball Court

Cenote
Xtoloc

The Market

180

Little Holes
(Chichan-Chob)

Hotel Mayaland

The Observatory
(El Caracol)

Steambath 1

Temple of Obscure Writing
(Akab Dzib)

Temple of the Sculptured Panels

Edifice of the Nuns
(Edificio de las Monjas)

Church

Hotel
Hacienda s Chichén Itzá
Chichén

Villas Arqueológica
Chichén

0   1/8 mi

0   125 meters

Uxmal Ruins

North Group
(Grupo Norte)

↑ To Mérida

0   330 feet

Hotel Hacienda
Uxmal

0   100 meters

Northwest Group
(Grupo Noroeste)

261

Platform of the Stelae
(Platforma de las Estelas)

Columns Group
*(Grupo de las
Columnas)*

Quadrangle of the Nuns
(Cuadrángulo de las Monjas)

To Puuc Route &
Campeche

Villa
Arqueológica
Uxmal

PARKING

Cemetery Group
(Grupo del Cementerio)

Pyramid of the Magician
(Pirámide del Advino)

House
of the Doves

Ball Court
(Juego de Pelota)

House of the Turtles
(Casa de las Tortugas)

West Group
(Grupo Oeste)

Governor's Palace
(Palacio del Gobenador)

South Temple
(Templo Sur)

Great Pyramid
(Gran Pirámide)

House of the Old Woman
(Pirámide de la Vieja)

To Chimez Temple ↙

To Temple of
the Phallus ↓

Information ⓘ

Frommer's®

Mexico

2006

by David Baird & Lynne Bairstow

Here's what the critics say about Frommer's:

"Amazingly easy to use. Very portable, very complete."

—*Booklist*

"Detailed, accurate, and easy-to-read information for all price ranges."
—*Glamour Magazine*

"Hotel information is close to encyclopedic."

—*Des Moines Sunday Register*

"Frommer's Guides have a way of giving you a real feel for a place."
—*Knight Ridder Newspapers*

WILEY
Wiley Publishing, Inc.

Published by:

Wiley Publishing, Inc.
111 River St.
Hoboken, NJ 07030-5774

ISBN-13: 978-0-7645-8795-5
ISBN-10: 0-7645-8795-1

Editor: Billy Fox
Production Editor: Suzanna R. Thompson
Cartographer: Anton Crane
Photo Editor: Richard Fox
Production by Wiley Indianapolis Composition Services

Front cover photo: Palenque: Temple of the Sun flanked by massive stone walls
Back cover photo: Food still life of tortillas, dip, chiles, and tequila

For information on our other products and services or to obtain technical support, please contact our Customer Care Department within the U.S. at 800/762-2974, outside the U.S. at 317/572-3993 or fax 317/572-4002.

Wiley also publishes its books in a variety of electronic formats. Some content that appears in print may not be available in electronic formats.

Manufactured in the United States of America

5   4   3   2   1

Contents

16   Mérida, Chichén Itzá & the Maya Interior   629

by David Baird

17   The Copper Canyon   682

by David Baird

18   Los Cabos & Baja California   702

by Lynne Bairstow

List of Maps

An Invitation to the Reader

In researching this book, we discovered many wonderful places—hotels, restaurants, shops, and more. We're sure you'll find others. Please tell us about them, so we can share the information with your fellow travelers in upcoming editions. If you were disappointed with a recommendation, we'd love to know that, too. Please write to:

Frommer's Mexico 2006
Wiley Publishing, Inc. • 111 River St. • Hoboken, NJ 07030-5774

An Additional Note

Please be advised that travel information is subject to change at any time—and this is especially true of prices. We therefore suggest that you write or call ahead for confirmation when making your travel plans. The authors, editors, and publisher cannot be held responsible for the experiences of readers while traveling. Your safety is important to us, however, so we encourage you to stay alert and be aware of your surroundings. Keep a close eye on cameras, purses, and wallets, all favorite targets of thieves and pickpockets.

About the Authors

David Baird is a writer, editor, and translator who doesn't much like writing about himself in the third person (too close to being an obituary). Texan by birth, Mexican by disposition, he has lived several years in different parts of Mexico. Now based in Austin, Texas, he spends as much time in Mexico as possible. At home his hobbies include painting, scraping, mowing, and patching drywall.

For **Lynne Bairstow,** Mexico has become more home than her native United States. She has lived in Puerto Vallarta for most of the past 13 years, where she has developed a true appreciation and respect for the customs, culture, and natural treasures of Mexico. Her travel articles on Mexico have appeared in the *New York Times, Los Angeles Times, Private Air* magazine, *Luxury Living* magazine, and Mexicana's and Alaska Airlines' in-flight magazines. In 2000, Lynne was awarded the Pluma de Plata, a top honor granted by the Mexican government to foreign writers, for her work in the Frommer's guidebook to Puerto Vallarta. She is appreciative of the invaluable contribution of her research assistant, **Alejandra Macedo**, in her work on this book.

Other Great Guides for Your Trip:

Frommer's Cancún, Cozumel & the Yucatán

Frommer's Portable Acapulco, Ixtapa & Zihuatanejo

Frommer's Portable Cancún

Frommer's Portable Los Cabos & Baja

Frommer's Portable Puerto Vallarta, Manzanillo & Guadalajara

The Unofficial Guide to Mexico's Best Beach Resorts

Frommer's Star Ratings, Icons & Abbreviations

Every hotel, restaurant, and attraction listing in this guide has been ranked for quality, value, service, amenities, and special features using a **star-rating system.** In country, state, and regional guides, we also rate towns and regions to help you narrow down your choices and budget your time accordingly. Hotels and restaurants are rated on a scale of zero (recommended) to three stars (exceptional). Attractions, shopping, nightlife, towns, and regions are rated according to the following scale: zero stars (recommended), one star (highly recommended), two stars (very highly recommended), and three stars (must-see).

In addition to the star-rating system, we also use **seven feature icons** that point you to the great deals, in-the-know advice, and unique experiences that separate travelers from tourists. Throughout the book, look for:

Finds	Special finds—those places only insiders know about
Fun Fact	Fun facts—details that make travelers more informed and their trips more fun
Kids	Best bets for kids, and advice for the whole family
Moments	Special moments—those experiences that memories are made of
Overrated	Places or experiences not worth your time or money
Tips	Insider tips—great ways to save time and money
Value	Great values—where to get the best deals

The following **abbreviations** are used for credit cards:

AE	American Express	DISC	Discover	V	Visa
DC	Diners Club	MC	MasterCard		

Frommers.com

Now that you have the guidebook to a great trip, visit our website at **www.frommers.com** for travel information on more than 3,000 destinations. With features updated regularly, we give you instant access to the most current trip-planning information available. At Frommers.com, you'll also find the best prices on airfares, accommodations, and car rentals—and you can even book travel online through our travel booking partners. At Frommers.com, you'll also find the following:

- Online updates to our most popular guidebooks
- Vacation sweepstakes and contest giveaways
- Newsletter highlighting the hottest travel trends
- Online travel message boards with featured travel discussions

What's New in Mexico

In 2004, tourism to Mexico grew 10.5%, to 20.6 million visitors compared to 2003, according to Mexican tourism ministry Sectur, while related revenues hit a historic high of $10.8 billion, up 14.6% over the year before. In addition, visitor spending grew 4.4%, the tourism industry's trade balance was 21.1% higher, airplane arrivals jumped 15.2%, and 15% more cruise ship passengers docked in Mexican ports. Tourism is expected to account for 8.2% of Mexico's economy in 2005.

For the past year the exchange rate between the U.S. dollar and the Mexican peso has been quite stable despite the dollar's decline against other major currencies. Over this same period, Mexico's rate of inflation has been relatively low. Prices have not risen sharply. These factors have increased Mexico's popularity with foreign tourists. For U.S. and Canadian travelers the country remains a moderately priced destination, while for Brits and Europeans it's a down right bargain. So if you've toyed with the idea of a Mexican vacation, you might want to act now.

PLANNING YOUR TRIP TO MEXICO **Frontier Airlines** (www.frontier airlines.com) is expanding its Mexico service outside its Denver hub, adding Kansas City as a departure point.

Continental Airlines (www.continental.com) announced new nonstop service four times a week between Houston's George Bush Intercontinental Airport and Huatulco. With the addition of Huatulco, Continental serves 29 cities in Mexico, more Mexican destinations from the U.S. than any other airline.

Fort Lauderdale, Florida–based **Spirit Airlines** (www.spiritair.com) began year-round Detroit-Cancún service. Connecting service to Cancún through Detroit includes flights from New York (LaGuardia), Las Vegas, and Los Angeles.

Alaska Airlines (www.alaskaair.com) launched twice-weekly nonstop service between Los Angeles and Loreto, its eighth destination in that country.

Mexicana Airlines (www.mexicana.com) launched nonstop service between Las Vegas and Los Cabos, operating three flights a week. Other new flights serving Los Cabos include **United**'s (www.united.com) daily service from San Francisco and three times a week service from Denver, and the expansion of **Frontier Airlines** (www.frontierairlines.com), service from Denver to Cabo to a daily flight.

MEXICO CITY For complete information, see chapter 4.

Accommodations The hip-and-happening Condesa neighborhood is about to have its first new hotel in a while: The 40-room **Condesa DF**, Av. Veracruz 102 (© **55/5282-3100;** www.condesadf.com) is scheduled to open at press time. Developed by the same group that brought Habita to Polanco, it promises to be the hot new place to stay upon opening. Housed in a 1928 triangular Beaux Arts building, it will have several rooms and bars that open onto an interior courtyard, with interiors by the French designer

India Mahdavi. The hotel will be managed by Jonathan Morr, the entrepreneur behind Townhouse hotel in Miami Beach and Bond Street restaurant in New York. Rooms will start at $195 double, and will include amenities like flatscreen TVs, video art, and iPods.

SILVER CITIES   For complete information, see chapter 6.

Querétaro   The beautiful historic center has always felt like an open-air museum, but it feels even more like it now that the tourism office is offering **self-guided audio tours** of the city. They supply the Walkman, you supply the legwork. But when listening to the descriptions of building facades and historical events, try not to get so distracted that you walk out in front of a car.

San Luis Potosí   The **National Mask Museum** will be closed for renovation for much of 2006.

MICHOACAN   For complete information, see chapter 7.

Continental is now offering **nonstop service** to and from Los Angeles.

GUADALAJARA   For complete information, see chapter 8.

The popular nightclub **La Feria** has closed.

PUERTO VALLARTA & THE CENTRAL PACIFIC COAST   For complete information, see chapter 9.

Accommodations   North of Puerto Vallarta, Punta Mita, currently home to the award-winning Four Seasons Resort, will welcome new neighbors, scheduled to open in 2006—the all-suite **Rosewood La Solana Resort,** and a **Starwood Luxury brand resort.**

Attractions   Vallarta   Adventures (© **866/256-2739;** www.vallartaadventures.com) launched an excursion to the mystical island village of **Mexcaltitan,** located just offshore of Nayarit coast.

From the air, Mexcaltitan looks strikingly similar to the Aztec sunstone, and is purported to be the birthplace of the Aztecs, prior to setting off on their quest to find the promised land.

Other new offerings by Vallarta Adventures includes a diving with sea lions program at its resort in Caletas, and a new interactive Dolphin Kids program, geared for children age 4 to 8. They have remodeled their dolphin center to include a viewing window into the dolphin tanks, where you can watch mother dolphins interacting with their newborns. Also added is their **Trainer for a Day** program, enabling you to work for a day alongside these skilled trainers.

For women who have been too intimidated to learn to sail, your prayers have been answered with the opening of **Coming About** (© **322/222-4119;** www. coming-about.com), a women-only sailing school that provides hands-on sailing instruction with day-sailing excursions, as well as weeklong sailing classes at a variety of skill levels. The owner and lead instructor is Pat Henry, who spent 8 years sailing around the globe, then wrote about it in her book *By the Grace of the Sea: A Woman's Solo Odyssey Around the World.* Dubbed "any woman's sailing school," the goal is to take away the fear and the mystery, and make the skill of sailing accessible to everyone. Courses range from a 1-day introductory course to a 9-day bareboat charter captain course.

Starwood Hotels & Resorts Latin America (www.starwood.com) partnered up with Nikki Beach (www.nikkibeach. com), a Miami-based family owned company that has created some of the hippest and most popular dining and bar locations in the world to open a new addition of their club at **Starwood**'s **Westin Regina Resort** in Puerto Vallarta. The restaurant offers out-of-the-ordinary cuisine and a relaxed ambience amid an alcove of tepees and fabric-draped bamboo beds.

PUEBLA   For complete information, see chapter 12.

Continental is now offering **nonstop service** to and from Houston.

At last the **Bello y González Museum** is open after 2 years of extensive renovations to the house that holds the collection.

Tlaxcala is offering more city tours now.

CANCUN   For complete information, see chapter 13.

Accommodations   Fiesta Americana hotels opened their most stylish resort to date: the **Aqua Cancún** (© 800/343-7821; www.fiestaamericana.com), which has been turning heads and creating a buzz prior to its opening in February 2005. The 370-room oceanfront Aqua is awash in blue hues and stylish design, launching it to the top of stylish accommodations in this resort town. Rooms are sleek and fitted with every possible amenity. Facilities include an expansive spa, several restaurants featuring menus by renowned chefs, and a lounge-style atmosphere in its lobby and pool areas.

The **Hilton Cancún Beach & Golf Resort** (© 998/881-8000; www.hilton cancun.com) opened its new spa in early 2005. The 3,700-sq.-m (40,000-sq.-ft.) spa features eight indoor and two beachside treatment areas, two saunas, and an outdoor whirlpool. The spa offers massages on the beach and yoga classes, as well as the traditional spa treatments. Hotel packages that bundle the resort's spa also are available.

Attractions   An impressive **Interactive Aquarium** opened at **La Isla Shopping Center** (© 998/883-0411; www. aquariumcancun.com.mx), with dolphin swims and the chance to feed a shark while immersed in the water in an acrylic cage.

The newest ecoadventure in the area is the half-day tour to **Chikin-Ha** (© 984/873-2036; www.alltournative.com), also known as the Mayan Canopy Tour. You have the option of hiking or biking through the landscape past a series of three *cenotes* (sinkholes) with deep-blue waters, with stops for swimming or traveling by zip-line over the *cenotes* and tropical landscape.

After Dark   In 2004 Avalon Resorts opened **The City** (© 998/848-8380; www.thecitycancun.com), a high-concept nightclub, beach bar, and lounge featuring a world-famous porterhouse grill. Meant to evoke a "city within a city," the property, located in the Hotel Zone, features a three-dimensional urban skyline of skyscrapers and city towers. It's already hosted the world's top DJs—Moby even played here—and the music is sizzling.

Glazz, at La Isla Shopping Village (© 998/883-1881; www.glazz.com/mx), is another new nocturnal offering in Cancún, combining a restaurant (China Bistro) with a sleek lounge and sophisticated, Miami-style nightclub for a complete evening of entertainment.

ISLA MUJERES & COZUMEL For complete information, see chapter 14.

Attractions   **Garrafón National Park** (www.garrafon.com) in Isla Mujeres offers Isla's newest attraction, the **Panoramic Tower.** At 50m (225 ft.) high, the tower offers visitors a birds' eye view of the entire island. The tower holds 20 visitors at a time, and rotates for 10 minutes while you can snap photos or simply enjoy the scenery. Adjacent to the tower, they've also installed **Sculptured Spaces,** an impressive and extensive garden of large sculptures donated to Isla Mujeres by internationally renowned sculptors as part of the 2001 First International Sculpture Exhibition. Nearby is the new **Caribbean Village,** with narrow lanes of colorful clapboard buildings that house cafes and shops displaying folkloric art. In addition, Garrafón Park also offers underwater museums, snorkeling through artificial reefs, and other activities.

Cozumel The **Plaza Las Glorias Hotel,** which was on the coast in the southern part of San Miguel, is now closed. It will reopen under new ownership as an all-inclusive property

THE RIVIERA MAYA For complete information, see chapter 15.

Playa del Carmen In Playa, two of our favorite economic hotels are being replaced with condos: **Villa Catarina** and the **Albatross Royale** are slated for closing. Demolition and construction will soon follow.

Costa Maya **Kailuum II,** the neoprimitive hotel that occupied a stretch of beach south of Puerto Morelos is moving to Majahual.

Río Bec Ruins Parts of the **ruins in Becán** remain closed for restoration.

MERIDA, CHICHEN ITZA & THE MAYA INTERIOR For complete information on this region, see chapter 16.

Mérida The construction of a **new city market** in the downtown area is now complete. It includes green space and better parking.

LOS CABOS & BAJA CALIFORNIA For complete information, see chapter 18.

Accommodations Los Cabos now has more than 9,200 hotel rooms, up from just over 8,000 in 2003. Although more growth is planned, Cabo has a building cap of 10,000 rooms.

In 2004, Ty Warner Hotels & Resorts purchased the 61-room **Las Ventanas al Paraíso Resort** in Los Cabos. The resort will continue to be managed by Rosewood Hotels and Resorts. Ty Warner is expected to invest a hefty sum expanding Las Ventanas's facilities, including its spa. Meanwhile, guests lounging by the pool at Las Ventanas can now request an iPod from the resort's pool butlers. The iPods will come preloaded with nearly a thousand songs in a number of categories, from jazz and classical to rock and hip hop. In addition to providing iPods, Las Ventanas' pool butlers offer guests towels, books and magazines, and complimentary sorbets, food, and beverages from the poolside bar.

And taking it one step farther, **One&Only Palmilla** is now making free PMDs (personal media devices) and iPods available to its guests. All one-bedroom suites at the 172-unit resort come equipped with both devices, preprogrammed with popular movies and music; guests can ask for programming with their own favorites before arrival. iPods are also available to all guests at the two pools, in the fitness center, and at Hammock Hill.

AmResorts opened the 308-room **Dreams Los Cabos Suites Golf Resort & Spa,** a conversion of a former Meliá property, in June 2004.

The **Marquis Los Cabos Beach, Golf, Spa and Casitas Resort,** established in 2003, opened a new spa and fitness center in April 2004. The 4,500-sq.-m (15,000-sq.-ft.) Spa Marquis has 10 treatment rooms, open-air Jacuzzis, and offers holistic treatments using indigenous ingredients. The fitness center has workout equipment and offers classes in yoga, Tai Chi, aerobics, and meditation.

The **Westin Regina Golf & Beach Resort Los Cabos** finished a $2-million upgrade. Renovated guest rooms now have high-speed Internet connectivity, and there is a new cybercafe business center. Wireless Internet access is available in the business center, meetings facilities, and all public areas. The resort also has a new tequila bar, sushi and martini bars, and a nine-hole putting green.

Attractions Trendy beach club franchise **Nikki Beach** opened its fifth tropical partying outlet at the 150-room Meliá San Lucas resort in Cabo in March 2005.

Loreto The Canadian nonprofit organization Trust for Sustainable Development has teamed up with Mexico's National Trust for Tourism Development (Fonatur) to develop **Loreto Bay Village** (www.loretobay.com), a $1.2-billion investment, which hopes to convert the sleepy seaside village of Loreto into a major tourist destination, with special emphasis placed on environment protection. Situated 240km (150 miles) north of La Paz and 1,125km (700 miles) south of San Diego, Loreto Bay Village is the last of five communities originally selected in the 1970s for development by Fonatur; the others were Cancún, Los Cabos, Ixtapa, and Huatulco. The planned village will occupy 5km (3 miles) of coastline on the Sea of Cortez, and will include the development of 5,000 residences, a town center, hotels, a beach club, spas, golf courses, a marina, cultural and recreational facilities, a nature preserve, and a solar farm.

1

The Best of Mexico

by David Baird & Lynne Bairstow

Across Mexico, in villages and cities, in mountains, tropical coasts, and jungle settings, enchanting surprises await travelers. These might take the form of a fantastic small-town festival, delightful dining in a memorable restaurant, or even a stretch of road through heavenly countryside. Below is a starter list of our favorites, to which you'll have the pleasure of adding your own discoveries.

1 The Best Beach Vacations

- **Puerto Vallarta:** Spectacularly wide Banderas Bay offers 42km (26 miles) of beaches. Some, like Playa Los Muertos—the popular public beach in town—abound with *palapa* restaurants, beach volleyball, and parasailing. The beaches of Punta Mita, the exclusive development north of Vallarta, are of the white-sand variety, with crystalline waters and coral reefs just offshore. Others around the bay nestle in coves, accessible only by boat. Puerto Vallarta is the only place where authentic colonial ambience mixes with true resort amenities. See "Puerto Vallarta" in chapter 9.

- **Puerto Escondido:** The best overall beach value in Mexico is principally known for its world-class surfing beach, Playa Zicatela. The surrounding beaches all have their own appeal; colorful fishing *pangas* dot the central town beach, parked under the shade of palms leaning so far over they almost touch the ground. Puerto Escondido offers unique accommodations at excellent prices, with exceptional budget dining and nightlife. See "Puerto Escondido" in chapter 10.

- **Ixtapa/Zihuatanejo:** These side-by-side resorts offer beachgoers the best of both worlds: serene simplicity and resort comforts. For those in search of a back-to-basics beach, the best and most beautiful is Playa La Ropa, close to Zihuatanejo. The wide beach at Playa Las Gatas, with its restaurants and snorkeling sites, is also a great place to play. The luxury hotels in Ixtapa, on the next bay over from Zihuatanejo, front Playa Palmar, a fine, wide swath of beach. See "Northward to Zihuatanejo & Ixtapa" in chapter 10.

- **Cancún:** In terms of sheer beauty, Mexico's best beaches are in Cancún and along the Yucatán's Quintana Roo coast, extending south almost all the way to the Belizean border. The powdery, white-sand beaches boast water the color of a Technicolor dream; it's so clear you can see through to the coral reefs below. Cancún offers the widest assortment of luxury beachfront hotels, with more restaurants, nightlife, and activities than any other resort destination in the country. See chapter 13.

- **Tulum:** Fronting some of the best beaches on Mexico's Caribbean coast, Tulum's small *palapa* hotels offer guests a little slice of paradise far from crowds and megaresorts. The bustling town lies inland; at the coast, things are quiet and will remain so because all these hotels are small and must generate their own electricity. If you can pull yourself away from the beach, nearby are ruins to explore and a vast nature preserve. See chapter 15.

- **Isla Mujeres:** There's only one small beach here—Playa Norte—but it's superb. From this island, you can dive El Garrafón reef, snorkel offshore, and take a boat excursion to the Isla Contoy national wildlife reserve, which features great birding and a fabulous, uninhabited beach. See "Isla Mujeres" in chapter 14.

- **Playa del Carmen:** "Playa" is Mexico's hip beach destination with a dash of third-world chic. Above all, it's easy and low key. You walk to the beach, you walk back to the hotel, you walk to one of the many good restaurants. Next day, you repeat. The beaches are white sand; the water is clear blue and perfect for swimming. If you feel the urge to be active, not far away are ancient Maya ruins, Cozumel, and the megaresort of Cancún, offering all the variety that you might want in a beach vacation. See chapter 15.

- **La Paz:** This state capital borders a lovely beach, dotted with colorful playgrounds and lively open-air restaurants. Take a cue from the local residents, though, and pass on swimming here in favor of the exquisite beaches just minutes from downtown. La Paz's beaches and the islets just offshore have transformed this tranquil town into a center for diving, sea kayaking, and other adventure pursuits. See "La Paz: Peaceful Port Town" in chapter 18.

- **Los Cabos:** Dramatic rock formations and crashing waves mix with wide stretches of soft sand and a rolling break. Start at Pueblo la Playa, just north of San José del Cabo, and work your way down the Cabo Corridor to the famed Playa de Amor at Land's End. Some beaches are more appropriate for contemplation than for swimming, which isn't all bad. See "Los Cabos: Resorts, Watersports & Golf" in chapter 18.

2 The Best Cultural Experiences

- **Passing Time in the Plazas & Parks:** All the world may be a stage, but some parts have richer backdrops than others. Town plazas are the perfect settings for watching everyday life unfold. Alive with people, these open spaces are no modern product of urban planners, but are rooted in the traditional Mexican view of society. Several plazas are standouts: **Veracruz**'s famous *zócalo* (see chapter 12) features nearly nonstop music and tropical gaiety. One look tells you how important **Oaxaca**'s *zócalo* (see chapter 11) is to the local citizenry; the plaza is remarkably beautiful, grand, and intimate all at once. **Mexico City**'s Alameda (see chapter 4) has a dark, dramatic history—heretics were burned at the stake here during the colonial period—but today it's a people's park where lovers sit, cotton-candy vendors spin their treats, and the sound of organ grinders drifts over the changing crowd. **San Miguel de Allende**'s Jardín (see chapter 6) is the focal point for meeting, sitting, painting, and sketching. During festivals, it fills with dancers, parades, and elaborate fireworks. **Guanajuato** and

Mexico

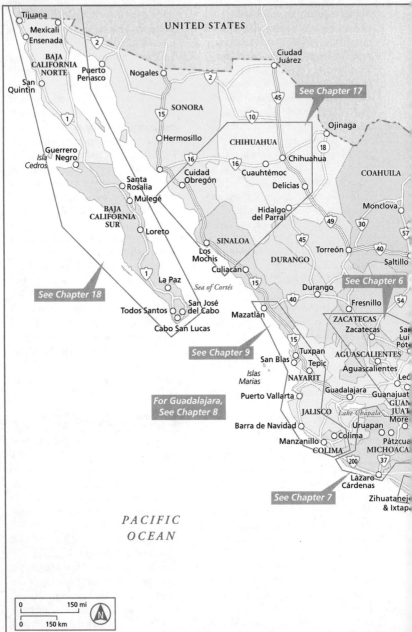

UNITED STATES

Tijuana
Mexicali
Ensenada
BAJA
CALIFORNIA
NORTE   Puerto
Penasco   Nogales
San
Quintin
Ciudad
Juárez

See Chapter 17

SONORA
Ojinaga
Hermosillo   CHIHUAHUA
Guerrero
Isla Negro
Cedros
Chihuahua
COAHUILA
Cuidad
Obregón   Cuauhtémoc
Santa
Rosalia
Mulegé
Delicias
Monclova
BAJA
CALIFORNIA
SUR
Hidalgo
del Parral
Loreto
SINALOA
Los
Mochis
Culiacán
DURANGO
Torreón
Saltillo
La Paz   Sea of Cortés
Durango

See Chapter 18

See Chapter 6

Todos Santos   San José
del Cabo
Cabo San Lucas
Mazatlán
Fresnillo
ZACATECAS
Zacatecas
Sa
Lui
Pot

See Chapter 9

Tuxpan   AGUASCALIENTES
San Blas
Tepic
Aguascalientes
Islas
Marias   NAYARIT
Puerto Vallarta   Guadalajara   Guanajuat
GUAN
JUAT
More

**For Guadalajara,
See Chapter 8**

JALISCO   Lake Chapala
Barra de Navidad   Uruapan   Pátzcua
Colima   MICHOACA
Manzanillo
COLIMA

Lázaro
Cárdenas

See Chapter 7

Zihuatanej
& Ixtap

PACIFIC
OCEAN

0   150 mi
0   150 km

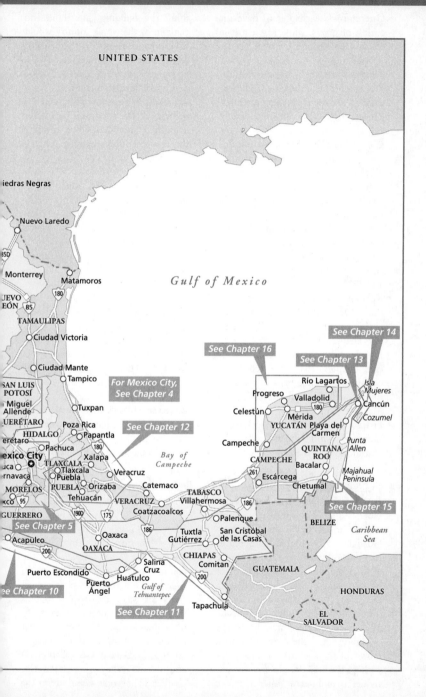

UNITED STATES

iedras Negras

Nuevo Laredo

85D

Monterrey   Matamoros

JEVO
EÓN   85

TAMAULIPAS

Ciudad Victoria

Ciudad Mante

SAN LUIS   Tampico
POTOSÍ

Miguel
Allende

UERÉTARO   Tuxpan

erétaro   Poza Rica
Papantla

Pachuca

exico City   Xalapa
uca   TLAXCALA
rnavaca   Tlaxcala
Puebla   Veracruz
MORELOS   PUEBLA   Orizaba
xco   95   Tehuacán   Catemaco

GUERRERO   VERACRUZ
1900   175   Coatzacoalcos

See Chapter 5

Acapulco   Oaxaca
200   OAXACA

Puerto Escondido

ee Chapter 10   Puerto   Huatulco
Ángel   Gulf of
Tehuantepec

Gulf of Mexico

For Mexico City,
See Chapter 4

See Chapter 12

Bay of
Campeche

See Chapter 16

Progreso
Celestún

Campeche

CAMPECHE
261   Escárcega

TABASCO
Villahermosa   186

Palenque

Tuxtla   San Cristóbal
Gutiérrez   de las Casas

CHIAPAS
Comitan
200

Salina
Cruz

See Chapter 11   Tapachula

Río Lagartos

Valladolid
180

Mérida
YUCATÁN   Playa del
Carmen

QUINTANA
ROO
Bacalar

Chetumal

See Chapter 13

See Chapter 14

Isla
Mujeres

Cancún

Cozumel

Punta
Allen

Majahual
Peninsula

See Chapter 15

BELIZE

GUATEMALA

EL
SALVADOR

Caribbean
Sea

HONDURAS

Querétaro (see chapter 6) have the coziest of plazas, while El Centro in **Mérida** (see chapter 16) on a Sunday can't be beat.

- *Música Popular:* Nothing reveals the soul of a people like music, and Mexico boasts many kinds in many different settings. You can find brassy, belt-it-out **mariachi** music in the famous Plaza de Garibaldi in Mexico City (see chapter 4), under the arches of El Parián in Tlaquepaque, and in other parts of Guadalajara (see chapter 8). Or perhaps you want to hear romantic **boleros** about love's betrayal sung to the strumming of a Spanish guitar, or what Mexicans call *música tropical* and related *cumbias,* mambos, and cha-cha-chas (see chapters 13 and 16).

- **Regional Folk Dancing:** Whether it's the Ballet Folklórico in Mexico City or the Ballet Folclórico in Guadalajara (see chapters 4 and 8), the almost-nightly park performances in Mérida (see chapter 16), or celebrations countrywide, these performances are diverse and colorful expressions of Mexican traditions.

- **Fireworks:** Mexicans have such a passion for fireworks and such a cavalier attitude toward them that it's a good thing the buildings are stone and cement, or the whole country would have burned down long ago. Many local traditions surround fireworks, and every festival includes a display. The most lavish are the large constructions known as *castillos,* and the wildest are the *toros* that men carry over their shoulders while running through the streets, causing festival-goers to dive for cover.

- **Strolling** *El Malecón:* Wherever there's a seafront road, you'll find *el malecón* bordering it. This is generally a wide sidewalk for strolling, complete with vendors selling pinwheels and cotton candy. In some places, it has supplanted the plaza as a centerpiece of town life. The best examples are in **Puerto Vallarta, Mazatlán** (see chapter 9), **La Paz** (see chapter 18), **Cozumel** (see chapter 14), and **Veracruz** (see chapter 12).

- **Regional Fairs:** Almost every city and town has its regional fair *(feria regional).* These fairs showcase the best products of the region—tequila or fruit liquors, livestock, intricately carved silver, or clay handicrafts. One of the most notable regional fairs is La Feria del Caballo in Texcoco, which takes place in late March or early April.

3 The Best Festivals & Celebrations

- **Festival de Nuestra Señora de Guadalupe:** This annual celebration leads up to Día de Nuestra Señora de Guadalupe, celebrated throughout Mexico on December 12. The Virgin of Guadalupe is the patron saint of Mexico, and is also identified with the Aztec earth goddess and mother of humankind. The basilica just outside of **Mexico City** features the largest celebration and the most impressive crowd of impassioned believers, but perhaps the best place to view the festivities is in **Puerto Vallarta,** where they continue around the clock for 12 days. It is a visual delight. See "Exploring Mexico City" in chapter 4, and "Puerto Vallarta" in chapter 9.

- **Days of the Dead:** People across the country celebrate *Los Días de los Muertos* (Oct 31–Nov 2); they erect altars for the dead, with marigolds (the flower of the dead) and offerings of food and drink. The most popular celebrations happen in the villages around **Pátzcuaro** (see chapter 7) and in the valley of **Oaxaca** (see chapter 11). People head out to the cemetery for all-night vigils and sing and pray for the souls of the dearly departed. During the day, markets sell crafts and special items made just for the festival.

- **Carnaval:** Mexico has two particularly notable celebrations. Festivities in **Veracruz** fill the 3 days before Ash Wednesday, with fabulous floats, dancing in the plaza, and live entertainment. **Mazatlán**'s party lasts a full week before Lent, with parades, strolling musicians, and crowds of revelers along the entire length of the *malecón*. See "Veracruz City" in chapter 12, and "Mazatlán" in chapter 9.

- **Holy Week:** The silver city of **Taxco** hosts one of the most compelling Holy Week commemorations in the country, beginning the Friday before Palm Sunday with nightly processions (and several during the day). On the evening of Holy Thursday, villagers carrying saints from the surrounding area march ahead of hooded members of a society of self-flagellating penitents. On the Saturday morning before Easter, the Plaza Borda fills for the Procession of Three Falls, which reenacts the three times Christ stumbled and fell while carrying the cross. See chapter 5. In **San Miguel de Allende, Pátzcuaro** and surrounding communities, and **Oaxaca,** the solemn weeklong commemoration involves nightly candlelit processions through the streets and other religious events. See chapters 6, 7, and 11.

- **La Fiesta de los Locos:** In **San Miguel de Allende,** a town known for celebrations, this one is the most fun for visitors. Young and old alike dress in grotesque costumes and parade around the center of town, or in dressed-up carts, to musical accompaniment. Keep an eye open for practical jokes. See "San Miguel de Allende" in chapter 6.

- **Guelaguetza:** On the last 2 Mondays in July, **Oaxaca** puts on a big show. Dance groups from communities across the state perform in the amphitheater on the hillside above the city. See "Oaxaca City" in chapter 11.

- **"Night of the Radishes":** Unique in the country, December 23 in **Oaxaca** is when the Oaxaqueños build fantastic sculptures out of radishes, flowers, and dried cornhusks. They go on display on the *zócalo.* On December 24, each Oaxacan church organizes a procession with music, floats, and crowds bearing candles. See "Oaxaca City" in chapter 11.

- **"Gourmet Festival":** This festival of fine dining held in **Puerto Vallarta** brings together some of the world's finest chefs creating magical menus in the town's top restaurants. Added attractions include a gourmet food expo, cooking classes, tequila and wine tastings, and an array of special events and parties. Dates vary, but the festival generally takes place for 10 days in mid-November. www.festival gourmet.com. See "Puerto Vallarta" in chapter 9.

4 The Best Archaeological Sites

- **Teotihuacán:** So close to Mexico City, yet centuries away. You can feel the majesty of the past in a stroll down the pyramid-lined Avenue of the Dead, from the Pyramid of the Sun to the Pyramid of the Moon. Imagine what a fabulous place this must have been when the walls were stuccoed and painted brilliant colors. See "A Side Trip to the Pyramids of San Juan Teotihuacán" in chapter 4.

- **Monte Albán:** A grand ceremonial city built on a mountaintop overlooking the valley of Oaxaca, Monte Albán offers the visitor panoramic vistas; a fascinating view of a society in transition, reflected in the contrasting methods of pyramid construction; and intriguing details in ornamentation. See "Oaxaca City" in chapter 11.

- **Palenque:** Like the pharaohs of Egypt, the rulers of Palenque built tombs deep within their pyramids. Imagine the magnificent ceremony in A.D. 683 when King Pacal was entombed in his magnificent burial chamber, which lay unspoiled until its discovery in 1952. See "Palenque" in chapter 11.

- **Ek Balam:** Archaeologists at this site have made the most astonishing discoveries of the decade. Ek Balam's main pyramid is taller than Chichén Itzá's, and it holds a sacred doorway bordered with elaborate stucco figures of priests and kings and rich iconography. See "Ek Balam: Dark Jaguar" in chapter 16.

- **Uxmal:** No matter how many times you see Uxmal, the splendor of its stone carvings is awe-inspiring. A stone rattlesnake undulates across the facade of the Nunnery complex, and 103 masks of the rain god Chaac project out from the Governor's Palace. See "The Ruins of Uxmal" in chapter 16.

- **Chichén Itzá:** Stand beside the giant serpent head at the foot of El Castillo pyramid and marvel at the architects and astronomers who positioned the building so precisely that shadow and sunlight form a serpent's body slithering from the peak to the earth at each equinox (Mar 21 and Sept 21). See "The Ruins of Chichén Itzá" in chapter 16.

5 The Best Active Vacations

- **Scuba Diving in Cozumel & along the Yucatán's Caribbean Coast:** The coral reefs off the island, Mexico's premier diving destination, are among the top five dive spots in the world. See chapter 14. The Yucatán's coastal reef is part of the second-largest reef system in the world and affords excellent diving. Especially beautiful is the Chinchorro Reef, 32km (20 miles) offshore from Majahual or Xcalak. You can also dive in the clear, cool water of the many caverns and *cenotes* (sinkholes, or natural wells) that dot the interior. See chapter 15. Other excellent dive sites are in and around **Puerto Vallarta** and off **Los Cabos.** See chapters 9 and 18.

- **Fly-Fishing off the Punta Allen Peninsula:** Serious anglers will enjoy the challenge of fly-fishing the saltwater flats and lagoons of Ascension Bay, near Punta Allen. See "Tulum, Punta Allen & Sian Ka'an" in chapter 15.

- **Hiking & Horseback Riding in the Copper Canyon:** Miles and miles of beautiful, remote, challenging canyon lands are paradise for the serious hiker or rider. **Canyon Travel** (© **800/ 843-1060** in the U.S.) can set hikers up with a Tarahumara Indian guide, who can take you deep into the canyons to places rarely viewed by tourists. Doug Rhodes of the **Paraíso del Oso** (© **800/884-3107** in the U.S.) leads tours of experienced horseback riders on a 12-day ride that tests a rider's skill in mountainous terrain. It has to be the most challenging ride in North America. See "The Copper Canyon Train and Stops Along the Way" in chapter 17.

- **Golf in Los Cabos & Puerto Vallarta:** Puerto Vallarta, with its seven championship courses, is *the* new destination for golfers to keep their eyes on. Added to the appeal of golf here are courses within easy driving distance along the

Pacific Coast at El Tamarindo, Isla Navidad, and Manzanillo. See chapter 9. The Corridor between San José del Cabo and Cabo San Lucas is one of the world's premier golf destinations, with five championship courses open and a total of 207 holes slated for the area. See chapter 18.

- **Surfing Zicatela Beach in Puerto Escondido:** This world-class break is a lure for surfers from around the globe. It challenges the best in the sport each September and October, when the waves peak and the annual surf competitions take place. See chapter 10. Other noted surf breaks in Mexico include Sayulita and Las Islitas Beach near **San Blas** (both north of Puerto Vallarta), and Playa Costa Azul, on the outskirts of **San José del Cabo.** See chapters 9 and 18.

- **Sportfishing in La Paz:** Billfishing for magnificent marlin and sailfish is a popular sport throughout southern Baja, and La Paz pulls in the most consistent share. See chapter 18. Fishing is also excellent in Los Cabos, Mazatlán, Manzanillo, and Zihuatanejo. See chapters 9, 10, and 18.

- **Sea Kayaking in the Sea of Cortez:** From Cabo San Lucas to La Paz, and continuing north, the Sea of Cortez is a sea kayaker's dream. It has dozens of tiny coves and impressive inlets to pull into and explore, under the watchful gaze of sea lions and dolphins. Professional outfitters provide gear, guides, and instruction for novices. See chapter 18.

6 The Best of Natural Mexico

- **Michoacán's Million Monarch March:** Mexico is an exotic land, and no place drives this home more forcefully than a mountain forest where you stand surrounded by the fluttering wings of millions of monarch butterflies—it's like being in a fairy tale. The setting is the rugged highlands of Michoacán, from mid- to late November through March. See "Morelia" in chapter 7.

- **Whale-Watching:** Each winter, between December and April, magnificent humpback and gray whales return to breed and instruct their young in the waters of Banderas Bay, fronting **Puerto Vallarta,** and in **Los Cabos.** See "Puerto Vallarta" in chapter 9, and "Los Cabos: Resorts, Watersports & Golf" in chapter 18.

- **Sea-Turtle Nesting Beaches:** Between June and November, sea turtles return to the beaches of their birth to lay their eggs in nests on the sand. With poaching and natural predators threatening these species, communities along Mexico's Pacific coast have established protected nesting areas. Many are open for public viewing and participation in the egg collection and baby-turtle release processes. Turtles are found along the Yucatán coast, in Baja Sur, on the Oaxaca coast, in Puerto Vallarta, and on Costa Alegre. See chapters 9, 11, 15, and 18.

- **Lago Bacalar** (Yucatán Peninsula): The waters of this crystal-clear, spring-fed lake—Mexico's second largest—are noted for their vibrant color variations, from pale blue to deep blue-green and turquoise. The area surrounding the lake is known for birding, with over 130 species identified. See "Lago Bacalar" in chapter 15.

- **The Rugged Copper Canyon:** The canyons known collectively as the Copper Canyon are beautiful, remote, and unspoiled. The entire network is larger than the Grand Canyon; it incorporates high waterfalls, vertical canyon walls, mountain forests in the canyon-rim country, and semiarid desert inside the canyons. This is the land of the Tarahumara Indians, who gained their legendary endurance from adapting to this wilderness. See chapter 17.

- **Desert Landscapes in Baja Sur:** The painted-desert colors and unique plant life are a natural curiosity in **Los Cabos,** where horseback, hiking, and ATV trips explore the area. The arid desert contrasts sharply with the intense blue of the strong sea surrounding the peninsula. See "Los Cabos: Resorts, Watersports & Golf" in chapter 18.

7 The Best Places to Get Away from It All

- **Costa Alegre:** Between Puerto Vallarta and Manzanillo, a number of superexclusive hotels cater to those with both time and money. These resorts—Hotelito Desconocido, Las Alamandas, Hotel Careyes, and El Tamarindo—are miles from civilization on private beaches. See "Costa Alegre: Puerto Vallarta to Barra de Navidad" in chapter 9.
- **San Sebastián:** A 15-minute flight from Puerto Vallarta takes you a century back in time. The colonial mountain town of San Sebastián used to be the center of Mexico's mining operations; today, it's simply a place of delicious seclusion in a magical mountain setting. See "Puerto Vallarta" in chapter 9.
- **Punta Mita:** Its ancient inhabitants considered the northern tip of the Bay of Banderas sacred ground. Today, the point where the Sea of Cortez, the Pacific Ocean, and Banderas Bay meet is evolving into Mexico's most exclusive residential resort development. The beaches are white and the waters crystalline. See "Puerto Vallarta" in chapter 9.
- **Riviera Maya & Punta Allen Peninsula:** Away from the popular resort of Cancún, the Riviera Maya's heavenly quiet getaways offer tranquillity at low prices on beautiful palm-lined beaches. South of the Tulum ruins,

Punta Allen's beachside budget inns offer some of the most peaceful getaways in the country. See chapter 15.
- **Lago Bacalar:** The spring-fed waters of Lake Bacalar—Mexico's second-largest lake—make an ideal place to unwind. South of Cancún, near Chetumal, there's nothing around for miles. If you want adventure, you can take a kayak out on the lake, follow a birding trail, or venture to Belize or the nearby Maya ruins. See "Lago Bacalar" in chapter 15.
- **Cerocahui:** Up in the high Sierra Tarahumara, far from where the large tours stop, you'll find a peaceful little town surrounding a former mission. Nearby are two small hotels that are even more peaceful—no phones, no crowds, no traffic, just beautiful mountains and canyons clothed in pine forest. See "The Copper Canyon Train and Stops Along the Way" in chapter 17.
- **Todos Santos:** Purportedly home of the original Hotel California: You can check out any time, but you may not want to leave once you unwind for a while in this artists' outpost, also known as "Bohemian Baja." But come soon, because it's gaining the attention of like-minded adventurers. See "Todos Santos: A Creative Oasis" in chapter 18.

8 The Best Art, Architecture & Museums

- **Museo Nacional de Antropología:** Among the world's most outstanding museums, the Museum of Anthropology in Mexico City contains riches representing 3,000 years of the country's past. Also on view are fabulous artifacts of still-thriving indigenous cultures. The building, designed by architect Pedro Ramírez Vázquez, is stunning. See p. 126.

- **Museo Frida Kahlo (Frida Kahlo House & Museum):** While perhaps not a world-class collection of works by Mexico's first couple of art, Frida Kahlo and Diego Rivera, this museum does contain a strong sampling of their works, plus their fascinating private collection. With rooms arranged as they were when the couple lived here, in the Mexico City suburb of Coyoacán, it also allows visitors to peek into the lives of these creative masters. This is also where much of the 2002 film *Frida* was shot. See p. 124.

- **Palacio Nacional:** Mexico's center of government and presidential office was originally built in 1692 on the site of Moctezuma's "new" palace, to be the home of Hernán Cortez. The top floor, added in the late 1920s, holds a series of stunning Diego Rivera murals depicting the history of Mexico. See p. 126.

- **Palacio de Bellas Artes in Mexico City:** The country's premier venue for the performing arts, this fabulous building is the combined work of several masters, including the Italian architect Adamo Boari. The theater's exterior is early-20th-century Art Nouveau, covered in marble; the interior is 1930s Art Deco. See p. 130.

- **The Templo Mayor's Aztec Splendor:** The Templo Mayor and Museo del Templo Mayor, in Mexico City, are an archaeological excavation and a museum with 6,000 objects on display. They showcase the variety and splendor of the Aztec Empire as it existed in the center of what is now Mexico City. See p. 128.

- **Catedral Metropolitana:** This towering cathedral, begun in 1573 and finished in 1788, blends baroque, neoclassical, and Mexican churrigueresque architecture, and was constructed primarily from the stones of destroyed Aztec temples. See p. 132.

- **Santa Prisca y San Sebastián Church:** One of Mexico's most impressive baroque churches, completed in 1758, this church in Taxco has an intricately carved facade, an interior decorated with gold-leafed saints and angels, and paintings by Miguel Cabrera, one of Mexico's most famous colonial-era artists. See p. 161.

- **Mexican Masks in Zacatecas:** Masks are a ubiquitous feature in Mexican festivals and folk art, and the Museo Rafael Coronel in Zacatecas has the greatest collection in the country. See p. 226.

- **Museo Virreinal de Guadalupe:** Six kilometers (4 miles) southeast of Zacatecas in the small town of Guadalupe, this Franciscan convent and art museum holds a striking collection of 17th- and 18th-century paintings by such masters as Miguel Cabrera and Cristóbal de Villalpando. The expressive, dramatic works will fascinate art lovers. See p. 227.

- **Morelia's Cathedral:** Sober lines, balanced proportions, a deft blending of architectural styles, and monumental height—Morelia's cathedral is the most beautiful in the country. It's built of brownish-pink stone that turns fiery rose in the late-afternoon sun. See p. 242.

- **Xalapa's Museo Antropología:** With the finest examples of Olmec and Totonac sculpture and ceramics, this museum includes the best collection of the Olmec megalithic heads. See p. 497.
- **Puebla's Capilla del Rosario:** Located in the church of Santo Domingo, this chapel is a tour de force of baroque

expression, executed in molded plaster, carved wood, Talavera tile, and gold leaf. The overall effect is to overpower the senses. See p. 504.

- **Puebla's Museo Amparo:** A magnificent collection of pre-Columbian and colonial art, beautifully displayed. See p. 506.

9 The Best Shopping

- **Bazar del Sábado in San Angel:** This festive weekly market in a colonial neighborhood south of Mexico City offers exceptional crafts, of a more sophisticated nature than you'll see in most *mercados*. Furnishings, antiques, and collectibles are also easy to find in surrounding garages and street plazas. See p. 144.
- **Polanco, Mexico City:** This fashionable neighborhood is noted for its designer boutiques, cigar shops, fine jewelers, and leather-goods offerings. See "Shopping" in chapter 4.
- **Contemporary Art:** Latin American art is surging in popularity and recognition. Galleries in Mexico City feature Mexico's masters and emerging stars, with Oaxaca, Puerto Vallarta, and San Miguel de Allende galleries also offering excellent selections. See chapters 4, 6, 9, and 11.
- **Taxco Silver:** Mexico's silver capital, Taxco, has hundreds of stores featuring fine jewelry and decorative objects. See "Taxco: Cobblestones & Silver" in chapter 5.
- **Talavera Pottery in Puebla & Dolores Hidalgo:** An inheritor of the Moorish legacy of ceramics, Puebla produces some of the most sought-after dinnerware in the world. The tiles produced there adorn building facades and church domes throughout the area. See chapter 12. Dolores Hidalgo, 40km (25 miles) northwest

of San Miguel de Allende, produces attractive, inexpensive Talavera of less traditional design. Almost every block has a factory or store outlet. See "San Miguel de Allende" in chapter 6.

- **San Miguel de Allende's Diverse Crafts:** Perhaps it's the influence of the Instituto Allende art school, but something has given storekeepers here real savvy about choosing their merchandise. The stores have fewer typical articles of Mexican handicrafts and more interesting and eye-catching works than you'll find in other towns. And the shopping experience is low-key. See "San Miguel de Allende" in chapter 6.
- **Pátzcuaro's Fine Crafts:** Michoacán is known for its crafts, and Pátzcuaro is at the center of it all. You can find beautiful cotton textiles, woodcarvings, pottery, lacquerware, woven straw pieces, and copper items in the market, or you can track the object to its source in one of the nearby villages. See "Pátzcuaro" in chapter 7.
- **Decorative Arts in Tlaquepaque & Tonalá:** These two neighborhoods of Guadalajara offer perhaps the most enjoyable shopping in Mexico. Tlaquepaque has attracted sophisticated and wide-ranging shops selling a wide variety of decorative art. In Tonalá, more than 400 artisans have workshops, and you can visit many of them on regular days; on market

days, wander through blocks and blocks of market stalls seeking that one perfect piece. See "Shopping" in chapter 8.

- **Huichol Art in Puerto Vallarta:** One of the last indigenous cultures to remain faithful to their customs, language, and traditions, the Huichol Indians come down from the Sierra Madre to sell their unusual art to Puerto Vallarta galleries. Inspired by visions received during spiritual ceremonies, the Huichol create their art with colorful yarn or beads pressed into wax. See "Shopping" in chapter 9.

- **Oaxacan Textiles:** The valley of Oaxaca produces the best weavings and naturally dyed textiles in Mexico; it's also famous for its pottery (especially the black pottery), and colorful, imaginative woodcarvings. See "Oaxaca City" in chapter 11.

- **The Markets of San Cristóbal de las Casas:** This city, deep in the heart of the Maya highlands, has shops, open plazas, and markets featuring distinctive waist-loomed wool and cotton textiles, as well as leather shoes, handsome pottery, genre dolls, and Guatemalan textiles. See "San Cristóbal de las Casas" in chapter 11.

10 The Hottest Nightlife

- **Polanco & Condesa, Mexico City:** Mexico City, like any world capital, has sizzling nightlife. Latin, Cuban, and alternative music rock in the Polanco neighborhood; Condesa is nicknamed the SoHo of Mexico City, due to its architecture and galleries. Its trendy club scene evokes the culture's roots in Madrid and Barcelona. Arrive fashionably late—the party doesn't start before midnight. See "Mexico City After Dark" in chapter 4.

- **Guadalajara's Sophisticated Scene:** Nightlife here extends to theater, classical music, jazz, and salsa, never forgetting mariachi music—which, when done properly, requires vocalists to really flaunt their talent. See "Guadalajara After Dark" in chapter 8.

- **Puerto Vallarta:** Of all the beach destinations, Puerto Vallarta enjoys the most sophisticated and varied nightlife. An excellent selection of small clubs features live jazz, blues, salsa, and good old rock 'n' roll. You'll also find mariachi, pre-Columbian, and traditional Mexican ballads. Heating up the scene are a new group of contemporary clubs and lounges with

DJs spinning house, trance, and chill. See "Puerto Vallarta" in chapter 9.

- **Acapulco Dance Clubs:** Nightlife can't possibly get more lavish, extravagant, or flashy than it is in Acapulco, Mexico's hands-down diva. This city's main cultural attractions are the clubs that jam until sunrise, several of which have walls of windows overlooking the bay. See "Acapulco" in chapter 10.

- **The Lively Offerings of San Cristóbal de las Casas:** Small though it may be, this city has a live-music scene that can't be beat for fun and atmosphere. It's inexpensive, too. This is the perfect place to do some barhopping: It offers variety, convenience (everything is within walking distance), and few if any cover charges. See "San Cristóbal de las Casas" in chapter 11.

- **Cancún's Clubs in Malls:** Cancún's wide-ranging hot spots include most of the name-brand nightlife destinations, concentrated in entertainment malls and festival shopping centers, as well as hotel-lobby bars with live music, and sophisticated dance clubs. Popular nightlife tours allow you to bypass lines and sample various clubs in a single night. The clubs here can accommodate up to 3,000, and there are plenty of options for staying out until the sun comes up. See "Cancún After Dark" in chapter 13.

- **Cabo San Lucas Beach Bars:** In the nightlife capital of Baja California, after-dark fun centers on the casual bars and restaurants that line the main drag, as well as those on the town's public Medano Beach. The place retains a rowdy, outlaw feel, despite the influx of tony hotels nearby. A new lounge scene is, thankfully, updating this lively town's nightlife. See "Los Cabos: Resorts, Watersports & Golf" in chapter 18.

11 The Best Luxury Hotels

- **Hotel Four Seasons** (Mexico City; ℭ 800/332-3442 in the U.S.): The standard of excellence in Mexico, and the most stylish choice in Mexico City, this hotel captures both serenity and elegance in a hacienda-style building that surrounds a picturesque courtyard. The gracious staff and offerings of unique cultural tours are bonuses. See p. 111.

- **W Mexico City** (Mexico City; ℭ 888/625-5144 in the U.S.): Stylish, comfortable, and high-tech, this dramatic new addition to Mexico City hotels has set the city abuzz. With its super-*caliente* red hues and lively bar scene, the W Mexico City has infused the country's capital with a dose of passion. Luxury extras include expansive bathrooms with circular tubs and walk-in showers with hanging hammocks. See p. 112.

- **Casa de Sierra Nevada Quinta Real** (San Miguel de Allende; ℭ 866/621-9288 in the U.S. and Canada): This luxury hotel has all the flavor of colonial Mexico; it's a collection of eight elegant colonial houses in one of the country's most appealing colonial towns. See p. 192.

- **Villa Montaña** (Morelia; ℭ 800/223-6510 in the U.S., or 800/448-8355 in Canada): The Villa Montaña defines perfection. From the layout of the grounds to the decoration of the rooms, every detail has been skillfully handled. The hotel perches on a ridge overlooking Morelia; from its terraces, guests can survey the city below. The restaurant is one of the city's best. See p. 245.

- **Four Seasons Resort Punta Mita** (north of Puerto Vallarta; ℭ 800/332-3442 in the U.S.): This luxury resort has soared in popularity since opening in 1999. It offers an unrivaled location (on a remote, pristine stretch of beach) and the stellar service characteristic of the Four Seasons chain. Also on-site are an expansive spa and a private Jack Nicklaus Signature golf course. See p. 329.

- **El Tamarindo** (between Manzanillo and Puerto Vallarta; ℭ 315/351-5032): The most exclusive remote resort in Mexico, this stylish place combines large private casitas facing the Pacific with a stunning private oceanfront golf course. Fellow guests are likely to be Hollywood celebrities and the well-to-do from around the world. It's about 1 hour north of Manzanillo along Costa Alegre. See p. 353.

- **Villa del Sol** (Zihuatanejo; ℭ 888/389-2645 in the U.S.): Few hotels meet the demanding standards of luxury and attention to detail required to be a member of the French Relais & Châteaux, but this small beachfront inn does. It's also a member of the Small Luxury Hotels of the World. See p. 406.

- **Hotel Camino Real** (Oaxaca; ✆ **800/ 722-6466** in the U.S.): No other hotel in Mexico captures the sense of antiquity as well as this one. It occupies a 16th-century convent in the middle of the best part of Oaxaca City and has several beautiful, tranquil courtyards where renovation efforts have carefully preserved the marks of time. See p. 447.

- **Ritz-Carlton Hotel** (Cancún; ✆ **800/ 241-3333** in the U.S. and Canada): In a resort known for high-rise luxury, this hotel is in a class of its own, with spectacular facilities fronting a perfect beach. You'll find spacious, beautifully furnished rooms, elegant dining, and exceptional service. See p. 526.

- **Le Méridien Cancún Resort & Spa** (Cancún; ✆ **800/543-4300** in the U.S. and Canada): In a resort known for high-rise luxury, this hotel is in a class of its own, with a more intimate, inviting ambience in its collection of services and rooms fronting a perfect beach. You'll find spacious, elegantly furnished rooms, delectable dining, and exceptional service. See p. 525.

- **Las Ventanas al Paraíso** (Los Cabos; ✆ **888/525-0483** in the U.S.): Stunning in its relaxed elegance, Las Ventanas comes complete with a deluxe European spa, excellent gourmet restaurant, and elegantly appointed rooms and suites. From fireplaces and telescopes to private pools and rooftop terraces, each suite is a private slice of heaven. See p. 716.

- **One&Only Palmilla** (Los Cabos; ✆ **800/637-2226** in the U.S.): Currently the most popular Mexican resort with the Hollywood crowd, the completely renovated Palmilla has regained its spot as the most deluxe hotel in this seaside playground known for sumptuous accommodations and great golf. The new, exceptional spa, fitness center, and yoga garden, as well as a restaurant by renowned chef Charlie Trotter are added bonuses. See p. 716.

12 The Best Unique Inns

- **Verana** (Yelapa; ✆ **800/677-5156**): The stylish Verana adds a dash of sophistication to funky Yelapa—a remote village accessible only by boat, about 45 minutes from Puerto Vallarta. Each of the six handcrafted *casas* has a unique architectural style that complements the expanse of vistas to the surrounding jungle and ocean. It's a perfect blend of style, romance, and nature. See p. 312.

- **Quinta María Cortez** (Puerto Vallarta; ✆ **888/640-8100** in the U.S.): This is one of the country's most original places to stay; it's an eclectic B&B uniquely decorated with antiques, curios, and original art. It sits on a beautiful cove on Conchas Chinas beach. See p. 311.

- **Hacienda San Angel** (Puerto Vallarta; ✆ **322/222-2692**): Once a villa owned by Richard Burton, this elegant B&B adds a sophisticated option to places to stay in this seaside resort. With a direct view to the signature Guadalupe church crown, the nine suites are exquisitely decorated in antiques, original art, and the finest in linens and amenities. Personalized service and its central location make it a true find in Mexico. See p. 309.

- **La Casa Que Canta** (Zihuatanejo; ✆ **888/523-5050** in the U.S.): This architecturally dramatic hotel incorporates wonderful Mexican adobe and folk art in grandly scaled rooms. It's a delightful place to unwind, read on the terrace overlooking the bay, and order room service. See p. 405.

- **Hotel Santa Fe** (Puerto Escondido; ℃ **954/582-0170**): This Spanish-colonial-style inn has a welcoming staff and comfortable rooms appointed with rustic wood furnishings. The hacienda-style buildings, splashed with bougainvillea, surround two courtyard swimming pools. Across the street is the famed surfing beach, Zicatela. The restaurant is one of the best on the Pacific coast. See p. 418.
- **Mesón de la Sacristía de la Compañía** (Puebla; ℃ **222/232-4513**): No other place captures the feel of colonial Mexico, or does it with as much fun, as this small hotel that doubles as a popular nightspot and antiques store. See p. 508.
- **Deseo Hotel + Lounge** (Playa del Carmen; ℃ **984/879-3620**): Perhaps it should be Hotel = Lounge. That might be an overstatement, but the lounge is at the center of everything, making Deseo the perfect fit for outgoing types who are into an alternative lodging experience. Enjoy a cocktail at the bar or on one of the large daybeds and chill to the modern lounge music. See p. 588.

- **Casa Mexilio Guest House** (Mérida; ℃ **800/538-6802** in the U.S.): An imaginative arrangement of rooms around a courtyard features a pool surrounded by a riot of tropical vegetation. The rooms are on different levels, connected by stairs and catwalks. Breakfast here provides extra incentive for getting out of bed. See p. 645.
- **Casa Natalia** (San José del Cabo; ℃ **888/277-3814** in the U.S.): This renovated historic home, now a charming inn, is an oasis of palms, waterfalls, and flowers against the desert landscape. Each room and suite is an artful combination of modern architecture and traditional Mexican touches. The restaurant is the hottest in town. See p. 711.
- **Posada Las Flores** (Loreto; ℃ **877/245-2860** in the U.S.): Adjacent to the main plaza in this town steeped in history, this inn is the perfect setting from which to explore—rooms are individually decorated in fine Mexican antiques and arts and crafts. It also boasts a rooftop glass-bottomed swimming pool. See p. 743.

13 The Best Inexpensive Inns

- **Best Western Hotel de Cortés** (Mexico City; ℃ **800/528-1234** in the U.S.): This historic building and former home of Augustinian friars offers exceptionally clean, comfortable, value-priced accommodations. It's on La Alameda park, near the Palace of Fine Arts and the Franz Mayer Museum. See p. 114.
- **Hotel Victoria** (Taxco; ℃ **762/622-0004**): With its pristine 1940s decor and fabulous hillside setting overlooking all of Taxco, this hotel gets special marks as an inexpensive inn that exudes all the charm of old-fashioned Mexico. See p. 163.

- **Hotel San Francisco Plaza** (Guadalajara; ℃ **33/3613-8954**): This two-story colonial-style hotel is a more agreeable place to stay than lodgings charging twice as much, and it's every bit as comfortable. It's in the downtown area, near the main plaza and several good restaurants and nightspots. See p. 270.
- **Hotel Flor de María** (Puerto Escondido; ℃ **954/582-0536**): This hotel is charming in every way, from the hospitable owners, Lino and María Francato, to the guest rooms individually decorated with Lino's fine artistic touches. The restaurant is the best in town. See p. 420.

- **Paraíso Escondido** (Puerto Escondido; ☎ 954/582-0444): This eclectic inn is a great bargain, especially for the originality of the decor, and the excellent service. It's a short walk to both the beach and the action along Puerto's main street. See p. 418.
- **Misión de los Arcos** (Huatulco; ☎ 958/587-0165): Just 1 block from the central plaza, this hotel has a similar style to the elegant Quinta Real, at a fraction of the cost. An all-white facade and intriguing decorative touches give it an inviting feel. There's shuttle service to the Huatulco beaches. See p. 431.
- **Las Golondrinas** (Oaxaca; ☎ 951/514-3298): We receive more favorable letters about this hotel than about any other in the country. It's small, simple, and colorful, with homey touches of folk art and pathways lined with abundant foliage. See p. 450.
- **Treetops** (Playa del Carmen; ☎ 984/873-0351): An economical, quiet hotel steps from both the beach and Avenida 5, Treetops could easily get by on location alone. But the owners have gone out of their way to create a distinctive lodging with plenty of amenities. The hotel has its own *cenote* and piece of shady jungle, making it a lovely place to relax after a trying day of strolling the beach and wandering the village streets. See p. 590.
- **Rey del Caribe Hotel** (Cancún; ☎ 998/884-2028): A unique oasis in downtown Cancun, this hotel has considered every detail to achieve the goal of living in an organic and environmentally friendly manner. Set in a tropical garden, the combination of sunny rooms, warm service, yoga and meditation classes, and healthful dining is a welcome respite to party-hearty Cancún. See p. 530.
- **Club Cabo Inn** (Cabo San Lucas; ☎ 624/143-3348): This former bordello is the best budget inn in the area. Rooms are small but extra clean and invitingly decorated, amenities are generous, and the owner-managers are friendly and helpful. Ideally located, close to town and near the marina, the inn caters to sportfishers. See p. 728.

14 The Best Spa Resorts

- **Hotel Spa Ixtapan** (Ixtapan; ☎ 800/638-7950 in the U.S.): In operation since 1939, this resort is a classic, traditional spa with consistently upgraded amenities and services. It's also close to the region's renowned thermal baths. See p. 166.
- **Misión Del Sol Resort & Spa** (Cuernavaca; ☎ 777/321-0999 in the U.S.): Mexico's finest spa resort, with every architectural and functional detail designed to soothe body and soul—from meditation rooms to reflexology showers to magnets under your mattress. The sumptuous, full-service spa and fitness center and delicious vegetarian cuisine make this a heavenly base for personal renewal. See p. 177.
- **Four Seasons Resort Punta Mita** (Punta Mita; ☎ 800/332-3442): The enticing spa at this posh resort is one of its principal appeals. The menu of spa services based on native Mexican therapies is an intriguing complement to the modern facilities and amenities. Located north of Puerto Vallarta. See p. 329.
- **Paradise Village** (Nuevo Vallarta; ☎ 800/995-5714): Excellent fitness facilities combined with pampering yet affordable spa services make this one of the best all-around spas in Mexico. It actively promotes the beneficial

properties of indigenous Mexican spa therapies and natural treatments. See p. 327.

- **Le Méridien Cancún Resort & Spa** (Cancún; ☎ **800/543-4300** in the U.S.): The Spa del Mar is a state-of-the-art, 1,400-sq.-m (15,000-sq.-ft.) facility bordering the brilliant Caribbean. It boasts the most complete spa in the area, with inhalation rooms, saunas, steam, Jacuzzis, cold plunges, Swiss showers, a cascading waterfall whirlpool, and 14 treatment rooms. There's also an expansive fitness center and salon services. See p. 525.

- **Ikal del Mar** (☎ **888/230-7330** in the U.S.); **Maroma** (☎ **866/454-9351** in the U.S.); and **Paraíso de la Bonita** (☎ **800/327-0200** in the U.S.): The area north of Playa del Carmen, around Puerto Morelos, is a hotbed of spa-resort luxury. These three establishments, in lovely settings, offer guests an impressive range of pampering treatments. And it's all just a half-hour or so from the Cancún airport. See p. 600.

- **El Tamarindo** (Costa Alegre; ☎ **315/351-5032**): Admittedly, the spa facilities at this resort are limited, but the spa director has creatively integrated the surrounding natural beauty and history into this spa—think massages on the beach, scrubs made from local volcanic mud, and their very special version of the ancient purification ritual, the *temazcal.* See p. 353.

- **Aqua** (Cancún; ☎ **800/343-7821** in the U.S.): This brand-new resort, part of the Fiesta Americana chain, was designed with the sense of "spa" *(salud por agua)* in mind—all colors and spaces carry a water theme. As for its actual spa, it's a 1,500 sq.-m (over 15,000-sq.-ft.) facility that blends Eastern, pre-Hispanic, and Western treatment philosophies. Tai Chi, yoga, and Pilates classes are offered, and you can indulge in a full array of massages and treatments. See p. 522.

- **Casa de los Sueños Resort & Spa Zenter** (Isla Mujeres; ☎ **998/877-0651**). This luxury B&B has a small but well-appointed spa and "Zenter," which is also accessible to nonguests. Highlights include yoga classes, massages, and holistic spa treatments, which take place either indoors or out, in one of the most tranquil places you'll find. See p. 555.

- **Las Ventanas al Paraíso** (Los Cabos; ☎ **888/525-0483** in the U.S.): This is an elegant and highly professional spa in one of the area's most exclusive resorts. See "The Best Luxury Hotels" above, and p. 716.

15 The Best Mexican Food & Drink

- **Fonda El Refugio, for Traditional Mexican Food** (Mexico City; ☎ **55/5207-2732**): This elegantly casual place prepares specialties from all over the country, including *manchamanteles* ("tablecloth stainers") on Tuesday and *albóndigas en chile chipotle* (meatballs in chipotle sauce) on Saturday. See p. 119.

- **El Nivel, to Experience a True Cantina** (Mexico City; ☎ **55/5522-9755**):

What a bar . . . this cantina has the honor of holding Mexico City liquor license #1, dating back 3 centuries. Once only the domain of men, cantinas in Mexico serve small plates of complimentary snacks as you continue to order rounds of drinks. El Nivel, located across from the Palacio de Gobierno, draws a crowd of politicians and journalists. See p. 120.

- **Adobe Fonda, for Inventive *Nueva Cocina*** (Tlaquepaque; ℂ 33/3657-2792): Delicious Mexican food served inside one of those gorgeous decorative arts stores that line Tlaquepaque's Calle Independencia. The point of departure for the food is some uncommon Mexican recipes, which are then given sparkling Italian and Argentine accents. See p. 271.

- **El Sacromonte, for Artful *Alta Cocina*** (Guadalajara; ℂ 33/3825-5447): Various dishes delight the senses with novel tastes and textures and skillful presentation. The menu describes each dish in Spanish couplets—a fun topic for conversation over an aperitif. See p. 272.

- **Arrayán, for Tacos Like You've Never Before Tasted** (Puerto Vallarta; ℂ 322/223-2963): The colorful atmosphere may be casual, funky, and fun, but the food is seriously and authentically Mexican. Prime beef filet tacos are just one specialty—others include Mexican duck confit, shrimp pozole, and homemade ice creams from indigenous fruits. See p. 316.

- **El Mirador, for Margaritas** (Acapulco, in the Hotel Plaza Las Glorias; ℂ 800/342-AMIGO in the U.S.): You can enjoy a great margarita at many places in Mexico, but this is the only one that serves them with a view of the spectacular La Quebrada cliff divers. See p. 387.

- **El Naranjo, for Oaxacan Cuisine** (Oaxaca; ℂ 951/514-1878): Oaxaca has an elaborate regional cuisine, and I am delighted by what El Naranjo does with it. Each day offers a different *mole* in addition to several uncommon dishes. This is a wonderful place for throwing caution to the wind—the owner is meticulous about cleaning and sterilizing foods. See p. 451.

- **Mariscos Villa Rica Mocambo, for Fresh Seafood, Veracruz Style** (Veracruz; ℂ 229/922-2113): Nobody else does seafood the way Veracruz does seafood, and this restaurant is the showcase for the region's cuisine. See p. 493.

- **100% Natural, for Licuados:** *Licuados,* drinks made from fresh fruit mixed with water or milk, are much more popular than soft drinks. This restaurant chain offers the widest selection, including innovative mixtures like the Cozumel (spinach, pineapple, and orange) and the Caligula (orange, pineapple, beet, celery, parsley, carrot, and lime juices)—a healthy indulgence. Branches in Puerto Vallarta, Acapulco, and Cancún.

2

Planning Your Trip to Mexico

A little planning can make the difference between a good trip and a great trip. When should you go? What's the best way to get there? How much should you plan on spending? What festivals or special events will occur during your visit? What safety or health precautions should you take? We'll answer these and other questions in this chapter. In addition to these basics, I highly recommend taking a little time to learn about the culture and traditions of Mexico. It can make the difference between simply getting away for a few days and truly adding cultural understanding to your trip. See appendix A for more details.

1 The Regions in Brief

BAJA CALIFORNIA A peninsula longer than Italy, Baja stretches 1,402km (876 miles) from its border with California at Mexico's northernmost city of **Tijuana** to **Cabo San Lucas** at its southern tip. On one side is the Pacific Ocean; on the other, the **Sea of Cortez.** Volcanic uplifting created the craggy desertscape you see today. Culturally and geographically, Baja sits apart from mainland Mexico, and it remained isolated for centuries. A vacation haven, it offers golf, fishing, diving, and whale-watching in beautiful settings and at posh resorts.

THE COPPER CANYON The Copper Canyon is the common name for a region of roughly 16,800 sq. km (6,500 sq. miles) in the northern state of Chihuahua, midway between the state's capital city and the Pacific coast. Here you'll find a network of canyons deeply etched into the volcanic rock of the **Sierra Tarahumara.** The dramatic canyon area is one of those rare places where one can sense the earth's creation. To get there, you ride the famous Chihuahua al Pacífico railroad. It starts at the seaport of Topolobampo, outside **Los Mochis,** and runs 620km

(390 miles) to **Chihuahua City,** climbing to 2,120m (7,000 ft.) above sea level in the process. The train skirts the edge of more than 20 canyons. Tours can accommodate any kind of traveler, from primitive camper to modern hotel patron.

THE PACIFIC COAST The Pacific coast has virtually every kind of beach and landscape imaginable. You can stay in modern resorts that offer inexhaustible arrays of amenities and activities, from sailing to scuba diving to golf, capped off by exuberant nightlife. Or you can stay in a sleepy coastal town where the scenery abounds with rustic charm, life is slower, and the beaches are quieter. By **Mazatlán,** the northern desert disappears, replaced by tropical vegetation and plantations of coconut and other fruit. At **Puerto Vallarta,** mountains covered in tropical forests meet the sea. For many, this is the most appealing place on the coast. From here, it's a 5-hour car ride inland to **Guadalajara,** the most Mexican of cities and a superb place to shop. Tropical forests interspersed with banana, mango, and coconut palm plantations cover the coast from Puerto Vallarta to **Manzanillo.**

Map Pointer

To locate these regions, please turn to the map of Mexico on p. 8.

Well south of Manzanillo, in the state of Guerrero, are the beach towns **Zihuatanejo** and **Ixtapa.** Tree-covered mountains remain around **Acapulco,** though hillside development has marred them. From Acapulco, a road leads inland to **Taxco,** a mountainside colonial city famed for its hundreds of silver shops. Farther south along the coast are the beach villages of **Puerto Escondido** and **Puerto Angel,** and beyond them, the nine gorgeous bays of **Huatulco.**

THE NORTH-CENTRAL REGION This funnel-shaped region stretches from the northern border with Texas and New Mexico to **Mexico City** and includes the beautiful colonial **silver cities.** The majority of this territory lies in the vast Chihuahua/Coahuila desert of the north between the two great **Sierra Madre ranges,** which meet in the south to form the central valley of Mexico. The colonial cities nestle in the mountains not far north and west of Mexico City.

THE GULF COAST Of all Mexico, this region is probably the least known, yet the whole coast, which includes the long, skinny state of Veracruz, holds marvelous pockets of scenery and culture. Highway 180 leads from **Matamoros** at the Texas border and offers a few glimpses of the Gulf of Mexico. Highlights of this region are the ruins of **El Tajín,** near the mountain village of Papantla; the mountain town of **Xalapa,** Veracruz's capital and home of the magnificent Museo de Antropología; and the lively, colorful port of **Veracruz.** This is a good region to visit if you're longing for the Mexico of yesteryear.

TARASCAN COUNTRY This region, in the state of Michoacán, presents two distinct visions of colonial architecture: **Pátzcuaro,** a town of tile roofs and adobe

walls painted traditional white with dark red borders; and **Morelia,** a stately city of stone mansions, broad plazas, and a monumental cathedral. The eastern part of the state consists of high mountains with large tracts of pine and fir forests. Every year, millions of **monarch butterflies** make the long journey to congregate in a small part of the forest here. The central part of the state, a land of lakes, is the homeland of the Purépecha or Tarascan Indians. The villages throughout this area specialize in crafts for which the region is well known. Farther west lie the hot lands and the coast. Tourists largely neglect Michoacán, except during the Days of the Dead.

OAXACA & CHIAPAS This is the southern land of the Zapotec, Mixtec, and Maya cultures. Most people fly around this region, but a toll highway from near Puebla to **Oaxaca City** makes the area more accessible by car. The valley of Oaxaca is one of the grandest places in Mexico: fascinating Indian villages everywhere, beautiful ruins, and a wonderful colonial city. **San Cristóbal de las Casas,** in Chiapas, is harder to get to, but definitely worth the effort. Approaching San Cristóbal from any direction, you see small plots of corn tended by colorfully clad Maya. Oaxaca and Chiapas are rich in craftspeople, from woodcarvers to potters to weavers.

THE YUCATAN PENINSULA Travelers to the peninsula have an opportunity to see pre-Hispanic ruins—such as **Chichén Itzá, Uxmal,** and **Tulum**—and the living descendants of the cultures that built them, as well as the ultimate in resort Mexico: **Cancún.** The peninsula borders the dull aquamarine Gulf of Mexico on the west and north, and the clear blue

Caribbean on the east. It covers almost 217,560 sq. km (84,000 sq. miles), with nearly 1,600km (1,000 miles) of shoreline.

Lovely rock-walled Maya villages and crumbling henequén haciendas dot the interior of the peninsula. The placid interior contrasts with the hubbub of the Caribbean coast. From Cancún south to **Chetumal,** the jungle coastline is spotted with all kinds of development, from posh to budget. It also boasts an enormous array of wildlife, including hundreds of species of birds. National parks near **Celestún** and **Río Lagartos** on the Gulf Coast are home to amazing flocks of flamingos.

2 Visitor Information

The **Mexico Hot Line** (© 800/44-**MEXICO**) is an excellent source for general information; you can request brochures on the country and get answers to the most common questions from the exceptionally well-trained, knowledgeable staff.

More information (15,000 pages' worth) about Mexico is available on the official site of Mexico's Tourism Promotion Board, **www.visitmexico.com**. The **U.S. State Department** (© 202/647-5225; www.travel.state.gov) offers **Travel Warnings** and a **Consular Information Sheet** on Mexico with safety, medical, driving, and general travel information gleaned from reports by its offices in Mexico, and consistently updated. You can also request the Consular Information Sheet by fax (© 202/647-3000). The **Centers for Disease Control and Prevention Hot Line** (© 800/311-3435 or 404/639-3534; www.cdc.gov) is a source of medical information for travelers to Mexico and elsewhere. For travelers to Mexico and Central America, the number with recorded messages is © 877/FYI-TRIP. The toll-free fax number for requesting information is © 888/232-3299. Information available by fax is also available at **www.cdc.gov/travel**. The U.S. State Department website (see above) also offers medical information for Americans traveling abroad and a list of air ambulance services.

The **Mexican Government Tourist Board** has offices in major North American cities, in addition to the main office in Mexico City (© 555/203-1103). In the **United States:** Chicago (© 312/606-9252), Houston (© 713/772-2581, ext. 105, or 713/772-3819), Los Angeles (© 310/282-9112), and New York (© 212/308-2110).

The **Mexican Embassy** in the United States is at 1911 Pennsylvania Ave. N.W., Washington, DC 20005 (© 202/728-1750). In Canada: 1 Place Ville-Marie, Suite 1931, Montreal, QUE, H3B 2C3 (© 514/871-1052); 2 Bloor St. W., Suite 1502, Toronto, ON, M4W 3E2 (© 416/925-0704); 999 W. Hastings, Suite 1110, Vancouver, BC, V6C 2W2 (© 604/669-2845). Embassy office: 1500-45 O'Connor St., Ottawa, ON, K1P 1A4 (© 613/233-8988; fax 613/235-9123).

3 Entry Requirements & Customs

ENTRY REQUIREMENTS

All travelers to Mexico are required to present **proof of citizenship,** such as an original birth certificate with a raised seal, a valid passport, or naturalization papers. Those using a birth certificate should also have current photo identification, such as a driver's license or official ID. If the last name on the birth certificate is different from your current name, bring a photo identification card *and* legal proof of the name change, such as the original marriage license or certificate. *Note:* Photocopies are *not* acceptable.

The best ID is a passport. Safeguard your passport in an inconspicuous, inaccessible place like a money belt, and keep a copy of the critical pages with your passport number in a separate place. If you lose your passport, visit the nearest consulate of your native country as soon as possible for a replacement.

For information on how to get a passport, go to "Passports" in the "Fast Facts" section of this chapter—the websites listed provide downloadable passport applications as well as the current fees for processing passport applications. For an up-to-date country-by-country listing of passport requirements around the world, go to the "Passports" section of the U.S. State Department's website (see above).

You must carry a **Mexican Tourist Permit (FMT),** the equivalent of a tourist visa, which Mexican border officials issue, free of charge, after proof of citizenship is accepted. Airlines generally provide the necessary forms aboard your flight to Mexico. The FMT is more important than a passport, so guard it carefully. If you lose it, you may not be permitted to leave until you can replace it—a bureaucratic hassle that can take anywhere from a few hours to a week.

The FMT can be issued for up to 180 days. Sometimes officials don't ask but just stamp a time limit, so be sure to say "6 months," or at least twice as long as you intend to stay. If you decide to extend your stay, you may request that additional time be added to your FMT from an official immigration office in Mexico.

In **Baja California,** immigration laws have changed; they allow FMTs for a maximum of 180 days per year, with a maximum of 30 days per visit. This is to encourage regular visitors, or those who spend longer periods in Mexico, to obtain documents that denote partial residency.

For travelers entering Mexico by car at the border of Baja California, note that FMTs are issued only in Tijuana, Tecate, and Mexicali, as well as in Ensenada and Guerrero Negro. If you travel anywhere beyond the frontier zone without the FMT, you will be fined $40. Permits for driving a foreign-plated car in Mexico are available only in Tijuana, Ensenada, Tecate, Mexicali, and La Paz.

Note: Children under age 18 traveling without parents or with only one parent must have a notarized letter from the absent parent(s) authorizing the travel.

CUSTOMS
WHAT YOU CAN BRING INTO MEXICO
When you enter Mexico, Customs officials will be tolerant as long as you have no illegal drugs or firearms. You're allowed to bring in two cartons of cigarettes or 50 cigars, plus 1 kilogram (2.2 lb.) of smoking tobacco; two 1-liter bottles of wine or hard liquor, and 12 rolls of film. A laptop computer, camera equipment, and sports equipment that could feasibly be used during your stay are also allowed. The underlying guideline is: Don't bring anything that looks as if it's meant to be resold in Mexico.

WHAT YOU CAN TAKE HOME
Returning **U.S. citizens** who have been away for at least 48 hours are allowed to bring back, once every 30 days, $800 worth of merchandise duty-free. You'll be charged a flat rate of 4% duty on the next $1,000 worth of purchases. Any dollar amount beyond that is dutiable at whatever rates apply. On mailed gifts, the duty-free limit is $200. Be sure to have your receipts or purchases handy to expedite the declaration process. *Note:* If you owe duty, you are required to pay on your arrival in the United States, by either cash, personal check, government or traveler's check, or money order, and in some locations, a Visa or MasterCard.

To avoid having to pay duty on foreign-made personal items you owned before you left on your trip, bring along a bill of sale, insurance policy, jeweler's appraisal, or receipts of purchase. Or you can register items that can be readily identified by a permanently affixed serial number or marking—think laptop computers, cameras, and CD players—with Customs before you leave. Take the items to the nearest Customs office or register them with Customs at the airport from which you're departing. You'll receive, at no cost, a Certificate of Registration, which allows duty-free entry for the life of the item.

With some exceptions, you cannot bring fresh fruits and vegetables into the United States. For specifics on what you can bring back, download the invaluable free pamphlet *Know Before You Go* online at **www.cbp.gov**. (Click on "Travel," and then click on "Know Before You Go.") Or contact the **U.S. Customs & Border Protection (CBP),** 1300 Pennsylvania Ave., NW, Washington, DC 20229 (© **877/ 287-8667**), and request the pamphlet.

For a clear summary of **Canadian** rules, write for the booklet *I Declare,* issued by the **Canada Customs and Revenue Agency** (© **800/461-9999** in Canada, or 204/983-3500; www.cra-arc. gc.ca). Canada allows its citizens a C$750 exemption, and you're allowed to bring back duty-free one carton of cigarettes, 1 can of tobacco, 40 imperial ounces of liquor, and 50 cigars. In addition, you're allowed to mail gifts to Canada valued at less than C$60 a day, provided they're unsolicited and don't contain alcohol or tobacco (write on the package "Unsolicited gift, under $60 value"). All valuables should be declared on the Y-38 form before departure from Canada, including serial numbers of valuables you already own, such as expensive foreign cameras. *Note:* The C$750 exemption can only be used once a year and only after an absence of 7 days.

U.K. citizens returning from **a non-E.U. country** have a customs allowance of: 200 cigarettes; 50 cigars; 250 grams of smoking tobacco; 2 liters of still table wine; 1 liter of spirits or strong liqueurs (over 22% volume); 2 liters of fortified wine, sparkling wine or other liqueurs; 60 cubic centimeters (ml) perfume; 250 cubic centimeters (ml) of toilet water; and £145 worth of all other goods, including gifts and souvenirs. People under 17 cannot have the tobacco or alcohol allowance. For more information, contact **HM Customs & Excise** at © **0845/010-9000** (020/8929-0152 from outside the U.K.), or consult the website at www.hmce. gov.uk.

The duty-free allowance in **Australia** is A$400 or, for those under 18, A$200. Citizens can bring in 250 cigarettes or 250 grams of loose tobacco, and 1,125 milliliters of alcohol. If you're returning with valuables you already own, such as foreign-made cameras, you should file form B263. A helpful brochure available from Australian consulates or Customs offices is *Know Before You Go.* For more information, call the **Australian Customs Service** at © **1300/363-263,** or log on to www. customs.gov.au.

The duty-free allowance for **New Zealand** is NZ$700. Citizens over 17 can bring in 200 cigarettes, 50 cigars, or 250 grams of tobacco (or a mixture of all three if their combined weight doesn't exceed 250g); plus 4.5 liters of wine and beer, or 1.125 liters of liquor. New Zealand currency does not carry import or export restrictions. Fill out a certificate of export, listing the valuables you are taking out of the country; that way, you can bring them back without paying duty. Most questions are answered in a free pamphlet available at New Zealand consulates and Customs offices: *New Zealand Customs Guide for Travellers, Notice no. 4.* For more information, contact **New Zealand Customs,** The Customhouse, 17–21 Whitmore St., Box 2218, Wellington (© **04/473-6099** or 0800/428-786; www.customs.govt.nz).

GOING THROUGH CUSTOMS

Mexican Customs inspection has been streamlined. At most points of entry, tourists are requested to press a button in front of what looks like a traffic signal, which alternates on touch between red and green. Green light and you go through without inspection; red light and your luggage or car may be inspected. If you have an unusual amount of luggage or an oversized piece, you may be subject to inspection anyway.

4 Money

CURRENCY

The currency in Mexico is the **peso.** Paper currency comes in denominations of 20, 50, 100, 200, and 500 pesos. Coins come in denominations of 1, 2, 5, 10, and 20 pesos, and 20 and 50 **centavos** (100 centavos = 1 peso). The current exchange rate for the U.S. dollar, and the one used in this book, is around 11 pesos; at that rate, an item that costs 11 pesos would be equivalent to US$1.

Getting **change** is a problem. Small-denomination bills and coins are hard to come by, so start collecting them early in your trip. Shopkeepers everywhere always seem to be out of change and small bills; that's doubly true in markets.

Many establishments that deal with tourists, especially in coastal resort areas, quote prices in dollars. To avoid confusion, they use the abbreviations "Dlls." for dollars and "M.N." (*moneda nacional*, or national currency) for pesos.

The rate of exchange fluctuates daily, so you probably are better off not exchanging too much currency at once. Don't forget to have enough pesos to carry you over a weekend or Mexican holiday, when banks are closed. In general, avoid carrying the U.S. $100 bill, the bill most commonly counterfeited in Mexico and therefore the most difficult to exchange, especially in smaller towns. Because small bills and coins in pesos are hard to come by in Mexico, the $1 bill is very useful for tipping. A tip of U.S. coins, which cannot be exchanged into Mexican currency, is of no value to the service provider.

The bottom line on exchanging money: Ask first, and shop around. Banks generally pay the top rates.

Casas de cambio (exchange houses) are generally more convenient than banks because they have more locations and longer hours; the rate of exchange may be the same as at a bank or slightly lower. Before leaving a bank or exchange-house window, count your change in front of the teller before the next client steps up.

Large airports have currency-exchange counters that often stay open whenever flights are operating. Though convenient, they generally do not offer the most favorable rates.

A hotel's exchange desk commonly pays less favorable rates than banks; however, when the currency is in a state of flux, higher-priced hotels are known to pay higher rates than banks, in an effort to attract dollars. *Note:* In almost all cases, you receive a better rate by changing money first, then paying.

It's a good idea to exchange at least some money—just enough to cover airport incidentals and transportation to your hotel—before you leave home (though don't expect the exchange rate to be ideal), so

Money Matters

The **universal currency sign ($)** is used to indicate pesos in Mexico. The use of this symbol in this book, however, denotes U.S. currency.

Tips A Few Words about Prices

The peso's value continues to fluctuate—at press time, it was roughly 11 pesos to the dollar. Prices in this book (which are always given in U.S. dollars) have been converted to U.S. dollars at 11 pesos to the dollar. Most hotels in Mexico— with the exception of places that receive little foreign tourism—quote prices in U.S. dollars. Thus, currency fluctuations are unlikely to affect the prices most hotels charge.

Mexico has a **value-added tax** of 15% (*Impuesto de Valor Agregado*, or IVA; pronounced "ee-vah") on most everything, including restaurant meals, bus tickets, and souvenirs. (Exceptions are Cancún, Cozumel, and Los Cabos, where the IVA is 10%; as ports of entry, they receive a break on taxes.) Hotels charge the usual 15% IVA, plus a locally administered bed tax of 2% (in most areas), for a total of 17%. In Cancún, Los Cabos, and Cozumel, hotels charge the 10% IVA plus 2% room tax. The prices quoted by hotels and restaurants do not necessarily include IVA. You may find that upper-end properties (three or more stars) quote prices without IVA included, while lower-priced hotels include IVA. Always ask to see a printed price sheet and always ask if the tax is included.

---

you can avoid lines at airport ATMs (automated teller machines). You can exchange money at your local American Express or Thomas Cook office or your bank. If you're far away from a bank with currency-exchange services, **American Express** offers travelers checks and foreign currency, though with a $15 order fee and additional shipping costs, at © **800/807-6233** or www.americanexpress.com.

BANKS & ATMs

Banks in Mexico are rapidly expanding and improving services. They tend to be open weekdays from 9am until 5pm, and often for at least a half day on Saturday. In larger resorts and cities, they can generally accommodate the exchange of dollars (which used to stop at noon) anytime during business hours. During times when the currency is in flux, a particular bank may not exchange dollars, so check before standing in line. Some, but not all, banks charge a service fee of about 1% to exchange traveler's checks. However, you can pay for most purchases directly with traveler's checks at the establishment's stated exchange rate. Don't even bother with personal checks drawn on a U.S.

bank—the bank will wait for your check to clear, which can take weeks, before giving you your money.

Travelers to Mexico can easily withdraw money from **ATMs** (automated teller machine) in most major cities and resort areas. The U.S. State Department has an advisory against using ATMs in Mexico for safety reasons, stating that they should only be used during business hours, but this pertains primarily to Mexico City, where crime remains a significant problem. In most resorts in Mexico, the use of ATMs is perfectly safe—just use the same precautions you would at any ATM. Universal bank cards (such as the Cirrus and PLUS systems) can be used. This is a convenient way to withdraw money and avoid carrying too much with you at any time. The exchange rate is generally more favorable than that at a *casas de cambio*. Most machines offer Spanish/English menus and dispense pesos, but some offer the option of withdrawing dollars. The **Cirrus** (© **800/424-7787**; www.mastercard.com) and **PLUS** (© **800/843-7587**; www.visa.com) networks span the globe; look at the back of your bank card to see which network you're on, then call or check online for ATM locations at your destination. Be sure you know your personal identification number (PIN) before you leave home and be sure to find out your daily withdrawal limit before you depart. Also keep in mind that many banks impose a fee every time a card is used at a different bank's ATM, and that fee can be higher for international transactions (up to $5 or more) than for domestic ones (where they're rarely more than $1.50). On top of this, the bank from which you withdraw cash may charge its own fee. To compare banks' ATM fees within the U.S., use www.bankrate.com. For international withdrawal fees, ask your bank.

You can also get cash advances on your credit card at an ATM. Keep in mind that credit card companies try to protect themselves from theft by limiting the funds someone can withdraw outside their home country, so call your credit card company before you leave home. And keep in mind that you'll pay interest from the moment of your withdrawal, even if you pay your monthly bills on time.

TRAVELER'S CHECKS

Traveler's checks are something of an anachronism from the days before the ATM made cash accessible at any time. Traveler's checks used to be the only sound alternative to traveling with dangerously large amounts of cash. They were as reliable as currency, but, unlike cash, could be replaced if lost or stolen.

These days, traveler's checks are less necessary because most cities have 24-hour ATMs that allow you to withdraw small amounts of cash as needed. However, keep in mind that you will likely be charged an ATM withdrawal fee if the bank is not your own, so if you're withdrawing money every day, you might be better off with traveler's checks—provided that you don't mind showing identification every time you want to cash one.

You can get traveler's checks at almost any bank. You can also get **American Express** traveler's checks over the phone by calling ⓒ **800/221-7282;** Amex gold and platinum cardholders who use this number are exempt from the 1% fee.

Visa offers traveler's checks at Citibank locations nationwide, as well as at several other banks. Call ⓒ **800/732-1322** for information. AAA members can obtain Visa checks without a fee at most AAA offices or by calling ⓒ **866/339-3378.** **MasterCard** also offers traveler's checks. Call ⓒ **800/223-9920** for a location near you.

If you choose to carry traveler's checks, be sure to keep a record of their serial numbers separate from your checks in the event that they are stolen or lost. You'll get a refund faster if you know the numbers.

CREDIT CARDS

Credit cards are a safe way to carry money: They also provide a convenient record of all your expenses, and they generally offer relatively good exchange rates. You can

---

⎛Tips Dear Visa: I'm Off to Cancún!

Some credit card companies recommend that you notify them of any impending trip abroad so that they don't become suspicious and block your charges when the card is used numerous times in a foreign destination. Even if you don't call your credit card company in advance, you can always call the toll-free emergency number (see "Fast Facts," later in this chapter) if a charge is refused—a good reason to carry the phone number with you. But perhaps the most important lesson is to carry more than one card on your trip; if one card doesn't work for any number of reasons, you'll have a backup.

also withdraw cash advances from your credit cards at banks or ATMs, provided you know your PIN. If you've forgotten yours, or didn't even know you had one, call the number on the back of your credit card and ask the bank to send it to you. It usually takes 5 to 7 business days, though some banks will provide the number over the phone if you tell them your mother's maiden name or some other personal information.

Keep in mind that when you use your credit card abroad, most banks assess a 2% fee above the 1% fee charged by Visa, MasterCard, or American Express for currency conversion on credit charges. But credit cards still may be the smart way to go when you factor in things like exorbitant ATM fees and higher traveler's check exchange rates (and service fees).

In Mexico Visa, MasterCard, and American Express are the most accepted cards. You'll be able to charge most hotel, restaurant, and store purchases, as well as almost all airline tickets, on your credit card. You generally can't charge gasoline purchases in Mexico. You can get cash advances of several hundred dollars on your card, but there may be a wait of 20 minutes to 2 hours.

Charges will be made in pesos, then converted into dollars by the bank issuing the credit card. Generally you receive the favorable bank rate when paying by credit card. However, be aware that some establishments in Mexico add a 5% to 7% surcharge when you pay with a credit card. This is especially true when using American Express. Many times, advertised discounts will not apply if you pay with a credit card.

For tips and telephone numbers to call if your wallet is stolen or lost, go to "Lost & Found" in the "Fast Facts" section of this chapter.

5 When to Go

SEASONS

Mexico has two principal travel seasons. **High season** begins around December 20 and continues to Easter; in some places it begins as early as mid-November. **Low season** is from the day after Easter to mid-December; during low season, prices may drop 20% to 50%. In beach destinations popular with Mexican travelers, such as Veracruz and Acapulco, prices will revert to high season during July and August, the traditional national summer vacation period. Prices in inland cities seldom fluctuate from high to low season, but may rise dramatically during the weeks of **Easter** and **Christmas.** Taxco and Pátzcuaro raise prices during their popular Easter-week celebrations. In Isla Mujeres and Playa del Carmen, on the Yucatán Peninsula, high season starts earlier than in the rest of the country and includes the month of August, when many European visitors and Mexican families arrive. The chapters that follow mention all of these exceptions and others.

Mexico has two main climate seasons: **rainy** (May to mid-Oct) and **dry** (mid-Oct to Apr). The rainy season can be of little consequence in the dry, northern region of the country. Southern regions typically receive tropical showers, which begin around 4 or 5pm and last a few hours. Though these rains can come on suddenly and be quite strong, they usually end just as quickly and cool off the air for the evening. **Hurricane season** particularly affects the Yucatán Peninsula and the southern Pacific coast, especially June through October. However, if no hurricanes strike, the light, cooling winds, especially September through November, can make it a perfect time to tackle the pre-Hispanic ruins that dot the interior of the peninsula.

Norte (**northern**) **season** runs from late November to mid-January, when the jet stream dips far south and creates northerly winds and showers in many resort areas. These showers usually only last for a couple of days.

June, July, and August are unrelentingly hot on the Yucatán Peninsula and in most coastal areas, though temperatures rise only into the mid-80s to 90°F (mid-20s to 32°C). Most of coastal Mexico experiences temperatures in the 80s°F (20s°C) in the hottest months. The northern states that border the United States experience very high summer temperatures.

Elevation is another important factor. High-elevation cities such as Mexico City and San Cristóbal de las Casas can be surprisingly cold. Temperatures can drop close to freezing at night in winter even in San Miguel de Allende and Guanajuato, which are at lower elevations.

MEXICO CALENDAR OF EVENTS

During national holidays, Mexican banks and governmental offices—including immigration—are closed.

January

Año Nuevo (New Year's Day). This national holiday is perhaps the quietest day in all of Mexico. Most people stay home or attend church. All businesses are closed. In traditional indigenous communities, new tribal leaders are inaugurated with colorful ceremonies rooted in the pre-Hispanic past. January 1.

Día de los Reyes (Three Kings Day), nationwide. This day commemorates the Three Kings' bringing of gifts to the Christ Child. On this day, children receive gifts, much like the traditional Christmas gift-giving in the United States. Friends and families gather to share the Rosca de Reyes, a special cake. Inside the cake is a small doll representing the Christ Child; whoever receives the doll must host a tamales-and-*atole* (a warm drink made of corn dough) party on February 2. January 6.

Regional Fair, León, Guanajuato. One of Mexico's largest fairs celebrates the founding of this shoemaking and leather-craft city. There are parades, theater, craft exhibits, music, and dance. www.ferialeon.com.mx. Month of January.

Feast of San Antonio Abad, Mexico City. This feast is celebrated through the Blessing of the Animals at the Santiago Tlatelolco Church on the Plaza of Three Cultures, at San Juan Bautista Church in Coyoacán, and at the Church of San Fernando, 2 blocks north of the Juárez-Reforma intersection. January 17.

February

Día de la Candelaria (Candlemas), nationwide. Music, dances, processions, food, and other festivities lead up to a blessing of seed and candles in a ceremony that mixes pre-Hispanic and European traditions marking the end of winter. Those who attended the Three Kings celebration reunite to share *atole* and tamales at a party hosted by the recipient of the doll found in the Rosca. February 2.

Día de la Constitución (Constitution Day). This national holiday is in honor of the current Mexican constitution, signed in 1917 as a result of the revolutionary war of 1910. It's celebrated through small parades. February 5.

Carnaval. Carnaval takes place the 3 days preceding Ash Wednesday and the beginning of Lent. The cities of Tepoztlán, Huejotzingo, Chamula, Veracruz, Cozumel, and Mazatlán celebrate with special gusto. In some places, such as Veracruz, Mazatlán, and Cozumel, the celebration resembles New Orleans's Mardi Gras, with a festive atmosphere and parades. In Chamula, the event harks back to pre-Hispanic times, with ritualistic running on flaming branches. On Shrove Tuesday in Tepoztlán and Huejotzingo, brilliantly clad masked dancers fill the streets. Transportation and hotels are packed, so it's best to make reservations 6 months in advance and arrive a couple of days ahead of the beginning of celebrations.

Ash Wednesday. The start of Lent and time of abstinence, this is a day of reverence nationwide; some towns honor it with folk dancing and fairs.

March

Annual Witches Conference, Lake Catemaco, Veracruz. Shamans, white witches, black witches, and practitioners of macumba, Caribbean, Afro, and Antillean ritualistic practices gather on the shores of the lake. Taking place the first Friday night of March every year, the annual gathering is a spectacle of witches, healers, magicians, and wizards. March 3.

Benito Juárez's Birthday. This national holiday is observed through small hometown celebrations countrywide, especially in Juárez's birthplace, Guelatao, Oaxaca. March 21.

Spring Equinox, Chichén Itzá. On the first day of spring, the Temple of Kukulkán—Chichén Itzá's main pyramid—aligns with the sun, and the shadow of the plumed serpent moves slowly from the top of the building down. When the shadow reaches the bottom, the body joins the carved stone snake's head at the base of the pyramid. According to ancient legend, at the moment that the serpent is whole, the earth is fertilized. Visitors come from around the world to marvel at this sight, so advance arrangements are advisable. March 21. (The shadow appears Mar 19–23.) Elsewhere, equinox festivals and celebrations welcome spring, in the custom of the ancient Mexicans, with dances and prayers to the elements and the four cardinal points. It's customary to wear white with a red ribbon.

April

Semana Santa (Holy Week). Mexico celebrates the last week in the life of Christ, from Palm Sunday to Easter Sunday, with somber religious processions almost nightly, spoofing of Judas, and reenactments of biblical events, plus food and craft fairs. Among the Tarahumara Indians in the Copper Canyon, celebrations have pre-Hispanic overtones. Pátzcuaro, Taxco, and Malinalco hold special celebrations. Businesses close during this traditional week of Mexican national vacations.

If you plan on traveling to or around Mexico during Holy Week, make your reservations early. Seats on flights into and out of the country will be reserved months in advance. Buses to these towns and to almost anywhere else in Mexico will be full, so try arriving on the Wednesday or Thursday before Good Friday. Easter Sunday is quiet, and the week following is a traditional vacation period. Early April.

San Marcos National Fair, Aguascalientes. Mexico's largest fair, first held in 1604, lasts 22 days. About a million visitors come for bullfights and rodeos as well as *ranchera* music and mariachis. There are craft and industrial exhibits, markets, fireworks, and folk dancing. April 12 to May 4.

Festival del Centro Historico (Annual Mexico City Festival), Mexico City. Regarded as one of Latin America's most vibrant celebrations of art and culture, this 2-week festival features diverse events including opera, concerts, theater, art exhibits, dance productions, and gourmet fare. Proceeds go toward the rescue and restoration of the art and architecture of Mexico City's historic downtown area. www.fchmexico.com. April 15 to 28.

May

Labor Day. National holiday. Workers' parades countrywide; everything closes. May 1.

Cinco de Mayo, Puebla and nationwide. This national holiday celebrates the defeat of the French at the Battle of Puebla. May 5.

Feast of San Isidro. A blessing of seeds and work animals honors the patron saint of farmers. May 15.

June

Día de la Marina (Navy Day). All coastal towns celebrate the holiday, with naval parades and fireworks. June 1.

Corpus Christi. This day, celebrated nationwide, honors the Body of Christ (the Eucharist) with processions, Masses, and food. Festivities include performances of *voladores* (flying pole dancers) beside the church and at the ruins of El Tajín, Veracruz. In Mexico City, children dressed as Indians and carrying decorated baskets of fruit for the priest's blessing gather with their parents before the National Cathedral.

Mulitas (mules), handmade from dried cornhusks and painted, are traditionally sold outside all churches on that day to represent a prayer for fertility. Dates vary.

National Ceramics Fair and Fiesta, Tlaquepaque, Jalisco. This pottery center on the outskirts of Guadalajara offers craft demonstrations and competitions as well as mariachis, dancers, and colorful parades. June 14 to July 14.

Día de San Pedro (St. Peter and St. Paul Day). This national feast day is celebrated wherever St. Peter is the patron saint; it also honors anyone named Pedro or Peter. It's especially festive at San Pedro Tlaquepaque, near Guadalajara, with numerous mariachi bands, folk dancers, and parades with floats. June 29.

July

Guelaguetza Dance Festival, Oaxaca. This is one of Mexico's most popular events. Villagers from the seven regions around Oaxaca gather in the city's amphitheater. They dress in traditional costumes, and many wear colorful "dancing" masks. The celebration dates from pre-Hispanic times. Make advance reservations—this festival attracts visitors from around the world. Call ✆ **800/44-MEXICO** for details and schedule. Late July.

August

Fiestas de la Vendimia (Wine Harvest Festival), Ensenada, Baja California. A food and wine festival celebrating the annual harvest, with blessings, seminars, parties, and wine tastings. Call ✆ **800/44-MEXICO** for details and schedule. Mid- to late August.

International Chamber Music Festival, San Miguel de Allende. Held since 1982 in this beautiful town, the festival features international award-winning classical music ensembles. August 1 to 15.

Fall of Tenochtitlán, Mexico City. The last battle of the Spanish Conquest took place at Tlatelolco, ruins that are now part of the Plaza of Three Cultures. Wreath-laying ceremonies there and at the Cuauhtémoc monument on Reforma commemorate the surrender of the last Aztec king, Cuauhtémoc, to Cortez, and the loss of thousands of lives. August 13.

Assumption of the Virgin Mary. This day is celebrated throughout the country with special Masses, and in some places with processions. In Huamantla, flower petals and colored sawdust carpet the streets. At midnight on August 15, a statue of the Virgin is carried through the streets; on August 16 is the running of the bulls. On August 15 in Santa Clara del Cobre, near Pátzcuaro, Our Lady of Santa Clara de Asis and the Virgen de la Sagrado Patrona are honored with a parade of floats, dancers on the main square, and an exposition of regional crafts. Buses to Huamantla from Puebla and Mexico City will be full, and there are few hotels in Huamantla. Plan to stay in Puebla and commute to the festivities. August 15 to 17.

September

Mariachi Festival, Guadalajara, Jalisco. These public concerts of mariachi music include visiting mariachi groups from around the world (even Japan!). Workshops and lectures focus on the history, culture, and music of the mariachi in Mexico. Call © **800/44-MEXICO** to confirm dates and schedule of performances. September 2 to 16.

Reto al Tepozteco (Tepozteco Challenge), Tepoztlan, Morelos. Performance depicting King Tepoztecatl's conversion to the Catholic religion. Procession leads toward the Tepozteco Pyramid, where people offer food and beverages. This event includes hypnotic *chinelo* dances, fireworks, and a food festival. September 7 to 8.

Independence Day. This national holiday celebrates Mexico's independence from Spain with parades, picnics, and family reunions. At 11pm on September 15, the president gives the famous independence *grito* (shout) from the National Palace in Mexico City. At least half a million people crowd into the *zócalo* (main plaza), and the rest of the country watches on TV or participates in local celebrations. Tall buildings downtown are draped in the national colors (red, green, and white), and the *zócalo* is ablaze with lights. Many people drive downtown at night to see the lights. Querétaro and San Miguel de Allende, where Independence conspirators lived and met, also celebrate elaborately; the schedule of events is exactly the same in every village, town, and city across Mexico. September 15 and 16.

Fall Equinox, Chichén Itzá. The same shadow play that occurs during the spring equinox repeats. September 21 and 22.

Sanmiguelada (Running of the Bulls at San Miguel), San Miguel de Allende. Also known as the Pamplonada because it is Mexico's imitation of Spain's running of the bulls, the Sanmiguelada is an annual festival usually taking place the third Saturday of September in honor of Saint Michael the Archangel. The event involves dances, concerts, fireworks and bulls running through town. Daring participants meet at high noon. www.sanmiguelguide.com/tour-pamplonada.htm. September 23.

October

Fiestas de Octubre (October Festivals), Guadalajara. This "most Mexican of cities" celebrates for a month with its trademark mariachi music. It's a bountiful display of popular culture and fine arts, and a spectacular spread of traditional food, Mexican beer, and wine. All month.

Festival Cervantino, Guanajuato. This festival began in the 1970s as a cultural event bringing performing artists from all over the world to this picturesque village northeast of Mexico City. Now the artists travel all over the republic after appearing in Guanajuato. Check local calendars or call ℂ **800/44-MEXICO** for details. www.festivalcervantino.gob.mx. Mid- to late October.

Oaxaca's Ninth Annual Food of the Gods Festival, Oaxaca, Oaxaca. A culinary exploration of the indigenous cultures of Oaxaca. Known globally for its culinary creativity, Oaxaca is the birthplace of chocolate. More information on this weeklong event is available at www.food-of-the-gods-festival.com. October 2 to 9.

Día de la Raza ("Ethnicity Day," or Columbus Day). This day commemorates the fusion of the Spanish and Mexican peoples. October 12.

November

Day of the Dead. This national holiday (Nov 1) actually lasts for 2 days: All Saints' Day—honoring saints and deceased children—and All Souls' Day, honoring deceased adults. Relatives gather at cemeteries countrywide, carrying candles and food, and often spend the night beside graves of loved ones. Weeks before, bakers begin producing bread in the shape of mummies or round loaves decorated with bread "bones." Sugar skulls emblazoned with glittery names are sold everywhere. Many days ahead, homes and churches erect altars laden with bread, fruit, flowers, candles, favorite foods, and photographs of saints and of the deceased. On both nights, costumed children walk through the streets, often carrying mock coffins and pumpkin lanterns, into which they expect money will be dropped.

The most famous celebration—which has become almost too well known—is on Janitzio, an island on Lake Pátzcuaro, Michoacán, west of Mexico City. Mixquic, a mountain village south of Mexico City, hosts an elaborate street fair, and around 11pm on both nights solemn processions lead to the cemetery in the center of town. Cemeteries around Oaxaca are well known for their solemn vigils, and some for their Carnaval-like atmosphere. November 1 and 2.

Fiestas de Noviembre (November Festivals), Puerto Escondido, Oaxaca. The events during this month include the annual Pipeline of Mexico, Zicatela Beach's International Surfing Tournament, the International Sailfish Tournament, and the Coastal Dance Festival. Check local calendars or call ℂ **800/44-MEXICO** for details. All month.

Second Annual Puerto Vallarta Film Festival of the Americas, Puerto Vallarta, Jalisco. Featuring a wide range of North American independent and Latin American productions, this elaborate showcase of feature-length films and documentaries includes gala events, art expos, and concerts, with celebrity attendees. www.puertovallartafilm.com. Check local calendars or call ℂ **800/44-MEXICO** for details. Mid-November, extending 10 days.

Gourmet Festival. Puerto Vallarta, Jalisco. In this culinary capital of Mexico, chefs from around the world join with local restaurateurs to create special menus, as well as host wine tastings, tequila tastings, cooking classes, a gourmet food expo, and other special events. For a detailed schedule and more information visit www.festivalgourmet.com. Dates vary, but the festival generally takes place for 10 days in mid-November.

Revolution Day. This national holiday commemorates the start of the Mexican Revolution in 1910 with parades, speeches, rodeos, and patriotic events. November 20.

Fifth Annual Yucatán Bird Festival, Mérida, Yucatán. Bird-watching sessions, workshops, and exhibits are the highlights of this festival designed to illustrate the special role birds play in our environment and in the Yucatán territory. www.yucatanbirds.org.mx. Call ℂ **800/44-MEXICO** for details. Mid-November.

National Silver Fair, Taxco. A competition of Mexico's best silversmiths and some of the world's finest artisans. There are exhibits, concerts, dances, and fireworks. Check local calendars or call ℂ **800/44-MEXICO** for details. Late November to early December.

December

Fifth Annual Hot Air Balloon Festival, León, Guanajuato. Largest festival in Latin America with more than 60 balloons and pilots from all over the globe participating. www.festivaldelglobo. com.mx. Call ℂ **800/44-MEXICO** for details. Early December.

Feast of the Virgin of Guadalupe. Religious processions, street fairs, dancing, fireworks, and Masses honor the patroness of Mexico. It is one of the country's most moving and beautiful displays of traditional culture. The Virgin of Guadalupe appeared to a young man, Juan Diego, in December 1531 on a hill near Mexico City. It's customary for children to dress up as Juan Diego, wearing mustaches and red bandanas. One of the most famous and elaborate celebrations takes place at the Basílica of Guadalupe, north of Mexico City, where the Virgin appeared. But every village celebrates this day, often with processions of children carrying banners, and with *charreadas* (rodeos),

bicycle races, dancing, and fireworks. In Puerto Vallarta, the celebration begins on December 1 and extends through December 12, with traditional processions to the church for a brief Mass and blessing. In the final days, the processions and festivities take place around the clock. There's a major fireworks exhibition on the feast day at 11pm. December 12.

Festival of San Cristóbal de las Casas, San Cristóbal de las Casas, Chiapas. This 10-day festival in Chiapas includes a procession by the Tzotzil and Tzetzal Indians, *marimba* music, and a parade of horses. December 12 to 21.

Christmas Posadas. On each of the 9 nights before Christmas, it's customary to reenact the Holy Family's search for an inn. Door-to-door candlelit processions pass through cities and villages nationwide, especially Querétaro and Taxco. Hosted by businesses and community organizations, these take the place of the northern tradition of a Christmas party. December 15 to 24.

Fiesta de los Rábanos (Festival of the Radishes), Oaxaca, Oaxaca. Local artisans and sculptors set up stalls around the main square to display their elaborate pieces of art—made entirely from radishes! The local crop is used for creating nativity scenes and famous Mexican figures. Balloons and birds crafted from local flowers add even more color. December 23.

Christmas. Mexicans often extend this national holiday and leave their jobs up to 2 weeks before Christmas, returning after New Year's. Many businesses close, and resorts and hotels fill. Significant celebrations take place on December 23 (see above). Querétaro has a huge parade. On the evening of December 24 in Oaxaca, processions culminate on the central plaza. On the same night, Santiago Tuxtla in Veracruz celebrates by dancing the *huapango* and with *jarocho* bands in the beautiful town square. December 24 and 25.

New Year's Eve. Like the rest of the world, Mexico celebrates New Year's Eve with parties, fireworks, and plenty of noise. Special festivities take place at Santa Clara del Cobre, near Pátzcuaro, with a candlelit procession of Christ, and at Tlacolula, near Oaxaca, with commemorative mock battles. December 31.

6 Travel Insurance

Check your existing insurance policies and credit card coverage before you buy travel insurance. You may already be covered for lost luggage, canceled tickets, or medical expenses. The cost of travel insurance varies widely, depending on the cost and length of your trip, your age and health, and the type of trip you're taking, but expect to pay between 5% and 8% of the vacation itself.

If you'll be driving in Mexico, see "Getting There: By Car" and "Getting Around Mexico: By Car," later in this chapter, for information on **collision** and **damage** and **personal accident insurance.**

TRIP-CANCELLATION INSURANCE
Trip-cancellation insurance helps you get your money back if you have to back out of a trip, if you have to go home early, or if your travel supplier goes bankrupt. Allowed reasons for cancellation can range from sickness to natural disasters to the State Department declaring your destination unsafe for travel. (Insurers usually won't cover vague fears, though, as many travelers discovered who tried to cancel their trips after the Sept 11, 2001, terrorist attacks because they were wary of flying.) In this unstable world, trip-cancellation insurance is a good buy if you're getting tickets well in advance—who knows what the state of the world, or of your airline, will be in 9 months? Insurance policy details vary, so read the fine print—and make sure that your airline or cruise line is on the list of carriers covered in case of bankruptcy. A good resource is **"Travel Guard Alerts,"** a list of companies considered high-risk by Travel Guard

International (see website below). Protect yourself further by paying for the insurance with a credit card—by law, consumers can get their money back on goods and services not received if they report the loss within 60 days after the charge is listed on their credit card statement.

Note: Many tour operators, particularly those offering trips to remote or high-risk areas, include insurance in the cost of the trip or can arrange insurance policies through a partnering provider, a convenient and often cost-effective way for the traveler to obtain insurance. Make sure the tour company is a reputable one, however: Some experts suggest you avoid buying insurance from the tour or cruise company you're traveling with, saying it's better to buy from a "third party" insurer than to put all your money in one place.

For more information, contact one of the following recommended insurers: **Access America** (© 866/807-3982; www.accessamerica.com); **Travel Guard International** (© 800/826-4919; www. travelguard.com); **Travel Insured International** (© 800/243-3174; www.travel-insured.com); and **Travelex Insurance Services** (© 888/457-4602; www.travelex-insurance.com).

MEDICAL INSURANCE For travel overseas, most health plans (including Medicare and Medicaid) do not provide coverage, and the ones that do often require you to pay for services upfront and reimburse you only after you return home. Even if your plan does cover overseas treatment, most out-of-country hospitals make you pay your bills up front, and send you a refund only after you've returned home and filed the necessary paperwork with your insurance company. As a safety net, you may want to buy travel medical insurance, particularly if you're traveling to a remote or high-risk area where emergency evacuation is a possible scenario. If you require additional medical insurance, try **MEDEX Assistance** (© 410/453-6300; www.medexassist.com) or **Travel Assistance International** (© 800/821-2828; www.travelassistance.com; for general information on services, call the company's Worldwide Assistance Services, Inc., at © 800/777-8710).

LOST-LUGGAGE INSURANCE   On domestic flights, checked baggage is covered up to $2,500 per ticketed passenger. On international flights (including U.S. portions of international trips), baggage coverage is limited to approximately $9.07 per pound, up to approximately $635 per checked bag. If you plan to check items more valuable than the standard liability, see if your valuables are covered by your homeowner's policy or get baggage insurance as part of your comprehensive travel-insurance package. Don't buy insurance at the airport, as it's usually overpriced. Be sure to take any valuables or irreplaceable items with you in your carry-on luggage, as many valuables (including books, money, and electronics) aren't covered by airline policies.

If your luggage is lost, immediately file a lost-luggage claim at the airport, detailing the luggage contents. For most airlines, you must report delayed, damaged, or lost baggage within 4 hours of arrival. The airlines are required to deliver luggage, once found, directly to your house or destination free of charge.

Keep in mind that in these uncertain times, insurers no longer cover some airlines, cruise lines, and tour operators. *The bottom line:* Always, always check the fine print before you sign; more and more policies have built-in exclusions and restrictions that may leave you out in the cold if something goes awry.

7 Health & Safety

STAYING HEALTHY
GENERAL AVAILABILITY OF HEALTH CARE

In most of Mexico's resort destinations, health care meeting U.S. standards is now available. Mexico's major cities are also known for their excellent health care, although the facilities available may be fewer, and equipment older than what is available at home. Prescription medicine is broadly available at Mexico pharmacies, however be aware that you may need a copy of your prescription, or obtain a prescription from a local doctor. This is especially true in the border towns, such as in Tijuana, where many Americans have been crossing into Mexico specifically for the purpose of purchasing lower priced prescription medicines.

Contact the **International Association for Medical Assistance to Travelers** (**IAMAT;** © 716/754-4883 or, in Canada, 416/652-0137; www.iamat.org) for tips on travel and health concerns in the countries you're visiting, and lists of local, English-speaking doctors. The U.S. **Centers for Disease Control and Prevention** (© 800/311-3435; www.cdc.gov) provides up-to-date information on health hazards by region or country and offers tips on food safety.

COMMON AILMENTS
HIGH-ALTITUDE HAZARDS   Travelers to certain regions of Mexico occasionally experience **elevation sickness,** which results from the relative lack of oxygen and the decrease in barometric pressure that characterizes high elevations

(more than 1,500m/5,000 ft.). Symptoms include shortness of breath, fatigue, headache, insomnia, and even nausea. Mexico City is at 2,100m (7,000 ft.) above sea level, as are a number of other central and southern cities, such as San Cristóbal de las Casas (even higher than Mexico City). At high elevations, it takes about 10 days to acquire the extra red blood corpuscles you need to adjust to the scarcity of oxygen. To help your body acclimate, drink plenty of fluids, avoid alcoholic beverages, and don't overexert yourself during the first few days. If you have heart or lung problems, talk to your doctor before going above 2,400m (8,000 ft.).

BUGS, BITES & OTHER WILDLIFE CONCERNS **Mosquitoes** and **gnats** are prevalent along the coast and in the Yucatán lowlands. *Repelente contra insectos* (insect repellent) is a must, and it's not always available in Mexico. If you'll be in these areas and are prone to bites, bring along a repellent that contains the active ingredient DEET. Avon's Skin So Soft also works extremely well. Another good remedy to keep the mosquitoes away is to mix citronella essential oil with basil, clove, and lavender essential oils. If you're sensitive to bites, pick up some antihistamine cream from a drugstore at home.

Most readers won't ever see an *alacrán* (scorpion). But if one stings you, go immediately to a doctor. In Mexico you can buy scorpion toxin antidote at any drugstore. It is an injection and it costs around $25. This is a good idea if you plan to camp in a remote area where medical assistance can be several hours away.

MORE SERIOUS DISEASES You shouldn't be overly concerned about tropical diseases if you stay on the normal tourist routes and don't eat street food. However, both dengue fever and cholera have appeared in Mexico in recent years. Talk to your doctor or to a medical specialist in tropical diseases about precautions you should take. You can also get medical bulletins from the U.S. State Department and the Centers for Disease Control and Prevention (see "Visitor Information," earlier in this chapter). You can protect yourself by taking some simple precautions: Watch what you eat and drink; don't swim in stagnant water (ponds, slow-moving rivers, or wells); and avoid mosquito bites by covering up, using repellent, and sleeping under netting. The most dangerous areas seem to be on Mexico's west coast, away from the big resorts.

WHAT TO DO IF YOU GET SICK AWAY FROM HOME

Any foreign consulate can provide a list of area doctors who speak English. If you get sick, consider asking your hotel concierge to recommend a local doctor—even his or her own. You can also try the emergency room at a local hospital. Many hospitals also have walk-in clinics for emergency cases that are not life-threatening; you may not get immediate attention, but you won't pay the high price of an emergency room visit. We list hospitals and emergency numbers under "Fast Facts," in each destination's chapter.

If you suffer from a chronic illness, consult your doctor before your departure. For conditions like epilepsy, diabetes, or

---

Tips Over-the-Counter Drugs in Mexico

Antibiotics and other drugs that you'd need a prescription to buy in the States are available over the counter in Mexican pharmacies. Mexican pharmacies also carry a limited selection of common over-the-counter cold, sinus, and allergy remedies.

heart problems, wear a **MedicAlert identification tag** (© 888/633-4298; www.medicalert.org), which will immediately alert doctors to your condition and give them access to your records through MedicAlert's 24-hour hot line.

Pack **prescription medications** in your carry-on luggage, and carry prescription medications in their original containers, with pharmacy labels—otherwise they won't make it through airport security. Also bring along copies of your prescriptions in case you lose your pills or run out. Don't forget an extra pair of contact lenses or prescription glasses. Carry the generic name of prescription medicines, in case a local pharmacist is unfamiliar with the brand name.

Contact the **International Association for Medical Assistance to Travelers** (see above under "Staying Healthy") for tips on travel and health concerns in Mexico and lists of local English-speaking doctors. The U.S. **Centers for Disease Control and Prevention** (see above) provides up-to-date information on necessary vaccines and health hazards by region or country.

EMERGENCY EVACUATION In extreme medical emergencies, a service from the United States will fly people to American hospitals. **Global Lifeline** (© 888/554-9729, or 01-800/305-9400 in Mexico) is a 24-hour air ambulance.

STAYING SAFE
CRIME

I have lived and traveled in Mexico for over a decade, have never had any serious trouble, and rarely feel suspicious of anyone or any situation. You will probably feel physically safer in most Mexican cities and villages than in any comparable place at home. However, crime in Mexico has received attention in the North American press over the past several years. Many feel this unfairly exaggerates the real dangers, but it should be noted that crime rates, including taxi robberies, kidnappings, and highway carjackings, have risen in recent years. The most severe problems have been concentrated in Mexico City, where even longtime foreign residents will attest to the overall lack of security. Isolated incidents have also occurred in Ixtapa, Baja, Cancún, and even traditionally tranquil Puerto Escondido. Check the U.S. State Department advisory before you travel for any notable "hot spots." See "Visitor Information," earlier in this chapter, for information on the latest **U.S. State Department advisories.**

Precautions are necessary, but travelers should be realistic. Common sense is essential. You can generally trust people whom you approach for help or directions—but be wary of anyone who approaches you offering the same. The more insistent the person is, the more cautious you should be. The crime rate is, on the whole, much lower in Mexico than in most parts of the United States, and the nature of crimes in general is less violent. Random, violent, or serial crime is essentially unheard of in Mexico.

Although these general comments on crime are basically true throughout Mexico, the one notable exception is in **Mexico City,** where violent crime is serious. Do not wear fine jewelry, expensive watches, or any other obvious displays of wealth. Muggings—day and night—are common. Avoid the use of the **green Volkswagen taxis,** many of which have been involved in "pirate" robberies, muggings, and even kidnappings. These taxis are also common in incidents where a passenger is "hijacked," and released only when the limit on their ATM bank cards have been withdrawn. Car theft and carjackings are also a common occurrence. More specific precautions appear in chapter 4. (See also "Emergencies" under "Fast Facts," later in this chapter.)

Tips Treating & Avoiding Digestive Trouble

It's called "travelers' diarrhea" or *turista*, the Spanish word for "tourist": persistent diarrhea, often accompanied by fever, nausea, and vomiting, that used to attack many travelers to Mexico. (Some in the U.S. call this "Montezuma's revenge," but you won't hear it called that in Mexico.) Widespread improvements in infrastructure, sanitation, and education have practically eliminated this ailment, especially in well-developed resort areas. Most travelers make a habit of drinking only bottled water, which also helps to protect against unfamiliar bacteria. In resort areas, and generally throughout Mexico, only purified ice is used. If you do come down with this ailment, nothing beats Pepto Bismol, readily available in Mexico. Imodium is also available in Mexico and is used by many travelers for a quick fix. A good high-potency (or "therapeutic") vitamin supplement and even extra vitamin C can help; yogurt is good for healthy digestion.

Since dehydration can quickly become life-threatening, the Public Health Service advises that you be careful to replace fluids and electrolytes (potassium, sodium, and the like) during a bout of diarrhea. Drink Pedialyte, a rehydration solution available at most Mexican pharmacies, or natural fruit juice, such as guava or apple (stay away from orange juice, which has laxative properties), with a pinch of salt added.

How to Prevent It: The U.S. Public Health Service recommends the following measures for preventing travelers' diarrhea: **Drink only purified water** (boiled water, canned or bottled beverages, beer, or wine). **Choose food carefully.** In general, avoid salads (except in first-class restaurants), uncooked vegetables, undercooked protein, and unpasteurized milk or milk products, including cheese. Choose food that is freshly cooked and still hot. In addition, something as simple as **clean hands** can go a long way toward preventing *turista*.

BRIBES & SCAMS

As is the case around the world, there are the occasional bribes and scams in Mexico, targeted at people believed to be naive—such as the telltale tourist. For years Mexico was known as a place where bribes—called *mordidas* (bites)—were expected; however, the country is rapidly changing. Frequently, offering a bribe today, especially to a police officer, is considered an insult, and it can land you in deeper trouble.

If you believe a **bribe** is being requested, here are a few tips on dealing with the situation. Even if you speak Spanish, don't utter a word of it to Mexican officials. That way you'll appear innocent, all the while understanding every word.

When you are crossing the border, should the person who inspects your car ask for a tip, you can ignore this request—but understand that the official may suddenly decide that a complete search of your belongings is in order. If faced with a situation where you feel you're being asked for a *propina* (literally, "tip"; colloquially, "bribe"), how much should you offer? Usually $3 to $5 or the equivalent in pesos will do the trick. Many tourists have the impression that everything works better in Mexico if you "tip"; however, in reality, this only perpetuates the *mordida* attitude. If you are pleased with a service, feel free to tip, but you shouldn't tip simply to attempt to get away with something illegal or inappropriate, whether it is crossing the border without having your car inspected or not getting a ticket that's deserved.

Whatever you do, **avoid impoliteness;** under no circumstances should you insult a Latin American official. Extreme politeness, even in the face of adversity, rules Mexico. In Mexico, *gringos* have a reputation for being loud and demanding. By adopting the local custom of excessive courtesy, you'll have greater success in negotiations of any kind. Stand your ground, but do it politely.

As you travel in Mexico, you may encounter several types of **scams,** which are typical throughout the world. One involves some kind of a **distraction** or feigned commotion. While your attention is diverted, a pickpocket makes a grab for your wallet. In another common scam, an **unaccompanied child** pretends to be lost and frightened and takes your hand for safety. Meanwhile the child or an accomplice plunders your pockets. A third involves **confusing currency.** A shoeshine boy, street musician, guide, or other individual might offer you a service for a price that seems reasonable—in pesos. When it comes time to pay, he or she tells you the price is in dollars, not pesos. Be very clear on the price and currency when services are involved.

8 Specialized Travel Resources

FAMILY TRAVEL

Children are considered the national treasure of Mexico, and Mexicans will warmly welcome and cater to your children. Many parents were reluctant to bring young children into Mexico in the past, primarily due to health concerns, but I can't think of a better place to introduce children to the exciting adventure of exploring a different culture. Some of the best destinations include Puerto Vallarta, Cancún, and La Paz. Hotels can often arrange for a babysitter.

Before leaving, ask your doctor which medications to take along. Disposable diapers cost about the same in Mexico but are of poorer quality. You can get Huggies Supreme and Pampers identical to the ones sold in the United States, but at a higher price. Many stores sell Gerber's baby foods. Dry cereals, powdered formulas, baby bottles, and purified water are easily available in midsize and large cities or resorts.

Cribs may present a problem; only the largest and most luxurious hotels provide them. However, rollaway beds are often available. Child seats or high chairs at restaurants are common.

Consider bringing your own car seat; they are not readily available for rent in Mexico.

Every country's regulations differ, but in general children traveling abroad should have plenty of documentation on hand, particularly if they're traveling with someone other than their own parents (in which case a notarized form letter from a parent is often required). For details on entry requirements for children traveling abroad, go to the U.S. State Department website (www.travel.state.gov); click on "International Travel," "Travel Brochures," and "Foreign Entry Requirements."

Throughout this book, the "Kids" icon distinguishes attractions, hotels, restaurants, and other destinations that are particularly attractive and accommodating to children and families.

Familyhostel (© **800/733-9753;** www.learn.unh.edu/familyhostel) takes the whole family, including kids ages 8 to

15, on moderately priced domestic and international learning vacations. Lectures, field trips, and sightseeing are guided by a team of academics.

Recommended family travel Internet sites include **Family Travel Forum** (www.familytravelforum.com), a comprehensive site that offers customized trip planning; **Family Travel Network** (www.familytravelnetwork.com), an award-winning site that offers travel features, deals, and tips; **Traveling Internationally with Your Kids** (www.travelwithyourkids.com), a comprehensive site offering sound advice for long-distance and international travel with children; and **Family Travel Files** (www.thefamilytravelfiles.com), which offers an online magazine and a directory of off-the-beaten-path tours and tour operators for families.

TRAVELERS WITH DISABILITIES

Mexico may seem like one giant obstacle course to travelers in wheelchairs or on crutches. At airports, you may encounter steep stairs before finding a well-hidden elevator or escalator—if one exists. Airlines will often arrange wheelchair assistance to the baggage area. Porters are generally available to help with luggage at airports and large bus stations, once you've cleared baggage claim.

Mexican airports are upgrading their services, but it is not uncommon to board from a remote position, meaning you either descend stairs to a bus that ferries you to the plane, which you board by climbing stairs, or you walk across the tarmac to your plane and ascend the stairs. Deplaning presents the same problem in reverse.

Escalators (and there aren't many in the country) are often out of order. Stairs without handrails abound. Few restrooms are equipped for travelers with disabilities; when one is available, access to it may be through a narrow passage that won't accommodate a wheelchair or a person on crutches. Many deluxe hotels (the most expensive) now have rooms with bathrooms for people with disabilities. Those traveling on a budget should stick with one-story hotels or hotels with elevators. Even so, there will probably still be obstacles somewhere. Generally speaking, no matter where you are, someone will lend a hand, although you may have to ask for it.

One exception is Puerto Vallarta, which has recently renovated the majority of its downtown sidewalks and plazas with ramps that accommodate wheelchairs (as well as baby strollers). Even the airport has ramps adjacent to all stairways, and special wheelchair lifts. A local disabled citizen deserves the credit for this impressive task—hopefully setting the stage for greater accessibility in other towns and resorts.

Most disabilities shouldn't stop anyone from traveling. There are more options and resources out there than ever before.

Many travel agencies offer customized tours and itineraries for travelers with disabilities. **Flying Wheels Travel** (© 507/451-5005; www.flyingwheelstravel.com) offers escorted tours and cruises that emphasize sports and private tours in minivans with lifts. **Access-Able Travel Source** (© 303/232-2979; www.accessable.com) offers extensive access information and advice for traveling around the world with disabilities. **Accessible Journeys** (© 800/846-4537 or 610/521-0339; www.disabilitytravel.com) caters specifically to slow walkers and wheelchair travelers and their families and friends.

Organizations that offer assistance to disabled travelers include **MossRehab** (www.mossresourcenet.org), which provides a library of accessible-travel resources online; **Society for Accessible Travel & Hospitality** (SATH; © 212/447-7284; www.sath.org; annual membership fees: $45 adults, $30 seniors and students), which offers a wealth of travel resources for all types of disabilities and informed recommendations on destinations, access guides, travel agents, tour operators, vehicle rentals, and companion services; and the **American Foundation for the Blind** (AFB; © 800/232-5463; www.afb.org), a referral resource for the blind or visually impaired that includes information on traveling with Seeing Eye dogs.

For more information specifically targeted to travelers with disabilities, the community website **iCan** (www.icanonline.net/channels/travel) has destination guides and several regular columns on accessible travel. Also check out the quarterly magazine **Emerging Horizons** ($15 per year, $20 outside the U.S.; www.emerginghorizons.com); and *Open World* magazine, published by SATH (see above; subscription: $13 per year, $21 outside the U.S.).

SENIOR TRAVEL

Mexico is a popular country for retirees. For decades, North Americans have been living indefinitely in Mexico by returning to the border and recrossing with a new tourist permit every 6 months. Mexican immigration officials have caught on, and now limit the maximum time in the country to 6 months within any year. This is to encourage even partial residents to acquire proper documentation.

Some of the most popular places for long-term stays are Guadalajara, Lake Chapala, Ajijic, and Puerto Vallarta, all in the state of Jalisco; San Miguel de Allende and Guanajuato in Guanajuato state; Cuernavaca in Morelos; and Alamos in Sinaloa.

AIM, Apartado Postal 31–70, 45050 Guadalajara, Jal., is a well-written, informative newsletter for prospective retirees. Issues have evaluated retirement in Aguascalientes, Puebla, San Cristóbal de las Casas, Puerto Angel, Puerto Escondido and Huatulco, Oaxaca, Taxco,

Tepic, Manzanillo, Melaque, and Barra de Navidad. Subscriptions are $18 to the United States and $21 to Canada. Back issues are three for $5.

Sanborn Tours, 2015 S. 10th St., Post Office Drawer 519, McAllen, TX 78505-0519 (© 800/395-8482), offers a "Retire in Mexico" orientation tour.

Mention the fact that you're a senior citizen when you make your travel reservations. Although all of the major U.S. airlines except America West have canceled their senior discount and coupon book programs, many hotels still offer discounts for seniors.

Members of **AARP** (formerly known as the American Association of Retired Persons), 601 E St. NW, Washington, DC 20049 (© 888/687-2277; www.aarp.org), get discounts on hotels, airfares, and car rentals. AARP offers members a wide range of benefits, including *AARP: The Magazine* and a monthly newsletter. Anyone over 50 can join.

Many reliable agencies and organizations target the 50-plus market. **Elderhostel** (© 877/426-8056; www.elderhostel.org) arranges study programs for those aged 55 and over (and a spouse or companion of any age) in the U.S. and in more than 80 countries around the world. Most courses abroad last 2 to 4 weeks, and many include airfare, accommodations in university dormitories or modest inns, meals, and tuition. **ElderTreks** (© 800/741-7956; www.eldertreks.com) offers small-group tours to off-the-beaten-path or adventure-travel locations, restricted to travelers 50 and older. **INTRAV** (© 800/456-8100; www.intrav.com) is a high-end tour operator that caters to the mature, discerning traveler, not specifically seniors, with trips around the world that include guided safaris, polar expeditions, private-jet adventures, and small-boat cruises down jungle rivers.

Recommended publications offering travel resources and discounts for seniors include: the quarterly magazine *Travel 50 & Beyond* (www.travel50andbeyond.com); *Travel Unlimited: Uncommon Adventures for the Mature Traveler* (Avalon); *101 Tips for Mature Travelers,* available from Grand Circle Travel (© **800/221-2610** or 617/350-7500; www.gct.com); and *Unbelievably Good Deals and Great Adventures That You Absolutely Can't Get Unless You're Over 50* (McGraw-Hill), by Joann Rattner Heilman.

GAY & LESBIAN TRAVELERS

Mexico is a conservative country, with deeply rooted Catholic religious traditions. Public displays of same-sex affection are rare and still considered shocking for men, especially outside of urban or resort areas. Women in Mexico frequently walk hand in hand, but anything more would cross the boundary of acceptability. However, gay and lesbian travelers are generally treated with respect and should not experience any harassment, assuming they give the appropriate regard to local culture and customs.

Puerto Vallarta is perhaps the most welcoming and accepting destination in Mexico. Susan Weisman's travel service **Bayside Properties** (© **322/223-4424;** www.baysidepuertovallarta.com) rents gay-friendly condos, villas, and hotels for individuals and large groups. Her services are customized to individual needs, and she can offer airport pickups and in-villa cooks.

The International Gay and Lesbian Travel Association (IGLTA; © **800/448-8550** or 954/776-2626; www.iglta.org) is the trade association for the gay and lesbian travel industry, and offers an online directory of gay- and lesbian-friendly travel businesses; go to their website and click on "Members."

Many agencies offer tours and travel itineraries specifically for gay and lesbian travelers. **Above and Beyond Tours** (© **800/397-2681;** www.abovebeyond tours.com) is the exclusive gay and lesbian tour operator for United Airlines. **Now,**

Tips Advice for Female Travelers

As a female traveling alone, I can tell you firsthand that I feel safer traveling in Mexico than in the United States. But I use the same common-sense precautions I use anywhere else in the world and am alert to what's going on around me.

Mexicans in general, and men in particular, are nosy about single travelers, especially women. If a taxi driver or anyone else with whom you don't want to become friendly asks about your marital status, family, and so forth, my advice is to make up a set of answers (regardless of the truth): "I'm married, traveling with friends, and I have three children." Saying you are single and traveling alone may send the wrong message. U.S. television—widely viewed now in Mexico—has given many Mexican men the image of American single women as being sexually promiscuous. Check out the award-winning website **Journeywoman** (www.journeywoman.com), a "real life" women's travel information network where you can sign up for a free e-mail newsletter and get advice on everything from etiquette and dress to safety; or the travel guide *Safety and Security for Women Who Travel* by Sheila Swan and Peter Laufer (Travelers' Tales, Inc.), offering common-sense tips on safe travel.

Voyager (© 800/255-6951; www.now voyager.com) is a well-known San Francisco–based gay-owned and -operated travel service. **Olivia Cruises & Resorts** (© 800/631-6277; www.olivia.com) charters entire resorts and ships for exclusive lesbian vacations and offers smaller group experiences for both gay and lesbian travelers.

The following travel guides are available at most travel bookstores and gay and lesbian bookstores, or you can order them from **Giovanni's Room** bookstore, 1145 Pine St., Philadelphia, PA 19107 (© 215/923-2960; www.giovannisroom.com); *Out and About* (© 800/929-2268; www.outandabout.com), which offers guidebooks and a newsletter ($20 per year; 10 issues) packed with solid information on the global gay and lesbian scene; *Spartacus International Gay Guide* (Bruno Gmünder Verlag; www.spartacusworld.com/gayguide) and *Odysseus: The International Gay Travel Planner* (Odysseus Enterprises Ltd.), both good, annual English-language guidebooks focused on gay men; the *Damron* guides (www.damron.com), with separate, annual books for gay men and lesbians; and *Gay Travel A to Z: The World of Gay & Lesbian Travel Options at Your Fingertips* by Marianne Ferrari (Ferrari International; Box 35575, Phoenix, AZ 85069), a very good gay and lesbian guidebook series.

STUDENT TRAVEL

Because Mexicans consider higher education more a luxury than a birthright, there is no formal network of student discounts and programs. Most Mexican students travel with their families rather than with other students, so student discount cards are not commonly recognized.

However, more hostels have entered the student travel scene. The **Mexican Youth Hostel Network,** or Red Mexicana de Albergues Juveniles (www.remaj.com), offers a list of hostels that meet international standards in Mexico City, Cuernavaca and surrounding areas, Oaxaca, and Veracruz. The **Mexican Youth Hostel Association (Asociación Mexicana de Albergues Juveniles;** www.hostels.com./en/mx.html), offers a list of hostels in Mexico City, Zacatecas, Guanajuato, Puerto Escondido, Uxmal, Palenque, Tulum, Cancún, and Playa del Carmen.

If you're a student planning to travel outside the U.S., you'd be wise to arm yourself with an **International Student Identity Card (ISIC),** which offers substantial savings on rail passes, plane tickets, and entrance fees. It also provides you with basic health and life insurance and a 24-hour help line. The card is available for $22 from **STA Travel** (© 800/781-4040 in North America; www.statravel.com), the biggest student travel agency in the world. If you're no longer a student but are still under 26, you can get an **International Youth Travel Card (IYTC)** for the same price from the same people, which entitles you to some discounts (but not on museum admissions). (*Note:* In 2002, STA Travel bought competitors **Council Travel** and **USIT Campus** after they went bankrupt. It's still operating some offices under the Council name, but it's owned by STA.) **Travel CUTS** (© 800/667-2887 or 416/614-2887; www.travelcuts.com) offers similar services for both Canadians and U.S. residents.

9 Planning Your Trip Online

SURFING FOR AIRFARES

The "big three" online travel agencies, **Expedia.com, Travelocity.com,** and **Orbitz.com,** sell most of the air tickets bought on the Internet. (Canadian travelers should try expedia.ca and Travelocity.ca;

> ### (Tips Frommers.com: The Complete Travel Resource
>
> For an excellent travel-planning resource, we highly recommend **Frommers. com** (www.frommers.com), voted Best Travel Site by *PC Magazine*. We're a little biased, of course, but we guarantee that you'll find the travel tips, reviews, monthly vacation giveaways, bookstore, and online-booking capabilities thoroughly indispensable. Among the special features are our popular **Destinations** section, where you'll get expert travel tips, hotel and dining recommendations, and advice on the sights to see for more than 3,500 destinations around the globe; the **Frommers.com Newsletter,** with the latest deals, travel trends, and money-saving secrets; our **Community** area featuring **Message Boards,** where Frommer's readers post queries and share advice (sometimes even our authors show up to answer questions); and our **Photo Center,** where you can post and share vacation tips. When your research is done, the **Online Reservations System** (www.frommers.com/book_a_trip) takes you to Frommer's preferred online partners for booking your vacation at affordable prices.

U.K. residents can go for expedia.co.uk and opodo.co.uk.). Each has different business deals with the airlines and may offer different fares on the same flights, so it's wise to shop around. Expedia and Travelocity will also send you **e-mail notification** when a cheap fare becomes available to your favorite destination. Of the smaller travel agency websites, **Side-Step** (www.sidestep.com) has gotten the best reviews from Frommer's authors. It's a browser add-on that purports to "search 140 sites at once," but in reality only beats competitors' fares as often as other sites do.

Also remember to check **airline websites,** especially those for low-fare carriers such as Southwest, whose fares are often misreported or simply missing from travel agency websites. Even with major airlines, you can often shave a few bucks from a fare by booking directly through the airline and avoiding a travel agency's transaction fee. But you'll get these discounts only by **booking online:** Most airlines now offer online-only fares that even their phone agents know nothing about. For the websites of airlines that fly to and from your destination, go to "Getting There," later in this chapter.

Great **last-minute deals** are available through free weekly e-mail services provided directly by the airlines. Most of these are announced on Tuesday or Wednesday and must be purchased online. Most are only valid for travel that weekend, but some (such as Southwest's) can be booked weeks or months in advance. Sign up for weekly e-mail alerts at airline websites or check megasites that compile comprehensive lists of last-minute specials, such as **SmarterTravel.com.** For last-minute trips, **site59.com** and **lastminutetravel.com** in the U.S. and **lastminute.com** in Europe often have better air-and-hotel package deals than the major-label sites. A website listing numerous bargain sites and airlines around the world is **www.itravelnet.com.**

If you're willing to give up some control over your flight details, use what is called an **"opaque" fare service** like **Priceline** (www.priceline.com, or www. priceline.co.uk for Europeans) or its smaller competitor **Hotwire** (www.hotwire.com). Both offer rock-bottom prices in exchange for travel on a "mystery airline" at a mysterious time of day, often with a mysterious change of planes en route. The mystery airlines are all major, well-known carriers—and the possibility of being sent from Philadelphia to Chicago via Tampa is remote; the airlines' routing computers have gotten a lot better than they used to be. But your chances of getting a 6am or 11pm flight are pretty high. Hotwire tells you flight prices before you buy; Priceline usually has better deals than Hotwire, but you have to play their "name our price" game. If you're new at this, the helpful folks at **BiddingForTravel** (www.biddingfortravel.com) do a good job of demystifying Priceline's prices and strategies. Priceline and Hotwire are great for flights within North America and between the U.S. and Europe. But for flights to other parts of the world, consolidators will almost always beat their fares. *Note:* In 2004 Priceline added nonopaque service to its roster. You now have the option to pick exact flights, times, and airlines from a list of offers—or opt to bid on opaque fares as before.

For much more about airfares and savvy air-travel tips and advice, pick up a copy of *Frommer's Fly Safe, Fly Smart* (Wiley Publishing, Inc.). See also "Flying for Less," later in this chapter.

SURFING FOR HOTELS

Shopping online for hotels is generally done one of two ways: by booking through the hotel's own website or through an independent booking agency (or a fare-service agency like Priceline; see above). These Internet hotel agencies have multiplied in mind-boggling numbers of late, competing for the business of millions of consumers surfing for accommodations around the world. This competitiveness can be a boon to consumers who have the patience and time to shop and compare the online sites for good deals—but shop they must, for prices can vary considerably from site to site. And keep in mind that hotels at the top of a site's listing may be there for no other reason than that they paid money to get the placement.

Of the "big three" sites, **Expedia** offers a long list of special deals and "virtual tours" or photos of available rooms so you can see what you're paying for (a feature that helps counter the claims that the best rooms are often held back from bargain booking websites). **Travelocity** posts unvarnished customer reviews and ranks its properties according to the AAA rating system. Also reliable are **Hotels.com** and **Quikbook.com**. An excellent free program, **TravelAxe** (www.travelaxe.net), can help you search multiple hotel sites at once, even ones you may never have heard of—and conveniently lists the total price of the room, including the taxes and service charges. Another booking site, **Travelweb** (www.travelweb), is partly owned by the hotels it represents (including the Hilton, Hyatt, and Starwood chains) and is therefore plugged directly into the hotels' reservations systems—unlike independent online agencies, which have to fax or e-mail reservation requests to the hotel, a good portion of which get misplaced in the shuffle. More than once, travelers have arrived at the hotel, only to be told that they have no reservation. To be fair, many of the major sites are undergoing improvements in service and ease of use, and Expedia will soon be able to plug directly into the reservations systems of many hotel chains—none of which can be bad news for consumers. In the meantime, it's a good idea to **get a confirmation number** and **make a printout** of any online booking transaction.

SURFING FOR RENTAL CARS

For booking rental cars online, the best deals are usually at rental-car company websites, although all the major online travel agencies also offer rental-car reservations services. Priceline and Hotwire work well for rental cars, too; the only "mystery" is which major rental company you get, and for most travelers the difference between Hertz, Avis, and Budget is negligible.

10 The 21st-Century Traveler

INTERNET ACCESS AWAY FROM HOME

Travelers have any number of ways to check their e-mail and access the Internet on the road. Of course, using your own laptop—or even a PDA (personal digital assistant) or electronic organizer with a modem—gives you the most flexibility. But even if you don't have a computer, you can still access your e-mail and even your office computer from cybercafes.

WITHOUT YOUR OWN COMPUTER

It's hard nowadays to find a city or town in Mexico that *doesn't* have a few cybercafes. The "Fast Facts" sections in this book list cybercafes in major destinations. Although there's no definitive directory for cybercafes—these are independent businesses, after all—three places to start looking are at **www.cybercaptive.com** and **www.cybercafe.com**.

Hotels that cater to business travelers often have **in-room dataports** and **business centers,** but the charges can be hefty—and downright frightful if you're trying to connect to a U.S.-based access number.

Most major airports now have **Internet kiosks** scattered throughout their gates. These kiosks, which you'll also see in shopping malls, hotel lobbies, and tourist information offices around the world, give you basic Web access for a per-minute fee that's usually higher than cybercafe prices. The kiosks' clunkiness and high price mean they should be avoided whenever possible.

To retrieve your e-mail, ask your **Internet service provider (ISP)** if it has a Web-based interface tied to your existing e-mail account. If your ISP doesn't have such an interface, you can use the free **mail2web** service (www.mail2web.com) to view and reply to your home e-mail. For more flexibility, you may want to open a free, Web-based e-mail account with **Yahoo! Mail** (mail.yahoo.com). Microsoft's **Hotmail** is another popular option, but Hotmail has severe spam problems. Your home ISP may be able to forward your e-mail to the Web-based account automatically.

If you need to access files on your office computer, look into a service called **GoToMyPC** (www.gotomypc.com). The service provides a Web-based interface for you to access and manipulate a distant PC from anywhere—even a cybercafe—provided your "target" PC is on and has an always-on connection to the Internet (such as with Road Runner cable). The service offers top-quality security, but if you're worried about hackers, use your own laptop rather than a cybercafe computer to access the GoToMyPC system.

WITH YOUR OWN COMPUTER

Wi-Fi (wireless fidelity) is the buzzword in computer access, and more and more hotels, cafes, and retailers are signing on as wireless "hotspots" from where you can get high-speed connection without cable wires, networking hardware, or a phone line (see below). You can get Wi-Fi connection one of several ways. Many laptops sold in the last year have built-in Wi-Fi capability (an 802.11b wireless Ethernet connection). Mac owners have their own networking technology, Apple AirPort. For those with older computers, an 802.11b/**Wi-Fi card** (around $50) can be plugged into your laptop. You sign up for wireless access service much as you do cellphone service, through a plan offered by one of several commercial companies that have made wireless service available in airports, hotel lobbies, and coffee shops, primarily in the U.S. (followed by the U.K. and Japan). **T-Mobile Hotspot** (www.t-mobile.com/hotspot) serves up wireless connections at more than 1,000 Starbucks coffee shops nationwide. **Boingo** (www.boingo.com) and **Wayport** (www.wayport.com) have set up networks in airports and high-class hotel lobbies. IPass providers (see below) also give you access to a few hundred wireless hotel lobby setups. Best of all, you don't need to stay at the Four Seasons to use the hotel's network; just set yourself up on a nice couch in the lobby. The companies' pricing policies can be byzantine, with a variety of monthly, per-connection, and per-minute plans, but in general you pay around $30 a month for limited access—and as more and more companies jump on the wireless bandwagon, prices are likely to get even more competitive.

There are also places that provide **free wireless networks** in cities around the world. To locate these free hotspots, go to www.personaltelco.net/index.cgi/wireless communities.

If Wi-Fi is not available at your destination, most business-class hotels throughout the world offer dataports for laptop modems, and many hotels are now offering free high-speed Internet access using an Ethernet network cable. You can bring your own cables, but most hotels rent them for around $10. **Call your hotel in advance** to see what your options are.

In addition, major Internet service providers (ISPs) have **local access numbers** around the world, allowing you to go online by simply placing a local call. Check your ISP's website or call its toll-free number and ask how you can use your current account away from home, and how much it will cost.

If you're traveling outside the reach of your ISP, the **iPass** network has dial-up numbers in most of the world's countries. You'll have to sign up with an iPass provider, who will then tell you how to set up your computer for your destination(s). For a list of iPass providers, go to www.ipass.com and click on "Individual Purchase." One solid provider is **i2roam** (© **866/811-6209** or 920/235-0475; www.i2roam.com).

Wherever you go, bring a **connection kit** of the right power and phone adapters, a spare phone cord, and a spare Ethernet network cable—or find out whether your hotel supplies them to guests.

USING A CELLPHONE

The three letters that define much of the world's **wireless capabilities** are GSM (Global System for Mobiles), a big, seamless network that makes for easy cross-border cellphone use throughout Europe and dozens of other countries worldwide, including Mexico. In the U.S., T-Mobile, AT&T Wireless, and Cingular use this quasi-universal system; in Canada, Microcell and some Rogers customers are GSM, and all Europeans and most Australians use GSM.

If your cellphone is on a GSM system, and you have a world-capable multiband phone such as many Sony Ericsson, Motorola, or Samsung models, you can make and receive calls across civilized areas on much of the globe, from Andorra to Uganda. Just call your wireless operator and ask for "international roaming" to be activated on your account. Unfortunately, per-minute charges can be high—usually $1 to $1.50 in western Europe and up to $5 in places like Russia and Indonesia.

That's why it's important to buy an "unlocked" world phone from the get-go. Many cellphone operators sell "locked" phones that restrict you from using any other removable computer memory phone chip card (called an SIM card) other than the ones they supply. Having an unlocked phone allows you to install a cheap, pre-paid SIM card (found at a local retailer) in your destination country. Show your phone to the salesperson; not all phones work on all networks. You'll get a local phone number—and much, much lower calling rates. Getting an already locked phone unlocked can be a complicated process, but it can be done; just call your cellular operator and say you'll be going abroad for several months and want to use the phone with a local provider.

For many, **renting** a phone is a good idea. (Even world phone owners will have to rent new phones if they're traveling to non-GSM regions, such as Japan or Korea.) While you can rent a phone from any number of overseas sites, including kiosks at airports and at car-rental agencies, we suggest renting the phone before you leave home. That way you can give loved ones and business associates your new number, make sure the phone works, and take the phone wherever you go— especially helpful for overseas trips through several countries, where local phone-rental agencies often bill in local currency and may not let you take the phone to another country.

Online Traveler's Toolbox

Veteran travelers usually carry some essential items to make their trips easier. Following is a selection of handy online tools to bookmark and use.

- **Airplane Seating & Food.** Find out which seats to reserve and which to avoid (and more) on all major domestic airlines at www.seatguru.com. And check out the type of meal (with photos) you'll likely be served on airlines around the world at www.airlinemeals.com.
- **Visa ATM Locator** (www.visa.com) and **MasterCard ATM Locator** (www.mastercard.com), for locations of PLUS (Visa) and Cirrus (MasterCard) ATMs worldwide.
- **Foreign Languages for Travelers** (www.travlang.com). Learn basic terms in more than 70 languages and click on any underlined phrase to hear what it sounds like.
- **Intellicast** (www.intellicast.com) and **Weather.com** (www.weather.com). Weather forecasts for all 50 states and cities around the world.
- **Universal Currency Converter** (www.xe.net). See what your dollar or pound is worth in more than 100 other countries.
- **Travel Warnings** (www.travel.state.gov, www.fco.gov.uk/travel, www.voyage.gc.ca, www.smartraveller.gov.au). These sites report on places where health concerns or unrest might threaten American, British, Canadian, and Australian travelers. Generally, U.S. warnings are the most paranoid; Australian warnings are the most relaxed.

Phone rental isn't cheap. You'll usually pay $40 to $50 per week, plus airtime fees of at least a dollar a minute. The bottom line: Shop around.

Two good wireless rental companies are **InTouch USA** (© **800/872-7626;** www.intouchglobal.com) and **RoadPost** (© **888/290-1606** or 905/272-5665; www.roadpost.com). Give them your itinerary, and they'll tell you what wireless products you need. InTouch will also, for free, advise you on whether your existing phone will work overseas; simply call © **703/222-7161** between 9am and 4pm EST, or go to www.intouchglobal.com/travel.htm.

For trips of more than a few weeks spent in one country, **buying a phone** becomes economically attractive, as many nations have cheap, no-questions-asked prepaid phone systems. In Mexico, both of the two major cell service providers, **TelCel** and **USACell** sell inexpensive phones that use prepaid cards.

Once you arrive at your destination, stop by a local cellphone shop and get the cheapest package; you'll probably pay less than $100 for a phone and a starter calling card. Local calls may be as low as 10¢ per minute, and in many countries incoming calls are free.

True wilderness adventurers, or those heading to less-developed countries, should consider renting a **satellite phone ("satphone"),** which is different from cellphones in that they connect to satellites rather than ground-based towers. A satphone is more costly than a cellphone but works where there's no cellular signal and no towers. You can rent satellite phones from **RoadPost** (© **888/290-1606** or 905/272-5665; www.roadpost.com). InTouch USA (see above) offers a wider range of satphones but at higher rates. Per-minute call charges can be even cheaper than roaming charges with a regular cellphone, but the phone itself is more expensive (up to $150 a week), and depending on the service you choose, people calling you may incur high long-distance charges. As of this writing, satphones were amazingly expensive to buy, so don't even think about it.

11 Getting There

BY PLANE

The airline situation in Mexico is rapidly improving, with many new regional carriers offering scheduled service to areas previously not served. In addition to regularly scheduled service, charter service direct from U.S. cities to resorts is making Mexico more accessible. For information about saving money on airfares using the Internet, see "Planning Your Trip Online," earlier.

THE MAJOR INTERNATIONAL AIRLINES The main airlines operating direct or nonstop flights from the United States to Mexico include **Aero California** (© 800/237-6225), **Aeromexico** (© 800/237-6639; www.aeromexico.com), **Air France** (© 800/237-2747; www.airfrance. com), **Alaska Airlines** (© 800/426-0333; www.alaskaair.com), **America West** (© 800/235-9292; www.americawest. com), **American Airlines** (© 800/433-7300; www.aa.com), **Continental** (© 800/525-0280; www.continental. com), **Frontier Airlines** (© 800/432-1359; www.frontierairlines.com), **Mexicana** (© 800/531-7921; www.mexicana. com), **Northwest/KLM** (© 800/225-2525; www.nwa.com), **Taca** (© 800/225-2272; www.taca.com), **United** (© 800/241-6522; www.united.com), and **US Airways** (© 800/428-4322; www.us airways.com). **Southwest Airlines** (© 800/435-9792; www.iflyswa.com) serves the U.S. border.

Tips   Luxury Bus Service from the Mexico City Airport

An airport-to-destination service to a number of cities in central Mexico takes the hassle out of travel. The deluxe buses serving these routes are air-conditioned and have video movies and a restroom. The price usually includes soft drinks (and passengers tend to stock up when they board).

If you're going to **Puebla** (see chapter 12), Estrella Roja buses ($12) depart hourly beginning at 6 or 7:30am from in front of the airport's Sala D (Gate D) exit. The bus runs every hour until midnight. Buses for **Querétaro, Toluca, Pachuca,** and **Cuernavaca** are in front of the covered concourse outside the terminal between exit doors for Gate D. If you have trouble locating them, ask for help at an information desk on the main concourse.

If precise scheduling is essential, call the **Airport Information Office** (© 555/ 786-9341, 555/786-9342, 555/786-9358, or 555/571-3600) to verify names of buses, where to find them, and current schedules.

The main departure points in North America for international airlines are Atlanta, Chicago, Dallas/Fort Worth, Denver, Houston, Las Vegas, Los Angeles, Miami, New York, Orlando, Philadelphia, Phoenix, Raleigh/Durham, San Antonio, San Francisco, Seattle, Toronto, and Washington, D.C.

GETTING THROUGH THE AIRPORT

With the federalization of security, procedures at U.S. airports are more stable and consistent than ever. Generally, you'll be fine if you arrive at the airport **1 hour** before a domestic flight and **2 hours** before an international flight; if you show up late, tell an airline employee and she'll probably whisk you to the front of the line.

Bring a **current, government-issued photo ID** such as a driver's license or passport. Keep your ID at the ready to show at check-in, the security checkpoint, and sometimes even the gate. (Children under 18 do not need government-issued photo IDs for domestic flights, but they do for international flights to most countries.)

In 2003, the TSA phased out **gate check-in** at all U.S. airports. And **e-tickets** have made paper tickets nearly obsolete. Passengers with e-tickets can beat the ticket-counter lines by using airport **electronic kiosks** or even **online check-in** from your home computer. Online check-in involves logging on to your airlines' website, accessing your reservation, and printing out your boarding pass—and the airline may even offer you bonus miles to do so! If you're using a kiosk at the airport, bring the credit card you used to book the ticket or your frequent-flier card. Print out your boarding pass from the kiosk and simply proceed to the security checkpoint with your pass and a photo ID. If you're checking bags or looking to snag an exit-row seat, you will be able to do so using most airline kiosks. Even the smaller airlines are employing the kiosk system, but always call your airline to make sure these alternatives are available. Note that at press time, these check-in services were not available at Mexico's airports, so plan on checking in the old-fashioned way—by standing in line. **Curbside check-in** is also a good way to avoid lines, although a few airlines still ban curbside check-in; call before you go.

Security checkpoint lines are getting shorter than they were during 2001 and 2002, but some doozies remain. If you have trouble standing for long periods of time, tell an airline employee; the airline will provide a wheelchair. Speed up security by **not wearing metal objects** such as big belt buckles. If you've got metallic body parts, a note from your doctor can prevent a long chat with the security screeners. Keep in mind that only **ticketed passengers** are allowed past security, except for folks escorting disabled passengers or children.

Federalization has stabilized **what you can carry on** and **what you can't.** The general rule is that sharp things are out, nail clippers are okay, and food and beverages must be passed through the X-ray machine—but that security screeners can't make you drink from your coffee cup. Bring food in your carry-on rather than checking it, as explosive-detection machines used on checked luggage have been known to mistake food (especially chocolate, for some reason) for bombs. Travelers in the U.S. are allowed one carry-on bag, plus a "personal item" such as a purse, briefcase, or laptop bag. Carry-on hoarders can stuff all sorts of things into a laptop bag; as long as it has a laptop in it, it's still considered a personal item. The Transportation Security Administration (TSA) has issued a list of restricted items; check its website (www.tsa.gov/public/index.jsp) for details.

Airport screeners may decide that your checked luggage needs to be searched by hand. You can now purchase luggage locks that allow screeners to open and relock a checked bag if hand-searching is necessary. Look for Travel Sentry certified locks at luggage or travel shops and Brookstone stores (you can buy them online at www.brookstone.com). These locks, approved by the TSA, can be opened by luggage inspectors with a special code or key. For more information on the locks, visit www.travelsentry.org. If you use something other than TSA-approved locks, your lock will be cut off your suitcase if a TSA agent needs to hand-search your luggage.

FLYING FOR LESS: TIPS FOR GETTING THE BEST AIRFARE

Passengers sharing the same airplane cabin rarely pay the same fare. Travelers who need to purchase tickets at the last minute, change their itinerary at a moment's notice, or fly one-way often get stuck paying the premium rate. Here are some ways to keep your airfare costs down.

- Passengers who can book their tickets **far in advance,** who can **stay over Saturday night,** or who **fly midweek** or **at less-trafficked hours** may pay a fraction of the full fare. If your schedule is flexible, say so, and ask if you can secure a cheaper fare by changing your flight plans.

- You can also save on airfares by keeping an eye out in local newspapers for **promotional specials** or **fare wars,** when airlines lower prices on their most popular routes. You rarely see fare wars offered for peak travel times, but if you can travel in the off-months, you may snag a bargain.

- Search the **Internet** for cheap fares (see "Planning Your Trip Online," earlier in this chapter).

- **Consolidators,** also known as bucket shops, are great sources for international tickets, although they usually can't beat the Internet on fares within North America. Start by looking in Sunday newspaper travel sections; U.S. travelers should focus on the *New York Times,* the *Los Angeles Times,* and the *Miami Herald.* For less-developed destinations, small travel agents who cater to immigrant communities in large cities often have the best deals. *Beware:* Bucket shop tickets are usually nonrefundable or rigged with stiff cancellation penalties, often as high as 50% to 75% of the ticket price, and some put you on charter airlines which may leave at inconvenient times and experience delays. Several reliable consolidators are worldwide and available on the Net. **STA Travel** (© **800/781-4040** in North America; www.statravel.com) is now the world's leader in student travel, thanks to their purchase of Council Travel. It also offers good fares for travelers of all ages. **ELTExpress** (© **800/TRAV-800;** www.eltexpress.com) started in Europe and has excellent fares worldwide, but particularly to that continent. It also has "local" websites in 12 countries. **FlyCheap** (© **800/FLY-CHEAP;** www.1800flycheap.com) is owned by package-holiday megalith MyTravel and so has especially good access to fares for sunny destinations. **Air Tickets Direct** (© **800/778-3447;** www.airticketsdirect.com) is based in Montreal and leverages the currently weak Canadian dollar for low fares; it'll also book trips to places that U.S. travel agents won't touch, such as Cuba.

- Join **frequent-flier clubs.** Accrue enough miles, and you'll be rewarded with free flights and elite status. It's free, and you'll get the best choice of seats, faster response to phone inquiries, and prompter service if your luggage is stolen, your flight is canceled or delayed, or if you want to change your seat. You don't need to fly to build frequent-flier miles—**frequent-flier credit cards** can provide thousands of miles for doing your everyday shopping.

- For many more tips about air travel, including a rundown of the major frequent-flier credit cards, pick up a copy of *Frommer's Fly Safe, Fly Smart* (Wiley Publishing, Inc.).

BY CAR

Driving is not the cheapest way to get to Mexico, but it is the best way to see the country. Even so, you may think twice about taking your own car south of the border once you've pondered the bureaucracy involved. One option is to rent a car once you arrive and tour around a specific region. Rental cars in Mexico are generally new, clean, and well maintained. Although they're pricier than in the United States, discounts are often available for rentals of a week or longer, especially when you make arrangements in advance from the United States. (See "Car Rentals," later in this chapter, for more details.)

Tips Carrying Car Documents

You must carry your temporary car-importation permit, tourist permit (see "Entry Requirements," earlier in this chapter), and, if you purchased it, your proof of Mexican car insurance (see below) in the car at all times. The temporary car-importation permit papers are valid for 6 months to a year, while the tourist permit is usually issued for 30 days. It's a good idea to overestimate the time you'll spend in Mexico, so that if you have to (or want to) stay longer, you'll avoid the hassle of getting your papers extended. Whatever you do, don't overstay either permit. Doing so invites heavy fines, confiscation of your vehicle (which will not be returned), or both. Also remember that 6 months does not necessarily equal 180 days—be sure that you return before the earlier expiration date.

If, after reading the section that follows, you have additional questions or you want to confirm the current rules, call your nearest Mexican consulate or the Mexican Government Tourist Office. Although travel insurance companies are generally helpful, they may not have the most accurate information. To check on road conditions or to get help with any travel emergency while in Mexico, call ✆ **01-800/903-9200,** or 555/250-0151 in Mexico City. English-speaking operators staff both numbers.

In addition, check with the **U.S. State Department** (see "Visitor Information," earlier in this chapter) for warnings about dangerous driving areas.

CAR DOCUMENTS

To drive your car into Mexico, you'll need a **temporary car-importation permit,** which is granted after you provide a required list of documents (see below). The permit can be obtained through Banco del Ejército (Banjercito) officials, who have a desk, booth, or office at the *aduana* (Mexican Customs) building after you cross the border into Mexico.

The following strict requirements for border crossing were accurate at press time:

- **A valid driver's license,** issued outside of Mexico.
- **Current, original car registration and a copy of the original car title.** If the registration or title is in more than one name and not all the named people are traveling with you, a notarized letter from the absent person(s) authorizing use of the vehicle for the trip is required; have it ready. The registration and your credit card (see below) must be in the same name.
- **A valid international major credit card.** With a credit card, you are required to pay only a $23 car-importation fee. The credit card must

be in the same name as the car registration. If you do not have a major credit card (American Express, Diners Club, MasterCard, or Visa), you must post a bond or make a deposit equal to the value of the vehicle. Check cards are not accepted.

- **Original immigration documentation.** This is either your tourist permit (FMT) or the original immigration booklet, FM2 or FM3, if you hold more permanent status.
- **A signed declaration promising to return to your country of origin with the vehicle.** Obtain this form *(Carta Promesa de Retorno)* from AAA or Sanborn's before you go, or from Banjercito officials at the border. There's no charge. The form does not stipulate that you must return by the same border entry through which you entered.
- **Temporary Importation Application.** By signing this form, you state that you are only temporarily importing the car for your personal use and will not be selling it. This is to help regulate the entry and restrict the resale of unauthorized cars and trucks. Make sure the permit is canceled when you return to the U.S.

If you receive your documentation at the border, Mexican officials will make two copies of everything and charge you for the copies. For up-to-the-minute information, a great source is the Customs office in Nuevo Laredo, or *Módulo de Importación Temporal de Automóviles, Aduana Nuevo Laredo* (✆ **867/712-2071**).

Important reminder: Someone else may drive, but the person (or relative of the person) whose name appears on the car-importation permit must *always* be in the car. (If stopped by police, a non-registered family member driving without the registered driver must be prepared to prove familial relationship to the registered driver—no joke.) Violation of this rule subjects the car to impoundment and the driver to imprisonment, a fine, or both. You can drive a car with foreign license plates only if you have a foreign (non-Mexican) driver's license.

MEXICAN AUTO INSURANCE

Liability auto insurance is legally required in Mexico. U.S. insurance is invalid; to be insured in Mexico, you must purchase Mexican insurance. Any party involved in an accident who has no insurance may be sent to jail and have his or her car impounded until all claims are settled. This is true even if you just drive across the border to spend the day. U.S. companies that broker Mexican insurance are commonly found at the border crossing, and several quote daily rates.

You can also buy car insurance through **Sanborn's Mexico Insurance,** P.O. Box 52840, 2009 S. 10th, McAllen, TX (© **956/686-3601;** fax 800/222-0158 or 956/686-0732; www.sanbornsinsurance. com). The company has offices at all U.S. border crossings. Its policies cost the same as the competition's do, but you get legal coverage (attorney and bail bonds if needed) and a detailed mile-by-mile guide for your proposed route. Most of the Sanborn's border offices are open Monday through Friday, and a few are staffed on Saturday and Sunday. **AAA** auto club (www.aaa.com) also sells insurance.

RETURNING TO THE UNITED STATES WITH YOUR CAR

You *must* return the car documents you obtained when you entered Mexico when you cross back with your car, or at some point within 180 days. (You can cross as many times as you wish within the 180 days.) If the documents aren't returned, heavy fines are imposed ($250 for each 15 days late), your car may be impounded and confiscated, or you may be jailed if you return to Mexico. You can only return the car documents to a Banjercito official on duty at the Mexican *aduana* (Customs) building *before* you cross back into the United States. Some border cities have Banjercito officials on duty 24 hours a day, but others do not; some do not have Sunday hours.

BY SHIP

Numerous cruise lines serve Mexico. Some (including whale-watching trips) cruise from California to the Baja Peninsula and ports of call on the Pacific coast, or from Houston or Miami to the Caribbean (which often includes stops in Cancún, Playa del Carmen, and Cozumel). Several cruise-tour specialists offer substantial discounts on unsold cabins if you're willing to take off at the last minute. One such company is **The Cruise Line,** 150 NW 168 St., North Miami Beach, FL 33169 (© **800/777-0707** or 305/ 521-2200).

BY BUS

Greyhound-Trailways (or its affiliates) offers service from around the United States to the Mexican border, where passengers disembark, cross the border, and buy a ticket for travel into Mexico. Many border crossings have scheduled buses from the U.S. bus station to the Mexican bus station.

12 Packages for the Independent Traveler

Before you start your search for the lowest airfare, you may want to consider booking your flight as part of a travel package. Package tours are not the same thing as escorted tours. Package tours are simply a way to buy the airfare, accommodations, and other elements of your trip (such as car rentals, airport transfers, and sometimes even activities) at the same time and often at discounted prices—kind of like one-stop shopping. Packages are sold in bulk to tour operators—who resell them to the public at a cost that usually undercuts standard rates.

You can buy a package at any time of the year, but the best deals usually coincide with high season—from mid-December to April—when demand is at its peak, and companies are more confident about filling planes. You might think that package rates would be better during low season, when room rates and airfares plunge. But the key is air access, which is much easier during the winter. Packages vary widely, with some companies offering a better class of hotels than others. Some offer the same hotels for lower prices. Some offer flights on scheduled airlines, while others book charters. In some packages, your choices of accommodations and travel days may be limited. Each destination usually has some packagers that are better than the rest because they buy in even bigger bulk. Not only can that mean better prices, it can mean more choices.

You are often required to make a large payment up front. On the plus side, packages can save you money, offering group prices but allowing for independent travel. Some even let you add on a few guided excursions or escorted day trips (also at prices lower than if you booked them yourself) without booking an entirely escorted tour.

Before you invest in a package tour, get some answers. Ask about the **accommodations choices** and prices for each. Then look up the hotels' reviews in a Frommer's guide and check their rates online for your specific dates of travel. You'll also want to find out what **type of room** you get. If you need a certain type

of room, ask for it; don't take whatever is thrown your way. Request a nonsmoking room, a quiet room, a room with a view, or whatever you fancy.

Finally, look for **hidden expenses.** Ask whether airport departure fees and taxes, for example, are included in the total cost.

Beyond those described below, travel packages are also listed in the travel section of your local Sunday newspaper. Or check ads in the national travel magazines such as *Arthur Frommer's Budget Travel Magazine, Travel & Leisure, National Geographic Traveler,* and *Condé Nast Traveler.*

WHERE TO BROWSE

- One specialist in Mexico vacation packages is **www.mexicotravelnet. com**, an agency that offers most of the well-known travel packages to Mexico beach resorts, plus offers last minute specials.

- Check out **www.2travel.com** and find the page with links to a number of the big-name Mexico packagers, including several of those listed here.

- For last-minute air-only or package bargains, check out **Vacation Hot Line** (www.vacationhotline.net). Once you find your deal, you'll need to call to make booking arrangements. This service offers packages from the popular Apple and Funjet vacation wholesalers.

- Several big **online travel agencies**—Expedia.com, Travelocity.com, Orbitz. com, Site59.com, and Lastminute. com—also do a brisk business in packages. If you're unsure about the pedigree of a smaller packager, check with the Better Business Bureau in the city where the company is based, or go online at www.bbb.org. If a packager won't tell you where they're based, don't fly with them.

RECOMMENDED PACKAGERS

- **Aeromexico Vacations** (© 800/ 245-8585; www.aeromexico.com) offers year-round packages to almost every destination it serves, including Acapulco, Cancún, Cozumel, Ixtapa/ Zihuatanejo, Los Cabos, and Puerto Vallarta. Aeromexico has a large (more than 100) selection of resorts in these destinations and more, in a variety of price ranges. The best deals are from Houston, Dallas, San Diego, Los Angeles, Miami, and New York, in that order.

- **Alaska Airlines Vacations** (© 800/ 468-2248; www.alaskaair.com) sells packages to Ixtapa/Zihuatanejo, Los Cabos, Manzanillo/Costa Alegre, Mazatlán, and Puerto Vallarta. Alaska flies direct from Los Angeles, San Diego, San Jose, San Francisco, Seattle, Vancouver, Anchorage, and Fairbanks. The website offers unpublished discounts that are not available through the phone operators.

- **American Airlines Vacations** (© 800/ 321-2121; www.aavacations.com) has year-round deals to Acapulco, Cancún, the Riviera Maya, Guadalajara, Los Cabos, Mexico City, and Puerto Vallarta. You don't have to fly with American if you can get a better deal on another airline; land-only packages include hotel, hotel tax, and airport transfers. American's hubs to Mexico are Dallas/Fort Worth, Chicago, and Miami. The website offers unpublished discounts that are not available through the operators.

- **America West Vacations** (© 800/ 356-6611; www.americawest vacations.com) has deals to Acapulco, Guadalajara, Ixtapa, Mazatlán, Manzanillo, Mexico City, Los Cabos, and Puerto Vallarta, mostly from its Phoenix gateway. Many packages to

Los Cabos include car rentals. The website offers discounted featured specials that are not available through the operators. You can also book hotels without air by calling the toll-free number.

- **Apple Vacations** (© 800/365-2775; www.applevacations.com) offers inclusive packages to all the beach resorts, and has the largest choice of hotels in Acapulco, Cancún, Cozumel, Huatulco, Ixtapa, Loreto, Los Cabos, Manzanillo, Mazatlán, Puerto Vallarta, and the Riviera Maya. Scheduled carriers for the air portion include American, United, Mexicana, Delta, US Airways, Reno Air, Alaska Airlines, Aero California, and Aeromexico. Apple perks include baggage handling and the services of a company representative at major hotels.

- **Classic Custom Vacations** (© 800/ 635-1333; www.classiccustom vacations.com) specializes in package vacations to Mexico's finest luxury resorts. It combines discounted first-class and economy airfare on American, Continental, Mexicana, Alaska, America West, and Delta with stays at the most exclusive hotels in Cancún, the Riviera Maya, Mérida, Oaxaca, Guadalajara, Mexico City, Puerto Vallarta, Mazatlán, Costa Alegre, Manzanillo, Ixtapa/Zihuatanejo, Acapulco, Huatulco, and Los Cabos. In many cases, packages also include meals, airport transfers, and upgrades. The prices are not for bargain hunters but for those who seek luxury, nicely packaged.

- **Continental Vacations** (© 800/ 301-3800; www.covacations.com) has year-round packages to Cancún, Cozumel, Puerto Vallarta, Cabo San Lucas, Acapulco, Ixtapa, Mazatlán, Mexico City, and Guadalajara. The

Finds **Out-of-the-Ordinary Places to Stay**

Mexico lends itself beautifully to the concept of small, private hotels in idyllic settings. They vary in style from grandiose estate to palm-thatched bungalow. **Mexico Boutique Hotels** (www.MexicoBoutiqueHotels.com) specializes in smaller places to stay with a high level of personal attention and service. Most options have less than 50 rooms, and the accommodations consist of entire villas, *casitas*, bungalows, or a combination. The Yucatán is especially noted for the luxury haciendas throughout the peninsula.

best deals are from Houston; Newark, N.J.; and Cleveland. You must fly Continental. The Internet deals offer savings not available elsewhere.

- **Delta Vacations** (© **800/221-6666;** www.deltavacations.com) has year-round packages to Acapulco, Los Cabos, Cozumel, and Cancún. Atlanta is the hub, so expect the best prices from there.

- **Funjet Vacations** (book through any travel agent; www.funjet.com for general information) is one of the largest vacation packagers in the United States. Funjet has packages to Acapulco, Cancún, Cozumel, the Riviera Maya, Huatulco, Los Cabos, Mazatlán, Ixtapa, and Puerto Vallarta. You can choose a charter or fly on American, Continental, Delta, Aeromexico, US Airways, Alaska Air, or United.

- **GOGO Worldwide Vacations** (© **888/636-3942;** www.gogowwv.com) has trips to all the major beach destinations, including Acapulco, Cancún, Mazatlán, Puerto Vallarta, and Los Cabos. It offers several exclusive deals from higher-end hotels. Book through any travel agent.

- **Mexicana Vacations,** or MexSeaSun Vacations (© **800/531-9321;** www.mexicana.com) offers getaways to all the resorts. Mexicana operates daily direct flights from Los Angeles to Los

Cabos, Mazatlán, Cancún, Puerto Vallarta, Manzanillo, and Ixtapa/Zihuatanejo.

- **Online Vacation Mall** (© **800/839-9851;** www.onlinevacationmall.com) allows you to search for and book packages offered by a number of tour operators and airlines to Acapulco, Cancún, Cozumel, Guaymas, Huatulco, Ixtapa/Zihuatanejo, La Paz, Los Cabos, Mazatlán, Mexico City, Puerto Vallarta, and the Riviera Maya.

- **Pleasant Mexico Holidays** (© **800/448-3333;** www.pleasantholidays.com) is one of the largest vacation packagers in the United States, with hotels in Acapulco, Cancún, Cozumel, Ixtapa/Zihuatanejo, Los Cabos, Mazatlán, and Puerto Vallarta.

REGIONAL PACKAGERS

From the East Coast: Liberty Travel (© **888/271-1584;** www.libertytravel.com), one of the biggest packagers in the Northeast, often runs a full-page ad in the Sunday papers, with frequent Mexico specials. You won't get much in the way of service, but you will get a good deal.

From the West: Suntrips (© **800/SUNTRIPS,** or 800/786-8747 for departures within 14 days; www.suntrips.com) is one of the largest West Coast packagers for Mexico, with departures from San Francisco and Denver; regular charters to Cancún, Cozumel, Los Cabos, and Puerto Vallarta; and a large selection of hotels.

From the Southwest: Town and Country (book through travel agents) packages regular deals to Los Cabos, Mazatlán, Puerto Vallarta, Ixtapa, Manzanillo, Cancún, Cozumel, and Acapulco with America West from the airline's Phoenix and Las Vegas gateways.

Resort Packages: The biggest hotel chains and resorts also sell packages. To take advantage of these offers, contact your travel agent or call the hotels directly.

13 The Active Traveler

Mexico has more than 120 **golf** courses, concentrated in the resort areas, with excellent options in Mexico City and Guadalajara. Los Cabos, in Baja Sur, has become the country's preeminent golf destination; the Puerto Vallarta area enjoys a growing reputation. For details on courses and events, see chapters 9 and 18. Visitors to Mexico can also enjoy **tennis, racquetball, squash, water-skiing, surfing, bicycling,** and **horseback riding. Scuba diving** is excellent, not only off the Yucatán's Caribbean coast (especially Cozumel), but also on the Pacific coast at Puerto Vallarta and Manzanillo, and off Baja in the Sea of Cortez. **Mountain and volcano climbing** is a rugged sport that allows you to meet like-minded folks from around the world. The top peaks are just 80km (50 miles) south of Mexico City—the snowcapped volcanoes Ixtaccihuatl (5,255m/17,342 ft.) and Popocatépetl (5,420m/17,887 ft.). Popocatépetl was not accepting visitors at press time, due to recent volcanic activity. For information on visiting and climbing the volcanoes, contact the **Club de Exploraciones de México** in Mexico City (© **555/740-8032**).

PARKS   Most national parks and nature reserves are understaffed or unstaffed. Reliable Mexican companies (such as AMTAVE members; see below) and many U.S.-based companies offer adventure trips.

OUTDOORS ORGANIZATIONS & TOUR OPERATORS   AMTAVE (Asociación Mexicana de Turismo de Aventura y Ecoturismo, A.C.) is an active association of ecotour and adventure tour operators. It publishes an annual catalog of participating firms and their offerings, all of which must meet certain criteria for security, quality, and training of the guides, as well as for sustainability of natural and cultural environments. For more information, contact AMTAVE (© **800/509-7678;** www.turismoaventura.com).

The **Archaeological Conservancy,** 5301 Central Ave. NE, Suite 402, Albuquerque, NM 87108 (© **505/266-1540;** www.americanarchaeology.org), presents one trip per year led by an expert, usually an archaeologist. The trips change from year to year and space is limited; make reservations early.

ATC Tours and Travel, Calle 16 de Septiembre 16, 29200 San Cristóbal de las Casas, Chis. (© **967678-2550** or 967/678-2557; fax 967/678-3145; www.atctours.com.mx), a Mexico-based tour operator with an excellent reputation, offers specialist-led trips, primarily in southern Mexico. In addition to trips to the ruins of Palenque and Yaxchilán (extending into Belize and Guatemala by river, plane, and bus if desired), ATC offers horseback tours to Chamula or Zinacantán, and day trips to the ruins of Toniná around San Cristóbal de las Casas; birding in the rain forests of Chiapas and

Guatemala (including in the El Triunfo Reserve of Chiapas); hikes to the shops and homes of native textile artists of the Chiapas highlands; and walks from the Lagos de Montebello in the Montes Azules Biosphere Reserve, with camping and canoeing. The company can also prepare custom itineraries.

Baja Expeditions, 2625 Garnet Ave., San Diego, CA 92109 (© **800/843-6967** or 858/581-3311; fax 858/581-6542; www.bajaex.com), offers natural-history cruises, whale-watching, sea kayaking, camping, scuba diving, and resort and day trips out of Loreto or La Paz, Baja California, and San Diego, California. Small groups and special itineraries are Baja Expeditions' specialty.

The **California Native,** 6701 W. 87th Place, Los Angeles, CA 90045 (© **800/ 926-1140** or 310/642-1140; www.cal native.com), offers small-group deluxe 7-, 8-, 9-, and 11-day escorted tours through the Copper Canyon. Many trips visit the towns of Batopilas, Urique, and Tejeban as well as the customary destinations of Creel, El Fuerte, Divisadero, Chihuahua, and Cerocahui. The guides are known throughout the area for their work with the Tarahumara Indians. In addition to escorted trips, the company offers a full range of custom itineraries.

Columbus Travel, 900 Rich Creek Lane, Bulverde, TX 78163-2872 (© **800/ 843-1060** in the U.S. and Canada, or 830/885-2000; fax 830/885-2010; www. canyontravel.com), specializes in the Copper Canyon and has a variety of adventures, from easy to challenging. It designs trips for special-interest groups of agriculturists, geologists, rock hounds, and birders, and custom trips to the Copper Canyon. The owner works with the Tarahumara Indians.

Culinary Adventures, 6023 Reid Dr. NW, Gig Harbor, WA 98335 (© **253/ 851-7676;** fax 253/851-9532), specializes in a short but select list of cooking tours in Mexico. They feature well-known cooks and travel to regions known for excellent cuisine. The owner, Marilyn Tausend, is the co-author of *Mexico the Beautiful Cookbook* and *Cocinas de la Familia* (Family Kitchens).

Far Flung Adventures, P.O. Box 377, Terlingua, TX 79852 (© **800/359-4138** or 915/371-2489; www.farflung.com), organizes specialist-led river trips to the Antigua, Actopan, and Filobobo rivers, in Veracruz.

Gorgas Science Foundation, 510 E. St. Charles, Brownsville, TX 78520 (© **956/504-6862**), offers weeklong trips once or twice a year (usually in June) to the northernmost tropical cloud forest in the Americas, and to the Rancho El Cielo in the remote El Cielo Biosphere Reserve, 80km (50 miles) south of Ciudad Victoria, Tamaulipas, in northern Mexico. The Gorgas Science Foundation of Texas Southmost College sponsors the trips. The area is rich in birds, orchids, and bromeliads and is home to endangered black bear, jaguar, and ocelot.

Expediciones México Verde, Homero 526-801, 11510 México, D.F. (© **555/ 255-4400;** www.raftingmexicoverde. com), under the leadership of Agustín Arroyo, offers a tour covering the original route of Cortez—though unlike Cortez and his henchmen, you're not on horseback or on foot. Highlights include the ruins of Zempoala; the cities of Veracruz (where you learn the local dance borrowed from Cuba, *danzón*), Xalapa and its excellent Museo de Antropología, Puebla, Tlaxcala, and Mexico City; river rafting (if you desire); plus cultural experiences in food, history, and literature. Trips can be customized.

Mexico Art Tours (© **888/783-1331,** or 480/730-1764 in the U.S., fax 480/ 730-1496; 1233 E. Baker Dr., Tempe, AZ 85282; www.mexicanarttours.com).

Led by Jean Grimm, a specialist in the arts and cultures of Mexico, these unique tours focusing on the authentic arts and cultures of Mexico are accompanied by compelling speakers who are themselves respected scholars and artists. Itineraries include visits to Oaxaca, Chiapas, Guadalajara and Puerto Vallarta, Mexico City, and other locales. Special tours include a Day of the Dead tour, and one on the Art of Mexican Masks.

Mexico Travel Link Ltd., 300-3665 Kingsway, Vancouver, BC V5R 5W2 Canada (© **604/454-9044;** fax 604/454-9088; www.mexicotravel.net), offers cultural, sports, and adventure tours to Mexico City and surrounding areas, Baja, Veracruz, the Copper Canyon, the Mayan Route, and other destinations.

Mexico Motorcycle Adventures, Inc., 697 18th St., Beaumont, TX 77706 (© **409/838-9983;** fax 409/833-2550), offers off-road motorcycle tours to the Copper Canyon, Baja, and La Cola de Caballo, outside Monterrey.

Mountain Travel Sobek, 6420 Fairmount Ave., El Cerrito, CA 94530 (© **800/227-2384,** 888/687-6235, or 510/527-8100; www.mtsobek.com), takes groups kayaking in the Sea of Cortez, whale-watching in Baja, and river rafting, hiking, and camping in Veracruz. Sobek is one of the world's leading ecotour outfitters.

Natural Habitat Adventures, 2945 Center Green Court, Suite H, Boulder, CO 80301 (© **800/543-8917** or 303/449-3711; www.nathab.com), offers naturalist-led natural history and adventure travel. Expeditions focus on monarch butterfly watching in Michoacán and gray whale–watching in Baja.

Naturequest, 30872 South Coast Hwy., Suite PMB, Laguna Beach, CA 92651 (© **800/369-3033** or 949/499-9561; www.naturequesttours.com), specializes in the natural history, culture, and wildlife of the Copper Canyon and the remote lagoons and waterways off Baja California. A 10-day hiking trip ventures into rugged areas of the canyon; a less strenuous trip goes to Creel and Batopilas, in the same area. Baja trips get close to nature, with special permits for venturing by two-person kayak into sanctuaries for whales and birds.

Oaxaca Reservations/Zapotec Tours, 4955 North Claremont Ave., Suite B, Chicago, IL 60625 (© **800/44-OAXACA** outside Illinois, or 773/506-2444; fax 773/506-2445; www.oaxacainfo.com), offers a variety of tours to Oaxaca City and the Oaxaca coast (including Puerto Escondido and Huatulco). Its specialty trips include Day of the Dead in Oaxaca and the Food of the Gods Tour of Oaxaca. The coastal trips emphasize nature, while the Oaxaca City tours focus on the immediate area, with visits to weavers, potters, markets, and archaeological sites. This is also the U.S. contact for several hotels in Oaxaca City that offer a 10% discount for reserving online.

One World Workforce, P.O. Box 3188, La Mesa, CA 91944 (© **800/451-9564**), arranges 1-week "hands-on conservation" trips that offer working volunteers a chance to help with sea-turtle conservation at Bahía de Los Angeles, in Baja (spring, summer, and fall), and along the Majahuas beach 100km (60 miles) south of Puerto Vallarta (summer and fall).

Tour Baja, P.O. Box 827, Calistoga, CA 94515 (© **800/398-6200** or 707/942-4550; fax 707/942-8017; www.tourbaja.com), offers sea-kayaking tours in the Loreto area. Owner Trudi Angell has guided these trips for more than 20 years. She and her guides offer firsthand knowledge of the area. Kayaking, mountain biking, and pack trips as well as sailing charters combine these elements with outdoor adventures.

Sea Kayak Adventures, 1036 Pine Avenue, Coeur d'Alene, ID 83814 (© **800/616-1943** or 208/765-3116; fax 208/765-5254; www.seakayakadventures.com), features kayak trios in both the Sea of Cortez and Magdalena Bay, with a focus on whale-watching. This company has the exclusive permit to paddle Magdalena Bay's remote northern waters, and they guarantee gray whale sightings. Trips combine paddling of 4 to 5 hours per day, with hiking across dunes and beaches, while nights are spent camping.

Sea Trek Sea Kayaking Center, P.O. Box 561, Woodacre, CA 94973 (© **415/488-1000;** fax 415/488-1707; www.SeaTrekKayak.com). Alternating sea-kayaking trips between Alaska and Baja for 20 years has given Sea Trek an intimate knowledge of the peninsula's coastline. Eight-day trips depart from and return to Loreto, and a 12-day expedition travels from Loreto to La Paz. An optional day excursion to Bahía Magdalena for gray whale–watching is available. Full boat support is provided, and no previous paddling experience is necessary.

Trek America, P.O. Box 189, Rockaway, NJ 07866 (© **800/221-0596** or 973/983-1144; fax 973/983-8551; www.trekamerica.com), organizes lengthy, active trips that combine trekking, hiking, van transportation, and camping in the Yucatán, Chiapas, Oaxaca, the Copper Canyon, and Mexico's Pacific coast, and a trip that covers Mexico City, Teotihuacán, Taxco, Guadalajara, Puerto Vallarta, and Acapulco.

Veraventuras, Santos Degollado 81-8, 91000 Xalapa, Ver. (© **228/818-9579,** or 01-800/712-6572 in Mexico; fax 228/818-9680; www.veraventuras.com.mx), uses specially trained leaders on well-organized and -outfitted adventures into the state of Veracruz, including rafting the rapids of the Antigua, Actopan, Barranca, and Filobobos rivers.

14 Tips on Accommodations

MEXICO'S HOTEL RATING SYSTEM

The hotel rating system in Mexico is called "Stars and Diamonds." Hotels may qualify to earn one to five stars, or five diamonds. Many hotels that have excellent standards are not certified, but all rated hotels adhere to strict standards. The guidelines relate to service, facilities, and hygiene more than to prices.

Five-diamond hotels meet the highest requirements for rating: The beds are comfortable, bathrooms are in excellent working order, all facilities are renovated regularly, infrastructure is top-tier, and services and hygiene meet the highest international standards.

Five-star hotels usually offer similar quality, but with lower levels of service and detail in the rooms. For example, a five-star hotel may have less luxurious linens, or perhaps room service during limited hours rather than 24 hours.

Four-star hotels are less expensive and more basic, but they still guarantee cleanliness and basic services such as hot water and purified drinking water. Three-, two-, and one-star hotels are at least working to adhere to certain standards: Bathrooms are cleaned and linens are washed daily, and you can expect a minimum standard of service. Two- and one-star hotels generally provide bottled water rather than purified water.

The nonprofit organization Calidad Mexicana Certificada, A.C., known as **Calmecac** (www.calmecac.com.mx), is responsible for hotel ratings. For additional details about the rating system, visit Calmecac's website or www.starsanddiamonds.com.mx.

HOTEL CHAINS

In addition to the major international chains, you'll run across a number of less-familiar brands as you plan your trip to Mexico. They include:

- **Brisas Hotels & Resorts** (www.brisas.com.mx). These were the hotels that originally attracted jet-set travelers to Mexico. Spectacular in a retro way, these properties offer the laid-back luxury that makes a Mexican vacation so unique.
- **Fiesta Americana** and **Fiesta Inn** (www.posadas.com). Part of the Mexican-owned Grupo Posadas company, these hotels set the country's midrange standard for facilities and services. They generally offer comfortable, spacious rooms and traditional Mexican hospitality. Fiesta Americana hotels offer excellent beach-resort packages. Fiesta Inn hotels are usually more business oriented. Grupo Posadas also owns the more luxurious Caesar Park hotels and the eco-oriented Explorean hotels.
- **Hoteles Camino Real** (www.caminoreal.com). The premier Mexican hotel chain, Camino Real maintains a high standard of service at its properties, all of which carry five stars (see "Mexico's Hotel Rating System," above). Its beach hotels are traditionally located on the best beaches in the area. This chain also focuses on the business market. The hotels are famous for their vivid and contrasting colors.
- **Hoteles Krystal NH** (www.nh-krystal.mexico-hoteles.com). Grupo Chartwell recently acquired this family-owned chain. The hotels are noted for their family-friendly facilities and five-star standards. The beach properties' signature feature is a pool, framed by columns, overlooking the sea.
- **Plaza Las Glorias** (www.sidek.com.mx/hotel/ing/glorias.asp). Sidek Situr

group, the company responsible for building the first mega-developments in Mexico's resort areas, built these hotels. The chain usually represents a more affordable option than its competitors but maintains international standards.

- **Quinta Real Grand Class Hotels and Resorts** (www.quintareal.com). These hotels, owned by Summit Hotels and Resorts, are noted for architectural and cultural details that reflect their individual regions. At these luxury properties, attention to detail and excellent service are the rule.

HOUSE RENTALS & SWAPS

House and villa rentals and swaps are becoming more common in Mexico, but no single recognized agency or business provides this service exclusively for Mexico. In the chapters that follow, we have provided information on independent services that we have found to be reputable.

With regard to general online services, the most extensive inventory of homes is found at **VRBO** (Vacation Rentals by Owner; www.vrbo.com). They have over 33,000 homes and condominiums worldwide, including a large selection in Mexico. Another good option is **VacationSpot** (www.vacationspot.com) owned by Expedia, and a part of its sister company, Hotels.com. It has fewer choices, but the company's criteria for adding inventory is much more selective, and often includes onsite inspections. They also offer toll-free phone support.

SAVING ON YOUR HOTEL ROOM

The **rack rate** is the maximum rate that a hotel charges for a room. Hardly anybody pays this price, however, except in high season or on holidays. To lower the cost of your room:

- **Ask about special rates or other discounts.** Always ask whether a room less expensive than the first one quoted is available, or whether any special rates apply to you. You may qualify for corporate, student, military, senior, or other discounts. Mention membership in AAA, AARP, frequent-flier programs, or trade unions, which may entitle you to special deals as well. Find out the hotel policy on children—do kids stay free in the room or is there a special rate?

- **Dial direct.** When booking a room in a chain hotel, you'll often get a better deal by calling the individual hotel's reservation desk rather than at the chain's main number.

- **Book online.** Many hotels offer Internet-only discounts, or supply rooms to Priceline, Hotwire, or Expedia at rates much lower than the ones you can get through the hotel itself. Shop around. And if you have special needs—a quiet room, a room with a view—call the hotel directly and make your needs known after you've booked online.

- **Remember the law of supply and demand.** Resort hotels are most crowded and therefore most expensive on weekends, so discounts are usually available for midweek stays. Business hotels in downtown locations are busiest during the week, so you can expect big discounts over the weekend. Many hotels have high-season and low-season prices, and booking the day after "high season" ends can mean big discounts.

- **Look into group or long-stay discounts.** If you come as part of a large group, you should be able to negotiate a bargain rate, since the hotel can then guarantee occupancy in a number of rooms. Likewise, if you're planning a long stay (at least 5 days), you might qualify for a discount. As a general rule, expect 1 night free after a 7-night stay.

- **Avoid excess charges and hidden costs.** When you book a room, ask whether the hotel charges for parking. Use your own cellphone, pay phones, or prepaid phone cards instead of dialing direct from hotel phones, which usually have exorbitant rates. And don't be tempted by the room's minibar offerings: Most hotels charge through the nose for water, soda, and snacks. Finally, ask about local taxes and service charges, which can increase the cost of a room by 15% or more. If a hotel insists upon tacking on a surprise "resort fee" for amenities you didn't use, you can often make a case for getting it removed.

- Consider the pros and cons of **all-inclusive** resorts and hotels. The term "all-inclusive" means different things at different hotels. Many all-inclusive hotels will include three meals daily, sports equipment, spa entry, and other amenities; others may include all or most drinks. In general, you'll save money going the "all-inclusive" way—as long as you use the facilities provided. The down side is that your choices are limited and you're stuck eating and playing in one place for the duration of your vacation.

- Carefully consider your hotel's meal plan. If you enjoy eating out and sampling the local cuisine, it makes sense to choose a **Continental Plan**

Tips Dial "E" for "Easy"

For quick directions on how to call Mexico, see "Telephone & Fax" in "Fast Facts," later in this chapter, or check out the "Telephone Tips" on the inside front cover of the book.

(CP), which includes breakfast only, or a **European Plan (EP)**, which doesn't include any meals and allows you maximum flexibility. If you're more interested in saving money, opt for a **Modified American Plan (MAP)**, which includes breakfast and one other meal, or the **American Plan (AP)**, which includes three meals. If you must choose a MAP, see if you can get a free lunch at your hotel if you decide to do dinner out.

- **Book an efficiency.** A room with a kitchenette allows you to shop for groceries and cook your own meals. This is a big money saver, especially for families on long stays.

- **Consider enrolling in hotel "frequent-stay" programs,** which reward repeat customers who accumulate enough points or credits to earn free hotel nights, airline miles, complimentary in-room amenities, or even merchandise. These are offered not only by many chain hotels and motels (Hilton HHonors, Marriott Rewards, Wyndham ByRequest, to name a few), but individual inns and B&Bs. Many chain hotels partner with other hotel chains, car-rental firms, airlines, and credit-card companies to give consumers additional ways to accumulate points in the program.

LANDING THE BEST ROOM

Somebody has to get the best room in the house. It might as well be you. You can start by joining the hotel's frequent-guest program, which may make you eligible for upgrades. A hotel-branded credit card usually gives it owner "silver" or "gold" status in frequent-guest programs for free. Always ask about a corner room. They're often larger and quieter, with more windows and light, and they often cost the same as standard rooms. When you make your reservation, ask if the hotel is renovating; if it is, request a room away from the construction. Ask about nonsmoking rooms, rooms with views, rooms with twin, queen- or king-size beds. If you're a light sleeper, request a quiet room away from vending machines, elevators, restaurants, bars, and dance clubs. Ask for a room that has been most recently renovated or redecorated.

If you aren't happy with your room when you arrive, ask for another one. Most lodgings will be willing to accommodate you.

In resort areas, ask the following questions before you book a room:

- What's the view like? Cost-conscious travelers may be willing to pay less for a back room facing the parking lot, especially if they don't plan to spend much time in their room.
- Does the room have air-conditioning or ceiling fans? Do the windows open? If they do, and the nighttime entertainment takes place al fresco, you may want to find out when show time is over.
- What's included in the price? If you're charged for beach chairs, towels, sports equipment, and other amenities, you could end up spending more than you bargained for.
- How far is the room from the beach and other amenities? If it's far, is there transportation to and from the beach, and is it free?

15 Getting Around Mexico

An important note: If your travel schedule depends on a vital connection—say, a plane trip or a ferry or bus connection— use the telephone numbers in this book or other resources to find out if the connection is still available.

BY PLANE

Mexico has two large private national carriers: **Mexicana** (✆ **01-800/366-5400** toll-free in Mexico), and **Aeromexico** (✆ **01-800/021-4000** toll-free in Mexico), in addition to several up-and-coming regional carriers. Mexicana and Aeromexico offer extensive connections to the United States as well as within Mexico.

Several new regional carriers are operated by or can be booked through Mexicana or Aeromexico. Regional carriers are Mexicana's **Aerocaribe** and **Aero Mar,** and Aeromexico's **Aerolitoral.** For points inside the state of Oaxaca only—Oaxaca City, Puerto Escondido, and Huatulco— contact **Zapotec Tours** (✆ **800/44-OAXACA,** or 773/506-2444 in Illinois). The regional carriers are expensive, but they go to difficult-to-reach places. In each applicable section of this book, we've mentioned regional carriers with all pertinent telephone numbers.

Because major airlines can book some regional carriers, read your ticket carefully to see if your connecting flight is on one of these smaller carriers—they may use a different airport or a different counter.

AIRPORT TAXES   Mexico charges an airport tax on all departures. Passengers leaving the country on international flights pay $18—in dollars or the peso equivalent. It has become a common practice to include this departure tax in your ticket price, but double-check to make sure so you're not caught by surprise at the airport. Taxes on each domestic departure within Mexico are around $13, unless you're on a connecting flight and have already paid at the start of the flight.

Mexico charges an $18 "tourism tax," the proceeds of which go into a tourism promotional fund. Your ticket price may not include it, so be sure to have enough money to pay it at the airport upon departure.

RECONFIRMING FLIGHTS   Although Mexican airlines say it's not necessary to reconfirm a flight, it's still a good idea. To avoid getting bumped on popular, possibly overbooked flights, check in for an international flight 1½ hours in advance of travel.

BY CAR

Most Mexican roads are not up to U.S. standards of smoothness, hardness, width of curve, grade of hill, or safety markings. Driving at night is dangerous—the roads are rarely lit; trucks, carts, pedestrians, and bicycles usually have no lights; and you can hit potholes, animals, rocks, dead ends, or uncrossable bridges without warning.

The spirited style of Mexican driving sometimes requires super vision and reflexes. Be prepared for new customs, as when a truck driver flips on his left turn signal when there's not a crossroad for miles. He's probably telling you the road's clear ahead for you to pass. Another custom that's very important to respect is turning left. Never turn left by stopping in the middle of a highway with your left signal on. Instead, pull onto the right shoulder, wait for traffic to clear, then proceed across the road.

GASOLINE   There's one government-owned brand of gas and one gasoline station name throughout the country— **Pemex** (Petroleras Mexicanas). There are two types of gas in Mexico: *magna,* 87-octane unleaded gas, and premium 93 octane. In Mexico, fuel and oil are sold by the liter, which is slightly more than a quart (40 liters equals about 11 gal.). Many franchise Pemex stations have bathroom facilities and convenience stores—a great improvement over the old ones.

Important note: No credit cards are currently accepted for gas purchases.

TOLL ROADS Mexico charges some of the highest tolls in the world for its network of new toll roads; as a result, they are rarely used. Generally speaking, though, using toll roads cuts travel time. Older toll-free roads are generally in good condition, but travel times tend to be longer.

BREAKDOWNS If your car breaks down on the road, help might already be on the way. Radio-equipped green repair trucks operated by uniformed English-speaking officers patrol major highways during daylight hours. These **"Green Angels"** perform minor repairs and adjustments free, but you pay for parts and materials.

Your best guide to repair shops is the Yellow Pages. For repairs, look under *Automóviles y Camiones: Talleres de Reparación y Servicio;* auto-parts stores are under *Refacciones y Accesorios para Automóviles.* To find a mechanic on the road, look for a sign that says TALLER MECANICO.

Places called *vulcanizadora* or *llantera* repair flat tires, and it is common to find them open 24 hours a day on the most traveled highways.

MINOR ACCIDENTS When possible, many Mexicans drive away from minor accidents, or try to make an immediate settlement, to avoid involving the police. If the police arrive while the involved persons are still at the scene, everyone may be locked in jail until blame is assessed. In any case, you have to settle up immediately, which may take days. Foreigners who don't speak fluent Spanish are at a distinct disadvantage when trying to explain their version of the event. Three steps may help the foreigner who doesn't wish to do as the Mexicans do: If you were in your own car, notify your Mexican insurance company, whose job it is to intervene on your behalf. If you were in a rental car, notify the rental company immediately and ask how to contact the nearest adjuster. (You did buy insurance with the rental, right?) Finally, if all else fails, ask to contact the nearest Green Angel, who may be able to explain to officials that you are covered by insurance. See also "Mexican Auto Insurance" in "Getting There," earlier in this chapter.

CAR RENTALS You'll get the best price if you reserve a car at least a week in advance in the United States. U.S. car-rental firms include **Advantage** (© 800/777-5500 in the U.S. and Canada; www.arac.com), **Avis** (© 800/331-1212 in the U.S., 800/TRY-AVIS in Canada; www.avis.com), **Budget** (© 800/527-0700 in the U.S. and Canada; www.budget.com), **Hertz** (© 800/654-3131 in the U.S. and Canada; www.hertz.com), **National** (© 800/CAR-RENT in the U.S. and Canada; www.nationalcar.com), and **Thrifty** (© 800/367-2277 in the U.S. and Canada; www.thrifty.com), which often offers discounts for rentals in Mexico. For European travelers, **Kemwel Holiday Auto** (© 800/678-0678; www.kemwel.com) and **Auto Europe** (© 800/223-5555; www.autoeurope.com) can arrange Mexican rentals, sometimes through other agencies. These and some local firms have offices in Mexico City and most other large Mexican cities. You'll find rental desks at airports, all major hotels, and many travel agencies.

Cars are easy to rent if you are 25 or over and have a major credit card, valid driver's license, and passport with you. Without a credit card you must leave a cash deposit, usually a big one. One-way rentals are usually simple to arrange but more costly.

Car-rental costs are high in Mexico because cars are more expensive. The condition of rental cars has improved greatly over the years, and clean new cars are the norm. The basic cost of the 1-day rental

Bus Hijackings

The U.S. State Department notes that bandits target long-distance buses traveling at night, but there have been daylight robberies as well. Buses are more common targets than individual cars—they offer thieves more bucks for the bang.

---

of a Volkswagen Beetle at press time, with unlimited mileage (but before 15% tax and $15 daily insurance), was $48 in Cancún, $52 in Mexico City, $44 in Puerto Vallarta, $48 in Oaxaca, and $38 in Mérida. Renting by the week gives you a lower daily rate. Avis was offering a basic 7-day rate for a VW Beetle (before tax or insurance) of $220 in Cancún and Puerto Vallarta, $180 in Mérida, and $250 in Mexico City. Prices may be considerably higher if you rent around a major holiday. Also double-check charges for insurance—some companies will increase the insurance rate after several days. Always ask for detailed information about all charges you will be responsible for.

Car-rental companies usually write credit-card charges in U.S. dollars.

Deductibles Be careful—these vary greatly; some are as high as $2,500, which comes out of your pocket immediately in case of damage. On a VW Beetle, Hertz's deductible is $1,000 and Avis's is $500.

Insurance Insurance is offered in two parts: **Collision and damage** insurance covers your car and others if the accident is your fault, and **personal accident** insurance covers you and anyone in your car. Read the fine print on the back of your rental agreement and note that insurance may be invalid if you have an accident while driving on an unpaved road.

Damage Always inspect your car carefully and note every damaged or missing item, no matter how minute, on your rental agreement, or you may be charged.

BY TAXI

Taxis are the preferred way to get around almost all of Mexico's resort areas, and around Mexico City. Fares for short trips within towns are generally preset by zone, and are quite reasonable compared with U.S. rates. (Los Cabos is one exception. Another is taxi service to the north side of the bay from Puerto Vallarta. Travelers are better off renting a car than paying these exorbitant taxi fares—$80 for a one-way trip to Punta Mita.) For longer trips or excursions to nearby cities, taxis can generally be hired for around $10 to $15 per hour, or for a negotiated daily rate. A negotiated one-way price is usually much less than the cost of a rental car for a day, and a taxi travels much faster than a bus. For anyone who is uncomfortable driving in Mexico, this is a convenient, comfortable alternative. A bonus is that you have a Spanish-speaking person with you in case you run into trouble. Many taxi drivers speak at least some English. Your hotel can assist you with the arrangements.

BY BUS

Except for the Baja peninsula, where bus service is not well developed, Mexican buses run frequently, are readily accessible, and can get you to almost anywhere you want to go. They're often the only way to get from large cities to other nearby cities and small villages. Don't hesitate to ask questions if you're confused about anything, but note that little English is spoken in bus stations.

Dozens of Mexican companies operate large, air-conditioned, Greyhound-type buses between most cities. Classes are *segunda* (second), *primera* (first), and *ejecutiva* (deluxe), which goes by a variety of names. Deluxe buses often have fewer seats than regular buses, show video movies, are air-conditioned, and make few stops. Many run express from point to point. They are well worth the few dollars more. In rural areas, buses are often of the school-bus variety, with lots of local color.

Whenever possible, it's best to buy your reserved-seat ticket, often using a computerized system, a day in advance on long-distance routes and especially before holidays. See appendix B for a list of helpful bus terms in Spanish.

16 Recommended Books & Films

Studying up on Mexico can be one of the most fun bits of "research" you'll ever do. If you'd like to learn more about this fascinating country before you go—which I encourage—these books and movies are an enjoyable way to do it.

BOOKS

HISTORY & CULTURE For an overview of pre-Hispanic cultures, pick up a copy of Michael D. Coe's *Mexico: From the Olmecs to the Aztecs* or Nigel Davies's *Ancient Kingdoms of Mexico.* Richard Townsend's *The Aztecs* is a thorough, well-researched examination of the Aztec and the Spanish conquest. For the Maya, Michael Coe's *The Maya* is probably the best general account. For a survey of Mexican history through modern times, *A Short History of Mexico* by J. Patrick McHenry (Doubleday) provides a complete, yet concise account.

John L. Stephens's *Incidents of Travel in the Yucatán, Vol. I and II* (Dover Publications) are considered among the great books of archaeological discovery, as well as being travel classics. The two volumes chart the course of Stephens's discoveries of the Yucatán, beginning in 1841. Before his expeditions, little was known of the region, and the Mayan culture had not been discovered. During his travels, Stephens found and described 44 Mayan sites, and his account of these remains the most authoritative in existence.

For a more modern exploration of the archaeology of the region, Peter Tompkins's *Mysteries of the Mexican Pyramids* is a visually rich book which explores not only the ruins of the Maya in the Yucatán, but the whole of Mexico's archaeological treasures.

For contemporary culture, start with Octavio Paz's classic, *The Labyrinth of Solitude,* which still generates controversy among Mexicans. For a recent collection of writings by Subcomandante Marcos, leader of the Zapatista movement, try *Our Word is Our Weapon.* Another source is *Basta! Land and the Zapatista Rebellion* by George Collier, et al. For those already familiar with Mexico and its culture, Guillermo Bonfil's *Mexico Profundo: Reclaiming a Civilization* is a rare bottom-up view of Mexico today.

Lesley Byrd Simpson's *Many Mexicos* (University of California Press) provides a comprehensive account of Mexican history with a cultural context. A classic on understanding the culture of this country is *Distant Neighbors,* by Alan Riding (Vintage).

ART & ARCHITECTURE *Art and Time in Mexico: From the Conquest to the Revolution,* by Elizabeth Wilder Weismann, covers religious, public, and private architecture. *Casa Mexicana,* by Tim Street-Porter, takes readers through the interiors of some of Mexico's finest homes-turned-museums, public buildings, and private homes.

Folk Treasures of Mexico, by Marion Oettinger, is the fascinating story behind the 3,000-piece Mexican folk-art collection amassed by Nelson Rockefeller over a 50-year period.

Maya Art and Architecture, by Mary Ellen Miller (Thames and Hudson) showcases the best of the artistic expression of this culture, with interpretations into its meanings.

For a wonderful read on the food of the Yucatán and Mexico, pick up *Mexico,* *One Plate at a Time,* by celebrity chef and Mexico aficionado Rick Bayless (Scribner).

NATURE *A Naturalist's Mexico,* by Roland H. Wauer, is a fabulous guide to birding. *A Hiker's Guide to Mexico's Natural History,* by Jim Conrad, covers flora and fauna and tells how to find the easy-to-reach as well as out-of-the-way spots he describes. *Peterson Field Guides: Mexican Birds,* by Roger Tory Peterson and Edward L. Chalif, is an excellent guide.

FAST FACTS: Mexico

Abbreviations Dept. (apartments); Apdo. (post office box); Av. (*avenida;* avenue); c/ (*calle;* street); Calz. (*calzada;* boulevard). "C" on faucets stands for *caliente* (hot), "F" for *fría* (cold). "PB" *(planta baja)* means ground floor; in most buildings the next floor up is the first floor (1).

Business Hours In general, businesses in larger cities are open between 9am and 7pm; in smaller towns many close between 2 and 4pm. Most close on Sunday. In resort areas it is common to find stores open at least in the mornings on Sunday, and for shops to stay open late, often until 8pm or even 10pm. Bank hours are Monday through Friday from 9 or 9:30am to anywhere between 3 and 7pm. Increasingly, banks open on Saturday for at least a half-day.

Cameras & Film Film costs about the same as in the United States. Tourists wishing to use a video or still camera at any archaeological site in Mexico or at many museums operated by the Instituto de Antropología e Historia (INAH) must pay $4 per camera at each site visited. (Listings for specific sites and museums note this fee.) Also, use of a tripod at any archaeological site requires a permit from INAH. It's courteous to ask permission before photographing anyone. It is never considered polite to take photos inside a church in Mexico. In some areas, such as around San Cristóbal de las Casas (see chapter 11), there are other restrictions on photographing people and villages.

Car Rentals See "Getting Around Mexico," earlier in this chapter.

Climate See "When to Go," earlier in this chapter.

Currency See "Money," earlier in this chapter.

Doctors & Dentists Every embassy and consulate can recommend local doctors and dentists with good training and modern equipment; some of the doctors and dentists speak English. See the list of embassies and consulates under "Embassies & Consulates," below. Hotels with a large foreign clientele can often recommend English-speaking doctors.

Driving Rules See "Getting Around Mexico," earlier in this chapter.

Drug Laws It may sound obvious, but don't use or possess illegal drugs in Mexico. Mexican officials have no tolerance for drug users, and jail is their solution, with very little hope of getting out until the sentence (usually a long one) is completed or heavy fines or bribes are paid. Remember, in Mexico the legal system assumes you are guilty until proven innocent. *Note:* It isn't uncommon to be befriended by a fellow user, only to be turned in by that "friend," who collects a bounty. Bring prescription drugs in their original containers. If possible, pack a copy of the original prescription with the generic name of the drug.

U.S. Customs officials are on the lookout for diet drugs that are sold in Mexico but illegal in the U.S. Possession could land you in a U.S. jail. If you buy antibiotics over the counter (which you can do in Mexico) and still have some left, U.S. Customs probably won't hassle you.

Drugstores Farmacias (pharmacies) will sell you just about anything, with or without a prescription. Most pharmacies are open Monday through Saturday from 8am to 8pm. The major resort areas generally have one or two 24-hour pharmacies. Pharmacies take turns staying open during off hours; if you are in a smaller town and need to buy medicine during off hours, ask for the *farmacia de turno.*

Electricity The electrical system in Mexico is 110 volts AC (60 cycles), as in the United States and Canada. In reality, however, it may cycle more slowly and overheat your appliances. To compensate, select a medium or low speed on hair dryers. Many older hotels still have electrical outlets for flat two-prong plugs; you'll need an adapter for any plug with an enlarged end on one prong or with three prongs. Many better hotels have three-hole outlets (*trifásicos* in Spanish). Those that don't may have loan adapters, but to be sure, it's always better to carry your own.

Embassies & Consulates They provide valuable lists of doctors and lawyers, as well as regulations concerning marriages in Mexico. Contrary to popular belief, your embassy cannot get you out of jail, provide postal or banking services, or fly you home when you run out of money. Consular officers can provide advice on most matters and problems, however. Most countries have an embassy in Mexico City, and many have consular offices or representatives in the provinces.

The Embassy of the **United States** in Mexico City is at Paseo de la Reforma 305, next to the Hotel María Isabel Sheraton at the corner of Río Danubio (© **55/ 5080-2000** or 555/511-9980); hours are Monday through Friday from 8:30am to 5:30pm. Visit www.usembassy-mexico.gov for addresses of the U.S. consulates inside Mexico. There are U.S. Consulates General at López Mateos 924-N, Ciudad Juárez (© **656/611-3000**); Progreso 175, Guadalajara (© **333/268-2100**); Av. Constitución 411 Pte., Monterrey (© **818/345-2120**); and Tapachula 96, Tijuana (© **664/622-7400**). In addition, there are consular agencies in Acapulco (© **744/ 469-0556**); Cabo San Lucas (© **624/143-3566**); Cancún (© **998/883-0272**); Cozumel (© **987/872-4574**); Hermosillo (© **662/217-2375**); Ixtapa/Zihuatanejo (© **755/ 553-2100**); Matamoros (© **868/812-4402**); Mazatlán (© **669/916-5889**); Mérida

(© 999/925-5011); Nogales (© 631/313-4820); Nuevo Laredo (© 867/714-0512); Oaxaca (© 951/514-3054); Puerto Vallarta (© 322/222-0069); San Luis Potosí (© 444/811-7802); and San Miguel de Allende (© 415/152-2357).

The Embassy of **Australia** in Mexico City is at Rubén Darío 55, Col. Polanco (© 55/51101-2200). It's open Monday through Friday from 9am to 1pm.

The Embassy of **Canada** in Mexico City is at Schiller 529, Col. Polanco (© 555/724-7900); it's open Monday through Friday from 9am to 1pm. At other times, the name of a duty officer is posted on the door. Visit www.dfait-maeci.gc.ca for addresses of consular agencies in Mexico. There are Canadian consulates in Acapulco (© 744/484-1305); Cancún (© 998/883-3360); Guadalajara (© 333/615-6215); Mazatlán (© 669/913-7320); Monterrey (© 818/344-2753); Oaxaca (© 951/513-3777); Puerto Vallarta (© 322/293-0098); San José del Cabo (© 624/142-4333); and Tijuana (© 664/684-0461).

The Embassy of **New Zealand** in Mexico City is at José Luis Lagrange 103, 10th floor, Col. Los Morales Polanco (© 55/5283-9460; kiwimexico@compuserve.com.mx). It's open Monday through Friday from 8am to 3pm.

The Embassy of the **United Kingdom** in Mexico City is at Río Lerma 71, Col. Cuauhtémoc (© 55/5242-8500; www.embajadabritanica.com.mx). It's open Monday through Friday from 8:30am to 3:30pm.

The Embassy of **Ireland** in Mexico City is at Bulevar Cerrada, Avila Camacho 76, 3rd floor, Col. Lomas de Chapultepec (© 55/5520-5803). It's open Monday through Friday from 9am to 5pm.

The **South African** Embassy in Mexico City is at Andrés Bello 10, 9th floor, Col. Polanco (© 55/5282-9260). It's open Monday through Friday from 8am to 3:30pm.

Emergencies In case of emergency, dial © 065 from any phone within Mexico. For police emergency numbers, turn to "Fast Facts" in the chapters that follow. The 24-hour **Tourist Help Line** in Mexico City is © 01-800/903-9200 or 555/250-0151. The operators don't always speak English, but they are always willing to help. The tourist legal assistance office (Procuraduría del Turista) in Mexico City (© 555/625-8153 or 555/625-8154;) always has an English speaker available. Though the phones are frequently busy, they operate 24 hours.

Holidays See "Mexico Calendar of Events," earlier in this chapter.

Internet Access In large cities and resort areas, a growing number of top hotels offer business centers with Internet access. You'll also find cybercafes in destinations that are popular with expats and business travelers. Even in remote spots, Internet access is common. Note that many ISPs automatically cut off your Internet connection after a specified period of time (say, 10 min.), because telephone lines are at a premium.

Language Spanish is the official language in Mexico. English is spoken and understood to some degree in most tourist areas. Mexicans are very accommodating with foreigners who try to speak Spanish, even in broken sentences. For basic vocabulary, refer to appendix B.

Legal Aid **International Legal Defense Counsel,** 111 S. 15th St., 24th floor, Packard Building., Philadelphia, PA 19102 (© **215/977-9982**), is a law firm specializing in legal difficulties of Americans abroad. See also "Embassies & Consulates" and "Emergencies," above.

Liquor Laws The legal drinking age in Mexico is 18; however, asking for ID or denying purchase is extremely rare. Grocery stores sell everything from beer and wine to national and imported liquors. You can buy liquor 24 hours a day, but during major elections, dry laws often are enacted for as much as 72 hours in advance of the election—and they apply to tourists as well as local residents. Mexico does not have laws that apply to transporting liquor in cars, but authorities are beginning to target drunk drivers more aggressively. It's a good idea to drive defensively.

It is not legal to drink in the street; however, many tourists do so. If you are getting drunk, you shouldn't drink in the street, because you are more likely to get stopped by the police.

Lost & Found To replace a **lost passport,** contact your embassy or nearest consular agent. You must establish a record of your citizenship and fill out a form requesting another FMT (tourist permit) if it, too, was lost. If your documents are stolen, get a police report from local authorities; having one *might* lessen the hassle of exiting the country without all your identification. Without the FMT, you can't leave the country, and without an affidavit affirming your passport request and citizenship, you may have problems at U.S. Customs when you get home. It's important to clear everything up *before* trying to leave. Mexican Customs may, however, accept the police report of the loss of the FMT and allow you to leave.

If you lose your **wallet** anywhere outside of Mexico City, before panicking, retrace your steps—you'll be surprised at how honest people are, and you'll likely find someone trying to find you to return your wallet.

If your wallet is stolen, the police probably won't be able to recover it. Be sure to notify all of your credit card companies right away, and file a report at the nearest police precinct. Your credit card company or insurer may require a police report number or record of the loss. Most credit card companies have an emergency toll-free number to call if your card is lost or stolen; these numbers are not toll-free within Mexico (see "Telephone & Fax," below, for instructions on calling U.S. toll-free numbers). The company may be able to wire you a cash advance off your credit card immediately, and, in many places, can deliver an emergency credit card in a day or two. **Visa**'s U.S. emergency number is © **800/847-2911** or 410/581-9994. **American Express** cardholders and traveler's check holders should call © **800/221-7282. MasterCard** holders should call © **800/307-7309** or 636/722-7111. For other credit cards, call the toll-free number directory at © **800/555-1212.**

If you need emergency cash over the weekend when all banks and American Express offices are closed, you can have money wired to you via **Western Union** (© **800/325-6000;** www.westernunion.com).

Identity theft or fraud are potential complications of losing your wallet, especially if you've lost your driver's license along with your cash and credit cards. Notify the major credit-reporting bureaus immediately; placing a fraud alert on your records may protect you against liability for criminal activity. The three major U.S. credit-reporting agencies are **Equifax** (© **800/766-0008;** www.equifax.com), **Experian** (© **888/397-3742;** www.experian.com), and **Trans-Union** (© **800/680-7289;** www.transunion.com). Finally, if you've lost all forms of photo ID call your airline and explain the situation; they might allow you to board the plane if you have a copy of your passport or birth certificate and a copy of the police report you've filed.

Mail Postage for a postcard or letter is 1 peso; it may arrive anywhere from 1 to 6 weeks later. A registered letter costs $1.90. Sending a package can be quite expensive—the Mexican postal service charges $8 per kilo (2.2 lb.)—and unreliable; it takes 2 to 6 weeks, if it arrives at all. The recommended way to send a package or important mail is through FedEx, DHL, UPS, or another reputable international mail service.

Newspapers & Magazines There currently is no national English-language newspaper. Newspaper kiosks in larger cities carry a selection of English-language magazines.

Passports **For Residents of the United States:** Whether you're applying in person or by mail, you can download passport applications from the U.S. State Department website at **www.travel.state.gov**. To find your regional passport office, either check the U.S. State Department website or call the **National Passport Information Center's** toll-free number (© **877/487-2778**) for automated information.

For Residents of Canada: Passport applications are available at travel agencies throughout Canada or from the central Department of Foreign Affairs and International Trade, Ottawa, ON K1A 0G3 (© **800/567-6868;** www.ppt.gc.ca).

For Residents of the United Kingdom: To pick up an application for a standard 10-year passport (5-year passport for children under 16), visit your nearest passport office, major post office, or travel agency or contact the **United Kingdom Passport Service** at © **0870/521-0410** or search its website at www.ukpa.gov.uk.

For Residents of Ireland: You can apply for a 10-year passport at the **Passport Office,** Setanta Centre, Molesworth Street, Dublin 2 (© **01/671-1633;** www.irlgov.ie/iveagh). Those under age 18 and over 65 must apply for a €12 3-year passport. You can also apply at 1A South Mall, Cork (© **021/272-525**) or at most main post offices.

For Residents of Australia: You can pick up an application from your local post office or any branch of Passports Australia, but you must schedule an interview at the passport office to present your application materials. Call the **Australian Passport Information Service** at © **131-232,** or visit the government website at www.passports.gov.au.

For Residents of New Zealand: You can pick up a passport application at any New Zealand Passports Office or download it from their website. Contact the **Passports Office** at © **0800/225-050** in New Zealand or 04/474-8100, or log on to www.passports.govt.nz.

Pets Taking a pet into Mexico is easy but requires a little planning. Animals coming from the United States and Canada need to be checked for health within 30 days before arrival in Mexico. Most veterinarians in major cities have the appropriate paperwork—an official health certificate, to be presented to Mexican Customs officials, that ensures the pet's vaccinations are up-to-date. When you and your pet return from Mexico, U.S. Customs officials will require the same type of paperwork. If your stay extends beyond the 30-day time frame of your U.S.-issued certificate, you'll need an updated Certificate of Health issued by a veterinarian in Mexico. To check last-minute changes in requirements, consult the Mexican Government Tourist Office nearest you (see "Visitor Information," earlier in this chapter).

Police In Mexico City, police are to be suspected as frequently as they are to be trusted; however, you'll find many who are quite honest and helpful. In the rest of the country, especially in the tourist areas, most are very protective of international visitors. Several cities, including Puerto Vallarta, Mazatlán, Cancún, and Acapulco, have a special corps of English-speaking Tourist Police to assist with directions, guidance, and more.

Restrooms See "Toilets," below.

Safety See "Health & Safety," earlier in this chapter.

Smoking Smoking is permitted and generally accepted in most public places, including restaurants, bars, and hotel lobbies. Nonsmoking areas and hotel rooms for nonsmokers are becoming more common in higher-end establishments, but they tend to be the exception rather than the rule.

Taxes The 15% IVA (value-added) tax applies on goods and services in most of Mexico, and it's supposed to be included in the posted price. This tax is 10% in Cancún, Cozumel, and Los Cabos. There is a 5% tax on food and drinks consumed in restaurants that sell alcoholic beverages with an alcohol content of more than 10%; this tax applies whether you drink alcohol or not. Tequila is subject to a 25% tax. Mexico imposes an exit tax of around $18 on every foreigner leaving the country (see "Airport Taxes" under "Getting Around Mexico: By Plane," earlier in this chapter).

Telephone & Fax Mexico's telephone system is slowly but surely catching up with modern times. All telephone numbers have 10 digits. Every city and town that has telephone access has a two-digit (Mexico City, Monterrey, and Guadalajara) or three-digit (everywhere else) area code. In Mexico City, Monterrey, and Guadalajara, local numbers have eight digits; elsewhere, local numbers have seven digits. To place a local call, you do not need to dial the area code. Many fax numbers are also regular telephone numbers; ask whoever answers for the fax tone (*"me da tono de fax, por favor"*). Cellular phones are very popular for small businesses in resort areas and smaller communities. To call a cellular number inside the same area code, dial 044 and then the number. To dial the cellular phone from anywhere else in Mexico, first dial 01, and then the three-digit area code and the seven-digit number. To dial it from the U.S., dial 011-52, plus the three-digit area code and the seven-digit number.

The **country code** for Mexico is **52.**

To call Mexico: If you're calling Mexico from the United States:

1. Dial the international access code: 011.
2. Dial the country code: 52.
3. Dial the two- or three-digit area code, then the eight- or seven-digit number. For example, if you wanted to call the U.S. consulate in Acapulco, the whole number would be 011-52-744-469-0556. If you wanted to dial the U.S. embassy in Mexico City, the whole number would be 011-52-55-5209-9100.

To make international calls: To make international calls from Mexico, first dial 00, then the country code (U.S. or Canada 1, U.K. 44, Ireland 353, Australia 61, New Zealand 64). Next, dial the area code and number. For example, to call the British Embassy in Washington, you would dial 00-1-202-588-7800.

For directory assistance: Dial ℂ **040** if you're looking for a number inside Mexico. *Note:* Listings usually appear under the owner's name, not the name of the business, and your chances to find an English-speaking operator are slim to none.

For operator assistance: If you need operator assistance in making a call, dial ℂ **090** to make an international call, and ℂ **020** to call a number in Mexico.

Toll-free numbers: Numbers beginning with 800 within Mexico are toll-free, but calling a U.S. toll-free number from Mexico costs the same as an overseas call. To call an 800 number in the U.S., dial 001-880 and the last seven digits of the toll-free number. To call an 888 number in the U.S., dial 001-881 and the last seven digits of the toll-free number. For a number with an 887 prefix, dial 882; for 866, dial 883.

Time Zone Central Time prevails throughout most of Mexico. The states of Sonora, Sinaloa, and parts of Nayarit are on Mountain Time. The state of Baja California Norte is on Pacific Time, but Baja California Sur is on Mountain Time. All of Mexico observes **daylight saving time.**

Tipping Most service employees in Mexico count on tips for the majority of their income, and this is especially true for bellboys and waiters. Bellboys should receive the equivalent of 50¢ to $1 per bag; waiters generally receive 10% to 20%, depending on the level of service. It is not customary to tip taxi drivers, unless they are hired by the hour or provide touring or other special services.

Toilets Public toilets are not common in Mexico, but an increasing number are available, especially at fast-food restaurants and Pemex gas stations. These facilities and restaurant and club restrooms commonly have attendants, who expect a small tip (about 50¢).

Useful Phone Numbers **Tourist Help Line,** available 24 hours (© 01-800/903-9200 toll-free inside Mexico). **Mexico Hot Line** (© 800/44-MEXICO). **U.S. Dept. of State Travel Advisory,** staffed 24 hours (© 202/647-5225). **U.S. Passport Agency** (© 202/647-0518). **U.S. Centers for Disease Control and Prevention International Traveler's Hot Line** (© 404/332-4559).

Water Most hotels have decanters or bottles of purified water in the rooms, and the better hotels have either purified water from regular taps or special taps marked *agua purificada.* Some hotels charge for in-room bottled water. Virtually any hotel, restaurant, or bar will bring you purified water if you specifically request it but will usually charge you for it. Drugstores and grocery stores sell bottled purified water. Some popular brands are Santa María, Ciel, and Bonafont. Evian and other imported brands are also widely available.

3

Suggested Mexico Itineraries

by David Baird

Mexico is a land of contrasts, which makes it the perfect destination for those seeking a little variety in their travels. Several of the suggested itineraries described below will take you through changing landscapes and both big-city and small-town Mexico. A few itineraries conclude at a beach resort so that you can relax a little at the end of your trip. But there's another reason for this: I wanted to make use of Mexico's major points of entry—the big international airports—and many of these happen to serve resorts. When I visit Mexico, I seldom book a round-trip ticket, preferring to enter through one airport and leave through another; usually I don't have to pay any extra for doing this. Times have changed and round-trip fares aren't what they used to be.

Once inside Mexico, most travel is by bus, rental car, or a hired car and driver. Domestic flights are expensive, and there is only one true passenger train still operating. This train runs along the Copper Canyon to Chihuahua City and works well for the surf-to-sierra approach that I like (see "Los Cabos to Copper Canyon," below). I've tried to keep time spent traveling to a minimum for obvious reasons. None of these can be called exhaustive explorations of Mexico, but neither are they exhausting. If you want to put together a tour linking all of Mexico's most famous sites, you can connect the central archaeological tour with the Ruta Maya. This would take 3 weeks and cover most of what Mexico is famous for.

Renting a car works really well for the Yucatán and a few other parts of the country. In other areas it can be confusing as road signs are not always posted. Hiring a car and driver or taking the bus for certain legs of the trip are reasonable options. Mexico has good buses with an array of categories of service. Once you're inside a town or city it's usually best to use taxis, which are for the most part cheap and plentiful.

1 Central Mexico's Pre-Columbian Treasures in a Week

Most of Mexico's great archaeological sites, aside from those left by the Maya, are located in the center of the country, from Mexico City to the east. This trip takes yo to the best of these and to the three most impressive archaeological museums in Mexico. The area in which all of this is located is relatively compact. It doesn't require a lot of travel time to cover, unless you add on a side trip to Oaxaca for the ruins of Monte Albán and Mitla.

Days ❶, ❷ & ❸: Arrive in Mexico City
If you arrive at an early hour, go straight to the very heart of the nation: Mexico's

zócalo or main square (p. 139). There, poetically situated between the nation's pre-eminent cathedral and its National Palace, are the ruins of the Aztec's **Templo Mayor**

Central Mexico's Pre-Columbian Treasures

(p. 128), left buried and forgotten until 1978. Explore the ruins and the museum. Dedicate your first full day of activity to the **Museo Nacional de Antropología** (p. 126). By the third day you may have adapted to the altitude and are ready for a day trip to **Teotihuacán** (p. 150), "City of the Gods," where you can explore palaces and pyramids and climb to the summit of the **Pyramid of the Sun** (p. 153).

Day ❹: Tlaxcala

Drive or take a bus to colonial Tlaxcala to view the vivid murals of **Cacaxtla** and the hilltop stronghold of **Xochitécatl** (p. 511). The murals are painted in an intriguing Maya style, with rich symbolism that invites speculation. Stay the night here and enjoy the slow rhythms and street life of the town. Though it is a state capital (in the smallest state in Mexico), Tlaxcala is small and off the beaten path. It still retains an unhurried, graceful air. Stroll over to the **Government Palace** (p. 511) to view the modern murals of artist Desiderio Hernández Xochitiotzin, which chronicle the history of the Tlaxcaltecans, ancient rivals of the Aztecs. See p. 511.

Day ❺: Puebla 🍴🍴 & Cholula

From Tlaxcala it's a quick car or bus ride to colonial **Puebla** (p. 500) and its satellite town, Cholula, which was the ancient religious center of central Mexico. In the afternoon, visit the **Museo Amparo** (p. 506) to see its stunning collection of pre-Hispanic art, then over to **Cholula** (p. 510) the next day to view the ruins of Mexico's largest pyramid with the beautiful volcano "El Popo" as a backdrop. If you have time, visit the local churches of **Tonantzintla** (p. 510) and **San Francisco Acatepec** (p. 511) for their beautiful Indian baroque design.

Day ❻: Xalapa

From Puebla it's on to bustling **Xalapa** (p. 494), a 3-hour drive from the dry central plateau to the misty slopes of the Sierra Madre Oriental. Visit the city's wonderful **Museo Antropología** (p. 497) with a collection of megalithic Olmec heads and expressive Totonac art.

Day ❼: Veracruz City 🍴

Next travel down to the old port city of **Veracruz** (p. 485). Enjoy a relaxing day in this lively town with its coffee shops, tropical music, and dance. From here, you can fly out directly or via Mexico City. To extend your trip, you can head north to see the ruins of **El Tajín** (p. 498) or south to **Oaxaca** (p. 435) to see Monte Albán and Mitla.

Mexico's Best Shopping

2 Mexico's Best Shopping in a Week

There's a lot of good shopping in Mexico, but this trip takes you to the most varied sites in the country. All the stops on this route are interesting for more than just shopping, so there will be plenty to keep everyone interested.

Days ① & ②: Arrive in Mexico City

The happy hunting grounds for curios, antiques, decorative objects and one-of-a-kind handicrafts are concentrated in the **Centro Histórico** and the **Zona Rosa** (p. 142). But just for kicks, check out the Saturday shopper's special at the **Bazar del Sábado** (p. 144) in the San Angel neighborhood. You never know what you'll find there.

Days ③ & ④: San Miguel de Allende ✪✪✪

This comfortable town in the highlands 3½ hours north of Mexico City is a pleasure to walk around in, with a great variety of sophisticated shops. Work you way though the streets in and around **El Jardín,** and make sure not to neglect the shops on **Zacateros** and **Hernández Macías** streets. If you're willing to extend your trip another day, hire a car and driver for a trip to **Dolores Hidalgo** (p. 198) to load up on inexpensive *talavera* pottery, and to **Guanajuato** (p. 199) to see the creations of local famous ceramists, Capelo and Gorky González.

From San Miguel you can have your things shipped back home. See p. 188.

Days ⑤ & ⑥: Guadalajara

Take the deluxe ETN bus for the 5-hour trip. Your objective will be the craft towns of **Tlaquepaque** (p. 279) and **Tonalá** (p. 281) for all manner of furniture, handicrafts, art, jewelry, and decorative objects. Walk up and down pedestrian-only **Independencia** and enter whatever shops strike your fancy; there are plenty to choose from, and everyone is helpful and low-key in approaching customers. If you want to be more methodical, get a list of shops from the tourism office. For bargains and to have something custom made, go to Tonalá, where nearly 400 local *talleres* (workshops) work with all manner of materials.

Day ⑦: Arrive in Puerto Vallarta ✪✪✪

Come for the galleries and the Huichol art; stay as long as you want to rest and relax. Then, when you're ready, fly back home. See p. 283.

The Best of Western Mexico

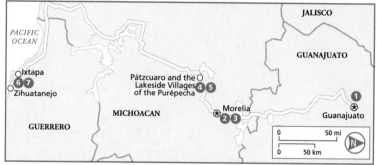

On this route you enter Mexico through the Leon/Guanajuato International airport and leave from Ixtapa-Zihuatanejo. In between you're treated to a variety of places and scenes—from the maze of streets and alleyways of the old mining town of Guanajuato, to the stately colonial city of Morelia, to the Indian town of Pátzcuaro to the modern resort hotels of Ixtapa and Zihuatanejo. From November to March you can add a day trip from Morelia to a magical place in the mountain forests east of the city where millions of monarch butterflies congregate in a yearly ritual that is one of the most intriguing of nature's mysteries.

Day ❶: Guanajuato ★★★

Take it easy until you get used to the altitude. Contract a taxi to give you a tour of the city by taking you along the panoramic highway that circles the narrow valley where the old city is nestled. Stop to take in the **view** from the statue of **El Pípila** (p. 203) before descending to the subterranean highway to see the houses cantilevered out over the road. Once you're ready for a stroll, try navigating through the jumble of streets surrounding the city's main plaza, taking time to visit a couple of the downtown **museums.** See p. 203.

Days ❷ & ❸: Morelia ★

Take a taxi or bus for the 2½-hour drive to **Morelia** (p. 239). Build in some time to enjoy the **cathedral** from one of the many vantage points offered by the cafes and restaurants that front Avenida Madero. This is best done in late afternoon/early

evening, when it appears to the casual visitor that no one in Morelia is at the office. Take a tour of the city the next day and enjoy coffee, a drink, or dinner on the terrace of the **Villa Montaña Hotel** (p. 245). In winter you can take a day trip to see the **monarch butterflies** (p. 249). Another option is a day trip to the dormant volcano **El Paricutín.** See p. 260.

Days ❹ & ❺: Pátzcuaro ★★★ & the Lakeside Villages of the Purépecha

From Morelia it's only an hour's drive to the picturesque town of **Pátzcuaro** (p. 250) and the heart of the Purépecha homeland. This is the Indian version of colonial Mexico. Enjoy a stroll around the two principal plazas of the town and pay a visit to the **House of Eleven Patios** (p. 253) and the **Museo de Artes e Industrias Populares** (p. 253) for a fascinating

Los Cabos to Copper Canyon

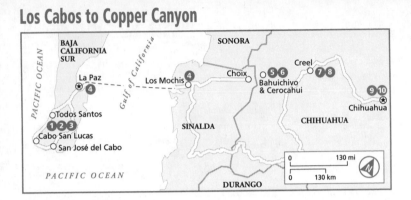

examination of all the different art forms practiced in the region. Next day hire a car or guide to take a tour of the lakeside villages and perhaps take a taxi to the town of **Santa Clara** (p. 258) to watch the coppersmiths at work.

Days ⑥ & ⑦: Ixtapa ✦ & Zihuatanejo

But for one large bridge, the new modern toll highway connecting the central highlands to the coast would be complete. Still, it saves hours over the old route. Relax for a couple of days and then catch a flight back home. See p. 394.

4 Los Cabos to Copper Canyon

This itinerary offers a great deal of contrast and starts in the resort area of Los Cabos. After enjoying any number of seaside activities, take a short tour of Southern Baja that includes bohemian Todos Santos before crossing the Sea of Cortez and boarding a train that climbs up through rugged Sierra Tarahumara, hugging the sides of the Copper Canyon. Stop here to enjoy the peace and the beauty, then reboard the train heading to the historical city of Chihuahua, which was home to Pancho Villa. This tour has been made easier by recent improvements to the ferry service between La Paz and Topolobampo.

Days ①, ② & ③: Cabo San Lucas, San José del Cabo & Todos Santos ✦✦

Spend your time enjoying the beauty of the area and the many activities offered in this large resort. Rent a car to drive along the coast and perhaps visit the town of **Todos Santos** (p. 732) to get a feel for the nonresort character of the region. See p. 702.

Day ④: La Paz ✦✦ to Los Mochis

Take a bus or *colectivo* to **La Paz** and, from there, to the ferry dock. After a 5-hour voyage you'll arrive at **Topolobampo** (p. 694), the port area of Los Mochis.

Days ⑤ & ⑥: Bahuichivo & Cerocahui ✦✦✦

The train departs early in the morning, and by late morning is snaking its way through some of the most beautiful canyon land on the trip. By midday you reach **Bahuichivo,** where you can get transportation to the town and mission of **Cerocahui.** This is a good place for hiking, horseback riding, and driving tours to the overlook of **Cerro Gallego.** See p. 688.

Days ⑦ & ⑧: Creel ✦

Continue by train on to **Creel,** where you can get a car to take you to the nearby

Copper Canyon Sierra Lodge (p. 693). Here you can enjoy the peace and quiet of the sierra, visit an old mission, hike to a nearby waterfall, and meet Tarahumara Indian women, who come to sell their pine needle baskets and other handicrafts. See p. 690.

Days ❾ & ❿: Chihuahua ⭐
You'll arrive at night. Use part of the next day to enjoy the historic downtown area and visit **Pancho Villa's house** (p. 699) before flying back home. See p. 696.

5 La Ruta Maya in 2 Weeks

This route, which connects all the major Maya sites in Mexico, could be done quickly in 2 weeks, or more slowly in a month, or perhaps broken up into two trips. There is a slight risk of overdosing on ruins by seeing too many in too short a time. I give you the fast-track approach, but that doesn't mean that I am encouraging you to move through this area that quickly. The best mode of travel would be a rental car: the highways are not terribly busy and are for the most part in good shape.

Day ❶: Arrive in Cancún
After you arrive, enjoy the remainder of the day with a swim in the Caribbean or a relaxing afternoon poolside. See p. 515.

Day ❷: Ek Balam ⭐⭐⭐ & Chichén Itzá ⭐⭐⭐
Get on the modern toll highway that heads toward Mérida and take the exit for Valladolid. Head north away from the town to visit the ruins of **Ek Balam** (p. 680). Highlights include a sacred doorway richly decorated with vivid figures of gods and men. Then it's back to the town of Valladolid for lunch before driving the short distance to **Chichén Itzá** (p. 670) on the old federal highway. Just outside of town, stop to see the *cenotes* **of Dzitnup** and **Sammulá** (p. 680). Farther on is the **cave of Balankanché** (p. 677). When you get to Chichén, check into your hotel, then go to the **ruins** later in the evening for the **sound-and-light show.** See p. 671.

Day ❸: Continuing to Uxmal ⭐⭐⭐
Spend more time at the **ruins of Chichén Itzá** in the morning, then continue west on toll highway toward Mérida, and turn off at Ticopó. Head south toward the town of **Acanceh** (p. 654) and Highway 18. Stop to see the small but interesting ruins in the middle of town, then proceed down Highway 18 to the ruins of **Mayapán** (p. 655). Afterward, continue through Ticul to Santa Elena and Uxmal. Experience the sound-and-light show. See p. 657.

Day ❹: Edzná
Visit **Uxmal** (p. 656) in the morning, then drive back toward Santa Elena and take Highway 261 south to Hopelchén and on to the impressive ruins of **Edzná** (p. 662). Nearby is a fancy hacienda turned hotel called **Uayamón** (p. 645; reservations can be made through Starwood hotels) or drive into the town of Campeche and stay at more modest digs.

Days ❺ & ❻: Palenque ⭐⭐, Bonampak & Yaxchilán
Stay on Highway 261 to Escárcega, then head west on Highway 186 toward Villahermosa then south on Highway 199 to the town of **Palenque** (p. 478) with its magnificent ruins. The next day go to the **ruins of Bonampak and Yaxchilán** (p. 484) using one of the local tour operators.

La Ruta Maya

Days ⑦ & ⑧: San Cristóbal de las Casas ✦✦

Keep south on Highway 199 toward **San Cristóbal** (p. 462). On the way, take a swimming break at **Agua Azul** (p. 484), and visit the ruins of **Toniná** outside of the town of Ocosingo. From San Cristóbal, go with one of the local guides to see the present-day Maya communities of **Chamula** and **Zinacantan** (p. 470). Spend sometime enjoying the town.

Day ⑨: En Route to Calakmul ✦✦✦

Retrace your steps to Escárcega and continue east on Highway 186. If there's time, visit the fascinating sculptures of **Balamkú** (p. 628). Spend the night at one of the hotels in the vicinity of the turnoff for Calakmul, one of the prime city-states of the classic age of the Maya, and not often visited.

Day ⑩: Calakmul & Becán ✦✦✦

Get to **Calakmul** (p. 626) early. Keep your eyes open for wildlife as you drive along a narrow jungle road. All the area surrounding the city is a **wildlife preserve.** For most of the city's history, Calakmul was the main rival to the city of Tikal, which is in present day Guatemala. It eventually defeated Tikal and subjugated it for a hundred years. Calakmul's **Structure 2** is the highest Maya pyramid in Mexico. Afterward, continue east on Highway 186 to see the ruins of **Becán,** a large ceremonial center with tall temples.

Also in the vicinity are **Xpujil** and **Chi-canná.** Spend the night on the shores of **Lake Bacalar,** where you can cool off in its blue waters. See p. 626.

Days ⓫ & ⓬: Tulum

Drive north on Highway 307 to **Tulum** and settle into one of the small beach hotels there. In the morning walk through the ruins and enjoy the lovely view of the coast. See p. 608.

Day ⓭: Back to Cancún

Drive back to Cancún. Depending on your schedule, you can enjoy some more beach time, or simply head to the airport (25 min. south of Cancún) and depart. See p. 515.

Mexico City

by Lynne Bairstow

Mexico City is experiencing a well-deserved renaissance in interest. In recent years, travelers dismissed Mexico's capital because of this grand city's problems with crime, pollution, and out-of-control growth. Now that these unsavory trends have been reversed, the culturally curious are rediscovering what originally led so many to this magnificent place. I love Mexico City, with all of its urban energy and historic and cultural treasures. Although many compare it to the great cities of Europe, I find it a singular experience. Along with city sophistication, you also find riots of color, a constant background of music, and an endearing mix of the majestically ancient with the irresistibly new.

Located 2,239m (7,347 ft.) high, on an enormous dry lakebed in a highland valley surrounded by mountains, this was the center of power of pre-Hispanic America, and it remains one of the most dynamic, fascinating, and charismatic cities in the world today.

For me, Mexico City is the only place where you can find true insight into this captivating country—veiled in mysticism, infused with an appreciation of the moment, and proud of its heritage. Founded more than 675 years ago as the ancient city of Tenochtitlán and capital of the Aztec Empire, today it has some 22 million inhabitants—making it a contender for the most populated city on the globe.

You only need to stand in the center of the *zócalo*—the central plaza—to visually comprehend the undisputed significance of this city. Here, the remains of an Aztec pyramid, a colonial church, and a towering modern office building face one another, a testament to the city's prominence in ancient and contemporary history. Located at the heart of the Americas, Mexico City has been a center of life and commerce for more than 2,000 years. The Teotihuacán, Toltec, Aztec, and European conquistadors all contributed to the city's fascinating evolution, art, and heritage. Although residents refer to their city as simply México (*meh*-hee-koh), its multitude of ancient ruins, colonial masterpieces, and modern architecture has prompted others to call it "The City of Palaces."

The central downtown area resembles a European city, dominated by ornate buildings and broad boulevards, and interspersed with public art, parks, and gardens. This sprawling city is thoroughly modern and, in places, unsightly and chaotic, but it never strays far from its historical roots. In the center are the partially excavated ruins of the main Aztec temple; pyramids rise just beyond the city.

The sheer number of residents trying to exist here, combined with economic malaise, high unemployment, and government corruption, has created an environment where petty crime (principally robberies) is common. Several years ago, Mexico City's notoriety came from its rising crime rate, a trend that—thankfully—is in reverse. Over the past several years,

Mexico City & Environs

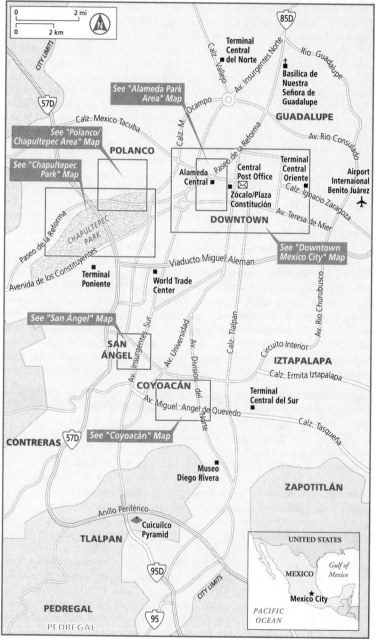

0 2 mi
0 2 km

CITY LIMITS

85D

57D

Terminal Central del Norte

Calz. Vallejo

Av. Insurgentes Norte

Rio Guadalupe

Basilíca de Nuestra Señora de Guadalupe

GUADALUPE

See "Alameda Park Area" Map

Ocampo

Calz. Mexico-Tacuba

See "Polanco/ Chapultepec Area" Map

Calz. M. Ocampo

POLANCO

See "Chapultepec Park" Map

Alameda Central

Paseo de la Reforma

Central Post Office

Zócalo/Plaza Constitución

Terminal Central Oriente

Calz. Ignacio Zaragoza

Av. Rio Consulado

Airport Internaional Benito Juárez

DOWNTOWN

Av. Teresa de Mier

Paseo de la Reforma

CHAPULTEPEC PARK

See "Downtown Mexico City" Map

Avenida de los Constituyentes

Viaducto Miguel Aleman

Terminal Poniente

World Trade Center

Av. Rio Churubusco

See "San Ángel" Map

Av. Insurgentes Sur

Av. Universidad

Av. Division del Norte

Calz. Tlalpan

Circuito Interior

IZTAPALAPA

Calz. Ermita Iztapalapa

SAN ÁNGEL

COYOACÁN

Av. Miguel Angel de Quevedo

Terminal Central del Sur

Calz. Tasqueña

CONTRERAS

57D

See "Coyoacán" Map

Museo Diego Rivera

ZAPOTITLÁN

Anillo Periférico

Cuicuilco Pyramid

TLALPAN

95D

CITY LIMITS

PEDREGAL

95

PEDREGAL

UNITED STATES

MEXICO

Gulf of Mexico

Mexico City

PACIFIC OCEAN

91

the city has achieved admirable progress in making visitors feel more secure, with special safety programs, faster response to reports of crime, a vastly increased police presence, and programs that are effectively combating corruption—including hiring Rudy Giuliani as an anti-corruption consultant. By 2002, Mexico City had reduced crime rates to 50% of 1994 levels, with only .02% related to visitors to the city.

Violent crime in Mexico is largely concentrated among drug traffickers and politicians, but kidnappings and murders of businesspeople, both Mexican and foreign, are numerous. Mexico City has many treasures to enjoy, but safety concerns demand that you dress and behave conservatively as you explore the city.

Technically, Mexico City is a "Federal District" (similar to Washington, D.C.), called the *Distrito Federal* (D.F.). One finds here a microcosm of all that is happening in the rest of the country—it's not only the seat of government, but in every way the dominant center of Mexican life.

You've undoubtedly heard about Mexico City's pollution. Major steps to improve the air quality (restricted driving, factory closings, emission-controlled buses and taxis) have worked wonders, but the problem persists. On some days you won't notice it; on other days it will make your nose run, your eyes water, and your throat rasp. If you have respiratory problems, be very careful; the city's elevation makes matters even worse. Minimize your exposure to the fumes by refraining from walking busy streets during rush hour. Sunday, when many factories are closed and many cars escape the city, should be your prime outdoor day. One positive note: In the evenings the air is usually deliciously cool and relatively clean. (See also "Pollution" under "Fast Facts," later in this chapter.)

Mexico City is a feast of urban energy, culture, dining, and shopping. The city has sidewalk cafes and cantinas; bazaars and boutiques; pyramids, monuments, and museums; and a multitude of entertainment options. And when you've had your fill of the city, memorable towns and historic national landmarks are only a couple of hours away in any direction.

1 Orientation

ARRIVING & DEPARTING

BY PLANE   For information on carriers serving Mexico City from the United States, see chapter 2.

Mexico City's **Benito Juárez International Airport** is something of a small city, where you can grab a bite, have an espresso (including Starbucks!), or buy clothes, books, gifts, and insurance, as well as exchange money or stay in a hotel.

Near Gate A is a guarded **baggage-storage area** (another is near Gate F). The key-operated metal lockers measure about .5×.5×.5m (2×2×1½ ft.) and cost $3 daily. Larger items are stored in a warehouse, which costs $3.50 to $8.50 for each 24 hours, depending on the size. You may leave your items for up to a month.

The Mexico City Hotel and Motel Association offers a **hotel-reservation service** for its member hotels. Look for its booths before you leave the baggage-claim area, or near Gate A on the concourse. Representatives will make the call according to your specifications for location and price. If they book the hotel, they require 1 night's advance payment and will give you a voucher, which you must present at the hotel. Ask about hotels with special deals. **Telephones** (Ladatel) are all along the public concourse; for instructions on how to use them, see chapter 2 and appendix B.

When you're getting ready to leave Mexico City and need local information on flights, times, and prices, contact the airlines directly; (most airlines in Mexico City have English-speaking personnel). Although airline numbers change frequently, the following may be useful:

- **Aero California** (℃ 55/5207-1392) serves Culiacán, Durango, Hermosillo, Matamoros, Mérida, Puebla, Puerto Vallarta, Torreón, Veracruz, Villa Hermosa, Guadalajara, Monterrey, Tijuana, Chihuahua, Ciudad Juárez, La Paz, Los Cabos, Loreto, Mazatlán, Manzanillo, León, Aguascalientes, San Luis Potosí, Tampico, Ciudad Victoria, Tepic, Colima, Los Mochis, Tucson, and Los Angeles.
- **Aeromexico** (℃ 55/5133-4000; www.aeromexico.com.mx) serves Guadalajara, Monterrey, Tijuana, Chihuahua, Ciudad Juárez, La Paz, Los Cabos, Loreto, Mazatlán, Manzanillo, León, Aguascalientes, Ixtapa-Zihuatanejo, Puerto Vallarta, Veracruz, Acapulco, Huatulco, Oaxaca, Tapachula, Campeche, Mérida, Cancún, Tuxtla Gutiérrez, New York, Chicago, Houston, Los Angeles, San Diego, Paris, Madrid, São Paulo, Santiago de Chile, and Lima.
- **American Airlines** (℃ 55/5209-1400; www.aa.com) has direct flights from inside Mexico to Dallas, San Francisco, Los Angeles, New York, Miami, and Chicago, and connecting flights to Orlando; Sacramento; Seattle; Washington, D.C.; Denver; Salt Lake City; Vancouver; Toronto; Montreal; São Paulo; Rio de Janeiro; London; Madrid; Paris; Manchester; Milan; and Tokyo.
- **Aviacsa** (℃ 55/5716-9005; www.aviacsa.com.mx) serves Cancún, León, Guadalajara, Mérida, Monterrey, Oaxaca, Tapachula, Tijuana, Tuxtla Gutierrez, Villa Hermosa, and Chetumal, and operates flights from Houston, Los Angeles, and Las Vegas.
- **Air Canada** (℃ 55/9138-0280; www.aircanada.ca) serves Toronto (direct flight), Montreal, Vancouver, London, Paris, Hong Kong, Taipei, and Tokyo from inside Mexico.
- **Continental** (℃ 55/5283-5500; www.continental.com) serves Houston, New York, and other U.S., Canadian, and European destinations.
- **Delta** (℃ 55/5279-0909; www.delta.com) serves Atlanta, Los Angeles, and New York.
- **Mexicana** (℃ 55/5448-0990; www.mexicana.com) has flights to Acapulco, Guadalajara, Puerto Vallarta, Monterrey, Ixtapa-Zihuatanejo, Mexicali, Tijuana, Hermosillo, Loreto, Los Cabos, Nuevo Laredo, Monterrey, Mazatlán, Zacatecas, Saltillo, Tampico, León, Morelia, Poza Rica, Manzanillo, Colima, Veracruz, Xalapa, Oaxaca, Puerto Escondido, Huatulco, Minatitlán, Villa Hermosa, Tuxtla Gutiérrez, San Cristóbal de las Casas, Tapachula, Ciudad del Carmen, Mérida, Cancún, Cozumel, Santiago de Chile, Buenos Aires, Sao Paulo, Rio de Janeiro, Bogotá, Caracas, Panamá, San José (Costa Rica), Santo Domingo, San Salvador, Guatemala, Havana, Miami, Orlando, San Antonio, Los Angeles, San Jose (California), Oakland, Las Vegas, Washington, Chicago, New York, Montreal, Toronto, and Frankfurt.
- **United** (℃ 55/5627-0222; www.ual.com) has flights to San José (Costa Rica); Los Angeles; San Francisco; Washington, D.C.; and Chicago.

Be sure to allow at least 45 to 60 minutes' travel time from the Zona Rosa or the *zócalo* (plaza) area to the airport—add about 30 minutes more if you're traveling during rush hour or bad weather. Check in at least 90 minutes before international flights and 60 minutes before domestic flights.

Getting to Town   Ignore those who approach you in the arrivals hall offering taxis; they are usually unlicensed and unauthorized. **Authorized airport taxis,** however, provide good, fast service. After exiting the baggage-claim area and before entering the public concourse (as well as near the far end of the terminal near Gate A), you'll see a booth marked TAXI. Staff members at these authorized taxi booths wear bright-yellow jackets or bibs emblazoned with TAXI AUTORIZADO (authorized taxi). Tell the ticket-seller your hotel or destination; the price is based on a zone system. Expect to pay around $17 for a *boleto* (ticket) to the Zona Rosa. Present your ticket outside to the driver. Taxi "assistants" who lift your luggage into the waiting taxi naturally expect a tip for their trouble. Putting your luggage in the taxi is the driver's job. (See also "Important Taxi Safety Precautions in Mexico City," below.)

The **Metro,** Mexico City's modern subway system, is cheap and faster than a taxi, but it seems to be gaining popularity among thieves who target tourists. If you try it, be forewarned: As a new arrival, you'll stand out. If you are carrying anything much larger than a briefcase, including a suitcase, don't even bother going to the station—they won't let you on with it. For Metro information, see "Getting Around," later in this chapter.

Here's how to find the Metro at the airport: As you come from your plane into the arrivals hall, turn left toward Gate A and walk all the way through the long terminal, out the doors, and along a covered sidewalk. Soon, you'll see the distinctive Metro logo that identifies the Terminal Aérea station, down a flight of stairs. The station is on Metro Line 5. Follow the signs for trains to Pantitlán. At Pantitlán, change for Line 1 ("Observatorio"), which takes you to stations that are just a few blocks south of the *zócalo* and La Alameda park: Pino Suárez, Isabel la Católica, Salto del Agua, and Balderas.

BY CAR   Driving in Mexico City is as much a challenge and an adventure as driving in any major metropolis. Here are a few tips. First, check whether your license-plate number permits you to drive in the city that day (break the rule, and the fine can be as much as $1,600). Traffic runs the course of the usual rush hours—to avoid getting tangled in traffic, plan to travel before dawn. Park the car in a guarded lot whenever possible.

Here are the chief thoroughfares for getting out of the city: Insurgentes Sur becomes Highway 95 to Taxco and Cuernavaca. Insurgentes Norte leads to Teoti-huacán and Pachuca. Highway 57, the Periférico (loop around the city), is also known as Bulevar Manuel Avila Camacho, to denote street addresses; it goes north and leads out of the city to Tula and Querétaro. Constituyentes leads west out of the city past Chapultepec Park and connects with Highway 15 to Toluca, Morelia, and Pátzcuaro. (Reforma also connects with Hwy. 15.) Zaragoza leads east to Highway 150 to Puebla and Veracruz.

BY BUS   Mexico City has a bus terminal for each of the four points of the compass: north, east, south, and west. You can't necessarily tell which terminal serves which area of the country by looking at a map, however.

Some buses leave directly from the **Mexico City airport.** Departures are from a booth located outside **Gate D (Sala D),** and buses also park there. Tickets to Cuer-navaca and Puebla each run about $12, with departures every 45 minutes. Other des-tinations include Querétaro, Pátzcuaro, and Toluca.

If you're in doubt about which station serves your destination, ask any taxi driver—they know the stations and the routes they serve. All stations have restaurants, money-exchange booths or banks, post offices, luggage storage, and long-distance telephone booths where you can also send a fax.

(Tips) Important Taxi Safety Precautions in Mexico City

There has been a marked increase in violent crime against both residents and tourists using taxis for transportation in Mexico City, concentrated among users of Volkswagen Beetle taxis. Robberies of taxi passengers have become increasingly violent, with beatings and even murders not uncommon. Victims have included U.S. citizens. Many times the robberies involve taking passengers to an ATM, where they are forced to withdraw whatever limit their card or cards will allow. These occurrences have become so common and so severe that, as of the time of this update, the U.S. State Department had issued a standing **travelers' advisory** concerning taxi travel in Mexico City.

If you plan to use a **taxi from the airport or bus stations,** use only an authorized airport cab with all the familiar markings: yellow car, white taxi light on the roof, and TRANSPORTACION TERRESTRE painted on the doors. Buy your ticket from the clearly marked taxi booth inside the terminal—nowhere else. After purchasing your ticket, go outside to the line of taxis, where an official taxi chief will direct you to the next taxi in line. Don't follow anyone else.

In Mexico City, *do not hail a passing taxi on the street.* Most hotels have official taxi drivers who are recognized and regulated by the terminal and city; they are considered safe taxis to use. These are known as **authorized** or *sitio* **taxis.** Hotels and restaurants can call the radio-dispatched taxis. **Official Radio Taxis (© 55/5271-9146, 55/5271-9058, or 55/5273-6125) are also considered safe. You can hire one of these taxis from your hotel; the driver will frequently act as your personal driver and escort you through your travels in the city. This is a particularly advisable option at night.

All official taxis, except the expensive "Turismo" cars, are painted predominantly yellow, orange, or green, have white plastic roof signs bearing the word TAXI, have TAXI or SITIO painted on the doors, and are equipped with meters. Look for all these indications, not just one or two of them. Even then, be cautious. The safest cars to use are sedan taxis (luxury cars without markings) dispatched from four- and five-star hotels. They are the most expensive, but worth it(taxi crime in Mexico City is very real.

Do not use VW Beetle taxis, which are frequently involved in robberies of tourists. Even though they are the least expensive taxis, you could be taking your life into your hands should you opt to use one. In any case, never get in a taxi that does not display a large 5×7-inch laminated **license card** with a picture of the driver on it; it's usually hanging from the door chain or glove box, or stuck behind the sun visor. *If there is no license, or if the photo doesn't match the driver, don't get in.* It's illegal for a taxi to operate without the license in view. No matter what vehicle you use for transportation, lock the doors as soon as you get in. Do not carry credit cards, your passport, or large sums of cash, or wear expensive jewelry when taking taxis.

The U.S. State Department advisory also specifies that taxis parked in front of the **Bellas Artes Theater** and in front of nightclubs, restaurants, or cruising tourist areas should be avoided.

Taxis from bus stations: Each station has a taxi system based on fixed-price tickets to various zones within the city, operated from a booth or kiosk in or near the entry foyer of the terminal. Locate your destination on a zone map or tell the seller where you want to go, and buy a *boleto* (ticket). See also the "Important Taxi Safety Precautions in Mexico City" box, above.

For bus riders' terms and translations, see appendix B.

Terminal Central de Autobuses del Norte   Called "Terminal Norte," "Central Norte" (© **55/5133-2444** or 55/5587-1552), Avenida de los Cien (100) Metros, is Mexico's largest bus station. It handles most buses coming from the U.S.-Mexico border. It also handles service to and from the Pacific Coast as far south as Puerto Vallarta and Manzanillo; the Gulf Coast as far south as Tampico and Veracruz; and such cities as Guadalajara, San Luis Potosí, Durango, Zacatecas, Morelia, and Colima. You can also get to the pyramids of San Juan Teotihuacán and Tula from here. By calling the above number, you can purchase tickets over the phone, charging them to a credit card. The operators can also provide exact information about prices and schedules, but few speak English.

To get downtown from the Terminal Norte, you have a choice: The **Metro** has a station (Terminal de Autobuses del Norte, or TAN) right here, so it's easy to hop a train and connect to all points. Walk to the center of the terminal, go out the front door and down the steps, and go to the Metro station. This is Línea 5. Follow the signs that say DIRECCION PANTITLAN. For downtown, you can change trains at La Raza or Consulado (see the Mexico City Metro map on the inside back cover). Be aware that if you change at La Raza, you'll have to walk for 10 to 15 minutes and will encounter stairs. The walk is through a marble-lined underground corridor, but it's a long way with heavy luggage. If you have heavy luggage, you most likely won't be allowed into the Metro in the first place.

Another way to get downtown is by **trolleybus.** The stop is on Avenida de los Cien Metros, in front of the terminal. The trolleybus runs down Avenida Lázaro Cárdenas, the "Eje Central" (Central Artery). Or try the CENTRAL CAMIONERA DEL NORTE–VILLA OLIMPICA buses, which go down Avenida Insurgentes, past the university. Just like the Metro, the trolley will not let you board if you are carrying anything larger than a small carry-on suitcase. Backpacks seem to be an exception, but not large ones with frames.

Terminal de Autobuses de Pasajeros de Oriente (© **55/5762-5210,** 55/5133-2424, 55/5542-9220, 55/5542-7156, or 55/5542-2009)   The terminal is known as **TAPO.** Buses going east (Puebla, Amecameca, the Yucatán Peninsula, Veracruz, Xalapa, San Cristóbal de las Casas, and others) and Oaxaca buses, which pass through Puebla, arrive and depart from here.

To get to TAPO, take a HIPODROMO–PANTITLAN bus east along Alvarado, Hidalgo, or Donceles; if you take the Metro, go to the San Lázaro station on the eastern portion of Line 1 (DIRECCION PANTITLAN).

Terminal Central de Autobuses del Sur (© **55/5689-9745**)   Mexico City's southern bus terminal is at Av. Taxqueña 1320, right next to the Taxqueña Metro stop, the last stop on Line 2. The Central del Sur handles buses to and from Cuernavaca, Taxco, Acapulco, Zihuatanejo, and intermediate points. The easiest way to get to or from the Central del Sur is on the Metro. To get downtown from the Taxqueña Metro station, look for signs that say DIRECCION CUATRO CAMINOS. Or take a trolleybus on Avenida Lázaro Cárdenas.

Terminal Poniente de Autobuses (© 55/5271-0038)   The western bus terminal is conveniently located right next to the Observatorio Metro station, at Sur 122 and Tacubaya.

This is the smallest terminal; it mainly serves the route between Mexico City and Toluca. It also handles buses to and from Ixtapan de la Sal, Valle de Bravo, Morelia, Uruapan, Querétaro, Colima, Ixtapa-Zihuatanejo, Acapulco, and Guadalajara. In general, if the Terminal Norte also serves your destination, you'd be better off going there. It has more buses and better bus lines.

VISITOR INFORMATION

The Federal District Department provides several information services for visitors. **Infotur** offices offer information in English and Spanish, including maps, a wide selection of brochures, and access to information from the Mexico Secretary of Tourism website. The most convenient office is in the Zona Rosa at Amberes 54, at the corner of Londres (© 55/5550-0123). Others are at the TAPO bus terminal and at the airport. They're open daily from 9am to 7pm.

SECTUR, Mexico's Secretary of Tourism, developed a website to address safety concerns about travel to this city and other areas in Mexico. The website, **www.sectur. gob.mx**, offers perhaps not-so-objective assessments of destinations, as well as travel safety tips. **The Mexico City Secretary of Tourism** also has a website, www.mexico city.gob.mx, which includes details on things to do, special events, and safety precautions, as well as a variety of other topics.

The **Mexico City Chamber of Commerce** (© 55/5592-2665) maintains an information office with a very friendly, helpful staff that can sell you detailed maps of the city or country and answer questions. It's conveniently located at Reforma 42—look for the Cámara Nacional de Comercio de la Ciudad de México. It's open Monday through Thursday from 9am to 2pm and 3 to 6pm; Friday from 9am to 2pm and 3 to 5:30pm.

Day and night diversions are listed in the Spanish-language magazine *Tiempo Libre,* which is published each Thursday, and is available at hotels and newsstands. It also has a website, **www.tiempolibre.com.mx**. A good English-language source of visitor information is the Mexico File (**www.mexicofile.com**), and current event information and visitor tips are offered on the excellent site **www.mexicocity.gob.mx**.

Mexico City has a special **Elite Police force,** with officers versed in the history and culture of the city—in English—as well as trained in crime prevention and traveler safety, especially to respond to the needs of the city's tourists.

CITY LAYOUT

FINDING AN ADDRESS   Despite its size, Mexico City is not hard to get a feel for. The city is divided into 350 *colonias,* or neighborhoods. Taxi drivers are notoriously ignorant of the city, including the major tourist sights and popular restaurants. Before getting into a taxi, always give a street address, *colonia,* and cross streets as a reference, and show the driver your destination on a map that you carry with you. Some of the most important colonias are Colonia Centro (historic city center); Zona Rosa (Colonia Juárez); Polanco (Colonia Polanco), a fashionable neighborhood immediately north of Chapultepec Park; colonias Condesa and Roma, south of the Zona Rosa, where there are many restaurants in quiet neighborhoods; and all the Lomas—including Lomas de Chapultepec and Lomas Tecamachalco—which are exclusive neighborhoods west of Chapultepec Park. In addresses, the word is abbreviated *Col.,* although the full *colonia* name is vital in addressing correspondence.

STREET MAPS   Should you want more detailed maps of Mexico City than the ones included in this guide, you can get them easily. The **Infotur** office (see "Visitor Information," above) generally has several free maps available. Bookstores carry several local map-guides, with greater detail. The best-detailed map is the *Guia Roji,* available at bookstores in Mexico City. It features all the streets in Mexico City and is updated annually.

THE NEIGHBORHOODS IN BRIEF

Centro Histórico The heart of Mexico City, its business, banking, and historic center, includes the areas in and around La Alameda and the *zócalo.* The Spaniards built their new capital city on top of the destroyed capital of the conquered Aztec, and today, it is home to over 1,500 buildings. This is where you'll find the historic landmarks, the most important public buildings, the partially unearthed Aztec ruins of the Great Temple, and numerous museums. There are restaurants, shops, and hotels in this area as well. In the past few years, public improvements have spurred the development of a few new hotels here, as well as a surge in nightlife and dining options, with some exquisite bars and clubs located in historic buildings.

A $300 million face-lift was completed in 2003 in honor of the city's 675th anniversary. In addition to a beautification program for the *zócalo*—including the addition of a grassy knoll—other elements of the program included the restoration and conversion of more than 80 18th- and 19th-century buildings.

This neighborhood is also undergoing a residential renaissance. Investors are subsidizing rents in rehabbed loft buildings for students—especially artists, Web designers, and other creative types, hoping to turn it into a Latin version of New York City's Meat-Packing District—and betting on a future escalation in real estate values. Accordingly, look for the hottest and hippest in nightlife here.

A special corps of police on horseback, outfitted in traditional *charro* attire, now patrols the Centro Histórico and Alameda Park. These mounted cops speak English, and they have been specially trained in the history and culture of the area they patrol.

Chapultepec Park & Polanco A large residential area west of the city center and Zona Rosa, it centers on Chapultepec Park. The largest green area in Mexico City, it was dedicated as a park in the 15th century by the Aztec ruler Netzahualcóyotl. Together with the neighboring *colonia* of Polanco (north of the park), this is Mexico City's most exclusive address. With its zoo, many notable museums, antiques shops, stylish shopping, fine dining, and upscale hotels, it's an ideal place for discovering contemporary Mexican culture, and is considered Mexico City's most upscale address for a visit. **Avenida Presidente Masaryk** is the main artery.

Condesa & Roma With their new moniker "the SoHo of Mexico City," these side-by-side bohemian neighborhoods, located just south of the Zona Rosa, are home to the current hip clubs and hot spots, from cutting-edge restaurants to offbeat shops, art galleries, and cafes. The neighborhoods are also known for their restored Art Deco buildings.

Coyoacán Eight kilometers (5 miles) from the city center, east of San Angel and north of the Ciudad Universitaria, Coyoacán (koh-yoh-ah-*kahn*) is an attractive, colonial-era suburb noted for its beautiful town square, cobblestone streets, fine old mansions, and several of the city's most interesting museums. This was the home of Frida Kahlo and Diego Rivera, and of Leon Trotsky after his exile from Stalin's USSR. It's a wonderful place to spend the day, but overnight accommodations are limited. Attractions in Coyoacán are listed in the section "Southern Neighborhoods," later in this chapter.

From downtown, Metro Line 3 can take you to the Coyoacán or Viveros station, within walking distance of Coyoacán's museums. IZTACALA–COYOACAN buses run from the center to this suburb. If you're coming from San Angel, the quickest and easiest way is to take a cab for the 15-minute ride to the Plaza Hidalgo. Sosa, a pretty street, is the main artery into Coyoacán from San Angel. Or you can catch the ALCANTARILLA–COL. AGRARISTA bus heading east along the Camino al Desierto de los Leones or Avenida Altavista, near the San Angel Inn. Get off when the bus reaches the corner of Avenida México and Xicoténcatl in Coyoacán.

San Angel Eight kilometers (5 miles) south of the city center, San Angel (sahn *ahn*-hehl) was once a village but has been absorbed by the city. It's a beautiful neighborhood of cobblestone streets and colonial-era homes, with several worthwhile museums. This is where the renowned Bazar del Sábado (Saturday Bazaar) is held. It's full of artistic and antique treasures, with excellent restaurants as well—a good place to spend a day. Other attractions in San Angel include a wonderful baroque fountain made of broken pieces of porcelain at the Centro Cultural Isidro Fabela, better known as the Casa del Risco (Plaza San Jacinto 15), and the ethereal Iglesia San Jacinto, a

16th-century church with an exquisite baroque altar, bordering the Plaza San Jacinto.

The nearest Metro station is M.A. Quevedo (Line 3). From downtown, take a *colectivo* (minibus) marked SAN ANGEL, or bus marked INDIOS VERDES–TLALPAN or CENTRAL NORTE–VILLA OLIMPICA, south along Insurgentes near the Zona Rosa. Ask to get off at La Paz. To the east is a pretty park, the Plaza del Carmen, and to the west is a Sanborn's, on the eastern side of Insurgentes.

Xochimilco Twenty-four kilometers (15 miles) south of the town center, Xochimilco (soh-chee-*meel*-coh) is noted for its famed canals and Floating Gardens, which have existed here since the time of the Aztec. Although the best-known attractions are the more than 80km (50 miles) of canals (see "Parks & Gardens," later in this chapter, for details), Xochimilco itself is a colonial-era gem: It seems small, with its brick streets, but they can become heavy with traffic—it has a population of 300,000. Restaurants are at the edge of the canal and shopping area, and historically significant churches are within easy walking distance of the main square. In the town of Xochimilco, you'll find a busy market, specializing in rugs, ethnic clothing, and brightly decorated pottery.

Xochimilco hosts an amazing 422 festivals annually, the most famous of which celebrate the **Niñopa,** a figure of the Christ Child that is believed to possess miraculous powers. The figure is venerated on January 6 (Three Kings' Day), February 2 (annual changing of the Niñopa's custodian), April 30 (Day of the Child), and from December 16 to December 24 (*posadas* for the Niñopa). Caring for the Niñopa is a coveted privilege, and the schedule of approved caretakers is filled through 2031. From March 28 to April 4 (dates vary slightly) is the *Feria de la Flor Más Bella del Ejido,* a flower fair when the most beautiful girl with Indian features and costume is selected. For more information and exact dates, contact the **Xochimilco Tourist Office (Subdirección de Turismo),** Pino 36, Barrio San Juan (© **55/5676-8879;** fax 55/5676-0810), next to VIPS, 2 blocks from the main square. It's open Monday through Sunday from 8am to 10pm. Attractions in Xochimilco are listed in the section "Southern Neighborhoods," later in this chapter.

To reach Xochimilco, take the Metro to Taxqueña, then the *tren ligero* (light train), which stops at the main plaza of Xochimilco. From there, take a taxi to the main plaza of the town of Xochimilco. Buses run all the way across the city from north to south to end up at Xochimilco, but they take longer than the Metro. Of the buses

coming from the center, the most convenient is LA VILLA–XOCHIMILCO, which you catch going south on Correo Mayor and Pino Suárez near the *zócalo,* or near Chapultepec on Avenida Vasconcelos, Avenida Nuevo León, and Avenida Division del Norte.

Zona Rosa West of the Centro, the "Pink Zone" was once the city's most exclusive residential neighborhood. It has given way to countless tourists, with a glittering array of luxury hotels, boutiques, popular dining, and nightlife—although in my opinion, it's beginning to turn toward the tacky side. Many of the streets here are pedestrian-only, making it an inviting place for shopping or taking in the sights over a cappuccino or aperitif at one of the numerous cafes. It's among the more popular places to stay, especially for business travelers, despite the fact that it has fewer real historic or cultural attractions than other parts of the city.

2 Getting Around

Mexico City has a highly developed and remarkably cheap public transportation system. It is a shame that the sharp increase in crime and resulting safety concerns have made these less comfortable options for travelers. The Metro, first- and second-class buses, *colectivos* (minibuses), and yellow or green VW Beetle taxis will take you anywhere you want to go for very little money—but the recent visitor warnings about the use of public transportation should be respected. Because even *sitio* taxis (official taxis registered to a specific locale or hotel) are relatively inexpensive, and are the safest way to travel today within the city, they are what I use when traveling solo in this city.

BY TAXI   Taxis operate under several distinct sets of rules. *Warning:* Read the cautionary box "Important Taxi Safety Precautions in Mexico City," earlier in this chapter, before using any taxi.

"Turismo" Taxis   These are by far the safest way to travel within Mexico City. The unmarked cabs, usually well-kept luxury cars assigned to specific hotels, have special license plates, and bags covering their meters. Although more expensive than the VW taxis, "turismo" taxis, along with radio-dispatched taxis, are the safest ones to use. The drivers negotiate rates with individual passengers for sightseeing, but rates to and from the airport are established. Ask the bell captain what the airport fare should be, and establish it before taking off. These drivers are often licensed English-speaking guides and can provide exceptional service. In general, expect to pay around $15 per hour for guided service, and about 15% more than metered rates for normal transportation.

Often, these drivers will wait for you while you shop or dine to take you back to the hotel, or they can be called to come back and pick you up.

Metered Taxis   Yellow or green VW Beetle and *sitio* (radio-dispatched) cabs provide low-cost service. Although you may encounter a gouging driver, or one who advances the meter or drives farther than necessary to run up the tab, most service is quick and adequate. These taxis operate strictly by the meter: If the driver says his meter isn't working, find another taxi. But then, you will be heeding the warnings, and won't be using one anyway . . . now, will you?

BY METRO   The subway system in Mexico City offers a smooth ride for one of the lowest fares anywhere in the world (20¢ per ride). Ten lines crisscross the sprawling city. Each train usually has nine cars.

As you enter the station, buy a *boleto* (ticket) at the glass *taquilla* (ticket booth). Insert your ticket into the slot at the turnstile and pass through; inside, you'll see two large signs showing the line's destination (for example, for Line 1, it's OBSERVATORIO and PANTIT-LAN). Follow the signs in the direction you want and *know where you're going;* there is usually only one map of the routes, at the entrance to the station. You'll see two signs everywhere: SALIDA (exit), and ANDENES (platforms). Once inside the train, you'll see above each door a map of the station stops for that line with symbols and names.

CORRESPONDENCIAS indicates transfer points. The ride is smooth, fast, and efficient (although hot and crowded during rush hours). The beautifully designed stations are clean and have the added attraction of displaying archaeological ruins unearthed during construction. A subterranean passage goes between the Pino Suárez and Zócalo stations, so you can avoid the crowds and rain along Pino Suárez. The Zócalo station features dioramas and large photographs of the different periods in the history of the Valley of México. At Pino Suárez you'll find the foundation of a pyramid from the Aztec Empire.

The Metro is crowded during daylight hours on weekdays and consequently pretty hot and muggy in summer. In fact, you may find it virtually unusable downtown between 4 and 7pm on weekdays, because of sardine-can conditions. At some stations, there are even separate lanes roped off for women and children; the press of the crowd is so great that someone might get molested. Buses, *colectivos,* and taxis are all heavily used during these hours, less so during off hours (like 10:30am–noon). Avoid the crowds by traveling during off-peak hours, or simply wait a few minutes for the next train.

Tips **The Subway Skinny**

The Metro system runs workdays from 5am to midnight, Saturday from 6am to 1am, and Sunday and holidays from 7am to midnight. Baggage larger than a small carry-on is not allowed on the trains. In practice, this means that bulky suitcases or backpacks will make you persona non grata. On an average day, Mexico City's Metro handles more than five million riders—leaving little room for bags! But in effect, if no one stops you as you enter, you're in.

Watch your bags and your pockets. Metro pickpockets prey on the unwary (especially foreigners) and are very crafty—on a crowded train, they've been known to empty a fanny pack from the front. Be careful, and carry valuables inside your clothing.

Downtown Mexico City

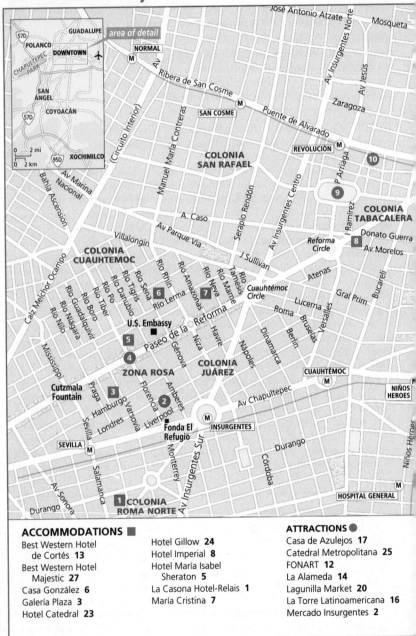

ACCOMMODATIONS ■

Best Western Hotel
  de Cortés **13**
Best Western Hotel
  Majestic **27**
Casa González **6**
Galería Plaza **3**
Hotel Catedral **23**

Hotel Gillow **24**
Hotel Imperial **8**
Hotel María Isabel
  Sheraton **5**
La Casona Hotel-Relais **1**
María Cristina **7**

ATTRACTIONS ●

Casa de Azulejos **17**
Catedral Metropolitana **25**
FONART **12**
La Alameda **14**
Lagunilla Market **20**
La Torre Latinoamericana **16**
Mercado Insurgentes **2**

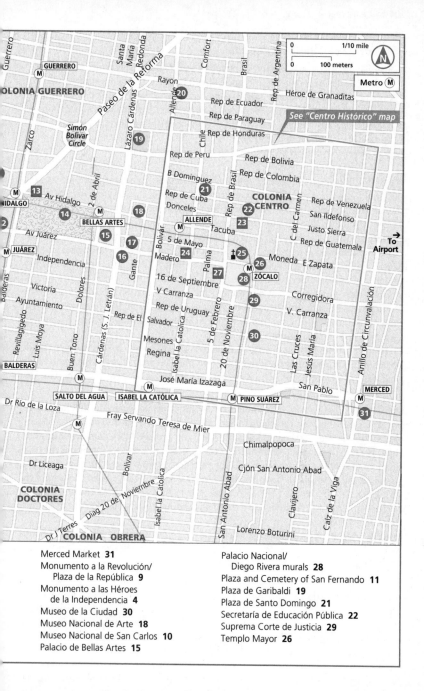

Merced Market **31**
Monumento a la Revolución/
    Plaza de la República **9**
Monumento a las Héroes
    de la Independencia **4**
Museo de la Ciudad **30**
Museo Nacional de Arte **18**
Museo Nacional de San Carlos **10**
Palacio de Bellas Artes **15**

Palacio Nacional/
    Diego Rivera murals **28**
Plaza and Cemetery of San Fernando **11**
Plaza de Garibaldi **19**
Plaza de Santo Domingo **21**
Secretaría de Educación Pública **22**
Suprema Corte de Justicia **29**
Templo Mayor **26**

Finds **Free Sunday Concerts**

Every Sunday, concerts organized by Mexico City's Cultural Institute take place at the Zócalo, generally around 6pm. They feature a changing array of traditional and classical Mexican talent—and can draw crowds of 5,000 or more to the historic central plaza. For more information, and listings of upcoming events, visit the Mexico City website, **www.mexicocity.gob.mx**. Listings also appear in *Tiempo Libre* magazine.

BY BUS   Moving millions of people through this sprawling urban mass is a gargantuan task, but the city officials do a pretty good job of it. Bus stops on the major tourist streets usually have a map posted with the full route description.

The large buses that used to run on the major tourist routes (**Reforma** and **Insurgentes**) tended to become overpacked and have been phased out in favor of smaller, more frequent buses. Crowding is now uncommon except perhaps during peak hours. The cost in pesos is the U.S. equivalent of 20¢ to 40¢. Although the driver usually has change, try to have exact fare or at least a few coins when you board.

One of the most important bus routes runs between the *zócalo* and the Auditorio (National Auditorium in Chapultepec Park) or the Observatorio Metro station. The route is Avenida Madero or Cinco de Mayo, Avenida Juárez, and Paseo de la Reforma. Buses marked ZOCALO run this route.

Another important route is **INDIOS VERDES–TLALPAN,** which runs along Avenida Insurgentes, connecting the northern bus terminal (Terminal Norte), Buenavista railroad station, Reforma, the Zona Rosa, and, far to the south, San Angel and University City.

BY COLECTIVO   Also called *peseros* or *combis,* these are sedans or minibuses, usually green and gray, that run along major arteries. They pick up and discharge passengers along the route, charge established fares, and provide more comfort and speed than the bus. Cards in the windshield display routes; often a Metro station is the destination. One of the most useful routes for tourists runs from the *zócalo* along **Avenida Juárez,** along **Reforma** to **Chapultepec,** and back again. Board a *colectivo* with a sign saying ZOCALO, not VILLA. (The Villa route goes to the Basílica de Guadalupe.) Some of the minibuses on this route have automatic sliding doors—you don't have to shut them.

As the driver approaches a stop, he may put his hand out the window and hold up one or more fingers. This is the number of passengers he's willing to take on (vacant seats are difficult to see if you're outside the car).

BY TOURIST BUS   A new, and increasingly popular way to see the city is on one of the red double-decker **Turibuses,** put into service in the fall of 2002 to see sights around the capitol. Each of the double-decker buses seats 75 and offers audio information in five languages, plus street maps. The buses operate from 9am to 9pm, with unlimited hop-on, hop-off privileges after paying $10 for a day pass. There are 25 stops at major monuments, museums, neighborhoods, and landmarks along the 35km (21-mile) route, which runs from the National Auditorium to the city center and from there to La Plaza de las Tres Culturas (Square of the Three Cultures), returning via Reforma Avenue towards the posh neighborhood of Polanco and finally to Museo del Niño (Children's Museum).

Tips **Festival del Centro Histórico**

In March of every year, a series of concerts, cultural events, art exhibits, and public performances takes place in—and in honor of—Mexico City's historic downtown district. For more information or a calendar of events, call the **Delegacíon Cuauhtémoc** (© **55/5702-1205** or 55/5535-5343).

RENTAL CARS   If you plan to travel to Puebla (see chapter 12) or a surrounding area, a rental car might come in handy. But using taxis and the Metro eliminates the risk of getting lost in an unsavory area. And due to high rates of auto theft, I don't recommend renting a car. But if you do, the least-expensive rental car is the (old-style) manual-shift Volkswagen Beetle, manufactured in Mexico. The price jump is considerable beyond the VW Beetle, and you pay more for automatic transmission and air-conditioning in any car. Hertz, Budget, National, and Avis, among other agencies, are represented at the airport, and each has several city offices as well. Daily rates and deductibles vary considerably. It's more economical to arrange the rental from your home country than to wait to rent one upon arrival. (See also "Getting Around Mexico" in chapter 2.)

If you still feel the need to rent a car in Mexico City, you can leave the driving to someone else—**Avis** offers chauffeur-driven rental cars at its nine locations in the Mexican capital. Prices begin at around $90 per day, which includes taxes, insurance, and unlimited mileage, with fuel extra. The chauffeur is on an 8-hour shift, but the car is available to the customer for 24 hours. For information and reservations, call Avis in the U.S. (© **800/331-1084**).

FAST FACTS: Mexico City

American Express   The Mexico City office is at Reforma 234 (© **55/5207-7282**), in the Zona Rosa. It's open for banking, the pickup of American Express clients' mail, and travel advice Monday through Friday from 9am to 6pm and Saturday from 9am to 1pm.

Banks   Banks are usually open Monday through Friday from 9am to 4pm; many now offer Saturday and even Sunday business hours. Bank branches at the airport are open whenever the airport is busy, including weekends. They usually offer ATMs and good rates of exchange. Banks and money-exchange offices line Avenida Reforma. The Centro Histórico downtown also has banks and money-exchange booths on almost every block, as does the Zona Rosa.

Bookstores   In Mexico City, **Sanborn's** always has a great selection of books in English, as well as magazines and newspapers.

About the most convenient foreign- and Spanish-language bookstore in Mexico City, with a good selection of guidebooks and texts on Mexico, is **Librería Gandhi**, Av. Juárez 4, near Avenida Lázaro Cárdenas (© **55/5510-4231**; www.gandhi.com.mx), right across from the Bellas Artes. It's open daily from 10am to 9pm. The **New Option**, Rosas Moreno 152 (© **55/5705-3332** or 55/5705-0585), is open Monday through Friday from 9am to 6pm and Saturday from 10am to

4pm. The **Museo Nacional de Antropología,** in Chapultepec Park (© 55/5553-1902 or 55/5211-0754), also has a fair selection of books on Mexico, particularly special-interest guides. It's open Tuesday through Sunday from 9am to 7pm. Also in Chapultepec, the bookstore **Otro Lugar de la Mancha,** Esopo 11 Chapultepec (© 55/5280-4826), offers a small but outstanding collection of books, music, and art, plus an upstairs cafe in a historic home. It's open Monday through Friday from 8am to 10pm, Saturday and Sunday from 9am to 10pm.

Currency Exchange The alternative to a bank is a currency-exchange booth, or *casa de cambio.* These often offer extended hours, with greater convenience to hotels and shopping areas, and rates similar to bank exchange rates. Usually, their rates are much better than those offered by most hotels. Use caution when exiting both banks and currency exchanges, which are popular targets for muggings.

Drugstores The drug departments at Sanborn's stay open late. Check the phone directory for the location nearest you. After hours, check with your hotel staff, which can usually contact a 24-hour drugstore.

Elevation Remember, you are now at an elevation of 2,239m (7,346 ft.)—over a mile in the sky. There's a lot less oxygen in the air than you're used to. If you run for a bus and feel dizzy when you sit down, it's the elevation. If you think you're in shape but huff and puff getting up Chapultepec Hill, it's the elevation. If you have trouble sleeping, it may be the elevation. If your food isn't digesting, again, it's the elevation. It takes about 3 days or so to adjust to the scarcity of oxygen. Go easy on food and alcohol the first few days in the city.

Emergencies The Mexico City government has an emergency number for visitors—dial © 060 for assistance 24 hours a day. The number is hard to reach, so have a local or Spanish speaker help you. In case of a crime or accident, contact the Procuraduría del Turista (© 55/5553-1260). A government-operated service, **Locatel** (© 55/5658-1111; www.df.gob.mx/servicios/locatel/seicios.html), is most often associated with finding missing persons anywhere in the country. With a good description of a car and its occupants, they'll search for motorists who have an emergency back home. **SECTUR** (Secretaría de Turismo; © 55/5250-0123, 55/5250-0493, 55/5250-0027, 55/5250-0151, 55/5250-0292, or 55/5250-0589; www.mexico-travel.com), staffs telephones 24 hours daily to help tourists in difficulty.

Hospitals The **American–British Cowdray (ABC) Hospital** is at Calle Sur 136, at the corner of Avenida Observatorio, Col. las Américas (© 55/5230-8000).

Hot Lines If you think you've been ripped off on a purchase, call the **consumer protection office,** the Procuraduría Nacional del Consumidor (© 55/5568-8722, 55/5272-9847, or 01-800/468-8722; www.profeco.gob.mx). SECTUR also sponsors Infotur, a 24-hour tourist-assistance line (© 55/5250-0123 or 55/5205-0493).

Internet Access Surprisingly enough, it is easier to find cybercafes in some resort areas than in Mexico City. However, most hotels that cater to business travelers offer Internet connections in their business centers. The **Java Chat Café Internet,** Genova 44, in the Zona Rosa (© 55/5525-6853), is open daily from 8am to 11:30pm. The price per hour of access is around $4.

Pollution September and October seem to be light months for pollution. Mid- to late November, December, and January are noted for heavy pollution. During January, schools may even close because of it, and restrictions on driving that are usually imposed only on weekdays may apply on weekends; be sure to check before driving into or around the city. (See "Rental Cars" under "Getting Around," earlier in this chapter.) Be careful if you have respiratory problems. Just before your visit, call the Mexican Government Tourist Board office nearest you (see "Visitor Information" in chapter 2 for the address) and ask for the latest information on pollution in the capital. Minimize your exposure to fumes by refraining from walking busy streets during rush hour. Make Sunday, when many factories are closed and many cars escape the city, your prime sightseeing day.

Post Office The city's main post office, the **Correo Mayor,** is a block north of the Palacio de Bellas Artes on Avenida Lázaro Cárdenas, at the corner of Tacuba (© 55/5512-0091). For general postal information, call **FonoPost** (© 55/5709-9600); the staff is very helpful, and a few operators speak English.

   If you need to mail a package in Mexico City, take it to the post office called Correos Internacional 2, Calle Dr. Andrade and Río de la Loza (Metro: Balderas or Salto del Agua). It's open Monday through Friday from 8am to noon. Don't wrap your package securely until an inspector examines it. Although postal service is improving, your package may take weeks, or even months, to arrive at its destination. (For a glossary of mail terms, see appendix B.)

Restrooms There are few public restrooms. Use those in the larger hotels and in cafes, restaurants, and museums. Seasoned travelers frequently carry their own toilet paper and hand soap. Many public restrooms at museums and parks have an attendant who dispenses toilet paper for a "tip" of 5 pesos, in lieu of a usage charge.

Safety Read the "Crime" and "Bribes & Scams" sections under "Health & Safety" in chapter 2, and the "Important Taxi Safety Precautions in Mexico City" box, earlier in this chapter. In response to rising crime, Mexico City has added hundreds of new foot and mounted police officers, and there's a strong military presence. But they can't be everywhere. Watch out for pickpockets. Crowded subway cars and buses provide the perfect workplace for petty thieves, as do major museums (inside and out), crowded outdoor markets and bullfights, and indoor theaters. The "touch" can range from light-fingered wallet lifting or purse opening to a fairly rough shove by two or three petty thieves. Be extra careful anywhere that attracts a lot of tourists: on the Metro, in Reforma buses, in crowded hotel elevators and lobbies, at the Ballet Folklórico, and at the Museo de Antropología.

   Robberies may occur in broad daylight on crowded streets in "good" parts of town, outside major tourist sights, and in front of posh hotels. The best way to avoid being mugged is to not wear any jewelry of value, especially expensive watches. If you find yourself up against a handful of these guys, the best thing to do is relinquish the demanded possession, flee, and then notify the police. (You'll need the police report to file an insurance claim.) If you're in a crowded place, you could try raising a fuss—whether you do it in Spanish or

English doesn't matter. A few shouts of *"¡Ladrón!"* ("Thief!") might put them off, but that could also be risky. Overall, it's wise to leave valuables in the hotel safe and to take only the cash you'll need for the day, and no credit cards. Conceal a camera in a shoulder bag draped across your body and hanging in front of you, not on the side.

Taxes Posted prices generally include Mexico's 15% sales tax; however, it may be added. If in doubt, ask *"¿Mas IVA?"* ("Plus tax?") or *"¿Con IVA?"* ("With tax?"). There are also airport taxes for domestic and international flights, but the price of your ticket usually includes them. (See "Getting Around Mexico" in chapter 2.)

Telephones Telephone numbers within Mexico City are eight digits; the first digit of the local phone number is always 5. Generally speaking, Mexico City's telephone system is rapidly improving (with new digital lines replacing old ones), offering clear, efficient service. Some of this improvement is resulting in numbers changing. As elsewhere in the country, the telephone company changes numbers without informing the telephone owners or the information operators. Business telephone numbers may be registered in the name of the corporation, which may be different than the name of a hotel or restaurant owned by the corporation. Unless the corporation pays for a separate listing, the operator uses the corporate name to find the number. The local number for **information** is ⓒ **040**, and you are allowed to request three numbers with each information call.

Coin-operated phones are prone to vandalism; **card-only Ladatel phones** have replaced most of them. Ladatel cards are usually available at pharmacies and newsstands near public phones. They come in denominations of 20, 50, and 100 pesos. **Long-distance calls** within Mexico and to foreign points can be surprisingly expensive. Consult "Fast Facts: Mexico" in chapter 2 and "Telephones & Mail" in appendix B for information on using phones.

Weather & Clothing Mexico City's high altitude means you'll need a warm jacket and sweater in winter. The southern parts of the city, such as the university area and Xochimilco, are much colder than the central part. In summer, it gets warm during the day and cool, but not cold, at night. From May to October is the rainy season (this is common all over Mexico)—take a raincoat or rain poncho.

3 Where to Stay

Not only is Mexico City one of the most exciting cities in the world, it can also be one of the most affordable when it comes to accommodations. For $30 to $50, you can find a double room in a fairly central hotel, complete with a bathroom and often such extras as air-conditioning and TV. Many hotels have their own garages where guests can park free.

The best hotel values concentrate in the downtown **Centro Histórico (historic district),** which has recently undergone a dining and nightlife renaissance. Luxury hotels are mostly in the two most popular areas for mainstream tourism: The **Zona Rosa** seems to attract predominantly those in the city for business or shopping,

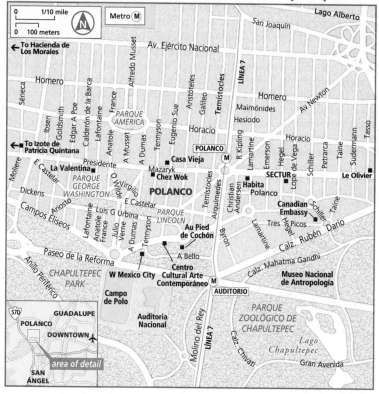

whereas the **Chapultepec Park** and **Polanco** neighborhood is ideally located near museums and other cultural attractions. This area is where you'll find Mexico City's hippest hotels, including the new **W Mexico City** and the acclaimed **Habita** (see below).

Hotels in these zones not only offer more deluxe accommodations and amenities, but also generally have their own fleets of taxis (see "By Taxi" under "Getting Around," earlier in this chapter) and secured entrances for guests. The crime rate, though on the decline, is still quite high; given this unfortunate reality, visitors should consider staying in the most secure accommodations they can afford.

The hip and happening **Condesa** neighborhood is about to have its first new hotel in a while, the 40-room **Condesa DF**, Av. Veracruz 102 (© **55/5282-3100;** www. condesadf.com), scheduled to open at press time. Developed by the same group that brought Habita to Polanco, it promises to be the hot new place to stay upon opening. Housed in a 1928 triangular Beaux Arts building it will have several rooms and bars that open onto an interior courtyard, with interiors by the French designer India Mahdavi. The hotel will be managed by Jonathan Morr, the entrepreneur behind Townhouse hotel in Miami Beach and Bond Street restaurant in New York. Rooms will start at $195 double, and will include amenities like flatscreen TVs, video art, and iPods.

CHAPULTEPEC PARK & POLANCO
VERY EXPENSIVE

Casa Vieja 🏵🏵   Pure Mexican style and service are the hallmarks of this luxury boutique hotel, a true gem known more to locals than tourists. Once a private residence, Casa Vieja is decorated with bold colors, unique handicrafts, exquisite antiques, and original furnishings. Each has a living and kitchen area, 36-inch TV, ample bedroom, and sizable bathroom with Jacuzzi tub. Notwithstanding the lovely decor, the real attraction is the highly personalized, gracious service. A rooftop bar and terrace serves made-to-order breakfasts (not included in the room rate). The only negative I can note is that in some rooms, you tend to overhear conversations in the halls and common areas, leading you to believe your own privacy may be compromised.

Eugenio Sue 45 (½ block from Av. Presidente Masaryk), Col. Polanco, 11560 Mexico D.F. 🕾 **55/5282-0067** or 55/5281-4468. Fax 55/5281-3780. www.casavieja.com. 10 suites. $390 junior suite; $650 master suite; $1,250 presidential suite. Rates include continental breakfast. AE, MC, V. Limited parking. Metro: Polanco. Children under 16 not accepted. **Amenities:** Bar and cafe w/light meal service; concierge; 24-hr. room service; laundry service; dry cleaning. *In room:* A/C, TV, VCR, fax, dataport, kitchenette, minibar, hair dryer, 3 phone extensions, air purifier, Internet access, Jacuzzi and steam-room, electronic safe-deposit box.

Habita 🏵🏵🏵   If you're into the hot and the hip, and don't mind attitude with your stay, this is your place in Mexico City. I give Habita high points for changing the Mexico City hotel scene. A boutique hotel of modernist design and minimalist interiors, Habita quickly became the hot hotel in the city's most stylish neighborhood, and still retains this distinction. The white and steel room decor is understated, with striking extras like flat-panel TV displays and elegant gray Mexican marble that lines the bathrooms from floor to ceiling. Beds are super-comfortable, with down comforters and pillows. It's one of the few hotels that offers high-speed Internet access in all rooms. Located on its rooftop terrace, the hotel's bar, AREA, is among the city's most popular nightspots. The lower level of the terrace features AREA's VIP section, along with a lap pool and small fitness center for guests. Adjacent to the lobby is an appropriately chic restaurant serving fusion cuisine, AURA, and a bar. It belongs to Small Luxury Hotels and design Hotels.

Av. Presidente Masaryk 201, Col. Polanco, 11560 Mexico, D.F. 🕾 **800/337-4685** in the U.S., or 55/5282-3100. Fax 55/5282-3101. www.hotelhabita.com. 36 units. $310 double; $369 junior suite. AE, MC, V. Valet parking $3.50. Metro: Polanco. **Amenities:** Restaurant; 2 bars; rooftop heated pool and solarium; small, well-equipped gym; Jacuzzi; sauna; steam room; concierge; tour services; business center; 24-hr. room service; massage; laundry service; dry cleaning. *In room:* A/C, TV, dataport, minibar, hair dryer, safe-deposit box, high-speed Internet access, bathrobes.

Hotel Camino Real 🏵🏵🏵   Long one of the capital's leading hotels, the Camino Real is itself a work of art, set amid Mexico's finest museums. A perennial favorite, it is one of the capital's hot spots for business and social entertaining, and frequently sells out. Designed by renowned architect Ricardo Legorreta, the building is a classic example of contemporary Mexican architecture; over 400 works of art by Mexican masters and other celebrated contemporary artists complement the design. A stunning Rufino Tamayo mural, *Man Facing Eternity,* greets visitors as they enter, a mural by José Luis Covarrubias graces the La Huerta restaurant, and an impressive sculpture by Alexander Calder dominates the foyer. The spacious rooms, all with brightly colored, modern decor and a sitting and desk area, contain armoires that conceal the TV and minibar. Executive Club rooms come with bathrobes; rates here include continental breakfast, evening cocktail hour, and daily newspaper. It is also home to a branch of the hot **China Grill** restaurant, as well as the first **Le Cirque** restaurant outside of the

U.S. The Lobby Bar—a water-themed space with cascading waterfall and chairs set on an acrylic floor over a pool—occasionally features some of Latin America's finest performers. The property's public areas were remodeled, and rooms upgraded in 2003.

Mariano Escobedo 700, Col. Anzúrez, 11590 Mexico, D.F. (C) **800/722-2646** in the U.S. and Canada, or 55/5263-8888. Fax 55/5250-6897. www.caminoreal.com/mexico. 714 units. $275 double; $525 suite; $360 Executive Club. AE, DC, MC, V. Metro: Chapultepec. **Amenities:** 5 restaurants; popular bar w/live entertainment; pool; 4 tennis courts; complete gym; sauna; steam room; concierge; travel agency; car rental; full-service business center; salon; 24-hr. room service; massage; laundry service; dry cleaning. *In room:* A/C, TV, minibar, dataport, hair dryer, safe-deposit box.

Hotel Four Seasons ⋆⋆⋆   One of the finest hotels in all of Mexico, and a personal favorite, the Four Seasons sets the standard for service with a staff noted for gracious manners. In the style of an elegant Mexican hacienda, the hotel's rooms surround a beautiful interior courtyard—a veritable sanctuary in this busy city. Although you're only steps from the busy Paseo de la Reforma, the grounds of the eight-story hotel seem more like the quiet countryside surrounding a gracious manor house. On one side of the large and inviting outdoor courtyard, there's umbrella-covered alfresco dining with colonnaded walkways all around; other dining rooms and bars face this pleasant scene.

The huge, airy rooms have high ceilings and are resolutely sumptuous. Each has plush bedspreads, beautiful Talavera lamps and bathroom accessories, Indonesian tapestries, and rich dark-wood furnishings, including a working desk. All rooms have bathrooms with separate shower and tub, dual sinks, and illuminated makeup mirrors. Most rooms face the interior courtyard, two deluxe suites have patios facing the courtyard, and most Executive Suites (with 1–2 separate bedrooms) overlook Reforma. About 100 rooms are reserved for nonsmokers. Expert-led private tours to many of the city's historic sites and museums are a unique offering; weekend guests have the option of one or two tours included in the price of the room—a true value. The Four Seasons is at the western end of the Zona Rosa, near Chapultepec Park and Polanco and opposite the Hotel Marquís Reforma.

Reforma 500, Col. Juárez, 06600 Mexico, D.F. (C) **800/332-3442** in the U.S., 800/268-6282 in Canada, or 55/5230-1818. Fax 55/5230-1817. www.fourseasons.com. 240 units. $290 double; $400–$480 suite. Special weekend cultural packages generally available. AE, DC, MC, V. Free valet parking. Metro: Sevilla. **Amenities:** 2 restaurants; 2 bars; heated rooftop swimming pool; spa w/complete gym; whirlpool; sauna; complete business center; salon; room service; massage; laundry service; dry cleaning; 1-hr. pressing service; 2 rooms for travelers w/disabilities. *In room:* A/C, TV, dataport, minibar, hair dryer, iron, safe-deposit box, bathrobes.

Hotel Marquís Reforma ⋆ *(Overrated)*   With a faux Art Deco exterior and an overdone combination of glass, marble, and dark mahogany within, the Marquís Reforma opened in 1991 and has been billed as one of the city's state-of-the-art luxury hotels. If superfluity is your style, you'll be thrilled here. If you prefer understated elegance, try another choice—you'll feel imposed upon here. It does have an excellent location, however, at the eastern end of Chapultepec Park opposite the Four Seasons at the western end of the Zona Rosa, which is why it's a favorite for business travelers. Rooms vary in shape and size. Some have terraces; some separate living rooms, dining rooms, and bedrooms; some an attached meeting room. Standard double rooms have king-size beds and small sitting areas. The units billed as business rooms lack a suitable desk and are smaller than normal for the type and price. The junior suites are very spacious, with dark wood paneling. A piano player entertains nightly in the lobby **Caviar Bar,** the highlight of the hotel, which serves tea, drinks, and light meals. As part of a multimillion-dollar renovation, a new spa, which features massage rooms, a complete gym, pool, and three outdoor Jacuzzis that overlook the city's dramatic skyline, opened in 2003.

Paseo Reforma 465, Col. Cuauhtémoc, 06500 Mexico, D.F. ⓒ **800/235-2387** in the U.S., or 55/5229-1200. Fax 55/5229-1212. www.marquisreforma.com. 208 units. $310 double; $395–$575 suite. AE, DC, MC, V. Free parking adjacent to hotel. Metro: Sevilla. **Amenities:** Restaurant; coffee shop; lobby bar; fitness center w/workout equipment, 3 whirlpools, sauna and steam rooms; car rental; complete business center; salon; room service; massage; laundry service. *In room:* A/C, TV, dataport, minibar, hair dryer, safe-deposit box.

W Mexico City ★★★★   In late 2003 the W Mexico City opened to overwhelmingly rave reviews, living up to its billing as the chicest spot to stay in Mexico. This dramatic 26-story business hotel—with an all-glass entrance—is a sophisticated mixture of style, comfort and technology. The entry encompasses a series of stepped lounge areas with koi ponds, the lobby-level Red Lounge and a three-story projection wall displaying fascinating images from around the world. The rooms are spectacular, decorated with brilliant cherry-red walls, white beds, terrazzo floors, and a spacious and comfortable work area. Bathrooms are stunning, and break with tradition by being located on the far end of the room and feature windows and walk-in showers with a hanging hammock inside. Some rooms have a large circular tub with massage jets. There are also nine high-ceiling "loft" suites, with views of Chapulapec Park, green-glass showers, and plasma TVs mounted on the ceiling above the beds. One Extreme WOW penthouse suite has two bedrooms, a terrace, kitchen and wet bar, plus a 16-jet shower and a pillow-covered playroom. Targeting business travelers, the W Mexico City also has nine high-tech conference rooms that seat up to 400, a complete business center, and specially equipped "cyber rooms" with printers, scanners, and fax. The hotel has its own full-service spa plus a glass-enclosed health club. Dining is available at Solea, a chic seafood restaurant with a Mexican and Asian flare, with al fresco terrace dining available for breakfast or lunch. It also contains the first of Rande Gerber's popular Whiskey Bars outside of the U.S., The Terrace, already considered the city's top nightspot.

Campos Eliseos 252 (corner of Andrés Bello), Col. Polanco, 11560 Mexico, D.F. ⓒ **888/625-5144** in the U.S., or 55/9138-1800. Fax 55/9138-1899. www.starwood.com/whotels. 237 units. $190–$290 double; $470 suite. AE, MC, V. Valet parking $5. Metro: Polanco. **Amenities:** Restaurant; 2 bars; full-service spa; concierge; tour services; business center; 24-hr. room service; laundry service; dry cleaning; CD and DVD library. *In room:* A/C, 27-in. TV, minibar w/munchie box, coffeemaker, hair dryer, safe-deposit box, wireless high-speed Internet access, CD players, cordless phones w/voice mail, bathrobes, featherbeds, down duvets.

ZONA ROSA & SURROUNDING AREAS
VERY EXPENSIVE

Galería Plaza ★★   In the heart of the Zona Rosa, the Galería Plaza has earned a reputation as one of the highest-quality hotels in Mexico City. It's immensely popular with business travelers. The large, bright rooms have light-colored wood and wicker furniture. All come with dual-line phones and purified tap water. Marble bathrooms have makeup mirrors and a telephone extension. Universal outlets accommodate a fax or computer, and electrical adapters are available from the concierge. The staff is professional, efficient, and accommodating. Executive Floor rates include free local calls, parking privileges, continental breakfast, and afternoon cocktails served in the Executive Lounge. Guest Office rooms contain a nearly complete office, including printer/fax/copier, desk, speakerphone with dataport, and special telephone rates that include free local calls and long-distance access, plus in-room faxing without a surcharge. Nonsmoking floors are also available.

Hamburgo 195, 06600 Mexico, D.F. ℂ **888/559-4329** toll-free in the U.S. and Canada, or 55/5230-1717. Fax 55/5207-5867. www.brisas.com.mx. 439 units. $185 double; $238 Executive Floor double. AE, DC, MC, V. Free covered guarded parking. Metro: Insurgentes. **Amenities:** 3 restaurants; lobby bar; heated rooftop swimming pool; fully equipped fitness center; 24-hr. concierge; travel agency; car rental; full-service business center; room service; laundry service; dry cleaning. Rooms for travelers w/disabilities are available. *In room:* A/C, TV, dataport, minibar, coffeemaker, hair dryer, iron, safe-deposit boxes.

Hotel Sheraton María Isabel ★★   The Sheraton María Isabel's location in front of the Monumento de la Independencia is ideal: It's next to the U.S. Embassy and across Reforma from the heart of the Zona Rosa. A favorite for business travelers, the hotel offers premium amenities in all its rooms. Tower suites, the most deluxe, occupy the fourth floor and have private check-in, butler service, and continental breakfast and evening canapés. The **Jorongo Bar,** a Mexico City institution, offers live entertainment nightly from 7pm to 1am. (See "Mexico City After Dark," later in this chapter.)

Paseo de la Reforma 325 (at Río Tiber), 06500 Mexico, D.F. ℂ **800/325-3535** in the U.S., or 55/5242-5555. Fax 55/5207-0684. www.sheraton.com. 755 units. $285 double; $330 Tower. AE, MC, V. Covered parking $5.50. Metro: Insurgentes (6 blocks away). **Amenities:** 3 restaurants; 2 bars; open-air pool; privileges at nearby golf course; 2 tennis courts; full-service fitness center; travel agency; complete business center; salon; 24-hr. room service; laundry service; dry cleaning. *In room:* A/C, TV, dataport, minibar, hair dryer, safe.

EXPENSIVE

La Casona Hotel-Relais ★★★ *(Finds)*   Reminiscent of a small European luxury hotel, this exquisite establishment opened in 1996 after restoration of a dilapidated 1923 building. It has since been designated an artistic monument by Mexico's National Institute of Fine Arts. Each luxuriously decorated room is unique; all have antique furniture. Tall interior shutter doors on guest-room windows keep out sound and light at night, and thick glass mutes street noise by day. Oriental-style rugs warm the hardwood floors throughout. A small wine cellar and bar below the lobby has been a popular gathering place for drinks and conversation. The hotel is 3 blocks south of the Diana Circle on Reforma, and 4 longish blocks west of the western edge of the Zona Rosa. Chapultepec Park is about a 20-minute walk to the northwest. More important than decor or location is the excellent service here—truly capable of giving you a pampered feeling.

Durango 280 (corner of Cozumel), Col. Roma, 06700 Mexico, D.F. ℂ **800/223-5652** in the U.S., or 55/5286-3001. Fax 55/5211-0871. www.hotellacasona.com.mx. 29 units. $166 double. Rates include American breakfast. AE, DC, MC, V. Gated parking $4. Metro: Sevilla (4 blocks away). **Amenities:** Restaurant; bar; small gym w/steam room; concierge; room service; laundry service; safe-deposit boxes; currency exchange. *In room:* A/C, TV, dataport.

MODERATE

Hotel Imperial ★ *(Value)*   This classic hotel, which dates from 1904 and has been designated a historic monument, is one of the most memorable buildings along the Avenida Reforma. It has been the home of one Mexican president, the site of the assassination of another, and, for years, the U.S. embassy. The Imperial changed hands several times before returning to its original name and status as a premier hotel in 1989. Popular with foreign—especially European—guests, it's one of the best values in the area. Rooms are extra large, with high ceilings and carpeting, although the traditional-style furnishings are a bit dated. All have either a king or two double beds, plus desks and sitting areas. Bathrooms are very large, with tubs and separate vanities. Each Master Suite, at the tip of one of the five floors of the building, has a unique triangular bedroom overlooking Avenida Reforma, living/dining room, bar, and whirlpool in the bathroom. All rooms are entered from a central atrium with staircase (there's also an elevator).

Paseo de la Reforma 64 (at Morelos), Col. Juárez, 06600 Mexico, D.F. © **55/5705-4911.** Fax 55/5703-3122. www.hotelimperial.com.mx. 65 units. $130 double; $145–$210 suite. AE, DC, MC, V. Weekend rates are discounted 40%. Free parking. Metro: Revolución or Juárez. **Amenities:** Noted Spanish restaurant and bar Gaudi, w/live music nightly; concierge; business center; room service; laundry service; dry cleaning. *In room:* A/C, TV, minibar, hair dryer, safe-deposit box.

INEXPENSIVE

Casa González Casa González is a two-story hostel made up of two converted mansions. The houses, with little grassy patios out back and a huge shade tree, contain rooms that are charming and homey—and heated for those chilly mornings. Each is unique, and some have a terrace or balcony. A dining room brightened by stained glass and international conversation serves (optional) meals. Casa González is especially good for women traveling alone, although there are only three single rooms. The warm, caring management ensures that each guest feels more like part of a shifting, growing family than just a passing visitor.

Río Sena 69 (between Río Lerma and Río Panuco), 06500 Mexico, D.F. © 55/5514-3302. Fax 55/5511-0702. 22 units. $40 double; $65 suite for 4. No credit cards. Limited parking $6. Metro: Insurgentes (4 blocks away). **Amenities:** Dining room.

María Cristina ⭐ This classic choice for budget travelers is conveniently located just a 10-minute walk from the Zona Rosa. Rooms are bright and have one king or two double beds, ample closets, and modern bathrooms. The large lobby with overstuffed couches and a fireplace makes a comfortable meeting place. A grassy courtyard offers lounge chairs for reading or relaxing. The hotel is at Río Neva, on the north side of Reforma.

Río Lerma 31, 06030 Mexico, D.F. © **55/5703-1212** or 55/5566-9688. Fax 55/5566-9194. www.hotelmariacristina. com.mx. 150 units. $60 double; $95 suite. AE, DC, MC, V. Free guarded parking. **Amenities:** Restaurant; El Ritiro Bar; travel agency; salon; private garden; Internet service. *In room:* TV, safe.

CENTRO HISTORICO & SURROUNDING AREAS
MODERATE

Best Western Hotel de Cortés ⭐⭐ *(Finds* This baroque-style hotel offers comfortable, modern accommodations in a fascinating historic building—a former home for Augustinian friars. The 18th-century stone structure features rooms on two floors surrounding a central colonial courtyard with a graceful fountain and Mexican restaurant. It's on La Alameda park, a short distance from the Palace of Fine Arts and the Franz Mayer Museum. Rooms vary in size and features, but all contain hand-woven bedspreads, carpeting, and a desk. The modern bathrooms have three-prong plugs and tile accents. Security boxes are available in the reception area.

Av. Hidalgo 85, 06300 Mexico, D.F. © **800/528-1234** in the U.S., or 55/5518-2184. Fax 55/5512-1863. www.hotel decortes.com.mx. 29 units. $120 double; $170 suite. AE, DC, MC, V. Valet parking available. Metro: Hidalgo. **Amenities:** Courtyard restaurant/bar; concierge; room service; babysitting; safe-deposit boxes. *In room:* TV, minibar.

Best Western Hotel Majestic ⭐⭐ This classic hotel's prime location, facing the *zócalo,* is reason enough to stay here. The Majestic is somewhat of a Mexico City institution that visitors should experience at least once. The comfortable lobby has a glass ceiling that is also the floor of a sitting area surrounded by rooms. Rooms that don't look onto the *zócalo* overlook Avenida Madero or the hotel's inner court. The lobby and courtyard are decorated with stone arches, beautiful tiles, and stone fountains.

Furnishings in the rooms are rather dated, and plans to upgrade them seem to continually stall. Tile bathrooms have tub/shower combos. In lower-floor rooms facing Avenida Madero, noise from the street may be a problem—quieter rooms look out onto the interior courtyard, which has its own aviary. Occupants of rooms facing the *zócalo* will get an unexpected jolt from the early-morning flag-raising ceremony, complete with marching feet, drums, and bugle. The popular Terazza rooftop cafe/restaurant with umbrella-shaded tables serves all three meals, and the Majestic also has a sidewalk cafe facing the *zócalo*. You can save quite a few dollars by booking directly with the hotel and by asking for promotional rates or discounts.

Av. Madero 73, Col. Centro Cp., 06000 Mexico, D.F. ℂ 55/5521-8600. Fax 55/5512-6262. www.majestic.com.mx. 85 units. $95–$105 double; $170–$220 suite. AE, MC, V. No parking available. Metro: Zócalo. **Amenities:** Restaurant/bar; travel agency; room service; babysitting. *In room:* TV, minibar, coffeemaker.

INEXPENSIVE

Hotel Catedral *Value*   This modern hotel in a stellar location is also probably the best bargain lodging in the city. One block north of Calle Tacuba is tree-shaded Calle Donceles, where you'll find the eight-story (with elevator) Hotel Catedral, half a block from the Templo Mayor and a block from the Museo San Ildefonso. Rooms are modern; all have purified drinking water from a special tap, good over-bed reading lights, and TVs with U.S. cable channels. Some have tub/shower combinations, and some have whirlpool tubs. Rooms on the upper floors afford views of Mexico City's mammoth cathedral. On the seventh floor, a terrace with small tables and chairs offers great views. The Catedral's location is ideal for sightseeing, and the central downtown district is experiencing a revival. Because heavily trafficked streets surround the hotel, add 45 minutes to your departure time if you go to the airport from here. In front of the big, marble-embellished lobby is the bustling restaurant. The cozy bar beyond the reception desk also serves food. Ask for a top-floor room with a view.

Calle Donceles 95 (between Brasil and Argentina), 06020 Mexico, D.F. ℂ 55/5521-6183. Fax 55/5512-4344. www.hotelcatedral.com. 116 units. $42–$53 double; $57 junior suite. AE, MC, V. Free parking. Metro: Zócalo. **Amenities:** Restaurant; bar; travel agency; room service; laundry service. *In room:* TV, hair dryer, safe-deposit box.

Hotel Gillow   The dignified-looking, seven-story Gillow is a modern hotel with six stories of rooms grouped around a long, glass-canopied, rectangular courtyard with a colonial fountain. Were it in the Zona Rosa, the Gillow could easily cost three times what it does. The well-kept, carpeted rooms have comfortable beds, tub/shower combinations, and excellent lighting. Some units are small, with one double bed and enough room for one person's luggage. Others are quite spacious, with a long carpeted bench for suitcases. Interior-room windows open to an airshaft; exterior rooms have small terraces with wrought-iron furniture. Request a room as far away from street noise as possible. The hotel is between Cinco de Mayo and Madero—a hard-to-beat downtown location.

Isabel la Católica 17, 06000 Mexico, D.F. ℂ 55/5518-1440. Fax 55/5512-2078. www.hotelgillow.com. 103 units. $48–$55 double; $61 suite. AE, MC, V. No parking available. Metro: Zócalo. **Amenities:** Restaurant; bar; concierge; tour desk; room service; laundry service. *In room:* TV.

NEAR THE AIRPORT

Hilton Airport Hotel *⋆*   This on-site hotel is the newest and nicest of the airport hotels in terms of service and facilities. The lobby bar is a popular gathering place, and if the restaurant happens to be closed, there's 24-hour room service. The staff is attentive and the rooms nicely furnished, though small. Each has color TV with U.S. channels, a nice-size work desk, and an ergonomic executive chair. It can't be beat for convenience and a guarantee of making an early-morning plane. To get there, exit the terminal near Gate A and walk right, down the corridor to Sala F and the international departure gates.

Carlos Capitán s/n (Sala F, 3rd floor), 15520 Mexico, D.F. © **800/228-9290** in the U.S., or 55/5133-0505. Fax 55/5133-0500. www.hilton.com 129 units. $190 double; $300 junior suite. AE, DC, MC, V. Covered and uncovered parking $1 per hr. **Amenities:** Restaurant; lobby bar; small health club; 24-hr. concierge; business center; 24-hr. room service; laundry and pressing service. *In room:* A/C, TV w/pay movies, dataport, minibar, coffeemaker, hair dryer, iron, safe-deposit box.

4 Where to Dine

As in most of the world's major cities, dining in Mexico City is sophisticated, with cuisine that spans the globe. From high chic to the Mexican standard of *comida corrida* (food on the go), the capital offers something for every taste and budget. The **Polanco** area in particular has become a place of exquisite dining options, with new restaurants rediscovering and modernizing classic Mexican dishes. The **Centro Histórico** led a resurgence of ultra-hip restaurants and clubs open for late-night dining and nightlife, which has spread to the **Condesa** and **Roma** neighborhoods—now known as the SoHo of Mexico City. Cantinas, until not so very long ago the privilege of men only, offer some of the best food and colorful local atmosphere.

Everybody eats out in Mexico City, regardless of social class. Consequently, you can find restaurants of every type, size, and price range scattered across the city. Mexicans take their food and dining seriously, so if you see a full house, that's generally recommendation enough. But those same places may be entirely empty if you arrive early—remember, here, lunch is generally eaten at 3pm, with dinner not seriously considered before 9pm.

CHAPULTEPEC PARK & POLANCO
VERY EXPENSIVE
Chez Wok ✿ HAUTE CHINESE   Opened in the fashionable Polanco area in 1992 with five chefs from Hong Kong and their incredible recipes, Chez Wok immediately became *the* place to feast on Chinese food. Years later, it hasn't lost its popularity, especially for power lunches. It's generally packed, and, although prices are high, most dishes serve two or three people. The dining area, with large and small sections, has a combination of booths and tables with an elegant but simple yellow, black, and beige decor. Main courses include steamed red snapper with white-wine sauce, chicken in shrimp paste with sesame and crab sauce, and the house specialty, Peking duck.

Tennyson 117, 2nd floor (at Av. Presidente Masaryk), Col. Polanco. © **55/5281-3410** or 55/5281-2921. Reservations recommended. Main courses $18–$55. AE, MC, V. Daily Mon–Sat 1:30–11pm; Sun 1:30–4pm. Valet and free parking available. Metro: Polanco.

Izote de Patricia Quintana ✿✿ MEXICAN HAUTE CUISINE   A new star of the city's superb dining scene, this latest venture of celebrated chef Patricia Quintana pays homage to the best of classic Mexican cooking. While the atmosphere is simple, what's on your plate will more than make up for it. Opened in 2002 on Mexico's version of Rodeo Drive, it quickly became the "must-dine" restaurant, so reservations are essential, often even at lunch. The menu is a compilation of modern versions of old *mestizo* (indigenous) dishes, and draws heavily on indigenous ingredients such as yucca flower, cactus, and *masa* (corn flour). Each dish is a delight. Try lobster enchiladas with pumpkinseed sauce, or lamb barbecued in a banana leaf. Endings are especially sweet here—save room for Tarta Zaachila, a chocolate pastry filled with nuts, accompanied by the traditional café de olla, coffee flavored with cinnamon and brown sugar. If you're curious, *izote* is the beautiful white flower that adorns the yucca plant.

My, what an inefficient way to fish.

Ring toss, good. Horseshoes, bad.

Faster! Faster! Faster!

We take care of the fiddly bits, from providing over 43,000 customer reviews of hotels, to helping you find our best fares, to giving you 24/7 customer service. So you can focus on the only thing that matters. Goofing off.

travelocity
You'll never roam alone.

Frommers.com

So many places, so little time?

TOKYO — 7766 miles
LONDON — 3818 miles
TORONTO — 4682 miles
SYDNEY — 5087 miles
NEW YORK — 4947 miles
LOS ANGELES — 2556 miles
HONG KONG — 5638 miles

Frommers.com makes the going fast and easy.

Find a destination. ✓ Buy a guidebook. ✓ Book a trip. ✓ Get hot travel dea
Enter to win vacations. ✓ Check out the latest travel news.
Share trip photos and memories. ✓ And much more.

Av. Presidente Masaryk 513 (between calles Sócrates and Platón), Col. Polanco. ℂ **55/5280-1671** or 55/5280-1265. Reservations recommended. Main courses $21–$55. AE, MC, V. Mon–Sat 1pm–midnight; Sun 1–6pm. Valet parking available. Metro: Polanco.

EXPENSIVE

Fonda del Claustro ★★★ TRADITIONAL MEXICAN/PUEBLA Previously called Fonda Santa Clara, and still under the same ownership, this is one of the city's fine dining establishments, presenting the best of Puebla's cuisine to a full house daily. The menu lists a full range of daily and seasonal specialties. The large serving of *manchamantel* (literally, "tablecloth stainer") is a sweet, smooth *mole* made by blending chiles, apricots, pears, apples, and bananas, served over pork or chicken—it's fabulous. The *sartenada ranchera* is enough to fill two diners. The feast is a combination plate of superbly seasoned and grilled meats, sausage, and bacon served with onions, salsa, and avocado. Service is refined and attentive. Arrive early, because every seat in its several dining areas will be filled, especially at lunch. If you happen to be visiting between September and October, you must try *chiles en nogada,* a delicious blend of poblano chiles stuffed with meat and fruit and covered in sweet walnut sauce, served chilled. This is one of the most baroque dishes in Mexican cuisine. Fonda del Claustro is a more expensive cousin of the Fonda de Santa Clara in Puebla, but the menus are almost identical.

Homero 1910 (between the Periférico Norte and Blas Pascal), Col. Polanco. ℂ **55/5557-6144.** Also at Av. San Jerónimo 775, Col. San Jerónimo Lídice. ℂ **55/5683-0730.** Reservations recommended. Main courses $20–$35. AE, DC, MC, V. Mon–Fri 7:30am–11pm; Sat 8:30am–midnight; Sun 8:30am–6pm. Metro: Polanco.

La Fonda del Recuerdo ★★ MEXICAN/SEAFOOD/VERACRUZ For an all-out good time, no other restaurant in the city compares to this one. Come here if you want to immerse yourself in Mexico and join people eating, drinking, singing, and having the time of their lives. Diners enjoy their platters of food amid a glorious din created by *jarocho* musicians from Veracruz (several groups rove around the restaurant at once). The menu is authentically Mexican, with an emphasis on seafood; specials match the culinary traditions of whichever Mexican holiday is closest. Arrive before 2:30pm for lunch or you'll have to wait in line, which nonetheless will be worth it if you have all afternoon. At night, it's just as festive, but try to make it before 9pm, if you care to avoid the crowd. It's near the corner of Bahía de Santa Bárbara—take a taxi.

Bahía de las Palmas 37, Col. Verónica Anzures. ℂ **55/5260-0545** or 55/9112-7476. www.fondadelrecuerdo.com. Reservations recommended. Main courses $10–$20. AE, DC, MC, V. Mon–Sat 1pm–midnight; Sun 1–6pm. Metro: Polanco.

La Valentina ★★ MEXICAN NOUVELLE CUISINE In the midst of posh Polanco, on the second floor of a small boutique-filled shopping center, is this dignified restaurant with an elegantly casual flair. Pale-apricot stucco walls, shiny wood floors, and wood-beamed ceilings set off the cozy nooks of immaculately set tables. The menu features specialties from some of the country's best Mexican cooks. For example, there's Marta Chapa's breaded shrimp with sesame, lettuce, herbs, and chiles; cilantro soup by Suzanna Palazuelos; and Patricia Quintana's filet in butter and salsa. The bar is worth a visit on its own, with an impressive selection of premium tequilas, a selection of fine art, live trio music, and an upscale cantina-style atmosphere.

Av. Presidente Masaryk 393 (near the corner of Lafontaine), Col. Polanco. ℂ **55/5282-2656** or 55/5282-2514. Reservations recommended. Main courses $20–$25. AE, DC, MC, V. Daily 2pm–2am. Valet parking $2.50. Metro: Polanco.

MODERATE

Au Pied de Cochon ✿ FRENCH/BISTRO   The *capitalaños* seem to be having a love affair with French bistros these days, and this is currently their top choice. A direct import from Paris, this always-busy bistro packs in the city's jet set and fashion forward for classic cafe fare. It's the best late-night dining option in the city. The main dining room is a spirited scene of activity and conversation, in multiple languages. Two service bars offer singles places to dine without feeling "solo," and other tables are packed in together. Pâtés, cheese plates, and exquisite salads are standard starters. Steak frites, steamed mussels, and the specialty of *pied de cochon* (pigs' feet) are menu favorites—meat dishes are especially popular. There's an excellent selection of French wines, as well as an ample choice of tequilas. Desserts are classically French and rich.

Campos Eliseos 218, in the Intercontinental Hotel, Col. Chapultepec. ℂ **55/5327-7700** or 55/5327-7756. Reservations recommended. Main courses $8–$20. AE, MC, V. Daily 24 hrs. Valet parking available. Metro: Auditorio.

Le Olivier ★★★ *(Finds* COUNTRY FRENCH/BISTRO   This bright, bustling bistro would be reminiscent of an authentic French cafe—were it not for the fact that its patrons tend to be business professionals rather than bohemians. Opened in 2000, this place packs in a crowd, and with good reason—the food is superb. Choices range from pâtés to soufflés (definitely plan ahead and save room for a chocolate soufflé!). There's an excellent representation of country French fare, including steak frites, cassoulets, and fricassees. The chef-owner, Oliver Lombard, is the former chef of Mexico City's Club de Industriales, a celebrated private club. The restaurant is 12 blocks from the Polanco station. You could venture in without reservations, but depending on the night, you might not get in without them. There is no bar to wait in.

Masaryk 49-C (at Torcuato Tasso), Col. Polanco. ℂ **55/5545-3133**. Reservations recommended. Main courses $15–$25. AE, MC, V. Daily 1:30–11pm. Valet parking $2.50. Metro: Polanco.

ZONA ROSA & SURROUNDING AREAS

If you're up for a culinary adventure, dine at the student-staffed Restaurante Escuela Monte Servino at the **Colegio Superior de Gastronomía,** Sonora 189, Condesa (ℂ **55/5584-3800**), the training ground for Mexico's up-and-coming chefs. It's in a lovely room overlooking the Parque México. The menu varies, and there are a few misses among the hits, but this is a great way to sample the latest culinary trends. The ever-changing five-course fixed-price lunch costs just $18. Wines by the glass are available. It's open weekdays, and reservations are a must.

EXPENSIVE

Cicero-Centenario ★★★ INTERNATIONAL/NOUVELLE MEXICAN   You'll either feel you've stepped into the set of *Frida,* or back in time to an elegant hacienda when you enter Cicero-Centenario. It's deservedly one of the most noted restaurants in the country. Stylish, eccentric, artistic, and whimsical all at once, this place offers not just excellent food but a complete dining experience *a la mexicana*. Tables in the intimate nooks of the restaurant's smart salons look out on a backdrop of stained glass, antiques, and flickering candlelight. Among the highlights on the menu are starters such as delectable cream of cilantro soup or crepes stuffed with squash-flower blossoms and Gruyère cheese in a mild poblano chile sauce. Main dishes include recipes developed for the restaurant by noted chef and author Patricia Quintana, such as chicken in rich almond sauce and her renowned *mole poblano*. There is another branch of the restaurant in the Historic Center of the city (see below).

Londres 195 (between Florencia and Amberes), Zona Rosa. ✆ **55/5533-3800** or 55/5533-4276. Reservations recommended. Main courses $10–$40. AE, DC, MC, V. Mon–Sat 1pm–1am. Valet parking available. Metro: Insurgentes.

Tezka ✿✿ SPANISH/MEXICAN HAUTE CUISINE The sister of the Michelin three-star restaurant Arzak in Spain's Basque country, Tezka is earning rave reviews of its own with innovative contemporary Spanish cuisine, with Mexican influences. The atmosphere is spacious and relaxing, with several dining rooms, including one table for four on its own level. Several tables are next to French windows that open to the street, one level below. Starters include amuse-bouche of cerviche of slivers of raw tuna and strawberries on tiny tostadas, and a mousse of foie gras wrapped in sliced mango. Entrees include sea bass in a pistachio sauce, lamb with a peanut sauce, served with peanuts and leeks, in thin slices of melon. For dessert, try the sweet-and-spicy chocolate-chile ice cream, or for more traditional palates, coconut soup with lemon ice cream. There's a $37 tasting menu that is a great bargain for epicures. The wine list has an excellent selection of Spanish wines, as well as better Mexican offerings.

Amberes 78, in the Hotel Royal, Zona Rosa. ✆ **55/5228-9918**. Reservations recommended. Main courses $30–$50. AE, DC, MC, V. Mon–Fri 1–5pm and 8-11pm; Sat 1–5pm. Metro: Insurgentes.

MODERATE
Fonda El Refugio ✿✿ MEXICAN More than 40 years of tradition have shaped the service, food, and atmosphere at Fonda El Refugio, making it a very special place for authentic Mexican dining. It's small and unusually congenial, with a large fireplace decorated with gleaming copper pots and pans. Rows and rows of culinary awards and citations hang behind the desk. The restaurant manages the almost impossible task of being both elegant and informal. The menu runs the gamut of Mexican cuisine, from *arroz con plátanos* (rice with fried bananas) to *enchiladas con mole poblano,* topped with the rich, thick, spicy chocolate sauce of Puebla. There's a daily specialty. Try chiles stuffed with ground beef or cheese, and for dessert have some coconut candy. Fonda El Refugio is very popular, especially on Saturday night, so get there early.

Liverpool 166 (between Florencia and Amberes), Col. Juárez Zona Rosa. ✆ **55/5207-2732** or 55/5525-8128. Main courses $7–$9. AE, MC, V. Mon–Sat 1–11pm; Sun 1–10pm. Valet parking $1. Metro: Insurgentes.

CENTRO HISTORICO & SURROUNDING AREAS
EXPENSIVE
Cicero-Centenario ✿✿✿ INTERNATIONAL/NUEVA COCINA MEXICANA This Cicero-Centenario shares an ambience of magical realism with its sister restaurant in the Zona Rosa. Tucked into the historic zone in an elegant two-story 18th-century mansion, it is among the most popular eating establishments in the city. At every meal, all the tables have reservation cards. The menu is essentially the same as at the other Cicero's—fish, beef, and chicken served with great sauces and seasonings. Each day there's a different special: on Friday, whitefish from Pátzcuaro; on Saturday, *man-chamanteles*—both traditional Mexican fare transformed into gourmet delights. From June to September you'll see *chiles en nogada;* during April and May, *gusanos de maguey.* The latter is a seasonal worm dish: Worms that live on the maguey leaves (the tequila plant) are a regional delicacy. They're served fried, accompanied with guacamole and tortillas. The restaurant is 5 blocks northeast of La Alameda, not far from the Santo Domingo Plaza and Church.

República de Cuba 79 (between República de Chile and Palma). ✆ **55/5521-7866**. Reservations recommended. Main courses $7–$30. AE, DC, MC, V. Mon–Sat 1pm–1am; Sun 1:30–7pm. Metro: Allende.

MODERATE

Café Tacuba 🍴🍴 MEXICAN   One of the city's most popular restaurants, Café Tacuba dates from 1912 and boasts a handsome colonial-era atmosphere. Guests are welcomed into one of two long dining rooms, with brass lamps, dark oil paintings, and a large mural of nuns working in a kitchen. The menu is authentic Mexican with traditional dishes, including tamales, enchiladas, chiles rellenos, *mole*, and *pozole.* Thursday through Sunday from 6pm until closing, a wonderful group of medieval-costumed singers entertains; their sound is like the melodious *estudiantina* groups of Guanajuato accompanied by mandolins and guitars. A trio plays on alternate Mondays and Tuesdays from 8 to 10pm.

Tacuba 28 (between República de Chile and Bolívar), Col. Centro. (C) 55/5512-8482 or 55/5518-4950. Breakfast $4–$10; main courses $9–$13; *comida corrida* $10–$15. AE, MC, V. Daily 8am–11:30pm. Metro: Allende.

Restaurant Danubio SEAFOOD/SPANISH/INTERNATIONAL   This place has been a Mexico City tradition since 1938, and it remains an excellent choice for lunch. Locals enjoy it on weekends with their families. The house specialty is *langostinos* (baby crayfish), and the menu offers a range of selections emphasizing seafood. Danubio is noted for its excellent wine cellar. The restaurant is south of La Alameda.

Uruguay 3 (near Lázaro Cárdenas). (C) 55/5512-0912. www.danubio.com. Main courses $15–$30. AE, DC, MC, V. Daily 1–10pm. Metro: Bellas Artes or Salto del Agua.

CANTINAS

Cantina La Guadalupana 🍴🍴 *Finds* MEXICAN   Opened in 1928, this cantina is in Coyoacán, the southern neighborhood that was once the home of the artists Diego Rivera and Frida Kahlo and the revolutionary Leon Trotsky. From the entrance—off a narrow, cobblestone, colonial street—to the antiquated bar, a sense of nostalgia permeates the comfortable, jovial cantina. The operation is as traditional as the menu. For those who are only drinking, waiters bring the customary small plates of complimentary snacks that range from crisp jicama (a root) slices with lime and chile to pigs' feet in a red sauce. It's easy to imagine the communist conversations that must have bounced off the walls here in Frida and Diego's day.

Higuera 14 (1 block from the central plaza), Coyoacán. (C) 55/5554-6253. Main courses $3.25–$5; mixed drinks $2.50–$8 (more for premium tequilas). AE, MC, V. Mon–Sat 1–11:30pm. Metro: Coyoacán.

El Nivel 🍴 *Finds* MEXICAN   With a distinction of holding liquor license #1, El Nivel better have it right, after 3 centuries of operation! Although the current business opened in 1855, it claims three centuries of service. Previously, it was the building where the water level in Mexico City was measured, hence the name, El Nivel, or the "level." Throughout its history, it has drawn a highly literary clientele, and still counts among its regular patrons the most distinguished writers, journalists, and political pundits in the capital. Location, no doubt, helps in the attraction—it's on the corner across from the Palacio de Gobierno, in the Centro Historico.

Moneda 2, Centro Histórico. (C) 55/5522-9755 or 55/5522-6184. Main courses $3.25–$10; mixed drinks $2.50–$8 (more for premium tequilas). AE, MC, V. Mon–Sat noon–midnight. Metro: Zócalo.

La Nueva Opera Bar 🍴🍴 *Moments* INTERNATIONAL   La Nueva Opera Bar, 3 blocks east of La Alameda, is the most opulent of the city's cantinas. Slide into a dark wood booth below gilded baroque ceilings, patches of beveled mirror, and exquisite small oil paintings. Or opt for a linen-covered table with a basket of fresh bread. La Opera is the Mexican equivalent of a London gentlemen's club, although it has

Moments ¡Café, Por Favor!

If you think espresso bars are a new phenomenon, or coffee drinks a development of recent years, you may be intrigued to learn that in Mexico, drinking good coffee has been considered an art form for generations. Some of the best coffee can be found in small cafes that have a crowd of regulars who congregate to catch up on the local *chisme* (gossip).

Café La Habana, downtown at Bucareli and Morelos, is one of the most famous, a longstanding cafe with a rich history—and a reputation for strong coffee, all roasted and ground in-house. Ask the waiter and he'll tell you how Fidel Castro and Ché Guevara planned the Cuban revolution while sipping an espresso *cortao.* It's open Monday through Saturday from 7:30am to 10pm.

More European-style coffeehouses are in the Zona Rosa, frequented by businesspeople and trendy urban residents. Some of the most popular are **Salón de Té Auseba** and **Duca d'Este,** both on Hamburgo near Florencia. They serve excellent coffee and scrumptious cakes, as well as a variety of herbal teas. The sidewalk cafe **Konditori,** Genova 61, is another good option, on a pedestrian-only street. Open daily 7am to midnight.

The Condesa neighborhood, east of Chapultepec Park, is another top cafe zone. **El Péndulo,** Nuevo León 115, close to Insurgentes, is a favorite. It combines its cafe setting with a book and music store, and so tends to draw intellectuals, writers, and students. It frequently hosts live music and poetry readings. It's open Monday through Friday from 8am to 11pm and weekends from 10am to 11pm.

become so popular for dining that fewer and fewer men play dominoes. In fact, you see people enjoying romantic interludes in cavernous booths—but tables of any kind are hard to find. Service is best if you arrive for lunch when it opens or go after 5pm when the throngs have diminished; the jacketed waiters cater to regulars at the expense of unknown diners. The Spanish and Mexican menu is sophisticated and extensive, and the atmosphere is excellent. Try the incredible Aperital Batido—the bartender's special aperitif—or a classic tequila. Specialties include Spanish tapas, Caesar salad, and Veracruz-style red snapper with olives and tomatoes. While you wait for your meal, look to the ceiling for the bullet hole that legend says Pancho Villa left when he galloped in on a horse. It's half a block toward the *zócalo* from Sanborn's House of Tiles.

Cinco de Mayo 10, Col. Centro. ☎ **55/5512-8959.** Reservations recommended at lunch. Main courses $4–$10; mixed drinks $3.50–$6. AE, MC, V. Mon–Sat 1–11:30pm; Sun 1–5:30pm. Metro: Bellas Artes.

5 Exploring Mexico City

The diverse attractions in Mexico City spring from its complex layers of history. From the simple pleasure of a stroll through a bustling *mercado* to museums filled with treasures of artistic and historic significance, Mexico City has much to explore.

Mexico City was built on the ruins of the ancient city of Tenochtitlán. A downtown portion of the city, comprising almost 700 blocks and 1,500 buildings, has

Mexico City Neighborhoods

Several of Mexico City's outlying neighborhoods are worth a visit. Outside the Historic Center, **San Angel, Coyoacán,** and **Xochimilco** have developed their own unique appeal and attractions. For a more extensive description and directions, see "Mexico City Neighborhoods in Brief," earlier in this chapter, and the neighborhood maps on the following pages.

been designated Centro Histórico (Historical Zone). The area has surged in popularity, and once-neglected buildings are rapidly being converted into chic clubs and trendy restaurants, recalling its former colonial charm.

Remember that this is a city, and a major one at that; dress is more professional and formal here than in other parts of the country. The altitude makes temperatures rather cool, which is often a surprise for travelers with preconceptions of Mexico as perpetually hot. In summer, always be prepared for rain, which falls almost daily. In winter, carry a jacket or sweater—stone museums are chilly inside, and when the sun goes down, the outside air gets quite cold.

THE TOP ATTRACTIONS

Basílica de Nuestra Señora de Guadalupe ★★　Within the northern city limits is the famous Basílica of Guadalupe—not just another church, but the central place of worship for Mexico's patron saint and the home of the image responsible for uniting pre-Hispanic Indian mysticism with Catholic beliefs. It is virtually impossible to understand Mexico and its culture without appreciating the national devotion for Our Lady of Guadalupe. The blue-mantled Virgin of Guadalupe is the most revered image in the country, and you will see her countenance wherever you travel.

The Basílica occupies the site where, on December 9, 1531, a poor Indian named Juan Diego reputedly saw a vision of a beautiful lady in a blue mantle. The local bishop, Zumarraga, was reluctant to confirm that Juan Diego had indeed seen the Virgin Mary, so he asked the peasant for evidence. Juan Diego saw the vision a second time, on December 12, and when he asked her for proof, she instructed him to collect the roses that began blooming in the rocky soil at his feet. He gathered the flowers in his cloak and returned to the bishop. When he unfurled his cloak, the flowers dropped to the ground and the image of the Virgin was miraculously emblazoned on the rough-hewn cloth. The bishop immediately ordered the building of a church on the spot, and upon its completion, the cloth with the Virgin's image was hung in a place of honor, framed in gold. Since that time, millions of the devout and the curious have come to view the miraculous image that experts, it is said, are at a loss to explain. So heavy was the flow of visitors—many approached for hundreds of yards on their knees—that the old church, already fragile, was insufficient to handle them. An audacious New Basílica, designed by Pedro Ramírez Vázquez, the same architect who designed the breathtaking Museo Nacional de Antropología, opened in 1987.

The miracle cloak hangs behind bulletproof glass above the altar. Moving walkways going in two directions transport the crowds a distance below the cloak. If you want to see it again, take the people-mover going in the opposite direction; you can do it as many times as you want.

A plaza with a visitor information center, museum, and auditorium were part of a $50-million face-lift and opened a couple of years ago.

Historic Downtown (Centro Histórico)

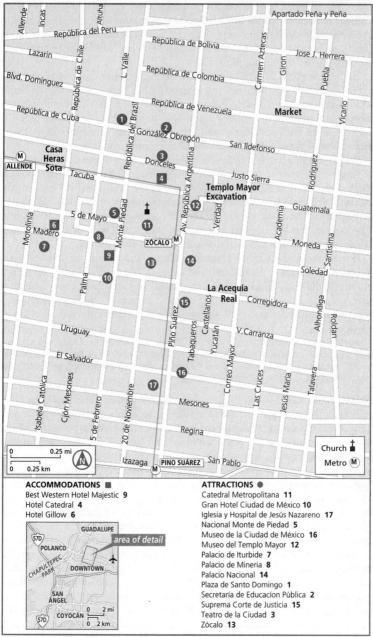

ACCOMMODATIONS ■
Best Western Hotel Majestic **9**
Hotel Catedral **4**
Hotel Gillow **6**

ATTRACTIONS ●
Catedral Metropolitana **11**
Gran Hotel Ciudad de México **10**
Iglesia y Hospital de Jesús Nazareno **17**
Nacional Monte de Piedad **5**
Museo de la Ciudad de México **16**
Museo del Templo Mayor **12**
Palacio de Iturbide **7**
Palacio de Mineria **8**
Palacio Nacional **14**
Plaza de Santo Domingo **1**
Secretaría de Educacíon Pública **2**
Suprema Corte de Justicia **15**
Teatro de la Ciudad **3**
Zócalo **13**

In 2002, the pope declared Juan Diego a saint, a very big deal in this predominantly Catholic country; he was the first Mexican to achieve sainthood. The achievement was not, however, without controversy—Juan Diego's images have increasingly taken on a "European" appearance, and native Mexicans insist that Juan Diego be portrayed as the dark-skinned indigenous peasant he was.

To the right of the modern basilica is the Old Basílica, actually the second one built to house the cloak—the first one is higher up on the hill. Restoration of the Old Basílica, which had been tilting precariously, has been ongoing for at least 10 years. Lately it has moved more rapidly—the building is now open to the public. To the back of it is the entrance to the Basílica Museum, with a very good display of religious art in restored rooms. One of the side chapels, with a silver altar, is adjacent to the museum.

Outside the museum is a garden commemorating the moment Juan Diego showed the cloak to the archbishop. Numerous photographers with colorful backdrops gather there to capture your visit on film. At the top of the hill, behind the basilica, is the **Panteón del Tepeyac,** a cemetery for Mexico's more infamous folk (Santa Anna among them), and several gift shops specializing in religious objects and other folk art. The steps up this hill are lined with flowers, shrubs, and waterfalls, and the climb, though potentially tiring, is worthwhile for the view from the top.

If you visit Mexico City on **December 12,** you can witness the grand festival in honor of the **Virgin of Guadalupe.** The square in front of the basilica fills with the pious and the party-minded as prayers, dances, and a carnival atmosphere attract thousands of the devout. Many visitors combine a trip to the basilica with one to the **ruins of Teotihuacán,** since both are out of the city center in the same direction.

Villa de Guadalupe. (✆ 55/5577-6022. Free admission; museum 55¢. Tues–Sun 10am–7pm. Free guided tours (in Spanish) Fri–Sat noon. Metro: Basílica or La Villa. From Basílica, take exit marked SALIDA AV. MONTIEL; walk a block or so north of the station to a major intersection (Montevideo; you'll know it by the VIPS and Denny's across the street to the left); turn right onto Av. Montevideo and cross the overpass; after about a 15-min. walk, you'll see the church ahead. From La Villa, walk north on Calzada de Guadalupe.

Museo Frida Kahlo ⭑⭑⭑   Although during her lifetime Frida Kahlo was known principally as the wife of muralist Diego Rivera, today her art surpasses his in popularity. Certainly the 2002 Salma Hayek movie *Frida* did much to bring this Mexican icon to the attention and appreciation of millions more. Kahlo dedicated her life to both her painting and her passionate, tortured love for her husband. Her emotional and physical pain—her spine was pierced during a serious streetcar accident in her youth—were the primary subjects of her canvases, many of which are self-portraits. Her paintings are now acknowledged as not only exceptional works of Latin American art, but as some of the purest artistic representations of female strength and struggle ever created. As her paintings have surged in renown and price, so has interest in the life of this courageous, provocative, and revolutionary woman.

Kahlo was born in this house on July 7, 1910, and lived here with Rivera from 1929 to 1954. During the 1930s and 1940s it was a popular gathering place for intellectuals. As you wander through the rooms of the cornflower-blue house, you'll get a glimpse of the life they led. Most of the rooms remain in their original state, with mementos everywhere. Tiny clay pots hang about; the names Diego and Frida are painted on the walls of the kitchen. In the studio upstairs, a wheelchair sits next to the easel with a partially completed painting surrounded by brushes, palettes, books, photographs, and other intimate details of the couple's art-centered lives. Contributing to its authenticity, much of the movie *Frida* was filmed in this house.

Chapultepec Park

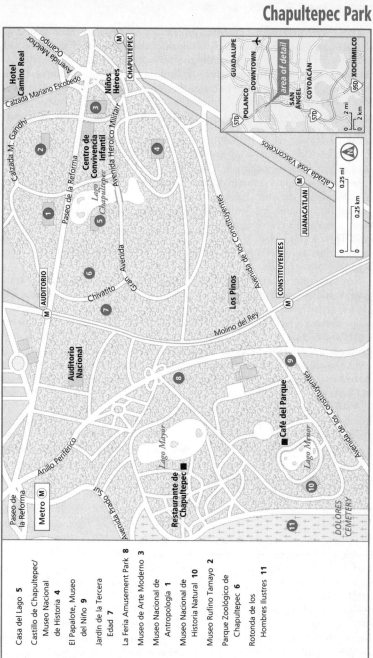

Casa del Lago **5**

Castillo de Chapultepec/
Museo Nacional
de Historia **4**

El Papalote, Museo
del Niño **9**

Jardín de la Tercera
Edad **7**

La Feria Amusement Park **8**

Museo de Arte Moderno **3**

Museo Nacional de
Antropología **1**

Museo Nacional de
Historia Natural **10**

Museo Rufino Tamayo **2**

Parque Zoológico de
Chapultepec **6**

Rotonda de los
Hombres Ilustres **11**

Frida and Diego collected pre-Columbian art, and many of the rooms contain jewelry and terra cotta figurines from Teotihuacán and Tlatelolco. Kahlo even had a mock-up of a temple built in the garden to exhibit her numerous pots and statues. On the back side of the temple are several skulls from Chichén Itzá. A cafe on the first floor serves light snacks, and the adjacent bookstore offers a full range of Kahlo and Rivera books and other commercialized memorabilia.

Londres 247, Coyoacán. *©* 55/5554-5999. Admission $2. No cameras allowed. Tues–Sun 10am–6pm. Metro: Coyoacán.

Museo Nacional de Antropología ★★★
Occupying 4,088 sq. m (44,000 sq. ft.), Mexico City's anthropology museum is regarded as one of the top museums in the world. It offers the single best introduction to the culture of Mexico.

Inside the museum is an open courtyard (containing the Chávez Morado fountain) with beautifully designed rooms running around three sides on two levels. The **ground-floor rooms** are devoted to history—from prehistoric days to the most recently explored archaeological sites—and are the most popular among studious visitors. These rooms include dioramas of Mexico City when the Spaniards arrived, and reproductions of part of a pyramid at Teotihuacán. The Aztec calendar stone "wheel" occupies a proud place.

Save some time and energy for the livelier and more readily comprehensible **ethnographic rooms** upstairs. This section is devoted to the way people throughout Mexico live today, complete with straw-covered huts, recordings of songs and dances, crafts, clothing, and lifelike models of village activities. This floor, a living museum, strikes me as vital to the understanding of contemporary Mexico because of the importance of pre-Hispanic customs in Mexican village life.

The museum has a lovely, moderately priced restaurant with cheerful patio tables. *Note:* Most of the museum is wheelchair accessible; however, assistance will be needed in places.

A sweeping restoration took place during 2000 and 2001. The $13-million refurbishment project was the first since the museum opened in 1964. Over 2,000 new artifacts and information garnered from some 200 recent digs have been incorporated throughout the 23 rooms. In addition, new computerized touch-screen technology with video images and sound depicting rituals and customs are on display, providing visitors with a richer, more interactive experience. Exhibit signs now display English as well as Spanish explanations.

Chapultepec Park. *©* 55/5553-6266. www.mna.inah.gob.mx. Admission $2.50; free Sun. Still camera $3, amateur video camera $4.50. No tripods or flash permitted. Tues–Sun 9am–7pm. Metro: Auditorio.

Palacio Nacional and the Diego Rivera Murals ★★
This complex of countless rooms, wide stone stairways, and numerous courtyards adorned with carved brass balconies is where the president of Mexico works. Even so, it's better known for the fabulous second-floor Diego Rivera murals depicting the history of Mexico. Begun in 1692 on the site of Moctezuma's "new" palace, this building became the site of Hernán Cortez's home and the residence of colonial viceroys. It has changed much in 300 years, taking on its present form in the late 1920s when the top floor was added. Just 30 minutes here with an English-speaking guide provides essential background for an understanding of Mexican history. The cost of a guide is negotiable: $8 or less, depending on your bargaining ability.

Enter by the central door, over which hangs the bell rung by Padre Miguel Hidalgo when he proclaimed Mexico's independence from Spain in 1810—the famous *grito*.

Coyoacán

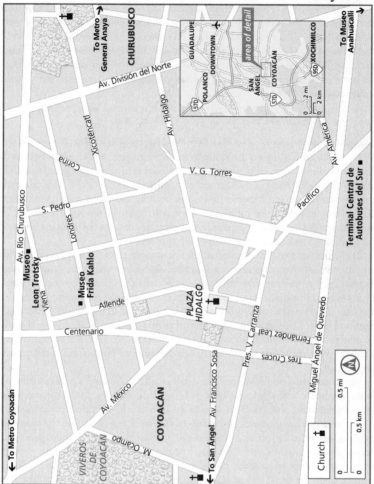

Each September 15, Mexican Independence Day, the president of Mexico stands on the balcony above the door to echo Hidalgo's cry to the thousands of spectators who fill the *zócalo*. Take the stairs to the Rivera murals, which were painted over a 25-year period. The *Legend of Quetzalcoatl* depicts the famous tale of the feathered serpent bringing a blond-bearded white man to the country. When Cortez arrived, many Aztecs, recalling this legend, believed him to be Quetzalcoatl. Another mural tells of the American Intervention, when American invaders marched into Mexico City during the War of 1847. It was on this occasion that the military cadets of Chapultepec Castle (then a military school) fought bravely to the last man. The most notable of Rivera's murals is the *Great City of Tenochtitlán,* a study of the original settlement in the Valley of Mexico. The city is but a small part of the mural; the remainder is filled with what appear to be four million extras left over from a Hollywood epic, including the lovely Xochiquetzal, goddess of love, with her crown of flowers and tattooed legs.

Diego Rivera, one of Mexico's legendary muralists, left an indelible stamp on Mexico City, his painted political themes affecting the way millions view Mexican history. Additional examples of Rivera's stunning and provocative interpretations are found at the Bellas Artes, the National Preparatory School, the Department of Public Education, the National School of Agriculture at Chapingo, the National Institute of Cardiology, and the Museo Mural Diego Rivera (which houses the mural formerly located in the now-razed Hotel del Prado).

Palacio Nacional, Av. Pino Suárez, facing the *zócalo*. Free admission, but visitor tags required; be prepared to leave a form of photo identification in exchange. Mon–Sat 9am–5:30pm. Metro: Zócalo.

Templo Mayor and Museo del Templo Mayor (Great Temple) ✪✪✪   In 1978, workmen digging on the east side of the Metropolitan Cathedral, next to the Palacio Nacional, unearthed an exquisite Aztec stone of the moon goddess Coyolxauhqui. Major excavations by Mexican archaeologists followed, and they uncovered interior remains of the Pyramid of Huitzilopochtli, also called the Templo Mayor (Great Temple)—the most important religious structure in the Aztec capital. What you see are the remains of pyramids that were covered by the great pyramid the Spaniards saw upon their arrival in the 16th century.

At the time of the 1521 Conquest, the site was the center of religious life for the city of 300,000. No other museum illustrates the variety and splendor of the Aztec Empire the way this one does. All 6,000 pieces came from the relatively small plot of excavated ruins just in front of the museum. Strolling along the walkways built over the site, visitors pass a water-collection conduit constructed during the presidency of Porfirio Díaz (1877–1911), as well as far earlier constructions. Shelters cover the ruins to protect traces of original paint and carving. Note especially the Tzompantli, or Altar of Skulls, a common Aztec and Maya design. Explanatory plaques with building dates are in Spanish.

The Museo del Templo Mayor (Museum of the Great Temple) opened in 1987. To enter it, take the walkway to the large building in the back portion of the site, which contains fabulous artifacts from on-site excavations. Inside the door, a model of Tenochtitlán gives a good idea of the scale of the vast city of the Aztec. The rooms and exhibits, organized by subject, occupy many levels around a central open space. You'll see some marvelous displays of masks, figurines, tools, jewelry, and other artifacts, including the huge stone wheel of the moon goddess Coyolxauhqui ("she with bells painted upon her face") on the second floor. The goddess ruled the night, the Aztec believed, but died at the dawning of every day, slain and dismembered by her brother, Huitzilopochtli, the sun god.

Look also for the striking jade-and-obsidian mask and the full-size terra-cotta figures of the *guerreros águilas*, or eagle warriors. A cutaway model of the Templo Mayor shows the layers and methods of construction.

Off the *zócalo*. ✆ **55/5542-0606.** Fax 55/5542-1717. www.conaculta.gob.mx/templomayor. Admission (valid for museum and ruins) $4; free Sun. Video camera permit $3.50; no flash photos. Tues–Sun 9am–5:50pm (last ticket sold at 5pm). Metro: Zócalo.

ARCHITECTURAL HIGHLIGHTS

Casa de los Azulejos   This "House of Tiles" is one of Mexico City's most precious colonial gems and popular meeting places. Covered in gorgeous blue-and-white tiles, it dates from the end of the 1500s, when it was built for the count of the Valley of

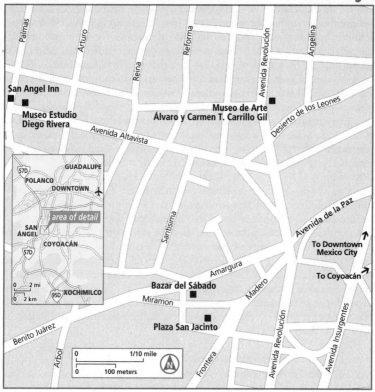

Orizaba. According to the oft-told story, during the count's defiant youth his father proclaimed: "You will never build a house of tiles." A tiled house was a sign of success, and the father was sure his son would amount to nothing. So when success came, the young count covered his house in tiles, a fine example of Puebla craftsmanship. The tiled murals in the covered courtyard, where the restaurant is located, were restored a few years back. Tile craftsmen from Saudi Arabia were brought in to ensure that the technique was true to the original 16th-century work. You can stroll through to admire the interior. Pause to see the Orozco mural, *Omniscience,* on the landing leading to the second floor (where the restrooms are).

Madero 4, Centro Histórico. ✆ **55/5518-6676.** Daily 7am–1am. Metro: Bellas Artes.

Gran Hotel Ciudad de México   Originally a department store, the Gran Hotel boasts one of the most splendid interiors of any downtown building. Step inside to see the lavish lobby with gilded open elevators on both sides, topped with a breathtaking 1908 stained-glass canopy by Jacques Graber.

On the fourth floor, overlooking the *zócalo,* El Mirador restaurant makes a great stop for a coffee or drink with a view.

Palma and Piedad, facing the *zócalo,* Centro Histórico. ✆ **55/1083-7700.** Free admission to view the lobby. Daily 24 hr. Metro: Zócalo.

Palacio de Bellas Artes 🎭🎭   Opulent and dramatic, the Bellas Artes is the masterpiece of theaters in this architecturally rich city. The exterior is early-20th-century Art Nouveau, built during the Porfiriato and covered in Italian Carrara marble. Inside, it's completely 1930s Art Deco. Since construction began in 1904, the theater (which opened in 1934) has sunk some 4m (12 ft.) into the soft belly of Lake Texcoco. The Palacio is the work of several masters: Italian architect Adamo Boari, who made the original plans; Antonio Muñoz and Federico Mariscal, who modified his plans considerably; and Mexican painter Gerardo Murillo ("Doctor Atl"), who designed the fabulous Art Nouveau glass curtain that was constructed by Louis Comfort Tiffany in the Tiffany Studios of New York. Made from nearly a million iridescent pieces of colored glass, the curtain portrays the Valley of Mexico with its two great volcanoes. You can see the curtain before important performances at the theater and on Sunday mornings.

In addition to being the concert hall, the theater houses permanent and traveling art shows. On the third level are famous murals by Rivera, Orozco, and Siqueiros. The controversial Rivera mural *Man in Control of His Universe* was commissioned in 1933 for Rockefeller Center in New York City. He completed the work there just as you see it: A giant vacuum sucks up the riches of the earth to feed the factories of callous, card-playing, hard-drinking white capitalist thugs—John D. Rockefeller himself among them—while all races of noble workers of the earth rally behind the red flag of socialism and its standard-bearer, Lenin. Needless to say, the Rockefellers weren't so keen on the new purchase. Much to their discredit, they had it painted over and destroyed. Rivera duplicated the mural here as *Man at the Crossing of the Ways* to preserve it. For information on tickets to performances of the **Ballet Folklórico,** see "Mexico City After Dark," later in this chapter.

Warning: The U.S. State Department advisory specifies that taxis parked in front of the Bellas Artes Theater should be avoided.

Calle López Peralta, east end of La Alameda, Centro Histórico. ℭ **55/5512-2593,** ext. 152. www.cnca.gob.mx/ museos.htm. Free admission to view building when performances are not in progress; museum $3. Tues–Sun 10am–6pm. Metro: Bellas Artes.

Palacio de Minería   Built in the 1800s, this "mining palace" is one of architect Manuel Tolsá's finest works and one of the capital's handsomest buildings. Formerly the school of mining, it's occasionally used today for concerts and cultural events. If it's open, step inside for a look at the patios and fabulous stonework.

Tacuba 5, Centro Histórico. ℭ **55/5521-4020.** Free admission. Mon–Fri 9am–8pm. Metro: Bellas Artes.

CEMETERIES

Rotonda de los Hombres Ilustres   The din of traffic recedes in the serene resting place where Mexico's military, political, and artistic elite are buried. It's more like an outdoor monument museum than a cemetery; the stone markers stand in a double circle around an eternal flame. A stroll here is a trip through who's who in Mexican history. Among the famous buried here are the artists Diego Rivera, David Alfaro Siqueiros, José Clemente Orozco, and Gerardo Murillo; presidents Sebastian Lerdo de Tejada, Valentín Gómez Farías, and Plutarco Calles; musicians Jaime Nuño (author of the Mexican national anthem), Juventino Rosas, and Agustín Lara; and outstanding citizens such as the philanthropist and writer Carlos Pellicer. Stop in the building at the entrance and the guard will give you a map with a list (in Spanish and English) of those buried here, which includes biographical information.

Constituyentes and Av. Civil Dolores, Dolores Cemetery, Chapultepec Park. Free admission. Daily 6am–6pm. Metro: Constituyentes.

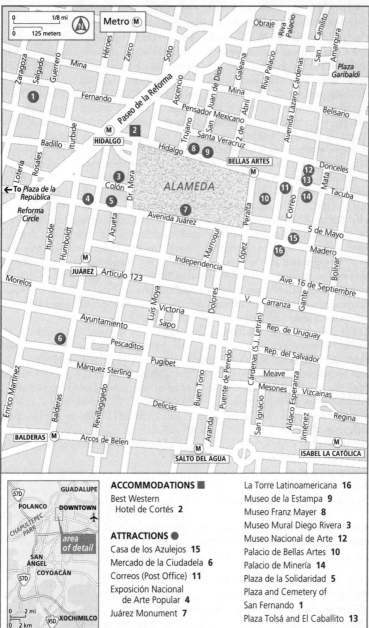

Metro Ⓜ

ACCOMMODATIONS ■

Best Western
  Hotel de Cortés **2**

ATTRACTIONS ●

Casa de los Azulejos **15**
Mercado de la Ciudadela **6**
Correos (Post Office) **11**
Exposición Nacional
  de Arte Popular **4**
Juárez Monument **7**

La Torre Latinoamericana **16**
Museo de la Estampa **9**
Museo Franz Mayer **8**
Museo Mural Diego Rivera **3**
Museo Nacional de Arte **12**
Palacio de Bellas Artes **10**
Palacio de Minería **14**
Plaza de la Solidaridad **5**
Plaza and Cemetery of
San Fernando **1**
Plaza Tolsá and El Caballito **13**

CHURCHES

Catedral Metropolitana ⭐⭐⭐ The impressive, towering cathedral, begun in 1567 and finished in 1788, blends baroque, neoclassic, and Mexican churrigueresque architecture. As you look around the cathedral and the Sagrario (chapel) next to it, note how the building has sunk into the soft lake bottom beneath. The base of the facade is far from level and straight, and when one considers the weight of the immense towers—127,000 tons—it's no surprise. Scaffolding has become almost a part of the structure, in place to stabilize the building. However, much to the credit of Mexico City and its preservation efforts, the Catedral Metropolitana came off the World Monuments Fund's list of 100 Most Endangered Sites in 2000, as a result of an extensive reconstruction of the building's foundation.

In Mexico, the sacred ground of one religion often becomes the sacred ground of its successor. Cortez and his Spanish missionaries converted the Aztec, tore down their temples, and used much of the stone to construct a church on the spot of the temples that preceded it. The church they built was pulled down in 1628 while the present Metropolitan Cathedral was under construction. The building today has 5 naves and 14 chapels. As you wander past the small chapels, you may hear guides describing some of the cathedral's outstanding features: the tomb of Agustín Iturbide, placed here in 1838; a painting attributed to the Spanish artist Bartolomé Esteban Murillo; and the fact that the stone holy-water fonts ring like metal when tapped with a coin. Like many huge churches, it has catacombs underneath. The much older-looking church next to the cathedral is the chapel known as the Sagrario, another tour de force of Mexican baroque architecture built in the mid-1700s.

The Metropolitan Cathedral contains many prized works of art from the colonial era, in a variety of artistic styles. Jerónimo de Balbas built and carved the Altar de los Reyes (Altar of Kings) and the Altar del Perdón (Altar of Pardon) in 1737.

A sound-and-light show, "Voices of the Cathedral," takes visitors on a candlelit stroll through the cathedral, accompanied by period music. Tickets are $25, and are available through Ticketmaster (© **55/5325-9000**). The schedule of English-language performances changes periodically; call © **55/5512-7096** for details. Even if the presentation is in Spanish, it is mostly about choral music, so the language is not crucial for most visitors. Each Wednesday, the *Reforma* newspaper publishes the dates for the next 3 months of presentations.

As you walk around the outside of the cathedral, you will notice a reminder of medieval trade life. The west side is the gathering place of carpenters, plasterers, plumbers, painters, and electricians who have no shops. Craftspeople display the tools of their trades, sometimes along with pictures of their work. In front of the cathedral, you can buy crystals, gemstones, and herbs, believed to provide special qualities of protection and cure from various afflictions.

The *zócalo*, on Cinco de Mayo, Centro Histórico. Free admission. Daily 7am–7pm. Metro: Zócalo.

Convent of San Bernardino de Siena This 16th-century building is noted for its flower petals carved in stone—a signature of the Indians who did most of the work—on 16th-century *retablos* (painted boards) including one of three such altarpieces in the country that has miraculously been preserved for more than 400 years. The last Indian governor of Xochimilco, Apoxquiyohuatzin, is buried here. Inside and to the right, the skull over the font is from a pre-Hispanic skull rack signifying an Indian-Christian mixture of the concept of life and death. Eight lateral *retablos* date from the 16th to the 18th centuries. The fabulous gilt main altar, also from the 16th century, is like an open book with sculpture and religious paintings. A profusion of cherubic angels decorates columns and borders. Some of the altar paintings are attributed to Baltasar Echave Orio the Elder. Over the altar, above the figure of Christ, is San Bernardino with the *caciques* (local authorities) dressed in clothing with Indian elements, and without shoes.

Pino and Hidalgo (facing the main square), Xochimilco. Free admission. Daily 8am–8pm. *Tren ligero* (light train): Xochimilco.

HISTORIC BUILDINGS & MONUMENTS
CHAPULTEPEC PARK & POLANCO
Castillo de Chapultepec/Museo Nacional de Historia   This site had been occupied by a fortress since the days of the Aztec, although the present palace wasn't built until 1784. When open, the castle offered a beautiful view of Mexico City. During the French occupation of the 1860s, Empress Carlota (who designed the lovely garden surrounding the palace) could sit up in bed and watch her husband, Maximilian, proceeding down Reforma on his way to work. Later, this was the official home of Mexico's president until 1939. In 2004, archaeologists discovered an ancient Teotihuacán settlement behind the landmark, and are currently working on excavations, which are expected to demonstrate that the Teotihuacán culture spread and influenced the area around Mexico City earlier than previously thought, to between A.D. 300 and 600. Although the site is currently closed to tourists, it's worth knowing what is to come here.

Chapultepec Park and Polanco. *©* **55/5241-3117** or 55/5241-3115. Metro: Chapultepec.

ZONA ROSA & SURROUNDING AREAS
Monumento a los Héroes de la Independencia ✮   Without a doubt, the Monument to the Heroes of Independence is the most noted of Mexico City's exceptional public sculptures and monuments. The "Angel" is both a landmark and homage to those who lost their lives fighting for independence. Set upon a tall marble shaft, the golden angel is an important and easily discerned guidepost for travelers. A creation of Antonio Rivas Mercado, the 7m-high (22-ft.) gold-plated bronze angel, cast in Florence, Italy, was completed in 1906 at a cost of $2.5 million. With its base of marble and Italian granite, the monument's total height is 45m (135 ft.).

Intersection of Paseo de la Reforma, Florencia, and Río Tiber, Reforma/Zona Rosa. Metro: Insurgentes.

CENTRO HISTORICO & SURROUNDING AREAS
Monumento a la Revolución and Museo Nacional de la Revolución   The Art Deco Monument to the Revolution, in the large **Plaza de la República,** has a curious history. The government of Porfirio Díaz, who was perennially "reelected" president of Mexico, began construction of what was intended to be a new legislative chamber. However, only the dome was raised by the time the Mexican Revolution (1910) put an end to his plans, not to mention his dictatorship. In the 1930s, after the revolutionary turmoil had died down, the dome was finished as a monument. The remains of two revolutionary presidents, Francisco Madero and Venustiano Carranza, were entombed in two of its pillars, and it was dedicated to the Revolution. Later, presidents Plutarco Elías Calles and Lázaro Cárdenas were also buried there.

Beneath the Monument to the Revolution is the **Museo Nacional de la Revolución** (enter directly across from the Frontón). It chronicles the tumultuous years from 1867 to 1917—when the present constitution was signed—in excellent exhibits of documents, newspaper stories, photographs, drawings, clothing, costumes, uniforms, weapons, and furnishings.

Av. Juárez and La Fragua. Plaza de la República s/n, Col. Tabacalera en el sótano del Monumento a la Revolución. © 55/5546-2115 or 55/5566-1902. www.arts-history.mx/museos/revolucion/historia.html. Admission 60¢. Tues–Sun 9am–5pm. From the Colón Monument on Reforma, walk 2 blocks north on I. Ramírez; the monument looms ahead. Metro: Revolución.

Secretaría de Educación Pública Originally built in 1922 as a convent, it became the home of the Secretary of Public Education in 1922, and was decorated with a great series of more than 200 Diego Rivera murals dating from 1923 and 1928, that cover over 1,500 sq. m (16,146 sq. ft.) of wall space. Other artists did a panel here and there, but the Rivera murals are the most outstanding.

República de Argentina 28, near República de Brasil. © 55/5512-1707 or 55/5328-1019. www.sep.gob.mx. Free admission. Daily 9am–3pm. Metro: Allende.

Suprema Corte de Justicia The Supreme Court of Justice, built between 1935 and 1941, is the highest court in the country. Inside, on the main staircase and its landings, are Orozco murals depicting a theme of justice.

Pino Suárez and Corregidora, Centro Histórico. No phone. Free admission. Mon–Fri 9am–5:30pm. Metro: Zócalo.

OTHER MUSEUMS & GALLERIES
CHAPULTEPEC PARK & POLANCO
El Papalote, Museo del Niño *(Kids* The Building of the Pyramids at this interactive children's museum holds most of the more than 350 exhibits, while two films alternate (10 shows daily) in the IMAX building. There's virtually nothing here that children can't touch; once they discover this, they'll want to stay a long time. As they say, adults must be accompanied by children, except on Thursday, when the museum opens until 11pm to give "big kids" a chance to enjoy it themselves.

Av. de los Constituyentes 268, Chapultepec Park, Section 2. © 55/5237-1700, 55/5237-1781, or 55/5237-1781. http://papalote.citaris.com. Admission to museum $5 adults, $4 children; admission to museum and IMAX show $6 adults, $5 children. Mon–Fri 9am–1pm and 2–6pm; Sat–Sun and holidays 10am–2pm and 3–7pm; Thurs 7–11pm. Metro: Constituyentes.

Museo de Arte Moderno *(★* The Museum of Modern Art is known for having the best permanent exhibition of painters and sculptors from the modern Mexican art movement. It also features some of the most important temporary exhibitions of national and international modern art in the world. Representing the Mexican muralist movement are significant works by the three greats: Diego Rivera, José Clemente Orozco, and David Alfaro Siqueiros. The main building is a round, two-story structure with a central staircase. Two of the museum's four spaces showcase the permanent collection, which also contains works by Mexico's other modern masters—Tamayo, José Luis Cuevas, Alejandro Colunga, Francisco Toledo, and Vladamir Cora. The remaining two spaces house visiting exhibitions. The museum's surrounding gardens exhibit large-scale public sculptures.

Chapultepec Park. © 55/5553-6233. www.arts-history.mx/museos/mam/home.html. Admission $2; discounts for students and teachers w/ID; free Sun. Tues–Sun 10am–5:30pm. Metro: Chapultepec.

Museo Nacional de Historia Natural *(Kids* The 10 interconnecting domes that form the Museum of Natural History contain stuffed and preserved animals and birds; tableaux of different natural environments with the appropriate wildlife; exhibits on geology, astronomy, biology, and the origin of life; and more. It's a fascinating place for anyone with the slightest curiosity about nature and is totally absorbing for youngsters.

Chapultepec Park, Section 2, s/n. © **55/5516-2848**. www.sma.df.gob.mx/mhn/mhn1.html. Admission $1.50; free Tues. Tues–Sun 10am–5pm. Metro: Constituyentes.

Museo Rufino Tamayo ★ Oaxaca-born painter Rufino Tamayo not only contributed a great deal to modern Mexican painting, but also collected pre-Hispanic, Mexican, and foreign works, including pieces by de Kooning, Warhol, Dalí, and Magritte. Tamayo's pre-Hispanic collection is in Oaxaca, but here you can see a number of his works and the remainder of his collection (unless a special exhibit has temporarily displaced them).

Chapultepec Park. © **55/5286-6529**. Fax 55/528-6519. info@museotamayo.org. Admission $1.50; free Sun. Tues–Sun 10am–6pm. Free guided 1-hr. tours available Sat–Sun 10am–2pm. Metro: Chapultepec.

CENTRO HISTORICO & SURROUNDING AREAS

Museo de la Ciudad de México Before you enter the Museum of Mexico City, go to the corner of República del Salvador and look at the enormous stone serpent head, a corner support at the building's base. The stone was once part of an Aztec pyramid. At the entrance, a stone doorway opens to the courtyard of this mansion, built in 1778 as the House of the Counts of Santiago de Calimaya. This classic building became the Museum of the City of Mexico in 1964; it's a must for anyone interested in the country's past. Dealing solely with the Mexico Valley, where the first people arrived around 8000 B.C., the museum contains some fine maps, pictographic presentations of the initial settlements, and outlines of the social organization as it developed, as well as models of several famous buildings. Upstairs is the studio of Mexican Impressionist Joaquín Clausell (1866–1935). There's a good bookstore, to the left after you enter.

Pino Suárez 30, Centro Histórico. © **55/5542-0487**. Admission $1.40. Tues–Sun 10am–6pm. Metro: Zócalo.

Museo Franz Mayer One of the capital's foremost museums, the Franz Mayer Museum opened in 1986 in a beautifully restored 16th-century building on Plaza de la Santa Veracruz on the north side of La Alameda. The extraordinary 10,000-piece collection of antiques, mostly Mexican objects from the 16th through 19th centuries, was amassed by one man: Franz Mayer. A German immigrant, he adopted Mexico as his home in 1905 and grew rich here. Before his death in 1975, Mayer bequeathed the collection to the country and arranged for its permanent display through a trust with the Banco Nacional. The pieces, mostly utilitarian objects (as opposed to pure art objects), include inlaid and richly carved furniture; an enormous collection of Talavera pottery; gold and silver religious pieces; sculptures; tapestries; rare watches and clocks (the oldest is a 1680 lantern clock); wrought iron; old-master paintings from Europe and Mexico; and 770 *Don Quixote* volumes, many of which are rare editions or typographically unique. There's so much here that it may take two visits to absorb it. In the central courtyard, a pleasant cafe serves coffee and light snacks.

Av. Hidalgo 45, facing La Alameda. © **55/5518-2265**. www.franzmayer.org.mx. Admission $1.50; free Tues. Tues–Sun 10am–5pm. Guided tours by appointment Mon–Sat 10:30, 11:30am, and 12:30pm. Metro: Hidalgo or Bellas Artes.

Museo José Luis Cuevas José Luis Cuevas is one of Mexico's leading contemporary artists, though early in his career, he was considered the *enfant terrible* of Mexican plastic arts. To this day, he can arouse controversy, and is known to draw throngs of women wherever he appears. The center that bears his name opened in 1992 and is filled with about 1,000 paintings, drawings, and sculptures donated by Cuevas, including many of his own. Don't miss the Erotic Room, a permanent exhibit of his erotic paintings, photographs, and erotic objects from the artist's personal collection. Housed in the 16th century Convento de Santa Inés, the museum includes many works by other contemporary Latin American artists, as well as a large collection of Picassos.

Calle Academia 13, 2 blocks northeast of the Palacio Nacional and across from the Academia de San Carlos. ℂ 55/5542-8959 or 55/5542-6198. Admission $1. Tues–Sun 9:30am–6pm. Metro: Zócalo.

Museo Mural Diego Rivera   This museum houses Diego Rivera's famous mural *Dream of a Sunday Afternoon in Alameda Park,* which was painted on a wall of the Hotel Prado in 1947. The hotel was demolished after the 1985 earthquake, but the precious mural, perhaps the best known of Rivera's works, was saved and transferred to its new location in 1986. The huge picture, 15m (45 ft.) long and 4m (12 ft.) high, chronicles the history of the park from the time of Cortez onward. Portrayed in the mural are numerous historical figures. More or less from left to right, but not in chronological order, they include: Cortez; a heretic suffering under the Spanish Inquisition; Sor Juana Inés de la Cruz, a brilliant, progressive woman who became a nun to continue her scholarly pursuits; Benito Juárez, seen putting forth the laws of Mexico's great *Reforma;* the conservative Gen. Antonio López de Santa Anna, handing the keys to Mexico to the invading American Gen. Winfield Scott; Emperor Maximilian and Empress Carlota; José Martí, the Cuban revolutionary; Death, with the plumed serpent (Quetzalcoatl) entwined about his neck; Gen. Porfirio Díaz, great with age and medals, asleep; a police officer keeping La Alameda free of "riffraff" by ordering a poor family out of the elitists' park; and Francisco Madero, the martyred democratic president who caused the downfall of Díaz, and whose betrayal and alleged murder by Gen. Victoriano Huerta (pictured on the right) resulted in years of civil turmoil.

Plaza de la Solidaridad (at Balderas and Colón), Centro Histórico–Alameda. ℂ **55/5510-2329** or 55/5512-0754. www.arts-history.mx/museos/mu. Admission $1.50; free Sun. Tues–Sun 10am–6pm. Metro: Hidalgo.

Museo Nacional de Arte   The National Art Museum's palacelike building, designed by Italian architect Silvio Contri and completed in 1911—a legacy of Europe-loving Porfirio Díaz's era—was built to house the government's offices of Communications and Public Works. Díaz occupied the opulent second-floor salon, where he welcomed visiting dignitaries. The National Museum of Art took over the building in 1982. Wander through the immense rooms with polished wooden floors as you view the wealth of paintings showing Mexico's art development, primarily covering the period from 1810 to 1950. There's a nice cafe on the second floor.

Tacuba 8, Centro Histórico. ℂ **55/5130-3400** or 55/5130-3410. Fax 55/5130-3401. Admission varies depending upon exhibition and is occasionally free; free Sun. Tues–Sun 10:30am–5:30pm. Metro: Allende.

Museo Nacional de la Estampa   *Estampa* means "engraving" or "printing," and this museum is devoted to understanding and preserving the graphic arts. The beautifully restored 16th-century building holds both permanent and changing exhibits. Displays include those from pre-Hispanic times, when clay seals were used for designs on fabrics, ceramics, and other surfaces. But the most famous works here are probably those of José Guadalupe Posada, Mexico's famous printmaker, who poked fun at death and politicians through his skeleton figure drawings. If your interest in this subject is deep, ask to see the video programs on graphic techniques—woodcuts, lithography, etchings, and the like.

Av. Hidalgo 39 (next door to the Museo Franz Mayer), Centro Histórico–Alameda. (C) **55/5521-2244**. Admission $1.50; free Sun. Tues–Sun 10am–5:30pm. Metro: Bellas Artes.

Museo Nacional de San Carlos The San Carlos Museum exhibits 15th- to 19th-century European paintings. The museum was once the Academy of San Carlos, an art school that some of the country's great painters—Rivera and Orozco among them—attended. Architect Manuel Tolsá built the beautiful mansion in the early 1800s; it was later the home of the Marqués de Buenavista. The rooms on the first and second floors hold some of Mexico's best paintings, by both Mexican and European artists. Another gallery holds prints and engravings. In the mansion's elliptical court are displays of 19th-century Mexican statuary and busts by Manuel Vilar and his pupils, and off to one side is a pretty garden court shaded by rubber trees.

Puente de Alvarado 50 (at Arizpe). (C) **55/5566-8085**, ext.124 or 131, or 55/5566-8342. Fax 55/5535-1256. www.mnsancarlos.inba.gob.mx. Admission $2.50; free Sun. Wed–Mon 10am–6pm. English tours available by reservation for nominal charge. Walk 5½ blocks west of La Alameda (2½ blocks west of San Fernando Plaza). Metro: Revolución.

SOUTHERN NEIGHBORHOODS

Archaeological Museum of Xochimilco The building dates from 1904, when it was the pump house for the springs. It houses artifacts from the area, many of them found when residents built their homes. These include 10,000-year-old mammoth bones; figures dating from the Teotihuacán period, including representations of Tlaloc (god of water and life), Ehecatl (god of the wind), Xipe Totec (god of renewal and of plants), and Huehueteotl (god of fire); polychrome pottery; carved abalone; and tombs showing funerary practices. One unique piece is a clay figure of a child holding a bouquet of flowers.

Av. Tenochtitlán and Calle La Planta, Santa Cruz Acalpixcan. (C)/fax **55/2157-1757**. Admission $1. Tues–Sun 10am–5pm. From Xochimilco (see "Mexico City Neighborhoods in Brief," earlier in this chapter), take a cab or microbus to Tulyehualco. The museum is at Tenochtitlán and La Planta, on the left.

Diego Rivera Anahuacalli Museum Not to be confused with the Museo Estudio Diego Rivera near the San Angel Inn (see below), this is probably the most unusual museum in the city. Designed by Rivera before his death in 1957, it's devoted to his works as well as his extensive collection of pre-Columbian art. With over 52,000 pieces, it is the largest private collection displayed in Mexico. Constructed of pedregal (the lava rock in which the area abounds), it resembles Maya and Aztec architecture. Anahuacalli means "House of Mexico;" *Anahuac* was the old name for the ancient Valley of Mexico.

In front of the museum is a reproduction of a Toltec ball court, and the entrance to the museum is a coffin-shaped door. Twenty-three display rooms are arranged in chronological order, with thousands of pieces stashed on the shelves, tucked away in corners, and peeking out of glass cases.

Upstairs, in a replica of Rivera's studio, you'll find the original sketches for some of his murals and two in-progress canvases. There's a photo of his first sketch (of a train), done at the age of 3, plus a color photograph of him at work later in life. Rivera (1886–1957) studied in Europe for 15 years and spent much of his life as a devoted Marxist. Yet he came through political scrapes and personal tragedies with no apparent diminution of creative energy. A plaque in the museum proclaims him "a man of genius who is among the greatest painters of all time."

Calle Museo 150, Col. San Pablo Tepetlapa. ℂ 55/5617-3797. anahuacalli@museo.com. Admission $3.50. Tues–Sun 10am–6pm. Metro: Taxqueña; then *tren ligero* (light train) to Xotepingo; go west on Xotepingo (Museo) 3 short blocks; cross División del Norte and go another 6 blocks.

Museo de Arte Alvar y Carmen T. Carrillo Gil　Sometimes called the Museo de la Esquina (Corner Museum)—it's at a major intersection on Avenida de la Revolución—this modern gallery features a collection that includes rooms dedicated to the works of José Clemente Orozco (1883–1949), Diego Rivera (1886–1957), David Alfaro Siqueiros (1896–1974), and other Mexican painters. The museum is not accessible by Metro.

Revolución 1608 (at Desierto de los Leones). ℂ 55/5550-1254 or 55/5550-3983. Admission $1.50; free Sun. Tues–Sun 10am–6pm.

Museo Dolores Olmedo Patiño 🏵　Art collector and philanthropist Olmedo left her former home, the grand Hacienda La Noria, as a museum featuring the works of her friend Diego Rivera. At least 137 of his works are displayed here, including his portrait of Olmedo, 25 paintings of Frida Kahlo, and 37 creations of Angelina Beloff (Rivera's 1st wife), many of them drawings and engravings. Among the notable Kahlo works here is her famed *The Broken Column,* which is considered the artistic embodiment of her physical suffering, the result of a trolley accident that pierced her spine when she was young. Besides the paintings, there are fine pre-Hispanic pieces on display, colonial furniture and other hacienda artifacts, and a collection of folk art. An excellent gift shop and a cafeteria are on the premises. Olmeda was the executor of both the Rivera and Kahlo estates, a close friend and former lover of Diego's, and a rival to Frida. Olmeda died in 2002, recognized as one of the most astute collectors of contemporary Mexican art.

Av. México 5843, Col. La Noria, Xochimilco. ℂ 55/5555-1016 or 55/5555-0891. Fax 55/5555-1642. www.arts-history. mx/museos/mdo/home.html. Admission $2. Tues–Sun 10am–6pm. Metro: Taxqueña; then *tren ligero* (light train) to Xochimilco. Get off at the La Noria station.

Museo Estudio Diego Rivera　Here, in the studio designed and built by Juan O'Gorman in 1928, Rivera drew sketches for his wonderful murals and painted smaller works. He died here in 1957. Now a museum, the Rivera studio holds some of the artist's personal effects and mementos, as well as changing exhibits relating to his life and work. (Don't confuse Rivera's studio with his museum, the Anahuacalli; see above.) The museum is not accessible by Metro.

Calle Diego Rivera and Av. Altavista (across from San Angel Inn), Col. San Angel. ℂ 55/5616-0996. Admission $1; free Sun. Tues–Sun 10am–6pm. By taxi, go up Insurgentes Sur to Altavista and make a left.

Museo León Trotsky　During Lenin's last days, Stalin and Trotsky fought a silent battle for leadership of the Communist Party in the Soviet Union. Trotsky stuck to ideology, while Stalin took control of the party mechanism. Stalin won, and Trotsky was exiled to continue his ideological struggle elsewhere. Invited by Diego Rivera, an ardent admirer of his work, he settled here on the outskirts of Mexico City to continue his writings on political topics and Communist ideology.

His ideas clashed with those of Stalin in many respects, and Stalin, wanting no opposition or dissension in the world Communist ranks, set out to have Trotsky assassinated. A first attempt failed, but it served as a warning to Trotsky, his wife, Natalia, and their household. The house became a veritable fortress, with watchtowers, thick steel doors, and round-the-clock guards, several of whom were Americans who sympathized with Trotsky's philosophies. Finally, a man thought to have been paid, cajoled, or blackmailed by Stalin, directly or indirectly, was able to gain admittance to the house by posing as a friend of Trotsky's and of his political views. On August 20, 1940, he put an ice pick into the philosopher's head. The assailant was caught, and Trotsky died of his wounds shortly afterward. Because Trotsky and Rivera had previously had a falling out—Trotsky was having an affair with Rivera's wife, Frida Kahlo—Rivera was a suspect for a short time.

You can visit Natalia's study, the communal dining room, and Trotsky's study—with worksheets, newspaper clippings, books, and cylindrical wax dictating records still spread around—as well as the fortresslike bedroom. Some of the walls bear the bullet holes left from the first attempt on his life. Trotsky's tomb, designed by Juan O'Gorman, is in the garden. You can recognize this house by the brick riflemen's watchtowers on top of the high stone walls.

Av. Río Churubusco 410 (between Gómez Farías and Morelos), Col. Del Carmen Coyoacán. ℂ 55/5658-8732 or 55/5554-0687. Admission $3. Tues–Sun 10am–5pm. Metro: Coyoacán. From Plaza Hidalgo, go east on Hidalgo 3 blocks to Morelos, then north 8 blocks to Churubusco. House is on the left.

OUTDOOR ART/PLAZAS

Plaza de las Tres Culturas   Three cultures converge here: Aztec, Spanish, and contemporary Mexican. Surrounded by modern office and apartment buildings are large remains of the **Aztec city of Tlatelolco,** site of the last battle of the conquest of Mexico. Off to one side is the **Church of Santiago.** During the Aztec Empire, Tlatelolco was on the edge of Lake Texcoco, linked to the Aztec capital by a causeway. Bernal Díaz de Castillo, in his *True Story of the Conquest of New Spain,* described the roar from the dazzling market there, and the incredible scene after the last battle of the conquest in Tlatelolco on August 13, 1521—the dead bodies were piled so deep that walking there was impossible. That night determined the fate of the country and completed the Spanish takeover of Mexico. It was also here, in October 1968, that government troops fired on thousands of protesters who had filled the square, killing hundreds.

View the pyramidal remains from raised walkways over the site. The church, off to one side, was built in the 16th century entirely of volcanic stone. The interior has been tastefully restored, preserving little patches of fresco in stark-white plaster walls, with a few deep-blue stained-glass windows and an unadorned stone altar. Sunday is a good day to combine a visit here with one to the Lagunilla street market (for details, see "Shopping," below), which is within walking distance, south across Reforma.

Lázaro Cárdenas and Flores Magón, Centro Histórico. Metro: Tlatelolco.

Plaza de Santo Domingo   This fascinating plaza—a wonderful slice of Mexican life—has arcades on one side, a Dominican church on another. A statue of the Corregidora of Querétaro, Josefa Ortiz de Domínguez, dominates the plaza. The plaza is best known for the scribes who compose and type letters for clients unable to do so. Years ago, it was full of professional writers clacking away on typewriters, and a few still ply their trade on ancient electric typewriters among a proliferation of small print shops and presses. Emperor Cuauhtémoc's palace once occupied this land, before Dominicans built their monastery here.

Bordered by República de Venezuela, República de Brasil, República de Cuba, and Palma, Centro Histórico. Metro: Tacuba.

Zócalo ⟨★★⟩   Every Spanish colonial city in North America was laid out according to a textbook plan, with a plaza at the center surrounded by a church, government buildings, and military headquarters. Because Mexico City was the capital of New Spain, its *zócalo* is one of the grandest, graced on all sides by stately 17th-century buildings.

Zócalo actually means "pedestal" or "plinth." A grand monument to Mexico's independence was planned and the pedestal built, but the project was never completed. Nevertheless, the pedestal became a landmark for visitors, and soon everyone was calling the square the *zócalo*, even after the pedestal was removed. (Its official name, which you will rarely hear, is Plaza de la Constitución.) It covers almost 4 hectares (10 acres) and is bounded on the north by Cinco de Mayo, on the east by Piño Suárez, on the south by 16 de Septiembre, and on the west by Nacional Monte de Piedad. The downtown district—especially north of the Templo Mayor, one of the oldest archaeological sites in the city—is currently undergoing an important restoration project that is renewing much of its colonial charm. Occupying the entire east side of the *zócalo* is the majestic red tezontle-stone Palacio National, seat of the Mexican national government, and on the northern border is the Catedral Metropolitana.

Juárez and 20 de Noviembre, Centro Histórico. Metro: Zócalo.

PARKS & GARDENS

Alameda Park   Today the lovely tree-filled Alameda Park attracts pedestrians, cotton-candy vendors, strollers, lovers, and organ grinders. Long ago, the site was an Aztec marketplace. When the conquistadors took over in the mid-1500s, heretics were burned at the stake here under the Spanish Inquisition. In 1592, the governor of New Spain, Viceroy Luis de Velasco, converted it to a public park. Within the park, known as La Alameda, is the **Juárez Monument,** sometimes called the *Hemiciclo* (hemicycle, or half-circle), facing Avenida Juárez. Enthroned as the hero he was, Juárez assumes his proper place here in the pantheon of Mexican patriots. European (particularly French) sculptors created most of the other statuary in the park in the late 19th and early 20th centuries.

Av. Juárez and Lázaro Cárdenas. Free admission. Metro: Bellas Artes.

Chapultepec Park   One of the biggest city parks in the world, 220-hectare (551-acre) Chapultepec Park is more than a playground; it's virtually the centerpiece of the city. Besides accommodating picnickers on worn-away grass under centuries-old trees, it has canoes on the lake; jogging and bridle paths; vendors selling balloons, souvenirs, and food; a miniature train; an auditorium; and **Los Pinos,** home of Mexico's president. The park is also home to the **City Zoo** and **La Feria** amusement park. Most important for tourists, it contains a number of interesting museums, including the Museo Nacional de Antropología.

Between Paseo de la Reforma, Circuito Interior, and Av. Constituyentes. Free admission. Daily 5am–5pm. Metro: Chapultepec.

Floating Gardens of Xochimilco ⊛   In the southern neighborhood of Xochimilco are more than 80km (50 miles) of canals known as the "Floating Gardens." They consist of two main parts. The first is the tourism-oriented area in the historic center of town, where colorful boats called *trajineras* take loads of tourists (some of them picnicking along the way) through a portion of the canals. Lively music, some of it provided by mariachi and trio musicians for hire who board the gondolas, is a staple. Historic buildings, restaurants, souvenir stands, curio sellers, and boat vendors border this area. The other section, north of the center of town, is the ecology-oriented area, or Parque Natural Xochimilco. On Sunday, Xochimilco (especially the tourist-oriented section) is jammed; on weekdays, it's nearly deserted. As you enter Xochimilco proper, you will see many places to board boats. Should you miss them, turn along Madero and follow signs that say LOS EMBARCADEROS (the piers).

Southern neighborhood of Xochimilco. ℂ 55/5673-7890. Admission to area $1.50. Boat rides $17 per boat, which 8–10 people may share. Mon–Fri 9am–6pm; Sat–Sun 9:30am–5pm.

BEST VIEW

La Torre Latinoamericana   From the observation deck on the 42nd floor of this soaring skyscraper, the Latin American Tower, you can take in fabulous views of the whole city. Buy a ticket for the deck at the booth as you approach the elevators. Tokens for the telescope are on sale here, too. You then take an elevator to the 37th floor, cross the hall, and take another elevator to the 42nd floor. An employee will ask for your ticket as you get off.

Madero and Lázaro Cárdenas, Centro Histórico. ℂ **55/5518-1710.** Admission $3.50 adults, $3 children. Daily 10am–11pm. Metro: Bellas Artes.

6 Organized Tours

Mexico City is a great place for looking around on your own, and in general this is the easiest and least expensive way to see what you like. If your time is limited, you may want to acclimate yourself quickly by taking a tour or two.

Among the noncommercial offerings are **free guided tours** sponsored by the **Mexico City Historical Center** (ℂ 55/5510-4737, ext. 1499), in the 18th-century home of Don Manuel de Heras y Soto, at Donceles and República de Chile. Groups meet each Sunday at 10:45am at a central gathering place for that day's tour, which varies from week to week. These tours might explore a historic downtown street, cafes and theaters, cemeteries, or the colonial churches of Xochimilco. Most tours, which last about 2 hours, are in Spanish; as many as 300 people may be divided among 10 guides. Visitors can ask a day in advance for a guide who speaks their language. The center's phone is almost always busy, so you may opt to visit the office, in the far back of the building, on the right and up a spiral staircase, to get a list of upcoming tours and gathering locations. Office hours are Monday through Friday from 9am to 3pm and 6 to 9pm.

If you're a guest of the **Hotel Four Seasons** (see "Where to Stay," earlier in this chapter), be sure to take advantage of its excellent weekend cultural tours, led by noted

---

Tips Tours: The Downside

Many readers have written to say they were unhappy with the sightseeing tours of this or that company. The reasons are myriad: The tour was too rushed; the guide knew nothing and made up stories about the sights; the tour group spent most of its time in a handicrafts shop (chosen by the tour company) rather than seeing the sights. Do tour companies get a kickback from souvenir shops? Of course! If you meet someone who has recently taken a guided tour and liked it, go with the same company. Otherwise, you might do well to see the sights on your own, following the detailed information in this book. Your hotel can arrange a private car by the hour or day—generally with a driver who is also an English-speaking guide. This can cost less or only slightly more than an organized tour, with greater flexibility and personalized service.

Kids A Mexico City Just for Kids

The **Ciudad de los Niños (City of Children)** is an innovative attraction for youthful visitors to Mexico City. It is a comprehensive fantasy village where children interact as part of a "virtual" economy and have the chance to experience adult life—complete with working, then choosing whether to spend or save their earnings. They first board an American Airlines replica plane for the "trip" to Ciudad de los Niños. When they "arrive," they enter the airport, pass through immigration, and receive some "money." They can choose to put this in the bank or spend it at various community establishments, which include restaurants, a gas station, a beauty shop, a racetrack, and other service providers. They can also choose to "work" at any of the above places and earn more "Niño money." Ciudad de los Niños is in the Santa Fe shopping mall, Vasco de Quiroga 3800 (**(** 55/5261-1099**)**, next to the Liverpool store. It's open Monday through Friday from 9am to 7pm, and Saturday and Sunday from 10am to 3pm and 4 to 9pm. Admission is $6 for children 2 to 3 years old and adults, $12 for children ages 4 to 16. Free for travelers with disabilities and seniors. Visa and MasterCard are accepted. **Note:** It's mostly Spanish-speaking, but go anyway—children seem to quickly move beyond any language barriers.

---

experts. These highly recommendable tours are available only to Four Seasons guests and are included in the price of the room.

The many commercial tours include a 4-hour city tour of such sites as the **Metropolitan Cathedral,** the **National Palace,** and **Chapultepec Park and Castle;** a longer tour to the **Shrine of Guadalupe** and nearby pyramids at **Teotihuacán;** and the Sunday tour that begins with the **Ballet Folklórico,** moves on to the **Floating Gardens of Xochimilco,** and may or may not include lunch and the afternoon bullfights. Almost as popular are 1-day and overnight tours to Puebla, Cuernavaca, Taxco, and Acapulco. There are also several nightclub tours. Book through your hotel concierge or tour desk.

7 Shopping

From handicrafts to the finest in designer apparel, Mexico City, like any major metropolitan area, is a marvelous place for shopping. From malls to *mercados,* numerous places display fascinating native products and sophisticated goods.

The two best districts for browsing are on and off **Avenida Presidente Masaryk,** in Polanco, and the **Zona Rosa.** Polanco's shops include Burberrys of London, Christian Dior, Gianni Versace, Gucci, Hermès, Luis Vuitton, Giorgio Armani, Tiffany's, and Cartier. Think New York's Madison Avenue, Beverly Hills's Rodeo Drive, or Chicago's Mag Mile, and you'll get the picture. The 12 square blocks at the heart of the Zona Rosa are home to antiques shops, boutiques, art galleries, silver shops, and fine jewelers. A few unique shops deserve particular mention.

Several government-run shops and a few excellent private shops have exceptionally good collections of Mexico's arts and crafts. Here's the rundown on the best places to shop, from small crafts shops to vast general markets.

SHOPPING A TO Z
ART
Artesanos de México   This shop in the Zona Rosa sells crafts from all over Mexico. It isn't large, but it's a good place to see handsome displays of pottery, textiles, and original art. It's open Monday through Friday from 11am to 7pm. Londres 117, Zona Rosa. ✆ 55/5525-6235 or 55/5514-7455. Metro: Insurgentes.

Arvil. Galería de Arte y Libros de Arte   Collectible works of art—auction-quality pieces—by Mexican masters. It's open by appointment only, Monday through Friday from 10am to 2:30pm and 4 to 7pm, and Saturday from 10am to 3pm. Cerrada de Hamburgo 7 and 9, Reforma/Zona Rosa. ✆ 55/5207-2647. Fax 55/5207-3994. Metro: Insurgentes.

Exposición Nacional de Arte Popular (FONART)   This store is usually loaded with crafts: papier-mâché figurines, textiles, earthenware, colorful candelabras, hand-carved wooden masks, straw goods, beads, bangles, and glass. The Fonda Nacional para el Fomento de las Artes (FONART), a government organization that helps village craftspeople, operates the store. It's open daily from 10am to 7pm. Juárez 89, Centro Histórico. ✆ 55/5521-0171. Metro: Hidalgo or Juárez.

FONART   Another branch of the government-operated store (see above) is in the heart of the Zona Rosa. Although it's in small, narrow, upstairs quarters, it is chock-full of folk art, much of it not available at the larger store on Juárez. It's open Monday through Saturday from 9am to 8pm. Londres 136A, Zona Rosa. ✆ 55/5598-5552 or 55/5598-1666. Metro: Insurgentes.

López Quiroga Gallery   Auction-quality works of art by contemporary Latin American masters, including Toledo, Tamayo, and Siqueiros. The gallery is not accessible by Metro. It's open Monday 7am to 10pm and Tuesday through Saturday from 10am to 2pm. Aristóteles 169, Polanco. ✆ 55/5280-1247. Fax 55/5280-3960. www.arte-mexico.com.

O.M.R. Gallery   This gallery has earned a reputation for discovering and introducing emerging talents and new artists from Latin America. It's open Monday through Friday from 10am to 3pm and 4 to 7pm, Saturday from 10am to 2pm. Plaza Río de Janeiro 54, Col. Roma. ✆ 55/5511-1179, 55/5525-3095, or 55/5207-1080. Fax: 55/5533-4244. Metro: Insurgentes.

Víctor Artes Populares Mexicanas   Owned by the Fosado family, which has been in the folk art business for more than 50 years, Victor, near La Alameda, is a shop for serious buyers and art collectors. The Fosados buy most of their crafts from Indian villages near and far, and supply various exhibits with native crafts. It's open Monday through Friday from 12:30 to 7pm, and Saturdays by appointment only. Fco. I. Madero 8 Y 10, 2nd floor, Room 305, Centro Histórico. ✆ 55/5512-1263. Metro: Bellas Artes or Allende.

JEWELRY
Besides the shops mentioned below, dozens of jewelry stores and optical shops are on Madero from Motolinia to the *zócalo*, in the portals facing the National Palace. **Nacional Monte de Piedad/National Pawn Shop,** also opposite the National Palace, has an enormous jewelry selection. The first Latin American branch of **Tiffany's** is on Avenida Presidente Masaryk in Polanco.

Bazar del Centro   Located between La Alameda and the *zócalo*, this colonial-era building was the palace of the Counts of Miravale. Now it houses shops selling jewelry, precious stones, and silver. It's open Monday through Friday from 10am to 7pm and Saturday from 10am to 3pm. Isabel la Católica 30, Centro Histórico. No phone. Metro: Zócalo.

Tane   Tucked in the lobby of the hotel Presidente InterContinental, this is one of the branches of one of Mexico's top silver designers, with other locations found only in the best hotels and shopping centers. The quantity of good-quality silver work is enormous. You'll see jewelry, platters, pitchers, plates, cutlery, frames, candlesticks, and even the signature china, by Limoges. There are also branches in the Polanco and San Angel neighborhoods, and at the airport. It's open Monday through Friday from 10am to 7pm and Saturday from 11am to 2:30pm. ℭ **55/5616-0165.** www.tane.com.mx.

MARKETS

Bazar del Sábado *(Moments*   A festive and unique shopping experience, the Bazar Sábado is held (as its name indicates) only on Saturday. Located in an expensive colonial-era suburb of cobblestone streets, mansions, and parks a few kilometers south of the city, it's my top recommendation for passing a Saturday afternoon in Mexico City. The actual bazaar building is an elegant two-story mansion built around a courtyard.

The central area houses an excellent, authentic, hectic Mexican cafe where waiters hustle to serve tacos hot off the grill and frosty margaritas, plus *antojitos* (finger foods) and traditional main dishes like enchiladas. Marimba music plays in the background. Dozens of small rooms surrounding the courtyard serve as permanent stalls featuring original works of high-quality decorative art. You'll find blown glass, original fine jewelry, papier-mâché figures, masks, and embroidered clothing. The prices are on the high side, but the quality is equally high, and the designs are sophisticated. On adjacent plazas, hundreds of easel artists display their paintings, and surrounding homes abound with antiques, fine rugs, and hand-carved furniture for sale. Members of indigenous groups from Puebla and elsewhere bring their folk art—baskets, masks, pottery, textiles, and so on—to display in the parks. Restaurants, some in mansions, line the streets and play host to leisurely diners seated at umbrella-shaded tables. Plan to spend Saturday touring the attractions on the southern outskirts of the city. (See also "San Angel" under "The Neighborhoods in Brief," earlier in this chapter.) It's open Saturday from 9am to 6pm. Plaza de San Jacinto, San Angel.

Centro Artesanal (Mercado de Curiosidades)   This rather modern building set back off a plaza consists of a number of stalls on two levels, selling everything from leather to tiles. They have some lovely silver jewelry and, as in most non-fixed-price stores, the asking price is high but the bargained result is often very reasonable. It's open Monday through Saturday from 10am to 5:30pm. Corner of Ayuntamiento and Dolores, Reforma North. Metro: Guerrero.

Lagunilla Market   This is one of the most interesting and unusual markets in Mexico—but watch out for pickpockets. It's only open on Sundays, when the Lagunilla becomes a colorful outdoor market filling the streets for blocks. Arrive around 9am. Vendors sell everything from axes to antiques. The two enclosed sections, on either side of a short street, Calle Juan Salvages, are open all week. They have different specialties: The one to the north is noted for clothes, *rebozos* (shawls), and blankets; the one to the south for tools, pottery, and household goods, such as attractive hanging copper lamps. This is also the area to find old and rare books, many at a ridiculously low cost, if you're willing to hunt and bargain. It's open Sundays from 10am to 3:30pm. 3 blocks east of Plaza de Garibaldi, at the corner of Francisco Bocanegra. Metro: Allende.

Mercado de La Ciudadela   An excellent place to get authentic arts and crafts, this market has hundreds of stalls with arts and crafts from all over Mexico. It's across from the Escuela Nacional de Artes. A few places take credit cards. It's open daily from 7am to 8pm. Balderas, between Reforma and Chapultepec. Metro: Balderas.

Mercado Insurgentes   Mercado Insurgentes is a full-fledged crafts market tucked into the Zona Rosa. Because of its address, you might expect exorbitant prices, but vendors in the maze of stalls are eager to bargain, and good buys aren't hard to come by. It's open Monday through Saturday from 9am to 5:30pm. Londres between Florencia and Amberes, Zona Rosa. Metro: Insurgentes.

Merced Market   This is the city's biggest market and among the most fascinating in the country; the intense activity and energy level are akin to those at Oaxaca's Abastos Market (see chapter 11). Officially it's housed in several modern buildings, but shops line the tidy, crowded streets all the way to the *zócalo*.

The first building is mainly for fruits and vegetables; the others contain about what you'd find if a department store joined forces with a discount warehouse—especially housewares, such as hand-held citrus juicers of all sizes, tinware, colorful spoons, and decorative oilcloth. The main market, east of the *zócalo* on Circunvalación between General Anaya and Adolfo Gurrión, is the place to stock up on Mexican spices. The easy 13-block walk from the *zócalo* zigzags past many shops. Or take the Metro; the stop is right outside the market. It's open Monday through Friday from 8am to 4pm, Saturday from 8am to 2pm. Circunvalación between General Anaya and Adolfo Gurrión. Metro: Merced.

Nacional Monte de Piedad (National Pawn Shop)   This building used to be a pawn shop for all sorts of items, but now is reserved for the more profitable and saleable jewelry, with a couple of small rooms set aside for art and antiques. The building is on the site of Moctezuma's old Axayácatl palace, where the captive emperor was accidentally killed. Cortez used the site to build a viceregal palace. Pedro Romero de Terreros, the Count of Regla, an 18th-century silver magnate from Pachuca, donated the present building so that Mexican people could get low-interest loans. It's open Monday through Friday from 8:30am to 6pm, Saturday from 8:30am to 3pm. Corner of Monte de Piedad and Cinco de Mayo, Centro Histórico. Metro: Zócalo.

MUSIC
Sanborn's, the popular Mexican variety store, with locations throughout the city, carries an excellent selection of traditional and popular Mexican music in most of its larger stores.

8 Mexico City After Dark

From mariachi, reggae, and opera to folkloric dance, classical ballet, and dinner shows, the choice of nighttime entertainment in Mexico City is enormous and sophisticated. Prices are much lower than those for comparable entertainment in most of the world's major cities. If you're willing to let *la vida mexicana* put on its own fascinating show for you, the bill will be even less. People-watching, cafe-sitting, music, and even a dozen mariachi bands all playing at once can be yours for next to nothing. For those looking for the hottest spots in dance clubs, head straight for the **Condesa** and **Roma** neighborhoods.

THE ENTERTAINMENT SCENE
Mexico City has a very impressive club scene, with great places for dancing to music ranging from salsa to house. In recent years, the **Centro Histórico** downtown has earned a reputation for a broad range of chic clubs concentrated within walking distance. The posh

> ⟨*Tips* **Crime at Night**
>
> Make sure to leave valuables—especially watches and jewelry—at your hotel, and bring only the cash you will need. While I list Metro stops, these should probably be used only for orientation; take only authorized *sitio* taxis (see the advisory "Important Taxi Safety Precautions in Mexico City," at the beginning of this chapter) or hire a private taxi by the hour and have an escort waiting for you as you sample the festivities of the city. Your hotel can help with these arrangements.

Polanco neighborhood is known for its perennial hot nightclub scene, but in recent years, the hippest clubs are found in the **Condesa** neighborhood (reputedly the SoHo of Mexico City, though the nightlife scene is more akin to New York's East Village). The **Zona Rosa** remains highly popular, and continues to be the most comfortable place for tourists. There the music tends to be more English-language than Spanish, and the masses of people strolling the sidewalks give the area a festive, friendly feel. Clubs and dinner-dance establishments don't even begin to get going until around 10 or 11pm and stay open until at least 3am. Many clubs operate only Thursday through Saturday.

Fiesta nights give visitors a chance to dine on typical Mexican food and see wonderful regional dancing, which seems always to be a treat no matter how many times you've seen it.

For lower-key nightlife and people-watching, outdoor cafes remain a popular option. Those on **Calle Copenhague,** in the thick of the Zona Rosa scene, are among the liveliest, but with one or two exceptions, they have become more expensive than they are good. Another tradition is **Garibaldi Square,** where mariachis tune up and wait to be hired, but *be especially careful*—it's now known as much for chronic street crime as for music.

Hotel lobby bars tend to have live entertainment of the low-key type in the late afternoon and into the evening. The exception is the lobby bar at the Camino Real, which occasionally books top-name Latin American talent.

THE PERFORMING ARTS

Mexico City's performing arts scene is among the finest and most comprehensive in the world. It includes opera, theater, ballet, and dance, along with concerts of symphonic, rock, and popular music.

For current information on cultural offerings, *Donde, Tiempo Libre,* and *Concierge,* free magazines found in hotels, are good sources for locating the newest places, though they don't have complete listings of changing entertainment or current exhibits. **Ticketmaster** (© **55/5325-9000**) usually handles ticket sales for major performances.

The **Ballet Folklórico de México (Folkloric Ballet of Mexico),** with its stunning presentation of regional dance, is perhaps the city's most renowned entertainment for visitors.

Note: The majority of the theatrical performances at the Palacio de Bellas Artes and in other theaters around the city are presented in Spanish.

FOLKLORIC BALLET

Palacio de Bellas Artes   Although various groups perform around the city, the finest offering is at the Palacio de Bellas Artes, where the famed **Ballet Folklórico de México** performs twice a week. The Ballet Folklórico is a celebration of pre- and post-Hispanic dancing. A typical program includes Aztec ritual dances, agricultural dances from Jalisco, a fiesta in Veracruz, a wedding celebration—all linked with mariachis, marimba players, singers, and dancers.

Because the Bellas Artes books many other events—visits by foreign opera companies, for instance—the Ballet Folklórico occasionally moves. In that case, it usually appears in the **National Auditorium** in Chapultepec Park. Check at the Bellas Artes box office. The show is popular and tickets sell rapidly (especially to tour agencies at twice the cost). The box office is on the ground floor of the Bellas Artes, main entrance. Ballet Folklórico performances are on Sunday at 9:30am and Wednesday at 8:30pm.

The Fine Arts theater not only offers the finest in performing arts, but is also architecturally worth a visit (see "Exploring Mexico City," earlier in this chapter). Open Monday through Saturday 11am to 7pm, and Sunday 8:30am to 7pm. *Note:* The U.S. State Department advisory specifies that taxis parked in front of this theater should be avoided. Eje Central and Av. Juárez, Centro Histórico–Alameda. © 55/5512-2593, ext. 152. www.cnca.gob.mx/palacio/ni.htm. Tickets $20–$30. Metro: Bellas Artes.

THE CLUB & MUSIC SCENE

This warning can't be reiterated enough: *Take an authorized* sitio *taxi or hire a car for transportation to all nightspots.* Metro stops are given merely as a point of reference.

MARIACHIS

Mariachis play the music of Mexico. Although the songs they play may be familiar—ranging from traditional *boleros* to Mozart to the Beatles—their style and presentation are unique to Mexico. Known for their distinctive dress, strolling presentation, and mix of brass and guitars, they epitomize the romance and tradition of the country. They look a little like Mexican cowboys dressed up for a special occasion—tight trousers studded with silver buttons down the outside of the legs, elaborate cropped jackets, embroidered shirts with big bow ties, and grandiose sombrero hats. The dress dates to the French occupation of Mexico in the mid–19th century, as does the name. *Mariachi* is believed to be an adaptation of the French word for marriage; this was the type of music commonly played at weddings in the 15th and 16th centuries. The music is a derivative of *fandango,* which was the most popular dance music of the elite classes in 16th-century Spain. In Mexico, fandango became the peasant's song and dance.

In Mexico City, the mariachis make their headquarters around the **Plaza de Garibaldi,** 5 blocks north of the Palacio de Bellas Artes—up Avenida Lázaro Cárdenas, at Avenida República de Honduras. Mariachi players are everywhere in the plaza. At every corner, guitars are stacked together like rifles in an army camp. Young musicians strut proudly in their outfits, on the lookout for señoritas to impress. They play when they feel like it, when there's a good chance to gather some tips, or when someone orders a song—the going rate is $1.50 to $3.25 per song.

Tips A Note of Caution in Garibaldi Square

Plaza de Garibaldi, *both day and night,* is increasingly populated by thieves looking to separate tourists from their valuables. Although the police presence has increased, it's still best to visit by private taxi. If you go, don't take credit cards or excess money with you. Go with a crowd of friends rather than alone, or take a tour that includes Garibaldi.

Should you want to enjoy mariachi music in a more tourist-friendly venue, I can recommend:

Jorongo Bar   For wonderful mariachi and trio music in plush surroundings, make your way to the Hotel María Isabel Sheraton, facing the Angel Monument. This bar has enjoyed a reputation for mariachi music for decades—it's an institution. Nightly from 7pm to midnight, you can enjoy the smooth and joyous sounds for the price of a drink ($5–$9) plus cover. Hotel María Isabel Sheraton, Reforma 325, Zona Rosa. ℂ 55/5242-5555. Cover $7. Metro: Insurgentes.

CLUBS & MUSIC BARS

AREA Bar and Terrace, at the Habita *Finds*   The rooftop bar of this oh-so-chic boutique hotel is also among Mexico City's hottest nightspots. Umbrellas top tables, but otherwise, you're under the stars—and, likely, surrounded by a few—in an ultra-trendy crowd sipping tequila cocktails and Cosmopolitans. If there's a chill in the air, the fireplace or veiled space heaters will take care of it. Decor is minimalist, of course, with a few white couches. Barstools set along the railing look out over the city. If you can make it past the bouncer and down the circular stairway to the lower terrace and pool area, you've really arrived—that's the super VIP section. Music is mainly Euro, chill, and house. It's open nightly from 7pm to 4am, and packed from Thursday to Saturday. Habita hotel, Av. Presidente Masaryk 201, Polanco. ℂ 55/5282-3100. Metro: Polanco.

Bar Cosmo   One of the top spots in the capitol for visiting international DJs, this is a favorite with those in their teens and 20s looking for the latest in techno, house, Drum & Bass, and other electronic music. It's open Friday and Saturday from 8pm to 4am. Av. Presidente Masaryk 410 (corner of Calderón de la Barca), Polanco. ℂ 55/5281-4412. $5 cover; 2-drink minimum. Metro: Polanco.

Bar Fly *Finds*   The talented house band—direct from Cuba—makes this small but stylish bar sizzle. By midnight the tiny dance floor is overflowing. It's on the second floor of an upscale shopping center. It's open Wednesday through Saturday from 8pm to 2am; live music starts at 11pm. Av. Presidente Masaryk 393, Polanco. ℂ 55/5282-2906 or 55/2514-2297. 2-drink minimum. Metro: Polanco.

Blu Bar   An intimate nightclub for lovers, and lovers of live music, this is an invit-ing spot where conversation is actually possible. The atmosphere is reminiscent of a New York bar, and martinis are the house specialty. The clientele is mid-30s and up, and live jazz is the most frequently featured music, but other soulful performers also take the stage. There's food service available, featuring Mediterranean fare. It's the best choice if you're staying south of the city. The club is not easily accessible by Metro. Open Monday through Saturday from 7pm to 2:30am. Av. de la Paz, local 1, Col. San Angel. ℂ 55/5616-4791. Reservation required for tables on weekends. Cover $6 and up.

Cinna Bar   This Condesa hot spot is immediately visible with its huge red glass win-dows. A "see and be seen" place, the bar runs the length of the room, and features elec-tronic music that's not too overbearing for a conversation. It's popular with a younger crowd on the weekends, but all ages enjoy it throughout the week. There's also a menu of Thai food. It's open daily from 7:30pm to 2:30am, often later on weekend nights. Nuevo León 67-1, ground floor of the Cine Plaza building, Col. Condesa. ℂ 55/5286-8456. Metro: Insurgentes.

Ligaya   Across the street from Cinna Bar is another Condesa hot spot that serves both food and drinks, but is really known for its hip bar scene. The all white mini-malist decor is the perfect backdrop for showing off the slinky fashions of the

20-something crowd that favors the place. A menu of nouveau Mexican cuisine is served. Open daily from 7:30pm to 2:30am, often later on weekend nights. Nuevo León 68, Col. Condesa. ℂ 55/5286-6268. Metro: Insurgentes.

Living Room and Box Among Mexico City's most popular gay clubs, this is one of the hottest, with weekends packing in both gay men and lesbians dancing to electronic music. Open weekends from 10pm until 3am. Paseo de la Reforma 483, Col. Cuauhtémoc. ℂ 55/5286-0069. www.living.com.mx. During special shows or events, cover charge of up to $20 may apply.

Rexo Credited with changing Mexico City's nightlife scene by leading people to Condesa, this bar, restaurant, and club still rules as the one of the city's hot spots. A cube walled in by glass, Rexo consists of three floors. The first is a bar, the second has a bar plus table service and dining available (classic tapas), while the third floor is for dancing. The crowd is 30-something, mostly single, and very stylish. The club is not easily accessible by Metro. It's open Tuesday through Saturday from 1pm to 2am, Sunday and Monday from 1pm to 1am. Saltillo 1 (corner of Nuevo León), Col. Condesa. ℂ 55/5553-5337.

Rioma Hard to get into, this VIP club currently commands the top spot for the ultrachic. A set of stairs leads down to the superhot dance floor, with tables, lit from the inside, surrounding it. There's a long bar along one wall. Music is Euro, house, and techno. The crowd is among the most fashionable in the city—models, young socialites, celebrities, and hard-core clubbers. On weekends there's often a line out the door and down the street. Plan to arrive late and stay into the early morning. It's open Wednesday through Saturday from 10pm to 4am. Insurgentes Sur 377 (near the corner of Michoacán), Col. Condesa. ℂ 55/5584-0613. Cover $10 and up. Metro: Insurgentes.

BARS

Caviar Bar While guests enjoy light meals and drinks in this stylish hotel's lobby bar, a string quartet plays in the evening. It's elegant and wonderfully soothing. It's open daily from noon to 12:45am. Hotel Marquís Reforma, Reforma 465, Col. Cuauhtémoc. ℂ 55/5229-1200, ext. 4074. Metro: Insurgentes.

La Casa de las Sirenas This bar serves 146 types of tequila—one of the widest selections available anywhere—in a stylish atmosphere. Although it also serves food, it's best known for its bar crowd and ambience. It becomes a popular club, playing recorded rock music, Thursday through Saturday evenings. It's in a 17th-century colonial building, with a courtyard filled with flowering plants and trees, almost in front of the Templo Mayor in the Historic Centro. It's open Monday from 1 to 6pm, Tuesday through Friday from 1 to 11pm, Saturday from 8am to 11pm, Sunday from 8am to 7pm. Guatemala 32, Centro Histórico, behind the cathedral. ℂ 55/5704-3345 or 55/5704-3225. Metro: Zócalo.

Whiskey Bar/The Terrace ★★ If this bar is too crowded to get in—which it often is—you can at least view the action you're missing through the floor-to-ceiling glass windows, visible from the street. Known as the place where the "beautiful people" go since opening in late 2003, this first international location of Rande Gerber's hot chain of bars has created a sensation, and is known as being the most *caliente* of the hot clubs in the city. Stunning design and the group's signature cool music are the features, but it's the buzz and the crowd that's the real attraction. There's also an outdoor terrace area, if things heat up too much. Open until 2am Sunday through Wednesday, until 4am Thursday through Saturday. At the W Mexico City hotel, Campos Eliseos 252, at Andrés Bello; ℂ 55/9138-1800. Metro: Polanco.

STRIP CLUBS

The Men's Club Mexico City Here you will find entertainment for men, including erotic shows and private dancing. Special parties are also featured; call for details. It's open Monday through Friday from 2pm to 2am, Saturday from 9:30pm to 2am. Varsovia 54, Col. Juárez, Zona Rosa. (✆ 55/5533-2224. www.mensclub.com.mx. Cover $18 Mon–Tues and Thurs–Sat; $24 Wed (package includes buffet and national wine 2–5pm). Metro: Insurgentes.

9 A Side Trip to the Pyramids of San Juan Teotihuacán ★★★

48km (30 miles) NE of Mexico City

The ruins of Teotihuacán are among the most remarkable in Mexico—indeed, they are among the most important ruins in the world. Mystery envelops this former city of 200,000; although it was the epicenter of culture and commerce for ancient Mesoamerica, its inhabitants vanished without a trace. *Teotihuacán* (pronounced "teh-oh-tee-wa-*khan*") means "place where gods were born," reflecting the Aztec belief that the gods created the universe here.

Occupation of the area began around 500 B.C., but it wasn't until after 100 B.C. that construction of the enormous Pyramid of the Sun commenced. Teotihuacán's rise coincided with the classical Romans' building of their great monuments, and with the beginning of cultures in Mexico's Yucatán Peninsula, Oaxaca, and Puebla.

Teotihuacán's magnificent pyramids and palaces covered 31 sq. km (12 sq. miles). At its zenith, around A.D. 500, the city counted more inhabitants than in contemporary Rome. Through trade and other contact, Teotihuacán's influence was known in other parts of Mexico and as far south as the Yucatán and Guatemala. Still, little information about the city's inhabitants survives: what language they spoke, where they came from, why they abandoned the place around A.D. 700. It is known, however, that at the beginning of the 1st century A.D., the Xitle volcano erupted near Cuicuilco (south of Mexico City) and decimated that city, which was the most prominent of the time. Those inhabitants migrated to Teotihuacán. Scholars believe that Teotihuacán's decline, probably caused by overpopulation and depletion of natural resources, was gradual, perhaps occurring over a 250-year period. In the last years, it appears that the people were poorly nourished and that the city was deliberately burned.

Ongoing excavations have revealed something of the culture. According to archaeoastronomer John B. Carlson, the cult of the planet Venus that determined wars and human sacrifices elsewhere in Mesoamerica was prominent at Teotihuacán as well. (Archaeoastronomy is the study of the position of stars and planets in relation to archaeology.) Ceremonial rituals were timed with the appearance of Venus as the morning and evening star. The symbol of Venus at Teotihuacán (as at Cacaxtla, 80km/50 miles away, near Tlaxcala) appears as a star or half-star with a full or half-circle. Carlson also suggests the possibility that people from Cacaxtla conquered Teotihuacán, since name glyphs of conquered peoples at Cacaxtla show Teotihuacán-like pyramids. Numerous tombs with human remains (many of them either sacrificial inhabitants of the city or perhaps war captives) and objects of jewelry, pottery, and daily life have been uncovered along the foundations of buildings. It appears that the primary deity at Teotihuacán was a female, called "Great Goddess" for lack of any known name.

Today, what remains are the rough stone structures of the three pyramids and sacrificial altars, and some of the grand houses, all of which were once covered in stucco

SAN MARTÍN

Entrance
Peripheral Highway

Parking

Avenue of the Dead

Parking

To San Juan
Teotihuacán

Parking

Terraced Road

Pyramid
Charlie's

La Cueva

Parking

Entrance

Río San Juan

Avenue of the Dead

Parking

Villas
Arqueológicas

To Mexico
City

Entrance

Parking

Peripheral Highway

Roadside
Food Stands

0   0.25 mi
0   0.25 km

1 Tepantitla
2 Pyramid of the Moon
3 Palace of Quetzalpapálotl
4 Palace of the Jaguars
5 El Corso
6 Pyramid of the Sun
7 The High Priest's Home
8 New Museum Location
9 The Viking Group
10 The Temple of
     Quetzalcoatl
11 La Ciudadela
12 Old Museum Building
13 La Ventilla
14 Atetelco
15 Tetitla
16 Zacuala
17 Yayahuala

and painted with brilliant frescoes (mainly in red). The Toltec, who rose in power after the city's decline, were fascinated with Teotihuacán and incorporated its symbols into their own cultural motifs. The Aztec, who followed the Toltec, were fascinated with the Toltec and with the ruins of Teotihuacán; they likewise adopted many of their symbols and motifs. For more information on Teotihuacán and its influence in Mesoamerica, see appendix A.

ESSENTIALS

GETTING THERE & DEPARTING   By Car   Driving to San Juan Teotihuacán on the toll Highway 85D or the free Highway 132D takes about an hour. Head north on Insurgentes to leave the city. Highway 132D passes through picturesque villages but can be slow due to the surfeit of trucks and buses. Highway 85D, the toll road, is less attractive but faster.

By Private Sedan or Taxi   If you prefer to explore solo or want more or less time than an organized tour allows, consider hiring a private car and driver for the trip. They can easily be arranged through your hotel or at the Secretary of Tourism (SECTUR) information module in the Zona Rosa; they cost about $10 to $15 an hour. The higher price is generally for a sedan with an English-speaking driver who doubles as a tour guide. Rates can also be negotiated for the entire day.

By Bus Buses leave daily every half hour (5am–10pm) from the Terminal Central de Autobuses del Norte; the trip takes 1 hour. When you reach the Terminal Norte, look for the AUTOBUSES SAHAGUN sign at the far northwest end, all the way down to the sign 8 ESPERA. Be sure to ask the driver where you should wait for returning buses, how frequently buses run, and especially the time of the last bus back.

ORIENTATION The ruins of Teotihuacán (© **59/4956-0276** or 59/4956-0052) are open daily from 7am to 6pm. Admission is $3.80. Using a video camera costs $3.

A small trolley-train that takes visitors from the entry booths to various stops within the site, including the Teotihuacán museum and cultural center, runs only on weekends and costs 60¢ per person.

Keep in mind that you're likely to be doing a great deal of walking, and perhaps some climbing, at an altitude of more than 2,120m (7,000 ft.). Take it slow, bring sunblock and drinking water, and during the summer be prepared for almost daily afternoon showers.

A good place to start is at the **Museo Teotihuacán** ✦. This excellent state-of-the-art museum holds interactive exhibits and, in one part, a glass floor on which visitors walk above mock-ups of the pyramids. On display are findings of recent digs, including several tombs, with skeletons wearing necklaces of human and simulated jaw-bones, and newly discovered sculptures.

The Layout The grand buildings of Teotihuacán were laid out in accordance with celestial movements. The front wall of the **Pyramid of the Sun** is exactly perpendicular to the point on the horizon where the sun sets at the equinoxes (twice annually). The rest of the ceremonial buildings were laid out at right angles to the Pyramid of the Sun.

The main thoroughfare, which archaeologists call the **Calzada de los Muertos (Avenue of the Dead),** runs roughly north to south. The **Pyramid of the Moon** is at the northern end, and the **Ciudadela (Citadel)** is on the southern part. The great street was several kilometers long in its prime, but only a kilometer or two has been uncovered and restored.

EXPLORING THE TEOTIHUACAN ARCHAEOLOGICAL SITE

LA CIUDADELA The Spaniards named the Ciudadela. This immense sunken square was not a fortress at all, although the impressive walls make it look like one. It was the grand setting for the Feathered Serpent Pyramid and the Temple of Quetzal-coatl. Scholars aren't certain that the Teotihuacán culture embraced the Quetzalcoatl deity so well known in the Toltec, Aztec, and Maya cultures. The feathered serpent is featured in the Ciudadela, but whether it was worshipped as Quetzalcoatl or a similar god isn't known. Proceed down the steps into the massive court and head for the ruined temple in the middle.

The Temple of Quetzalcoatl was covered over by an even larger structure, a pyramid. As you walk toward the center of the Ciudadela's court, you'll approach the Feathered Serpent Pyramid. To the right, you'll see the reconstructed temple close behind the pyramid, with a narrow passage between the two structures.

Early temples in Mexico and Central America were often covered by later ones. The Pyramid of the Sun may have been built up in this way. Archaeologists have tunneled deep inside the Feathered Serpent Pyramid and found several ceremonially buried human remains, interred with precise detail and position, but as yet no royal personages. Drawings of how the building once looked show that every level was covered with faces of a feathered serpent. At the Temple of Quetzalcoatl, you'll notice at once the fine, large carved serpents' heads jutting out from collars of feathers carved in the stone walls; these weigh 4 tons. Other feathered serpents are carved in relief low on the walls.

AVENUE OF THE DEAD   The Avenue of the Dead got its strange and forbidding name from the Aztec, who mistook the little temples that line both sides of the avenue for tombs of kings or priests.

As you stroll north along the Avenue of the Dead toward the Pyramid of the Moon, look on the right for a bit of wall sheltered by a modern corrugated roof. Beneath the shelter, the wall still bears a painting of a jaguar. From this fragment, you might be able to reconstruct the breathtaking spectacle that must have been visible when all the paintings along the avenue were intact.

PYRAMID OF THE SUN   The Pyramid of the Sun, on the east side of the Avenue of the Dead, is the third-largest pyramid in the world. The first and second are the Great Pyramid of Cholula, near Puebla, and the Pyramid of Cheops on the outskirts of Cairo, Egypt. Teotihuacán's Pyramid of the Sun is 221m (730 ft.) per side at its base—almost as large as Cheops. But at 64m (210 ft.) high, the Sun pyramid is only about half as high as its Egyptian rival. No matter—it's still the biggest restored pyramid in the Western Hemisphere, and an awesome sight. Although the Pyramid of the Sun was not built as a great king's tomb, it is built on top of a series of sacred caves, which aren't open to the public.

The first structure of the pyramid was probably built a century before Christ, and the temple that used to crown the pyramid was completed about 400 years later (A.D. 300). By the time the pyramid was discovered and restoration was begun (early in the 20th c.), the temple had disappeared, and the pyramid was just a mass of rubble covered with bushes and trees.

It's a worthwhile 248-step climb to the top. The view is extraordinary and the sensation exhilarating.

PYRAMID OF THE MOON   The Pyramid of the Moon faces a plaza at the northern end of the avenue. The plaza is surrounded by little temples and by the Palace of Quetzalpapalotl or Quetzal-Mariposa (Quetzal-Butterfly) on the left (west) side. You have about the same range of view from the top of the Pyramid of the Moon as you do from its larger neighbor, because the moon pyramid is built on higher ground. The perspective straight down the Avenue of the Dead is magnificent.

PALACE OF QUETZALPAPALOTL   The Palace of Quetzalpapalotl lay in ruins until the 1960s, when restoration work began. Today, it reverberates with its former glory, as figures of Quetzal-Mariposa (a mythical, exotic bird-butterfly) appear painted on walls or carved in the pillars of the inner court.

Behind the Palace of Quetzalpapalotl is the Palace of the Jaguars, complete with murals showing jaguars and some frescoes.

WHERE TO DINE

Vendors at the ruins sell drinks and snacks, but many visitors choose to carry a box lunch—almost any hotel or restaurant in the city can prepare one for you. A picnic in the shadow of this impressive ancient city allows extended time and perspective to take it all in. There is a **restaurant** in the new Museo Teotihuacán, which is the most convenient place for a snack or a meal.

5

Silver, Spas & Spiritual Centers: From Taxco to Tepoztlán

by Lynne Bairstow

It may seem as if the small towns in this region of Mexico are trying to capitalize on recent trends in travel toward spas and self-exploration, but in reality, they've helped define them. From the restorative properties of thermal waters and earth-based spa treatments to the mystical and spiritual properties of gemstones and herbs, the treasures and knowledge in these towns have existed for years—and, in some cases, for centuries.

This is only a sampling of towns south and west of Mexico City. They are fascinating in their diversity, history, and mystery, and make for a unique travel experience, either on their own or combined. They vary in character from mystical villages to sophisticated spa towns, with archaeological and colonial-era attractions in the mix. And with their proximity to Mexico City, all are within easy reach by private car or taxi—or by inexpensive bus—in under a few hours.

The legendary silver city of **Taxco,** on the road between Acapulco and Mexico City, is renowned for its museums, picturesque hillside colonial-era charm, and, of course, its silver shops. North of Taxco and southwest of Mexico City, over the mountains, are the venerable thermal spas at **Ixtapan de la Sal,** as well as their more modern counterparts in **Valle de Bravo.** Verdant **Cuernavaca,** known as the land of eternal spring, has gained a reputation for its exceptional spa facilities and its wealth of cultural and historic attractions. Finally, **Tepoztlán,** with its enigmatic charms and legendary pyramid, captivates the few travelers who find their way there.

1 Taxco: Cobblestones & Silver ★★

178km (111 miles) SW of Mexico City; 80km (50 miles) SW of Cuernavaca; 296km (185 miles) NE of Acapulco

In Mexico and around the world, the town of Taxco de Alarcón—most commonly known simply as Taxco (*tahs*-koh)—is synonymous with silver. The town's geography and architecture are equally precious: Taxco sits at nearly 1,515m (5,000 ft.) on a hill among hills, and almost any point in the city offers fantastic views.

Hernán Cortez discovered Taxco as he combed the area for treasure, but its rich caches of silver weren't fully exploited for another 2 centuries. In 1751, the French prospector Joseph de la Borda—who came to be known locally as José—commissioned the baroque Santa Prisca Church that dominates Taxco's *zócalo* (Plaza Borda) as a way of giving something back to the town. In the mid-1700s, Borda was considered the richest man in New Spain.

The fact that Taxco has become Mexico's most renowned center for silver design, even though it now mines only a small amount of silver, is the work of an American,

William Spratling. Spratling arrived in the late 1920s with the intention of writing a book. He soon noticed the skill of the local craftsmen and opened a workshop to produce handmade silver jewelry and tableware based on pre-Hispanic art, which he exported to the United States in bulk. The workshops flourished, and Taxco's reputation grew.

Today, most of the residents of this town are involved in the silver industry in some way. Taxco is home to hundreds (some say up to 900) of silver shops and outlets, ranging from sleek galleries to small stands in front of stucco homes. You'll find silver in all of its forms here—the jewelry basics, tea sets, silverware, candelabras, picture frames, and napkin holders.

The tiny one-man factories that line the cobbled streets all the way up into the hills supply most of Taxco's silverwork. "Bargains" are relative, but nowhere else will you find this combination of diversity, quality, and rock-bottom prices. Generally speaking, the larger shops that most obviously cater to the tourist trade will have the highest prices—but they may be the only ones to offer "that special something" you're looking for. For classic designs in jewelry or other silver items, shop around, and wander the back streets and smaller venues.

You can get an idea of what Taxco is like by spending an afternoon, but there's much more to this picturesque town of 120,000 than just the Plaza Borda and the shops surrounding it. Stay overnight, wander its steep cobblestone streets, and you'll discover little plazas, fine churches, and, of course, an abundance of silversmiths' shops.

The main part of town is relatively flat. It stretches up the hillside from the highway, and it's a steep but brief walk up. White VW minibuses, called *burritos,* make the circuit through and around town, picking up and dropping off passengers along the route, from about 7am until 9pm. These taxis are inexpensive (about 50¢), and you should use them even if you arrive by car, because parking is practically impossible. Also, the streets are so narrow and steep that most visitors find them nerve-racking. Find a secured parking lot for your car or leave it at your hotel, and forget about it until you leave.

Warning: Self-appointed guides will undoubtedly approach you in the *zócalo* (Plaza Borda) and offer their services—they get a cut (up to 25%) of all you buy in the shops they take you to. Before hiring a guide, ask to see his SECTUR (Tourism Secretary) credentials. The Department of Tourism office on the highway at the north end of town can recommend a licensed guide.

ESSENTIALS

GETTING THERE & DEPARTING   By Car   From Mexico City, take Paseo de la Reforma to Chapultepec Park and merge with the Periférico, which will take you to Highway 95D on the south end of town. From the Periférico, take the Insurgentes exit and merge until you come to the sign for Cuernavaca/Tlalpan. Choose either CUERNAVACA CUOTA (toll) or CUERNAVACA LIBRE (free). Continue south around Cuernavaca to the Amacuzac interchange, and proceed straight ahead for Taxco. The drive from Mexico City takes about 3½ hours.

From Acapulco you have two options: Highway 95D is the toll road through Iguala to Taxco, or you can take the old two-lane road (Hwy. 95) that winds more slowly through villages; it's in good condition.

By Bus   From Mexico City, buses depart from the Central de Autobuses del Sur station (Metro: Taxqueña) and take 2 to 3 hours, with frequent departures.

Side Trips from Mexico City

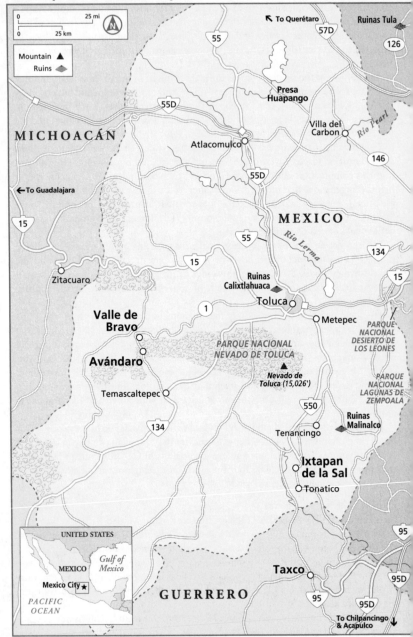

0 ____ 25 mi
0 ____ 25 km

Mountain ▲
Ruins ◈

↖ To Querétaro

Ruinas Tula

57D

126

55

Presa
Huapango

Villa del
Carbon

Río Pearl

MICHOACÁN

55D

Atlacomulco

146

55D

← To Guadalajara

MEXICO

15

55

Río Lerma

134

15

15

Zitacuaro

Ruinas
Calixtlahuaca

Toluca

Metepec

PARQUE
NACIONAL
DESIERTO DE
LOS LEONES

Valle de
Bravo

1

PARQUE NACIONAL
NEVADO DE TOLUCA

Avándaro

▲
Nevado de
Toluca (15,026')

PARQUE
NACIONAL
LAGUNAS DE
ZEMPOALA

Temascaltepec

550

Ruinas
Malinalco

134

Tenancingo

Ixtapan
de la Sal

Tonatico

95

UNITED STATES

Gulf of
Mexico

MEXICO

Mexico City ★

PACIFIC
OCEAN

GUERRERO

Taxco

95D

95

95D

To Chilpancingo
& Acapulco ↓

Spanish & Art Classes in Taxco

The **Universidad Nacional Autónoma de México (UNAM;** ✆ **762/622-0124** for the Spanish school, or 762/622-3690 for the art school) is on the grounds of the Hacienda del Chorrillo, formerly part of the Cortez land grant. Here, students learn silversmithing, Spanish, drawing, composition, and history under the supervision of UNAM instructors. Classes are small, and courses generally last 3 months. The school provides a list of prospective town accommodations that consist primarily of hotels. More reasonable accommodations for a lengthy stay are available, but best arranged once you're there. At many locations all over town, you'll find notices of furnished apartments or rooms for rent. For information about the school, contact either the Dirección de Turismo (tourist office) in Taxco (see "Visitor Information," above), or write the school directly at Hacienda del Chorrillo, 40200 Taxco, Gro.

Taxco has two bus stations. Estrella de Oro buses arrive at their own station on the southern edge of town. Estrella Blanca service, including *Futura* executive-class buses, and Flecha Roja buses arrive at the station on the northeastern edge of town on Avenida Los Plateros ("Avenue of the Silversmiths," formerly Av. Kennedy). Taxis to the *zócalo* cost around $2.

VISITOR INFORMATION The **State of Guerrero Dirección de Turismo** (✆/fax **762/622-6616** or 762/622-2274) has offices at the arches on the main highway at the north end of town (Av. de los Plateros 1), which is useful if you're driving into town. The office is open Monday through Friday from 8am to 3:30pm, and Saturday from 8am to noon. To get there from the Plaza Borda, take a ZOCALO-ARCOS *combi* and get off at the arch over the highway. As you face the arches, the tourism office is on your right.

CITY LAYOUT The center of town is the tiny **Plaza Borda,** shaded by perfectly manicured Indian laurel trees. On one side is the imposing twin-towered, pink-stone **Santa Prisca Church;** whitewashed, red-tile buildings housing the famous silver shops and a restaurant or two line the other sides. Beside the church, deep in a crevice of the mountain, is the **wholesale silver market**—absolutely the best place to begin your silver shopping, to get an idea of prices for more standard designs. You'll be amazed at the low prices. Buying just one piece is perfectly acceptable, and buying in bulk can lower the per-piece price. One of the beauties of Taxco is that its brick-paved and cobblestone streets are completely asymmetrical, zigzagging up and down the hillsides. The plaza buzzes with vendors of everything from hammocks and cotton candy to bark paintings and balloons.

FAST FACTS The telephone area code is **762.** The main post office, Benito Juárez 6, at the City Hall building (✆ **762/622-8596**), is open Monday through Friday from 9am to 3pm. The older branch of the post office (✆ **762/622-0501**) is on the outskirts, on the highway to Acapulco. It's in a row of shops with a black-and-white CORREO sign.

Taxco

To Mexico City, Cuernavaca,
Ixtapan de la Sal & Toluca ↑

Church ✝

HIDALGO

0   50 mi
0   50 km

MICHOACÁN

MEXICO

★ **Mexico City**

PUEBLA

MORELOS

GUERRERO   • **Taxco**

Tourism Office

Aqueduct

Avenida J.F. Kennedy

Calle la Garita

Punte Ramonet

0   330 feet
0   100 meters

Calle Reforma

Avenida J.F. Kennedy

✝ **Chavarrieta**

Ex Convento

✝ **Guadalupe**

Plazuela de Bernal   Calle Juan Ruiz de Alarcón   **3**   **4**

2

1 ■ **City Hall**

Plaza Borda

■ **Silver Museum**   **5**

Veracruz

Flecha Roja
■ **Bus Station**

7 ✝ **6**   Calle de la Veracruz & San Sebastián

Santa Prisca

8

Mercado de Artesanías

Calle San Agustín

Bank ■

Calle Santa Ana

Bank ■

Plazuela San Juan

Calle Cena Obscuras

Calle San Nicolás   **La Santisima** ✝

✝ **San Nicolás**

Calle San Miguel

9

✝ **San Miguel** ■

11 →

← **To Panoramic Road**

Calle Luis Montes de Oca

Estrella de Oro
■ **Bus Station**

12 →

10

↓ **To Ixateopan**

To Iguala & Acapulco →

ATTRACTIONS ●

Casa de la Cultura de Taxco (Casa Borda) **1**
Humboldt House/Museo Virreinal de Taxco **4**
Mercado Central **6**
Museo de Taxco Guillermo Spratling **5**
Santa Prisca y San Sebastián Church **7**
Wholesale Silver Market **8**
Workshops: Los Castillo & Spratling **12**

ACCOMMODATIONS ■

Hacienda del Solar **11**
Hotel Los Arcos **2**
Hotel Posada Emilia Castillo **3**
Hotel Santa Prisca **9**
Hotel Victoria **10**

EXPLORING TAXCO

Shopping for jewelry and other items is the major pastime for tourists. Prices for silver jewelry at Taxco's shops are about the best in the world, and everything is available, from $1 trinkets to artistic pieces costing hundreds of dollars.

In addition, Taxco is the home of some of Mexico's finest stone sculptors and is a good place to buy masks. However, beware of so-called "antiques"—there are virtually no real ones for sale.

Viajes Sibely, Miguel Hidalgo 24 (✆/fax **762/622-8080** or 762/622-3808), offers daily tours to the Cacahuamilpa Caves and the ruins of Xochicalco for $59, including transportation, ticket, and the services of a guide. It also sells bus tickets to Acapulco, Chilpancingo, Iguala, and Cuernavaca. The agency is to the left of La Hamburguesa. Another agency offering similar services is **Turismo Garlum,** next to the Santa Prisca Church (✆ **762/622-3021** or 762/627-3500). It offers daily tours to the Cacahuamilpa Caves and the Santa Prisca Church for $18, which includes transportation, ticket, and the services of a guide. Both agencies are open Monday trough Friday from 9am to 7pm and Saturday from 9am to 2pm.

SPECIAL EVENTS & FESTIVALS   January 18 marks the annual celebration in honor of Santa Prisca, with public festivities and fireworks displays. **Holy Week** 🤿🤿 in Taxco is one of the most poignant in the country, beginning the Friday a week before Easter with processions daily and nightly. The most riveting, on Thursday evening, lasts almost 4 hours and includes villagers from the surrounding area carrying statues of saints, followed by hooded members of a society of self-flagellating penitents, chained at the ankles and carrying huge wooden crosses and bundles of thorny branches. On Saturday morning, the Plaza Borda fills for the **Procession of Three Falls,** reenacting the three times Christ stumbled and fell while carrying the cross.

Taxco's **Silver Fair** starts the last week in November and continues through the first week in December. It includes a competition for silver works and sculptures among the top silversmiths. At the same time, **Jornadas Alarconianas** features plays and literary events in honor of Juan Ruiz de Alarcón (1572–1639), a world-famous dramatist who was born in Taxco—and for whom Taxco de Alarcón is named. Art exhibits, street fairs, and other festivities are part of the dual celebration.

SIGHTS IN TOWN

Casa de la Cultura de Taxco (Casa Borda)   Diagonally across from the Santa Prisca Church and facing Plaza Borda is the home José de la Borda built for his son around 1759. Now the Guerrero State Cultural Center, it houses classrooms and exhibit halls where period clothing, engravings, paintings, and crafts are on display. The center also books traveling exhibits.

Plaza Borda 1. ✆ **762/622-6617** or 762/622-6632. Fax 762/662-6634. Free admission. Tues–Sun 10am–5pm.

Humboldt House/Museo Virreinal de Taxco   Stroll along Ruiz de Alarcón (the street behind the Casa Borda) and look for the richly decorated facade of the Humboldt House, where the renowned German scientist and explorer Baron Alexander von Humboldt (1769–1859) spent a night in 1803. The museum houses 18th-century memorabilia pertinent to Taxco, most of which came from a secret room discovered during the recent restoration of the Santa Prisca Church. Signs with detailed information are in Spanish and English. As you enter, to the right are very rare *tumelos* (three-tiered funerary paintings). The bottom two were painted in honor of Charles III of

Spain; the top one, with a carved phoenix on top, was supposedly painted for the funeral of José de la Borda.

Another section presents historical information about Don Miguel Cabrera, Mexico's foremost 18th-century artist. Fine examples of clerical garments decorated with gold and silver thread hang in glass cases. Excellently restored Cabrera paintings hang throughout the museum. And, of course, a small room is devoted to Humboldt and his sojourns through South America and Mexico.

Calle Juan Ruiz de Alarcón 12. ☎ 762/622-5501. Admission $2 adults, $1.50 students and teachers with ID. Tues–Sat 10am–5pm; Sun 10am–3pm.

Mercado Central   Located to the right of the Santa Prisca Church, behind and below Berta's, Taxco's central market meanders deep inside the mountain. Take the stairs off the street. In addition to a collection of wholesale silver shops, you'll find numerous food stands, always the best place for a cheap meal.

Plaza Borda. Shops daily 10am–8pm; food stands daily 7am–6pm.

Museo Arqueológico Guillermo Spratling   A plaque in Spanish explains that most of the collection of pre-Columbian art displayed here, as well as the funds for the museum, came from William Spratling. You'd expect this to be a silver museum, but it's not—for Spratling silver, go to the Spratling Ranch Workshop (see "Nearby Attractions," below). The entrance floor and the one above display a good collection of pre-Columbian statues and implements in clay, stone, and jade. The lower floor holds changing exhibits.

Calle Porfirio A. Delgado 1. ☎ 762/622-1660. Admission $3 adults, free for children under 12; free to all Sun. Tues–Sat 9am–6pm; Sun 9am–3pm. Leaving Santa Prisca Church, turn right and right again at the corner; continue down the street, veer right, then immediately left. The museum will be facing you.

Santa Prisca y San Sebastián Church ★★   This is Taxco's centerpiece parish church; it faces the pleasant Plaza Borda. José de la Borda, a French miner who struck it rich in Taxco's silver mines, funded the construction. Completed in 1758, it's one of Mexico's most impressive baroque churches. The ultracarved facade is eclipsed by the interior, where the intricacy of the gold-leafed saints and cherubic angels is positively breathtaking. The paintings by Miguel Cabrera, one of Mexico's most famous colonial-era artists, are the pride of Taxco. The sacristy (behind the high altar) contains more Cabrera paintings.

Guides, both children and adults, will approach you outside the church offering to give a tour. Make sure the guide's English is passable, and establish whether the price is per person or per tour.

Plaza Borda. ☎ 762/622-0184. Free admission. Daily 6:30am–8pm.

Silver Museum   The Silver Museum, operated by a local silversmith, is a relatively recent addition to Taxco. After entering the building next to Santa Prisca (upstairs is Sr. Costilla's restaurant; p. 164), look for a sign on the left; the museum is downstairs. It's not a traditional public museum; nevertheless, it does the much-needed job of describing the history of silver in Mexico and Taxco, as well as displaying some historic and contemporary award-winning pieces. Time spent here seeing quality silver work will make you a more discerning shopper. At press time, it was in the process of upgrading the exhibits.

Plaza Borda 1. ☎ 762/622-0658. Admission $1. Daily 10am–5:30pm.

NEARBY ATTRACTIONS

The impressive **Grutas de Cacahuamilpa** ✦, known as the Cacahuamilpa Caves or Grottoes (© **734/346-1716**), are 20 minutes north of Taxco. Hourly guided tours run daily at the caverns, which are truly sensational and well worth the visit. To see them, you can join a tour from Taxco (see "Exploring Taxco," above) or take a *combi* from the Flecha Roja terminal in Taxco; the one-way fare is $2.50. For more information, see "Sights near Tepoztlán," later in this chapter.

Los Castillo   Don Antonio Castillo was one of hundreds of young men to whom William Spratling taught silversmithing in the 1930s. He was also one of the first to branch out with his own shops and line of designs, which over the years have earned him a fine reputation. Castillo has shops in several Mexican cities. Now, his daughter Emilia creates her own noteworthy designs, including decorative pieces with silver fused onto porcelain. Emilia's work is for sale on the ground floor of the Posada de los Castillo, just below the Plazuela Bernal.

8km (5 miles) south of town on the Acapulco Hwy. Also at Plazuela Bernal, Taxco. © **762/622-1016** or ©/fax 762/622-1988 (workshop). Free admission. Workshop Mon–Fri 8am–2pm and 3–6pm; open to groups at other hours by appointment only.

Spratling Ranch Workshop   William Spratling's hacienda-style home and workshop on the outskirts of Taxco still bustles with busy hands reproducing unique designs. A trip here will show you what distinctive Spratling work was all about, for the designs crafted today show the same fine work. Although the prices are higher than at other outlets, the designs are unusual and considered collectible. There's no store in Taxco, and unfortunately, most of the display cases hold only samples. With the exception of a few jewelry pieces, most items are by order only. Ask about U.S. outlets.

10km (6 miles) south of town on the Acapulco Hwy. No phone. Free admission. Mon–Sat 9am–5pm. The *combi* to Iguala stops at the ranch; fare is 70¢.

WHERE TO STAY
MODERATE
Hacienda del Solar ✦✦   This hotel comprises several Mexican-style cottages, all on a beautifully landscaped hilltop with magnificent views of the surrounding valleys and the town. The decor is slightly different in each cottage, but most contain lots of beautiful handicrafts, red-tile floors, and bathrooms with handmade tiles. Several rooms have vaulted tile ceilings and private terraces. Others come equipped with more modern amenities, like televisions. Standard rooms have no terraces and only showers in the bathrooms; deluxe rooms have sunken tubs (with showers) and terraces. Junior suites are the largest and most luxurious accommodations. All rooms are priced the same, so if you want one of the larger ones (suites), make sure to ask for it when you check in.

Paraje del Solar s/n (Apdo. Postal 96), 40200 Taxco, Gro. (©/fax **762/622-0587**). 22 units. $120 double. Take Hwy. 95 toward Acapulco 4km (2½ miles) south of the town center; look for signs on the left and go straight down a narrow road until you see the hotel entrance. **Amenities:** Restaurant (w/spectacular city view; see "Where to Dine," below); heated outdoor pool; tennis court; travel desk; room service; laundry service.

INEXPENSIVE
Hotel los Arcos ✦   Los Arcos occupies a converted 1620 monastery. The handsome inner patio is bedecked with Puebla pottery surrounding a central fountain. The rooms are nicely but sparsely appointed, with natural tile floors and colonial-style furniture.

You'll feel immersed in colonial charm and blissful quiet. To find the hotel from the Plaza Borda, follow the hill down (with Hotel Agua Escondida on your left) and make an immediate right at the Plazuela Bernal; the hotel is a block down on the left, opposite the Hotel Posada (see below).

Juan Ruiz de Alarcón 4, 40200 Taxco, Gro. © **762/622-1836.** Fax 762/622-7982. 21 units. $35 double; $40 triple; $45 quad; $50 junior suite. No credit cards. **Amenities:** Tour desk.

Hotel Posada Emilia Castillo ⚑   Each room in this delightful small hotel is simply but beautifully appointed with handsome carved doors and furniture; bathrooms have either tubs or showers. The manager, Don Teodoro Contreras Galindo, is a true gentleman and a fountain of information about Taxco.

Juan Ruiz de Alarcón 7, 40200 Taxco, Gro. ©/fax **762/622-1396.** 15 units. $30 double; $40 double with TV. MC, V. From the Plaza Borda, go downhill a short block to the Plazuela Bernal and make an immediate right; the hotel is a block farther on the right, opposite the Hotel los Arcos (see above). *In room:* TV.

Hotel Santa Prisca ⚑⚑ *(Value)*   The Santa Prisca, 1 block from the Plaza Borda on the Plazuela San Juan, is one of the older and nicer hotels in town. Rooms are small but comfortable, with standard bathrooms (showers only), tile floors, wood beams, and a colonial atmosphere. For longer stays, ask for a room in the adjacent new addition, where the rooms are sunnier, quieter, and more spacious. There is a reading area in an upstairs salon overlooking Taxco, as well as a lush patio with fountains.

Cenaobscuras 1, 40200 Taxco, Gro. © **762/622-0080** or 762/622-0980. Fax 762/622-2938. 34 units. $46 double; $52 superior double; $64 suite. AE, MC, V. Limited free parking. **Amenities:** Dining-room-style restaurant and bar; room service; laundry service; safe-deposit boxes.

Hotel Victoria ⚑⚑   The Victoria clings to the hillside above town, with stunning views from its flower-covered verandas. It exudes the charm of old-fashioned Mexico. The comfortable furnishings, though slightly run-down, evoke the hotel's 1940s heyday. In front of each standard room, a table and chairs sit out on the tiled common walkway. Each deluxe room has a private terrace; each junior suite has a bedroom, a nicely furnished large living room, and a spacious private terrace overlooking the city. Deluxe rooms and junior suites have TVs. Even if you don't stay here, come for a drink in the comfortable bar and living room, or sit on the terrace to take in the fabulous view. Formerly known as Rancho Taxco Victoria, the hotel underwent a change in management in 2002.

Carlos J. Nibbi 5 and 7 (Apdo. Postal 83), 40200 Taxco, Gro. © **762/622-0004.** Fax 762/622-0010. 63 units. $55 standard double; $89 deluxe double; $100 junior suite. AE, MC, V. Free parking. From the Plazuela San Juan, go up Carlos J. Nibbi, a narrow, winding cobbled street. The hotel is at the top of the hill. **Amenities:** Restaurant; bar; small outdoor pool.

WHERE TO DINE

Taxco gets a lot of day-trippers, most of whom choose to dine close to the Plaza Borda. Prices in this area are high for what you get. Just a few streets back, you'll find some excellent, simple *fondas* (tavern) or restaurants.

VERY EXPENSIVE

Toni's ⚑ STEAKS/SEAFOOD   High on a mountaintop, Toni's is an intimate, classic restaurant enclosed in a huge, cone-shaped *palapa* with a panoramic view of the city. Eleven candlelit tables sparkle with crystal and crisp linen. The menu, mainly shrimp or beef, is limited, but the food is superior. Try tender, juicy prime roast beef, which comes with Yorkshire pudding, creamed spinach, and baked potato. Lobster is sometimes available. To reach Toni's, it's best to take a taxi. Note that it's open for dinner only.

In the Hotel Monte Taxco. ✆ 762/622-1300. Reservations recommended. Main courses $14–$22. AE, MC, V. Mon–Sat 7pm–1am.

MODERATE

Café Sasha ⟨⟨ INTERNATIONAL/VEGETARIAN   One of the cutest places to dine in town, Café Sasha is very popular with locals, and offers a great array of vegetarian options—like falafel and vegetarian curries, as well as Mexican and international classics. Try their Thai chicken or a hearty burrito. Open for breakfast, lunch, and dinner, it's also a great place for a cappuccino and pastry, or an evening cocktail. The music is hip, and the atmosphere inviting and chic. Local artists often exhibit here.

Calle Juan Ruiz de Alarcón 1, just down from Plazuela de Berna. No phone. cafesasha@hotmail.com. Breakfast $2–$7; main courses $5–$15. No credit cards. Daily 8am–11:30pm.

La Terraza Café-Bar INTERNATIONAL   One of two restaurants at the Hotel Agua Esondida (on the *zócalo*), the rooftop La Terraza is a popular place for lunch, with wonderful views and tasty food. The menu is ample—there's something for every taste—as well as classic Mexican dishes. You can get anything from soup to roast chicken, enchiladas, tacos, steak, and dessert, as well as frosty margaritas or a great cappuccino. During the day, cafe umbrellas shade the sun, but you can stargaze at night here.

Plaza Borda 4. ✆ 762/622-0663. Main courses $7.50–$14. MC, V. Daily noon–10pm.

La Ventana de Taxco ⟨ ITALIAN   The spectacular view of the city from this restaurant makes it one of the best places to dine in Taxco. The changing menu of standard Italian fare is also quite good. The pasta dishes are the most recommendable. Lasagna is a big favorite, and Sicilian steak is also popular.

In the Hacienda del Solar hotel, Paraje del Solar s/n. ✆/fax 762/622-0587. Breakfast $3–$7; main courses $10–$20. MC, V. Daily 8–11am and 1–10:30pm.

Sotavento Restaurant Bar Galería ⟨⟨ ITALIAN/INTERNATIONAL   Paintings decorate the walls of this stylish restaurant, and a variety of linen colors dot the tables. The menu features many Italian specialties—try deliciously fresh spinach salad and large pepper steak for a hearty meal, or Spaghetti Bárbara, with poblano peppers and avocado, for a vegetarian option.

Juárez 8, next to City Hall. No phone. Main courses $3–$8. No credit cards. Tues–Sun 1pm–midnight. From the Plaza Borda, walk downhill beside the Hotel Agua Escondida, then follow the street as it bears left (don't go right on Juan Ruiz de Alarcón) about 1 block. The restaurant is on the left just after the street bends left.

Sr. Costilla's MEXICAN/INTERNATIONAL   The offbeat decor at "Mr. Ribs" includes a ceiling decked out with an assortment of cultural curios. Several tiny balconies hold a few minuscule tables that afford a view of the plaza and church, and they fill up long before the large dining room does. The menu is typical of Carlos Anderson chain restaurants, with Spanglish sayings and a large selection of everything from soup, steaks, sandwiches, and spareribs to desserts and coffee. The restaurant serves wine, beer, and drinks.

Plaza Borda 1 (next to Santa Prisca, above Patio de las Artesanías). ✆/fax 762/622-3215. Main courses $8–$20. MC, V. Daily noon–midnight.

INEXPENSIVE

Fonda Ethel MEXICAN/INTERNATIONAL   This family-run place is opposite the Hotel Santa Prisca, 1 block from the Plaza Borda. It has colorful cloths on the tables and a tidy, homey atmosphere. The hearty *comida corrida* consists of soup or pasta, meat (perhaps a small steak), dessert, and good coffee.

Plazuela San Juan 14. (*C*) 762/622-0788. Breakfast $4.45–$5.55; main courses $5.15–$6.30; *comida corrida* (served 1–5pm) $5.80. No credit cards. Daily 9am–9pm.

TAXCO AFTER DARK

Paco's (no phone) is the most popular place overlooking the square for cocktails, conversation, and people-watching, all of which continue until midnight daily. Taxco's version of a disco, **Windows,** is high up the mountain in the **Hotel Monte Taxco** (*C* 762/622-1300). The whole city is on view, and music runs the gamut from the hit parade to hard rock. For a cover of $7, you can dance away Saturday night from 10pm to 3am.

Completely different in tone is **Berta's** (no phone), next to the Santa Prisca Church. Opened in 1930 by a lady named Berta, who made her fame on a drink of the same name (tequila, soda, lime, and honey), it's the traditional gathering place of the local gentry and more than a few tourists. Spurs and old swords decorate the walls. A Berta (the drink, of course) costs about $2; rum, the same. It's open daily from 11am to around 10pm.

National drinks (not beer) are two-for-one nightly between 6 and 8pm at the terrace bar of the **Hotel Victoria** (*C* 762/622-0004), where you can also drink in the fabulous view. The gay-friendly **Aztec Disco** (*C* 762/627-3833) features drag shows and dancing. It's located at Av. de los Plateros 184, and is open from 10pm until late.

2 Ixtapan de la Sal: A Thermal Spa Town

120km (75 miles) SW of Mexico City

The whitewashed town of Ixtapan de la Sal (not to be confused with Ixtapa, on the Pacific coast) is known for its thermal mud baths—this is an original spa town, with generations of healing traditions.

Hotels in Ixtapan (pronounced "*eeks*-tah-pahn") de la Sal tend to be full on weekends and Mexican holidays, as the town is a popular retreat from Mexico City. Cuernavaca, Taxco, and Toluca are all easy side trips.

ESSENTIALS

GETTING THERE & DEPARTING   By Car   From Mexico City, take Highway 15 to Toluca. In Toluca, Highway 15 becomes Paseo Tollocan. Follow Tollocan south until you see signs pointing left to Ixtapan de la Sal. After the turn, continue straight for around 16km (10 miles). Just before the town of Tenango del Valle, you have a choice of the free road to Ixtapan de la Sal or the toll road. The free road winds through the mountains and takes 1½ hours. The inexpensive two-lane toll road has fewer mountain curves and takes around an hour—it's worth taking. The toll road stops about 16km (10 miles) before Ixtapan; the rest of the trip is on a curvy mountainous drive.

By Bus   From Mexico City's Terminal Poniente, buses leave for Ixtapan de la Sal every few minutes. Request a bus that's taking the toll road, which cuts the travel time by 30 to 60 minutes, to about 2½ hours. To return, take a bus marked MEXICO DIRECTO, which leaves every 10 minutes and usually stops in Toluca. Buses from here also go to Cuernavaca and Taxco every 40 minutes.

A PUBLIC SPA

The **Balneario Ixtapan** (© 721/143-0331), next to the Hotel Spa Ixtapan, is the town's original public spa and bathhouse. It's not a modern, pampering spa, but a spa in the traditional manner—think Turkish baths. Over the years, the *balneario* has melded its traditional thermal waters with some features that make it more of an aquatic park. In addition to the large pools of varying temperatures, it offers modern features such as water slides, a slow-moving river, and other attractions. Entrance is $14 for adults, $6 for children between .9 and 1.2m (3–4 ft.) tall; children under .9m (3 ft.) tall enter free. The *balneario* has restaurants, so you can spend the day. The entrance fee gives you access to all of the pools and rides. Lockers are 50¢ and dressers are $1. Open daily from 7am to 7pm. The traditional spa amenities and services are next door, where you can take private thermal water baths or choose among massages, facials, hair treatments, paraffin wraps, pedicures, and manicures. Prices range from $15 to $50. When you purchase a spa treatment you can include access to the *balneario* for $6. The spa is open daily from 7am to 8pm during holiday periods; at other times, Monday through Friday from 8am to 8pm, Saturday and Sunday from 7am to 8pm. For a spa menu, call Sra. Silvia Rivas at © **55/5254-0500.**

WHERE TO STAY & DINE

Hotel Spa Ixtapan ✿✿ (Value The town's only first-class hotel sits on 14 manicured and flower-filled hectares (35 acres). It's been in operation since 1939, and though it's continually upgraded, some areas that have been left untouched provide guests with the nostalgic feel of the original resort. When you compare this spa's comfort, weight-loss programs, good food, and relaxing pace to the offering at other spas, you'll understand its continued popularity. It's one of the best spa values in Mexico, although very expensive for Ixtapan. The resort offers golf, tennis, riding, swimming, and miles of trails for walking, jogging, or biking. It also has freshwater and thermal mineral swimming pools, an outdoor whirlpool, and a host of spa facilities for body treatments. The guest rooms are large, comfortable, and stylishly furnished. You have your choice of two dining areas. One serves a menu geared for weight loss, with vegetarian options; the other offers a more traditional international menu. The hotel offers first-run movies, classical concerts, and folkloric ballet and live musical performances. The spa week goes from Monday to Friday, with Sunday arrival preferred. Spa facilities are closed on Sunday. Hotel guests not on the spa program can use the facilities on a per-treatment basis, and there's no daily admission charge. Round-trip taxi transportation from the Mexico City airport can be arranged at the time of reservation for around $260, which can be shared by up to four people. There are about 10 different package options.

Bulevar San Román s/n, Ixtapan de la Sal, 51900 Edo. de México. © **800/638-7950** in the U.S., or 721/143-2440. Fax 721/143-0856. www.spamexico.com. 220 units, including 45 villas. $150 double or villa. 4-day spa package $701 per person double; 7-day spa package $1,247 per person double; 21-day spa package $3,853 per person double; 28-day spa package $4,140 per person double. Rates include meals. AE, MC, V. **Amenities:** 2 dining rooms; private 18-hole golf course; 2 tennis courts; full-service spa w/fully equipped gym, aerobics room and classes, steam room, solarium, 2 indoor whirlpools, 2 outdoor pools, sauna; mountain bikes; tour desk; Internet room; room service; laundry service; hiking trails. *In room:* TV, minibar.

Ixtapan de la Sal

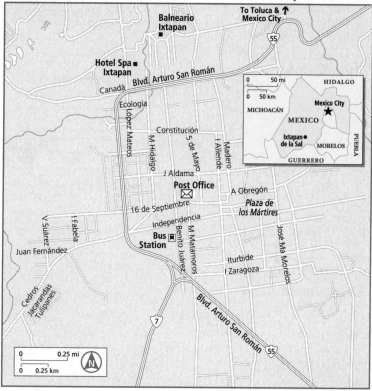

3 Valle de Bravo & Avándaro: Mexico's Switzerland

152km (95 miles) SW of Mexico City

At 1,040m (6,070 ft.), Valle de Bravo has aptly been called the "Switzerland of Mexico." Ringed by pine-forested mountains and set beside a beautiful man-made lake, Valle de Bravo is a 16th-century village with cobblestone streets and colonial structures built around a town plaza. Like San Miguel de Allende, Taxco, and Puerto Vallarta, Valle de Bravo is a National Heritage village; new construction must conform to the colonial style of the original village.

The village's cobbled streets, small restaurants, hotels, spas, and shops are full on weekends—this is a very popular retreat from Mexico City. Some shops and restaurants may be closed weekdays. The crafts market, 3 blocks from the main square, is open daily from 10am to 5pm, and colorfully dressed Mazahua Indians sell their handmade tapestries daily around the town plaza.

Sailing, windsurfing, bass fishing, and water-skiing are popular on the lake. Excursions from here include a trip to the nesting grounds of the monarch butterfly between November and February. It can be very rainy and chilly September through December, in addition to the summer rainy season.

Valle de Bravo & Avándaro

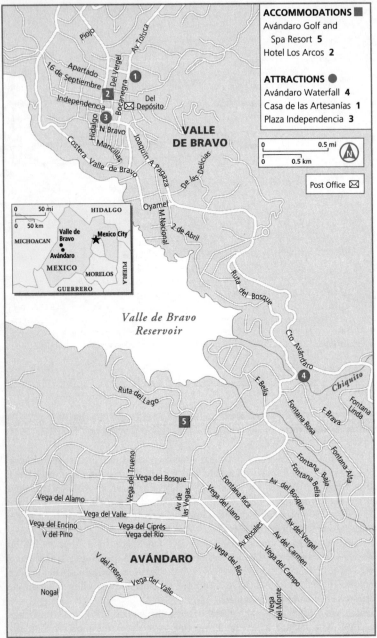

ACCOMMODATIONS ■
Avándaro Golf and
  Spa Resort **5**
Hotel Los Arcos **2**

ATTRACTIONS ●
Avándaro Waterfall **4**
Casa de las Artesanías **1**
Plaza Independencia **3**

Post Office ⊠

VALLE
DE BRAVO

Valle de Bravo
Reservoir

HIDALGO
MICHOACAN
Valle de
Bravo
Mexico City
Avándaro
MEXICO
MORELOS
PUEBLA
GUERRERO

AVÁNDARO

The neighboring town of Avándaro, 6km (4 miles) away, is a popular place for weekend homes for well-to-do residents of Mexico City.

ESSENTIALS

GETTING THERE & DEPARTING **By Car** From Mexico City, the quickest and most direct route is Highway 15 to Toluca. In Toluca, Highway 15 becomes Paseo Tollocan. Follow Tollocan south until you see signs pointing left to Highway 134 and Valle de Bravo, Francisco de los Ranchos, and Temascaltepec. After the turn, continue on Highway 142 until Francisco de los Ranchos, where you bear right, following signs to Valle de Bravo. The drive from this point takes about 1½ to 2 hours.

By Bus From Mexico City's Terminal Poniente, buses leave every 20 minutes for the 3-hour journey. First-class buses depart hourly.

WHERE TO STAY & DINE

Avándaro Golf and Spa Resort ★★ Nestled on 118 hectares (296 acres) amid large estates, lushly forested mountains, and a gorgeous, rolling 18-hole golf course, this resort occupies one of the loveliest settings in Mexico. Rooms come in two categories: large, beautifully furnished deluxe suites, and small, less luxurious cabañas. All have fireplaces and terraces or balconies overlooking the grounds, and all were upgraded in 2000 and 2001. Transportation from Mexico City can be arranged.

Fraccionamiento Avándaro, 51200 Valle de Bravo, Edificio de México. ⓒ 726/266-1651; reservations 555/280-1532, 555/282-0954, 555/280-5532, or 555/282-0578 in Mexico City. www.grupoavandaro.com.mx. 82 units. $167 double cabaña; $400 deluxe suite. 7-day spa or golf package available. AE, MC, V. **Amenities:** 2 restaurants; 25m (80-ft.) junior Olympic-size pool; 18-hole golf course; 7 tennis courts; weight-training equipment; ultramodern spa w/well-trained staff and full range of services, including massage, wraps, facials, aerobics, exercise classes, and body treatments; hot and cold whirlpools; sauna; steam rooms; room service. *In room:* TV, hair dryer, safe-deposit box.

Hotel los Arcos The Hotel los Arcos, close to the main square, has views of the village and mountains. Two stories of rooms on one side and three stories on the other surround a swimming pool. Nineteen rooms have fireplaces, an important feature in winter here. Some rooms have balconies, and most have glass walls with views.

Bocanegra 310, 51200 Valle de Bravo, Edificio de México. ⓒ/fax 726/262-0042, 726/262-0531, or 726/262-0168. 24 units. Mon–Thurs $71–$96 double; Fri–Sun $115–$135 double. AE, MC, V. **Amenities:** Restaurant/bar; outdoor pool. *In room:* TV.

---

4 Cuernavaca: Land of Eternal Spring ★★★

102km (64 miles) S of Mexico City; 80km (50 miles) N of Taxco

Often called the "land of eternal spring," Cuernavaca is known these days as much for its rejuvenating spas and spiritual sites as it is for its perfect climate and flowering landscapes. Spa services are easy to find, but more than that, Cuernavaca exudes a sense of deep connection with its historical and spiritual heritage. Its palaces, walled villas, and elaborate haciendas are home to museums, spas, and extraordinary guesthouses.

Wander the traditional markets and you'll see crystals, quartz, onyx, and tiger's eye, in addition to tourist trinkets. These stones come from the Tepozteco Mountains— for centuries considered an energy source—which cradle Cuernavaca to the north and east. This area is where Mexico begins to narrow, and several mountain ranges converge. East and southeast of Cuernavaca are two volcanoes, also potent symbols of

Cuernavaca

earth energy, Ixaccihuatl (the Sleeping Woman) and the recently active Popocatépetl (the Smoking Mountain).

Cuernavaca, capital of the state of Morelos, is also a cultural treasure, with a past that closely follows the history of Mexico. So divine are the landscape and climate that both the Aztec ruler Moctezuma and colonial Emperor Maximilian built private retreats here. Today, the roads between Mexico City and Cuernavaca are jammed almost every weekend, when city residents seek the same respite. Cuernavaca even has a large American colony, plus many students attending the numerous language and cultural institutes.

Emperor Charles V gave Cuernavaca to Hernán Cortez as a fief, and in 1532 the conquistador built a palace (now the Museo de Cuauhnahuac), where he lived on and off for half a dozen years before returning to Spain. Cortez introduced sugar cane cultivation to the area, and African slaves were brought in to work in the cane fields, by way of Spain's Caribbean colonies. His sugar hacienda at the edge of town is now the impressive Hotel de Cortez.

After Mexico gained independence from Spain, powerful landowners from Mexico City gradually dispossessed the remaining small landholders, imposing virtual serfdom on them. This condition led to the rise of Emiliano Zapata, the great champion of agrarian reform, who battled the forces of wealth and power, defending the small farmer with the cry of *"¡Tierra y Libertad!"* (Land and Liberty!) during the Mexican Revolution following 1910.

Today, Cuernavaca's popularity has brought an influx of wealthy foreigners and industrial capital. With this commercial growth, the city has also acquired the less desirable by-products of increased traffic, noise, and air pollution.

ESSENTIALS

GETTING THERE & DEPARTING   By Car   From Mexico City, take Paseo de la Reforma to Chapultepec Park and merge with the Periférico, which will take you to Highway 95D, the toll road on the far south of town that goes to Cuernavaca. From the Periférico, take the Insurgentes exit and continue until you come to signs for Cuernavaca/Tlalpan. Choose either the CUERNAVACA CUOTA (toll) or CUERNAVACA LIBRE (free) road on the right. The free road is slower and very windy, but is more scenic.

By Bus   *Important note:* Buses to Cuernavaca depart directly from the Mexico City airport. (See "Getting There," in chapter 2, for details.) The trip takes an hour. The Mexico City Central de Autobuses del Sur exists primarily to serve the Mexico City–Cuernavaca–Taxco–Acapulco–Zihuatanejo route. Pullman has two stations in Cuernavaca: downtown, at the corner of Abasolo and Netzahualcoyotl (© 777/318-0907 or 777/312-6063), 4 blocks south of the center of town; and Casino de la Selva (© 777/312-9473), less conveniently located at Plan de Ayala 14, near the railroad station.

Autobuses Estrella Blanca, Elite, Futura, and Flecha Roja also depart from the Central del Sur (© 777/312-2626), with 33 buses daily from Mexico City. They arrive in Cuernavaca at Morelos 329, between Arista and Victoria, 6 blocks north of the town center. Here, you'll find frequent buses to Toluca, Chalma, Ixtapan de la Sal, Taxco, Acapulco, the Cacahuamilpa Caves, Querétaro, and Nuevo Laredo.

Estrella de Oro (© 777/312-3055), Morelos 900, serves Iguala, Chilpancingo, Acapulco, and Taxco.

Estrella Roja (© 777/318-5934), a second-class station at Galeana and Cuauhtemotzin in Cuernavaca, about 8 blocks south of the town center, serves Cuautla, Yautepec, Oaxtepec, and Izúcar de Matamoros.

VISITOR INFORMATION   Cuernavaca's **State Tourist Office** is at Av. Morelos Sur 187, between Jalisco and Tabasco (© 777/314-3881; ©/fax 777/314-3872 or 777/314-3920; www.morelostravel.com), half a block north of the Estrella de Oro bus station and about a 15- to 20-minute walk south of the cathedral. It's open Monday through Friday from 8am to 5pm. There's also a **City Tourism kiosk** (© 777/318-7561 or 777/318-6498), on Morelos beside the El Calvario Church. It's open daily from 8am to 5pm.

CITY LAYOUT   In the center of the city are two contiguous plazas. The smaller and more formal, across from the post office, has a Victorian gazebo (designed by Gustave Eiffel, of Eiffel Tower fame) at its center. This is the **Alameda.** The larger, rectangular plaza with trees, shrubs, and benches is the **Plaza de Armas.** These two plazas are known collectively as the *zócalo* and form the hub for strolling vendors selling balloons, baskets, bracelets, and other crafts from surrounding villages. It's all easy-going, and one of the great pleasures of the town is hanging out at a park bench or table in a nearby restaurant. On Sunday afternoons, orchestras play in the gazebo. At the eastern end of the Alameda is the **Cortez Palace,** the conquistador's residence, now the Museo de Cuauhnahuac.

Note: The city's street-numbering system is extremely confusing. It appears that the city fathers, during the past century or so, imposed a new numbering system every 10 or 20 years. An address given as "no. 5" may be in a building that bears the number "506," or perhaps "Antes no. 5" (former no. 5).

FAST FACTS: Cuernavaca

American Express   The local representative is **Viajes Marín,** Edificio las Plazas, Loc. 13 (© **777/314-2266** or 777/318-9901; fax 777/312-9297). It's open daily from 9am to 2pm and 4 to 7pm.

Area Code   The telephone area code is **777.**

Banks   Bank tellers (9am–3 or 5pm, depending on the bank), ATMs, and *casas de cambio* change money. The closest bank to the *zócalo* is **Bancomer,** Matamoros and Lerdo de Tejada, cater-cornered to Jardín Juárez (across López Rayón from the Alameda). Most banks are open until 6pm Monday through Friday and a half-day on Saturday.

Elevation   Cuernavaca sits at 1,533m (5,058 ft.).

Hospital   **Clínica Londres,** Calle Cuauhtémoc 305, Col. Lomas de la Selva (© 777/311-2482, -2483, or -2484).

Internet Access   **Café Internet Net-Conn,** Morelos Norte 360-A, Col. Carolina (© **777/317-9496**), offers high-speed access for $2.50 per hour, as well as color laser printers, Web cams, scanners, and other equipment. They also serve coffee, and have an adjoining bookstore. It's open Monday through Saturday from 8am to 11pm, closed Sunday.

Pharmacy   **Farmacias del Ahorro** (© 777/322-2277) offers hotel delivery service, but you must ask the front desk of your hotel to place the order, because the pharmacy requires the name of a hotel employee. It has 12 locations around the city, but the individual pharmacies have no phone. They are open daily from 7am to 8pm.

Population   Cuernavaca has 400,000 residents.

Post Office   The *correo* (© 777/312-4379) is on the Plaza de Armas, next door to Café los Arcos. It's open Monday through Friday from 8am to 6pm, Saturday from 9am to 1pm.

Spanish Lessons   Cuernavaca is known for its Spanish-language schools. Generally, the schools will help students find lodging with a family or provide a list of places to stay. Rather than make a long-term commitment in a family living situation, try it for a week, then decide. Contact the **Center for Bilingual Multicultural Studies,** San Jerónimo 304 (Apdo. Postal 1520), 62000 Cuernavaca, Morelos (© 777/317-1087 or 777/317-2488, www.spanish.com.mx); **Instituto de Idioma y Cultura en Cuernavaca** (© 777/317-8947; fax 777/317-0455); or **Universal Centro de Lengua y Comunicación Social A.C. (Universal Language School),** J. H. Preciado 171 (Apdo. Postal 1-1826), 62000 Cuernavaca, Morelos (© 777/318-2904 or 777/312-4902; www.universal-spanish.com). Note that the whole experience, from classes to lodging, can be quite expensive; the school may accept credit cards for the class portion.

EXPLORING CUERNAVACA

On weekends, the whole city (including the roads, hotels, and restaurants) fills with people from Mexico City. This makes weekends more hectic, but also more fun. You can spend 1 or 2 days sightseeing pleasantly enough. If you've come on a day trip, you may not have time to make all the excursions listed below, but you'll have enough time to see the sights in town. Also notable is the traditional *mercado* **(public market)** adjacent to the Cortez Palace. It's open daily from 10am to 10pm, and the colorful rows of stands are a lively place for testing your bargaining skills as you purchase pottery, silver jewelry, crystals, and other trinkets. Note that the Cuauhnahuac museum is closed on Monday.

Catedral de la Asunción de María ⋆ *(Moments*   As you enter the church precincts and pass down the walk, try to imagine what life in Mexico was like in the old days. Construction on the church began in 1529, a mere 8 years after Cortez conquered Tenochtitlán (Mexico City) from the Aztec, and was completed in 1552. The churchmen could hardly trust their safety to the tenuous allegiance of their new converts, so they built a fortress as a church. The skull and crossbones above the main door is a symbol of the Franciscan order, which had its monastery here. The monastery is still here, in fact, and open to the public; it's on the northwest corner of the church property. Also visible on the exterior walls of the main church are inlaid rocks, placed there in memory of the men who lost their lives during its construction.

Once inside, wander through the sanctuaries and the courtyard, and pay special attention to the impressive frescoes painted on the walls, in various states of restoration. The frescoes date from the 1500s and have a distinct Asian style.

The main church sanctuary is stark, even severe, with an incongruous modern feeling (it was refurbished in the 1960s). Frescoes on these walls, discovered during the refurbishing, depict the persecution and martyrdom of St. Felipe de Jesús and his companions in Japan. No one is certain who painted them. In the churchyard, you'll see gravestones marking the tombs of the most devout—or wealthiest—of the parishioners. Being buried on the church grounds was believed to be the most direct route to heaven.

At the corner of Hidalgo and Morelos (3 blocks southwest of the Plaza de Armas). Free admission. Daily 8am–2pm and 4–10pm.

Jardín Borda   Across Morelos Street from the cathedral is the Jardín Borda (Borda Gardens). José de la Borda, the Taxco silver magnate, ordered a sumptuous vacation house built here in the late 1700s. When he died in 1778, his son Manuel inherited the land and transformed it into a botanical garden. The large enclosed garden next to the house was a huge private park, laid out in Andalusian style, with kiosks and an artificial pond. Maximilian took it over as his private summer house in 1865. He and Empress Carlota entertained lavishly in the gardens and held frequent concerts by the lake.

The gardens were completely restored and reopened in 1987 as the Jardín Borda Centro de Artes. In the gateway buildings, several galleries hold changing exhibits and large paintings showing scenes from the life of Maximilian and from the history of the Borda Gardens. One portrays the initial meeting between Maximilian and La India Bonita, a local maiden who became his lover.

On your stroll through the gardens, you'll see the little man-made lake on which Austrian, French, and Mexican nobility rowed small boats in the moonlight. Ducks have taken the place of dukes, however. There are rowboats for rent. The lake is now artfully adapted as an outdoor theater, with seats for the audience on one side and the stage on the other. A cafe serves refreshments and light meals, and a weekend market inside the *jardín* sells arts and crafts.

Morelos 271, at Hidalgo. ℂ **777/318-1038** or 777/318-1052. Fax 777/318-3706. Admission $1.50; free Sun. Tues–Sun 10am–5:30pm.

Jardín Botánico y Museo de Medicina Tradicional y Herbolaria ✸✸   This museum of traditional herbal medicine, in the south Cuernavaca suburb of Acapantzingo, occupies a former resort residence built by Maximilian, the Casa del Olvido. During his brief reign, the Austrian-born emperor came here for trysts with La India Bonita, his Cuernavacan lover. The building was restored in 1960, and the house and gardens now preserve the local wisdom of folk medicine. The shady gardens are lovely to wander through, and you shouldn't miss the 200 orchids growing near the rear of the property.

Matamoros 14, Acapantzingo. ℂ **777/312-5955**, 777/312-3108, or 777/314-4046. www.inah.gob.mx Free admission. Daily 9am–4:30pm. Take a taxi, or catch *combi* no. 6 at the mercado on Degollado. Ask to be dropped off at Matamoros near the museum. Turn right on Matamoros and walk 1½ blocks; the museum will be on your right.

Museo Casa Robert Brady ✸✸   This museum in a private home contains more than 1,300 works of art. Among them are pre-Hispanic and colonial pieces; oil paintings by Frida Kahlo and Rufino Tamayo; and handicrafts from America, Africa, Asia, and India. Robert Brady, an Iowa native with a degree in fine arts from the Art Institute of Chicago, assembled the collections. He lived in Venice for 5 years before settling in Cuernavaca in 1960. The wildly colorful rooms are exactly as Brady left them. Admission includes a guide in Spanish; English and French guides are available if requested in advance.

Calle Netzahualcoyotl 4 (between Hidalgo and Abasolo). ℂ **777/318-8554**. Fax 777/314-3529. www.geocities.com/bradymuseum/bradyspanish.html. Admission $3. Tues–Sun 10am–6pm.

Museo de Cuauhnahuac The museum is in the Cortez Palace, the former home of the greatest of the conquistadors, Hernán Cortez. Construction started in 1530 on the site of a Tlahuica Indian ceremonial center and was finished by the conquistador's son Martín. The palace later served as the legislative headquarters for the state of Morelos.

In the east portico on the upper floor is a large Diego Rivera mural commissioned by Dwight Morrow, U.S. ambassador to Mexico in the 1920s. It depicts the history of Cuernavaca from the coming of the Spaniards to the rise of Zapata (1910). On the lower level, the excellent bookstore is open daily from 10am to 8pm. Tour guides in front of the palace offer their services in the museum, and for other sights in Cuernavaca, for about $10 per hour. Make sure you see official SECTUR (Tourism Secretary) credentials before hiring one of these guides. This is also a central point for taxis in the downtown area.

In the Cortez Palace, Leyva 100. © 777/312-8171. www.morelostravel.com/cultura/museo7.html. Admission $3.30; free Sun. Tues–Sun 9am–6pm.

ACTIVITIES & EXCURSIONS

GOLF With its perpetually springlike climate, Cuernavaca is an ideal place for golf. The **Tabachines Golf Club and Restaurant,** Km 93.5 Carr. Mexico-Acapulco (© 777/314-3999), the city's most popular course, is open for public play. Percy Clifford designed this 18-hole course, surrounded by beautifully manicured gardens blooming with bougainvillea, gardenias, and other flowers. The elegant restaurant is a popular place for breakfast, lunch, and especially Sunday brunch. Greens fees are $80 during the week and $160 on weekends. American Express, Visa, and MasterCard are accepted. It's open Tuesday through Sunday from 7am to 6pm; tee times are available from 7am to 2pm.

Also in Cuernavaca is the **Club de Golf Hacienda San Gaspar,** Avenida Emiliano Zapata, Col. Cliserio Alanis (© 777/319-4424), an 18-hole golf course designed by Joe Finger. It's surrounded by more than 3,000 trees and has two artificial lagoons, plus beautiful panoramic views of Cuernavaca, the Popocatepetl and Iztacihuatl volcanoes, and the Tepozteco Mountains. Greens fees are $45 on weekdays, $89 on weekends; carts cost an additional $28 for 18 holes, and a caddy is $17 plus tip. American Express, Visa, and MasterCard are accepted. Additional facilities include a gym with whirlpool and sauna, pool, four tennis courts, and a restaurant and snack bar. It's open Wednesday through Monday from 7am to 7pm.

LAS ESTACAS Either a side trip from Cuernavaca or a destination on its own, Las Estacas, Km 6.5 Carretera Tlaltizapán–Cuautla, Morelos (© 777/312-4412 or 777/312-7610 in Cuernavaca, or 734/345-0350 or 734/345-0159; www.lasestacas.com) is a natural water park. Its clear spring waters reputedly have healing properties. In addition to the crystal-clear rivers, Las Estacas has two pools, wading pools for children, horseback riding, and a *balneario* (traditional-style spa), open daily from 8am to 6pm. Several restaurants serve such simple food as quesadillas, fruit with yogurt, sandwiches, and *tortas*. Admission is $19 for adults, $12 for children under 4 feet tall. A small, basic hotel charges $91 to $140 for a double room; rates include the entrance fee to the *balneario* and breakfast. Cheaper lodging options are available, including a trailer park; you can rent an adobe or straw hut with two bunk beds for $15. Visit the website for more information. MasterCard and Visa are accepted. On weekends, the place fills with families.

Las Estacas is 36km (23 miles) east of Cuernavaca. To get there, take Highway 138 to Yautepec, then turn right at the first exit past Yautepec.

PYRAMIDS OF XOCHICALCO ⭐ This beautiful ceremonial center provides clues to the history of the whole region. Artifacts and inscriptions link the site to the mysterious cultures that built Teotihuacán and Tula, and some of the objects found here would indicate that residents were also in contact with the Mixtec, Aztec, Maya, and Zapotec. The most impressive building in Xochicalco is the Pirámide de la Serpiente Emplumada (Pyramid of the Plumed Serpent), with its magnificent reliefs of plumed serpents twisting around seated priests. Underneath the pyramid is a series of tunnels and chambers with murals on the walls. There is also an observatory, where from April 30 to August 15 you can follow the trajectory of the sun as it shines through a hexagonal opening. The pyramids (© **777/314-3920** for information) are 36km (23 miles) southwest of Cuernavaca. They're open daily from 6am to 5pm. Admission is $3.80.

WHERE TO STAY
EXPENSIVE
Camino Real Sumiya ⭐⭐ About 11km (7 miles) south of Cuernavaca, this unusual resort, whose name means "the place of peace, tranquillity, and longevity," was once the home of Woolworth heiress Barbara Hutton. Using materials and craftsmen from Japan, she constructed the estate in 1959 for $3.2 million on 12 wooded hectares (30 acres). The main house, a series of large connected rooms and decks, overlooks the grounds and contains restaurants and the lobby. Sumiya's charm is in its relaxing atmosphere, which is best midweek (escapees from Mexico City tend to fill it on weekends). The guest rooms, which cluster in three-story buildings bordering manicured lawns, are simple in comparison to the striking Japanese architecture of the main house. Rooms have subtle Japanese accents, with austere but comfortable furnishings and scrolled wood doors. Hutton built a Kabuki-style theater and exquisite Zen meditation garden, which are now used only for special events. The theater contains vividly colored silk curtains and gold-plated temple paintings protected by folding cedar and mahogany screens. Strategically placed rocks in the garden represent the chakras, or energy points of the human body.

Cuernavaca is an inexpensive taxi ride away. Taxis to the Mexico City airport cost $112 one-way.

Interior Fraccionamiento Sumiya s/n, Col. José Parres, 62550 Jiutepec, Mor. © **01-800/901-2300** or 777/329-9888. Fax 777/329-9889. www.caminoreal.com/sumiya. 163 units. $200 double; $385 suite. Low-season packages and discounts available. AE, DC, MC, V. Free parking. From the freeway, take the Atlacomulco exit and follow signs to Sumiya. Ask directions in Cuernavaca if you're coming from there; the route is complicated. **Amenities:** 2 restaurants; poolside snack bar; outdoor pool; golf privileges nearby; 10 tennis courts; business center; room service; convention facilities w/simultaneous translation capabilities. *In room:* A/C, TV, minibar, dual-line phones w/dataport, hair dryer, iron, safe, ceiling fans.

Las Mañanitas *(Overrated)* This has been Cuernavaca's most renowned luxury lodging for years. Although it is impeccably maintained, Las Mañanitas has an overly formal feeling to it, which may take away from some guests' comfort. The rooms are formal in a style that was popular 15 years ago, with gleaming polished molding and brass accents, large bathrooms, and rich fabrics. Rooms in the original mansion, called terrace suites, overlook the restaurant and inner lawn; the large rooms in the patio section each have a secluded patio; and those in the luxurious, expensive garden section each have a patio overlooking the pool and emerald lawns. Thirteen rooms have fireplaces, and the hotel also has a heated pool in the private garden. The hotel is one of only two in Mexico associated with the prestigious Relais & Châteaux chain. Transportation to and from the Mexico City airport can be arranged through the hotel for $240 round-trip. The restaurant overlooking the gardens is one of the country's premier dining places (see "Where to Dine," below). It's open to nonguests for lunch and dinner only.

Ricardo Linares 107 (5½ long blocks north of the Jardín Borda), 62000 Cuernavaca, Mor. ℂ **777/314-1466** or 777/312-4646. Fax 777/318-3672. www.lasmananitas.com.mx. 20 units. Weekday $190–$390 double; weekend $220–$425 double. Rates include breakfast. AE, MC, V. Free valet parking. **Amenities:** Restaurant; outdoor pool; concierge; room service; laundry service. *In room:* TV upon request, hair dryer.

Misión Del Sol Resort & Spa ✿✿✿ *Finds*   This adults-only hotel and spa offers an experience that rivals any in North America or Europe—and is an exceptional value. You feel a sense of peace from the moment you enter the resort, which draws on the mystical wisdom of the ancient cultures of Mexico, Tibet, Egypt, and Asia. Guests and visitors are encouraged to wear light-hued clothes to contribute to the harmonious flow of energy.

Architecturally stunning adobe buildings that meld with the natural environment house the guest rooms, villas, and common areas. Streams border the extensive gardens. Such group activities as reading discussions, chess club, and painting workshops take place in the salon, where films are shown on weekend evenings. Rooms are large and peaceful; each looks onto its own garden or stream and has three channels of ambient music. Some have air-conditioning. Bathrooms are large, with sunken tubs, and the dual-headed showers have river rocks set into the floor, as a type of reflexology treatment. Beds contain magnets for restoring proper energy flow. Villas have two separate bedrooms, plus a living/dining area and a meditation room. The spa has a menu of 32 services, with an emphasis on water-based treatments. Elegant relaxation areas are interspersed among the treatment rooms and whirlpool. Airport transfers from Mexico City are available for $180 one-way.

Av. General Diego Díaz González 31, Col. Parres, 62550 Cuernavaca, Mor. ℂ **01-800/999-9100** toll-free inside Mexico, or 777/321-0999. Fax 777/320-7981. www.misiondelsol.com.mx. 42 units, plus 12 villas. $262 deluxe double; $551 villa (up to 4 persons); $610 Villa Magnolia (up to 4 persons). Special spa and meal packages available. AE, MC, V. Free parking. Children under 13 not accepted. **Amenities:** Restaurant; 2 tennis courts; well-equipped gym; spa services, including massages, body wraps, scrubs, facial treatments, *temazcal* (pre-Hispanic sweat lodge), Janzu, phototherapy; daily meditation, yoga, Tai Chi classes/sessions; Ping-Pong table. *In room:* Safe-deposit box; bathrobes.

MODERATE

Hotel Posada María Cristina ✿✿   The María Cristina's high walls conceal many delights: a small swimming pool, lush gardens with fountains, a good restaurant, and patios. Guest rooms vary in size; all are exceptionally clean and comfortable, with firm beds and colonial-style furnishings. Bathrooms have inlaid Talavera tiles and skylights. Suites are only slightly larger than normal rooms; junior suites have Jacuzzis. La Calandria, the handsome little restaurant on the first floor, overlooks the gardens and serves excellent meals based on Mexican and international recipes. Even if you don't stay here, consider having a meal. The Sunday brunch ($13 per person) is especially popular. The hotel is half a block from the Palacio de Cortez.

Leyva 20, at Abasolo (Apdo. 203), 62000 Cuernavaca, Mor. ℂ **777/318-6984** or 777/318-5767. Fax 777/312-9126 or 777/318-2981. www.maria-cristina.com. 19 units. $110 double; $135–$160 suite or cabaña. AE, MC, V. Free parking. **Amenities:** Restaurant; bar; outdoor pool; concierge; tour desk. *In room:* A/C, TV, hair dryer, ceiling fan.

INEXPENSIVE

Hotel Juárez   Low rates and a prime location (downtown, 1 block from the Casa Borda) make the Juárez a good choice for those intent on exploring the town's cultural charms. Each of the simple rooms is old-fashioned but well kept.

Netzahualcoyotl 19, 62000 Cuernavaca, Mor. ℂ 777/314-0219. 12 units. $30 double. No credit cards. Limited street parking. From the Cathedral, go east on Hidalgo, then turn right on Netzahualcoyotl. The hotel is 1 block down on the left. **Amenities:** Outdoor pool; tour desk. *In room:* TV, fan.

WHERE TO DINE
VERY EXPENSIVE

Restaurant Las Mañanitas *Overrated* MEXICAN/INTERNATIONAL   Las Mañanitas has set the standard for sumptuous, leisurely dining in Cuernavaca, but lately its reputation has surpassed the reality. The setting is exquisite and the service superb, but the food is not as noteworthy as one would expect. Tables are on a shaded terrace with a view of gardens, strolling peacocks, and softly playing violinists or a romantic trio. Service is extremely attentive. The cuisine is Mexican with an international flair, drawing on seasonal fruits and vegetables and offering a full selection of fresh seafood, beef, pork, veal, and fowl, but in standard preparations. Try cream of watercress soup, filet of red snapper in curry sauce, and black-bottom pie, the house specialty.

In Las Mañanitas hotel, Ricardo Linares 107 (5½ long blocks north of the Jardín Borda). ℂ 777/314-1466 or 777/312-4646. www.lasmananitas.com.mx. Reservations recommended. Main courses $16–$32. AE, MC, V. Daily 1–5pm and 7–11pm.

MODERATE

Casa Hidalgo ★★★ GOURMET MEXICAN/INTERNATIONAL   In a beautifully restored colonial building across from the Palacio de Cortez, this is a relatively recent addition to Cuernavaca dining. The food is more sophisticated and innovative than that at most places in town. Specialties include cream of Brie soup, smoked rainbow trout, and the exquisite Spanish-inspired filet Hidalgo—breaded and stuffed with serrano ham and *manchego* cheese. There are always daily specials, and bread is baked on the premises. Tables on the balcony afford a view of the action in the plaza below. The restaurant is accessible by wheelchair.

Calle Hidalgo 6. ℂ 777/312-2749. Reservations recommended on weekends. Main courses $13–$20. AE, MC, V. Mon–Thurs 1:30–11pm; Fri–Sat 1:30pm–midnight; Sun 1:30–11:30pm. Valet parking available.

Restaurant La India Bonita ★★ MEXICAN   Housed among the interior patios and portals of the restored home of former U.S. Ambassador Dwight Morrow, La India Bonita is a gracious haven where you can enjoy the setting as well as the food. Specialties include *mole poblano* (chicken with a sauce of bitter chocolate and fiery chiles) and *fillet a la parrilla* (charcoal-grilled steak). There are also several daily specials. A breakfast mainstay is *desayuno Maximiliano,* a gigantic platter featuring enchiladas.

Morrow 15 (between Morelos and Matamoros), Col. Centro, 2 blocks north of the Jardín Juárez. ℂ 777/318-6967 or 777/312-5021. Breakfast $4.15–$6.50; main courses $6.70–$14. AE, MC, V. Tues–Sat 9am–9pm; Sun–Mon 9am–5pm.

INEXPENSIVE

La Universal ★★ *Value* MEXICAN/PASTRIES   This is a busy place, partly because of its great location (overlooking both the Alameda and Plaza de Armas), partly because of its traditional Mexican specialties, and partly because of its reasonable prices. It's open to the street and has many outdoor tables, usually filled with older men discussing the day's events or playing chess. These tables are perfect for watching the parade of street vendors and park life. The specialty is a Mexican grilled sampler plate, including *carne asada,* enchilada, pork cutlet, green onions, beans, and tortillas, for $10. A full breakfast special ($4) is served Monday through Friday from 9:30am to noon. There's also a popular happy hour on weekdays from 8 to 10pm.

Guerrero 2. ℭ 777/318-6732 or 777/318-5970. Breakfast $4–$7.50; main courses $4–$15; *comida corrida* $8.90. AE, MC, V. Daily 9:30am–midnight.

CUERNAVACA AFTER DARK

Cuernavaca has a number of cafes right off the Jardín Juárez where people gather to sip coffee or drinks till the wee hours. The best are La Parroquia and La Universal (see "Where to Dine," above). There are band concerts in the Jardín Juárez on Thursday and Sunday evenings.

A recent—and welcome—addition is **La Plazuela,** a short, pedestrian-only stretch across from the Cortez Palace. Here, coffee shops alternate with tattoo parlors and live-music bars. It's geared toward a 20-something, university crowd.

5 Tepoztlán ✯✯

72km (45 miles) S of Mexico City; 45km (28 miles) NE of Cuernavaca

Tepoztlán is one of the strangest and most beautiful towns in Mexico. Largely undiscovered by foreign tourists, it occupies the floor of a broad, lush valley whose walls were formed by bizarrely shaped mountains that look like the work of some abstract expressionist giant. The mountains are visible from almost everywhere in town; even the municipal parking lot has a spectacular view.

Tepoztlán is small and steeped in legend and mystery—it is adjacent to the alleged birthplace of Quetzalcoatl, the Aztec serpent god—and comes about as close as you're going to get to an unspoiled, magical mountain hideaway. Though the town is tranquil during the week, escapees from Mexico City overrun it on the weekends, especially Sunday. Most Tepoztlán residents, whether foreigners or Mexicans, tend to be mystically or artistically oriented—although some also appear to be just plain disoriented.

Aside from soaking up the ambience, two things you must do are climbing up to the Tepozteco pyramid and hitting the weekend crafts market. In addition, Tepoztlán offers a variety of treatments, cures, diets, massages, and sweat lodges. Some of these are available at hotels; for some, you have to ask around. Many locals swear that the valley possesses mystical curative powers.

If you have a car, Tepoztlán provides a great starting point for traveling this region of Mexico. Within 90 minutes are Las Estacas, Taxco, las Grutas de Cacahuamilpa, and Xochicalco (some of the prettiest ruins in Mexico). Tepoztlán is 20 minutes from Cuernavaca and only an hour south of Mexico City, which—given its lost-in-time feel—seems hard to believe.

ESSENTIALS

GETTING THERE & DEPARTING By Car From Mexico City, the quickest route is Highway 95 (the toll road) to Cuernavaca; just before the Cuernavaca city limits, you'll see the clearly marked turnoff to Tepoztlán on 95D and Highway 115. The slower, free federal Highway 95D, direct from Mexico City, is also an option, and may be preferable if you're departing from the western part of the city. Take 95D south to Km 71, where the exit to Tepoztlán on Highway 115 is clearly indicated.

Cooking Classes in Tepoztlán

An engaging new cooking school called **Cocinar Mexicano** offers weeklong programs in Mexican cuisine. The founder, Magda Bogin, conducts class from her large, sunny outdoor kitchen, tiled in blue-and-white Talavera. Participants study recipes typical of the festival that coincides with their visit. During the Day of the Dead workshop, for example, students learn to make tamales, the traditional dish that families bring to the gravesites of deceased love ones. For other festivals the focus is *mole,* a typical fiesta food often made with chocolate and chiles that's arguably the most complex dish in Mexican cuisine. Cost for the class is $1,695, which includes round-trip transportation from Mexico City and most meals but not airfare or accommodations. Frommer's readers receive a $100 discount. For more information, visit www.cocinarmexicano.com.

By Bus   From Mexico City, buses to Tepoztlán run regularly from the Terminal de Sur and the Terminal Poniente. The trip takes an hour.

In addition, you can book round-trip transportation to the Mexico City airport through **Marquez Sightseeing Tours** (© 777/320-9109 and 777/315-5875; marquez tours@hotmail.com) and two hotels: the **Posada del Tepozteco** (© 739/395-0010), and **Casa Iccemayan** (© 739/395-0899). The round-trip cost varies between $125 and $200.

EXPLORING TEPOZTLAN

Tepoztlán's **weekend crafts market** is one of the best in central Mexico. More crafts are available on Sunday, but if you can't stand the multitudes, Saturday is quite good, too. Vendors sell all kinds of ceramics, from simple fired clay works resembling those made with pre-Hispanic techniques, to the more commercial versions of Majolica and pseudo-Talavera. There are also puppets, carved wood figures, and some textiles, especially thick wool Mexican sweaters and jackets made out of *jerga* (a coarse cloth). Very popular currently is the "hippie"-style jewelry that earned Tepoztlán its fame in the '60s and '70s. The market is also remarkable for its variety of food stands.

The other primary activity is hiking up to **Tepozteco pyramid.** The climb is steep but not difficult. Dense vegetation shades the trail (actually a long natural staircase), which is beautiful from bottom to top. Once you arrive at the pyramid you are treated to remarkable views and, if you are lucky, a great show by a family of *coatis* (tropical raccoons), who visit the pyramid most mornings to beg for food; they especially love bananas. The pyramid is a Tlahuica construction that predates the Náhuatl (Aztec) domination of the area. It was the site of important celebrations in the 12th and 13th centuries. The main street in Tepoztlán, Avenida 5 de Mayo, takes you to the path that leads you to the top of the Tepozteco. The trail begins where the name of Avenida 5 de Mayo changes to Camino del Tepozteco. The hike is about an hour each way, but if you stop and take in the scenery and really enjoy the trail, it can take up to 2 hours each way.

Also worth visiting is the **former convent Dominico de la Navidad,** just east of the main plaza. Built between 1560 and 1588, it is now a museum.

SIGHTS NEAR TEPOZTLAN

Many nearby places are easily accessible by car. One good tour service is **Marquez Sightseeing Tours,** located in Cuernavaca (© 777/320-9109 or 777/315-5875). Marquez has four- and seven-passenger vehicles, very reasonable prices, and a large variety of set tours. The dependable owner, Arturo Marquez Diaz, speaks better than passable English and will allow you to design your own tour. He also offers transportation to and from Mexico City airport for approximately $150.

Two tiny, charming villages, **Santo Domingo Xocotitlán** and **Amatlán,** are only a 20-minute drive from Tepoztlán and can be reached by minibuses, which depart regularly from the center of town. There is nothing much to do in these places except wander around absorbing the marvelous views of the Tepozteco Mountains and drinking in the magical ambience.

Las Grutas de Cacahuamilpa ✿, known as the Cacahuamilpa Caves or Grottoes (© **555/150-5031**), is an unforgettable system of caverns with a wooden walkway for easy access. As you pass from chamber to chamber you'll see spectacular illuminated rock formations. Admission for 2 hours is $3.50; a guide for groups, which can be assembled on the spot, costs an additional $8. The caverns are open daily from 10am to 5pm, and are 90 minutes from Tepoztlán.

About 40 minutes southeast of Tepoztlán is **Las Estacas,** an ecological resort with a cold-water spring that is said to have curative powers (p. 175). The ruins of **Xochicalco** (see "Cuernavaca," earlier in this chapter), and the colonial town of **Taxco** (earlier in this chapter) are easily accessible from Tepoztlán.

WHERE TO STAY

The town gets very busy on the weekends, so if your stay will include Friday or Saturday night, make reservations well in advance. In addition to the choices noted below, consider two other excellent options just outside of town. **Casa Bugambilia** ✿✿✿, Callejón de Tepopula 007, Valle de Atongo (© **739/395-0158;** www.casabugambilia.com), is a new 11-room hotel property not far from El Telón, the local dance club. Don't confuse this hotel with Posada Bugambilia, a modest hotel in town. The spacious rooms are elegantly furnished with high-end, carved Mexican furniture, and every room has a fireplace. Doubles average $180 to $250. **Las Golondrinas** ✿✿✿, Callejón de Términas 4 (© **739/ 395-0649;** homepage.mac.com/marisolfernandez/LasGolondrinas), is a B&B so off the beaten track that even cab drivers have trouble finding the place—in the area behind Ixcatepec church. But owner Marisol Fernández has imbued the house with her tranquil, down-to-earth charm; three of the four guest rooms open onto a wraparound terrace that overlooks the garden, a small pool, and the Tepozteco Mountains beyond. Doubles are $109, including breakfast.

Hotel Nilayam ✿   Formerly Hotel Tepoztlán, this holistic-oriented retreat is in a colonial building, but the decor has been brightened up considerably. Suites, with hydromassage tubs and terraces, are the most spacious option. Stays here encourage

---

Moments **Tepoznieves: A Taste of Heaven**

Don't leave town without a stop at **Tepoznieves,** Av. 5 de Mayo 21 (© **739/395-3813**), the sublime local ice cream shop. The store's slogan, "Nieve de dioses" (Ice cream of the gods), doesn't exaggerate. More than 120 types of ice cream and sorbet, made only with natural ingredients, come in flavors familiar (vanilla, bubble gum), exotic (tamarind, mango studded with chile piquin), and off the wall (beet, lettuce, corn).

self-exploration: The gracious, helpful staff offers complete detox programs and a full array of services, including yoga, reflexology, spinal-column exercises, meditation, music therapy, and more. The hotel has a great view of the mountain. The restaurant features a creative menu of vegetarian cuisine.

Industrias 6, 62520 Tepoztlán, Mor. © **739/395-0522.** Fax 739/395-0522. www.nilayam.com 36 units. $85 double; $175 suite. AE, MC, V. **Amenities:** Restaurant; pool; tennis court; spa services; private *temazcal* (pre-Hispanic sweat lodge). *In room:* TV.

Posada del Tepozteco ⭐⭐   This property looks out over the town and down the length of the spectacular valley; the views from just about anywhere are superb. Rooms are tastefully furnished in rustic Mexican style. All but the least expensive have terraces and views. All suites have small whirlpool tubs. The grounds are exquisitely land-scaped, and the atmosphere intimate and romantic.

Paraíso 3 (2 blocks from the town center), 62520 Tepoztlán, Mor. © **739/395-0010.** Fax 739/395-0323. www.posadadeltepozteco.com. 20 units. $145–$225 double. Rates include breakfast. AE, MC, V. Free parking. **Amenities:** Restaurant w/stunning view; small outdoor pool.

WHERE TO DINE

In addition to the two choices listed below, El Chalchi restaurant at the **Hotel Nilayam** (see above) offers some of the best vegetarian fare in the area. It's 3 blocks from the main square, with main courses priced around $5.

El Ciruelo Restaurant Bar ⭐ MEXICAN GOURMET   This picturesque restaurant, surrounded by beautiful flowering gardens and adobe walls, offers a sampling of Tepoztlán's essence in one place. The service is positively charming, and the food divine. House specialties include chalupas of goat cheese, chicken with *huitlacoche*, and a regional treat: milk candies.

Zaragoza 17, Barrio de la Santísima, in front of the church. © **739/395-1203.** Dinner $7.50–$25. AE. Sun–Thurs 1–7pm; Fri–Sat 1pm–midnight.

Restaurant Axitla ⭐⭐⭐ *Finds* GOURMET MEXICAN/INTERNATIONAL Axitla is not only the best restaurant in Tepoztlán, but also one of the finest in Mexico for showcasing the country's cuisine. Gourmet Mexican delicacies are made from scratch using the freshest local ingredients. Specialties include chicken breast stuffed with wild mushrooms in a *chipotle chile* sauce, *chiles en nogada,* and exceptional *mole.* There are also excellent steaks and fresh seafood. As if the food weren't enough—and believe me, it is—the setting will make your meal even more memorable. The restaurant is at the base of the Tepozteco Pyramid, surrounded by 1.2 hectares (3 acres) of junglelike gardens that encompass a creek and lily ponds. The views of the Tepozteco Mountains are magnificent. Memo and Laura, the gracious owners, speak excellent English and are marvelous sources of information about the area.

Av. del Tepozteco, at the foot of the trail to the pyramid. © **739/395-0519.** Lunch $5–$10; dinner $5–$20. MC, V. Wed–Sun 10am–7pm.

6

San Miguel de Allende & the Colonial Silver Cities

by David Baird

Mexico's colonial silver mining cities—San Miguel, Querétaro, San Luis Potosí, Guanajuato, and Zacatecas—lie northwest of Mexico City in the rugged mountains of the Sierra Madre Occidental. The towns, in colonial settings with backdrops of high mountains, feature an ideal climate, local handicrafts, good food, and many memorable sites.

San Miguel de Allende is the smallest of the cities. Its cobblestone streets and fanciful church set it apart from the rest, as do its numerous restaurants and interesting shops. For many years it has supported a resident population of artists, writers, and expatriates. **Guanajuato** and **Zacatecas,** with their winding streets and alleys and diminutive plazas, seem more like medieval towns than products of the Renaissance. In contrast, **Querétaro** and **San Luis Potosí** have stately colonial centers of broad plazas and monumental civil and religious architecture.

Travel through these parts is easy and relaxing; there is little crime, and the inhabitants are gracious. The region is a good introduction to Mexico's interior and is well suited for a family vacation. All Mexicans, but especially those in this region, are family-oriented and warm up quickly when they see a family traveling together.

The colonial silver cities are close to the Mexican capital by modern standards, but at the time of their founding, this land was the frontier. In pre-Columbian times, the great civilizations of central Mexico never established more than a tenuous sway here. Mountainous and arid, this was the land of the Chichimeca, a large nation of nomadic tribes that occasionally banded together for raids upon their civilized neighbors to the south. After the Spanish conquest of the Aztec empire in 1521, the conquistadors turned their attention to this region in search of precious metals. The Chichimecans resisted the encroachers, but epidemic diseases brought from Europe soon decimated the native population. The Spanish established mining cities in quick succession, stretching from Querétaro (established in 1531) north all the way to Zacatecas (1548) and beyond. They found quantities of gold, but silver proved so plentiful that it made Mexico world-famous as a land of riches.

For 3 centuries of colonial rule, much of the mines' great wealth went to build urban centers of impressive and lasting architecture. It's wonderful to walk leisurely through these cities and view them, not one building at a time, but in broad views of colonial cityscapes. Of the five cities, three (Guanajuato, Querétaro, and Zacatecas) have been designated World Heritage Sites by UNESCO.

Life remains civilized here; it is savored and enjoyed at a relaxed pace. Many people have ancestors who lived here at least a

The Colonial Silver Cities

century ago. They maintain a broad network of kinfolk, friends, and acquaintances. I've walked down streets with locals who would greet every third or fourth person we passed. Often, I've had conversations in which I mention someone from a completely different context, only to hear something like, "Oh, he's married to my cousin." This is the kind of intimate and close-knit world you enter when visiting these cities.

EXPLORING THE SILVER CITIES

The most common ways of getting here are flying into Mexico City and taking the bus that goes directly from the airport to Querétaro, or flying into the León-Guanajuato airport. Zacatecas and San Luis Potosí also have international airports that receive a few flights from the U.S. Or you can get to this region by car or bus on one of the superhighways that run from the U.S. border. From Texas, the first of the silver cities you reach will be San Luis Potosí (which, by the way, bills itself to the rest of Mexico as the "Gateway to the United States").

Once in the region, you'll find the roads are good, but the smaller ones are poorly marked. Driving within these towns can be maddening due to convoluted, narrow streets and bizarre traffic routing (especially in Guanajuato and Zacatecas). If you ever have difficulty navigating into the center of town, simply hail a cab to lead the way. Parking can also be a problem; we have included, when possible, good motels where you can park and leave your car for the length of your visit. If you prefer to travel by bus, you'll find frequent, inexpensive first-class buses connecting all these cities, which are only a few hours apart from each other.

The region has a short rainy season from June through September, which is a good time to come. I also like late fall, winter, and early spring. The hottest month is May (and sometimes early June before the rains arrive). May can also be smoky because it's when many farmers burn the stubble in their corn fields before the next planting. As to how and where to spend your time, much depends on your interests. If your chief goal is to relax and enjoy the good life, spend more time in San Miguel. If it is to be active and do some exploring, spend more time in Guanajuato and Zacatecas. If you're already comfortable running around Mexico and are looking for cultural immersion, I would point you to Querétaro and San Luis Potosí. But whichever cities you elect to visit, I recommend a stay of at least 3 days per destination—a good part of their charm will go unappreciated if you're pressing too much to see everything.

1 San Miguel de Allende ✮✮✮

288km (180 miles) NW of Mexico City; 120km (75 miles) E of Guanajuato; 64km (40 miles) NW of Querétaro

San Miguel de Allende mixes the best aspects of small-town life with the cosmopolitan pleasures of a big city. It is the smallest of the cities covered here and perhaps the most relaxed, but it offers such a variety of restaurants, shops, and galleries that urbanites find themselves quite at home. Most of the buildings in the central part of the town date from the colonial era or the 19th century; the law requires newer buildings to conform to existing architecture, and the town has gone to some lengths to retain its cobblestone streets.

Living in San Miguel is a large community of Americans: some retired, some attending art or language school, and some who have come here to live simply and follow their creative muses—painting, writing, and sculpting. The center of this community is the public library in the former convent of Santa Ana. It is a good place to find information on San Miguel or just to sit in the patio and read.

A notable aspect of San Migueleña society is the number of festivals it celebrates. In a country that needs only the barest of excuses to hold a fiesta, it is known far and wide for them. Most of these celebrations are of a religious character and are meant to combine social activity with religious expression. People practice Catholicism with great fervor—going on religious pilgrimages, attending all-night vigils, ringing church bells at the oddest times throughout the night (something that some visitors admittedly might not find so amusing). See "Special Events & Festivals," below.

ESSENTIALS

GETTING THERE & DEPARTING   By Plane   The two major airports are the Mexico City airport, which is 3½ hours away (and has direct bus transportation to nearby Querétaro) and the León-Guanajuato airport, 1½ hours away.

By Car   You have a choice of two routes for the 3½-hour trip from Mexico City—a Querétaro bypass or via Celaya. The former is shorter—take Highway 57, a four-lane freeway, north toward Querétaro. Past the Tequisquiapan turnoff is an exit on the right marked A SAN MIGUEL. This toll road bypasses Querétaro and crosses Highway 57 again north of town. Here it narrows to two lanes and becomes Highway 111. Some 32km (20 miles) farther is San Miguel.

From Guanajuato, the quick route is to go south from the city a short distance on Highway 110, then east on a secondary, paved road passing near the village of Joconoxtle. For the long but scenic route, which passes through Dolores Hidalgo, go northeast on Highway 110 through Dolores, then south on Highway 51. If you drive this route, take a break and experience a slice of rural Mexican life near the small community of Santa Rosa, where a few restaurants serve the local *mezcal de la sierra.*

By Bus   AeroPlus buses (© **55/5786-9357**) leave the Mexico City airport for Querétaro about every hour and cost $22. You'll find the buses just outside the doors in front of Gate D (Sala D). From Querétaro, local buses ($4) run to San Miguel every 20 minutes. The **bus station** in San Miguel is 2km (1½ miles) west of town on the westward extension of Calle Canal. Taxis to town are cheap ($2–$3) and available at all hours. An office in the center of San Miguel sells tickets for AeroPlus buses from Querétaro to the Mexico City airport, as well as for all other buses operated by Primera Plus or Servicios Coordinados. It's around the corner from the Jardín, at Calle Sollano 11 (© **415/152-5043**). Office hours are from 9am to 3:45pm Monday through Saturday, and Sunday from 9am to 2pm.

The trip to San Miguel from Mexico City's "Terminal Norte" takes 4 hours on a first-class bus (with one stop in Querétaro). The company ETN has the best service, with wide seats that recline far back (four buses per day). It's also the most expensive ($25 one-way). Primera Plus has two buses per day ($20). Regular service is handled by Flecha Amarilla ($16) with buses leaving every 40 minutes.

If you arrive in Querétaro by first-class bus you'll be in Terminal A. Go out the door, turn right, and walk to Terminal B. Buses for San Miguel leave every 20 minutes, alternating between Flecha Amarilla and Herradura de Plata. The trip takes a little over an hour and costs $4.

ETN has two nonstop superdeluxe buses per day to Guanajuato ($9). Primera Plus/Servicios Coordinados has four nonstop buses per day ($7).

To/from Nuevo Laredo: A first-class bus belonging to **Autobuses Americanos** (© **415/152-2237**) leaves at 6:30pm, arriving in San Miguel de Allende between 8 and 9am the next day. The return bus leaves San Miguel at 5:30pm and arrives in Nuevo Laredo around 7am. You can buy a ticket all the way through Nuevo Laredo to any of several major Texas cities, changing buses in San Luis Potosí.

VISITOR INFORMATION   The state **tourist information office** is in a small office to the left of the Parroquia (© **415/152-6565**). Office hours are Monday through Friday from 10am to 5pm, Saturday and Sunday from 10am to 1pm. Also, there are a couple of free monthly publications for tourists. These have a lot of advertising, but also some useful info and a calendar of events.

CITY LAYOUT   Groomed Indian laurel trees shade San Miguel's central square, **El Jardín.** The center of city life, El Jardín is the point of reference for all places in the middle of town and is bounded by Correo (Post Office St.), San Francisco, Hidalgo, and Reloj.

Where to Stay in San Miguel de Allende

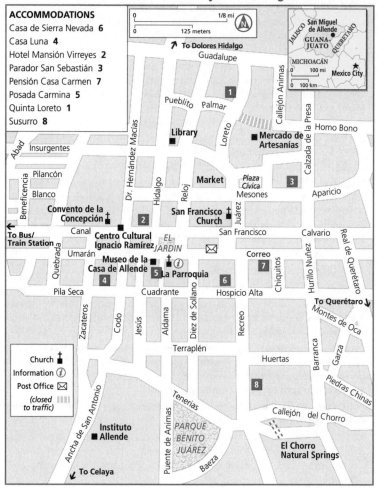

ACCOMMODATIONS
Casa de Sierra Nevada **6**
Casa Luna **4**
Hotel Mansión Virreyes **2**
Parador San Sebastián **3**
Pensión Casa Carmen **7**
Posada Carmina **5**
Quinta Loreto **1**
Susurro **8**

GETTING AROUND   Buses to outlying villages (La Taboada thermal pool, for example) leave from the little plaza by the *mercado*. Taxis to places inside town should not cost more than $2 or $3, unless ordered from a hotel.

FAST FACTS: San Miguel de Allende

American Express   The local representative is **Viajes Vertiz**, Hidalgo 1 (*C* **415/152-1856**; fax 415/152-0499), open Monday through Friday from 9am to 2pm and 4 to 6:30pm, Saturday from 10am to 2pm.

Area Code   The telephone area code is **415**.

Climate San Miguel can be warm in summer and cold enough for wool clothing in winter, especially at night or occasionally when a norther (a strong, sudden north wind) makes its way this far south.

Communication & Shipping Services Several services offer packing and shipping, mail boxes, telephone messages, long distance, faxes, and the like. One is **Border Crossings,** Correo 19, Int. 2 (© 415/152-2497; fax 415/152-3672). **Pack 'n' Mail** has sizable space at Calle Jesús 2-A (©/fax **415/152-3191**). The hours for both are weekdays from 9am to 6pm, Saturday from 10am to 3pm.

Consular Office It's located at Hernández Macías 72, Int. 111. (© **415/152-2357**). Hours are Monday to Friday 9am to 1pm.

Currency Exchange Two convenient places near El Jardín change money. **Dicambio,** Correo 13, is open Monday through Friday from 9am to 4pm and Saturday from 9am to 2pm. Next door is **Intercam,** open Monday through Friday from 9am to 8pm, Saturday from 9am to 2pm. There are cash machines at several banks—one on the corner of the Jardín in the Casa del Conde, and a few on San Francisco Street.

Drugstore Try the **Farmacia Agundus** (© **415/152-1198**), Canal 26 at Macías. It's open daily from 10am to midnight.

Elevation San Miguel sits at 1,862m (6,143 ft.).

Internet Access There are places offering Internet access all over the town. These businesses come and go so fast it's not worth listing them. Ask at your hotel for the nearest cybercafe.

Library The **Biblioteca Pública (Public Library),** Insurgentes 25 (© 415/152-0293), is a social institution for the American community. It has a good selection of books in Spanish and English. Hours are Monday through Friday from 10am to 2pm and 4 to 7pm; Saturday from 10am to 2pm.

Newspaper An English-language paper, *Atención,* carries local news as well as full listings of what to see and do.

Parking San Miguel is congested, and street parking is scarce. *Note:* White poles, signs, or both at the ends of streets mark the stopping point for parking (so that other cars can make a turn). Police are vigilant about parking and ticket with glee.

Population San Miguel has 110,000 residents.

Post Office The *correo,* Calle Correo 16, is open Monday through Friday from 9am to 2pm for all services (and sells stamps until 5pm), Saturday from 9am to 1pm.

Seasons Because of the fast freeway access from Mexico City, San Miguel is popular with weekenders from the capital. Arrive early on Friday or make a reservation ahead of time for weekends, especially long weekends. There's also a squeeze on rooms around the Christmas and Easter holidays and around the feast of San Miguel's patron saint, on September 29.

SPECIAL EVENTS & FESTIVALS

San Miguel celebrates 30 to 40 festivals a year. These are just the standouts: January 17 is the **Blessing of the Animals.** In the morning, locals bring their decorated pets and farm animals to the town's churches to be doused with holy water. The first Friday in March celebrates **Our Lord of the Conquest,** and the day before is filled with music, fireworks, and decorated teams of oxen. After a celebratory Mass, there is dancing by the *concheros* (traditional Aztec dancers). Two weeks before Holy Week is the procession of **Our Lord of the Column.** Between then and Easter Sunday there are more processions, and altars are set up in honor of **La Virgen Dolorosa.** In May is the **Festival of the Holy Cross.** In June around Saint Anthony's Day is the **Fiesta de los Locos (Festival of the Madmen)** 🌟🌟, when many dress up in carnavalesque costumes and go cavorting about the center of town. August begins the preparatory festivals for September 29, the festival of San Miguel's **patron saint.** Parades, fireworks, and band concerts continue throughout September. On one weekend in September the town holds a *pamplonada* (running of the bulls)—it produces a lot of public drunkenness and carousing in the central part of town. I would avoid it. At the beginning of November is the **Day of the Dead,** followed by the **Christmas fiestas.** In addition to all of this, you have the **Chamber Music Festival** in summer, **Jazz Music Festival** in the fall, and a couple of arts fairs that occur on varying dates.

EXPLORING SAN MIGUEL

It's difficult to be bored in San Miguel. The shopping is excellent, and you'll run out of time before you can try all the restaurants. The town is well situated for side trips to Dolores Hidalgo, Querétaro, and Guanajuato. It's also popular for Spanish and art classes.

The colonial architecture tends more toward domestic than monumental and offers much to see—fine courtyards, beautiful interiors, and rich architectural details. Of particular note are the town's lovely streetscapes with narrow cobblestone lanes that invite aimless strolling and make it advisable to wear walking shoes with thick soles.

THE TOP ATTRACTIONS

Centro Cultural Ignacio Ramírez (Bellas Artes/El Nigromante) Housed in the former Convento de la Concepción (1755), 2 blocks west of El Jardín, the Centro is a branch of the Palacio de Bellas Artes of Mexico City. The two-story cloister, surrounding an enormous courtyard with large trees and a gurgling fountain, houses art exhibits and classrooms for drawing, painting, sculpture, lithography, textiles, ceramics, dramatic arts, ballet, regional dance, piano, and guitar. A mural by David Alfaro Siqueiros and some of his memorabilia are worth seeing. A bulletin board lists concerts and lectures at this institute and elsewhere in the city. You can also dine in these pleasant surroundings at the restaurant **Las Musas,** which serves pasta dishes, salads, sandwiches, and desserts. Before you leave, take a look at the magnificent dome behind the convent. It belongs to the Iglesia de la Concepción and was designed by the same unschooled architect who designed the Parroquia (see below).

Hernández Macías 75 (between Canal and Insurgentes). 📞 **415/152-0289.** Free admission. Mon–Fri 10am–5:30pm; Sat 10am–2pm.

La Parroquia 🌟🌟🌟 Looking nothing like any other church in Mexico, La Parroquia has become the emblem of San Miguel. The church is an object of great pride for the citizenry and a source of discomfort for architectural purists. Originally built in the colonial style, it was remade in the late 19th century by a local builder named Zeferino Gutiérrez, who reconstructed the towers and facade. Gutiérrez was supposedly unlettered but had seen picture postcards of European Gothic churches and worked from these alone, drawing his designs in the sand. I find the finished product fascinating—a very personal vision of the Gothic style that owes more to the builder's imagination and fancy than to the European churches that were its inspiration. The inside is not nearly so much fun as the outside; the church was looted on several occasions during times of social upheaval, and this kind of art criticism puts a damper on commissioning more paintings and decoration. Still, there are things to see. My favorite, and one often missed, is the crypt beneath the altar. You get to it through a door on the right side. You'll have to seek out the caretaker, who can unlock the door (for a small tip).

South side of El Jardín. No phone. Free admission. Daily 8am–2pm and 5–9pm.

Learning at the Source: Going to School in San Miguel

San Miguel is known for its Spanish-language and art schools. These schools cater to English speakers and often provide a list of apartments for long-term stays. Rates for language classes are usually hourly and get lower the more hours you take.

Instituto Allende, Calle Ancha de San Antonio 20, 37700 San Miguel de Allende, Gto. (© 415/152-0190; fax 415/152-4538; www.instituto-allende. edu.mx), put San Miguel on the map in the 1930s. Its founders were Enrique Fernández Martínez, the former governor of the state of Guanajuato, and Stirling Dickinson, an American. Today, it thrives in the 18th-century home of the former counts of Canal, a beautiful place with elegant patios and gardens, art exhibits, and murals. You can wander past classrooms where weavers, sculptors, painters, ceramists, photographers, and students are at work. Much of the craftwork that San Miguel is known for sprang from this institute. The language office maintains a list of local families who rent rooms for stays of a month or more. The institute offers an MFA degree, and the school's credits are transferable to at least 300 colleges and universities in the United States and Canada; noncredit students are also welcome.

Academia Hispano Americana, Mesones 4 (Apdo. Postal 150), 37700 San Miguel de Allende, Gto. (© 415/152-0349; fax 415/152-2333; www.ahaspeak spanish.com), has a reputation for being a comparatively tougher language school with an emphasis on grammar as well as conversation. Classes are limited to 12 people. The work is intensive, and the school is particularly interested in students who plan to use Spanish in their careers or who feel the need to communicate and understand the other Americas. The school has a continuous program of study of 12 4-week sessions for 35 hours a week. Private lessons are available. It's a member of the International Association of Language Centers.

Sazón, Correo 22, 37700 San Miguel de Allende, Gto. (© 415/154-7671; www.sazonsanmiguel.com), a cooking school and store, offers cooking classes and weekly market tours, with the occasional special event thrown in. Visitors to San Miguel can sign up for classes at the store, open Monday to Saturday 10am to 6pm and Sunday 11am to 3pm.

Also see the **Centro Cultural Ignacio Ramírez** in "The Top Attractions," above.

Museo Casa de Allende   The house of San Miguel's most famous son and name-sake, the independence leader Ignacio Allende, is now a museum. It is of the genre known as *museos regionales* that you will find across Mexico. The objective of these museums is to present a view of the local area from prehistoric times to recent history; to explain what roles the region played in the context of national development; and to give some idea of how the great historical movements that swept across Mexico ran their courses at the local level. For the sake of context, this museum goes back a tad too far, starting with the creation of the solar system and the beginning of time, but from there it quickly moves to the meat of the matter—the way of life in the region from pre-Hispanic to late colonial times.

Featured is a small biographical exhibit on Allende as one of the initiators of the independence movement, which began in nearby Dolores Hidalgo, and on what national independence meant for San Miguel and the local area. Explanations are in Spanish only, but the artifacts—including fossils, pre-Hispanic pottery, colonial-era furnishings, and articles of daily life—and the beauty of the house are worth the price.

Southwest corner of El Jardín. No phone. Admission $3. Tues–Sun 10am–4pm.

MORE ATTRACTIONS

The **House and Garden Tour** ⏰, sponsored by the Biblioteca Pública, is universally enjoyed. The tour opens the doors of some of the city's most interesting colonial and contemporary houses. Tours leave Sunday at 11:30am from the library, Insurgentes 25 (© **415/152-0293**), and last about 2 hours. A $15 donation goes to support various library projects benefiting the youth of San Miguel.

The **Centro de Crecimiento,** Zamora Ríos 6, a donation-supported school for children with disabilities, conducts Saturday tours (10am–3pm) to interesting places in the countryside around San Miguel. Donations are $15 per person; tickets are available at Casa Maxwell, a store at Canal 14.

A couple of the most enjoyable walks in town are to the lookout point **El Mirador,** especially at sunset, which colors the whole town and the lake beyond, and to **Parque Juárez,** a large and shady park.

NEARBY ATTRACTIONS

Just outside of San Miguel are several hot mineral springs that have been made into bathing spots. They're all just off the road leading to Dolores Hidalgo. **La Taboada, La Gruta,** and **Escondido** lie close to one another, just 8 to 10km (5–6 miles) outside San Miguel. La Gruta is perhaps the nicest, but La Taboada has a quiet, old hotel reminiscent of an earlier Mexico and makes for a relaxing stay.

Near these hot springs is the sanctuary of **Atotonilco el Grande,** a complex of chapels, dormitories, and dining rooms, and a fascinating church. World Monuments Watch ranks the church among the world's most important buildings meriting preservation. Father Luis Felipe Neri Alfaro, an austere priest and mystic, founded the church in 1740. He chose this spot for his sanctuary because it was here that he was granted an ecstatic vision of Christ. Alfaro thought the area in dire need of a religious presence, since many people would gather at the thermal springs to bathe publicly and immodestly, leading to licentious behavior. He commissioned a local artist, Martínez Pocasangre, to paint murals illustrating the instructive verses that Alfaro wrote, with much emphasis on the dangers lying in wait for the human soul. The murals and accompanying verses cover the entire ceiling and walls. They are vivid and moving, and add brightness and color to an otherwise dark and severe structure.

The church and adjoining buildings still function throughout the year as a religious retreat for people who come from all over the country for a week of prayer, penance, and mortification. These spiritual exercises are conducted quietly, in private, with no public display. You can get to Atotonilco by cab or by taking the EL SANTUARIO bus at the market. It passes every hour on the hour, and goes through Taboada on its way to Atotonilco.

SHOPPING

San Miguel is a town of artists; you'll find art for sale not only in galleries but also in restaurants, offices, and just about anywhere there's space in a public area. San Miguel is also a town of artisans working mainly with clay, iron, brass, tin, blown glass, and papier-mâché. And San Miguel is a town of shopkeepers who sell locally produced items as well as folk art and decorative objects from across Mexico. There are so many stores, and they are so different from each other, that a list would not be helpful. The best advice I can give shoppers is to explore the area around the main square. If you're looking for something in particular (say, gold-leaf candlesticks or a Huichol ceremonial mask), ask the shopkeepers you meet. Most of them have a good idea of what's out there.

Stores are usually open Monday through Saturday from 9am to 2pm and 4 to 7 or 8pm. Most stores close on Sunday. If you're interested in Talavera pottery, consider going to nearby Dolores Hidalgo (see "A Side Trip to Dolores Hidalgo," later in this chapter). There are a lot of new and interesting shops on and around calles Hernández Macías and Zacateros. Also, you can find some fun knickknacks at the **Mercado de Artesanías (handicrafts market),** but it will require hunting through lots of goods that are either too tacky or not tacky enough. The *mercado* occupies a walkway 3 blocks long that descends from the municipal market past the Hotel Quinta Loreto.

WHERE TO STAY

For a long stay (a month or more), check at the instituto or the academia (see "Learning at the Source: Going to School in San Miguel," above) and other bulletin boards around town for lists of apartments or rooms to rent, or check the following Web pages: www.internetsanmiguel.com, www.infosma.com, or www.portal-sanmiguel.com. Most apartments have kitchens and bedding; some come with maid service. San Miguel is a popular weekend getaway for residents of the capital, and a several hotels raise rates on weekends. Secured parking is at a premium; if your hotel doesn't provide it, you'll pay around $12 to $15 daily in a guarded lot. Most places can arrange airport transportation. The rates listed below already include taxes, which are 17%.

VERY EXPENSIVE

Casa de Sierra Nevada Quinta Real ★★★   This handsome hotel occupies several 16th-century town houses on a couple of streets just above El Jardín. With picturesque terraces and courtyards bedecked in flowers and plants, some affording charming views and considerable privacy, this place feels like a true getaway from the modern world. Rooms vary in shape and design; most have private patios or secluded entrances and working fireplaces. All have decorative antiques and tile floors with area rugs. The newest rooms are apart from the rest, down by the Parque Juárez, and have their own restaurant on the premises, which is less formal than the one in the main complex. The hotel is 2 blocks southeast of El Jardín. Transportation from either airport is available.

Hospicio 35 (between Diez de Sollano and Recreo), 37700 San Miguel de Allende, Gto. © **866/621-9288** in the U.S. and Canada, or 415/152-7040. Fax 415/152-1436. www.casadesierranevada.com. 33 units. $258–$292 double; $363–$450 suite. AE, MC, V. Free valet parking. Children not accepted. **Amenities:** 2 restaurants; 2 bars; large heated pool; spa; concierge; tour and activities desk; room service until 11pm; in-room massage; laundry service; dry cleaning. *In room:* TV, minibar, fridge, hair dryer, safe.

La Puertecita Boutique Hotel ★★ (Kids)

Those who can't find the charm in church bells and firecrackers going off at odd hours of the night will appreciate this hotel, as will those who are traveling with children. Set on the side of a narrow canyon (which it has all to itself), the hotel is above and a little removed from the central part of town. A fence surrounds the grounds, with terraced gardens and the ruined remains of an aqueduct for a touch of local character. Rooms, especially deluxe units and suites, are large; many have vaulted brick ceilings, small terraces, and beautifully tiled large bathrooms. They are furnished and decorated in modern Mexican style. The junior and one-bedroom suites have living areas and, in some cases, a dining area for four. Six suites have kitchenettes. Superior rooms and villas come with a king or a queen bed; the deluxe rooms and suites have a king or two queen beds. There are also two-bedroom suites, which are the equivalent of a one-bedroom suite with a deluxe room attached.

Santo Domingo 75, 37740 San Miguel de Allende, Gto. © **415/152-5011.** Fax 415/152-5505. www.la puertecita.com. 32 units. $205–$264 double; $295–$324 suite. AE, MC, V. Free guarded parking. **Amenities:** Restaurant; bar; 2 small outdoor pools (1 heated); golf and tennis at local club; exercise equipment; outdoor whirlpool; game room; concierge; tour desk; courtesy car; room service until 9pm; in-room massage; babysitting; laundry service; dry cleaning; nonsmoking rooms. *In room:* TV, dataport, hair dryer, safe, bathrobe.

EXPENSIVE

Casa de la Cuesta ★★★

In an upper *barrio* (neighborhood) stands this magnificent house, an example of how colonial architecture can be rethought in modern terms. The combined effect of architecture and location is dramatic. The entrance to the house is through a long tunnel-like passage that abruptly opens up to the first of two courtyards. On three sides are structures of different heights, which make use wherever possible of rooftop terraces. In one of these structures is a studio and gallery, which the owners (who are art dealers) use for shows or workspace. Guest rooms encircle the arcaded rear courtyard, with a lot of terraces and common space, much of which has a fine view of the central part of town. Rooms are large and comfortable, with king-size beds, lots of color and detail, and a mix of modern and colonial furnishings. The casa is about a 10-minute walk to the center of town, and the return is uphill. Breakfasts are great, and the hosts, Heidi and Bill Levasseur, are helpful and entertaining.

Cuesta de San José 32, 37700 San Miguel de Allende, Gto. ©/fax **415/154-4324.** www.casadelacuesta.com. 6 units. $130–$150 double. Rates include full breakfast. MC, V (for deposits). **Amenities:** In-room massage; laundry service; nonsmoking rooms.

Casa Luna/Casa Luna Quebrada ★★★

Casa Luna and the new Casa Luna Quebrada are both striking to look at and fun to stay in. Both are just a few blocks below the main square. The new house on Calle Quebrada is a large property, enjoys lots of open space, and is designed in the hacienda style. The original house on Pila Seca is more playful and has lovely nooks and crannies and riotous vegetation. Guest rooms in both houses are roughly the same in size and amenities. They are great fun—lots of color, lots of detail. Most have some Mexican theme but not exclusively. The owner, Dianne Kushner, has a real talent for bringing together disparate design elements and making them look like they naturally belong together. Most rooms are large and come with a king bed or two twins, down comforters, gas fireplaces, and large bathrooms with shower/tub combinations. Most have private patios. The common areas are lovely and relaxing and get you right into that "mañana" attitude. Breakfasts are delicious, and cooking classes are sometimes offered.

Pila Seca 11, 37700 San Miguel de Allende, Gto. © 210/200-8758 in the U.S., or 415/152-1117. www.casaluna.com. 12 units. $135–$155 double. Rates include full breakfast. MC, V (for deposits). Children under 16 not accepted. **Amenities:** Bar; Jacuzzi; tour information; massage; nonsmoking rooms. *In room:* Safe.

Susurro ★★ *(Finds)* Spend any amount of time in places like San Miguel or Cuernavaca, and you realize that the domestic architecture is all about the creation of serene, private spaces. Susurro (which in Spanish refers to the sound made by whispering wind and trickling water) has elegant interior spaces, and with only four guest rooms, you'll find plenty of time to enjoy these all to yourself. The soft sounds of flowing water can be heard all around the house. Three of the rooms are large and come with separate terraces. The fourth, the garden room, is small but has a lovely patio area in the rear garden. All rooms have either a queen or a king bed and come beautifully decorated. The house is just a few blocks from the main square. Robert Waters, the owner, is an easy-going, agreeable man who makes an excellent host.

Recreo 78, 37700 San Miguel de Allende, Gto. © 310/943-7163 in the U.S., or 415/152-1065. www.susurro-sma. com. 4 units. $120–$175 double. Rates include full breakfast. AE. Children under 13 not accepted. **Amenities:** Jacuzzi; in-room massage; laundry service; nonsmoking rooms. *In room:* TV, hair dryer.

MODERATE
Hotel Mansión Virreyes Judicious remodeling has raised the comfort level in this three-story colonial hotel a half-block off the Jardín. Once a private home, it became the first hotel in San Miguel soon after the Mexican Revolution ended. The rooms are simple and comfortable but can be a little breezy. Almost all face the interior courtyard and hold two full beds and carpeted floors. Bathrooms are small to medium. Three suites with kitchenettes are quite large and usually rented out from January to March.

Canal 19, 37700 San Miguel de Allende, Gto. © 415/152-3355 or 415/152-0851. Fax 415/152-3865. mansionvirreyes@ prodigy.net.mx. 25 units. Fri–Sun $85 double, Mon–Thurs $75 double; $120–$160 suite. Rates include full breakfast. AE, MC, V. **Amenities:** Restaurant; room service until midnight. *In room:* TV.

Pensión Casa Carmen ★ Every B&B has its own feel, and this one feels like a friendly Mexican household. A pretty little Mexican patio with orange trees and a fountain; large rooms that are comfortably but simply furnished; and a gracious, helpful landlady who speaks English—all help set you at ease. All rooms have gas heaters and come with either two twins or one queen-size bed. Of these, the penthouse is perhaps the most comfortable, but the ones in the first courtyard have the most character. Bathrooms vary in size. Breakfast (daily) and the afternoon meal (Mon–Sat) are served in a pleasant dining room; the cooking is good. You can reserve rooms by the day, week, or month, with discounts for extended stays. The hotel is 2½ blocks east of the Jardín.

Correo 31, near Recreo (Apdo. Postal 152), 37700 San Miguel de Allende, Gto. ©/fax **415/152-0844**. ccarmen@unisono.net.mx. 11 units. $80 double. Rates include breakfast and lunch (breakfast only Sun). No credit cards. Children under 14 not accepted.

Posada Carmina ★ This centrally located hotel is comfortable, beautiful, and well managed. It's a half-block south of the plaza, next to the Parroquia, in a large colonial mansion made from the same stone as the church. The two floors of rooms surround a stately courtyard with orange trees growing around a stone fountain, and bougainvillea and llamarada creeping up the walls. Rooms are ample and well furnished. Most of the bathrooms are comfortably sized but simple, with small mirrors (and, in some, little counter space) and plenty of hot water. Light sleepers will find that the bells of the Parroquia prove a nuisance in the front rooms. The new section in back is quieter. Rooms there are midsize with well-lit bathrooms and firm mattresses.

Cuna de Allende 7, 37700 San Miguel de Allende, Gto. ✆ **415/152-0458**. Fax 415/152-1036. www.posadacarmina. com. 24 units. $75–$85 double. MC, V. **Amenities:** Restaurant; room service until 6pm. *In room:* TV.

INEXPENSIVE

Parador San Sebastián *(Value* The San Sebastián is a modest colonial house turned hotel with surprisingly spacious, attractive rooms for the price. Standard rooms are simple, quiet, and comfortable. Apartments come with kitchen and living/dining area. There are tables and chairs in the courtyard and on the rooftop terrace. This *parador* (inn) doesn't take reservations, so you have to try your luck. It's 3½ blocks northeast of the Jardín.

Mesones 7 (between Colegio and Núñez), 37700 San Miguel de Allende, Gto. ✆ **415/152-7084**. 27 units. $27 double; $40 apt. No credit cards. Free parking.

Quinta Loreto *(Value* This motel-like *quinta* (country house) is a good place to stay whether traveling by car or not. It has good rooms for the price, a lovely garden, and a friendly atmosphere. Rooms come with ceiling fans and heaters. The cheaper rooms, without phones or televisions, are smaller than the others. Most rooms contain one double and one twin bed. The food is good and the laundry service a bargain. Make reservations—the Loreto is very popular and often books up weeks in advance. Nonguests can come for breakfast ($3–$5) and for lunch ($8). The *quinta* is on a small street below the crafts market off Calle Loreto, about 7 blocks from the main square.

Calle Loreto 15, 37700 San Miguel de Allende, Gto. ✆ **415/152-0042**. Fax 415/152-3616. hqloreto@ cybermatsa.com.mx. 40 units. $45–$55 double. Weekly and monthly discounts available. AE, MC, V. Free parking. **Amenities:** Restaurant; small pool; tour desk; laundry service. *In room:* TV.

WHERE TO DINE

Competition among restaurants is fierce; new places open all the time, while established restaurants close or change ownership with unsettling frequency. In San Miguel vegetarians will have no problem—most restaurants have legitimate meat-free main courses. Reservations generally aren't necessary except during festival times. For the best baked goods (pastries, French bread, croissants, and cakes), try **El Petit Four,** Calle Mesones 99-1, down the street from the Angela Peralta Theater. It's open Tuesday through Saturday from 10am to 9pm, Sunday from 10am to 6pm. There's a small seating area, or you can take your baked goods with you. The shop also sells coffee.

For a dining experience a bit different from that offered by the following restaurants, try the local cooking at **Cenaduría La Alborada** at Sollano 11 (✆ **415/513-0577**) by the main square. It's a traditional sort of supper place where you can get a nourishing bowl of *pozole* or a plate of enchiladas. It's open Monday to Saturday from 2pm to 1am.

EXPENSIVE

Bella Italia ✿✿ ITALIAN This restaurant is the best thing the Hotel Sautto has going for it. The chef, Anselmo, does wonders. If you have time, order risotto, which takes a little while but is well worth it; it comes with asparagus, boletus mushrooms, or shrimp, depending on what's available. The chef's specials are good bets—duck breast with blueberry sauce, or crabmeat pasta would be an excellent choice. Pastas include fresh spinach ravioli. The restaurant is on the same street as Bellas Artes.

In the Hotel Sautto, Hernández Macías 59. 🕐 415/152-4989. Reservations recommended on weekends and during festivals. Main courses $13–$21. AE, MC, V. Daily 1–10:30pm.

MODERATE

Chamonix ECLECTIC   Dine on a lovely little patio on any number of dishes that seem to span the globe. The owners refuse to be limited to a particular cooking tradition—or, for that matter, even a particular continent. They do have some preferences—when it comes to European cooking, country-style over haute cuisine; with the Far East, Southeast Asian over Mandarin. Pastas are popular, and there are usually a couple of Asian or European options on the menu. But I was in the mood for something more substantial and ordered Sri Lankan curry—try it if it's on the menu. The Sunday brunch looks particularly good. There are two dining areas—one is nonsmoking.

Sollano 12-A. 🕐 415/154-8363. Reservations recommended on weekends and during festivals. Main courses $7–$15. MC, V. Tues–Sat 1:30–10pm; Sun brunch 11am–3pm.

El Market Bistro ⭐⭐⭐ FRENCH   Despite what the name might suggest, there is no postmodern jumble of cooking styles here—the food is traditional French. The main dining area is in a country-style courtyard just beyond the small, popular wine bar. Off the courtyard are interior dining rooms in case the night is chilly. The place has an informal feel, with none of the pretentiousness that often accompanies French food in Mexico. There are two menus: full and light. The full menu is full indeed; dishes include chateaubriand béarnaise, tournedos montagnarde, braised sweetbreads, and salmon a la Provençale.

Hernández Macías 95. 🕐 415/152-3229. Reservations recommended during high season. Main courses $7–$20. AE, MC, V. Daily 1–11pm.

L'Invito ⭐⭐⭐ ITALIAN   Silvia Bernardini, L'Invito's owner and chef, seems to prefer dishes that rely upon preparation rather than on liberal use of spices and herbs for their flavors. Good examples of this are *brasato* (beef cooked in delicately flavored vegetable gravy) and chicken alla Rossini (with creamy lemon sauce). Her tastes run toward rich and subtle flavors and away from showiness. She offers a variety of salads and dishes with pasta, some of which she makes on the premises. For dessert, there's tiramisu.

Calle Ancho de San Antonio 20 (inside the Instituto Allende). 🕐 415/152-7333. Main courses $8–$16. AE, MC, V. Daily 1–11pm.

Restaurant/Bar Bugambilia ⭐⭐⭐ MEXICAN   One can ask little more of a restaurant—delicious and attractive dishes, a large menu, good service, well-spaced tables, and a choice between dining in an elegant plant-filled courtyard and a large dining room, which in cool weather holds a roaring fire. Señora Arteaga offers a delicious variation on *chiles en nogada* (stuffed poblano chile with walnut cream sauce)—she marinates the pepper and serves it cold, not fried in batter. The *chiles en nogada* has been the object of many innovations, but most fail because they don't preserve the essence of this baroque dish, which balances opposites like the point and counterpoint of a fugue. Too spicy or too sweet, too strong a taste of meat or onions, and the magic is lost. Something simpler, perhaps? Start with the *caldo Xochitl* (the perfect soup for an irritable stomach), followed by traditional *enchiladas del portal* cooked in *chile ancho* sauce.

Hidalgo 42. ℭ **415/152-0127.** Reservations recommended on weekends. Main courses $10–$17. MC, V. Daily noon–11pm. From the Jardín, walk 2½ blocks north on Hidalgo.

Romanos ⚘ *Value* ITALIAN   This restaurant is run by an American restaurateur who moved to San Miguel to slow his life down but couldn't manage to get restaurants out of his system. He found a beautiful location that offers indoor and outdoor dining and has turned it into a popular spot serving great food in generous portions. The ingredients are fresh (organic when possible) and most of the pastas are made on the premises. Pizzas and fresh bread are baked in a wood-burning brick oven. Among the locals, the extrathick grilled pork chops earn lots of remarks, as do the pasta dishes or the pizzas.

Hernández Macías 9. ℭ **415/152-7454.** Reservations recommended. Main courses $8–$16. No credit cards. Tues–Sat 5–11pm.

INEXPENSIVE

El Correo ⚘ MEXICAN   The new owner has made changes to the menu, which are all for the good. He has decreased the number offerings and concentrated on producing quality renditions of Mexican standards. On my last visit I tried the *sopes* for an appetizer, a *caldo tlalpeño* (chicken, rice, and vegetable soup) for the soup course, and the *enchiladas del portal* (enchiladas with chile sauce). All were delicious. Other offerings include *mole, arrachera a la tampiqueña* (steak with an array of side dishes), and *corundas* (similar to tamales with no filling). This restaurant is opposite the post office, a half-block east of the Jardín. It's small and homey, with a limited number of tables.

Correo 23. ℭ **415/152-4951.** Reservations accepted. Breakfast $4–$5; main courses $7–$10. MC, V. Wed–Mon 8am–11pm.

El Pegaso Restaurant & Bar INTERNATIONAL   Decorated in a cheerful, colorful style, and with a friendly, helpful staff, this restaurant is popular with expatriates and visitors. It's particularly good for breakfast. The wide array of dishes includes eggs Benedict. For lunch or dinner you can order sandwiches, soups, or salads. The daily specials include Asian dishes. The restaurant is 1 block east of the Jardín.

Corregidora 6 (at Correo). ℭ **415/152-1351.** Breakfast $4–$8; soups, salads, sandwiches $5–$7; main courses $5–$15. MC, V. Mon–Sat 8:30am–10pm.

Olé Olé MEXICAN   Festive and friendly, this small restaurant is a riot of red and yellow streamers and bullfight memorabilia. The small menu specializes in grilled main courses—beef or chicken fajitas, shrimp brochettes, and *arrachera* (skirt steak). It also includes dishes such as *champiñones al ajillo* (mushrooms in garlic and *guajillo* chile) and *chistorra* (Spanish-style sausage).

Loreto 66. ℭ **415/152-0896.** Main courses $5–$12. No credit cards. Daily 1–9pm. From the San Francisco Plaza on Juárez, walk north and cross Mesones; jog left, then right where the street becomes Loreto, and continue for 3 or 4 blocks. Look for a yellow building on the left with a small sign.

SAN MIGUEL AFTER DARK

To see a calendar of events, find a copy of the local paper, *Atención,* or one of the free monthly periodicals for visitors. Bellas Artes and the Angela Peralta Theater also post announcements of performances around town. Local regulations favor restaurant-bars over simple bars, so live-music acts often perform in restaurants. Clubs and dance clubs tend to spring up and then die off quickly. One club that has persisted is **La Cava de la Princesa,** Recreo 3 (ℭ **415/152-1403**). It books a lot of live acts playing different kinds of music, as well as impersonators of Mexican pop stars. The cover charge is $3 to $8. A couple of restaurants are popular nightspots: **Tío Lucas** (© **415/ 512-4996**) is a fun place to hear jazz, have a few drinks and perhaps a bite of dinner. It's located at Mesones 105 across from the Teatro Peralta. **Mama Mía,** Umarán 8, between Jesús and Hernández Macías (© **415/152-2063**), has a bar area where salsa and jazz bands play on the weekends. There is a $4 cover. In the summer you can enjoy the late afternoon and early evening from its rooftop terrace. If you don't feel like hearing music, how about a drink and a movie? The **Cine Bar** at the Hotel Jacaranda (© **415/152-1015**), Calle Aldama 53, shows recently released American movies on a large screen and includes popcorn and a drink with the $6 price of admission. Waiters come to your table with drinks and will bring the dinner menu as well. The film starts rolling at 7:30pm. A couple of bars near El Jardín are good places if you just want to enjoy a drink with friends. One is **La Fragua,** next to Allende's house.

A SIDE TRIP TO DOLORES HIDALGO: FINE POTTERY & SHRIMP ICE CREAM

Dolores Hidalgo lies 40km (25 miles) northwest of San Miguel on Highway 35. Most people go there to shop at the Talavera companies, but the town itself merits a visit. It remains a quiet, provincial place with a lovely main square and parish church; on the church steps, Father Hidalgo proclaimed the independence of Mexico. The church has a charming facade that, if pressed, I would label late Mexican baroque, but that doesn't do it justice. The interior of the church was plundered at various times but retains a couple of altarpieces that are worth a peek.

The main square has a quaint, small-town feel to it. Vendors sell ice cream in exotic flavors—tequila, shrimp, and *pulque* (beer) are just a few enticing examples—as well as mango, *guanábana,* and other more familiar standbys. It all started 30 years ago on a dare, and then caught on for the notoriety it gave the vendors. Ask for some impossibly bad flavor like cilantro-mezcal-chocolate-chip or chicken *mole* swirl, and, without batting an eye, they'll tell you they're fresh out and to come back tomorrow. Most of these ice creams are known as *nieves* and are low in fat; for a richer ice cream ask for a *mantecado.* If you're hungry, there is a restaurant, El Patio, on the east side of the square.

Dolores has two small museums. The **Casa de Hidalgo** (admission $2) is filled with letters and historical artifacts having to do with Father Hidalgo, and will be of

---

Tips Recommended Day-Trip Tours

Dolores Hidalgo is the most popular destination for day-trippers from San Miguel. Some people make a day trip of Guanajuato or Querétaro. It's a hurried way of seeing them, but it can be done. Several tour guides and companies in San Miguel make trips to all of these places. **Leandro Delgado** (© **415/152-0155;** leandrotours@hotmail.com) is an independent tour guide who is well informed and conscientious. He speaks English, is a good driver, and is familiar with the artisans of Dolores Hidalgo and Guanajuato. Another tour agency is **PMC,** Hidalgo 18 (© **415/152-0121;** www.pmexc.com). It offers several options for day trips and walking tours of San Miguel, too. Both of these businesses offer trips to see the **monarch butterflies,** 5 hours away in the state of Michoacán (see chapter 7). This is an exhausting trip; do it in 2 days, overnighting in the town of Angangueo, if you can. The season runs from mid- to late November to March.

most interest to history buffs. The **Museo de la Independencia** (admission 50¢), a more dramatic approach to the theme of independence, also has a small collection of memorabilia of José Alfredo Jiménez, the king of *ranchera* music.

SHOPPING FOR TALAVERA

The **Talavera** pottery produced in Dolores is quite handsome and colorful, if less traditional than Talavera produced elsewhere. It is also cheaper and more plentiful. You can find all kinds of objects, from sink basins to napkin rings to hand-painted tiles. The pieces are formed with molds and then painted freehand. Prices here are considerably lower than those in San Miguel. Workshops are usually open from 10am to 6pm, but may or may not close for the afternoon meal. Almost all are closed on Sunday.

The first couple of Talavera workshops you'll encounter aren't even in town, but are on the highway just before you get there. **Talavera San Gabriel** (© **418/185-5037**) has a warehouse full of large and small decorative objects, including picture frames, candlesticks, and ginger jars. And **Talavera Mora** (© **418/185-9002**) has more dinnerware, including the popular blue-and-yellow fish pattern.

Once you get into town, you're best off just asking directions for different stores and factories. There are a lot of shops and each seems to have a different specialty. At the entrance to the town, on the left side of the first roundabout is **Hacienda Style** (© **418/182-2064** or 602/288-9122 in the U.S.; www.haciendastyle.net). It is the outlet for two factories that produce tiles and sink basins and decorative objects in traditional and contemporary patterns. Another that specializes in decorative objects is **Talavera Cortés** (© **418/182-0900**), at the corner of Distrito Federal and Tabasco streets. **Azulejos Talavera Vázquez** (© **418/182-0630**) has a large store at the corner of Puebla and Tamaulipas streets. It has a bit of everything, and at that same intersection are a couple of other stores with lots of dinnerware.

2 Guanajuato ★★★

354km (221 miles) NW of Mexico City; 56km (35 miles) SE of León; 93km (58 miles) W of San Miguel de Allende; 208km (130 miles) SW of San Luis Potosí; 163km (102 miles) N of Morelia; 280km (175 miles) SE of Zacatecas

If you're going to Mexico to lose yourself, you'll have no problem doing so on the streets of Guanajuato (gwah-nah-*whah*-toh). They seem designed for just that purpose as they curl this way and that, becoming alleys or stairways, and intersecting each other at different angles. At times it can seem like the Twilight Zone; I've heard of people hurriedly passing by a curious-looking shop intending to return later, and then never being able to locate it again. To make matters worse, the streets are filled with things that can draw your attention away from the business of getting from one place to another. The town is so photogenic; everywhere you look is postcard material. Most buildings, like the streets, are irregular in shape, creating a jumble of walls, balconies, and rooftops meeting at anything but a right angle. The churches are the exception, having regular floor plans, but even they show asymmetry—despite the best efforts of their builders, none has two matching towers, which only adds to their charm.

Founded in 1559, Guanajuato soon became a fabulously rich town, with world-famous mines (such as La Valenciana, Mineral de Cata, and Mineral de Rayas) that earned their owners titles of nobility. Along with Zacatecas and San Luis Potosí, Guanajuato was one of Mexico's most important mining cities. From the 16th through the 18th centuries, the mines in these towns produced a third of all the silver in the world, and Guanajuato bloomed with elaborate churches and mansions. Floods plagued the city until the citizenry finally diverted the river, leaving a bed for what has become a subterranean highway with cantilevered houses jutting out high above the road. To improve traffic flow, the city has opened an impressive network of tunnels (it is, after all, a mining town).

Still, on the surface Guanajuato seems like an old Spanish city dumped into a Mexican highland valley. It's one of Mexico's hidden gems, explored by relatively few foreign tourists, but popular with Mexicans. Picturesque and laden with atmosphere, Guanajuato should be high on your list of places to visit.

ESSENTIALS

GETTING THERE & DEPARTING   By Plane   Air access is good, with frequent flights in and out of the León-Guanajuato (also known as León/Bajío) airport, 27km (17 miles) from downtown Guanajuato. The taxi ride costs about $30. The airport has an ATM, pharmacy, and gift store. It also has the following car-rental counters: **Avis** (© 477/713-3003), **Budget** (© 477/713-1404), **Hertz** (© 477/771-5050), **National** (© 477/771-3371), and **Thrifty** (© 477/713-8522).

American Airlines's number in Mexico is © 01-800/904-6000; **Continental**'s is © 01-800/900-5000; **Delta**'s is © 01-800/902-2100. **Aeromexico** (© 01-800/021-4000) and its affiliate, **Aerolitoral,** fly to and from Los Angeles, Tijuana, Mexico City, Puerto Vallarta, Monterrey, and Ciudad Juárez. **Mexicana** (© 01-800/502-2000) flies to and from Chicago, Oakland, Los Angeles, Denver, San Jose, Guadalajara, Mexico City, and Tijuana. **AeroMar** (© 01-800/704-2900) flies to and from Saltillo and Puebla.

There are airline ticket offices in León and at the airport. In Guanajuato, travel agencies can arrange flights.

By Car   From Mexico City there are two routes. The faster one (4½ hr.), is Highway 57 north and northwest to Highway 45D at Querétaro, west through Salamanca to Irapuato, where you follow Highway 45 north to Silao and then take Highway 110 east. The route is a four-lane road almost all the way. The slower route continues north on Highway 57 past Querétaro, then west on Highway 110 through Dolores Hidalgo, and continues to Guanajuato. From San Luis Potosí, the quickest way to Guanajuato is through Dolores Hidalgo (3 hr.).

By Bus   The bus station in Guanajuato is 6km (3½ miles) southwest of town. From **Mexico City's Terminal Norte,** you'll have no trouble finding a *directo* (nonstop bus) to Guanajuato. **Servicios Coordinados/Primera Plus** (© 55/5567-4388) and **Estrella Blanca** (© 55/5729-4388) run express buses (5 hr.). You shouldn't have to wait more than a half-hour. Try to catch one of **ETN**'s (© 55/5785-1576) superdeluxe buses with extrawide seats that recline far back (eight per day). They're worth the extra money.

From **San Miguel de Allende,** ETN has two nonstop buses, Primera Plus/Servicios Coordinados has five, and Herradura de Plata has a couple. These go *vía la Presa* (the short route—1¼ hr.). Don't take buses that go via Dolores Hidalgo. There is also service to Guadalajara (4 hr.), Morelia (2½ hr.), and elsewhere.

ORIENTATION   Arriving by Plane   The only transportation from the León-Guanajuato airport, 27km (17 miles) from downtown, is a **private taxi.** You pay for the cab ($30) inside the airport. There is no shuttle service.

Arriving by Car   Try not to lose your sanity while finding a place to park. Such a winding, hilly town defies good verbal or written directions. Be alert for one-way streets. Consider parking your car until you leave town, because the frustration of driving in the city could spoil your visit.

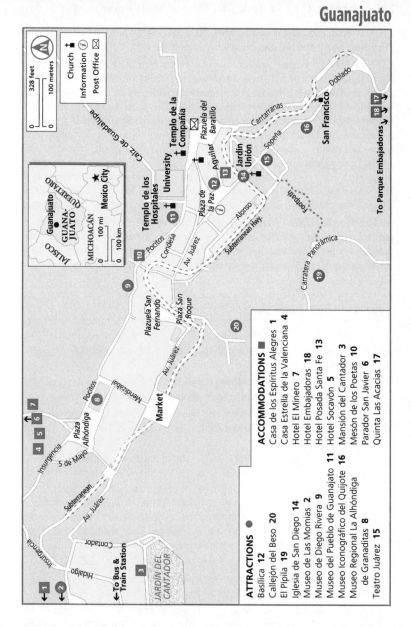

Guanajuato

N

| 0 | 328 feet |
| 0 | 100 meters |

† Church
ⓘ Information
⊠ Post Office

ATTRACTIONS ●
Basílica **12**
Callejón del Beso **20**
El Pípila **19**
Iglesia de San Diego **14**
Museo de Las Momias **2**
Museo de Diego Rivera **9**
Museo del Pueblo de Guanajuato **11**
Museo Iconográfico del Quijote **16**
Museo Regional La Alhóndiga
  de Granaditas **8**
Teatro Juárez **15**

ACCOMMODATIONS ■
Casa de los Espíritus Alegres **1**
Casa Estrella de la Valenciana **4**
Hotel El Minero **7**
Hotel Embajadoras **18**
Hotel Posada Santa Fe **13**
Hotel Socavón **5**
Mansión del Cantador **3**
Mesón de los Poetas **10**
Parador San Javier **6**
Quinta Las Acacias **17**

Arriving by Bus   The bus station is about 6km (3½ miles) southwest of town, on the road to Celaya. Cabs are easy to come by and should cost about $3.

VISITOR INFORMATION   The state **tourism information office** is at Plaza de la Paz 14, across from the basilica (© **473/732-0397,** ext. 107). It's open Monday through Wednesday from 9am to 7pm, Thursday and Friday from 9am to 8pm, Saturday from

10am to 4pm, and Sunday and holidays from 10am to 2pm. It has a knowledgeable English-speaking staff and distributes a free map of the city.

CITY LAYOUT   Guanajuato is a town of narrow streets, alleys, and stairs and small, picturesque plazas. The hilly terrain and tangle of streets are difficult to represent on a map. You'll soon learn that maps aren't drawn to scale, nor do they show every street and stairway. The best way to get oriented to the major sights is to get the *Mapa Turístico* published by the state tourism office. It represents the city as it would appear from the overlook at Pípila's statue. Then visit the overlook (see "The Top Attractions," below) and compare what you see with the map. This will help you get your bearings.

The **Jardín Unión,** known as the cheese wedge for its shape, the small plaza at the center of the city—is the place where students, locals, and visitors gather. Facing the Jardín from the direction of El Pípila are both the **Teatro Juárez** and **Templo de San Diego.** From this plaza, you are within walking distance of many of the major sights.

GETTING AROUND   Walking is the only way to get to know the historic district of this labyrinthine town. For longer stretches, taxis are reasonably priced and abundant, except between 2 and 4pm when office workers are trying to get home for the midafternoon meal. As usual, you should establish the price before setting out.

FAST FACTS: Guanajuato

Area Code   The telephone area code is **473.**

Climate   The city has temperatures that are mild in summer, cool in winter, with the occasional freeze at night.

Elevation   Guanajuato sits at 2,008m (6,700 ft.).

Emergency & Police   Seguridad Pública (© **473/732-0266**).

Hospital   You have two reasonable choices: **Centro Médico La Presa,** Paseo de la Presa 85 (© **473/731-1074**), and **Clínica Plaza Mayor,** in the western part of the city (© **473/732-2305**).

Internet Access   There are several Internet cafes in the downtown area, with a lot of turnover. Just keep your eyes peeled for any sign that says INTERNET or CYBERCAFE.

Language School   There are five language schools in Guanajuato. The best known is **Academia Falcón,** Paseo de la Presa 80 (© **473/731-0745**; www.academiafalcon. com; mailing address: Callejón de la Mora 158, 36000 Guanajuato, Gto.). The institute provides skilled and dedicated tutors for those at all levels, and gets high marks from students. It can also arrange boarding with local families.

Pharmacy   **Farmacia Embajadoras,** Paseo Madero 10 (© **473/732-0996**), or **Farmacia La Perla,** Juárez 146 (© **473/732-1175**).

Population   Guanajuato has 135,000 residents.

Post Office   The *correo,* on the corner of Ayuntamiento and Carcamanes, near the Templo de la Compañía, is open Monday through Friday from 9am to 6pm.

Seasons   The rainy season is June through September. Occasionally the rain is hard, but mostly it's afternoon showers and presents no problems for travelers. The coldest part of the year is December and January; the hottest is April, May, and some of June, before the rains come.

SPECIAL EVENTS & FESTIVALS

Every year in October, the state of Guanajuato sponsors the **Festival Cervantino (International Cervantes Festival)** ⭐⭐, 2 weeks of performing arts from all over the world. In recent years, the festival has featured marionettes from the Czech Republic, the Eliot Feld Ballet from New York, the Kiev Ballet, and a host of Mexican artists. The shows are held in open plazas and theaters all over town. Book rooms well in advance during the festival; if Guanajuato is full, consider staying in San Miguel de Allende.

For ticket information and a schedule, contact Festival Cervantino, Plaza San Francisquito 1, 36000 Guanajuato, Gto. (℅ **473/731-1221**). Once you know the schedule, you can order tickets through **Ticketmaster** in Mexico City (℅ **55/5325-9000**). Keep your confirmation number; you'll need it to pick up your tickets in Guanajuato. The best time to be at the festival is during the week; on weekends it's absolute madness.

EXPLORING GUANAJUATO
THE TOP ATTRACTIONS

El Pípila   This is the best vantage point in Guanajuato for photographs—the whole city unfolds below you, with great views in every direction. A funicular railway runs up the hill from behind the church of San Diego. You can also climb the hill on foot up a rugged winding pathway. Just look for signs that read AL PIPILA (to El Pípila).

The statue is the city's monument to José de los Reyes Martínez, better known as El Pípila. According to the story, El Pípila (if he existed) was a brave young miner in Father Hidalgo's ragtag army of peasants and workers fighting for Mexican independence. Guanajuato was the first real battle of the war. The royalist forces took up their position inside the Alhóndiga de Granaditas. It seemed impregnable to Hidalgo's army, which lacked artillery. But El Pípila managed to breach the Spanish defenses by tying a flagstone to his back as protection, crawling to the fortress doors, and setting them ablaze. Today, El Pípila's statue raises a torch high over the city in everlasting vigilance; the inscription at his feet proclaims AUN HAY OTRAS ALHONDIGAS POR INCENDIAR (There still remain other *alhóndigas* to burn).

Free admission. Daily 24 hr.

Museo del Pueblo de Guanajuato ⭐⭐   Just north of the Plaza de la Paz is this 17th-century mansion that once belonged to the Marqués San Juan de Rayas. The first and third floors display traveling exhibits; the second holds a fascinating collection of colonial-era civil and religious pieces gathered by distinguished local muralist José Chávez Morado. As a collector, Chávez Morado had an eye for the macabre, acquiring death portraits, some even eerier portraits of the living, and religious paintings on the subject of mortality. Also in the collection are some paintings by the gifted Hermenegildo Bustos, a portrait artist of the 19th century. There is a small collection of pre-Hispanic artifacts and several folk-art testimonials dedicated to the miraculous powers of various saints. The museum contains a couple of Chávez's murals; other works can be found at La Alhóndiga, down the street.

Calle Positos 7. ℅ **473/732-2990**. Admission $2. Tues–Sat 10am–6:30pm; Sun 10am–2:30pm.

Museo Iconográfico del Quijote ⭐ *(Finds)*   There are only a few truly universal characters in the world of literature: Hamlet, Faust, Don Juan, and Don Quixote come to mind. Writers far and wide have taken up these characters and reworked their stories, but Don Quixote much more than the others has become a favorite subject of artists. The list includes Dalí, Picasso, Miró, Raul Angiano, José Guadalupe Posada, Daumier, José Moreno Carbonero, and Pedro Coronel. This museum, a long block southeast of the Jardín Unión, holds a fascinating collection of art based upon Don Quixote—all Quixote, all the time! Particularly forceful are the sculptures and murals, but the sheer variety of forms and thematic treatment is what makes a stroll through this museum so entertaining.

Manuel Doblado 1. ℂ 473/732-6721. Free admission. Tues–Sat 10am–6:30pm; Sun 10am–2:30pm.

Museo Regional La Alhóndiga de Granaditas ★★ On the same street as the Rivera Museum, 2 blocks farther down, is La Alhóndiga de Granaditas, which was built between 1798 and 1809 as the town granary—hard to believe, because it is such a beautiful building. The Spanish took refuge here in 1810 when El Pípila (see above) and company captured Guanajuato. A slaughter ensued that Father Hidalgo was unable to stop. This convinced many people who had been leaning toward independence to remain loyal to Spain, although when the Spanish forces under Félix Calleja retook Guanajuato, they exacted an equally horrible revenge on the locals suspected of collusion. (The exhibits tell the story.) By the next year, the royalist forces triumphed, and the heads of the insurrectionists Hidalgo, Allende, Aldama, and Jiménez adorned the four corners of the building, where they remained until 1821 as a dissuasive reminder.

The old granary now houses a *museo regional* (regional museum). The interior courtyard is large and beautiful and shouldn't be missed. Two floors of rooms hold exhibits of pre-Columbian artifacts, displays on colonial history, and regional crafts. Adorning the two stairways to the second floor are the vivid murals of José Chávez Morado, who donated his pre-Hispanic art collection to the museum (and whose colonial-era collection is in the Museo del Pueblo de Guanajuato). The exhibits that follow take you through the region's colonial era and its role in the struggle for independence, all the way up to the Mexican Revolution. Explanatory text is in Spanish only, but the artifacts are interesting and well displayed. Down the hill from the Alhóndiga is the Mercado Hidalgo (see "Shopping," below).

Mendizábal 6. ℂ 473/732-1112. Admission $3.25, free for students with ID. Video camera $3. Tues–Sat 10am–2pm and 4–6pm; Sun 10am–3pm.

Museum Birthplace of Diego Rivera ★★ From the Museo del Pueblo, walk 1½ blocks farther down the street, and you'll find the house where the artist Diego Rivera was born on December 8, 1886. It has been restored and converted into a museum. The first floor is furnished as it might have been in the era of Rivera's birth. Upstairs there's a pretty good collection of his early works. He began painting when he was 10 years old and eventually moved to Paris, where he became a Marxist during World War I. The house contains a few sketches of some of the earlier murals that made his reputation, and paintings from 1902 to 1956. The fourth floor holds a small auditorium for lectures and conferences, and there you'll find a large representation of one of Rivera's most famous murals, *Un Sueño Dominical en la Alameda*.

Calle Positos 47. ℂ 473/732-1197. Admission $2. Tues–Sat 10am–6:30pm; Sun 10am–2:30pm.

Teatro Juárez Built in 1903 during the opulent era of the Porfiriato, this theater is now the venue for many productions, especially during the Festival Cervantino. The exterior is starkly at odds with its surroundings—Greco-Roman portico adorned with fin-de-siècle bronze lions and lanterns. The interior is especially eye-catching. Box seats rise up four stories along the walls of the theater, and there's not a bad seat in the house.

Jardín de la Unión. ℰ 473/732-0183. Admission $1. Still camera $1, video camera $2. Tues–Sun 9am–1:45pm and 5–7:45pm.

MORE ATTRACTIONS

The **Church of San Diego,** on the Jardín Unión, stands almost as it did in 1633, when it was built under the direction of Franciscan missionaries. A flood in 1760 nearly destroyed it. The reconstruction was completed in 1786, largely at the expense of the Count of La Valenciana. The pink cantera-stone facade is a fine example of the Mexican baroque.

The **Plazuela del Baratillo,** just behind the Jardín Unión, has a beautiful fountain (a gift from Emperor Maximilian) at its center. You'll always find people sitting around it peacefully, some in the shade and others in the sun. Its name derives from its former role as a weekly *tianguis* (market); vendors would yell *"¡Barato!"* ("Cheap!").

Just west of Baratillo is the **Church of the Compañía.** Built in 1747 by the Jesuit order, it was the biggest of their churches. It dominates the street. The churrigueresque decoration lightens it somewhat, but the interior, which was restored in the 19th century, is neoclassical. This church was built as part of a Jesuit university, which was founded in 1732 on orders of Philip V. It's the last of 23 universities the Jesuit order built in Mexico. The main building of the **university** is on the same block as the church. Its entrance was rebuilt in 1945 in imposing neoclassical style.

Farther west, between the main street, Juárez, and Calle Positos are three plazas almost connected to each other and worth seeing: **Plaza San Roque, Jardín de la Reforma,** and **Plaza San Fernando,** where you can sit at one of the outdoor tables and enjoy coffee in a perfectly charming setting. This plaza is an increasingly popular hangout, and it's a good area to find an Internet cafe.

NEARBY ATTRACTIONS

The following attractions are all a short distance above the city, and the best way to get to them is by taxi. You can hire one for $10 per hour. I would recommend taking the panoramic highway around the city, which allows you to pass by La Valenciana, La Cata, and La Raya; each has a mine and a church. The highway circles around to El Pípila. The drive is enjoyable and lasts about an hour, with a couple of stops and a quick drive along the submerged highway to view the houses that are perched precariously above the road.

La Valenciana ✦✦✦   The area around La Valenciana mine holds several attractions, shopping destinations, and a good restaurant. You might want to allot several hours for a visit, but keep in mind that everything closes by 6pm. The star attraction is the magnificent **church of San Cayetano,** built toward the end of the colonial period in the opulent style of Mexican baroque. The interior is a dazzling affair, with gilded carvings and *retablos* (altarpieces). The best time to see it is midafternoon, when sunlight pours through the windows, illuminating the golden carvings.

In the church plaza are an excellent folk-art store called **Ojo de Venado** (see "Shopping," below) and a rock-and-mineral shop. Guides offer (in Spanish only) a short, so-so **tour of the mine** ($1) and explain something of its operation. Zacatecas has a more interesting mine tour. Look for a sign that says BOCAMINA–LA VALENCIANA.

Across the road from the church is the house of the Count of La Valenciana, which now holds a restaurant, **La Casa del Conde de la Valenciana** (see "Where to Dine," later in this chapter) and a shop (see "Shopping," below). La Valenciana silver mine is still in operation. The mining operations are a couple of hundred yards west of the house. It's an eight-sided vertical shaft (500m/1,650 ft. deep) surrounded by a tall stone wall in the shape of a crown with large wooden doors and a miner's chapel at the entrance. The miners extract silver and about 50 other minerals and metals.

If you keep climbing on the road that runs alongside La Valenciana, you will shortly see the driveway up to Casa de Capelo (see "Shopping," below) and to Cerámica La Cruz. Continue for a few miles farther and you come to the small town of Santa Rosa, where you can see yet more beautiful ceramics at Mayólica Santa Rosa (see "Shopping," below).

Templo de la Valenciana, Valenciana. Free admission. Daily 9am–6pm.

Museo de Los Momias (Mummy Museum)   First-time visitors find this museum grotesque or fascinating or both: Mummified remains of the dead, some of whom wear tattered clothing from centuries past, are on display. Dryness and the earth's gases and minerals in this particular *panteón* (pantheon) have halted decomposition. Because graveyards have limited space, bodies are eventually exhumed in Mexico to make room for newcomers. Those on display were exhumed between 1865 and 1985. The mummies stand or recline in glass cases, grinning, choking, or staring, while tour guides tell crowds of visitors macabre stories in Spanish of the fates of some of the deceased. Are they true? *¿Quién sabe?* But it's impossible to resist the temptation to go up and look at them, and this is the only graveyard I've seen with souvenir stands. They mostly sell sugar skulls and effigies of the mummies. Next to the mummy museum is a small exhibit called "El Culto a la Muerte" (Worship of the Dead) which is a bad mix of morbid and hokey.

Esplanada del Panteón. (📞) 473/732-0639. Admission $2. Still camera $1, video camera $2. Daily 9am–6pm. At the northwest end of town, the steep Esplanada del Panteón leads up to the municipal cemetery.

Templo de Cata   Up above the city, perched on the mountain to the north, is this small, elaborate "miners' church." Cata is also the name of the mine nearby and the *barrio* (neighborhood) that surrounds the church. A lovely baroque facade, with just one tower standing, decorates the outside. Until a couple of years ago, this church held an enormous number of personal testimonials that covered the walls from floor to ceiling. Most of these took the traditional form of small square sheets of metal with painted scenes (in a primitive folk style) and explanatory text describing the miracles performed by the church's Señor de Villaseca. "El Trigueñito" (roughly translated as "the olive-skinned one"), as he is affectionately called, is a popular figure in Guanajuato, especially with miners and truck and taxi drivers. The testimonials were a touching display of the highly personal relationship these people have with El Trigueñito. What has become of all these testimonials is now the question. At first, the removal of the testimonials was supposed to be temporary, but I suspect they might not be coming back.

Carretera Panorámica. Free admission. Daily 9am–5pm.

A NEARBY MUSEUM   Surrounding Guanajuato were more than 150 haciendas of wealthy colonial mine owners. Most are now either in ruins or restored and privately owned, but one has been made into the **Museo Exhacienda San Gabriel de Barrera** (✿). About 3km (2 miles) from town on the road to Marfil, it's a lovely place noted for its elaborate gardens in different styles (Moorish, English, and Spanish, for example). The hacienda house presents a good picture of 18th-century life in the grand style. As is often the case, the hacienda has its own chapel (baroque, of course), with a key identifying the various figures depicted in the *retablo* (altarpieces). There is also a state-run shop displaying all the handicrafts produced in the state. The grounds are open daily from 9am to 6pm; admission is $2.50, plus $1 for a still camera or $1.50 for a video camera. The store's hours are Wednesday through Sunday from 10am to 5pm.

SHOPPING

Stores in Guanajuato keep the usual hours—Monday through Saturday from 10am to 2pm and 4 to 8pm. The **Mercado Hidalgo,** or municipal market, is one of the most orderly in Mexico. You can browse on the main floor or watch the action from the raised walkway that encircles it. Aside from food and vegetable stalls, there's lots of pottery and ceramic ware.

Artesanías Vázquez   Outlet for a factory in Dolores Hidalgo, this place is small but loaded with the colorful Talavera-style pottery for which Dolores is famous. You'll see plates, ginger jars, frames, cups and saucers, serving bowls, and the like. Cantarranas 8. © 473/732-5231.

Casa de Capelo   Famous ceramist Javier de Jesús Hernández, known simply as Capelo, has his workshop and showroom high above Guanajuato, past La Valenciana church. You'll see signs for the store, which point to a dirt road that climbs steeply to the left of the highway. It's open Monday through Friday from 10am to 6pm. Carretera a Dolores Hidalgo s/n. © 473/732-8964.

Cerámica La Cruz   If you're on your way up to see Capelo's store, stop here, just below Capelo's, to view another style of ceramic ware that plays a lot with glazes producing crackleware, among other things. Its hours are Monday through Friday from 10am to 6pm. Carretera a Dolores Hidalgo s/n. © 473/732-9037.

The Gorky González Workshop   This prize-winning ceramist has dedicated himself to bringing back the traditional Talavera of Guanajuato. The workshop is a short cab ride from the historic center. The showroom is open Monday through Friday from 10am to 2pm and 4 to 6pm, Saturday from 10am to 1pm. Call first. Calle Pastita Ex Huerta de Montenegro (by the baseball field). © 473/731-0389.

La Casa del Conde de la Valenciana   In the same building as the restaurant in La Valenciana, this small shop carries an eye-catching selection of ceramics and furnishings from all over Mexico. It's open daily from 10am to 6pm. Across from the church of San Cayetano. © 473/732-2550.

Mayólica Santa Rosa   In the small town of Santa Rosa, on the way to Dolores Hidalgo, is this factory store. It carries high-quality mayólica for much less money than in Guanajuato. It's open Monday through Friday from 8am to 5pm. On the highway. © 473/739-0572.

Ojo de Venado   A knowledgeable dealer of folk art sells wonderful pieces from Michoacán and areas near Guanajuato. He specializes in unique, highly expressive works. The store is open daily from 10am to 6pm. Below the church of San Cayetano. © 473/734-1435.

Rincón Artesanal   Objects in carved wood, wax, papier-mâché, pewter, and ceramic, produced in different workshops throughout the state of Guanajuato, stock this store. It also carries items from farther afield, including beautiful *catrina calaveras* (skeleton statues in fancy dress) from the state of Michoacán. The mother and daughter who own and run the place are very helpful. It's open daily from 10am to 9pm. Sopeña 5 (1 block east of Jardín Unión). © 473/732-8632.

WHERE TO STAY

Hotels have high-season rates for Christmas, Easter, and the Festival Cervantino. High season at moderate and inexpensive hotels also includes July and August, when schools are out and families vacation and any long weekend. During the Festival Cervantino, in October, rooms are virtually impossible to find without a reservation, and even then it's good to claim your room early in the day. Some visitors have to stay as far away as León or San Miguel de Allende. Rates quoted here include the 17% tax.

VERY EXPENSIVE

Casa Estrella de la Valenciana 🏠🏠🏠 This is a beautiful modern house perched on the mountain side above La Valenciana church. It's constructed in contemporary Mexican style in such a way as to take full advantage of the panoramic view of the city and surrounding valley. The owners—two American women, one of whom lives on the premises—have taken pains to create comfortable, spacious interiors decorated with the tiles, pottery, and arts of the area. The bathrooms, the fixtures, the linens—everything has been handled with meticulous attention. Guest rooms are named after local mines. All have their own balcony or terrace; two are handicap accessible. The two most expensive are quite large and have special amenities such as a private Jacuzzi (La Valenciana) or a steam locker (La Sirena). Each comes with a king bed. Another oversize room, the San Bernabé, comes with two queens and has both a tub and a shower. The others have either a queen or a king bed. La Cata is the smallest, most economical but is still of a good size. It has a lovely boveda ceiling. Common areas include a living room and an upstairs terrace and a poolside patio. These are attractive and inviting, and there's a library and an honor bar.

Callejón Jalisco 10, Col. La Valenciana 36240 Guanajuato, Gto. © 866/983-8844 in the U.S., or 473/732-1748. Fax 563/430-0648 in the U.S. www.mexicaninns.com. 6 units. $175 double; $199–$210 suite; $234 master suite. Rates include full breakfast and beverages. AE. Free parking. Small pets allowed. In the colonia above La Valenciana church. **Amenities:** Heated outdoor pool; Jacuzzi; in-room massage; babysitting; overnight laundry; nonsmoking rooms. *In room:* TV, DVD/VCR, hair dryer, iron, safe, no phone.

Quinta Las Acacias 🏠🏠 To stay here is to go back in time, not to the colonial period as with so many hotels, but to the late 19th century, when architecture and design in Mexico were borrowing heavily from French (called *afrancesado*) and Victorian styles. This elegant house, like so many on the Paseo de la Presa, was built then and has been painstakingly remodeled. The rooms are decorated and furnished with period furniture, wallpaper, and wainscoting. I prefer the three suites on the second floor (in Mexico, this is the first floor) to the three on the third floor. Behind the house are three larger, modern suites that have Jacuzzis. Rooms contain one king or two queen beds and have spacious, well-equipped bathrooms. Breakfast can be served in the dining room, on the terrace, or in the guest's room. The cocktail area serves drinks until 10pm. The higher rates listed here are for high season.

Paseo de la Presa 168. 36000 Guanajuato, Gto. © 888/497-4129 in the U.S., or 473/731-1517. Fax 473/731-1862. www.quintalasacacias.com.mx. 10 units. $220–$240 suite; $263–$295 suite with Jacuzzi; $315 master suite. AE, MC, V. Rates include breakfast. Free limited parking. Children under 14 not accepted. **Amenities:** Restaurant; bar; large outdoor Jacuzzi; tour desk; laundry service; dry cleaning. *In room:* A/C, TV, hair dryer, safe.

EXPENSIVE

Casa de Espíritus Alegres B&B ★★★ *Moments*   Folk art and atmosphere abound in this idiosyncratic "house of happy spirits," a 16th-century colonial hacienda. The rooms are decorated and furnished in a vivacious and attractive style. Each fulfills the promise of "a skeleton in every closet," and each has its own fireplace. The grounds are so lovely you don't want to leave.

Breakfast, served overlooking the garden, features Californian and Mexican food, with generous helpings of fresh fruit. Check out the hand-painted chairs (decorated by artist friends of the owners); one pays homage to Frida Kahlo. Guests have use of the folk-art-decorated living room, and may borrow history, travel, and art books as well as paperback novels. The B&B is 3km (2 miles) from downtown (10 min. by taxi). The bilingual staff can set you up with a guide.

La Exhacienda la Trinidad 1, 36250 Marfil, Gto. ℂ/fax 473/733-1013. www.casaspirit.com. 8 units. $158–$181 double. Rates include breakfast. No credit cards. Free guarded parking. **Amenities:** Tour info; massage; laundry service; nonsmoking rooms. *In room:* Hair dryer, no phone.

Parador San Javier ★★ *Kids*   Created from a former silver-mining hacienda, the San Javier is built around lovely tree-shaded grounds (completely walled in) about 5 blocks above the Alhóndiga. Rooms in the six-story back section are large, carpeted, quiet, and comfortable. They have good lighting and usually come with two double beds. My favorites are four standard rooms in the original structure, with vaulted brick ceilings. They have more character and go for the same price. The suites are quite large and better furnished; most come with a king-size bed. The regular suites have separate sitting rooms. The "senior suite" has two bedrooms with four double beds, two bathrooms, and a very large living room. A lovely pool is open during the season. Beneath the hotel bar is a cave with a natural spring that was the water source for the original hacienda.

Plaza Aldama 92, 36020 Guanajuato, Gto. ℂ **473/732-2222** or 473/732-0626. www.paradorsanjavier.com.mx. 114 units. $100–$110 double; $120–$140 suite; $270 2-bedroom suite. AE, MC, V. Free guarded parking. **Amenities:** Restaurant; 2 bars; large heated pool; wading pool; room service until 11pm; babysitting; laundry service; dry cleaning; nonsmoking rooms. *In room:* TV, dataport, safe.

MODERATE

Hotel Embajadoras   I liked this hotel a lot more before the owners raised the rates by about 40%. Still, you might want to call for a price check. The location is good— right on Parque Embajadoras, a tree-lined square that's a 10-minute walk east of the main square (not much climbing). The rooms are plain but quiet. They come with carpeted floors, and midsize bathrooms. A reasonably priced restaurant with pleasant outdoor dining area takes care of meals.

Parque Embajadoras, 36000 Guanajuato, Gto. ℂ 473/731-0105. Fax 473/731-0063. hotelembajadoras@hotmail.com. 27 units. $55–$65 double. MC, V. Free parking. **Amenities:** Restaurant; travel agency; room service until 9:30pm. *In room:* TV.

Hotel Posada Santa Fe ★   Right on the Jardín Unión, this hotel is for those who want to be in the thick of things from the moment they step out the door. It dates from the 1860s, having survived both the reform wars and the revolution, and the old lobby is a great place to have a drink. The hotel recently underwent extensive remodeling, and the wiring and plumbing in most of the building was replaced, which was money well spent. But the size of the rooms was one thing that couldn't be changed.

They're small, except for the suites and some of the rooms with exterior views. They are, however, attractive, well kept, and comfortable. Standard rooms hold either one double or two twin beds. Exterior-view rooms and suites have larger bathrooms and fancier furniture; most have king-size beds. Prices vary considerably for seasons.

Jardín Unión, 36000 Guanajuato, Gto. ℂ 473/732-0084. Fax 473/732-4653. www.posadasantafe.com. 48 units. $90–$120 double; $140–$210 suite and exterior views. AE, MC, V. Free limited valet parking. **Amenities:** Restaurant; 2 bars; whirlpool; room service until 10pm; laundry service. *In room:* TV.

Mesón de los Poetas   I love hotels that are unself-conscious expressions of their city, and this is just such a place. Set against a hillside, it makes the most of its space by clever positioning of rooms in an irregular jumble. Following the stairs and walk-ways that led to my room, I thought for a moment I was trapped in a M. C. Escher drawing. Only a native architect would have hit upon such a solution.

Standard rooms are decorated in the attractive modern Mexican style. They vary in size, and a few come with kitchenettes. The largest hold two double beds. Others come with only one double or a double and a twin. The lighting in all the rooms is good. The bathrooms are adequate. Suites have king-size beds, but I prefer the two-bedroom suites, which have a spacious, attractive living room with dining table and chairs, a sitting area, and a nice kitchenette. The bedrooms hold a double bed or two twins. (Kitchenettes come with little in the way of cooking implements, but ask for some and you may get them.) The hotel is right downtown by the Diego Rivera museum.

Positos 35, 36000 Guanajuato, Gto. ℂ/fax **473/732-6657** or 473/732-0705. www.mexonline.com/poetas.htm. 31 units. $80–$95 double; $150 2-bedroom suite; $140–$160 suite. Extra person $9. MC, V. Limited off-site parking. **Amenities:** Tour info; laundry service; nonsmoking rooms. *In room:* TV, coffeemaker on request.

INEXPENSIVE

Hotel El Minero 🄵*Value*   Only 3 blocks above the Museo Alhóndiga, this four-story (no elevator) hotel has a rare commodity: cheap rooms that aren't ugly or small. New tile floors, attractive paint jobs, ceiling fans, and cleanliness are the high points. The location is good, and the back rooms are quiet, but the lighting is just okay, the bathrooms are small, and the TVs don't add much to the experience of staying here. Most rooms have a double and a single bed. A major inconvenience was having to hike out to get coffee and breakfast.

Alhóndiga 12-A, 36000 Guanajuato, Gto. ℂ **473/732-5251**. Fax 473/732-4739. 20 units. $35–$45 double. MC, V. **Amenities:** Restaurant. *In room:* TV.

Hotel Socavón   *Socavón* means "mine shaft," and that's something of the feel you get when you walk from the door to the reception area. Farther back, up a couple of flights of stairs (no elevator), are four floors of rooms around a small colonial-style courtyard. Rooms have tile floors, fans, cable TV with a few English channels, and small bathrooms. All are quiet and have either two full beds or a full and a twin. The lighting is poor.

Alhóndiga 41-a, 36000 Guanajuato, Gto. ℂ **473/732-4885**. Fax 473/732-7344. hotelsocavon@hotmail.com. 38 units. $36–$55 double. AE, MC, V. Free sheltered parking. **Amenities:** Restaurant; bar; room service until 11pm; laundry service. *In room:* TV.

Mansión del Cantador   For a no-frills hotel, I like this choice. It offers large, cheerful rooms on the Jardín del Cantador for a good price. Being on this square cuts down on noise, and yet it's still close to the market and the Alhóndiga. Most rooms come with two double beds. The standard midsize bathrooms are in good repair.

Cantador 19, 36000 Guanajuato, Gto. © **473/732-6888**. hmcr84@hotmail.com. 41 units. $45–$59 double. Rates include full breakfast. V. **Amenities:** Restaurant; bar.

WHERE TO DINE

The quality of restaurants in the downtown area is inexplicably poor. I list three below where one can get a decent meal. In addition, try an outdoor table at the restaurant of the **Hotel Posada Santa Fe** (see above), which is a wonderful way of enjoying the Jardín de la Union. The Jardín has a closed, intimate feel; if you want something more open with longer vistas, try the Plaza de la Paz, a block away. Here you can sit, have a drink, and perhaps nibble on an appetizer at one of the outdoor cafes in front of Guanajuato's cathedral. If you're in search of coffee, the best in town is at the **Café Dada** on the Plaza del Baratillo. It's open from 9am to 11pm daily.

EXPENSIVE

Casa del Conde de la Valenciana ★★ MEXICAN/INTERNATIONAL   Dine in the former home of the count of La Valenciana, across the street from his other creation, La Valenciana church. You can eat on the patio or in one of the dining rooms. The menu is a combination of old standards and original recipes. For an appetizer, try a fresh salad or refreshing gazpacho served in a vessel encased in ice. For a main course, you can choose one of Mexico's traditional dishes, such as chicken *mole* (or *enmoladas*), or perhaps chicken breast *a la flor de calabaza* (in a mild, satisfying cream sauce of blended squash flowers and poblano chile). The shady patio is so relaxing and the chairs so comfortable that many linger here over coffee and dessert.

Carretera Guanajuato-Dolores Km 5, opposite La Valenciana church. ©/fax **473/732-2550**. Main courses $7–$12. MC, V. Mon–Wed noon–6pm; Thurs–Sat noon–10pm.

Chez Nicole ★★ INTERNATIONAL   In the Marfil area outside Guanajuato proper, next to the Casa de Espíritus Alegres (see "Where to Stay," above), this shady outdoor restaurant offers leisurely dining in a garden setting. The owner, Nicole, is French but has lived in Mexico for a long time. Things to try include oyster mushrooms with garlic and parsley as an appetizer and the fondue *tequileño* (tequila with three Mexican cheeses: Manchego, Chihuahua, and asadero) for a main course. Or try the farm-raised trout, *trucha salmonada,* prepared three different ways. I enjoyed it with *xoconostle* (a sour fruit). Another specialty is *civet de lapin* (rabbit in a wine sauce), which was quite good. If you order tequila, have it with Nicole's special sangrita, a wonderful variation on the traditional stuff. You can also order steaks and fine fresh salads with a choice of dressings. To get there, it's best to take a cab.

Arcos de Guadalupe 3, Marfil. © **473/733-1148**. Main courses $7–$12. AE, MC, V. Tues–Sun 1:20–6:30pm.

MODERATE

El Claustro MEXICAN/ANTOJITOS   A lot of locals really like this downtown hole-in-the-wall. Tables are outside on the square or inside in what was once the bodega of the building now occupied by the restaurant. My favorite things to eat here are the enchiladas, especially the *rojas* and the *enmoladas.* The *pollo con mole* (chicken with *mole* sauce) is good, too. Other dishes include various *antojitos* (small plates) and main dishes. The restaurant is within 50 paces of Avenida Juárez, almost across from the market.

Jardín de la Reforma 13-B. No phone. Main courses $4–$7. No credit cards. Daily 8am–10pm.

El Gallo Pitagórico ITALIAN   Lasagna with a view—getting here from the main square is roughly the equivalent of climbing a few flights of stairs. Look for a deep-blue house on the hill behind San Diego church, well below the statue of El Pípila. It's not hard to find. Dining on the upper terrace at night, with the city lights for a backdrop, is the star attraction here. Besides the lasagna, house specialties include a variety of pastas, *filetto alla italiana,* and crostini.

Constancia 10-A. © 473/732-6758. Reservations recommended. Main courses $5–$10. MC, V. Tues–Sun 2–11:30pm.

Truco 7 ★ MEXICAN   With its economical prices and warm atmosphere, this place is a solid choice for any meal. The three dining rooms are small and a bit crowded, yet nicely decorated with leather *equipal* (a rustic Mexican style) tables and chairs and paintings by local artists. The restaurant occupies an 18th-century structure originally built for members of the Valenciana silver family. Calle Truco, a short street south of the basilica, runs between the Jardín Unión and the Plaza de la Paz.

Truco 7. © 473/732-8374. Reservations not accepted. Breakfast $2–$4; *comida corrida* (served 2–4pm) $3; main courses $4–$7. No credit cards. Daily 8:30am–11:30pm.

GUANAJUATO AFTER DARK

If city planners had known the **Jardín Unión** would be so popular, they might have made it larger. This tiny plaza, shaded by Indian laurel trees, is the heart of the city and the best hangout. No other spot in town rivals its benches and sidewalk restaurants.

You can catch some worthwhile free **theater** in Plazuela de San Roque at 8pm on Sunday when the university is in session. Students perform short theatrical pieces known as *entremeses* (literally, "intermissions"). These are usually costumed period pieces that rely more on action than dialogue, so you don't need to understand too much Spanish to get the point. The costumes are great and look curiously appropriate in this *plazuela.*

More conventional nightspots—such as dance clubs—aren't difficult to find; ask at your hotel. A different kind of place is **La Dama de las Camelias,** Sopeña 32, an

---

Moments   The Redolent Mexican Cantina

If you're curious about Mexican cantinas, swinging saloon doors and all, Guanajuato is a good place to do your fieldwork. You should know, however, that most of these are *men-only* drinking dives.

The town's favorite son is José Alfredo Jiménez, the undisputed master of *ranchera* music. This is the quintessential drinking music (long laments punctuated by classic Mexican yelps) that drives most non-Mexicans screaming from the building. But after downing a few *copitas,* you may warm up to it, and after asking about Jiménez, you'll probably get a few more drinks on the house. Around the Jardín Unión are a couple of cantinas that aren't bad; I enjoyed a few shots at one called **El Incendio (The Fire),** Cantarranas 15. Unlike most cantinas, this place welcomes women. El Incendio opens at 10am and closes at 4am.

You may be surprised to see an open urinal at the end of the bar. While this is a standard feature in cantinas and part of the, er, authentic flavor, you still may wish to opt for a seat at the opposite end.

unpretentious second-floor bar that doesn't get going until late in the evening. The music is all classic recordings of *danzón,* mambo, *son cubano,* and salsa. It opens at 8pm, starts getting busy around midnight, and closes at 4am. Another salsa bar is behind the San Diego church at the foot of the hill where El Pípila stands.

3 Santiago de Querétaro ★★★

213km (133 miles) NW of Mexico City; 96km (60 miles) SE of San Miguel Allende; 200km (125 miles) S of San Luis Potosí

Querétaro is the oldest city in this chapter, and the most historic. During the colonial era, it played a central role in the conquest and evangelization of northern Mexico. In later times, it was at the center of events in the three wars that forged the Mexican nation: *La Independencia, La Reforma,* and *La Revolución.* Downtown Querétaro is lively, pedestrian-friendly, and filled with eye-opening colonial splendor. The local government has spruced up the city, keeps it neat with impressive round-the-clock cleaning crews, and provides street vendors with attractive stands, closely regulating them so that they don't obstruct public streets and walkways. In the evenings, the downtown area fills with people who stroll about the plazas and *andadores* (pedestrian walkways), eat at one of the outdoor restaurants or at one of the stands, and perhaps listen to the municipal band play in the Jardín Zenea or one of the other plazas. The next morning you won't find a scrap of paper on the ground. Since the city is only an hour by bus from San Miguel, it makes an easy day trip, and you can stay into the evening. But once you do, you'll be tempted to stay longer to further your acquaintance with this lovely city.

The Spanish founded Querétaro (1531) during their first large-scale expedition into the vast northern stretches of their new territory. It occurred after a battle with the Chichimeca in which Santiago (St. James) appeared in the clouds. Santiago is the patron saint of Spain and of La Reconquista, the seven-century struggle to expel the Moors from Spain, which had ended barely 40 years earlier. It is no wonder that the Spanish hoped he would again lend a hand in this new struggle for territory. For his appearance, Santiago also became the patron saint of Querétaro. (When you visit the Jardín Zenea at the center of town, look up at the facade of the church of San Francisco, and you will see a forceful depiction of Santiago in battle, lopping off the turbaned head of a Moor.) In time, the city became the base of operations for all expeditions headed north.

While the conquistadors were setting out to conquer lands for the crown, the religious orders were setting out to convert souls for Christ. The Franciscans established a large community in Querétaro and eventually a college for the propagation of the faith, the first such institution in the New World. From here, the missionaries set out (always on foot, as the Franciscan Rule forbade riding on horseback or in carriages) to evangelize and establish missions as far away as Texas and California. Some of their histories are nothing short of astounding.

Centuries later, Mexican independence began in Querétaro with the conspiracy of 1810 (of which Father Hidalgo was a member). A little more than 50 years after that, Querétaro was again in the thick of it when Emperor Maximilian made his last stand here and was defeated and executed. Another 50 years passed, and the city became the site of the laborious constitutional convention during the Mexican Revolution. The document that it produced, the Constitution of 1917, remains the law of the land.

Santiago de Querétaro

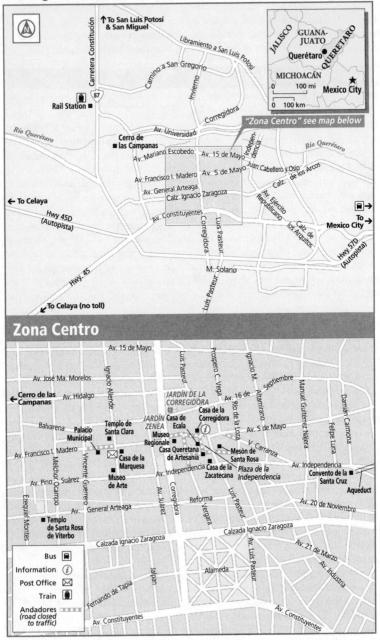

Zona Centro

To San Luis Potosí & San Miguel

Carretera Constitución

Libramiento a San Luis Potosí

Camino a San Gregorio

57

Rail Station

Río Querétaro

Invierno

Corregidora

Av. Universidad

Cerro de las Campanas

Av. Mariano Escobedo

Av. 15 de Mayo

Av. Francisco I. Madero

Av. 5 de Mayo

Independencia

Juan Caballero y Osio

Río Querétaro

Av. General Arteaga

Calz. Ignacio Zaragoza

Calz. de los Arcos

"Zona Centro" see map below

← To Celaya

Hwy 45D (Autopista)

Av. Constituyentes

Corregidora

Luis Pasteur

Av. Ejército Republicano

Calz. los Arquitos

To Mexico City →

Hwy 57D (Autopista)

Hwy 45

M. Solano

Luís Pasteur

To Celaya (no toll)

Zona Centro

Av. 15 de Mayo

Luis Pasteur

Próspero C. Vega

Ignacio M.

Septiembre

Manuel Gutiérrez Nájera

Damián Carmona

Av. José Ma. Morelos

Ignacio Allende

Av. 16 de

Altamirano

Felipe Luna

Cerro de las Campanas

Av. Hidalgo

JARDÍN DE LA CORREGIDORA

Río de la Loza

Casa de la Corregidora

Balvarena

Palacio Municipal

Templo de Santa Clara

JARDÍN ZENEA

Casa de Ecala

Av. 5 de Mayo

Vicente Guerrero

Museo Regionale

V. Carranza

Av. Francisco I. Madero

Melchor Ocampo

Casa de la Marquesa

Casa Queretana de Artesanía

Mesón de Santa Rosa

Av. Pino Suárez

Museo de Arte

Av. Independencia

Casa de la Zacatecana

Plaza de la Independencia

Av. Independencia

Convento de la Santa Cruz

Aqueduct

Ezequiel Montes

Av. General Arteaga

Corregidora

Av. Juárez

Reforma

Vergara

Luis Pasteur

Av. 20 de Noviembre

Templo de Santa Rosa de Viterbo

Calzada Ignacio Zaragoza

Calzada Ignacio Zaragoza

Av. Luis Pasteur

Av. 21 de Marzo

Av. Industria

Bus	🚌
Information	ⓘ
Post Office	✉
Train	🚆
Andadores (road closed to traffic)	▦

Jalpan

Alameda

Fernando de Tapia

Av. Constituyentes

Av. Constituyentes

Inset Map

JALISCO

GUANA-JUATO

QUERÉTARO

Querétaro

MICHOACÁN

Mexico City

0   100 mi

0   100 km

← To Celaya

To Mexico City →

ESSENTIALS

GETTING THERE & DEPARTING   By Plane   Fly to Mexico City. At the airport, exit through the doors facing Gate D (Sala D), and you will find direct bus service to Querétaro (3 hr.). Buses leave about every hour and cost $22.

By Car   From Mexico City, take the super toll road 57D (2½ hr.). From San Miguel, take Highway 111 to 57D, then turn right (1 hr.). From San Luis Potosí, take 57D south (2½ hr.).

By Bus   From the Mexico City airport, see above. From Mexico City's northern bus terminal (Central del Norte), buses leave every 15 minutes. Make sure you get a *directo* (nonstop). From San Miguel, second-class buses leave every 20 minutes. The bus station is south of town. Look for a booth in the terminal that sells cab tickets. A cab ride downtown costs $3.

VISITOR INFORMATION   There is a good **tourism information office** at Pasteur Norte 4, just off the Plaza de la Independencia on the north side. It's open daily from 9am to 8pm. The phone numbers are © **442/238-5000**, ext. 5067 or ext. 5212 or toll free from the U.S. 888/811-6130 or visit www.queretaro.gob.mx/turismo. The office conducts 1-hour tours of the city in a trolley-style bus. Buy tickets at the tourism office: $5 for adults, $3 for children 3 to 12. Tours follow one of three routes and leave at 9, 10, and 11am, and 4, 5, and 6pm. If there are enough English speakers, the tour is done in English. These abbreviated trips necessarily leave out a lot, but they're good for getting an idea of the city's layout. If you would like a more detailed tour of the downtown area, you have the option of a self-guided audio tour. At the information office, you can rent a Walkman for $5 per day plus a credit card voucher for a deposit.

CITY LAYOUT   The heart of downtown is the Jardín Zenea, at the intersection of the main north-south and east-west streets, Corregidora and Madero. Just east is the Plaza de Armas, and farther east are the Convento de la Cruz and the famous aqueduct. West of Jardín Zenea are several plazas, churches, convents, and museums.

FAST FACTS: Querétaro

American Express The local representative is **Agencia Turismo Beverly,** Av. Tecnológico 118, Col. San Angel (© **442/216-1500**). Office hours are Monday through Friday from 9am to 2pm and 4 to 6pm, Saturday from 9am to noon.

Area Code The telephone area code is **442.**

Climate The average temperature in summer is 75°F (24°C), in winter 56°F (13°C).

Elevation Querétaro sits at 1,818m (6,000 ft.).

Emergency The central emergency number (similar to 911) is © **066.**

Hospital The local hospital is the **Hospital General de Querétaro** (© **442/216-2036**).

Internet Access Cybercafes and Internet access providers are everywhere in the central historic district.

Parking To find parking in the downtown area, look for white square signs with the capital letter E in light blue. There are a couple of places at Pino Suárez 45 and 17. Rates run about $1 for the first hour, 25¢ for every hour after that.

Population Querétaro has 640,000 residents.

Post Office The *correo,* Arteaga 5, is open Monday through Saturday from 9am to 2:30pm.

A STROLL AROUND THE HISTORIC CENTER

In the center of Querétaro, you'll notice right away how many lovely plazas, churches, and convents there are. If you're really observant, you'll notice that the plazas are frequently next to the churches. In fact, most of these plazas were formed at the cost of the convents, which lost much of their real estate to the government after the Reform Law. This is true of the town's most important plaza, **Jardín Zenea,** where we will begin. This plaza used to be part of the atrium of San Francisco Church and Convent, which you see facing the park across Corregidora Street. This park is popular every night, but especially on Sunday, when the municipal band plays dance music of the '40s, '50s, and '60s. (Great fun.) The old bandstand dates from 1900.

Turn toward **San Francisco Church,** and you will see on the facade the depiction of St. James mentioned earlier. From the beginning, this church was the most important in town; it remains so today, the more recent cathedral notwithstanding. It and the attached cloister are all that remain of a large complex that included several chapels and an orchard that extended a few blocks east and south. Inside the church, you will see a few interesting remains of baroque decoration. The main altar is a rather uninteresting piece of neoclassicism that replaced what reputedly was a masterpiece of baroque design. This is a common story with churches in Querétaro. Many of the baroque *retablos* (altarpieces) escaped the plunderers, only to fall prey to the "improvers," as was the case here.

Next door to the church is the cloister, which is now the **Museo Regional** ☆. It's open Tuesday through Sunday from 10am to 7pm. Admission is $3. Exhibits include artifacts from pre-Hispanic, colonial, and republican times. The architecture shows common traits of Franciscan design in the simplicity of its lines and decoration, which you can contrast with the rich decoration (caryatids and all) of the former convent of San Agustín, now a museum of colonial art (see below).

Leaving the museum, turn left and then left again and you'll be on the pedestrians-only Andador Libertad. This leads to the small Plaza de Independencia or Plaza de Armas, with its carefully hedged Indian laurel trees, outdoor restaurants, and colonial mansions. Before you get to it, you'll pass the **Casa Queretana de Artesanía,** Andador Libertad 52 (© **442/214-1235**), a handicrafts store run by the state. It's on the right and has no sign. It sells weavings, clothing, pottery, hand-carved furniture, onyx, opals, and jewelry, all from Querétaro, and also carries items from other states. It's open Tuesday through Friday from noon to 2pm and 4 to 8pm, Saturday from 11:30am to 9pm, and Sunday from 11:30am to 5pm.

If you keep walking, in just a few yards you'll arrive at the Plaza de Independencia. At the far end of the plaza is the **Casa de la Corregidora.** As you walk toward it, you will pass the **Casa de Ecala** on your left. A mansion built in magisterial baroque style with beautiful balconies and wrought iron, it dates from the 18th century. The fountain in the middle of the plaza honors Querétaro's greatest benefactor, a Spanish grandee named Don Juan Antonio de Urrutia y Arana, who built a large aqueduct to bring water to the city.

La Corregidora (the mayor's wife) is the honorable title of Doña Josefa Ortiz de Domínguez, a heroine of the War of Independence. She was a member of the conspiracy to liberate Mexico from Spain and, as the wife of Querétaro's mayor, was in a useful position for gathering information. The conspiracy was discovered, and she was put under house arrest but still managed to warn Father Hidalgo. He eluded capture and rushed to Dolores, where he gave the famous *grito* (the cry for independence). For her actions, La Corregidora was imprisoned several times between 1810 and 1817. She died impoverished and forgotten, but was later remembered when she became the first woman to appear on a Mexican coin. Around the corner, on Calle Pasteur, is the tourism office.

To view the aqueduct, continue east on Andador Libertad. It ends in 1 block, so you must dogleg to the next eastbound street, either Independencia or Carranza. In 3 blocks you will arrive at a plaza, church, and convent. This is the **Convento de La Santa Cruz** ☆☆, where missionaries were trained to evangelize the heathens as far away as California and Nicaragua. It is a simple monastery in the Franciscan style. You can take a short tour, which shows how the water from the aqueduct arrived here and how it fed a system of fountains known as *cajas de agua* that provided water throughout the old city. From these, the citizens of Querétaro would fill their buckets. You will also be shown a thorn tree said to have grown from the walking stick of Friar Antonio Margil de Jesús, a famous missionary who covered vast territories on foot. This thorn tree is considered miraculous because its thorns grow in the shape of the cross.

Behind the church is a small plaza where the city's most illustrious are buried; it affords a good view of the 74 arches of the **aqueduct** that connects two prominences across an expanse of bottomland. This feat of engineering was begun in 1726 and finished in 1738.

To get back to the Jardín Zenea, you can work your way through some of the *andadores* around Plaza de la Independencia, or stay on Calle Independencia all the way to Calle Corregidora. If you go this way, you'll pass a small museum on your right after you cross Río de la Losa. Called **La Casa de la Zacatecana** (look for a banner), it presents a vision of what many colonial mansions were like in Querétaro, with period furnishings and decor. It's open Tuesday to Sunday 11am to 7pm. Associated with this house (as with a couple of others in town) is a tale of illicit love, crime, and final retribution. Colonial Mexico is a fertile land for gothic tales, and in my travels I have heard many.

Back at Jardín Zenea, head west on Calle Madero. At the first corner, just before the street becomes an *andador,* is **La Casa de la Marquesa** ☆☆☆, an opulent colonial residence turned hotel. Walk in and check out the courtyard lobby, which has elaborate *mudéjar*-style (a style with Moorish origins) arches and patterned walls. Cater-corner from this hotel is a fountain of Neptune by one of Mexico's most famous architects, Eduardo Tresguerras, who is responsible for much of Querétaro's 19th-century neoclassical architecture.

The **church and former Convent of Santa Clara** ☆☆☆ is behind the fountain. The church is a must-see; inside are five astonishing baroque *retablos* (altarpieces) and a choir loft, all gilded and each a self-contained composition. In prominent positions are sculptures and paintings of saints; here and there, the faces of angels appear out of the enveloping, thickly textured ornament. Gazing upon these is like gazing upon a mandala. The juxtaposition of straight lines and multiple facets with overflowing curves that move inward and outward make the *retablos* appear fluid and structured at

> ## *Tips* Shopping for Opals
>
> The small state of Querétaro is one of the two principal places in the world that mine opals commercially (the other is southern Australia). The opal is a soft stone noted for its iridescent play of color. Prices vary depending on size, color, shape, and transparency. A few stores in Querétaro, usually called *lapidarias,* sell locally mined opals and other semiprecious stones. One is the **Lapidaria de Querétaro,** Corregidora Norte 149-A, a few blocks north of Jardín Zenea (© **442/214-2140**). It's open Monday through Friday from 10am to 2pm and 5 to 7:30pm. Or stop by **El Artesano,** a little shop at Corregidora Norte 42, near the Jardín Zenea and across from Sears. Owner Alfredo Vázquez, who carves miniatures out of opals and other semi-precious stones, speaks mostly Spanish, and is a fountain of information on opals and the trade. He keeps interesting store hours: 12:30 to 5pm and 6 to 10pm Monday through Saturday. Another source is **Lapidaria Ramírez,** Pino Suárez 98.

the same time. The key to enjoying these *retablos* is not to look for proportion, balance, or the underlying reason behind them, but to look at them as the exultant expression of a religious sentiment that defies these very concepts.

For a greater acquaintance with the colonial religious mind, walk south 1 block on Allende. On your right will be the **Museo de Arte** ✶✶✶ (© **442/212-3523**), in the former **convent of San Agustín.** Admission is $2; free on Tuesday. The museum is open Tuesday through Sunday from 10am to 6pm. It contains one of the great collections of Mexican colonial art, but the architecture of the former convent alone is worth the price of admission. In contrast to the Franciscan convents, highly stylized human forms, complex geometric lines, and vegetal motifs are everywhere. The art is organized by style of painting. The collection has works by Europeans, but its focus is on painters in New Spain, including the most famous of the land.

If you're still in the mood for colonial splendor, continue south 1 block to Arteaga Street, turn right, and head west for 3 blocks to the **church and former convent of Santa Rosa de Viterbo** ✶✶✶. Like Santa Clara, it is a masterpiece of baroque architecture. On the outside, notice the fanciful flying buttresses (a style that as far as I know is unique to Querétaro) and the imaginative tower. Inside, the church is much like Santa Clara, with magnificent gilt *retablos* occupying all available wall space. Also like Santa Clara, the main altar failed to escape the "improvers."

Farther west is the **Cerro de las Campanas (Hill of Bells),** where Maximilian was executed. To get there you'll have to take a cab. You'll find a large, ugly statue of Juárez that was built by the Mexican government to counter a small, sad memorial chapel for Maximilian built by his brother, Emperor Franz Josef of Austria.

WHERE TO STAY

Rates below include the 17% tax. Most of the downtown hotels have high and low season. High season is Easter, July, August, December, and any long weekend. The city is a favorite weekend getaway from Mexico City; it's much easier to find a room during the week.

Hotel Mesón de Santa Rosa ★★   With its large open courtyards, clean lines, and simple stone and iron work, this hotel presents a colonial architecture that contrasts sharply with La Casa de la Marquesa. There are three courtyards variously holding a heated pool, a fountain, and a stone trough for watering your horses (a vestige of the original tavern, which served wagon and mule drivers). Rooms are quiet, large, and comfortable, with high ceilings and carpeted floors. The furniture and decoration are simple. The bathrooms are large and come with either two doubles or a king-size bed. Superior rooms are much larger. Higher rates are for remodeled rooms with air-conditioning. The hotel is on the southwest corner of the Plaza de Independencia—a perfect spot.

Pasteur 17 Sur, 76000 Querétaro, Qro. © **442/441-5000.** Fax 442/212-5522. www.mesonsantarosa.com. 21 units. $110–$120 standard double; $150–$160 superior double. AE, DC, DISC, MC, V. Valet parking $6. **Amenities:** Restaurant; bar; midsize heated outdoor pool; room service until 11pm; babysitting; laundry service; dry cleaning. *In room:* TV, dataport, minibar, coffeemaker, hair dryer, safe.

Hotel Señorial   This is a simple hotel with plainly furnished and carpeted rooms. The beds (usually two twins or two doubles) are comfortable. The bathrooms have recently been remodeled. Rooms with air-conditioning are about $5 extra. The important thing is to reserve an even-numbered room. Odd-numbered rooms are in the south wing, which has plumbing so noisy you think it will bring down the building.

Guerrero Norte 10-A, 76000 Querétaro, Qro. ©/fax **442/214-3700.** 54 units. $43–$60 double. MC, V. Free secure parking. From the Jardín Zenea, walk west on Madero, turn right at the Plaza Guerrero and walk 2 blocks. **Amenities:** Restaurant; room service until 10pm. *In room:* TV.

La Casa de la Marquesa ★★★   Few hotels in Mexico can match this one for sheer colonial opulence. Even if you don't stay here, make a point of walking into the courtyard lobby. Built for the widow of the Marqués de Urrutia, the house, with Moorish-inspired arches, tiles, and painted walls, has an Andalusian feel. Rooms are large, have all the amenities, and are furnished with period pieces and Persian rugs. Bed choices include one queen-size, two queen-size, or one king-size. Some rooms are across the street in another colonial house, La Casa Azul. These go for less. The hotel, a member of the Small Luxury Hotels of the World, prides itself on the attention it gives its guests. The location is excellent.

Madero 41, 76000 Querétaro, Qro. © **442/212-0092.** Fax 442/212-0098. www.LaCasaDeLaMarquesa.com. 25 units. $155 deluxe; $185 royal suite; $280 imperial suite. Rates include continental breakfast. AE, MC, V. Free valet parking. **Amenities:** Restaurant; bar; membership at local spa; concierge; tour desk; room service until 11pm; in-room massage; laundry service; dry cleaning. *In room:* A/C, TV, dataport, coffeemaker, hair dryer.

Mesón de la Luna *Value*   This three-story hotel with quiet rooms is off Calle Guerrero 2 blocks past the Hotel Señorial. The cheerful, midsize rooms have tile floors, one or two double beds, and small bathrooms. The junior suites are larger and come with two queen-size beds, a small fridge, carpeting, and roomier bathrooms. Some of the staff is bilingual (uncommon in inexpensive hotels).

Mariano Escobedo 104 (between Guerrero and Ocampo), 76000 Querétaro, Qro. © **442/212-4378.** 40 units. $35 double; $47 junior suite. MC, V. Free secure parking. **Amenities:** Restaurant; room service until 11pm; laundry service. *In room:* TV.

Mesón del Obispado   For better or worse, this hotel is in the middle of the most popular part of downtown. For better, it's on a pedestrian *andador* and is close to just about everything. For worse, it's by the plaza, which doesn't settle down on weekends until well after midnight. The rooms in front have balconies overlooking the *andador* and are popular with the vacationing crowd that isn't going to bed early anyway. I had a room in back that looked out toward the courtyard of the hotel, and it was perfectly quiet. The attractively furnished rooms are medium to large in size, usually with two double beds and a midsize bathroom.

Andador 16 de Septiembre 13, 76000 Querétaro, Qro. ⓒ 442/224-2464. 16 units. $60 double. AE, MC V. **Amenities:** Restaurant; tour info; room service until 3am. *In room:* TV.

WHERE TO DINE

The restaurants listed below are in the *centro histórico.* If you don't like any of these options, there's a restaurant district in the area by the aqueduct, where you'll find just about anything. You can also eat well at the Mesón de Santa Rosa on the Plaza Independencia.

Cafetería Bisquets ⓡ (Value) MEXICAN   This modest restaurant serves inexpensive *comida casera* (home cooking) on a lovely little patio and in adjoining dining rooms. One of the specialties is paper-thin *milanesa* (lightly breaded round steak) served with green enchiladas on the side. For breakfast, avoid the *bisquet*—something like an American biscuit, but larger and heavier—and try the *chilaquiles con pollo y crema* or any of the egg dishes and the *café con leche* (coffee with milk). The *menú del día* (daily menu) is a bargain.

Pino Suárez 7 (½ block west of the southwest corner of Plaza de la Constitución). ⓒ 442/214-1481. Main courses $3–$7; menu del día $4–$6. No credit cards. Daily 7:30am–11pm.

Cafetería La Mariposa MEXICAN   This coffee shop, sweet shop, and restaurant is a popular hangout. The breakfasts are probably better at Bisquets, but this place makes its own sweets, cakes, ice cream, and yogurt, which makes it a good stop for a lunch or afternoon snack. The menu has several Mexican standards. To the left when you enter is the retail area.

Angela Peralta 7. ⓒ 442/212-1166. Main courses $3–$7. No credit cards. Daily 8am–9:30pm. From the Jardín Zenea, walk north 2 blocks along Corregidora and turn left.

Restaurante Bar 1810 ⓡ MEXICAN/INTERNATIONAL   This is one of the restaurants on the Plaza de Armas across from the house of La Corregidora. It has a large and varied menu, and is the perfect place to enjoy an afternoon or evening meal. There is indoor dining as well. Your best bet is to stick with traditional Mexican specialties, which are well prepared; the soups are wonderful. Sunday brunch is especially popular.

Andador Libertad 62. ⓒ 442/214-3324. Reservations recommended on weekends and holidays. Main courses $7–$15. AE, MC, V. Daily 8am–midnight.

San Miguelito ⓡⓡ MEXICAN   The least you should do is go for a drink and a view of the surroundings. The restaurant occupies the newly restored Casa de los Cinco Patios, a landmark colonial house that had been closed to the public for years. The first patio (which is the main dining area) impresses me with the height of its arches and the fine wrought-iron work. It's beautifully lit at night, too. For an appetizer, try *huesitos* (ribs) with *chile morita* (a dried chile) and tamarind. For a main course, steaks are available with a variety of sauces, and there's a chicken nicely done in chipotle sauce.

Andador 5 de Mayo 39. ⓒ 442/224-2760. Reservations recommended on weekends. Main courses $10–$16. AE, MC, V. Tues–Sat 1–11pm; Sun 2–6pm.

SIDE TRIPS FROM QUERETARO

In the northern part of the small state of Querétaro is a mountain range known as the **Sierra Gorda.** It makes a good 2- or 3-day trip whether you're in the mood to see beautiful mountain landscapes with pine forests and old Spanish missions or to simply get away from all the people. There are some comfortable, inexpensive hotels in the towns of Jalpan and Concá, among others. Tours to the region from Querétaro are a bargain. A company called **Promotur** (© 442/212-8940) operates a recommended tour.

4 Zacatecas ★★★

627km (392 miles) NW of Mexico City; 198km (124 miles) NW of San Luis Potosí; 322km (201 miles) NE of Guadalajara; 298km (186 miles) SE of Durango

Zacatecas, like Guanajuato, owes its beauty to the wealth of silver extracted from its mines. The farthest flung of the silver cities, it is a jewel in the rough. High over the town center looms a steep mountain that's accessible by cable car. From there, you can gaze over the city and beyond to the wild and desolate surroundings. The scene makes you realize what a frontier town Zacatecas must have been, and after you have been in town for a few days, you appreciate its present sophistication all the more. In this city out in the middle of nowhere, you will find startlingly good museums, beautiful architecture, and wonderful restaurants. There also seems to be a high degree of civic pride, judging from the fact that the city has gone to the enormous trouble of hiding all of its power and telephone cables. This adds greatly to the beauty of the town and makes strolling along the streets a pleasure.

ESSENTIALS

GETTING THERE & DEPARTING   By Plane   Mexicana (© 800/531-7921 in the U.S., 01-800/502-2000 in Mexico, or 492/922-7429 locally) flies nonstop to and from Chicago, Denver, and Los Angeles. Seats are hard to come by around Christmas, when native Zacatecans fly home in large numbers. Within Mexico, Mexicana flies nonstop to and from León/Guanajuato, Mexico City, and Tijuana.

Transportation from the airport, 29km (18 miles) north of Zacatecas, is about $15 by taxi.

By Car   From the south, you can take Highway 45D, a toll road in various spots, from Querétaro through Irapuato, León, and Aguascalientes. It's expensive (about $20) but fast. Highway 54 heads northeast to Saltillo and Monterrey (a 5- to 6-hr. drive) and southeast to Guadalajara (a 4½-hr. drive). Highway 49 leads north to Torreón (4 hr.) and southeast to San Luis Potosí (2½ hr.). Highway 45 heads to Durango (4 hr.).

By Bus   Omnibus de México, Estrella Blanca, and their many affiliates handle first-class bus travel to and from Zacatecas. Together, they operate 30 buses a day to Guadalajara and to San Luis Potosí, more than that to Mexico City (via Querétaro), and 10 per day to Guanajuato. I usually don't buy a ticket ahead of time unless I'm traveling during a national holiday or during December and August (vacation months), or I'm going all the way to the border. The **Central Camionera** (bus station) is on a hilltop a bit out of town. The taxi ride costs about $3.

VISITOR INFORMATION   The downtown office is at Hidalgo 403, second floor (© 492/924-4047); it's open Monday to Friday from 8am to 8pm; Saturday and Sunday from 10am to 6pm. If you would like a calendar of events, ask for an *agenda cultural.*

CITY LAYOUT   Understanding traffic circulation in the middle of town requires an advanced degree in chaos theory. I either walk or let the cab driver handle it. The city's main axis is Hidalgo. From the **Plaza de Armas (main square),** it goes 8 blocks southwest to the Enrique Estrada Park and Hotel Quinta Real (changing names as it goes); in the opposite direction it reaches another 8 blocks to the Rafael Coronel Museum (again making a name change). The historical center of town extends several blocks on either side of this 1-mile stretch of Hidalgo.

GETTING AROUND   I enjoy walking around Zacatecas, but the terrain is hilly and the air is thin. Cabs are inexpensive and readily available. Their availability declines somewhat between 2 and 4pm, when office workers snag them to get home for the midafternoon meal.

FAST FACTS: Zacatecas

American Express Visit travel agent **Viajes Mazzoco,** Enlace 115 (© **492/ 922-0859** or 492/922-5159; fax 492/924-0277). Hours are Monday through Friday from 9am to 6pm, Saturday from 9am to 2pm.

Area Code The telephone area code is **492.**

Climate It's cool enough year-round to require a sweater or other warm wrap.

Elevation The city is at a lofty 2,485m (8,200 ft.). The air is always crisp and cool but a tad thin for some people.

Emergency & Police The emergency number is © 066.

Hospital The two hospitals in town are **Clínica Santa Elena,** Av. Guerrero 143 (© **492/922-6861**), and **Hospital San José,** Cuevas Cancino 208, near the clinic (© **492/922-3892**).

Internet Access Internet cafes are cheap and very popular with the young crowd. To find one all you have to do is ask at your hotel or get directions from any young person you meet on the street.

Population Zacatecas has 230,000 residents.

Post Office The *correo,* at Allende 111, a half-block from Avenida Hidalgo, is open Monday through Friday from 9am to 3pm, Saturday from 10am to 2pm.

SPECIAL EVENTS & FESTIVALS

During Semana Santa (Holy Week), Zacatecas hosts an **international cultural festival** that the town hopes will eventually rival the Festival Cervantino in Guanajuato. Painters, poets, dancers, musicians, actors, and other artists converge on the town.

The annual **Feria de Zacatecas,** which celebrates the founding of the city, begins the Friday before September 8 and lasts for 3 weeks, incorporating the national Fiestas Patrias (independence celebration). Cockfights, bullfights, sporting events, band concerts, and general hoopla prevail. Famous bullfighters appear, and the cheap bullfight tickets go for around $8.

EXPLORING ZACATECAS

SIGHTS   In town you can visit museums and churches, tour an **abandoned silver mine,** ride a cable car up to the **Cerro de la Bufa,** perhaps take in a concert, and partake

Zacatecas

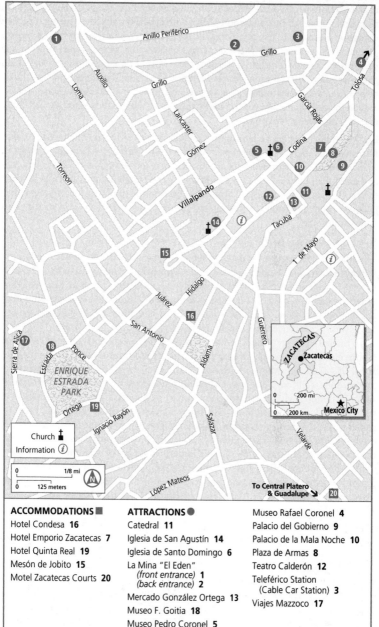

ACCOMMODATIONS ■
Hotel Condesa **16**
Hotel Emporio Zacatecas **7**
Hotel Quinta Real **19**
Mesón de Jobito **15**
Motel Zacatecas Courts **20**

ATTRACTIONS ●
Catedral **11**
Iglesia de San Agustín **14**
Iglesia de Santo Domingo **6**
La Mina "El Eden"
  (front entrance) **1**
  (back entrance) **2**
Mercado González Ortega **13**
Museo F. Goitia **18**
Museo Pedro Coronel **5**

Museo Rafael Coronel **4**
Palacio del Gobierno **9**
Palacio de la Mala Noche **10**
Plaza de Armas **8**
Teatro Calderón **12**
Teleférico Station
  (Cable Car Station) **3**
Viajes Mazzoco **17**

of an old tradition called *callejoneadas*. On Saturday night, people go strolling and singing with tambourines, drums, and a burro laden with mezcal through the winding streets and *callejones* (alleyways) of the city. Zacatecas remains largely neglected by foreign tourists, though it is popular with Mexicans. Consequently, the various sights provide little descriptive material in English. If you don't speak Spanish, you might want to hire a bilingual tour guide. Try contacting **Viajes Mazzoco** (see "American Express" in "Fast Facts," above). It offers several tours that you can choose from for a fixed price. Some take you around the city; others take you to **nearby ruins** or to some of the old towns near Zacatecas, such as **Jerez** or **Fresnillo.**

SHOPPING   **Zacatecan handicrafts** include stone-carving, leatherwork, and silver. Examples can be found in shops inside the old **Mercado González Ortega** on Hidalgo, next to the cathedral. A few other stores on Hidalgo and Tacuba sell crafts and antiques. Huichol Indians occasionally sell their crafts around the Plaza Independencia. Of all its handicrafts, Zacatecas is best known for its stone carvings. Many architects and builders from the United States come to Zacatecas when they need fancy stonework.

A STROLL AROUND TOWN

The **Plaza de Armas,** the town's main square on Avenida Hidalgo, is where you'll find the **cathedral** ✮✮✮, with its famous facade. Nowhere else in Mexico is there anything like this; the depth of relief in the carving (4 in. and more) and sheer wealth of detail create the impression that the images are formed not in stone but in some softer material, such as cake icing. The cathedral took 23 years to build (1729–52), and the final tower wasn't completed until 1904.

To the left of the cathedral, on the Plaza de Armas, is the 18th-century **Palacio de Gobierno,** where viceregal-era governors lived. By the time of Mexico's revolt against Spain in 1810, Don Miguel de Rivera (Count of Santiago de la Laguna), owned it. Since 1834, it's been a government building. Inside is a modern **mural** (1970) by Antonio Pintor Rodríguez showing the history of Zacatecas. It is a fairly straightforward chronological presentation of history from left to right, except for the center panel, which represents prominent Zacatecans. Below it is a stone frieze depicting the economic underpinning that supports society and drives historical events. It flows into the mural's central panel, tying society's leaders to the soil of their motherland.

To the left of the Palacio de Gobierno is the **Residencia de Gobernadores,** with its multicolor stonework; the governor lived here until 1950. Across the street from the plaza are the **Palacio de la Mala Noche (Palace of the Bad Night)** and the Hotel Emporio. The palace's name comes from the mine that brought great wealth to its original owner, Manuel de Rétegui, a philanthropic Spaniard. In case you're thinking that such fine stonework is becoming a lost art, look at the hotel's facade, which was done within the last 40 years.

Climb the small street next to the Palacio de la Mala Noche, and you'll face the massive walls of the church of **Santo Domingo,** which fronts an open space that it shares with the Museo Pedro Coronel (see "Museums," below). This church and the building that houses the museum belonged to the Jesuits until their expulsion in 1767. Afterward, the Dominicans occupied the church and convent. Inside are some lovely baroque gilt *retablos* (altarpieces).

Two blocks south of Santo Domingo, on Calle Dr. Hierro (the mostly level street that parallels Hidalgo), is another grand church, **San Agustín.** This one is in partial ruins. During the Reform Wars, Zacatecas's liberal leaders kicked out the Augustinian friars, converted church and convent into a hotel and gambling casino, and destroyed the reportedly beautiful gilt altarpieces. The bishop of Zacatecas promptly excommunicated these Philistines. Twenty years later, a Presbyterian missionary society bought the property and dismantled the ultrabaroque facade that decorated the east door. Again, excommunication of all involved quickly followed. Now the government owns the building, and some restoration has taken place. You'll see lots of odd bits of masonry crammed into any available niche, waiting for someone to figure out just where they go.

Turn and go downhill, and you'll be back on Avenida Hidalgo. Walk back toward the cathedral (left), and you'll pass on your left the **Teatro Calderón** (inaugurated first in 1836 and again in 1891 after a fire). A stately building with lovely stained-glass windows, it is also a favorite spot for people to sit and watch passers-by. The opera star Angela Peralta sang here several times in the 1800s. Zacatecas has a flourishing music school, and occasionally it offers performances here. A little farther down Hidalgo, a block before the cathedral on the same side of the street, is the 19th-century **Mercado Jesús González Ortega,** which used to be the town's main market. A pleasant, old-fashioned market, it now holds small stores selling handicrafts and some of the region's wines.

Backtrack along Hidalgo, and over the next few blocks you will pass by some lovely buildings and climb up to **Enrique Estrada Park** (the street changes names and becomes Av. General Jesús González Ortega). The **equestrian statue** (1898) portrays none other than the general himself, hero of the Battle of Calpulalpan. Behind it are a gazebo with marvelous acoustics and a pleasant, shady park that is a romantic spot for young couples at night. Beginning at Estrada Park and extending southward are the lovely arches of the **Aqueduct of Zacatecas.** Two of these arches frame the doorway to the Quinta Real Hotel, which you can enter to see the town's old bullring, a lovely sight. Go to the hotel bar and order a margarita—another lovely sight.

A RIDE UP CERRO DE LA BUFA ★★★

To get to the cable car station from the Plaza de Armas, you must climb one of the streets or alleys that lead up the hill that faces the cathedral. But first, glance up to see if the cars are running; if it's windy, they won't be. The first cross street will be Villalpando or Hierro; go right, and make a left when you get to the Callejón (alley) de García Roja. If you're unaccustomed to the thin air, this is quite a climb. An easier way to get there is to catch bus no. 7, which you can pick up along Juárez, or take a cab. The cable car (© **492/922-5694**) is a great ride up to the Cerro de la Bufa. The view from the top is best in the late afternoon and early evening, when the sun is low in the sky; if you intend to ride the cable car down, you can't stay too late. It operates only from 10am to 6pm, but the walk down isn't too bad should you want to stay later. A one-way ticket is $2.75, round-trip is $5.

On Cerro de la Bufa is the **Museo de la Toma de Zacatecas,** which will be of most interest to Spanish-speaking history buffs. It displays artifacts and enlarged newspaper articles about the capture of Zacatecas by Pancho Villa. This was a decisive battle of La Revolución, and one of Villa's greatest victories. The museum is in need of investment; admission is $2. Beside the museum is the beautiful church **La Capilla de la Virgen del Patrocinio,** patroness of Zacatecas. Around the far side of the *cerro* (hill) is the **Mausoleo de los Hombres Ilustres de Zacatecas,** where many of the city's heroes are entombed.

MUSEUMS

La Mina "El Edén" ⭐ This mine is a giant gash carved diagonally through the core of a mountain following the trail of a silver vein deeper and deeper underground. To see this gash and think that all the stone and ore that once occupied this space was mined and extracted by hand provokes a sense of wonder. The mine opened in 1586, using forced Indian labor. Accidents, tuberculosis, and silicosis caused the workers' early deaths. The mine was extremely rich, yielding gold, copper, zinc, iron, and lead in addition to silver, but it eventually closed when an attempt to use explosives resulted in an inundation of water in the lower levels. Unfortunately, there are no English-speaking guides here, although the tour is eye-opening even for those who don't speak Spanish. Manikins illustrate some of the mining process. A visit also includes a short, unremarkable train ride.

The mine's back entrance is only a block from the cable-car terminal. I prefer this entrance because most people start at the main entrance, so you can avoid the crowds. When you get to the ticket office, buy your ticket right then. According to the rules, a tour must begin within 15 minutes after the first ticket is purchased. On my last two visits I've had the guide all to myself (a tip is appreciated). After the tour is over, you can exit by the front entrance, which puts you on Juárez, just a few blocks above Hidalgo.

For directions on getting to the front entrance, see "El Malacate" below, under "Zacatecas After Dark."

Cerro Grillo. ☏ 492/922-3002. Admission $2 (includes train and tour). Daily 10am–6pm.

Museo F. Goitia ⭐⭐ I don't expect anyone to believe what he reads about modern art, and because my credentials as a critic are nil, I'll be brief. I was surprised by this small museum and the work of Goitia and his Zacatecan comrades. I walked in expecting it to be a display of regional chauvinism, but I found the works moving, serious, and meaningful. Francisco Goitia (1882–1960) is famous in Mexico, and the brothers Rafael and Pedro Coronel amassed great collections that became the basis for two highly touted museums. The other artists are Julio Relas and José Kuri Brença.

Enrique Estrada 102, Col. Sierra de Alica. ☏ 492/922-0211. Admission $3. Tues–Sun 10am–5pm. Walk 7 short blocks south of the cathedral on Hidalgo, cross Juárez, and continue up the hill. Turn right on Manuel Ponce (look for the aqueduct) and walk 2 more short blocks. Look for the imposing white "palace" behind the park.

Museo Pedro Coronel ⭐⭐ Pedro Coronel, in addition to being an artist, was a collector of inspired tastes. He acquired works from all over the world, but the strongest parts of the collection are the works of European modern masters (Dalí, Picasso, Miró, Kandinsky, Braque, Rouault), pre-Columbian Mesoamerica, and West Africa. All but a few of the pieces of modern art are illuminating. Many date from early in the artist's career, and some display a seminal character that points in the direction of later works. This collection is not large; after a while you drift into the Mesoamerican room—beautiful stuff, and seeing it so quickly after the modern art gets your mind working out strange and improbable connections. There is no filler here; all of the pieces are outstanding. The same can be said of the African material, but in this case the connections with modern art are tangible.

Plaza de Santo Domingo. ☏ 492/922-8021. Admission $3. Fri–Wed 10am–5pm. Facing the cathedral, walk left to the next street, De Veyna, turn left, and walk 1 block up to Plaza de Santo Domingo and the museum.

Museo Rafael Coronel ⭐⭐⭐ First stroll through the tranquil gardens and ruins of the former Franciscan convent, filled with trailing blossoms and framed by crumbling arches and the open sky. A small wing contains Coronel's drawings on paper. Once you step inside the mask museum, you'll be dazzled by the sheer number of fantastic masks. There are 4,500 of them from all over Mexico, and they're so exotic and dissimilar that you would think that they came from all over the world. One wing of the museum is dedicated to puppets. There are dioramas showing a bullfight, battling armies, and even a vision of hell. The puppets are some of the hundreds created during the last century by the famous Rosete-Aranda family of Huamantla, Tlaxcala, where there is also a puppet museum. Also in the museum, to the left after you enter, is the Ruth Rivera room, where some of Diego Rivera's drawings are on display. Ruth Rivera is the daughter of Diego Rivera and the wife of Rafael Coronel.

Calle Chevano, between Juan de Tolosa and Vergel Nuevo. © 492/922-8116. Admission $3. Thurs–Tues 10am–5pm. Facing the cathedral, walk left up Hidalgo to the Founder's Fountain (about 2 blocks), then take the left fork (Calle Abasolo) 2 more short blocks; at the large yellow-ocher building and traffic triangle, take the right fork. You'll spot the large, old temple ahead.

A SIDE TRIP TO NEARBY GUADALUPE

In the nearby town of Guadalupe, now almost a suburb of Zacatecas, is a large Franciscan convent and evangelical college founded by a famous member of the evangelical college of Querétaro, Fray Antonio Margil de Jesús. It remains an active monastery, but a large part of the convent houses a wonderful museum of colonial art, which will impress anyone interested in art and painting of any kind. Some people might skip this one because they suppose colonial art to be staid, scholastic, and full of arcane symbolism. Not true. The paintings, mostly from the 1700s, are by some of the greatest painters of New Spain—Cabrera, Villalpando, Correa, and others. They are detailed, expressive, dramatic, and eye-catching for their use of anachronisms and fantastical themes. There is also a smaller museum displaying antique carriages from colonial times and classic cars. Zacatecas had a lively carriage-building industry in the colonial era.

A taxi to Guadalupe runs about $10. Transportes de Guadalupe buses go to Guadalupe from the Central Camionera in Zacatecas. If you're driving, take López Mateos east, and follow the signs. When you enter the town, ask anyone for directions to the convent. The convent's church has a lovely facade and holds the famous 19th-century Capilla de Nápoles, a chapel in the shape of a cross with lots of gilding and beautiful designs. You cannot enter the chapel, but you can see it from the ground floor of the church or from the organ loft, which is accessible from the museum.

Convento de Guadalupe/Museo Virreinal de Guadalupe ✪✪✪ To a dedicated museumgoer, seeing these paintings exhibited in galleries with open air circulation and no climate control is a little unsettling. But with Zacatecas's climate, there may not be much cause for concern. The museum has about 350 works. On the first floor are over 20 portraits depicting scenes of St. Francis's life. The stairway to the second floor has some large, striking paintings, including Cabrera's *Virgin of the Apocalypse* and Arnáez's *The Triumph of the Sweet Light of Jesus,* which is an amusing propagandistic work showing the victory of Rome over the pagans and the Reformation. Highlights on the second floor include the organ loft, 14 oval paintings by Cabrera, 4 by Villalpando, and the surprising work of a local artist named Gabriel José de Ovalle, who distorts space and deforms human features in a style that seems much more modern than the 1700s. Guides are available for a tour of the museum and to view the Capilla de Nápoles (if the resident monks aren't celebrating Mass).

Jardín Juárez, Oriente, Guadalupe. © 492/923-2089 or 492/923-2386. Admission $3. Daily 10am–4:30pm.

Museo Regional de la Historia   This museum, to the right of the convent, contains examples of carriages and antique cars. Collected from all over Mexico, they formerly belonged to ex-presidents and famous historical figures.

Jardín Juárez, Guadalupe. ✆ **492/923-2386** or 492/923-2089. Free admission. Tues–Sun 10am–4:30pm.

WHERE TO STAY

Zacatecas has a great selection of hotels. In the fall and winter, heat can come in handy. Of the hotels listed here, all but the Condesa have heaters in the rooms, but many hotels in Zacatecas do not. Prices quoted here include the 17% tax. Rates go up for festivals and high season—Easter, and August to September.

VERY EXPENSIVE

Hotel Quinta Real ★★★   Mexico is littered with hotels made from former colonial mansions, convents, and haciendas, but how many have risen from bullrings? And yet, it's the beauty, not the novelty, that makes this hotel so great. It has won several design awards, undoubtedly because the architects knew enough to leave the beautiful old bullring intact and keep the hotel small enough to be unobtrusive. A few of the graceful arches that remain from the town's colonial aqueduct frame the entrance. Inside the lobby, you can survey the whole arena, with its arches and stepped levels. On one side is the restaurant, below it a bar, and to the left are shops. The rooms were built along the outside of the bullring, and their windows open onto a small courtyard. Rooms are large, with spacious, well-equipped bathrooms, a writing desk, and a couch. Master suites are one room with a king or two double beds; *gran clase* suites are a good bit larger and have a sitting area and a whirlpool tub.

Av. Rayón 434, 98000 Zacatecas, Zac. ✆ **800/445-4565** in the U.S. and Canada, or 492/922-9104. Fax 492/922-8440. www.quintareal.com. 49 suites. $290 master suite; $315 *gran clase* suite. AE, DC, MC, V. Free guarded parking. **Amenities:** Restaurant; bar; golf and health club privileges at local club; concierge; tour desk; business center; secretarial service; room service until 11pm; in-room massage; babysitting; laundry service; dry cleaning; nonsmoking rooms. *In room:* A/C, TV, dataport, hair dryer, iron.

EXPENSIVE

Hotel Emporio Zacatecas ★★   A comfortable colonial-style hotel across from the Plaza de Armas, it is a popular choice with Mexican tourists and businesspeople. The spacious rooms on its six floors are carpeted and well furnished. Rooms in the back are quiet. The rooms in front, mostly junior suites, are sunny and have balconies with good views of the cathedral and Cerro de la Bufa. The ones I like most are those on the fourth floor, which have terraces. These are set back a little and offer more shielding from street noise. The rooms in back face a small interior patio, complete with gurgling fountain. They contain one king or two double beds. Bathrooms are midsize, with a decent amount of counter space.

Av. Hidalgo 703, Col. Centro, 98000 Zacatecas, Zac. ✆ **492/922-6183**. Fax 492/922-6245. www.hotelesemporio.com.mx. 113 units. $170 double; $200 junior suite. AE, MC, V. Free secure parking. **Amenities:** Restaurant; bar; golf and tennis at local club; fitness center; tour desk; car rental; secretarial services; room service until 11pm; babysitting; laundry service; dry cleaning; nonsmoking rooms. *In room:* TV, hair dryer, iron.

Mesón de Jobito ★★   This two-story hotel occupies a traditional *vecindad,* which was a common form of housing for the lower classes in olden days. The buildings ramble back from the entrance, forming private alleys decorated with ornamental plants and flowers and painted in traditional Mexican colors. The hotel has an intimate feel. The rooms are large, carpeted, and nicely furnished, with queen- or king-size beds and large bathrooms. A couple of the junior suites are large and stylishly decorated. Rates vary seasonally and are highest from September to December and during festival times. The hotel is 5 blocks from the cathedral and a block above Hidalgo.

Jardín Juárez 143, 98000 Zacatecas, Zac. ℂ/fax **492/924-1722,** or 01-800/021-0040 in Mexico. www.mesondejobito. com.mx. 53 units. $165 double; $175–$190 suite. AE, MC, V. Free valet parking. **Amenities:** 2 restaurants; bar; tour desk; car rental; room service until 1am; babysitting; laundry service; dry cleaning; nonsmoking rooms. *In room:* A/C, TV, coffeemaker, hair dryer.

INEXPENSIVE

Hotel Condesa *Value* The good location, well-kept rooms, and economical price are the main attractions here. Many rooms, especially on the lower floors, have been remodeled and have modern furniture, cheerful paint, and new bathroom tile. These rooms have interior views. Rooms on the third floor haven't been remodeled, but those facing east overlook Cerro de la Bufa and the market below the hotel. Some remodeled rooms contain king-size beds; other units have a double or two twins.

Av. Juárez 102, 98000 Zacatecas, Zac. ℂ/fax **492/922-1160.** 60 units. $40 double. AE, MC, V. **Amenities:** Restaurant; cafe/bar; tour desk; room service; laundry service. *In room:* TV.

Motel Zacatecas Courts Rooms have carpeting, hot water 24 hours a day, and comfortable beds. It is a 10-minute walk from the main square. Be sure to get a room in the back, away from the street. Also, you must ask to have the heat turned on in the room, and ask for extra blankets in winter.

López Velarde 602, 98000 Zacatecas, Zac. ℂ **492/922-0328.** Fax 492/922-1225. 92 units. $45 double. AE, MC, V. Free enclosed parking. **Amenities:** Restaurant; tour info; room service. *In room:* TV.

WHERE TO DINE

The dining in Zacatecas is good. In addition to the establishments listed below, the restaurants at the Quinta Real and Mesón del Jobito have good reputations. Gorditas might be considered the state food of Zacatecas, and the most popular gordita place is **Gorditas Doña Julia,** which operates three or four locations. The best coffee in town is at **Café San Patricio,** below the tourism office. It doesn't open until 9am.

Café Nevería Acrópolis MEXICAN This restaurant and coffee shop with a soda fountain is a popular meeting spot for breakfast, afternoon coffee, or dessert. The kitchen does itself credit with breakfast, enchiladas, and *chile relleno zacatecas* (a poblano chile stuffed with cheese sitting on top of spicy *picadillo*). Behind the cash register are photos and signatures of famous patrons, including Gregory Peck and Jane Fonda.

Av. Hidalgo and Rinconada de Catedral. ℂ **492/922-1284.** Breakfast $4–$6; main courses $5–$9. MC, V. Daily 8am–10pm.

La Cantera Musical Restaurant Bar ⋆ MEXICAN/REGIONAL This restaurant is best known for its regional cooking, especially typical dishes such as *asado de bodas* (a pork dish made with cinnamon and ancho and *guajillo* chiles) and *mole zacatecano* (a sweet and spicy chicken dish). You can also get a number of Mexican standards. The dining room is attractive. The restaurant is below the Mercado González Ortega, by the cathedral.

Tacuba 2, Centro Comercial El Mercado. ℂ **492/922-8828.** Main courses $3–$10. AE, MC, V. Mon–Fri 1pm–midnight; Sat–Sun 9am–11pm.

La Cuija ⋆⋆ INTERNATIONAL/REGIONAL This stylish restaurant under the Centro Comercial has comfortable, attractively set tables in a heavily colonnaded room. Appetizers are referred to as "something to open the mouth," and the *quesadillas de flor de calabaza* (squash-blossom quesadillas) are especially good reasons for doing so. The restaurant has its own vineyards. The menu features a good selection of dishes, including *chile mestizo,* which is an ancho chile stuffed with *huitlacoche,* with a sauce of ground corn, cream, and a bit of aged cheese. Friday and Saturday nights, a guitar trio plays.

Tacuba T-5, Centro Comercial El Mercado. © **492/922-8275.** Reservations not accepted during Semana Santa. Main courses $8–$15. AE, MC, V. Daily 2pm–midnight.

Los Dorados de Villa 🐎🐎 MEXICAN   If your grandmother were Mexican, this is how you would want her to cook. The green *pozole* (soup with chicken, hominy, lettuce, and radishes) is excellent, as are the enchiladas, which come in many varieties (I recommend the *zacatecanas* and the *rojas*). Other menu items include tostadas, tacos, soups, and guacamole. The name of the place refers to "the golden ones"—Pancho Villa's honor guard of fearless soldiers. The owner is a collector of memorabilia—artifacts and reproductions from La Revolución cover the walls of the small dining room. Decorative paper cutouts hang from the ceiling, making the room feel even smaller, but festive, too. Los Dorados is not far from the Rafael Coronel Museum; walk north several blocks on Hidalgo, keeping to the left each time the street forks.

Plazuela de García 1314. © **492/922-5722.** Reservations recommended on weekends. Main courses $5–$7. No credit cards. Daily 2:30pm–midnight.

ZACATECAS AFTER DARK

El Malacate   Disco music in a mine deep inside the earth—does "Disco Inferno" ring a bell? Whose life could be considered complete without having made the scene here? Call in advance if you want to reserve a table. The entrance is at the end of Calle Dovali. From Hidalgo, walk up Juárez, which turns into Torreón. Just past the Seguro Social building on Avenida Torreón, you'll find Dovali; turn right. Take a cab if you don't want to be so bushed that you can't boogie. The club is open Thursday through Sunday from 9:30pm to 2am. Mina El Edén, Calle Dovali. © **492/922-3727.** Cover $14.

5 San Luis Potosí

418km (261 miles) N of Mexico City; 346km (216 miles) NE of Guadalajara; 202km (126 miles) N of Querétaro; 189km (118 miles) E of Zacatecas

San Luis Potosí, more than a mile high in central Mexico's high-plains region, was among the country's most picturesque and prosperous mining cities. It is now the largest and most industrial of the silver cities, with almost a million inhabitants, but you would never know it if you stayed in the historic central district. It has rich colonial architecture and is known for its great plazas. Capital of the state of the same name, San Luis Potosí was named for Louis IX, saintly king of France; *potosí,* the Quechua word for "richness," was borrowed from the incredibly rich Bolivian Potosí mines, which San Luis's mines were thought to rival.

ESSENTIALS

GETTING THERE & DEPARTING   By Plane   AeroMar (© 888/627-0207 in the U.S., or 444/817-7936) offers a direct flight on Sunday to and from San Antonio; **Continental** (© 800/231-0856 in the U.S., or 01-800/900-5000 in Mexico) flies to and from Houston. AeroMar, **Mexicana** (© 444/833-5326), **Aero California** (© 444/ 811-8050), and **Aerolitoral** (© 444/822-2229) operate domestically.

San Luis Potosí

ATTRACTIONS ●
Cathedral **6**
FONART store **2**
Museo Nacional
de la Máscara **8**
Palacio del Gobierno **5**
Teatro de la Paz **9**
Templo de San Francisco **1**
Templo del Carmen **10**

ACCOMMODATIONS ■
Hotel Filher **7**
Hotel María Cristina **11**
Hotel Panorama **4**
Hotel Real Plaza **3**

The **airport** is about 11km (7 miles) from downtown. A taxi to the city center is $19. A *colectivo* van is more economical, but don't tarry in the terminal, because they leave quickly.

By Car   From Mexico City, take Highway 57D; from Guadalajara, take Highway 80. If you're coming from the north, it takes 6 to 7 hours to drive the 536km (335 miles) from Monterrey.

By Bus   The large Central Camionera is 3km (2 miles) east of downtown on Guadalupe Torres at Diagonal Sur. City buses marked CENTRAL go to the bus station from the Alameda park for around 25¢. Taxis cost about $5. Most of the bus travel is through Estrella Blanca and its many affiliates, which occupy the counters to the left as you enter. You can buy a ticket for any of the affiliates from any counter. To the right as you enter are three other first-class bus companies: ETN (mostly to Mexico City and Guadalajara), Primera Plus (to Mexico City and Querétaro), and Omnibus de Mexico (to Mexico City, Guadalajara, and Querétaro).

VISITOR INFORMATION   The **State Tourism Office** (© **444/812-9939** or 444/812-9943; fax 444/812-6769) is at Obregón 520, a block west of Plaza Fundadores in an old mansion built in the French style. The information office has a helpful staff, a good map of the city and historic district, and, of course, lots of brochures. It's open Monday through Friday from 8am to 9pm, Saturday from 9am to 2pm. Plaza Fundadores is a block from the northwest corner of the Plaza de Armas.

CITY LAYOUT   The **Plaza de Armas** (or Jardín Hidalgo) is the center of the historic district. All the streets bordering it are pedestrian only. The principal pedestrian street runs north-south in front of the plaza; the southern part (called **Zaragoza**) extends 8 blocks to the Jardín Colón, and the northern part (called **Hidalgo**) runs 5 blocks to the main market. The city also has many plazas and a large downtown park called the **Alameda. Avenida Carranza** heads east from the Plaza de Armas, passes by the Plaza de Fundadores, and extends to the prosperous residential section of the city. Fronting this street are many banks, clubs, and restaurants.

FAST FACTS: San Luis Potosí

American Express   The local representative is **Grandes Viajes**, Av. Carranza 1077 (© **444/817-6004**; fax 444/811-1166). Hours are Monday through Friday from 9am to 2pm and 4 to 7pm, Saturday from 10am to 1pm.

Area Code   The telephone area code is **444**.

Climate   San Luis is on the high plateau more than a mile above sea level, but the weather can get hot during May, June, and sometimes July. In winter it occasionally drops to freezing at night. Rain is rare, with an average total of 14 inches per year; it falls between May and November, mostly in August.

Currency Exchange   Four *casas de cambios* near the main post office offer better rates and better service than the banks. Two are in the arcade on Julián de los Reyes, and two are on Mariano Escobedo. This is just a few blocks northeast of the Plaza de Armas. All are open Saturday. The historic district has many ATMs.

Emergency   San Luis's central emergency number is © **060**.

Hospital The **Hospital Centro Médico**, Antonio Aguilar 155 (© **444/813-3797**), is one of the best in the country.

Post Office The *correo*, Morelos 235, 4 blocks north-northeast of the Plaza de Armas, is open Monday through Friday from 8am to 3pm, Saturday 9am to 1pm. Look for a narrow one-story building made of gray stone.

Population San Luis Potosí has 850,000 residents.

EXPLORING SAN LUIS POTOSI
A STROLL AROUND THE HISTORIC CENTER

San Luis has more streets designated solely for pedestrian use than any of the other silver cities. The center of town is the **Plaza de Armas** or Jardín Hidalgo, dating from the mid-1700s and shaded by magnolia and flamboyant trees. The **bandstand** in the center of the plaza was built in 1947 (in colonial style), using pink volcanic stone. Free band concerts usually begin on Thursday and Sunday at around 7:30 or 8pm. On the west side of the plaza is the **Palacio de Gobierno.** It has been much repaired, restored, and added to through the centuries—the back and the south facade were redone as recently as 1973. The front of the building retains much of the original 18th-century decoration, at least on the lower floors. On the second floor, you'll find the rooms that Juárez occupied when he established his temporary capital here. It's worth a peek.

Across the plaza from the Government Palace is the **cathedral.** The original building had only a single bell tower; the one on the left was built in 1910 to match, although today the newer tower looks older. The Count of Monterrey built the **Palacio Municipal,** on the north side of the cathedral, in 1850. He filled it with paintings and sculptures, few of which survived the city's stormy history. When the count died in 1890, the palace was taken over by the bishop, and in 1921 by the city government. Since then, it has been San Luis's city hall. On January 1, 1986, it was firebombed in a moment of social unrest. It was restored and functions again.

Southeast of the Jardín Hidalgo is one of the city's most famous squares, **Plazuela del Carmen,** named for the **Templo del Carmen** 🏛 church. From the jardín, walk east along Madero-Othón to Escobedo and the plazuela. The entire area you see was once part of the extensive grounds of the 18th-century Carmelite monastery. The church survives from that time and is perhaps the Potosinos' favorite place of worship. The **Teatro de la Paz** and the **Museo Nacional de la Máscara** also face the plaza. The museum is closed for much of 2006 for remodeling.

Attached to the Teatro de la Paz (enter to the right of the theater's main entrance) is the **Sala German Gedovius** (© **444/812-2698**). It has four galleries for exhibitions of international and local art. It's open Tuesday through Sunday from 10am to 2pm and 4 to 6pm. Admission is free.

The square is a fine place to rest before heading a couple of blocks east to get to the shady, cool **Alameda,** the city's largest downtown park. Vendors sell handicrafts, fruits, and all manner of snacks. Just across Negrete is the magnificent **Templo de San José,** with lots of ornate gold decorations, huge religious paintings, and *El Señor de los Trabajos,* a miracle-working statue with many *retablos* testifying to the wonders it has performed.

PLAZAS

San Luis Potosí has more plazas than any other colonial city in Mexico. The two most famous ones are mentioned above. **Plaza de San Francisco** is southeast of the Plaza de Armas along Aldama, between Guerrero and Galeana. This shady square takes its name from the Franciscan monastery on the south side of the plaza and the church on the west side. It holds some beautiful stained glass, many colonial-era statues and paintings, and a crystal chandelier shaped like a sailing ship. This is San Luis society's favorite church for weddings.

Another square is **Plaza de los Fundadores (Founders' Square),** at the intersection of Obregón and Aldama, northwest of the Jardín Hidalgo. Facing it is the **Loreto Chapel,** with its exquisite baroque facade. The neighboring church of **El Sagrario** belonged to the Jesuits before the order was expelled from Mexico.

SHOPPING

The best one-stop shopping in San Luis is at the government-operated **FONART** crafts store (© **444/814-3868**) on the Plaza de San Francisco. The building was originally part of the Convent of San Francisco, founded in 1590. Today it houses the offices of the Casa de la Cultura, and a branch of FONART on the ground floor. This one is especially well stocked with some of the country's best crafts. It's open Monday through Friday from 9am to 2pm and 4 to 7pm, Saturday 10am to 5 pm. Another place to try is the state-run store **La Casa del Artesano,** Carranza 540 (no phone), 5 blocks west of Jardín Hidalgo. The store carries examples of every kind of craft made in the state. Each room in the store is dedicated to the crafts of one of the cultural or climatic zones of the state. The store is open Monday through Saturday from 10am to 2pm and 4 to 8pm.

Several blocks along the pedestrian Calle Hidalgo from the Jardín Hidalgo, you'll find the city's **Mercado Hidalgo,** a mammoth building devoted mostly to food, but also offering, among other things, baskets, *rebozos* (shawls), and straw furniture.

The walk along Hidalgo is an introduction to the city's commercial life. Hardware stores, crafts shops, shoe stores, groceries, and taverns crowd the street. Past the Mercado Hidalgo is another big market, the Mercado República.

A well-loved local chocolate factory is **Constanzo,** which has several outlets throughout the city, including three on Carranza. Most outlets are open Monday through Saturday from 10am to 1:30pm and 4 to 8:30pm.

WHERE TO STAY

There are no luxury hotels in the historic center. Most of them (the María Dolores, Real de Minas, and Holiday Inn) are to the east, where the highway from Mexico City enters the town. The Westin is to the west, along the highway to Guadalajara. All rates listed below include the 17% tax.

VERY EXPENSIVE

Westin San Luis Potosi ★★   Certainly the loveliest hotel in San Luis, the Westin offers comfort and service in surroundings that exemplify how contemporary Mexican architects have worked the elements of colonial architecture to achieve an aesthetic that is new without being divorced from its past. The rooms are along a three-story stone arcade that surrounds a broad courtyard. All are large, carpeted, and decorated with flair. They come with either two full- or one king-size bed, a writing table, and a small dining table. Bathrooms are very large, with marble tiles, countertops, and shower/tub combinations. Suites are even larger and offer a stereo with a CD player, a large whirlpool tub, a safe, and bathrobes. I prefer the rooms that have an interior view of the courtyard. The center of town is 15 to 20 minutes away by car.

Real de Lomas 1000, 78210 San Luis Potosí, S.L.P. Ⓒ 800/228-3000 in the U.S., or 444/825-0125. Fax 444/825-0200. www.westin.com. 123 units. $290 double; $300–$315 suite. Rates include airport transfers and breakfast buffet. Children under 12 stay free in parent's room. AE, MC, V. Free valet parking. **Amenities:** Restaurant; bar; small heated pool; access to nearby health club w/tennis and racquetball; fitness center; kids' club; concierge; tour desk; car rental; airport transportation; business center; executive business services; 24-hr. room service; babysitting; laundry service; dry cleaning; nonsmoking rooms. *In room:* A/C, TV, dataport, minibar, hair dryer, iron.

MODERATE

Hotel Panorama   Aptly named, this hotel is in a 10-story glass building near the Plaza Fundadores. Many years ago, it was *the* hotel in San Luis, but newer, fancier competitors and a certain amount of decay changed that. Rooms vary in size from medium to large; none feel cramped. Bathrooms are a little small. Most rooms come with two full-size beds, but some have a king. All have an exterior view. Five floors of guest rooms have been completely remodeled. The difference in the remodeled rooms is substantial; they have air-conditioning, high-speed Internet, hair dryers, marble bathrooms with plenty of counter space, modern mahogany-stained furniture, and much better lighting. Even if you don't stay here, visit the hotel's rooftop restaurant and bar in the evening (Mon–Sat 7pm–2am) and catch the view of the city.

Av. Carranza 315, 78000 San Luis Potosí, S.L.P. Ⓒ 444/812-1777. Fax 444/812-4591. www.hotelpanorama.com.mx. 126 units. $70 standard double; $80 executive level. AE, MC, V. Free secure parking. **Amenities:** Restaurant; cafe; 2 bars (1 rooftop); dance club; midsize heated pool; Jacuzzi; tour desk; car rental; room service until 11pm; babysitting; laundry service; dry cleaning; nonsmoking rooms; executive-level rooms. *In room:* A/C in remodeled rooms, TV, high-speed Internet.

Hotel Real Plaza   A modern nine-story hotel 8 blocks from the Plaza de Armas, the Real Plaza offers comfort and quiet at a good price. The midsize rooms are carpeted and well lit but have no style. They are preferable, however, to the unremodeled rooms at the Panorama. Bathrooms are a little larger than at the Panorama, but some rooms have no view. It's probably worth doing a little price comparison, keeping in mind that you'll have to do a little more walking if you stay here.

Av. Carranza 890, 78250 San Luis Potosí, S.L.P. Ⓒ 444/814-6969. Fax 444/814-6639. www.realplaza.com.mx. 268 units. $62 double. AE, MC, V. Free secure parking. **Amenities:** Restaurant; bar; tour desk; business center; room service until 10pm; babysitting; laundry service. *In room:* A/C, TV, high-speed Internet.

INEXPENSIVE

Hotel Filher ⒱ⱥˡᵘᵉ   Good location and medium to large rooms painted in cheerful colors are the high points of this economical three-story hotel. If you want quiet, request a room on the third floor; if you want a window and a firm new mattress, book a room on the second. Rates are higher for second-floor rooms. Of these, I like the ones facing the pedestrian-only Zaragoza. They have balconies with a good view, and though there may be street noise, you don't get the noise that reverberates through the rather loud lobby. This hotel is a good choice in warm weather because the rooms are airy and have tile floors rather than carpeting. They also have ceiling fans. Hot water can take as long as 5 minutes to get to the rooms.

Av. Universidad 375 (at Zaragoza), 78000 San Luis Potosí, S.L.P. Ⓒ 444/812-1562. Fax 444/812-1564. 50 units. $45 double. AE, MC, V. Parking 1 block away. **Amenities:** Restaurant; bar; limited room service. *In room:* No phone.

Hotel María Cristina   The María Cristina is in a narrow nine-story building around the corner from the Plaza del Carmen. It's next door to (and often confused with) the Hotel Nápoles. Rooms have "French-style" side tables and headboards and comfortable mattresses. All rooms are small and have a ceiling fan, and most don't offer much of a view. The bathrooms are small, with little counter space, but they offer filtered water from the faucet (a rarity in this price range). More good news is that the rooms are quiet, carpeted, and warmer in the winter than the rooms at the Filher. Rooms contain one full or two twin beds.

Juan Sarabia 110, 78000 San Luis Potosí, S.L.P. ✆ 444/812-9408. Fax 444/812-8823. 74 units. $60 double. AE, MC, V. Free guarded parking. **Amenities:** 2 restaurants; bar; tour info; room service until 11:30pm. *In room:* TV.

WHERE TO DINE

The local cooking in downtown San Luis is represented by a number of restaurants. Try the **Posada del Virrey** on the Plaza de Armas, the large 24-hour **Café Pacífico** (not the small one) near the Plaza del Carmen on Constitución, or **La Parroquia** on the Plaza Fundadores. For something a little more special, try one of the following.

MODERATE

El Callejón de San Francisco ✦✦ MEXICAN   If the night air is comfortable, there's no lovelier place for dinner than this restaurant's rooftop terrace, with San Francisco's cupola and bell towers for a backdrop. Even if it's a tad too chilly, you can still enjoy yourself; just ask the waiter for a *jorongo* (hoh-*rohn*-goh), a traditional woolen wrap for the shoulders. There's also a dining room downstairs. The menu has a number of Mexican standards at reasonable prices. The *enchiladas potosinas* (which are in the appetizer section) make a full meal. Other specialties are *chiles en nogada* and *pechuga Doña Luz* (chicken breast in poblano cream sauce). The restaurant is on a pedestrian street beside San Francisco church and behind FONART.

Callejón de Lozada 1. ✆ 444/812-4508. Reservations recommended on weekends. Main courses $6–$10. AE, MC, V. Tues–Sat 1:30pm–midnight; Sun 1:30–6pm.

La Corriente Restaurant Bar ✦ REGIONAL   It's hard to categorize this place because its specialties run in three directions: down-home country Mexican dishes, using mostly beef; a large selection of blended fruit and vegetable drinks, conventional and unconventional; and *antojitos* (Mexican supper foods served after 7pm). Of the main dishes, I liked *chamorro pibil* (pork cooked in a Huastecan *mole*) and *puntas al chipotle* (beef in a spicy chipotle sauce). The juices are filling—don't make the mistake of getting one and a main course or a full breakfast; try an appetizer such as the *quesadillas de huitlacoche*. The restaurant is in a large old house with a roofed patio and several dining rooms with high ceilings.

Carranza 700 (at Reforma). ✆ 444/812-9304. Main courses $5–$10; blended juices $3. AE, MC, V. Mon–Sat 8am–midnight; Sun 10am–6pm.

La Gran Vía ✦ SPANISH/INTERNATIONAL   Ask any prosperous Potosino for the best restaurant in town, and he or she will tell you La Gran Vía. On walking in, you certainly get the feel of a restaurant that's been around a long time and doesn't need to impress. It has polish, but nothing fancy in its decor (except some lovely Talavera pieces). Spanish specialties include *lechón asado* (roast suckling pig) and *cocido* (traditional Spanish potage made with garbanzo beans). I would go for either of these or the chef's special over the international menu, which seemed a little weak. The soups are also worthy—a mushroom and cilantro, and the classic Spanish garlic. In the afternoons and evenings, there's live piano music in the dining room to the left—choose your table accordingly.

Av. Carranza 560. ℂ **444/812-2899**. Reservations accepted. Main courses $7–$15. AE, MC, V. Mon–Sat 1pm–midnight; Sun 1–7pm.

Restaurant Orizatlán ★★ HUASTECAN   This colorful restaurant specializes in the traditional Huastecan cooking of eastern San Luis Potosí. If you are hungry, try the *parrillada a la Huasteca* for two. A large sampling of typical dishes, it includes portions of the *zacahuil,* Mexico's largest *tamal.* The waiters will keep the Huastecan enchiladas coming until you beg them to stop. Less ambitious eaters can order a la carte. After dinner, the restaurant serves complimentary home-style cordials made from several fruits and puts on a mini Huastecan fandango, with music and dance.

Pascual M. Hernández 240. ℂ **444/814-6786**. Breakfast $4; main courses $5–$10. AE. Mon–Sat 8am–11pm; Sun 8am–7pm. 8 blocks south of Plaza de Armas on Zaragoza, turn left at Jardín Colón; restaurant is about 30m (100 ft.) down.

SAN LUIS AFTER DARK

The most popular clubs in town are those where you can sit down to a late supper or drinks and hear guitarists and vocalists. Most of the music is romantic—*trovas,* or ballads. In the downtown area, a number of bars offer this kind of entertainment. They include **La Compañía,** Mariano Arista 350 (ℂ **444/812-9693**); **Viejo San Luis,** Carranza 485-A (ℂ **444/814-0801**); and **Restaurant Bar 1913,** Galeana 205 (ℂ **444/812-8352**). **Staff,** Carranza 423 (ℂ **444/814-7034**), is a popular dance club for 20-somethings.

7

Michoacán

by David Baird

West of Mexico City and southeast of Guadalajara lies the state of Michoacán (mee-choh-ah-*kahn*), the homeland of more than 200,000 Tarascan Indians, properly known as the Purépecha. The land is mountainous in the east, north, and center, but in the south and west it drops to a broad lowland plain that meets the Pacific. The state gets more rain and is consequently greener than its neighbors Jalisco and Guanajuato, and many Mexicans consider it the most beautiful state in their country. And yet, it remains relatively unvisited by foreign tourists.

High in the mountains, in the northeastern part of the state, a miraculous ritual occurs every year. Millions of monarch butterflies congregate in an isolated highland forest. They are the final link in a migratory chain stretching as far away as Canada. During peak season (Dec–Mar), the tree limbs bend under their cumulative weight, and the undulation of so many wings creates a dazzling spectacle. (See "Michoacán's Monarch Migration," later in this chapter.) In central Michoacán are highland lakes and colorful Indian towns that evoke the Mexico of old. These towns are well known for their handicrafts and the syncretic celebrations honoring their ancestors on the Day of the Dead. Farther west and south is the famous volcano Paricutín, the only major volcano born in modern times (1943).

The two most important cities in Michoacán, **Morelia** and **Pátzcuaro**, offer the visitor contrasting visions of the colonial past. Morelia is a city built of chiseled stone, planned with architectural considerations, and possessed of a clear-cut geometry. While Pátzcuaro is all about undulating adobe walls, crooked red tile roofs, and narrow meandering streets. The former is proud of its Spanish heritage; the latter remains rooted in its Indian origins.

The native Purépecha are an intriguing people. Where they came from and how they got here we don't know. Their language is unlike any other in Mexico; the closest linguistic connection being with native peoples in Ecuador. Their civilization developed contemporaneously with that of the Aztec, and they successfully defeated Aztec expansionism—the only highland civilization to do so.

Since they were not vassals of the Aztec, they didn't simply submit to Spanish rule after the collapse of the Aztec empire. In the history of the conquest and conversion of the Purépecha, two men represent the extremes of Spanish attitudes toward the Indians. One was the conquistador Nuño de Guzmán, a man whose rapaciousness and cruelty made him infamous even among fellow conquistadors, eventually earning him a prison cell in Spain. The other was Vasco de Quiroga, a humanist who believed in the ideas of Erasmus and Thomas More. He joined the church late in life and came to Michoacán as the first bishop of the Purépecha, establishing his see in Pátzcuaro. Here, he strove to build a utopian society of cooperative communities, organizing and instructing each village in the practice of a specific craft. To this day, his organization of crafts among the different villages is largely followed.

EXPLORING MICHOACAN

Travel between the major cities of Michoacán takes only an hour or 2 at most, and public transportation is frequent. You should plan 3 days in **Morelia** (more if you intend to see the butterflies) and a minimum of 3 days in **Pátzcuaro,** but more like a week if you're interested in taking day trips to the lakes and the villages in the region and want to look into the local handicrafts. **Uruapan,** another important town, is an easy day trip from either city, although you may want to stay longer to visit the **Paricutín volcano.** During Easter week or Day of the Dead observances (Nov 1–2), the Plazas Grandes in Pátzcuaro and Uruapan overflow with regional crafts. Reserve rooms well in advance for these holidays. With the new highway from Ixtapa, it's possible to plan a vacation that combines the lovely colonial cities of Michoacán with quality beach time.

1 Morelia ⟨★⟩

312km (195 miles) NW of Mexico City; 365km (228 miles) SE of Guadalajara

The first Viceroy of Mexico ordered the founding of the city in 1541 under the name Valladolid. The name was later changed to Morelia to honor the revolutionary hero José María Morelos, who was born here.

Morelia was intended as a bastion of Spanish culture for the region's large population of Indians. The adjective people most frequently use to describe Morelia is "aristocratic." And indeed, the city's greatest appeal lies in its grand colonial architecture.

ESSENTIALS

GETTING THERE & DEPARTING   By Plane Continental has direct flights from Houston and Los Angeles. **Mexicana** (② 443/324-3808) has flights to and from the U.S. Flights from San Francisco, Oakland, San Jose, Los Angeles, and Chicago are either one-stop or nonstop, depending on the day of the flight. Mexicana also flies direct to several destinations within Mexico. **Aeromexico/Aerolitoral** (② 443/324-2424 or 443/324-3604) flies to and from Mexico City, Guadalajara, Querétaro, Tepic, and Tijuana, with connections to U.S. destinations.

Morelia's airport is **Aeropuerto Francisco J. Mújica,** a 45-minute drive from the city center on Km 27 of the Carretera Morelia-Zinapécuaro. Taxis meet each flight. **Budget** has a car-rental office there (② 800/527-0700 in the U.S. and Canada, or 443/313-3399).

By Car Using the modern **toll highway** running between Mexico City and Guadalajara, the trip to Morelia from either city takes 4 hours. **Highway 15** (the long route) runs west from Mexico City and east and south from Guadalajara. Both sections of Highway 15 are mountainous and slow, with beautiful vistas. From Mexico City, the toll highway goes to Toluca, then through Atlacomulco and Marvatío. From Guadalajara, it goes through La Barca (northeast of Lake Chapala). Tolls run close to $20. Coming from either direction, you will see the very large Lake Cuitzeo; then look for the intersection with Highway 43 and turn south. **Highway 43** is a fairly direct route from Guanajuato (2½ hr.) and from San Miguel de Allende (3 hr.). Four-lane **Highway 120** connects Pátzcuaro and Morelia; the trip takes about 50 minutes.

Morelia

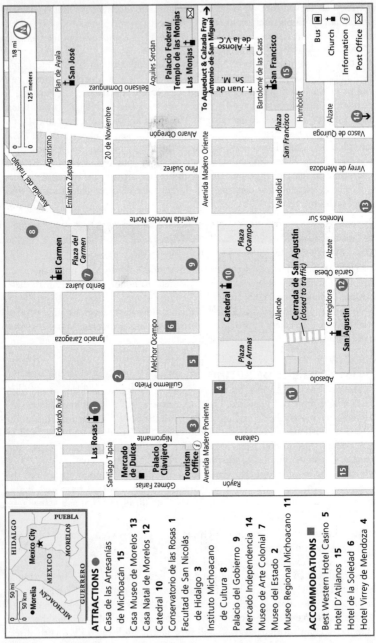

ATTRACTIONS

Casa de las Artesanías de Michoacán **15**

Casa Museo de Morelos **13**

Casa Natal de Morelos **12**

Catedral **10**

Conservatorio de las Rosas **1**

Facultad de San Nicolás de Hidalgo **3**

Instituto Michoacano de Cultura **8**

Palacio del Gobierno **9**

Mercado Independencia **14**

Museo de Arte Colonial **7**

Museo del Estado **2**

Museo Regional Michoacano **11**

ACCOMMODATIONS

Best Western Hotel Casino **5**

Hotel D'Atilanos **15**

Hotel de la Soledad **6**

Hotel Virrey de Mendoza **4**

(Midway, you'll see a turnoff for Tupátaro and Cuanajo, covered in "Side Trips from Pátzcuaro," later in this chapter.) By the time you read this, the new highway from Ixtapa/Zihuatanejo to Michoacán's highlands should be completely finished, which should cut traveling time to 6 hours.

By Bus   You will arrive at the new **Central Camionera** in the far northwest side of town, near the soccer stadium. First-class and deluxe bus service to and from Morelia uses terminal A, and regional service to and from Pátzcuaro uses terminal B. From Mexico City, take a bus from the Terminal Poniente, or Observatorio station. ETN, Pegasso, Primera Plus/Servicios Coordinados, and Autovías all go to Morelia. Make sure to request a *directo* or "via autopista." The trip takes 4 hours, and there are usually three or four departures every hour. ETN offers the best service. These bus lines also go to Guadalajara and together offer 25 arrivals and departures per day. Travel time is 3½ hours. From Guanajuato, your best bet is Primera Plus and Servicios Coordinados (a total of six departures per day).

In Morelia there are a few travel agencies that sell bus tickets. At the corner of 20 de Noviembre and Obregón is one called **GAP** (© **443/317-2828**), and it sells tickets for ETN and Primera Plus.

VISITOR INFORMATION   The city government, in association with local guides, has a tourist information kiosk on the Plaza de Armas (main square). It's open from 9am until 8pm weekdays, until 3pm on Saturday and Sunday. The main office at Guillermo Prieto 56, around the corner from Avenida Madero. Office hours are Monday through Friday from 10am to 2pm and 5 to 8pm. The city operates a website (**www.visitmorelia.com**) and prints a free quarterly magazine with calendar of events (**La Guía de Morelia**), which is handy.

CITY LAYOUT   The heart of the city is the **cathedral,** with the Plaza de Armas on its left and the Plaza Melchor Ocampo on its right. The wide street passing in front of the cathedral is **Avenida Madero,** the city's main street. It meets the lovely colonial aqueduct .8km (½ mile) east of the cathedral. This segment of Madero, along with several blocks to either side, is the old part of town (see "Other Attractions," below.) From the fountain, the **aqueduct** heads southeast toward what has become the fashionable part of town.

GETTING AROUND   Taxis are a bargain here. Still, you should settle the fare before you enter the cab.

FAST FACTS: Morelia

American Express   The local representative is **Gran Turismo Viajes**, Av. Camelinas 3233, Int. 102–103, Fracc. Las Américas (© **443/324-0484**; fax 443/324-0495). Hours are Monday through Saturday from 9am to 2pm and 4 to 6pm.

Area Code   The telephone area code is **443**.

Climate   Morelia can be a bit chilly in the morning and evening, especially from November through February.

Elevation   Morelia sits at 1,950m (6,435 ft.).

Emergencies   The local number for emergencies is © **066**.

Hospital The best in town is the **Sanatorio de la Luz,** Calle Bravo 50, in the Chapultepec Norte neighborhood ((© **443/314-4568,** 443/314-4464, or 443/315-2966).

Internet Access You can find Internet service without much effort in the *centro histórico* (historic district). The usual cost is about $2 per hour.

Population Morelia has 540,000 residents.

Post Office &Telegraph Office Both are in the Palacio Federal, on the corner of Madero and Serapio Rendón, 5 blocks east of the cathedral.

SPECIAL EVENTS & FESTIVALS

The International Guitar Festival attracts musicians from all over the world. Dates vary; last year it took place in August. In May, the city holds the **International Organ Festival** (linked to the variable feast day of Corpus Christi). The cathedral has what might be the largest pipe organ in this hemisphere—if you like organ music, consider attending this festival. The **International Festival of Music** is in November. September is the month of the *fiestas patrias;* on **Independence Day** (Sept 16) and **Morelos's Birthday** (Sept 30), there are large *castillos* (fireworks displays), parades, and a good deal of celebrating.

EXPLORING MORELIA

A STROLL THROUGH THE COLONIAL CENTER

Downtown Morelia is a good town for walking. One comes across interesting details on just about any street, and crime poses little problem. The walk outlined below could take a whole day. The museums open at 9am; you'll find a lot of places closed on Mondays, holidays, and between 2 and 4pm. For a guided tour of the city, contact either of the guides mentioned in the section on the monarch butterfly migration. They can give a lot of local color and provide fascinating details about the city's history and architecture. They also offer tours to the local villages and the ruins around Lake Pátzcuaro.

The **cathedral** *★★★* is the place to begin. Built with the pink volcanic stone (*cantera* in Spanish) that Morelia is famous for, it's the most beautiful cathedral in Mexico. Notice how Avenida Madero widens as it passes in front of the cathedral, and how a cross street lines up with its facade. You'll see this arrangement repeated with other churches. Morelia's planners sought to lend prominence to the city's churches by the placement of plazas and the alignment of streets to allow good views. This cathedral took the place of an earlier one; construction began in 1640 and ended in 1745. The new cathedral incorporated the finest features of the styles of religious architecture already in the city, including plateresque, mannerist, and a native style of baroque characterized by sobriety and restraint—qualities that came naturally to Morelianos. The cathedral's impressive size and monumental proportions were necessary to place it at the top of the hierarchy of the city's temples, and to make plain Morelia's superiority to rival Pátzcuaro. The Italian architect who designed it worked closely with the different authorities of Morelia's sizable religious community, and he did a masterful job balancing the architectural elements in the facade and shaping the proportions of the towers. The inside is stately, but the cathedral's most valuable possessions were plundered. Things to look for include the beautiful **organ** *★* with 4,600 pipes (see "Special Events & Festivals," above); the silver baptismal font where Mexico's first emperor, Agustín de Iturbide, was baptized; and the elegant choir with carved wooden stalls.

Across Avenida Madero from the cathedral is a two-story stone building with little decoration on its exterior walls, yet topped with fanciful, Oriental-style decorations and finials. This is the **Palacio del Gobierno,** built in 1732 as a seminary. It now holds sweeping murals depicting the history of Michoacán and Mexico. Some are the work of a well-known local artist, Alfredo Zalce.

As you leave the *palacio,* turn left and walk down Madero for 2 blocks. Turn right at a small church on your right with a tall wrought-iron fence. The name of the street is Vasco de Quiroga. Walk 1 block, and to your left you'll see a broad plaza and the **church and convent of San Francisco** ★★. This is one of the two oldest religious buildings in Morelia. It draws on the Spanish Renaissance architectural style known as plateresque (already antiquated by the time of construction) because the builders wanted to accentuate their Spanish heritage. The convent is quite striking; it has elegant, Moorish windows on the second floor, borrowed from Spanish Mudéjar architecture. The interior courtyard, unlike any other in Morelia, has a medieval feel. Instead of being broad and open with light arches, it is closed and narrow, with heavy columns set closely together and thick buttressing. The former convent now houses a local **handicrafts museum** and the best shopping in Morelia (see "Shopping," below).

Morelia's **city market** is 5 blocks south of San Francisco in a plain, warehouselike structure. It's much like other Mexican city markets, and a good place to observe details of local life. If you want to skip the market, take the street that lines up with the front door of San Francisco, and turn left at the second intersection on Calle Morelos Sur. One block down on your left is the Casa Museo de Morelos (see below).

To get to the market, continue downhill along Calle Vasco de Quiroga. Just before you get there you will see a little plaza and the **Templo de las Capuchinas.** It's a precious little baroque church with a gilt *retablo* (altarpiece) inside. Unfortunately, it is often closed; the best time to try is from 8 to 9am and from 5 to 6pm, when the priest opens the church for Mass. One block further is the market—a good place to pick up sombreros, huaraches, and such.

From the market, backtrack to the church and turn left (west) on the street that runs in front of the church (Ortega y Montáñez). Walk 2 blocks to Morelos Sur. Turn right (uphill) and after 1 long block, look for the **Casa Museo de Morelos,** Morelos Sur 323 (© **443/313-2651**), on your right. This is where José María Morelos lived as an adult. It's a grand house, with furniture and personal effects that belonged to the independence leader, as well as a period kitchen. For history buffs, there is an exhibition on his four campaigns against Spanish royalist forces. The museum is open daily from 9am to 7pm; admission is $2.50.

The next place to see is the **Museo Regional Michoacano** ★, at the intersection of Allende and Abasolo (© **443/312-0407**). To get there, walk uphill toward Madero, turn left when you get to the plaza next to the cathedral (1 block before Madero), and walk through the stone arcades behind the cathedral. At the end of the arcades and across the street, cater-cornered to the Plaza de Armas, is the museum. It provides a colorful view of the state from prehistoric times to Mexico's Cardenist period of the 1930s. Isidor Huarte, father of Ana Huarte, Emperor Iturbide's wife, originally owned the building, which was finished in 1775. The museum is open Tuesday through Saturday from 9am to 7pm, Sunday from 9am to 4pm. Admission is $2.

To take a break, sit at one of the outdoor cafes under the stone arches facing the front of the cathedral and order refreshments.

From the arches, go west on Madero for 1 block until you get to the corner of Nigromante. On the right corner, you'll find the **College of San Nicolás de Hidalgo,** a beautiful colonial-era building that claims to house the oldest university in the New World. Founded in Pátzcuaro in 1540, the university moved to Morelia in 1580 and became the University of Michoacán in 1917. On the other corner is another of Morelia's oldest church structures, the **Iglesia de la Compañía de Jesús,** built by the Jesuits. It is now a lovely library. Through a doorway to the right of the church is the state's **tourist information office.** Attached to the church is the former convent, now called the **Palacio Clavijero.** To see the graceful arches and rose-colored stone of its broad interior courtyard (the most photographed in Morelia), turn down Nigromante and follow it to the main entrance. The former convent now houses state government offices. Once you've seen the palacio, continue down the street to the little park. Facing the park is the **Conservatorio de las Rosas,** a former Dominican convent. It became a music school in 1785 and is now the home of the internationally acclaimed **Morelia Boys Choir.** The choir practices on weekday afternoons. If you would like to attend a concert, ask for information inside.

Cater-cornered from the conservatory, at the junction of Santiago Tapia and Guillermo Prieto, is the **Museo del Estado** (📞 443/313-0629). Exhibits include a display on the archaeology and history of the area and a 19th-century apothecary shop. The museum is open Monday through Friday from 9am to 2pm and 4 to 8pm, Saturday and Sunday from 9am to 2pm and 4 to 7pm. Admission is free. Look for or ask about concerts and other goings-on.

To visit another interesting museum, continue east on Santiago Tapia 2 blocks to Benito Juárez and turn north (left). The **Museo de Arte Colonial** ⚡, Av. Benito Juárez 240 (📞 443/313-9260), is a colonial mansion that houses a large collection of religious art from the 16th to the 18th centuries. One section displays Christ figures made from the paste of corn stalks. This was a pre-Columbian artistic technique among the Purépecha, and the missionaries soon had their Indian converts using it to create the Christ figures and saints that adorn many churches in Mexico. The museum is open Tuesday through Sunday from 10am to 2pm and 5 to 8pm. Admission is free.

Just around the corner from this museum (turn right as you exit) is the **Plaza del Carmen.** Across the plaza, behind a heavy wrought-iron fence, is the church and former convent of **El Carmen.** The entrance to the convent is on the opposite side of the block from the church, on Morelos Norte. The building is home to the state's **Instituto Michoacano de Cultura** (📞 443/313-1320), which has made this a comfortable and utilitarian destination; you can examine the calendars posted at the entrance to see whether a concert, film, or exhibition is happening during your stay. You can also sit down and have coffee while viewing the large stone courtyard built in the style often used by the Carmelites. In and about the courtyard are a museum of native masks, a large bookstore, and a gallery. Entrance is free. The institute is open daily from 10am to 8pm.

OTHER ATTRACTIONS

If you enjoy walks, try going east on Madero from the cathedral. After a couple of blocks, you'll reach the **Templo de las Monjas (Nuns' Temple),** a lovely old church with a unique twin facade and B-shaped floor plan. Beside it is the massive **Palacio Federal,** which houses, among many other official bureaus, the post and telegraph offices. Continue and you'll reach the colonial **aqueduct.** The graceful arches of the aqueduct stretch from here about a kilometer (less than a mile) eastward. A beautiful stone walkway, lined with trees and long stone benches, starts from one of the arches in front of the fountain. This is **La Calzada Fray Antonio de San Miguel** ⚡, and it leads to the **church of San Diego** ⚡. The most ornate church in Morelia, San Diego is also known as **El Santuario de Guadalupe.** Don't miss the interior, which looks like a jewel box. This was the product of a remodeling job done a century ago. In early December, food stands fill the entire plaza in front of the church, and a festival is held to celebrate the feast day of the Virgin of Guadalupe (Dec 12).

The distance from the cathedral to San Diego is about a kilometer (less than a mile). You can take a taxi back or, if you still feel like walking, return by crossing the large plaza with the statue of Morelos on horseback. Go under the aqueduct, and enter the park known as **El Bosque (The Woods).** Continue west and work your way back to the center of town. If you get turned around here, note that if you're walking on level ground, you're parallel to or heading toward Madero; if you're walking downhill, you're heading away from it.

SHOPPING

Casa de las Artesanías 🐨🐨 This is both a museum and one of the best crafts shops in Mexico. In the showroom on the right as you enter, you'll find an array of objects produced in the Indian villages of Michoacán's central highlands, including carved-wood furniture from Cuanajo, pottery from Tzintzuntzan, wood masks from Tócuaro, lacquerware from Pátzcuaro and Uruapan, cross-stitch embroidery from Tarecuato, copperware from Santa Clara, guitars from Paracho, and close-woven hats from Jarácuaro. Straight ahead in the interior courtyard are showcases laden with the best regional crafts. Upstairs, individual villages have sales outlets. Sometimes you'll find artisans demonstrating their craft. The shop and museum are open daily from 9am to 2pm and 5 to 8pm. Exconvento de San Francisco, Plaza Valladolid. © **443/312-1248.**

Mercado de Dulces Occupying the back part of the former Jesuit convent is the sweets market—a collection of stalls selling the typical sweets that Morelia is famous for, such as *ates* (a thick fruit paste), candied fruit wedges, jelly candies, honey, strawberry jam, pralines, toasted coconut, and milk candies. A shop upstairs has all kinds of regional *artesanías* (crafts) and hundreds of picture postcards from all over Michoacán. The *mercado* is open daily from 7am to 10pm. Behind the Palacio Clavijero, along Valentín Gómez Farías. No phone. From the cathedral, head west on Madero and turn right on Gómez Farías; entrance is ½ block down on the right.

WHERE TO STAY

Rates listed here include the 17% tax. Many hotels have high-season and low-season rates. High season includes Easter, July through August, Days of the Dead, Christmas, and long weekends (called *puentes* in Mexico).

VERY EXPENSIVE

Villa Montaña 🐨🐨🐨 High above the city on the Santa María Ridge, this hotel radiates beauty and tranquillity. Rooms are in a small complex of buildings on a hillside, separated by gardens and connected by footpaths. The buildings are at different levels; this, as well as the placement of the entrances, allows for privacy. Villa Montaña, a member of the Small Luxury Hotels of the World, has no rough edges. Rooms are large, impressively furnished, and have working fireplaces. Most come with two doubles or a king-size bed. Bathrooms are large, with tub/shower combinations and lots of counter space. Most of the junior suites have a separate living area and a small terrace with table and chairs. Master suites have a lot of architectural details. The restaurant does a great job with local dishes, and having a drink on the terrace overlooking the city is one of the delights of staying here. Service is attentive, and the hotel has recently opened a spa.

Patzimba 201, Col. Vista Bella 58090 Morelia, Mich. ℂ **800/223-6510** in the U.S., 800/448-8355 in Canada, 443/314-0231, or 443/314-0179. Fax 443/315-1423. www.villamontana.com.mx. 36 units. $211 double; $293–$355 suite; $460 2-bedroom suite. Internet specials sometimes available. Weekday discounts available. AE, MC, V. Free secure parking. **Amenities:** Restaurant; terrace bar; heated outdoor pool; golf at local country club; lighted tennis court; spa; fitness room; concierge; tour desk; business center; executive business services; room service until 11pm; in-room massage; babysitting; laundry service; dry cleaning. *In room:* TV, dataport, hair dryer, safe.

EXPENSIVE

Hotel Virrey de Mendoza ★★ This is one of the old-style grand hotels one occasionally finds in Mexico's colonial cities. Unlike others, this one was not allowed to decay; it is beautifully kept and most impressive. It's also right on the Plaza de Armas. Furnishings vary, but all rooms are comfortable. They have lots of character—wood floors with area rugs, period furniture, old-fashioned tile bathrooms with tub/shower combinations. Bed choices include two twins, one full, two queen-size, or one king-size. Standard rooms are midsize; of the eight exterior rooms, two have balconies. Suites are large, and master suites have separate sitting rooms. The *suite virreinal* (viceroy suite) is really grand, with a large third-floor terrace that looks out over the Plaza de Armas to the cathedral. Rooms have double-glazed windows, but traffic noises still leak in. If you crave quiet, avoid the exterior rooms, especially those facing Madero. Interior rooms are lovely, as are the fourth-floor rooms in rear courtyard.

Av. Madero Poniente 310, 58000 Morelia, Mich. ℂ/fax **443/312-4940**. www.hotelvirrey.com. 55 units. $170 double; $190–$350 suite. Internet specials available. AE, MC, V. Free valet parking. **Amenities:** Restaurant; lobby bar; tour desk; car rental; business center; room service until 11pm; in-room massage; babysitting; laundry service; dry cleaning; nonsmoking rooms. *In room:* TV, dataport, hair dryer.

MODERATE

Best Western Hotel Casino (Value) A colonial hotel that's not as striking as the Hotel de la Soledad, the Best Western should still be considered for its location—across the street from the cathedral—comfort, and price. The owners continue to invest money in improvements and upgrades. They've opened three new rooms on the top floor that are large, sunny, and quite comfortable. Most rooms are midsize and furnished and carpeted. They are, for the most part, more comfortable than the rooms at the Soledad. There are second-floor rooms in front that have a balcony and view of the cathedral, but they aren't as quiet as the rest. Many rooms have two double beds or one double and one twin.

Portal Hidalgo 229, 58000 Morelia, Mich. ℂ **800/528-1234** in the U.S., or 443/313-1328. Fax 443/312-1252. www.hotelcasino.com.mx. 43 units. $80–$90 double. AE, MC, V. Free valet parking. **Amenities:** Restaurant; bar; tour desk; car rental; business center; room service until 9:30pm; laundry service; dry cleaning; nonsmoking rooms. *In room:* TV, dataport, coffeemaker, hair dryer, iron.

Hotel de la Soledad ★ Past the massive wooden doors of this colonial hotel is a large, beautiful courtyard with antique carriages parked beneath stone arches. Some rooms have fireplaces and balconies. Standard rooms vary quite a bit and come with two twin beds, one double, or one king-size. The price depends on whether the room faces the more elegant front courtyard (these rooms are generally bigger) or the rear courtyard. Rooms have rugs or carpeting, Spanish-style furniture, and high ceilings. Bathrooms vary in size and quality; most are ample, and many contain tub/shower combinations. The location is great—1 block north of the cathedral.

Ignacio Zaragoza 90, 58000 Morelia, Mich. ℂ **443/312-1888** or 443/313-0627. www.hsoledad.com. 58 units. $90–$100 double; $110–$120 suite. AE, MC, V. **Amenities:** Restaurant; bar; tour desk; car rental; room service until 10pm; laundry service; dry cleaning. *In room:* TV, hair dryer on request, safe.

INEXPENSIVE

Hotel D'Atilanos   This is the only decent inexpensive hotel in the downtown area. Two floors of rooms surround a simple patio. The rooms are simply furnished, with one or two double beds, two twins, or one king bed (king rooms are more expensive). Most rooms are midsize, but bathrooms are small. I prefer the downstairs rooms, which have high ceilings. Lighting is poor.

Corregidora 465, 58000 Morelia, Mich. © **443/313-3309** or 443/312-0121. 27 units. $40–$48 double. No credit cards. *In room:* TV.

WHERE TO DINE

For light, cheap fare, there are several options worth exploring. Go to the **Cerrada de San Agustín,** which is a 1-block, pedestrian-only street behind the cathedral. There you will find **Gazpachos La Cerrada,** a popular hole in the wall serving great fruit salads (finely chopped, juicy fruit salads are called gazpacho in Michoacán) made of jicama (a root vegetable), mango, and pineapple, with orange juice, lime juice, salt, and powdered chile. Next door to it is an inexpensive restaurant that serves enchiladas and such called **La Guarecita.** If you have a sweet tooth, walk back toward the cathedral and at the corner under the arches to your right, you will find an ice cream vendor (if he hasn't moved) called **Nieves del Correo.** It's a third-generation business. The specialty is fruit-flavored ice cream. Another dining option is 2 blocks away, at the corner of Valladolid and Morelos Sur. It's called **Trico.** Downstairs is a Mexican-style deli, and upstairs is a comfortable dining room that serves mostly soups and sandwiches.

Michoacán is known for a dish of slowly cooked pork called *carnitas.* To try it, you have to go to a *carnitas* establishment. Restaurants don't offer it. Probably the best known is **Los Tabachines,** in the colonia Ventura Puente. The address is Laguna de la Magdalena 430, but the taxi driver will know where it is. You can eat the *carnitas* there or buy them to go.

Cenaduría Lupita ☽ ANTOJITOS   Translated literally, *antojitos* means "little cravings." This is the traditional supper food of most Mexicans, but they usually eat it at home or in greasy-spoon joints whose cleanliness is doubtful. A good-looking, comfortable restaurant that specializes in *antojitos* is a rarity; rarer still is one that does such a good job. Take your pick of tacos dorados, tostadas, tamales, *huchepos* (like *tamales,* but made with fresh corn), and *pozole* prepared Michoacán style. The restaurant is a half-block off Avenida Lázaro Cárdenas; take a cab.

Sánchez de Tagle 1004. © **443/312-1340.** *Antojitos* $3–$5. DC, DISC, MC, V. Wed–Mon 7–11pm (Sun to 10pm).

La Casa del Portal ☽ REGIONAL/INTERNATIONAL   This upstairs restaurant is in a beautiful stone mansion facing the Plaza de Armas (entrance is on the side street). The floors, walls, and ceilings of the old house have remained virtually intact, including the antique wallpaper and other details. There are several dining rooms, and on occasion the rooftop terrace is open for dining. Most of the furniture comes from the owner's workshop—his colorful designs make use of many furniture-making traditions of the region. The restaurant doubles as a sort of factory outlet, and all the furniture is for sale. What's for dinner? The menu includes several regional standards, such as *enchiladas del portal* (Michoacán-style enchiladas) and *arrachera valladolid,* a skirt steak accompanied by a few Mexican sides.

Guillermo Prieto 30 (cater-cornered from Virrey de Mendoza; entrance is on the side street). © **443/313-4899.** Main courses $6–$15. AE, MC, V. Daily 8:30am–10pm.

La Conspiración ★★ SEAFOOD/STEAKS   At this new downtown restaurant you can enjoy a variety of Mexican seafood specialties and a smattering of original dishes. The mussels, clams, and oysters are flown in daily from a farm in Baja California and are guaranteed fresh. You'll also find Argentine-style empanadas with a good dipping sauce and fish tacos. I tried two delicious soups: the regional *sopa tarasca* and the spicy *sopa del alcalde*. The main dining area is upstairs and has balconies facing out toward the cathedral from across Avenida Madero, but the entrance is around the corner on Morelos Norte.

Av. Morelos Norte 33 (corner of Av. Madero). © 443/317-6300. Reservations accepted. Main courses $10–$17. MC, V. Mon–Sat noon–10pm.

Las Trojes STEAKS/REGIONAL   A *troje* is the traditional dwelling of the highland Purépecha Indians, constructed of rough-cut wood planks. This restaurant is made of seven connected *trojes,* with picture windows added for light. For starters, try *sopa tarasca* (bean soup). Main courses include *cecina* (beef or pork sliced thin, spiced, and dried), a good steak *a la tampiqueña* (marinated and grilled), rib-eye, *chistorra* (Spanish-style sausage), and chicken stuffed with cheese en brochette. Take a cab.

Juan Sebastián Bach 51, Col. La Loma. © 443/314-7344. Main courses $9–$16. AE, MC, V. Mon–Sat 1pm–midnight; Sun 1–6pm. Valet parking available.

Los Mirasoles ★★ REGIONAL   Good regional cooking including fish tacos, corundas, and enchiladas placeras. Good steaks, too. Lots of kinds of beer and a large wine selection. The dining rooms are lovely, especially at night. Los Mirasoles is a few blocks west of the main square.

Av. Madero Poniente 549. © 443/317-5775. Reservations recommended on weekends. Main courses $5–$10; seafood/steaks $10–$18. AE, MC, V. Daily 1–11pm. From cathedral, walk 4 blocks west on Madero.

San Miguelito ★★ *Finds* MEXICAN   Perhaps the most popular restaurant in town, San Miguelito has a winning combination of an inventive menu, attentive service, and a setting loaded with icons of Mexican culture. The bar and waiting area is a miniature bullring dedicated to the Silvetis, a Mexico dynasty of bullfighters. One part of the main dining room is the Rincón de las Solteronas (the bachelorette corner), where many images of Saint Anthony hang upside down—the custom in Mexico when a girl is petitioning him for a boyfriend or husband. Guests are welcome to make a petition; the staff will be happy to show you how. The menu includes ribs marinated in tamarind and *chile morita,* a dish of *huitlacoche* with roasted squash and fresh farmer's cheese, mushroom soup, and fish steamed in a banana leaf. There are several steak dishes, including one in tequila, *guajillo* chile, and orange sauce. For dessert there's a delicious version of cherries jubilee. Take a cab.

Av. Camelinas (at Ventura Puente). © 443/324-2300. Reservations recommended. Main courses $10–$15. AE, MC, V. Mon–Wed 2–11pm; Thurs–Sat 2pm–1am; Sun 2–5pm.

MORELIA AFTER DARK

For nighttime entertainment, be sure to check the calendar of events at the **Instituto Michoacano de Cultura** (see "A Stroll Through the Colonial Center," earlier in this chapter). In addition, you can sit at one of the cafes under the stone arches across from the Plaza de Armas to do some people-watching (a very Moreliano thing to do). Aside from the dance clubs that are mostly on the fashionable east side, there are few nightlife options. The following are my favorites. For dancing, go to **La Casa de la Salsa** (© 443/313-9362), a large dance hall facing Plaza Morelos at the end of the

(Moments) Michoacán's Monarch Migration

A visit to the winter nesting grounds of the monarch butterfly, high in the mountains of northeast Michoacán, is a stirring experience. It might be the highlight of your trip. The season lasts from mid- to late November to March. Tour operators in Morelia offer a day trip to see the butterflies for $50 to $60 per person. The tour takes 10 to 12 hours and involves hiking up a mountain at a high altitude. You shouldn't consider doing this if you're not in decent physical condition.

The best time to see the butterflies is on a sunny day, when they flutter through the air in a blizzard of orange and black. At the center of the group, the branches of the tall fir trees bow under their burden of butterflies, whose wings undulate softly as the wind blows through the forest; it's quite a spectacle.

From Morelia, you'll have no difficulty finding a tour; most hotels and all travel agencies can put you in contact with one. I particularly recommend guides **Luis Miguel López Alanís** (© 443/340-4632) and **Alfredo de la Cruz Ibarra** (© 443/331-4473). They speak English, are federally licensed, and belong to a small cooperative of guides called Mex Mich Guías (www.mmg.com.mx). The easiest way to contact them is through their website. Most tours provide transportation, guide, soft drinks, and usually lunch. A good guide is important, if only to answer all the questions that these butterflies and their strange migration provoke.

Two butterfly sanctuaries are open to the public. (The monarchs congregate at seven sites, but five are closed to visitors.) They are **El Rosario** (admission $2; daily 10am–5 or 6pm) and the newer **Chincua** (same admission and hours as El Rosario). It is less of a drive, but usually more of a walk to the nucleus of the butterfly group—but not always. Throughout the season, the groups shift, moving up and down the mountains and making for a longer or shorter climb. A good guide will be aware of which is the shorter walk.

If you're driving, take the *autopista* to Mexico City, exit at Maravatio and go right. Keep right after going through Maravatio and take the narrow two-lane road toward Angangueo. When you get to a T-junction, go right, toward San Felipe. Enter the town of Ocampo and look for a small sign pointing left to get to Rosario, where you will find a parking lot near the trail head. If you want to make this a leisurely trip, spend the night in the nearby town of Angangueo at **Hotel Don Bruno** (© 715/156-0026; $55 double). It's a pretty hotel but a little overpriced, so you should ask to see the room before you accept it.

Travel agencies from **San Miguel de Allende** also book monarch tours, which take 2 days. See chapter 6 for details.

Calzada Fray Antonio de San Miguel. It's open Tuesday through Saturday from 9pm to 3am. It books live music on Friday and Saturday ($4 cover). You can call ahead to reserve a table; the band plays a lot of salsa, merengue, and mambo.

If you want to hear live Latin American folk music, have a drink, and eat something, try **Peña Colibrí** (© 443/312-2261), Galeana 36, behind the Virrey de Mendoza. It opens daily at 8pm and closes around midnight. There is another *peña* (bar where folk music is played) close by at Allende 3, **Bohemia V** (no phone). The food isn't good, but the music is great.

2 Pátzcuaro ⟨★⟨★⟨★

370km (231 miles) NW of Mexico City; 285km (178 miles) SE of Guadalajara; 69km (43 miles) SW of Morelia

Pátzcuaro is perhaps the loveliest town in Mexico. Crooked cobblestone streets, smooth stucco walls painted white with dark red borders, blackened tile roofs that join to form ramshackle rooflines—it is a town meant to be photographed and painted. During the rainy season, when low clouds roll in and curl through the tall trees, and water drips from the low-slung overhangs, a sweet melancholy descends upon the town.

Pátzcuaro is in the heart of the Purépecha homeland. Beside it is Lake Pátzcuaro (one of the world's highest at 2,200m/7,250 ft.), whose shores border dozens of Indian villages. In these villages and in town, visitors frequently hear the soft sounds of the Purépechan language in the background as they take in the sights. Although distinct regional costumes are seldom seen today, Indian women still braid their hair with ribbons and wear the blue *rebozos* (long woolen wraps) that serve them in so many ways.

ESSENTIALS

GETTING THERE & DEPARTING   By Car   See "Getting There & Departing" under "Morelia," earlier in this chapter, for information from Mexico City, Guadalajara, San Miguel de Allende, and Morelia. From Morelia there are two routes to Pátzcuaro; the faster is the new four-lane **Highway 120,** which passes near Tiripetío and Tupátaro/Cuanajo (see "Side Trips from Pátzcuaro," later in this chapter). The longer route, **Highway 15,** takes a little more than an hour and passes near the pottery-making village of Capula and then through Quiroga, where you follow signs to Pátzcuaro (see "Side Trips from Pátzcuaro," later in this chapter).

By Bus   The bus station is on the outskirts of Pátzcuaro, 5 minutes away by taxi ($2). If you're going anywhere outside of Michoacán, it's usually best to go to Morelia first. If you're going straight to Mexico City, the Pegaso bus company offers nonstop service. Buses between Morelia and Pátzcuaro run every 10 minutes. To visit any of the lakeside villages or nearby towns, public transportation is a viable option. From the Pátzcuaro bus station, there are buses to Tócuaro and Erongarícuaro every 20 minutes; to Tupátaro and Cuanajo every hour; to Tzintzuntzan and Quiroga every 40 minutes; and to Santa Clara del Cobre every hour. For Ihuatzio, you can pick up a minivan or a bus from the Plaza Chica.

VISITOR INFORMATION   The **Tourism Office,** Cuesta Buenavista 7 (© 434/342-1214), near the basilica, is open Monday through Saturday from 9am to 3pm and 4 to 7pm, and Sunday from 9am to 2pm. Although you might not find someone who speaks English, the staff can give you maps and point you in the right direction. There's also an office on the west side of the Plaza Grande (no phone). It keeps the same hours as the main office.

CITY LAYOUT   In a way, Pátzcuaro has two town centers, both plazas a block apart. **Plaza Grande,** also called Plaza Principal or Plaza Don Vasco de Quiroga, is picturesque and tranquil, with a fountain and a statue of Vasco de Quiroga. Hotels,

Pátzcuaro

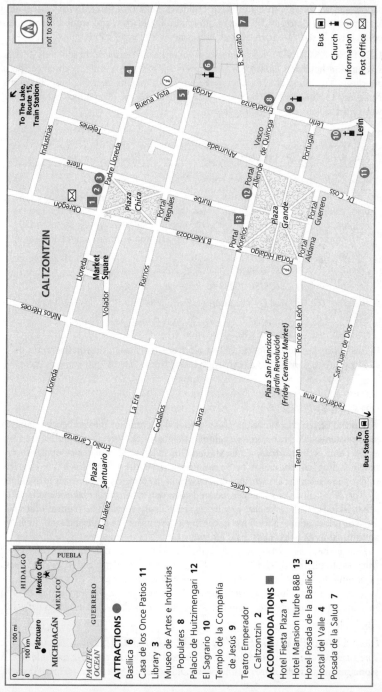

Bus 🚌   **Church** ✝   **Information** *i*   **Post Office** ⊠

CALTZONTZIN

To The Lake,
Route 15,
Train Station

To
Bus Station

not to scale

ATTRACTIONS ●

Basílica **6**
Casa de los Once Patios **11**
Library **3**
Museo de Artes e Industrias
  Populares **8**
Palacio de Huitzimengari **12**
El Sagrario **10**
Templo de la Compañía
  de Jesús **9**
Teatro Emperador
  Caltzontzin **2**

ACCOMMODATIONS ■

Hotel Fiesta Plaza **1**
Hotel Mansión Iturbe B&B **13**
Hotel Posada de la Basílica **5**
Hostal del Valle **4**
Posada de la Salud **7**

HIDALGO
PUEBLA
Mexico City ★
MICHOACÁN
GUERRERO
Pátzcuaro ●
PACIFIC OCEAN

0   100 mi
0   100 km

shops, and restaurants in colonial-era buildings flank this plaza. **Plaza Chica,** also known as Plaza Gertrudis Bocanegra, flows into the market, and around it swirls the commercial life of Pátzcuaro. Plaza Chica is north of Plaza Grande.

GETTING AROUND With the exception of Lake Pátzcuaro, the lookout, the bus station, and hotels on Lázaro Cárdenas, everything is within walking distance. Taxis are cheap. The lake is about a kilometer (less than a mile) from town; buses make the run every 15 minutes from both the Plaza Grande and the Plaza Chica, going all the way to the *embarcadero* or *muelle* (pier).

FAST FACTS: Pátzcuaro

Area Code The telephone area code is **434.**

Climate The climate is delightful most of the year, but occasional blustery days bring swirls of chilled air from across the lake, causing everyone to retreat indoors. October through April, it's cold enough for a heavy sweater, especially in the morning and evening. Few hotels have fireplaces or any source of heat in the rooms.

Elevation Pátzcuaro sits at an altitude of 2,200m (7,250 ft.).

Emergency Dial *©* **434/349-0209** for emergency assistance.

Hospital The **Hospital Civil Dr. Gabriel García** is at Calle Romero 18 (*©* **434/342-0285**).

Population Pátzcuaro has 70,000 residents.

Post Office The *correo,* located a half-block north of Plaza Chica, on the right side of the street, is open Monday through Friday from 10am to 2pm and 4 to 8pm.

SPECIAL EVENTS

The island of **Janitzio** has achieved international celebrity for the candlelight vigil that local residents hold at the cemetery during the nights of November 1 and 2, the Days of the Dead. **Tzintzuntzan,** a village 16km (10 miles) away, also hosts popular festivities, including folkloric dances in the main plaza and in the nearby *yácatas* (pre-Hispanic ruins), concerts in the church, and decorations in the cemetery. If you want to avoid the crowds, skip Janitzio and Tzintzuntzan and go to one of the smaller **lakeside villages or other islands** on the lake that also have extraordinary rituals. The tourism office (see "Visitor Information," above) has a schedule of events for the entire area and publishes an explanatory booklet, *Días de los Muertos.*

During the week surrounding **Days of the Dead,** artisans and vendors from all over Michoacán fill the Plaza Grande in Pátzcuaro with regional crafts. **Easter week,** beginning the Friday before Palm Sunday, is special, too. Most activity centers on the basilica. There are processions involving the surrounding villages almost nightly, and in Tzintzuntzan, there's a reenactment of the betrayal of Christ and a ceremonial washing of the feet.

EXPLORING PATZCUARO: A STROLL AROUND TOWN

The **Plaza Grande** is in the middle of town, surrounded by colonial-era buildings. A **stone fountain** in the center of the plaza holds a large figure of the beloved Vasco de

---

Tips **Festival Hotel Crunch**

Make hotel reservations months in advance for Holy Week or Days of the Dead. Most hotels require a 3-night minimum stay during these events. There are some other, less popular festivals in Pátzcuaro and surrounding towns; check with the tourist office to see if any will occur during your visit.

Quiroga, "Tata Vasco," depicted in a benevolent posture. On the north side of the plaza is the **Palacio de Huitziméngari,** built by the Spaniards for the Tarascan emperor. Local Indian artisans now occupy the slowly deteriorating building.

One long block north is the **Plaza Chica,** crisscrossed by walkways and adorned with the statue of Gertrudis Bocanegra, a heroine of Mexican independence. This is the commercial center of town. On the west side of the plaza are **market** stalls selling pottery, copper, *rebozos,* serapes (a small woolen blanket that is sometimes carried over the shoulder), and food. On some days, the stalls extend a couple of blocks up the street. What was once San Agustín church is on the north side of the plaza. The cloister was remodeled in the 20th century and converted into the **Teatro Emperador Caltzontzin,** the municipal theater. The old church is now the public library; inside, all the way to the back, you'll find an early work of Juan O'Gorman—a large mural stretching the width and height of the nave.

Don Vasco built the **basilica,** on a hill just east of the Plaza Chica, although he died before it was inaugurated in 1554. It was designated a basilica by papal decree in 1907. Now reconstructed, it has survived many catastrophes, human and natural—from earthquakes to the civil war of the mid–19th century. Be sure to visit the main altar to see the **Virgen de la Salud.** She is a sacred figure to the Indians of this region, who come from the villages to pay homage to her and petition her healing power on the eighth day of each month.

Two blocks south of the basilica is the **Museo de Artes e Industrias Populares** ★★ (© **434/342-1029**). It occupies yet another beautiful colonial building (1540), originally Don Vasco's College of San Nicolás. The rooms, filled with fine examples of regional popular art such as crafts and costumes, open to a central courtyard. The museum guides are well informed about the various crafts. The museum is open Tuesday through Saturday from 9am to 7pm, Sunday from 9am to 12:30pm. Admission is $3.50. Behind the museum are some recent excavations of Purépechan ruins.

Of the many old churches in Pátzcuaro, one of the most interesting is the **Templo de la Compañía de Jesús,** just south of the museum. This church was Don Vasco's cathedral before the basilica; afterward, it was given to the Jesuits. The buildings across the street from the church were once part of the complex, containing the hospital, soup kitchen, and living quarters for religious scholars.

The **Casa de los Once Patios (House of Eleven Patios)** ★, between José María Cos and Enseñanza, is another achievement of the colonial period. Formerly a convent belonging to the Catherine nuns, today it houses the **Casa de las Artesanías de Michoacán,** with every type of local artistry for sale (see "Shopping," below).

SHOPPING

Pátzcuaro is one of Mexico's best shopping towns: It has terrific textiles, copper, woodcarvings, lacquerwork, and straw weavings made in the region. Most shops are on the **Plaza Grande** and the streets leading from it to the **Plaza Chica,** the place of choice for copper vendors. There are also a couple of shops on the street facing the basilica. If you're interested in investigating a particular craft, you can find out which village or villages specialize in it, and if the villages have shops or a market. Tzintzuntzan, Ihuatzio, Cuanajo, Tupátaro, and Santa Clara del Cobre all have shops (see "Side Trips from Pátzcuaro," below).

Casa de las Artesanías de Michoacán/Casa de los Once Patios This is the best one-stop shopping in the village. Small shops sell textile arts, pottery and ceramic dishes, lacquerwork, paintings, woodcarvings, jewelry, copper work, and musical instruments (including the famous Paracho guitars). Much of the merchandise was produced in the region. Most shops are open daily from 9am to 2pm and 4 to 6pm. Calle Madrigal de las Altas Torres, between Dr. Coss and Lerín. No phone.

Diseño Artesano Owner Esperanza Sepúlveda designs one-of-a-kind clothing using locally made fabrics. Her shop, on the west side of the Plaza Grande, is open daily from 10am to 8pm. Dr. Coss 1. No phone.

Friday Pottery Market *Finds* Early each Friday morning this plaza, 1 block west of the Plaza Grande, fills with vendors of various styles of regionally made pottery, most of it not for sale in Pátzcuaro on other days. This is a market for locals that few tourists seem to hear about. Prices are *cheap*. Plaza San Francisco, Ponce de León at Federico Teña. No phone.

Galería del Arcángel Across from the Museo Regional, this store ("the Archangel's Gallery") offers a fine collection of quality regional pottery and hand-carved furniture, plus some of the best crafts from other parts of Mexico. It's open daily from 9am to 7pm. Arciga 30. ©/fax **434/342-1774.**

Galería Iturbe Most of the artwork here is by local painters, mask makers, and other artists. You might also find a typical Day of the Dead altar. There's a small selection of books on Mexican art and culture. Enter through the Hotel Iturbe (go all the way to the back) or from Calle Iturbe, off the Plaza Grande. It's open daily from 10am to 8pm. Portal Morelos 59. © **434/342-0368.**

Mantas Típicas *Value* A factory outlet for the company's textile mill, this is one of several textile outlets on the Plaza Grande. Colorful foot-loomed tablecloths, napkins, bedspreads, and bolts of fabric cover the shelves. It's open daily from 9am to 7pm. Dr. Coss 5. © **434/342-1324.** Fax 434/342-0527.

Market Plaza The House of Eleven Patios (see above) should be your first stop and this your second. The entire plaza fronting the food market holds covered stalls selling crafts, clothing, rugs, *rebozos,* and more. Locally knitted sweaters are a good buy. Streets surrounding the plaza churn with exuberant sellers of fresh vegetables and caged birds. West of Plaza Chica. No phone.

Palacio Huitziméngari On the north side of the Plaza Grande, in a colonial house, are a few shops run by folk from neighboring towns. Most of the merchandise is pottery and woodcarvings. Open daily from 8am to 10pm. Plaza Grande. No phone.

WHERE TO STAY

In addition to the hotels listed below, you can also contact Casa Santiago, which rents rooms in Ihuatzio, one of the lakeside villages in the area. See below.

Hacienda Las Mariposas ★★★ *Kids*   This hotel is a retreat into the Mexican countryside. Most of the rooms are in separate bungalows. The rooms are big and the bathrooms are spacious and well equipped. Master suites come with Jacuzzi tubs. Emphasis is on personal attention and ecological practices. The hotel has plenty of educational activities for kids including collecting eggs and other farm activities, hiking, and pony rides. The entire hotel is nonsmoking. Breakfasts feature healthy versions of regional specialties, and there is a separate dining area with a low-fat menu. This is the first hotel in Mexico to be certified as ecological by the Mexican government.

Carretera Pátzcuaro–SantaClara Km 3, 61600 Pátzcuaro, Mich. © 434/342-4728. www.haciendamariposas.com. 27 units. $175 junior suite; $230 master suite; $290 2-bedroom master suite. Rates include full breakfast, horseback rides, spa, and afternoon *antojitos*. AE, MC, V. Free secure parking. **Amenities:** Restaurant; bar; spa; Jacuzzi; steam room; children's activities; tours; business center; room service until 11pm; in-room massage; babysitting; laundry service; nonsmoking rooms. *In room:* Minibar w/organic snacks; hair dryer, safe, CD player and music library.

Hostal del Valle   Operated by a friendly, English-speaking couple from Guadalajara, this small hotel offers attractive rooms decorated with crafts from the region. They are small to midsize. Most come with one double bed or two twins. The common area is a large roofed patio with a sitting area. Free coffee is always available.

Padre Lloreda 27, 61600 Pátzcuaro, Mich. ©/fax 434/342-0512. www.hostaldelvalle.com. 8 units. $60 double. MC, V. Free secure parking. **Amenities:** Restaurant; laundry service. *In room:* TV.

Hotel Fiesta Plaza   Fiesta Plaza has three stories of rooms (no elevator) around an open courtyard. In character with the region, it has dark wood columns and beams and a tile roof, but it's not an old building. Wrought-iron banisters border wide arcades that hold attractive sitting areas. The comfortable rooms have pine furniture, carpets, and small, tiled bathrooms. All have windows that open onto the courtyard. The hotel faces the north side of the Plaza Chica.

Plaza Bocanegra 24, 61600 Pátzcuaro, Mich. © 434/342-2515 or ©/fax 434/342-2516. www.hotelplaza.com. 60 units. $105 double. MC, V. Free parking. **Amenities:** Restaurant; bar; room service until 10:30pm; babysitting; laundry service. *In room:* TV.

Hotel Mansión Iturbe Bed and Breakfast ★★   Located on the north side of the Plaza Grande, this 17th-century mansion has kept more of its original character than any of the other colonial buildings-turned-hotels. The owners have worked hard to keep the old local touches, such as raised thresholds. Rooms are on the second floor and have the original plank flooring, along with heavy, dark, Spanish-style wooden furniture and fresh-cut flowers. Exterior rooms have double-glazed windows to keep the noise down. Most bathrooms are large. All rooms are nonsmoking. Purified ice, instant coffee, and hot water are available. The free cocktail hour every night allows guests to make acquaintances and share experiences. Guests have the use of a solarium, a library, and a study.

Tips **If Pátzcuaro's Packed Solid . . .**

During Easter week and Days of the Dead, Pátzcuaro's hotels fill up; visitors should be aware of three inexpensive hotels in the nearby town of Santa Clara. The **Hotel Oasis,** Portal Allende 144 (© 434/343-0040), is the better of the two on the town's main plaza; **Hotel Real del Cobre,** Portal Hidalgo 19 (© 434/343-0205), has a restaurant. The third hotel, **Camino Real** (© 434/343-0281), is a few blocks away and is comparable to the Oasis.

Portal Morelos 59, 61600 Pátzcuaro, Mich. ℂ **434/342-0368** or 434/342-3628. Fax (in Morelia for reservations) 443/313-4593. www.mexonline.com/iturbe.htm. 14 units. $90–$130 double. Rates include full breakfast. 4th night free (some restrictions apply). Ask about special promotions. AE, MC, V. Free secure parking. **Amenities:** 2 restaurants; 2 bars; bike rental; tour desk; same-day laundry. *In room:* TV, hair dryer on request.

Hotel Posada de la Basílica

This colonial-style hotel in a great location across from the basilica has a lovely patio. The rooms, which border the patio on three sides, have tile floors and fireplaces. Seven have small balconies overlooking the street. Bathrooms don't have enough light, but the rooms have been remodeled this year and new plumbing installed. The restaurant has a fabulous view of the mountains, the tile rooftops, and the lake. Rooms come with one or two double beds.

Arciga 6 (at La Paz), 61600 Pátzcuaro, Mich. ℂ **434/342-1108.** Fax 434/342-0659. www.mexonline.com/michoacan/posadalabasilica-esp.htm. 12 units. $85–$95 double. AE, MC, V. Free secure parking. **Amenities:** Restaurant; children's activities; tour info; airport transfer; limited room service; babysitting; laundry service; dry cleaning. *In room:* TV, hair dryer.

Posada de la Salud (Value

This *posada* (inn) offers two floors of quiet, basic rooms built around an attractive courtyard. Rooms are clean and have simple wooden furniture. Two units have fireplaces. Rooms have one double bed, two double beds, two twins, or one twin and one double. The location is great—on the southeast side of the basilica, a long half-block up on the right.

Serrato 9, 61600 Pátzcuaro, Mich. ℂ **434/342-0058.** 15 units. $30 double. No credit cards.

WHERE TO DINE

Restaurants open late and close early; don't plan on hot coffee if you're up early, but do plan ahead for late-evening hunger pangs. For inexpensive eats, try the **tamal and atole** vendors in front of the basilica and by the market. Housewives also sell steamy cups of *atole,* hot *corundas* (triangular tamales with no filling), and tamales.

In the evenings at the Plaza Chica, you can get a meal of chicken with simple enchiladas and heaps of fried potatoes and carrots. Look for a stand called **Don Emilio.** You can also get *buñuelos,* giant corn flakes that drip with cane syrup.

El Patio MEXICAN/REGIONAL

High ceilings, good lighting, and paintings of local scenes make this a pleasant place to dine. Specialties include *sopa tarasca* (bean soup to which you add cheese, fried tortilla strips, and toasted chiles), *trucha salmonada al vino blanco* (farm-raised trout—fed on special foods that turn the flesh salmon-colored—cooked in white-wine sauce). Standard Mexican dishes include enchiladas and more. El Patio is on the south side of Plaza Grande.

Plaza Grande 19. ℂ **434/342-0484.** Breakfast $4–$6; main courses $7–$9. MC, V. Daily 8am–10pm.

El Primer Piso MEXICAN/INTERNATIONAL

El Primer Piso, which means "the first floor" (second floor in American usage), offers a bit of everything but focuses mostly on dishes of its own creation: *pechuga enogada* (chicken breast in walnut cream sauce) with cashews, for instance, and *pescado en salsa negra* (fish in a three-chile vinaigrette). These are good, as are the appetizers. The soups are more conventional—Tarascan, French onion, and Provençal. The restaurant is on the same block as El Patio.

Vasco de Quiroga 29. ℂ **434/342-0122.** Main courses $8–$10. AE, MC, V. Mon and Wed–Sat 1–10pm; Sun 1–8pm.

Restaurant Doña Paca ⭐ MICHOACAN

This is one of the best places to try regional Michoacán cuisine. It serves fish in several ways, including in a cilantro sauce, *al mojo de ajo* (this is the most popular way of eating fish in Mexico—it's griddled with tiny toasted bits of garlic) or cooked in herbs. This is one of the few places featuring *churipo*, a regional beef and vegetable stew served with *corundas* (tamales without filling). The restaurant also serves a fixed-price menu, which includes a glass of wine. For dessert, try a *buñuelo* topped with ice cream. Margarita Arriaga, the English-speaking owner, prides herself on her coffee, with good reason. The dining room is in the colonial Hotel Iturbe and is comfortable and welcoming. In the afternoon the kitchen serves light fare at the tables outside under the archway.

Hotel Iturbe, Portal Morelos 59. © **434/342-3628.** Breakfast $6–$10; main courses $9–$14. AE, MC, V. Daily 8:30–11:30am, 2–5pm, and 6–9pm. (Closed for Sun dinner during low season.)

PATZCUARO AFTER DARK

Generally speaking, Pátzcuaro closes down before 10pm, so bring a good book or plan to rest up. Late-night music lovers can go to **Viejo Gaucho** to hear Latin American folk music. The small restaurant serves food like salads and hamburgers. It's in the Hotel Iturbe, Portal Morelos 59 (© **434/342-3627**); enter from Calle Iturbe. It's open Wednesday through Saturday from 6pm to midnight. Music starts between 8:30 and 9pm. After the music starts, there's a $2.50 cover charge.

SIDE TRIPS FROM PATZCUARO

EL ESTRIBO: A SCENIC OVERLOOK   For a good view of the town and the lake, head for the lookout at El Estribo, on the hill 3km (2 miles) west of town. Driving from the main square on Calle Ponce de León and following the signs takes 10 to 15 minutes on an unpaved road. Walking up the steep hill will take about 45 minutes. Once you reach the gazebo, you can climb more than 400 steps to the summit of the hill. The gazebo area is great for a picnic; there are barbecue pits and sometimes a couple selling soft drinks and beer.

JANITZIO   No visit to Pátzcuaro would be complete without a trip on the lake to one or more of the islands. A hilltop statue of José María Morelos dominates the island of **Janitzio** 👀. The village church is famous for the annual **Days of the Dead** ceremony, held at midnight on November 1. Villagers climb to the churchyard carrying lit candles in memory of their dead relatives, then spend the night in graveside vigil. The long day begins October 30 and lasts through November 2.

The cheapest way to get to Janitzio is by *colectivo* launch, which makes the trip when enough people have gathered to go, about every 20 to 30 minutes from about 7:30am to 6pm. It's best to go during the week when fewer travelers are around. Round-trip fare is $3.50; children under 5 ride free. A private boat costs around $55 for a trip to Janitzio for 1 hour and then a cruise by the other 3 islands. Sometimes the cooperative has launches available for significantly cheaper. The **ticket office** on the pier, or *embarcadero* (© **434/342-0681**), is open daily from 8am to 6pm. The pier is less than a kilometer (about a half-mile) from the main square, and the 5-minute taxi ride costs $2.50.

At the ticket office, a map of the lake posted on the wall details boat trips to various islands and lakeshore towns. Launches will take you wherever you want to go. Up to 20 people can split the cost.

TZINTZUNTZAN: RUINS & HANDICRAFTS   Tzintzuntzan (tzeen-*tzoon*-tzahn) is an ancient village 15km (10 miles) from Pátzcuaro on the road to Quiroga (see "By Bus" under "Getting There & Departing," earlier in this chapter). In earlier centuries, Tzintzuntzan was the capital of the Purépechan kingdom (a confederation of more than 100 towns and villages). On a hill on the right before you enter town, pyramids, called *yácatas,* remind visitors of the town's past. There is also an interesting church and monastery dating from the time of Don Vasco. Today, the village is known for its straw handicrafts—mobiles, baskets, and figures (skeletons, airplanes, reindeer, turkeys, and the like)—as well as pottery and woven goods. Several open-air **wood-carving workshops,** full of life-size wooden saints and other figures, are across from the basket market.

LAKESIDE VILLAGES: A PORTRAIT OF INDIAN LIFE   For a close-up view of the Purépecha, contact Kevin Quigley or Arminda Flores, who live in Ihuatzio (see below) or **Francisco Castilleja** (© **434/344-0167**), an English-speaking Mexican who lives in Erongarícuaro. Mr. Castilleja conducts tours of the villages that explain their daily life, customs, and beliefs. He passes through the Restaurant Doña Paca in the Hotel Iturbe at 10am every day but Sunday and takes people to the villages of **Erongarícuaro, Uricho,** and **Tócuaro** to visit households, small workshops, and a well-known mask maker. The cost depends on the size of the group.

SANTA CLARA DEL COBRE: COPPER SMITHERY   About 30 minutes away by car (a $10 taxi ride), **Santa Clara del Cobre** ⊛ is a good side trip if you want to purchase copper items or see how copper is worked. Although the copper mines of pre-Conquest times have disappeared, local artisans still make copper vessels using the age-old method of hammering pieces out by hand. They don't work on Sunday and are strict observers of "San Lunes"—taking Monday off to recover from the weekend. On other days, the sound of hammering fills the air. If you want to see someone practicing the craft, go to one of the larger stores and ask if you can visit the *taller* (studio). You can also visit the **Museo del Cobre (Copper Museum),** a half-block from the main plaza at Morelos and Pino Suárez. The museum section of the building displays copper pieces that date to pre-Columbian times. A sales showroom to the left of the entrance features the work of local craftsmen. Admission is 50¢; the museum is open Tuesday through Sunday from 10:30am to 3pm and 5 to 7pm.

The **National Copper Fair** is held here each August. It coincides with the **Festival de Nuestra Señora de Santa Clara de Asis** (Aug 12) and the **Festival of the Virgin of the Sacred Patroness** (Aug 15), with folk dancing and parades. For information, call the tourism office in Morelia.

Buses for Santa Clara leave every few minutes from the Pátzcuaro bus station. If you want to spend the night in town, see "If Pátzcuaro's Packed Solid . . . " on p. 255.

TUPATARO & CUANAJO: A HISTORIC CHURCH & HAND-CARVED FUR-NITURE   The turnoff for these colonial-era villages is approximately 32km (20 miles) northwest of Pátzcuaro, off Highway 120 on the way to Morelia (see "Getting There & Departing," earlier in this chapter). The narrow paved road passes first through tiny **Tupátaro** (pop. 600), which in Tarascan means "place of tule of Chuspata" (*tule* means "reed").

Just opposite the small main plaza is the **Templo del Señor Santiago Tupátaro,** with its beautifully painted 18th-century ceiling—a rare surviving detail. Restored in 1994, it's still the parish church but is overseen by the Institute of Anthropology and History. The church was built in 1775 after the miraculous discovery of a crucifix formed in a pine tree. Indian artists painted the entire wood-plank ceiling with scenes of the life and death of Christ and Mary. The magnificent gilt *retablo* (altarpiece) still intact behind the altar, features Solomonic columns and paintings. Santiago (St. James) is in the center of the *retablo,* and the face of the Eternal Father is above him. The sign of the dove crowns the *retablo.* There's no admission charge, and photography is not permitted. The church is open daily from 8am to 8pm. Days of religious significance include the Tuesday of Carnaval week and July 25, which honors Santiago.

Cuanajo (pop. 8,000) is 8km (5 miles) farther. It's a village devoted to hand-carved pine furniture and weaving. On the road as you enter, and around the pleasant, tree-shaded main plaza, you'll see storefronts with **colorful furniture** inside and on the street. Parrots, plants, the sun, the moon, and faces are carved on the furniture, which is painted in bright colors. Furniture is also sold at a **cooperative** on the main plaza. Here you'll also find soft-spoken women who weave tapestries and thin belts on waist looms. Everything is for sale. It's open daily from 9am to 6pm. A new highway runs directly to Cuanajo from Pátzcuaro.

Festival days in Cuanajo include March 8 and September 8, both of which honor the patron saint Virgin María de la Natividad.

IHUATZIO: TULE FIGURES & PRE-HISPANIC ARCHITECTURE   This little lakeside village is renowned for its **weavers of tule figures**—fanciful animals such as elephants, pigs, and bulls, made from a reed that grows on the edge of the lake—and for some ruins widespread through the area. Kevin Quigley, an American from San Francisco, and Arminda Flores, a Purépecha, live just outside the village (Casa Santiago; ℰ **434/344-0880;** mananawood@ml.com.mx). They rent comfortable rooms to guests, usually small groups, and Kevin, who has lived in the area for many years, takes people around the area, explaining the local culture, the society, and the local crafts. The turnoff to Ihuatzio is a paved road a short distance from the outskirts of Pátzcuaro on the road to Tzintzuntzan.

ZIRAHUEN: A PRISTINE LAKE   If you want to visit one of the few lakes in Mexico that remains more or less in its natural state, make the trip to **Zirahuén,** about 11km (7 miles) west of Pátzcuaro on the road to Uruapan. There's no regular bus service, so getting to Zirahuén without a car is difficult. Lakeside restaurants serve fish—but make sure it's fresh.

3 Uruapan: Handicrafts & Volcanoes

61km (38 miles) W of Pátzcuaro

Uruapan has long been a large commercial center for western Michoacán. It's a larger, busier town than Pátzcuaro. For tourists, the best feature is the **Parque Nacional Eduardo Ruiz,** a lovely botanical garden with flowing water everywhere you look. Uruapan is also useful as a base for several interesting side trips, the most famous of which is to the **Paricutín volcano** and the lava-covered church and village near **Angahuan.** See "Angahuan, Paricutín Volcano," below.

ESSENTIALS

The **tourist office** (ℰ **452/524-7199**) is at Juan Ayala 16. It's open Monday through Saturday from 9am to 2pm and 4 to 7pm.

The main plaza, **Jardín Morelos/Plaza de los Mártires,** is actually a long, narrow rectangle running east to west, with the churches and La Huatápera Museum on the north side and a few hotels on the south. Everything you need is within 1 or 2 blocks of the square, including the market, which is behind the churches.

WHERE TO STAY & DINE

The best hotel in town is the **Hotel Cupatitzio** (© 452/523-2022), next to the national park. It has plenty of amenities, including a good restaurant, a large pool, and a lovely garden. A room for two people costs $97 (American Express, MasterCard, and Visa are accepted). Also consider two inexpensive hotels by the main plaza: The comfortable **Hotel Villa de Flores,** Emiliano Carranza 15 (© 452/524-2800; MasterCard and Visa are accepted), and the slightly less desirable, slightly cheaper **Hotel Nuevo Alameda,** Av. 5 de Febrero 11 (© 452/523-3635; MasterCard and Visa are accepted). Rooms go for $30 to $40. Both have restaurants, and there are restaurants on and near the plaza.

EXPLORING URUAPAN & BEYOND

Uruapan's main plaza fills with artisans and craft sellers from around the state before and during **Easter week.** There's an unbelievable array of wares.

La Huatápera ✸, attached to the church on the main square, is a good museum of regional crafts. It occupies a former hospital built in 1533 by Fray Juan de San Miguel, a Franciscan. It's open daily from 9:30am to 1:30pm and 3:30 to 6pm. Admission is free.

For the finest in foot-loomed, brilliantly colored tablecloths, napkins, and other **textiles,** take a taxi to **Telares Uruapan** ✸✸ (© 452/524-0677 or 452/524-6135), in the **Antigua Fábrica de San Pedro,** Calle Miguel Treviño s/n. Call ahead, and the English-speaking owners may be able to give you a tour of the factory.

When you enter the **Parque Nacional Eduardo Ruiz,** a botanical garden 8 blocks west of the main plaza, you'll feel as if you're deep in the tropics. This semitropical paradise contains jungle paths, deep ravines, rushing water, and clear waterfalls. The garden is open daily from 8am to 6pm, and there is a small admission fee.

A WATERFALL OUTSIDE OF URUAPAN

Eight kilometers (5 miles) outside of town is the **Tzaráracua** waterfall. The falls are pretty but not spectacular, and sometimes they smell bad. The real reason to come here is for the walk—a descent that takes you from cool pine forest to warm subtropical vegetation in no time. The return ascent takes 40 minutes, and the trail is good, with handrails in the steeper areas. You can catch a bus from Uruapan's bus station or take a cab, which costs only $5. Either one will drop you off at the trail head.

ANGAHUAN, PARICUTIN VOLCANO ✸✸

About 34km (21 miles) from Uruapan is **Angahuan,** a village, which is the point of departure for trips to **Paricutín volcano.** The volcano was born in 1943 and grew quickly, eventually enveloping portions of a village in lava. Autotransportes Galeana buses leave every 30 minutes from Uruapan's Central Camionera for the hour-long trip. To return, pick up the bus where it dropped you off. A taxi costs $15.

THE ERUPTION STORY   If you don't know the tale of Paricutín's volcanic blast, stop by the plaza in Angahuan and look at the carved wooden door of a house that faces the church (around the stone fence to the right, two doors down). In the afternoon of February 20, 1943, a local man was plowing his cornfield in the valley when the ground began to boil and fissures opened up emitting steam. At first he tried to plug it up; when that proved impossible, he fled. By that evening, the earth was spitting fire and smoke. Some villagers fled that night; others, days later. The volcano remained active, continually spewing, until March 6, 1952, when it ceased as suddenly as it had begun.

USING A GUIDE   Angahuan has a little tourist center that rents cabins and runs a small cafeteria (© 452/520-8786). It allows a good view of the volcano and the tower of the **Church of San Juan Parangaricutiro** (try saying that five times fast), which is half-buried in lava. You will undoubtedly be offered a guide and horses for a trip to either or both places. Although a horse is not necessary, a guide is advisable.

CLIMBING THE VOLCANO   Allow at least 8 hours from Angahuan. The round-trip is about 22km (14 miles). *Take plenty of food and water—they are not available along the way.* The hike is mostly flat, with some steeper rises toward the end. Climbing the steep crater takes about 40 minutes for those who exercise regularly. Count on more time to walk around the crater's rim on top (1.5–3km/1–2 miles) and enjoy the view.

The trip to the volcano takes 6 to 7 hours on horseback, including the time spent climbing the crater, which you must do on foot. On the way, you can pass by the old church tower of Parangaricutiro. The asking price for a horse is around $20, and you'll need to pay for one for a guide. A good guide will climb to the top of the crater with you and point out various interesting features, including steaming fumaroles. Acting as a volcano guide is one of the conspicuously poor Angahuan villagers' few opportunities to earn money. Just withhold payment until the ride is over, and services are delivered as promised. Plan to spend an entire day for this outing.

8

Guadalajara

by David Baird

Guadalajara is the second-largest city in Mexico (with 3.5 million inhabitants, it's a very distant second to Mexico City), but because it's the homeland of mariachi music, the *jarabe tapatío* (the Mexican hat dance), and tequila, many consider it the most Mexican of cities. Despite its size, Guadalajara isn't hard to navigate, and the people are friendly and helpful. And unlike in Mexico City, vis-itors can enjoy big-city pleasures with-out big-city hassles.

While here, you'll undoubtedly come across the word *tapatío* (or *tapatía*). In the early days, people from the area were known to trade in threes, called *tapatíos*. Gradually, the locals came to be called Tapatíos, too, and the word now signifies Guadalajaran when referring to a thing, a person, or a manner of doing something.

1 Orientation

GETTING THERE

BY PLANE Guadalajara's international airport is a 25- to 45-minute ride from the city. Taxi tickets to Guadalajara, priced by zone, are for sale in front of the airport ($15 to downtown area). Taxis are the only transport.

Major Airlines See chapter 2 for a list of toll-free numbers for international airlines serving Mexico. Numbers in Guadalajara are: **AeroMar** (© 33/3615-8509), **Aeromexico** (© 01-800/021-4010), **American** (© 01-800/904-6000), **Continental** (© 01-800/900-5000), **Delta** (© 33/3630-3530), **Mexicana** (© 01-800/502-2000), and **United** (© 33/3616-9489).

Of the smaller airlines, **Aviacsa** (© 33/3123-1751) connects to Los Angeles, Las Vegas, Houston, and Chicago. **Aero California** (© 33/3616-2525) connects to Tijuana, Mexico City, Los Mochis, La Paz, and Puebla. **Azteca** (© 33/3630-4615) offers service to and from Mexico City, and from there to several cities in Mexico. **Allegro** (© 33/3647-7799) operates flights to and from Oakland and Las Vegas via Tijuana. **Alaska Airlines** (© 01-800/426-0333) flies to Los Angeles and Reno.

BY CAR Guadalajara is at the hub of several four-lane toll roads (called *cuotas* or *autopistas*), which cut travel time considerably but are expensive. From Nogales on the **U.S. border,** follow Highway 15 south (21 hr.). From **Tepic,** a quicker route is toll road 15D (5 hr., $37). From **Puerto Vallarta,** go north on Highway 200 to Compostela; toll road 68D heads east to join the Tepic toll road. Total time is 5½ hours, and the tolls add up to $28. From **Barra de Navidad,** on the coast southeast of Puerto Vallarta, take Highway 80 northeast (4½ hr.). From **Manzanillo,** you might also take

Greater Guadalajara

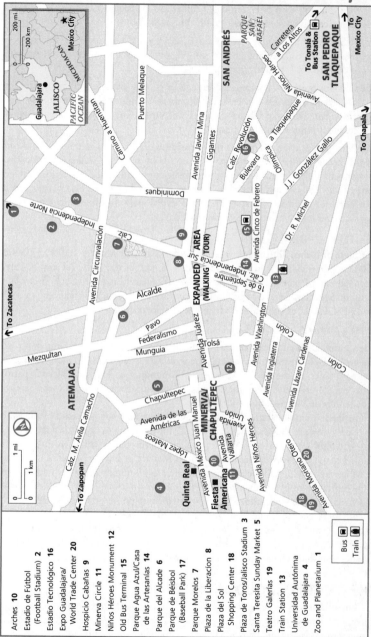

Arches **10**
Estadio de Fútbol
  (Football Stadium) **2**
Estadio Tecnológico **16**
Expo Guadalajara/
  World Trade Center **20**
Hospicio Cabañas **9**
Minerva Circle **11**
Niños Héroes Monument **12**
Old Bus Terminal **15**
Parque Agua Azul/Casa
  de las Artesanías **14**
Parque del Alcade **6**
Parque de Béisbol
  (Baseball Park) **17**
Parque Morelos **7**
Plaza de la Liberación **8**
Plaza del Sol
  Shopping Center **18**
Plaza de Toros/Jalisco Stadium **3**
Santa Teresita Sunday Market **5**
Teatro Galerías **19**
Train Station **13**
Universidad Autónoma
  de Guadalajara **4**
Zoo and Planetarium **1**

Bus
Train

this road, but toll road 54D through Colima to Guadalajara (3½ hr., $25) is faster. From **Mexico City,** take toll road 15D (7 hr., $48).

BY BUS   Two bus stations serve Guadalajara. The old one, south of downtown, is for buses to Lake Chapala and other nearby areas; the new one, 10km (6 miles) southeast of downtown, is for longer trips.

The Old Bus Station   For destinations within 100km (60 miles) of town, including the Lake Chapala area, go to the old bus terminal, on Niños Héroes off Calzada Independencia Sur. For Lake Chapala, take **Transportes Guadalajara-Chapala,** which runs frequent buses and *combis* (minivans).

The New Bus Station   The **Central Camionera** is 15 to 30 minutes from downtown. The station has seven terminals connected by a covered walkway. Each terminal contains different bus lines, offering first- and second-class service for different destinations. You can buy bus tickets from several travel agents in Guadalajara. Ask at your hotel for the closest to you. There are several major bus lines. The best service (big seats and lots of room) is provided by **ETN.**

VISITOR INFORMATION

The **State of Jalisco Tourist Information Office** is at Calle Morelos 102 (© **33/3668-1600** or 33/3668-1601; http://visita.jalisco.gob.mx) in the Plaza Tapatía, at Paseo Degollado and Paraje del Rincón del Diablo. It's open Monday through Friday 9am to 8pm; Saturday, Sunday, and festival days 10am to 2pm. You can get maps, a monthly calendar of cultural events, and good information.

CITY LAYOUT

The **Centro Histórico (city center),** with all its plazas, churches, and museums, will obviously be of interest to the visitor. The **west side** is Guadalajara's modern, cosmopolitan district. In the northwest corner is **Zapopan,** home of Guadalajara's patron saint. On the opposite side of the city from Zapopan, in the southeast corner, are the craft centers of **Tlaquepaque** and **Tonalá.**

The main artery for traffic from downtown to the west side is **Avenida Vallarta.** It starts downtown as **Juárez.** The main arteries for returning to downtown are **Mexico** and **Hidalgo,** both north of Vallarta. Vallarta heads due west, where it intersects another major artery, **Avenida Adolfo López Mateos,** at **Fuente Minerva** (or simply La Minerva, or Minerva Circle). Minerva Circle, a 15-minute drive from downtown, is the central point of reference for the west side. To go to Zapopan from downtown, take **Avenida Avila Camacho,** which you can pick up on Alcalde; it takes 20 minutes by car. To Tlaquepaque and Tonalá, take **Calzada Revolución.** Tlaquepaque is 8km (5 miles) from downtown and takes 15 to 20 minutes by car; Tonalá is 5 minutes farther. Another major viaduct, **Calzada Lázaro Cárdenas,** connects the west side to Tlaquepaque and Tonalá, bypassing downtown.

THE NEIGHBORHOODS IN BRIEF

Centro Histórico   The heart of the city contains many plazas, the cathedral, and several historic buildings and museums. Here, too, are the striking murals of José Clemente Orozco, one of the great Mexican muralists. Theaters, restaurants, shops, and clubs dot the area, and an enormous market rounds out the attractions. All of this is in a space roughly 12 blocks by 12 blocks, an easy area for a good walker to explore and enjoy the several plazas and pedestrian-only areas. To the south is a large green space called Parque Agua Azul.

West Side This is the swanky part of town, with the fine restaurants, luxury hotels, boutiques, and galleries, as well as the American, British, and Canadian consulates. It's a large area best navigated by taxi.

Zapopan Founded in 1542, Zapopan is a suburb of Guadalajara. In its center is the 18th-century basilica, the home of Guadalajara's patron saint, the Virgin of Zapopan. The most interesting part of Zapopan is clustered around the temple and can be explored by foot. It has a growing arts and nightlife scene.

Tlaquepaque This was a village of artisans (especially potters) that grew into a market center. In the last 30 years, it has attracted designers from all over Mexico. Every major form of art and craft is for sale here: furniture, pottery, glass, jewelry, woodcarvings, leather goods, sculptures, and paintings. The shops are sophisticated, yet Tlaquepaque's center retains a small-town feel that makes door-to-door browsing enjoyable and relaxing.

Tonalá This has remained a town of artisans. Plenty of stores sell mostly local products from the town's more than 400 workshops. You'll see wrought iron, ceramics, blown glass, and papier-mâché. A busy street market operates each Thursday and Sunday.

2 Getting Around

BY TAXI Taxis are the easiest way to get around town. Almost all have meters, and, though some drivers are reluctant to use them, you can insist that they do. There are three rates: for day, night, and suburbia. On my last visit typical fares were the following: downtown to the west side, $6 to $8; downtown or west side to Tlaquepaque, $6 to $9; to new bus station, $7; to airport, $14 to $18.

BY CAR Keep in mind the several main arteries (see "City Layout," above). Several important freeway-style thoroughfares crisscross the city. **González Gallo** leads south from the town center and connects with the road to Lake Chapala. **Avenida Vallarta** continues past La Minerva and eventually feeds onto **Highway 15,** bound for Tequila and Puerto Vallarta.

BY BUS There are various city bus lines that offer different grades of service. The best buses are the **Turquesa buses,** which can be identified by the large capital letters TUR. They are air-conditioned and comfortable and carry only as many passengers as there are seats; they are worth the price (about 60¢ for most destinations). For the visitor, the handiest route is the **706 TUR,** which runs from the Centro Histórico southeast to Tlaquepaque, the Central Camionera (the new bus station), and Tonalá. For more information on Tlaquepaque and Tonalá, see "Shopping," later in this chapter. You can catch this bus on Avenida 16 de Septiembre. The same bus runs in the reverse direction back to the downtown area.

The electric bus is handy for travel between downtown and the Minerva area. It bears the sign PAR VIAL and runs east along Hidalgo and west along the next street to the north, Calle Independencia (not Calzada Independencia). Hidalgo passes along the north side of the cathedral. The Par Vial goes as far east as Mercado Libertad and as far west as Minerva Circle. The city also has a light rail system, **Tren Ligero,** but it doesn't serve areas that are of interest to visitors.

FAST FACTS: Guadalajara

American Express The local office is at Av. Vallarta 2440, Plaza los Arcos, Local A-1 (© **33/3818-2323**); it's open Monday through Friday from 9am to 6pm, Saturday from 9am to noon.

Area Code The telephone area code is **33**.

Books, Newspapers & Magazines **Gonvil,** a popular bookstore chain, has a branch across from Plaza de los Hombres Ilustres on Avenida Hidalgo, and another a few blocks south at Av. 16 de Septiembre 118 (Alcalde becomes 16 de Septiembre south of the cathedral). It carries few English selections. **Sanborn's,** at the corner of Juárez and 16 de Septiembre, does a good job of keeping English-language periodicals in stock, but most are specialty magazines. Many newsstands sell the two English local papers, the *Guadalajara Reporter* and the *Guadalajara Weekly.* For the widest selection of English-language books, try **Sandi Bookstore,** Av. Tepeyac 718 (© **33/3121-0863**), in the Chapalita neighborhood on the west side.

Business Hours Store hours are Monday through Saturday from 10am to 2pm and 4 to 8pm.

Climate & Dress Guadalajara is mild year-round, with the occasional freak cold spell. Generally, from November through March, you'll need a sweater in the evening. The warmest months, April and May, are hot and dry. From June through September, the city gets afternoon and evening showers that keep the temperature a bit cooler. Dress in Guadalajara is conservative; attention-getting sportswear (short shorts, halters, and the like) is out of place.

Consulates The **American consular offices** are at Progreso 175 (© **33/3268-2200** or 33/3268-2100). Other consulates include the **Canadian consulate,** Hotel Fiesta Americana, Local 31 (© **33/3615-6215**); the **British consulate,** Calle Jesús Rojas 20, Col. Los Pinos (© **33/3343-2296**); and the **Australian consulate,** López Cotilla 2018, Col. Arcos Vallarta (© **33/3615-7418**). These offices all keep roughly the same hours: Monday through Friday from 8am to 1pm.

Currency Exchange The best rates are found 3 blocks south of the cathedral on López Cotilla, between Corona and Degollado. There are more than 20 *casas de cambio* on these 2 blocks. Almost all post their rates, which are better than the banks', without the long lines.

Elevation Guadalajara sits at 1,700m (5,576 ft.).

Emergencies The emergency phone number is © **080.**

Hospitals For medical emergencies, visit the **Hospital México-Americano,** Cólomos 2110 (© **33/3642-7152**).

Internet Access Ask at your hotel for the closest Internet access. Most of the big hotels have business centers that you can use. In the Centro Histórico, there are many. All you have to do is ask around.

Language Classes Foreigners can study Spanish at the **Foreign Student Study Center,** University of Guadalajara, Calle Tomás V. Gómez 125, 44100 Guadalajara, Jal. (© **33/3616-4399**). **IMAC** is a private Spanish school at Donato Guerra 180 in the Centro Histórico (© **33/3613-1080**).

Luggage Storage & Lockers You can store luggage in the main bus station, the Central Camionera, and at the Guadalajara airport.

Police Tourists should first try to contact the Jalisco tourist information office in Plaza Tapatía (© **33/3658-1600**). If you can't reach the office, call the municipal police at © **33/3617-6060**.

Post Office The *correo* is at the corner of Carranza and Calle Independencia, about 4 blocks northeast of the cathedral. Standing in the plaza behind the cathedral, facing the Degollado Theater, walk to the left and turn left on Carranza; walk past the Hotel Mendoza, cross Calle Independencia, and look for the post office on the left. It's open Monday through Thursday from 9am to 5pm, Saturday from 10am to 2pm.

Safety Guadalajara doesn't have the violent crime that Mexico City does. Crimes against tourists and foreign students are infrequent and most often take the form of pickpocketing and purse snatching. Criminals usually work in teams and target travelers in busy places, such as outdoor restaurants: One will create a distraction while the other slips off with whatever the tourist has set down. Purse-snatchers usually target unaccompanied women at night and rarely in places with crowds. The same is true of necklace snatching (the assailant grabs a necklace, especially if it has a gold chain, and pulls hard, hoping it will break). Be especially alert if someone spills something on you—this is a common trick.

3 Where to Stay

Rates shown are the standard rack rates and include the 17% tax. In slow periods, look for discounts; the big hotels often give business discounts.

Almost all of the luxury hotels in Guadalajara are on the west side, which has the majority of the shopping malls, boutiques, fashionable restaurants, and clubs. There is also a lot to do in the Centro Histórico, making it a good place to stay. Finally, Tlaquepaque is a comfortable suburb and is perfect for shoppers; the only drawback is that almost everything shuts down by 7 or 8pm. Chain hotels not included below are the Hilton, Marriott, Camino Real, Howard Johnson, Crowne Plaza, and Best Western.

VERY EXPENSIVE

Hotel Presidente InterContinental ✦✦✦ Housed in a 14-story glass building with an atrium lobby, this hotel offers the most comprehensive list of services and amenities in Guadalajara. There is little turnover in staff, and the concierge has proven more capable and knowledgeable than any other in the city. The recently remodeled rooms are comfortable and quiet, with modern furnishings that include a desk and a small table with two chairs. Club rooms have discreet check-in and are on limited-access hallways; rates include continental breakfast, newspaper, and evening cocktails. The extra privacy and services are good for Mexican soap opera stars or repeat guests who like having their preferences known in advance. If you're neither of these, opt for one of the other rooms. The lobby bar is popular; during the season, bullfighters relax here after the *corrida.* The hotel sits across from the Plaza del Sol shopping center in western Guadalajara.

Av. López Mateos Sur and Moctezuma, 45050 Guadalajara, Jal. © **800/327-0200** in the U.S. and Canada, or 33/3678-1234. Fax 33/3678-1222. www.interconti.com. 409 units. $192–$249 double, $204–$261 deluxe; $227–$285 club; $305 and up for suite. Rates include breakfast buffet. AE, DC, MC, V. Valet parking $4. **Amenities:** 2 restaurants; lobby bar; outdoor heated pool; golf at nearby clubs; health club w/saunas, steam rooms, and whirlpools; concierge; tour desk; car rental; large business center; executive business services; salon; 24-hr. room service; massage; babysitting; laundry service; dry cleaning; nonsmoking rooms; executive-level rooms. *In room:* A/C, TV w/pay movies, minibar, hair dryer, iron, safe, high-speed wireless Internet.

Quinta Real ★★★   This chain specializes in building properties that are suggestive of Mexico's heritage, in contrast to the comfortable but generic luxury hotel. No glass skyscraper here—two four-story buildings made of stone, wood, plaster, and tile occupy lush grounds. Rooms vary quite a bit: Eight have brick cupolas, some have balconies, and four are equipped with a whirlpool tub in the bathroom. All are large, with a split-level layout and antique decorative touches. And all come with large, fully equipped bathrooms with tub/shower combinations and excellent water pressure. You can choose between two doubles or one king-size bed. The hotel is 2 blocks from Minerva Circle in western Guadalajara. Ask for a room that doesn't face López Mateos.

Av. México 2727 (at López Mateos), 44680 Guadalajara, Jal. © **800/445-4565** in the U.S. and Canada, or 33/3669-0600. Fax 33/3669-0601. www.quintareal.com. 75 suites. $357 master suite; $387 grand-class suite. AE, DC, MC, V. Free secure parking. **Amenities:** Restaurant; bar; small outdoor heated pool; golf at local club; access to nearby health club; concierge; tour desk; car rental; business center; executive business services; room service until midnight; babysitting; laundry service; dry cleaning; nonsmoking rooms. *In room:* A/C, TV, dataport, minibar, hair dryer, iron, safe.

Villa Ganz ★★★   This small, stylish hotel on the near west side of the city is one of the most comfortable places to stay in Guadalajara. Rooms are big, comfortable, and decorated with flair. Each holds a basket of fruit and a small bottle of wine on check-in. Bathrooms are large and well lit—some have tubs, others just showers. Bed choices include a king, a queen, or two twins. Beds come with down comforters (hypoallergenic option available). Rooms facing the garden are the quietest, but those facing the street are set back from the traffic and have double-glazed windows. The common rooms and rear garden are agreeable places to relax. Service is personal and helpful. Guests can contract with a guide or taxi driver at the hotel. In-room dining can be arranged with one of three nearby restaurants or arrangements can be made to bring in a chef. Villa Ganz is a member of the Boutique Hotels of Mexico. Villa Ganz has opened a bed-and-breakfast in central Guadalajara and it also offers apartments for extended stays; see the website for more information.

López Cotilla 1739, 44140 Guadalajara, Jal. © **877/278-8018** in the U.S., 866/818-8342 in Canada, or 33/3120-1416. www.villaganz.com. 10 suites. $235–$2278 suites. Rates include continental breakfast. AE, MC, V. Free secure parking. Children under 12 not accepted. **Amenities:** Golf and tennis at local club; concierge; tour desk; airport transfer; 24-hr. room service; laundry service; dry cleaning. *In room:* A/C, TV, hair dryer, iron on request, safe, high-speed Internet.

EXPENSIVE

Fiesta Americana ★★   A sharp 22-story hotel, similar to the Presidente Inter-Continental but with fewer amenities, the Fiesta Americana caters mainly to business travelers. The location is excellent—in front of Minerva Circle, in western Guadalajara—and service is great. Request floors 4 through 10, which have been remodeled. Rooms are large and carpeted, with two doubles or one king and a soundproof door. The large, well-equipped bathrooms hold shower/tub combinations. The furniture is modern and understated.

Aurelio Aceves 225, Glorieta Minerva, 44100 Guadalajara, Jal. © **800/FIESTA-1** in the U.S. and Canada, or 33/3825-3434. Fax 33/3630-3725. www.fiestaamericana.com. 391 units. $145–$185 double; $190 Fiesta Club double;

$281–$624 suite. AE, DC, MC, V. Free secure parking. **Amenities:** Restaurant; lobby bar; heated midsize pool; golf privileges at local club; 2 lighted tennis courts; exercise room; children's activities (Fiesta kids' program on Sun); concierge; tour desk; business center; executive business services; salon; 24-hr. room service; massage; babysitting; laundry service; dry cleaning; nonsmoking rooms; executive-level rooms; 1 room equipped for guests w/disabilities. *In room:* A/C, TV w/pay movies, dataport, minibar, coffeemaker, hair dryer.

Holiday Inn Hotel and Suites Centro Histórico ★★

This six-story hotel has the most comfortable lodging in the downtown area. Its location, a few blocks from the main square, is good, too. Standard rooms are carpeted and decorated in Mexican architectural colors. The furniture is modern Mexican with a few wrought-iron pieces—the overall effect is cheerful. The size and lighting are good; bathrooms are midsize and well equipped, with ample counter space. For quiet, ask for a room off the street. The suites are larger, but otherwise not worth the extra cost. Room rates include transportation to (but not from) the airport.

Av. Juárez 211, 44100 Guadalajara. Jal. © 800/HOLIDAY in the U.S. and Canada, 01-800/009-9900 in Mexico, or 33/3613-1763. www.holiday-inn.com. 90 units. $180 double; $200 suite. Ask about promotional rates. AE, MC, V. Free secure parking. **Amenities:** Restaurant; bar; fitness room; business center; room service until 10:30pm; laundry service; dry cleaning; nonsmoking rooms. *In room:* A/C, TV, dataport, minibar, coffeemaker, hair dryer, iron.

Hotel de Mendoza ★

On a quiet street next to the Degollado Theater and Plaza Tapatía, 2 blocks from the cathedral, the Mendoza has the best location of any downtown hotel. The decor would best be described as a stab at old Spanish, with wood paneling and old-world accents. Standard rooms are midsize and comfortable. Bed choices are one queen, two full, or two queens. Bathrooms are midsize, with ample counter space. Suites have an additional sitting area and larger bathrooms. Rooms face the street, an interior courtyard, or the pool. *Note:* The bath towels are the narrowest I've ever seen—obviously the brainchild of a demented cost-cutting expert. If the hotel hasn't changed these, ask for a couple extra after you check in.

Carranza 16, 44100 Guadalajara, Jal. © 800/221-6509 in the U.S., or 33/3613-4646. Fax 33/3613-7310. www.demendoza.com.mx. 104 units. $120 double; $142 suite. Discounts sometimes available. AE, MC, V. Secure parking $4. **Amenities:** Restaurant; bar; small pool; fitness room; Jacuzzi; tour desk; room service until 10:30pm; laundry service; dry cleaning; nonsmoking rooms. *In room:* A/C, TV, dataport.

MODERATE

El Aposento Hotel ★ *Value*

This small hotel in a colonial house in the Centro Histórico has handsomely furnished rooms decorated in muted tones. In price, comfort, and location, it is roughly the equal of the other downtown bargain in this category—the Hotel Cervantes—but rooms here are larger and have more character (but maybe not as much light). Add the full breakfast, and you have a winner. To avoid street noise, ask for a room facing away from the street (especially Madero). Rooms come with a king or two doubles. Most bathrooms are large; half come with a shower/tub combination.

Francisco Madero 545, 44100 Guadalajara, Jal. ©/fax 33/3614-1612. www.elaposento.com. 28 units. $65 double. Rates include full breakfast. AE, MC, V. Free sheltered parking. **Amenities:** Tour info; massage; nonsmoking rooms. *In room:* A/C, TV.

Hotel Cervantes ★ *Value*

This six-story downtown hotel offers modern amenities at a great price. The rooms are attractive and midsize. They have wall-to-wall carpeting and tile bathrooms with ample sink areas and shower/tub combinations. The lower price is for one double bed; the higher price, for a king or two doubles. This is not a particularly noisy hotel, but if you require absolute quiet, request an interior room. The Cervantes is 6 blocks south and 3 blocks west of the cathedral.

Prisciliano Sánchez 442, Col. Centro Histórico, 44100 Guadalajara, Jal. ©/fax **33/3613-6686.** 100 units. $65–$75 double. AE, MC, V. Free secure parking. **Amenities:** Restaurant; lobby bar; small outdoor heated pool; tour desk; room service until 10pm; babysitting; laundry service; dry cleaning. *In room:* A/C, TV.

La Villa del Ensueño ★★   This B&B in central Tlaquepaque is a lovely alternative to big-city hotels. A modern interpretation of traditional Mexican architecture, it is a delight to the eye—small courtyards and beautiful gardens bordered by old stucco walls, which have been painted in muted shades of orange oxide or covered in carefully trimmed ivy, with an occasional wrought-iron balcony or stone staircase. The rooms are individually decorated and have more character than most hotel lodgings. All contain ceiling fans and wireless Internet connections. Doubles have either two twin or two double beds. Guests receive a complimentary cocktail on arrival. The hotel is about 8 blocks from the main plaza.

Florida 305, 45500 Tlaquepaque, Jal. © **800/220-8689** in the U.S., or 33/3635-8792. Fax 818/597-0637 in the U.S. www.villadelensueno.com. 18 units. $88 double; $100 deluxe double; $117 2-bedroom unit; $140 suite. Rates include full breakfast, light laundry service. AE, MC, V. Free valet parking. **Amenities:** Bar; indoor and small outdoor pool; laundry service. *In room:* A/C, TV, dataport, hair dryer.

Quinta Don José ★★ *Value*   Good value, great location, friendly English-speaking owners—there are a lot of reasons to like this small establishment just 2 blocks from Tlaquepaque's main square. Rooms run the gauntlet from midsize to extralarge. They are comfortable, attractive, and quiet, with some nice local touches. Most of the standard and deluxe doubles have a king or two double beds and an attractive, midsize bathroom. A couple have small private outdoor spaces. Some of the suites in back come with a full kitchen and lots of space—more than twice the size of the usual suite, with one king and one double bed. The breakfasts are good, and would you believe high-speed wireless Internet connection? Some lodgings just have a good feel to them, and this is one.

Reforma 139, 45500 Tlaquepaque, Jal. © **866/629-3753** in the U.S. and Canada, or 33/3635-7522. Fax 33/3659-9315. www.quintadonjose.com. 15 units. $88–$99 double; $117–$152 suite. Rates include full breakfast, wireless Internet access, airport and bus station pickup for longer stays. AE, MC, V. Free secure parking. **Amenities:** Restaurant; bar; heated outdoor pool; tour info; in-room massage; babysitting; laundry service; nonsmoking rooms. *In room:* A/C, TV, hair dryer, iron, high-speed wireless Internet.

INEXPENSIVE

Hotel San Francisco Plaza *Value*   This colonial-style downtown hotel is both pleasant and a bargain. Its rooms are big and comfortable, with attractive furnishings. All have rugs or carpeting, and most have tall ceilings (except in the remodeled area behind the reception desk). The hotel is built in colonial style around four courtyards, which contain fountains and potted plants. Rooms along the Sánchez Street side are much quieter now that the management has installed double windows. Some units along the back wall of the rear patio have small bathrooms. The San Francisco Plaza is 6 blocks south and 2 blocks east of the cathedral.

Degollado 267, 44100 Guadalajara, Jal. © **33/3613-8954** or 33/3613-8971. Fax 33/3613-3257. www.sanfrancisco hotel.com.mx. 76 units. $47 double. AE, MC, V. Free parking. **Amenities:** Restaurant; limited room service; babysitting; laundry service; dry cleaning; ironing service. *In room:* A/C, TV.

Plaza Los Reyes *Value*   Rooms in this 10-story downtown hotel are midsize and come with either two doubles or a king-size bed. Those on the mezzanine level are larger and often cost the same. Ask for a room facing away from the busy Calzada Independencia. Midsize bathrooms are clean and come with showers. The air-conditioning units are minisplits, which are quiet and effective. Good for the money.

Calzada Independencia Sur 168, 44100 Guadalajara, Jal. ℭ **33/3613-9770** or 33/3613-9775. 189 units. $55 double. AE, MC, V. Free valet parking. **Amenities:** Restaurant; bar; outdoor heated pool; tour info; room service until midnight; laundry service; nonsmoking rooms. *In room:* A/C, TV.

4 Where to Dine

Guadalajara has many excellent restaurants for fine dining and for typical local fare. Most of the fine-dining spots are on the west side. Those in the Centro Histórico are uniformly bad, excepting **La Fonda de San Miguel.** Tlaquepaque has some good choices, but they all close around 8pm. Popular eateries serving good local fare are abundant, especially in the Centro Histórico. Local dishes include *birria* (goat, lamb, or pork covered in maguey leaves and roasted). It comes in a tomato-based broth or with the broth on the side. To get it properly prepared, go to one of the many *birrierías.* There are about a half-dozen in Las Nueve Esquinas neighborhood, downtown; in Tlaquepaque, try **Birriería El Sope.** Another local favorite is *torta ahogada,* a sandwich with a pork filling bathed in a tomato sauce. Jalisco-style *pozole* is chicken-and-hominy soup to which you add lime juice, onion, Mexican oregano, and chiles.

For a quick meal, there are several **Sanborn's** in the city. This is a popular national chain of restaurants and coffee shops; the traditional dish is *enchiladas suizas* (enchiladas in cream sauce). It's a good idea to keep your guidebook handy when taking a taxi; many drivers are unfamiliar with even the most popular places and require an address. Make reservations in the evening, especially for restaurants on the west side.

EXPENSIVE

Chez Nené ★★★ FRENCH   In a small and pleasant open-air dining room, you can enjoy a quiet and leisurely meal of delicious French food. After doing just this, I had to meet the owner to see who was behind such work. He turned out to be a French expatriate (whose Mexican wife, Nené, is the restaurant's namesake) with clear ideas about food and dining. What I had seen and tasted confirmed everything he said. Shorn of all fads and pretense, his cooking aims at the essential in a dish. Freshness and quality of ingredients are what matter for him, and everything (except stews and such) is cooked to order. The daily menu is on a chalkboard and depends on what the owner finds that morning at the market. There are always at least a dozen main courses. The waiter answered every question I put to him and gave excellent service.

Juan Polomar y Arias 426 (continuación Rafael Sauzio), west side. ℭ **33/3673-4564.** Reservations recommended on weekends. Main courses $10–$20. AE, MC, V. Tues 4–11pm; Wed–Sat 1–5:30pm and 7:30–11:30pm; Sun 1–6pm.

MODERATE

Adobe Fonda ★★★ NUEVA COCINA   This charming restaurant shares space with a large store on pedestrian-only Independencia. The space is open and airy. The menu is inventive and thoughtfully designed. Homemade bread and tostadas come to the table with an olive oil–based chile sauce, pico de gallo, and *requezón de epazote* (ricotta-like cheese with a Mexican herb). Among the soups are *crema de cilantro* and an interesting mushroom soup with a dark beer broth. The main courses present some difficult decisions, with intriguing combinations of Mexican, Italian, and Argentine ingredients: shrimp quesadillas accompanied by *chimichurri* with *nopal* cactus; filet in creamy ancho sauce. The daily specials can be very good. Sample the margaritas, too.

Francisco de Miranda 27, corner of Independencia, Tlaquepaque. ℭ **33/3657-2792.** Reservations recommended on weekends. Main courses $9–$17. AE, MC, V. Daily 12:30–6:30pm.

El Sacromonte ★★★ ALTA COCINA   The food here is so exquisite that I try to dine here every time I'm in Guadalajara. El Sacromonte emphasizes artful presentation and design: Order "Queen Isabel's crown," and you'll be served a dish of shrimp woven together in the shape of a crown and covered in divine lobster-and-orange sauce. Or try quesadillas with rose petals in a deep-colored strawberry sauce. For soup, consider *el viejo progreso* for its unlikely combination of flavors (blue cheese and chipotle chile). The menu features amusing descriptions in verse. The main dining area is a shaded, open-air patio. The restaurant isn't far from the downtown area, on an eastbound street just 2 blocks north of Avenida Vallarta.

In the building next door, the owners have opened an updated version of the classic Mexican bar where one drinks, while snacking on complimentary *botanas* (the Mexican equivalent of tapas). There is also a menu, which is simpler than the restaurant's. The place is called **El Duende.**

Pedro Moreno 1398, corner of Colonias, west side. ✆ 33/3825-5447 or 33/3827-0663. Reservations recommended. Main courses $9–$17. MC, V. Mon–Sat 1:30pm–midnight.

Hostería del Angel ★★ TAPAS/SPANISH-ITALIAN DELI   Sip wine and munch on a few tapas in this comfortable and casual restaurant and wine bar just a few blocks from the basilica in Zapopan. The chef-owner cooked for years in Spain and Italy, where he became fascinated with the making of cheeses and deli meats such as prosciutto and Spanish *jamón Serrano.* He serves a variety of tapas, and his baguette sandwiches are very popular with the locals. The menu doesn't do a good job of explaining the dishes, so don't hesitate to ask the waitperson for explanations. The house specialty is the *rotolata*—vegetables and cold cuts surrounded by a thin layer of crispy cheese. Live music plays from 9 to 11pm Monday through Saturday. The restaurant is a half-block off the pedestrian-only *calzada,* which leads to the plaza in front of the basilica.

5 de Mayo 295, Zapopan, west side. ✆/fax 33/3656-9516. Reservations recommended. Menu items $4–$9. MC, V. Tues–Sat 9am–midnight; Sun 9am–8pm.

I Latina FUSION   Warehouse chic with a porcine motif (the owner tells me that the pig is a symbol of abundance in Thailand) is the setting here. Naturally, the menu must exhibit sophistication, which it does with carpaccio here, portobellos there—you probably get the picture. But the food was well prepared. I had a stir-fry of chicken flavored with ginger, and a salad with greens, fried rice noodle, and citrus-flavored dressing. I also enjoyed people-watching. The furniture—metal and plastic—is completely in character yet comfortable. There's live music Thursday from 9 to 11pm and Sunday afternoon. Go early if you want to avoid the rush, and make reservations—this restaurant is *popularísimo.*

Av. Inglaterra, west side. ✆ 33/3647-7774. Reservations recommended. Main courses $9–$15. MC, V. Wed–Sat 7:30pm–1am; Sun 2–6pm.

La Destilería ★★ MEXICAN   You know that with a name like "The Distillery," tequila will somehow be involved. Although this museum-restaurant abounds with artifacts and photos depicting every stage of the tequila-making process, the food is what really pulls in the *tapatíos.* This place is sure to please everyone. Specialties include *molcajete de la casa*—steaming fajitas, *rajas* (chile strips), cheese, onion, and avocado in a large, sizzling *molcajete* (three-legged stone mortar). The steak dish *medallones a la poblana* is memorable, as is the delicately flavored fish in parsley sauce. You can order salads here without hesitation (all greens are washed in antimicrobial solution), and the dessert menu includes such favorites as *pastel de tres leches.* And, with its vast selection of tequilas, it's the perfect place to do a little tasting. La Destilería is 5 blocks northwest of Fuente Minerva.

Av. México 2916 (corner of Nelson), Fracc. Terranova, west side. © 33/3640-3440 or 33/3640-3110. Reservations recommended. Main courses $9–$15. AE, MC, V. Mon–Sat 1pm–midnight; Sun 1–6pm.

La Fonda de San Miguel ★★ *(Moments* MEXICAN

My favorite way to enjoy a good meal in Mexico is to have it in an elegant colonial courtyard. I love the contrast between the bright, noisy street and the cool, shaded patio. This restaurant is in the former convent of Santa Teresa de Jesús. While you enjoy the stone arches and gurgling fountain, little crisp tacos, homemade bread, and mildly spiced butter awaken the appetite. For main courses, try *chiles en nogada* (a combination of spicy and sweet) if it's in season, or perhaps a traditional *mole poblano*. The restaurant is 4 blocks west and 1 block south of the cathedral, between Pedro Moreno and Morelos. Thursday to Saturday musicians perform from 3 to 5 and 9 to 11pm.

Donato Guerra 25, downtown. © 33/3613-0809. Reservations recommended on weekends. Breakfast $4–$8; main courses $9–$16. AE, MC, V. Sun–Mon 8am–6pm; Tues–Sat 8am–midnight.

La Trattoria Pomodoro Ristorante ★ ITALIAN

Good food, good service, and moderate prices make this restaurant perennially popular. The price of pastas and main courses includes a visit to the well-stocked salad bar. Recommendable menu items include the combination pasta plate (lasagna, fettuccini Alfredo, and spaghetti), shrimp linguine, and chicken parmigiana. The Italian owner likes to stock lots of wines from the motherland. The dining room is attractive and casual, with comfortable furniture and separate seating for smokers and nonsmokers. Reservations are not accepted during holidays.

Niños Héroes 3051, west side. © 33/3122-1817. Reservations recommended. Pasta $7–$9; main courses $8–$10. AE, MC, V. Daily 1pm–midnight. Free parking.

Mariscos Progreso SEAFOOD

On a large, open patio shaded by trees and tile roofs, waiters navigate among the tables carrying large platters of delicious seafood. Mexicans do a wonderful job with seafood, and this popular restaurant does the tradition proud. Grilling over charcoal is the specialty here, but the kitchen's repertoire includes all the Mexican standards. For a sampling of grilled favorites, try the *parrillada* (a platter of grilled dishes) for two. Sometimes there's quite a bit of ambience, with mariachis adding to the commotion. At other times, the crowd thins and one can rest peacefully from the exertions of shopping with a cold drink. It's a half-block from the Parián.

Progreso 80, Tlaquepaque. © 33/3657-4995. Reservations not accepted. Main courses $7–$14. AE, MC, V. Daily 11am–7pm.

INEXPENSIVE

Café Madrid MEXICAN

This little coffee shop is like many coffee shops used to be—a social institution where people come in, greet each other and the staff by name, and chat over breakfast or coffee and cigarettes. Change comes slowly here. For example, despite the fact that it's an informal place, the waiters wear white jackets with black bow ties, as they did 20 years ago. The coffee and Mexican breakfasts are good, as is the standard Mexican fare served in the afternoon. The front room opens to the street, with a small lunch counter and another room in the back.

Juárez 264, downtown. © 33/3614-9504. Breakfast $2–$4; main courses $3–$6. No credit cards. Daily 7:30am–10:30pm. From the Plaza de Armas, walk 1 block on Corona to Juárez and turn right; the cafe is on the right.

La Chata Restaurant REGIONAL/MEXICAN This popular downtown spot offers good standards at reasonable prices. Aromas waft into the street from the kitchen in front, where women with their heads wrapped in bandanas busily stir, chop, and fry. Past this is a large dining area. Local dishes include *pozole* (chicken, pork, and hominy in a broth to which you add onions, radishes, chile, and oregano) and *torta ahogada* (a spicy pork sandwich bathed in sauce). If you're very hungry, the sampler platter of *antojitos* for four people will fill the bill. Or try the *plato combinado* (*mole*, chile relleno, rice, and beans).

Corona 126 (between Juárez and López Cotilla), downtown. ☎ 33/3613-0588. Reservations not accepted. Breakfast $3–$5; main courses $4–$7. AE, DC, MC, V. Daily 8am–11:30pm. From the Plaza de Armas, walk 1½ blocks south on Corona; La Chata is on the right.

La Fonda de la Noche ★★ *Finds* MEXICAN For a host of reasons this is my favorite place in the city for a simple supper. The limited menu is excellent, the surroundings are comfortable and inviting, the lighting is perfect, and there's a touch of nostalgia for the Mexico of the '40s, '50s, and '60s. It's not far from downtown or the west side; take a cab to the intersection of Jesús and Reforma, and, when you get there, look for a door behind a small hedge. There's no sign. It's a house with five dining rooms. I like best the bar immediately to your right as you enter. Only Spanish is spoken, but the menu is simple. To try a little of everything, order the *plato combinado,* which comes with an *enchilada de "medio mole,"* an empanada called a *media luna,* a tostada, and a *sope* (soup). The owner is Carlos Ibarra, an artist originally from the state of Durango. He has decorated the place with traditional Mexican pine furniture and cotton tablecloths and his personal collection of paintings, mostly the works of close friends.

Jesús 251, corner with Reforma, Col. El Refugio. ☎ 33/3827-0917. Reservations not accepted. Main course $5–$7. No credit cards. Tues–Sun 7pm–midnight.

Los Itacates Restaurant ★ *Value* MEXICAN The Mexican equivalent of down-home cooking at reasonable prices. Office workers pack the place between 2 and 4pm weekdays, and there's a good crowd weekend nights, but at other times there's no problem finding a table. You can dine outdoors in a shaded sidewalk area or in one of the three dining rooms. The atmosphere is bright and colorful. Specialties include *pozole* (chicken-and-hominy soup) *lomo adobado* (baked pork in dark chile sauce), and chiles rellenos. *Pollo Itacates* is a quarter of a chicken, two cheese enchiladas, potatoes, and rice. Los Itacates is 5 blocks north of Avenida Vallarta. In the evenings they serve tacos and other *antojitos.*

Chapultepec Norte 110, west side. ☎ 33/3825-1106 or 33/3825-9551. Reservations accepted on weekends and holidays. Breakfast buffet $6; tacos $1; main courses $5–$7. MC, V. Mon–Sat 8am–11pm; Sun 8am–7pm.

5 Exploring Guadalajara

SPECIAL EVENTS

There's always something going on from September to December. In September, when Mexicans celebrate independence from Spain, Guadalajara goes all out, with a full month of festivities. The celebrations kick off with the **Encuentro Internacional del Mariachi** (www.mariachi-jalisco.com.mx), in which mariachi bands from around the world play before knowledgeable audiences and hold sessions with other mariachis. Bands come from as far as Japan and Russia, and the event takes on a curious postmodern hue. There are concerts in several venues. In the Degollado Theater, you can hear orchestral arrangements of classic mariachi songs with solos by famous mariachis.

Downtown Guadalajara

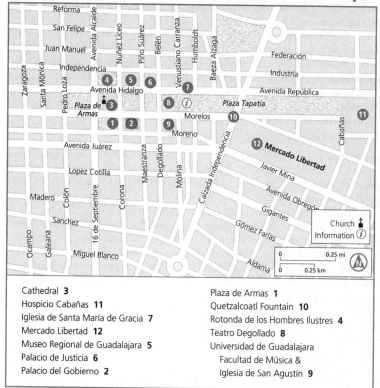

Cathedral **3**
Hospicio Cabañas **11**
Iglesia de Santa María de Gracia **7**
Mercado Libertad **12**
Museo Regional de Guadalajara **5**
Palacio de Justicia **6**
Palacio del Gobierno **2**

Plaza de Armas **1**
Quetzalcoatl Fountain **10**
Rotonda de los Hombres Ilustres **4**
Teatro Degollado **8**
Universidad de Guadalajara
  Facultad de Música &
  Iglesia de San Agustín **9**

You might be acquainted with many of the classics without even knowing it. The culmination is a parade of thousands of mariachis and *charros* (Mexican cowboys) through downtown. It starts the first week of September.

On **September 15,** a massive crowd assembles in front of the Governor's Palace to await the traditional *grito* (shout for independence) at 11pm. The *grito* commemorates Father Miguel Hidalgo de Costilla's cry for independence in 1810. The celebration features live music on a street stage, spontaneous dancing, fireworks, and shouts of *"¡Viva México!"* and *"¡Viva Hidalgo!"* The next day is the official Independence Day, with a traditional parade; the plazas downtown resemble a country fair and market, with booths, games of chance, stuffed-animal prizes, cotton candy, and candied apples. Live entertainment stretches well into the night.

On **October 12,** a **procession** ★★ honoring Our Lady of Zapopan celebrates the feast day of the Virgin of Zapopan. Around dawn, her small, dark figure begins the 5-hour ride from the Cathedral of Guadalajara to the suburban Basilica of Zapopan (see "Other Attractions," below). The original icon dates from the mid-1500s; the procession began 200 years later. Today, crowds spend the night along the route and vie for position as the Virgin approaches. She travels in a gleaming new car (virginal in that it must never have had the ignition turned on), which her caretakers pull through the streets. During the previous months, the figure visits churches all over the city. You will likely see neighborhoods decorated with paper streamers and banners honoring the Virgin's visit to the local church.

The celebration has grown into a month-long event, **Fiestas de Octubre,** which kicks off with an enormous parade, usually on the first Sunday or Saturday of the month. Festivities include performing arts, *charreadas* (rodeos), bullfights, art exhibits, regional dancing, a food fair, and a Day of Nations incorporating all the consulates in Guadalajara. By the time this is over, you enter the **holiday season of November and December,** with Revolution Day (Nov 20), the Virgin of Guadalupe's feast day (Dec 12), and several other celebrations.

DOWNTOWN GUADALAJARA

The most easily recognized building in the city is the **cathedral** ✦, around which four open plazas make the shape of a Latin cross. Later, a long swath of land was cleared to extend the open area from the cathedral east to the Instituto Cultural Cabañas, creating **Plaza Tapatía.**

Construction on the cathedral started in 1561 and continued into the 18th century. Over such a long time, it was inevitable that remodeling would take place before the building was ever completed. The result is an unusual facade that is an amalgam of several architectural styles, including baroque, neoclassical, and Gothic. An 1818 earthquake destroyed the original large towers; their replacements were built in the 1850s, inspired by designs on the bishop's dinner china. Blue and yellow are Guadalajara's colors. The nave is open, airy, and majestic. Items of interest include a painting in the sacristy ascribed to the 17th-century Spanish artist Bartolomé Estaban Murillo (1617–82).

To the cathedral's left is the **Plaza de Armas,** the oldest and loveliest of the plazas. A cast-iron Art Nouveau bandstand is its dominant feature. Made in France, it was a gift to the city from the dictator Porfirio Díaz in the 1890s. The female figures on the bandstand exhibited too little clothing for conservative Guadalajarans, who clothed them. The dictator, recognizing when it's best to let the people have their way, said nothing.

Facing the plaza is the **Palacio del Gobierno** ✦✦, a broad palace two stories high, built in 1774. The facade blends Spanish and Moorish elements and holds several details that catch the eye. Inside the central courtyard, above the staircase to the right, is a spectacular mural of Hidalgo by the modern Mexican master José Clemente Orozco. The Father of Independence appears high overhead, bearing directly down on the viewer and looking as implacable as a force of nature. On one of the adjacent walls Orozco painted *The Carnival of Ideologies,* a dark satire on the prevailing fanaticisms of his day. Another of his murals is inside the second-floor chamber of representatives, depicting Hidalgo again, this time in a more conventional posture, writing the proclamation to end slavery in Mexico. The *palacio* is open daily from 10am to 8pm.

In the plaza on the opposite side of the cathedral from the Plaza de Armas is the **Rotonda de los Hombres Ilustres.** Sixteen white columns, each supporting a bronze statue, stand as monuments to Guadalajara's and Jalisco's distinguished sons. Across the street from the plaza you will see a line of horse-drawn buggies. A spin around the Centro Histórico lasts about an hour and costs $20 for one to four people.

Facing the east side of the rotunda is the **Museo Regional de Guadalajara,** Liceo 60 (✆ 33/3614-9957). Originally a convent, it was built in 1701 in the churrigueresque (Mexican baroque) style and contains some of the region's important archaeological finds, fossils, historic objects, and art. Among the highlights are a giant reconstructed mammoth's skeleton and a meteorite weighing 1,715 pounds, discovered in Zacatecas in 1792. On the first floor, there's a fascinating exhibit of pre-Hispanic pottery, and some exquisite pottery and clay figures recently unearthed near Tequila during the construction of the toll road. On the second floor is a small ethnography exhibit of the contemporary dress of the state's indigenous peoples, including the Coras, Huicholes, Mexicaneros, Nahuas, and Tepehuanes. It's open Tuesday through Sunday from 9am to 5pm. Admission is $3 for adults, $1 for children.

Behind the Cathedral is the Plaza de la Liberación, with the **Teatro Degollado** (deh-goh-*yah*-doh) on the opposite side. This neoclassical 19th-century opera house was named for Santos Degollado, a local patriot who fought with Juárez against Maximilian and the French. Apollo and the nine muses decorate the theater's pediment, and the interior is famous for both the acoustics and the rich decoration. It hosts a variety of performances during the year, including the Ballet Folclórico on Sunday at 10am. It's open Monday through Friday from 10am to 2pm and during performances.

To the right of the theater, across the street, is the sweet little **church of Santa María de Gracia,** built in 1573 as part of a convent for Dominican nuns. On the opposite side of the Teatro Degollado is the **church of San Agustín.** The former convent is now the **University of Guadalajara School of Music.**

Behind the Teatro Degollado begins the Plaza Tapatía, which leads to the Instituto Cabañas. It passes between a couple of low, modern office buildings. The Tourism Information Office is in a building on the right-hand side.

Beyond these office buildings, the plaza opens into a large expanse, now framed by department stores and offices and dominated by the abstract modern **Quetzalcoatl Fountain.** This fluid steel structure represents the mythical plumed serpent Quetzalcoatl, who figured so prominently in pre-Hispanic religion and culture, and exerts a presence even today.

At the far end of the plaza is the Hospicio Cabañas, formerly an orphanage and known today as the **Instituto Cultural Cabañas** ★★, Cabañas 8 (② **33/3617-4322**). This vast structure is impressive for both its size (more than 23 courtyards) and its grandiose architecture, especially the cupola. Created by the famous Mexican architect Manuel Tolsá, it housed homeless children from 1829 to 1980. Today, it's a thriving cultural center offering art shows and classes. The interior walls and ceiling of the main building display murals painted by Orozco in 1937. His *Man of Fire,* in the dome, is said to represent the spirit of humanity projecting itself toward the infinite. Other rooms hold additional Orozco works, as well as excellent contemporary art and temporary exhibits.

Just south of the Hospicio Cabañas (to the left as you exit) is the **Mercado Libertad** ★, Guadalajara's gigantic covered central market, the largest in Latin America. This site has been a market plaza since the 1500s; the present buildings date from the early 1950s (see "Shopping," below).

OTHER ATTRACTIONS

At **Parque Agua Azul (Blue Water Park),** plants, trees, shrubbery, statues, and fountains create a perfect refuge from the bustling city. Many people come here to exercise early in the morning. The park is open daily from 7am to 6pm. Admission is $1 for adults, 50¢ for children.

Across Independencia from the park, cater-cornered from a small flower market, is the **Museo de Arqueología del Occidente de México,** Calzada Independencia at Avenida del Campesino. It houses a fine collection of pre-Hispanic pottery from

Jalisco, Nayarit, and Colima. The museum is open Tuesday through Sunday from 10am to 2pm and 4 to 7pm. There's a small admission charge.

The state-run **Casa de las Artesanías** (© 33/3619-4664) is at the Instituto de la Artesanía Jalisciense, just past the park entrance at Calzada Independencia and González Gallo (for details, see "Shopping," below).

Also near the park is Guadalajara's rodeo arena, **Lienzo Charro de Jalisco** (© 33/3619-0315). Mexican cowboys, known as *charros,* are famous for their riding and lasso work, and the arena in Guadalajara is considered the big time. There are shows and competitions every Sunday at noon. The arena is at Av. Dr. R. Michel 577, between González Gallo and Las Palomas.

The Basilica of the Virgin of Zapopan ✿

A wide promenade several blocks long leads to a large, open plaza and the basilica. This is the religious center of Guadalajara. On the Virgin's feast day (see "Special Events," above) the plaza fills with thousands of *tapatíos.* The 18th-century church is a lovely (and somewhat anachronistic) combination of baroque and plateresque styles. The cult of the Virgin of Zapopan practically began with the foundation of Guadalajara itself. She is much revered and the object of many pilgrimages. In front of the church are several stands selling religious figures and paraphernalia. On one side of the church is a lovely museum and store dedicated to the betterment of the Huichol Indians. It is well worth a visit.

Main Plaza, Zapopan (10km/6 miles northwest of downtown). No phone. Free admission. Daily 7am–7pm; museum daily 10am–7pm.

Museo de las Artes de la Universidad de Guadalajara

Inside the main lecture hall of this building are some more murals by Orozco. On the wall behind the stage is a bitter denunciation of corruption called *The People and Their False Leaders.* But in the cupola is a more optimistic work—*The Five-fold Man,* who works to create a better society and better self. There is also a small permanent collection of modern art, which will look all too familiar because the works seem so derivative of many of the modern masters.

Juárez 975 (enter on López Cotilla). © 33/3134-2222. Free admission. Tues–Sun 10am–8pm.

Museo de la Ciudad

This museum opened in 1992 in a former convent. It chronicles Guadalajara's past. The eight rooms, beginning on the right and proceeding in chronological order, cover the period from just before the city's founding to the present. Unusual artifacts, including rare Spanish armaments and equestrian paraphernalia, give a sense of what day-to-day life was like. Descriptive text is in Spanish only.

Independencia 684 (at M. Barcena). © 33/3658-2531. Free admission. Tues–Sun 10am–5pm.

6 Shopping

Many visitors to Guadalajara come specifically for the shopping in Tlaquepaque and Tonalá (see below). If you have little free time, try the government-run **Instituto de la Artesanía Jalisciense** ✿, González Gallo 20 at Calzada Independencia (© 33/3619-4664), in Parque Agua Azul, just south of downtown. This place is perfect for one-stop shopping, with two floors of pottery, silver jewelry, dance masks, glassware, leather goods, and regional clothing from around the state and the country. As you enter, on the right are museum displays showing crafts and regional costumes from the state of Jalisco. The craft store is open Monday through Friday from 10am to 6pm, Saturday from 10am to 5pm, Sunday from 10am to 3pm.

Guadalajara is known for its shoe industry; if you're in the market for a pair, try the **Galería del Calzado,** a shopping center made up exclusively of shoe stores. It's on the west side, about 6 blocks from Minerva Circle, at avenidas Mexico and Yaquis.

Mariachis and *charros* come to Guadalajara from all over Mexico to buy their highly worked belts and boots, wide-brimmed sombreros, and embroidered shirts. Several tailor shops and stores specialize in these outfits. One is **El Charro,** which has a store in the Plaza del Sol shopping center, across the street from the Hotel Presidente Inter-Continental, and one downtown on Juárez.

To view a good slice of what constitutes the material world for most Mexicans, try the mammoth **Mercado Libertad** ⌖ downtown. Besides food and produce, you'll see crafts, household goods, clothing, magic preparations, and more. Although it opens at 7am, the market isn't in full swing until around 10am. Come prepared to haggle.

SHOPPING IN TLAQUEPAQUE & TONALA

Almost everyone who comes to Guadalajara for the shopping has Tlaquepaque (tlah-keh-*pah*-keh) and Tonalá in mind. These two suburbs are traditional handicraft centers that produce and sell a wide variety of *artesanía* (crafts).

TLAQUEPAQUE

Located about 20 minutes from downtown, **Tlaquepaque** ⌖⌖⌖ has the best shopping for handicrafts and decorative arts in all of Mexico. Over the years, it has become a fashionable place, attracting talented designers in a variety of fields. Even though it's a suburb of a large city, it has a cozy, small-town feel; it's a pleasure simply to stroll through the central streets from shop to shop. No one hassles you; no one does the hard sell. There are some excellent places to eat (see "Where to Dine," earlier in this chapter), or you can grab some simple fare at **El Parián,** a building in the middle of town that houses a number of small eateries.

A taxi from downtown Guadalajara costs $5, or you can take one of the deluxe **Turquesa buses** that make a fairly quick run from downtown to Tlaquepaque and Tonalá (see "Getting Around," earlier in this chapter).

The **Tlaquepaque Tourism Office,** Juárez 238 (ⓒ **33/3635-1220,** ext. 104 or 113), has a helpful, English-speaking staff. It's open Monday through Friday from 9am to 3pm. Most stores in Tlaquepaque close between 2 and 4pm and stay open until 7 or 8pm. Most are closed or have reduced hours on Sunday.

If you are interested in pottery and ceramics, two museums are worth a visit. The **Regional Ceramics Museum,** Independencia 237 (ⓒ **33/3635-5404**), displays several aspects of traditional Jalisco pottery as produced in Tlaquepaque and Tonalá. The examples date back several generations and are grouped according to the technique used to produce them. Note the crosshatch design known as *petatillo* on some of the pieces; it's one of the region's oldest traditional motifs and is, like so many other motifs, a real pain to produce. Look for the wonderful old kitchen and dining room, complete with pots, utensils, and dishes. The museum is open Tuesday through Saturday from 10am to 6pm, Sunday from 10am to 3pm; admission is free. The **Museo Pantaleón Panduro** ⌖⌖⌖ (ⓒ **33/3635-1089,** ext. 17) is at P. Sánchez 191, at Florida. It is a must-see. Named after a famous local 19th-century artisan, it displays prize-winning pieces from the national ceramics contest held each year in Tlaquepaque. Many of the pieces exhibit an astounding virtuosity. Categories include miniatures, traditional designs, and original designs. It's open Tuesday through Sunday from

---

> ### ⌒Tips Packing It In
>
> If you need your purchases packed safely so that you can check them as extra baggage, or if you want them shipped, talk to **Margaret del Río**. She is an American who runs a large packing and shipping company at Juárez 347, Tlaquepaque (𝄐 **33/3657-5652**). Paying the excess baggage fee usually is cheaper than shipping, but less convenient.

10am to 6pm; admission is free. If you still haven't had your fill, the Museo Nacional de Cerámica is in Tonalá (see below).

A number of workshops permit visitors to watch artisans at work. A popular workshop is **La Rosa de Cristal,** Contreras Medillín 173, a glassblowing factory. It's open Monday through Saturday from 10am to 7pm. If you're interested in a particular craft, talk to the city tourism office; the staff can help locate workshops that are open to the public.

The following list of Tlaquepaque shops will give you an idea of what to expect. This is just a small fraction of what you'll find; the best approach might be to just follow your nose. The main shopping is along **Independencia,** a pedestrian-only street that starts at El Parián. You can go door-to-door visiting the shops until the street ends, then work your way back on **Calle Juárez,** the next street over, north of Independencia.

Agustín Parra   So you bought an old hacienda and are trying to restore its chapel—where do you go to find traditional baroque sculpture, religious art, gold-leafed objects, and even entire *retablos* (altarpieces)? Parra is famous for exactly this kind of work, and the store is lovely. It's open Monday through Saturday from 10am to 7pm. Independencia 158. 𝄐 **33/3657-8530.**

Bazar Hecht   One of the village's longtime favorites. Here you'll find wood objects, handmade furniture, and a few antiques. It's open Monday through Saturday from 10am to 2:30pm and 3:30 to 7pm. Juárez 162. 𝄐 **33/3657-0316.**

Casa Canela   One of the most elegant stores in Tlaquepaque, this is a feast for the eyes. Browse through rooms full of furniture and decorative objects. It's open Monday through Friday from 10am to 2pm and 3 to 7pm, Saturday from 10am to 6pm, Sunday from 11am to 3pm. Independencia 258, near Calle Cruz Verde. 𝄐 **33/3635-3717.**

Sergio Bustamante   Sergio Bustamante's imaginative, original bronze, ceramic, and papier-mâché sculptures are among the most sought-after in Mexico—as well as the most copied. He also designs silver jewelry. This exquisite gallery showcases his work. It's open Monday through Saturday from 10am to 7pm, Sunday from 11am to 4pm. Independencia 236 at Cruz Verde. 𝄐 **33/3639-5519.**

Tete Arte y Diseño   Architectural decorative objects mix with pottery, antiques, glassware, and paintings at this shop. It's open Monday through Saturday from 10am to 7pm. Juárez 173. 𝄐 **33/3635-7347.**

Tierra Tlaquepaque   Here you'll find unusual, rustic, and finely finished pottery, as well as wood sculptures, table textiles, and decorative objects. Open Monday through Saturday from 10am to 7pm, Sunday from 11am to 5pm. Independencia 156. 𝄐 **33/3635-9770.**

TONALA: A TRADITION OF POTTERY MAKING

Tonalá ✰✰ is a pleasant town 5 minutes from Tlaquepaque. The streets were paved only recently, and there aren't any fancy shops. The village has been a center of pottery making since pre-Hispanic times; half of the more than 400 workshops here produce a wide variety of high- and low-temperature pottery. Other local artists work with forged iron, cantera stone, brass and copper, marble, miniatures, papier-mâché, textiles, blown glass, and gesso. This is a good place to look for custom work in any of these materials; you can locate a large pool of craftspeople by asking around a little.

Market days are Thursday and Sunday. Expect large crowds, and blocks and blocks of stalls displaying locally made pottery and glassware, as well as cheap manufactured goods, food, and all kinds of bric-a-brac. "Herb men" sell a rainbow selection of dried medicinal herbs from wheelbarrows; magicians entertain crowds with sleight-of-hand; and craftspeople spread their colorful wares on the plaza's sidewalks. I prefer to visit Tonalá on non-market days, when it's much easier to get around and see the glass and pottery stores. This is the place for buying sets of margarita glasses, the widely seen blue-rimmed rustic glassware, as well as the pottery typically associated with Mexico and finely painted *petatillo* ware.

The **Tonalá Tourism Office** (✆ **33/3683-1740;** fax 33/3683-0590) is in the Artesanos building, set back from the road at Atonaltecas 140 Sur (the main street leading into Tonalá) at Matamoros. Hours are Monday through Friday from 9am to 3pm, Saturday from 9am to 1pm. The office offers free walking tours on Monday, Tuesday, Wednesday, and Friday at 9am and 2pm, Saturday at 9am and 1pm. They include visits to artisans' workshops (where you'll see ceramics, stoneware, blown glass, papiermâché, and the like). Tours last 3 to 4 hours and require a minimum of five people. Visitors can request an English-speaking guide. Also in Tonalá, cater-cornered from the church, you'll see a small tourism information kiosk that's staffed on market days and provides maps and useful information.

Tonalá is also the home of the **Museo Nacional de Cerámica,** Constitución 104, between Hidalgo and Morelos (✆ **33/3683-0494**). The museum occupies a two-story mansion and displays work from Jalisco and all over the country. There's a large shop in the front on the right as you enter. The museum is open Tuesday through Friday from 10am to 5pm, Saturday and Sunday from 10am to 2pm. Admission is free; the fee for using a video or still camera is $8.50 per camera.

7 Guadalajara After Dark

MARIACHIS

You can't go far in Guadalajara without coming across some mariachis, but seeing really talented performers takes some effort. Try **Casa Bariachi,** Av. Vallarta 2221 (✆ **33/3615-0029**). In Tlaquepaque, go to **El Parián,** the building on the town square where mariachis serenade diners under the archways.

THE CLUB & MUSIC SCENE

Guadalajara, as you might expect, has a lot of variety in entertainment. For the most extensive listing of clubs and performances, get your hands on a copy of *Ocio,* the weekly insert of *Público.* You'll find listings in the back, categorized by type of music.

Bar Copenhagen 77   On weekends, this snug little den with upholstered walls and wood trim is the perfect setting for catching a little modern jazz. The house band of three to five musicians plays bebop and Latin jazz on Friday and Saturday nights. You

Tequila: The Name Says It All

Tequila is an entertaining (and intoxicating) town, well worth a day trip from Guadalajara. Several taxi drivers charge about $55 to take you to the town, get you into a tour of a distillery, take you to a restaurant, and haul you back to Guadalajara. A few of them speak English. One driver is named José Gabriel Gómez (℃ 33/3649-0791; jgabriel-taxi@hotmail.com); he has a new car and drives carefully. Call him in the evening. Tour companies also arrange bus trips to Tequila; see a travel agency in Guadalajara.

Tequila has many distilleries, including the famous brands **Sauza** and **José Cuervo**. All the distilleries—the big, modern ones and the small, more traditional ones—offer tours. If you're on your own, a good place to hook up with a tour is at the little booth outside the city hall on the main square. Two young women who speak English run tours to any of the local factories. The tour costs only $5 and lasts about 2 hours. All tours show how tequila is made, what traditions the process follows, and what differences exist between tequilas; they end, of course, with a tasting. Avenida Vallarta runs straight to the highway to Tequila, which is about an hour outside of Guadalajara.

Another approach is to take the **Tequila Express** ★★ to the town of Amatitán, home of the Herradura distillery. It leaves from the train station on Friday and Saturday, and sometimes on Sunday during vacation and holiday season. You need to be there by 10am. The Guadalajara Chamber of Commerce (Cámara de Comercio), at Vallarta and Niño Obrero (℃ 33/3880-9099), organizes this trip. Buy tickets ahead of time at the main office; at the small office in the Centro Histórico at Morelos 395, at Calle Colón (no phone); or through Ticketmaster (℃ 33/3818-3800). Office hours are Monday through Friday from 9am to 2pm and 4 to 6pm. Tickets cost $65 for adults, $35 for children 6 to 12. The tour includes an open bar with tequila tasting that begins on the train, a visit to the Hacienda San José del Refugio, a tour of a distillery, dinner, and, of course, mariachis. It returns to Guadalajara at about 8pm. Travel time is 1¾ hours each way. For more information, see www.tequila express.com.mx.

can have just drinks, or you can order from the small, well-thought-out menu; the specialty is paella. Monday through Thursday it's classical guitar. The club faces the Parque de la Revolución (along Juárez, 9 blocks west of the Plaza de Armas), on your left as you walk down López Cotilla. The restaurant is open Monday through Saturday 2pm to 1am; music begins at 9pm. Marcos Castellanos 140-Z. ℃ 33/3826-7306.

El Cubilete   El Cubilete ("the dice cup") is a small club tucked away in an old downtown neighborhood called Las Nueve Esquinas (The Nine Corners). This up-and-coming area has a couple of other clubs that are worth checking out. The house band, Son de Cuba, plays a number of salsa and *cumbia* standards from Wednesday to Saturday from 10:30pm to 1am. The club is open Monday through Saturday 2pm to 1am. Gral. Río Seco 9. ℃ 33/3658-0406 or 33/3613-2096. $5 cover on weekends.

9

Puerto Vallarta & the Central Pacific Coast

by Lynne Bairstow

Known as the Mexican Riviera, Mexico's Pacific coastline—with its palm-studded jungles sweeping into the deep blue of the ocean—is a spectacular backdrop for some of the country's most modern resort cities. From Mazatlán through Puerto Vallarta and curving down to Manzanillo, modern hotels, easy air access, and a growing array of activities and adventure tourism attractions have transformed this region into a premier resort area. And for those seeking an experience off the beaten track, the villages that border this stretch of coastline remain largely undiscovered.

Puerto Vallarta, with its traditional Mexican architecture and gold-sand beaches bordered by jungle-covered mountains, is the second most visited resort in Mexico (trailing only Cancún). Vallarta maintains a small-town charm despite boasting sophisticated hotels, great restaurants, a thriving arts community, active nightlife, and a growing variety of ecotourism attractions. **Mazatlán** may be the greatest resort value in Mexico, luring

visitors with exceptional fishing, a historic downtown, and the recent addition of championship golf facilities. **Manzanillo** is surprisingly relaxed; even though it's one of Mexico's most active commercial ports, it also offers great fishing and golf. And along **Costa Alegre,** between Puerto Vallarta and Manzanillo, pristine coves are home to unique luxury and value-priced resorts that cater to travelers seeking seclusion and privacy. Just north of Puerto Vallarta is **Punta Mita,** home of the first Four Seasons resort in Latin America and a Jack Nicklaus golf course. With four luxury resorts—including Rosewood and St. Regis resorts coming soon—and two golf courses on tap, it is emerging as Mexico's most exclusive luxury address.

Villages such as **Rincón de Guayabitos, Barra de Navidad,** and **Melaque** are laid-back and almost undiscovered. Starkly different from the spirited resort towns, they offer travelers a glimpse into local culture. Excursions to these smaller villages make easy day trips or extended stays.

1 Puerto Vallarta ★★★

885km (553 miles) NW of Mexico City; 339km (212 miles) W of Guadalajara; 285km (178 miles) NW of Manzanillo; 447km (278 miles) SE of Mazatlán; 239km (149 miles) SW of Tepic

No matter how extensively I travel in Mexico, Puerto Vallarta remains my favorite part of this colorful country, for its unrivaled combination of simple pleasures and sophisticated charms. No other place in Mexico offers both the best of the country's natural beauty and an authentic dose of its vibrant culture.

Puerto Vallarta's seductive innocence captivates visitors, beckoning them to return—and to bring friends. Beyond the cobblestone streets, graceful cathedral, and welcoming atmosphere, Puerto Vallarta offers a wealth of natural beauty and man-made pleasures. Hotels of all classes and prices, over 250 restaurants, a sizzling nightlife, and enough shops and galleries to tempt even jaded consumers, make this town a perennial favorite.

Ecotourism activities flourish—from mountain biking the Sierra foothills to whale-watching, ocean kayaking, and diving with giant mantas in Banderas Bay. Forty-two kilometers (26 miles) of beaches, many in pristine coves accessible only by boat, extend around the bay. High in the Sierra Madre, the mystical Huichol Indians still live in relative isolation in an effort to protect their centuries-old culture from outside influences.

Vallarta (as locals refer to it) was never the "sleepy little fishing village" that many proclaim. It began life as a port for processing silver brought down from mines in the Sierra Madre—then was forever transformed by a movie director and two star-crossed lovers. In 1963, John Huston brought stars Ava Gardner and Richard Burton here to film the Tennessee Williams play *Night of the Iguana.* Burton's new love, Elizabeth Taylor, came along to ensure the romance remained in full bloom—even though both were married to others at the time. Titillated, the international paparazzi arrived, and when they weren't shooting photos of the famous couple—or of Gardner water-skiing back from the set, surrounded by a bevy of beach boys—they photographed the beauty of Puerto Vallarta.

Luxury hotels and shopping centers have sprung up north and south of the original town, allowing Vallarta to grow into a city of 250,000 without sacrificing its considerable charms. It boasts the services and infrastructure of a modern city as well as the authenticity of a colonial Mexican village.

Cool breezes flow down from the mountains along the Río Cuale, which runs through the center of town. Fanciful public sculptures grace the boardwalk, or *malecón,* which is bordered by lively restaurants, shops, and bars. The *malecón* is a magnet for both residents and visitors, who stroll the main walkway to take in an ocean breeze, a multihued sunset, or a moonlit, perfect wave.

If I sound partial, it's not just because Puerto Vallarta is my favorite of Mexico's sunny resorts; this has been my home for the past 14 years. I live here in good company—there's a considerable colony of American, Canadian, and European residents. Perhaps they feel as I do: that the surrounding mountains offer the equivalent of a continual, comforting embrace, adding to that sense of welcome that so many visitors feel as well.

ESSENTIALS

GETTING THERE & DEPARTING **By Plane** For a list of international carriers serving Mexico, see chapter 2. Local numbers of some international carriers serving Puerto Vallarta are **Alaska Airlines** (② **322/221-1350** or 322/221-1353), **American Airlines** (② **322/221-1799** or 322/221-1927), **America West** (② **322/221-1333,** or 01-880/235-9292 inside Mexico), and **Continental** (② **322/221-1025** or 322/221-2212), **Frontier** (② **800/432-1359**), and **Ted** (United's lower-cost carrier offers direct service from San Francisco and Denver; ② **800/225-5833** in the U.S.).

Aeromexico (② **322/224-2777** or 322/221-1055) flies from Los Angeles, San Diego, Aguascalientes, Guadalajara, La Paz, León, Mexico City, Morelia, and Tijuana. **Mexicana** (② **322/224-8900** or 322/221-1266) has direct or nonstop flights from Chicago, Los Angeles, Guadalajara, Mazatlán, and Mexico City.

Puerto Vallarta: Hotel Zone & Beaches

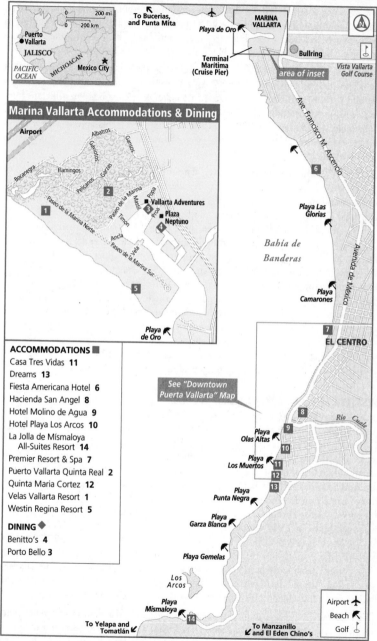

200 mi
200 km

Puerto Vallarta
JALISCO
PACIFIC OCEAN
MICHOACAN
Mexico City

To Bucerias, and Punta Mita

Playa de Oro

MARINA VALLARTA

Terminal Maritima (Cruise Pier)

Bullring

Vista Vallarta Golf Course

area of inset

Marina Vallarta Accommodations & Dining

Airport

Albatros
Gaviotas
Garbos
Flamingos
Pelicanos
Garzas
Bocanegra
Paseo de la Marina Norte
Paseo de la Marina
Popa
Proa
Mastil
Timon
Ancla
Paseo de la Vela
Paseo de la Marina Sur

Vallarta Adventures
Plaza Neptuno

Playa de Oro

Ave. Francisco M. Ascencio

Playa Las Glorias

Bahía de Banderas

Avenida de México

Playa Camarones

EL CENTRO

See "Downtown Puerta Vallarta" Map

Río Cuale

Playa Olas Altas

Playa Los Muertos

Playa Punta Negra

Playa Garza Blanca

Playa Gemelas

Los Arcos

Playa Mismaloya

To Yelapa and Tomatlán

To Manzanillo and El Eden Chino's

ACCOMMODATIONS ■

Casa Tres Vidas **11**
Dreams **13**
Fiesta Americana Hotel **6**
Hacienda San Angel **8**
Hotel Molino de Agua **9**
Hotel Playa Los Arcos **10**
La Jolla de Mísmaloya
 All-Suites Resort **14**
Premier Resort & Spa **7**
Puerto Vallarta Quinta Real **2**
Quinta Maria Cortez **12**
Velas Vallarta Resort **1**
Westin Regina Resort **5**

DINING ◆

Benitto's **4**
Porto Bello **3**

Airport ✈
Beach ☚
Golf ⛳

By Car The coastal **Highway 200** is the only choice from Mazatlán (6 hr. north) or Manzanillo (3½–4 hr. south). Highway 15 from Guadalajara to Tepic takes 6 hours; to save as much as 2 hours, take Highway 15A from Chapalilla to Compostela, bypassing Tepic, then continue south on Highway 200 to Puerto Vallarta.

By Bus The bus station, **Central Camionera de Puerto Vallarta,** is just north of the airport, approximately 11km (7 miles) from downtown. It offers overnight guarded parking and baggage storage. Most major first-class bus lines operate from here, with transportation to points throughout Mexico, including Mazatlán, Tepic, Manzanillo, Guadalajara, and Mexico City. Taxis into town cost approximately $7.50 and are readily available; public buses operate from 7am to 11pm and regularly stop in front of the arrivals hall.

ORIENTATION **Arriving by Plane** The airport is close to the north end of town near the Marina Vallarta, about 10km (6 miles) from downtown. **Transportes Terrestres** minivans and **Aeromovil** taxis make the trip. They use a zone pricing system, with fares clearly posted at the ticket booths. Fares start at $10 for a ride to Marina Vallarta and go up to $30 for the south shore hotels. Federally licensed airport taxis exclusively provide transportation from the airport, and their fares are more than three times as high as city (yellow) taxi fares. A trip to downtown Puerto Vallarta costs $20, whereas a return trip using a city taxi costs only $6. Only airport cabs may pick up passengers leaving the airport. However, if you don't have too much baggage, you can cross the highway using the new overpass, and there you'll find yellow cabs lined up. Note that now when you arrive at the International Arrivals gate, after you collect your baggage, you enter into an enclosed area with colorful wall displays and an aggressive group of seemingly helpful greeters—beware—these are timeshare hustlers, and their goal, often in the guise of offering you free or discounted transportation, is to get you to attend a timeshare presentation. Keep walking, just outside this booth are the bona fide taxi and transportation alternatives.

VISITOR INFORMATION Prior to arrival, a great source of general information is the **Puerto Vallarta Tourism Board** ⓒ 888/384-6822 in the U.S.; www.visitpuerto vallarta.com. If you have questions after you arrive, visit the **Municipal Tourism Office** at Juárez and Independencia (ⓒ 322/223-2500, ext. 230), a corner of the white Presidencia Municipal building (city hall) on the northwest end of the main square. In addition to offering a listing of current events and promotional brochures for local activities and services, the employees can also assist with specific questions—there's usually an English speaker on staff. This is also the office of the tourist police. It's open Monday through Friday from 8am to 4pm. During low season it may close for lunch between 2 and 4pm.

The **State Tourism Office,** Plaza Marina L 144, second floor (ⓒ 322/221-2676 or -2677; fax 322/221-2678), also offers brochures and can assist with specific questions about Puerto Vallarta and other points in the state of Jalisco, including Guadalajara, Costa Alegre, the town of Tequila, and the program that promotes stays in authentic rural haciendas. It's open Monday through Friday from 9am to 5pm.

CITY LAYOUT The seaside promenade, the *malecón,* is a common reference point for giving directions. It's next to **Paseo Díaz Ordaz** and runs north-south through the central downtown area. From the waterfront, the town stretches back into the hills a half-dozen blocks. The areas bordering the **Río Cuale** are the oldest parts of town— the original Puerto Vallarta. The area immediately south of the river, called **Olas Altas**

after its main street (and sometimes Los Muertos after the beach of the same name), is home to a growing selection of sidewalk cafes, fine restaurants, espresso bars, and hip nightclubs. In the center of town, nearly everything is within walking distance both north and south of the river. **Bridges** on Insurgentes (northbound traffic) and Ignacio Vallarta (southbound traffic) link the two sections of downtown.

AREA LAYOUT Beyond downtown, Puerto Vallarta has grown along the beach to the north and south. Linking downtown to the airport is **Avenida Francisco Medina Ascencio.** Along this main thoroughfare are many luxury hotels (in an area called the **Zona Hotelera,** or Hotel Zone), plus several shopping centers with casual restaurants.

Marina Vallarta, a resort city within a city, is at the northern edge of the Hotel Zone not far from the airport. It boasts modern luxury hotels, condominiums and homes, a huge marina with 450 yacht slips, a golf course, restaurants and bars, and several shopping plazas. Because it was originally a swamp, the beaches are the least desirable in the area, with darker sand and seasonal inflows of cobblestones. The Marina Vallarta peninsula faces the bay and looks south to the town of Puerto Vallarta.

Nuevo Vallarta is a planned resort north of the airport, across the Ameca River in the state of Nayarit (about 13km/8 miles north of downtown). It also has hotels, condominiums, and a yacht marina, with a limited selection of restaurants and shopping, although the new Paradise Plaza mall is bringing in new options. Most hotels there are all-inclusive, with some of the finest beaches in the bay, but guests usually travel into Puerto Vallarta (about a $13 cab ride) for anything other than poolside or beach action. Regularly scheduled public bus service costs about $1.50 and runs until 10pm.

Bucerías, a small beachside village of cobblestone streets, villas, and small hotels, is farther north along Banderas Bay, 30km (19 miles) beyond the airport. Past Bucerías, following the curved coastline of Banderas Bay to the end of the road is **Punta Mita.** Once a rustic fishing village, it is in the process of development as a luxury destination. In the works are a total of five exclusive luxury boutique resorts, private villas, and three golf courses. The site of an ancient celestial observatory, it is an exquisite setting, with white-sand beaches and clear waters. The northern shore of Banderas Bay is emerging as the area's most exclusive address for luxury villas and accommodations.

In the other direction from downtown is the southern coastal highway, home to more luxury hotels. Immediately south of town lies the exclusive residential and rental district of **Conchas Chinas.** Ten kilometers (6 miles) south, on **Playa Mismaloya** (where *Night of the Iguana* was filmed), lies the Jolla de Mismaloya resort. There's no road on the southern shoreline of Banderas Bay, but three small coastal villages are popular attractions for visitors to Puerto Vallarta: **Las Animas, Quimixto,** and **Yelapa,** all accessible only by boat. The tiny, pristine cove of **Caletas,** site of John Huston's former home, is a popular day- or nighttime excursion (see "Boat Tours," later in this chapter).

GETTING AROUND **By Taxi** Taxis are plentiful and relatively inexpensive. Most trips from downtown to the northern Hotel Zone and Marina Vallarta cost

---

Tips **Steer Clear of the Rambo Bus!**

Buses in Vallarta tend to be rather aggressive, and some even sport names—including "Terminator," "Rambo," and "Tornado." Don't tempt fate by assuming these buses will stop for pedestrians. Although Vallarta has an extremely low crime rate, bus accidents are frequent—and frequently fatal.

$3.50 to $7; to or from Marina Vallarta to Mismaloya Beach (to the south) costs $10. Rates are charged by zone and are generally posted in the lobbies of hotels. Taxis can also be hired by the hour or day for longer trips. Rates run $12 to $15 per hour, with discounts available for full-day rates—consider this an alternative to renting a car.

By Car   Rental cars are available at the airport and through travel agencies, but unless you're planning a distant side trip, don't bother. Car rentals are expensive, averaging $66 per day, and parking around town is difficult. If you see a sign for a $10 jeep rental or $20 car rental, be aware that these are lures to get people to attend timeshare presentations. Unless you are interested in a timeshare, stopping to inquire will be a waste of your time.

By Bus   City buses, easy to navigate and inexpensive, will serve just about all your transportation needs. They run from the airport through the Hotel Zone along Morelos Street (1 block inland from the *malecón*), across the Río Cuale, and inland on Vallarta, looping back through the downtown hotel and restaurant districts on Insurgentes and several other downtown streets. To get to the northern hotel strip from old Puerto Vallarta, take the ZONA HOTELES, IXTAPA, or LAS JUNTAS bus. These buses may also post the names of hotels they pass, such as Krystal, Fiesta Americana, Sheraton, and others. Buses marked MARINA VALLARTA travel inside this area, stopping at the major hotels there.

Other buses operate every 10 to 15 minutes south to either Mismaloya Beach or Boca de Tomatlán (a sign in the front window indicates the destination) from Constitución and Basilio Badillo, a few blocks south of the river.

Buses run generally from 6am to 11pm, and it's rare to wait more than a few minutes for one. The fare is about 50¢.

By Boat   The cruise ship pier *(muelle)*, also called Terminal Marítima, is where **excursion boats** to Yelapa, Las Animas, Quimixto, and the Marietas Islands depart. It's north of town near the airport, an inexpensive taxi or bus ride from town. Just take any bus marked IXTAPA, LAS JUNTAS, PITILLAL, or AURORA and tell the driver to let you off at the Terminal Marítima. *Note:* Odd though it may seem, you must pay a $1.50 fee (this is a federal tax) to gain access to the pier—and your departing excursion boat.

Water taxis to Yelapa, Las Animas, and Quimixto leave at 10:30 and 11am from the pier at Los Muertos Beach (south of downtown), on Rodolfo Rodríguez next to the Hotel Marsol. Another water taxi departs at 11am from the beachside pier at the northern edge of the *malecón*. A round-trip ticket to Yelapa (the farthest point) costs $25. Return trips usually depart between 3 and 4pm, but confirm the pickup time with your water taxi captain. Other water taxis depart from Boca de Tomatlán, about 30 minutes south of town by public bus. These water taxis are the better option if you want more flexible departure and return times from the southern beaches. Generally, they leave on the hour for the southern shore destinations, or more frequently if there is traffic. Prices run about $12 round-trip, with rates now clearly posted on a sign on

---

⎛Tips Don't Let Taxi Drivers Steer You Wrong

Beware of restaurant recommendations offered by taxi drivers—many receive a commission from restaurants where they discharge passengers. Be especially wary if a driver tries to talk you out of a restaurant you've already selected.

the beach. A private water taxi costs $35 to $55 (depending on your destination) and allows you to choose your own return time. They'll take up to eight people for that price, so often people band together at the beach to hire one.

FAST FACTS: Puerto Vallarta

American Express The local office is at Morelos 660, at the corner of Abasolo (© **01-800/504-0400** and 01-800/333-3211 in Mexico, or 322/223-2955). It's open Monday through Friday from 9am to 6pm, Saturday from 9am to 1pm. It offers excellent, efficient travel agency services in addition to money exchange and traveler's checks.

Area Code The telephone area code is **322**.

Climate It's warm all year, with tropical temperatures; however, evenings and early mornings in the winter can turn quite cool. Summers are sunny, with an increase in humidity during the rainy season, between May and October. Rains come almost every afternoon in June and July, and are usually brief but strong—just enough to cool off the air for evening activities. In September, heat and humidity are least comfortable and rains heaviest.

Consumer Assistance Tourists with complaints about taxis, stores, abusive timeshare presentations, or other matters should contact **PROFECO**, the consumer protection office (© **322/225-0000**; fax 322/225-0018). The office is open Monday through Friday from 8:30am to 3:30pm and may not have fluent English-speaking staff.

Currency Exchange Banks are found throughout downtown and in the other prime shopping areas. Most banks are open Monday through Friday from 9am to 5pm, with shorter hours on Saturday. ATMs are common throughout Vallarta, including the central plaza downtown. They are becoming the most favorable way to exchange currency, with bank rates plus 24-hour convenience. Money exchange houses *(casas de cambio),* located throughout town, offer longer hours than the banks with only slightly lower exchange rates.

Embassies & Consulates The consulates are in a building on the southern border of the central plaza (you'll see the U.S. and Canadian flags). The **U.S. Consular Agency** office (© **322/222-0069**; fax 322/223-0074, 24 hr. a day for emergencies) is open Monday through Friday from 10am to 2pm. The **Canadian Consulate** (© **322/293-0099** or 322/293-0098; 24-hr. emergency line 01-800/706-2900) is open Monday through Friday from 9am to 3pm.

Emergencies **Police** emergency, © **060**; local police, © **322/290-0513** or -0512; intensive care **ambulance,** © **322/225-0386** (*Note:* English-speaking assistance is not always available at this number); **Red Cross,** © **322/222-1533; Global Life Ambulance Service** (provides both ground and air ambulance service), © **322/226-1010,** ext. 304.

Hospitals The following offer U.S.-standards service and are available 24 hours: **Ameri-Med Urgent Care,** Avenida Francisco Medina Ascencio at Plaza Neptuno, Local D-1, Marina Vallarta (© **322/221-0023**; fax 322/221-0026; www.amerimed-hospitals.com); and **San Javier Marina Hospital,** Av. Francisco Medina Ascencio 2760, Zona Hotelera (© **322/226-1010**).

Internet Access Puerto Vallarta is probably the most wired destination in Mexico. **The Net House,** Ignacio L. Vallarta 232 (© 322/222-6953; info@vallartacafes. com), 2 blocks past the southbound bridge, has 15 computers with fast connections and English keyboards. It's open daily from 8am to 2am and charges $3.50 per hour. **Café.com** (© 322/222-0092), Olas Altas 250, at the corner of Basilio Badillo, charges $2 for 30 minutes. It offers complete computer services, a full bar, and food service. It's open daily from 8am to 2am. Some hotels have lobby e-mail kiosks, but they're more expensive than the Net cafes.

Newspapers & Magazines **Vallarta Today,** a daily English-language newspaper (© **322/225-3323** or 322/224-2829), is a good source for local information and upcoming events. The bilingual quarterly city magazine **Vallarta Lifestyles** (© **322/221-0106**) is also very popular. Both are for sale at area newsstands and hotel gift shops. The weekly English-language *P.V. Tribune* (© **322/223-0585**) is distributed free throughout town and offers an objective local viewpoint.

Pharmacies **CMQ Farmacia,** Basilio Badillo 365 (© **322/222-1330**), is open 24 hours and makes free deliveries to hotels between 11am and 10pm with a minimum purchase of $20. **Farmacias Guadalajara,** Emiliano Zapata 232 (© **322/ 224-1811**), is also open 24 hours.

Post Office The *correo* is at Mina 188 (© **322/222-1888**). It's open Monday through Friday from 9am to 6pm, Saturday from 9am to 1pm. A second location, on Colombia St., behind Hidalgo park, is open the same hours.

Safety Puerto Vallarta enjoys a very low crime rate. Public transportation is safe to use, and Tourist Police (dressed in white safari uniforms with white hats) are available to answer questions, give directions, and offer assistance. Most encounters with the police are linked to using or purchasing drugs—so don't (see chapter 2). *Note:* The tourist police conduct random personal searches for drugs. Although there is some question about their right to do this, the best course of action if they want to frisk you is to comply—objecting will likely result in a free tour of the local jail. However, you are within your rights to request the name of the officer. Report any unusual incidents to the local consular office.

BEACHES, ACTIVITIES & EXCURSIONS

Travel agencies can provide information on what to see and do in Puerto Vallarta and can arrange tours, fishing trips, and other activities. Most hotels have a tour desk on-site. Of the many travel agencies in town, I highly recommend **Tukari Servicios Turísticos,** Av. España 316 (© **322/224-7177;** fax 322/224-2350), which specializes in ecological and cultural tours. Another source is **Xplora Adventours** (© **322/223-0661**), in the Huichol Collection shop on the *malecón*. It has listings of all locally available tours, with photos, explanations, and costs; however, be aware that a timeshare resort owns the company, so part of the information you receive will be an invitation to a presentation, which you may decline. **American Express Travel Services,** Morelos 660 (© 322/223-2955), also has a varied selection of high-quality, popular tours. One of the tour companies with the largest—and best quality—selection of boat cruises and land tours is **Vallarta Adventures** ✦✦✦ (© **866/256-2739** toll-free in the U.S., or 322/297-1212, ext. 3;

(Moments) Special Events in Puerto Vallarta

Each November, the annual **Gourmet Festival** (www.festivalgourmet.com) is a standout reason to come here, with an agenda filled with culinary exhibitions, wine tastings, and guest chefs preparing special menus at area restaurants. In its second year, the **Film Festival of the Americas** (www.puertovallartafilm.com) features film screenings, panel discussions with celebrity guests, and gala events. Dates vary; call the Tourism Board ((©) **888/384-6822** in the U.S.) for dates and schedule. From December 1 to December 12, the **Festival of the Virgin of Guadalupe** ⚜—Mexico's patron saint—inspires one of the most authentic displays of culture and community in Mexico. Businesses, neighborhoods, associations, and groups make pilgrimages (called *peregrinaciones*) to the church, where they exchange offerings for a brief blessing by the priest. These processions, especially those created by hotels, often include floats, Aztec dancers, and mariachis, and are followed by fireworks. Hotels frequently invite guests to participate in the walk to the church. It's an event not to be missed.

www.vallarta-adventures.com). I can highly recommend any of their offerings. Book with them directly and get a 10% discount when you mention Frommer's.

THE BEACHES

For years, beaches were Puerto Vallarta's main attraction. Although visitors today are exploring more of the surrounding geography, the sands are still a powerful draw. Over 42km (26 miles) of beaches extend around the broad Bay of Banderas, ranging from action-packed party spots to secluded coves accessible only by boat.

IN TOWN   The easiest to reach is **Playa Los Muertos** (also known as Playa Olas Altas or Playa del Sol), just off Calle Olas Altas, south of the Río Cuale. The water can be rough, but the wide beach is home to a wide array of *palapa* restaurants that offer food, beverage, and beach-chair service. The most popular are the adjacent El Dorado and La Palapa, at the end of Pulpito Street. On the southern end of this beach is a section known as "Blue Chairs"—the most popular gay beach. Vendors stroll Los Muertos, and beach volleyball, parasailing, and jet-skiing are all popular pastimes. The **Hotel Zone** is also known for its broad, smooth beaches, accessible primarily through the hotel lobbies.

SOUTH OF TOWN   **Playa Mismaloya** is in a beautiful sheltered cove about 10km (6 miles) south of town along Highway 200. The water is clear and beautiful, ideal for snorkeling off the beach. Entrance to the public beach is just to the left of the **Jolla de Mismaloya All-Suites Resort** ((©) **322/226-0600**). The movie *Night of the Iguana* was filmed at Mismaloya, and the resort has a restaurant on the restored film set—**La Noche de la Iguana Set Restaurant,** open daily from noon to 11pm. The movie runs continuously in a room below the restaurant, and still photos from the filming hang in the restaurant. The restaurant is accessible by land on the point framing the south side of the cove. Just below the restaurant is **John Huston's Bar & Grill,** serving drinks and light snacks daily from 11am to 6pm.

The beach at **Boca de Tomatlán,** just down the road, has numerous *palapa* restaurants where you can relax for the day—you buy drinks, snacks, or lunch, and you can use their chairs and *palapa* shade.

The two beaches are accessible by public buses, which depart from the corner of Basilio Badillo and Insurgentes every 15 minutes from 5:30am to 10pm and cost just 50¢.

Las Animas, Quimixto, and **Yelapa** beaches offer a true sense of seclusion; they are accessible only by boat (see "Getting Around," above, for information about water-taxi service). They are larger than Mismaloya, offer intriguing hikes to jungle water-falls, and are similarly set up, with restaurants fronting a wide beach. Overnight stays are available at Yelapa (see "Side Trips from Puerto Vallarta," later in this chapter).

NORTH OF TOWN The beaches at **Marina Vallarta** are the least desirable in the area, with darker sand and seasonal inflows of stones.

The entire northern coastline from Bucerías to Punta Mita is a succession of sandy coves alternating with rocky inlets. For years the beaches to the north, with their long, clean breaks, have been the favored locale for surfers. The broad, sandy stretches at **Playa Anclote, Playa Piedras Blancas,** and **Playa Destiladeras,** which all have *palapa* restaurants, have made them favorites with local residents looking for a quick getaway. At Playa Anclote you'll find a broad, sandy beach with protected swimming areas and a few great *palapa* (thatched roof) restaurants. Of the restaurants, El Anclote and El Dorado have been the long-standing favorites, but **Mañana,** by Chef Roger (© **329/291-6374**), is raising the culinary bar of this casual dining area. It's open Tuesday through Sunday 10am to 9pm, in summer 1 to 9pm. All have beach chairs available for your postmargarita nap in the sun.

You can also hire a *panga* (small motorized boat) at Playa Anclote from the fisher-man's cooperative on the beach and have the captain take you to the **Marietas Islands** ✦✦✦ just offshore. These uninhabited islands are a great place for bird-watching, diving, snorkeling, or just exploring. Blue-footed booby birds (no joke) can be spotted all along the islands' rocky coast, and giant mantas, sea turtles, and colorful tropical fish swim among the coral cliffs. The islands are honeycombed with caves and hidden beaches—including the stunning Playa de Amor (beach of love) that only appears at low tide. You enter a shallow passageway to access this semicir-cular stretch of sand. There's also a cave 12m (40 ft.) below the surface with an air pocket where divers can dispose of their regulators and have an underwater conver-sation! Humpback whales congregate around these islands during the winter months, and *pangas* can be rented for a do-it-yourself whale-watching excursion. Trips cost about $20 per hour. You can also visit these islands aboard one of the numerous day cruises that depart from the cruise-ship terminal in Puerto Vallarta.

The stellar white-sand beach at **Punta Mita,** home of the Four Seasons, is closed to road access, except for guests of this residential resort development.

One option for visiting a north shore beach is to spend a day at the **Los Veneros Beach Club** (© **329/291-7082,** ext. 123 or 125, or 329/291-7085), 32km (20 miles) north of Puerto Vallarta, just past Destiladeras beach on the highway to Punta Mita. To get there, take a taxi, a public bus bound for Punta Mita. Two pools—one reserved for adults—and marble bathrooms with changing rooms and showers complement an exquisite beach. There's also a *palapa*-topped restaurant and bar, gym, kids' play area with water slides and splashes, and small shopping area. The entrance fee of $12 for adults, $8 for children, includes towel service, and the use of all the facilities for the day. Extra charges apply for food, drinks, horseback riding, or massage. It's open daily from 10am to 6pm.

ORGANIZED TOURS

BOAT TOURS Puerto Vallarta offers a number of boat trips, including sunset cruises and snorkeling, swimming, and diving excursions. They generally travel one of two routes: to the **Marietas Islands,** a 30- to 45-minute boat ride off the northern shore of Banderas Bay, or to **Yelapa, Las Animas,** or **Quimixto** along the southern shore. The trips to the southern beaches make a stop at **Los Arcos,** an island rock formation south of Puerto Vallarta, for snorkeling. Don't base your opinion of under-water Puerto Vallarta on this, though—dozens of tour boats dump quantities of snorkelers overboard at the same time each day, exactly when the fish know *not* to be there. It is, however, an excellent site for night diving. When comparing boat cruises, note that some include lunch, while most provide music and an open bar on board. Most leave around 9:30am, stop for 45 minutes of snorkeling, and arrive at the beach destination around noon for a 2½-hour stay before returning around 3pm. At Quim-ixto and Yelapa, visitors can take a half-hour hike to a jungle waterfall or rent a horse for the ride. Prices range from $45 for a sunset cruise or a trip to one of the beaches with open bar, to $85 for an all-day outing with open bar and meals.

One boat, the *Marigalante* (© 322/223-0309; www.marigalante.com.mx), is an exact replica of Columbus's ship the *Santa María,* built in honor of the 500th anniversary of his voyage to the Americas. It features a daytime "pirate's cruise" ($65 per person), complete with picnic barbecue and treasure hunt, and a sunset dinner cruise ($70 per person) with fireworks and disco dance. Children ages 3 to 8 are half-price.

One of the best trips is a day trip to **Caletas** ⭑⭑, the cove where John Huston made his home for years. **Vallarta Adventures** (© 866/256-2739 toll-free in the U.S., or 322/297-1212, ext. 3; www.vallarta-adventures.com) holds the exclusive lease on the private cove and has done an excellent job of restoring Huston's former home, adding exceptional day-spa facilities and landscaping the beach, which is wonderful for snorkeling. They also have a colony of sea lions that play with the visiting divers! You'll have a hard time deciding whether to kayak, take a yoga class, hike through sur-rounding trails, or simply relax in the hammocks strung between palms on the beach. The facilities and relative privacy have made this excursion ($75 per person; $38 for children under 12) one of the most popular. The evening cruise includes dinner and a spectacular contemporary dance show, "Rhythms of the Night" (see "Puerto Vallarta After Dark," later in this chapter).

Travel agencies sell tickets and distribute information on all cruises. If you prefer to spend more time at Yelapa or Las Animas without snorkeling and cruise entertain-ment, see the information about travel by water taxis, earlier in this chapter, under "Getting Around."

Whale-watching tours become more popular each year. Viewing humpback whales is almost a certainty from mid- to late November to March. The majestic whales have migrated to this bay for centuries (in the 17th c. it was called "Hump-back Bay") to bear their calves. The noted local authority is **Open Air Expeditions,** Guerrero 339 (©/fax 322/222-3310; www.vallartawhales.com). It offers ecologically oriented, oceanologist-guided 4-hour tours on the soft boat *Prince of Whales,* the only boat in Vallarta specifically designed for whale-watching. Cost is $80, and travel is in a group of up to 12. Twice-daily departures (8:30am and 2:30pm) include a healthful snack. **Vallarta Adventures** (© 866/256-2739 toll-free in the U.S., or 322/297-1212, ext. 3; www.vallarta-adventures.com) offers a variety of whale-watching excur-sions that may combine time for snorkeling, or simply focus on photographing these exquisite mammals. Prices range from $65 to $80, and offer a choice of boat, ranging from small boats to bring you closest for photos, to graceful sailboats. All trips include a predeparture briefing on whale behaviors.

LAND TOURS **Tukari Servicios Turísticos** (see "Beaches, Activities & Excursions," above) can arrange trips to the fertile birding grounds near **San Blas,** 3 to 4 hours north of Puerto Vallarta in the state of Nayarit, and shopping trips to **Tlaquepaque** and **Tonalá** (6 hr. inland, near Guadalajara). A day trip to **Rancho Altamira,** a 20-hectare (50-acre) working ranch, includes a barbecue lunch and horseback riding, then a stroll through **El Tuito,** a small nearby colonial-era village. The company can also arrange an unforgettable morning at **Terra Noble Art & Healing Center** ★★ (© 322/223-3530 or 322/222-5400), a mountaintop day spa and center for the arts where participants can get a massage, *temazcal* (ancient, indigenous sweat lodge), or treatment, work in clay and paint, and have lunch in a heavenly setting overlooking the bay. Call ahead for reservations, and make sure to advise if you want to have lunch there.

Hotel travel desks and travel agencies, including Tukari and American Express, can also book the popular **Tropical Tour** or **Jungle Tour** ($25), a basic orientation to the area. These excursions are expanded city tours that include a drive through the workers' village of Pitillal, the affluent neighborhood of Conchas Chinas, the cathedral, the market, the Taylor-Burton houses, and lunch at a jungle restaurant. Any stop for shopping usually means the driver picks up a commission for what you buy.

The **Jeep Safari** is another excellent tour offered by **Vallarta Adventures** (© 866/256-2739 toll-free in the U.S., or 322/297-1212, ext. 3; www.vallarta-adventures. com). The daily excursion travels in Mercedes all-terrain vehicles north of Puerto Vallarta through jungle trails, stops at a small town, ventures into a forest for a brief nature walk, and winds up on a pristine secluded beach for lunch and swimming. The $75 outing is worthwhile because it takes tourists on exclusive trails into scenery that would otherwise be off-limits.

AIR TOURS Speaking of off-limits, you can explore some of the most remote and undiscovered reaches of the Sierra Madre mountains in Vallarta Adventures' **San Sebastián Air Expedition** (© 866/256-2739 toll-free in the U.S., or 322/297-1212, ext. 3; www.vallarta-adventures.com). A 15-minute flight aboard a 14-seat turbo-prop Cessna Caravan takes you into the heart of the Sierra Madre. The plane is equipped with raised wings, which allow you to admire—and photograph—the mountain scenery. The plane arrives on a gravel landing strip in the old mining town of San Sebastián, a beautiful village that dates from 1603. One of the oldest mining towns in Mexico, it reached its prosperous peak in the 1800s, with over 30,000 inhabitants. Today, San Sebastián remains an outstanding example of how people lived and worked in a remote Mexican mountain town—it's a living museum. The half-day adventure costs $130, which covers the flight, a walking tour of the town (including a stop at the old Hacienda Jalisco, a favored getaway of John Huston, Liz and Dick, and their friends), and brunch in town. Other excursions include overnight stays and return trips by bike or horseback. There's also a **Jeep tour** to San Sebastián, which costs $75 per person, for up to four people per Jeep, and includes a guide. This tour departs at 9am and returns at 5pm. Call Pacific Travel (© **322/225-2270**) to make reservations.

Vallarta Adventures (© **866/256-2739** toll-free in the U.S., or 322/297-1212, ext. 3; www.vallarta-adventures.com) also offers a similar—yet different—air tour to the mountain villages of **Mascota** and **Talpa de Allende** ★★, where you'll learn about the religious significance of these traditional towns. In Mascota, stroll the cobblestone streets lined with adobe houses and colonial haciendas, stopping at the majestic town church, dedicated to the Virgin de los Dolores (Virgin of Sorrows), which was completed in 1880 and took over 100 years to construct. You'll stop for lunch and tour a local raicilla distillery to sample this locally popular beverage before traveling on to Talpa. Talpa is known for being home to one of Mexico's most revered icons, the Virgin Rosario de Talpa, believed to grant miracles with her healing powers. Ask for one yourself, as you visit the Gothic church that bears her name, or simply wander around this pastoral village, set in a valley that is surrounded by pine covered mountains. The 6-hour adventure includes airfare and lunch, for $140 per person. Departures are daily, except Wednesdays and Sundays, at 10:30am, from Aerotron.

Anyone up for a taste of Tequila? We're talking about the town, and a sampling of the best of the spirit of Mexico. Vallarta Adventures (see above) offers a trip that takes you to the classic town, where you visit one of the original haciendas and tequila (agave) fields. A comfortable 35-minute flight aboard a private 16-passenger plane takes you to the town of **Tequila.** This is the only region in the world where the legendary spirit is distilled. The visit centers around Herradura Tequila's impressive 18th-century Hacienda San José, where you learn about the myth and the tradition of producing tequila from the stately plants that line the hillsides of the town. From Tequila, you'll travel by plane on to Guadalajara, one of Mexico's largest cities, with a rich colonial heritage, for some time to shop at the world-renown markets of Tlaquepaque. Departures are every Thursday at 10am from the Aerotron private airport (adjacent to the Puerto Vallarta International Airport); the group returns to Puerto Vallarta by 8pm. Cost is $290, which includes all air and ground transportation, tours, lunch, and beverages.

Vallarta Adventures also offers air tours to remote mountain villages where the **Huichol Indians** live, as well as to the **Copper Canyon,** and the mystical village of **Mexcaltitan,** all departing from Puerto Vallarta. Details and online booking options are available at www.vallarta-adventures.com.

TOURS IN TOWN Every Wednesday and Thursday in high season (late Nov to Easter), the **International Friendship Club** (© 322/222-5466) offers a **private home tour** of four villas in town. It costs $30 per person, with proceeds donated to local charities. Arrive early, because this tour sells out quickly. It starts at the Hotel Molino de Agua, Av. Ignacio L. Vallarta 130, adjacent to the southbound bridge over the Río Cuale. Get there at 10am, and you can buy breakfast while you wait for the group to gather. The tour departs at 11am and lasts approximately 2½ hours.

You can also tour the **Taylor/Burton villas** (Casa Kimberley; © 322/222-1336), at Calle Zaragoza 445. Tours of the two houses owned by Elizabeth Taylor and Richard Burton cost $8. Call ahead daily between 9am and 6pm, and if the manager is available, he will take you through the house.

STAYING ACTIVE

DIVING Underwater enthusiasts from beginner to expert can arrange scuba diving through **Vallarta Adventures** (© 866/256-2739 toll-free in the U.S., or 322/297-1212, ext. 3; www.vallarta-adventures.com), a five-star PADI dive center. Dives take place at Los Arcos, a company-owned site at Caletas Cove (where you'll dive in the company of sea lions!), Quimixto Coves, the Marietas Islands, or the offshore La Corbeteña, Morro, and Chimo reefs. The company also offers a full range of certification courses (through Instructor). **Chico's Dive Shop,** Díaz Ordaz 772–5, near Carlos O'Brian's (© 322/222-1895; www.chicos-diveshop.com), offers similar dive trips and is also a PADI five-star dive center. Chico's is open daily from 8am to 10pm and has branches at the Marriott, Las Palmas, Holiday Inn, Fiesta Americana, Krystal, San Marino, Villa del Palmar, Paradise Village, and Playa Los Arcos hotels.

ECOTOURS & ACTIVITIES   **Open Air Expeditions** (②/fax **322/222-3310;** www. vallartawhales.com) offers nature-oriented trips, including birding and ocean kayaking in Punta Mita. **Ecotours de México,** Ignacio L. Vallarta 243 (②/fax **322/222-6606**), has eco-oriented tours, including seasonal (Aug–Nov) trips to a turtle preservation camp where you can witness hatching baby Olive Ridley turtles.

Vallarta's newest adventure activity is **Canopy Tours.** You glide from treetop to treetop, getting an up-close-and-personal look at a tropical rainforest canopy and the trails far below. Expert guides assist you to the special platforms, and you move from one to another using pulleys on horizontal traverse cables, while the guides explain the tropical flora surrounding you. They also offer assistance—and moral support!—as you rappel back down to the forest floor. Tours depart from the **Vallarta Adventures** (② **866/ 256-2739** toll-free in the U.S., or 322/297-1212, ext. 3; www.vallarta-adventures. com) offices in both Marina Vallarta and Nuevo Vallarta at 8am, returning at 2pm. The price ($65 for adults, $33 for children 8–12) includes the tour, unlimited nonalcoholic beverages, and light snacks.

A second option is available in the southern jungles of Vallarta, over the Orquidias River, through **Canopy Tours de Los Veranos** (② **322/223-6060;** www.canopytours-vallarta.com). This tour will pick you up at the Canopy office, near the south side Pemex station to transport you to their facilities upriver from Mismaloya. Departures are at 9, 10, and 11am, noon, and 1 and 2pm. In addition to the 13 cables—the longest being a full 350m (115 ft.)—it also offers climbing walls, waterslides, and horseback riding. The guides here are noted for helping even the faintest of heart propel through the treetops. Price is $80 for adults, or $46 for children. Use of the natural-granite climbing wall (helmets and climbing shoe use included) is $18; the 1½-hour jungle horseback riding tour costs $35.

FISHING   Arrange fishing trips through travel agencies or through the **Cooperativa de Pescadores (Fishing Cooperative),** on the *malecón* north of the Río Cuale, next door to the Rosita Hotel (② **322/222-1202** or 322/224-7886). Fishing charters cost $90, for one to eight people; or select from other options where the price varies with the size of the boat. Although the posted price at the fishing cooperative is the same as you'll find through travel agencies, you may be able to negotiate a lower price at the cooperative, which does not accept credit cards. It's open Monday through Saturday from 7am to 10pm, but make arrangements a day ahead. You can also arrange fishing trips at the Marina Vallarta docks, or by calling **Fishing with Carolina** (② **322/ 224-7250;** cell 044-322/292-2953; fishingwithcarolina@hotmail.com), which uses a 9m (30-ft.) Uniflite sportsfisher, fully equipped with an English-speaking crew. Fishing trips cost $350 for up to six people and include equipment and bait, but drinks, snacks, and lunch are optional, at $10 per person. If you mention Frommer's when you make your reservation, they'll offer a free lunch with your booking.

GOLF   Puerto Vallarta is an increasingly popular golf destination; five courses have opened in the past 4 years, bringing the total in the region to nine. The Joe Finger–designed private course at the **Marina Vallarta Golf Club** (② **322/221-0073**) is an 18-hole, par-74 course that winds through the Marina Vallarta peninsula and affords ocean views. It's for members only, but most luxury hotels in Puerto Vallarta have memberships for their guests. Greens fees are $136 in high season, $115 in low season. Fees include golf cart, range balls, and tax. Hiring a caddy costs $8 to $10. Club rentals, lessons, and special packages are available.

North of town in the state of Nayarit, about 16km (10 miles) beyond Puerto Vallarta, is the 18-hole, par-72 **Los Flamingos Club de Golf** (© 329/296-5006). It features beautiful jungle vegetation and has just undergone a renovation and upgrade of the course. It's open from 7am to 5pm daily, with a snack bar (but no restaurant) and full pro shop. The greens fee is $95 and includes the use of a golf cart; hiring a caddy costs $12 plus tip, and club rental is $27 to $44. A free shuttle runs from downtown Puerto Vallarta; call for pickup times and locations.

The breathtaking Jack Nicklaus Signature course at the **Four Seasons Punta Mita** ★★★ (© 329/291-6000; fax 329/291-6060) has eight oceanfront holes and an ocean view from every hole. Its hallmark is the optional Hole 3B, the "Tail of the Whale," with a long drive to a green on a natural island—the only natural-island green in the Americas. It requires an amphibious cart to take you over when the tide is high, and there's an alternate hole for when the ocean or tides are not accommodating. It's open only to guests of the Four Seasons resort or to members of other golf clubs with a letter of introduction from their pro. Selected other area hotels also have guest privileges—ask your concierge. Greens fees for nonguests are $260, including cart, with (Calloway) club rentals for $60. Lessons are also available.

A second Jack Nicklaus course is at the **Vista Vallarta Golf Club** (© 322/290-0030), along with one designed by Tom Weiskopf. These courses were the site of the 2002 PGA World Cup Golf Championships. It's in the foothills of the Sierra Madre, behind the bullring in Puerto Vallarta. A round costs $167 per person, including cart.

The Robert von Hagge–designed **El Tigre** course at Paradise Village (© 322/297-0773; www.paradisevillage.com), in Nuevo Vallarta, opened in March 2002. The 7,239-yard course is on a relatively flat piece of land, but the design incorporates challenging bunkers, undulating fairways, and water features on several holes. El Tigre also offers lessons and has an expansive clubhouse. This seems to be the favored course of local pros. Greens fees are $185 a round, or $85 if you play after 2pm.

HORSEBACK-RIDING TOURS   Travel agents and local ranches can arrange guided horseback rides. **Rancho Palma Real,** Carretera Vallarta, Tepic 4766 (© 322/222-0501), has an office 5 minutes north of the airport; the ranch is in Las Palmas, approximately 40 minutes northeast of Vallarta. It is by far the nicest horseback riding tour in the area. The horses are in excellent condition, and you enjoy a tour of local farms on your way to the ranch. The price ($62; American Express only) includes breakfast and lunch.

Another excellent option is **Rancho El Charro,** Av. Francisco Villa 895 (© 322/224-0114; cell 322/294-1689; www.ranchoelcharro.com), which has beautiful well-cared for horses, and a variety of rides for all levels, departing from their ranch at the base of the Sierra Madre Mountains. Rides range in length from 3 hours to 8 hours, and in price from $47 to $100. There's even the $60 Wild Ride, where you gallop along a ridge to a jungle waterfall—too often, riders are disappointed with only trotting along well-marked trails on these excurions, and this ride allows experienced riders much more freedom. Rancho El Charro also has multiple-day rides, check their web site for details. **Rancho Ojo de Agua,** Cerrada de Cardenal 227, Fracc. Las Aralias (©/fax 322/224-0607), also offers high-quality tours, from its ranch located 10 minutes by taxi north of downtown toward the Sierra Madre foothills. The morning and sunset rides last 3 hours and take you up into the mountains overlooking the ocean and town. The cost is $52. Both of the ranches listed above have their own comfortable base camp for serious riders who want to stay out overnight.

SAILING   The newest addition to Vallarta's sailing scene is most impressive—**Coming About** ✦✦ (© **322/222-4119;** www.coming-about.com) is a women-only sailing school that provides hands-on sailing instruction for day-sailing excursions, as well as week-long sailing classes at a variety of skill levels. Owned and operated by Pat Henry, who spent 8 years sailing around the globe, then wrote about it in her book *"By the Grace of the Sea: A Woman's Solo Odyssey Around the World"* the classes are challenging, inspiring, and entertaining, as Pat shares her adventures with participants. Dubbed "any woman's sailing school," the goal is to take away the fear and the mystery, and make the skill of sailing accessible to everyone. Courses range from a 1-day introductory course to a 9-day bareboat charter captain course. Fees for the 1-day course are $475 for four people; $2,800 to $3,600 for the 9-day course, including hotel.

Vallarta Adventures (© **866/256-2739** toll-free in the U.S., or 322/297-1212, ext. 3; www.vallarta-adventures.com) offers two beautiful sailboats for charter or small-group sails (up to 12 people). Daytime sailing charters are priced at $80 per person, where sunset sails are $60 per person. The service is superb, as is the quality of the food and beverages, making it, in my opinion, one of the very best ways to spend a Vallarta evening. These are known as the boats that are most frequently under sail—many other sailing charters prefer to motor around the bay.

SWIMMING WITH DOLPHINS   Ever been kissed by a dolphin? Take advantage of a unique opportunity to swim with Pacific bottlenose dolphins in one of two facilities—a clear lagoon or a special swim facility that's part of the Vallarta Adventures offices. **Dolphin Adventure** ✦✦✦ (© **866/256-2739** toll-free in the U.S., or 322/ 297-1212, ext. 3; www.vallarta-adventures.com) operates an interactive dolphin-research facility—considered the finest in Latin America—that allows limited numbers of people to swim with dolphins Monday through Saturday at scheduled times. Cost for the swim is $145. Reservations are required, and they generally sell out at least a week in advance. You may prefer the **Dolphin Encounter** ($60), which allows you to touch and learn about the dolphins in smaller pools, so you're ensured up-close-and-personal time with them. You can even be a **Trainer for a Day,** a special 7-hour program of working alongside the more experienced trainers and the dolphins, for a cost of $250. The new **Dolphin Kids** program, for children ages 4 to 8, is a gentle introduction to dolphins, featuring the Dolphin Adventure baby dolphins and their mothers interacting with the children participants ($60). I give this my highest recommendation. Not only does the experience leave you with an indescribable sensation, but it's also a joy to see these dolphins—they are well cared for, happy, and spirited. The program is about education and interaction, not entertainment or amusement, and is especially popular with children 10 and older.

Tips **A Spectator Sport**

Bullfights are held December through April beginning at 5pm on Wednesday at the La Paloma bullring, across the highway from the town pier. Travel agencies can arrange tickets, which cost around $25.

Tips **A Spectacular Sight**

Performances of the **Papantla Flyers (Voladores de Papantla),** take place every Saturday and Sunday nights at 6, 6:30, 8, 8:30, 9 and 10pm, on the *malecón,* adjacent to the "Boy on a Seahorse" statue. In this pre-Columbian religious ritual four men are suspended from the top of a tall pole, circling around it (as if in flight), while another beats a drum and plays a flute while balancing himself at the top. It signifies the four cardinal points, and the mystic "center" of the self, a sacred direction for ancient Mexican cultures.

TENNIS   Many hotels in Puerto Vallarta offer excellent tennis facilities; they often have clay courts. The full-service **Canto del Sol Tennis Club** (© **322/224-0123**) is at the Canto del Sol hotel in the Hotel Zone. It offers indoor and outdoor courts (including a clay court), full pro shop, lessons, clinics, and partner matches.

PARASAILING   Parasailing and other watersports are available at many beaches along the Bay of Banderas. The most popular spot is at Los Muertos Beach. WaveRunners, banana boats, and parasailing are available by the hour, half-day, or full day. Be forewarned, however, that the swiftly shifting winds in Banderas Bay can make this a dangerous proposition. Fly at your own risk!

A STROLL THROUGH TOWN

Puerto Vallarta's cobblestone streets are a pleasure to explore; they're full of tiny shops, rows of windows edged with curling wrought iron, and vistas of red-tile roofs and the sea. Start with a walk up and down the *malecón.*

Among the sights you shouldn't miss is the **municipal building** on the main square (next to the tourism office), which has a large Manuel Lepe mural inside in its stairwell. Nearby, right up Independencia, sits the picturesque **Parish of Nuestra Señora de Guadalupe church,** Hidalgo 370 (© **322/222-1326**), topped with a curious crown held in place by angels—a replica of the one worn by Empress Carlota during her brief time in Mexico as Emperor Maximilian's wife. On its steps, women sell religious mementos; across the narrow street, stalls sell native herbs for curing common ailments. Services in English are held each Saturday at 5pm, and Sunday at 10am. Regular hours are Monday through Saturday from 7:30am to 8:30pm, Sunday from 6:30am to 8:30pm. Note that entrance is restricted to those properly attired—no shorts or sleeveless shirts allowed. Three blocks south of the church, head east on Libertad, lined with small shops and pretty upper windows, to the **municipal market** by the river. (It's the Río Cuale Mercado, but I recently overheard a tourist ask for the "real quality" market!) After exploring the market, cross the bridge to the island in the river; sometimes a painter is at work on its banks. Walk down the center of the island toward the sea, and you'll come to the tiny **Museo Río Cuale** (no phone; Mon–Sat 10am–4pm; free admission), which has a small but impressive permanent exhibit of pre-Columbian figurines.

Retrace your steps to the market and Libertad, and follow Calle Miramar to the brightly colored steps up to Zaragoza. Midway is a magnificent view over rooftops to the sea, plus a cute cafe, **Graffiti** (no phone), where you can break for a cappuccino and a snack. Up Zaragoza to the right 1 block is the famous **pink arched bridge** that once connected Richard Burton's and Elizabeth Taylor's houses. In this area, known as **"Gringo Gulch,"** many Americans have houses.

SHOPPING

Shopping in Puerto Vallarta is generally concentrated in small, eclectic, independent shops rather than impersonal malls. You can find excellent **folk art,** original **clothing** designs, fine jewelry, and creative home accessories at great prices. Vallarta is known for having the most diverse and impressive selection of **contemporary Mexican fine art** outside Mexico City. It also has an abundance of tacky T-shirts and the ubiquitous **silver jewelry.**

THE SHOPPING SCENE

There are a few key shopping areas: central downtown, the Marina Vallarta *malecón,* the popular *mercados,* and on the beach—where the merchandise comes to you. Some of the more attractive shops are 1 to 2 blocks in **back of the *malecón.*** Start at the intersection of Corona and Morelos streets—interesting shops spread out in all directions from here. **Marina Vallarta** has two shopping plazas, Plaza Marina and Neptuno Plaza, on the main highway from the airport into town, which offer a limited selection of shops, with Plaza Neptuno primarily featuring home décor shops. Although still home to a few interesting shops, the marina boardwalk *(marina malecón)* is dominated by real estate companies, timeshare vendors, restaurants, and boating services.

Puerto Vallarta's **municipal market** is just north of the Río Cuale, where Libertad and A. Rodríguez meet. The *mercado* sells clothes, jewelry, serapes, shawls, leather accessories and suitcases, papier-mâché parrots, stuffed frogs and armadillos, and, of course, T-shirts. Be sure to comparison-shop, and definitely bargain before buying. The market is open daily from 9am to 7pm. Upstairs, a **food market** serves inexpensive Mexican meals—for more adventurous diners, it's probably the best value and most authentic dining experience in Vallarta. An **outdoor market** is along Río Cuale Island, between the two bridges. Stalls sell crafts, gifts, folk art, and clothing. New to downtown is the **Small Vallarta** (© **322/222-7530**) on Paseo Díaz Ordaz 928, on the eastern side, just before the start of the *malecón.* It is a "small mall" featuring tourist-friendly shops and dining options, including Carl Junior's burgers, Häagen-Dazs ice cream, Swatch watch shop, El Mundo de Tequila, and a Diamonds International jewelry store.

Along any public beach, walking **vendors** will probably approach you. Their merchandise ranges from silver jewelry to rugs and T-shirts to masks. "Almost free!" they'll call out. If you're too relaxed to think of shopping in town, this can be an entertaining alternative for picking up souvenirs, and remember: Bargaining is expected. The most reputable beach vendors concentrate at Los Muertos Beach in front of the El Dorado and La Palapa restaurants (on Calle Pulpito).

In most of the better shops and galleries, shipping, packing, and delivery to Puerto Vallarta hotels are available. Some will also ship to your home address. Note that while

---

Tips **Beware the Silver Scam**

Much of the silver sold on the beach is actually alpaca, a lower-quality silver metal (even though many pieces are stamped with the designation ".925," supposedly indicating true silver). Prices for silver on the beach are much lower, as is the quality. If you're looking for a more lasting piece of jewelry, you're better off in a silver shop.

Downtown Puerto Vallarta

ATTRACTIONS ●
Gringo Gulch (neighborhood) **19**
Isla del Río Cuale **20**
Main Square **12**
Parish of Nuestra Señora de
   Guadalupe **13**
Terra Noble Center for the Arts **1**

ACCOMMODATIONS ■
Hacienda San Angel **14**
Hotel Molino de Agua **23**
Hotel Playa Los Arcos **27**

RESTAURANTS ◆
Adobe Grill **11**
Archie's Wok **29**
Arrayán **6**
Barcelona Tapas **5**
Bianca **22**
Café des Artistes/
   Thierry Blouet
   Cocina del Autor **7**
Café Kaiser Maximilian **27**
Café San Angel **28**
Daiquiri Dick's **26**
de Santos **3**
Espresso **24**

Fajita Republic **25**
Kit-Kat **30**
La Bodeguita del Medio **2**
La Esquina de los Capricios **16**
La Palapa **31**
Las Palomas **8**
La Taberna de San Pascual **10**
Le Bistro **21**
Planet a Vegetariano **15**
Red Cabbage Café **32**
Rito's Baci **4**
Trio **18**
Vitea **17**
Xitomates **9**

bargaining is expected in the *mercados* and with beach vendors, stores generally charge fixed—and fair—prices for their wares.

THE LOWDOWN ON HUICHOL INDIAN ART

Puerto Vallarta offers the best selection of Huichol art in Mexico. Descendants of the Aztec, the Huichol are one of the last remaining indigenous cultures in the world that has remained true to its ancient traditions, customs, language, and habitat. The Huichol live in adobe structures in the high Sierras (at an elevation of 1,394m/4,600 ft.) north and east of Puerto Vallarta. Due to the decreasing fertility (and therefore productivity) of the land surrounding their villages, they have come to depend more on the sale of their artwork for sustenance.

Huichol art has always been cloaked in a veil of mysticism—probably one of the reasons serious collectors seek out this form of *artesanía.* Colorful, symbolic yarn "paintings," inspired by visions experienced during spiritual ceremonies, characterize Huichol art. In the ceremonies, artists ingest peyote, a hallucinogenic cactus, which induces brightly colored visions; these are considered messages from their ancestors. The visions' symbolic and mythological imagery influences the art, which encompasses not only yarn paintings but also fascinating masks and bowls decorated with tiny colored beads.

The Huichol might be geographically isolated, but are learning the importance of good business, and have adapted their art to meet consumer demand. Original Huichol art, therefore, is not necessarily traditional. Iguanas, jaguars, sea turtles, frogs, eclipses, and eggs appear in response to consumer demand. For more traditional works, look for pieces that depict deer, scorpions, wolves, or snakes.

The Huichol have also had to modify their techniques to create more pieces in less time and meet increased demand. Patterned fill-work, which is faster to produce, sometimes replaces the detailed designs that used to fill the pieces. The same principle applies to yarn paintings. While some are beautiful depictions of landscapes and even abstract pieces, they are not traditional themes.

You may see Huichol Indians on the streets of Vallarta—they are easy to spot, dressed in white clothing embroidered with colorful designs. A number of fine Huichol galleries are in downtown Puerto Vallarta (see individual listings under "Crafts & Gifts" and "Decorative & Folk Art," below).

One place to learn more about the Huichol is **Huichol Collection,** Morelos 490, across from the sea-horse statue on the *malecón* (© **322/223-2141**). Not only does this shop offer an extensive selection of Huichol art in all price ranges, but it also has a replica of a Huichol adobe hut, informational displays explaining more about their fascinating way of life and beliefs, and usually a Huichol artist at work. However, note that this is a timeshare sales location, so don't be surprised if you're hit with a pitch for a "free" breakfast and property tour.

CLOTHING

Vallarta's single true department store is **LANS,** with branches at Juárez 867 (© **322/ 226-9100;** www.lans.com.mx), and in Plaza Caracol, next door to the supermarket Gigante, in the Hotel Zone (© **322/226-0204**). Both offer a wide selection of name-brand clothing, accessories, footwear, cosmetics, and home furnishings. Along with the nationally popular **LOB, Carlos 'n' Charlie's,** and **Bye-Bye** brands, Vallarta offers a distinctive shop featuring original designs.

Fun Fact **A Huichol Art Primer: Shopping Tips**

Huichol art falls into two main categories: yarn paintings and beaded pieces. All other items you might find in Huichol art galleries are either ceremonial objects or items used in everyday life.

Yarn paintings are made on a wood base covered with wax and meticulously overlaid with colored yarn. Designs represent the magical vision of the underworld, and each symbol gives meaning to the piece. Paintings made with wool yarn are more authentic than those made with acrylic; however, acrylic yarn paintings are usually brighter and have more detail because the threads are thinner. It is normal to find empty spaces where the wax base shows. Usually the artist starts with a central motif and works around it, but it's common to have several independent motifs that, when combined, take on a different meaning. A painting with many small designs tells a more complicated story than one with only one design and fill-work on the background. Look for the story of the piece on the back of the painting. Most Huichol artists write in pencil in Huichol and Spanish.

Beaded pieces are made on carved wooden shapes depicting different animals, wooden eggs, or small bowls made from gourds. The pieces are covered with wax and tiny *chaquira* beads are applied one by one to form designs. Usually the beaded designs represent animals; plants; the elements of fire, water, or air; and certain symbols that give a special meaning to the whole. Deer, snakes, wolves, and scorpions are traditional elements; other figures, such as iguanas, frogs, and any animals not indigenous to Huichol territory, are incorporated by popular demand. Beadwork with many small designs that do not exactly fit into one another is more time-consuming and has a more complex symbolic meaning. This kind of work has empty spaces where the wax shows.

---

de Santos Boutique   Hip and sultry fashions, direct from South America are the specialties of this small but well-stocked boutique. It's open Monday to Saturday 11am to 9:30pm. Morelos 771, adjacent to the de Santos Club and restaurant. ℂ **322/223-5326** or 322/223-3052.

Laura López Labra Designs   The most comfortable clothing you'll ever enjoy. LLL is renowned for her trademark all-white (or natural) designs in 100% cotton or lace. Laura's fine gauze fabrics float in her designs of seductive skirts, romantic dresses, blouses, beachwear, and baby dolls. Men's offerings include cotton drawstring pants and lightweight shirts. Other designs include a line of precious children's clothing and some pieces with elaborate embroidery based on Huichol Indian designs. Personalized wedding dresses are also available. Open Monday through Saturday from 10am to 3:30pm; Fridays and Saturdays also from 5 to 9pm. Basilio Badillo 329. ℂ **322/222-3074**.

Mar de Sueños ⭐⭐   This small shop carries stunning swimsuits and exquisite lingerie. Without a doubt, the finest women's beachwear, intimate apparel, and evening wear in Vallarta for those special occasions—or just to make you feel extra special. The shop also stocks a selection of fine linen clothing—and it's one of the few places in Mexico that carries the renowned Italian line La Perla. Other name brands include Gottex, D&G, and DKNY. Open Monday through Saturday from 10am to 2pm and 5 to 9pm. Leona Vicario 220-C. ℂ **322/222-2662.**

CONTEMPORARY ART

Known for sustaining one of the stronger art communities in Latin America, Puerto Vallarta has an impressive selection of fine galleries featuring quality original works. Several dozen galleries get together to offer art walks almost every week between November and April.

Corsica   Among the newest and bests of Vallarta's galleries, Corsica features an exquisite collection of sculptures, installations and paintings, from world-renown contemporary artists from Mexico. They offer professional packing and worldwide shipping with purchases. There are three locations—all within a few blocks of one another—at Guadalupe Sánchez 735, Leona Vicario 230, and Pipila 268. Open Monday through Saturday 11am to 2pm, and by appointment 5 to 11pm. ℂ **322/223-1821** or 322/222-9260. www.galeriacorsica.com.

Galería AL (Arte Latinoamericano)   This gallery showcases contemporary works created by young, primarily Latin American artists, as well as Vallarta favorite Marta Gilbert. Feature exhibitions take place every 2 weeks during high season. The historic building (one of Vallarta's original structures) has exposed brick walls; small rooms of exhibition spaces on the second and third floors surround an open courtyard. It's also rumored to have a friendly resident ghost, who partner Susan Burger says has been quite welcoming. Open Monday through Saturday from 10:30am to 9pm. Josefa Ortiz Domínguez 155. ℂ/fax **322/222-4406.**

Galería des Artistes   This stunning gallery features contemporary painters and sculptors from throughout Mexico, including the renowned original "magiscopes" of Feliciano Bejar. Paintings by Vallarta favorite Evelyn Boren, as well as a small selection of works by Mexican masters, including Diego Rivera and Orozco, can be found here, among the exposed brick walls and stylish interior spaces. It's open Monday to Saturday 11am to 10pm Leona Vicario 248; ℂ **322/223-0006.** Just across the street, affiliate **Galleria Omar Alonso** exhibits photography by internationally renowned artists. Leona Vicario 249. ℂ **322/222-5587.** www.galeriaomaralonso.com.

Galería Pacífico   Since opening in 1987, Galería Pacífico has been considered one of the finest in Mexico. On display is a wide selection of sculptures and paintings in various media by midrange masters and up-and-comers alike. The gallery is 1½ blocks inland from the fantasy sculptures on the *malecón*. Among the artists whose careers Galería Pacífico has influenced are rising talents Rogelio Díaz and Brewster Brockman, internationally renowned sculptor Ramiz Barquet, and Patrick Denoun. Open Monday through Saturday from 10am to 8pm Sunday by appointment. Between May and October, check for reduced hours or vacation closings. Aldama 174, 2nd floor. ℂ **322/222-1982.** Fax 322/222-5502. galeriapacifico@prodigy.net.mx.

Galería Uno   One of Vallarta's first galleries, the Galería Uno features an excellent selection of contemporary paintings by Latin American artists, plus a variety of posters and prints. During the high season, featured exhibitions change every 2 weeks. In a classic adobe building with open courtyard, it's also a casual, *salón*-style gathering place for friends of owner Jan Lavender. Open Monday through Saturday from 10am to 10pm. A branch, **Arte de las Américas** (© 322/221-1985), is at Marina Vallarta between La Taberna and the Yacht Club. It exhibits some of the same artists but has a decidedly more abstract orientation. It's open Monday through Saturday from 10am to 2pm and 5 to 9pm. Morelos 561 (at Corona). © 322/222-0908.

Galleria Dante This gallery-in-a-villa showcases contemporary art as well as sculptures and classical reproductions of Italian, Greek, and Art Deco bronzes—against a backdrop of gardens and fountains. Located on the "Calle de los cafés," the gallery is open during the winter Monday through Saturday from 10am to 5pm, and by appointment. Basilio Badillo 269. © 322/222-2477. Fax 322/222-6284. www.galleriadante.com.

Studio Cathy Van Rohr This lovely studio showcases the work of Cathy Von Rohr, one of the most respected artists in the area. For years, Cathy lived in the secluded cove of Majahuitas, on the bay's southern shore, and much of her work reflects the tranquillity and deep connection with the natural world that resulted. Paintings, prints, and sculptures are featured. It's open by appointment and does not accept credit cards. Manuel M. Diéguez 321. © 866/256-2739 toll-free in the U.S., or 322/222-5875. www.cathyvonrohr.com.

CRAFTS & GIFTS

Alfarería Tlaquepaque Opened in 1953, this is Vallarta's original source for Mexican ceramics and decorative crafts, all at excellent prices. Talavera pottery and dishware, colored glassware, birdcages, baskets, and wood furniture are just a few of the many items in this warehouse-style store. Open Monday through Saturday, 9am to 9pm, and Sundays from 9am to 3pm. Av. México 1100. © 322/223-2121.

La Casa del Feng Shui I am enchanted by this shop's selection of crystals, candles, talismans, fountains, and wind chimes—along with many more items designed to keep the good energy flowing in your home, office, or personal space. Why not take home something to add more harmony to your life? Open Monday through Saturday, 10am to 7pm. Corona 165, around the corner from Morelos. © 322/222-3300.

Safari Accents Flickering candles glowing in colored-glass holders welcome you to this highly original shop overflowing with creative gifts, one-of-a-kind furnishings, and reproductions of paintings by Frida Kahlo and Botero. Open daily from 10am to 11pm. Olas Altas 224, Local 5. © 322/223-2660.

DECORATIVE & FOLK ART

Banderas Bay Trading Company 𝕲 This shop features fine antiques and one-of-a-kind decorative objects for the home, including contemporary furniture, antique wooden doors, religious-themed items, *retablos* (painted scenes on tin backgrounds depicting the granting of a miracle), original art, beeswax candles in grand sizes, hand-loomed textiles, glassware, and pewter. This unique selection is handpicked by one of the area's most noteworthy interior designers, Peter Bowman. Open Monday to Saturday 9am to 9pm. Cárdenas 263 (near Ignacio L. Vallarta). © 322/223-4352.

Lucy's CuCu Cabaña and Zoo *Finds* Owners Lucy and Gil Givens have assembled an exceptionally entertaining, eclectic, and memorable collection of Mexican folk art—about 70% of which is animal-themed. Each summer they travel Mexico and personally select the handmade works created by over 100 indigenous artists and artisans. Items include metal sculptures, Oaxacan wooden animals, *retablos,* and fine Talavera ceramics. Open Monday through Saturday from 10am to 10pm. The store is closed from May 15 to October 15. Basilio Badillo 295. No phone.

Olinala Two floors of fine indigenous Mexican crafts and folk art, including an impressive collection of museum-quality masks and original contemporary art by gallery owner Brewster Brockman. Open Monday through Friday from 10am to 2pm and 5 to 8pm, Saturday from 10am to 2pm. Cárdenas 274. © 322/222-4995.

Puerco Azul Set in a space that actually has a former pig-roasting oven, Puerco Azul features a whimsical and eclectic selection of art and home accessories, much of it created by owner and artist Lee Chapman (aka Lencho). You'll find many animal-themed works in bright colors, including his signature "blue pigs" *(puercos azules)*. Open Monday to Saturday from 10am to 8pm, closed on Sunday. Constitución 325, just off Basilio Badillo's "restaurant row." © 322/222-8647.

Querubines *Finds* This is my personal favorite for the finest-quality artisanal works from throughout Mexico. Owner Marcella García travels across the country to select the items, which include exceptional artistic silver jewelry, embroidered and hand-woven clothing, bolts of loomed fabrics, tin mirrors and lamps, glassware, pewter frames and trays, high-quality wool rugs, straw bags, and Panama hats. Open Monday through Saturday from 9am to 9pm. Under the same ownership and open the same hours, **Serafina,** Basilio Badillo 260 (© 322/223-4594), features a more extensive selection of cotton clothing and handmade jewelry. Juárez 501A (corner of Galeana). © 322/223-1727.

JEWELRY & ACCESSORIES

Mosaique It's a potpourri of global treasures—an extensive selection of silk, cotton, and cashmere pareos and shawls, plus resort bags, jewelry, and home decor items. You'll also see blouses, tops, and wrap skirts in mix-and-match colors. The emphasis here is on handmade and hand-dyed, richly colored natural fabrics. There's a second location at Juárez 279 (© 322/223-3183). Both are open Monday through Saturday from 10am to 9pm, Sunday from 10am to 6pm. Basilio Badillo 277. © 322/223-3146.

Viva *✦✦✦ Finds* At Viva, both the shop and the jewelry are stunning. You enter through a long corridor lined with displays showcasing exquisite jewelry from over 450 international designers, including Mexico's finest silversmiths. The main room, under a large pyramid-shaped skylight, holds comfy couches surrounded by memorable jewelry displays. Viva also features the largest selection of authentic French espadrilles and ballet slippers in Latin America, plus an inspired selection of beach hats, sunglasses, and accessories. Open daily from 10am to 11pm. Basilio Badillo 274. © 322/222-4078. www.vivacollection.com.

TEQUILA & CIGARS

La Casa del Habano This fine tobacco shop has certified quality cigars from Cuba, Mexico, and the Dominican Republic, along with humidors, cutters, elegant lighters, and other smoking accessories. It's also a local cigar club, with a walk-in humidor for regular clients. In the back, you'll find comfy leather couches, TV sports, and full bar service—in other words, a manly place to take a break from shopping. Open Monday through Saturday from noon to 9pm. Aldama 170. © 322/223-2758.

La Casa del Tequila *✦* Here you'll find an extensive selection of premium tequilas, plus information and tastings. Also available are cigars from Cuba and Veracruz, books, tequila glassware, humidors, and other tequila-drinking and cigar-smoking accessories. The shop has recently been downsized to accommodate the **Adobe Grill**

(see "Where to Dine," later in this chapter) in the back, but now you can enjoy tasty Mexican fare and margaritas while you shop! Open Monday through Saturday from noon to 11pm. Morelos 589. © **322/222-2000.**

WHERE TO STAY

Beyond a varied selection of hotels and resorts, Puerto Vallarta offers many alternative accommodations. Oceanfront or marina-view condominiums and elegant private villas can offer families and small groups a better value and more ample space than a hotel. For more information on short-term rentals, check out **www.virtualvallarta.com**. Prices start at $99 a night for nonbeachside condos and go to $1,000 for penthouse condos or private villas. Susan Weisman's **Bayside Properties,** Francisco Rodríguez 160, corner of Olas Altas (© **322/223-4424;** www.puertovallartabayside.com), rents condos, villas, and hotels for individuals and large groups, including gay-friendly accommodations. She can arrange airport pickup and in-villa cooks. Another reputable option is the full-service travel agency, **Holland's** (© **415/841-1194** or 618/236-2787; www.PuertoVallarta Villas.com). For the ultimate, indulge in a Punta Mita Villa rental within this exclusive resort. Contact **Punta Mita Properties** (© **888-647-0979** or 329/291-6500; www. punta-mitaproperties.com).

This section lists hotels in directional order, moving south along Banderas Bay from the airport.

MARINA VALLARTA

Marina Vallarta is the most modern and deluxe area of hotel development in Puerto Vallarta. Located immediately south of the airport and just north of the cruise-ship terminal, it's a planned development whose centerpiece is a 450-slip modern marina.

The hotels reviewed below are on the beachfront of the peninsula. The beaches here are much less attractive than beaches in other parts of the bay; the sand is darker, firmly packed, and, during certain times of the year, quite rocky. These hotels compensate with oversize pool areas and exotic landscaping. This area suits families and those looking for lots of centralized activity. Marina Vallarta is also home to an 18-hole **golf course** designed by Joe Finger.

In addition to the hotels reviewed below, an excellent choice is the **Puerto Vallarta Quinta Real,** on the golf course at Pelicanos 311 (© **322/221-0800;** fax 322/221-0801; www.quintareal.com). The elegant, boutique-style hotel has extra large rooms, an on-site spa, and a lovely pool. Although it is not located on the beach, it has a beach club, with shuttle service for guests. High-season rates average $250.

Due to traffic (rather than distance), a taxi from the Marina to downtown takes 20 to 30 minutes.

Velas Vallarta Grand Suite Resort ★★★ ⓚ️ᵢ𝒹ₛ   The beachside Velas Vallarta is an excellent choice for families. Each suite offers a full-size, fully equipped kitchen, ample living and dining areas, separate bedroom or bedrooms, and a large balcony with seating. Following a complete makeover in 2003, the suites are now decorated in a sophisticated, modern design featuring jewel-tone colors, Huichol art and Mexican textiles, feather beds with goose down comforters, texturized wall coverings, new 27-inch flatscreen TVs, modern kitchen appliances, and teak wood furniture on balconies and terraces. Special extras include a pillow menu and luxury bathroom amenities. This property is part hotel, part full-ownership condominiums, which means each suite is the size of a residential unit. The suites all have partial ocean views; they face a central area where three freeform swimming pools, complete with bridges and waterfalls, meander through tropical gardens. A full range of services means you'd never need to leave the place if you don't want to. The Marina Vallarta Golf Club is across the street, and special packages are available for Velas guests. Guests may pay an extra fee for the Gold Crown All-Inclusive option, which is one of the most premium all-inclusive programs in Mexico.

Paseo de la Marina 485, Marina Vallarta, 48354 Puerto Vallarta, Jal. ℂ **800/659-8477** in the U.S. and Canada, or 322/221-0091. Fax 322/221-0755. www.velasvallarta.com. 361 units. High season $258 double; $325–$650 suite. All-inclusive option (per person, based on double occupancy) is an additional $170 studio; $215 suite. AE, DC, MC, V. Free indoor parking. **Amenities:** 2 restaurants; poolside snack bar; lobby bar; 3 pools; golf privileges at Marina Vallarta Golf Club; 3 lighted tennis courts; fitness center w/spa and massage; beach w/watersports equipment rental; bicycle rentals; activities program for children and adults; concierge; travel agency; car rental; salon; room service; laundry service; minimarket; deli. In room: A/C, TV, dataport, full kitchen w/coffeemaker, hair dryer, iron, safe.

Westin Regina Resort 👍👍 Stunning architecture and vibrant colors are the hallmark of this award-winning property, considered Puerto Vallarta's finest. Although the grounds are large—over 8.4 hectares (21 acres) with 258m (850 ft.) of beachfront—the warm service and gracious hospitality create the feeling of an intimate resort. Hundreds of tall palms surround the spectacular central freeform pool. You'll find hammocks strung between the palms closest to the beach, where there are also private beach cabañas. Rooms are contemporary in style, with oversize wood furnishings, tile floors, original art, and tub/shower combinations. Balconies have panoramic views. Eight junior suites and some double rooms have Jacuzzis, and the five grand suites and presidential suite are two-level, with ample living areas. Two floors of rooms make up the Royal Beach Club, with VIP services, including private concierge. The fitness center is one of the most modern, well-equipped facilities in Vallarta, with regularly scheduled spinning and yoga classes. **Nikki Beach** (www.nikkibeach.com), a renowned haven for the hip, opened an onsite, beachfront restaurant and club in 2004, complete with big white bed-size lounges for taking in the sun, or enjoying libations anytime from noon until the early morning hours. Their Sunday champagne brunch is especially popular.

Paseo de la Marina Sur 205, Marina Vallarta, 48321 Puerto Vallarta, Jal. ℂ **800/228-3000** in the U.S., or 322/221-1100. Fax 322/221-1121. www.westinpv.com. 280 units. High season $258–$295 double, $585–$802 suite; low season $217–$234 double, $480–$600 suite. AE, DC, MC, V. Free parking. **Amenities:** 2 restaurants; 2 poolside bars; lobby bar; ocean-side pool; Nikki Beach Club; golf privileges at Marina Vallarta Golf Club; 3 lighted grass tennis courts; full-service, state-of-the-art health club w/treadmills, StairMasters, resistance equipment, sauna, steam room, solarium, whirlpool, massage, and salon; Kids' Club; travel agency; car rental; shopping arcade; 24-hr. room service; laundry service. In room: A/C, TV, dataport, minibar, coffeemaker, hair dryer, iron, safe-deposit box.

THE HOTEL ZONE

The main street running between the airport and town is Avenida Francisco Medina Ascencio. The hotels here offer excellent, wide beachfronts with generally tranquil waters for swimming. From here it's a quick taxi or bus ride to downtown.

Fiesta Americana Puerto Vallarta 👍 The Fiesta Americana's towering, three-story, thatched *palapa* lobby is a landmark in the Hotel Zone, and the hotel is known for its excellent beach and friendly service. An abundance of plants, splashing fountains, constant breezes, and comfortable seating areas in the lobby create a casual South Seas ambience. The nine-story terra-cotta-colored building embraces a large plaza with a pool facing the beach. Marble-trimmed rooms in neutral tones with pastel accents contain carved headboards and comfortable rattan and wicker furniture. All have private balconies with ocean and pool views.

Av. Francisco Medina Ascencio Km 2.5, 48300 Puerto Vallarta, Jal. ℭ **322/224-2010.** Fax 322/224-2108. www.fiesta
americana.com. 291 units. High season $180 double; low season $120–$160 double. Year-round $256–$819 suite.
AE, DC, MC, V. Limited free parking. **Amenities:** 3 restaurants; lobby bar w/live music nightly; large pool w/activities
and children's activities in high season; travel agency; salon; room service; laundry service. *In room:* A/C, TV, minibar,
hair dryer, safe.

Premier Hotel & Spa ✮✮   You couldn't ask for a better location to be close to all
that Vallarta's vibrant *centro* has to offer. Located on a wide swathe of golden sand
beach—and just a few blocks north of the start of the *malecón*—the Premier is easy
walking distance or a quick taxi ride to the downtown restaurants, shops, galleries, and
clubs. One of the newer hotels in Vallarta (opened 1999), the architecture is contemporary, but its size gives it an intimate feel. With a first-rate spa and a policy that
restricts guests to ages 16 and older, it's a place that caters to relaxation. Four types of
rooms are available, but all are decorated in warm colors with tile floors and light
wood furnishings. Deluxe rooms have ocean views, a respectable seating area with
comfortable chairs, plus a sizable private balcony—request one of several that has an
outdoor whirlpool. There are also seven suites that have a separate living room plus a
dining area with private bar, and a spacious terrace. These rooms also have a double
whirlpool tub, and separate glass-enclosed shower. The top-of-the-line master suites
have all that the above suites offer, plus an outdoor whirlpool on the spacious balcony.
The stunning bi-level spa is the real attraction of this hotel—scented with aromatherapy and glowing with candlelight, it uses top-notch, 100% natural products, most
based on Mexico's natural treasures like coconut, aloe, and papaya. If you're not
tempted by the nearby and accessible dining choices in downtown Vallarta, the premier also offers an all-inclusive option, with all meals and drinks included.

San Salvador 117, behind the Buenaventura Hotel, Col. 5 de Diciembre, 48350Puerto Vallarta, Jal. ℭ **877/886-9176**
toll-free in the U.S., or 322/226-7001. Fax: 322/226-7043. www.premiereonline.com.mx. 83 rooms and suites. Room
only rates: high season $135–$374 double; low season $121–$325 double. All-inclusive rates: high season
$224–$299 per person, based on double occupancy; low season $167–$224 per person, double. For ages 16 and
older only. AE, MC, V. **Amenities:** 3 restaurants; small pool; fitness center; full spa; travel agency; salon; 24-hr. room
service; laundry service. *In room:* A/C, TV, minibar, coffeemaker, hair dryer, safe, bathrobes.

DOWNTOWN TO LOS MUERTOS BEACH

This part of town has recently undergone a renaissance; economical hotels and good-
value guesthouses dominate. Several blocks off the beach, you can find numerous
budget inns offering clean, simply furnished rooms; most offer discounts for long-
term stays. Much of Vallarta's nightlife activity now centers in the areas south of the
Río Cuale and along Olas Altas.

Hacienda San Angel ✮✮✮ *Finds*   This enchanting boutique hotel may not be on
the beach, but you'll hardly miss it, you'll be so pampered in the stunning suites, or
satisfied enjoying the view from the rooftop heated pool or Jacuzzi and sun deck.
Once Richard Burton's home in Puerto Vallarta, it's located just behind Puerto Vallarta's famed church, making it easy walking distance to all of the restaurants, shopping, and galleries of downtown. The Hacienda is comprised of three villas; the first
two are joined to the third villa by a path that winds through a lovely terraced garden
filled with tropical plants, flowers, statuary and a charming fountain. A large, heated
pool and deck offer panoramic views of the city and Bay of Banderas, while a second
sun deck with Jacuzzi literally overlooks the church's crown, across to the water
beyond. Each of the Hacienda's nine elegant suites is individually decorated, accented

with exquisite antiques and original art. Bed linens and coverings are of the finest quality, with touches like Venetian lace and goose-down pillows. Each morning, you'll awake to continental breakfast served outside your suite at your requested hour. From Monday through Saturday, guests are invited to a cocktail hour, where one of the Hacienda's signature drinks (like the Celestial Sin—a wicked blend of vodka and blue Curacao) are served, accompanied by snacks. Sophisticated style, coupled with casual Vallarta charm, make Hacienda San Angel the newest "find" in Mexico for the discriminating traveler.

Miramar 336, Col. Centro, 48300 Puerto Vallarta, Jal. ℂ **322/222-2692**. www.haciendasanangel.com. 9 suites. High season $250–$475 double; low season $200–$370 double. All rates include daily continental breakfast. Rates for the entire Hacienda or separate villas consisting of 3 suites each are also available. MC, V. Very limited street parking available. **Amenities:** Menu of full breakfasts, lunches, and dinner, or private chef available; 2 pools; rooftop sun deck w/Jacuzzi; concierge; tour services; complimentary Internet access. *In room:* A/C, TV with DVD/CD player, hair dryer, safe-deposit box, bathrobes.

Hotel Molino de Agua 🌟   With an unrivaled location adjacent to both the Río Cuale and the ocean, this hotel is a mix of stone and stucco-walled bungalows and small beachside buildings, spread out among winding walkways and lush tropical gardens. It's immediately past the Río Cuale—after crossing the southbound bridge, it's on your right. Although it's centrally located on a main street, open spaces, big trees, birds, and lyrical fountains lend it tranquillity. The individual bungalows are in the gardens between the entrance and the ocean. They are well maintained and simply furnished, with a wooden desk and chair, Mexican tile floors, beamed ceilings, and beautiful tile bathrooms. Wicker rocking chairs grace the private patios. Rooms and suites in the two small two- and three-story buildings on the beach have double beds and private terraces, and are decorated in rustic Mexican style.

Vallarta 130 (Apdo. Postal 54), 48380 Puerto Vallarta, Jal. ℂ **322/222-1957**. Fax 322/222-6056. www.molino deagua.com. 60 units. High season garden bungalow $100 double, oceanfront room or suite $143–$175 double; low season bungalow $88 double, oceanfront room or suite $106–$132 double. AE, MC, V. Free secured parking. **Amenities:** Restaurant; bar; beachside pool; pool w/whirlpool; tour desk; car-rental desk. *In room:* A/C.

Hotel Playa Los Arcos 🌟🌟   This is one of Vallarta's perennially popular hotels and a favorite of mine, with a stellar location in the heart of Los Muertos Beach, central to the Olas Altas sidewalk-cafe action and close to downtown. The four-story structure is U-shaped, facing the ocean, with a small swimming pool in the courtyard. Rooms with private balconies overlook the pool. The 10 suites have ocean views; 5 of these have kitchenettes. The standard rooms are small but pleasantly decorated and immaculate, with carved wooden furniture painted pale pink. On the premises are a *palapa* beachside bar with occasional live entertainment, a gourmet coffee shop, and the popular Kaiser Maximilian's gourmet restaurant. It's 7 blocks south of the river.

Olas Altas 380, 48380 Puerto Vallarta, Jal. ℂ **800/648-2403** in the U.S., or 322/222-1583. Fax 322/222-2418. www.playalosarcos.com. 175 units. High season $116–$140 double, $166 suite; low season $85 double, $127 suite. AE, MC, V. Limited street parking. **Amenities:** 2 restaurants; lobby bar; pool; tour desk; car-rental services; babysitting; laundry; safe-deposit boxes; money exchange at front desk. *In room:* A/C, TV.

SOUTH TO MISMALOYA

Casa Tres Vidas 🌟🌟 *Value*   Terraced down a hillside to Conchas Chinas Beach, Casa Tres Vidas is three individual villas that make great, affordable lodgings for families or groups of friends. Set on a stunning private cove, Tres Vidas gives you the experience of your own private villa, complete with service staff. It offers outstanding value for the location—close to town, with panoramic views from every room—as well as for the excellent service. Each villa has at least two levels and over 465 sq. m (5,000 sq. ft.) of mostly open living areas, plus a private swimming pool, heated whirlpool, and air-conditioned bedrooms. The Vida Alta penthouse villa has three bedrooms, plus a rooftop deck with pool and bar. Vida Sol villa's three bedrooms sleep 10 (two rooms have two king-size beds each). Directly on the ocean, Vida Mar is a four-bedroom villa, accommodating eight. The staff prepares gourmet meals in your villa twice a day—you choose the menu and pay only for the food. If you're planning a wedding, Tres Vidas and its adjacent sister property, Quinta María Cortez, do a stunning job.

Sagitario 134, Playa Conchas Chinas, 48300 Puerto Vallarta, Jal. ℂ **888/640-8100** or 801/531-8100 in the U.S., or 322/221-5317. Fax 322/221-53-27. www.casatresvidas.com. 3 villas. High season $625 villa; low season $450 villa. Rates include services. Special summer 1- or 2-bedroom rates available; minimum 3 nights. AE, MC, V. Very limited street parking. **Amenities:** 2 prepared daily meals; private pool; concierge; tour desk; car rental. *In room:* Kitchen facilities, safe-deposit box.

Dreams Puerto Vallarta Resort & Spa 🌟🌟 Formerly the Camino Real, this original luxury hotel in Puerto Vallarta was taken over by AMResorts in 2004 and turned into the premium all-inclusive Dreams Resort. It has the nicest beach of any Vallarta hotel, with soft white sand in a private cove. Set apart from other properties, with a lush mountain backdrop, it retains the exclusivity that made it popular from the beginning—yet it's only a 5- to 10-minute ride to town. The hotel consists of two buildings: the 250-room main hotel, which curves gently with the shape of the Playa Las Estacas, and the newer 11-story Club Tower, also facing the beach and ocean. An ample pool fronts the main building, facing the beach. Standard rooms in the main building are large; some have sliding doors opening onto the beach, and others have balconies. Club Tower rooms (from the sixth floor up) feature balconies with whirlpool tubs. The top floor consists of six two-bedroom suites, each with a private swimming pool, and with special concierge services. All rooms feature ocean views, and are decorated in vibrant colors, with marble floors. In 2004, all rooms were completely renovated, with additions including two new swimming pools (including an adults-only tranquillity pool), a wedding gazebo, and upgraded health club and spa.

Carretera Barra de Navidad Km 3.5, Playa Las Estacas, 48300 Puerto Vallarta, Jal. ℂ **866/237-3267** in the U.S. and Canada, or 322/221-5000. Fax 322/221-6000. www.dreamsresorts.com. 337 units. All-inclusive rates include all meals, premium drinks, activities, airport transfers, tips, and taxes. Rates: $298–$333 double, $598–$633 junior suite; $1,012–$1,500 suite. AE, DC, MC, V. Free secured parking. **Amenities:** 5 restaurants; lobby bar; pool bar; swimming pool; 2 lighted grass tennis courts; fully equipped health club and spa; children's program (Easter and Christmas vacations); travel agency; car rental; convenience store; 24-hr. room service; laundry service; beach *palapas* w/chair, towel, and dining service; nightly entertainment. *In room:* A/C, TV, dataport, minibar, hair dryer, iron, safe-deposit box.

Quinta María Cortez 🌟🌟🌟 *(Finds* A sophisticated, imaginative B&B on the beach, this is Puerto Vallarta's most original place to stay—and one of Mexico's most memorable inns. Most of the seven large suites, uniquely decorated with antiques, whimsical curios, and original art, have a kitchenette and balcony. Sunny terraces, a small pool, and a central gathering area with fireplace and *palapa*-topped dining area (where an excellent full breakfast is served) occupy different levels of the seven-story house. A rooftop terrace offers another sunbathing alternative—and is among the best sunset-watching spots in town. The quinta is on a beautiful cove on Conchas Chinas beach. A terrace fronting the beach accommodates chairs for taking in the sunset.

The Quinta María wins my highest recommendation (in fact, I enjoyed living here for a few years when it still accepted long-term stays), but admittedly it's not for everyone. Air-conditioned areas are limited, due to the open nature of the suites and common areas. Those who love it return year after year, charmed by this remarkable place and by the consistently gracious service.

A new and very popular specialty of QMC and its adjacent sister property Casa Tres Vidas (see above) is planning and hosting weddings.

Sagitario 132, Playa Conchas Chinas, 48300 Puerto Vallarta, Jal. © **888/640-8100** or 801/536-5850 in the U.S., or 322/221-5317. Fax 322/221-53-27. www.quinta-maria.com. 7 units. High season $100–$235 double; low season $85–$175 double. Rates include breakfast. AE, MC, V. Very limited street parking. Children not accepted. **Amenities:** Small pool; concierge. *In room:* Dataport, minifridge, coffeemaker, hair dryer, safe-deposit box, CD player.

YELAPA

Verana ★★★ *(Moments)*   The magical Verana is my current favorite place to stay in Mexico. It has an unparalleled ability to inspire immediate relaxation and a deep connection with the natural beauty of the spectacular coast. Although Yelapa is 30 minutes by water taxi from town, even those unfamiliar with the village should consider it. Verana has six rustic yet sophisticated suites, set into a hillside with sweeping views of the mountains and ocean. Each is a work of art, hand-crafted with care and creativity by owners Heinz Leger, a former film production designer, and prop stylist Veronique Lieve. Each has a private terrace and two beds—but you won't find TVs, telephones, stereos, or other distractions. My favorite suite is the Studio; it's the most contemporary, with a wall of floor-to-ceiling windows that perfectly frame the spectacular view. The European-trained chef prepares scrumptious creations—global cuisine with a touch of Mexico. Compare this to the prices of the other rustic-chic resorts along Mexico's Pacific coast, and you'll find it's a true value. Adventurous travelers should not miss a stay at this unique place.

Domicilio conocido, 48300 Yelapa, Jal. © **800/677-5156** or 661/946-7477 in the U.S., or 322/222-2360; mobile 322/227-5420. www.verana.com. 6 villas. High season $200-$450 per night per villa, 5-night minimum; 3-bedroom Casa Grande $400 per night, all based on double occupancy; extra person $95 per night. Mandatory daily breakfast and dinner charge $65 per person. Lunch and beverages extra. Shorter stays based on availability. AE, MC, V. Management helps arrange transportation from Puerto Vallarta to Boca, where a private boat runs to Yelapa; from there, Verana is a gentle hike or mule ride. **Amenities:** Restaurant/bar; 2 prepared daily meals; pool; spa w/massage services; morning yoga classes; tours and excursions; library.

WHERE TO DINE

Puerto Vallarta has the most exceptional dining scene of any resort town in Mexico. Over 250 restaurants serve cuisines from around the world, in addition to fresh seafood and regional dishes. Chefs from France, Switzerland, Germany, Italy, and Argentina have come for visits and stayed to open restaurants. In celebration of this diversity, Vallarta's culinary community hosts a 2-week-long gourmet dining festival each November.

Dining is not limited to high-end options—there are plenty of small, family-owned restaurants, local Mexican kitchens, and vegetarian cafes. Vallarta also has branches of the world food-and-fun chains: Hard Rock Cafe, Outback Steakhouse, and even Hooters. I won't bother to review these restaurants, where the quality and decor are so familiar.

Of the inexpensive local spots, one favorite is **El Planeta Vegetariano,** Iturbide 270, just down from the main church (© **322/222-3073**), serving an inexpensive, bountiful, and delicious vegetarian buffet, which changes for breakfast and lunch/dinner. It's open Monday through Saturday. Breakfast ($3.50) is served from 8 to 11am; the lunch and dinner buffets ($5.50) are served from 11:30am to 10pm; no credit cards. A second location with the same prices and hours of service is now in Marina Vallarta (② **322/209-0555**), located in Marina del Rey, local L-4.

MARINA VALLARTA

Contrary to conventional travel wisdom, most of the best restaurants in the Marina are in hotels. Especially notable are **Andrea** (fine Italian cuisine), at Velas Vallarta, and **Nikki Beach** (fusion), on the beachfront of the Westin Regina Resort. (See "Where to Stay," earlier in this chapter, for more information.) Other choices are along the boardwalk bordering the marina yacht harbor. A notable stop is the **Café Max,** next to the Vallarta Adventures offices in Condominiums Marina Golf, Local 11 (② **322/221-0362**). It serves excellent coffee and espresso drinks, plus pastries and light snacks. Open Monday through Saturday from 8am to 1pm, and 4 to 10:30pm.

Benitto's ⊛ CAFE   Wow! What a sandwich! Benitto's food would be reason enough to come to this tiny, terrific cafe inside the Plaza Neptuno—but added to that are the original array of sauces and the very personable service. This place is popular with locals for light breakfasts, filling lunches, and fondue and wine in the evenings. It's the best place in town to find pastrami, corned beef, or other traditional (gringo) sandwich fare, all served on your choice of gourmet bread. Draft beer and wine are available, as are the cafe's specialty infused waters.

Inside Plaza Neptuno. ② 322/209-0287. benittosdeli@prodigy.net.mx. Breakfast $3–$6; main courses $5–$7. No credit cards. Daily 8:30am–10:30pm.

Porto Bello ⊛⊛ ITALIAN   One of the first restaurants in the marina, Porto Bello remains a favorite for its authentically flavorful Italian dishes and exceptional service. For starters, fried calamari is delicately seasoned, and grilled vegetable antipasto could easily serve as a full meal. Signature dishes include fusilli prepared with artichokes, black olives, lemon juice, basil, olive oil, and Parmesan cheese, and sautéed fish filet with shrimp and clams in saffron tomato sauce. The elegant indoor dining room is air-conditioned, and there's also marina-front seating. The restaurant occasionally schedules live music in the evening.

Marina Sol, Local 7 (Marina Vallarta *malecón*). ② 322/221-0003. Main courses $7–$19. AE, MC, V. Daily noon–11pm.

DOWNTOWN
Expensive
Café des Artistes/Thierry Blouet Cocina del Autor ⊛⊛⊛ FRENCH/INTER-NATIONAL   This sophisticated restaurant is known as the place in town for that very special evening. Creative in its menu and innovative in design, the dinner-only restaurant rivals those in any major metropolitan city for its culinary sophistication, and may soon become a reason in itself to visit Vallarta. The award-winning chef and owner, Thierry Blouet, is both a member of the French Academie Culinaire and a Maitre Cuisinier de France. In late 2003, the singular dining experience of the Café evolved into a trio of special places, expanding to add the upscale Bar Constantini lounge, and separate, but connected Theirry Blouet, Cocina del Autor dining area. All are located in a restored house that resembles a castle. The interior of the original Café des Artistes combines murals, lush fabrics, and an array of original works of art, with both an interior dining area as well as a lushly landscaped terraced garden area, open only during the winter and spring. The menu of this section is a changing delight of French gourmet bistro fare, which draws heavily on Chef Blouet's French training, yet uses regional specialty ingredients. A few of the noteworthy entrees include sea bass

filet served with polenta, and the renowned roasted duck glazed with honey, soy, ginger, and lime sauce, and served with a pumpkin risotto. At the Cocina del Autor, the atmosphere is sleek and stylish, and the fixed-priced tasting menu (prices depend on the number of plates you select, from three to six) offers you a choice of the chef's most creative and sumptuous creations, with each dish creatively combining ingredients to present one memorable "flavor"—choose any combination of starters, entrees or desserts. They also provide perfect wine pairings, if desired. After, you're invited to the cognac and cigar room, an exquisite blend of old adobe walls, flickering candles, and elegant leather chairs. Or, move on to the adjacent Bar Constantini, with its live jazz music and plush sofas, for a fitting close to a memorable meal. It's without a doubt worth the splurge.

Guadalupe Sánchez 740. © **322/222-3228,** -3229, or -3230. www.cafedesartistes.com. Main courses $9–$31. Cocina del Autor tasting menu ranges $25–$68. AE, MC, V. Daily 6–11:30pm.

Moderate

Daiquiri Dick's 👍👍 MODERN AMERICAN   A Vallarta dining institution, Daiquiri Dick's has been around for over 20 years, evolving its winning combination of decor, service, and scrumptious cuisine. The menu is among Vallarta's most sophisticated, and the genuinely warm staff and open-air location fronting Los Muertos Beach add to the feeling of casual comfort. As lovely as the restaurant is, though, and as notorious as the fresh-fruit daiquiris are, the food is the main attraction. It incorporates touches of Tuscan, Thai, and Mexican. Start with grilled asparagus wrapped in prosciutto and topped with shaved Asiago cheese, then try an entree such as sesame-crusted tuna, grilled rare and served with wild greens; pistachio chicken served with polenta; or my favorite, simple yet indulgent lobster tacos. Chocolate banana bread pudding makes a perfect finish. Daiquiri Dick's is a great place for groups—as well as for a romantic dinner. It's one of the few places that is equally enjoyable for breakfast, lunch, or dinner.

Olas Altas 314. © **322/222-0566.** www.ddpv.com Main courses $6.50–$21. AE, MC, V. Daily 9am–10:30pm. Closed Sept.

de Santos 👍 MEDITERRANEAN   After it opened a few years ago, de Santos quickly became the hot spot in town for late-night dining and bar action. Although the food initially didn't live up to the atmosphere and music, now it does. It's Mediterranean-inspired; best bets include lightly breaded calamari, paella Valenciana, and excellent thin-crust pizza. Also ask about nightly specials. The cool, refined interior feels more urban than resort, and it boasts the most sophisticated sound system in town—including a DJ who spins to match the mood of the crowd. It probably helps that one of the partners is also a member of the wildly popular Latin group Mana. There's open-air terrace dining in the back. Prices are extremely reasonable for the quality and overall experience of an evening here. Be sure to stay and check out the adjacent club—simply the hottest nightspot in town (see "Puerto Vallarta After Dark," below). We hear an expansion is planned for summer 2005, adding even more dining tables in the club area during peak evening hours.

Morelos 771, Centro. © **322/223-3052.** www.desantos.com.mx. Reservations recommended during high season. Main courses $5–$20. AE, MC, V. Daily 5pm–1am; bar closes at 4am on weekends.

Las Palomas 👍 MEXICAN   One of Puerto Vallarta's first restaurants, this is the power-breakfast place of choice—and a popular hangout for everyone else throughout the day. Authentic in atmosphere and menu, it's one of Puerto Vallarta's few genuine

Mexican restaurants, with the atmosphere of a gracious home. Breakfast is the best value. The staff pours mugs of steaming coffee spiced with cinnamon as soon as you're seated. Try classic *huevos rancheros* or *chilaquiles* (tortilla strips, fried and topped with red or green spicy sauce, cream, cheese, and fried eggs). Lunch and dinner offer traditional Mexican specialties, plus a selection of stuffed crepes. The best places for checking out the *malecón* and watching the sunset while sipping an icy margarita are the spacious bar and upstairs terrace.

Paseo Díaz Ordaz 610. ℂ **322/222-3675.** Breakfast $3.50–$10; lunch $8.50–$20; main courses $8.50–$22. AE, MC, V. Daily 8am–11pm.

Rito's Baci ★★ ITALIAN If the food weren't reason enough to come here (and it definitely is!), then Rito himself would be. He directs gentle, devoted attention to every detail of this cozy trattoria. His grandfather emigrated from Italy, and the recipes and tradition of Italian food come naturally to him. So does his passion for food—it's obvious as he describes the specialties, which include lasagna (vegetarian, *verde*, or meat-filled); ravioli stuffed with spinach and ricotta; spaghetti with garlic, anchovy, and lemon zest; or a side of homemade Italian sausage. Everything is made by hand from fresh ingredients. Pizza-lovers favor the Piedmonte, with that famous sausage and mushrooms, and the Horacio, a cheeseless version with tomatoes, oregano, and basil. Sandwiches come hot or cold; arrive hungry—they're a two-handed operation. Because Rito offers home and hotel delivery, I enjoy his food more than any other restaurant's. It's 1½ blocks off the *malecón*.

Domínguez 181 (between Morelos and Juárez). ℂ **322/222-6448.** Pasta $7–$17; salads and sandwiches $2.50–$7; pizza $13–$17. MC, V. Daily 1–11pm.

Trío ★★★ *Finds* INTERNATIONAL Trio is the darling of Vallarta restaurants, with diners beating a path to the modest but stylish cafe where chef-owners Bernhard Güth and Ulf Henricksson both share an undeniable passion for food, which imbues each dish. Trio is noted for its perfected melding of Mexican and Mediterranean flavors; memorable entrees include San Blas shrimp in a fennel-tomato vinaigrette served over broiled *nopal* cactus, herb risotto with toasted sunflower seeds and quail, and pan-roasted sea bass with glazed grapes, mashed potatoes and sauerkraut in a white pepper sauce. These dishes may not be on the menu when you arrive, though—it's a constantly changing work of art. The atmosphere is always comfortable and welcoming, and the chefs regularly chat with guests at the end of the evening. The rooftop bar area allows for a more comfortable wait for a table or for after-dinner coffee. A real treat!

Guerrero 264. ℂ **322/222-2196.** Reservations recommended. Main courses $14–$26. AE, MC, V. Year-round daily 6pm–midnight; high season Mon–Fri noon–3:30pm.

Xitomates ★★ MEXICAN Located in the heart of downtown, this creative Mexican restaurant has earned raves for its intimate atmosphere and Chef/owner Luis Fitch's exceptionally creative versions of the country's culinary treasures. It's named for one of Mexico's contributions to gastronomy—the tomato (Xitomatl, in the ancient Aztec language of Náhuatl). The menu mixes Mexican with Caribbean, Asian, and Mediterranean influences, and the presentation is as creative as the preparation. Starters include their signature coconut shrimp in a tangy tamarind sauce, thinly sliced scallops with cucumber and jicama julienne, or mushrooms stuffed with shrimp or huitlacoche (a mushroom that grows on corn stalks). Main courses range from grilled salmon filet in a poblano chile sauce, to a tender rib-eye steak with mushrooms, delicately flavored with the Mexican herb, epazote. The house specialty dessert is a

Tapas Anyone?

Certainly, much of modern Mexico's culture draws on the important influence of Spain, so it only makes sense that culinary traditions would be evident as well. Within the last several years, dining on tapashas soared in popularity here. Of the many options, these are my favorites: the long-standing **Barcelona Tapas**, Matamoros and 31 de Octobre streets ((C) **322/222-0510**), a large and lovely restaurant on a terrace built high on a hillside, with sweeping views of the Bay. They serve tapas and a selection of Spanish entrees, including paella, from 5pm to midnight. **La Taberna de San Pascual,** Corona 186 ((C) **322/223-9371;** Mon–Sat 5pm–midnight, with bar service extending to 2am; closed Sun) is a cozy eatery, rich with brick walls and dark wood accents, located on popular Corona Street, in the center of downtown. All ingredients are imported from Spain, and there's a selection of excellent Spanish wines to accompany their flavorful tapas. **La Esquina de los Caprichos,** Miramar 402, corner of Iturbide ((C) **322/222-0911;** Mon–Sat 1–11pm) is a tiny tapas place, known as having the most reasonably priced ($1.50–$6) tapas in town, and perhaps the tastiest.

Toluca ice cream cake. The warmly decorated dining room is accented with tin star lamps and flickering candles. An excellent wine list and full bar complement the exquisite dining.

Morelos 570, across from Galería Uno. (C) **322/222-1695.** www.losxitomates.com. Main courses $8–$22. AE, MC, V. Daily 7–11:30pm.

Inexpensive

Adobe Grill (F) MEXICAN   Opening its doors in late 2004, Adobe Grill took over most of the space at the Casa de Tequila, where it's located in the back, in a beautiful garden setting, within this classic Hacienda-style building in central downtown. The space has been put to excellent use: This cafe serves modern, casual Mexican cuisine and is an ideal spot to stop for a snack or a margarita while shopping. Start with an order of chiles anchos, stuffed with cream cheese and raisins, or the *antijotos mexicana,* a sampler of Mexican snacks including sopes, quesadillas, a tamale, and guacamole. Favorite main courses include *mole poblano,* or the beef filet in a chile pasilla gravy, served with mashed sweet potatoes and grilled watermelon. For a sweet finish, don't miss their chocolate truffle with coconut foam in a strawberry salsa. All tortillas are handmade, as are the savory salsas. An elegant bar borders the room, serving undoubtedly Vallarta's most original selection of fine tequilas, many from small distilleries. In addition to the tequilas and fresh fruit margaritas, Adobe Grill also serves a selection of fine Mexican wines.

Morelos 589. (C) **322/222-2000.** Main courses: $6–$17. MC, V. Mon–Sat noon–11pm.

Arrayán (F)(F)(F) *Finds* MEXICAN   The traditional but original Arrayán is the pot of gold at the end of the rainbow for anyone in search of authentic Mexican cuisine. Owner Carmen Porras enlisted Mexico City chef Carmen Titita (praised by James Beard for her culinary work) to assist in the design of the kitchen and creation of the restaurant's concise menu, which features genuine Mexican food of the region. The open-air (but covered) dining area surrounds a cozy courtyard, while its exposed brick walls, and funky-chic decor showcase a modern view of Mexican classics—tin tubs serve as sinks in the bathrooms, while colorful plastic tablecloths and primitive art enliven the dining room. Start with an order of sumptuous plantain fritters filled with black beans, or an unusual salad of diced *nopal* cactus paddles with fresh cheese. Favorite main courses include their tacos filled with prime beef filet, or a Mexican duck confit, served in an arrayán-orange sauce. (Arrayán—the namesake of the place, is a small bittersweet fruit native to the region.) Homemade, fresh-fruit ice creams are an especially tasty finish to your meal. The full bar offers an extensive selection of tequilas and regional liquors, while nonalcoholic beverages center around *aguas frescas,* a blended drink of fresh fruit and water. You can't miss the pink facade with the large bell at the entry. The excellent service is a plus to this can't-miss dining experience.

Allende 344, just past the corner with Matamoros. ℂ 322/223-2963. carmyp@prodigy.net.mx. Main courses $8–$12. No credit cards. Daily 1–11pm.

Vitea ★★★ *Finds* INTERNATIONAL   This beachfront bistro was opened in late 2004 by the Chef/owners of Trio, and their recipe for success took hold from day one—the place is already bustling at any hour, and has become the new favorite among local residents. Due to strategically-placed mirrors on the back wall, every seat has a view of the ocean, while the eclectic interior is cheerful and inviting. Seating is at small bistro-style tables, along a banquette that runs the length of the back wall, or at the small but beautiful bar. The long, narrow bistro faces the waterfront between the central plaza and river, which is currently undergoing a restoration—the *malecón* is being extended and will soon pass by Viteo, certain to be joined by other cafes. But enough about looks—what counts here is the exceptional fare, which is both classic and original. Starters include a tomato and Roquefort salad with pecans, foie gras with Spanish plum sauce, and an exquisite bistro salad with bacon. Quiche is always on the menu, with changing selections, and main courses include chickpea ravioli with portobello mushrooms, Wiener schintzel with salad, or a traditional steak frites. Lunch offers lighter fare, including heavenly deli sandwiches. You won't be disappointed here, no matter what you order! There's a full bar with an excellent selection of wines, and the service is exceptional.

Libertad 24, at the *malecón.* ℂ 322/222-8703 or 322/222-8695. Reservations recommended during peak dining hours. Main courses $7–$19. MC, V. Daily noon–midnight.

SOUTH OF THE RIO CUALE TO OLAS ALTAS

South of the river is the densest restaurant area, where you'll find the street Basilio Badillo, nicknamed "Restaurant Row." A second main dining drag has emerged along Calle Olas Altas, with a variety of cuisines and price categories. Cafes and espresso bars, generally open from 7am to midnight, line its wide sidewalks.

Expensive

Café Kaiser Maximilian ★★ INTERNATIONAL   This bistro-style cafe has a casually elegant atmosphere with a genuinely European feel. It's the prime place to go if you want to combine exceptional food with great people-watching. Austrian-born owner Andreas Rupprechter is always on hand to ensure that the service is as impeccable as the food is delicious. Indoor, air-conditioned dining is at cozy tables; sidewalk tables are larger and great for groups of friends. The cuisine merges old-world European preparations with regional fresh ingredients. My favorite is filet of trout with watercress and beet sauce—so much so that I've never tried any other dish, although friends tell me mustard chicken with mashed potatoes is excellent, and the rack of lamb with polenta, endives, and lima beans is simply divine. The restaurant also offers northern European classics like *Rahmschnitzel* (sautéed pork loin and homemade noodles in creamy mushroom sauce). Desserts are especially tempting, as are gourmet coffees—Maximilian has an Austrian cafe and pastry shop next door.

Olas Altas 380-B (at Basilio Badillo, in front of the Hotel Playa Los Arcos), Zona Romántica. ✆ 322/223-0760. Reservations recommended in high season. Main courses $16–$26. AE, MC, V. Mon–Sat 6–11pm.

Le Bistro ✿ MEXICAN/INTERNATIONAL   A long-standing favorite, Le Bistro is especially enjoyable for breakfast. I consider a morning meal here one of Vallarta's best values. Le Bistro is known for its elegant decor, great recorded jazz music, and open-air setting on the island in the midst of the Río Cuale—all creating a singular experience that blends sophistication with a typically Vallarta atmosphere. Favorite choices at breakfast are eggs Benedict and eggs *motuleño* style (sunny side up, smothered in tomato-based sauce and served with cheese, peas, and fried plantains). The specialty is crepes, which come in a variety of flavors for breakfast, lunch, or dinner. Especially scrumptious are those filled with chicken breast and squash blossoms (a Mexican delicacy) in hollandaise sauce. The menu also has an excellent selection of innovative Mexican cuisine, including duck in Oaxacan black *mole,* and rock Cornish hen stuffed with herbed rice, dried tropical fruits, and nuts, finished in mango cilantro sauce. The vegetarian offerings are more creative than most. An impressive wine list and ample selection of specialty coffees complement the menu.

Isla Río Cuale 16-A (just east of northbound bridge). ✆ 322/222-0283. www.lebistro.com.mx. Reservations recommended in high season. Breakfast $5–$8; main courses $19–$25. AE, MC, V. Mon–Sat 9am–midnight.

Moderate

Archie's Wok ✿✿✿ *Finds* ASIAN/SEAFOOD   Since 1986, Archie's has been legendary in Puerto Vallarta for serving original cuisine influenced by the intriguing flavors of Thailand, China, and the Philippines. Archie was Hollywood director John Huston's private chef during the years he spent in the area. Today his wife Cindy upholds his legacy at this tranquil retreat. The Thai mai tai and other tropical drinks, made from only fresh fruit and juices, are a good way to kick off a meal, as are the consistently crispy and delicious Filipino spring rolls. The popular Singapore fish filet features lightly battered filet strips in sweet-and-sour sauce; Thai garlic shrimp are prepared with fresh garlic, ginger, cilantro, and black pepper. Vegetarians have plenty of options, including broccoli, tofu, mushroom, and cashew stir-fry in black bean and sherry sauce. Finish with the signature Spice Islands coffee or a slice of lime cheese pie. Thursday through Saturday from 8 to 11pm, there's live classical harp and flute in Archie's Oriental garden.

Francisco Rodríguez 130 (½ block from the Los Muertos pier). ✆ 322/222-0411. awok@pvnet.com.mx. Main courses $6–$21. AE, MC, V. Mon–Sat 2–11pm. Closed Sept–Oct.

Espresso ✿✿ ITALIAN   This popular eatery is Vallarta's best late-night dining option. The two-level restaurant is on one of the town's busiest streets—across from El Torito's sports bar, and cater-cornered from the lively Señor Frog's—meaning that traffic noise is a factor, though not a deterrent. The food is superb, the service attentive, and the prices more than reasonable. Owned by a partnership of lively Italians, it serves food that is authentic in preparation and flavor, from thin-crust, brick-oven pizzas to savory homemade pastas. My favorite pizza is the "Quattro Stagioni," topped with artichokes, black olives, ham, and mushrooms. Excellent calzones and pannini (sandwiches) are also options. I prefer the rooftop garden area for dining, but many patrons gravitate to the pool table in the air-conditioned downstairs, which features major sports and entertainment events on satellite TV. Espresso also has full bar service and draft beer. Espresso is especially popular with *vallartenses* (locals).

Ignacio L. Vallarta 279. © 322/222-3272. Main courses $6.50–$13. AE, MC, V. Daily noon–4am.

La Palapa ★★ SEAFOOD/MEXICAN   This colorful, open-air, *palapa*-roofed restaurant on the beach is a decades-old local favorite, and with each recent visit, I have found the quality of both the food and service keeps improving. It's an exceptional dining experience, day or night. Enjoy a tropical breakfast by the sea, lunch on the beach, cocktails at sunset, or a romantic dinner (on a cloth-covered table in the sand). For lunch and dinner, seafood is the specialty; featured dishes include macadamia-and-coconut-crusted prawns, and poached red snapper with fresh cilantro sauce. Its location in the heart of Los Muertos Beach makes it an excellent place to start or end the day; I favor it for breakfast or, even better, a late-night sweet temptation and specialty coffee, while watching the moon over the bay. A particular draw is the all-you-can-eat Sunday brunch, which entitles you to a spot on popular Los Muertos beach for the day. A plus at lunch is you can enjoy the extra-comfortable beach chairs for postlunch sunbathing. A new classy bar area features acoustic guitars and vocals nightly from 8 to 11pm, generally performed by the owner, Alberto. La Palapa had a complete makeover in 2002 yet retained its charm and gracious service.

Pulpito 103. © 322/222-5225. Reservations recommended for dinner in high season. Breakfast $2.50–$12; main courses $7–$25; salad or sandwiches $5–$12. AE, MC, V. Daily 8am–11pm.

Inexpensive

Café San Angel CAFE   This comfortable, classic sidewalk cafe is a local gathering place from sunrise to sunset. For breakfast, choose a burrito stuffed with eggs and *chorizo* sausage, a three-egg Western omelet, crepes filled with mushrooms, Mexican classics like *huevos rancheros* and *chilaquiles,* or a tropical fruit plate. Deli sandwiches, crepes, and pastries round out the small but ample menu. The cafe also serves exceptional fruit smoothies, like the Yelapa—a blend of mango, banana, and orange juice—and perfectly made espresso drinks. Note that the service is reliably slow and frequently frustrating, so choose this place if you have time on your side—and keep in mind that it offers the best people-watching in the area. Bar service and Internet access are available.

Olas Altas 449 (at Francisco Rodríguez). © 322/223-1273. Breakfast $3.50–$6; main courses $3.50–$6. No credit cards. Daily 8am–1am.

Fajita Republic ★★ MEXICAN/SEAFOOD/STEAKS   Fajita Republic is consistently popular—and deservedly so. It has hit on a winning recipe: delicious food, ample portions, welcoming atmosphere, and low prices. The specialty is, of course, fajitas, grilled to perfection in every variety: steak, chicken, shrimp, combo, and vegetarian. All come with a generous tray of salsas and toppings. This "tropical grill" also serves sumptuous barbecued ribs, Mexican *molcajetes* with incredibly tender strips of marinated beef filet, and grilled shrimp. Starters include fresh guacamole served in a giant spoon and the ever-popular Mayan cheese sticks (breaded and deep-fried). Try an oversize mug or pitcher of Fajita Rita Mango Margaritas—or another spirited temptation. This is a casual, fun, festive place in a garden of mango and palm trees. A new, second location in Nuevo Vallarta, across from the Grand Velas Resort is drawing equal raves, with the same menu and prices.

Pino Suárez 321 (at Basilio Badillo), 1 block north of Olas Altas. ℂ **322/222-3131.** Breakfast $3.60–$4.70; main courses $9–$17. MC, V. Daily 9am–midnight.

Red Cabbage Café (El Repollo Rojo) ★★ (Finds) MEXICAN   The tiny, hard-to-find cafe is worth the effort—a visit here will reward you with exceptional traditional Mexican cuisine and a whimsical crash course in contemporary culture. The small room is covered wall-to-wall and table-to-table with photographs, paintings, movie posters, and news clippings about the cultural icons of Mexico. Frida Kahlo figures prominently in the decor, and a special menu duplicates dishes she and husband Diego Rivera prepared for guests.

Specialties from all over Mexico include divine *chiles en nogada* (poblanos stuffed with ground beef, pine nuts, and raisins, topped with sweet cream sauce and served cold), intricate chicken *mole* from Puebla, and hearty *carne en su jugo* (steak in its juice). In addition, the vegetarian menu is probably the most diverse and tasty in town (the owner offers cooking classes for groups of four or more). This is not the place for an intimate conversation, however—the poor acoustics cause everyone's conversations to blend together, although generally what you're hearing from adjacent tables are raves about the food. Also, this is a nonsmoking restaurant—the only one I'm aware of in town.

Calle Rivera del Río 204A (across from Río Cuale). ℂ **322/223-0411.** Main courses $5–$20. No credit cards. Daily 5–10:30pm.

JUNGLE RESTAURANTS

One of the unique attractions of Puerto Vallarta is its "jungle restaurants," south of town toward Mismaloya. They offer open-air dining in a tropical setting by the sea or beside a mountain river. The many varieties of "jungle" and "tropical" tours (see "Organized Tours," earlier in this chapter) include a stop for swimming and lunch. If you travel on your own, a taxi is the best transportation—the restaurants are quite a distance from the main highway. Taxis are usually waiting for return patrons.

The most recommendable of the jungle restaurants is the ecologically sensitive **El Nogalito** ★ (ℂ/fax **322/221-5225**). Located beside a clear jungle stream, the exceptionally clean, beautifully landscaped ranch serves lunch, beverages, and snacks on a shady, relaxing terrace. Several hiking routes depart from the grounds, and the restaurant provides a guide (whom you tip) to point out the native plants, birds, and wildlife. It's much closer to town than the other jungle restaurants: To find it, travel to Punta Negra, about 8km (5 miles) south of downtown Puerto Vallarta. A well-marked sign points up Calzada del Cedro, a dirt road, to the ranch. It's open daily from noon to 5:30pm. No credit cards.

Just past Boca de Tomatlán, at Highway 200 Km 20, is **Chico's Paradise** (ℂ **322/ 223-6005;** chicosp@prodigy.net.mx). It offers spectacular views of massive rocks—some marked with petroglyphs—and the surrounding jungle and mountains. There are natural pools and waterfalls for swimming, plus a small *mercado* selling pricey trinkets. The menu features excellent seafood as well as Mexican dishes. The quality is quite good, and the portions are generous, although prices are higher than in town—remember, you're paying for the setting. Open daily from 10am to 6pm. No credit cards.

PUERTO VALLARTA AFTER DARK

Puerto Vallarta's spirited nightlife reflects the town's dual nature: part resort, part colonial town. In years past, Vallarta was known for its live music scene, but in recent years the nocturnal action has shifted to DJ clubs, spinning an array of eclectic, contemporary music. A concentration of nightspots lies along Calle Ignacio L. Vallarta (the extension of the main southbound road) after it crosses the Río Cuale. Along one 3-block stretch you'll find a live blues club, sports bar, live mariachi music, gay dance club, steamy live salsa dance club, and the obligatory **Señor Frog's.** Walk from place to place and take in a bit of it all!

The *malecón,* which used to be lined with restaurants, is now known more for hip dance clubs and a few more relaxed options, all of which look out over the ocean. You can first stroll the broad walkway by the water's edge and check out the action at the various clubs, which extend from **Bodeguita del Medio** on the north end to **Hooters** just off the central plaza.

Marina Vallarta's clubs offer a more upscale, indoor, air-conditioned atmosphere. South of the Río Cuale, the **Olas Altas** zone's small cafes and martini bars buzz with action. In this zone, there's also an active gay and lesbian club scene.

PERFORMING ARTS & CULTURAL EVENTS

Truth be told, cultural nightlife beyond the **Mexican Fiesta** is limited. Culture centers on the visual arts; the opening of an exhibition has great social and artistic significance. Puerto Vallarta's gallery community comes together to present almost weekly **art walks,** where new exhibits are presented, featured artists attend, and complimentary cocktails are served. These social events alternate between the galleries along the Marina Vallarta *malecón* and those in the central downtown area. Check listings in the daily English-language newspaper, *Vallarta Today,* or the events section of www.virtual vallarta.com, to see what's on the schedule during your stay. Also of note are the free musical performances in the downtown plaza's gazebo—check with the municipal tourism office for current schedule.

FIESTA NIGHTS

Major hotels in Puerto Vallarta feature frequent fiestas for tourists—extravaganzas with open bars, Mexican buffet dinners, and live entertainment. Some are fairly authentic and make a good introduction for first-time travelers to Mexico; others can be a bit cheesy. Shows are usually held outdoors but move indoors when necessary. Reservations are recommended.

NH Krystal Vallarta   One of the best fiesta nights is here on Tuesday and Saturday at 7pm. These things are difficult to quantify, but Krystal's program is probably less tacky than those at most of its counterparts. Av. de las Palmas, north of downtown off the airport road. © 322/224-1041. kvallart@krystal.com.mx. Cover $48.

Rhythms of the Night (Cruise to Caletas) ★★★ *Moments*   This is an unforgettable evening under the stars at John Huston's former home at the pristine cove called Las Caletas. The smooth, fast Vallarta Adventures catamaran travels here, entertaining guests along the way. Tiki torches and native drummers greet you at the dock. There's no electricity—you dine by the light of candles, the stars, and the moon. The buffet dinner is delicious—steak, seafood, and generous vegetarian options. Everything is first-class. The entertainment showcases indigenous dances in contemporary style. The cruise departs at 6pm and returns by 11pm. Departs from Terminal Marítima. © 866/256-2739 toll-free in the U.S., or 322/297-1212, ext 3. www.vallarta-adventures.com. Cost $70 (includes cruise, dinner, open bar, and entertainment).

THE CLUB & MUSIC SCENE
Restaurant/Bars
Bar Constantini ⚝⚝ The newest and most sophisticated lounge in Vallarta is set in the elegant eatery, Café des Artistes. Opened in late 2003, it's become a popular option for those looking for a lively yet sophisticated option for after dinner drinks. The plush sofas are welcoming, and the list of champagnes by the glass, signature martinis, and specialty drinks are suitably tempting. Live jazz and blues in an intimate atmosphere are drawing crowds. An ample appetizer and dessert menu make it appropriate for a late-night dining-and-drinks option. Open from 6pm to 2am. Guadalupe Sánchez 740. ℂ **322/222-3229.**

Bianco ⚝ Among the more popular choices for sophisticated nightlife in Vallarta is the sleek Bianco. It has a long glass-top bar and cozy seating areas where conversation is possible. This is the spot—finally—for anyone over 30 who wants to enjoy an evening out, listening to contemporary music. The air-conditioned lounge also features occasional live music, notably salsa on Thursday nights. You can't miss the dramatic entrance, and the lounge even has valet parking—a first in Vallarta. Open daily from 5pm to 4am. Insurgentes 109, Col. Emiliano Zapata. ℂ **322/222-2748.**

Carlos O'Brian's Vallarta's original nightspot was once the only place for an evening of revelry. Although the competition is stiffer nowadays, COB's still packs them in—especially the 20-something set. The late-night scene resembles a college party. Open daily from noon to 2am; happy hour is from noon to 6pm. Paseo Díaz Ordaz (*malecón*) 786, at Pípila. ℂ **322/222-1444** or 322/222-4065. Weekend cover $11 (includes 2 drinks).

Kit Kat Club ⚝ It's swank and sleek and reminiscent of a New York club, but don't be fooled—the Kit Kat Club also has a terrific sense of humor. In the golden glow of candlelight, lounge around on cushy leopard-patterned chairs or cream-colored overstuffed banquettes, listening to swinging tunes while you sip a martini. Not only does the place attract a very hip, generally gay crowd, but it also serves good food, with especially tasty appetizers—which can double as light meals—and scrumptious desserts. Michael, the owner, describes his air-conditioned lounge and cafe as cool, crazy, wild, jazzy, and sexy. Often, in high season, you'll be treated to a cabaret-style floorshow performed by a cross-dressing songstress. Open daily from 6pm to 2am. Pulpito 120, Playa Los Muertos. ℂ **322/223-0093.**

La Bodeguita del Medio This authentic Cuban restaurant and bar is known for its casual energy, terrific live music, and mojitos. It is a branch of the original Bodeguita in Havana (reputedly Hemingway's favorite restaurant there), which opened in 1942. If you can't get to that one, the Vallarta version has successfully imported the essence—and has a small souvenir shop that sells Cuban cigars, rum, and other items. The downstairs has large wooden windows that open to the *malecón* street action, while the upstairs offers terrific views of the bay. Walls throughout are decorated with old photographs and patrons' signatures—if you can, find a spot and add yours! I feel the food is less memorable here than the music and atmosphere, so I recommend drinks and dancing, nothing more. Open daily from 11:30am to 2am. Paseo Díaz Ordaz (*malecón*), at Allende. ℂ **322/223-1585.**

La Cantina de los Remedios Cantinas are a centuries-old Mexican tradition, and this one has retained the fundamentals while updating the concept to a hip club. Cantinas serve little complimentary plates of food as your table orders drinks. La Cantina does this from 1 to 5pm; dishes might include *carne con chile* (meat in chile sauce), soup of the day, or quesadillas. In the evenings, recorded music alternates between sultry boleros and the hottest in Mexican rock, at a volume that permits conversation, creating a romantic, clubby atmosphere. If you require more stimulation, play a board game in one of the smaller rooms or on the larger open-air patio. Beers cost $1.50, bar drinks $2.50. Open Sunday through Wednesday from noon to 2am, Thursday through Saturday from noon to 4am. No credit cards. Morelos 709, downtown. © 322/222-7701.

Rock, Jazz & Blues

Club Roxy   A popular live-music club in Vallarta, Club Roxy features a hot house band led by club owner Pico, playing a mix of reggae, blues, rock, and anything by Santana. Live music jams between 10pm and 2am Monday through Saturday nights. It's open daily from 6pm to 2am. Ignacio L. Vallarta 217 (between Madero and Cárdenas, south of the river). No phone.

El Faro Lighthouse Bar 🏅   A circular cocktail lounge at the top of the Marina lighthouse, El Faro is one of Vallarta's most romantic nightspots. Live or recorded jazz plays, and conversation is manageable. Drop by at twilight for the magnificent panoramic views, but don't expect anything other than a drink and, if you get lucky, some popcorn. Open daily from 5pm to 2am. Royal Pacific Yacht Club, Marina Vallarta. © 322/221-0541 or 322/221-0542. elfaropv@pvnet.com.mx.

Mariachi Loco   This lively mariachi club features singers belting out boleros and ranchero classics. The mariachi show begins at 9pm—the mariachis stroll and play as guests join in impromptu singing—and by 10pm it gets going. After midnight the mariachis play for pay, which is around $10 for each song played at your table. There's Mexican food from 7 to 10:30pm. Open daily from 1pm to 4am. Cárdenas 254 (at Ignacio Vallarta). © 322/223-2205.

Clubs & Discos

A few of Vallarta's clubs or discos charge admission, but generally you pay just for drinks—$4 for a margarita, $2.50 for a beer, more for whiskey and mixed drinks. Keep an eye out for discount passes frequently available in hotels, restaurants, and other tourist spots. Most clubs are open from 10pm to 4am.

Christine   This dazzling club draws a crowd with an opening laser-light show, pumped-in dry ice, flashing lights, and a dozen large-screen video panels. Once a disco—in the true sense of the word—it received a needed face-lift in 2003, and is now a more modern dance club, with techno, house, and hip-hop the primary tunes played. The sound system is truly amazing, and the mix of music can get almost anyone dancing. Dress code: No shorts for men, tennis shoes, or thongs. Open daily from 10pm to 4am; the light show begins at 11pm. In the Krystal Vallarta hotel, north of downtown off Av. Francisco Medina Ascencio. © 322/224-0202. Cover free–$6.

de Santos 🏅🏅🏅   Vallarta's chicest dining spot is known more for the urban, hip crowd the bar draws—it is *the* local hot spot. In 2003 it added a stunning state-of-the-art club, which quickly became the place for the superchic to party. The lower level holds an air-conditioned bar and dance floor, where a DJ spins the hottest of house and techno. Upstairs, there's an open-air rooftop bar with chill-out music and acid jazz. Enjoy the tunes and the fresh air while lounging around on one of the several oversize beds. One partner, a member of the superhot Latin rock group Mana, uses Vallarta as a home base for writing songs. The crowd, which varies in age from 20s on up, shares a common denominator of cool style. The restaurant bar is open daily from

5pm to 1am; the club is open Wednesday through Saturday from 10pm to 6am, and often waives the cover charge for women. Wednesday nights—Ladies' Night—draws a particularly large crowd. Morelos 771. **(C) 322/223-3052** or -3053. Cover usually $10 (includes 1 drink).

Emporium by Collage   A multilevel monster of nighttime entertainment, Collage includes a pool salon, video arcade, bowling alley, and the always-packed Disco Bar, with frequent live entertainment. It's just past the entrance to Marina Vallarta, air-conditioned, and very popular with a young, mainly local crowd. Open daily from 10am to 6am. Calle Proa s/n, Marina Vallarta. **(C) 322/221-0505** or 322/221-0861. Cover $5.50–$25, but call ahead as cover varies depending on the theme—Mardi Gras, Foam Party, Black Light party, and so on.

Hilo   You'll recognize Hilo by the giant-sized sculptures that practically reach out the front entrance and pull you into this high-energy club, which has become a favorite with the 20-something set. Music ranges from house and electronic to rock. It seems the later the hour, the more crowded the place becomes. Open daily from 10am to 6am. *Malecón*, between Aldama and Abasolo sts. **(C) 322/223-5361.** Cover $7, weekends and holidays.

J & B Salsa Club   This is the locally popular place to go for dancing to Latin music—from salsa to samba, the dancing is hot! On Fridays, Saturdays, and holidays the air-conditioned club features live bands. Open Monday through Saturday from 10pm to 6am. Av. Francisco Medina Ascencio Km 2.5 (Hotel Zone). **(C) 322/224-4616.** Cover $9.

Nikki Beach   This haven of the hip hails from South Beach, Miami, and St. Tropez, and has brought its ultracool vibe to Vallarta. White-draped bed-size lounges scatter the outdoor lounge area, under a canopy of tall palms and umbrellas. Indoor dining and lounge areas are also available. The music is the latest in electronic, house, and chill, with visiting DJs often playing on weekend nights. Sundays feature their signature beach brunch, and Thursday evenings feature "Beautiful People" night. It's a great choice for catching rays during the day while sipping tropical drinks, but its real appeal is the nocturnal action. Open Sunday to Wednesday from 11am to 1am (food service stops at 11pm); Thursday to Saturday from 11am to 3am (food service stops at 1am.). On the beach at the Westin Regina Resort, Marina Vallarta. **(C) 322/221-0252** or 322/226-1150. www.nikkibeach.com.

The Palm Video & Show Bar   The big screen above the dance floor of this colorful, lively club plays the most danceable videos in town. They're certain to get you moving. The pool table is regularly in play, and the air-conditioned club frequently books live shows featuring female impersonators. This is a gay-friendly but not exclusively gay club, with a spirited, festive atmosphere. Open daily from 7pm to 2am. Olas Altas 508. **(C) 322/223-4813.** www.thepalmbar.com. Cover $5 on show nights only.

Señor Frog's   The sheer size of this outpost of the famed Carlos 'n' Charlie's chain is daunting, but it fills up and rocks until the early morning hours. Cute waiters are a signature of the chain, and one never knows when they'll assemble on stage and call on a bevy of beauties to join them in a tequila-drinking contest. Occasionally live bands appear. Although mainly popular with the 20s set, all ages will find the air-conditioned club fun. There's food service, but it's better known for its dance-club atmosphere. Open daily from 11am to 4am. Ignacio L. Vallarta and Venustiano Carranza. **(C) 322/222-5171** or 322/222-5177. Cover–$11 (includes 2 drinks).

Zoo   Your chance to be an animal and get wild in the night. Zoo even has cages to dance in if you're feeling unleashed. This popular club has a terrific sound system and a great variety of dance music, including techno, reggae, and rap. Every hour's happy hour, with two-for-one drinks. It opens daily at noon and closes in the wee hours. Paseo Díaz Ordaz (*malecón*) 630. ✆ **322/222-4945.** Cover $11 (includes 2 drinks).

A SPORTS BAR
Micky's No Name Cafe   With a multitude of TVs and enough sports memorabilia to start a mini-museum, Micky's is a great venue for catching your favorite game. It shows all NBA, NHL, NFL, and MLB broadcast events, plus pay-per-view. Mickey's also serves great barbecued ribs and USDA imported steaks. It's open daily from 9am to midnight. Morelos 460 (*malecón*), at Mina. ✆ **322/223-2508.**

GAY & LESBIAN CLUBS
Vallarta has a vibrant gay community with a wide variety of clubs and nightlife options, including special bay cruises and evening excursions to nearby ranches. The free *Gay Guide Vallarta* (✆ **322/299-0936;** www.gayguidevallarta.com) specializes in gay-friendly listings, including weekly specials and happy hours.

Club Paco Paco   This combination disco, cantina, and rooftop bar stages a spectacular "Trasvesty" transvestite show every Thursday, Friday, Saturday, and Sunday night at 1:30am. It's open daily from 1pm to 6am and is air-conditioned. Ignacio L. Vallarta 278. ✆ **322/222-1899.** www.pacopaco.com. Cover $6 (includes 1 drink) after 10pm or start of 1st show, whichever is earlier.

Garbos   This small, cozy club is gay friendly, but not exclusively gay, and features great recorded music and occasional live music on weekends. It's open daily from 6pm to 2am and is air-conditioned. Pulpito 142. ✆ **322/229-7309.**

Los Balcones   One of the original gay clubs in town, this air-conditioned bi-level space boasts several dance floors and an excellent sound system. It earned a few chuckles when *Brides* magazine listed it as one of the most romantic spots in Vallarta. It posts nightly specials, including exotic male dancers. Open from 9pm to 4am, daily November through March, closed Sunday in the off season. Juárez 182. ✆ **322/222-4671.**

Ranch Disco Bar   This place is known for the nightly "Ranch Hand's Show," at 11:30pm and 2am. The club also has a new dance floor. Open daily from 9pm to 6am. Venustiano Carranza 239 (around the corner from Paco Paco, and can also be accessed directly from Paco Paco). ✆ **322/223-0537.** Cover $6 (includes 1 drink).

SIDE TRIPS FROM PUERTO VALLARTA
YELAPA: ROBINSON CRUSOE MEETS JACK KEROUAC 🏆   It's a cove straight out of a tropical fantasy, and only a 45-minute trip by boat from Puerto Vallarta. Yelapa has no cars, has one sole paved (pedestrian-only) road, and got electricity only in the past 3 years. It's accessible only by boat. Its tranquillity, natural beauty, and seclusion have made it a popular home for hippies, hipsters, artists, writers, and a few expats (looking to escape the stress of the world, or perhaps the law). A seemingly strange mix, but you're unlikely to ever meet a stranger—Yelapa remains casual and friendly.

To get there, travel by excursion boat or inexpensive water taxi (see "Getting Around," earlier in this chapter). You can spend an enjoyable day, but I recommend a longer stay—it provides a completely different perspective.

Once you're in Yelapa, you can lie in the sun, swim, snorkel, eat fresh grilled seafood at a beachside restaurant, or sample the local moonshine, *raicilla.* The local beach vendors specialize in the most amazing pies you've ever tasted (coconut, lemon, or chocolate). Equally amazing is how the pie ladies walk the beach while balancing the pie plates on their heads; they sell crocheted swimsuits, too. You can also tour this tiny town or hike up a river to see one of two waterfalls. The closest to town is about a 30-minute walk from the beach. *Note:* If you use a local guide, agree on a price before you start out. Horseback riding, guided birding, fishing trips, and paragliding are also available.

For overnight accommodations, local residents frequently rent rooms, and there's also the rustic **Hotel Lagunita** ☆ (© 322/209-5056 or -5055; www.hotel-lagunita. com). Its 32 cabañas have private bathrooms, and the hotel has electricity, a saltwater pool, primitive spa with massage, an amiable restaurant and bar, as well as the Baracuda Beach lounge and brick-oven pizza cafe, plus a gourmet coffee shop. Though the prices are high for what you get, it is the most accommodating place for most visitors. Double rates run $95 during the season and $75 in the off season (MasterCard and Visa are accepted). Lagunita has become a popular spot for yoga retreats, and regularly features yoga classes.

A stylish alternative is the fashionable **Verana** ☆☆☆ (© 800/677-5156 or 322/222-2360; www.verana.com). See "Where to Stay," earlier, for details.

If you stay over on a Wednesday or Saturday during the winter, don't miss the regular dance at the **Yelapa Yacht Club** ☆ (no phone). Typically tongue-in-cheek for Yelapa, the "yacht club" consists of a cement dance floor and a disco ball, but the DJ spins a great range of tunes, from Glenn Miller to Eminem, attracting all ages and types. Dinner ($5–$12) is a bonus—the food may be the best anywhere in the bay. The menu changes depending on what's fresh. Ask for directions; it's in the main village, on the beach.

NUEVO VALLARTA & NORTH OF VALLARTA: ALL-INCLUSIVES

Many people assume Nuevo Vallarta is a suburb of Puerto Vallarta, but it's a stand-alone destination over the state border in Nayarit. It was designed as a megaresort development, complete with marina, golf course, and luxury hotels. Although it got off to a slow start, it is finally coming together, with a collection of mostly all-inclusive hotels on one of the widest, most attractive beaches in the bay. The biggest resort, Paradise Village, has a growing marina and an 18-hole golf course inland from the beachside strip of hotels. The Mayan Palace also recently opened an 18-hole course. The Paradise Plaza shopping center, next to Paradise Village, adds much to the area's shopping, dining, and services. It's open daily from 10am to 10pm. To get to the beach, you travel down a lengthy entrance road from the highway, passing by fields (great for birding) and nearby lagoons (great for kayaking).

Also worthwhile is a day spent at the **Etc. Beach Club,** Paseo de los Cocoteros 38, Nuevo Vallarta (© 322/297-0174). This beach club has a volleyball net, showers, restroom facilities, and food and drink service on the beach, both day and night. To get there, take the second entrance to Nuevo Vallarta coming from Puerto Vallarta and turn right on Paseo de los Cocoteros; it is past the Vista Bahía hotel. It's open daily during the winter from 11am to 10:30pm, summer from 11am to 7pm. Drinks cost $2.50 to $7, entrees $4.50 to $17; cash only.

A trip into downtown Puerto Vallarta takes about 30 minutes by taxi, costs about $15, and is available 24 hours a day. The ride is slightly longer by public bus, which costs $1.20 and operates from 7am to 11pm.

Marival Grand & Club Suites This all-inclusive hotel sits almost by itself at the northernmost end of Nuevo Vallarta. Done in Mediterranean style, it offers a complete vacation experience, from its beautiful beach to adjacent disco. There are a large variety of room types, ranging from standard units with no balconies to large master suites with whirlpools. The master suites have minibars and hair dryers. The broad white-sand beach is one of the real assets here—it stretches over 450 m (1,500 ft.). There is also an extensive activities program, including fun for children.

Paseo de los Cocoteros and Bulevar Nuevo Vallarta s/n, 63735 Nuevo Vallarta, Nay. ℂ 322/297-0100. Fax 322/297-0262. www.gomarival.com. 495 units. High season $246 double; low season $230 double. Upgrade to junior suite $50 per day, to master suite with whirlpool $300 per day. Rates are all-inclusive. Ask for seasonal specials. AE, MC, V. From the Puerto Vallarta airport, enter Nuevo Vallarta from the 2nd entrance; Club Marival is the 1st resort to your right on Paseo de los Cocoteros. **Amenities:** 6 restaurants; 8 bars; 3 pools and a whirlpool for adults; 2 pools and a water park for children; 4 lighted tennis courts; spa; business center; salon. *In room:* A/C, TV, safe-deposit boxes.

Paradise Village ⭐⭐ Truly a village, this self-contained resort on an exquisite stretch of beach offers a full array of services, from an on-site disco to a full-service European spa and health club. The collection of pyramid-shaped buildings, designed in Maya-influenced style, houses well-designed all-suite accommodations in studio, one-bedroom, and two-bedroom configurations. All have sitting areas and kitchenettes, making the resort ideal for families or groups of friends. The Maya theme extends to both oceanfront pools, with mythical creatures forming water slides and waterfalls. The exceptional spa is reason enough to book a vacation here, with treatments, hydrotherapy, massage (including massage on the beach), and fitness and yoga classes. Special spa packages are always available. A new and compelling attraction is their El Tigre golf course (details earlier in this chapter, under "Golf"), and their onsite marina continues to draw a growing number of boats and yachts.

Paseo de los Cocoteros 001, 63731 Nuevo Vallarta, Nay. ℂ 800/995-5714 in the U.S., or 322/226-6770. Fax 322/226-6713. www.paradisevillage.com. 490 units. High season $164–$308 junior or 1-bedroom suite; 2-bedroom suite $340-$388, 3-bedroom suite $565-$599; low season $137–$246 junior or 1-bedroom suite; 2-bedroom suite $246-$267, 3-bedroom suite $514-$546. AE, DC, MC, V. **Amenities:** 2 restaurants; 2 beachside snack bars; theme nights; nightclub; 2 beachside swimming pools; lap pool; championship golf club w/18-hole course; 4 tennis courts; European spa and complete fitness center; watersports center; Kid's Club; travel services desk; guests-only rental-car fleet; basketball court; beach volleyball; petting zoo; full marina. *In room:* A/C, TV, dataport, minibar, coffeemaker, hair dryer, iron, safe-deposit box.

BUCERIAS: A COASTAL VILLAGE ⭐

Only 18km (11 miles) north of the Puerto Vallarta airport, Bucerías ("boo-seh-*ree*-ahs," meaning "place of the divers") is a small coastal fishing village of 10,000 people in Nayarit state on Banderas Bay. It's caught on as an alternative to Puerto Vallarta for those who find the pace of life there too invasive. Bucerías offers a seemingly contradictory mix of accommodations—trailer-park spaces and exclusive villa rentals tend to dominate, although there's a small selection of hotels as well.

To reach the town center by car, take the exit road from the highway and drive down the shaded, divided street that leads to the beach. Turn left when you see a line of minivans and taxis (which serve Bucerías and Vallarta). Go straight ahead 1 block to the main plaza. The beach, with a lineup of restaurants, is a half-block farther. You'll see cobblestone streets leading from the highway to the beach, and hints of villas and town homes behind high walls. Second-home owners and about 1,500 transplanted Americans have already sought out this peaceful getaway; tourists have discovered its relaxed pace as well.

If you take the bus to Bucerías, exit when you see the minivans and taxis to and from Bucerías line up on the street that leads to the beach. To use public transportation from Puerto Vallarta, take a minivan or bus marked BUCERIAS (they run from

6am–9pm). The last minivan stop is Bucerías's town square. There's also 24-hour taxi service.

Exploring Bucerías   Come here for a day trip from Puerto Vallarta just to enjoy the long, wide, uncrowded beach, along with the fresh seafood served at the beachside restaurants or at one of the unusually great cafes listed below. If you are inclined to stay a few days, you can relax inexpensively and explore more of Bucerías. Sunday is street-market day, but it doesn't get going until around noon, in keeping with the town's casual pace.

The **Coral Reef Surf Shop,** Heroe de Nacozari 114-F (© **329/298-0261**), sells a great selection of surfboards and gear, and offers surfboard and boogie board rentals, surf lessons, and ATV and other adventure tours to surrounding areas.

Where to Stay   Unfortunately, I cannot recommend any of the hotels in Bucerías; they're run-down, and most people who choose to stay here opt for a private home rental. Check out the villa rental bulletin board at **www.sunworx.com**. **Las Palmas** in Bucerías (© **329/298-0060;** fax 329/298-1100) will book accommodations, including villas, houses, and condos. Call ahead, or ask for directions to the office when you get to Bucerías. It's open Monday through Friday from 9am to 2pm and 4 to 6pm, Saturday from 9am to 2pm.

Where to Dine   Besides those mentioned below, there are many seafood restaurants fronting the beach. The local specialty is *pescado zarandeado,* a whole fish smothered in tasty sauce and slow-grilled.

Cafe Magaña 🌟🌟 BARBECUED RIBS   Famous for its ribs and chicken, Cafe Magaña gives you a choice of 10 original homemade sauces, including the "legendary" Salsa Magaña. Flavors have mythological names and contain creative ingredients like ginger, garlic, oranges, apples, cinnamon, and chiles. The sauces have been such a hit that British owner Jeff Rafferty also sells bottled versions and says to look for them commercially soon. This casual, colorful cafe and take-out restaurant also features TV sports and an occasional live band.

Calle Lázaro Cárdenas 40. © **329/298-1761**. www.sunworx.com/salsa. Main courses $7–$12. No credit cards. Daily 5–11pm.

Karen's Place 🌟 INTERNATIONAL/MEXICAN   This casual oceanside restaurant offers classic cuisine, plus Mexican favorites in a style that appeals to North American appetites. Known for Sunday Champagne brunch (9am–3pm), it is a perfect place to enjoy a light beach lunch, or a romantic dinner. The best-selling entree is a Parmesan herb-crusted fish filet with a salad of baby greens. The casual, comfortable restaurant features live music on Tuesday and Thursday. It also has a terrace dining area with spectacular views, and a sushi menu.

On the beach at the Costa Dorada, Calle Lázaro Cárdenas. © **329/229-6892** or 329/298-0832. www.all.at/karens. Breakfast $4.50–$5.50; Sun brunch (9am–3pm) $12; main courses $5.50–$13. No credit cards. Tues–Sun 9am–9pm.

Le Fort 🌟🌟🌟 FRENCH   What an unforgettable dining experience! It's more than dinner—the evening consists of watching as Chef Gilles Le Fort prepares your gourmet meal and teaches you how to re-create it. The U-shaped bar in the intimate kitchen accommodates diners, who sip fine wines and nibble on pâté while the master works. Chef Le Fort is the winner of numerous culinary awards, and his warm conviviality is the real secret ingredient of this unusual experience. Once dinner is served, the chef and his wife, Margarita, will join the table, entertaining with stories of their experiences in Mexico. The first group of six to book for the evening chooses the menu; the maximum class size is 16, so groups often blend together. Le Fort has probably the most extensive wine cellar in the bay—some 4,000 bottles. Hand-rolled Cuban cigars, homemade sausages, pâtés, and more delicacies are available in the adjoining shop.

Calle Lázaro Cárdenas 71, 1 block from the Hotel Royal DeCameron. (€ 329/298-1532. www.lefort.com.mx. Reservations required. 3-course dinner, wines, and recipes $45 per person. No credit cards. Daily 8–10:30pm; cooking classes available 10am–1:30pm.

Mark's ★★ *(Finds)* ITALIAN/STEAK/SEAFOOD   It's worth a special trip to Bucerías just to eat at this covered-patio restaurant. The most popular American hangout in town, Mark's offers a great assortment of thin-crust pizzas and flatbread, baked in its brick oven and seasoned with fresh herbs grown in the garden. Everything has exquisite flavorings—some favorites include shrimp in angel-hair pasta, pesto-crusted fish filet, Ahi tuna served rare, and filet mignon with bleu-cheese ravioli. Multitalented chef Jan Marie (Mark's charming wife and partner) runs an adjacent boutique, featuring elegant home accessories and unique gift items. The bar televises all major sporting events.

Calle Lázaro Cárdenas 56, ½ block from the beach. (€ 329/298-0303. Pasta $8.70–$19; main courses $13–$22. MC, V. High season daily 5–11pm; low season daily 5–10pm. From the highway, turn left just after bridge, where there's a small sign for Mark's. Double back left at next street (immediately after you turn left) and turn right at next corner. Mark's is on the right.

PUNTA MITA: EXCLUSIVE SECLUSION ★★★

At the northern tip of the bay is an arrowhead-shaped, 600-hectare (1,500-acre) peninsula bordered on three sides by the ocean, called Punta Mita. Considered a sacred place by the Indians, this is the point where Banderas Bay, the Pacific Ocean, and the Sea of Cortez come together. It's magnificent, with white-sand beaches and coral reefs just offshore. Stately rocks jut out along the shoreline, and the water is a dreamy translucent blue. Punta Mita is evolving into one of Mexico's most exclusive developments. The master plan calls for a total of five luxury hotels, several high-end residential communities, and three championship golf courses. It is the first luxury residential development in Mexico intended for the foreign market. Today, all you'll find is the elegant Four Seasons Resort and its Jack Nicklaus Signature golf course, but by next year, a new 68-unit all-suite Rosewood resort will open, and shortly after that, a St. Regis resort will open, along with Punta Mita's second Jack Nicklaus golf course.

Four Seasons Resort Punta Mita ★★★   The Four Seasons Resort has brought a new standard of luxury to Mexico's Pacific Coast. The boutique hotel artfully combines seclusion and pampering service with a welcoming sense of comfort. Accommodations are in three-story *casitas* surrounding the main building, which holds the lobby, cultural center, restaurants, and pool. Every guest room offers breathtaking views of the ocean from a large terrace or balcony. Most suites also offer a private plunge pool, a separate sitting room, a bar, and a powder room. Room interiors are typical Four Seasons—plush and spacious, with a king or two double beds, a seating area, and an oversized bathroom with a deep soaking tub, separate glass-enclosed shower, and dual vanity sink. More than the stylish luxury, this hotel boasts unerring service that is both warm and unobtrusive. At least 45 minutes from Puerto Vallarta's activities, it's the perfect get-away—but then, most guests feel so relaxed and at ease, it's hard to think of venturing beyond the resort at all. The full-service spa, tennis center, and private championship golf course seem to be options enough.

63734 Bahía de Banderas, Nay. ⓒ 800/332-3442 in the U.S., or 329/291-6000. Fax 329/291-6060. www.fourseasons. com. 140 units. High season $691–$796 double, $1,814–$2,048 suite; low season $457–$656 double, $1,170– $1,287 suite. AE, DC, MC, V. Free valet parking. **Amenities:** 2 restaurants; lobby bar; heated infinity pool surrounded by private cabañas; tennis center w/4 courts of various surfaces; full-service fitness center; European-style spa; *temazcal;* watersports equipment including sea kayaks, Windsurfers, surfboards, and sunfish sailboats; Kids for All Seasons children's activity program; game room, 24-hr. concierge service; tour desk; 24-hr. room service; daily activity agenda; cultural center w/lectures and activities; complimentary video library. *In room:* A/C, TV/VCR, dataport, minibar, coffeemaker, hair dryer, iron, safe-deposit box, high-speed Internet access.

Casa Las Brisas ★★ *(Finds)*   Although not technically in Punta Mita, Casa Las Brisas is near enough to get the sense of relaxed seclusion of this area, in an intimate setting. It's located on the back road that runs from Punta Mita to Sayulita, on the small, pristine Careyerros Bay. The six rooms are set in a villa, overlooking the exquisite beach. The villa itself is a work of white stucco walls, tile floors and patios, thatch and tile roofs and guayaba wood balcony detailing. Patios and intimate indoor-outdoor seating areas on varying levels are ideal for an afternoon read or an evening cocktail. Interiors of the guest rooms are simple and elegant, with touches such as carved armoires, headboards and doors from Michoacan. The colorful bathrooms feature large showers lined with hand-painted tiles. Private balconies with ocean views surround the pool, which features submerged sunning chairs and a small fountain. There are no TVs or telephones, but a cellphone in the lobby is available for guests. A big plus here is the delicious dining, included in the price of your stay.

Playa Careyero, 63734 Punta de Mita, Nay. ⓒ 877/278-8018 in the U.S., 322/306-2122, or 322/225-4364. www. mexicoboutiquehotels.com/casalasbrisas/index.html. 7 suites. High season $385–$445 suite; low season $335–$395 suite. Rates include all meals and drinks, minimum 3-night stay required. Credit cards for deposit only; cash payment upon booking. **Amenities:** Restaurant; small pool; universal gym station; spa services; tour services; entertainment room w/TV, DVD, and VCR. *In room:* Remote-controlled A/C, minibar, safe-deposit box, bathrobes.

SAYULITA: MUCH MORE THAN A GREAT SURF SPOT   Sayulita is only 40km
(25 miles) northwest of Puerto Vallarta, on Highway 200 to Tepic, yet it feels like worlds away. It captures the simplicity and tranquillity of beach life that has long since left Vallarta—but hurry, because it seems this place is on the verge of exploding in popularity. For years, Sayulita has been principally a surfers' destination—the main beach in town is known for its consistent break and long, rideable waves. Recently, visitors and locals who find Vallarta becoming too cosmopolitan have started to flock to here.

An easygoing attitude seems to permeate the air in this beach town. Yet despite its simplicity, niceties are popping up all over among the basic accommodations, inexpensive Mexican food stands, and handmade, hippie-style baubles. It's quickly becoming gentrified with new restaurants, cafes, and elegant villas for rent.

Sayulita is a popular stage for surfing tournaments; on any given weekend you might encounter perfect-swell-seeking surfers—or a Huichol Indian family that has come down to sell their wares. This eclectic mix of the cool, the unusual, and the authentic Mexican makes Sayulita such a special place.

To get to Sayulita, you can rent a car, or take a taxi from the airport or downtown Vallarta. The rate is about $50 to get to the town plaza. You can also take a taxi back to Vallarta. The stand is on the main square, or you can call for pickup at your hotel. The trip from the airport to Sayulita costs $55. Guides also lead tours to Puerto Vallarta, Punta Mita, and other surrounding areas, including a Huichol Indian community.

Where to Stay   Sayulita offers several private homes for rent. Your best option is to contact **Upi Viteri** (upiviteri@prodigy.net.mx), who has access to some of the nicest rental properties.

Villa Amor   Villa Amor is a collection of inviting, airy, perfectly appointed guest rooms—think of it as your private villa by the sea. Owner Rod Ingram and his design team have carefully crafted each space and individual suite into something truly special. The exterior walls curve invitingly and open up to breathtaking views all around. The one- and two-bedroom suites have fully equipped kitchenettes, plus open-air seating or dining areas (or both), and some have plunge pools. TVs are available on request. Construction of 24 new villas is under way; it makes the place a bit unsightly from the road, but once you're there, you'll find the peace and beauty you came for.

Camino Playa Los Muertos s/n, 63732 Sayulita, Nay. ⓒ 329/291-3010. Fax 329/291-3018. www.villaamor.com. 21 units. $85 double; $135–$195 1-bedroom villa, $275–$350 2-bedroom villa. No credit cards. **Amenities:** Restaurant; kayaks; boogie boards; surfboards; bicycles; concierge; tour desk; room service; massage. *In room:* Fan.

Where to Dine   If you are in Sayulita, chances are you heard about it because of **Don Pedro's,** the most popular restaurant in town, in the heart of the main beach.

Don Pedro's INTERNATIONAL   Many say it's Don Pedro's that has brought so much attention to Sayulita in recent years—Vallarta area visitors came for the food, then booked their next vacation in this funky town. Choose between a two-level indoor dining area, or shaded tables on the beach for breakfast, lunch or dinner. Starters include crispy calamari, spring rolls, and fresh salads. Main courses include thin-crust pizzas, fresh fish artfully prepared, and a changing selection of savory pasta and chicken dishes, such as chicken Provençal, a whole chicken marinated in garlic and herbs, served with sautéed spinach and roasted tomatoes and white beans. Grilled Ahi tuna with mashed potatoes is also a favorite. In the bar area, TVs broadcast sporting events of any relevance, from the Super Bowl to Mexican soccer. I enjoy a relaxing lunch here, then staying for the beach action. Full bar service also available.

Marlin 2, on the beachfront. ⓒ 329/291-3090. www.donpedros.com. Main courses $4–$14. MC, V. Daily 8am–11pm.

L'Ultima Spiaggia ITALIAN   Paolo, an Italian chef, runs this tiny restaurant by the seashore. The menu is simple and classic, with salads, pizzas, and pastas. Paolo picks the freshest ingredients at the market every morning for his daily specials. They usually include fresh fish and seafood pasta dishes. Start with dorado carpaccio. The pizzas, baked in a wood-burning oven, have thin, crispy crusts. Don't miss the gnocchi, homemade fresh every day. The restaurant has a table out by the sea, which is perfect for romantic dinners. Breakfast features European-style offerings, including light omelets and fresh fruit. The espressos and cappuccinos are by far the best in Sayulita.

Camino Playa Los Muertos s/n, downstairs from Villa Amor. ⓒ 322/100-6879. Breakfast $3–$8; pizza $7–$11; main courses $8–$17. No credit cards. Tues–Sun 8:30–11am and 6–11pm.

Rollie's ★★ (Finds BREAKFAST   Breakfast heaven! This family restaurant emanates a happy aura that puts its patrons in a good mood. The menu reflects the tone of the place, with options such as Rollie's Delight (blended fresh orange and banana), Adriana's Rainbow (an omelet with cheese, tomatoes, green peppers, and onions), and my personal favorite, Indian Pipe Pancakes. All dishes come with Rollie's famous potatoes (lightly seasoned pan-fried new potatoes).

Av. Revolución, 2 blocks west of the main square. ⓒ 329/291-3053. Breakfast $3–$8. No credit cards. Daily Nov–Apr 8am–noon. Closed May–Oct.

SAN SEBASTIÁN: AN AUTHENTIC MOUNTAIN HIDEAWAY ★★★   If you

haven't heard about San Sebastián yet, it probably won't be long—its remote location and historic appeal have made it the Mexican media's new darling destination.

Originally discovered in the late 1500s and settled in 1603, the town peaked as a center of mining operations, swelling to a population of over 30,000 by the mid-1800s. Today, with roughly 600 year-round residents, San Sebastián retains all the charm of a village locked in time, with an old church, a coffee plantation, an underground tunnel system—and wholly without a T-shirt shop.

Getting There   By car, it's a 2½-hour drive up the Sierra Madre from Puerto Vallarta on an improved road, but it can be difficult during the summer rainy season, when the road washes out frequently. **Vallarta Adventures** (© 866/256-2739 toll-free in the U.S., or 322/297-1212, ext. 3; www.vallarta-adventures.com) runs a daily plane service for half-day tours and can occasionally accommodate overnight visitors. The small private airport can arrange flights. **Aerotrón** (© 322/221-1921) charges about $130 round-trip, **Aéro Taxis de la Bahía** (© 322/221-1990) about $92 round-trip, depending on the type of plane and number of passengers. For more information on air tours and horseback-riding excursions, see the "Organized Tours" section, earlier in this chapter.

Where to Stay   There are two places to stay in San Sebastián. The first is the very basic **El Pabellón de San Sebastián,** which faces the town square. Its nine simply furnished rooms surround a central patio. Don't expect extras here; rates run $40 per double. The town's central phone lines handle reservations—you call (© 322/297-0200) and leave a message or send a fax, and hopefully the hotel will receive it. More reliable is e-mail: ssb@pvnet.com.mx. Except on holidays, there is generally room at this inn. No credit cards.

A more enjoyable option is the stately **Hacienda Jalisco** 🏇🏇 (© 322/223-1695; www.haciendajalisco.com), built in 1850 and once the center of mining operations in this mining town. The beautifully landscaped, rambling old hacienda is near the airstrip a 15-minute walk from town. Proprietor Bud Acord has welcomed John Huston, Liz Taylor, Richard Burton, Peter O'Toole, and a cast of local characters over the years.

The 10 extra-clean rooms have wood floors, rustic furnishings and antiques, and working fireplaces; some are decorated with pre-Columbian reproductions. The ample bathrooms are beautifully tiled and have skylights. Hammocks grace the upstairs terrace, while a sort-of museum on the lower level attests to the celebrity guests and importance the hacienda has enjoyed over the years. Because of its remote location, all meals are included. Rates are $80 per person per night, and includes full breakfast and dinner; alcoholic beverages are extra. Reserve through e-mail (pmt15@hotmail.com or info@haciendajalisco.com), through the town telephone listed above, or on their website. Group rates and discounts for longer stays are available. No credit cards. Guided horseback, walking, or mine tours can be arranged through the Hacienda.

2 Mazatlán ⍟

1,078km (674 miles) NW of Mexico City; 502km (314 miles) NW of Guadalajara; 1,561km (976 miles) SE of Mexicali

Mazatlán is comfortable, casual, value-packed Mexico at its best. More than any other beach resort in the country, it probably best represents the golden beaches, fresh seafood, and inexpensive accommodations that typified Mexico's appeal to travelers in the first place. Although some developments are edging Mazatlán into the golf-playing, manicured resort that typifies most of Mexico today, it is going there grudgingly—most of Mazatlán remains refreshingly simple.

Mazatlán Area

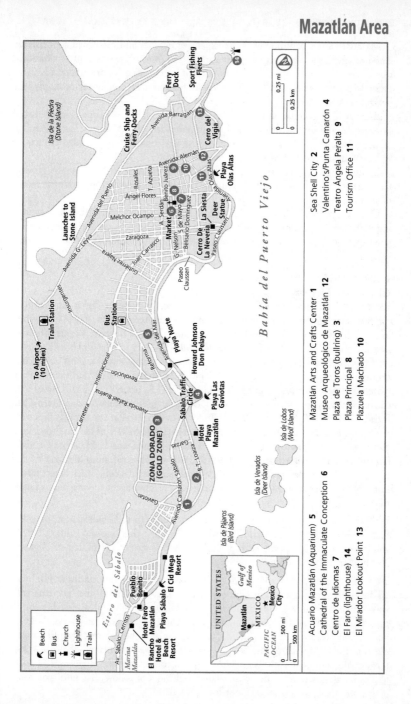

Acuario Mazatlán (Aquarium) **5**
Cathedral of the Immaculate Conception **6**
Centro de Idiomas **7**
El Faro (lighthouse) **14**
El Mirador Lookout Point **13**

Mazatlán Arts and Crafts Center **1**
Museo Arqueológico de Mazatlán **12**
Plaza de Toros (bullring) **3**
Plaza Principal **8**
Plazuela Machado **10**

Sea Shell City **2**
Valentino's/Punta Camarón **4**
Teatro Ángela Peralta **9**
Tourism Office **11**

Mazatlán's lures continue to be its expansive beaches and renowned sportfishing. The evolving golf scene, luxury yacht harbor, and growing selection of accommodations have yet to catch the attention of enough tourists to drive prices to the levels of other Mexican resorts, and that's good news for travelers looking for economy in a beach resort.

A city with a population of nearly 500,000, Mazatlán is the largest port between Los Angeles and the Panama Canal. Elegant reminders of its history, 27km (17 miles) of sandy beaches, and a geographically diverse environment are all added attractions in Mazatlán's efforts to become a premier beach resort.

Limited flight availability is the principal factor holding back Mazatlán's growth. Charter operators have picked up some of the slack and are the predominant means of arrival here.

Once known as a spring break haven and a place to party, Mazatlán is now attracting more families, mature travelers, and other tourists with an eye for value. It enjoys strong repeat business and positive word of mouth, as it continues to offer exceptional vacation values.

ESSENTIALS
GETTING THERE
BY PLANE A number of airlines operate direct or nonstop flights to Mazatlán, though charters predominate. From the United States, **Aeromexico** (© **800/237-6639** in the U.S., or 01-800/021-4000 in Mexico) flies from Los Angeles, Atlanta, Phoenix, and Tucson, via Mexico City. **Mexicana** (© **800/531-7921** in the U.S.) has direct service from Denver, Chicago, Los Angeles, Miami, and San Antonio, most connecting through Mexico City. **Aero California** (© **800/237-6225** in the U.S.) flies from Los Angeles. **Alaska Airlines** (© **800/426-0333** in the U.S., or 669/985-2730) serves Vancouver, Seattle, Portland, San Francisco, and Los Angeles. Within Mexico, **Aero California** (© **669/985-2557,** 669/981-5970, or 669/985-3434 at the airport) flies from La Paz, Guadalajara, and Mexico City. **Aeromexico** (© **669/914-1111**) has flights from Hermosillo, Durango, Monterrey, Puerto Vallarta, Tijuana, and León, all via Guadalajara or Mexico City. **Mexicana** (© **669/982-2888**) offers service from Mexico City and Los Cabos. **Aero Calafia** (© **669/985-4300;** www.aerocalafia.com) offers direct service from Puerto Vallarta and Los Cabos. Check with a travel agent for the latest **charter flights.**

By Bus First-class and deluxe buses connect Mazatlán to Guadalajara (7 hr., $35 first class one-way) and Mexico City (14½ hr., $67 first class one-way) almost hourly, and less often to other points within Mexico. The bus terminal is located on Highway 200 N. Km 1203; © **669/982-8351.**

BY CAR To reach Mazatlán from the United States, take **International Highway 15** from Nogales, Arizona, to Culiacán. At Culiacán, change to the four-lane **tollway**—it costs about $40 but is the only road considered safe and in drivable condition. On the tollway, total trip time from the United States to Mazatlán is about 10 hours. Consider an overnight stop, because driving at night in Mexico can be dangerous. From Puerto Vallarta, the 560km (350-mile) drive is not easy—the road winds through the mountains, but is in generally good condition. Take Highway 200 north to Las Varas. There it becomes four-lane Highway 68; follow that until you see a detour for Highway 15. Take 15 north to Mazatlán.

BY FERRY   Passenger ferries now operate as a private business, run between Mazatlán and La Paz, Baja California. The ferry leaves daily at 3pm and carries cars, with Thursday reserved for cargo and seated passengers (no cabins). The trip takes 18 hours. Seats cost $75, tourist-class service with two beds $125, cabin class with two beds and a private bathroom $195, and special class $240. Prices for cars vary, depending on size. For example, an economy car like a Volkswagen Golf costs $450. For information, call toll-free within Mexico ✆ **01-800/696-9600,** or 669/981-7020. Tickets for the ferry must be purchased in advance at the ferry office on Carnaval Street or through travel agents; MasterCard and Visa are accepted. To find the ferry office, go south on Olas Altas and turn left on Alemán; Carnaval is the second street. Turn right and you'll find the office in the middle of the block. Ferries return from La Paz to Mazatlán daily.

ORIENTATION

ARRIVING   The Rafael Buelna International Airport (airport code: MZT) is 27km (17 miles) southeast of the hotel-and-resort area of town. The following rental-car companies have counters in the airport, open during flight arrivals and departures: **Hertz** (✆ **800/623-3650** in the U.S., or 669/985-0845), **Budget** (✆ **800/322-9976** in the U.S., or 669/913-2000), and **National** (✆ **800/227-7368** in the U.S., or 669/982-4000). Daily rates run $65 to $145. A car is desirable if you want to explore the surrounding coastline and villages, but it is not essential in Mazatlán.

Taxis and *colectivo* minivans run from the airport to hotels; taxis cost about twice as much as the *colectivo,* which runs $20 to $28, depending on the location of your hotel. Only taxis make the return trip to the airport; they cost $20 to $30. The **Central de Autobuses** (main bus terminal) is at Río Tamazula and Chachalacas. To get there from Avenida del Mar, walk 3 blocks inland on Río Tamazula; the station is on your right. Taxis line up in front of the bus station.

VISITOR INFORMATION   The extremely helpful and professional **City and State Tourism Office** is on Calle Carnaval 1317, corner of Mariano Escobedo, at the Plaza Machado (✆ **669/981-8886** or 669/981-8887; fax 669/981-8884; www.sinaloa-travel.com). The office is open Monday through Friday from 9am to 5pm; the staff speaks English. To preview what's going on in Mazatlán before you arrive, check the website for the local English-language newspaper; www.pacificpearl.com, or pick up a copy of their very helpful publication upon arrival, for a complete schedule of current activities. Three other very helpful guides in English are the **Welcome Digest** (✆ **669/982-1977;** www.welcomedigest.com.mx), **Viejo Mazatlan** (✆ **669/985-3781**), and **Mazatlan Interactivo** (✆ **669/981-8435;** www.mazatlaninteractivo.com).

CITY LAYOUT   Mazatlán extends north from the peninsula port area along Avenida Gabriel Leyva and Avenida Barragan, where the cruise ships, sportfishing boats, and ferries dock. Downtown begins with the historic area of **Old Mazatlán (Viejo Mazatlán)** and **Playa Olas Altas** to the south. A curving seaside boulevard, or *malecón,* runs 27km (17 miles) along the waterfront, all the way from Playa Olas Altas to **Playa Norte,** changing names often along the way. Traveling north, it begins as Paseo Olas Altas and becomes Paseo Claussen parallel to the commercial downtown area. The name changes to Avenida del Mar at the beginning of the Playa Norte area.

About 6km (4 miles) north of downtown lies the Sábalo traffic circle in the **Zona Dorada (Golden Zone)** near the **Punta Camarón,** a rocky outcropping over the water. The Zona Dorada begins where Avenida del Mar intersects Avenida Rafael Buelna and becomes **Avenida Camarón Sábalo,** which leads north through the abundant hotels and fast-food restaurants of the tourist zone. From here, the resort hotels, including the huge El Cid resort complex, spread northward along and beyond **Playa Sábalo.** The **Marina Mazatlán** development has changed the landscape north of the Zona Dorada considerably; hotels, condo complexes, and private residences rise around the new marina. This area north of the Marina El Cid is increasingly known as Nuevo Mazatlán. North of here is **Los Cerritos (Little Hills),** the northern limit of Mazatlán.

GETTING AROUND

The downtown transportation center for buses, taxis, and *pulmonías* (see below) is on the central Plaza Principal, facing the cathedral.

BY TAXI   Eco Taxis are green-and-white cabs with posted set fares, but generally are about $3 or $5 per trip. Taxis are easy to flag around town and can also be rented by the day or by the hour. Agree on a price in advance. Fares between the Zona Dorada and Old Mazatlán average $4.50 to $6.50; within the Zona Dorada, you should pay about $3.50. To request a taxi, call **©️ 669/986-1111** or 669/985-2828.

BY *Pulmonía*   These open-air vehicles resembling overgrown golf carts carry up to three passengers. *Pulmonías* (literally "pneumonias") have surreylike tops and open sides. As a rule, they're slightly more expensive than taxis at about $5 per starting fare, but they're part of the Mazatlán experience.

BY BUS   Buses, some with air-conditioning, cover most of the city and are relatively easy to use, although knowing some Spanish is helpful. The fare is 80¢ for local routes. The SABALO CENTRO line runs from the Golden Zone along the waterfront to downtown near the market and the central plaza; at Avenida Miguel Alemán, the buses turn and head south to Olas Altas. The CERRITOS-JUAREZ line starts near the train station, cuts across town to the *malecón* beside the Golden Zone, and heads north to Los Cerritos and back. The SABALO COCOS line runs through the Golden Zone, heads inland to the bus station, and goes on to downtown (also stopping at the market) by a back route. The PLAYA SUR line goes to the area where the sportfishing and tour boats depart. Buses run daily from 6am to 10:30pm. Fares are about 75¢ for air-conditioned green buses, or 35¢ for the yellow buses.

FAST FACTS: Mazatlán

American Express   The office is on Avenida Camarón Sábalo in the Centro Comercial Balboa shopping center, Loc. 15 and 16 (©️ **669/913-0600;** fax 669/916-5908), between the traffic circle and the El Cid resort. It's open Monday through Friday from 9am to 6pm, Saturday from 9am to 1pm.

Area Code   The telephone area code for Mazatlán is **669.**

Banks   Most banks are generally open Monday through Friday from 9am to 6pm, and some have limited hours on Saturday.

Climate   As the northernmost major beach resort on the mainland, Mazatlán can be cooler in summer than the resorts farther south. The wettest month is September.

Emergencies Dial (C) 060. For medical emergencies, contact the **Sharp Hospital,** Rafael Buelna and Las Cruces ((C) 669/986-5676 or 669/986-5678).

Internet Access Numerous places offer access. **Cyber Cafe,** Av. Camarón Sábalo 204, Suite 9, near Domino's Pizza ((C) 669/914-0008; cybercafe@mazatlan.com.mx) has 10 workstations plus a color printer. Charges are 10 hours of time for $25, or $4 per hour. Open from 9am to 10pm Monday through Saturday, 10am to 10pm Sunday. They also have free coffee and Coke, and always have someone on hand who speaks English. **Internet Café Netscape** (Av. Camarón Sábalo 222, between Farmacia Benavides and Taco Loco), is open daily, including holidays, from 8am to 11pm. Access costs $3 per hour; $1.50 for 30 minutes ((C) 669/990-1289). **Mailboxes Etc.,** Av. Camarón Sábalo 202, local 4, on the corner of Sierra de Venados ((C) 669/916-4010; fax 669/916-4011; mbe15@mzt.megared.net.mx), charges $3 for 30 minutes and $1 per printed page. It's open Monday through Friday from 9am to 6.30pm, Saturday and Sunday from 9am to 2pm.

Language Classes Spanish-language classes begin every Monday at the **Centro de Idiomas** ((C) 669/985-5606; fax 669/982-2053; www.spanishlink.org), 3 blocks west of the cathedral near 21 de Marzo and Canizales. In addition to small-group (maximum 10 students) and individual instruction, the language center offers a home-stay program and a person-to-person program that matches students with local people. On Friday at 7pm, the center holds free Spanish and English conversation groups open to both visitors and locals. For more information, call or write Dixie Davis, Belisario Domínguez 1908, Mazatlán, Sin.

Pharmacy **Farmacias Hidalgo,** Herman R. Hidalgo s/n ((C) 669/985-4545 or 669/985-4646), is open 24 hours and delivers to hotels. **Boiron Homeopathy** ((C) 669/981-4615) offers all-natural medicines and products, and also delivers to hotels. It's located at Plaza Azcona, Av. Cruz Lizarraga 604, Local 1.

Police The local police number is (C) 669/983-4510 or 669/983-6585, local 066. The Tourist Police can be reached at (C) 669/914-8444.

Post Office The *correo* is downtown on Benito Juárez just off Angel Flores, on the east side of the main plaza ((C) 669/981-2121). Hours are Monday through Friday from 8am to 6pm, Saturday from 9am to 1pm.

ACTIVITIES ON & OFF THE BEACH

To orient yourself, walk up and enjoy the panoramic view from **El Faro,** the famous lighthouse on the point at the south end of town. It's the second-highest lighthouse in the world (only Gibraltar's is higher), towering 135m (447 ft.) over the harbor. Begin at the end of Paseo Centenario, near the sportfishing docks. There's a refreshment stand at the foot of the hill. Allow about 45 minutes for the climb. The view is nearly as spectacular from the top of **Cerro del Vigía (Lookout Hill),** which is accessible by car from Paseo Olas Altas.

BEACHES   At the western edge of downtown is rocky, pebbly **Playa Olas Altas,** a lovely stretch of pounding surf, but not suitable for swimming. Around a rocky promontory north of Olas Altas is **Playa Norte,** which offers several kilometers of good sand beach.

At the Sábalo traffic circle, Punta Camarón juts into the water, and on either side of the point is **Playa Las Gaviotas.** Farther north, **Playa Sábalo** is perhaps the best beach in Mazatlán. The next point jutting into the water is Punta Sábalo, beyond which you'll find a bridge over a channel that flows in and out of a lagoon. Beyond the marina, more beaches stretch all the way to Los Cerritos. Remember that all beaches in Mexico are public property, so you have the right to enjoy the beach of your choice.

Mazatlán is one of only a few resorts in Mexico where surfing is common on central town beaches. The waves are best at **Los Pinos,** north of the fort—known in surfing circles as "the Cannon"—and at Playa Las Gaviotas and Playa Sábalo. Waves are most notable and consistent from May to September. Other notable surf breaks are found at Olas Altos, Cerritos, Isla de la Piedra, and El Camaron, at Playa Norte. For surf gear, board rentals, lessons, and surf reports, visit the **Mazatlan Surf Center** (© 669/ 913-1821; www.mazatlassurfcenter.com) in the Golden Zone, at Camaron S. Abalo, 500-4, next to the Dairy Queen. Boogie boards are widely available for rent on the beaches in front of the Golden Zone, for about $3 per hour.

A good beach that makes a great day trip is on the ocean side of **Isla de la Piedra (Stone Island).** From the center of town, board a Circunvalación or Playa Sur bus from the north side of the Plaza Principal for the ride to the boat landing, Embarcadero–Isla de la Piedra. Small motorboats make the 5-minute trip to the island every 15 minutes or so from 7am to 6pm for a modest price. When you arrive on the island, walk through the rustic little village to the ocean side, where the pale-sand beaches, bordered by coconut groves, stretch for miles. On Sunday afternoons, the *palapa* restaurants on the shore have music and dancing, attracting mainly Mexican families; on other days the beach is almost empty. **Carmelita's** has delicious fish called *lisamacho;* it's grilled over an open fire and served slightly blackened with fresh, hot corn tortillas and salsa. It's open daily from 10am to 6pm and doesn't accept credit cards.

The local gay beach is on **Isla de las Chivas.** Transportation to the island is by launches, which you can catch at the Muelle Puntilla, located next to the docks where the ferry to La Paz departs.

CRUISES & BOAT RENTALS   The **Kolonahe Sailing Adventure** departs for Isla de Venados (Deer Island) Tuesday through Sunday from Marina El Cid. Reserve through any travel agent or through El Cid directly (see below). This excursion sails aboard a 15m (50-ft.) trimaran to the island, where guests enjoy a picnic lunch and beverages, plus the use of snorkel equipment, boogie boards, kayaks, and canoes for a cost of $35 per person. Departure is at 9:15am, with the boat returning at 3:30pm.

Anfibios, amphibious vehicles that operate on land and in the water, head for Isla de Venados (Deer Island), one of three big islands off the coast. Trips last 2 to 2½ hours; they leave from the beaches of the **El Cid resort** (© 669/913-3333, ext. 3341) daily at 10am, noon, and 2pm. Round-trip tickets cost $8, plus $8 for snorkeling gear.

DEEP-SEA FISHING   Mazatlán claims to be the billfish and shrimp capital of the world, and whether or not it's a valid claim, deep-sea fishing in Mazatlán is generally less expensive than in other parts of Mexico. If you request it (please do!), your captain will practice "catch and release." Rates are around $250 per day for a 7.2m (24-ft.) *lancha* for up to three persons and $430 per day for an 11m (36-ft.) cruiser for up to four passengers; rates do not include fishing licenses, drinks, or gratuities. Try the **Flota Estrella** (©/fax 669/982-3878) or the **Aries Fleet** located at the Marina El Cid harbormaster's office (© 669/916-3468). Locals suggest making fishing reservations for October through January at least a month in advance; at the very least, do it the minute you arrive in town. You may also choose to rent a *panga* (a small, uncovered, fiberglass boat with an outboard motor) at a rate of $40 per hour, with a minimum of 4 hours—it's the way the locals fish.

OTHER WATERSPORTS Among the best places to rent watersports equipment, from snorkeling gear to kayaks, are the Aqua Sport Center at the **El Cid resort** (② 669/ 913-3333; www.mazatlan-aquasports.com) and the Ocean Sport Center at the **Hotel Faro Mazatlán** (② 669/913-1111).

SPECIAL EVENTS IN NEARBY VILLAGES On the weekend of the first Sunday in October, **Rosario,** a small town 45 minutes south on Highway 15, holds a **festival honoring Our Lady of the Rosary.** Games, music, dances, processions, and festive foods mark the event. From May 1 to May 10, Rosario holds its **Spring Festival.**

In mid-October, the village of **Escuinapa,** south of Rosario on Highway 15, holds a **Mango Festival.**

For more information, call the State Tourism Office at ② **669/981-8886.**

SPECTATOR SPORTS There's a bullring (Plaza de Toros) on Rafael Buelna about a mile from the Golden Zone. From December to early April, **bullfights** take place every Sunday and on holidays at 4pm; locals recommend arriving by 2pm. Tickets range from $12 for general admission (ask for the shady side—*la sombra*) to $30 for the front of the shaded section; most travel agencies and tour desks sell advance tickets.

Rodeos, or *charreadas,* take place at the Lienzo Charro (bullring) of the Asociación de Charros de Mazatlán (② **669/986-3510**) on Saturday or Sunday beginning at 4pm. Tickets (around $4.50) are available through local travel agents and hotel concierge desks, which will have the current schedule.

At Playa Olas Altas, daring **cliff divers** take to the rock ledges of **El Mirador** and plunge into the shallow, pounding surf below, a la Acapulco. The divers perform sporadically during the day as tour buses arrive near their perch, sometimes diving with torches at 7pm. After the dive, they collect donations from spectators. Follow the *malecón* to the esplanade and look for the mermaid statue to find El Mirador.

TENNIS, GOLF & OTHER OUTDOOR SPORTS Mazatlán has more than 100 tennis courts. Try the **El Cid resort,** on Camarón Sábalo (② **669/913-3333**), although hotel guests have priority, or the **Racquet Club Gaviotas, Ibis,** and **Río Bravo** in the Golden Zone (② **669/913-5939**). Many larger hotels in Mazatlán also have courts.

Mazatlán is probably the best **golf** value in Mexico. Try the 27-hole course at the **El Cid resort** (② **669/913-3333**). Nine holes designed by Lee Trevino complement the 18 holes designed by Robert Trent Jones Jr. It's open to the public, with preference given to hotel guests. Tee times book up quickly. Greens fees for nonguests range from $60 for 9 holes, plus $17 for the caddy, to $75 for 18 holes, plus $17 for the caddy. El Cid guests get a discount of 15%. El Cid's facilities include a John Jacobs golf school, the only one in Mexico.

Another option is the 9-hole course at the **Club Campestre Mazatlán** (② **669/ 980-1570**), which is open to the public. Greens fees are $18 for 9 holes, $25 for 18 holes; a caddy costs an extra $8 and $15, a cart $12 and $22, respectively. It's on Highway 15 on the outskirts of downtown.

Mazatlán's newest course is at the **Estrella del Mar Golf Club** (② **669/982-3300;** www.estrelladelmar.com). The 18-hole, 7,004-yard course, also designed by Robert Trent Jones Jr., stretches along 3km (2 miles) of coastline on Isla de la Piedra, a peninsula just south of downtown Mazatlán. There's a PGA pro on staff, and daily clinics. Greens fees run $110 ($69 after 1pm), including cart, but no caddies are available at present. It's open daily from 7:30am to sunset. Also on site are a golf shop, restaurant, and bar. Clubs are available for rent for $30 plus tax.

You can go **horseback riding** on Isla de la Piedra for $6 per hour. Ask your hotel's travel agent to arrange a **kayaking excursion** on El Verde Comacho Ecological Lagoon, or take a trip to Teacapán for **birding** in one of Mexico's largest estuaries (see "Road Trips from Mazatlán," later in this chapter).

Kelly's Bicycle Shop, Av. Camarón Sábalo 204 L-10 (© **669/914-1187**), in the Zona Dorada, arranges mountain-bike tours and rents aluminum-frame bikes with full suspension. A half-day guided tour costs $25; rentals are $5 per half-day, $10 per full day. Bike rentals include water bottle, snack, map, and general route information.

ATV and other motorbike tours are available through **Adventours Outdoor Excursions,** Av. Camarón Sábalo 7B, Golden Zone, in front of Bancomer (© **669/916-6672** and 669/916-6673). Their 6-hour Moto Tour costs $125 and travels off-road through a coconut plantation as well as to local beaches, and includes lunch and open bar at a restaurant, plus two beach activities of your choice (banana boat, snorkeling, horseback riding, kayaking, or boogie-boarding).

EXPLORING MAZATLAN

Mazatlán may be best known for its wide, sandy beaches and sporting activities, but visitors who neglect to sample the city's cultural events and attractions are missing out on a multidimensional destination.

MUSEUMS

Acuario Mazatlán *Kids* Children and adults interested in the sea will love the Mazatlán Aquarium. With over 200 species of fish, including sharks, eels, and sea horses, it is one of the largest and best in Mexico. Next to the aquarium are a playground and

---

Moments **Mazatlán's Carnaval: A Weeklong Party**

The week before Lent (usually in Feb) is Mazatlán's famous Carnaval, or Mardi Gras. People come from all over the country and abroad for this flamboyant celebration, topped in size and revelry only by those in Río de Janeiro and New Orleans. Highlights of the event include parades, special shows, the coronation of the Carnaval queen, outdoor concerts, more than 150 food and beverage vendors, all-night parties, and extravaganzas all over town. For event information, check with the major hotels or the tourism office, or look for posters around town. Every night during Carnaval week, all along the Olas Altas oceanfront drive in the southern part of town, the streets fill with music from roving mariachi groups, local traditional *bandas sinaloenses* (sporting lots of brass instruments), and electrified bands under tarpaulin shades. The crowd increases each day until the last night, Shrove Tuesday, when musicians, dancers, and people out for a good time pack the *malecón*. The following day, Ash Wednesday, the party is over. People receive crosses of ashes on their foreheads at church, and Lent begins.

Tips **The Mazatlán Hotel Crunch**

Mazatlán hotels fill quickly during Carnaval, Easter week, and spring break; some of the choicest rooms are reserved a year in advance, and room rates generally rise 30% to 40%. High season in Mazatlán, as in the rest of Mexico, is from December 20 to Easter; low season begins the day after Easter and extends to December 19.

---

a botanical garden, with an aviary and a small crocodile exhibit. Staff members feed the sea lions, birds, and fish at shows almost hourly. The staff is helpful and knowledgeable about the different species on exhibit.

Av. de los Deportes 111, ½ block off Av. del Mar. ℂ 669/981-7815 or 669/981-7817. Admission $6 adults, $3 children 3–11. Daily 9:30am–6pm.

Museo Arqueológico de Mazatlán   This small, attractive archaeological museum displays both pre-Hispanic artifacts and a permanent contemporary art exhibit. From Olas Altas, walk inland on Sixto Osuna 1½ blocks; the museum is on your right. Art exhibits sometimes take place in the Casa de la Cultura across the street from the museum.

Sixto Osuna 76, 1½ blocks from Paseo Olas Altas. ℂ 669/981-1455. Free admission. Mon–Sat 9am–6pm.

ARCHITECTURAL HIGHLIGHTS

Two blocks south of the central plaza stands the lovely **Teatro Angela Peralta** (ℂ 669/982-4447; www.teatroangelaperalta.com), a national historic monument. Built between 1869 and 1874, it most recently underwent renovation in 1998. The 841-seat Italian-style theater has three levels of balconies, two facades, and, in true tropical style, a lobby with no roof. The theater was named for one of the world's great divas, who, along with the director and 30 members of the opera, died in Mazatlán of cholera in an 1863 epidemic. Some city tours stop here; if you're visiting on your own, the theater is open daily from 9am to 6pm. The fee for touring the building is $1. It regularly schedules folkloric ballets, along with periodic performances of classical ballet, contemporary dance, symphony concerts, opera, and jazz. For information, call or check at the theater box office. This theater is the home of Delfos, one of the most important contemporary dance companies in Mexico.

The 20-block historic area near the theater, including the small square **Plazuela Machado** (bordered by Frías, Constitución, Carnaval, and Sixto Osuna), abounds with beautiful old buildings and colorful town houses trimmed with wrought iron and carved stone; many buildings were restored as part of the 1998–99 downtown beautification program—although much remains to be done. Small galleries are beginning to move into the area as the neighborhood becomes the center of Mazatlán's artistic community. Check out the **town houses** on Libertad between Domínguez and Carnaval and the two lavish **mansions** on Ocampo at Domínguez and at Carnaval. For a rest stop, try the **Café Pacífico** (decorated with historic pictures of Mazatlán) on the Plazuela Machado.

The **Plaza Principal,** also called Plaza Revolución, is the heart of the city, filled with vendors, shoeshine stands, and people of all ages out for a stroll. At its center is a Victorian-style, wrought-iron bandstand with a diner-type restaurant underneath. Be sure to take in the **Cathedral of the Immaculate Conception,** built in the 1800s, with its unusual yellow-tiled twin steeples and partially tiled facade. It's on the corner of Calle 21 de Marzo and Nelson.

ORGANIZED TOURS

In addition to 3-hour **city tours** ($20), tour operators offer excursions to many colorful and interesting villages nearby, such as Concordia and Copala (see below). Some towns date from the 16th-century Spanish Conquest; others are modest farming or fishing villages. Information and reservations are available at any travel agency or major hotel, and all accept American Express, MasterCard, and Visa. The premier provider of these, and other tours, is **Pronatours** (© 669/916-7720 or 669/916-3333; www.pronatures.elcid. com.mx), yet another part of the El Cid megacomplex of activities. In addition to the city tour, they offer a 5-hour Tequila Tour, visiting a distillery ($33), a 5-hour sailing excursion to Deer Island ($42), and a seasonal tour to visit protected turtle hatcheries ($45). Two other recommended tour agencies are the very helpful **Marlin Tours** (© 669/913-5301) and **Olé Tours** (© 669/916-6287).

COPALA-CONCORDIA   This popular countryside tour stops at several mountain villages where artisans craft furniture and other items. Copala is a historic mining village with a Spanish-colonial church. The tour ($45), also known as the "Mountain Tour" or "Country Tour" includes lunch and soft drinks. For more about Copala, see "Road Trips from Mazatlán," later.

MAZATLAN JUNGLE TOUR   Some might say that David Pérez's **Jungle Tour** (© 669/914-1444; fax 669/914-0451) is misnamed, but it's still worthwhile. It consists of a 1½-hour boat ride past a Mexican navy base, Mazatlán's shrimp fleet and packing plants, and into the mangrove swamps to Isla de la Piedra (Stone Island). There's a 3-hour stop at a pristine beach that has what could be the world's largest sand dollars (though fewer and fewer are left). Horseback rides on the beach are $6 for a half-hour. After the beach stop, feast on *pescado zarandeado* (fish cooked over coconut husks, green mangrove, and charcoal). Tours run from 9am to 3pm and cost $42 per person. Days vary, so call for dates and reservations. MasterCard and Visa are accepted.

WHERE TO STAY

The hotels in downtown Mazatlán are generally older and less expensive than those along the beachfront heading north. As a rule, room rates rise the farther north you go from downtown. The three major areas to stay are Olas Altas and downtown, the Playa Norte (North Beach), and the Zona Dorada.

THE ZONA DORADA AND NORTH

The Golden Zone is an elegant arc of gold sand linked by a palm-lined boulevard and bordered by the most deluxe hotels and a sprinkling of elaborate beach houses. A bonus here is the sunset view. Many hotels along this beach cut their prices from May through September.

El Cid Mega Resort ✧✧✧   El Cid Mega Resort is as much a destination as it is a hotel—with *mega* being the operative word. Although it is large, bordering on imposing, El Cid offers every service and convenience you can think of, from deluxe rooms to ecotours. Both a hotel and a residential development, El Cid has three beachside buildings, private villas, and a 27-hole golf course on 360 hectares (900 acres). The main 17-story beachside tower, Castilla, was renovated in 1999; there's also the 28-story, all-suite El Moro Tower and the lower-rise, lower-priced Granada, near the golf course. Although room layouts vary, most are heavily detailed in marble and feature private balconies and contemporary, upscale furnishings. *Mega* also applies to extra services at El Cid, where a program called "Active Learning Vacations" encourages more involved vacations, priced as special packages. There are opportunities to improve your golf, tennis, or sailing skills or indulge in a Fit for Life program through the on-site spa. Small boats are available, with departures every ten minutes, to take guests to nearby beaches. All-inclusive options are also available; ask for special deals. This resort has something for every type of traveler and is especially ideal when size matters.

Av. Camarón Sábalo s/n (between Av. Rodolfo T. Loaiza and Circuito Campeador), 82110 Mazatlán, Sin. ✆ 800/525-1925 in the U.S., or 669/913-3333. Fax 669/914-131. www.elcid.com. 1,320 units. High season $106–$281 double, $281 junior suite, $396–$536 suite; low season $89–$244 double, $244 junior suite, $343–$465 suite. All-inclusive program $180 double occupancy, children 3–11 $30. AE, DC, MC, V. Free guarded parking. **Amenities:** 11 restaurants; 8 bars; glitzy disco; 8 swimming pools (including 1 saltwater pool); 9 tennis courts; complete spa and fitness center; watersports equipment; "Mega Kids Club"; concierge; tour desk; car-rental desk; business center; shopping arcade; salon; room service; babysitting; laundry service; dry cleaning; marina; sailing school; tennis academy. *In room:* A/C, TV, hair dryer, iron, safe-deposit box.

El Rancho Hotel & Beach Resort ★★ *(Kids)*

Book a room at El Rancho, and you'll book yourself an apartment suite, complete with kitchen, making it a top choice for families. An intimate group of villas, the resort is located on a beautiful stretch of soft-sand beach, immediately to the north of the Golden Zone. All units feature the same traditional Mexican-style decor, with colorful fabric accents, and are very well maintained. The difference in price depends on your view—garden, pool, or ocean. Each features two levels, with two spacious bedrooms (one with a king-size bed, the other with two queen-size beds) as well as two bathrooms, a fully-equipped kitchen, and a living/dining area. The gardens are lovely, and the onsite restaurant is one level up, making it an ideal spot for watching sunsets. Note that this is also a timeshare resort, so be prepared for a sales pitch if you stay here.

Av. Sábalo-Cerritos 3000, 82110 Mazatlán, Sin. ✆ 888/596-5760 toll-free in the U.S., or 01-800/717-1991 in Mexico. www.elrancho.com.mx. 28 units. High season $135–$200; low season $110–$170 per 2-bedroom suite, sleeps up to 6. Rates include free airport pickup and daily continental breakfast. AE, MC, V. Free parking. **Amenities:** Restaurant; pool; Jacuzzi; tour desk; laundry service. *In room:* A/C, TV.

Hotel Faro Mazatlán ★★

Formerly known as the Camino Real, this grande dame of Mazatlán hotels changed management in 2004, and underwent a much-needed renovation. Considered the most sophisticated place to stay in town, it's the best choice for those seeking seclusion. I feel it has the best location in Mazatlán, on a rocky cliff overlooking the sea, and the beach edges a small cove that's perfect for swimming. Marble-floored hallways lead to rooms decorated in light, neutral colors, each with bathtubs and showers, large closets, and vanity tables. Junior suites have king-size beds and comfy couches. The hotel is about a 10-minute drive from the heart of the Golden Zone. Higher rates are for rooms with an ocean view; other rooms have a marina view.

Punta de Sábalo s/n, 82100 Mazatlán, Sin. ✆ 800/716-9757 in the U.S., or 669/913-1111. Fax 669/916-5144. 169 units. High season $104–$195 double, $220 junior suite; low-season discounts and special packages available. All-inclusive package $95 per person, with discounts available for families. AE, MC, V. Free guarded parking. **Amenities:** 2 restaurants; lobby bar; small heated pool; 2 tennis courts; gym; travel agency; business center; room service. *In room:* A/C, TV, minibar.

Pueblo Bonito ★★

The all-suite Pueblo Bonito continues to be a favored place to stay in Mazatlán. The kitchenettes and ample seating areas, along with architectural touches that include curved ceilings, arched windows, and tiled floors, make you feel more at home than traditional hotels do. The extra space means it's a good choice for families or friends traveling together. The grounds are gorgeous—peacocks and flamingos stroll lush lawns, a waterfall cascades into a large pool, and a row of *palapas* lines the beachfront. A second Pueblo Bonito resort, **Emerald Bay** (© **669/989-0525**), mirrors the refined style and all-suite concept of this resort. It has 78 suites and a luxury spa. It's about 15 minutes north of town at Av. Ernesto Coppel Campaña s/n, Camino al Delfín, Zona Nuevo Mazatlán.

Av. Camarón Sábalo 2121 (Apdo. Postal 6), 82110 Mazatlán, Sin. © **01-800/699-9000** in Mexico, or 669/989-8900. Fax 669/914-1723. www.pueblobonito.com. 250 units. $202 junior suite, $240 1-bedroom suite for 2 adults and 2 children. AE, MC, V. Free guarded parking; valet parking. **Amenities:** 3 restaurants (1 w/popular Sun brunch); 2 large pools; gym; whirlpool; sauna; concierge; tour desk; sightseeing desk; car-rental desk; room service; massage; babysitting; laundry service. *In room:* A/C, TV.

PLAYA NORTE

The waterfront between downtown and the Golden Zone is Mazatlán's original tourist hotel zone. Moderately priced hotels and motels line the street across from the beach. Señor Frog's, Mazatlán's most famous restaurant, is in this neighborhood, as is the bus station. From May to September, many hotels cut their prices.

Hotel Playa Mazatlán ★★ *Kids*   The most happening place on this stretch of the Golden Zone, the Hotel Playa Mazatlán is enduringly popular with families, tour groups, and regulars who return annually for winter vacations or spring break. The quietest rooms are in the three-story section surrounding the well-tended interior gardens; those by the terrace restaurant and beach can be noisy. All rooms are decorated in bright colors, with dark wood furnishings and colonial accents. The beach is one of the liveliest in town. The hotel hosts popular Mexican fiestas on Tuesday, Thursday, and Saturday, and a fireworks display on Sunday.

Av. Playa Gaviotas 202 gold zone, 82110 Mazatlán, Sin. © **800/762-5816** in the U.S., or 669/989-0555. Fax 669/914-0366. www.playamazatlan.com.mx. 423 units. $110 garden-view double; $130 oceanview double. AE, MC, V. Free guarded parking. **Amenities:** 2 restaurants; bar; 3 pools; gym; 2 outdoor whirlpools; watersports rental equipment; tour desk; small gift shop/pharmacy; room service; laundry service; in-house doctor. *In room:* A/C, TV, coffeemaker, hair dryer, iron.

Howard Johnson Don Pelayo   The Don Pelayo remains a top choice among budget inns. It's on the North Beach at the edge of the *malecón*. The very clean, regularly updated waterfront rooms have small balconies; all rooms have satellite TV, a king-size bed or two double beds, and central air-conditioning (without individual controls). Lighting and furnishings are gradually being improved. Suites have minibars. When you call to book, ask about seasonal specials; quite often you can get a junior suite for a substantial discount. The hotel is very popular with families and has ample RV parking.

Av. del Mar 1111 (Apdo. Postal 1088), 82000 Mazatlán, Sin. © **669/983-2221** or 669/983-1888. Fax 669/984-0799. 165 units. $68 double; $104 junior suite. AE, MC, V. Free enclosed parking. **Amenities:** Restaurant; bar; swimming pool; wading pool w/slide; whirlpool. *In room:* A/C, TV.

DOWNTOWN SEAFRONT/PLAYA OLAS ALTAS

The old section of Mazatlán spreads around a picturesque beach a short walk from downtown. Movie stars of the 1950s and 1960s came here for sun and surf, and the hotels where they stayed are still here. There are a few seafront restaurants here, making it easy to dine near your hotel.

Hotel La Siesta ✦   The historic La Siesta occupies a well-maintained building surrounded by the old mansions of Mazatlán. Inside, three levels encircle a central courtyard; rooms facing the ocean have balconies opening to sea breezes and pounding waves. Guest rooms at the back of the hotel are quieter but less charming; all have two beds, a small table and chair, good lighting, and dependably hot water. For such functional accommodations, there's a surprising array of guest services. A bonus is the popular **El Shrimp Bucket** restaurant, in the courtyard, where live marimbas and recorded music play until 11pm. This is one of the most popular hotels in Old Mazatlán and fills up quickly. Reservations are strongly advised.

Av. Olas Altas 11 Sur, 82000 Mazatlán, Sin. © **669/981-2640** or 669/981-2334. Fax 669/982-2633. www.lasiesta.com.mx. 57 units. $58 ocean-view double, $40 interior double. AE, MC, V. Street parking. From the deer statue on Olas Altas, go right 1 block. **Amenities:** Restaurant; bar; concierge; room service; in-room massage; laundry service; money exchange; safe-deposit boxes. *In room:* A/C, TV.

WHERE TO DINE

Mazatlán boasts one of the largest shrimp fleets in the world, so it's no surprise that shrimp and seafood are the specialties. Most restaurants are very casual and moderately priced, offering good value. A cheap-eats treat is to stop in one of the many *loncherías* scattered throughout the downtown area. Here you can get a *torta* (a sandwich on a small French roll) stuffed with a variety of meats, cheeses, tomatoes, onions, and chiles for around $2. Also recommendable is the **Deli 28 Centro,** Belisario Domínguez 1503, Historic Downtown (© **669/981-1577**), serving gourmet baguettes, focaccia, brioche and a selection of quality deli meats and cheeses, as well as pizzas.

THE ZONA DORADA
Expensive

Angelo's ✦ ITALIAN/SEAFOOD   Even locals consider this hotel restaurant one of the best in town, as much for its ambience as for its food. Beveled glass doors reveal a dining room gleaming with brass, polished wood, and crystal chandeliers. A pianist plays in the background as formally dressed waiters present menus featuring homemade pastas; shrimp dishes, including superb scampi; and a large selection of imported wines. The dress code forbids beachwear, jeans, tennis shoes, and flip-flops.

In the Pueblo Bonito hotel, Av. Camarón Sábalo 2121. © **669/989-8900**, ext. 8608. Reservations required. Main courses $8–$24. AE, MC, V. Daily 6–11:30pm.

Papagayo Restaurant ✦ INTERNATIONAL   Nestled on the beach, diners at Papagayo enjoy the natural beauty of the sea, with a choice of beach or open-air patio seating, and a view across the water to Las Tres Islas, the three imposing islands just offshore. The food is consistent and elegantly presented, with an extensive menu of international fare; favorites are shrimp CocoLoco, and tournedos Rossini in wild mushroom sauce.

The Inn at Mazatlán, Av. Camarón Sábalo 6291. © **669/913-4151**. Main courses $9.50–$28. AE, MC, V. Daily 7am–11pm.

Señor Pepper's ✦✦ INTERNATIONAL   Managing to be both elegant and comfortable, this restaurant is known for serving the best steaks in Mazatlán. Potted plants, candlelight, and lots of polished crystal, silver, and brass give the dining room a romantic feeling, and some nights it seems as if all the diners are old friends. The enormous Sonoran beef steaks are grilled over mesquite; lobster and shrimp are also big hits. The nightly special includes appetizer, steak or seafood, vegetables, and soup or salad; those having only drinks at the bar receive a complimentary appetizer.

Av. Camarón Sábalo s/n, across from the Hotel Faro Mazatlan. © 669/914-0101. Main courses $20–$39. AE, MC, V. Daily 5–11pm; bar daily 5pm–2am.

Moderate
No Name Café ★★ INTERNATIONAL   The 30 TVs are one of the main attractions of this restaurant and sports bar, the best place in town to watch sports. Memorabilia—including pennants, posters, team photos, and baseball card collections—covers every square inch of the place. Between games, rousing rock 'n' roll and country music will lure you onto the dance floor. Renowned for having the best barbecue ribs in town, the cafe also has seating on a tree-covered courtyard surrounded by *palapas*.

The menu is as oriented to the good ol' USA as the setting, with outdoor-grilled steaks, spare ribs, pork chops, thick hamburgers, and barbecued chicken—plus grilled shrimp, a touch of Mazatlán. For dessert, the homemade banana-coconut cream pie is sumptuous.

Av. Rodolfo T. Loaiza 4178, Zona Dorada. © 669/913-2031. Main courses $5.50–$20. AE, MC, V. Daily noon–12:30am.

Terraza Playa MEXICAN/INTERNATIONAL   During the day, diners enjoy the action on the beach plus a view across to Isla de Venados (Deer Island). After sundown, the stars overhead (in the open terrace) and the sound of the surging waves are a backdrop to live music and dancing from 7pm to midnight. The menu is standard international fare, well prepared, with excellent, friendly service. Especially popular is the breakfast buffet.

In the Hotel Playa Mazatlán, Av. Rodolfo T. Loaiza 202. Breakfast $3.50–$7; Mexican plates $4.50–$9.50; seafood and meat $7.50–$15. AE, MC, V. Daily 6am–midnight.

Inexpensive
Jungle Juice ★★ (Finds) MEXICAN/STEAKS/SEAFOOD   This comfortable patio and upstairs bar has a definite Mexican flair that gives the partially open-air restaurant a festive touch. Grilled meats and lobster are the specialties at this juice-and-smoothie joint, which has evolved into a full-fledged grill and bar. Smoothies and juices are still the specialties, as are vegetarian plates and meat dishes grilled over mesquite on the patio. This casual spot also serves good breakfasts and makes a nice stop after shopping in the Golden Zone. Look for daily specials on the blackboard.

Las Garzas 101. © 669/913-3315. Main courses $5–$20. AE, MC, V. Daily 7am–11pm; bar daily 6pm–2am. From Pastelería Panamá, take Sábalo and turn right on Las Garzas; it's 1 block down on your right. Heading north on Loaiza, Las Garzas and the Pastelería Panamá are on the right after the Sábalo traffic circle, before the Mazatlán Arts and Crafts Center.

Pura Vida I ★ VEGETARIAN/HEALTH FOOD   Nearly hidden behind thick plants, Pura Vida has several small seating sections with wood picnic tables and white canvas umbrellas. A perfect morning spot, it specializes in juices and smoothies, from kelp to papaya. The energetic staff serves omelets and whole-wheat pancakes for breakfast, and burgers, purified salads, soups, and Mexican specialties for lunch. There are plenty of vegetarian dishes, like soy burgers. The veggie and white-chicken sandwiches served on whole-wheat rolls are fabulous.

Bugambilia 100. © 669/916-5815. Main courses $2–$6. No credit cards. Daily 8am–10pm. From Pastelería Panamá on Sábalo, turn right on Las Garzas, then left 1 block down onto Laguna. The cafe is on your right.

DOWNTOWN & PLAYA NORTE
Moderate

Copa de Leche ★★ *Moments* MEXICAN   This shaded sidewalk cafe on the water-front at Playa Olas Altas feels the way Mazatlán must have in the 1930s, and the food is consistently as good as the ocean view. The menu includes *pechugas en nogada* (chicken breast in pecan-and-pomegranate sauce); shrimp in tamarind sauce; tradi-tional *alambre* barbecue (beef cooked with onion, peppers, mushrooms, ham, and bacon); wonderful seafood soup loaded with squid, shrimp, and chunks of fish; and great shrimp with *chipotle* sauce. Inside, the decor is updated Mexican, the bar is an old wooden boat, and the dining tables are covered with linen cloths.

Av. Olas Altas 1220 A Sur. ⓒ 669/982-5753. Fax 669/983-3325. Breakfast $4–$8; main courses $5.50–$17. AE, MC, V. Daily 7am–11pm. From El Shrimp Bucket (at Mariano Escobedo and Olas Altas), turn south and walk ½ block down Olas Altas; the cafe is on your left.

El Shrimp Bucket ★ MEXICAN/SEAFOOD   El Shrimp Bucket is among the most popular restaurants in town. The specialty is Mazatlán's famous shrimp, in the air-conditioned dining room or under umbrellas in the center courtyard. For wining, dining, and dancing, this is a great place for a rousing time, another testament to the success of the Carlos Anderson chain formula.

In the Hotel La Siesta, Av. Olas Altas 111 (at Mariano Escobedo). ⓒ 669/981-6350 or 669/982-8019. Mexican plates $4.50–$10; seafood and steak $9–$22. AE, DISC, MC, V. Daily 6:30am–11pm.

Señor Frog's INTERNATIONAL   A sign over the door says JUST ANOTHER BAR AND GRILL, but once inside you'll know that's just another of the Carlos Anderson chain's infamous understatements. The decor is delightfully wacky, the food consis-tently tasty, and the loud music extremely danceable. With an atmosphere this friendly and lively, revelers have been known to dance on the tables late into the night. Try the tasty ribs, Caesar salad, or caramel crepes. The restaurant is on the waterfront drive at Playa Norte.

North Beach *malecón*, Av. del Mar s/n. ⓒ 669/985-1110 or 669/982-1925. Main courses $7–$22. AE, MC, V. Daily noon–1:30am.

SHOPPING

Mazatlán shopping runs the gamut from precious stones to seashells—with plenty of T-shirts in between. Most stores are open Monday through Saturday from 9 or 10am to 6 or 8pm. Very few close for lunch, and many stores are open on Sunday afternoon.

   La Zona Dorada is the best area for shopping. For a huge selection of handicrafts from all over Mexico, visit the **Mazatlán Arts and Crafts Center,** Calle Gaviotas and Avenida Rodolfo T. Loaiza. It accepts cash only. Nearby **Sea Shell City,** Avenida Playa Gaviotas 407 (ⓒ 669/913-1301) is exactly what the name implies—more shell-cov-ered decorative items than you ever dreamed could exist, from the tacky to the sub-lime. It's open daily, 9am to 8pm. **Gallery Michael,** Av. Las Garzas 18, off Avenida Camarón Sábalo (ⓒ 669/916-7816, www.michaelgallerymexico.com), has an excel-lent selection of Tlaquepaque crafts and fine silver jewelry. It is near the Dairy Queen and does not accept credit cards.

   For fine jewelry, seek out **Pardo Jewellers,** Av. Rodolfo T. Loaiza 411 (ⓒ 669/914-3354), and **Rubio Jewellers,** in the Costa de Oro Hotel, Avenida Camarón Sábalo (ⓒ 669/914-3167). Shops throughout the Golden Zone carry a good selection of clothing, fabrics, silver jewelry, leather, art, and crafts.

The **Centro Mercado** in Old Mazatlán is another kind of shopping experience. Here you'll find women selling fresh shrimp under colorful umbrellas; open-air food stalls; and indoor shops stacked with pottery, clothing, and crafts (mostly of lesser quality). Small galleries and shops are beginning to appear in Old Mazatlán; one of the nicest is **NidArt Galería,** Av. Libertad 45 and Carnaval (© **669/981-0002,** or 669/985-5991 for after-hours appointments; www.nidart.com), next to the Angela Peralta Theater. It features changing exhibits of contemporary art. Open Monday through Saturday from 10am to 3pm, or after hours, by appointment.

La Gran Plaza is a large shopping mall 3 blocks from the waterfront on Avenida de los Deportes. The plaza has a large supermarket, department stores, and specialty shops. A good place for buying basic items, it's open daily from 10am to 9pm.

MAZATLAN AFTER DARK

Mazatlán is known for its vibrant Mexican fiestas and equally colorful local bar scene, where dancing on bars, atop tables, and inside cages can be a nightly event. Traditional mariachi groups, *tambora* bands, and live romantic music create a festive mood in many restaurants and hotel bars.

Happy hour specials abound in value-oriented Mazatlán. One particular favorite is **El Adobe,** in the Costa de Oro hotel (© **669/913-5344,** ext. 1166, or 669/913-5043). This three-level restaurant and bar has views to the Pacific, overlooking the cascading waterfalls and hotel gardens. From 6 to 10pm, El Adobe serves two-for-one tropical drinks in oversize brandy snifters.

A free **fireworks** show takes place every Sunday at 8pm on the beach fronting the Hotel Playa Mazatlán, Av. Rodolfo T. Loaiza 202, in the Golden Zone (© **669/913-5320** or 669/989-0555). The display is visible from the beach and from the hotel's Terraza Playa restaurant (see "Where to Dine," above).

The same hotel presents Mazatlán's most popular **Fiesta Mexicana,** complete with buffet, open bar, folkloric dancing, and live music. Fiestas begin at 7pm on Tuesday, Thursday, and Saturday year-round; try to arrive by 6pm to get a good table. Tickets are $32.

CLUBS & BARS

Coliseo's Disco Forum   If the Roman's knew how to party to excess, this theme club aims to follow in their footsteps. The newest club in Mazatlan, it caters to a more sophisticated crowd, with electronic and dance music. It's open daily from 11am to 2am. Av. Del Mar 406, 1 block south of the Golden Zone. No phone. Cover is $9, and includes a drink, or opt for an open bar cover charge.

Joe's Oyster Bar   Beer, burgers, fresh oysters, and high-volume dance music are the house specialties at this casual, *palapa*-topped, open-air disco. It's open daily from 11am to 2am. On the beachfront at Los Sábalos Hotel, Av. Rodolfo T. Loaiza 100. © 669/983-5333.

Valentino's & the Fiestaland Complex   The popularity of the Valentino's club has resulted in its expansion to a whole array of nocturnal options. The centerpiece remains Valentino's, dramatically perched on a rocky outcropping overlooking the sea, in an all-white, Moorish-looking building, and features a good high-tech light show complete with green laser beams. For a break from the pulsating dance floor, there are pool tables in another room, and some (relatively) quiet areas for talking. Foam parties are the feature every Thursday night. Part of the complex is the Bora Bora, a pub-style bar complete with volleyball court and surfing simulator, and Mikonos and

Canta Bar, with karaoke. Open daily from 9pm to 4am. Punta Camarón, near the Camarón Sábalo traffic circle. ℭ 669/984-1666. Cover $5–$10.

ROAD TRIPS FROM MAZATLAN
TEACAPAN: ABUNDANT WILDLIFE & A RUSTIC VILLAGE

Just 2 hours (131km/82 miles) south of Mazatlán is the fishing village of Teacapán, at the tip of an isolated peninsula that extends 29km (18 miles) down a coastline of pristine beaches. Mangrove lagoons and canals border its other side. Palm and mango groves, cattle ranches, and an occasional cluster of houses dot the peninsula, which ends at the Boca de Teacapán, a natural marina separating the states of Sinaloa and Nayarit. Shrimping boats line the beach at the edge of the marina, which backs up to the worn houses and dirt streets of town. A rugged place, it's recommended for those interested in birding.

Birders hire local fishermen to take them out around the lagoons, where they can see herons, flamingos, Canadian ducks, and countless other species. Inland, the sparsely populated land is a haven for deer, ocelot, and wild boars. There's talk of making the entire peninsula into an ecological preserve, and thus far, residents have resisted attempts by developers to turn the area into a large-scale resort. For now, visitors to Teacapán find the ultimate peaceful refuge.

GETTING THERE   By Car   Drive south from Mazatlán on the highway to Escuinapa. There are no signs marking the right turn for the road to Teacapán; ask for directions in Escuinapa. If you're arriving from the south, turn left at the Bancomer building.

By Bus   Autotransportes Escuinapa runs several second-class buses daily to Escuinapa; the fare is about $5. From there you can transfer to Teacapán (about $3). The second-class bus station is behind the first-class station, across the lot where the buses park.

Where to Stay

Villas Maria Fernanda   This small resort offers a selection of villas and one larger *casa* that sleeps up to 10 people. All are spacious, with simple, traditional furnishings in a colorful Mexican style, plus full kitchen facilities. Boat tours, bird-watching tours, and horseback riding are available. The hotel is adjacent to a small restaurant, which serves all meals. It's at the entrance to the estuary, making it ideal for bird-watchers who want to explore the area.

Domicilio Conocido Teacapán, Sin. ℭ 695/954-5393. Fax 695/953-1343. www.villasmariafernanda.com. 6 units. Villas $65 double, houses $160. AE. **Amenities:** Restaurant; pool; Jacuzzi; water slide; children's playground *In room:* A/C, TV, full kitchen.

COPALA: AN OLD SILVER TOWN

Popular tours from Mazatlán stop here for lunch only, but Copala is well worth an overnight stay. The town was founded in 1565, and from the late 1880s to the early 1900s it was the center of the region's silver-mining boom. When the mines closed, the town was nearly deserted. Today, it's a National Historic Landmark with 600 full-time residents and a part-time community of retired Canadian and U.S. citizens devoted to Copala's picturesque solitude.

Every building in town is painted white, and most have red-tile roofs splashed with bougainvillea. Cobblestone streets wind from the entrance to town up slight hills to the main plaza and the 1610 Cathedral of San José. The town kicks into high gear (relatively speaking) around noon, when tour buses arrive and visitors stroll the streets surrounded by small boys selling geodes extracted from the local hills. By 3pm, most of the outsiders have left. You can wander the streets in peace and visit the century-old cemetery, the ruins of haciendas, and the neighborhoods of white villas.

GETTING THERE Tours go to Copala and Concordia (see "Organized Tours," earlier in this chapter). Copala is an easy 2-hour drive from Mazatlán; drive south for about 25 minutes until you get to the detour for Durango, then turn west and drive to Concordia. From there, follow the signs for Copala; it's about 22km (14 miles). The Autotransportes Concordia bus service runs four buses daily from the second-class bus station, behind the first-class bus station. The fare is $4; check the schedule carefully before departing so you don't get stranded in Copala.

3 Costa Alegre: Puerto Vallarta to Barra de Navidad ★★★

Costa Alegre is one of Mexico's most spectacular coastal areas, a 232km (145-mile) stretch that connects tropical forests with a series of dramatic cliff-lined coves. Tiny outpost towns line the coast, while dirt roads trail down to a succession of magical coves with pristine beaches, most of them steeped in privileged exclusivity. Considered one of Mexico's greatest undiscovered treasures, this area is becoming a favored hideaway for publicity-fatigued celebrities and those in search of natural seclusion.

The area is referred to as **Costa Alegre (Happy Coast)**—the marketer's term—and **Costa Careyes (Turtle Coast),** after the many sea turtles that nest here. It is home to an eclectic array of the most captivating and exclusive places to stay in Mexico, with a selective roster of activities that includes championship golf and polo. Along the line, however, you will encounter the funky beach towns that were the original lure for travelers who discovered the area.

Stops along Highway 200, as it meanders between Puerto Vallarta to the north and Manzanillo to the south, can be an enjoyable day trip, but travelers usually make the drive en route to a destination along the coast.

EXPLORING COSTA ALEGRE Costa Alegre is more an ultimate destination than a place to rent a car and take a drive. Most of the beaches are tucked into coves accessible by dirt roads that can extend for miles inland. If you do drive along this coast, Highway 200 is safe, but it's not lit and it curves through the mountains, so travel only during the day. A few buses travel this route, but they stop only at the towns that line the highway; many of them are several kilometers inland from the resorts along the coast.

ALONG COSTA ALEGRE (NORTH TO SOUTH)
CRUZ DE LORETO'S LUXURY ECORETREAT

Hotelito Desconocido ★★★ *(Moments)* The fact that the Hotelito Desconocido ("little unknown hotel") is ecologically minded is a bonus, but it's not the principal appeal. A cross between *Out of Africa* and *Blue Lagoon,* it is among my favorite places in Mexico. Think camping out with luxury linens, romantic candles everywhere, and a symphony performed by cicadas, birds, and frogs.

The rustic, open-air rooms, called *palafitos,* are in cottages perched on stilts over a lagoon. A grouping of suites is on the ample sand bar that separates the tranquil estuary from the Pacific Ocean. However, these are the least desirable units, and are often damp from the ocean air. Also here is a saltwater pool—the ocean is too aggressive for even seasoned swimmers.

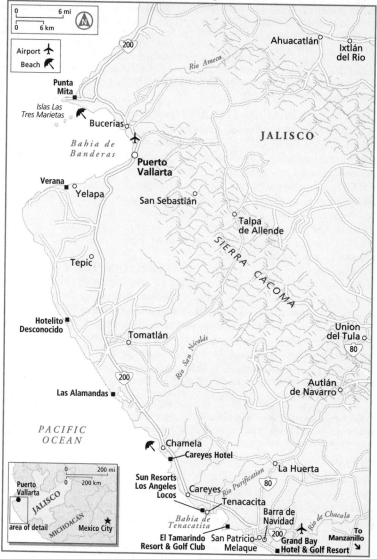

The rooms have cotton sheets, oversize bath towels, and gauzy mosquito nets. Ceiling fans cool the air, and water is solar-heated. It's easy to disconnect here. In fact, it's mandatory: There's no electricity, no phones, no neighboring restaurants, nightclubs, or shopping—only delicious tranquillity. What the service lacks in polish it makes up for in enthusiasm. Rates do not include meals or drinks; a meal plan is mandatory, because there are no other options nearby (making the whole package somewhat pricey)—but it's a unique experience.

Playón de Mismaloya s/n, Cruz de Loreto, 48360 Tomatlán, Jal. ✆ **800/851-1143** in the U.S. and Canada. Reservations ✆ **01-800/013-1313** in Mexico, 322/281-4010, or 322/222-2546. Fax 322/281-4130. www.hotelito.com. 30 units. High season *palafito* double $370–$450, *palafito* suite $490–$670; low season *palafito* double $290–$340, *palafito* suite $390–$530. Mandatory daily meal plan $90 per person. Not appropriate for children. AE, MC, V. Take Hwy. 200 south for 1 hr., turn off at exit for Cruz de Loreto, and continue on clearly marked route on unpaved road for about 25 min. **Amenities:** 2 restaurant/bars; primitive-luxury spa w/massage and spa treatments, sauna, and whirlpool; windsurfing; kayaking; mountain biking; birding tours; hiking; horseback riding; billiards; beach volleyball. All activities are subject to an extra charge.

LAS ALAMANDAS: AN EXCLUSIVE LUXURY RESORT

Las Alamandas ✦✦✦   Almost equidistant between Manzanillo (1½ hr.) and Puerto Vallarta (1¾ hr.) lies Mexico's original ultra-exclusive resort. A dirt road winds for about a mile through a tiny village to the guardhouse of Las Alamandas, on 28 hectares (70 acres) set against low hills that are part of a 600-hectare (1,500-acre) estate. The resort, owned by Isabel Goldsmith, daughter of British financier Sir James Goldsmith, consists of villas and *palapas* spread among four beaches, gardens, lakes, lagoons, and a bird sanctuary. It's designed for privacy—to the point that guests rarely catch a glimpse of one another. The resort has air-conditioning, telephones, and a new beachside massage *palapa,* yet manages to keep the experience as natural as possible. The resort accommodates only 22 guests.

The six spacious villas have tiled verandas with ocean views. They have several bedrooms (each with its own bathroom) and can be rented separately; guests who rent whole villas have preference for reservations. Some villas are on the beach, others across a cobblestone plaza. TVs with VCRs are available on request, but there's no outside reception. Van transportation to and from Manzanillo ($293 one-way) and Puerto Vallarta ($289 one-way) can be arranged when you reserve your room. Air transport from Puerto Vallarta is also available; call for details.

Hwy. 200, 48800 Manzanillo–Puerto Vallarta, Jal. Mailing address: Domicilio Conocido Costa Alegre QUEMARO Jalisco, Apdo. Postal 201, 48980 San Patricio Melaque, Jal. ✆ **888/882-9616** in the U.S. and Canada, or 322/285-5500. Fax 322/285-5027. www.alamandas.com. 14 units. High season $567–$1,998 double, $2,039–$4,235 villa; low season $495–$1,312 double, $1,496–$2,978 villa. Meal plans available. AE, MC, V. **Amenities:** Restaurant; 18m (60-ft.) pool; lighted tennis court; weight room; mountain bikes; concierge; tour desk; room service; horses; hiking trails; boogie boards; birding boat tours; book and video library; landing strip (make advance arrangements). *In room:* A/C, dataport, minibar.

CAREYES

The Careyes Hotel ✦✦   The Careyes is a gem of a resort nestled on a small, pristine cove between dramatic cliffs that are home to the exclusive villas of Careyes. This area has practically defined the architectural style that defines Mexico beach chic— bold washes of vibrant colors, open spaces, and gardens that showcase the tropical flowers and palms indigenous to the area.

The hotel, a Starwood Luxury Collection property, recently completed significant upgrades in services and facilities. The pampering accommodations all face the ocean and are stylishly simple. Although guests come here for isolation, you can enjoy many services, including a full European spa and polo. It's both rustic and sophisticated, with the room facades awash in scrubbed pastels forming a U around the center lawn and freeform pool. Rooms have a dramatic feel, from the plantation shutters and white-tile floors to the handsome loomed bedspreads and colorful pillows. Some units have balconies; all have ocean views. Twenty rooms have private pools, and villas are available for rent. The hotel is popular for weddings and small corporate retreats.

The hotel offers a number of special-interest activities for guests. Named after the hawksbill turtle (*carey* in Spanish), the hotel sponsors a Save the Turtle program in which guests can participate between July and December.

The hotel is roughly 160km (100 miles) south of Puerto Vallarta. It's about a 2-hour drive north of Manzanillo on Highway 200, and about a 1-hour drive from the Manzanillo airport. Taxis from the Manzanillo airport charge around $100 one-way. There are car-rental counters at the Manzanillo and Puerto Vallarta airports. A car would be useful only for exploring the coast—Barra de Navidad and other resorts, for example—and the hotel can make touring arrangements.

Hwy. 200 Km 53.5, 48970 Careyes, Jal. CP. Mailing address: Apdo. Postal 24, 48970 Cihuatlán, Jal. © **800/525-4800** in the U.S. and Canada, 315/351-0000, or 315/351-0606. Fax 315/351-0100. www.elcareyesresort.com or www.luxury collection.com. 51 units. High season $265 double, $415–$485 suite; low season $225 double, $350–$450 suite. AE, MC, V. **Amenities:** Restaurant; bar; deli; large beachside pool; privileges at exclusive El Tamarindo resort (40km/25 miles south), w/18-hole mountaintop golf course; 2 tennis courts; fully equipped, state-of-the-art spa w/massage, hot and cold plunge pools, steam, sauna, weight equipment; kayaks; windsurf boards; Aquafins; "Just for Kids" children's activity program (during Christmas and Easter vacations); room service; laundry service; paddle court; book and video library, Internet access room. *In room:* A/C, TV/VCR, minibar, small fridge, hair dryer, bathrobes.

TENACATITA BAY

Located 60 minutes (53km/33 miles) north of the Manzanillo airport, this jewel of a bay is accessible by an 8km (5-mile) dirt road that passes through a small village set among banana plants and coconut palms. Sandy, serene beaches dot coves around the bay (frolicking dolphins are a common sight), and exotic birds fill a coastal lagoon. Swimming and snorkeling are good, and the bay is a popular stop for luxury yachts. Just south of the entrance to Tenacatita is a sign for the all-inclusive **Sun Resorts Los Angeles Locos,** as well as the exclusive **El Tamarindo** resort and golf club. There is no commercial or shopping area, and dining options outside hotels are limited to a restaurant or two that may emerge during the winter months (high season). Relax—that's what you're here for.

El Tamarindo ★★★ *(Finds* A personal favorite, El Tamarindo is a gem that combines stunning jungle surroundings with exquisite facilities, gracious service, and absolute tranquillity. The area's most luxurious resort, part of Starwood Hotels' Luxury Collection, it comes complete with its own golf course.

The bungalows exude an air of exclusivity—each thatched-roof villa has a splash pool and whirlpool, hammock, plus lounging and dining areas that overlook a private lawn and complement the stunning bedrooms. What they don't have are televisions. Service throughout the resort is exceptional. The bedrooms—with dark hardwood floors and furnishings—can be closed off for air-conditioned comfort, but the remaining areas are open to the sea breezes and heady tropical air.

The categories of bungalows denote their location—Beachfront (on a calm cove, but not as private as the others), Palm Tree, Garden, and Forest. The non-beachside bungalows all have similar decor and amenities but feature more closed-in areas. Anyone squeamish about creepy-crawlies may be uncomfortable in the beginning, but listening to the life around you is a spectacular sensation. On 800 hectares (2,000 acres) of tropical rainforest bordering the Pacific Ocean, you'll feel as if you've found your own personal bit of heaven.

El Tamarindo has a championship 18-hole golf course; the approach to the first hole is through a forest of palms so tall they block the sun. The course has seven oceanside holes and dramatic views. Equally exceptional is their spa services, with most massages and treatments provided in beachfront *cabañas*. Their twice-weekly *temazcal*, a 2½-hour indigenous purification ritual, gets my highest recommendation—a combination of steam bath and spiritual experience, it's generally led by their spa director, Reto. Swiss-born, Reto has studied with Mexican shamans and other soulful teachers, and brings a unique and highly gifted approach to rejuvenating experiences.

The resort restaurant is the only dining option, but you won't be disappointed. The menu, which changes daily, has ample selections of fresh seafood selections, as well as pastas and beef, and all are artfully prepared. You can't leave without trying the resort's Tamarind Margarita.

Carretera Melaque–Puerto Vallarta Km 7.5, 48970 Cihuatlán, Jal. ℭ **315/351-5032.** Fax 315/351-5070. www. eltamarindoresort.com or www.luxurycollection.com. 29 bungalows. High season Ocean Front Villa $695, Palm Tree Villa $559; 2-bedroom Palm Tree Villa $805, Mountain Villa $589; low season Ocean Front Villa $615, Palm Tree Villa $485; 2-bedroom Palm Tree bungalow $685, Mountain Villa $375. AE, MC, V. From Puerto Vallarta (3 hr.) or the Manzanillo airport (40 min.), take Hwy. 200, then turn west at the clearly marked exit for El Tamarindo. Follow signs for about 25 min. **Amenities:** Restaurant; bar; large beachside pool w/whirlpool; 2 clay tennis courts; spa services; windsurfing; kayaking; aquafin sailboats; mountain biking; horseback riding; estuary bird-watching tours; hiking; en-suite dining; yoga classes; *temazcal* (pre-Hispanic sweat lodge), TV and Internet-access room below Lobby. *In room:* A/C, dataport, hair dryer, safe, bathrobes.

Sun Resorts Los Angeles Locos ★

On a 4.8km (3-mile) stretch of sandy beach, Los Angeles Locos offers an abundance of activities and entertainment. An extensive activities program and an ample selection of dining and entertainment options offer guests excellent value. It's a good choice for families and groups of friends. All rooms have ocean views, with either balconies or terraces. The three-story hotel is basic in decor and amenities, but comfortable. The attraction here is the wide array of on-site activities, plus a "Jungle River" cruise excursion (included in the room rate). **La Lagarta Disco** is a little on the dark and smoky side but can really rock, depending on the crowd—it's basically the only option on the bay.

Carretera Federal 200 Km 20, Tenacatita 48989, Municipio de la Huerta, Jal. ℭ **315/351-5020** or 315/351-5100. Fax 315/351-5020. www.losangeleslocos.com. 204 units. High season $140 double; low season $95 double. Children 5–12 $30 year-round. Rates are all-inclusive. Ask about family specials. AE, MC, V. **Amenities:** 2 restaurants and snack bar (w/buffets and a la carte dining); 3 bars; disco; nightly shows and entertainment; adult pool; kids' pool adjacent to the beach; 3 tennis courts; exercise room; windsurfing; kayaks; Hobie cats; Kid's Club; massage; babysitting; laundry service; pool tables; horseback riding; basketball court. *In room:* A/C, TV.

BARRA DE NAVIDAD & MELAQUE

This pair of rustic beach villages (only 5km/3 miles apart) have been attracting travelers for decades. Only 30 minutes north of Manzanillo's airport, and 104km (65 miles) north of downtown Manzanillo, Barra has a few brick or cobblestone streets, good budget hotels and restaurants, and funky beach charm. All of this lies incongruously next to the superluxurious Grand Bay Hotel, which sits on a bluff across the inlet from Barra. Melaque offers budget hotels on and off the beach, fewer restaurants, and little in the way of charm, although the beach is as wide as and more beautiful than Barra's. Both villages appeal to those looking for a quaint, quiet, inexpensive retreat rather than a modern, sophisticated destination.

In the 17th century, Barra de Navidad was a harbor for the Spanish fleet; from here, galleons first set off in 1564 to find China. Located on a crescent-shaped bay with curious rock outcroppings, Barra de Navidad and neighboring Melaque are connected by a continuous beach on the same wide bay. It's safe to say that the only time Barra

Barra de Navidad Bay Area

355

and Melaque hotels are full is during Easter and Christmas weeks. **Barra de Navidad** has more charm, more tree-shaded streets, better restaurants, more stores, and more conviviality between locals and tourists. Barra is very laid-back; faithful returnees adore its lack of flash. Other than the Grand Bay Hotel, on the cliff across the waterway in what is called Isla Navidad (although it's not on an island), nothing is new or modern. But there's a bright edge to Barra, with more good restaurants and limited—but existent—nightlife.

Melaque, on the other hand, is larger, rather sun-baked, treeless, and lacking in attractions. It does, however, have plenty of cheap hotels available for longer stays, and a few restaurants. Although the beach between the two is continuous, Melaque's beach, with deep sand, is more beautiful than Barra's.

Isla Navidad Resort has a manicured 27-hole golf course and the super-luxurious Grand Bay Hotel, but the area's pace hasn't quickened as fast as expected. The golf is challenging and delightfully uncrowded, with another exceptional course at nearby El Tamarindo. It's a serious golfer's dream.

ESSENTIALS

GETTING THERE   Buses from Manzanillo frequently run up the coast along Highway 200 on their way to Puerto Vallarta and Guadalajara. The fare is about $3.50. Most stop in the central villages of Barra de Navidad and Melaque. From the Manzanillo airport, it's only around 30 minutes to Barra, and taxis are available. The fare from Manzanillo to Barra is around $40; from Barra to Manzanillo, $30. From Manzanillo, the highway twists through some of the Pacific Coast's most beautiful mountains. Puerto Vallarta is a 3-hour (by car) to 5-hour (by bus) ride north on Highway 200 from Barra.

VISITOR INFORMATION   The **tourism office** for both villages is at Jalisco 67 (between Veracruz and Mazatlán), Barra (✆/fax **315/355-5100;** www.barradenavidad. com). The office is open daily from 9am to 5pm. The **Travel Agency Isla Navidad Tours,** Veracruz 204-A, Barra de Navidad (✆ **315/355-5666** or 315/355-5667), can handle arrangements for plane tickets and sells bus tickets from Manzanillo to Puerto Vallarta and Guadalajara. It's open Monday through Friday from 11am to 8pm and Saturday from 11am to 6pm.

ORIENTATION   In Barra, hotels and restaurants line the main beachside street, **Legazpi.** From the bus station, beachside hotels are 2 blocks straight ahead, across the central plaza. Two blocks behind the bus station and to the right is the lagoon side. More hotels and restaurants are on its main street, **Morelos/Veracruz.** Few streets are marked, but 10 minutes of wandering will acquaint you with the village's entire layout. There's a taxi stand at the intersection of Legazpi and Sinaloa streets. Legazpi, Jalisco, Sinaloa, and Veracruz streets border Barra's **central plaza.**

ACTIVITIES ON & OFF THE BEACH

Swimming and enjoying the attractive beach and views of the bay take up most tourists' time. You can hire a small boat for a coastal ride or fishing in two ways. Go toward the *malecón* on Calle Veracruz until you reach the tiny boatmen's cooperative, with fixed prices posted on the wall, or walk two buildings farther to the water taxi ramp. The water taxi is the best option for going to Colimilla (5 min., $2) or across the inlet (3 min., $1) to the Grand Bay Hotel. Water taxis make the rounds regularly, so if you're at Colimilla, wait, and one will be along shortly. At the cooperative, a 30-minute **lagoon tour** costs $20, and a **sea tour** costs $25. **Sportfishing** is $80 for up to four people for a half-day in a small *panga* (open fiberglass boat, like the ones used for water taxis).

Surfing along Costa Alegre is gaining ground, thanks in large part to Germaine Badke, and the **South Swell Mex Surf Shop** (© **314/338-7152;** www.southswellmex. com), which he owns and operates. The shop offers boogie board and surfboard rentals, surfboard and surf supply sales, and will also create a custom-designed board. Surf lessons are also available. They're located in Suite 2 of the Hotel Alondra.

The Grand Bay Hotel's beautiful and challenging 27-hole, 7,053-yard, par-72 **golf course** is open to the public. Hotel guests pay greens fees of $166 for 18 holes, $192 for 27 holes; nonguests pay $216 and $240, respectively. Prices include a motorized cart. Caddies are available, as are rental clubs. The Crazy Cactus (see below) can arrange golf at El Tamarindo's gorgeous mountaintop course, about 32km (20 miles) north of Barra.

Beer Bob's Books, Ave. Tampico, between Sinaloa and Guanajuato, is a book-lover's institution in Barra and a sort of community service that the rather grouchy Bob does for fun. His policy of "leave a book if you take one" allows vacationers to select from hundreds of neatly shelved paperbacks, as long as they leave a book in exchange. It's open Monday through Friday from noon to 3pm and occasionally in the evenings. "Beer Bob" got his name because in earlier days, when beer was cheap, he kept a cooler stocked, and book browsers could sip and read. (When beer prices went up, Bob put the cooler away.)

WHERE TO STAY

Low season in Barra is any time except Christmas and Easter weeks. Except for those 2 weeks, it doesn't hurt to ask for a discount at the inexpensive hotels. To arrange **real estate rentals,** contact **The Crazy Cactus,** Jalisco 8, a half-block inland from the town church on Legazpi (©/fax **315/355-6099;** crazycactusmx@yahoo.com). The store may be closed May through October.

Very Expensive

Grand Bay Hotel Wyndham Resort ★ *Overrated*   Across the yacht channel from Barra de Navidad, this luxurious hotel opened in 1997 on 480 hectares (1,200 acres) next to its 27-hole golf course. Now operated by Wyndham Resorts, it overlooks the village, bay, Pacific Ocean, and Navidad lagoon. The hotel's beach is narrow and on the lagoon. A better beach is opposite the hotel on the bay in Barra de Navidad. The spacious rooms are sumptuously outfitted with marble floors, large bathrooms, and hand-carved wood furnishings. Prices vary according to view and size of room, but even the modest rooms are large; all have cable TV. Each comes with a king-size or two double beds, a glass-top desk, ceiling fans plus air-conditioning, and a balcony. All suites have a steam sauna and telephones in the bathroom as well as a sound system. The hotel is a short water-taxi ride across the inlet from Barra de Navidad; it is also on a paved road from Highway 200. Although the hotel bills itself as being on the Island of Navidad at Port Navidad, the port is the marina, and the hotel is on a peninsula.

Isla Navidad, Col. 45110. © **01-800/996-3426,** 315/355-5050, or 314/331-0500 in Mexico, or 310/536-9278 in the U.S. Fax 315/355-6070. www.islaresort.com.mx; www.wyndham.com. 199 units. High season $220–$460 double, $550–$680 suite; low season $160–$321 double, $468–$614 suite. Ask about tennis, golf, fishing, and honeymoon packages. Rates include round-trip transportation to and from Manzanillo airport. AE, DC, DISC, MC, V. **Amenities:** 2 restaurants; 2 bars; golf club w/food and bar service; swimming pool w/water slides and swim-up bar; 27-hole, par-72 golf course designed by Robert Von Hagge; golf club w/pro shop and driving range; 3 lighted grass tennis courts w/stadium seating; small but sufficient workout room; Kid's Club w/activity program; 24-hr. concierge; business center; salon; room service; babysitting; laundry service; dry cleaning; 150-slip marina w/private yacht club; fishing, boat tours, and other excursions can be arranged. *In room:* A/C, TV, dataport, minibar, hair dryer, iron, safe-deposit box, bathrobes.

Moderate

Hotel Cabo Blanco ✫✫ Located on the point where you cross over to Isla Navidad, the Cabo Blanco is an outstanding option for family vacations or longer-term stays. Rooms are pleasantly rustic, with tile floors, large tile tubs, separate dressing areas, and stucco walls. The hotel overlooks the bay, but it's a 5-minute walk to the beach. The beamed-ceiling lobby is in its own building; rooms are in hacienda-style buildings surrounded by gardens. The atmosphere is generally tranquil, except during weekends and Mexican holidays, when this hotel tends to fill up. Because the Cabo Blanco doesn't front the beach, it has an affiliated beach club and restaurant, Mar y Tierra (see "Where to Dine," below).

Armada y Bahía de la Navidad s/n, 48987 Barra de Navidad, Jal. ✆ 315/355-5103 or 315/355-5136. Fax 315/355-6494. 101 units. $130 double; $256 suite with kitchenette. All-inclusive plans also available. AE, MC, V. **Amenities:** 2 restaurants; 4 pools (2 adults only); 2 tennis courts; concierge; tour desk; car-rental desk; laundry service. *In room:* A/C, TV.

Inexpensive

Hotel Barra de Navidad ✫ At the northern end of Legazpi, this popular, comfortable beachside hotel is among the nicest in the town. It has friendly management, and some rooms with balconies overlooking the beach and bay. Other, less expensive rooms afford only a street view. Only the oceanview rooms have air-conditioning. A nice swimming pool is on the street level to the right of the lobby.

Legazpi 250, 48987 Barra de Navidad, Jal. ✆ 315/355-5122. Fax 315/355-5303. 59 units. $50–$72 double. MC, V. **Amenities:** Pool.

Hotel Delfín One of Barra's better-maintained hotels, the four-story (no elevator) Delfín is on the landward side of the lagoon. It offers pleasant, basic, well-maintained, and well-lit rooms. Each has red-tile floors and a double, two double, or two single beds. The tiny courtyard, with a small pool and lounge chairs, sits in the shade of an enormous rubber tree. From the fourth floor, there's a view of the lagoon. A breakfast buffet is served from 8:30 to 10:30am (see "Where to Dine," below).

Morelos 23, 48987 Barra de Navidad, Jal. ✆ 315/355-5068. Fax 315/355-6020. 24 units. $49 double; ask about low-season discounts. MC, V. Free parking. **Amenities:** Restaurant; pool.

Hotel Sands The colonial-style Sands, across from the Hotel Delfín (see above) on the lagoon side at Jalisco, offers small but homey rooms with red-tile floors and windows with both screens and glass. The remodeled bathrooms have new tiles and fixtures. Lower rooms look onto a public walkway and wide courtyard filled with greenery and singing birds; upstairs rooms are brighter. Twelve rooms (suites or bungalows) have air-conditioning and kitchenette facilities. The hotel is known for its warm hospitality and high-season happy hour (2–6pm) at the pool terrace bar beside the lagoon. On weekends from 9pm to 4am, an adjacent patio "disco" plays recorded music for dancing. Breakfast is served from 7:30am to noon. Fishing trips can be arranged, and tours to nearby beaches are available.

Morelos 24, 48987 Barra de Navidad, Jal. ✆/fax 315/355-5018. 42 units. High season $61 double; low season $42 double. Rates include breakfast. Room-only rates $10 less. Discounts for stays of 1 week or more. MC, V (6% surcharge). **Amenities:** Restaurant; bar; pool w/whirlpool overlooking lagoon beach; children's play area; tour desk.

WHERE TO DINE

El Manglito ✫ SEAFOOD/INTERNATIONAL On the placid lagoon, with a view of the palatial Grand Bay Hotel, El Manglito serves home-style Mexican food to a growing number of repeat diners. The whole fried fish accompanied by drawn garlic butter, boiled vegetables, rice, and french fries, is a crowd-pleaser. Other entice-ments include boiled shrimp, chicken in orange sauce, and shrimp salad.

Veracruz, near the boatmen's cooperative. No phone. Main courses $5–$10. No credit cards. Daily 9am–11pm.

Hotel Delfín INTERNATIONAL   The second-story terrace of this small hotel is a pleasant place to begin the day. The self-serve buffet offers an assortment of fresh fruit, juice, granola, yogurt, milk, pastries, and unlimited coffee. The price includes made-to-order eggs and delicious banana pancakes—for which the restaurant is known.

Morelos 23. ℂ 315/355-5068. Breakfast buffet $4. No credit cards. Daily 8:30am–noon.

Mar y Tierra INTERNATIONAL   Hotel Cabo Blanco's beach club is also a popu-lar restaurant and bar, and a great place to spend a day at the beach. On the beach, there are shade *palapas* and beach chairs, and a game of volleyball seems constantly in progress. The colorful restaurant is decorated with murals of mermaids. Perfectly sea-soned shrimp fajitas come in plentiful portions.

Legazpi s/n (at Jalisco). ℂ 315/355-5028. Main courses $10–$17. AE, MC, V. Wed–Sun 2–10pm; closes at 6pm on Sun (opens at 10am Wed–Mon for hotel guests).

Restaurant Bar Ambar CREPES/SPANISH/FRENCH   This cozy, thatched-roof, upstairs restaurant is open to the breezes. The crepes are named after towns in France; the delicious *crêpe Paris,* for example, is filled with chicken, potatoes, spinach, and green sauce. Sweet dessert crepes are also available. International main dishes include imported (from the U.S.) rib-eye steak in Dijon mustard sauce, mixed brochettes, quiche, and Caesar salad. Ambar serves Spanish-style tapas from noon until 6pm, and adds French specialties during dinner.

Av. Veracruz 101-A (at Jalisco). No phone. Crepes $5–$13; main courses $5–$15. No credit cards. Daily noon–mid-night (happy hour 1pm–midnight). Closed July–Oct.

Restaurant Bar Ramón 🏵 *Value* SEAFOOD/MEXICAN   It seems that everybody eats at Ramón's, where the chips and fresh salsa arrive unbidden, and service is prompt and friendly. The food is especially good—however, most options are fried. Try fresh fried shrimp with french fries, or any daily special that features vegetable soup or chicken-fried steak. Great value!

Legazpi 260. ℂ 315/355-6435. Main courses $6–$10. MC, V. Daily 7am–11pm.

Seamaster SEAFOOD/INTERNATIONAL   This cheery, colorful restaurant on the beach facing the ocean is a great place for sunsets and margaritas, or a meal any-time. Specialties include steamed shrimp (peeled or unpeeled), fried calamari, barbe-cue chicken, ribs, steak, chicken wings, hamburgers, and other sandwiches. During high season, it turns into a popular disco at night.

Legazpi (at Yucatán). No phone. Main courses $5–$15. No credit cards. Daily noon–midnight.

BARRA DE NAVIDAD AFTER DARK

When dusk arrives, visitors and locals alike find a cool spot to sit outside, sip cock-tails, and chat. Many outdoor restaurants and stores in Barra accommodate this relax-ing way to end the day, adding extra tables and chairs for drop-ins.

During high season, the **Hotel Sands** poolside and lagoon-side bar has happy hour from 2 to 6pm. The colorful **Sunset Bar and Restaurant,** facing the bay at the cor-ner of Legazpi and Jalisco, is a favorite for sunset watching, and then a game of ocean-side pool or dancing to live or taped music. It's most popular with travelers ages 20 to

30. In the same vein, **Chips Restaurant,** on the second floor facing the ocean at the corner of Yucatán and Legazpi near the southern end of the *malecón,* has an excellent sunset vista. Live music follows the last rays of light, and patrons stay for hours. **Piper's Lover Bar & Restaurant,** Legazpi 254 (© **315/355-6747;** www.piperlover. com) is done in the style of the Carlos Anderson's chain—but it's not one of them. Still, it is lively, with pool tables and occasional live music.

At the **Disco El Galeón,** in the Hotel Sands on Calle Morelos, cushioned benches and cement tables encircle the round dance floor. It's all open-air, and about as stylish as you'll find in Barra. It serves drinks only. Admission is $6, and it's open Friday and Saturday from 9pm to 4am.

A VISIT TO MELAQUE (SAN PATRICIO)

For a change of scenery, you may want to wander over to Melaque (aka San Patricio), 5km (3 miles) from Barra on the same bay. You can walk on the beach from Barra or take one of the frequent local buses from the bus station near the main square in Barra. The bus is marked MELAQUE. To return to Barra, take the bus marked CIHUATLAN.

Melaque's pace is even more laid-back than Barra's, and though it's a larger village, it seems smaller. It has fewer restaurants and less to do. Although there are more hotels, or "bungalows," as they are usually called, few manage the charm of those in Barra; if Barra hotels are full on a holiday weekend, Melaque would be a second choice. The paved road ends where the town begins. A few yachts bob in the harbor, and the palm-lined beach is gorgeous.

If you come by bus from Barra, you can exit anywhere in town or stay on until the last stop, which is the bus station in the middle of town a block from the beach. Restaurants and hotels line the beach. Coming into town from the main road, you'll be on the town's main street, **Avenida López Matéos.** You'll pass the main square on the way to the waterfront, where there's a trailer park. The street going left (southeast) along the bay is **Avenida Gómez Farías;** the one going right (northwest) is **Avenida Miguel Ochoa López.**

WHERE TO DINE At the north end of Melaque beach is **Los Pelícanos** (© **315/ 355-5415**). It serves the usual seafood specialties; the tender fried squid is delectable. In addition, you can find burritos, nachos, and hamburgers. Many Barra guests come here to stake a place on the beach and use the restaurant as headquarters for sipping and nipping. Open daily from 8am to 10pm, it's a peaceful place to watch the pelicans bobbing. The restaurant is at the far end of the bay before the **Hotel Legazpi** (© **315/355-5397**), a pleasant place to stay. It has 20 rooms, charges $32 for a double, and doesn't accept credit cards.

In addition to the Los Pelícanos, there are many rustic *palapa* **restaurants** on the beach and farther along the bay at the end of the beach.

4 Manzanillo ⍟

256km (160 miles) SE of Puerto Vallarta; 267km (167 miles) SW of Guadalajara; 64km (40 miles) SE of Barra de Navidad

Manzanillo has long been known as a resort town with wide, curving beaches, legendary sportfishing, and a highly praised diversity of dive sites. Golf is also an attraction here, with two popular courses in the area.

One reason for its popularity could be Manzanillo's enticing tropical geography—vast groves of tall palms, abundant mango trees, and successive coves graced with smooth sand beaches. To the north, mountains blanketed with palms rise alongside

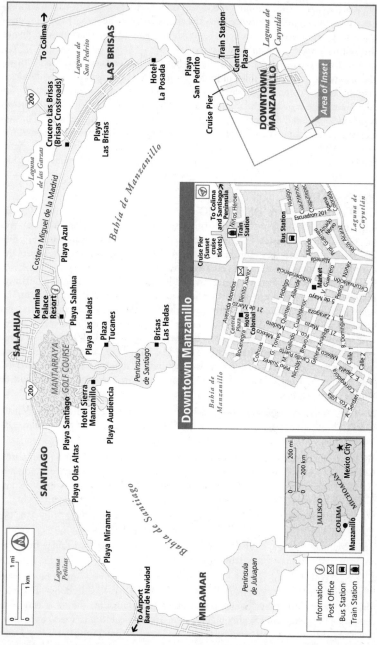

Manzanillo Area

To Colima →

LAS BRISAS

Laguna de San Pedro

Hotel La Posada

Playa San Pedrito

Train Station

Central Plaza

Laguna de Cuyutlán

Cruise Pier

DOWNTOWN MANZANILLO

Area of Inset

Crucero Las Brisas (Brisas Crossroads)

Playa Las Brisas

Bahía de Manzanillo

Costera Miguel de la Madrid

Laguna de las Garzas

Playa Azul

SALAHUA

Karmina Palace Resort i

Playa Salahua

Playa Las Hadas

Plaza Tucanes

Brisas Las Hadas

Hotel Sierra Manzanillo

Playa Audiencia

MANTARRAYA GOLF COURSE

Playa Santiago

Península de Santiago

SANTIAGO

Playa Olas Altas

Laguna Peñitas

Playa Miramar

Bahía de Santiago

To Airport Barra de Navidad →

MIRAMAR

Península de Juluapan

Downtown Manzanillo

Bahía de Manzanillo

Cruise Pier (Sunset cruise tickets)

To Colima and Santiago Peninsula →

Niños Héroes

Train Station

Bus Station

Hidalgo

Cuauhtémoc

Chapultepec

Escuadron 201

Av. Amado Nervo

Jesús Arreaza

Colorada

Laguna de Cuyutlán

Allende

Prol. Gala Nava

Alameda

Pedro Núñez

Circunvalación

V. Guerrero

Market

Independencia

Hotel Colonial

Avenida Morelos

Central Plaza

Bocanegra

Benito Juárez

21 de Marzo

Hidalgo

5 de Mayo

Quintero

Allende

Cuauhtémoc

Madero

I. Zaragoza

México

B. Domínguez

Colimas

G. Torres

G. Galindo

Fco. Bravo

Nicolás Bravo

Cuauhtémoc

Juan Puerto

General Anaya

21 de Marzo

Pino Suárez

Calle 1

Corregidora

E. Zapata

Calle 2

Villa

A. Serdán

Fco.

200 mi

200 km

★ Mexico City

JALISCO

COLIMA

Manzanillo

MICHOACÁN

1 mi

1 km

i Information

☒ Post Office

Bus Station

Train Station

the shoreline. And over it all lies the veneer of perfect weather, with balmy temperatures and year-round sea breezes. Even the approach by plane into Manzanillo showcases the promise—you fly in over the beach and golf course. Once on the ground, you exit the airport through a palm grove.

Manzanillo is a dichotomous place—it is both Mexico's busiest commercial seaport and a tranquil, traditional town of multicolor houses cascading down the hillsides to meet the central commercial area of simple seafood restaurants, shell shops, and a few salsa clubs. The activity in Manzanillo divides neatly into two zones: the downtown commercial port and the luxury Santiago Peninsula resort zone to the north. The busy harbor and rail connections to Mexico's interior dominate the downtown zone. A visit to the town's waterfront *zócalo* provides a glimpse into local life. The exclusive Santiago Peninsula, home to the resorts and golf course, separates Manzanillo's two golden sand bays.

ESSENTIALS

GETTING THERE & DEPARTING **By Plane** **Alaska Airlines** (© 800/426-0333 in the U.S., or 314/334-2211) offers service from Los Angeles; **America West** (© 800/235-9292 in the U.S.) flies from Phoenix; and **Aero California** (© 800/237-6225 in the U.S. and Canada, or 314/334-1414) has flights from Los Angeles. Ask a travel agent about the numerous **charters** from the States in the winter.

The **Playa de Oro International Airport** is 40km (25 miles; 45 min.) northwest of town. *Colectivo* (minivan) airport service is available from the airport; hotels arrange returns. Make reservations for return trips 1 day in advance. The *colectivo* fare is based on zones and runs $8 to $10 for most hotels. Private taxi service between the airport and downtown area is around $25. **Budget** (© 800/527-0700 in the U.S., or 314/333-1445) and **AutoRentas** (© 314/333-2580) have counters in the airport open during flight arrivals; they will also deliver a car to your hotel. Daily rates run $58 to $78. You need a car only if you plan to explore surrounding cities and the Costa Alegre beaches.

By Car **Coastal Highway 200** leads from Acapulco (south) and Puerto Vallarta (north). From Guadalajara, take Highway 54 through Colima into Manzanillo. Outside Colima you can switch to a toll road, which is faster but less scenic.

By Bus Buses run to Barra de Navidad (1½ hr. north), Puerto Vallarta (5 hr. north), Colima (1½ hr. east), and Guadalajara (4½ hr. north), with deluxe service and numerous daily departures. Manzanillo's **Central Camionera** (bus station) is about 12 long blocks east of town. If you follow Hidalgo east, the station will be on your right.

VISITOR INFORMATION The **tourism office** (© 314/333-2277 or 314/333-2264; fax 314/333-2264) is on the Costera Miguel de la Madrid 4960, Km 8.5. It's open Monday through Thursday from 9am to 3pm and 5 to 7pm Friday from 9am to 3pm. and Saturday from 10am to 2pm.

CITY LAYOUT The town lies at one end of an 11km-long (7-mile) beach facing Manzanillo Bay and its commercial harbor. The beach has four sections—**Playa Las Brisas, Playa Azul, Playa Salahua,** and **Playa Las Hadas.** At the other end of the beaches is the high, rocky **Santiago Peninsula.** Santiago is 11km (7 miles) from downtown; it's the site of many beautiful homes and the best hotel in the area, Las Hadas, as well as the hotel's Mantarraya Golf Course. The peninsula juts out into the bay, separating Manzanillo Bay from Santiago Bay. Playa Las Hadas is on the south side of the peninsula, facing Manzanillo Bay, and **Playa Audiencia** is on the north side, facing Santiago Bay. The inland town of **Santiago** is opposite the turnoff to Las Hadas.

Activity in downtown Manzanillo centers on the **central plaza,** or *zócalo,* officially known as the Jardín Alvaro Obregón. A railroad, shipyards, and a basketball court with constant pickup games separate it from the waterfront. The plaza has flowering trees, a fountain, twin kiosks, and a view of the bay. It is a staple of local life, where people congregate on park benches to swap gossip and throw handfuls of rice to the ever-present *palomas* (doves—really just pigeons). Large ships dock at the pier nearby. **Avenida México,** the street leading out from the plaza's central gazebo, is the town's principal commercial thoroughfare. This area is currently undergoing a government-funded renaissance, so look for new improvements.

Once you leave downtown, the highway (the **Costera Miguel de la Madrid,** or just Costera Madrid) runs through the neighborhoods of Las Brisas, Salahua, and Santiago to the **hotel zones** on the Santiago Peninsula and at Miramar. Shell shops, mini-malls, and several restaurants are along the way.

There are two main lagoons. **Laguna de Cuyutlán,** almost behind the city, stretches south for miles, paralleling the coast. **Laguna de San Pedrito,** north of the city, parallels the Costera Miguel de la Madrid; it's behind Playa Las Brisas beach. Both are good birding sites. There are also two bays. **Manzanillo Bay** encompasses the harbor, town, and beaches. The Santiago Peninsula separates it from the second bay, **Santiago.** Between downtown and the Santiago Peninsula is **Las Brisas,** a flat peninsula with a long stretch of sandy golden beach, a lineup of inexpensive but run-down hotels, and a few good restaurants.

GETTING AROUND   By Taxi   Taxis in Manzanillo are plentiful. Fares are fixed by zones; rates for trips within town and to more distant points should be posted at your hotel. Daily rates can be negotiated for longer drives outside the Manzanillo area.

By Bus   The local buses *(camionetas)* make a circuit from downtown in front of the train station, along the Bay of Manzanillo, to the Santiago Peninsula and the Bay of Santiago to the north; the fare is 10¢. The ones marked LAS BRISAS go to the Las Brisas crossroads, to the Las Brisas Peninsula, and back to town; MIRAMAR, SANTIAGO, and SALAHUA buses go to outlying settlements along the bays and to most restaurants mentioned below. Buses marked LAS HADAS go to the Santiago Peninsula and pass the Las Hadas resort and the Sierra Manzanillo and Plaza Las Glorias hotels. This is an inexpensive way to see the coast as far as Santiago and to tour the Santiago Peninsula.

FAST FACTS: Manzanillo

American Express   There is no local office for American Express in Manzanillo. However a highly recommendable agency (and American Express's former representative) is **Bahías Gemelas Travel Agency,** Km 10 Costera Miguel de la Madrid (✆ **314/333-1000;** fax 314/333-0649). It's open Monday through Friday from 10am to 2pm and 4 to 6pm, Saturday from 10am to 2pm.

Area Code   The telephone area code is **314.**

Bank   **Banamex,** just off the plaza on Avenida México, downtown (✆ **314/332-0115**), is open Monday through Friday from 9am to 4pm.

Hospital Contact the **Cruz Roja (Red Cross)** at ℭ **314/336-5770,** or the **General Hospital** at ℭ **314/332-1903.**

Internet Access **Digital Center,** Blvd. Miguel de la Madrid 96-B (ℭ **314/333-9191),** is located in the hotel zone, near the Hotel Marbella and Fiesta Americana hotels. It charges $2 per hour, and also has printers and copiers. It's open Monday through Friday from 9am to 8pm, Saturday from 9am to 2pm. They also have computer repair services available.

Police Both the general police and Tourism Police are available by calling ℭ **314/332-1004.**

Post Office The *correo,* Dr. Miguel Galindo 30, opposite Farmacia de Guadalajara, downtown (ℭ **314/332-0022),** is open Monday through Friday from 9am to 2pm.

ACTIVITIES ON & OFF THE BEACH

Activities in Manzanillo revolve around its golden sand beaches, which frequently accumulate a film of black mineral residue from nearby rivers. Most of the resort hotels are completely self-contained. Manzanillo's public beaches provide an opportunity to see more local color and scenery. They are the daytime playground for those staying at places off the beach or without pools.

BEACHES **Playa Audiencia,** on the Santiago Peninsula, offers the best swimming as well as snorkeling, but **Playa San Pedrito,** shallow for a long way out, is the most popular beach for its proximity to downtown. **Playa Las Brisas** offers an optimal combination of location and good swimming. **Playa Miramar,** on the Bahía de Santiago past the Santiago Peninsula, is popular with bodysurfers, windsurfers, and boogie boarders. It's accessible by local bus from town. The major part of **Playa Azul** drops off sharply but is noted for its wide stretch of golden sand.

BIRDING Several lagoons along the coast offer good birding. As you go from Manzanillo past Las Brisas to Santiago, you'll pass **Laguna de Las Garzas (Lagoon of the Herons),** also known as Laguna de San Pedrito, where you can see many white pelicans and huge herons fishing in the water. They nest here in December and January. Directly behind downtown is the **Laguna de Cuyutlán** (follow the signs to Cuyutlán), where you'll usually find birds in abundance; species vary between summer and winter.

DIVING **Underworld Scuba** 🐟🐟 (ℭ/fax **314/333-0642;** cell 314/358-0327; www.gomanzanillo.com), owned by longtime resident and local diving expert Susan Dearing, conducts highly professional diving expeditions and classes. Susan's warm enthusiasm and intimate knowledge of the area make this one of my top recommendations for dive outfitters in Mexico. Many locations are so close to shore that there's no need for a boat. Close-in dives include the jetty with coral growing on the rocks at 14m (45 ft.), and a nearby sunken frigate downed in 1959 at 8m (28 ft.). Divers can see abundant sea life, including coral reefs, seahorses, giant puffer fish, and moray eels. A dive requiring a boat costs $60 per person for one tank (with a three-person minimum), or $70 for two tanks ($10 discount if you have your own equipment). You can also rent weights and a tank for beach dives for $10. A three-stop snorkel trip costs $35. All guides are certified divemasters, and the shop offers certification classes

(PADI, YMCA, and CMAS) in very intensive courses of various durations. The owner offers a 10% discount on your certification when you mention Frommer's. Master-Card and Visa are accepted.

ESCORTED TOURS Because Manzanillo is so spread out, you might consider a city tour. Reputable local tour companies include **Hectours** (© 314/333-1707) and **Bahías Gemelas Travel Agency** (© 314/333-1000; fax 314/333-0649). Schedules are flexible; a half-day city tour costs around $25. Other tours include the daylong Colima Colonial Tour ($67), which stops at a sugar-cane plantation, Colima's Archaeological Museum, and principal colonial buildings, and passes the active volcano. Offerings change regularly, so ask about new tours.

FISHING Manzanillo is famous for its fishing, particularly sailfish. Marlin and sailfish are abundant year-round. Winter is best for dolphin fish and dorado (mahimahi); in summer, wahoo and rooster fish are in greater supply. The international sailfish competition is held around the November 20 Revolution Day holiday, and the national sailfish competition is in February. You can arrange fishing through travel agencies or directly at the fishermen's cooperative (© 314/332-1031), located downtown where the fishing boats moor. Call from 7am to 7pm. A fishing boat is approximately $40 to $65 per hour, with most trips lasting about 5 hours.

GOLF The 18-hole **La Mantarraya Golf Course** (© 314/331-0101) is open to nonguests as well as guests of Las Hadas. At one time, La Mantarraya was among the top 100 courses in the world, but newer entries have passed it. Still, the compact, challenging 18-hole course designed by Roy and Pete Dye is a beauty, with banana trees, blooming bougainvillea, and coconut palms at every turn. A lush and verdant place (12 of the 18 holes are played over water), it remains a favored of Mexico's 125 courses.

When the course was under construction, workers dug up pre-Hispanic ceramic figurines, idols, and beads where the 14th hole now lies. It is believed to have been an important ancient burial site. The course culminates with its signature 18th hole, with a drive to the island green off El Tesoro (the treasure) beach, directly in front of the Karminda Palace Resort. Local lore says this beach still may hold buried treasure from Spanish galleons, whose crews were the first to recognize the perfection of this natural harbor, and who used it during the 16th century as their starting point for voyages to the Pacific Rim. Greens fees are $122 for 18 holes, $73 for 9 holes; cart rental costs $50.

The fabulous 27-hole golf course associated with the **Grand Bay Hotel** in Barra de Navidad, an easy distance from Manzanillo, is also open to the public. The Robert Von Hagge design is long and lovely, with each hole amid rolling, tropical landscapes. It is wide open, with big fairways and big greens, and features plenty of water (2 lagoon holes, 13 lakeside holes, and 8 holes along the Pacific). The greens fees are $166 for 18 holes, $192 for 27 holes for hotel guests, $216 and $240, respectively, for nonguests, including a motorized cart. Barra is about a 1- to 1½-hour drive north of Manzanillo on Highway 200. (See "Activities On & Off the Beach" under "Barra de Navidad & Melaque," earlier in this chapter.)

A MUSEUM The **Museum of Archaeology and History** (© 314/332-2256) is a small but impressive structure that houses exhibits depicting the region's history, plus rotating displays of contemporary Mexican art. It's on Avenida Niños Héroes at Avenida Teniente Azueta, on the road leading between the downtown and Las Brisas areas. Every Friday evening, the museum hosts free cultural events, which might be a trio playing romantic ballads or a chamber music ensemble. Performances begin at

8pm. Hours are Tuesday through Saturday from 10am to 2pm and 5 to 8pm, Sunday from 10am to 1pm. The museum is undergoing a complete renovation, scheduled to be completed in November 2006.

SHOPPING   Manzanillo has a selection of shops carrying Mexican crafts and clothing, mainly from nearby Guadalajara. Almost all are downtown on the streets near the central plaza. Shopping downtown is an experience—for example, you won't want to miss the shop bordering the plaza that sells a combination of shells, religious items (including shell-framed Virgin of Guadalupe nightlights), and orthopedic supplies. The Plaza Manzanillo is an American-style mall on the road to Santiago, and there's a traditional *tianguis* (outdoor) market in front of the entrance to Club Maeva, with touristy items from around Mexico. Most resort hotels also have boutiques or shopping arcades.

SUNSET CRUISES   To participate in this popular activity, buy tickets from a travel agent or your hotel tour desk. Most cost around $25. The trips vary in their combinations of drinks, music, and entertainment and last 1½ to 2 hours. Departing from Las Hadas is the **El Explorer** (✆ **314/352-4882**) and **Antares** (✆ **314/376-0144**).

WHERE TO STAY

Manzanillo's strip of coastline consists of three areas: **downtown,** with its shops, markets, and commercial activity; **Las Brisas,** the hotel-lined beach area immediately north of the city; and **Santiago,** the town and peninsula, now virtually a suburb, to the north at the end of Playa Azul. Transportation by bus or taxi makes all three areas fairly convenient to each other. Reservations are recommended during the Easter, Christmas, and New Year's holidays.

DOWNTOWN

Hotel Colonial ⚐   An old favorite, this three-story colonial-style hotel is in the central downtown district. Popular for its consistent quality, ambience, and service, it has beautiful blue-and-yellow tile, and colonial-style carved doors and windows in the lobby and restaurant. Rooms are decorated with minimal furniture, red-tile floors, and basic comforts. The hotel is 1 block inland from the main plaza at the corner of Juárez and Galindo.

Av. México 100 and González Bocanegra, 28200 Manzanillo, Col. ✆ **314/332-1080**, 314/332-0668, 314/332-1230, or 314/332-1134. 42 units. $34 double. MC, V. **Amenities:** Restaurant; bar; tour desk. *In room:* A/C, TV.

LAS BRISAS

Some parts of the Las Brisas area look run-down, however, it still lays claim to one of the best beaches in the area and is known for its constant gentle sea breezes—a pleasure in the summer.

Hotel La Posada ⚐   This small inn has a bright-pink stucco facade with a large arch that leads to a broad tiled patio right on the beach. The rooms have exposed brick walls and simple furnishings with Mexican decorative accents. It remains popular with longtime travelers to Manzanillo. The atmosphere is casual and informal—help yourself to beer and soft drinks, and at the end of your stay, owners Juan and Lisa Martínez will count the bottle caps you deposited in a bowl labeled with your room number. The restaurant, which is open to nonguests, is open daily during high season from 8 to 11am and 1:30 to 8pm. A meal costs around $7. During low season, the restaurant is open from 8am to 3pm. Stop by for a drink at sunset; the bar's open until 9pm all year. The hotel is at the end of Las Brisas Peninsula, closest to downtown, and is on the local Las Brisas bus route.

Av. Lázaro Cárdenas 201, Las Brisas (Apdo. Postal 135), 28200 Manzanillo, Col. ℭ/fax **314/333-1899**. www.hotel-la-posada.info or www.mexonline.com/laposada.htm. 23 units. High season $78 double; low season $58 double. Rates include full breakfast. MC, V. **Amenities:** Restaurant; bar; Internet cafe; laundry service; money exchange; safe-deposit boxes.

SANTIAGO

Five kilometers (3 miles) north of Las Brisas is the wide Santiago Peninsula. The settlement of Salahua is on the highway where you enter the peninsula to reach the hotels Las Hadas, Plaza Las Glorias, and Sierra Manzanillo, as well as the Mantarraya Golf Course. Buses from town marked LAS HADAS pass by these hotels every 20 minutes. Past the Salahua turnoff, at the end of the settlement of Santiago, an obscure road on the left is marked ZONA DE PLAYAS and leads to the hotels on the other side of the peninsula and Playa de Santiago.

Brisas Las Hadas Golf Resort & Marina 𝔈𝔈   For me, Las Hadas is synonymous with a visit to Manzanillo. This elegant beachside resort is built in Moorish style into the side of the rocky peninsula. The service is gracious, warm, and unobtrusive. Rooms, which, admittedly, need some updating, are spread over landscaped grounds and overlook the bay; cobbled lanes lined with colorful flowers and palms connect them. The resort is large but maintains an air of seclusion. (Motorized carts are on call for transportation within the property.)

Views, room size, and amenities differentiate the six types of accommodations, which can vary greatly. If you're not satisfied with your room, ask to be moved—

> **Film Fact**
> The movie *10* featured Manzanillo's signature property, Las Hadas— along with Bo Derek.

a few of the rooms are significantly less attractive than others. Understated and spacious, the better units have white-marble floors, sitting areas, and large, comfortably furnished balconies. Nine suites have private pools. The lobby is a popular place for curling up in one of the overstuffed seating areas or, at night, for enjoying a drink and live music. Pete and Roy Dye designed La Mantarraya, the hotel's 18-hole, par-71 golf course.

Av. de los Riscos s/n, Santiago Peninsula, 28200 Manzanillo, Col. ℭ **888/559-4329** in the U.S. and Canada, or 314/331-0101. www.brisas.com.mx. 233 units. High season $250–$300 double, $462–$557 Fantasy Suite; low season $190–$232 double, $395–$495 Fantasy Suite. AE, DC, MC, V. Free guarded parking. **Amenities:** 3 restaurants, including the elegant Legazpi (see "Where to Dine," below); 3 lounges and bars; 2 pools; small workout room; scuba diving, snorkeling, water-skiing, sailing, and trimaran cruises; concierge; tour desk; travel agency; car rental; shopping arcade; 24-hr. room service; in-room massage; babysitting; laundry service; dry cleaning; marina for 70 vessels; shade tents on the beach. *In room:* A/C, TV, dataport, minibar, hair dryer, safe-deposit box, bathrobes.

Hotel Sierra Manzanillo 𝔈 *Kids*   This hotel, with all-inclusive package options, has 21 floors overlooking La Audiencia beach, and a full program of activities, dining, and entertainment. Its excellent kids' program makes it a top choice for families. Architecturally, it mimics the white Moorish style of Las Hadas that has become so popular in Manzanillo. Inside, it's palatial in scale and awash in pale-gray marble. Room decor picks up the pale-gray theme with armoires that conceal the TV and minibar. Most standard rooms have two double beds or a king-size bed, plus a small table, chairs, and desk. Several rooms at the end of most floors are small, with one double bed, small porthole-size windows, no balcony, and no view. Most rooms, however, have balconies and ocean or hillside views. The 10 honeymoon suites have sculpted shell-shaped head-boards, king-size beds, and chaises. Junior suites have a sitting area with couch, and large bathrooms. Scuba-diving lessons take place in the pool, and excellent scuba-diving sites are within swimming distance of the shore.

Av. La Audiencia 1, Los Riscos, 28200 Manzanillo, Col. © 800/564-7556 in the U.S., or 314/333-2000. Fax 314/333-2611. 332 units. High season $342 double, $392–$412 suite; low season $175 double, $248–$308 suite. Rates are all-inclusive. AE, MC, V. **Amenities:** 3 restaurants; 4 bars; grand pool on the beach; children's pool; 4 lighted tennis courts; health club w/exercise equipment, aerobics, hot tub, men's and women's sauna and steam rooms; travel agency; salon w/massage; room service; laundry service; 24-hr. currency exchange. *In room:* A/C, TV, dataport, minibar, hair dryer.

Karmina Palace 🟊🟊🟊 (Kids) The quality of rooms and services at this all-inclusive resort makes the newest of Manzanillo's hotels probably one of the area's best values. It's the best choice for families in Manzanillo. The buildings resemble Maya pyramids, and even though the architecture at first might seem a little overdone, somehow it works. Rooms are all very large suites, with rich wood accents, comfortable recessed seating areas with pull-out couches, and two 27-inch TVs in each room. The extralarge bath-rooms have marble floors, twin black marble sinks, separate tubs, and glassed-in show-ers. Most rooms have terraces or balconies with views of the ocean, overlooking the tropical gardens and swimming pools. Master suites have spacious sun terraces with private splash pools, plus a full wet bar, full refrigerator, and a large living room area with 42-inch TV. Two full-size bedrooms close off from the living/dining area.

The Kid's Club offers a host of activities, while adults have numerous choices for fun—all included in the price. There's also an exceptionally well-equipped gym and European-style spa.

Av. Vista Hermosa 13 Fracc. Península de Santiago, 28200 Manzanillo, Col. © 888/234-6222 in the U.S and Canada, 314/334-1300, 314/331-1313, or 01-800/234-6222 in Mexico. Fax 314/334-1108. www.karminapalace.com. Reservations: reservations@karminapalce.com. 324 units. $364–$384 double; $850–$1,000 2-bedroom suites for quad occupancy. Rates are all-inclusive. Special packages and Web specials available. 2 children under 8 stay free in parent's room. Ask about seasonal specials. AE, MC, V. **Amenities:** 2 restaurants; snack bar; 5 bars; 8 connected swimming pools; tennis courts; health club w/treadmills and Cybex equipment; full spa facilities, including men's and women's sauna and steam rooms; kids' activity program; 24-hr. concierge; car rental; 24-hr. room service; beach volleyball; windsurfing; money exchange; safe-deposit box in reception area. *In room:* A/C, TV, dataport, minibar, hair dryer, iron, safe-deposit box ($2).

Plaza Tucanes 🟊 The sunset-colored walls of this pueblolike hotel ramble over a hillside on the Santiago Peninsula. The restaurant on top and most rooms afford a broad vista of other red-tiled rooftops and either the palm-filled golf course or the bay. It's one of Manzanillo's undiscovered resorts, known more to wealthy Mexicans than to Americans. Originally conceived as private condominiums, the accommodations were designed for living; each spacious unit is stylishly furnished, and very comfort-able. Each has a huge living room; a small kitchen/bar; one, two, or three large bed-rooms with tile or brick floors; large Mexican-tiled bathrooms; huge closets; and large furnished private patios with views. Some units contain whirlpool tubs, and a few rooms can be partitioned off and rented by the bedroom only. Rooms can be a long walk from the main entrance, through a succession of stairways and paths. If stair climbing bothers you, try to get a room by the restaurant and pool—you'll have a great view, and a hillside rail elevator goes straight from top to bottom.

Av. de Tesoro s/n, Santiago Peninsula. 28200 Manzanillo, Col. © 314/334-1098. Fax 314/334-0090. www.plazatucanes.com. 103 units. $75–$95 double. Packages available. AE, MC, V. **Amenities:** 2 restaurants, including

Argentine steakhouse; pool; kids' club; mini golf, "recreational park," game area; room service; babysitting (w/advance notice); beach club on Las Brisas beach, w/pool and small restaurant; transportation to and from beach club (once daily in each direction). *In room:* A/C, TV, safe-deposit box.

WHERE TO DINE
DOWNTOWN

Roca del Mar MEXICAN/INTERNATIONAL   Join the locals at this informal cafe facing the plaza. The large menu includes club sandwiches, hamburgers, *carne asada a la tampiqueña* (thin grilled steak served with rice, poblano pepper, an enchilada, and refried beans), fajitas, fish, shrimp, and vegetable salads. A specialty is its *paella* (served on Sun and Tues), and the economical *pibil* tacos are outstanding. This cafe is very clean and offers sidewalk dining.

21 de Marzo 204 (across from the plaza). © **314/332-0302.** Main courses $3–$12. No credit cards. Daily 7:30am–noon.

LAS BRISAS

The Hotel La Posada (see "Where to Stay," above) offers breakfast to nonguests at its beachside restaurant; it's also a great place to mingle with other tourists and enjoy the sunset and cocktails.

La Toscana ★★★ *Finds* SEAFOOD/INTERNATIONAL   You're in for a treat at La Toscana (by the same owner of the now-closed Willy's), one of Manzanillo's most popular restaurants, located on the beach in Las Brisas. It's homey, casual, and small, so reservations are highly recommended. The exquisite cuisine belies the atmosphere, with starters that include escargot and salmon carpaccio. Among the grilled specialties are shrimp imperial wrapped in bacon, red snapper tarragon, dorado basil, sea bass with mango and ginger, and tender fresh lobsters (four to a serving). Live music frequently sets the scene.

Bulevar Miguel de la Madris 3177, 100m (300 ft.) from Hotel Fiesta Mexicana. © **314/333-2515.** Reservations required. Main courses $8–$17. MC, V. Daily 6pm–2am.

SANTIAGO ROAD

The restaurants below are on the Costera Madrid between downtown and the Santiago Peninsula, including the Salahua area.

Benedetti's Pizza PIZZA   There are several branches in town, so you'll probably find a Benedetti's not far from where you are staying. The variety is extensive; add some *chimichurri* sauce to your sesame-crust pizza to enhance the flavor. Benedetti's specializes in seafood pizzas, such as smoked oyster and anchovy. You can also select from pastas, sandwiches, burgers, fajitas, salads, Mexican soups, cheesecake, and apple pie.

Bulevar Miguel de la Madrid, near the Las Brisas Glorietta on the ocean side (west). © **314/333-1592** or 314/334-0141. Pizza $9–$12; main courses $2–$5.55. AE, MC, V. Daily 1–11:30pm.

Bigotes II *Finds* SEAFOOD   Locals flock to this large, breezy restaurant (the name translates as "Mustaches") by the water for the good food and festive atmosphere. Strolling singers serenade diners, who dig into large portions of grilled seafood.

Puesta del Sol 3. © **314/333-1236.** Main courses $9.50–$23. MC, V. Daily noon–10pm. From downtown, follow the Costera Madrid past the Las Brisas turnoff; the restaurant is behind the Penas Coloradas Social Club, across from the beach.

SANTIAGO PENINSULA

Legazpi ★★ INTERNATIONAL   This is a top choice in Manzanillo for sheer elegance, gracious service, and outstanding food. The candlelit tables are set with silver and flowers. Enormous bell-shaped windows on two sides show off the sparkling bay below. The sophisticated menu includes prosciutto with melon marinated in port wine, crayfish bisque, broiled salmon, roast duck, lobster, veal, and flaming desserts from crepes to Irish coffee.

In the Brisas Las Hadas hotel, Santiago Peninsula. ℂ **314/331-0101.** Main courses $8.50–$16. AE, MC, V. High season daily 7–11:30pm. Closed low season.

MANZANILLO AFTER DARK

Nightlife in Manzanillo is much more exuberant than you might expect, but then Manzanillo is not only a resort town—it's a thriving commercial center. Clubs and bars tend to change from year to year, so check with your concierge for current hot spots. Some area clubs have a dress code prohibiting shorts or sandals, principally applying to men.

El Bar de Félix, between Salahua and Las Brisas by the Avis rental-car office (ℂ **314/333-1875),** is open Tuesday through Sunday from 2pm to midnight, and has an $8 minimum consumption charge. Music ranges from salsa and ranchero to rock and house—it's the most consistently lively place in town. **Vog Disco** (ℂ **314/333-1875),** Bulevar Costera Miguel de la Madrid Km 9.2, features alternative music in a cavernous setting; it's Manzanillo's current late-night hot spot, open until 5am, but only on Friday and Saturday. The cover charge for women is $10, for men $15. Also very popular—with a built-in crowd—is the nightclub at the **Club Maeva Hotel & Resort** (ℂ **01-800/523-8450),** on the inland side of the main highway, north of the Santiago Peninsula. It's open Tuesday, Thursday, and Saturday from 11pm to 2am. Couples are given preferential entrance. Nonguests are welcome but must pay an entrance fee, after which all drinks are included. Note that when Club Maeva is fully booked, entrance to nonguests may be difficult, or impossible—ask your hotel front desk if they can secure a pass for you. The fee varies depending on the night of the week and the time of year.

A SIDE TRIP TO COLIMA & ITS VOLCANO

The city of Colima makes an interesting and accessible day trip from Manzanillo. It's about an hour's drive along the well-maintained, four-lane Highway 54 to this charming colonial city, the capital of Colima state. Well-preserved colonial buildings, such as the city's 1527 **cathedral** and the **Palacio de Gobierno,** with its murals depicting Mexican history, are key attractions in the city's center.

Colima has several interesting museums, including the **Museo de las Culturas del Occidente,** which displays an impressive permanent collection of pre-Columbian pottery and artifacts. It's open Tuesday through Sunday from 10am to 5pm; admission is free. The **Casa de la Cultura** hosts changing exhibitions of contemporary art and offers free art, music, and dance classes. It's open Tuesday through Sunday from 10:30am to 5:30pm; admission is free.

Two imposing volcanoes (one still active) border the town. The **Volcán de Fuego** is 24km (15 miles) north, next to the taller, extinct **Nevado de Colima.** In 1999, the Volcán de Fuego became active, sometimes blowing smoke and ash up to 5km (3 miles) high, but it has since settled down.

Acapulco & the Southern Pacific Coast

by Lynne Bairstow

The exotic tropical beaches and rich jungle scenery of this part of Mexico first captured the imagination of travelers to this country. Although the geography of southern Pacific Mexico may be uniform, the resorts along this coast couldn't be more varied. They range from high-energy seaside cities to pristine, primitive coves.

Spanish conquistadors came to this coast for its numerous sheltered coves and protected bays, from which they set sail to the Far East. Centuries later, Mexico's first tourists found the same elements appealing, but for different reasons—they were seeking escape, and stretches of blue coves nicely complemented the tropical landscape of the adjacent mountains.

Over the years, the area developed a diverse selection of resorts. Each is distinct, and together they offer an ideal attraction for almost any type of traveler. The region encompasses the country's oldest resort, **Acapulco;** its newest, the **Bahías de Huatulco;** and a side-by-side pair of opposites, modern **Ixtapa** and the simple fishing village of **Zihuatanejo.** Between Acapulco and Huatulco lies **Puerto Escondido,** a laid-back beach town on a picturesque bay with stellar waves.

This chapter covers coastal towns in two Mexican states, Guerrero and Oaxaca. Stunning coastline and tropical mountains grace the whole region. Outside the urban centers, few roads are paved, and these two states remain among Mexico's poorest despite decades of tourist dollars (and many other currencies).

EXPLORING THE SOUTHERN PACIFIC COAST

Time at the beach used to be the top priority for most travelers to this part of Mexico. Today, ecotourism, adventure tourism, and more culturally oriented travel are gaining ground. Each of the beach towns in this chapter is capable of satisfying your sand and surf needs. You could also combine several coastal resorts into a single trip, or mix the coastal with the colonial—say, Puerto Escondido and Oaxaca (see chapter 11), or Acapulco and Taxco (see chapter 5).

The resorts have distinct personalities, but you get the beach wherever you go, whether you choose a city that offers virtually every luxury imaginable or a rustic town providing little more than seaside relaxation.

The largest and most decadent of Mexican resorts, **Acapulco** leapt into the international spotlight in the late 1930s when movie stars made it their playground. Today, though increasingly challenged by other seaside destinations, Acapulco still lures visitors with its glitzy nightlife and sultry beaches (even if the Hollywood celebrities who made it a household name have long since moved on). Of all the resorts, Acapulco has the best airline connections, the broadest range of late-night entertainment, the most savory dining, and the widest range of accommodations. The beaches are generally wide and clean, and although the ocean itself remains suspect, it's cleaner than in past years.

The resort of **Ixtapa** and its neighboring seaside village, **Zihuatanejo,** offer beach-bound tourist attractions on a smaller, less hectic scale than Acapulco. They attract travelers with their complementary contrasts—sophisticated high-rise hotels in one, local color and leisurely pace in the other. Their excellent beaches front clean ocean waters. To get there, many people fly into Acapulco, then make the 4- to 5-hour trip north by rental car or bus.

Puerto Escondido, noted for its celebrated surf break, laid-back village ambience, attractive and inexpensive inns, and nearby nature excursions, is a worthy destination and an exceptional value. It's 6 hours south of Acapulco on coastal Highway 200. Most people fly from Mexico City or drive up from Huatulco.

The **Bahías de Huatulco** encompass a total of nine bays—each lovelier than the last—on a pristine portion of Oaxaca's coast. Development of the area has been grad-ual and well planned, with great ecological sensitivity. The town of **Huatulco,** 128km (80 miles) south of Puerto Escondido, is emerging as Mexico's most authentic adven-ture tourism haven. In addition to an 18-hole golf course and a handful of resort hotels, it offers a growing array of soft adventures that range from bay tours to diving, river rafting, and rappelling. Dining and nightlife remain limited, but the setting is beautiful and relaxing.

1 Acapulco ★★

366km (229 miles) S of Mexico City; 272km (170 miles) SW of Taxco; 979km (612 miles) SE of Guadalajara; 253km (158 miles) SE of Ixtapa/Zihuatanejo; 752km (470 miles) NW of Huatulco

I like to think of Acapulco as a diva—maybe a little past her prime, perhaps overly made up, but still capable of captivating an audience. It's tempting to dismiss Aca-pulco as a passé resort, but the town's temptations are hard to resist. Where else do bronzed men dive from cliffs into the sea at sunset, and where else does the sun shine 360 days a year? Though most beach resorts are made for relaxing, Acapulco has non-stop, 24-hours-a-day energy. Its perfectly sculpted bay is an adult playground filled with water-skiers in *tanga* swimsuits and darkly tanned, mirror-shaded studs on jet skis. Visitors play golf and tennis with intensity, but the real sport is the nightlife, which has made this city famous for decades. Back in the days when there was a jet set, they came to Acapulco—filmed it, sang about it, wrote about it, and lived it.

It's not hard to understand why: The view of Acapulco Bay, framed by mountains and beaches, is breathtaking day or night. And I dare anyone to take in the lights of the city and not feel the pull to go out and get lively.

Though a few years ago tourism to Acapulco was in a state of decline, it's now attempting a renaissance, in a style reminiscent of Miami's South Beach. Classic hotels are slowly being renovated and areas gentrified. Clean-up efforts have put a whole new face on a place that was once aging less than gracefully.

International travelers began to reject Acapulco when it became clear that the cost of development was the pollution of the bay and surrounding areas. The city govern-ment responded, and invested over $1 billion in public and private infrastructure improvements. In addition, a program instituted in the early 1990s has cleaned up the water—whales have even been sighted offshore.

Acapulco tries hard to hold on to its image as the ultimate extravagant party town. It's still the top choice for those who want to have dinner at midnight, dance until dawn, and sleep all day on a sun-soaked beach.

ESSENTIALS
GETTING THERE & DEPARTING

BY PLANE See chapter 2 for information on flying from the United States or Canada to Acapulco. Local numbers for major airlines with nonstop or direct service to Acapulco are **Aeromexico** (© **744/485-1625**), **American** (© **744/466-9232,** or 01-800/904-6000 inside Mexico for reservations), **Continental** (© **744/466-9063**), **Mexicana** (© **744/466-9121** or 744/486-7586), and **America West** (© **744/466-9257**).

Aeromexico flies from Guadalajara, Mexico City, and Tijuana; **Mexicana** flies from Mexico City. Check with a travel agent about **charter** flights.

The airport (airport code: ACA) is 22km (14 miles) southeast of town, over the hills east of the bay. Private **taxis** are the fastest way to get downtown; they cost $30 to $50. The major **rental-car** agencies all have booths at the airport. **Transportes Terrestres** has desks at the front of the airport where you can buy tickets for minivan *colectivo* transportation into town ($10). You must reserve return service to the airport through your hotel.

BY CAR From Mexico City, take either the curvy toll-free Highway 95D south (6 hr.) or scenic Highway 95, the four- to six-lane toll highway (3½ hr.), which costs around $50 one-way. The free road from Taxco is in good condition; you'll save around $40 in tolls from there through Chilpancingo to Acapulco. From points north or south along the coast, the only choice is Highway 200, where you should (as on all Mexican highways) always try to travel by day.

BY BUS The **Ejido/Central Camionera station,** Ejido 47, is on the far northern end of the bay and north of downtown (Old Acapulco). It's far from the hotels; however, it serves more bus lines and routes than any other Acapulco bus station. It also has a hotel-reservation service.

From this station, **Turistar, Estrella de Oro,** and **Estrella Blanca** have almost hourly service for the 5- to 7-hour trip to Mexico City ($42), and daily service to Zihuatanejo ($14). Buses also serve other points in Mexico, including Chilpancingo, Cuernavaca, Iguala, Manzanillo, Puerto Vallarta, and Taxco.

ORIENTATION

VISITOR INFORMATION The **State of Guerrero Tourism Office** operates the **Procuraduría del Turista** (©/fax **744/484-4583** or 744/484-4416), on street level in

---

Tips Car & Bus Travel Warning Eases

Car robberies and bus hijackings on Highway 200 south of Acapulco on the way to Puerto Escondido and Huatulco used to be common, and you may have heard warnings about the road. The trouble has all but disappeared, thanks to military patrols and greater police protection. However, as in most of Mexico, it's advisable to travel the highways during daylight hours only—not so much for personal safety, but because highways are unlit, and animals can wander on them.

Acapulco Bay Area

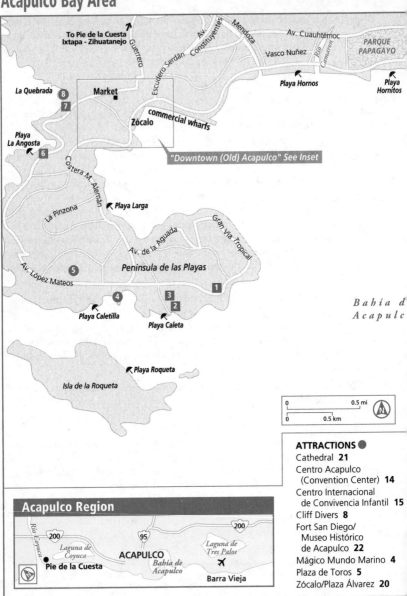

To Pie de la Cuesta
Ixtapa - Zihuatanejo

Guerrero

Av. Constituyentes

Mendoza

Av. Cuauhtémoc

Escudero Serdán

Vasco Nuñez

Río Camarón

PARQUE PAPAGAYO

La Quebrada **8 7**

Market

Playa Hornos

Playa Hornitos

Zócalo

commercial wharfs

Playa
La Angosta **6**

"Downtown (Old) Acapulco" See Inset

Costera M. Alemán

Playa Larga

La Pinzona

Gran Via Tropical

Av. de la Aguada

Peninsula de las Playas

Av. López Mateos **5**

1

*Bahía d
Acapulc*

4

3
2

Playa Caletilla

Playa Caleta

Playa Roqueta

Isla de la Roqueta

0 ____ 0.5 mi
0 ____ 0.5 km

ATTRACTIONS ●

Cathedral **21**
Centro Acapulco
(Convention Center) **14**
Centro Internacional
de Convivencia Infantil **15**
Cliff Divers **8**
Fort San Diego/
Museo Histórico
de Acapulco **22**
Mágico Mundo Marino **4**
Plaza de Toros **5**
Zócalo/Plaza Álvarez **20**

Acapulco Region

Río Coyuca

200

95

200

Laguna de
Coyuca

ACAPULCO

Laguna de
Tres Palos

Pie de la Cuesta

*Bahía de
Acapulco*

✈

Barra Vieja

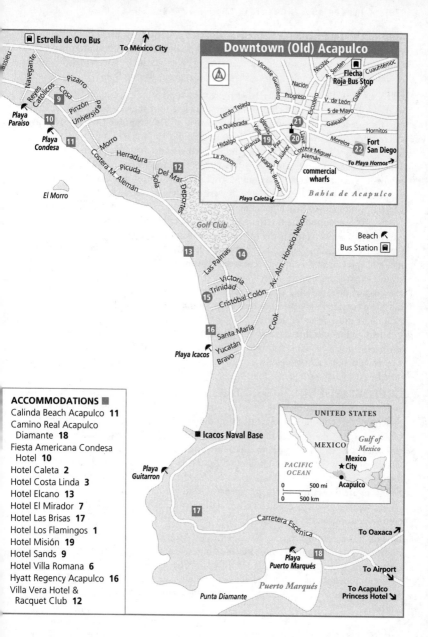

Estrella de Oro Bus

To México City

Navegante
Reyes Católicos
Pizarro
Casa
Pinzón
Universidad

Playa Paraíso

9

10

Playa Condesa

11

Morro

Herradura

Picuda

Costera M. Alemán

Del Mar

Sola

Deportes

El Morro

12

Golf Club

13

Las Palmas

14

Victoria

Trinidad

15

Cristóbal Colón

Av. Alm. Horacio Nelson

Cook

16

Santa María

Yucatán

Bravo

Playa Icacos

Downtown (Old) Acapulco

Vicente Guerrero
Nicolás
A. Serdán
Nación
Cuauhtémoc

Flecha Roja Bus Stop

Progreso
Escudero
V. de León
5 de Mayo
Galeana

Lerdo Tejada
La Quebrada
Iglesias
Valle
La Paz
B. Juárez
Carranza
Antigua
Bretón

Hidalgo
La Pinzón

Hornitos

Morelos

Costera Miguel Alemán

21

19

20

22

Fort San Diego

To Playa Hornos

commercial wharfs

Bahía de Acapulco

Playa Caleta

Beach
Bus Station

Icacos Naval Base

Playa Guitarrón

UNITED STATES

MEXICO

Gulf of Mexico

PACIFIC OCEAN

Mexico ★ City

Acapulco

0   500 mi
0   500 km

17

Carretera Escénica

To Oaxaca

Playa Puerto Marqués

18

Puerto Marqués

Punta Diamante

To Airport

To Acapulco Princess Hotel

front of the **International Center,** a convention center set back from the main Costera Alemán, down a lengthy walkway with fountains. The office offers maps and information about the city and state, as well as police assistance for tourists; it's open Monday to Saturday from 8am to 11pm, Sunday from 8am to 8pm.

CITY LAYOUT Acapulco stretches more than 6km (4 miles) around the huge bay, so trying to take it all in by foot is impractical. The tourist areas are roughly divided into three sections: On the western end of the bay is **Old Acapulco (Acapulco Viejo),** the original town that attracted the jet-setters of the 1950s and 1960s—and today it looks as if it's still locked in that era, though a renaissance is slowly getting under way. The second section, in the center of the bay, is the **Hotel Zone (Zona Hotelera);** it follows the main boulevard, **Costera Miguel Alemán** (or just "the Costera"), as it runs east along the bay from downtown. Towering hotels, restaurants, shopping centers, and strips of open-air beach bars line the street. At the far eastern end of the Costera lie the golf course and the International Center (a convention center).

Avenida Cuauhtémoc is the major artery inland, running roughly parallel to the Costera. The third major area begins just beyond the Hyatt Regency Hotel, where the name of the Costera changes to **Carretera Escénica (Scenic Hwy.),** which continues all the way to the airport. The hotels along this section of the road are lavish, and extravagant private villas, gourmet restaurants, and flashy nightclubs built into the hillside offer dazzling views. The area fronting the beach here is **Acapulco Diamante,** Acapulco's most desirable address.

Street names and numbers in Acapulco can be confusing and hard to find—many streets are not well marked or change names unexpectedly. Street numbers on the Costera do not follow logic, so don't assume that similar numbers will be close together.

GETTING AROUND **By Taxi** Taxis are more plentiful than tacos in Acapulco—and practically as inexpensive, if you're traveling in the downtown area only. Just remember that you should always establish the price with the driver before starting out. Hotel taxis may charge three times the rate of a taxi hailed on the street, and nighttime taxi rides cost extra, too. Taxis are also more expensive if you're staying in the Diamante section or south. The minimum fare is $2 per ride for a roving VW Bug–style taxi in town; the fare from Puerto Marqués to the hotel zone is $8, or $10 into downtown. *Sitio* taxis are nicer cars, but more expensive, with a minimum fare of $4.

The fashion among Acapulco taxis is flashy, with Las Vegas–style lights—the more colorful and pulsating, the better.

By Bus Even though the city has a confusing street layout, using city buses is amazingly easy and inexpensive. Two kinds of buses run along the Costera: pastel color-coded buses and regular "school buses." The difference is the price: New air-conditioned tourist buses (Aca Tur Bus) are 50¢; old buses, 35¢. Covered bus stops are all along the Costera, with handy maps on the walls showing routes to major sights and hotels.

The best place near the *zócalo* to catch a bus is next to Sanborn's, 2 blocks east. CALETA DIRECTO or BASE-CALETA buses will take you to the Hornos, Caleta, and Caletilla beaches along the Costera. Some buses return along the same route; others go around the peninsula and return to the Costera.

For expeditions to more distant destinations, there are buses to **Puerto Marqués** to the east (marked PUERTO MARQUES–BASE) and **Pie de la Cuesta** to the west (marked

ZOCALO–PIE DE LA CUESTA). Be sure to verify the time and place of the last bus back if you hop on one of these.

By Car   Rental cars are available at the airport and at hotel desks along the Costera. Unless you plan on exploring outlying areas, trust me, you're better off taking taxis or using the easy and inexpensive public buses.

FAST FACTS: Acapulco

American Express   The main office is in the Gran Plaza shopping center, Costera Alemán 1628 (© **744/435-2200**). It's open Monday through Friday from 9am to 6pm and Saturday 9am to 1pm.

Area Code   The telephone area code is **744**.

Climate   Acapulco boasts sunshine 360 days a year, with average daytime temperatures of 80°F (27°C). Humidity varies, with approximately 59 inches of rain per year. June through October is the rainy season, though July and August are relatively dry. Tropical showers are brief and usually occur at night.

Consular Agents   The **United States** has an agent at the Hotel Club del Sol, Costera Alemán at Reyes Católicos (© **744/481-1699** or 744/469-0556), across from the Hotel Acapulco Plaza; the office is open Monday through Friday from 10am to 2pm. The **Canadian** office is at the Centro Comercial Marbella, Local 23 (© **744/484-1305**). The toll-free emergency number inside Mexico is © **01-800/706-2900**. The office is open Monday through Friday from 9am to 5pm. The **United Kingdom** office is at the Las Brisas Hotel on Carretera Escénica near the airport (© **744/481-2533** or 744/484-1735). Most other countries in the European Union also have consulate offices in Acapulco.

Currency Exchange   Numerous banks along the Costera are open Monday through Friday from 9am to 6pm, Saturday from 10am to 1:30pm. Banks and their ATMs generally have the best rates. *Casas de cambio* (currency-exchange booths) along the street may have better rates than hotels.

Hospital   Try **Hospital Magallanes,** Av. Wilfrido Massieu 2, Fracc. Magallanes (© **744/485-6194** or 744/485-6197), which has an English-speaking staff and doctors, or **Hospital Pacífico,** Calle Fraile y Nao 4, Fracc. La Bocana (© **744/487-7180** or 744/487-7161). For local emergencies, call the **Red Cross,** Av. Ruiz Cortines s/n (© **065** or 744/445-5912).

Internet Access   **@canet,** Costera Alemán 1632 Int., La Gran Plaza, Local D-1, lower floor ((©/fax **744/486-9186** or 744/486-8182), is open daily from 10:30am to 9pm. Internet access costs $1.50 per hour. This is a computer shop that also offers Internet access and has a very helpful staff. Also along the Costera strip is the **Santa Clara Cafe,** Costera Alemán 136, serving coffee, pastries, ice cream, along with Internet service for 90¢ for 20 minutes. It's open 9 am to 11 pm.

Parking   It is illegal to park on the Costera at any time. Try parking along side streets, or in one of the few covered parking lots, such as in Plaza Bahía and in Plaza Mirabella.

Pharmacy One of the largest drugstores in town is **Farmacia Daisy,** Francia 49, across the traffic circle from the convention center (℃ 744/484-7664). Sam's Club and Wal-Mart, both on the Costera, have pharmacy services and lower prices on medicine.

Post Office The *correo* is next door to Sears, close to the Fideicomiso office. It's open Monday through Friday from 9am to 5pm, Saturday from 9am to 1pm. Other branches are in the Estrella de Oro bus station on Cuauhtémoc, inland from the Acapulco Qualton Hotel, and on the Costera near Caleta Beach.

Safety Riptides claim a few lives every year, so pay close attention to warning flags posted on Acapulco beaches. Red or black flags mean stay out of the water, yellow flags signify caution, and white or green flags mean it's safe to swim.

As is the case anywhere, tourists are vulnerable to thieves. This is especially true when shopping in a market, lying on the beach, wearing jewelry, or visibly carrying a camera, purse, or bulging wallet.

Telephone Acapulco phone numbers seem to change frequently. The most reliable source for telephone numbers is the **Procuraduría del Turista,** on the Costera in front of the convention center (℃ 744/484-4583), which has an exceptionally friendly staff.

Tourist Police Policemen in white and light blue uniforms belong to the Tourist Police (℃ 065 for emergencies, or 744/485-0490), a special corps of English-speaking police established to assist tourists.

ACTIVITIES ON & OFF THE BEACH

Acapulco is known for its great beaches and watersports, and few visitors bother to explore its traditional downtown area. But the shaded *zócalo* (also called Plaza Alvarez) is worth a trip, to experience a glimpse of local life and color. Inexpensive cafes and shops border the plaza. At its far north end is the **cathedral Nuestra Señora de la Soledad,** with blue, onion-shaped domes and Byzantine towers. Though reminiscent of a Russian Orthodox church, it was originally (and perhaps appropriately) built as a movie set, then later adapted into a house of worship. From the church, turn east along the side street going off at a right angle (Calle Carranza, which doesn't have a marker) to find an arcade with newsstands and more shops. The hill behind the cathedral provides an unparalleled view of Acapulco. Take a taxi to the top of the hill from the main plaza, and follow signs to **El Mirador (lookout point).**

Local travel agencies book city tours, day trips to Taxco, cruises, and other excursions and activities. Taxco is about a 3-hour drive inland from Acapulco (see chapter 5 for more information).

THE BEACHES   Here's a rundown on the beaches, going from west to east around the bay. **Playa la Angosta** is a small, sheltered, often-deserted cove just around the bend from **La Quebrada** (where the cliff divers perform).

South of downtown on the Península de las Playas lie the beaches **Caleta** and **Caletilla.** Separating them is a small outcropping of land that contains the aquarium and water park **Mágico Mundo Marino** (daily 9am–7pm). You'll find thatched-roofed restaurants, watersports equipment for rent, and brightly painted boats that

---

Tips **To Swim or Not to Swim in the Bay?**

In the past decade, the city has gone to great lengths (and great expense) to clean up the waters off Acapulco. Nevertheless, this is an industrial port that was once heavily polluted, so many choose to stick to the hotel pool. You may notice the fleet of power-sweeper boats that skim the top of the bay each morning to remove debris and oil.

Among the bay beaches that remain popular with visitors and locals are **Caleta** and **Caletilla beaches,** as well as **Playa Puerto Marqués.**

---

ferry passengers to **Roqueta Island.** You can rent beach chairs and umbrellas for the day. Mexican families favor these beaches because they're close to several inexpensive hotels. In the late afternoon, fishermen pull their colorful boats up on the sand; you can buy the fresh catch of the day and, occasionally, oysters on the half shell.

Pleasure boats dock at **Playa Manzanillo,** south of the *zócalo.* Charter fishing trips sail from here. In the old days, the downtown beaches—Manzanillo, Honda, Caleta, and Caletilla—were the focal point of Acapulco. Today, beaches and resort developments stretch along the 6.4km (4-mile) length of the shore.

East of the *zócalo,* the major beaches are **Hornos** (near Papagayo Park), **Hornitos, Paraíso, Condesa,** and **Icacos,** followed by the naval base (La Base) and **Punta del Guitarrón.** After Punta del Guitarrón, the road climbs to the legendary Las Brisas hotel. Past Las Brisas, the road continues to the small, clean bay of **Puerto Marqués,** followed by **Punta Diamante,** about 19km (12 miles) from the *zócalo.* The fabulous Acapulco Princess, the Quinta Real, and the Pierre Marqués hotels dominate the landscape, which fronts the open Pacific.

Playa Puerto Marqués, in the bay of Puerto Marqués, is an attractive area for swimming. The water is calm and the bay sheltered. Water-skiing can also be arranged. Past the bay lies **Revolcadero Beach,** a magnificent wide stretch of beach on the open ocean, where many of Acapulco's grandest resorts are found.

Other beaches are farther north and best reached by car, though buses also make the trip. **Pie de la Cuesta** is 13km (8 miles) west of town. Buses along the Costera leave every 5 or 10 minutes; a taxi costs about $22. The water is too rough for swimming, but it's a great spot for checking out big waves and the spectacular sunset, especially over *coco locos* (drinks served in fresh coconuts with the tops whacked off) at a rustic beachside restaurant. The area is known for excellent birding and surrounding coconut plantations.

If you're driving, continue west along the peninsula, passing **Coyuca Lagoon** on your right, until almost to the small air base at the tip. Along the way, various private entrepreneurs, mostly young boys, will invite you to park near different sections of beach. You'll also find *colectivo* boat tours of the lagoon offered for about $10.

BAY CRUISES & ROQUETA ISLAND   Acapulco has virtually every kind of boat to choose from—yachts, catamarans, and trimarans (single- and double-deckers). Cruises run morning, afternoon, and evening. Some offer buffets, open bars, and live music; others just snacks, drinks, and taped music. Prices range from $24 to $60. Cruise operators come and go, and their phone numbers change so frequently from year to year that it's pointless to list them here; to find out what cruises are currently operating, contact any Acapulco travel agency or your hotel's tour desk, and ask for brochures or recommendations.

Boats from Caletilla Beach to **Roqueta Island**—a good place to snorkel, sunbathe, hike to a lighthouse, visit a small zoo, or have lunch—leave every 15 minutes from 7am until the last one returns at 7pm. There are also primitive-style glass-bottom boats that circle the bay as you look down at a few fish and watch a diver swim down to the underwater sanctuary of the Virgin of Guadalupe, patron saint of Mexico. The statue of the Virgin—created by sculptor Armando Quesado—was placed there in 1958, in memory of a group of divers who lost their lives at the spot. You can purchase tickets ($5) directly from any boat that's loading.

WATERSPORTS & BOAT RENTALS An hour of **water-skiing** can cost as little as $35 or as much as $65. Caletilla Beach, Puerto Marqués Bay, and Coyuca Lagoon have facilities. The **Club de Esquís,** Costera Alemán 100 (℃ **744/482-2034**), charges $50 per hour.

Scuba diving costs $40 for 1½ hours of instruction if you book directly with the instructor on Caleta Beach. It costs $45 to $55 if you book through a hotel or travel agency. Dive trips start at around $40 per person for one dive. One reputable shop, near Club de Esquís, is **Divers de México** (℃ **744/482-1398**). Another recommended company, both PADI and NAUI-certified, is the **Acapulco Scuba Center,** Tlacopanocha 13–14, Paseo del Pescador, downtown Acapulco (℃ **744/480-1962**). They offer a variety of dives from half-day (9am–2pm) shallow dives for beginners to instructor training. Prices for two-tank dives are $70, and include transportation from your hotel, onboard lunch, boat, and gear. **Boat rentals** are cheapest on Caletilla Beach, where an information booth rents inner tubes, small boats, canoes, paddleboats, and chairs. It also arranges water-skiing and scuba diving (see "Bay Cruises & Roqueta Island," above).

For **deep-sea fishing** excursions, go to the boat cooperative's pink building opposite the *zócalo,* or book a day in advance (℃ **744/482-1099**). Charter trips run $200 to $300 for 6 hours, tackle and bait included, with an extra charge for ice, drinks, and lunch. Credit cards are accepted, but you're likely to get a better deal by paying cash. Boats leave at 7am and return at 2pm. If you book through a travel agent or hotel, prices start at around $200 for four people. Also recommendable is Fish-R-Us, Costera Alemán 100 (℃ **877/347-4787** toll-free in the U.S., or 744/482-8282). In addition to traditional fishing charters, they also offer private yacht charters, scuba diving, and a 3-hour Night of Delight cruise, complete with dinner served on board. Prices vary with the service requested, and number of people, so call for details.

Parasailing, though not free from risk (the occasional thrill-seeker has collided with a palm tree or even a building), can be brilliant. Floating high over the bay hanging from a parachute towed by a motorboat costs about $25. Most of these rides operate

---

(Tips **Tide Warning**

Each year, at least one or two unwary swimmers drown in Acapulco because of deadly riptides and undertow (see "Safety" in "Fast Facts," above). Swim only in Acapulco Bay or Puerto Marqués Bay—and be careful of the undertow no matter where you go. If you find yourself caught in the undertow, head back to shore at an angle instead of trying to swim straight back.

on Condesa Beach, but they also can be found independently operating on the beach in front of most hotels along the Costera.

Skydiving over Acapulco Bay is now possible. Following a 20-minute orientation, take a thrilling leap, attached to a tandem instructor from an altitude of 3,000m (10,000 ft.). The cost is $220 for the 45-second freefall and 5-minute dive, and a video of the experience is an extra $90. For experienced divers, the price drops to $27, with packages available. Contact **Skydive Acapulco,** Costera Alemán 130, Local 4, Hotel Romano Palace (ⓒ/fax **744/484-6672;** www.skydiveacapulco.com). They're open from 8am to sunset.

GOLF, TENNIS, RIDING & BULLFIGHTS   Both the **Acapulco Princess** (ⓒ 744/ **469-1000**) and **Pierre Marques** (ⓒ **744/466-1000**) hotels have top-notch courses. The Princess's course is a rather narrow, level, Ted Robinson design. The Marques course, redesigned by Robert Trent Jones Sr. in 1972 for the World Cup Golf Tournament, is longer and more challenging. A round of 18 holes at either course costs $125 for guests and $145 for nonguests; American Express, Visa, and MasterCard are accepted. Tee times begin at 7:35am, and reservations should be made a day in advance. Club rental is available and costs an extra $21. The **Mayan Palace Golf Club,** Geranios 22 (ⓒ **744/469-6043** or 744/469-0221), designed by Latin American golf great Pedro Guericia, lies farther east. Greens fees are $115, and caddies are available for an additional $15. At the **Club de Golf Acapulco,** off the Costera next to the convention center (ⓒ **744/484-0781**), you can play 9 holes for $40 and 18 holes for $60, with equipment renting for $16.

The newest addition to Acapulco's golf scene is the spectacular Robert von Hagge–designed course at the exclusive **Tres Vidas Golf Club,** Carretera a Barra Vieja Km 7 (ⓒ **744/444-5138** or 744/444-5135). The par-72, 18-hole course, right on the edge of the ocean, is landscaped with nine lakes, dotted with palms, and home to a flock of ducks and other birds. The club is open only to members, guests of members, and guests at Tres Vidas. Greens fees are $144, including cart; a caddy costs $20. Also here is a clubhouse with a restaurant (daily 7:30am–7:30pm), as well as a pool and beach club. American Express, Visa, and MasterCard are accepted.

The **Club de Tenis Hyatt,** Costera Alemán 1 (ⓒ **744/484-1225**), is open daily from 7am to 11pm. Outdoor courts cost $8 during the day, $15 per hour at night. Rackets rent for $3.50 and a set of balls for $3.50. Many of the hotels along the Costera have tennis facilities for guests; the best are at the Acapulco Princess, Pierre Marqués, Mayan Palace, and Las Brisas hotels. Tennis is also available at both the Club de Golf Acapulco and Tres Vidas golf clubs (above).

You can go **horseback riding** along the beach. Independent operators stroll the Hotel Zone beachfront offering rides for about $20 to $40 for 1 to 2 hours. Horses are also commonly found on the beach in front of the Acapulco Princess Hotel. There is no phone; you go directly to the beach to make arrangements.

Traditionally called Fiesta Brava, **bullfights** are held during Acapulco's winter season at a ring up the hill from Caletilla Beach. Tickets purchased through travel agencies cost around $17 to $40 and usually include transportation to and from your hotel. You can also buy a general admission ticket at the stadium for $4.50. Be forewarned that this is a true bullfight—meaning things generally do not fare well for the bull. The festivities begin at 5:30pm each Sunday from December to March.

A MUSEUM & A WATER PARK   The original **Fuerte de San Diego,** Costera Alemán, east of the *zócalo* (ⓒ **744/482-3828**), was built in 1616 to protect the town

Moments Death-Defying Divers

High divers perform at La Quebrada each day at 12:30, 7:15, 8:15, 9:15, and 10:15pm. Admission is $2.50. From a spotlit ledge on the cliffs, divers (holding torches for the final performance) plunge into the roaring surf of an inlet that's just 7m (20 ft.) wide, 4m (12 ft.) deep, and 40m (130 ft.) below—after wisely praying at a small shrine nearby. To the applause of the crowd, divers climb up the rocks and accept congratulations and gifts of money from onlookers. This is the quintessential Acapulco experience. No visit is complete without watching the cliff divers—and that goes for jaded travelers as well. To get there from downtown, take the street called La Quebrada from behind the cathedral for 4 blocks.

The public areas have great views, but arrive early, because performances quickly fill up. Another option is to watch from the lobby bar and restaurant terraces of the **Hotel Plaza Las Glorias/El Mirador.** The bar imposes a $9.50 cover charge, which includes two drinks. You can get around the cover by having dinner at the hotel's **La Perla restaurant.** Reservations (© **744/483-1155,** ext. 802) are recommended during high season.

---

from pirate attacks. At that time, the port reaped considerable income from trade with the Philippine Islands (which, like Mexico, were part of the Spanish Empire). The fort you see today was rebuilt after considerable earthquake damage in 1776, and most recently underwent renovation in 2000. The structure houses the **Museo Histórico de Acapulco (Acapulco Historical Museum)** ✸✸, with exhibits that tell the story of Acapulco from its role as a port in the conquest of the Americas to a center for local Catholic conversion campaigns and for exotic trade with the Orient. Other exhibits chronicle Acapulco's pre-Hispanic past, the coming of the conquistadors (complete with Spanish armor), and Spanish imperial activity. Temporary exhibits are also on display. Admission to the museum is $3, free on Sunday. It's open Tuesday through Sunday from 9:30am to 6:30pm. The new **Foro Cultural Multimedia,** a spectacular light-and-sound show, starts at 8pm in Spanish, with special accommodations and shows available for groups in English afterward. Enter at 7pm to have enough time to tour the museum before the show; the $10 charge includes museum admission. Call in advance to make group reservations for English shows.

To reach the fort, follow Costera Alemán past Old Acapulco and the *zócalo;* the fort is on a hill on the right.

The **Centro Internacional de Convivencia Infantil (CICI)** ✸, Costera Alemán at Colón (© **744/484-8033**), is a sea-life and water park east of the convention center. It offers guests swimming pools with waves, water slides, and water toboggans, and has a cafeteria and restrooms. The park, which recently underwent a $3-million renovation, is open daily from 10am to 6pm. General admission is $10 and free for children under 2. There are **dolphin shows** (in Spanish) weekdays at 2pm, and weekends at 2 and 4pm. There's also a dolphin swim program, which includes 30 minutes of introduction and 30 minutes of swim time. The cost for this option is $95 for a half-hour swim, $120 for an hour, and they are by prior reservation only. Shows are at 10am, 12:30, and 4pm. Reservations are required; there is a 10-person maximum per show for the dolphin swim option. The minimum age is 4 years.

SHOPPING

Acapulco is not among the best places to buy Mexican crafts, but it does have a few interesting shops, and the Costera is lined with places to buy tourist souvenirs, including silver jewelry, Mexico knickknacks, and the ubiquitous T-shirt.

The shopkeepers aren't pushy, but they'll test your bargaining mettle. The starting price will be steep, and dragging it down may take some time. Before buying silver, examine it carefully and look for ".925" stamped on the back. This supposedly signifies that the silver is 92.5% pure, but the less expensive silver metal called "alpaca" may also bear this stamp. (Alpaca is generally stamped MEXICO or MEX, often in letters so tiny that they are hard to read and look similar to the three-digit ".925"). The market is open daily from 9am to 6pm.

Sanborn's, a good department store and drugstore chain, offers an array of staples, including cosmetics, music, clothing, books, and magazines. It has a number of locations in Acapulco including downtown at Costera Miguel Alemán 209, across from the boat docks (© **744/484-4413**); Costera Miguel Alemán 1226 at the Condo Estrella Tower, close to the convention center (© **744/484-2025**), and also on Costera Miguel Alemán 163, at the Hotel Calinda (© **744/481-2426** or 744/484-4465).

Acapulco also has a Sam's Club and a Wal-Mart located on the inland side of the main highway just prior to its ascent to Las Brisas.

Boutiques selling resort wear crowd the Costera Alemán. These stores carry attractive summer clothing at prices lower than you generally pay in the United States. If there's a sale, you can find incredible bargains. One of the nicest air-conditioned shopping centers on the Costera is **Plaza Bahía,** Costera Alemán 125 (© **744/485-6939** or 744/485-6992), which has four stories of shops, movie theaters, a bowling alley, and small fast-food restaurants. The center is just west of the Costa Club Hotel. The bowling alley, **Aca Bol in Plaza Bahía** (© **744/485-0970** or 744/485-7464), is open Monday through Sunday from noon to 1:30am. Another popular shopping strip is the **Plaza Condesa,** adjacent to the Fiesta Americana Condesa, with shops that include Guess, Izod, and Bronce Swimwear. **Olvida Plaza,** near the restaurant of the same name, has Tommy Hilfiger and Aca Joe.

Acapulco has a few notable fine-art galleries. My favorite, **Galería Espacio Pal Kepenyes** ★★, Costera Guitarrón 140, on the road to the Radisson (© **744/484-3738**), carries the work of Pal Kepenyes, whose stunning bronzes are among Acapulco's most notable public sculptures. The gallery shows smaller versions, as well as signature pieces of jewelry in brass, copper, and silver, by appointment only.

WHERE TO STAY

The listings below begin with the very expensive resorts south of town (nearest the airport) and continue along Costera Alemán to the less expensive, more traditional hotels north of town, in the downtown or "Old Acapulco" part of the city. Especially in the "very expensive" and "expensive" categories, inquire about promotional rates or check with the airlines for air-hotel packages. During Christmas and Easter weeks, some hotels double their normal rates.

Private **villas** are available for rent all over the hills south of town; staying in one of these palatial homes is an unforgettable experience. **Se Renta** (www.acapulcoluxury villas.com) handles some of the most exclusive villas.

SOUTH OF TOWN

Acapulco's most exclusive and renowned hotels, restaurants, and villas nestle in the steep forested hillsides here, between the naval base and Puerto Marqués. This area is several kilometers from the heart of Acapulco; you'll pay the $12 to $20 round-trip taxi fare every time you venture off the property into town.

Very Expensive

Camino Real Acapulco Diamante ★★★ *(Kids)* Tucked in a secluded location on 32 hectares (81 acres), this relaxing, self-contained resort is an ideal choice for families, or for those who already know Acapulco and don't care to explore much. I consider it one of Acapulco's finest places in terms of contemporary decor, services, and amenities. I like its location on the Playa Puerto Marqués, which is safe for swimming, but you do miss out on compelling views of Acapulco Bay. From Carretera Escénica, a handsome brick road winds down to the hotel, overlooking Puerto Marqués Bay. The lobby has an enormous terrace facing the water. The spacious rooms have balconies or terraces, small sitting areas, marble floors, ceiling fans (in addition to air-conditioning with remote control), and comfortable, classic furnishings.

Carretera Escénica Km 14, Baja Catita s/n, Pichilingue, 39867 Acapulco, Gro. ⓒ **744/435-1010.** Fax 744/435-1020. www.caminoreal.com/acapulco. 157 units. High season $429 double; $611 master suite. Rates include American breakfast. Ask about low-season and midweek discounts. AE, MC, V. **Amenities:** 2 restaurants; lobby bar; 3 pools (1 for children); tennis court; health club w/aerobics, spa treatments, massage, and complete workout equipment (extra charge); watersports equipment rentals; children's activities; concierge; tour desk; car-rental desk; shopping arcade; salon; 24-hr. room service; babysitting; laundry service. *In room:* A/C, TV, dataport, minibar, hair dryer, iron, safe-deposit box.

Las Brisas ★★★ *(Moments)* This is a local landmark, often considered Acapulco's signature hotel, and my personal favorite. Perched on a hillside overlooking the bay, Las Brisas is known for its tiered pink stucco facade, private pools, and 175 pink Jeeps rented exclusively to guests. If you stay here, you ought to like pink, because the color scheme extends to practically everything. Las Brisas is also known for inspiring romance and is best enjoyed by couples indulging in time together—alone.

The hotel is a community unto itself: The simple, marble-floored rooms are like separate villas sculpted from a terraced hillside, with panoramic views of Acapulco Bay from a balcony or terrace. Each room has a private or semiprivate swimming pool. Las Brisas has a total of 250 pools. The spacious Regency Club rooms, at the apex of the property, offer the best views. You stay at Las Brisas more for the panache and setting than for luxury amenities, though rooms have been upgraded. Early each morning, continental breakfast arrives in a cubbyhole. If you tire of your own pool, Las Brisas has a beach club about a half-mile away, on Acapulco Bay; continuous shuttle service departs from the lobby. The club offers casual dining, a large swimming pool, and a natural saltwater pool—actually a rocky inlet. Mandatory service charges cover shuttle service from the hillside rooms to the lobby and from the lobby to the beach club,

---

(Fun Fact) Acapulco, Queen of the Silver Screen

Along with hosting some of the legendary stars of the silver screen, Acapulco has also played a few starring roles. Over 250 films have been shot here, including 1985's *Rambo II,* which used the Pie de la Cuesta lagoon as its backdrop.

and all tips. The hotel is on the southern edge of the bay, overlooking the road to the airport and close to the hottest area nightclubs.

Apdo. Carretera Escénica 5255, Las Brisas, 39868 Acapulco, Gro. ℂ 800/228-3000 in the U.S., or 744/469-6900. Fax 744/446-5332. 263 units. High season $330 shared pool, $435 private pool, $540 Royal Beach Club; low season $230 shared pool, $345 private pool, $432 Royal Beach Club. $20 per day service charge plus 17% tax. Rates include continental breakfast. AE, DC, MC, V. **Amenities:** 2 restaurants; deli; breakfast delivery; private beach club w/fresh- and saltwater pools; 5 tennis courts; access to nearby gym; concierge; guest-only tours and activity program; tour desk; car-rental desk; Jeeps for rent; 24-hr. shuttle transportation around the resort; shopping arcade; salon; room service; in-room massage; babysitting; laundry service; dry cleaning. *In room:* A/C, TV, minibar, hair dryer, safe-deposit box.

COSTERA HOTEL ZONE
Expensive

Fiesta Americana Condesa Acapulco 🐾   Once the Condesa del Mar, the Fiesta Americana Condesa Acapulco is a long-standing favorite deluxe hotel located in the heart of the beach-bar action. The 18-story structure towers above Condesa Beach, just east and up the hill from the Glorieta Diana traffic circle. The unremarkable, but comfortable rooms have marble floors, and can be loud if you're overlooking the pool area. Each has a private terrace or balcony with ocean view. The more expensive rooms have the best bay views, and all have purified tap water. The hilltop swimming pool affords one of the city's finest views. The location is great for enjoying the numerous beach activities, shopping, and more casual nightlife of Acapulco.

Costera Alemán 97, 39690 Acapulco, Gro. ℂ 800/FIESTA-1 in the U.S., or 744/484-2355. Fax 744/484-1828. www.fiestamericana.com. 500 units. High season $220 double, $315 suite; low season $90–$124 double, $253 suite. Ask about "Fiesta Break" packages, which include meals. AE, DC, MC, V. **Amenities:** 2 restaurants; coffee shop; lobby bar; theme nights w/buffet dinner; adults-only hilltop swimming pool; smaller children's pool; travel agency; shopping arcade; salon; room service; laundry service; pharmacy. *In room:* A/C, TV, minibar, safe-deposit box.

Hotel Elcano 🐾🐾🐾 *Finds*   An Acapulco classic, the Elcano is another personal favorite. It offers exceptional service and a prime location—on a broad stretch of beach in the heart of the hotel zone. The retro-style, turquoise-and-white lobby, and beachside pool area are the closest you can get to a South Beach Miami atmosphere in Acapulco, and its popular open-air restaurant adds to the lively waterfront scene. On the whole, the Elcano reminds me of a set from a classic Elvis-in-Acapulco movie. Rooms are continually upgraded, bright, and very comfortable. They feature classic navy-and-white tile accents, ample oceanfront balconies, and tub/shower combinations. The very large junior suites, all on corners, have two queen-size beds and huge closets. Studios are small but adequate, with king-size beds and small sinks outside the bathroom area. In the studios, a small portion of the TV armoire serves as a closet, and there are no balconies, only large sliding windows. All rooms have purified tap water. This is an ideal place if you're attending a convention or simply want the best of all possible locations, between hillside nightlife and the Costera beach zone. It's an excellent value.

Costera Alemán 75, 39690 Acapulco, Gro. ℂ 800/972-2162 in the U.S., or 744/435-1500. Fax 744/484-2230. http:// hotel-elcano.com. 182 units. $176 studio; $208 standard double; $240 junior suite, $299 master suite. Ask about promotional discounts. AE, DC, MC, V. **Amenities:** 3 restaurants; beachside pool; small workout room; video-game room; travel agency; shopping arcade; salon; 24-hr. room service; massage; babysitting; laundry service. *In room:* A/C, TV, minibar, hair dryer, safe-deposit box.

Hyatt Regency Acapulco 🐾🐾   A sophisticated oasis, the Hyatt is one of the largest and most modern of Acapulco's hotels—which still isn't as modern as other resorts. A freeform pool fronts a broad stretch of beautiful beach, one of the most inviting in Acapulco. The sleek lobby encloses a sitting area and bar where there's live music every evening. The stylishly decorated rooms are large, with sizable balconies overlooking the pool and ocean. Some contain kitchenettes. Regency Club guests receive continental breakfast, afternoon canapés, and other upgraded amenities. Children are not allowed in Regency Club rooms. This hotel caters to a large Jewish clientele and has a full-service kosher restaurant, synagogue, and Sabbath elevator.

Costera Alemán 1, 39869 Acapulco, Gro. ⓒ 800/233-1234 in the U.S. and Canada, 01-800/005-0000 in Mexico, or 744/469-1234. Fax 744/484-3087. www.hyattacapulco.com.mx. 646 units. High season $234 double, $260 Regency Club, $338 suite; low season $208 double, $234 Regency Club, $312 suite. AE, DC, MC, V. **Amenities:** 3 restaurants; cantina; lobby bar; 2 large, shaded free-form pools; 3 lighted tennis courts; access to a nearby gym; children's programs; concierge; tour desk; car-rental desk; business center; shopping arcade; salon; room service; in-room massage; babysitting; laundry service; dry cleaning; safe-deposit box in lobby. *In room:* A/C, TV, minibar, hair dryer, iron, safe-deposit box, bathrobes.

Villa Vera Hotel & Racquet Club ★★★ *Finds*

The legendary Villa Vera started off as a private home with adjacent villas for houseguests. It continues to offer the closest experience to Acapulco villa life that you'll find in a public property. After a while, it became a popular hangout for stars such as Liz Taylor, who married Mike Todd here. This hotel is also where Richard and Pat Nixon celebrated their 25th wedding anniversary and where Elvis's film *Fun in Acapulco* was shot. Lana Turner even made it her home for 3 years.

Villa Vera has undergone significant renovations and upgrades in facilities in recent years that have transformed it into an exclusive boutique-style hotel. The spa offers world-class services 7 days a week. Rooms are tastefully decorated in sophisticated light tones. The complex has 14 pools, including 8 private pools for the six villas and two houses. Most other rooms share pools; guests in standard rooms have the use of the large public pool across from the restaurant. The hotel is several blocks from the Condesa beach, up a hill.

Lomas del Mar 35, Fracc. Club Deportivo, 39693 Acapulco, Gro. ⓒ 1-800/710-9300 in Mexico, 744/484-0334, or -0335. Fax 744/484-7479. www.clubregina.com. hotel_villavera_aca@clubregina.com. 69 units, 2 houses. High season $246 studio, $246 double, $340–$405 suite, $481 villa, $1,222 Casa Teddy (4 people), $1,261 Casa Julio (6 people). Ask about low-season rates. AE, MC, V. **Amenities:** Restaurant; pool bar; pool; 2 clay tennis courts; gym; complete European spa; travel agency; car rental; 2 lighted racquetball courts. *In room:* A/C, TV, minibar, safe-deposit box.

Moderate

Calinda Acapulco

You'll see this tall cylindrical tower rising at the eastern edge of Condesa Beach. Each room has a view, usually of the bay. Though not exceptionally well furnished, guest rooms are large and comfortable; most have two double beds. It's the most modern of the reasonably priced lodgings along the strip of hotels facing popular Condesa Beach. Package prices are available, and the hotel frequently offers promotions, such as rates that include breakfast; otherwise it is expensive for what it provides.

Costera Alemán 1260, 39300 Acapulco, Gro. ⓒ 800/228-5151 in the U.S., or 744/484-0410. Fax 744/484-4676. www.hotelescalinda.com.mx. 357 units. $169 double. Ask about promotional specials. AE, DC, MC, V. Limited free parking. **Amenities:** 3 restaurants; poolside snacks; lobby bar w/live music; swimming pool; concierge; travel agency; shopping arcade; salon; room service; babysitting; laundry service; pharmacy. *In room:* A/C, TV, safe-deposit boxes.

Hotel Sands ★ *Kids* *Value*

A great option for budget-minded families, this unpretentious, comfortable hotel nestles on the inland side, opposite the giant resort hotels and away from the din of Costera traffic. A stand of umbrella palms and a pretty garden restaurant—with terrific, authentic Mexican food at reasonable prices—lead into the lobby. The rooms are light and airy in the style of a good modern motel, with basic furnishings and wall-to-wall carpeting. Some units have kitchenettes, and all have a terrace or balcony. The rates are reasonable, the accommodations satisfactory, and the location excellent.

Costera Alemán 178, 39670 Acapulco, Gro. (*C*) **744/484-2260.** Fax 744/484-1053. www.sands.com.mx. 93 units. $62 standard double; $50 bungalow. Rates include coffee in the lobby and are higher during Christmas, Easter, and other major holidays. AE, MC, V. Limited free parking. **Amenities:** Restaurant; 2 swimming pools (1 for children); children's playground; concierge; babysitting; laundry service; dry cleaning; squash court; volleyball; Ping-Pong area. *In room:* A/C, TV, minibar.

DOWNTOWN (ON LA QUEBRADA) & OLD ACAPULCO BEACHES

Numerous budget hotels dot the streets fanning out from the *zócalo*. They're among the best values in town, but be sure to check your room first to see that it meets your needs. Several hotels in this area are close to Caleta and Caletilla beaches, or on the back of the hilly peninsula, at Playa la Angosta.

Moderate

El Mirador Acapulco ✦

One of the landmarks of Old Acapulco, the El Mirador Hotel overlooks the famous cove where the cliff divers perform. Renovated with tropical landscaping and lots of Mexican tile, this hotel offers attractively furnished rooms. Each holds double or queen-size beds, a small kitchenette area with minifridge and coffeemaker, and a large bathroom with marble counters. Most have a separate living room, some have a whirlpool tub, and all are accented with colorful Saltillo tile and other Mexican decorative touches. Ask for a room with a balcony or ocean view.

A set-price dinner ($29) offers great views of the cliff-diving show. The large, breezy lobby bar is a favorite spot to relax as day fades into night on the beautiful cove and bay. Nearby is a protected cove with good snorkeling.

Quebrada 74, 39300 Acapulco, Gro. (*C*) **744/483-1221** or 744/484-0909 for reservations. Fax 744/482-4564. www.hotelmiradoracapulco.com.mx. 132 units. High season $185 double, $231 suite with whirlpool; low season $108 double, $135 suite with whirlpool. Add $13 for kitchenette. AE, MC, V. Street parking. **Amenities:** Restaurant; coffee shop; lobby bar; 3 pools, including 1 rather rundown saltwater pool; travel agency; room service; laundry service. *In room:* A/C, TV.

Hotel Caleta ✦

The all-inclusive Hotel Caleta (formerly the Grand Meigas) is more familiar to Mexican travelers than to their U.S. counterparts. This high-quality, nine-floor resort, adjacent to one of the liveliest beaches in Old Acapulco, offers excellent value. Stay here if you seek the authentic feel of a Mexican holiday, with all its boisterous, family-friendly charms. The hotel is built into a cliff on the Caleta peninsula, overlooking the beach. Rooms surround a plant-filled courtyard, topped by a glass ceiling. All have large terraces with ocean views, although some connect to the neighboring terrace. The simply decorated rooms are very clean and comfortable, with a large closet and desk. Each room has two queen beds with firm mattresses, and cable TV.

A succession of terraces holds tropical gardens, restaurants, and pools. A private beach and boat dock are down a brief flight of stairs. The resort has a changing agenda of theme nights and evening entertainment.

Cerro San Martín 325, Fracc. Las Playas, 39390 Acapulco, Gro. (*C*) **744/483-9940** or 744/483-9140. Fax 744/483-9125. meigaca@prodigy.net.mx. 255 units. High season $188 double; low season $90 double. Rates are all-inclusive. Room-only prices sometimes available. AE, DC, MC, V. Free private parking. **Amenities:** 3 restaurants; snack bar; bars; large fresh- and saltwater pools; tour desk; car-rental desk; shopping arcade. *In room:* A/C, TV, fan.

Inexpensive

Hotel Costa Linda Budget-minded American and Mexican couples are drawn to the sunny, well-kept rooms of the Costa Linda, one of the best values in the area. All rooms have individually controlled air-conditioning and a minifridge, and some have a small kitchenette (during low season there is a $5 charge for using the kitchenette). Closets and bathrooms are ample in size, and mattresses are firm. Cozy as the Costa Linda is, it is adjacent to one of the busier streets in Old Acapulco, so traffic noise can be bothersome. It's just a 1-block walk down to lively Caleta beach.

Costera Alemán 1008, 39390 Acapulco, Gro. ℂ 744/482-5277 or 744/482-2549. Fax 744/483-4017. 44 units. High season $89 double; low season $35 double. 2 children under 8 stay free in parent's room. MC, V. Free parking. **Amenities:** Restaurant; bar; small pool; tennis court; tour desk. *In room:* A/C, TV, minibar.

Hotel Los Flamingos ★★★ *Finds* An Acapulco landmark, this hotel, perched on a cliff 152m (500 ft.) above Acapulco Bay, once entertained John Wayne, Cary Grant, Johnny Weissmuller, Fred McMurray, Errol Flynn, Red Skelton, Roy Rogers, and others. In fact, the stars liked it so much that at one point they bought it and converted it into a private club. The place is a real find—it's in excellent shape and exceptionally clean, offering visitors a totally different perspective of Acapulco as it maintains all the charm of a grand era. All rooms have dramatic ocean views and a large balcony or terrace, but most of them are not air-conditioned (those that are also have TVs). Still, the constant sea breeze is cooling enough. Rooms are colorful, with mosaic-tile tables and mirrors. Thursdays at Los Flamingos are especially popular, with a *pozole* party and live music by a Mexican band that was probably around in the era of Wayne and Weissmuller—note the seashell-pink bass. Even if you don't stay here, plan to at least come for a margarita at sunset and a walk along the dramatic lookout point.

López Mateos s/n, Fracc. Las Playas, 39300 Acapulco, Gro. ℂ 744/482-0690. Fax 744/483-9806. 40 rooms. High season $85 double, $91 double with A/C, $130 junior suite; low season $65 double, $78 double with A/C, $91 junior suite. AE, MC, V. **Amenities:** Restaurant; bar; pool; tour desk; car rental; room service; laundry service.

Hotel Misión Enter this hotel's plant-filled brick courtyard, shaded by two enormous mango trees, and you'll retreat into an earlier, more peaceful Acapulco. This tranquil 19th-century hotel lies 2 blocks inland from the Costera and the *zócalo*. The original L-shaped building is at least a century old. The rooms have colonial touches, such as colorful tile and wrought iron, and come simply furnished, with a fan and one or two beds with good mattresses. Unfortunately, the promised hot water is not reliable—request a cold-water-only room and receive a small discount. Breakfast is served on the patio. The hotel is 2 blocks inland from the fishermen's wharf, main square, and La Quebrada.

Felipe Valle 12, 39300 Acapulco, Gro. ℂ 744/482-3643. Fax 744/482-2076. 27 units. $56 double. No credit cards. **Amenities:** Restaurant.

Hotel Villa Romana This is one of the most comfortable inns in the area for a long stay. Some rooms are tiled and others carpeted; nine have small kitchens with refrigerators. Terraces face Playa la Angosta. The small, plant-filled terrace on the second floor holds tables and chairs; the fourth-floor pool offers a great view of the bay.

Av. López Mateos 185, Fracc. Las Playas, 39300 Acapulco, Gro. ℂ 744/482-3995. www.aca-novenet.com.mx/villa romana. 9 units. High season $55 double; low season $45 double. MC, V. Street parking. *In room:* A/C, TV.

WHERE TO DINE

Diners in Acapulco enjoy stunning views and fresh seafood. The quintessential setting is a candlelit table with the glittering bay spread out before you. If you're looking for a romantic spot, Acapulco brims with such inviting places; most sit along the southern coast, with views of the bay. If you're looking for simple food or an authentic local dining experience, you're best off in Old Acapulco.

A deluxe establishment in Acapulco may not be much more expensive than a mass-market restaurant. The proliferation of U.S. franchise restaurants has increased competition, and even the more expensive places have reduced prices. Trust me—the locally owned restaurants offer the best food and the best value.

SOUTH OF TOWN: LAS BRISAS AREA
Very Expensive

Baikal ★★★ FUSION/FRENCH/ASIAN   The exquisite and ultrahot Baikal is the best place in Acapulco for an over-the-top dining experience. You enter from the street then descend a spiral staircase into the stunning bar and restaurant, awash in muted tan and cream colors of luxurious fabrics and natural accents of stone, wood, and water. The restaurant itself is constructed into the cliff, providing sweeping views of Acapulco Bay's glittering lights. The large dining room, with a two-story ceiling, has comfortable seating, including sofas that border the room. The creative menu combines fusion fare, then adds a dash of Mexican flare. Start with the scallops in a chipotle vinaigrette, or the black bean soup with duck fois gras. Notable entrees include steamed red snapper with lobster butter sauce, chicken breast rolled and stuffed with asparagus in a white whine reduction, or medallions of New Zealand lamb in a sweet garlic sauce. The service is as impeccable as the presentation. There's also an extensive selection of wines, as well as live piano music nightly. Periodically during the evening, large projector screens descend over the floor-to-ceiling glass windows, and show short films of Old Acapulco or cavorting whales and dolphins, providing a brief reprise from conversation and dining. A fashionably late dining spot (expect a crowd at midnight), the attire is chic resort wear, as most patrons are headed to the clubs following dinner. Baikal also has wheelchair access, a private VIP dining room, a wine cellar, and an amble bar, ideal for enjoying a sunset cocktail or after-dinner drink. It's located east of town on the scenic highway just before the entrance to the Las Brisas hotel.

Carretera Escénica 16 and 22. (*Ç* **744/446-6845** or 744/446-6867. www.baikal.com.mx. Reservations required. Main courses: $20–$60. AE, MC, V. Daily 7pm–2am. Closed Mon during the summer.

Casa Nova ★★ GOURMET ITALIAN   Enjoy an elegant meal and a fabulous view of glittering Acapulco Bay at this spot east of town. The cliff-side restaurant offers several elegantly appointed dining rooms awash in marble and stone accents, and outdoor terrace dining with a stunning view. If you arrive before your table is ready, have a drink in the comfortable lounge. This is a long-standing favorite of Mexico City's elite; dress tends toward fashionable, tropical attire. The best dishes include veal scaloppine and homemade pastas, such as linguine with fresh clams. A changing tourist menu offers a sampling of the best selections for a fixed price. There's also an

---

Moments Dining with a View

Restaurants with unparalleled views of Acapulco include **Baikal, Madeiras, Spicey, Mezzanotte,** and **Casa Nova** in the Las Brisas area, **El Olvido** along the Costera, **Su Casa** on a hill above the convention center, and the **Bella Vista Restaurant** at the Las Brisas hotel.

ample selection of reasonably priced national and imported wines. And there's live piano music nightly.

Carretera Escénica 5256. ℂ **744/446-6237.** Reservations required. Main courses $28–$50; fixed-price 4-course meal $39. AE, MC, V. Daily 7–11:30pm.

Mezzanotte Acapulco ✪ ITALIAN/FRENCH/MEXICAN   Mezzanotte offers a contemporary blending of classic cuisines, but its strongest asset is the view of the bay. This location has changed hands several times; it currently offers a mix of trendy international dishes served in an atmosphere that tries a bit too hard to be upscale and fashionable. Music is loud and hip, so if you're looking for a romantic evening, this is probably not the place. It's a better choice if you want a taste of Mexican urban chic. The view of the bay remains outstanding, though the food still strives for consistency. Dress up a bit for dining here. Mezzanotte is in the La Vista complex near the Las Brisas hotel.

Plaza La Vista, Carretera Escénica a Puerto Márquez 28-2, 39880 Acapulco, Guerrero. ℂ **744/446-5727** or 744/446-5728. Reservations required. Main courses $20–$35. AE, MC, V. Daily 6:30pm–midnight. Closed Mon during low season.

COSTERA HOTEL ZONE
Very Expensive

El Olvido ✪✪ NUEVA COCINA   Once you make it past the entrance of this handsome terrace restaurant, you'll almost forget that it's in a shopping mall. It gives you all the glittering bay-view ambience of the posh Las Brisas restaurants, without the taxi ride. The menu is one of the most sophisticated in the city. It's expensive, but each dish is delightful in both presentation and taste. Start with 1 of the 12 house specialty drinks, such as Olvido, made with tequila, rum, Cointreau, tomato juice, and lime juice. Soups include delicious cold melon, and thick black bean and sausage. Among the innovative entrees are quail with honey and *pasilla* chiles, and thick sea bass with a mild sauce of cilantro and avocado. For dessert, try chocolate fondue or *guanábana* (a tropical fruit) mousse in a rich *zapote negro* (black tropical fruit) sauce. El Olvido is in the Plaza Mirabella shopping center fronting Diana Circle. Walk into the passage to the right of Aca Joe and bear left; it's at the back.

Glorieta Diana traffic circle, Plaza Marbella. ℂ **744/481-0203,** 744/481-0256, 744/481-0214, or 744/481-0240. Reservations recommended. Main courses $14–$33. AE, MC, V. Daily 6pm–midnight.

Su Casa/La Margarita ✪ INTERNATIONAL   Relaxed elegance and terrific food at reasonable prices are what you get at Su Casa. Owners Shelly and Angel Herrera created this pleasant, breezy, open-air restaurant on the patio of their hillside home overlooking the city. Both are experts in the kitchen and are on hand nightly to greet guests on the patio. The menu changes often. Some items are standard, such as shrimp *a la patrona* in garlic; grilled fish, steak, and chicken; and flaming *filet al Madrazo,* a delightful brochette marinated in tropical juices. Most entrees come with garnishes of cooked banana or pineapple. The margaritas are big and delicious. Su Casa is the hot-pink building on the hillside above the convention center.

V. Anahuac 110. ℂ **744/484-4350** or 744/484-1261. Fax 744/484-0803. Reservations recommended. Main courses $14–$50. MC, V. Daily 6pm–midnight.

Moderate

El Cabrito NORTHERN MEXICAN   With its hacienda-inspired entrance, waitresses in white dresses and *charro*-style neckties, and location in the heart of the Costera, this restaurant targets tourists. But its authentic, well-prepared specialties

---

Moments If There's *Pozole,* It Must Be Thursday

If you're visiting Acapulco on a Thursday, indulge in the local custom of eating *pozole,* a bowl of white hominy and meat in broth, garnished with sliced radishes, shredded lettuce, onions, oregano, and lime. The traditional version includes pork, but a newer chicken version has also become a standard. You can also find green *pozole,* which is made by adding a paste of roasted pumpkin seeds to the traditional *pozole* base. Green *pozole* is also traditionally served with a side of sardines. For a singular Acapulco experience, enjoy your Thursday *pozole* at the cliff-side restaurant of the Hotel Los Flamingos (see above).

---

attract Mexicans in the know—a comforting stamp of approval. Among its specialties are *cabrito al pastor* (roasted goat), *charro* beans, Oaxaca-style *mole,* and *burritos de machaca.* It's on the ocean side of the Costera, south of the convention center.

Costera Alemán 1480. (*C* 744/484-7711. Main courses $5–$15. AE, MC, V. Mon–Sat 2pm–1am; Sun 2–11pm.

Inexpensive

Ika Tako ★★★ *(Finds* SEAFOOD/TACOS   This is my favorite place to eat in Acapulco, and I never miss it. Perhaps I have simple tastes, but these fresh fish, shrimp, and seafood tacos (served in combinations that include grilled pineapple, fresh spinach, grated cheese, garlic, and bacon) are so tasty that they're addicting. Unlike most inexpensive places to eat, the setting is also lovely, with a handful of tables overlooking tropical trees and the bay below. The lighting may be bright, the atmosphere occasionally hectic, and the service dependably slow, but the tacos are delectable. You can also order beer, wine, soft drinks, and dessert. This restaurant is along the Costera, next to Beto's lobster restaurant. A branch across from the Hyatt Regency hotel lacks the atmosphere of this one.

Costera Alemán 99. No phone. Main courses $2.50–$5. No credit cards. Daily 6pm–5am.

DOWNTOWN: THE *ZOCALO* AREA

The old downtown area abounds with simple, inexpensive restaurants serving tasty eats. It's easy to pay more elsewhere and not get food as consistently good as you'll find in this part of town. To explore this area, start at the *zócalo* and stroll west along Juárez. After about 3 blocks, you'll come to Azueta, lined with small seafood cafes and streetside stands.

Moderate

El Amigo Miguel ★★ *(Finds* MEXICAN/SEAFOOD   Locals know that El Amigo Miguel is a standout among downtown seafood restaurants—you can easily pay more elsewhere but not eat better. Impeccably fresh seafood reigns; the large, open-air dining room, 3 blocks west of the *zócalo,* is usually brimming with seafood lovers. When it overflows, head to a branch across the street, with the same menu. Try delicious *camarones borrachos* (drunken shrimp), in a sauce made with beer, applesauce, ketchup, mustard, and bits of fresh bacon—it tastes nothing like the individual ingredients. *Filete Miguel* is red snapper filet stuffed with seafood and covered in a wonderful chipotle pepper sauce. Grilled shrimp with garlic and whole red snapper *(mojo de ajo)* are served at their classic best.

Juárez 31, at Azueta. (*C* 744/483-6981. Main courses $2.20–$23. AE, MC, V. Daily 10am–11pm.

Mariscos Pipo ⚓ SEAFOOD   Check out the photographs of Old Acapulco on the walls while relaxing in this airy dining room decorated with hanging nets, fish, glass buoys, and shell lanterns. The English-language menu lists a wide array of seafood, including *ceviche,* lobster, octopus, crayfish, and baby-shark quesadillas. This local favorite is 2 blocks west of the *zócalo* on Breton, just off the Costera. Another bustling branch, open daily from 1 to 9:30pm, is at Costera Alemán and Canadá (© **744/484-0165**).

Almirante Breton 3. © **744/482-2237**. Main courses $5.60–$33. AE, MC, V. Daily noon–8pm.

ACAPULCO AFTER DARK

SPECIAL ATTRACTIONS   The **"Gran Noche Mexicana"** combines a performance by the Acapulco Ballet Folklórico with one by Los Voladores from Papantla (see chapter 12). It takes place in the plaza of the convention center Monday, Wednesday, and Friday at 7pm. With dinner and open bar, the show costs $62; general admission (including three drinks) is $42. Call for reservations (© **744/484-7046**) or consult a local travel agency. Many major hotels also schedule Mexican fiestas and other theme nights that include dinner and entertainment. Local travel agencies will have information.

NIGHTCLUBS & DISCOS   Acapulco is even more famous for its nightclubs than for its beaches. Because clubs frequently change ownership—and, often names—it's difficult to give specific and accurate recommendations. But some general tips will help. Every club seems to have a cover charge of around $20 in high season and $10 in low season; drinks can cost anywhere from $3 to $10. Women can count on paying less or entering free. Don't even think about going out to one of the hillside discos before 11pm, and don't expect much action until after midnight. But it will keep going until 4 or 5am.

Many discos periodically waive their cover charge or offer some other promotion to attract customers. Look for promotional materials in hotel reception areas, at travel desks or concierge booths, in local publications, and on the beach.

The high-rise hotels have their own bars and sometimes discos. Informal lobby or poolside cocktail bars often offer free live entertainment.

THE BEACH BAR ZONE   Prefer a little fresh air with your nightlife? The young, hip crowd favors the growing number of open-air oceanfront dance clubs along Costera Alemán, most of which feature techno or alternative rock. There's a concentration of them between the Fiesta Americana and Continental Plaza hotels. An earlier and more casual option to the glitzy discos, these clubs include the jamming **Disco Beach** ⚓⚓ (© **744/484-8230**), **El Sombrero** (you'll know it when you see it), **Tabú,** and the pirate-themed **Barbaroja.** These mainly charge a cover (around $10) and offer an open bar. Women frequently drink free with a lesser charge (men may pay more, but then, this is where the beach babes are). Disco Beach is the most popular of the bunch, and occasionally—such as during spring break—has live bands on the beachfront stage. Their Friday night foam parties are especially popular. Most of the smaller establishments do not accept credit cards; when they do, MasterCard and Visa are more widely accepted than American Express.

If you are brave enough—or inebriated enough—there's a **bungee jump** in the midst of the beach bar zone at Costera Alemán 101 (© **744/484-7529**). For $62 you get one jump, plus a T-shirt, diploma, and membership. Additional jumps are $28, and your fourth jump is free. For $67, you can jump as many times as you like from 4 to 11pm.

Alebrijes   This high-tech club boasts an exterior of reflection pools, gardens, and flaming torches. Inside, stadium seating, booths and round tables surround the vast dance floor—the disco (capacity 1,200) doubles as a venue for concerts and live performances by some of Mexico's most notable singers. The dress code forbids shorts, T-shirts, tennis shoes, sandals, and jeans. Average age here is late teens to early 20s. Open daily from 11pm to 5am. Costera Alemán 3308, across from the Hyatt Regency Acapulco. ⓒ 744/484-5902. Cover (including open bar with national drinks) $5–$25 for women, $8–$35 for men.

Baby-O ★★ This longtime Acapulco favorite is a throwback to the town's heady disco days, although the music is exceptionally contemporary. The mid-to-late-20s crowd dances to everything from house to hip-hop, techno to dance. Located across from the Romano Days Inn, Baby-O has a dance floor surrounded by several tiers of tables and sculpted, cavelike walls, serviced by five bars. Drinks cost $4 to $5. Three-dimensional laser shows and H_2O cooling effects keep the dancing going strong. Service is excellent. This is a great choice for those who shun mammoth clubs in favor of a more intimate setting—although there's generally a good crowd. It opens at 10:30pm. Costera Alemán 22. ⓒ 744/484-7474 or 744/481-1035. www.babyo.com.mx. Cover $5–$17 for women, $10–$35 for men.

Carlos 'n' Charlie's For fun, danceable music and good food, you can't go wrong with this branch of the Carlos Anderson chain. It's always packed. Come early and get a seat on the terrace overlooking the Costera. This is a great place to go for late dinner and a few drinks before moving on to a club. It's east of the Glorieta Diana traffic circle, across the street from the Fiesta Americana Condesa. It's open daily from 1pm to 1am. Costera Alemán 999. ⓒ 744/484-1285 or 744/484-0039.

Hard Rock Cafe If you like your music loud, your food trendy, and your entertainment international, you'll feel at home in Acapulco's branch of this chain bent on world domination. Elvis memorabilia greets you in the entry area, and among other numerous mementos is the Beatles' gold record for "Can't Buy Me Love." There's a bandstand for live music—played every night between 10pm and 2am—and a small dance floor. It's on the seaward side toward the southern end of the Costera, south of the convention center and opposite El Cabrito. Open daily from noon to 2am. Costera Alemán 37. ⓒ 744/484-0047.

Mandara ★★ (Moments) Venture into this stylish chrome-and-neon extravaganza (formerly Enigma) perched on the side of the mountain for a true Acapulco nightlife experience. The plush, dim club has a sunken dance floor and panoramic view of the lights of Acapulco Bay. The club also has an intimate piano bar upstairs overlooking the disco, called Siboney, with a special champagne menu, which draws a more mature and moneyed crowd. The after-hours lounge Privado, also in the same building, opens its doors at 3am. Downstairs, there's pumped-in mood smoke, alternating with fresh oxygen to keep you dancing. Tight and slinky is the norm for women; no shorts for men. The club opens nightly at 10:30pm; fireworks rock the usually full house at 3am, which is when a stylized dance performance takes place on weekends in the style of Euro clubs. Call to find out if you need reservations, this club tends to be busiest on Friday nights. Carretera Escénica, between Los Rancheros Restaurant and La Vista Shopping Center. ⓒ 744/446-5711 or -5712. Fax 744/446-5726. Cover $26 for women, $32 for men, includes open bar; or pay $10 for entrance to Siboney, and pay for drinks separately.

Palladium ★★ This cliff-side club currently reins as the top spot in town, and is found just down the road from Mandara. Generally, it welcomes a younger, rowdier crowd that enjoys the equally fabulous views and the dancing platforms set in the 48m-wide (160-ft.) glass windows overlooking the bay. Around 3am, Silver Man, complete with an Aztec headdress, performs, followed by a spray of fireworks outside the windows. Palladium has welcomed the world's finest DJs as special guests. The layout of the club is more open, which makes meeting people most accessible. Carretera Escénica. ✆ **744/481-0330** or 744/446-5483; www.palladium.com.mx. Cover $26 for women, $36 for men, includes open bar.

Pepe's Piano Bar Pepe's has surely been one of the most famous piano bars in the hemisphere, although it appears those days may be numbered. It has inspired patrons of all ages to sing their hearts out for more than 40 years, and it still draws a crowd, though it now caters to karaoke instead of piano—a big mistake, in my opinion. I keep hoping the owners will come to their senses and return to their roots. It's open Wednesday to Sunday from 10pm to 4am. Carretera Escénica, Comercial La Vista, Local 5. ✆ **744/446-5736.**

Salon Q This place bills itself as "the cathedral of salsa," and it's a fairly accurate claim—Salon Q is *the* place to get down and enjoy the Latin rhythms. Frequently, management raises the cover and features impersonators of top Latin American musical acts. Open daily from 10pm to 4am. Costera Alemán 3117. ✆ **744/481-0114.** Cover $13–$25.

ZUCCA This club offers a fantastic bay view. It caters to a more mature crowd—it allegedly admits only those over 25, though the attendants seem to bend the rules for women—and is particularly popular with the moneyed Mexico City set. The club periodically projects a laser show across the bay. The dress code prohibits shorts, jeans, T-shirts, or sandals. Reservations are recommended. It's open nightly from 10:30pm to 2:30am, until 4am on weekends and when the crowd demands it. In the La Vista Shopping Center, Carretera Escénica 28. ✆ **744/446-5690** or -5691. Cover $5–$10.

2 Northward to Zihuatanejo & Ixtapa ✦

576km (360 miles) SW of Mexico City; 565km (353 miles) SE of Manzanillo; 253km (158 miles) NW of Acapulco

Side-by-side beach resorts, Ixtapa and Zihuatanejo share geography, but they couldn't be more different in character. Ixtapa is a model of modern infrastructure, services, and luxury hotels, while Zihuatanejo—"Zihua" to the locals—is the quintessential Mexican beach village. For travelers, this offers the intriguing possibility of visiting two distinct destinations in one vacation. Those looking for luxury should opt for Ixtapa (eex-*tah*-pah). You can easily and quickly make the 6.5km (4-mile) trip into Zihuatanejo for a sampling of the simple life in a *pueblo* by the sea. Those who prefer a more rustic retreat with real personality should settle in Zihuatanejo (see-wah-tah-*neh*-hoh). It's known for its long-standing community of Swiss and Italian immigrants, and its legendary beach playboys.

The area, with a backdrop of the Sierra Madre and a foreground of Pacific Ocean waters, provides a full range of activities and diversions. Scuba diving, deep-sea fishing, bay cruises to remote beaches, and golf are among the favorites. Nightlife in both towns borders on subdued; Ixtapa is the livelier.

This dual destination is the choice for the traveler looking for a little of everything, from resort-style indulgence to unpretentious simplicity. These two resorts are more welcoming to couples and adults than families, with a number of places that are off-limits to children under 16—something of a rarity in Mexico.

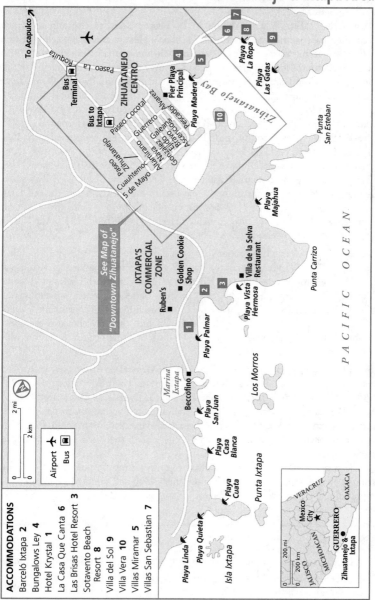

Zihuatanejo & Ixtapa Area

To Acapulco

Paseo La Roquita

Bus Terminal

Bus to Ixtapa

Paseo Cocotal

ZIHUATANEJO CENTRO

Paseo Zihuatanejo

Pescador
Alvarez
Ejido
Galeana
Bravo
Ascencio
Guerrero
N. Bravo
Gonzalez
Nava
Altamirano
Cuauhtemoc
5 de Mayo

Pier Playa Principal

Playa Madera

4

5

6

7

8

9

Playa La Ropa

Playa Las Gatas

10

Zihuatanejo Bay

Punta San Esteban

Playa Majahua

See Map of "Downtown Zihuatanejo"

IXTAPA'S COMMERCIAL ZONE

Golden Cookie Shop

Ruben's

Villa de la Selva Restaurant

2

3

Playa Vista Hermosa

Playa Palmar

1

Marina Ixtapa

Beccofino

Playa San Juan

Playa Casa Blanca

Playa Cuata

Punta Ixtapa

Los Morros

Punta Carrizo

PACIFIC OCEAN

Playa Linda

Playa Quieta

Isla Ixtapa

Airport

Bus

0   2 mi

0   2 km

ACCOMMODATIONS

Barceló Ixtapa **2**
Bungalows Ley **4**
Hotel Krystal **1**
La Casa Que Canta **6**
Las Brisas Hotel Resort **3**
Sotavento Beach
  Resort **8**
Villa del Sol **9**
Villa Vera **10**
Villas Miramar **5**
Villas San Sebastian **7**

VERACRUZ

Mexico City

JALISCO

MICHOACAN

GUERRERO

OAXACA

Zihuatanejo & Ixtapa

0   200 mi

0   200 km

ESSENTIALS

GETTING THERE & DEPARTING   By Plane   These destinations tend to be even more seasonal than most resorts in Mexico. Flights are available year-round from U.S. gateways, but they operate less frequently in the summer. See chapter 2, "Planning Your Trip to Mexico," for information on flying to Ixtapa/Zihuatanejo from the United States and Canada. Both **Aeromexico** and **Mexicana** fly daily from Mexico City and Guadalajara, and less often from Acapulco. Here are the local numbers of some international carriers: **Aeromexico** (© 755/554-2018 or -2019), **Alaska Airlines** (© 755/554-8457), **America West** (© 755/554-8634), **Continental** (© 755/554-4219), and **Mexicana** (© 755/554-2208 or -2209). Ask your travel agent about **charter** flights and packages.

Arriving: The **Ixtapa-Zihuatanejo airport** (© 755/554-2070) is about 11km (7 miles) and 15 minutes south of Zihuatanejo. Taxi fares are $12 to $19. **Transportes Terrestres** *colectivo* minivans transport travelers to hotels in Zihuatanejo and Ixtapa and to Club Med; buy tickets ($3–$6) just outside the baggage-claim area. Car-rental agencies with booths in the airport include **Hertz** (© 800/654-3131 in the U.S., or 755/554-2952), and **Budget** (© 800/527-0700 in the U.S., or 755/553-0397).

By Car   From Mexico City (about 7 hr.), the shortest route is Highway 15 to Toluca, then Highway 130/134 the rest of the way. On the latter road, highway gas stations are few. The other route is the four-lane Highway 95D to Iguala, then Highway 51 west to Highway 134. A new toll road, Highway 37 from Morelia to Ixtapa, was almost completed at press time, and should make the trip between these two cities about 4 hours.

From Acapulco (2½–3 hr.) or Manzanillo (11 hr.), the only choice is the coastal Highway 200. The ocean views along the winding, mountain-edged drive from Manzanillo can be spectacular.

By Bus   Zihuatanejo has two bus terminals: the **Central de Autobuses,** Paseo Zihuatanejo at Paseo la Boquita, opposite the Pemex station and IMSS Hospital (© 755/554-3477), from which most lines operate, and the **Estrella de Oro** station (© 755/554-2175), a block away. At the Central de Autobuses, several companies offer daily service to and from Acapulco, Puerto Escondido, Huatulco, Manzanillo, Puerto Vallarta, and other cities. At the other station, first-class Estrella de Oro buses run daily to Acapulco.

The trip from Mexico City to Zihuatanejo (bypassing Acapulco) takes 9 hours; from Acapulco, 4 to 5 hours. From Zihuatanejo, it's 6 or 7 hours to Manzanillo, and an additional 6 hours to Puerto Vallarta.

Tips Motorist Advisory

Motorists planning to follow Highway 200 northwest up the coast from Ixtapa or Zihuatanejo toward Lázaro Cárdenas and Manzanillo should be aware of reports of car and bus hijackings on that route, especially around Playa Azul, with bus holdups more common than car holdups. Before heading in that direction, ask locals and the tourism office about the status of the route. Don't drive at night. According to tourism officials, police and military patrols of the highway have recently been increased, and the number of incidents has dropped dramatically.

VISITOR INFORMATION   The **State Tourism Office** (℃/fax **755/553-1967** or -1968) is in the La Puerta shopping center in Ixtapa, across from the Presidente Inter-Continental Hotel; it's open Monday through Friday from 8am to 8:30pm and Saturday from 8am to 2pm. This is mainly a self-service office to collect brochures; the staff is less helpful than that at other offices in Mexico. The **Zihuatanejo Tourism Office Module** (no phone; www.ixtapa-zihuatanejo.com) is on the main square by the basketball court at Alvarez; it's open Monday through Friday from 9am to 3pm and serves basic tourist-information purposes. The administrative office, in City Hall (℃ 755/554-2355), is open Monday through Friday from 8am to 4pm. The **Convention and Visitor's Bureau** is another source of information, it's located in Ixtapa at Paseo de Las Gaviotas 12 (℃ 755/553-1270; www.ixtapa-zihuatanejo.org).

CITY LAYOUT   The fishing village and resort of **Zihuatanejo** spreads out around the beautiful Bay of Zihuatanejo, framed by downtown to the north and a beautiful long beach and the Sierra foothills to the east. The heart of Zihuatanejo is the water-front walkway **Paseo del Pescador** (also called the *malecón*), bordering the Municipal Beach. Rather than a plaza as in most Mexican villages, the town centerpiece is a **basketball court,** which fronts the beach. It's a point of reference for directions. The main thoroughfare for cars is **Juan Alvarez,** a block behind the *malecón.* Sections of several of the main streets are designated *zona peatonal* (pedestrian zone).

A cement-and-sand walkway runs from the *malecón* in downtown Zihuatanejo along the water to **Playa Madera.** The walkway is lit at night. Access to Playa La Ropa (Clothing Beach) is by the main road, **Camino a Playa La Ropa.** Playa La Ropa and Playa Las Gatas (Cats Beach) are connected only by boat.

A good highway connects Zihua to **Ixtapa,** 6km (4 miles) northwest. The 18-hole **Ixtapa Golf Club** marks the beginning of the inland side of Ixtapa. Tall hotels line Ixtapa's wide beach, **Playa Palmar,** against a backdrop of lush palm groves and mountains. Access is by the main street, **Bulevar Ixtapa.** On the opposite side of the main boulevard lies a large expanse of small shopping plazas (many with air-conditioned shops) and restaurants. At the far end of Bulevar Ixtapa, **Marina Ixtapa** has excellent restaurants, private yacht slips, and an 18-hole golf course. Condominiums and private homes surround the marina and golf course, and more developments of exclusive residential areas are rising in the hillsides past the marina on the road to Playa Quieta and Playa Linda. Ixtapa also has a paved bicycle track that begins at the marina and continues around the golf course and on toward Playa Linda.

GETTING AROUND   **Taxi** fares are reasonable, but from midnight to 5am, rates increase by 50%. The average fare between Ixtapa and Zihuatanejo is $4.50. Within Zihua, the fare runs about $2.50; within Ixtapa it averages $2.50 to $5. Radio cabs are available by calling ℃ 755/554-3680 or 755/554-3311, however taxis are available from most hotels. A **shuttle bus** (35¢) runs between Zihuatanejo and Ixtapa every 15 or 20 minutes from 5am to 11pm daily, but is almost always very crowded with commuting workers. In Zihuatanejo, it stops near the corner of Morelos/Paseo Zihuatanejo and Juárez, about 3 blocks north of the market. In Ixtapa, it makes numerous stops along Bulevar Ixtapa.

Note: The road from Zihuatanejo to Ixtapa is a broad, four-lane highway, which makes driving between the towns easier and faster than ever. Street signs are becoming more common in Zihuatanejo, and good signs lead in and out of both towns. However, both locations have an area called the "Zona Hotelera" (Hotel Zone), so if you're trying to reach Ixtapa's Hotel Zone, signs in Zihuatanejo pointing to that village's Hotel Zone may be confusing.

FAST FACTS: Zihuatanejo & Ixtapa

American Express The main office is in Av. Colegio Heróico Militar 38 in Plaza San Rafael, Local 7, Centro (© 755/544-6242; fax 755/544-6242). It's open Monday through Friday from 9am to 6pm.

Area Code The telephone area code is **755**.

Banks Ixtapa's banks include **Bancomer,** in the La Puerta Centro shopping center. The most centrally located of Zihuatanejo's banks is **Banamex,** Cuauhtémoc 4. Banks change money during normal business hours, which are generally Monday through Friday from 9am to 3 or 5pm, Saturday from 10am to 1pm. Automatic tellers and currency exchange are available during these and other hours.

Climate Summer is hot and humid, though tempered by sea breezes and brief showers; September is the peak of the tropical rainy season, with showers concentrated in the late afternoons.

Hospital **Hospital de la Marina Ixtapa** is at Bulevar Ixtapa s/n, in front of the Hotel Aristos (© 755/553-0499). In Zihuatanejo, there's the **Clinica Maciel** (© 755/554-2380; La Palmas 12), or **Hospital Hernández Montejano,** Juan Alvarez s/n (© 755/554-5404). Dial © 065 from any phone for emergencies.

Internet Access Ixtapa has many Internet cafes. **Dolfy's Internet Café** (© 755/553-1177) is in the Los Patios Shopping Center in Ixtapa, on the second floor, next to the Golden Cookie Shop. The cost of Internet access is $3 for 20 minutes, and $1 for each additional minute. It's open daily from 8am to 9pm. Access is cheaper in Zihuatanejo, the most popular is **Zihuatanejo Bar Net,** Agustín Ramírez 9, on the ground floor of the Hotel Zihuatanejo Centro (© 755/554-3661). Offering high-speed access for $1 per 30 minutes, it's open from 9am to 11pm daily.

Pharmacy There's a branch of **Farmacias Coyuca** in each town. They are open 24 hours a day, and will deliver. The Ixtapa branch doesn't have a phone number; in Zihuatanejo, call © 755/554-5390.

Post Office The *correo* is in the SCT building, Edificio SCT, behind El Cacahuate in Zihuatanejo (© 755/554-2192). It's open Monday through Friday from 8am to 6pm, Saturday from 9am to 1pm.

ACTIVITIES ON & OFF THE BEACH

The **Museo de Arqueología de la Costa Grande** (no phone) traces the history of the area from Acapulco to Ixtapa/Zihuatanejo (the Costa Grande) from pre-Hispanic times, when it was known as Cihuatlán, through the colonial era. Most of the museum's pottery and stone artifacts give evidence of extensive trade with far-off cultures and regions, including the Toltec and Teotihuacán near Mexico City, the Olmec on the Pacific and Gulf coasts, and areas known today as the states of Nayarit, Michoacán, and San Luis Potosí. Local indigenous groups gave the Aztec tribute items, including cotton *tilmas* (capes) and *cacao* (chocolate), representations of which can be seen here. This museum, in Zihuatanejo near Guerrero at the east end of Paseo

> **Tips** Beach Safety
>
> All beaches in Zihuatanejo are safe for swimming. Undertow is rarely a prob-
> lem, and the municipal beach is protected from the main surge of the Pacific.
> Beaches in Ixtapa are more dangerous for swimming, with frequent undertow
> problems.

del Pescador, easily merits the half-hour or less it takes to stroll through; signs are in Spanish, but an accompanying brochure is available in English. Admission is $1, and it's open Tuesday through Sunday from 9am to 6pm.

THE BEACHES   In Zihuatanejo   At Zihuatanejo's town beach, **Playa Munici-pal,** the local fishermen pull their colorful boats up onto the sand, making for a fine photo op. The small shops and restaurants lining the waterfront are great for people-watching and absorbing the flavor of daily village life. **Playa Madera (Wood Beach),** just east of Playa Municipal, is open to the surf but generally peaceful. A number of attractive budget lodgings overlook this area.

South of Playa Madera is Zihuatanejo's largest and most beautiful beach, **Playa La Ropa** ✸✸, a long sweep of sand with a great view of the sunset. Some lovely small hotels and restaurants nestle in the hills; palm groves edge the shoreline. Although it's also open to the Pacific, waves are usually gentle. A taxi from town costs $3. The name Playa La Ropa (*ropa* means clothing) comes from an old tale of the sinking of a *galeón* during a storm. The silk clothing that it was carrying back from the Philippines washed ashore on this beach—hence the name.

The nicest beach for swimming, and the best for children, is the secluded **Playa Las Gatas (Cats Beach),** across the bay from Playa La Ropa and Zihuatanejo. The small coral reef just offshore is a nice spot for snorkeling and diving, and a little dive shop on the beach rents gear. Shop owner Jean Claude is a local institution—and the only full-time resident of Las Gatas. He claims to offer special rates for female divers and has a collection of bikini tops on display. The waters at Las Gatas are exceptionally clear, without undertow or big waves. Open-air seafood restaurants on the beach make it an appealing lunch spot. Small *pangas* (launches) with shade run to Las Gatas from the Zihuatanejo town pier, a 10-minute trip; the captains will take you across when-ever you wish between 8am and 4pm. Usually the last boat back leaves Las Gatas at 6:30pm, but check to be sure.

Playa Larga is a beautiful, uncrowded beach between Zihuatanejo and the airport, with several small *palapa* restaurants, hammocks, and wading pools.

In Ixtapa   Ixtapa's main beach, **Playa Palmar,** is a lovely white-sand arc on the edge of the Hotel Zone, with dramatic rock formations silhouetted in the sea. The surf can be rough; use caution, and don't swim when a red flag is posted. Several of the nicest beaches in the area are essentially closed to the public. Although by law all Mex-ican beaches are open to the public, it is common practice for hotels to create artifi-cial barriers (such as rocks or dunes).

Club Med and Qualton Club have largely claimed **Playa Quieta,** on the mainland across from Isla Ixtapa. The remaining piece of beach was once the launching point for boats to Isla Ixtapa, but it is gradually being taken over by a private development. Isla Ixtapa–bound boats now leave from the jetty on **Playa Linda,** about 13km (8 miles) north of Ixtapa. Inexpensive water taxis ferry passengers to Isla Ixtapa. Playa

Linda is the primary out-of-town beach, with watersports equipment and horse rentals available. **Playa las Cuatas,** a pretty beach and cove a few miles north of Ixtapa, and **Playa Majahua,** an isolated beach just west of Zihuatanejo, are both being transformed into resort complexes. Lovely **Playa Vista Hermosa** is framed by striking rock formations and bordered by the Las Brisas Hotel high on the hill. All of these are very attractive beaches for sunbathing or a stroll but have heavy surf and strong undertow. Use caution if you swim here.

WATERSPORTS & BOAT TRIPS   Probably the most popular boat trip is to **Isla Ixtapa** for snorkeling and lunch at the El Marlin restaurant, one of several on the island. You can book this outing as a tour through local travel agencies, or go on your own from Zihuatanejo by following the directions to Playa Linda above and taking a boat from there. Boats leave for Isla Ixtapa every 10 minutes between 11:30am and 5pm, so you can depart and return as you like. The round-trip boat ride is $3. Along the way, you'll pass dramatic rock formations and see in the distance **Los Morros de Los Pericos islands,** where a great variety of birds nest on the rocky points jutting out into the blue Pacific. On Isla Ixtapa, you'll find good snorkeling; diving, and other watersports. Gear is available for rent on the island. Be sure to catch the last water taxi back at 5pm, and double-check that time upon arrival on the island.

Local travel agencies can usually arrange day trips to Los Morros de Los Pericos islands for **birding,** though it's less expensive to rent a boat with a guide at Playa Linda. The islands are offshore from Ixtapa's main beach.

Sunset cruises on the sailboat *Nirvana,* arranged through **Yates del Sol** (© 755/554-2694 or 755/554-8270), depart from the Zihuatanejo town pier at Puerto Mío. The cruises cost $49 per person and include an open bar and hors d'oeuvres. There's also a day trip to **Playa Manzanillo** on the very comfortable, rarely crowded sailboat. It begins at 10am, costs $78 per person, and includes an open bar, lunch, and snorkeling gear. Schedules and special trips vary, so call for current information.

You can arrange **fishing trips** with the **boat cooperative** (© 755/554-2056) at the Zihuatanejo town pier. They cost $130 to $300, depending on boat size, trip length, and so on. Most trips last about 7 hours. The cooperative accepts Visa and Master-Card; paying cash saves you 20% tax, but don't expect a receipt. The price includes 10 soft drinks, 10 beers, bait, and fishing gear, but not lunch. You'll pay more for a trip arranged through a local travel agency. The least expensive trips are on small launches called *pangas;* most have shade. Both small-game and deep-sea fishing are offered. The fishing is adequate, though not on par with that of Mazatlán or Baja. Other trips combine fishing with a visit to the near-deserted ocean beaches that extend for miles along the coast. Sam Lushinsky at **Ixtapa Sport-fishing Charters,** 19 Depue Lane, Stroudsburg, PA 18360 (© **570/688-9466;** fax 570/688-9554; www.ixtapasport fishing.com), is a noted outfitter. Prices range from $295 to $445 per day, for 8.4 to 13m (28–42 ft.) custom cruisers, fully equipped.

Boating and fishing expeditions from the new **Marina Ixtapa,** a bit north of the Ixtapa Hotel Zone, can also be arranged. As a rule, everything available in or through the marina is more expensive and more "Americanized."

Sailboats, Windsurfers, and other **watersports equipment** rentals are usually available at stands on Playa La Ropa, Playa las Gatas, Isla Ixtapa, and at the main beach, Playa Palmar, in Ixtapa. There's **parasailing** at La Ropa and Palmar. **Kayaks** are available for rent at hotels in Ixtapa and some watersports operations on Playa La Ropa.

The PADI-certified **Carlo Scuba,** on Los Gatos Beach (© 755/554-6003; www. carloscuba.com), arranges **scuba-diving trips.** Fees start at $55 for a one-tank dive, or $80 for two dives, including all equipment and lunch. This shop has been around since 1962, and is very knowledgeable about the area, which has nearly 30 different dive sites, including walls and caves. Diving takes place year-round, though the water is clearest from May through December, when visibility is 30m (100 ft.) or better. The nearest decompression chamber is in Acapulco. Advance reservations for dives are advised during Christmas and Easter.

Surfing is particularly good at **Petacalco Beach** north of Ixtapa.

LAND SPORTS & ACTIVITIES   In **Ixtapa,** the **Club de Golf Ixtapa Palma Real** (© 755/553-1062 or 755/553-1163), in front of the Sheraton Hotel, has an 18-hole course designed by Robert Trent Jones Jr. The greens fee is $75; caddies cost $19 for 18 holes, $13 for 9 holes; electric carts are $35; and clubs are $25. Tee times begin at 7am, but the course doesn't take reservations. The **Marina Ixtapa Golf Course** (© 755/ 553-1410; fax 755/553-0825), designed by Robert von Hagge, has 18 challenging holes. The greens fee is $85 and includes a cart; caddies cost $22, club rental $30. The first tee time is 7am. Call for reservations 24 hours in advance. Both courses accept American Express, MasterCard, and Visa.

In Ixtapa, the **Club de Golf Ixtapa** (© 755/553-1062 or 755/553-1163) and the **Marina Ixtapa Golf Course** (© 755/553-1410; fax 755/553-0825 or 755/553-1400) both have lighted public **tennis courts,** and both rent equipment. Fees are $6 to $20 an hour during the day, $9 to $30 at night. Call for reservations. The **Dorado Pacífico** and most of the other better hotels on the main beach in Ixtapa have courts.

For **horseback riding,** the largest local stable is located on **Playa Linda** (no phone), offering guided trail rides from the Playa Linda beach (about 13km/8 miles north of Ixtapa). It's just next to the pier where the water taxis debark to Isla Ixtapa. Groups of three or more riders can arrange their own tour, which is especially nice around sunset (though you'll need mosquito repellent). Riders can choose to trace the beach to the mouth of the river and back through coconut plantations, or hug the beach for the whole ride (which usually lasts 1–1½ hr.). The fee is around $30, cash only. Travel agencies in either town can arrange your trip but will charge a bit more for transportation. Reservations are suggested in high season. Another good place to ride is in Playa Larga. There is a ranch on the first exit coming from Zihuatanejo (no phone, but you can't miss it—it is the first corral to the right as you drive toward the beach). The horses are in excellent shape. The fee is $30 for 45 minutes. To arrange riding in advance, call Ignacio Mendiola, at © 755/559-8884 (cellphone, so locally, dial 044 before the number).

SHOPPING
ZIHUATANEJO

Zihuatanejo has its quota of T-shirt and souvenir shops, but it's becoming a better place to buy crafts, folk art, and jewelry. Shops are generally open Monday through Saturday from 10am to 2pm and 4 to 8pm. Many better shops close Sunday, but some smaller souvenir stands stay open, and hours vary.

The **artisans' market** on Calle Cinco de Mayo is a good place to start shopping before moving on to specialty shops. There's also a **municipal market** on Avenida Benito Juárez (about 5 blocks inland from the waterfront), but most vendors offer the same things—huaraches, hammocks, and baskets. The market sprawls over several

Downtown Zihuatanejo

ACCOMMODATIONS ■
Apartamentos
  Amueblados Valle **5**
Bungalows Ley **10**
Casa Cuitalateca **15**
Hotel Susy **8**
La Casa Que Canta **12**
Posada Citlalli **7**

Sotavento Beach Resort **14**
Villas Miramar **11**
Villas San Sebastián **16**
Villa del Sol **17**
Villa Vera Porto Mio **1**

ATTRACTIONS ●
Museo de Arqueologia **9**

RESTUARANTS ◆
Casa Puntarenas **2**
Coconuts **6**
Kau-Kan **13**
La Perla **18**
La Sirena Gorda **3**
Nueva Zelanda **4**

↑ To Ixtapa ↗

Main Bus Terminal

Avenida Morelos
Paseo Zihuatanejo
Tres Estrellas Bus Terminal
Paseo del Palmar
Cuauhtémoc
I. Altamirano
Avenida Nava
Benito Juárez
Municipal Market
5 de Mayo
C. González
Kioto   Plaza
Galeana
Ejido
Camino a Playa la Ropa
Artisan's Market
Vicente Guerrero
Paseo de la Boquita
Canal
Calle Adelita
N. Bravo
Pedro Ascencio
Avenida Ramírez
Calle Mateos
Álvarez del Pescador
J.N. Paseo
Playa Madera
Las Salinas
Playa Municipal
Playa Madera
Muelle Pier
Playa La Ropa
Bahía de Zihuatanejo
Punta Godomia
Bus ▣
Post Office ✉
Playa Las Gatas

| 0 | 330 feet |
| 0 | 100 meters |

---

blocks. Spreading inland from the waterfront some 3 or 4 blocks are numerous small shops well worth exploring.

Besides the places listed below, check out **Alberto's,** Cuauhtémoc 12 and 15 (no phone), for jewelry. Also on Cuauhtémoc, 2 blocks down from the Nueva Zelanda Coffee Shop, is a small shop that looks like a market stand and sells beautiful tablecloths, napkins, and other linens, all handmade in Aguascalientes.

Casa Marina This small complex extends from the waterfront to Alvarez near Cinco de Mayo and houses four shops, each specializing in handcrafted wares from all over Mexico. Items include handsome rugs, textiles, masks, colorful woodcarvings, and silver jewelry. Café Marina, the small coffee shop in the complex, sells shelves and shelves of used paperback books in several languages. Open daily from 9am to 9pm during the high season, 10am to 2pm and 4 to 8pm the rest of the year. Paseo del Pescador 9. ℂ 755/554-2373. Fax 755/554-3533.

Coco Cabaña Collectibles   Located next to Coconuts Restaurant, this impressive shop carries carefully selected crafts and folk art from across the country, including fine Oaxacan woodcarvings. Owner Pat Cummings once ran a gallery in New York, and the inventory reveals her discriminating eye. If you make a purchase, she'll cash your dollars at the going rate. Open Monday through Saturday from 10am to 2pm and 4 to 8pm; closed August and September. Guerrero and Alvarez, opposite the Hotel Citali. ℂ 755/554-2518.

Viva Zapatos   This shop carries bathing suits for every taste and shape, great casual and not-so-casual resort wear, sunglasses, and everything else for looking good in and out of the water. The store is three doors down from Amueblados Valle. It's open Monday through Saturday from 10am to 2pm and 5 to 9pm. Vicente Guerrero 33. No phone.

IXTAPA

Shopping in Ixtapa is not especially memorable, with T-shirts and Mexican crafts the usual wares. **Ferroni, Bye-Bye, Aca Joe,** and **Navale** sell brand-name sportswear. All of these shops are in the same area on Bulevar Ixtapa, across from the beachside hotels, and most are open daily from 9am to 2pm and 4 to 9pm.

La Fuente   This terrific shop carries gorgeous Talavera pottery, jaguar-shaped wicker tables, hand-blown glassware, masks, tin mirrors and frames, hand-embroidered clothing from Chiapas, and wood and papier-mâché miniatures. Open daily from 9am to 10pm during high season, daily from 10am to 2pm and 5 to 9pm in low season. Los Patios Center, Bulevar Ixtapa. ℂ 755/553-0812.

WHERE TO STAY

Larger, more expensive hotels, including many well-known chains, dominate accommodations in Ixtapa and on Playa Madera. There are only a few choices in the budget and moderate price ranges. If you're looking for lower-priced rooms, Zihuatanejo offers a better selection and better values. Many long-term guests in Ixtapa and Zihuatanejo rent apartments and condos. **Lilia Valle** (ℂ **755/554-2084** or 755/554-4649) is an excellent source for apartment and villa rentals. All lodgings in both towns offer free parking.

ZIHUATANEJO

Hotels in Zihuatanejo and its nearby beach communities are more economical than those in Ixtapa. The term "bungalow" is used loosely—it may mean an individual unit with a kitchen and bedroom, or just a bedroom. It may also be like a hotel, in a two-story building with multiple units, some of which have kitchens. It may be cozy or rustic, with or without a patio or balcony. Accommodations in town are generally very basic, though clean and comfortable.

Playa Madera and Playa La Ropa, separated by a craggy shoreline, are both accessible by road. Prices tend to be higher here than in town, but the value is much better, and people tend to find that the beautiful, tranquil setting is worth the extra cost. The town is 5 (by taxi) to 20 (on foot) minutes away.

In Town

Apartamentos Amueblados Valle ★★   These well-furnished apartments cost only as much as an inexpensive hotel room. Five one-bedroom units accommodate up to three people; the three two-bedroom apartments fit four comfortably. Units that do not face the street are less noisy than those that do. Each airy apartment is different; all have ceiling fans, private balconies, and kitchenettes. There's daily maid service, and a paperback-book exchange in the office. Owner Guadalupe Rodríguez and her son Luis Valle are good sources of information about cheaper apartments elsewhere, for long-term visitors. Reserve well in advance during high season. It's about 2 blocks from the waterfront.

Vicente Guerrero 33 (between Ejido and N. Bravo), 40880 Zihuatanejo, Gro. ⓒ 755/554-2084. Fax 755/554-3220. 8 units. High season $60 1-bedroom apt, $90 2-bedroom apt; low season $40 1-bedroom apt, $60 2-bedroom apt. Ask about low-season and long-term discounts. No credit cards. *In room:* Fan, kitchenette.

Hotel Susy   This two-story hotel, with lots of plants along a shaded walkway set back from the street, offers small rooms with fans and screened louvered-glass windows. Upper-floor rooms have balconies overlooking the street.

Juan Alvarez 3 (at Guerrero), 40880 Zihuatanejo, Gro. ⓒ 755/554-2339. 18 units. High season $78 double; low season $34 double. MC, V. Facing away from the water at the basketball court on the *malecón,* turn right and walk 2 blocks; the hotel is on your left. *In room:* TV.

Posada Citlali   In this pleasant, three-story hotel, small rooms with fans surround a shaded, plant-filled courtyard that holds comfortable rockers and chairs. It's a good value for the price. Bottled water is in help-yourself containers on the patio. The stairway to the top two floors is narrow and steep.

Vicente Guerrero 3 (near Alvarez), 40880 Zihuatanejo, Guerrero. ⓒ 755/554-2043. citlali@zihuatanejo.com.mx. 19 units. $39 double. No credit cards.

Playa Madera

Madera Beach is a 15-minute walk along the street, a 10-minute walk along the beach pathway, or a cheap taxi ride from Zihuatanejo. Most of the accommodations are on Calle Eva S. de López Mateos, the road overlooking the beach. Most hotels are set against the hill and have steep stairways.

Bungalows Ley ⭐   No two suites are the same at this small complex, one of the nicest on Playa Madera. If you're traveling with a group, you may want to book the most expensive suite (Club Madera); it has a rooftop terrace with a tiled hot tub, outdoor bar and grill, and spectacular view. All the units are immaculate; the simplest are studios with one bed and a kitchen in the same room. All rooms have terraces or balconies just above the beach, and all are decorated in Miami Beach colors. Bathrooms, however, tend to be small and dark. Guests praise the management and the service.

Calle Eva S. de López Mateos s/n, Playa Madera (Apdo. Postal 466), 40880 Zihuatanejo, Gro. ⓒ 755/554-4087. Fax 755/554-4563. 8 units. $103 double with A/C; $162 2-bedroom suite with kitchen (up to 4 persons) or $212 (up to 6 persons). AE, MC, V. Follow Mateos to the right up a slight hill; it's on your left. *In room:* TV.

Villas Miramar ⭐⭐⭐   This lovely hotel with beautiful gardens offers a welcoming atmosphere, attention to detail, and superb cleanliness. Some of the elegant suites are around a shady patio that doubles as a restaurant. Those across the street center on a lovely pool and have private balconies and sea views. A terrace with a bay view has a bar that features a daily happy hour (5–7pm). TVs get cable channels, and the restaurant serves a basic menu for breakfast, lunch, and dinner.

Calle Adelita, Lote 78, Playa Madera (Apdo. Postal 211), 40880 Zihuatanejo, Gro. ⓒ 755/554-2106 or 755/554-3350. Fax 755/554-2149. www.prodigyweb.net.mx/villasmiramar. 18 units. High season $95 suite, $100 oceanview suite, $135 2-bedroom suite; low season $60 suite, $70 oceanview suite, $106 2-bedroom suite. AE, MC, V. Free enclosed parking. Follow the road leading south out of town toward Playa La Ropa, take the 1st right after the traffic circle, and go left on Adelita. **Amenities:** Restaurant; bar; pool. *In room:* A/C, TV.

Playa La Ropa

Playa La Ropa is a 20- to 25-minute walk south of town on the east side of the bay, or a $2 taxi ride.

Casa Cuitlateca   This exclusive B&B is the perfect place for a romantic holiday. It's on the hillside across from La Ropa beach, with stunning views. Rooms are carefully decorated with handicrafts and textiles from all over Mexico, especially from Michoacán, Puebla, and Oaxaca. One suite has a large terrace, another a very nice sitting area and small private garden but no view. Two smaller units have private terraces and sitting areas. The bar, on the first level behind the pool, is open to the public from 4:30 to 8pm. On the top level, there is a sun deck and a hot tub for guests' use. From the entrance, a well-designed yet steep 150-step staircase leads to the B&B. The driveway is also very steep. A hanging bridge connects the parking lot to the house.

Calle Playa La Ropa, Apdo. Postal 124, 40880 Zihuatanejo, Gro. (C) **755/554-2448.** U.S. reservations (C) 877/541-1234 or 406/252-2834. Fax 406/252-4692. www.casacuitlateca.com. 4 suites. $397 double. Extra person $50. Rates include breakfast and round-trip airport transportation. Children under 15 not accepted. AE, MC, V. **Amenities:** Bar; small pool; Jacuzzi. In room: A/C.

La Casa Que Canta ✶✶✶   "The House that Sings" opened in 1992, and in looks alone, it's a very special hotel. It sits on a mountainside overlooking Zihuatanejo Bay, and its striking molded-adobe architecture typifies the rustic-chic style known as Mexican Pacific. Individually decorated rooms have handsome natural-tile floors, unusual painted Michoacán furniture, antiques, and stretched-leather *equipales*, with hand-loomed fabrics throughout. All units have large, beautifully furnished terraces with bay views. Hammocks hang under the thatched-roof terraces. Most of the spacious units are suites, and 10 of them have private pools. Rooms meander up and down the hillside, and while no staircase is terribly long, there are no elevators. An adjacent private villa, El Murmello, holds four suites, all with private plunge pools. A new "well-being" center has been added, offering massage, spa services, and yoga. La Casa Que Canta is a member of the Small Luxury Hotels of the World. It's on the road leading to Playa La Ropa, but not on any beach. The closest stretch of beach (not Playa La Ropa) is down a steep hill.

Camino Escénico a Playa La Ropa, 40880 Zihuatanejo, Guerrero. (C) **888/523-5050** in the U.S., 755/555-7000, 755/555-7030, or 755/554-6529. Fax 755/554-7900. www.lacasaquecanta.com.mx. 28 units. High season $330–$680 double; low season $290–$525 double. AE, MC, V. Children under 16 not accepted. **Amenities:** Small restaurant; bar; freshwater pool on main terrace; saltwater pool on bottom level; room service; laundry service. In room: A/C, minibar.

Sotavento Beach Resort ✶✶   Perched on a hill above the beach, this hotel is for people who want to relax near the ocean in a beautiful, simple setting without being bothered by televisions or closed up in air-conditioned rooms. A throwback to the style of the 1970s, when Zihua was first being discovered by an international jet set, the Sotavento is made up of two multistory buildings. Quite a variety of rooms are available to choose from—ask to see a few different rooms to find something that suits you. My favorites are the doubles on the upper floors of the Sotavento, which are about three times the size of normal doubles. They are simply and comfortably furnished. Each has an oceanview terrace that is half-sheltered, with hammocks, and half-open, with chaises for taking the sun. Screened windows catch the ocean breezes, and ceiling fans keep the rooms airy. One curious feature of the Sotavento is that the floors are slightly slanted—by design. This hotel is on the side of a hill and is not for people who mind climbing stairs.

Playa La Ropa, 40880 Zihuatanejo, Gro. © 755/554-2032. Fax 755/554-2975. www.beachresortsotavento.com. 126 units. $60–$110 standard double; $75–$130 terrace suite. AE, DC, MC, V. Take the highway south of Zihuatanejo about a mile, turn right at the hotel's sign, and follow the road. **Amenities:** Restaurant; lobby bar; pool w/whirlpool.

Villa del Sol ★★★   This exquisite inn is known as much for its unequivocal attention to luxurious detail as it is for its exacting German owner, Helmut Leins. A tranquil, magnificently designed spot that caters to guests looking for complete privacy and serenity, it sits on a 180m-long (600-ft.) private beach. Spacious, split-level suites have one or two bedrooms, plus a living area and a large terrace. Some have a private minipool, and all have CD players and fax machines, with satellite TVs or DVD players brought upon request. White netting drapes king-size beds, and comfy lounges and hammocks beckon at siesta time. Standard rooms are smaller and lack TV and telephone, but are appointed with Mexican artistic details. There are nine beachside suites, but I prefer the individually designed original rooms. This is one of only two hotels in Mexico that meet the demanding standards of the French Relais & Châteaux, and is a member of the Small Luxury Hotels of the World. Villa del Sol does not accept children under 12 during high season, and generally has a "no children" and "no excess noise" feel. This may make it less enjoyable for travelers who relish a more welcoming ambience. The meal plan (breakfast and dinner) is mandatory during the winter season.

Playa la Ropa (Apdo. Postal 84), 40880 Zihuatanejo, Gro. © 888/389-2645 in the U.S., or 755/555-5500. Fax 755/554-2758. www.hotelvilladelsol.com. 45 units. High season $300–$1,000 double; low season $250–$750 double. Meal plan $60 per person, during high season (mandatory) or an optional $45 during summer season. AE, MC, V. **Amenities:** Open-air beachside restaurant and bar; 3 pools (including 18m/60-ft. lap pool); 2 tennis courts; tour desk; car rental; salon; room service; massage; art gallery; doctor on call. *In room:* A/C, TV, minibar, hair dryer, bathrobes.

Villas San Sebastián   On the mountainside above Playa La Ropa, this nine-villa complex offers great views of Zihuatanejo's bay. The villas surround tropical vegetation and a central swimming pool. Each has a kitchenette and a spacious private terrace, and some have air-conditioning. The personalized service is one reason these villas come so highly recommended; owner Luis Valle, whose family has lived in this community for decades, is always available to help guests with any questions or needs.

Bulevar Escénico Playa La Ropa (across from the Dolphins Fountain). © 755/554-4154. Fax 755/554-3220. 11 units. High season $155 1-bedroom villa, $255 2-bedroom villa; low season $105 1-bedroom villa, $165 2-bedroom villa. No credit cards. **Amenities:** Pool.

Playa Zihuatanejo
Villa Vera Puerto Mío ★★   Located on 10 hectares (25 acres) of beautifully landscaped grounds, this resort sits apart from the rest of the hotels in Zihuatanejo, at the farthest end of the bay, almost directly across from Las Gatas beach. Casa de Mar, the cliff-side mansion near the main entrance, holds most of the rooms. Other units are in the Peninsula area, on the tip of the bay; a more secluded area holds two suites with ample sitting areas, beautiful views, and no TVs. Three suites between Casa de Mar and the Peninsula have private pools; the upper-level unit is largest. All rooms were renovated recently and are nicely decorated with handcrafted details from around Mexico. They enjoy beautiful views of either Zihuatanejo's bay or the Pacific Ocean. Golf carts provide transportation to areas around the property. The resort accepts children under 16 only during the summer, and recommends that you call in advance to check. The private beach is accessible only through the hotel, and there's a sailboat available for charters.

Paseo del Morro 5, 40880 Zihuatanejo, Gro. © 01-800/021-6566 in Mexico, 755/553-8165, -8166, or -8167. Fax 755/553-8168. 22 units. High season $291 double, $316 suite, $819 top-level suite with pool, $954 master suite; low season $252 double, $252 suite, $670 top-level suite with pool, $819 master suite. AE, MC, V. **Amenities:** 2 restaurants; concierge; tour desk; car rentals; small marina w/sailboat. *In room:* A/C, minibar, safe-deposit box, bathrobes.

IXTAPA
Very Expensive
Las Brisas Ixtapa ★★★   Set above the high-rise hotels of Ixtapa on its own rocky promontory, Las Brisas is the most stunning of Ixtapa's hotels, and the most noted for gracious service. The austere but luxurious public areas, all in stone and stucco, exude an air of exclusivity. Minimalist luxury also characterizes the rooms, which have Mexican-tile floors and private, plant-decked patios with hammocks and lounges. All rooms face the hotel's cove and private beach, which, though attractive, is dangerous for swimming. The six master suites come with private pools, and the 16th floor is reserved for nonsmokers.

Bulevar Ixtapa, 40880 Ixtapa, Gro. © 800/228-3000 in the U.S., or 755/553-2121. Fax 755/553-1091. 423 units. High season $285 deluxe double, $490 Royal Beach Club; low season $196 deluxe double, $230 Royal Beach Club. AE, MC, V. **Amenities:** 5 restaurants; 3 bars (including lobby bar w/live music at sunset); 4 swimming pools (1 for children); 4 lighted tennis courts w/pro on request; fitness center; travel agency; car rental; shopping arcade; salon; room service; massage; babysitting; laundry service; elevator to secluded beach; 3 units are equipped for travelers w/disabilities. *In room:* A/C, TV, minibar, hair dryer, safe-deposit box.

Expensive
Barceló Ixtapa ★★   This grand 12-story resort hotel (formerly the Sheraton) has large, handsomely furnished public areas facing the beach; it's an inviting place to sip a drink and people-watch. Most rooms have balconies with views of the ocean or the mountains. Nonsmoking rooms are available. Gardens surround the large pool, which has a swim-up bar and separate section for children. It's an excellent value and a great choice for families.

Bulevar Ixtapa, 40880 Ixtapa, Gro. © 800/325-3535 in the U.S. and Canada or 755/553-1858. Fax 755/553-2438. www.barcelo.com. 331 units. High season $245 double all-inclusive, $180 double with breakfast only; low season $225 double all-inclusive. AE, DC, MC, V. **Amenities:** 4 restaurants; nightclub; lobby bar; weekly Mexican fiesta w/buffet and live entertainment; beachside pool; 4 tennis courts; fitness room; concierge; travel agency; car rental; salon; room service; laundry service; pharmacy/gift shop; rooms equipped for travelers w/disabilities are available. *In room:* A/C, TV, minibar.

NH Krystal Ixtapa ★★★ *Kids*   Krystal hotels are known in Mexico for quality rooms and service, and this was the original hotel in the chain. It upholds its reputation for welcoming, exceptional service. Many staff members have been with the hotel for its 20-some years of operation, and are on hand to greet return guests. It is probably the best hotel in the area for families. This large, V-shaped hotel has ample grounds and a terrific pool area, expanded in 2004. Each spacious, nicely furnished room has a balcony with an ocean view, game table, and tile bathroom. Master suites have large, furnished, triangular balconies. Some rates include a breakfast buffet. The center of Ixtapa nightlife is here, at Krystal's famed **Christine** disco.

Bulevar Ixtapa s/n, 40880 Ixtapa, Gro. © 800/231-9860 in the U.S., or 755/553-0333. Fax 755/553-0216. www. nh-hotels.com. 257 units. High season $190 double, $280 suite; low season $170 double, $255 suite. 2 children under 12 stay free in parent's room. Ask about special packages. AE, DC, MC, V. **Amenities:** 5 restaurants; lobby bar; nightclub; pool; tennis court; gym; kids' club; travel agency; car rental; salon; room service; massage; laundry service; racquetball court. *In room:* A/C, TV, minibar.

WHERE TO DINE

ZIHUATANEJO

Zihuatanejo's **central market,** on Avenida Benito Juárez about 5 blocks inland from the waterfront, will whet your appetite for cheap and tasty food. It's best at breakfast and lunch, before the market activity winds down in the afternoon. Look for what's hot and fresh. The market area is one of the best on this coast for shopping and people-watching.

The town has several excellent **bakeries.** At **El Buen Gusto,** Guerrero 4, a half-block inland from the museum (© **755/554-3231**), you'll find banana bread, French bread, doughnuts, and cakes. It's open daily from 8:00am to 10pm.

Expensive

Coconuts ★★★ *Finds* INTERNATIONAL/SEAFOOD   What a find! Not only is the food innovative and delicious, but the restaurant is also in a historic building—the oldest in Zihuatanejo. This popular restaurant in a tropical garden was the weigh-in station for Zihua's coconut industry in the late 1800s. "Fresh" is the operative word on this creative, seafood-heavy menu. Chef Patricia Cummings checks what's at the market, then uses only top-quality ingredients in dishes like seafood pâté and grilled filet of snapper Coconuts. The bananas flambé has earned a loyal following, with good reason. Expect friendly, efficient service here.

Augustín Ramírez 1 (at Vicente Guerrero). © **755/554-2518** or 755/554-7980. Main courses $11–$34. AE, MC, V. High season daily 6–11pm. Closed during rainy season.

Kau-Kan ★★★ NUEVA COCINA/SEAFOOD   A stunning view of the bay is one of the many attractions of this refined restaurant. Stucco and whitewashed walls frame the simple, understated furniture. Head chef Ricardo Rodriguez supervises every detail, from the ultra-smooth background music that invites after-dinner conversation to the spectacular presentation of all the dishes. Baked potato with baby lobster and mahimahi *carpaccio* are two of my favorites, but I recommend you consider the daily specials—Ricardo always uses the freshest seafood and prepares it with great care. For dessert, pecan and chocolate cake served with dark chocolate sauce is simply delicious.

Camino a Playa La Ropa. © **755/554-8446**. Main courses $9–$25. AE, MC, V. Daily 5–11:30pm. From downtown on the road to La Ropa, Kau-Kan is on the right side of the road past the 1st curve.

Inexpensive

Casa Puntarenas MEXICAN/SEAFOOD   A modest spot with a tin roof and nine wooden tables, Puntarenas is one of the best places in town for fried whole fish served with toasted *bolillos* (crusty white-bread miniloaves), sliced tomatoes, onions, and avocado. The place is renowned for chiles rellenos, mild and stuffed with plenty of cheese; the meat dishes are less flavorful. Although it may appear a little too rustic for less experienced travelers, it is very clean, and the food is known for its freshness.

Calle Noria, Col. Lázaro Cárdenas. No phone. Main courses $4.50–$8.50. No credit cards. Daily 6:30–9pm. From the pier, turn left on Alvarez and cross the footbridge on your left. Turn right after you cross the bridge; the restaurant is on your left.

La Sirena Gorda MEXICAN   For one of the most popular breakfasts in town, head to La Sirena Gorda. It serves a variety of eggs and omelets, hotcakes with bacon, and fruit with granola and yogurt. The house specialty is seafood tacos—fish in a variety of sauces, plus lobster—but I consider them overpriced, at $4.50 and $25 respectively. A taco is a taco. I'd recommend something from the short list of daily specials, such as blackened red snapper, steak, or fish kebabs. The food is excellent, and patrons enjoy the casual sidewalk-cafe atmosphere.

Paseo del Pescador. ✆ **755/554-2687.** Breakfast $2–$5.50; main courses $4.50–$12. MC, V. Thurs–Tues 7am–10pm. From the basketball court, face the water and walk to the right; La Sirena Gorda is on your right just before the town pier.

Nueva Zelanda MEXICAN This open-air snack shop serves rich cappuccino sprinkled with cinnamon, fresh-fruit *licuados* (milkshakes), and pancakes with real maple syrup. The mainstays of the menu are *tortas* and enchiladas, and service is friendly and efficient. There's a second location in Ixtapa, in the back section of the Los Patios shopping center (✆ **755/553-0838**).

Cuauhtémoc 23 (at Ejido). ✆ **755/554-2340.** Tortas $3.50; enchiladas $5; *licuados* $2.50; cappuccino $2.50. No credit cards. Daily 8am–10pm. From the waterfront, walk 3 blocks inland on Cuauhtémoc; the restaurant is on your right.

Playa Madera & Playa La Ropa

La Perla SEAFOOD There are many *palapa*-style restaurants on Playa La Ropa, but La Perla, with tables under the trees and thatched roof, is the most popular. Somehow, the long stretch of pale sand and the group of wooden chairs under *palapas* combine with mediocre food and slow service to make La Perla a local tradition. Rumor has it that it is so hard to get the waiters' attention that you can get takeout food from a competitor and bring it here to eat, and they'll never notice. Still, it's considered the best spot for tanning and socializing.

Playa La Ropa. ✆ **755/554-2700.** Breakfast $4–$6.50; main courses $7.50–$24. AE, MC, V. Daily 9am–10pm; breakfast served 10am–noon. Near the southern end of La Ropa Beach, take the right fork in the road; there's a sign in the parking lot.

IXTAPA
Very Expensive
Villa de la Selva ✹ MEXICAN/CONTINENTAL Clinging to the edge of a cliff overlooking the sea, this elegant, romantic restaurant enjoys the most spectacular sea and sunset view in Ixtapa. The candlelit tables occupy three terraces; try to come early to get one of the best vistas, especially on the lower terrace. The cuisine is delicious, artfully presented, and classically rich. Filet Villa de la Selva is red snapper topped with shrimp and hollandaise sauce. Cold avocado soup or hot lobster bisque makes a good beginning; finish with chocolate mousse or bananas Singapore.

Paseo de la Roca. ✆ **755/553-0362.** Reservations recommended during high season. Main courses $15–$44. AE, MC, V. Daily 6–11:30pm.

Expensive
Beccofino ✹✹✹ NORTHERN ITALIAN This restaurant is a standout in Mexico. Owner Angelo Rolly Pavia serves the flavorful northern Italian specialties he grew up knowing and loving. The menu is strong on pasta. Ravioli, a house specialty, comes stuffed with seafood (in season). The garlic bread is terrific, and there's an extensive wine list. A popular place in a breezy marina location, the restaurant tends to be loud when it's crowded, which is often. It's also an increasingly popular breakfast spot.

Marina Ixtapa. ✆ **755/553-1770.** Breakfast $5–$7; main courses $14–$30. AE, MC, V. Daily 9:30am–midnight.

Moderate
Golden Cookie Shop ✹✹ PASTRIES/INTERNATIONAL Although the name is misleading—there are more than cookies here—Golden Cookie's freshly baked goods beg for a detour, and the coffee menu is the most extensive in town. Although prices

are high for the area, the breakfasts are noteworthy, as are the deli sandwiches. Large sandwiches on fresh soft bread come with a choice of sliced meats. Chicken curry is among the other specialty items. An air-conditioned area is reserved for nonsmokers.

Los Patios Center. © 755/553-0310. Breakfast $4–$6; sandwiches $4–$6; main courses $6–$8.50. MC, V. Daily 8am–3pm. Walk to the rear of the shopping center as you face Mac's Prime Rib; walk up the stairs, turn left, and you'll see the restaurant on your right.

Ruben's ★★★ *Finds* BURGERS/VEGETABLES   The choices are easy here—you can order either a big, juicy burger made from top sirloin grilled over mesquite, or a foil-wrapped packet of baked potatoes, chayote, zucchini, or sweet corn. Ice cream, beer, and soda fill out the menu, which is posted on the wall by the kitchen. It's kind of a do-it-yourself place: Patrons snare a waitress and order, grab their own drinks from the cooler, and tally their own tabs. Still, because of the ever-present crowds, it can be a slow process.

Plaza Los Portales. © 755/553-0055 or 755/553-0538. Burgers $4–$5; vegetables $2; ice cream $1.50. No credit cards. Daily noon–midnight.

ZIHUATANEJO & IXTAPA AFTER DARK

With an exception or two, Zihuatanejo nightlife dies down around 11pm or midnight. For a good selection of clubs, discos, hotel fiestas, special events, and fun watering holes with live music and dancing, head for Ixtapa. Just keep in mind that the shuttle bus stops at 11pm, and a taxi to Zihuatanejo after midnight costs 50% more than the regular price. During the off season (after Easter and before Christmas), hours vary: Some places open only on weekends, while others close completely. The most popular hangout for local residents and expats is **Paccolo,** around the corner from Amueblados Valle. It's the one place where you can find a lively crowd of locals almost every night.

THE CLUB & MUSIC SCENE

Many discos and dance clubs stay open until the last customers leave, so closing hours depend upon revelers. Most discos have a "ladies' night" at least once a week—admission and drinks are free for women.

Carlos 'n' Charlie's   Knee-deep in nostalgia, bric-a-brac, silly sayings, and photos from the Mexican Revolution, this restaurant-nightclub offers party ambience and good food. The eclectic menu includes iguana in season (with Alka-Seltzer and aspirin on the house). Out back by the beach is a partly shaded open-air section with a raised wooden platform for "pier dancing" at night. The recorded rock 'n' roll mixes with sounds of the ocean surf. The restaurant is open daily from 10am to midnight; pier dancing is nightly from 9pm to 3am. Bulevar Ixtapa, just north of the Best Western Posada Real, Ixtapa. © 755/553-0085. Cover (including drink tokens) after 9pm $10. No cover Sun–Fri during off season.

Christine   This glitzy street-side disco is famous for its midnight light show, which features classical music played on a mega sound system. A semicircle of tables in tiers overlooks the dance floor. No sneakers, sandals, or shorts are allowed, and reservations are recommended during high season. Open daily at 10pm during high season. Off-season hours vary. In the NH Krystal, Bulevar Ixtapa, Ixtapa. © 755/553-0456. Cover free–$20.

Señor Frog's   A companion restaurant to Carlos 'n' Charlie's, Señor Frog's has several dining sections and a warehouse-like bar with raised dance floors. Large speakers play rock 'n' roll, sometimes even prompting dinner patrons to shimmy by their tables between courses. The restaurant is open daily from 6pm to midnight; the bar is open until 3am. In the La Puerta Center, Bulevar Ixtapa, Ixtapa. © **755/553-2282**.

HOTEL FIESTAS & THEME NIGHTS

Many hotels hold Mexican fiestas and other special events that include dinner, drinks, live music, and entertainment for a fixed price (generally $36). The **Barceló Ixtapa** (© **755/555-2000**) stages a popular Wednesday night fiesta; the **NH Krystal** (© **755/553-0333**) and **Dorado Pacífico** (© **755/553-2025**) in Ixtapa also hold good fiestas. Only the Barceló Ixtapa offers them in the off season. Call for reservations or visit a travel agency for tickets, and be sure you understand what the price covers (drinks, tax, and tip are not always included).

3 Puerto Escondido ★★★

368km (230 miles) SE of Acapulco; 240km (150 miles) NW of Salina Cruz; 80km (50 miles) NW of Puerto Angel

I consider Puerto Escondido (*pwer*-toh es-cohn-*dee*-doh) the best overall beach value in Mexico, from hotels to dining. Although it used to be known only as one of the world's top surf sites, today it's broadening its appeal. Think alternative therapies, great vegetarian restaurants, hip nightlife, awesome hotel and dining values, and some of the best coffee shops in Mexico. It's a place for those whose priorities include the dimensions of the surf break (big), the temperature of the beer (cold), the strength of the coffee (espresso), and the "OTA" (beach speak for "optimal tanning angle"). The young and very aware crowd that comes here measures time by the tides, and the pace is relaxed.

The location of "Puerto," as the locals call it, makes it an ideal jumping-off point for ecological explorations of neighboring jungle and estuary sanctuaries, as well as indigenous mountain settlements. Increasingly, it attracts those seeking both spiritual and physical renewal, with abundant massage and bodywork services, yoga classes, and exceptional and varied healthful dining options.

People come from the United States, Canada, and Europe to stay for weeks and even months—easily and inexpensively. Expats have migrated here from Los Cabos, Acapulco, and Puerto Vallarta seeking what originally attracted them to their former homes—stellar beaches, friendly locals, and low prices. Added pleasures include an absence of beach vendors and time-share sales, an abundance of English speakers, and terrific, inexpensive dining and nightlife.

This is a real place, not a produced resort. A significant number of visitors are European travelers, and it's common to hear a variety of languages on the beach and in the bars. Solo travelers will probably make new friends within an hour of arriving. There are still surfers here, lured by the best break in Mexico, but espresso cafes and live music are becoming just as ubiquitous.

The city has been dismissed as a colony of former hippies and settled backpackers, but it's so much more. I have a theory that those who favor "Puerto" are just trying to keep the place true to its name (*escondido* means "hidden") and undiscovered by tourists. Don't let them trick you—visit, and soon, before it, too, changes.

ESSENTIALS

GETTING THERE & DEPARTING   By Plane   Aerocaribe (© **954/582-2023** or 954/582-3676), and **Aerovega** (© **954/582-2024** or -2023) operate daily flights to and from Oaxaca and Mexico City on small planes. Aerocaribe runs a morning and evening flight during high season; the fare is about $140 each way to Oaxaca. Aerovega flies to and from Oaxaca once daily. The price is about $100 each way. **Rodimar Travel** (see "Arriving," below) sells tickets to both.

If flights to Puerto Escondido are booked, you have the (possibly less expensive) option of flying into **Huatulco** on a scheduled or charter flight. This is especially viable if your destination is Puerto Angel, which lies between Puerto Escondido and Huatulco. An airport taxi costs $60 to Puerto Angel, $85 to Puerto Escondido. If you can find a local taxi, rather than a government-chartered cab, you can reduce these fares by about 50%, including the payment of a $5 mandatory airport exit tax. There is frequent bus service between the three destinations. **Budget** (© 958/581-9000) at the Huatulco airport, has cars available for one-way travel to Puerto Escondido, with an added drop charge of about $10. In Puerto Escondido, Budget is at the entrance to Bacocho (© **954/582-0312**).

Arriving: The Puerto Escondido **airport** (airport code: PXM) is about 4km (2½ miles) north of the center of town, near Playa Bacocho. The *colectivo* **minibus** to hotels costs $2.25 per person. **Aerotransportes Terrestres** sells *colectivo* tickets to the airport through **Rodimar Travel,** on pedestrian-only Avenida Pérez Gasga (© **954/ 582-0734;** fax 954/582-0737), next to Hotel Casa Blanca. The minibus will pick you up at your hotel.

By Car   From Oaxaca, Highway 175 via Pochutla is the least bumpy road. The 242km (150-mile) trip takes 5 to 6 hours. Highway 200 from Acapulco is also a good road and should take about 5 hours to travel. However, this stretch of road has been the site of numerous car and bus hijackings and robberies in recent years—travel only during the day.

From Salina Cruz to Puerto Escondido is a 4-hour drive, past the Bahías de Huatulco and the turnoff for Puerto Angel. The road is paved but can be rutty during the rainy season. The trip from Huatulco to Puerto Escondido takes just under 2 hours; you can easily hire a taxi for a fixed rate of about $50 an hour.

By Bus   Buses run frequently to and from Acapulco and Oaxaca, and south along the coast to and from Huatulco and Pochutla, the transit hub for Puerto Angel. Puerto Escondido's several bus stations are all within a 3-block area. For **Gacela** and **Estrella Blanca,** the station is just north of the intersection of the coastal highway and Pérez Gasga. First-class buses go from here to Pochutla, Huatulco, Acapulco, Zihuatanejo, and Mexico City. A block north at Hidalgo and Primera Poniente is **Transportes Oaxaca Istmo,** in a small restaurant. Several buses leave daily for Pochutla, Salina Cruz (5 hr.), and Oaxaca (10 hr. via Salina Cruz). The terminal for **Líneas Unidas, Estrella del Valle,** and **Oaxaca Pacífico** is 2 blocks farther down on Hidalgo, just past Oriente 3. They serve Oaxaca via Pochutla. From Primera Norte 207, **Cristóbal Colón** buses (© **954/582-1073**) serve Salina Cruz, Tuxtla Gutiérrez, San Cristóbal de las Casas, and Oaxaca.

Arriving: Minibuses from Pochutla or Huatulco will let you off anywhere, including the spot where Pérez Gasga leads down to the pedestrians-only zone.

VISITOR INFORMATION   The **State Tourist Office, SEDETUR** (© **954/582-0175**), which has a very helpful staff, is about a half-mile from the airport at the corner of Carretera Costera and Bulevar Benito Juárez. It's open Monday through Friday from 9am to 5pm, Saturday from 9am to 2pm. A kiosk at the airport is open for incoming flights during high season; another, near the west end of the paved tourist zone, is open Monday through Saturday from 9am to 1pm.

Puerto Escondido

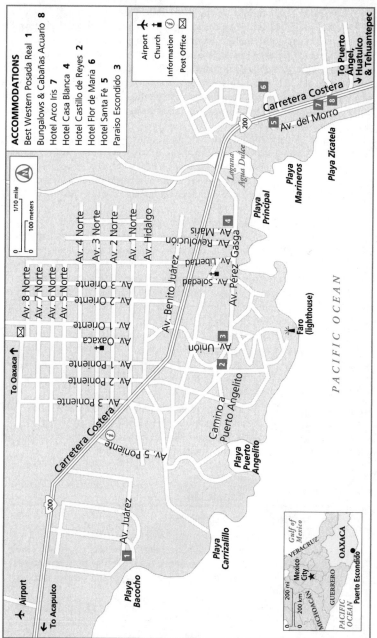

ACCOMMODATIONS

Best Western Posada Real **1**
Bungalows & Cabañas Acuario **8**
Hotel Arco Iris **7**
Hotel Casa Blanca **4**
Hotel Castillo de Reyes **2**
Hotel Flor de Maria **6**
Hotel Santa Fé **5**
Paraíso Escondido **3**

Airport ✈
Church ✝■
Information ⓘ
Post Office ☒

0   1/10 mile
0   100 meters

CITY LAYOUT   Looking out on the Bahía Principal and its beach, to your left you'll see the eastern end of the bay, consisting of a small beach, **Playa Marineros,** followed by rocks jutting into the sea. Beyond this is **Playa Zicatela,** unmistakably the main surfing beach. Zicatela Beach has come into its own as the most popular area for visitors, with restaurants, bungalows, surf shops, and hotels, well back from the shoreline. The west side of the bay, to your right, is about a mile long, with a lighthouse and a long stretch of fine sand. Beaches on this end are not quite as accessible by land, but hotels are overcoming this difficulty by constructing beach clubs reached by steep private roads and Jeep shuttles.

The town of Puerto Escondido has roughly an east-west orientation, with the long Zicatela Beach turning sharply southeast. Residential areas behind (east of) Zicatela Beach tend to have unpaved streets; the older town (with paved streets) is north of the Carretera Costera (Hwy. 200). The streets are numbered; Avenida Oaxaca divides east *(oriente)* from west *(poniente),* and Avenida Hidalgo divides north *(norte)* from south *(sur).*

South of this is the original **tourist zone,** through which Avenida Pérez Gasga makes a loop. Part of this loop is a paved pedestrians-only zone, known locally as the *Adoquín,* after the hexagonal bricks used in its paving. Hotels, shops, restaurants, bars, travel agencies, and other services are all here. In the morning, taxis, delivery trucks, and private vehicles may drive here, but at noon it closes to all but foot traffic.

Avenida Pérez Gasga angles down from the highway at the east end; on the west, where the Adoquín terminates, it climbs in a wide northward curve to cross the highway, after which it becomes Avenida Oaxaca.

The beaches—Playa Principal in the center of town and Marineros and Zicatela, southeast of the town center—are connected. It's easy to walk from one to the other, crossing behind the separating rocks. Puerto Angelito, Carrizalillo, and Bacocho beaches are west of town and accessible by road or water. Playa Bacocho is where you'll find the few more expensive hotels.

GETTING AROUND   Almost everything is within walking distance of the Adoquín. **Taxis** around town are inexpensive; call ℂ **954/582-0990** for service.

It's easy to hire a boat, and possible to walk beside the sea from the Playa Principal to the tiny beach of Puerto Angelito, though it's a bit of a hike.

FAST FACTS: Puerto Escondido

Area Code   The telephone area code is **954.**

Currency Exchange   Banamex, Bancomer, Bancrear, and Banco Bital all have branches in town, and all will change money during business hours; hours vary, but you can generally find one of the above open Monday through Saturday from 8am to 7pm. Automatic tellers are also available, as are currency-exchange offices.

Hospital   **Unidad Médico–Quirúrgica del Sur,** Av. Oaxaca 113 (ℂ **954/582-1288**), offers 24-hour emergency services and has an English-speaking staff and doctors.

Internet Access   The restaurant **Un Tigre Azul,** on the Adoquín, has an excellent cybercafe on its second floor (ℂ **954/582-2855**). It charges $2 for 30 minutes,

$4 per hour for Internet access. It's open Monday through Friday from 8am to 10pm, Saturday and Sunday from 8 to 10pm. On Zicatela Beach, **Cyber-café** is a small, extremely busy Internet service at the entrance to the Bungalows & Cabañas Acuario, Calle de Morro s/n (© **954/582-0357**). It's open daily from 8am to 9pm and charges just $1.50 for 15 minutes, $3 for a half-hour, $5 per hour.

Pharmacy **Farmacia de Más Ahorro,** Avenida 1 Norte at Avenida 2 Poniente (© **954/582-1911**), is open until 2am.

Post Office The *correo*, on Avenida Oaxaca at the corner of Avenida 7 Norte (© **954/582-0959**), is open Monday through Friday from 8am to 3pm.

Safety Depending on whom you talk to, you need to be wary of potential beach muggings, primarily at night. New lighting at Playa Principal and Playa Zicatela has caused the crime rate to drop considerably. Local residents say most incidents happen after tourists overindulge and then go for a midnight stroll along the beach. Puerto is so casual that it's an easy place to let your guard down. Don't carry valuables, and use common sense and normal precautions.

Also, respect the power of the magnificent waves here. Drownings occur all too frequently.

Seasons Season designations are somewhat arbitrary, but most consider high season to be from mid-December to January, around and during Easter week, July and August, and other school and business vacations.

Telephones Numerous businesses offer long-distance telephone service. Many are along the Adoquín; several accept credit cards. The best bet remains a pre-paid Ladatel phone card.

BEACH TIME

BEACHES **Playa Principal,** where small boats are available for fishing and tour services, and **Playa Marineros,** adjacent to the town center on a deep bay, are the best swimming beaches. Beach chairs and sun shades rent for about $2, which may be waived if you order food or drinks from the restaurants that offer them. **Playa Zicatela,** which has lifeguards, adjoins Playa Marineros and extends southeast for several kilometers. The surfing part of Zicatela, with large curling waves, is about 2.5km (1½ miles) from the town center. Due to the size and strength of the waves, it's not a swimming beach, and only experienced surfers should attempt to ride Zicatela's powerful waves. Stadium-style lighting has been installed in both of these areas, in an attempt to crack down on nighttime beach muggings. It has diminished the appeal of the Playa Principal restaurants—patrons now look into the bright lights rather than at the sea. Lifeguard service has recently been added to Playa Zicatela.

Barter with one of the fishermen on the main beach for a ride to **Playa Manzanillo** and **Puerto Angelito,** two beaches separated by a rocky outcropping. Here, and at other small coves just west of town, swimming is safe and the overall pace is calmer than in town. You'll also find *palapas,* hammock rentals, and snorkeling equipment. The clear blue water is perfect for snorkeling. Local entrepreneurs cook fresh fish, tamales, and other Mexican dishes right at the beach. Puerto Angelito is also accessible by a dirt road that's a short distance from town, so it tends to be busier. **Playa**

Ecotours & Other Adventurous Explorations

An exceptional provider of ecologically oriented tour services is **Ana's Eco Tours** 🐾🐾, in Un Tigre Azul restaurant, on the Adoquín (© **954/582-2001**). Ana Marquez was born in the small nearby mountain village of Jamiltepec, and has an intimate knowledge of the customs, people, flora, and fauna of the area. She and her expert guides lead small groups on both eco-adventures and cultural explorations. Tours into the surrounding mountains include a 5-hour horseback excursion up to the jungle region of the Chatino natives' **healing hot springs,** or to **Nopala,** a Chatino mountain village, and a neighboring coffee plantation. An all-day trip to **Jamiltepec** (a small, traditional Mixtex village) offers the opportunity to experience day-to-day life in an authentic village. It includes a stop at a market, church, and cemetery, and visits to the homes of local artisans.

Turismo Dimar Travel Agency, on the landward side just inside the Adoquín (© **954/582-0734;** fax 954/582-1551; daily 8am–10pm), is another excellent source of information and can arrange all types of tours and travel. Manager Gaudencio Díaz speaks English and can arrange individualized tours or more organized ones, such as **Michael Malone's Hidden Voyages Ecotours.** Malone, a Canadian ornithologist, leads dawn and sunset trips to **Manialtepec Lagoon,** a bird-filled mangrove lagoon about 19km (12 miles) northwest of Puerto Escondido. The tour ($32) includes a stop on a secluded beach for a swim.

One of the most popular all-day tours offered by both companies is to **Chacahua Lagoon National Park,** about 67km (42 miles) west. It costs $38 with Dimar, $25 with Ana's. These are true ecotours—small groups treading lightly. You visit a beautiful sandy spit of beach and the lagoon, which has incredible bird life and flowers, including black orchids. Locals provide fresh barbecued fish on the beach. If you know Spanish and get information from the tourism office, it's possible to stay overnight under a small *palapa,* but bring plenty of insect repellent.

Fishermen keep their colorful *pangas* (small boats) on the beach beside the Adoquín. A **fisherman's tour** around the coastline in a *panga* costs about $39, but a ride to Zicatela or Puerto Angelito beaches is only $5. Most hotels offer or will gladly arrange tours to meet your needs.

Bacocho is on a shallow cove farther northwest and is best reached by taxi or boat, rather than on foot. It's also the location of Coco's Beach Club at the Posada Real Hotel. A charge of $2.50 gives you access to pools, food and beverage service, and facilities.

SURFING Zicatela Beach, 2.5km (1½ miles) southeast of Puerto Escondido's town center, is a world-class surf spot. A surfing competition in August and Fiesta Puerto Escondido, held for at least 3 days each November, celebrate Puerto Escondido's renowned waves. The tourism office can supply dates and details. Beginning surfers often start out at Playa Marineros before graduating to Zicatela's awesome waves.

NESTING RIDLEY TURTLES   The beaches around Puerto Escondido and Puerto Angel are nesting grounds for the endangered Ridley turtle. During the summer, tourists can sometimes see the turtles laying eggs or observe the hatchlings trekking to the sea.

Escobilla Beach near Puerto Escondido and **Barra de la Cruz Beach** near Puerto Angel seem to be the favored nesting grounds of the Ridley turtle. In 1991, the Mexican government established the Centro Mexicano la Tortuga, known locally as the **Turtle Museum.** On view are examples of all species of marine turtles living in Mexico, plus six species of freshwater turtles and two species of land turtles. The center (no phone) is on **Mazunte Beach** ✿, near the town of the same name. Hours are from 10am to 4:30pm Tuesday through Saturday, from 10am to 2pm Sunday; admission is $2.50. The museum has a unique shop that sells excellent naturally produced shampoos, bath oils, and other personal-care products. All are made and packaged by the local community as part of a project to replace lost income from turtle poaching. Buses go to Mazunte from Puerto Angel about every half-hour, and a taxi ride is around $5.50. You can fit this in with a trip to Zipolite Beach (see "A Trip to Puerto Angel," later in this chapter). Buses from Puerto Escondido don't stop in Mazunte; you can cover the 65km (40 miles) in a taxi or rental car.

AN UNUSUAL SPA EXPERIENCE   For terrific massage services—the ideal answer to a day spent in pounding surf—**Espacio Meditativo Temazcalli,** Calle Temazcalli, corner with Av. Infraganti (✆ **954/582-1023;** www.temazcalli.com) is the place to go. A variety of therapeutic massages range in price from $15 to $32. There are also Body Beauty treatments ($27–$33) and facials ($27), designed to minimize the effects of too much sun. Bioenergetic Balance Techniques and the indigenous Mexican Temazcal steam bath (both individual and group), are added treatments, designed to purify body and soul. The center is a tranquil haven, lushly landscaped, with the sound of the nearby ocean prevalent in the treatment areas. On full moon nights, they feature a special group Temazcal ceremony, a truly fascinating experience!

SHOPPING

During high season, businesses and shops are generally open all day. During low season, they close between 2 and 5pm.

The Adoquín holds a row of tourist shops selling straw hats, postcards, and T-shirts, plus a few excellent shops featuring Guatemalan, Oaxacan, and Balinese clothing and art. You can also get a tattoo or rent surfboards and boogie boards. Interspersed among the shops, hotels, restaurants, and bars are pharmacies and minimarkets. The largest of these is **Oh! Mar,** Av. Pérez Gasga 502. It sells anything you'd need for a day at the beach, plus phone (Ladatel) cards, stamps, and Cuban cigars, has a mail drop box, and arranges fishing tours.

Highlights along the Adoquín include **Central Surf,** which has a shop on the Adoquín (✆ **954/582-0568;** www.centralsurfshop.com) and another on Zicatela Beach, Calle del Morro s/n (✆ **954/582-2285**). They rent and sell surfboards, offer surf lessons, and sell related gear. **Un Tigre Azul,** Av. Pérez Gasga s/n (✆ **954/582-2954**), is the only true art gallery in town, with quality work and a cafe-bar, plus Internet service upstairs.

Also of interest is **Bazar Santa Fe** ✿✿, Hotel Santa Fe lobby, Calle del Morro s/n, Zicatela Beach (✆ **954/582-0170**), which sells antiques, including vintage Oaxacan embroidered clothing, jewelry, and religious artifacts. At **Bikini Brazil,** Calle del

Morro s/n (no phone), you'll find the hottest bikinis under the sun imported from Brazil, land of the *tanga* (string bikini). **ego Hardcore Wear,** located on Zicatela Beach, between Bugalows Acali and Hotel Arco Iris, has the hottest selection of surf and babe-wear. It's open daily from 10am to 8pm; no phone. Adjacent to ego is the **360 Surf Shop,** which sells everything for your out-of-town surf needs, as well as sells, trades, and rents boards. Board rentals start at $10 per day, with lessons available for $20. They don't have a phone number, but you can contact them by e-mailing 360@puertoconnection.com. In front of the Rockaway Resort on Zicatela Beach, there's a 24-hour **mini-super** (no phone) that sells the necessities: beer, suntan lotion, and basic food.

WHERE TO STAY
MODERATE

Best Western Posada Real *Kids*   On a cliff top overlooking the beach, the expanse of manicured lawn that backs this hotel is one of the most popular places in town for a sunset cocktail. The smallish standard rooms are less enticing than the hotel grounds. A big plus here is Coco's Beach Club, with a half-mile stretch of soft-sand beach, large swimming pool, playground, and bar with occasional live music. A shuttle ride (or a lengthy walk down a set of stairs) will take you there. This is a great place for families, and it's open to the public (nonguests pay $2.50 to enter). The hotel is 5 minutes from the airport and about the same from Puerto Escondido's tourist zone, but you'll need a taxi to get to town.

Av. Benito Juárez 1, Fracc. Bacocho, 71980 Puerto Escondido, Oax. ✆ **800/528-1234** in the U.S., or 954/582-0133. Fax 01-800/719-5236. 100 units. High season $120 double; low season $104 double. AE, MC, V. **Amenities:** 2 restaurants; lobby bar; beach club w/food service; 2 swimming pools; wading pool; putting green; tennis courts; travel agency; car rental; laundry service. *In room:* A/C, TV, hair dryer, safe-deposit box.

Hotel Santa Fe *★★★* *Finds*   If Puerto Escondido is the best beach value in Mexico, then the Santa Fe is without a doubt one of the best hotel values in Mexico. It boasts a winning combination of unique Spanish-colonial style, a welcoming staff, and comfortable rooms. The hotel has grown up with the surfers who came to Puerto in the 1960s and 1970s and nostalgically return today. It's a half-mile southeast of the town center, off Highway 200, at the curve in the road where Marineros and Zicatela beaches join—a prime sunset-watching spot. The three-story hacienda-style buildings have clay-tiled stairs, archways, and blooming bougainvillea. They surround two courtyard swimming pools. The ample but simply stylish rooms feature large tile bathrooms, colonial furnishings, hand-woven fabrics, Guerrero pottery lamps, and both air-conditioning and ceiling fans. Most have a balcony or terrace, with ocean views from upper floors. Bungalows are next to the hotel; each has a living room, kitchen, and bedroom with two double beds. The restaurant (see "Where to Dine," below) is one of the best on the southern Pacific coast.

Calle del Morro (Apdo. Postal 96), 71980 Puerto Escondido, Oax. ✆ **954/582-0170** or 954/582-0266. Fax 954/582-0260. info@hotelsantafe.com.mx. 61 units, 8 bungalows. High season $100 double, $120 bungalow; low season $78 double, $100 bungalow. AE, MC, V. Free parking. **Amenities:** Restaurant; bar; swimming pool; lap pool; tour service; massage; babysitting; laundry. *In room:* A/C, TV, safe-deposit box.

Paraíso Escondido *★★★* *Finds*   This eclectic inn is hidden away on a shady street a couple of short blocks from the Adoquín and Playa Principal. A curious collection of Mexican folk art, masks, religious art, and paintings make this an exercise in Mexican magic realism, in addition to a tranquil place to stay. An inviting pool—surrounded by gardens, Adirondack chairs, and a fountain—affords a commanding view of the bay. The immaculate rooms each have one double and one twin bed, built-in desks, and a cozy balcony or terrace with French doors. The suites have much plusher decor than the rooms, with recessed lighting, desks set into bay windows, living areas, and large private balconies. The penthouse suite has a whirlpool tub and kitchenette, a tile chessboard inlaid in the floor, and murals adorning the walls—it is the owners' former apartment.

Calle Unión 10, 71980 Puerto Escondido, Oax. ℂ **954/582-0444**. 25 units. $45–$77 double; $150 suite. No credit cards. Limited free parking. **Amenities:** Restaurant; bar; pool; tour desk. *In room:* A/C.

INEXPENSIVE

Bungalows & Cabañas Acuario ★
Facing Zicatela Beach, this surfer's sanctuary offers cheap accommodations plus an on-site gym, surf shop, vegetarian restaurant, and Internet cafe. The two-story hotel and bungalows surround a pool shaded by great palms. Rooms are small and basic; bungalows offer fundamental kitchen facilities but don't have air-conditioning. The cabañas are more open and have hammocks. The adjoining commercial area has public telephones, money exchange, a pharmacy, and a vegetarian restaurant. The well-equipped gym costs an extra $1 per day, $15 per month. If you're traveling during low season, you can probably negotiate a better deal than the rates listed below once you're there.

Calle del Morro s/n, 71980 Puerto Escondido, Oax. ℂ **954/582-0357** or 954/582-1027. 40 units. High season $55 double, $70 double with A/C, $93 bungalow; low season $25 double, $34 double with A/C, $40 bungalow. No credit cards. **Amenities:** Restaurant; gym.

Hotel Arco Iris ★ *Value*
Rooms at the Arco Iris are in a three-story colonial-style house that faces Zicatela Beach. Each is simple yet comfortable, with a spacious terrace or balcony with hangers for hammocks—all have great views, but the upstairs ones are better. Beds are draped with mosquito nets, and bedspreads are made with beautifully worked Oaxacan textiles. La Galera bar has one of the most popular happy hours in town, daily from 5 to 7pm, with live music during high season. Ample free parking for cars and campers is available.

Calle del Morro s/n, Playa Zicatela, 71980 Puerto Escondido, Oax. ℂ **954/582-0432**. Fax 954/582-2963. www.puerto connection.com/arco.html. 26 units, 8 bungalows. $42–$46 double; $46–$50 double with kitchen. Extra person $4. Rates 10%–20% higher at Easter and Christmas. MC, V. **Amenities:** Restaurant; bar; pool; wading pool; TV/game room w/foreign channels; tour desk; drugstore; on-call medical services.

Hotel Casa Blanca ★ *Value*
If you want to be in the heart of the Adoquín, this is your best bet for excellent value and ample accommodations. The courtyard pool and adjacent *palapa* restaurant make great places to hide away and enjoy a margarita or a book from the hotel's exchange rack. The bright, simply furnished rooms offer a choice of bed combinations, but all have at least two beds and a fan. Some rooms have both air-conditioning and a minifridge. The best rooms have a balcony overlooking the action in the street below, but light sleepers should consider a room in the back. Some rooms accommodate up to five ($60). This is an excellent and economical choice for families.

Av. Pérez Gasga 905, 71980 Puerto Escondido, Oax. ℂ **954/582-0168**. 21 units. $29 double; $84 double with A/C. MC, V. **Amenities:** Restaurant; pool; tour desk; car rental; room service; in-room massage; safe-deposit boxes; money exchange. *In room:* TV.

Hotel Castillo de Reyes
Proprietor Don Fernando has a knack for making his guests feel at home. Guests chat around tables on a shady patio near the office. Most of the bright, white-walled rooms have a special touch—perhaps a gourd mask or

carved coconut hanging over the bed, plus over-bed reading lights. The rooms are shaded from the sun by palms and cooled by fans. The "castle" is on your left as you ascend the hill on Pérez Gasga, after leaving the Adoquín (you can also enter Pérez Gasga off Hwy. 200). This hotel is on one of Puerto's busiest streets, so traffic noise is a consideration.

Av. Pérez Gasga s/n, 71980 Puerto Escondido, Oax. © 954/582-0442. 18 units. High season $25 double; low season $15 double. No credit cards. **Amenities:** Safe-deposit box; money exchange.

Hotel Flor de María   Though not right on the beach, this hotel offers a welcoming place to stay. This cheery, three-story hotel faces the ocean, which you can see from the rooftop. Built around a garden courtyard, each room is colorfully decorated with beautiful trompe l'oeil still lifes and landscapes. Two rooms have windows with a view, and the rest face the courtyard. All have double beds with orthopedic mattresses. The roof has a small pool, a shaded hammock terrace, and an open-air bar (open 5–9pm during high season) with a TV that receives American channels—all in all, a great sunset spot. The hotel is a third of a mile from the Adoquín, 60m (200 ft.) up a sandy road from Marineros Beach on an unnamed street at the eastern end of the beach.

Playa Marineros, 71980 Puerto Escondido, Oax. ©/fax 954/582-0536. 24 units. $35–$50 double. Ask about off-season long-term discounts. MC, V. **Amenities:** Restaurant; bar; small pool.

WHERE TO DINE

In addition to the places listed below, a Puerto Escondido tradition is the *palapa* restaurants on Zicatela Beach, for early-morning surfer breakfasts or casual dining and drinking at night. One of the most popular is **Los Tíos**, offering very reasonable prices and surfer-sized portions. After dinner, enjoy homemade Italian ice cream from **Gelateria Giardino.** It has two locations, on Calle del Morro at Zicatela Beach, and Pérez Gasga 609, on the Adoquín (© **954/582-2243**).

MODERATE

Art & Harry's SEAFOOD/STEAKS   About 1.2km (¾ mile) southeast of the Hotel Santa Fe, on the road fronting Zicatela Beach, this robust watering hole is great for taking in the sunset, especially if you're having a giant hamburger or grilled shrimp dinner. Late afternoon and early evening here affords the best portrait of Puerto Escondido. Watch surfers, tourists, and the resident cat all slip into lazy silhouette as the sun dips into the ocean.

Av. Morro s/n. No phone. Main courses $4.50–$15. No credit cards. Daily 10am–10pm.

Cabo Blanco ★★ INTERNATIONAL   "Where Legends are Born" is the logo at this beachside restaurant, and the local crowd craves Gary's special sauces, which top his grilled fish, shrimp, steaks, and ribs. Favorites include dill–Dijon mustard, wine-fennel, and Thai curry sauces. But you can't count on them, because Gary creates based on what's fresh. A bonus is that Cabo Blanco turns into a hot Zicatela Beach bar, with live music Thursday and Saturday after 11pm. Gary's wife, Roxana, and a top-notch team of bartenders keeps the crowd well served and well behaved.

Calle del Morro s/n. © 954/582-0337. Main courses $7–$45. V. Dec–Apr daily 6pm–2am. Closed May–Nov.

Restaurant Santa Fe ★★★ *Finds* INTERNATIONAL   The atmosphere here is classic and casual, with great views of the sunset and Zicatela Beach. Big pots of palms are scattered around and fresh flowers grace the tables, all beneath a lofty *palapa* roof. The shrimp dishes are a bargain for the rest of the world, at $15, but a little higher-priced than elsewhere in town. Perfectly grilled tuna, served with homemade french-fried pota-toes and whole-grain bread, is an incredible meal for under $10. A *nopal* (cactus leaf) salad on the side ($2.50) is a perfect complement. Vegetarian dishes are reasonably priced and creatively adapted from traditional Mexican and Italian dishes. A favorite is the house specialty, chiles rellenos. The bar offers an excellent selection of tequilas.

In the Hotel Santa Fe, Calle del Morro s/n. © **954/582-0170.** Breakfast $4.50–$6; main courses $5–$15. AE, MC, V. Daily 7am–11pm.

INEXPENSIVE

Arte la Galería ⭐⭐ INTERNATIONAL/SEAFOOD   At the east end of the Ado-quín, La Galería offers a satisfying range of eats in a cool, creative setting. Dark-wood beams tower above, contemporary works by local artists grace the walls, and jazz music plays. Specialties are homemade pastas and brick-oven pizzas, but burgers and steaks are also available. Cappuccino and espresso, plus desserts such as baked pineapples, finish the meal. Two years ago, La Galería opened a second location in Playa Zicatela (next to Casa Babylon and Arco Iris Hotel, see above; no phone). Beautifully deco-rated with tiny mosaic tiles on the bar and in the bathrooms, the second Galería serves up the same great fare in a beautiful garden setting.

Av. Pérez Gasga. © **954/582-2039.** Breakfast $2.50–$3; main courses $4–$13. No credit cards. Daily 8am–midnight.

Carmen's Cafecito ⭐⭐ *Value* FRENCH PASTRY/SEAFOOD/VEGETARIAN/ COFFEE   Carmen's second shop opened a few years ago on Zicatela Beach, with the motto "Big waves, strong coffee!" Featuring all the attractions of Carmen's La Patisserie (below), it also serves lunch and dinner. This restaurant spans two facing corners. The northern corner is set up for coffee or a light snack, with oceanfront bistro-style seating. The southern corner, a more relaxed setting, has wicker chairs and Oaxacan cloth–topped tables under a *palapa* roof. Giant shrimp dinners cost less than $6, and creative daily spe-cials are always a sure bet. An oversize mug of cappuccino is $1.20, and a mango éclair—worth any price—is a steal at $1.

Calle del Morro s/n, Playa Zicatela. © **954/582-0516.** Pastries 50¢–$1.50; main courses $2.10–$5.70. No credit cards. Wed–Mon 6am–10pm.

Carmen's La Patisserie ⭐⭐ FRENCH PASTRY/SANDWICHES/COFFEE This tiny, excellent cafe and bakery attracts a loyal clientele. Carmen's baked goods are unforgettable and sell quickly, so arrive early for the best selection. She also provides space for an English-speaking AA group. La Patisserie is across the street from the Hotel Flor de María.

Playa Marineros. No phone. Pastries 60¢–$1.50; sandwiches $2.10–$2.70. No credit cards. Mon–Sat 7am–3pm; Sun 7am–noon.

El Jardín ⭐⭐ *Value* VEGETARIAN/COFFEE   Located in front of the Bungalows Acuario, this popular vegetarian restaurant (formerly El Gota Vida) facing Zicatela Beach is generally packed. It's known for its healthy food, ample portions, and low prices. Under a *palapa* roof, it offers an extensive menu that includes fruit smoothies, espresso drinks, herbal teas, and a complete juice bar. The restaurant makes its own tempeh, tofu, pastas, and whole-grain breads. Creative vegetarian offerings are based on Mexican favorites, like chiles rellenos, cheese enchiladas, and bean tostadas. El Jardin also features fresh seafood.

Calle del Morro s/n, Playa Zicatela. No phone. Main courses $1.80–$5.40. No credit cards. Daily 10am–11pm.

Herman's Best (Value) MEXICAN/SEAFOOD   This small restaurant's atmosphere is about as basic as it comes, but clearly Herman's is putting all its attention into the kitchen—offering simply delicious, home-style cooking. The menu changes daily, but generally includes a fresh fish filet, rotisserie chicken, and Mexican staples like enchiladas—all served with beans, rice, and homemade tortillas. Herman's Best is just outside the pedestrian-only zone at the eastern end of the Adoquín.

Av. Pérez Gasga s/n. No phone. Main courses $1.80–$4.20. No credit cards. Mon–Sat 5–10pm.

Un Tigre Azul SANDWICHES/COFFEE/MEXICAN   This place is primarily known for its lower-level art gallery and Internet access, but climb on up to the third floor and enjoy the view overlooking Playa Principal and the ambience of the casual, colorful cafe. It's near the western entrance to the Adoquín. The light fare includes quesadillas, nachos, fruit smoothies, and sandwiches. There's also excellent coffee and a full bar. Happy hour is every night from 7 to 8pm.

Av. Pérez Gasga s/n. © 954/582-2954. Breakfast $2–$4; sandwiches $2–$5. AE, MC, V. Mon–Fri 11am–11pm; Sat–Sun 3–11pm.

PUERTO ESCONDIDO AFTER DARK

Sunset-watching is a ritual to plan your days around, and good lookout points abound. Watch the surfers at Zicatela and catch up on local gossip at **La Galera,** on the third floor of the Arco Iris hotel. It has a nightly happy hour (with live music during high season) from 5 to 7pm. Other great sunset spots are the **Hotel Santa Fe,** at the junction of Zicatela and Marineros beaches, and the rooftop bar of **Hotel Flor de María.** For a more tranquil, romantic setting, take a cab or walk a half-hour or so west to the cliff-top lawn of the **Hotel Posada Real.**

Puerto's nightlife will satisfy anyone dedicated to late nights and good music. Most nightspots are open until 3am or until the customers leave. **El Son y la Rumba** features live jazz, by its house band, each night from 8 to 11pm. It switches over to DJ's playing house music Wednesdays through Saturdays, after 11pm. The cover is $1.20. It's beneath the Un Tigre Azul, on the western end of the Adoquín. Also downtown is **Tequila Sunrise,** a spacious two-story disco overlooking the beach. It plays Latino, reggae, *cumbia,* tropical, and salsa. It's a half-block from the Adoquín on Avenida Marina Nacional. A small cover charge ($1.20–$2.40) generally applies.

The Adoquín offers an ample selection of clubs. Among the favorites are **BarFly,** and located across the street, **Wipeout,** a multilevel club that packs in the crowds until 4am. **The Blue Iguana,** and **Rayos X** cater to a younger surf crowd with alternative and techno tunes. **Montezuma's Revenge** has live bands that usually play contemporary Latin American music. **El Tubo** is an open-air beachside disco just west of Restaurant Alicia on the Adoquín.

On Zicatela Beach, don't miss **Cabo Blanco** (see "Where to Dine," above), where local musicians get together and jam on Thursday and Saturday during high season, alternating with DJs. An added draw are the complimentary snacks with drink purchase, in the style of Mexico's cantina tradition. **Split Coco,** a few doors down, has live music on Tuesday and Friday, and TV sports on other nights. It has one of the most popular happy hours on the beach, and also serves barbecue.

A TRIP TO PUERTO ANGEL: BACKPACKING BEACH HAVEN

Eighty kilometers (50 miles) southeast of Puerto Escondido and 48km (30 miles) northwest of the Bays of Huatulco is the tiny fishing port of **Puerto Angel** (*pwer*-toh *ahn*-hehl). Puerto Angel, with its beautiful beaches, unpaved streets, and budget

---

(*Tips* **Important Travel Note**

Although car and bus hijackings along Highway 200 north to Acapulco have greatly decreased (thanks to improved security measures and police patrols), you're still wise to travel this road only during the day.

---

hotels, is popular with the international backpacking set and those seeking an inexpensive and restful vacation. Repeated hurricane damage and the 1999 earthquake took its toll on the village, driving the best accommodations out of business, but Puerto Angel continues to attract visitors. Its small bay and several inlets offer peaceful swimming and good snorkeling. The village's way of life is slow and simple: Fishermen leave very early in the morning and return with their catch before noon. Taxis make up most of the traffic, and the bus from Pochutla passes every half-hour or so.

ESSENTIALS

GETTING THERE & DEPARTING   By Car   North or south from Highway 200, take coastal Highway 175 inland to Puerto Angel. The road is well marked with signs to Puerto Angel. From Huatulco or Puerto Escondido, the trip should take about an hour.

By Taxi   Taxis are readily available to take you to Puerto Angel or Zipolite Beach for a reasonable price, or to the Huatulco airport or Puerto Escondido.

By Bus   There are no direct buses from Puerto Escondido or Huatulco to Puerto Angel; however, numerous buses leave Puerto Escondido and Huatulco for Pochutla, 11km (7 miles) north of Puerto Angel. Take the bus to Pochutla, then switch to a bus going to Puerto Angel. If you arrive in Pochutla from Huatulco or Puerto Escondido, you may be dropped at one of several bus stations that line the main street; walk 1 or 2 blocks toward the large sign reading POSADA DON JOSE. The buses to Puerto Angel are in the lot just before the sign.

ORIENTATION   The town center is only about 4 blocks long, oriented more or less east-west. There are few signs in the village, and off the main street much of Puerto Angel is a narrow sand-and-dirt path. The navy base is toward the west end of town, just before the creek crossing toward Playa Panteón (Cemetery Beach).

Puerto Angel has several public (Ladatel) telephones that use widely available prepaid phone cards. The closest bank is **Bancomer** in Pochutla, which changes money Monday through Friday from 9am to 6pm, Saturday from 9am to 1pm. The **post office** *(correo),* open Monday through Friday from 9am to 3:30pm, is on the curve as you enter town.

BEACHES, WATERSPORTS & BOAT TRIPS

The golden sands and peaceful village life of Puerto Angel are all the reasons you'll need to visit. Playa Principal, the main beach, lies between the Mexican navy base and the pier that's home to the local fishing fleet. Near the pier, fishermen pull their colorful boats onto the beach and unload their catch in the late morning while trucks wait to haul it off to processing plants in Veracruz. The rest of the beach seems light years from the world of work and commitments. Except on Mexican holidays, it's relatively deserted. It's important to note that Pacific Coast currents deposit trash on Puerto Angel beaches. The locals do a fairly good job of keeping it picked up, but the currents are constant.

Playa Panteón is the main swimming and snorkeling beach. Cemetery Beach, ominous as that sounds, is about a 15-minute walk from the center, straight through town on the main street that skirts the beach. The *panteón* (cemetery), on the right, is worth a visit—it holds brightly colored tombstones and equally brilliant blooming bougainvillea.

In Playa Panteón, some of the *palapa* restaurants and a few of the hotels rent snorkeling and scuba gear and can arrange boat trips, but they tend to be expensive. Check the quality and condition of gear—particularly scuba gear—that you're renting.

Playa Zipolite (see-poh-*lee*-teh) and its village are 6km (4 miles) down a paved road from Puerto Angel. Taxis charge less than $2. You can catch a *colectivo* on the main street in the town center and share the cost.

Zipolite is well known as a good surf break and as a nude beach. Although public nudity (including topless sunbathing) is technically illegal, it's allowed here—this is one of only a handful of beaches in Mexico that permits it. This sort of open-mindedness has attracted an increasing number of young European travelers. Most sunbathers concentrate beyond a large rock outcropping at the far end of the beach. Police will occasionally patrol the area, but they are much more intent on drug users than on sunbathers. The ocean and currents here are quite strong (that's why the surf is so good!), and a number of drownings have occurred over the years—know your limits. There are places to tie up a hammock and a few *palapa* restaurants for a light lunch and a cold beer.

Hotels in Playa Zipolite are basic and rustic; most have rugged walls and palapa roofs. Prices range from $10 to $50 a night.

Traveling north on Highway 175, you'll come to another hot surf break and a beach of spectacular beauty: **Playa San Augustinillo.** One of the pleasures of a stay in Puerto Angel is discovering the many hidden beaches nearby and spending the day. Local boatmen and hotels can give details and quote rates for this service.

You can stay in Puerto Angel near Playa Principal in the tiny town, or at Playa Panteón. Most accommodations are basic, older, cement-block style hotels, not meriting a full-blown description. Between Playa Panteón and town are several bungalow and guesthouse setups with budget accommodations.

4 Bahías de Huatulco

64km (40 miles) SE of Puerto Angel; 680km (425 miles) SE of Acapulco

Huatulco has the same unspoiled nature and laid-back attitude as its neighbors to the north, Puerto Angel and Puerto Escondido, but with a difference. In the midst of natural splendor, you'll also encounter indulgent hotels and modern roads and facilities.

Pristine beaches and jungle landscapes can make for an idyllic retreat from the stress of daily life—and when viewed from a luxury hotel balcony, even better. Huatulco is for those who want to enjoy the beauty of nature during the day, then retreat to well-appointed comfort by night.

Undeveloped stretches of pure white sand and isolated coves await the promised growth of Huatulco, but it's not catching on as rapidly as Cancún, the previous resort planned by FONATUR, Mexico's Tourism Development arm. FONATUR development of the Bahías de Huatulco is an ambitious project that aims to cover 21,000 hectares (52,000 acres) of land, with over 16,000 hectares (40,000 acres) to remain ecological preserves. The small local communities have been transplanted from the coast into Crucecita. The area consists of three sections: **Santa Cruz, Crucecita,** and **Tangolunda Bay** (see "City Layout," below).

Though Huatulco has increasingly become known for its ecotourism attractions—including river rafting, rappelling, and hiking jungle trails—it has yet to develop a true personality. There's little shopping, nightlife, or even dining outside the hotels, and what is available is expensive for the quality. However, the service in the area shines.

The planned opening of a new cruise ship dock in Santa Cruz Bay may change the level of activity in Huatulco, providing the sleepy resort with an important business boost. The new dock's plans call for it to handle up to two 3,000-passenger cruise ships at a time (passengers are currently ferried to shore aboard tenders). Also slated to open soon is a new "ecoarchaeological" park, Punta Celeste. This new development is all being handled with ecological sensitivity in mind.

If you're drawn to snorkeling, diving, boat cruises, and simple relaxation, Huatulco nicely fits the bill. Nine bays encompass 36 beaches and countless inlets and coves. Huatulco's main problem has been securing enough incoming flights. It relies heavily on charter service from the United States and Canada.

ESSENTIALS

GETTING THERE   By Plane   Mexicana flights (© **800/531-7921** in the U.S.; 958/587-0223 or 958/587-0260 at the airport) connect Huatulco with Cancún, Chicago, Guadalajara, Los Angeles, Miami, San Antonio, San Francisco, San Jose, and Toronto by way of Mexico City.

From Huatulco's international airport (airport code: HUX; © **958/581-9004** or -9005), about 19km (12 miles) northwest of the Bahías de Huatulco, private **taxis** charge $40 to Crucecita, $42 to Santa Cruz, and $48 to Tangolunda. **Transportes Terrestres** (© **958/581-9014**) *colectivo* minibus fares are $8 to $10 per person. When returning, make sure to ask for a taxi, unless you have a lot of luggage. Taxis to the airport run $40, but unless specifically requested, you'll get a Suburban, which costs $54.

Budget (© **800/322-9976** in the U.S., 958/587-0010, or 958/581-9000) has an office at the airport that is open for flight arrivals. Daily rates run around $71 for a VW sedan, $104 for a Sentra or Geo Tracker, and $123 for a Jeep Ranger. **Dollar** also has rental offices at the Royal, Barceló, and downtown, and offers one-way drop service if you're traveling to Puerto Escondido. Because Huatulco is so spread out and has excellent roads, you may want to consider a rental car, at least for 1 or 2 days, to explore the area.

By Car   Coastal Highway 200 leads to Huatulco (via Pochutla) from the north and is generally in good condition. The drive from Puerto Escondido takes just under 2 hours. The road is well maintained, but it's windy and doesn't have lights, so avoid travel after sunset. Allow at least 6 hours for the trip from Oaxaca City on mountainous Highway 175.

By Bus   There are three bus stations in Crucecita, all within a few blocks, but none in Santa Cruz or Tangolunda. The **Gacela** and **Estrella Blanca** station, at the corner of Gardenia and Palma Real, handles service to Acapulco, Mexico City, Puerto Escondido, and Pochutla. The **Cristóbal Colón** station (© **958/587-0261**) is at the corner of Gardenia and Ocotillo, 4 blocks from the Plaza Principal. It serves destinations throughout Mexico, including Oaxaca, Puerto Escondido, and Pochutla. The **Estrella del Valle** station, on Jasmin between Sabali and Carrizal, serves Oaxaca.

VISITOR INFORMATION   The **State Tourism Office,** or Oficina del Turismo (© **958/581-0176;** fax 958/581-0177; www.BaysofHuatulco.com.mx), has an information module in Tangalundo Bay, near the Grand Pacific hotel. It's open from 9am to 3pm and 6 to 8pm.

CITY LAYOUT The overall resort area is called **Bahías de Huatulco** and includes nine bays. The town of Santa María de Huatulco, the original settlement in this area, is 27km (17 miles) inland. **Santa Cruz Huatulco,** usually called Santa Cruz, was the first developed area on the coast. It has a central plaza with a bandstand kiosk, which has been converted into a cafe that serves regionally grown coffee. It also has an artisans' market on the edge of the plaza that borders the main road, a few hotels and restaurants, and a marina where bay tours and fishing trips set sail. **Juárez** is Santa Cruz's 4-block-long main street, anchored at one end by the Hotel Castillo Huatulco and at the other by the Meigas Binniguenda hotel. Opposite the Hotel Castillo is the marina, and beyond it are restaurants in new colonial-style buildings facing the beach. The area's banks are on Juárez. It's impossible to get lost and you can take in almost everything at a glance. This bay will be the site of Huatulco's new cruise ship dock.

About 3km (1½ miles) inland from Santa Cruz is **Crucecita,** a planned city that sprang up in 1985. It centers on a lovely grassy plaza. This is the residential area for the resorts, with neighborhoods of new stucco homes mixed with small apartment complexes. Crucecita has evolved into a lovely, traditional town where you'll find the area's best, and most reasonably priced, restaurants, plus some shopping and several less expensive hotels.

Until other bays are developed, **Tangolunda Bay,** 5km (3 miles) east, is the focal point of development. Over time, half the bays will have resorts. For now, Tangolunda has an 18-hole golf course, as well as the Las Brisas, Quinta Real, Barceló Huatulco, Royal, Casa del Mar, and Camino Real Zaashila hotels, among others. Small strip centers with a few restaurants occupy each end of Tangolunda Bay. **Chahué Bay,** between Tangolunda and Santa Cruz, is a small bay with a beach club, and other facilities under construction along with houses and a few small hotels.

GETTING AROUND Crucecita, Santa Cruz, and Tangolunda are too far apart to walk, but **taxis** are inexpensive and readily available. Crucecita has taxi stands opposite the Hotel Grifer and on the Plaza Principal. Taxis are readily available through hotels in Santa Cruz and Tangolunda. The fare between Santa Cruz and Tangolunda is roughly $2.50; between Santa Cruz and Crucecita, $2; between Crucecita and Tangolunda, $3. To explore the area, you can hire a taxi by the hour (about $15 per hr.) or for the day.

There is **minibus service** between towns; the fare is 50¢. In Santa Cruz, catch the bus across the street from Castillo Huatulco; in Tangolunda, in front of the Grand Pacific; and in Crucecita, cater-cornered from the Hotel Grifer.

FAST FACTS: **Bahías de Huatulco**

Area Code The area code is **958.**

Banks All three areas have banks with ATMs, including the main Mexican banks, Banamex and Bancomer. They change money during business hours, Monday through Friday from 9am to 5pm, Saturday from 10am to 1pm. Banks are along Calle Juárez in Santa Cruz, and surrounding the central plaza in Crucecita.

Emergencies **Police emergency** (© 060); **local police** (© 958/587-0815); **transit police** (© 958/587-0186); and **Red Cross,** Bulevar Chahué 110 (© 958/587-1188).

Medical Care **Dr. Ricardo Carrillo** (☎ **958/587-0687** or 958/587-0600) speaks English.

Information The **State Tourism Office** (Oficina del Turismo; ☎ **958/581-0176** or -0177; sedetur6@oaxaca.gob.mx) has an information module in Tangolunda Bay near the Grand Pacific hotel, and another inside the Gala Resort.

Internet Access An Internet cafe is located on the ground-floor level of the **Hotel Plaza Conejo,** Av. Guamuchil 208, across from the main plaza (☎ **958/587-0054** or 958/587-0009; www.turismo.conejo.com).

Pharmacy **Farmacia del Carmen,** just off the central plaza in Crucecita (☎ **958/587-0878**), is one of the largest drugstores in town. **Farmacia La Clínica** (☎ **958/587-0591**), Sabalí 1602, Crucecita, offers 24-hour service and delivery.

Post Office The *correo*, at Bulevar Chahué 100, Sector R, Crucecita (☎ **958/587-0551**), is open Monday through Friday from 8am to 3pm, Saturday from 9am to 1pm.

BEACHES, WATERSPORTS & OTHER THINGS TO DO

Attractions around Huatulco concentrate on the nine bays and their watersports. The number of ecotours and interesting side trips into the surrounding mountains is growing. Though it isn't a traditional Mexican town, the community of Crucecita is worth visiting. Just off the central plaza is the **Iglesia de Guadalupe,** with a large mural of Mexico's patron saint gracing the entire ceiling of the chapel. The image of the Virgin is set against a deep blue night sky, and includes 52 stars—a modern interpretation of Juan Diego's cloak.

You can dine in Crucecita for a fraction of the price in Tangolunda Bay, with the added benefit of some local color. Considering that shopping in Huatulco is generally poor, you'll find the best choices here, in the shops around the central plaza. They tend to stay open late, and offer a good selection of regional goods and typical tourist takehomes, including *artesanía,* silver jewelry, Cuban cigars, and tequila. A small, free trolley train takes visitors on a short tour of the town.

BEACHES   A section of the beach at Santa Cruz (away from the small boats) is an inviting sunning spot. Beach clubs for guests at non-oceanfront hotels are here. In addition, several restaurants are on the beach, and *palapa* umbrellas run down to the water's edge. For about $15 one-way, *pangas* from the marina in Santa Cruz will ferry you to **La Entrega Beach,** also in Santa Cruz Bay. There you'll find a row of *palapa* restaurants, all with beach chairs out front. Find an empty one, and use that restaurant for your refreshment needs. A snorkel equipment rental booth is about midway down the beach, and there's some fairly good snorkeling on the end away from where the boats arrive.

Between Santa Cruz and Tangolunda bays is **Chahué Bay.** The beach club has *palapas,* beach volleyball, and refreshments for an entrance fee of about $2. However, a strong undertow makes this a dangerous place for swimming.

Tangolunda Bay beach, fronting the best hotels, is wide and beautiful. Theoretically, all beaches in Mexico are public; however, nonguests at Tangolunda hotels may have difficulty entering the hotels to get to the beach.

BAY CRUISES & TOURS Huatulco's major attraction is its coastline—a magnificent stretch of pristine bays bordered by an odd blend of cactus and jungle vegetation right at the water's edge. The only way to really grasp its beauty is to take a cruise of the bays, stopping at **Organo** or **Maguey Bay** for a dip in the crystal-clear water and a fish lunch at a *palapa* restaurant on the beach.

One way to arrange a bay tour is to go to the **boat-owners' cooperative** (© 958/587-0081) in the red-and-yellow tin shack at the entrance to the marina. Prices are posted, and you can buy tickets for sightseeing, snorkeling, or fishing. Beaches other than La Entrega, including Maguey and San Agustín, are noted for offshore snorkeling. They also have *palapa* restaurants and other facilities. Several of these beaches, however, are completely undeveloped, so you will need to bring your own provisions. Boatmen at the cooperative will arrange return pickup at an appointed time. Prices run about $15 for 1 to 10 persons at La Entrega, and $35 for a trip to Maguey and Organo bays. The farthest bay is San Agustinillo; that all-day trip will run $80 in a private *panga*.

Another option is to join an organized daylong bay cruise. Any travel agency can easily make arrangements. Cruises are about $30 per person, with an extra charge of $5 for snorkeling-equipment rental and lunch. One excursion is on the *Tequila,* complete with guide, drinks, and on-board entertainment. Another, more romantic option is the *Luna Azul,* a 44-foot sailboat that also offers bay tours and sunset sails. Call © **958/587-2276** for reservations.

Ecotours are growing in both popularity and number throughout the Bays of Huatulco. The mountain areas surrounding the Copalita River are also home to other natural treasures worth exploring, including the **Copalitilla Cascades.** Thirty kilometers (19 miles) north of Tangolunda at 394m (1,300 ft.) above sea level, this group of waterfalls—averaging 20 to 25m (65–80 ft.) in height—form natural whirlpools and clear pools for swimming. The area is also popular for horseback riding and rappelling.

An all-day **Coffee Plantation Tour** takes you into the mountains east of Huatulco, touring various coffee plantations. You'll learn how Oaxacan coffee is cultivated and learn about life on the plantations. Lunch and refreshments are included. Cost for the day is $50; contact Paraíso Tours (© **958/581-0218;** paraisohuatulco@prodigy.net.mx) for reservations.

Guided **horseback riding** through the jungles and to Conejos and Magueyito beach makes for a wonderful way to see the natural beauty of the area. The ride lasts 3½ hours, with departures at 9:45am and 1:45pm, and costs $45. Available through **Caballo del Mar Ranch** (© **958/589-9387**).

For **bird-watchers,** local expert field guide Pedro Gasca will take you to several sites, depending on the season, to view a variety of species from parrots to pygmy owls (www.tomzap.com/h_bird.html). Contact him at © **333/854-7007** or at outdoors_huatulco@hotmail.com. The cost for birding expeditions vary from $20 to $80 depending on the length of the tour and the sites to be visited; each is individually designed for the client's preferences, and include land or aquatic transportation, a birding list, trip report, and beverages.

Another highly recommended guide is Laura Gonzalez, of **Nature Tours Huatulco** (© **958/583-4047;** lauriycky@hotmail.com), for both **hiking** and bird-watching. Choices include a hike around Punta Celeste with views of the river, open sea, and forest, for sightings of terrestrial and aquatic birds. The 3½-hour tour can be made in the early morning or late afternoon, and costs $45. An 8-hour excursion to the Ventanilla

Lagoons takes you by boat through a mangrove to view birds, iguanas, and crocodiles. The cost is $80, and lunch is included. Tours include transportation, binoculars, specialized bird guide, and beverages.

GOLF & TENNIS The 18-hole, par-72 **Tangolunda Golf Course** (✆ **958/581-0037**) is adjacent to Tangolunda Bay. It has tennis courts as well. The greens fee is $73, and carts cost $37. Tennis courts are also available at the **Barceló** hotel (✆ **958/581-0055**).

SHOPPING Shopping in the area is limited and unmemorable. It concentrates in the **Santa Cruz Market,** by the marina in Santa Cruz, and in the **Crucecita Market,** on Guamuchil, a half-block from the plaza. Both are open daily 10am to 8pm (no phones). Among the prototypical souvenirs, you may want to search out regional specialties, which include Oaxacan embroidered blouses and dresses, and *barro negro,* pottery made from dark clay exclusively found in the Oaxaca region. Also in Crucecita is the Plaza Oaxaca, adjacent to the central plaza. Its clothing shops include **Poco Loco Club/Coconut's Boutique** (✆ **958/587-0279**), for casual sportswear; and **Mic Mac** (✆ **958/587-0565**), for beachwear and souvenirs. **Coconuts** (✆ **958/587-0057**) has English-language magazines, books, and music.

WHERE TO STAY

Moderate- and budget-priced hotels in Santa Cruz and Crucecita are generally more expensive than similar hotels in other Mexican beach resorts. The luxury hotels have comparable rates, especially when they're part of a package that includes airfare. The trend here is toward all-inclusive resorts, which in Huatulco are an especially good option, given the lack of memorable dining and nightlife options. Hotels that are not oceanfront generally have an arrangement with a beach club at Santa Cruz or Chahué Bay, and offer shuttle service. Low-season rates apply August through November only.

EXPENSIVE

Camino Real Zaashila ✿✿✿ One of the original hotels in Tangolunda Bay, the Camino Real Zaashila is on a wide stretch of sandy beach secluded from other beaches by small rock outcroppings. The calm water, perfect for swimming and snorkeling, makes it ideal for families. The white stucco building is Mediterranean in style and washed in colors on the ocean side. The boldly decorated rooms are large and have an oceanview balcony or terrace and a large bathroom with a marble tub/shower combination. Each of the 41 rooms on the lower levels has its own sizable dipping pool. The main pool is a freeform design that spans 121m (400 ft.) of beach, with chaises built into the shallow edges. Well-manicured tropical gardens surround it and the guest rooms.

Bulevar Benito Juárez 5, Bahía de Tangolunda, 70989 Huatulco, Oax. ✆ **800/722-6466** in the U.S., or 958/581-0460. Fax 958/581-0461. www.camino-zaashila.com. 135 units. High season $215 double, $265 Club Room, $460 suite; low season $165 double, $200 Club Room, $350 suite. AE, DC, MC, V. **Amenities:** 3 restaurants (1 Oaxacan); lobby bar w/live music; large pool; lighted tennis court; outdoor whirlpool; beachside watersports center; tour and travel agency services; room service. *In room:* A/C, TV, minibar, safe.

Quinta Real ✿✿✿ Double Moorish domes mark this romantic, relaxed hotel, known for its richly appointed cream-and-white decor and complete attention to detail. From the welcoming reception area to the luxurious beach club below, the staff emphasizes excellence in service. The small groupings of suites are built into the sloping hill to Tangolunda Bay and offer spectacular views of the ocean and golf course. Rooms on the eastern edge of the resort sit above the highway, which generates some traffic noise. Interiors are elegant and comfortable, with stylish Mexican furniture, original art, wood-beamed ceilings, and marble tub/shower combinations with whirlpool tubs. Telescopes grace many of the suites. Balconies have overstuffed seating areas and stone-inlay floors. Eight Grand Class Suites and the Presidential Suite have private pools. The Quinta Real is perfect for weddings, honeymoons, or small corporate retreats.

Bulevar Benito Juárez Lt. 2, Bahía de Tangolunda, 70989 Huatulco, Oax. © 888/561-2817 in the U.S., 958/581-0428, or 958/581-0430. Fax 958/581-0429. www.quintareal.com/huatulco-eng.htm. 28 units. High season $386 Master Suite, $371 Grand Class Suite, $546 suite with private pool; low season $206 Master Suite, $351 Grand Class Suite, $416 suite with private pool. AE, DC, MC, V. **Amenities:** Restaurant (breakfast, dinner); poolside restaurant (lunch); bar w/stunning view; beach club w/2 pools (1 for children); concierge; tour desk; room service; in-room massage; laundry service; dry cleaning; beach *palapas*. *In room:* A/C, TV, dataport, minibar, hair dryer, safe-deposit box, bathrobes.

MODERATE

Gala Resort ★ *Kids*   With all meals, drinks, entertainment, tips, and a slew of activities included in the price, the Gala is a value-packed experience. It caters to adults of all ages (married and single) who enjoy both activity and relaxation. An excellent kids' activity program makes it probably the best option in the area for families. Rooms have tile floors and Oaxacan wood trim, large tub/shower combinations, and ample balconies, all with views of Tangolunda Bay.

Bulevar Benito Juárez s/n, Bahía de Tangolunda, 70989 Huatulco, Oax. © 800/GO-MAEVA in the U.S., or 958/581-0000. Fax 958/581-0220. www.gala-resort-huatulco.com. 290 units. $180–$291 double, $280–$388 junior suite. Child 12–15 an extra $54-$70; child 7–11 $60. Children under 7 stay free in parent's room. Ask about special promotions. AE, MC, V. **Amenities:** 4 restaurants (buffet, a la carte); 4 bars; 5 swimming pools, including a large free-form pool; 3 lighted tennis courts; full gym; complete beachside watersports center; theme nights. *In room:* A/C, TV, minibar, hair dryer, safe-deposit box.

Hotel Meigas Binniguenda ★   Huatulco's first hotel retains the charm and comfort that originally made it memorable. Rooms have Mexican-tile floors, foot-loomed bedspreads, and colonial-style furniture; French doors open onto tiny wrought-iron balconies overlooking Juárez or the pool and gardens. Newer rooms, added during an expansion in 2000, have more modern teak furnishings and are generally much nicer—request this section. A nice shady area surrounds the small pool in back of the lobby. The hotel is away from the marina at the far end of Juárez, only a few blocks from the water. It offers free transportation every hour to the beach club at Santa Cruz Bay.

Bulevar Santa Cruz 201, 70989 Santa Cruz de Huatulco, Oax. © 958/587-0077 or -0078. Fax 958/587-0284. binniguenda@prodigy.net.mx. 165 units. Year-round rates $250 double. Children under 7 stay free in parent's room. AE, MC, V. **Amenities:** Large, *palapa*-topped restaurant; small pool; travel agency; shuttle to beach. *In room:* A/C, TV, safe-deposit box.

INEXPENSIVE

Hotel Las Palmas   The central location and accommodating staff add to the appeal of the bright, basic rooms at Las Palmas. Located a half-block from the main plaza, it's connected to the popular El Sabor de Oaxaca restaurant (see "Where to Dine," below), which offers room service to guests. Rooms have tile floors, cotton textured bedspreads, tile showers, and cable TV.

Av. Guamuchil 206, 70989 Bahías de Huatulco, Oax. © 958/587-0060. Fax 958/587-0057. www.tomzap.com/huatulco.html. 25 units. High season $45 double; low season $28 double. AE, MC, V. Free parking. **Amenities:** Travel-agency services; tobacco shop; money exchange; safe-deposit boxes. *In room:* A/C, TV.

Misión de los Arcos ★★ *Finds*   This hotel, just a block from the central plaza, is similar in style to the elegant Quinta Real—but at a fraction of the cost. The hotel is completely white, accented with abundant greenery, giving it a fresh, inviting feel. Rooms continue the theme, washed in white, with cream and beige bed coverings and upholstery. Built-in desks, French windows, and minimal but interesting decorative accents give this budget hotel a real sense of style. At the entrance level, an excellent cafe offers high-speed Internet access, Huatulco's regionally grown coffee, tea, pastries, and ice cream. It's open from 7:30am to 11:30pm. Although there's no pool, the guests have the use of a beach club, to which the hotel provides a complimentary shuttle. The gym offers day passes for nonguests. The hotel is cater-cornered from La Crucecita's central plaza, close to all the shops and restaurants.

Gardenia 902, La Crucecita, 70989 Huatulco, Oaxaca. ℂ 958/587-0165. Fax 958/587-1904. www.misiondelosarcos. com. 13 units. High season $40 double without A/C, $45 double with A/C, $50-$95 suite; low season $30 double without A/C, $35 double with A/C, $40-$85 suite. Rates increase over Christmas and Easter holiday periods. AE, MC, V. **Amenities:** Full gym; tour desk; shuttle to beach club; laundry service. *In room:* TV, safe-deposit box.

WHERE TO DINE

El Sabor de Oaxaca ★★★ OAXACAN   This is the best place in the area to enjoy authentic, richly flavorful Oaxacan food, among the best of traditional Mexican cuisine. This colorful restaurant is a local favorite that also meets the quality standards of tourists. Among the most popular items are mixed grill for two, with a Oaxacan beef filet, tender pork tenderloin, *chorizo* (zesty Mexican sausage), and pork ribs; and the Oaxacan special for two, a generous sampling of the best of the menu, with tamales, Oaxacan cheese, pork *mole,* and more. Generous breakfasts include eggs, bacon, ham, beans, toast, and fresh orange juice. There's lively music, and the restaurant books special group events.

Av. Guamuchil 206, Crucecita. ℂ 958/587-0060. Fax 958/587-0057. Breakfast $3.90; main courses $5-$17. AE, MC, V. Daily 7am–midnight.

Noches Oaxaqueñas/Don Porfirio ★ SEAFOOD/OAXACAN   This dinner show presents the colorful, traditional folkloric dances of Oaxaca in an open-air courtyard reminiscent of an old hacienda (but in a modern strip mall). The dancers clearly enjoy performing traditional ballet under the direction of owner Celicia Flores Ramírez, wife of Don Willo Porfirio. The menu includes the *plato oaxaqueño,* a generous, flavorful sampling of traditional Oaxacan fare, with a tamale, a *sope,* Oaxacan cheese, grilled filet, pork enchilada, and a chile relleno. Other house specialties include shrimp with *mezcal,* and spaghetti marinara with seafood. Meat lovers can enjoy American-style cuts or a juicy *arrachera* (skirt steak). Groups are welcome.

Bulevar Benito Juárez s/n (across from Royal Maeva), Tangolunda Bay. ℂ 958/581-0001. Show $12. Main courses $12-$35. AE, MC, V. Fri–Sun noon–10pm. Show starts at 8:30 and 10pm Tues, Thurs, and Sat.

Restaurant Avalos Doña Celia SEAFOOD   Doña Celia, an original Huatulco resident, remains in business in the same area where she started her little thatch-roofed restaurant years ago. In a new building at the end of Santa Cruz's beach, she serves the same good eats. Among her specialties are *filete empapelado* (foil-wrapped fish baked with tomato, onion, and cilantro) and *filete almendrado* (fish filet covered with hotcake batter, beer, and almonds). The *ceviche* is terrific—one order is plenty for two— as is *platillo a la huatulqueño* (shrimp and young octopus fried in olive oil with chile and onion, served over white rice). The restaurant is basic, but the food is the reason for its popularity. If you dine here during the day, there are beach chairs and shade, so you can make your own "beach club" in a traditional and accessible part of Huatulco.

Santa Cruz Bay. ℂ **958/587-0128.** Breakfast $2.50–$3.50; seafood $4–$25. MC, V. Daily 8:30am–11pm.

Tostado's Grill MEXICAN   This traditional family-oriented Mexican restaurant serves typical Mexican fare, in a casual, friendly atmosphere. It's the place to dine if you're looking for a dose of local color with your meal, and want something authentically Mexican. Especially delectable is their Aztec soup (tortilla soup), and their beef is known for its tenderness. It is one of the few restaurants in La Crucecita that is open late during low season.

Flamboyan 306. Located in front of La Crucesita's central plaza. ℂ **958/587-1697.** Prices vary $2.20–$20. AE, MC, V. Daily 7pm–midnight.

HUATULCO AFTER DARK

There's a very limited selection of dance clubs around Huatulco—meaning that's where everyone goes. Huatulco seems to have the least consistent nightlife of any resort in Mexico, and clubs seem to change ownership—and names—almost annually. Check with your hotel concierge to see if any new places have opened. The current hot spot is **La Crema,** in Crucecita (about 4 blocks south of the *zócalo,* at the corner of Bugambilia and La Ceiba), playing predominantly reggae, but also a mix of dance tunes from the '60s and '70s. With bamboo-covered walls and batik hangings, it has a "just back from the beach" vibe to it. Nearby is **Café Dublin,** Carrizal 504 (1 block east and a half-block south from the *zócalo*), an Irish pub with a book exchange. On the east side of the *zócalo* is **Bar La Iguana,** playing rock music and featuring televised sports. During the high season, La Iguana has live tropical music. The bar is open from noon to 4am.

In Tangolunda, closer to the resort hotels, you'll find **Savage,** this area's hottest nightspot. It's across from the Barcelo hotel, and draws a more sophisticated crowd—meaning the T-shirts worn don't generally have advertising on them. The club plays techno dance music, with an impressive multi-media and light show. Each Wednesday, the Barcelo Resort hosts its **Fiesta Mexicana** from 7 to 11pm, featuring folkloric dances, mariachi music, and a buffet of Mexican food and drinks.

The Southernmost States:
Oaxaca & Chiapas

by David Baird

Oaxaca and Chiapas have larger Indian populations than the other states in Mexico. These Indians don't just keep to their own little villages; you see them everywhere. Over the centuries, their practices, beliefs, and customs have shaped the local culture, making these two states fascinating places to visit.

In **Oaxaca,** there is a large population of Zapotec and Mixtec Indians in the central highlands surrounding Oaxaca City. It is a beautiful land of mountains and valleys checkered with cornfields, at its prettiest during the rainy season (June–Oct), when the corn is green. The villages here are famous for their crafts and attract visitors from all over the world. For many families, selling handicrafts now contributes more to their livelihood than growing corn. But growing corn carries much more weight in their ordering of things. It's wrapped up in their identity.

Their ancestors established agriculture and civilization in these valleys centuries ago. They were the ones who built and rebuilt the magnificent ceremonial center of **Monte Albán** high upon a mountaintop above Oaxaca City. There you'll find an intriguing collection of buildings, ball courts, and plazas whose design is different from those of the Maya to the east and the many cultures of central Mexico to the northwest.

My favorite part of a trip here is visiting the **city of Oaxaca,** a beautiful colonial city with plazas, courtyards, and pedestrian walkways. With the pleasures of elegant surroundings, good food, and warm, welcoming people, I find myself very much at home here.

Chiapas, too, has a central highland area that produces beautiful handicrafts. Its center is the town of **San Cristóbal de las Casas,** which is higher, cooler, and wetter than Oaxaca. It's best to come here during the relatively dry season (late Oct to May). San Cristóbal is much smaller and offers a provincial version of colonial architecture—narrow cobblestone streets, tile roofs, old adobe walls, and wooden balconies. It looks less monumental and more Indian.

Aside from the beauty of the mountains and the many handicrafts, what brings people here are the villages of the highland Maya, a people who cling so tenaciously to their beliefs and traditions that for a long time the area attracted more anthropologists than tourists. These communities have a high degree of autonomy in religious and social practices; a visit to the church in **San Juan Chamula** will bring this home in a way no description can.

North and east of San Cristóbal are the lowlands, where you can visit the famous ruins of **Palenque,** a Maya city of the

Oaxaca Area

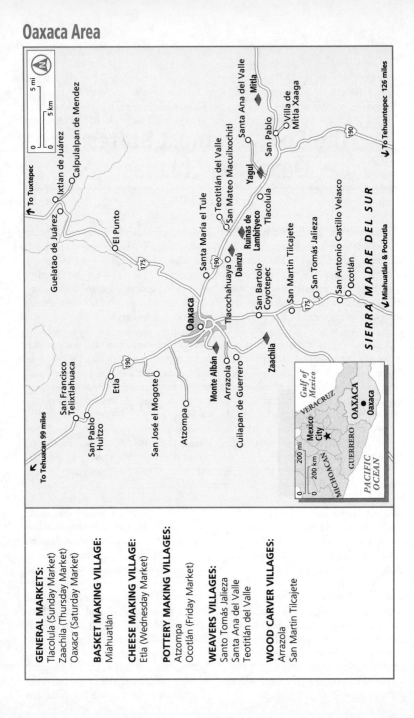

GENERAL MARKETS:
Tlacolula (Sunday Market)
Zaachila (Thursday Market)
Oaxaca (Saturday Market)

BASKET MAKING VILLAGE:
Miahuatlán

CHEESE MAKING VILLAGE:
Etla (Wednesday Market)

POTTERY MAKING VILLAGES:
Atzompa
Ocotlán (Friday Market)

WEAVERS VILLAGES:
Santo Tomás Jalieza
Santa Ana del Valle
Teotitlán del Valle

WOOD CARVER VILLAGES:
Arrazola
San Martin Tilcajete

Classic age. Thanks to the deciphering work of epigraphers, we know much about the history of Palenque and its kings. One was King Pacal, who lay buried for centuries inside his pyramid until an archaeological team discovered him in the 1950s.

In 1994, Chiapas made headlines when the Zapatista Liberation Army launched an armed rebellion and captured San Cristóbal. This forced the Mexican government to recognize the political and economic problems in Chiapas. Political violence erupted again in the winter of 1997–98 with a massacre in Acteal, near San Cristóbal. Sporadic violence occurs in the outlying towns from time to time, but no foreigners have been attacked, and no restrictions have been placed on travel to Palenque or the San Cristóbal region. Social unrest remains latent in the area. In 2003, a small lodge outside of Ocosingo owned by an American couple was invaded by the neighboring village. The couple was displaced, and the situation remains unresolved. The U.S. State Department has not issued a travel advisory for the region, but it has put out announcements. Before you go, get the most current information by checking the State Department website, **http://travel. state.gov**.

EXPLORING OAXACA & CHIAPAS

Airline and bus service to this area have improved a lot in the past few years. Most people arrive and depart through Oaxaca, Villahermosa (2 hr. from Palenque), or Tuxtla Gutiérrez (1½ hr. from San Cristóbal). A direct flight daily connects San Cristóbal and Mexico City.

You can see **Palenque** in a day. A couple of worthwhile side trips would add 1 or 2 days. **Oaxaca City** and **San Cristóbal** and their neighborhoods have so much to offer that I would consider 4 days in either place the minimum. Keep in mind, too, that Oaxaca's coastal resorts—including Puerto Escondido and Puerto Angel—are not far away. See chapter 10 for more information.

1 Oaxaca City ✶✶✶

520km (325 miles) SE of Mexico City; 230km (144 miles) SE of Tehuacán; 269km (168 miles) NE of Puerto Escondido

What you see today when you walk through the historic district of Oaxaca (wah-*hah*-kah) is largely the product of 3 centuries of colonial society. The city is famous for its green building stone and for its own particular style of colonial architecture—an adaptation to the frequent earthquakes that plagued the city in colonial times and still occasionally shake things up. Building walls and facades are thick and broad with heavy buttressing, colonnades are low and spaced closely, and bell towers are squat with relatively wide bases. The cumulative impression of this architectural style is one of mass and substantiality.

Before the arrival of the Spanish, the central valley of Oaxaca was an important and populous region. Olmec influence reached the area around 1200 B.C.; by 800 B.C. the Zapotec (the original builders of Monte Albán) occupied the valley. Their civilization flourished about the same time as Teotihuacán in central Mexico. Trade between the two areas intensified and remained important until the Conquest. There was also trade with the Maya to the east. In early post-Classic times, the Mixtec first appeared in the region and slowly, through war and conquest, gained ascendancy over much of the Zapotec homeland before both peoples were humbled by the Aztec and later the

Spaniards. To this day, the two principal ethnic groups in Oaxaca remain the Zapotec and Mixtec, whose tonal languages are closely related to each other but far different from the Aztec language Náhuatl.

The city of Oaxaca, originally called Antequera, was founded just a few years after the Spanish vanquished the Aztec. Most of Oaxaca's central valley was granted to Hernán Cortez for his services to the crown. Three centuries of colonial rule followed, during which the region remained calm.

In the years following independence, there was more or less continuous upheaval. From the 1830s to the 1860s, the Liberals and Conservatives fought for control of Mexico's destiny, with the French eventually intervening on the side of the Conservatives. One man, a Zapotec Indian from Oaxaca, led the resistance against the French and played the key role in shaping Mexico's future. He was Benito Juárez, and his handiwork is known to history as *La Reforma.*

Born in the village of Guelatao, north of Oaxaca City, Juárez was adopted by a wealthy Oaxacan family who clothed and educated him in return for his services as a houseboy. He fell in love with the daughter of his benefactor and promised he would become rich and famous and return to marry her. He did all three and became president of the republic in 1861. Juárez is revered throughout Mexico.

ESSENTIALS
GETTING THERE & DEPARTING
BY PLANE **Continental** (© **800/231-0856** in the U.S., or 01-800/900-5000 in Mexico) has nonstop service to/from Houston. **Mexicana** (© **800/531-7921** in the U.S., or 951/516-8414) and **Aeromexico** (© **800/237-6639** in the U.S., or 951/516-1066) have several flights daily to and from Mexico City. **Aerocaribe,** a Mexicana affiliate (© **951/516-0229** or 951/516-0266), flies to Puerto Escondido, Tuxtla Gutiérrez, Huatulco, and Ixtepec. **Aviacsa** (© **01-800/006-2200** in Mexico, or 951/514-5187) flies once a day to Mexico City and Hermosillo. **Aerovega** (© **951/516-4982** or 951/516-2777) flies a six-passenger twin-engine Aero-Commander to and from Puerto Escondido and Bahías de Huatulco once daily (twice if there are enough passengers). Make arrangements for AeroVega at the Monte Albán Hotel facing the Alameda (next to the *zócalo,* or town square).

BY CAR It's a 5-hour drive from Mexico City on the toll road, Highway 135D, which begins at Cuacnoapalan, about 80km (50 miles) east-southeast of Puebla, and runs south, terminating in Oaxaca; the one-way toll is $29. For adventurous souls, the old federal Highway 190 winds through the mountains and offers spectacular views; it takes 9 to 10 hours.

BY BUS First-class and deluxe buses to and from Mexico City use the *autopista* (superhighway toll road) which takes 6 hours. A few make a short stop in Nochistlán, which isn't much of a delay. Almost all buses leave from Mexico City's **TAPO (east) bus station.** There is less frequent service to and from Mexico City's Central del Norte (north), and the Central del Sur (south, also called Taxqueña). There is no service from the Mexico City airport.

ADO (Autobuses del Oriente) and its affiliates handle most of the first-class and deluxe bus service. Your options are: *primera clase* (ADO), with almost hourly departures and a one-way fare of $26; *de lujo* (ADO GL) with seven or more departures per day for $35 one-way; and *servicio ejecutivo* (UNO), with five-plus departures per day and $49 one-way. *De lujo* has the same seats as first class, but more legroom, free soda

Downtown Oaxaca

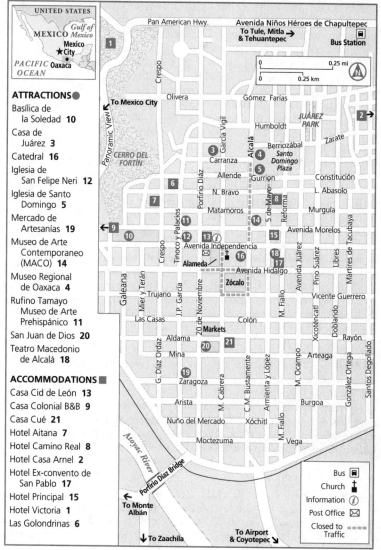

and bottled water, and a better bathroom. *Servicio ejecutivo* has all this plus superwide seats that recline far back. During holidays, you need to reserve a seat. Native Oaxaqueños living outside the state fill the buses for the Days of the Dead, Holy Week, and Christmas. It's possible to reserve seats over the Internet for the higher levels of service, and to check departure times and prices at **www.adogl.com.mx** and **www. uno.com.mx**.

In Oaxaca, the **ADO station** is on Calzada Niños Héroes. Buses serve Tuxtla Gutiérrez (five a day); San Cristóbal de las Casas (two overnight buses); Puebla (10 a day); Tehuacán (four a day); Tapachula (one a day); Veracruz (three a day); Villahermosa (two a day); and Huatulco, Pochutla, and Puerto Escondido on the coast (two a day, stopping at all three towns). These last buses take 9 hours to reach Puerto Escondido because they go by way of Huatulco; for a faster trip, see below.

Most of these buses are first-class; some are deluxe. When you walk through the station's main door, the passage to the buses is in front of you. The long counter to the right sells first-class tickets, and the shorter counter to the left sells deluxe. You can buy your tickets ahead of time at an agency downtown called **Ticket Bus,** 20 de Noviembre 103-D, near the corner of Hidalgo, 1 block from the *zócalo* (© 951/514-6655). Office hours are Monday through Saturday from 9am to 10pm, Sunday from 9am to 4pm.

The **Viajes Atlántida** agency, La Noria 101, near Armenta y López (© 951/514-7077), offers daily service to Pochutla in Suburbans. It's much faster than the bus. There are eight runs daily (4 hr.; $14). From Pochutla you can catch a *colectivo* (Volkswagon van) to **Puerto Escondido, Huatulco,** or **Puerto Angel** (which run 1–1½ hr.). You should buy your tickets in advance. The agency is open daily from 5:30am to 11:30pm.

The speediest buses to Puerto Escondido—6 hours away over a tortuous road— leave from the *terminal de segunda clase* (second-class terminal) Armenta y López 721, across from the Red Cross. Two lines serve the route. Pacífico Oaxaca buses leave daily at 8:30am and 10:30pm. One Estrella del Valle bus leaves at 11pm daily. Many people who go to Puerto Escondido on these buses say that if they had it to do over, they'd fly. Motion sickness is the main reason because of the hundreds of curves through the mountains.

ORIENTATION

ARRIVING BY PLANE   The airport is south of town; it's about a 20-minute cab ride. Buy a ticket at the window on your left as you exit the airport. A private cab is $10; a *colectivo* is $2.50 per person for downtown locations, more for outlying areas.

The same company provides service from the town to the airport. Go to **Transportes Aeropuerto Oaxaca** (© 951/514-4350), on the Alameda, in the building facing the cathedral. It doesn't accept phone reservations, so drop by Monday through Saturday from 9am to 2pm or 5 to 8pm to buy your ticket and arrange hotel pick-up. The cost is $2.50 from downtown hotels, $5.50 and up from outlying hotels, and more if you have extra luggage.

ARRIVING BY BUS   The ADO first-class bus station is a short distance north of the center of town. A taxi ride to downtown is $2 to $3. If you're coming from the Pacific coast, you may arrive at the Central Camionera de Segunda Clase (second-class bus terminal) next to the Abastos Market. It's 10 long blocks southwest of the *zócalo.*

VISITOR INFORMATION   The **State Tourist Office** is at Calle Independencia 607, corner of García Vigil, in front of the Alameda (©/fax **951/516-0123**). It's open daily from 8am to 8pm. The information booth at the airport keeps the same hours. The **Oficina de Turismo (Municipal Tourist Office)** is at García Vigil 517; it's open Monday through Friday from 9am to 3pm and 6 to 9pm.

CITY LAYOUT   Oaxaca's east-west axis is **Independencia.** When streets cross Independencia and the north-south axis, **Alcalá/Bustamante,** their names change. The city's center is the *zócalo,* a large square surrounded by stone archways, and the **Alameda,** a smaller plaza attached to the northwest part of the *zócalo.* Oaxaca's cathedral faces the

Alameda; its Palacio del Gobierno faces the *zócalo*. A few blocks to the north is the **Plaza de Santo Domingo.** The area between these two open spaces holds most of the historic district's shops, hotels, and restaurants. Two of the streets that run from Santo Domingo toward the *zócalo*—**Alcalá** and **Cinco de Mayo**—are partly closed to traffic.

GETTING AROUND   By Car   If you want to rent a car, try **Arrendadora Express,** 20 de Noviembre 103-B (© **951/516-6776**). Rental cars in Oaxaca are expensive, and the process is not exactly streamlined.

By Taxi   If you want to reach some of the outlying villages, I recommend hiring a taxi or signing up for a tour. Most taxi drivers have set hourly rates for touring the Oaxacan valleys. A trustworthy and careful taxi driver who speaks English is **Tomás Ramírez** (© **951/511-5061** (home); tomasramirez@prodigy.net.mx).

By Bus   Buses to the outlying villages of Guelatao, Teotitlán del Valle, Tlacolula, and Mitla leave from the second-class station just north of the Abastos Market. *Colectivos* leave for nearby villages from Calle Mercaderes, on the south side of the Abastos Market.

FAST FACTS: Oaxaca

American Express   The office, in **Viajes Micsa,** is at Valdivieso and Hidalgo, at the northeast corner of the *zócalo* (© **951/516-2700**; fax 951/516-7475). American Express office hours are Monday through Friday from 9am to 2pm and 4 to 6pm, Saturday from 9am to 1pm. The travel agency stays open later and doesn't close for lunch.

Area Code   The telephone area code is **951.**

Books, Newspapers & Magazines   **Amate Books,** Alcalá 307-2, a few steps from Santo Domingo (© **951/516-6960**), has perhaps the best selection anywhere of books in English about Mexico. It stocks English-language magazines as well as a number of books about Oaxacan handicrafts. Hours are Monday through Saturday from 10:30am to 2:30pm and 3:30 to 7:30pm. A couple of monthly freebies, the English-language *Oaxaca Times* and the trilingual (English, Spanish, and French) *OAXACA,* circulate through the city and have information for tourists.

Consulates   The **Canadian consulate,** Pino Suárez 700-11B (© **951/513-3777**), is open daily from 11am to 2pm. The **U.S. Consular Agency** is at Alcalá 407, Int. 20 (©/fax **951/514-3054**). Hours are Monday through Friday from 10am to 3pm.

Currency Exchange   *Casas de cambio* cluster on the streets at the northeast corner of the *zócalo,* at Alcalá and Valdivieso. These places post their rates, have short lines, and keep better hours than banks. Several exchange Canadian dollars.

Doctor   Dr. Carlos Arnaud Carreño is a reputable internist at Calle Reforma 905 (© **951/515-4053**). Hours are from noon to 2pm and 4 to 8pm Monday through Friday.

Emergencies   The phone number for emergencies is © **060.**

Internet Access   In the downtown area, there are more than 20 Internet access services and cybercafes. Most are along Alcalá and around the *zócalo* and the Plaza Santo Domingo.

Population Oaxaca has 380,000 residents.

Post Office The *correo* is at the corner of Independencia and Alameda Park. It is open Monday through Friday from 8am to 5pm, Saturday from 9am to 1pm.

Safety By any standard, Oaxaca is a safe town for tourists. A government agency, **CEPROTUR,** helps tourists who have been robbed or feel service providers have cheated them. It has compiled several years worth of data showing that the incidence of crime against tourists in the city is remarkably low. Most of it is simple theft, which commonly happens in crowded areas such as the markets. One method is to slice open a tourist's backpack; another method is to distract someone who has set down a bag while a partner makes away with it. Should you lose any documents or possessions covered by insurance, contact CEPROTUR, in the same building as the state tourism office on the north side of the Alameda (© **951/514-2155**). It can document your losses and facilitate paperwork.

Seasons April and May are the hottest, driest months. (Also in May, rural teachers invade the *zócalo* and create havoc in the downtown area while they demonstrate for higher wages.) The rains come in June and improve things considerably. June through March the city is most enjoyable. High seasons for tourists, when you can expect higher hotel rates, are late July and August (especially around the Guelaguetza), early November (around the Days of the Dead), the entire month of December, and during Easter.

Shipping The cheapest way to transport your goods is to have them packed securely so that you can check them as extra baggage on your flight home. Another way is to ship them. Many stores will pack and ship their own merchandise but not other stores' goods. Recommended shippers are **Corazón del Pueblo** and **ARIPO** (see "Shopping," later in this chapter).

SPECIAL EVENTS & FESTIVALS

Oaxaca is famous for its exuberant traditional festivals. The most important ones are **Holy Week,** the **Guelaguetza** in July, **Días de los Muertos** in November, and the **Night of the Radishes** and **Christmas** in December. Make hotel reservations at least 2 months in advance if you plan to visit during these times.

Note: If you want to come for Christmas or the Guelaguetza but rooms and transportation are booked, consider using **Sanborn's Tours,** 2015 S. 10th St., McAllen, TX 78503 (© **800/395-8482** in the U.S., or 956/682-9872).

At festival time in Oaxaca, sidewalk stands near the cathedral sell *buñuelos,* a thin, crisp, sweet snack food. It is the custom to serve *buñuelos* in cracked or otherwise flawed dishes; after you've finished eating, you smash the crockery on the sidewalk for good luck. Don't be timid! You can wash down the *buñuelos* with hot *ponche* (a steaming fruit punch) or *atole.*

HOLY WEEK During Holy Week, figurines made of palm leaves are sold on the streets. On Palm Sunday, the Sunday before Easter, there are colorful parades. On the following Thursday, Oaxaca residents follow the Procession of the Seven Churches. Hundreds of the pious walk from church to church, praying at each one. The next day, Good Friday, many of the *barrios* (neighborhoods) have *encuentros:* Groups depart separately from the church, carrying religious figures through the neighborhoods, then "encounter" each other back at the church. Throughout the week, each church sponsors concerts, fireworks, fairs, and other entertainment.

FIESTA GUELAGUETZA   On the last two Mondays in July, Oaxaca holds the Fiesta Guelaguetza. In the villages of central Oaxaca, a *guelaguetza* (literally, a gift) is a celebration by a family in need of assistance to hold a wedding or some other community celebration. Guests bring gifts, which the family repays when they attend other *guelaguetzas*. The Fiesta Guelaguetza, begun in 1974, brings dancers from all the state's various ethnic groups to Oaxaca. For many communities, participation has become a matter of intense civic pride, and an opportunity to show people in the state capital and those from other ethnic groups the beauty of their traditional clothing and dance. Some 350 different *huipiles* (women's overblouses) and dresses can be seen during the performances. In the afternoon, there is an interpretive dance of the legend of Princess Donají.

The performances take place in the stadium that crowns the Cerro del Fortín each Monday from 10am to 1pm. Admission ranges from free (in Section C) to $50 to $75 (in Section A). Reserve tickets in advance—no later than May—through the State Tourism Office. A travel agency may be able to help you. I recommend Sections 5 and 6 in Palco (gallery) A for the best seating. The ticket color matches the color of your seat. You will be sitting in strong sunlight, so wear a hat and long sleeves.

Even if you don't attend the dances, you can enjoy the festival atmosphere that engulfs the city. There are fairs, exhibits, and a lot of gaiety. On the Sunday nights before the Guelaguetza, university students present an excellent program in the Plaza de la Danza at the Soledad church. The production, the *Bani Stui Gulal,* is an abbreviated history of the Oaxaca valley. The program begins at 9pm; arrive early, because the event is free and seating is limited.

DIAS DE LOS MUERTOS   This Mexican festival (Nov 1–2) has garnered worldwide attention. It is celebrated across Oaxaca with more enthusiasm than in the rest of Mexico, which says quite a lot. Markets brim with marigolds—the flower of the underworld—and every household fills an altar with them and the favorite dishes, drinks, and cigarettes of the deceased. People visit relatives and friends, and anyone who visits is offered food. This is also the time to pay one's respects at the graveyard. Try to take one of the nocturnal cemetery tours offered around this time. **Hotel Casa Arnel** (© 951/515-2856) runs one. Another common form of celebrating is for young men to dress up in macabre outfits and frolic in the streets in Carnaval-like fashion.

DECEMBER FESTIVALS   The December Festivals begin on the 12th with the **Fiesta de la Virgen de Guadalupe (Festival of the Virgin of Guadalupe)** and continue on the 16th with a *calenda,* or procession, to many of the older churches in the *barrios* (neighborhoods), all accompanied by dancing and costumes. Festivities continue on the 18th with the **Fiesta de la Soledad** in honor of the Virgen de la Soledad, patroness of Oaxaca state. A large fireworks construction known as a *castillo* is erected in Plaza de la Soledad. When it is ignited, look out. December 23 is **La Noche de Rábanos** (the Night of the Radishes), when Oaxaqueños build fantastic sculptures out of enormous radishes, flowers, and cornhusks. Displays on three sides of the *zócalo* are set up from 3pm on. By 6pm, when the show officially opens, lines to see the figures are 4 blocks long. It's well organized and overseen by a heavy police presence. On December 24, around 8:30pm, each Oaxacan church organizes a procession with music, floats, enormous papier-mâché dancing figures, and crowds bearing candles, all of which converge on the *zócalo.*

EXPLORING OAXACA

There is so much sightseeing to do inside and outside Oaxaca that you have to be sure to allow some idle time for enjoying the *zócalo.* In the traffic-free square, you can relax while getting a feel for the town and a good glimpse of Oaxacan society. I recommend going in the late afternoon and taking a seat at the outdoor cafe with the best view of the cathedral. You can get a beer or order a bowl of the traditional drink of Oaxaca: chocolate. The afternoon light filters through the shiny green leaves of the laurel trees, heightening the color of the cathedral's green stone. As dusk comes, a small drill corps enters stage left and performs a flag-lowering ceremony with much pomp and circumstance. Then the *marimba* or the municipal band usually strikes up in the central bandstand.

The city contains museums worth visiting, some interesting churches, and colorful markets. Outside town are the famous ruins of Monte Albán and Mitla, and area villages known for their arts and crafts. It is sometimes best to check these out on market day; see "Shopping Splendor: Oaxaca's Market Villages," later in this chapter.

MUSEUMS

Museo de Arte Contemporáneo de Oaxaca The MACO, 2½ blocks north of the *zócalo,* exhibits the work of contemporary artists, primarily from Oaxaca state (which has produced some of Mexico's most famous painters). It also books traveling exhibitions. A small bookstore is to your right as you enter. The 18th-century building housing the museum merits a visit for its own sake. It's called the Casa de Cortés, and some say that it was built by order of Hernán Cortez after he received the title of Marqués of the Valley of Oaxaca (in reality, it was built 2 centuries too late for that).

Alcalá 202, between Murguía and Morelos. ✆ 951/514-2228. Admission $1. Wed–Mon 10:30am–8pm.

Museo Regional de Oaxaca ✦✦✦ Next to the Santo Domingo Church (6 blocks north of the *zócalo*) is the most impressive museum in the city, housed in a former Dominican convent—one of the greatest of colonial Mexico. Construction was largely completed by the early 1600s. The government has spent millions to renovate the former convent, and it shows. The stairs, the arches, the cupolas—everywhere you look, there are lovely details in stone or in the remnants of colonial-era murals. The museum is an ambitious project that displays the course of human development in the Oaxaca valley from earliest times to the 20th century.

The most treasured possessions are the artifacts from Monte Albán's Tomb 7, which were discovered in 1932. The tomb contained 12 to 14 corpses and some 500 pieces of jewelry and art, making use of almost 8 pounds of gold and turquoise, conch shell, amber, and obsidian. This is part of a larger collection of artifacts from Monte Albán, which you would do well to see before going up to the ruins. In the many ceramics and carvings you can see definite Olmec and Teotihuacán influences, yet they display a style distinctly different from either culture. Other rooms are dedicated to the present-day ethnographic make-up of Oaxaca and a brief history of the efforts of the Dominican order in the region. Attached to the convent is the Santo Domingo Church (see "Churches," below). From some points on the north side of the convent you can look down over the recently opened botanical garden. Admission to the garden is free but by guided tour only (at 1 and 6pm). Sign up at the front desk of the museum the same day of the tour. There are two tours a week in English; ask for info at the front desk.

Gurrión at Alcalá. ⓒ 951/516-2991. Admission $4.25. Tues–Sun 10am–7:45pm.

Rufino Tamayo Museo de Arte Prehispánico de México ⭐⭐⭐   The artifacts displayed in this museum were chosen "solely for the aesthetic rank of the works, their beauty, power, and originality." The result is a striking collection of pre-Hispanic art. The famed Oaxacan artist Rufino Tamayo amassed the collection over a 20-year period. The artifacts range from the pre-Classic period up to the Aztec, from far northwest Nayarit to southeastern Chiapas: terra-cotta figurines, scenes of daily life, lots of female fertility figures, Olmec and Totonac sculpture from the Gulf Coast, and Zapotec long-nosed figures. The beautifully displayed works reveal the great variety of styles of pre-Columbian art in Mexico.

Av. Morelos 503, north of the *zócalo* between Tinoco y Palacios and Porfirio Díaz. ⓒ 951/516-4750. Admission $3. Mon and Wed–Sat 10am–2pm and 4–7pm; Sun 10am–3pm. Closed holidays.

CHURCHES

Basílica de la Soledad ⭐⭐   The Basílica is the most important religious center in Oaxaca, and its Virgin is the patroness of the entire state. Adjoining the church is a former convent with a small but charming museum in back. A huge celebration on and around December 18 honors the Virgin, attracting penitents from all over Oaxaca. She is famous for her vestments, which are encrusted with pearls. (Until a few years ago, she had a crown of silver and jewels, which was stolen.) As with most Virgins, there is a story behind her. The short version is that her figure (actually just her hands and face) was found in a box on the back of a burro that didn't belong to anyone. The burro sat down on an outcropping of rock and refused to get up. This was the spot where the Virgin revealed herself and, consequently, where the basilica (completed in 1690) was constructed. You can still see the outcropping of rock, surrounded by a cage of iron bars, immediately to your right along the wall as you enter the church.

The concave facade of the church projecting forward from the building is unique in Mexico's religious architecture. The way the top is rounded and the tiers are divided suggests an imitation in stone of the traditional carved wooden *retablos* (altarpieces) common in Mexican churches. The interior is most impressive, too, but what I really like is the museum, which contains a curious blend of pieces—some museum-quality, others mere trinkets that might as well have come from my grandmother's attic.

The Basílica's upper plaza is an outdoor patio and theater (Plaza de la Danza) with stone steps that serve as seats. Here, spectators view the famous Bani Stui Gulal (see "Fiesta Guelaguetza" under "Special Events & Festivals," above). When visiting the Basílica, it is traditional to eat ice cream; there are vendors in the lower plaza in front of the church.

Independencia at Galeana. No phone. Museum: Admission 30¢. Mon–Sat 10am–2pm and 4–6pm; Sun 11am–2pm. Basilica: Daily 7am–2pm and 4–9pm.

Catedral de Oaxaca ⭐⭐   The cathedral was built in 1553 and reconstructed in 1773. Its elaborate 18th-century baroque facade is an excellent example of the Oaxacan style. The central panel above the door depicts the assumption of the Virgin. Note the heavy, elaborate frame around the picture and the highly stylized wavelike clouds next to the cherubs—these elements, repeated in other churches in the region, are telltale signs of Oaxacan baroque. An uncommon and quite lovely detail is how the Virgin's

cape and its folds are depicted in angular lines and facets. The cathedral's interior is not as interesting as its exterior because it was plundered during the Wars of Reform.

Fronting the Parque Alameda. No phone. Free admission. Daily 7am–9pm.

Iglesia de San Felipe Neri   This church, 2½ blocks northeast of the *zócalo,* was built in 1636 and displays all the architectural opulence of that period: The altar and nave are covered with ornately carved, gilded wood, and the walls are frescoed. In the west transept and chapel is a small figure of St. Martha and the dragon; the faithful have bedecked her with ribbons in hopes of obtaining her assistance.

Tinoco y Palacios at Independencia. No phone. Free admission. Daily 8am–11pm.

Iglesia de Santo Domingo 😖😖😖 *Moments*   There are 27 churches in Oaxaca, but none can equal the splendor of this one's interior. The church was started in the 1550s by Dominican friars and finished a century later; it contains the work of all the best artists of that period. Ornate plaster statues and flowers cover the extravagantly gilded walls and ceiling. When the sun shines through the yellow stained-glass window, it casts a golden glow over the whole interior and looks like a baroque vision of heaven. If you are there around 11am on Monday through Saturday, you are likely to hear the lovely sound of the gift-shop operator singing her devotions. Just as you enter, look up at the ceiling formed by the choir loft. Notice the beautifully depicted genealogical tree of the Dominican order, which starts with Don Domingo de Guzmán, Saint Dominic himself.

Corner of Gurrión and Alcalá. No phone. Free admission. Daily 7am–2pm and 4–11pm.

San Juan de Dios   This is the oldest church in Oaxaca, originally built in 1521 or 1522 of adobe and thatch. Construction of the present structure started during the mid-1600s and included a convent and hospital (where the 20 de Noviembre Market is now). The exterior is sweetly simple; the interior has an ornate altar and Urbano Olivera paintings on the ceiling. Oaxaqueños especially revere the glass shrine to the Virgin near the entrance, as well as one dedicated to Christ (off to the right). Because it's by the market, 1 block west and 2 blocks south of the *zócalo,* many of the people who visit the church are villagers who have come to Oaxaca to buy and sell.

20 de Noviembre s/n (corner of Aldama and Arteaga). No phone. Free admission. Daily 6am–11pm.

MORE ATTRACTIONS

Besides visiting the places mentioned below, try to get to the **Casa de Cortés,** which houses the Museo de Arte Contemporáneo (see above), and the former convent of **Santa Catalina,** home of the Hotel Camino Real (see below).

Casa de Juárez   This modest museum occupies the house where Benito Juárez first lived when he came to the city as a servant boy. It doesn't have any of his personal effects or any furniture belonging to the house, but it shows how a typical 19th-century household would have looked.

García Vigil 609. 🕐 **951/516-1860.** Admission $3. Tues–Sat 10am–7pm; Sun 10am–5pm.

Cerro del Fortín   To capture Oaxaca in a glance, take a cab to the top of this hill on the west side of town for a panoramic view. It's especially pretty just before sunset. Atop the hill are the statue of Benito Juárez and a stadium built to hold 15,000 spectators. The annual Fiesta Guelaguetza is held here. You can walk to the hill: Head up Díaz Ordaz/Crespo and look for the Escaleras del Fortín (Stairway to the Fortress) shortly after you cross Calle Delmonte; the 218 steps (interrupted by risers) are a challenge, but the view is worth it.

Díaz Ordaz at Calle Delmonte. No phone.

Teatro Macedonio de Alcalá   This beautiful 1903 Belle Epoque theater, 2 blocks east of the *zócalo*, holds 1,300 people and is still used for concerts and performances in the evening. Peek through the doors to see the marble stairway and Louis XV vestibule. Sometimes, a list of events is posted on the doors.

Independencia at Armenta y López. No phone. Open only for events.

SHOPPING

Oaxaca and the surrounding villages are wonderful hunting grounds for handcrafted pottery, woodcarvings, and weavings. The hunt itself may be the best part. Specialties include the shiny **black pottery** for which Oaxaca is famous, **woolen textiles** with the deep reds and purples produced using the natural dye *cochineal*, and highly imaginative *alebrijes* **(woodcarvings).**

For a list of market days in outlying villages and directions to the important crafts villages, see "Shopping Splendor: Oaxaca's Market Villages," later in this chapter.

SHOPS & GALLERIES

Most of the shops, galleries, and boutiques are in the area between **Santo Domingo** and the *zócalo*, comprising the streets of **Alcalá, Cinco de Mayo,** and **García Vigil** and the **cross streets.** Customary store hours are from 10am to 2pm and 4 to 7pm Monday through Saturday.

Artesanías e Industrias Populares del Estado de Oaxaca   ARIPO is a government store with a broader range of goods than most shops, including masks, baskets, clothing, furniture, and cutlery. The staff speaks English and will ship anywhere. Open Monday through Friday from 9am to 8pm, Saturday from 10am to 6pm, and Sunday from 11am to 4pm. It is 2 blocks above the Benito Juárez house. García Vigil 809 (at Cosijopi). ✆ 951/514-4030.

Arte y Tradición   Four blocks north of the *zócalo*, a brightly painted doorway leads into this attractive arcade of shops with an open patio in the center. Each shop functions as a cooperative, with articles on consignment from various villages, such as Teotitlán del Valle and Arrazola. Individuals from the villages are on hand to explain the crafts (weaving, woodcarving, and the like) practiced by their townspeople. You'll also find a restaurant serving Oaxacan food, the Belaguetza Travel Agency, and a small bookstore. The store is open daily from 9am to 8pm; individual shop hours vary. García Vigil 406. ✆ 951/516-3552.

Corazón del Pueblo *(Finds*   A buyer for museum gift shops recommended this store to me for the sophistication and quality of its wares. The owners, it turned out, used to be wholesale exporters of Mexican folk art and handicrafts. They know what they're doing. You'll find plenty of Oaxacan pottery, woodcarving, and weavings, as well as crafts you won't commonly see elsewhere. Alcalá 307, local 9, 2nd floor. ✆ 951/516-6960.

Galería Arte de Oaxaca   This gallery represents some of the state's leading contemporary artists. It's 2 blocks north and 1 block east of the *zócalo*. Murguía 105. ✆ 951/514-0910 or 951/514-1532.

Galería Quetzalli   A modest-looking art gallery behind the Church of Santo Domingo and next to Los Pacos restaurant, Galería Quetzalli represents some of the big names in Mexican art—Francisco Toledo, José Villalobos—and some up-and-coming artists. Quetzalli also has a gallery at Murguía 400. Constitución 104. ✆ **951/514-0030.**

Indigo   Beautiful and uncommon (and expensive) objects can be found here. The store can really test your resolution not to buy more artwork; go in and take a peek. Allende 104. ✆ **951/514-8338.**

La Mano Mágica   Come here to see some of the best rug weaving in Oaxaca (by Arnulfo Mendoza) before you head to Teotitlán to see the work of other weavers. In the back rooms you can find well-chosen pieces of regional folk art. Shipping is available. The store is opposite the MACO. Alcalá 203 (between Morelos and Matamoros). ✆ **951/516-4275.**

MARKETS

There are two market areas: one just south of the *zócalo,* and the newer Abastos Market, about 10 blocks west. Both areas bustle with people and are surrounded by small shops selling anything from hardware to leather goods to fabrics.

A few shops specialize in chocolate (not for eating, but for making hot chocolate) and *mole* paste. The neighboring state of Tabasco grows most of the cacao beans used for the chocolate. They are ground with almonds and cinnamon and pressed into bars or tablets. To prepare the drink, you dissolve the chocolate in hot milk or water (the more traditional drink) and beat until frothy. *Mole* paste, which contains chocolate, is used to make the classic Oaxacan dishes *mole negro* and *mole rojo.* A good place to hunt for chocolate and *mole* paste is along Mina street, on the south side of the 20 de Noviembre Market (see listing below). Here you'll find **Chocolate Mayordomo** and **Chocolate La Soledad.** Both offer a variety of preparations to fit American and European tastes, but I like the traditional Mexican best.

Benito Juárez Market   One block south of the *zócalo,* this covered market is big and busy; stalls sell vegetables, flowers, medicinal preparation, meats, cheeses, and even clothing. Between calles Las Casas, Cabrera, Aldama, and 20 de Noviembre.

Mercado Abastos   The Abastos Market is open daily but is most active on Saturday, when Indians from the villages come to town to sell and shop. You'll see dried chiles, herbs, vegetables, crafts, bread, and even burros for sale at this bustling market. 10 blocks west of zócalo, between Calle Mercaderes and the periférico.

Mercado de Artesanía   Located 1 block south and 1 block west of the 20 de Noviembre Market, this market sells mostly textiles and articles of clothing at cheap prices. J. P. García and Zaragoza.

20 de Noviembre Market   This market is just south of the Benito Juárez market, across Aldama. There are a lot of food stalls, but also some arts and crafts. On the south side, along Mina, are stores selling chocolate and *mole* paste. Between calles Aldama, Cabrera, Mina, and 20 de Noviembre.

OTHER THINGS TO DO

COOKING CLASSES   **Iliana de la Vega** (✆ **951/514-1878;** www.elnaranjo.com.mx), owner of El Naranjo (see "Where to Dine," below), offers Oaxacan cooking classes. She comes highly recommended. **Susana Trilling** (✆ **951/518-7726;** www.seasonsofmyheart.com), author of the cookbook *Seasons of My Heart,* operates a cooking school of the same name just outside Oaxaca.

SPANISH CLASSES   Oaxaca has about a half-dozen language schools. With prior notice, most can arrange homestays with a Mexican family for students looking for total immersion. With little notice, most can arrange a week of classes for visitors to brush up their language skills. The **Instituto Cultural Oaxaca A.C.,** Av. Juárez 909 (Apdo. Postal 340), 68000 Oaxaca, Oax. (© 951/515-3404; www.instculturaloax. com.mx), has the biggest name and perhaps the least flexibility. Besides language skill, classes focus on Oaxaca's history, archaeology, anthropology, and botany—a good choice for those who find themselves asking questions about their surroundings. The **Instituto de Comunicación y Cultura,** Alcalá 307–312, 68000 Oaxaca, Oax. (©/fax 951/516-3443; www.iccoax.com), provides group and private instruction and uses music, art, and handicrafts to get students into the swing of things. Classes are small. This school has been around for some time and comes recommended by former students. **Becari Language School,** M. Bravo 210, 68000 Oaxaca, Oax. (© 951/514-6076; www.becari.com.mx) was founded in 1994, and I'm hearing more and more good things from students.

HIKING & BIKING   Northwest of the city of Oaxaca is a mountain range known as the Sierra Norte that is cooler and wetter than the valley. The native communities offer guides and simple lodging for active sorts who are interested in seeing yet another side of Mexico. Several ecotourism outfits work with these communities. For information, ask at the State Tourism Office. **Bicicletas Bravo,** García Vigil 409-C, 68000 Oaxaca, Oax. (© 951/516-0953; www.bikeoaxaca.com), does bike tours. This outfit also leads bike tours of the valley, which avoid car traffic and are less challenging than biking the mountains.

WHERE TO STAY

High season includes Easter, July, August, early November, and most of December. You should have no difficulty finding a room the rest of the time, and promotional rates are usually available. The prices listed below include the 17% tax. Most evenings are cool enough that you don't need air-conditioning, but for about 60 days a year, mostly from April to June, it comes in handy, and not every hotel has it.

VERY EXPENSIVE

Casa Cid de León ★★★   Casa Cid de León has easily the largest suites in downtown Oaxaca. Each is extravagantly decorated in colonial style, with a few modern touches and fresh-cut flowers. The one that garners the most attention (La Bella Epoca) has three balconies facing the street and a large sitting room. The two-story, two-bathroom suite (El Mío Cid) would be perfect for a family. One of the downstairs suites, La Dominica, is my favorite for its space and comfort. Guests have access to a rooftop terrace. The location, 2 blocks north of the *zócalo,* is excellent, and Señora Cid de León is a most accommodating hotel owner. The hotel offers custom tours of the city and surrounding valley.

Av. Morelos 602, 68000 Oaxaca, Oax. © 951/514-1893. Fax 951/514-7013. www.casaciddeleon.com. 4 units. $211–$258 suite. Rates include juice, coffee, airport transfer, tour of city. AE, MC, V. Valet parking $10. **Amenities:** Tour and limo service; business services; in-room salon services; room service until 11pm; in-room massage; babysitting; laundry service. *In room:* A/C, TV, hair dryer, bathrobe.

Hotel Camino Real ★★★   A magnificent hotel in a 16th-century landmark convent, this is the place to cloister yourself when in Oaxaca. Several beautiful courtyards with age-old walls bring to mind the original purpose of the building. The rooms, however, do not. All are comfortable, well furnished, and have the conveniences you would expect in a hotel of this caliber (no small feat given the constraints imposed by the infrastructure). Exterior rooms have triple-glazed windows to reduce noise. Higher prices are for interior rooms with views of the courtyards. The main difference between "deluxe" and "club" is the size of the room. Service is good. The location—between the *zócalo* and Santo Domingo on a pedestrian-only street—is ideal.

On Friday evenings the hotel holds a *Guelaguetza*, a regional dance show with dinner buffet ($30); on Saturday evenings there's a mariachi show with dinner buffet ($17).

Cinco de Mayo 300, 68000 Oaxaca, Oax. ℂ **800/722-6466** in the U.S. and Canada, or 951/501-6100. Fax 951/516-0732. www.caminoreal.com/oaxaca. 91 units. $260–$280 deluxe; $310–$360 club; $400 junior suite. Children under 12 stay free in parent's room. AE, DC, MC, V. Valet parking $22. **Amenities:** Restaurant; 2 bars; large outdoor swimming pool; association with local health club; children's activities in high season; tour desk; car rental; 24-hr. room service; babysitting; laundry service; dry cleaning; nonsmoking rooms. *In room:* A/C, TV, minibar, hair dryer, safe.

EXPENSIVE

Hotel Ex-convento de San Pablo ★★
Yes, another former convent turned hotel. Covering colonial Mexico, as I do, the novelty of these places has worn off some, but I admire this particular establishment. I liked it better when it was kept a bit dark and felt more monastic, but even now it has wonderful character. There is an idiosyncrasy in the rooms that is fun, and these are furnished with more flair and just as much comfort as at the Camino Real. What the San Pablo doesn't have are the other's expansive courtyards, the grounds, the pool, or the large staff and hence the service, but there's a big price advantage, which in my book more than makes up for the lack of 24-hour room service—but then again, I'm inured to such hardship. All the rooms here are large suites with either a king or two double beds. The owners are supposed to be installing A/C in them this year, so if that's important to you, inquire when you make a reservation. Get an interior room for the sake of quiet. The hotel is 2 blocks from the *zócalo*.

Fiallo 102, 68000 Oaxaca, Oax. ℂ **951/516-4914** or 951/516-2553. Fax 951/514-0860. www.hotelsanpablo.com. 21 units. Low season $115–$130 double; high season $190. AE, DC, MC, V. Free secure parking. **Amenities:** Restaurant; bar; tour desk; car rental; room service until 10:30 pm; in-room massage; laundry service; dry cleaning. *In room:* TV, minibar, coffeemaker, hair dryer, safe.

Hotel Victoria ★★ *Finds*
High above the downtown area, the Hotel Victoria offers that rare combination of proximity and the feeling of distance. It is ideal for those who want a little more peace than staying downtown can offer. And you're only a couple of minutes away on the hotel's shuttle bus. The Victoria also has a lovely view. You can enjoy it from a room or suite in one of the main buildings (three stories, no elevator), or you can stay in one of the villas distributed about the grounds, each with its own terrace. Rooms are large and carpeted, and have modern furnishings.

Lomas del Fortín 1, 68070 Oaxaca, Oax. ℂ **951/515-2633.** Fax 951/515-2411. www.hotelvictoriaoax.com.mx. 149 units. $160 standard double; $195 villa; $260 junior suite. AE, MC, V. Free parking. **Amenities:** Restaurant; bar; large outdoor swimming pool; tennis court; complimentary shuttle to downtown; babysitting; laundry service; dry cleaning; nonsmoking rooms. *In room:* A/C, TV, minibar, hair dryer, safe.

MODERATE

Casa Colonial Bed and Breakfast
The casual and comfortable setting created by attentive hosts Jane and Thornton Robison promptly sets guests at ease. This is an especially attractive place for first-timers to Oaxaca, who can tap into the owners' knowledge of the area and perhaps even tour some villages with them. The good-size rooms open to a large garden with tall jacaranda trees; they are simply but comfortably furnished. Breakfast is substantial: fresh fruit, yogurt, hot cereal, eggs, bacon, juice, and coffee. The hotel is farther from downtown than most of the others listed

here. Rooms are not available for the Day of the Dead season or Christmas. Live music occasionally on Sunday afternoons. The casa is closed for May.

Negrete 105 (Apdo. Postal 640), 68000 Oaxaca, Oax. © **800/758-1697** in the U.S., or ©/fax 951/516-5280. www. mexonline.com/colonial.htm. 15 units. $105 double. Rates include full breakfast. MC, V. Free parking. Walk past La Soledad church on Av. Morelos, and angle right for a couple of blocks; the green house with purple trim (there's no sign) will be on your left.

Casa Cué *Value* A modern hotel 2 blocks from the *zócalo,* Casa Cué has good air-conditioning, good service, and bathrooms with instant hot water. The lovely terrace on top of the three-story building (there's no elevator) has patio furniture and a good view of the mountains. The midsize standard rooms are attractively furnished and well lit; most contain two twin beds. Junior suites are large and come with a sofa, coffee table, and writing table; most hold two double beds (some have one king and one double). The suites are still larger, and the second bedroom makes them perfect for a family. The hotel is well managed. It's across the street from the market, which can be a little noisy, but the double-glazed windows do a good job of blocking it out.

Aldama 103, 68000 Oaxaca, Oax. ©/fax **951/516-1336.** www.mexonline.com/casacue.htm. 23 units. High season $72 double, $92 junior suite, $130 suite; low season $65 double, $79 junior suite, $96 suite. AE, MC, V. Free covered, secure parking. **Amenities:** Restaurant; bar; exercise equipment; tour info; car rental; room service until 10pm; laundry service; dry cleaning. *In room:* A/C, TV.

Hotel Aitana *⚡ Finds* Offering the most attractive, comfortable rooms in this price range, this stylish hotel is a good choice. It is only 8 blocks from the *zócalo* and 6 blocks from Santo Domingo, but it is about 30m (100 ft.) uphill on a noisy street. All the rooms are away from the street, however, past a courtyard restaurant. The well-lit, beautifully decorated rooms hold two twin beds; a few rooms have either two doubles or a king. Bathrooms are attractive and spacious, with shower/tub combinations.

Crespo 313, 68000 Oaxaca, Oax. © **951/514-3788** or 951/514-3839. Fax 951/516-9856. www.hotelaitanaoaxaca. com. 23 units. High season $84–$110 double; low-season $65–$75. Low season rates include full breakfast and often 3rd night is free. MC, V. **Amenities:** Restaurant; bar; tour info; room service until 10:30pm; laundry service; dry cleaning. *In room:* TV, dataport, coffeemaker, hair dryer.

INEXPENSIVE

Hotel Casa Arnel *Value Kids* Not far from the bus station, this budget hotel is less than a kilometer (about a half-mile) from the *zócalo* but still within walking distance of most sights. It's a great choice for those traveling with kids: The Cruz family lives here with a couple of their children, and parrots hang out in the shady garden. From the rooftop terrace, you can admire the view and soak up some sun. Most rooms are plain but comfortable; some share bathrooms. Across the street in the new wing are three additional rooms with double beds and private bathrooms, plus four furnished, full-service apartments with fully equipped kitchens. Breakfast, at extra cost, is served on the patio. At Christmas, the family involves guests in the traditional Mexican celebrations or *posadas,* which are held during the 12 nights before Christmas. Rates rise 30% for Easter, Guelaguetza, Día de los Muertos, and Christmas.

Aldama 404, Col. Jalatlaco, 68080 Oaxaca, Oax. ©/fax **951/515-2856.** www.casaarnel.com.mx. 40 units. $25–$30 double without bathroom; $35–$40 double with bathroom; $60–$70 suite; apt $380–$450 monthly. No credit cards. Parking $3. **Amenities:** Laundry service; tours of local destinations; Internet access.

Hotel Principal The Principal, 1 block east and 2½ blocks north of the *zócalo,* is a longtime favorite of budget travelers. The location—near shops, museums, and restaurants—is great. Rooms are simply furnished and not well lit and a little worn. Three have balconies over the street; the rest are off the interior patio. Most have a double bed. Except for the three rooms with balconies, all of the rooms are quiet.

Cinco de Mayo 208, 68000 Oaxaca, Oax. ©/fax **951/516-2535**. 14 units. $45 double. No credit cards. Street parking.

Las Golondrinas ★★ This charming one-story hotel sits amid rambling patios with roses, fuchsia, bougainvillea, and mature banana trees. Owned and managed by Guillermina and Jorge Velasco, Las Golondrinas (The Swallows) is very popular, so make reservations in advance. The simply furnished rooms, with windows and doors opening onto courtyards, all have tile floors and a small desk and chairs. Each holds either one full or two twin beds. A few rooms have a king-size bed and go for a higher price. Breakfast is served between 8 and 10am in a small tile-covered cafe in a garden setting ($3–$7); nonguests are welcome. The hotel is 6½ blocks north of the *zócalo*.

Tinoco y Palacios 411 (between Allende and Bravo), 68000 Oaxaca, Oax. © **951/514-3298** or ©/fax 951/514-2126. lasgolon@prodigy.net.mx. 29 units. $46–$55 double. MC, V. Limited free parking. **Amenities:** Laundry service.

Finds **Oaxacan Street Food**

Unless it's during a festival, don't be surprised to find many restaurants empty. Oaxaqueños do not frequent restaurants but do like eating in market and street stalls. They favor foods such as tacos, tamales, *tlayudas* (12-in. tortillas, slightly dried, with a number of toppings), and quesadillas (in Oaxaca, large tortillas heated on the *comal*—a flat, earthenware pan—or among the coals, with several types of fillings). For adventurous diners, here are my picks for enjoying the people's food.

Quesadillas are a morning food, and the best place to eat them is in **La Merced** market (on Murguía, about 10 blocks east of Alcalá), where you'll find a number of food stalls. Everyone has a favorite; mine is **La Florecita,** and my favorite quesadilla comes with *huitlacoche.* The following places open only at night. For tacos, a little *taquería* (taco stand) called **Tacos Sierra** (on Morelos, a half-block west of Alcalá) is a Oaxacan institution. It makes simple tacos with pork filling and a spicy salsa, but I can never order enough. It closes when the pork runs out, usually by 10pm. Don't expect these tacos to come cheap. Another *taquería* is **El Mesón,** which is across from the northeast corner of the *zócalo* at Hidalgo 805. It offers *tacos de la parrilla* (grill) and *de olla* (clay pot). For *tlayudas,* seek out a hole-in-the-wall on Constitución around the corner from Libres, **El Chepil.** They come with a number of toppings, and with *tasajo* (dried beef) or *cecina* (pork rubbed with red chile) on the side. If you don't like lard, tell them that you want yours *sin asiento.* For tamales, find the woman who sets up her little stand on Avenida Hidalgo and 20 de Noviembre, in front of the pharmacy. She often doesn't get there until 7:30pm, but when she does, she quickly draws a crowd that buys tamales to go—six flavors, and my favorite is always the last one I've eaten. Since you're in Oaxaca, you might want to ask for a *tamal* made with *mole negro, mole amarillo,* or *chepil* (an herb).

WHERE TO DINE

Oaxacan cooking has a great reputation in Mexico. It makes use of more ingredients from the lowlands than central Mexican cooking. It's known for its *moles,* and for a wide variety of chiles, many of which you don't find in other parts of the country.

If you're curious to know more about Oaxacan cooking, **Zapotec Tours** (*C*) **800/446-2922** in the U.S.) organizes a weeklong trip to the city in early October. The "Food of the Gods Festival" includes dining at different restaurants, cooking classes, a tour of the market, and field trips. For good coffee, espresso or other, go to **Café Nuevo Mundo** (*C* 951/501-2122) at M. Bravo 206. For excellent ice cream go to **Gelateria Giardino** (*C* 951/516-9673) at Hidalgo 814-B, just off the *zócalo.*

EXPENSIVE

El Ché *★* STEAKS   Need a break from spicy Mexican food? Have a steak and salad in attractive surroundings, and wash it down with a classic margarita. The restaurant offers both American and Argentine cuts of beef; the rib-eye and the *churrasco* are the most popular. Salads include Caesar and Roquefort prepared at the table.

5 de Mayo 413. *C* 951/514-2122. Reservations recommended during special festivals. Steaks $13–$23. MC, V. Daily 1–11pm.

MODERATE

El Asador Vasco INTERNATIONAL/MEXICAN   Of the restaurants circling the *zócalo,* this is the best bet. It certainly offers the most pleasant dining area: Tables overlook the *zócalo* from a second-floor stone archway. Take your pick of purely Mexican specialties *(chiles rellenos, moles, carne asada)* or dishes with a European twist (snapper filet cooked in olive oil and *guajillo* chile).

Portal de Flores 11. *C* 951/514-4755. Main courses $8–$18. MC, V. Daily 1–11:30pm.

El Naranjo *★★★* (*Moments*) OAXACAN/MEXICAN   El Naranjo, where the emphasis is on Oaxacan specialties, is my favorite restaurant in the city. The owner and chef, Iliana de la Vega, prepares dishes that she grew up cooking and eating. She has added some others and made alterations, such as reducing the fat, to bring out the flavors of the vegetables, herbs, and chiles. If you have a craving for a salad but have been reluctant, this is your chance—all is safe here. For a main dish, try the featured *mole* of the day. For an especially exotic flavor, try fish cooked in the leaves of *hoja santa* (an herb) with a tangy sauce made from the *guajillo* chile. For something spicier, try the *pasilla oaxaqueño,* a chile stuffed with string cheese. A milder choice is poblano chile stuffed with squash blossoms. The restaurant occupies the roofed courtyard of a colonial house 1½ blocks from the southwest corner of the *zócalo.* El Naranjo also hosts cooking classes (see "Other Things to Do," earlier in this chapter).

Trujano 203. *C* 951/514-1878. Main courses $8–$15. Reservations recommended. AE, MC, V. Mon–Sat 1–10pm.

Marco Polo *★* SEAFOOD   If the weather's nice, you can enjoy dining outdoors in Marco Polo's shaded patio. The ceviche tostadas or the seafood cocktails are great starters (if you like your cocktail less tomato-y, tell the waiter you want it "a la marinera"). The specialty is the oven-baked fish (whole or filet) prepared several ways—I like their basic method, with just a chile guajillo marinade. For dessert, try the baked bananas. Marco Polo is just north of the central downtown area; it fronts the park known as Paseo Juárez.

Pino Suárez 806. *C* 951/513-4308. Breakfast $3; main courses $9–$15. AE, MC, V. Wed–Mon 8am–6pm.

María Bonita OAXACAN/MEXICAN What I like best about this restaurant is that it offers some simple, classic Oaxacan dishes that are spurned by other restaurants in the city. The appetizer section, for example, has *tlayudas* and *memelitas* (the Oaxacan name for *sopes*), both rarely seen on restaurant menus. The soups are good as are the Oaxacan main courses. María Bonita occupies a house on Alcalá, 2 blocks north of the Santo Domingo. The three dining rooms are all simple, colorful, and attractive, with plain wooden chairs and tables.

Macedonio Alcalá 706-B. © 951/516-7233. Main courses $6–$12. AE, MC, V. Tues–Sun 7am–8pm.

Yu Ne Nisa ⊛ OAXACAN ISTHMUS In the hot lowlands of eastern Oaxaca, an area called the isthmus, a different kind of cooking is practiced, and you can sample some of the region's specialties at this restaurant located in a residential part of the Colonia Reforma, which is north of the centro histórico. Start off with some *garnachas* for appetizers—little corn patties covered in sauce—and then try one of the regional specialties like shrimp *mole* or another kind of *mole* called *gucheguiña.* Seafood is a big part of isthmus cooking, and the menu offers seafood cocktails and soups.

Amapolas 1425, Col. Reforma. © 951/515-6982. Reservations accepted. Main courses $7–$14. No credit cards. Daily 1–8pm.

INEXPENSIVE

Doña Elpidia (Finds OAXACAN The phrase "home-style cooking" is bandied about a lot, but in this case it really means something. For the traveler, it means a meal just like the main dinner in a well-run Mexican home. Finding this place is a bit of a trick; it's 5½ blocks south of the *zócalo.* Look for a small sign saying only RESTAURANT. When you enter, a chalkboard in front of you lists the day's meal. You will find some tables behind the overgrown garden. There is also indoor dining. The *comida corrida* includes a basket of bread, an appetizer, vegetable or pasta soup, rice, a meat or enchilada course, and dessert. Beer and other beverages are available.

Miguel Cabrera 413 (between Arista and Nuño del Mercado). © 951/516-4292. Fixed-price lunch $5. No credit cards. Daily 1–5pm.

Itanoni (Finds MEXICAN/REGIONAL This business began as a tortilla shop. The owner then decided to branch out into making other things with his *masa* (mortar) besides tortillas. He is fascinated with the different forms of native corn and makes use of their varying characteristics in the cooking. The dishes are simple, traditional *antojitos* such as tacos, quesadillas, *memelitas,* and a couple I had never heard of: *tetelas,* and his own *"de ese."* I like these last two a lot. You can get them with a variety of fillings, including bean, cheese, mushrooms, *huitlacoche,* and others.

Belisario Domínguez 513, Col. Reforma. © 951/513-9223. Antojitos $1. No credit cards. Mon–Sat 7:30am–4pm; Sun 8am–2pm.

OAXACA AFTER DARK

If you are interested in seeing the region's traditional dances, you can check out the small-scale **Guelaguetza** performed by professional dancers at the Hotel Camino Real on Friday from 7 to 10pm. The cost ($30) includes a buffet. **La Casa de Cantera,** Murguía 102 (© 951/514-7585), offers something similar. The $11 cover is for the show only, which runs every night from 8:30 to 10:15pm. Drinks and supper cost extra. Call for reservations.

Concerts and dance programs take place all year at the **Teatro Macedonio de Alcalá,** Independencia and Armenta y López. Schedules are often posted by the front doors of the theater. In the early evening, the *zócalo* is a happening place, with all sorts of people out and about. The municipal brass band and marimba players perform free concerts on alternating nights. As the night wears on, usually you'll find some mariachis hanging about.

One of my favorite places to hear music is **El Sol y La Luna,** Reforma 502 (© **951/514-8069**). The owner books a lot of good bands from Mexico City—mainly jazz and blues acts—and some interesting performers from Veracruz and other neighboring states. You never know what you'll find, but it's usually good. There's often a cover of around $5, and you can order food (mostly pizza). For salsa, go to **La Candela,** Murguía 413 (© **951/514-2010**), which offers live music Thursday through Saturday from 10:30pm to 2am. The cover is usually $3.

ROAD TRIPS FROM OAXACA

The countryside around Oaxaca is dotted with small archaeological sites and villages, and the most important are easy to reach. The landmark ruins in the region are **Monte Albán** (30 min.) and **Mitla** (1 hr.). If you're heading toward Mitla, you can make some interesting stops (see "The Road to Mitla: Ruins & Rug Weavers," below). A number of interesting villages in other directions make good day trips from Oaxaca. The State Tourism Office will give you a map that shows nearby villages where beautiful handicrafts are made. The visits are fun excursions by car or bus. If you would like a guided tour of archaeological ruins or crafts villages, contact **Juan Montes Lara.** He is the thinking-person's guide to this area, as well as to most of southern Mexico. He speaks English and conducts tours for small groups throughout Oaxaca and Chiapas. He stays pretty busy, so contact him well in advance—the best way is by e-mail at jmonteslara@yahoo.com (or call © **951/515-7731**).

Many villages have, in the past several years, developed fine small municipal museums. **San José El Mogote,** site of one of the earliest pre-Hispanic village-dweller groups, has a display of carvings and statues found in and around the town, and a display model of an old hacienda. **Teotitlán del Valle** also has a municipal museum; it features displays on the weaving process. Ask at the State Tourism Office for more information.

MONTE ALBAN: RUINS WITH A VIEW

Had I been the priest-king of a large Indian nation in search of the perfect site on which to build a ceremonial center, this would have been it. **Monte Albán** sits on a mountain that rises from the middle of the valley floor—or, rather, divides two valleys. From here you can see all that lies between you and the distant mountains.

Starting around 2000 B.C., village-dwelling peoples of unknown origin inhabited the Oaxaca valleys. Between 800 and 500 B.C., a new ceramic style appeared, indicating an influx of new peoples, now called Zapotec. Around 500 B.C., these peoples began the monumental exercise of leveling the top of a mountain, where they would build Monte Albán (*mohn*-teh ahl-*bahn*).

Very little of the original structures remain; they've either been obscured beneath newer construction or had their stones reused for other buildings. The **Danzantes friezes** (see below) date from this period.

A center of Zapotec culture, Monte Albán was also influenced by contemporary cultures outside the valley of Mexico. You can see Olmec influence in the early sculptures; more recent masks and sculptures reflect contact with the Maya. When Monte Albán was at its zenith in A.D. 300, it borrowed architectural ideas from Teotihuacán.

Monte Albán

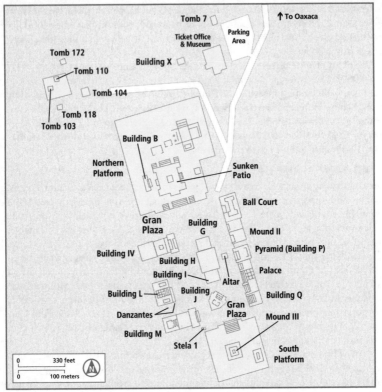

By around A.D. 800, the significance of Monte Albán in Zapotec society began to wane. Although most likely never completely abandoned, it became a shadow of its former grandeur. At the beginning of the 13th century, the Mixtec appropriated Monte Albán. The Mixtec, who had long coexisted in the area with the Zapotec, began expanding their territory. At Monte Albán, they added little to the existing architecture; however, they seem to have considered it an appropriate burial ground for their royalty. They left many tombs, including **Tomb 7,** with its famous treasure.

Monte Albán centers on the **Great Plaza,** a man-made area created by flattening the mountaintop. From this plaza, aligned north to south, you can survey the Oaxacan valley. The excavations at Monte Albán have revealed more than 170 tombs, numerous ceremonial altars, stelae, pyramids, and palaces.

Begin your tour of the ruins on the eastern side of the Great Plaza at the I-shaped **ball court.** This ball court differs slightly from Maya and Toltec ball courts in that there are no goal rings, and the sides of the court slope. Also on the east side of the plaza are several **altars** and **pyramids** that were once covered with stucco. Note the sloping walls, wide stairs, and ramps; all are typical of Zapotec architecture and reminiscent of the architecture of Teotihuacán. The building, slightly out of line with the plaza (not on the north-south axis), is thought by some to have been an observatory; it was probably aligned with the heavenly bodies rather than with the points of the compass.

The south side of the plaza has a large **platform** that bore several stelae, most of which are now in the National Museum of Anthropology in Mexico City. There's a good view of the surrounding area from the top of this platform.

The west side has more ceremonial platforms and pyramids. On top of the pyramid substructure are four columns that probably supported the roof of the temple at one time.

The famous building of **Los Danzantes (the dancers)** on the west side of the plaza, is the earliest known structure at Monte Albán. This building is covered with large stone slabs that have distorted naked figures carved into them (the ones you see are copies; the originals are protected in the site museum). There is speculation about who carved these figures and what they represent, although there is a distinct resemblance

---

Moments **Shopping Splendor: Oaxaca's Market Villages**

You could spend a full week in Oaxaca just visiting the various markets in nearby villages. Each has its specialty—cheese, produce, livestock, weaving, and pottery—and unique character. To pick a village or villages to visit, crack open a copy of *Mexican Folk Art from Oaxacan Artist Families* by Arden and Anya Rothstein. It has lots of photos that give a good idea of what to look for. In Oaxaca, look for it at **Amate Books**, Alcalá 307-2 (© **951/ 516-6960**).

Market days in the villages are as follows:

Day	Market
Wednesday	**Etla,** known for its cheese; 15km (9½ miles) north.
Thursday	**Zaachila,** ruins and agriculture; 16km (10 miles) southwest.
	Ejutla, agriculture; 64km (40 miles) south.
Friday	**Ocotlán,** pottery, textiles, and food; 30km (19 miles) south.
Saturday	**Oaxaca,** Abastos Market.
Sunday	**Tlacolula,** agriculture and crafts (visit the chapel as well); 31km (20 miles) southeast.

You can get to any of these craft villages by bus from the second-class station, 8 blocks west of the *zócalo* on Trujano. On market days, passengers cram these buses. If you get off a bus between destinations—say, at Cuilapan (see below) on the way to Zaachila—but want to continue to the next place, return to the highway and hail a passing bus.

It's also possible to take a *colectivo* (minibus) to the villages that don't have bus service. To find a *colectivo,* head to the south end of the Abastos Market. On Calle Mercaderes you'll see dozens of maroon-and-white *colectivo* taxis. The town each one serves is written on the door, trunk, or windshield. Posted metal signs also give destinations. *Colectivos* fill up relatively fast and are an economical way to reach the villages. Be sure to go early; by afternoon the *colectivos* don't fill up as fast, and you'll have to wait.

One of the many tour operators in the city can easily arrange tours to all the markets as well as the craft villages and ruins. Go to any travel agent or ask at your hotel.

to the Olmec baby faces at La Venta, in Tabasco state. The distorted bodies and pained expressions might connote disease. Clear examples of figures representing childbirth, dwarfism, and infantilism are visible. Because of the fluid movement represented in the figures, they became known as Los Danzantes—merely a modern label for these ancient and mysterious carvings.

The **Northern Platform** is a maze of temples and palaces interwoven with subterranean tunnels and sanctuaries. Take time to wander here, for there are numerous reliefs, glyphs, paintings, and friezes along the lintels and jambs as well as the walls. In this section of the ruins, you are likely to see vendors discreetly selling "original" artifacts found at the site. These guys come from the nearby town of Arrazola, where the fabrication of "antiquities" is a long-standing cottage industry. I like to buy a piece from them occasionally and pretend I'm getting the real thing just to get an opportunity to talk with them.

Leaving the Great Plaza, head north to the **cemetery** and **tombs.** If you have a day to spend at Monte Albán, be sure to visit some of the tombs, which contain magnificent glyphs, paintings, and stone carvings of gods, goddesses, birds, and serpents. Lately, the tombs have been closed to the public, but check anyway. Of the tombs so far excavated, the most famous is **Tomb 7,** next to the parking lot. It yielded some 500 pieces of gold, amber, and turquoise jewelry, as well as silver, alabaster, and bone art objects. This amazing collection is on display at the Regional Museum of Oaxaca.

As you enter the site, you'll see a museum, a shop with guidebooks to the ruins, a cafe, and a craft shop. I recommend purchasing a guidebook. Video camera permits cost $5. The site is open daily from 8am to 6pm. Admission to the ruins is $4. Licensed guides charge $15 per person for a walking tour.

To get to Monte Albán, take a bus from the Hotel Mesón del Angel, Mina 518, at Mier y Terán. **Autobuses Turísticos** makes seven runs daily, at 8:30, 9:30, 10:30, and 11:30am and 12:30, 1:30, and 3:30pm. Return service leaves the ruins at 11am, noon, 1, 2, 3, 4, and 5:30pm. The round-trip fare is $4. The ride takes a half-hour, and your scheduled return time is 2 hours after arrival. It's possible to take a later return for an additional $1 (though you won't be guaranteed a seat); inform the driver of your intent. During high season there are usually additional buses. If you're driving from Oaxaca, take Calle Trujano out of town. It becomes the road to Monte Albán, about 10km (6 miles) away.

THE ROAD TO MITLA: RUINS & RUG WEAVERS

East of Oaxaca, the Pan American Highway (Hwy. 190) leads to Mitla and passes several important archaeological sites, markets, and craft villages. You can visit the famous El Tule tree, an enormous, ancient cypress; the church at Tlacochahuaya, a lovely example of a 17th-century village church; the ruins at Dainzú, Lambityeco, and Yagul; the weaver's village of Teotitlán del Valle; and the village of Tlacolula, with its famous Dominican chapel.

There are a lot of little stops on this route, and some are a bit off the highway, so I recommend hiring a taxi, renting a car, or signing up with a small tour rather than using local bus transportation. If you take a tour, ask which sites it includes. To get to the highway, go north from downtown to Calzada Niños Héroes and turn right. This feeds directly on to the highway. All the sites are listed in order, from west (Oaxaca) to east (Mitla).

SANTA MARIA DEL TULE'S 2,000-YEAR-OLD TREE Santa María del Tule is a small town 8km (5 miles) outside Oaxaca. It's famous for the immense **El Tule Tree,**

an *ahuehuete* (Montezuma cypress, akin to the bald cypress) standing in a churchyard just off the main road. Now over 2,000 years old, it looks every bit its age, the way large cypresses do. However, this one is the most impressive tree I've ever seen for the sheer width of its trunk and canopy. It is said to have the broadest trunk of any tree in the world. When the tree was younger, the entire region around Santa María del Tule was marshland; in fact, the word *tule* means "reed." Now, the water table has dropped, so to protect the tree, a private foundation waters and takes care of it. The 25¢ admission fee goes toward these efforts.

The **Iglesia de San Jerónimo Tlacochahuaya,** 6km (4 miles) farther along, is the next stop. You'll see a sign pointing right; go less than another kilometer (about a half-mile) into town. Inside the church are an elaborately carved altar and a crucifix fashioned out of a ground paste made from the corn plant. The murals decorating the walls were the work of local artists of the 18th century and are a sweet mix of Spanish and Indian aesthetics. Make a point of seeing the beautifully painted baroque organ in the choir loft. The church is usually open daily from 10am to 2pm and 4 to 8pm.

DAINZU'S ZAPOTEC RUINS   Three kilometers (2 miles) farther, visible from the highway (26km/16 miles from Oaxaca), you'll see a sign pointing to the right. It's less than a kilometer (under a mile) to the ruins, which were first excavated in the 1960s. Dainzú is a pre-Classic site that dates from between 700 and 600 B.C. Increasingly sophisticated building continued until about A.D. 300. The site occupies the western face of a hill, presumably for defense. The main building is a platform structure whose walls were decorated with carvings resembling Monte Albán's Danzantes. These carvings are now in a protective shed; a caretaker will unlock it for interested parties. These figures show Olmec influence but differ from the Danzantes because they wear the trappings of the "ball game," which make them in all likelihood the earliest representations of the ball game in Mexico. And, in fact, a partially reconstructed ball court sits below the main structure. The site provides an outstanding view of the valley. Admission is $3.

TEOTITLAN DEL VALLE'S BEAUTIFUL RUGS   The next major turnoff you come to is 2km (1½ miles) farther along, 3km (2 miles) from the highway. This is Teotitlán, famous for weaving, and now an obviously prosperous town, to judge by all the current development. This is where you'll want to go for rugs, and you'll find no shortage of weavers and stores. Most weavers sell out of their homes and give demonstrations. The prices are considerably lower than in Oaxaca.

The church in town is well worth a visit. The early friars used pre-Hispanic construction stones to build the church and then covered them with adobe. When the townspeople renovated the church, they rediscovered these stones with carved figures, and now proudly display them. You'll see them in odd places in the walls of the church and sacristy. Teotitlán also has a small community museum, opposite the artisans' market and adjacent to the church. The museum has an interesting exhibit on natural dye-making, using herbs, plants, and *cochineal* (a red dye derived from insects).

For a bite to eat, consider the **Restaurant Tlamanalli,** Av. Juárez 39 (© **951/524-4006**), run by three Zapotec sisters who serve Oaxacan cuisine. Its reputation attracts lots of foreigners. It's on the right on the main street as you approach the main part of town, in a red brick building with black wrought-iron window covers. It's open Monday through Friday from 1 to 4pm. A bit farther on, there's another nice restaurant on the left where the main street intersects with the town center.

LAMBITYECO'S RAIN GOD   Getting back to the highway and continuing eastward, in 3km (2 miles) you'll see a turnoff on the right for the small archaeological site of Lambityeco. Of particular interest are the two beautifully executed and preserved **stucco masks** of the rain god Cocijo. At Lambityeco, a major product was salt, distilled from saline groundwaters nearby. Admission is $3.

TLACOLULA'S FINE MARKET & UNIQUE CHAPEL   Located about 32km (20 miles) from Oaxaca (1.5km/1 mile past Lambityeco), Tlacolula is in mezcal country, and along the road from here to Mitla, you'll see a couple of small distilleries and distillery outlets advertising their product. Feel free to stop by any one of them to taste their wares. Mezcal is distilled from a species of agave different from that of tequila. Most mezcal has a very strong smell and may or may not come with a worm in the bottle. Many of these small distilleries flavor their mezcal in much the same way that Russians flavor vodka.

Sunday is market day in Tlacolula, with rows of textiles fluttering in the breeze and aisle after aisle of pottery and baskets. If you don't go on market day, you have the advantage of not competing with crowds. The **Capilla del Mártir** of the parochial church is a stunning display of virtuosity in wrought iron. The doorway, choir screen, and pulpit, with their baroque convolutions, have no equals in Mexico's religious architecture. Also eye-catching are the realistic, almost life-size sculptures of the 12 apostles in their various manners of martyrdom. A few years ago, a secret passage was found in the church, leading to a room that contained valuable silver religious pieces. The silver was hidden during the Revolution of 1916, when there was a tide of anticlerical sentiment; the articles are now back in the church.

YAGUL'S ZAPOTEC FORTRESS   Yagul, a fortress city on a hill overlooking the valley, is a couple of kilometers (about 1½ miles) farther on down the highway. You'll see the turnoff to the left; it's less than a kilometer (about ½ mile) off the road. The setting is spectacular, and because the ruins are not as fully reconstructed as those at Monte Albán, you're likely to have the place to yourself. It's a good place for a picnic lunch.

The city was divided into two sections: the fortress at the top of the hill and the palaces lower down. The center of the palace complex is the plaza, surrounded by four temples. In the center is a ceremonial platform, under which is the **Triple Tomb.** The door of the tomb is a large stone slab decorated on both sides with beautiful hieroglyphs. The tomb may be open for viewing; if there are two guards, one can leave the entrance to escort visitors.

Look for the beautifully restored, typically Zapotec **ball court.** North of the plaza is the **palace** structure built for the chiefs of the city. It's a maze of rooms and patios decorated with painted stucco and stone mosaics. Visible here and there are ceremonial mounds and tombs decorated in the same geometric patterns found in Mitla. The panoramic view of the valley from the fortress is worth the rather exhausting climb.

Admission is $3. Still cameras are free, but use of a video camera costs $5. The site is open daily from 8am to 5:30pm.

It's just a few kilometers farther southeast to Mitla. The turnoff comes at a very obvious fork in the road.

MITLA'S LARGE ZAPOTEC & MIXTEC SITE   Mitla is 4km (2¾ miles) from the highway; the turnoff terminates at the **ruins** by the church. If you've come here by bus, it's less than a kilometer (about ½ mile) up the road from the dusty town square to the ruins; if you want to hire a cab, there are some in the square.

The Zapotec settled Mitla around 600 B.C., and it became a Mixtec bastion in the late 10th century. This city was still flourishing at the time of the Spanish Conquest, and many of the buildings were used through the 16th century.

Tour groups often bypass the **town of Mitla** (pop. 7,000), but it is worth a visit. The University of the Americas maintains the **Museum of Zapotec Art** (previously known as the Frissell collection) in town. It contains some outstanding Zapotec and Mixtec relics. Admission is $3. Be sure to look at the Leigh collection, which contains some real treasures. The museum is in a beautiful old hacienda.

You can easily see the most important buildings in an hour. Mixtec architecture is based on a quadrangle surrounded on three or four sides by patios and chambers, usually rectangular. The chambers are under a low roof, which is excellent for defense but makes the rooms dark and close. The stone buildings are inlaid with small cut stones to form geometric patterns.

There are five groups of buildings, divided by the Mitla River. The most important buildings are on the east side of the ravine. The **Group of the Columns** consists of two quadrangles, connected at the corners with palaces. The building to the north has a long chamber with six columns and many rooms decorated with geometric designs. The most common motif is the zigzag pattern, the same one seen repeatedly on Mitla blankets. Human and animal images are rare in Mixtec art. In fact, only one **frieze** has been found (in the Group of the Church, on the north patio). Here, you'll see a series of figures painted with their name glyphs.

Admission to the site is $3. Use of a video camera costs $5. Entrance to the museum is included in the price. It's open daily from 8am to 5pm.

Outside the ruins, vendors will hound you. The moment you step out of a car or taxi, every able-bodied woman and child for miles around will come charging over with shrill cries and a basket full of bargains—heavily embroidered belts, small pieces of pottery, fake archaeological relics, and cheap earrings. Offer to pay half the price the vendors ask. There's a modern handicrafts market near the ruins, but prices are lower in town.

SOUTH OF MONTE ALBAN: ARRAZOLA, CUILAPAN & ZAACHILA

ARRAZOLA: WOODCARVING CAPITAL   Arrazola lies in the foothills of Monte Albán, about 24km (15 miles) southwest of Oaxaca. The tiny town's most famous resident is **Manuel Jiménez,** the septuagenarian grandfather of the resurgence in wood-carving-as-folk-art. Jiménez's polar bears, anteaters, and rabbits carved from copal wood are shown in galleries throughout the world; his home is a magnet for folk-art collectors. Now the town is full of other carvers, all making fanciful creatures painted in bright, festive colors. Little boys will greet you at the outskirts offering to guide you to individual homes for a small tip. Following them is a good way to get to know the town, and after a bit you can take your leave of them.

If you're driving to Arrazola, take the road out of Oaxaca City that goes to Monte Albán, then take the left fork after crossing the Atoyac River and follow the signs for Zaachila. Turn right after the town of Xoxo and you will soon reach Arrazola. You can also take a bus from the second-class station near the Abastos Market.

CUILAPAN'S DOMINICAN MONASTERY   Cuilapan (kwi-*lah*-pan) is about 15km (10 miles) southwest of Oaxaca. The Dominican friars inaugurated their second **monastery** here in 1550. Parts of the convent and church were never completed due to political complications in the late 16th century. The roof of the monastery has fallen in, but the cloister and the church remain. The church, which is still in use, is being restored. There are three naves with lofty arches, large stone columns, and many frescoes. It is open daily from 10am to 6pm; entry is $5.50, plus $4 for a video camera. The monastery is visible on the right a short distance from the main road to Zaachila, and there's a sign as well. The bus from the second-class station stops within a few hundred feet of the church.

ZAACHILA: MARKET TOWN WITH MIXTEC TOMBS Farther on from Cuilapan, 24km (15 miles) southwest of Oaxaca, Zaachila (sah-*chee*-lah) has a **Thursday market;** baskets and pottery are sold for local household use, and the produce market is always full. Also take note of the interesting livestock section and a **mercado de madera (wood market)** just as you enter town.

Behind the church is the entrance to a small **archaeological site** containing several mounds and platforms and two interesting tombs. The artifacts found here now reside in the National Museum of Anthropology in Mexico City, but **Tomb 1** contains carvings that are worth checking out.

At the time of the Spanish Conquest, Zaachila was the last surviving city of the Zapotec rulers. When Cortez marched on the city, the Zapotec offered no resistance, and he formed an alliance with them. This outraged the Mixtec, who invaded Zaachila shortly afterward. The site and tombs are open daily from 9am till 4pm, and the entrance fee is $3.

To return to Oaxaca, your best option is to line up with locals to take one of the *colectivo* taxis on the main street across from the market. If you're driving, see the directions for Arrazola, above.

SOUTH ALONG HIGHWAY 175

SAN BARTOLO COYOTEPEC'S POTTERY San Bartolo is the home of the famous **black pottery** sold all over Oaxaca. It's also one of several little villages named Coyotepec in the area. Buses frequently operate between Oaxaca and this village, about 15km (10 miles) south on Highway 175. In 1953, a native woman named Doña Rosa invented the technique of smoking the pottery during firing to make it black and rubbing the fired pieces with a piece of quartz to produce a sheen. Doña Rosa died in 1979, and her son, **Valente Nieto Real,** carries on the tradition. Watching Valente change a lump of coarse clay into a work of art with only two crude plates (used as a potter's wheel) is an almost magical experience. The family's home and factory is a few blocks off the main road; you'll see the sign as you enter town. It's open daily from 9am to 5:30pm.

You can buy black pottery at many shops on the little plaza or in the artists' homes. Villagers who make pottery often place a piece of their work near their front door, by the gate, or on the street. It's their way of inviting prospective buyers to come in.

SAN MARTIN TILCAJETE: WOODCARVING VILLAGE San Martín Tilcajete, about 15km (10 miles) past San Bartolo, is home to **woodcarvers** who produce *alebrijes*—fantastical, brightly painted animals and imaginary beasts—much like those produced in Arrazola. You can wander from house to house viewing the amazing collections of hot-pink rabbits; 1.2m (4-ft.), bright-blue twisting snakes; and two-headed Dalmatians.

SANTO TOMAS JALIETZA About 2km (1½ mile) beyond San Martín, you'll see a sign on the left for this village of **weavers** who use backstrap looms. The village

Tips An Excellent Website for Chiapas

The Net Traveler (www.thenettraveler.com) specializes in information about the Yucatán, Quintana Roo (home state of Cancún), Chiapas, and other areas in the old Maya empire. Its information on archaeological sites and on diving in the region's caves and *cenotes* (sinkholes) is especially good.

cooperative runs a market in the middle of town. Prices are fixed; you'll find the greatest variety of goods on Friday.

OCOTLAN Twenty minutes farther on Highway 175 brings you to this fairly large market town. This city is notable for a few reasons: One is the **Aguilar sisters** (Josefina, Guillermina, Irene, and Concepción) and their families, who produce red clay pottery figures that are colorful, sometimes humorous, and prized by collectors. You'll see their row of home-workshops on the right as you enter. There are pottery figures on the fence and roof. (Don't go around town asking for the Aguilar family. Most of the town's inhabitants are named Aguilar.)

Ocotlán is also the home of **Rodolfo Morales,** a painter who, upon becoming wealthy and famous, took an active role in aiding his hometown with renovation projects. Two projects worth visiting are the parish church and former convent. Inside the convent, you can see some of the original decorations of the Dominicans. The noticeable sheen of the stucco walls is produced using the viscous innards of the *nopal* cactus. The convent is now a community museum.

Friday is market day in Ocotlán, and the town fills with people and goods. It's a very good market where you can find a variety of things at reasonable prices.

NORTH OF OAXACA

GUELATAO: BIRTHPLACE OF BENITO JUAREZ High in the mountains north of Oaxaca, this lovely town has become a living monument to its favorite son, Benito Juárez. Although usually peaceful, the town comes to life on **Juárez's birthday** (Mar 21). The museum, statues, and plaza all attest to the town's obvious devotion to the patriot.

A second-class bus departs from Oaxaca's first-class station six times daily. There are also several departures from the second-class station. The trip takes at least 2 hours, through gorgeous mountain scenery. Buses return to Oaxaca every 2 hours until 8pm.

EN ROUTE TO SAN CRISTOBAL DE LAS CASAS

Tuxtla Gutiérrez, the boomtown capital of the wild, mountainous state of Chiapas, is about 10 hours from Oaxaca on Highway 190, about 1½ hours before San Cristóbal. If you need to stop for a night's rest, try the **Hotel Bonampak Tuxtla,** Bulevar Domínguez 180 (© 961/613-2050), on the outskirts of town, or the less expensive but sometimes loud **Gran Hotel Humberto,** Av. Central 180 (© 961/612-2080), downtown.

On the highway to San Cristóbal 10 minutes outside of Tuxtla, you get a good view of majestic canyon walls rising from a wide river. This is the **Sumidero Canyon** ✦✦, and a boat trip through it makes a fun outing. Boats leave from a dock where Highway 190 crosses the river and from **Chiapa de Corzo,** a pleasant town just off the highway a couple of minutes down the road. A boat leaves when enough people are waiting. Cost per person is about $9; the trip takes 2 hours. You can get to Chiapa de Corzo from Tuxtla by *colectivo* for about $1.50. One leaves every 10 minutes from the corner of Calles 3 Oriente and 3 Sur.

2 San Cristóbal de las Casas ⋆⋆

229km (143 miles) SW of Palenque; 80km (50 miles) E of Tuxtla Gutiérrez; 74km (46 miles) NW of Comitán; 166km (104 miles) NW of Cuauhtémoc; 451km (282 miles) E of Oaxaca

San Cristóbal is a colonial town of white stucco walls and red-tile roofs, of cobblestone streets and narrow sidewalks, of graceful arcades and open plazas. It lies in a lush valley nearly 2,120m (7,000 ft.) high. The city owes part of its name to the 16th-century cleric Fray Bartolomé de las Casas, who was the town's first bishop and spent the rest of his life waging a political campaign to protect the indigenous peoples of the Americas.

Surrounding the city are many villages of Mayan-speaking Indians who display great variety in their language, dress, and customs, making this area one of the most fascinating in Mexico. San Cristóbal is the principal market town for these Indians, and their point of contact with the outside world. Most of them trek down from the surrounding mountains to sell goods and perform errands; some even live in San Cristóbal because they have been expelled from their villages for religious reasons.

Probably the most visible among the local indigenous groups are the **Chamula.** The men wear baggy thigh-length trousers and white or black *sarapes,* while the women wear blue *rebozos,* gathered white blouses with embroidered trim, and black wool wraparound skirts.

Another local Indian group is the **Zinacantecan,** whose men dress in light-pink overshirts with colorful trim and tassels and, sometimes, short pants. Hat ribbons (now a rare sight) are tied on married men, while ribbons dangle loosely from the hats of bachelors and community leaders. Zinacantecan women wear beautiful, brightly colored woven shawls and black wool skirts. You may also see **Tenejapa** men clad in knee-length black tunics and flat straw hats, and Tenejapa women dressed in beautiful reddish and rust-colored *huipiles.* Women of all groups go barefoot, while men wear handmade sandals or cowboy boots.

Several Indian villages lie within reach of San Cristóbal by road: **Chamula,** with its weavers and highly unorthodox church; **Zinacantán,** whose residents practice their own syncretic religion; **Tenejapa, San Andrés,** and **Magdalena,** known for brocaded textiles; **Amatenango del Valle,** a town of potters; and **Aguacatenango,** known for embroidery. Most of these "villages" consist of little more than a church and the municipal government building, with homes scattered for miles around and a general gathering only for church and market days (usually Sun).

Evangelical Protestant missionaries have converted large numbers of indigenous peoples, and some villages expel new converts from their homelands; in Chamula, for example, as many as 30,000 people have been cast out. Many of these people, *los expulsados* ("the expelled ones"), have taken up residence in new villages on the outskirts of San Cristóbal de las Casas. They still wear traditional dress. Other villages, such as Tenejapa, allow the Protestant church to exist and villagers to attend it without prejudice.

Although the influx of outsiders is nothing new, and in the last 20 years has been increasing, it hasn't created in most Indians a desire to adopt mainstream customs and dress. It's interesting to note that the communities closest to San Cristóbal are the most resistant to change. The greatest threat to the cultures in this area comes not from tourism but from the action of large market forces, population pressures, environmental damage, and poverty. The Indians aren't interested in acting or looking like the foreigners they see. They may steal glances or even stare at tourists, but mainly they pay little attention to outsiders, except as potential buyers for handicrafts.

San Cristóbal de las Casas

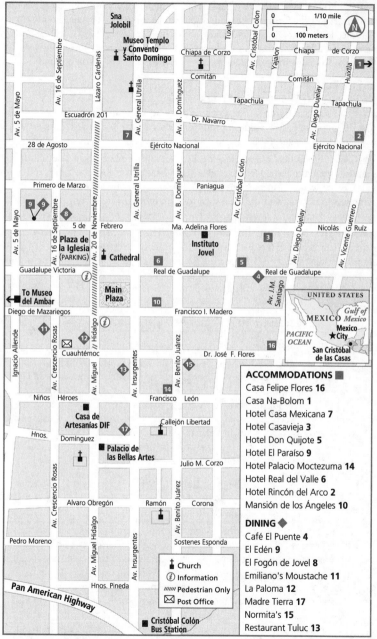

ACCOMMODATIONS ■
Casa Felipe Flores **16**
Casa Na-Bolom **1**
Hotel Casa Mexicana **7**
Hotel Casavieja **3**
Hotel Don Quijote **5**
Hotel El Paraíso **9**
Hotel Palacio Moctezuma **14**
Hotel Real del Valle **6**
Hotel Rincón del Arco **2**
Mansión de los Ángeles **10**

DINING ◆
Café El Puente **4**
El Edén **9**
El Fogón de Jovel **8**
Emiliano's Moustache **11**
La Paloma **12**
Madre Tierra **17**
Normita's **15**
Restaurant Tuluc **13**

✝ Church
ⓘ Information
▨▨▨ Pedestrian Only
✉ Post Office
■ Cristóbal Colón
Bus Station

You'll hear the word *ladino* here; it refers to non-Indian Mexicans. It may be used derogatorily or descriptively, depending on who is using the term and how.

Other local lingo you should know about includes *Jovel,* San Cristóbal's original name, used often by businesses, and *coleto,* meaning someone or something from San Cristóbal. You'll see signs for *tamales coletos, coleto* bread, and *coleto* breakfast.

ESSENTIALS
GETTING THERE & DEPARTING

BY PLANE   San Cristóbal has a new airport. **AeroMar** (© **967/674-3014** or 967/674-3003) operates daily flights to and from Mexico City, but these flights are subject to cancellation on short notice.

BY CAR   From Tuxtla Gutiérrez, the 1½-hour trip winds through beautiful mountain country. From Palenque, the road is just as beautiful (if longer—5 hr.), and it provides jungle scenery, but portions of it may be heavily potholed or obstructed during rainy season. Check with the local state tourism office before driving.

BY TAXI   Taxis from Tuxtla Gutiérrez to San Cristóbal cost around $50. Another way to travel to and from Tuxtla is by *combi.* The Volkswagen vans, which can get extremely crowded, make the run every 15 to 30 minutes and cost $3. They can be found just off the highway by the bus station. You'll have to ask someone to point them out to you because there isn't a sign.

The Zapatista Uprising & Lingering Tensions

In January 1994, Indians from this area rebelled against the *ladino*-led towns and Mexican government over health care, education, land distribution, and representative government. Their organization, the **Zapatista Liberation Army,** known as EZLN (Ejército Zapatista de Liberación Nacional), and its leader, Subcomandante Marcos, have become emblematic of the problems Mexico has with social justice. Since the revolt, discussions between government officials and the leadership of the EZLN have stalled. Progress has been made, but the principal issues remain unresolved, and tension remains. In 1997 and 1998 there were more killings, but these have been attributed to local political division rather than the tension between Zapatistas and the national government. We may never know the truth.

When in San Cristóbal, you'll see little evidence of social tension. There might be a political demonstration or perhaps a strike; you will see some political graffiti here and there, and, of course, you'll find little Subcomandante Marcos dolls, replete with black ski masks, offered for sale by street vendors (a hot-selling item, by the way). Locals don't seem concerned, and tourists are showing up in substantial numbers.

One of the first actions that Vicente Fox took on assuming the presidency of Mexico was to withdraw most of the military forces from the region and offer an olive branch to the Zapatistas. But direct talks between Zapatistas and members of the national legislature ended in stalemate. Before traveling to Chiapas, check your news sources and see if the State Department has issued any advisories: **http://travel.state.gov**.

BY BUS   The two bus stations in town are directly across the Pan American Highway from each other. The smaller one belongs to Transportes Rodolfo Figueroa, which provides first-class service to and from Tuxtla (every 40 min.) and Palenque (four buses per day, with a stop in Ocosingo—cheaper than the competition). For other destinations, go to the large station run by ADO and its affiliates, Altos, Cristóbal Colón, and Maya de Oro. This company offers service to and from Tuxtla (12 buses per day), Palenque (almost every hour), and several other destinations: Mérida (two buses per day), Villa-hermosa (two buses per day), Oaxaca (two buses per day), and Puerto Escondido (two buses per day). To buy a bus ticket without going down to the station, go to the **Ticket Bus** agency, Av. Belisario Domínguez 8 (© **967/678-0291**). Hours are Monday to Saturday from 9am to 2pm and 4 to 7pm, Sunday from 9am to 5pm.

ORIENTATION

ARRIVING   To get to the main plaza if you're arriving by car from Oaxaca and Tuxtla, turn left on **Avenida Insurgentes** (there's a traffic light); if you're coming from Palenque and Ocosingo, turn right. From the bus station, the main plaza is 9 blocks north up Avenida Insurgentes (a 10-min. walk, slightly uphill). Cabs are cheap and plentiful.

VISITOR INFORMATION   The **State Tourism Office** is just off the southwest corner of the main plaza, at Av. Hidalgo 1-B (© **967/678-6570**); it's open Monday to Friday from 8am to 8pm, Saturday from 9am to 8pm, and Sunday from 9am to 2pm. The **Municipal Tourism Office** (©/fax **967/678-0665**) is in the town hall, west of the main square. Hours are Monday to Saturday from 9am to 8pm. Check the bulletin board here for apartments, shared rides, cultural events, and local tours. Both offices are helpful, but the state office is open an hour later and is better staffed.

CITY LAYOUT   San Cristóbal is laid out on a grid; the main north-south axis is **Insurgentes/Utrilla,** and the east-west axis is **Mazariegos/Madero.** All streets change names when they cross either of these streets. The *zócalo* (main plaza) lies where they intersect. **Real de Guadalupe** seems to have become a principal street for tourism-related businesses. The market is 7 blocks north of the *zócalo* along Utrilla.

Take note that this town has at least three streets named Domínguez and two streets named Flores. There's Hermanos Domínguez, Belisario Domínguez, and Pantaleón Domínguez, and María Adelina Flores and Dr. José Flores.

GETTING AROUND   Most of the sights and shopping in San Cristóbal are within walking distance of the plaza.

Urbano buses **(minibuses)** take passengers between town and the residential neighborhoods. All buses pass by the market and central plaza on their way through town. Utrilla and Avenida 16 de Septiembre are the two main arteries; all buses use the market area as the last stop. Any bus on Utrilla will take you to the market.

Colectivos **(minibuses)** to outlying villages depart from the public market at Avenida Utrilla. Buses late in the day are usually very crowded. Always check to see when the last or next-to-last bus returns from wherever you're going, and then take the one before that—those last buses sometimes don't materialize, and you might be stranded. I speak from experience!

Rental cars come in handy for trips to the outlying villages and may be worth the expense when shared by a group, but keep in mind that insurance is invalid on unpaved roads. Try **Optima Car Rental,** Av. Mazariegos 39 (© **967/674-5409**). Office hours are daily from 9am to 1pm and 5 to 8pm. You'll save money by arranging the rental from your home country; otherwise, a day's rental with insurance will cost around $60 for a VW Beetle with manual transmission, the cheapest car available.

Bikes are another option for getting around the city; a day's rental is about $8. **Los Pingüinos,** Av. Ecuador 4-B (© 967/678-0202; pinguinosmex@yahoo.com), offers bike tours to a few out-of-town locations. Tours in the valley around San Cristóbal last 4 to 6 hours and cost $20 to $25. It's open daily from 10am to 2:30pm and 4 to 7pm.

FAST FACTS: San Cristóbal de las Casas

Area Code The telephone area code is **967**.

Books *Living Maya,* by Walter Morris, with photography by Jeffrey Fox, is the best book to read to understand the culture, art, and traditions surrounding San Cristóbal de las Casas, as well as the unresolved social, economic, and political problems that gave rise to the 1994 Chiapas Indian uprising. *The People of the Bat: Mayan Tales and Dreams from Zinacantán,* by Robert M. Laughlin, is a priceless collection of beliefs from that village near San Cristóbal. Another good book with a completely different view of today's Maya is *The Heart of the Sky,* by Peter Canby, who traveled among the Maya to chronicle their struggles (and wrote his book before the Zapatista uprising).

Bookstore For the best selection of new and used books and reading material in English, go to **La Pared,** Av. Hidalgo 2 (© **967/678-6367**). The owner, Dana Gay Burton, keeps a great collection of books on the Maya, and Mexico in general, both fiction and nonfiction.

Bulletin Boards Because San Cristóbal is a cultural crossroads for travelers from all over the world, several places maintain bulletin boards with information on Spanish classes, local specialty tours, rooms or houses to rent, rides needed, and so on. These include boards at the **Tourism Office, Café El Puente, Madre Tierra,** and **Casa Na-Bolom.**

Climate San Cristóbal can be chilly when the sun isn't out, especially during the winter. It's 2,200m (7,200 ft.) above sea level. Most hotels are not heated, although some have fireplaces. There is always a possibility of rain, but I would avoid going to San Cristóbal from late August to late October, during the height of the rainy season.

Currency Exchange There are at least five *casas de cambio* on Real de Guadalupe near the main square, and a couple under the colonnade facing the square. Most are open until 8pm, and some are open Sunday. There are also a number of ATMs.

Doctor The only doctor worth seeing is **Dr. Roberto Lobato,** Av. Belisario Domínguez 17, at Calle Flavio A. Paniagua (© **967/678-7777**). Don't be unsettled by the fact that his office is next door to Funerales Canober.

Internet Access **The Cyberc@fe** (© **967/678-7488**) is in the little concourse that cuts through the block just east of the main square. Look for the entrance on Real de Guadalupe or Francisco Madero. It is one of the largest Internet cafes I have seen in Mexico, with several well-connected machines and a few other toys.

Parking If your hotel does not have parking, use the *estacionamiento* (underground public lot) in front of the cathedral, just off the main square on 16 de Septiembre. Entry is from Calle 5 de Febrero.

Population San Cristóbal has 132,000 residents.

Post Office The *correo* is at Crescencio Rosas and Cuauhtémoc, a block south and west of the main square. It's open Monday to Friday from 8am to 7pm, Saturday from 9am to 1pm.

Spanish Classes The **Instituto Jovel,** María Adelina Flores 21 (Apdo. Postal 62), 29250 San Cristóbal de las Casas, Chi. (℃/fax **967/678-4069**), gets higher marks for its Spanish courses than the competition. It also offers courses in weaving and cooking. The **Centro Bilingüe,** at the Centro Cultural El Puente, Real de Guadalupe 55, 29250 San Cristóbal de las Casas, Chi. (℃ **800/303-4983** in the U.S., or ℃/fax 967/678-3723), offers classes in Spanish. Both schools can arrange home stays for their students.

Telephone The best price for long-distance telephone calls and faxing is at **La Pared** bookstore (see "Bookstore," above) at Av. Hidalgo 2, across the street from the State Tourism Office.

EXPLORING SAN CRISTOBAL

With its beautiful scenery, clean air, and mountain hikes, San Cristóbal draws many visitors. However, the town's biggest attraction is its colorful, centuries-old indigenous culture. The Chiapanecan Maya, attired in their unique native garb, can be seen anywhere in San Cristóbal, but most travelers take at least one trip to the outlying villages to get a close-up of Maya life. Don't neglect to meander through the San Cristóbal market. It's behind the Santo Domingo church (see "Attractions in Town," below) and is open almost every day, but never on Sunday. You can witness scenes of everyday local life, plus some that aren't so everyday.

ATTRACTIONS IN TOWN

Casa Na-Bolom 🌟🌟   If you're interested in the anthropology of the region, you'll want to visit this house museum. Stay here, if you can. The house, built as a seminary in 1891, became the headquarters of anthropologists Frans and Trudy Blom in 1951, and the gathering place of outsiders interested in studying the region. Frans Blom led many early archaeological studies in Mexico, and Trudy was noted for her photographs of the Lacandón Indians and her efforts to save them and their forest homeland. A room at Na-Bolom contains a selection of her Lacandón photographs, and postcards of the photographs are on sale in the gift shop (daily 9am–2pm and 4–7pm). A tour of the home covers the displays of pre-Hispanic artifacts collected by Frans Blom; the cozy library, with its numerous volumes about the region and the Maya (weekdays 10am–2pm); and the gardens Trudy Blom started for the ongoing reforestation of the Lacandón jungle. The tour ends with a showing of *La Reina de la Selva,* an excellent 50-minute film on the Bloms, the Lacandón, and Na-Bolom. Trudy Blom died in 1993, but Na-Bolom continues to operate as a nonprofit public trust.

The 12 guest rooms, named for surrounding villages, are decorated with local objects and textiles. All rooms have fireplaces and private bathrooms. Prices for rooms (including breakfast) are $50 single, $60 double.

> ### ⟮*Tips*⟯ Photography Warning
>
> Photographers should be cautious about when, where, and at whom or what they point their cameras. In San Cristóbal, taking a photograph of even a chile pepper can be a risky undertaking; locals just do not like having people take pictures. Especially in the San Cristóbal market, people who think they or their possessions are being photographed may angrily pelt photographers with whatever object is at hand—rocks or rotten fruit. Be respectful and ask first. Young handicrafts vendors will sometimes offer to be photographed for money.
>
> Nearby villages have strict rules about photography. Villages around San Cristóbal, especially Chamula and Zinacantán, require visitors to go to the municipal building upon arrival and sign an agreement (written in Spanish) not to take photographs. The penalty for disobeying these regulations is stiff: confiscation of your camera and perhaps even a lengthy stay in jail. And they mean it!

Even if you're not a guest here, you can come for a meal, usually a delicious assortment of vegetarian and other dishes. Just be sure to make a reservation at least 2½ hours in advance, and be on time. The colorful dining room has one large table, and the eclectic mix of travelers sometimes makes for interesting conversation. Breakfast costs $3 to $7; lunch and dinner cost $10 each. Dinner is served at 7pm. Following breakfast (8–10am), a guide not affiliated with the house offers tours to San Juan Chamula and Zinacantán (see "The Nearby Maya Villages & Countryside," below).

Av. Vicente Guerrero 3, 29200 San Cristóbal de las Casas, Chi. ℂ 967/678-1418. Fax 967/678-5586. Group tour and film $5. Tours daily 11:30am and 4:30pm. Leave the square on Real de Guadalupe, walk 4 blocks to Av. Vicente Guerrero, and turn left; Na-Bolom is 5½ blocks up Guerrero.

Catedral San Cristóbal's main cathedral was built in the 1500s. It has little of interest inside besides a lovely, uncommon beam ceiling and a carved wooden pulpit.

Calle 20 de Noviembre at Guadalupe Victoria. No phone. Free admission. Daily 7am–6pm.

Museo del Ambar 𝒜 If you've been in this town any time at all, you know what a big deal amber is here. Chiapas is the third-largest producer of amber in the world, and many experts prefer its amber for its colors and clarity. A couple of stores tried calling themselves museums but they didn't fool anybody. Now a real museum moves methodically through all the issues surrounding amber—mining, shaping, the differences between real and fake amber, variations of the mineral you'll find in different parts of the world. It's interesting, it's cheap, and you get to see the restored area of the old convent it occupies. There are a couple of beautiful pieces of worked amber that are on permanent loan. Make sure you see them. In mid-August, the museum holds a contest for local artisans who work amber. Check it out.

Exconvento de la Merced, Diego de Mazariegos s/n. ℂ 967/678-9716. Admission $1. Tues–Sun 10am–2pm and 4–7pm.

Museo Templo y Convento Santo Domingo Inside the front door of the carved-stone plateresque facade, there's a beautiful gilded wooden altarpiece built in 1560, walls with saints, and gilt-framed paintings. Attached to the church is the former Convent of Santo Domingo, which houses a small museum about San Cristóbal and Chiapas. The museum has changing exhibits and often shows cultural films. It's 5 blocks north of the *zócalo,* in the market area.

Av. 20 de Noviembre. ℂ **967/678-1609.** Free admission to church; museum $2. Museum Tues–Sun 10am–5pm.

Palacio de las Bellas Artes   Be sure to check out this building if you are interested in the arts. It periodically hosts dance events, art shows, and other performances. The schedule of events is usually posted on the door if the Bellas Artes is not open. There's a public library next door. Around the corner, the Centro Cultural holds a number of concerts and other performances; check the posters on the door to see what's scheduled.

Av. Hidalgo, 4 blocks south of the plaza. No phone.

Templo de San Cristóbal   For the best view of San Cristóbal, climb the seemingly endless steps to this church and *mirador* (lookout point). A visit here requires stamina. By the way, there are 22 more churches in town, some of which also demand strenuous climbs.

At the very end of Calle Hermanos Domínguez.

HORSEBACK RIDING

The **Casa de Huéspedes Margarita,** Real de Guadalupe 34, and **Hotel Real del Valle** (see "Where to Stay," below) can arrange horseback rides for around $15 for a day,

---

Moments   Special Events in & near San Cristóbal

In nearby Chamula, **Carnaval,** the big annual festival that takes place in the days before Lent, is a fascinating mingling of the Christian pre-Lenten ceremonies and the ancient Maya celebration of the 5 "lost days" at the end of the 360-day Maya agricultural cycle. Around noon on Shrove Tuesday, groups of village elders run across patches of burning grass as a purification rite. Macho residents then run through the streets with a bull. During Carnaval, roads close in town, and buses drop visitors at the outskirts.

During this time, nearby villages (except Zinacantán) also have celebrations, although perhaps not as dramatic. Visiting these villages, especially on the Sunday before Lent, will round out your impression of Carnaval in all its regional varieties. In Tenejapa, the celebration continues during the Thursday market after Ash Wednesday.

During Easter and the week after, for the annual **Feria de Primavera (Spring Festival),** San Cristóbal is ablaze with lights and excitement and gets hordes of visitors. Activities include carnival rides, food stalls, handicraft shops, parades, and band concerts. Hotel rooms are scarce and more expensive.

Another spectacle is staged from July 22 to 25, during the annual **Fiesta de San Cristóbal,** honoring the town's patron saint. The steps up to the San Cristóbal church are lit with torches at night. Pilgrimages to the church begin several days earlier, and on the 24th, there's an all-night vigil.

For the **Día de Guadalupe,** on December 12, honoring Mexico's patron saint, the streets are gaily decorated, and food stalls line the streets leading to the church on a hill where she is honored.

including a guide. Reserve your steed at least a day in advance. A horseback-riding excursion might go to San Juan Chamula, to nearby caves, or just up into the hills.

THE NEARBY MAYA VILLAGES & COUNTRYSIDE

The Indian communities around San Cristóbal are fascinating worlds unto themselves. If you are unfamiliar with these indigenous cultures, you will understand and appreciate more of what you see by visiting them with a guide, at least for your first foray out into the villages. Guides are acquainted with members of the communities and are viewed with less suspicion than newcomers. These communities have their own laws and customs—and visitors' ignorance is no excuse. Entering these communities is tantamount to leaving Mexico, and if something happens, the state and federal authorities will not intervene except in case of a serious crime.

The best guided trips are the locally grown ones. Three operators go to the neighboring villages in small groups. They all charge the same price ($10 per person), use minivans for transportation, and speak English. They do, however, have their own interpretations and focus.

Pepe leaves from **Casa Na-Bolom** (see "Attractions in Town," above) for daily trips to San Juan Chamula and Zinacantán at 10am, returning to San Cristóbal between 2 and 3pm. Pepe looks at cultural continuities, community relationships, and, of course, religion.

Mercedes Hernández Gómez, a very opinionated *mestiza* woman, leads a tour from the main plaza at 9am. She always carries an umbrella by which you can identify her. Mercedes, a largely self-trained ethnographer, is informed about the history and folkways of the villages, and her opinions make for a good tour. Lately, clients have reported that she's been behaving erratically and dictatorially, and has offended a few of those she has taken on tour.

Alex and Raúl can be found in front of the cathedral between 9:15 and 9:30am. They are quite personable and get along well with the Indians in the communities. They focus on cultural values and their expression in social behavior, which provides a glimpse of the details and the texture of life in these communities (and, of course, they talk about religion). Their tour is very good.

The above-mentioned guides (especially Alex and Raúl) can be persuaded to go to other communities besides Chamula and Zinacantán.

CHAMULA & ZINACANTAN A side trip to the village of San Juan Chamula will really get you into the spirit of life around San Cristóbal. Sunday, when the market is in full swing, is the best day to go for shopping; other days, when you'll be less impeded by eager children selling their crafts, are better for seeing the village and church.

The village, 8km (5 miles) northeast of San Cristóbal, has a large church, a plaza, and a municipal building. Each year, a new group of citizens is chosen to live in the municipal center as caretakers of the saints, settlers of disputes, and enforcers of village rules. As in other nearby villages, on Sunday local leaders wear their leadership costumes, including beautifully woven straw hats loaded with colorful ribbons befitting their high position. They solemnly sit together in a long line somewhere around the central square. Chamula is typical of other villages in that men are often away working in the "hotlands," harvesting coffee or cacao, while women stay home to tend the sheep, the children, the cornfields, and the fires. It's almost always the women's and children's work to gather firewood, and you see them along roadsides bent under the weight.

Don't leave Chamula without seeing the **church interior.** As you step from bright sunlight into the candlelit interior, you feel as if you've been transported to another country. Pine needles scattered amid a sea of lighted candles cover the tile floor. Saints line the walls, and before them people are often kneeling and praying aloud while passing around bottles of Pepsi-Cola. Shamans are often on hand, passing eggs over sick people or using live or dead chickens in a curing ritual. The statues of saints are similar to those you might see in any Mexican Catholic church, but beyond sharing the same name, they mean something completely different to the Chamulas. Visitors can walk carefully through the church to see the saints or stand quietly in the background and observe.

Carnaval, which takes place just before Lent, is the big annual festival. The Chamulas are not a wealthy people, but the women are the region's best wool weavers, producing finished pieces for themselves and for other villages.

In Zinacantán, a wealthier village than Chamula, you must sign a rigid form promising *not to take any photographs* before you see the two side-by-side **sanctuaries.** Once permission is granted and you have paid a small fee, an escort will usually show you the church, or you may be allowed to see it on your own. Floors may be covered in pine needles here, too, and the rooms are brightly sunlit. The experience is an altogether different one from that of Chamula.

AMATENANGO DEL VALLE   About an hour's ride south of San Cristóbal is Amatenango, a town known mostly for its **women potters.** You'll see their work in San Cristóbal—small animals, jars, and large water jugs—but in the village, you can visit the potters in their homes. Just walk down the dirt streets. Villagers will lean over the walls of family compounds and invite you in to select from their inventory. You may even see them firing the pieces under piles of wood in the open courtyard or painting them with color derived from rusty iron water. The women wear beautiful red-and-yellow *huipiles,* but if you want to take a photograph, you'll have to pay.

To get here, take a *colectivo* from the market in San Cristóbal. Before it lets you off, be sure to ask about the return-trip schedule.

AGUACATENANGO   This village 15km (10 miles) south of Amatenango is known for its **embroidery.** If you've visited San Cristóbal's shops, you'll recognize the white-on-white and black-on-black floral patterns on dresses and blouses for sale. The locals' own regional blouses, however, are quite different.

TENEJAPA   The **weavers** of Tenejapa, 28km (17 miles) from San Cristóbal, make some of the most beautiful and expensive work you'll see in the region. The best time to visit is on market day (Sun and Thurs, though Sun is better). The weavers of Tenejapa taught the weavers of San Andrés and Magdalena—which accounts for the similarity in their designs and colors. To get to Tenejapa, try to find a *colectivo* in the very last row by the market, or hire a taxi. On Tenejapa's main street, several stores sell locally woven regional clothing, and you can bargain for the price.

THE HUITEPEC CLOUD FOREST   Pronatura, Av. Benito Juárez 11-B (© 967/678-5000), a private, nonprofit, ecological organization, offers environmentally sensitive tours of the cloud forest. The forest is a haven for **migratory birds,** and more than 100 bird species and 600 plant species have been discovered here. Guided tours run from 9am to noon Tuesday to Sunday. They cost $25 per group of up to eight people. Make reservations a day in advance. To reach the reserve on your own, drive on the road to Chamula; the turnoff is at Km 3.5. The reserve is open Tuesday to Sunday from 9am to 4pm.

SHOPPING

Many Indian villages near San Cristóbal are noted for **weaving, embroidery, brocade work, leather,** and **pottery,** making the area one of the best in the country for shopping. You'll see beautiful woolen shawls, indigo-dyed skirts, colorful native shirts, and magnificently woven *huipiles,* all of which often come in vivid geometric patterns. Working in leather, the craftspeople are artisans of the highest caliber. Tie-dyed *jaspe* from Guatemala comes in bolts and is made into clothing. The town is also known for **amber,** sold in several shops and at La Pared bookstore (see "Bookstore" in "Fast Facts," earlier in this chapter). Shops line the streets leading to the market. Calle Real de Guadalupe has more shops than any other street.

CRAFTS

Casa de Artesanías   This fine showroom is in one of the city's old houses. Here you'll find such quality products as lined woolen vests and jackets, pillow covers, amber jewelry, and more. In back, a fine little museum shows costumes worn by villagers who live near San Cristóbal. It's open Tuesday to Saturday from 9am to 2pm and 5 to 8pm. Niños Héroes at Hidalgo. © 967/678-1180.

Central Market   The market buildings and the surrounding streets offer just about anything you need. The market in San Cristóbal is open every morning except Sunday (when each village has its own local market), and you'll probably enjoy observing the sellers as much as the things they sell. See "Photography Warning," earlier in this chapter, regarding picture-taking here. The *mercado* is north of the Santo Domingo church, about 7 blocks from the *zócalo.* Av. Utrilla. No phone.

El Encuentro   You should find some of your best bargains here—at a minimum, you'll think that the price is fair. The shop carries many regional ritual items, such as new and used men's ceremonial hats, false saints, and iron rooftop adornments, plus many *huipiles* and other textiles. It's open Monday to Saturday from 9am to 8pm. Calle Real de Guadalupe 63-A (between Diego Dujelay and Vicente Guerrero). © 967/678-3698.

La Alborada, Centro Desarrollo Comunitario DIF   At this government-sponsored school, young men and women from surrounding villages come to learn how to hook Persian-style rugs, weave fabric on foot looms, sew, make furniture, construct a house, cook, make leather shoes and bags, forge iron, and grow vegetables and trees for reforestation. Probably the most interesting crafts for the general tourist are the rugs and woven goods. Artisans from Temoaya in Mexico state learned rug making from Persians, who came to teach this skill in the 1970s. The Temoaya artisans, in turn, traveled to San Cristóbal to teach the craft to area students, who have taught others. The beautiful rug designs come from brocaded and woven designs used to decorate regional costumes. Visitors should stop at the entrance and ask for an escort. You can visit the various areas and see students at work, or go straight to the weavers. A small outlet at the entrance sells newly loomed fabric by the meter, leather bags, rugs, and baskets made at another school in the highlands. La Alborada is in a far southern suburb of the city off the highway to Comitán, to the right. To get there, take a cab. The school may be closed; midmorning is the likeliest time to find it open. Barrio María Auxiliadora. No phone.

La Galería   This lovely gallery beneath a cafe shows the work of well-known national and international painters. Also for sale are paintings and greeting cards by Kiki, the owner, a German artist who has found her niche in San Cristóbal. There are some Oaxacan rugs and pottery, plus unusual silver jewelry. It's open daily from 10am to 9pm. In the evenings, the bar opens and a jazz band plays from 9 to 10pm; afterward, another band plays Latin dance music. Hidalgo 3. ✆ **967/678-1547.**

Taller Leñateros   Paper making isn't all they do here, but it's executed with enough creativity and diversity of materials to warrant mention on that alone. This shop and workshop is a cooperative effort by six women: five Maya Indians and one American. They also make paper creations, silk screens, woodcuts, and binding, and they've put all those talents together to produce their own magazine. This shop is open Monday to Friday from 8:30am to 8pm, Saturday from 8:30am to 1:30pm; if you want to see paper being made, show up before 4pm. Flavio A. Paniagua 54. ✆ **967/678-5174.**

TEXTILES

Kun Kun SC   The name means "little by little." This cooperative society to aid local native artisans sells mostly ceramic tiles, weavings, and pottery. The weavings are made of locally produced wool that has been spun, dyed, and woven by members. Kun Kun holds workshops for artisans on such things as working with floor looms, which you can watch at the store. The tiles are wonderful. Also, if you're interested, ask about classes in using a backstrap loom. The workshop and store are open Monday to Saturday from 9am to 3pm. Another store, at Real de Guadalupe 55, closer to the plaza, stays open until 8pm. Real de Mexicanos 21. ✆ **967/678-1417.**

Plaza de Santo Domingo   The plazas around this church and the nearby Templo de Caridad fill with women in native garb selling their wares. Here you'll find women from Chamula weaving belts or embroidering, surrounded by piles of loomed woolen textiles from their village. Their inventory includes Guatemalan shawls, belts, and bags. There are also some excellent buys on Chiapanecan-made wool vests, jackets, rugs, and shawls, similar to those at Sna Jolobil (described below), if you take the time to look and bargain. Vendors arrive between 9 and 10am and begin to leave around 3pm. Av. Utrilla. No phone.

Sna Jolobil   Meaning "weaver's house" in Mayan, this place is in the former convent of Santo Domingo, next to the Templo de Santo Domingo. Groups of Tzotzil and Tzeltal craftspeople operate the cooperative store, which has about 3,000 members who contribute products, help run the store, and share in the moderate profits. Their works are simply beautiful; prices are high, as is the quality. Be sure to take a look. It's open Monday to Saturday from 9am to 2pm and 4 to 6pm; credit cards are accepted. Calzada Lázaro Cárdenas 42 (Plaza Santo Domingo, between Navarro and Nicaragua). ✆ **967/678-2646.**

Unión Regional de Artesanías de los Altos   Also known as J'pas Jolovlletic, this cooperative of weavers is smaller than Sna Jolobil (described above) and not as sophisticated in its approach to potential shoppers. It sells blouses, textiles, pillow covers, vests, sashes, napkins, baskets, and purses. It's near the market and worth looking around. Open Monday to Saturday from 9am to 2pm and 4 to 7pm, Sunday from 9am to 1pm. Av. Utrilla 43. ✆ **967/678-2848.**

WHERE TO STAY

Among the most interesting places to stay in San Cristóbal is the seminary-turned-hotel-museum **Casa Na-Bolom;** see "Attractions in Town," earlier in this chapter, for details.

Hotels in San Cristóbal are inexpensive by comparison with most of Mexico. You can do pretty well for $20 to $30 per night per double. Rates listed here include taxes. High season is Easter week, July to August, and December.

EXPENSIVE

Casa Felipe Flores ⭐⭐   This beautifully restored colonial house is the perfect setting for getting the feel of San Cristóbal. The patios and common rooms are relaxing and comfortable, and their architectural details are so very *coleto*. The guest rooms are nicely furnished and full of character. And they are warm in winter. The owners, Nancy and David Orr, are gracious people who enjoy sharing their appreciation and knowledge of Chiapas and the Maya. Their cook serves up righteous breakfasts.

Calle Dr. Felipe Flores 36, 29230 San Cristóbal de las Casas, Chi. ℭ/fax **967/678-3996**. www.felipeflores.com. 5 units. $85–$95 double. Rates include full breakfast. 10% service charge. No credit cards. **Amenities:** Tour info; laundry service; library.

Hotel Casa Mexicana ⭐⭐   Created from a large mansion, this beautiful hotel with a colonial-style courtyard offers comfortable lodging. Rooms, courtyards, the restaurant, and the lobby are decorated in modern-traditional Mexican style, with warm tones of yellow and red. The rooms are carpeted and come with two double beds or one king-size. They have good lighting, electric heaters, and spacious bathrooms. Guests are welcome to use the sauna, and inexpensive massages can be arranged. The hotel handles a lot of large tour groups; it can be quiet and peaceful one day and full and bustling the next. There is a new addition to the hotel across the street, but I like the doubles in the original section better. This hotel is 3 blocks north of the main plaza.

28 de Agosto 1 (at Utrilla), 29200 San Cristóbal de las Casas, Chi. ℭ **967/678-1348** or 967/678-0698. Fax 967/678-2627. www.hotelcasamexicana.com. 55 units. High season $95 double, $150 junior suite, $180 suite; low season $85 double, $140 junior suite, $170 suite. AE, MC, V. Free secure parking 1½ blocks away. **Amenities:** Restaurant; bar; sauna; tour info; room service until 10pm; massage; babysitting; laundry service. *In room:* TV, dataport, hair dryer on request.

MODERATE

Hotel Casavieja   The Casavieja is aptly named: It has a charming old feel that is San Cristóbal to a tee. Originally built in 1740, it has undergone restoration and new construction faithful to the original design in essentials such as wood-beam ceilings. One nod toward modernity is carpeted floors, a welcome feature on cold mornings. The rooms also come with electric heaters. Bathrooms vary, depending on what section of the hotel you're in, but all are adequate. The hotel's restaurant, Doña Rita, faces the interior courtyard, with tables on the patio and inside, and offers good food at reasonable prices. The hotel is 3½ blocks northeast of the plaza.

María Adelina Flores 27 (between Cristóbal Colón and Diego Dujelay), 29200 San Cristóbal de las Casas, Chi. ℭ/fax **967/678-6868** or 967/678-0385. www.casavieja.com.mx. 39 units. $75 double. AE, MC, V. Free parking. **Amenities:** Restaurant; bar; room service until 10:30pm; laundry service. *In room:* TV.

Hotel El Paraíso   For the independent traveler, this is a safe haven from the busloads of tour groups that can upset the atmosphere and service at other hotels. Rooms are small but beautifully decorated. They have comfortable beds and good reading lights; some rooms even have a ladder to a loft holding a second bed. Bathrooms are small, too, but the plumbing is good. The entire hotel is decorated in terra cotta and blue, with beautiful wooden columns and beams supporting the roof. The hotel's restaurant, El Edén (see "Where to Dine," below) may be the best in town.

Av. 5 de Febrero 19, 29200 San Cristóbal de las Casas, Chi. ℭ **967/678-0085** or 967/678-5382. Fax 967/678-5168. www.hotelposadaparaiso.com. 14 units. $70 double. AE, MC, V. **Amenities:** Restaurant; bar; tour info; room service until 11pm; laundry service. *In room:* TV.

Hotel Rincón del Arco   This well-run hotel has comfortable rooms at a good price. The original section of the former colonial-era home surrounds a small interior patio and dates from 1650. Rooms in this part are spacious, with tall ceilings and carpet over hardwood floors. The adjacent new section looks out across a grass yard to the mountains and the valley. These rooms are nicely furnished, and the thick bedspreads come from the family factory, which you can visit next door. Some rooms have small balconies; all have fireplaces. There's a restaurant just behind the lobby. The only downside is that it's a bit of a walk from the main plaza (8 blocks northeast).

Ejército Nacional 66 (at Av. Vicente Guerrero), 29220 San Cristóbal de las Casas, Chi. ✆ 967/678-1313. Fax 967/678-1568. www.rincondelarco.com. 50 units. $70 double. MC, V. Free parking. **Amenities:** Restaurant; room service; laundry service. *In room:* TV.

INEXPENSIVE

Hotel Don Quijote   Rooms in this three-story hotel (no elevator) are small but quiet, carpeted, and well lit. All have two double beds with reading lamps over them, tiled bathrooms, and plenty of hot water. There's complimentary coffee in the mornings. It's 2½ blocks east of the plaza.

Cristóbal Colón 7 (near Real de Guadalupe), 29200 San Cristóbal de las Casas, Chi. ✆ 967/678-0920. Fax 967/678-0346. 24 units. $25–$40 double. MC, V. Free secure parking 1 block away. *In room:* TV.

Hotel Real del Valle *Value*   The Real del Valle is just off the main plaza. The 24 recently added rooms in the back three-story section have new bathrooms, big closets, and tile floors. In addition to a rooftop solarium, you'll find a small cafeteria and an upstairs dining room with a double fireplace.

Real de Guadalupe 14, 29200 San Cristóbal de las Casas, Chi. ✆ 967/678-0680. Fax 967/678-3955. hrvalle@mundomaya.com.mx. 36 units. $30–$45 double. No credit cards. **Amenities:** Restaurant; laundry service. *In room:* TV, no phone.

Hotel Palacio de Moctezuma   This three-story hotel is more open and lush with greenery than other hotels in this price range. Fresh-cut flowers tucked around tile fountains are its hallmark. The rooms have carpeting and modern tiled showers; many are quite large but, alas, can be cold in winter. The restaurant looks out on the interior courtyard. On the third floor is a solarium with comfortable tables and chairs and great city views. The hotel is 3½ blocks southeast of the main plaza.

Juárez 16 (at León), 29200 San Cristóbal de las Casas, Chi. ✆ 967/678-0352 or 967/678-1142. Fax 967/678-1536. 42 units. $25 double. No credit cards. Free limited parking. **Amenities:** Restaurant. *In room:* TV, no phone.

Mansión de los Angeles   This well-managed hotel offers good service and tidy rooms and public areas. Guest rooms come with either a single and a double bed or two double beds, and the well-kept bathrooms are modern; windows open onto a pretty courtyard with a fountain. The rooftop sun deck is a great siesta spot.

Calle Francisco Madero 17, 29200 San Cristóbal de las Casas, Chi. ✆ 967/678-1173 or 967/678-4371. Fax 967/678-2581. hotelangeles@prodigy.net.com. 20 units. $50–$60 double. MC, V. *In room:* TV.

WHERE TO DINE

San Cristóbal is not known for its cuisine, but you can eat well at several restaurants. **El Fogón de Jovel** (see review below) is the place to try typical Chiapanecan fare. Some interesting local dishes include tamales, *butifarra* (a type of sausage), and *pox* (pronounced "posh"—the local firewater). For baked goods, try the **Panadería La**

Hojaldra, Mazariegos and 5 de Mayo (☎ **967/678-4286**). It's open daily from 8am to 9:30pm. In addition to the restaurants listed below, consider making reservations for dinner at Casa Na-Bolom (see "Attractions in Town," earlier in this chapter).

MODERATE

El Edén ✿✿ INTERNATIONAL   This is a small, quiet restaurant where it is obvious that somebody who enjoys the taste of good food prepares the meals; just about anything except Swiss rarebit is good. The meats are especially tender, and the margaritas are especially dangerous (one is all it takes). Specialties include Swiss cheese fondue for two, Edén salad, and brochette. This is where locals go for a splurge. It's 2 blocks from the main plaza.

In the Hotel El Paraíso, Av. 5 de Febrero 19. ☎ **967/678-5382**. Breakfast $5; main courses $6–$15. AE, MC, V. Daily 8am–9pm.

El Fogón de Jovel CHIAPANECAN   The waiters here wear local costumes, and Guatemalan and Chiapanecan prints and folk art hang on the walls. The menu, which is available in English, explains each dish and regional drink. A basket of warm handmade tortillas with six filling condiments arrives before the meal. Among the specialties are corn soup, *mole chiapaneco,* pork or chicken *adobado* in a chile sauce, and *pipián,* a dish of savory chile-and-tomato sauce served over chicken. For a unique dessert, try the *changleta,* which is half of a sweetened, baked *chayote* (a squash-like vegetable). Cooking classes for small groups can be arranged, but make reservations well in advance. The restaurant is a block northwest of the plaza.

16 de Septiembre 11 (at Guadalupe Victoria/Real de Guadalupe). ☎ **967/678-1153**. Main courses $5–$10. No credit cards. Daily 12:30–10pm.

La Paloma INTERNATIONAL/MEXICAN   La Paloma is San Cristóbal's newest, hippest restaurant and bar. I particularly like it in the evening, when the lighting shows off the modern design to best advantage. The menu has a lot of the classic Mexican dishes. For starters, I enjoyed the quesadillas cooked Mexico City style (small fried packets of *masa*—dough—stuffed with a variety of fillings). Don't make my mistake of trying to share them with your dinner companion; it will only lead to a quarrel over the last one. The *tampiqueña* (steak with an enchilada, guacamole, beans, and rice) is a good bet for a main course if you're hungry. Less ambitious appetites might go for the chicken in peanut sauce. Avoid the profiteroles.

Hidalgo 3. ☎ **967/678-1547**. Main courses $8–$12. MC, V. Daily 9am–11pm.

Madre Tierra INTERNATIONAL/VEGETARIAN   For vegetarians and meat-eaters alike, Madre Tierra is a good place for a cappuccino and pastry or an entire meal. The *comida corrida* is very filling; or try the chicken curry, lasagna, and fresh salads. The bakery specializes in whole-wheat breads, pastries, pizza by the slice, quiche, grains, granola, and dried fruit. The restaurant is in an old mansion with wood-plank floors, long windows looking onto the street, and tables covered in colorful Guatemalan *jaspe* (a hand-woven cloth). Madre Tierra is 3½ blocks south of the plaza.

Av. Insurgentes 19. ☎ **967/678-4297**. Main courses $4–$8; *comida corrida* (served after noon) $6. No credit cards. Restaurant daily 8am–9:45pm; bakery Mon–Sat 9am–8pm, Sun 9am–2pm.

INEXPENSIVE

Café el Puente ✿ MEXICAN/AMERICAN   El Puente is more than a cafe; it's a center for cultural activities where tourists and locals can converse, take Spanish classes, arrange a homestay, leave a message on the bulletin board, and send and receive faxes. Movies are presented nightly in a back courtyard and meeting room. The front courtyard holds a pleasant cafe, the kind of place where a Brandenburg concerto accompanies waffles for breakfast, and sub sandwiches or brown rice and vegetables for lunch. There is Mexican fare as well. The long bulletin board is well worth checking out if you're looking for a ride, a place to stay, or information on out-of-the-way destinations. It's 2½ blocks east of the plaza.

Real de Guadalupe 55 (between Diego Dujelay and Cristóbal Colón). No phone. Breakfast $2–$4; main courses $5–$10. No credit cards. Mon–Sat 8am–11pm; Sun 3–11pm.

Emiliano's Moustache *(Finds)* MEXICAN/TACOS   Like any right-thinking tourist, I initially avoided this place on account of its unpromising name and some cartoonlike *charro* (cowboy) figures by the door. But a conversation with some local folk tickled my sense of irony, and I overcame my prejudice. Sure enough, the place was crowded with *coletos* enjoying the restaurant's highly popular *comida corrida* and delicious tacos, and there wasn't a foreigner in sight. The daily menu is posted by the door; if it isn't appealing, you can choose from a menu of taco plates (a mixture of fillings cooked together and served with tortillas and a variety of hot sauces).

Crescencio Rosas 7. Ⓒ 967/678-7246. Main courses $4–$8; *comida corrida* $4. No credit cards. Daily 8am–midnight.

Normita's MEXICAN   Normita's is famous for its *pozole*, a hearty chicken and hominy soup to which you add a variety of things. It also offers cheap, dependable, short-order Mexican mainstays. It's an informal "people's" restaurant; the open kitchen takes up one corner of the room, and tables sit in front of a large paper mural of a fall forest scene from some faraway place. It's 2 blocks southeast of the plaza.

Av. Juárez 6 (at Dr. José Flores). No phone. Breakfast $2–$2.50; *comida corrida* (served 1:30–7pm) $4; *pozole* $3; tacos $1. No credit cards. Daily 7am–11pm.

Restaurant Tuluc *(Value)* MEXICAN/INTERNATIONAL   A real bargain here is the popular *comida corrida*—it's delicious and filling. Tuluc also has that rarest of rarities in Mexico: a nonsmoking section. Other popular items are sandwiches and enchiladas. The house specialty is *filete Tuluc,* a beef filet wrapped around spinach and cheese served with fried potatoes and green beans; while not the best cut of meat, it's certainly priced right. The Chiapaneco breakfast is a filling quartet of juice, toast, two Chiapanecan tamales, and your choice of tea, coffee, cappuccino, or hot chocolate. Tuluc is 1½ blocks south of the *zócalo.*

Av. Insurgentes 5 (between Cuauhtémoc and Francisco León). Ⓒ 967/678-2090. Breakfast $2–$3; main courses $4–$5; *comida corrida* (served 2–4pm) $3.75. No credit cards. Daily 7am–10pm.

COFFEEHOUSES

Because Chiapas-grown coffee is highly regarded, it's natural to find a proliferation of coffeehouses here. Most are concealed in the nooks and crannies of San Cristóbal's side streets. Try **Café La Selva,** Crescencio Rosas 9 (Ⓒ 967/678-7244), for coffee served in all its varieties and brewed from organic beans. It's well known for its baked goods, and open daily from 9am to 11pm. A more traditional-style cafe, where locals meet to talk over the day's news, is **Café San Cristóbal,** Cuauhtémoc 1 (Ⓒ **967/678-3861**). It's open Monday to Saturday from 9am to 10pm, Sunday from 9am to 9pm.

SAN CRISTOBAL AFTER DARK

San Cristóbal is blessed with a variety of species of nightlife, both resident and migratory. There is a lot of live music, which is surprisingly good and varied. The bars and restaurants are cheap—none charges a cover, and only one imposes a minimum. And they are easy to get to: You can hit all the places mentioned here without setting foot in a cab. Weekends are best, but on any night you'll find something going on.

You can start at **El Cocodrilo** (© 967/678-0871), on the main plaza in the Hotel Santa Clara. It gets going the earliest, with a variety of live acts playing original arrangements of cover tunes—nothing with an edge. The music shuts down by 11pm for the sake of hotel guests. If you want to continue the mellow tone, walk down Real de Guadalupe to no. 34—when I've been there, **La Margarita** (no phone) has had some good guitarists playing Latin jazz and flamenco. The setting is casual, cozy, and softly lit. If you want to dance, you have two choices, both on Francisco Madero: **Las Velas** (© 967/678-7584) at no. 14, and **Latino's** (© 967/678-2083), across the way and down a bit at no. 23. Las Velas usually attracts a younger crowd, while people of all ages go to Latino's. Both have Latin music—salsa, merengue, and such. Sometimes it's live, sometimes canned.

3 Palenque ★★

142km (89 miles) SE of Villahermosa; 229km (143 miles) NE of San Cristóbal de las Casas

The ruins of Palenque look out over the jungle from a tall ridge that juts out from the base of steep, thickly forested mountains. It is a dramatic sight colored by the mysterious feel of the ruins themselves. The temples here are in the Classic style, with high-pitched roofs crowned with elaborate combs. Inside many are representations in stone and plaster of the rulers and their gods, which give evidence of a cosmology that is—and perhaps will remain—impenetrable to our understanding. This is one of the grand archaeological sites of Mexico.

Eight kilometers (5 miles) from the ruins is the town of Palenque. There you can find lodging and food, as well as make travel arrangements. Transportation between the town and ruins is cheap and convenient.

ESSENTIALS
GETTING THERE & DEPARTING
BY PLANE   There is no regular commercial air service to Palenque.

BY CAR   The 229km (143-mile) trip from San Cristóbal to Palenque takes 5 hours and passes through lush jungle and mountain scenery. Take it easy, though, and watch out for potholes and other hindrances. Highway 186 from Villahermosa should take about 2 hours. You may encounter military roadblocks that involve a cursory inspection of your travel credentials and perhaps your vehicle.

BY BUS   The two first-class bus stations are 2 blocks apart. Both are on Palenque's main street between the main square and the turnoff for the ruins. The smaller company, Transportes Rodolfo Figueroa, offers good first-class service four times a day to and from San Cristóbal (5 hr.) and Tuxtla (6½ hr.). Cristóbal Colón offers service to those destinations and to Campeche (six per day, 5 hr.), Villahermosa (nine per day, 2 hr.), and Mérida (two per day, 9 hr.).

ORIENTATION
VISITOR INFORMATION   The **State Tourism Office** (©/fax **916/345-0356**) is a block from the main square, where Avenida Juárez intersects Abasolo. The office is open Monday to Saturday from 9am to 9pm, Sunday from 9am to 1pm.

Palenque Archaeological Site

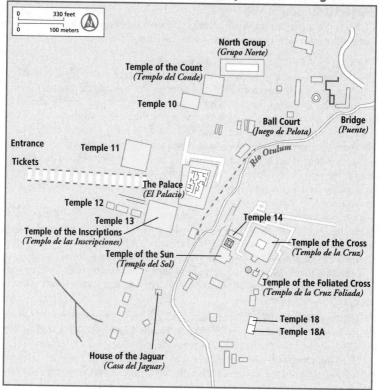

CITY LAYOUT **Avenida Juárez** is Palenque's main street. At one end of it is the **zócalo (main plaza)**; at the other is the oversize sculpture of the famous Maya head that was discovered here. To the right of the statue is the entrance to the Cañada; to the left is the road to the ruins, and straight ahead past the statue are the airport and the highway to Villahermosa. The distance between the town's main square and the monument is about 1.5km (1 mile).

La Cañada is a restaurant and hotel zone tucked away in a small piece of the forest. Aside from the main plaza area, this is the best location for travelers without cars, because the town is within a few blocks, and the buses that run to the ruins pass right by.

GETTING AROUND The cheapest way to get back and forth from the ruins is on the white **VW buses** that run down Juárez every 10 minutes from 6am to 6pm. The buses pass La Cañada and hotels along the road to the ruins and can be flagged down at any point, but they may not stop if they're full. The cost is $1 per person.

FAST FACTS The telephone area code is **916.** As for the **climate,** Palenque's high humidity is downright oppressive in the summer, especially after rain showers. During the winter, the damp air can occasionally be chilly in the evening. Rain gear is important at any time of year. Internet service and ATMs are easily available.

EXPLORING PALENQUE

The reason to come here is the ruins; although you can tour them in a morning, many people savor Palenque for days. There are no must-see sights in town.

PARQUE NACIONAL PALENQUE ✸✸✸

The archaeological site of Palenque underwent several changes in 1994, culminating in the opening of a **museum and visitor center** not far from the entrance to the ruins. The complex includes a large parking lot, a refreshment stand serving snacks and drinks, and several shops. Though it's not large, the museum is worth the time it takes to see; it's open Tuesday to Sunday from 10am to 5pm and is included in the price of admission. It contains well-chosen and artistically displayed exhibits, including the jade contents of recently excavated tombs. (The museum was robbed in 1996, but most of the jade pieces have been recovered.) Explanatory text in Spanish and English explains the life and times of this magnificent city. New pieces are often added as they are uncovered in ongoing excavations.

The **main entrance,** about 1km (½ mile) beyond the museum, is at the end of the paved highway. There you'll find a large parking lot, a refreshment stand, a ticket booth, and several shops. Among the vendors selling souvenirs by the parking lot are Lacandón Indians wearing white tunics and hawking bows and arrows.

Admission to the ruins is $5. The fee for using a video camera is $5. Parking at the main entrance and at the visitor center is free. The site and visitor center shops are open daily from 8am to 4:45pm.

TOURING THE RUINS Pottery shards found during the excavations show that people lived in this area as early as 300 B.C. By the Classic period (A.D. 300–900), Palenque was an important ceremonial center. It peaked around A.D. 600 to 700.

When John Stephens visited the site in the 1840s, the ruins that you see today were buried under centuries of accumulated earth and a thick canopy of jungle. The dense jungle surrounding the cleared portion still covers unexcavated temples, which are easily discernible in the forest even to the untrained eye. But be careful not to drift too far from the main paths. In the past there have been a few incidents where solitary tourists venturing into the rain forest were assaulted.

Of all Mexico's ruins, this is the most haunting, because of its majesty; its history, recovered by epigraphers; and its mysterious setting. Scholars have identified the rulers and constructed their family histories, putting visitors on a first-name basis with these ancient people etched in stone. You can read about it in *A Forest of Kings,* by Linda Schele and David Freidel.

As you enter the ruins, the building on your right is the **Temple of the Inscriptions,** named for the great stone hieroglyphic panels found inside. (Most of the panels, which portray the family tree of King Pacal, are in the National Anthropological Museum in Mexico City.) This temple is famous for the crypt of King Pacal deep inside the pyramid, but the crypt is closed to the public. The archaeologist Alberto Ruz Lhuller discovered the tomb in the depths of the temple in 1952—an accomplishment many scholars consider one of the great discoveries of the Maya world. In exploratory excavations, Ruz Lhuller found a stairway leading from the temple floor deep into the base of the pyramid. The original builders had carefully concealed the entrance by filling the stairway with stone. After several months of excavation, Ruz Lhuller finally reached King Pacal's crypt, which contained several fascinating objects, including a magnificent carved stone sarcophagus. Ruz Lhuller's own gravesite is opposite the Temple of the Inscriptions, on the left as you enter the park.

Just to your right as you face the Temple of the Inscriptions is **Temple 13,** which is receiving considerable attention from archaeologists. In the mid-1990s they discovered the burial of another richly adorned personage, accompanied in death by an adult female and an adolescent. Some of the artifacts found there are on display in the museum.

Back on the main pathway, the building directly in front of you is the **Palace,** with its unique tower. The explorer John Stephens camped in the Palace when it was completely covered in vegetation, spending sleepless nights fighting off mosquitoes. A pathway between the Palace and the Temple of the Inscriptions leads to the **Temple of the Sun,** the **Temple of the Foliated Cross,** the **Temple of the Cross,** and **Temple 14.** This group of temples, now cleared and in various stages of reconstruction, was built by Pacal's son, Chan-Bahlum, who is usually shown on inscriptions with six toes. Chan-Bahlum's plaster mask was found in Temple 14 next to the Temple of the Sun. Archaeologists have begun probing the Temple of the Sun for Chan-Bahlum's tomb. Little remains of this temple's exterior carving. Inside, however, behind a fence, a carving of Chan-Bahlum shows him ascending the throne in A.D. 690. The panels depict Chan-Bahlum's version of his historic link to the throne.

To the left of the Palace is the North Group, also undergoing restoration. Included in this area are the **Ball Court** and the **Temple of the Count,** where Count Waldeck camped in the 19th century. At least three tombs, complete with offerings for the underworld journey, have been found here, and the lineage of at least 12 kings has been deciphered from inscriptions left at this site.

Just past the North Group is a small building (once a museum) now used for storing the artifacts found during the restorations. It is closed to the public. To the right of the building, a stone bridge crosses the river, leading to a pathway down the hillside to the new museum. The rock-lined path descends along a cascading stream on the banks of which grow giant ceiba trees. Benches are placed along the way as rest areas, and some small temples have been reconstructed near the base of the trail. In the early morning and evening, you may hear monkeys crashing through the thick foliage by the path; if you keep noise to a minimum, you may spot wild parrots as well. Walking downhill (by far the best way to go), it will take you about 20 minutes to reach the main highway. The path ends at the paved road across from the museum. The *colectivos* going back to the village will stop here if you wave them down.

WHERE TO STAY

English is spoken in all the expensive hotels and about half of the inexpensive ones. The quoted rates include the 17% tax. High season in Palenque is Easter week, July to August, and December.

MODERATE

Chan-Kah Ruinas ⋆ This hotel is a grouping of comfortable, roomy bungalows that offer privacy and quiet in the surroundings of a tropical forest. Because the town of Palenque isn't particularly worth exploring, you might as well stay here. The grounds are beautifully tended, and there is an inviting pool made to look like a lagoon. A broad stream runs through the property. Some of the bungalows can have a musty smell. The hotel is on the road between the ruins and the town. Christmas prices will be higher than those quoted here, and you may be quoted a higher price if you reserve a room in advance from the United States. The outdoor restaurant and bar serves only passable Mexican food. Room service is pricey.

Carretera Las Ruinas Km 3, 29960 Palenque, Chi. ℂ **916/345-1100.** Fax 916/345-0820. www.chan-kah.com.mx. 73 units. High season $125 double; low season $110 double. MC, V. Free parking. **Amenities:** Restaurant; bar; 3 pools (1 large w/natural spring); game room; room service until 10pm; laundry service. *In room:* A/C.

Hotel Ciudad Real   This three-story hotel is your best bet for creature comforts and modern convenience. Though in no way fancy, it does the important things right—the rooms are large, quiet, and well lit, with good air-conditioning. They are comfortably, if plainly, furnished in modern style. Suites have a sitting room in addition to a standard room. Most units hold two double beds; some king-size beds are available. All rooms have a balcony, which in the best case overlooks an attractive garden and pool area. When making a reservation, be sure that the reservation-taker understands that it's for the hotel in Palenque. The hotel is at the edge of town in the direction of the airport.

Carretera a Pakal-Na Km 1.5, 29960 Palenque, Chi. ℂ **916/345-1343,** or 967/678-4400 for reservations. www.ciudad real.com.mx. 72 units. High season $110 double, $130 suite; low season $100 double, $115 suite. AE, MC, V. Free secure parking. **Amenities:** Restaurant; bar; large pool; baby pool; game room; travel agency; car rental; room service until 11pm; laundry service; nonsmoking rooms. *In room:* A/C, TV, hair dryer, iron.

Hotel Maya Tucán   Get a room in back, and you will have a view of the hotel's natural pond. The cheerfully decorated rooms are adequate in size; they come with double beds and large bathrooms but could use better lighting. Suites are larger and have king-size beds. The air conditioner is quiet and gets the job done. Sometimes the hotel operates a dance club when large tour groups are present (which might bear asking about before checking in), but that won't disturb you if you book a room in back. The grounds are well tended and lush; scarlet macaws kept by the hotel fly about the parking lot. The Maya Tucán is a stone's throw from the Ciudad Real on the highway to the airport.

Carretera-Palenque Km 0.5, 29960 Palenque, Chi. ℂ **916/345-0443.** Fax 916/345-0337. www.hoteles-tucan.com. 56 units. High season $100 double, $130 suite; low season $70 double, $90 suite. MC, V. Free secure parking. **Amenities:** Restaurant; bar; pool; room service until 11pm; laundry service. *In room:* A/C, TV, hair dryer.

Hotel Maya Tulipanes   The Maya Tulipanes keeps refurbishing rooms and does a good job with upkeep. The best units are the "plus" rooms in the modern wing in back—these are worth the extra money. They are large and come mostly with two double beds, a tile floor, and a midsize bathroom. Surrounding the hotel is the Cañada, lending tropical-forest shade. You can walk the 2 blocks to the road and pick up a van to the ruins from there. The travel agency operates daily tours to Bonampak and Misol Ha.

Calle Cañada 6, 29960 Palenque, Chi. ℂ **916/345-0201** or 916/345-0258. Fax 916/345-1004. www.mayatulipanes. com.mx. 72 units. High season $93 standard, $99 standard plus; low season $65–$80 standard, $70–$90 standard plus. Internet specials and promotional rates available. AE, MC, V. Free secure parking. **Amenities:** Restaurant; bar; pool; travel agency; ground transportation to/from Villahermosa airport; room service until 11pm; laundry service; nonsmoking rooms. *In room:* A/C, TV.

INEXPENSIVE

Hotel Kashlan   This dependable choice is the closest hotel to the bus station. The tidy rooms have interior windows opening onto the hall, marble floors, soft bedspreads, tile bathrooms, small vanities, and luggage racks. Show owner Ada Luz Navarro your Frommer's book, and you'll receive a 20% discount. Higher prices are for rooms with air-conditioning—there are 27, and some of the new units are quite comfortable. The ceiling fans in the rest of the rooms are powerful. The hotel restaurant features vegetarian food. The hotel offers trips to Agua Azul and Misol Ha.

5 de Mayo 105, 29960 Palenque, Chi. (C) **916/345-0297.** Fax 916/345-0309. kashlan@hotmail.com. 59 units. $23–$50 double. 20% Frommer's discount. Rates include coffee all day. No credit cards. **Amenities:** Restaurant; bar; tour desk; laundry service.

Hotel Xibalba This small two-story hotel has fanciful Maya architecture that makes staying here fun. The midsize rooms are bright and cheerful, with good air-conditioning. I prefer the upstairs units. The restaurant is pleasant and reliable, and you can arrange a trip to Bonampak or Misol Ha with the hotel management, which owns a long-standing travel agency, Viajes Shivalva (pronounced like Xibalba: "shee-*bahl*-bah"). Take the time to walk down the street to view the full-size replica of the giant stone slab that was the lid to King Pacal's sarcophagus.

Calle Merle Green 9, Col. La Cañada, 29960 Palenque, Chi. (C) **916/345-0411** or 916/345/0822. Fax 916/345-0392. www.palenquemx.com/shivalva. 14 units. $35–$45 double. MC, V. **Amenities:** Restaurant; bar; travel agency; limited room service; laundry service. *In room:* A/C, TV.

WHERE TO DINE

Palenque and, for that matter, the rest of backwater Chiapas, is not for gourmets. Who'd a thunk? But the situation has been improving, and you can get some decent Mexican food. I had an easy time eliminating a number of restaurants that didn't even seem to be keeping up the appearance of serving food.

MODERATE

La Selva ✵ MEXICAN/INTERNATIONAL At La Selva (the jungle), you dine under a large, attractive thatched roof beside well-tended gardens. The menu includes seafood, freshwater fish, steaks, and Mexican specialties. The most expensive thing on the menu is *pigua,* freshwater lobster that is caught in the large rivers of southeast Mexico. These can get quite large—the size of small saltwater lobsters. This and the finer cuts of meat have been frozen, but you wouldn't want otherwise in Palenque. I liked fish stuffed with shrimp, and *mole* enchiladas. La Selva is on the highway to the ruins, near the statue of the Maya head.

Carretera Palenque Ruinas Km 0.5. (C) **916/345-0363.** Main courses $8–$17. MC, V. Daily 11:30am–11:30pm.

INEXPENSIVE

Café de Yara MEXICAN A small, modern-style cafe and restaurant with a comforting, not overly ambitious menu, this is a dependable place for salads, sandwiches, something like *queso fundido* (a melted cheese dish served with tortillas as an appetizer), or a Mexican entree. Try beef or chicken milanesa or chicken with a *chile pasilla* sauce. The furniture and surroundings are comfortable.

Av. Hidalgo 66 (at Abasolo). (C) **916/345-0269.** Main courses $4–$7. MC, V. Daily 7am–11pm.

Restaurant Maya ✵ MEXICAN/STEAKS A popular place among tourists and locals, Restaurant Maya faces the main plaza on the northwest corner. The dining area is breezy and open. At breakfast there are free refills of strong coffee. I like the *consomé,* a chicken soup with rice and vegetables (be sure to add a little lime juice), or *sopa azteca,* a tortilla soup flavored with a little *guajillo* chile (add lime juice to this, too). Chicken breast is available in a number of ways that are good, if not terribly original. The plantains fried Mexican style are wonderful. You can also try *tascalate,* a pre-Hispanic drink not commonly seen at restaurants. It is made of water, *masa,* chocolate, and *achiote,* and served room temperature or cold. This restaurant was awarded a national prize for quality and service. There's a branch in the Cañada, called Maya Cañada.

Av. Independencia s/n. (✆) 916/345-0042. Breakfast $4–$5; main courses $6–$12. AE, MC, V. Daily 7am–11pm.

ROAD TRIPS FROM PALENQUE
SPECTACULAR WATERFALLS AT AGUA AZUL & MISOL HA

The most popular excursion from Palenque is a day trip to the Misol Ha waterfall and Agua Azul. **Misol Ha** is about 20km (12 miles) from Palenque, just off the Ocosingo road (there's a sign pointing to the right). Visitors can swim in the waters below the falls and scramble up slippery paths to smaller falls beside the large one, which drops about 30m (90 ft.) before spraying its mist on the waters below. There's a small restaurant run by the *ejido* (cooperative) that owns the site. Entrance costs around $3 per person.

Approximately 40km (24 miles) beyond Misol Ha on the same road are the **Agua Azul waterfalls,** a spectacular series of beautiful cascades tumbling into a wide river. Seeing both is a full day trip. Visitors can picnic and relax (bring something to sprawl on), swim, or clamber over the slippery cascades and go upstream for a look at the jungle encroaching the water. Agua Azul is prettiest after 3 or 4 consecutive dry days; heavy rains can make the water murky. Check with guides or other travelers about the water quality before you decide to go. The cost to enter is around $3.50. Trips can usually be arranged through your hotel, **Viajes Shivalva Tours,** or the **Hotel Kashlan.** They cost about $12 per person for the day.

BONAMPAK & YAXCHILAN: RUINS & RUGGED ADVENTURE

Intrepid travelers may want to consider the day trip to the Maya ruins of Bonampak and Yaxchilán. The **ruins of Bonampak,** southeast of Palenque on the Guatemalan border, were discovered in 1946. The site is important for the vivid **murals** of the Maya on the interior walls of one temple. Particularly striking is an impressive battle scene, perhaps the most important painting of pre-Hispanic Mexico. Reproductions of these murals are on view in the Regional Archaeology Museum in Villahermosa.

Several tour companies offer a day trip. The drive to Bonampak is 3 hours. From there you continue by boat to the ruins of Yaxchilán, famous for its highly ornamented buildings. Bring rain gear, boots, a flashlight, and bug repellent. All tours include meals and cost about $50. No matter what agency you sign up with, the hours of departure and return are the same because the vans of the different agencies caravan down and back for safety. You leave at 6am and return at 7pm.

Try **Viajes Na Chan Kan** (✆ 916/345-2154), at the corner of avenidas Hidalgo and Jiménez, across from the main square, or **Viajes Shivalva,** Calle Merle Green 1 (✆ 916/345-0411; fax 916/345-0392). A branch of Viajes Shivalva (✆ 916/345-0822) is a block from the *zócalo* (main plaza) at the corner of Juárez and Abasolo, across the hall from the State Tourism Office. It's open Monday to Saturday from 9am to 9pm.

12

Veracruz & Puebla:
On the Heels of Cortez

by David Baird

The region of Veracruz and Puebla, in the east-central part of the country, was, for Hernán Cortez and his conquistadors, the door to Mexico. The region also played that role for most of the visitors who came to the area during colonial and early republic times. But today only a small fraction of the multitudes that flock to Mexico each year passes through here.

This is a shame, for the area has much to recommend it. For adventure travelers, it offers excellent white-water rafting, challenging climbs that include Mexico's highest mountain—a dormant volcano called the Pico de Orizaba—and

scuba diving along Veracruz's coastal reefs. For the culture crowd, the region has three fascinating ruins, some excellent museums and historical sites, and great food.

Veracruz is a fun town for music and food, and for soaking up the easy-going rhythms of the tropics. **Puebla** has the ideal highland climate, even better food, and a great historic district. The ruins in the area feature the startlingly vivid pre-Columbian murals of Cacaxtla, the great ceremonial center of El Tajín, and the New World's largest man-made structure, the great pyramid of Cholula.

1 Veracruz City ⋆

232km (145 miles) E of Mexico City; 109km (68 miles) SE of Xalapa

Veracruz has a reputation as a town with a rich history but little to show for it. True enough, because much of that rich history involved sackings by pirates, heavy bombardment by three different foreign powers (including during the wonderfully named French Pastry War), and epidemics of malaria, yellow fever, and cholera. One might not necessarily want to preserve such a history, even when those same events didn't destroy artifacts. For this reason, and for the character of the natives, Veracruz (unlike Puebla) is better suited to cafe-goers than museum-goers. With the exception of the old fort of San Juan de Ulúa and perhaps the aquarium, the museums can be missed. You come here for the feel of the tropics, the balmy air, and the carefree attitude of the locals.

Veracruz brings to mind other Gulf and Caribbean port cities—part New Orleans, part Maracaibo. Even more than in the rest of Mexico, things such as schedules are managed rather loosely. If you expect punctuality and order, you'll just be banging your head against a wall. Here, you relax: you get your coffee in the morning at the

Café de la Parroquia, you stroll down the *malecón* (boardwalk) in the evening, you take in the party scene at the *zócalo* (town square) at night. The city attracts a lot of Mexicans, who come to take a break from the social constraints of their hometowns. In many parts of Mexico, for instance, a woman walking into a bar by herself would be frowned upon; not here.

Music is important to Veracruz. Specific to the port city are *marimba, danzonera,* and *comparsa* (carnavalesque) music. Just south of the city begins the Jarocha region of the state, whose music is rhythmic, with sexually suggestive lyrics that depend on double meanings. This is the home of "La Bamba," popularized by Ritchie Valens. In the northern part of the state is the Huasteca region. Its music, the *huapango huasteco,* involves a violin, a couple of small strumming guitars, and harmonized singing. Xalapa, the state's highland capital, is home to the largest and best music school in the country.

Cortez first landed a bit north of where the port is now, and his name for the place gives you an idea of what was on his mind: Villa Rica de la Vera Cruz ("Rich town of the true cross"). In colonial times, the Spanish galleons sailed for Spain from here, loaded with silver and gold. Pirates repeatedly attacked, and on occasion captured, the city. The citizens defended themselves, eventually constructing a high wall around the old town and a massive fort, San Juan de Ulúa. The walls surrounding the city are gone now, but the fort remains.

ESSENTIALS

GETTING THERE & DEPARTING **By Plane** **Continental** (© **800/231-0856** in the U.S., or 01-800/900-5000 in Mexico) has nonstop service to and from Houston. **Aeromexico** (© **800/237-6639** in the U.S., or 01-800/021-4000, 229/935-0283, or 229/934-1534) and **Mexicana** (© **800/531-7921** in the U.S., 229/932-2242, or 229/938-0008) operate frequent flights from Mexico City, with connecting service to the U.S. The smaller airlines **Aerolitoral** (© **800/237-6639** in the U.S., or 229/935-0142), an Aeromexico affiliate, and **Aerocaribe/Aerocozumel** (© **229/922-5212** or 229/922-5210) have direct flights to several Mexican cities.

The **airport** is 11km (7 miles) from the town center. Getting there by **taxi** costs about $12. Major car-rental agencies with counters at the airport and locations in downtown hotels include **Avis** (© **800/331-1212** in the U.S., or 229/931-1580), **Dollar** (© **800/800-4000** in the U.S., or 229/935-5231), and **National** (© **800/328-4567** in the U.S., or 229/931-7556).

By Car From Mexico City (6 hr.) and Puebla (4 hr.), take the *autopista* (toll Hwy. 150D) into Veracruz. From Xalapa (1½ hr.), take Highway 140 to coastal toll Highway 180 south.

By Bus The ADO first-class bus station is 20 blocks south of the town center on Díaz Mirón between calles Orizaba and Molina. There is frequent service to Mexico City, Puebla, Xalapa, and other cities. Taxis wait in front of the terminal; the trip to the center costs $3 or less. DIAZ MIRON city buses go to and from the town center. Catch them going outbound on Avenida 5 de Mayo (2 blocks west of the *zócalo*). You can buy a bus ticket downtown at the **Ticket Bus** agency (© **01-800/102-8000**) at Mario Molina between Independencia and Zaragoza. It's open Monday through Saturday from 11am to 2:30pm and 3 to 7pm.

VISITOR INFORMATION The **tourism office** (©/fax **229/989-8817** or 229/989-8800, ext. 158), is downtown by the *zócalo,* on the ground floor of the Palacio

Downtown Veracruz

Municipal (City Hall). It is open Monday through Saturday from 8am to 8pm, Sunday from 10am to 6pm.

CITY LAYOUT Downtown Veracruz is a jumble of streets. The social center of town is the *zócalo,* or town square (formally Plaza de Armas), where you'll find the tourism office. Two short blocks away is another landmark, *el malecón,* a long promenade fronting the harbor. Starting at the *malecón* and running south along the coast is **Bulevar Avila Camacho,** known as *el bulevar.* It connects downtown to Veracruz's hotel and restaurant zone, which stretches along the coast all the way to the onetime village of **Boca del Río.**

GETTING AROUND Taxis are plentiful. **City buses** are cheap (25¢–50¢) and not hard to use. There are **sightseeing trolleys**—imitations of the originals that ran in Veracruz until the early 1980s. They leave from the corner of 16 de Septiembre and the *malecón* around every hour (weather permitting) from 10am to 11:30pm, making an hour-long tour ($3–$4) down the Bulevar Avila Camacho and back. On weekends other trolleys depart from the *zócalo* and run around the main plazas and some of the port facilities. Everything is in Spanish.

FAST FACTS: Veracruz

American Express **Viajes Reptur** represents American Express. The main office is at Serdán 690-B (✆ 229/931-0838). Office hours for American Express–related business are Monday through Friday from 9am to 1:30pm and 4 to 6pm (but you can reach the staff during the lunch hour), and Saturday from 9am to 1pm.

Area Code The telephone area code is **229**.

Climate Veracruz is hot and humid most of the year, but the hottest months are May and June. In the winter, strong winds known as *nortes* occasionally bring cool, even chilly, weather.

Consulate The American consulate is closed, and there is no Canadian consulate. The **British Consulate** is at Independencia 1394 (✆/fax **229/931-6694**). It's open Monday through Friday from 9am to 1pm.

Emergencies Dial ✆ **060.**

High Season The peak tourist times are Carnaval, Easter, July and August, and December. Veracruz is more popular with Mexican nationals than with foreigners.

Hospital The **Hospital de María** is at Alacio Pérez 1004, between Carmen Serdán and 20 de Noviembre (✆ **229/931-3626** or 229/931-3619).

Pharmacy **Farmacia Las Torres,** Av. Díaz Mirón 295, between Abasolo and Paso y Toncoso (✆ **229/932-2885**), is open daily 24 hours.

Police In Veracruz ✆ **229/938-0664**; in Boca del Río ✆ **229/986-1997.**

Post Office The *correo,* on Avenida de la República near the Maritime Customs House, is open Monday through Saturday from 8am to 4pm.

EXPLORING VERACRUZ

The *zócalo* 🌟🌟🌟 is the social hub, where locals hang out in the cafes chatting with friends while the *marimbas, Jarocha* bands, and mariachis make a lively scene, playing well into the night. Bordering the *zócalo* are the **cathedral** and the **Palacio Municipal (City Hall).** There always seems to be some kind of performance on the square: exhibitions of *danzón* (see "Music, Dance & Carnaval," below), clown acts, band concerts, and comedy sketches.

One block east is the **Plaza de la República,** a long plaza where you'll find the **post office,** the old **customs house,** and the civil registry, all built around the turn of the 19th century. On the north side is the old train station, **Estación de Ferrocarriles,** with its remarkable yellow-and-blue tile facade. From the east side of this plaza, you can board a bus to Veracruz's most famous tourist attraction, the fortress of **San Juan de Ulúa.** Around the corner from the south side of the plaza is the *malecón* (boardwalk), where you can take a boat ride or have coffee at the city's most popular gathering spot, **El Café de la Parroquia.**

MUSIC, DANCE & CARNAVAL

Hang out in the *zócalo* and you'll be serenaded with *danzonera, marimba, Jarocha,* mariachi, and *norteño* music playing to a large crowd of Veracruzanos who've stopped to drink some coffee or beer and chat with friends. On Tuesday, Thursday, and Saturday a band plays in front of the Palacio Municipal for couples dancing the *danzón*. It's a stately affair: they alternate between dancing perfectly erect in a slow rumba-like fashion and promenading arm in arm while the women wave their fans. The *danzón* came to Veracruz from Cuba in the 1890s; today you won't often see it elsewhere. On Wednesday you can see more *danzón* at 8pm at the **Plaza de la Campana** for free.

If you would like to see more styles of traditional dance, inquire at the tourist office in the *zócalo* (see above) about performances by the **Ballet Tradiciones de México.** Several times throughout the year, the company appears at the **Teatro Clavijero** (𝒞 **229/931-0574,** or 229/932-6693 for reservations). Tickets cost $5 to $7. The shows are fun and colorful.

In the week before Ash Wednesday, Veracruz explodes with **Carnaval,** one of the best in Mexico. By local tradition, Carnaval begins with the ritual burning of "ill humor" and ends with the funeral of "Juan Carnaval." Visitors flood in from all over the country, packing the streets and hotels.

Carros alegóricos (floats) are made with true Mexican flair—bright colors, papiermâché figures, flowers, and live entertainment. Groups from neighboring villages dance in peacock- and pheasant-feathered headdresses. Draculas, drag queens, and women in sparkling dresses fill the streets. The parades follow Bulevar Avila Camacho; most of the other activities center in the *zócalo* and begin around noon, lasting well into the night.

On the Sunday before Ash Wednesday, the longest and most lavish of the Carnaval parades takes place on the *malecón*. Parades on Monday and Tuesday are scaled-down versions of the Sunday parade (ask at the tourist office about these routes); by Wednesday, it's all over.

THE TOP ATTRACTIONS

Baluarte Santiago   Built in 1635, this bastion is all that remains of the wall and fortifications that encircled the city. It was one of the nine original bastions protecting the wall. A small collection of pre-Hispanic gold jewelry, recovered several years ago by a fisherman along the coast some kilometers north of Veracruz, is on permanent display here.

Calle Canal, between Gómez Farías and 16 de Septiembre. 𝒞 **229/931-1059.** Admission $3. Tues–Sun 10am–4:30pm.

El Acuario 𝒦 *Kids*   For most Mexican visitors, the aquarium is one of the city's major attractions. The largest aquarium in Latin America, with 9 freshwater and 15 saltwater tanks, it's an impressive attraction that can hold its own with American public aquariums. The doughnut-shaped *gran pecera* (large tank) gives the illusion of being surrounded by the ocean and its inhabitants. The even larger shark tank also impresses. To reach it, take a cab.

Plaza Acuario Veracruzano, Bulevar M. Avila Camacho. 𝒞 **229/932-7984.** Admission $6 adults, $3 children 2–12. Daily 10am–7pm.

Fort of San Juan de Ulúa 𝒦𝒦𝒦   Built to ward off pirates and foreign invasions, the fortress was repeatedly enlarged throughout the colonial period until it became the massive work you see today. After independence, the fort served as a prison noted for its harsh conditions and for the famous people incarcerated there, among them Benito Juárez. It's a formidable example of colonial military architecture, with crenellated walls projecting straight up some 11m (35 ft.) from the water's edge, and bastions at each corner. Inside is a large courtyard, with wide ramps along the inside walls, storehouses,

---

> ⸢ *Fun Fact* **A Piece of Film History**
>
> The Fort of San Juan de Ulúa was the site of the spooky "alligator scene" toward the end of the Michael Douglas and Kathleen Turner movie *Romancing the Stone.*

---

barracks, and old prison cells. English-speaking guides are available at the entrance. A narrow stretch of landfill connects the onetime island to the mainland.

ⓒ 229/938-5151. Admission $3.50. Tues–Sun 9am–4:30pm. Bus: San Juan de Ulúa (30¢) from Av. de la República in front of the Customs House (15 min.). A taxi charges $4. By car, cross the bridge that heads north between Av. de la República and Av. Morelos, then turn right past the container storage and piers.

Museo de la Ciudad   On the ground floor of a 19th-century building is this small city museum. The exhibits concern the history of the city and its social evolution from colonial times to the present. Text and audio are in Spanish; most of the exhibits are photos or dioramas.

Zaragoza 397. ⓒ 229/989-8872. Admission $3. Tues–Sun 10am–6pm. From the Palacio Municipal, walk 5 blocks south on Zaragoza; it's on the right.

Museo Histórico Naval   This museum occupies the building that once housed Mexico's naval academy. Exhibits concern the history of navigation, including nautical paraphernalia, the history of the naval academy, and Mexico's struggles with other countries. In the courtyard, the foundations of the old wall that used to encircle the city are visible. As you enter, look for uniformed guides, who will show you around free.

Calle Arista between Landero y Coss and Gómez Farías. ⓒ 229/931-4078. Free admission. Tues–Sun 10am–5pm.

MORE ATTRACTIONS

BOAT TRIPS   Boats tour the harbor (most narration is in Spanish only), around the tankers and ships docked in the port and San Juan de Ulúa fortress, and out to the Isle of Sacrifices. Departures are sporadic (depending on the weather and demand) from the *malecón* in front of the Hotel Emporio. The cost is $7 for adults and $4 for children ages 2 to 8.

BEACHES   Veracruz has beaches, but they mostly have brown sand, and the Gulf water is a dull green. The nearest true beach is at the **Villa del Mar,** a little ways down *el bulevar,* followed by **Costa de Oro** and then **Mocambo** beach.

EXCURSIONS   Popular day trip destinations include **La Antigua;** the Totonac ruins at **Zempoala; Xalapa,** the state capital and home of an excellent anthropology museum; and the archaeological site at **El Tajín.** For prices and reservations, contact **VIP Tours** (ⓒ **229/922-3315** or 229/922-1918) or **Centro de Reservaciones de Veracruz** (ⓒ **229/935-6422**).

For the actively inclined, **river rafting, mountain climbing,** and **diving** are all options. River rafting centers outside Xalapa (see "Xalapa: Museums & White Water," below). **Divers** can explore series of reefs and shipwrecks south of town toward Boca del Río. Contact **Dorado Divers** (ⓒ **229/931-4305**) for details.

SHOPPING   Veracruz excels in one category of shopping and no other. It has sublimely **tacky souvenirs,** which make perfect payback for coworkers who have burdened you with white elephants. On the *malecón* across from Café de la Parroquia, you'll find a long row of small souvenir shops that constitute Veracruz's version of San Francisco's Fisherman's Wharf. Another place of interest (not so much for buying as for looking) is the **city market** at the corner of Madero and Cortez. It carries just about anything, from parrots and iguanas to medicinal shrubs.

WHERE TO STAY

Most hotels have high- and low-season rates. High-season rates apply during Carnaval, Easter, July and August, December, and long weekends. Low season is the rest of the year. Prices quoted include the 17% tax.

VERY EXPENSIVE

Fiesta Americana Veracruz 🏨 *Kids*   Veracruz's most resortlike hotel is six stories high and very long, stretching out across a wide beachfront. Spacious and decorated in muted colors, most rooms have either terraces or balconies, and all have ocean views. Each contains two full beds or one king. It's on the Playa Costa de Oro, one of Veracruz's nicest beaches, but there is also a large and inviting pool area, with an ample shaded section.

Bulevar Avila Camacho s/n, 94299 Boca del Río, Ver. ✆ **800/FIESTA-1** in the U.S. and Canada, or 229/989-8989. Fax 229/989-8909. www.fiestaamericana.com. 233 units. $211–$257 double; $240–$270 junior suite. AE, DC, MC, V. Free secure parking. **Amenities:** 3 restaurants; poolside snack bar; bar; 2 large pools (1 indoor); lighted tennis court; health club; spa; 2 whirlpools; watersports equipment; children's activities; concierge; tour desk; car rental; business center; salon; 24-hr. room service; babysitting; laundry service; dry cleaning; nonsmoking rooms; executive-level rooms; rooms for those w/limited mobility. *In room:* A/C, TV, dataport, minibar, coffeemaker, hair dryer, iron, safe.

EXPENSIVE

Hotel Emporio 🏨   Across from the *malecón* by the old lighthouse, the Emporio occupies an excellent location. Most of the rooms in the nine-story building have a view of the harbor. Some have balconies, others simply a large window. All are carpeted and have well-equipped bathrooms and double-glazed windows to keep out the noise. The suites are a bit larger and better lit. Rooms are furnished with rattan chairs and tables, with a choice of two double beds or one king. Sunday brunch on the top floor of the hotel is a popular event. In low season, a promotional rate is usually offered.

Paseo del Malecón s/n, 91700 Veracruz, Ver. ✆ **229/932-0020** or 01-/800-295-3000 in Mexico. Fax 229/931-2261. www.hotelesemporio.com.mx. 203 units. High season $170–$190 double, $210 junior suite; low season $150–$170 double, $190 junior suite. AE, MC, V. Free guarded parking. **Amenities:** 2 restaurants; bar; 2 large outdoor pools; heated indoor pool; health club; game room; activities desk; car rental; business center; executive services; room service until midnight; babysitting; laundry service. *In room:* A/C, TV, hair dryer.

Hotel Lois 🏨   Perched on the coast south of downtown, at the beginning of the hotel zone, this 10-story hotel is something of a monument to frivolity, with outlandish decor that mixes many colors and shapes. The aim is to get guests into vacation mode. And it works; the lobby bar is a popular hangout with guests and locals. Rooms are competitively priced and comfortable, though the standard units are staid compared to the rest of the hotel. They are midsize, with two double beds or one king, ample lighting, and good-size bathrooms with plenty of counter space. The suites are more in character with the rest of the hotel. They're larger, with larger bathrooms, and some contain Jacuzzi tubs. The large, attractive pool area, on the third floor, affords a good view of the coastline.

Calzada Ruiz Cortines 10, 91590 Boca del Río, Ver. ℂ **229/937-8290**, or 01-800/712-9136 in Mexico. www.hotel lois.com. 116 units. High season $110–$150 double, $130–$170 suite; low season $80–$100 double, $100–$120 suite. AE, MC, V. Free parking. **Amenities:** Restaurant; cafe; bar; large pool; health club w/sauna, massage; Jacuzzi; game room; travel agency; tour desk; room service until 11:30pm; laundry service; dry cleaning; squash court. *In room:* A/C, TV, minibar, safe.

Hotel Mocambo ★★ *Kids*　The Mocambo, built in 1932, was the city's first resort hotel, playing host to presidents and movie stars during the 1940s and 1950s. It overlooks some of Veracruz's finest beaches along the hotel zone south of downtown. In contrast to the bunched rooms and boxy corridors of the modern glass-enclosed hotels, its low buildings make luxurious use of space, with wide, breezy open-air walkways and terraces that look out over the ocean, the gardens, and the coconut palms. The grounds and a small play area are fenced in so kids can't escape, and there's a water slide at the pool. The architecture and decor are simple and elegant. The hotel may show its age, but it echoes Mexico's Belle Epoque with stylish touches such as the Art Deco indoor pool. Most of the simply furnished rooms are large, with sea views and tile floors. My favorite rooms are those on the upper floors, which have balconies. The hotel serves good Saturday and Sunday brunches on the restaurant terrace.

Boca del Río (Apdo. Postal 263), 91700 Veracruz, Ver. ℂ **229/922-0205**. Fax 229/922-0212. www.hotelmocambo. com.mx. 103 units. High season $165 junior suite; low season $100–$120 junior suite. AE, MC, V. Free guarded parking. **Amenities:** 2 restaurants; 2 bars; 3 pools (1 indoor); lighted tennis court; gym w/sauna and steam room; spa; whirlpool; children's activities (high season); tour desk; car rental; room service until 11pm; babysitting; laundry service; dry cleaning; nonsmoking rooms. *In room:* A/C, TV.

MODERATE

Hotel Colonial　Two hotels sit next door to each other on the *zócalo:* the Hotel Colonial (which isn't so colonial), and the Hotel Imperial (which isn't so imperial). In terms of rooms, services, and price, they are much the same—comfortable, but not fancy. The location is great: you can enjoy the music and party atmosphere in the *zócalo* and then retire to your room (preferably an interior one). The Colonial has two sections. Rooms in the new section are bright and comfortable, with tile floors and better air-conditioning; rooms in the old section are darker and more worn. Outside rooms, which are noisier and more expensive, have small balconies overlooking the plaza. The Imperial's lobby is more impressive, but the pool emits a slight smell of chlorine to parts of the hotel, and the Colonial seems to be better managed. Still, I think of these hotels for the most part as interchangeable. If you can't get a room at the Colonial, try the Imperial (ℂ **229/932-1204**). Lower rates are for the old section.

Miguel Lerdo 117, 91700 Veracruz, Ver. ℂ/fax **229/932-0193**. 174 units. $60–$78 double. AE, MC, V. Covered guarded parking $3. **Amenities:** Sidewalk cafe and bar; indoor pool. *In room:* A/C, TV.

WHERE TO DINE

The restaurants on the *zócalo* are the best spots for drinking a beverage and taking in the scene. While more expensive than places a few blocks away, their prices are still reasonable. If you want to have seafood with the locals, go to the city fish market on Lendero y Coss around the corner from the *malecón.* Facing the street are several small restaurants. Find the one called **La Cría.**

Seafood and coffee are two readily available commodities. You will find *pescado a la veracruzana* (fish cooked in a sauce of tomatoes, onions, olives, garlic, and chiles) on menus across Mexico. And the mountains surrounding Xalapa, Orizaba, and Córdoba provide the ideal climate for growing coffee.

EXPENSIVE

Restaurant El Cacharrito ☆ STEAKS Midway between downtown and Mocambo beach is this family-run, Argentine-style steakhouse. The steaks are expertly cooked and served Argentine style—on wooden boards. Order the *bife de chorizo* (ribeye) and wash it down with some of the good house red wine. Take a taxi here, and be sure to have the address handy.

Bulevar Ruiz Cortines 15. ℂ **229/937-7027**. Reservations recommended during Carnaval. Steaks $18–$25. MC, V. Daily 2–11pm.

MODERATE

Gran Café del Portal *(Value* MEXICAN In the *portales* that face the front door of the cathedral is this dependable restaurant with good prices and local color. In the evenings a parade of strolling troubadours, harpists, marimba players, and shoeshine men passes by. For the midafternoon meal, the *comida del día* (meal of the day) provides lots of food at a reasonable price and a choice of dishes for each course. Avoid the overcooked pasta and most beef dishes, which are tough. The exception is the tenderized *milanesa* (breaded beef cutlet), done very well in the Mexican style. For seafood, ask the waiter what's freshest. The enchiladas and the soups are good, and the *flan napolitano* could feed a family of four.

Independencia at Zamora. ℂ **229/931-2759**. Main courses $6–$10; *comida del dia* $6–$8. No credit cards. Daily 6am–midnight.

Mariscos Villa Rica Mocambo ☆☆☆ SEAFOOD This establishment prides itself on cooking Veracruz style. The menu includes all the seafood standards, plus a few dishes that are harder to come by in Mexico, let alone north of the border. Everything I tried, I enjoyed enormously. For starters, try a classic seafood cocktail. Veracruzano specialties include *pampano al acuyo* (pompano cooked in a sauce of green herbs), conch filet *al ajillo* (with toasted strips of *guajillo* peppers), and *steak de camarón a la naranja* (shrimp pressed together and cooked in orange sauce). Service is excellent. Look for an open-air thatched structure below the Mocambo hotel.

Calzada Mocambo 527. ℂ **229/922-2113**. Main courses $8–$17. AE, MC, V. Daily noon–10pm.

INEXPENSIVE

Gran Café de la Parroquia ☆☆ MEXICAN/COFFEE More than a coffeehouse, La Parroquia is an institution. Making the scene here for morning or afternoon coffee is practically mandatory on any trip to Veracruz. The action takes place in a large, bustling dining area facing the *malecón*. There's nothing fancy about it; white tiles cover the floor and walls, and the furniture is simple but comfortable. The thing to order is *café lechero,* which is so good I would pit it against any other coffee-and-milk drink. You'll get two fingers of dark coffee in a glass. Then, to get the attention of the waiter who circulates with the kettle of steaming milk, you tap the glass with your spoon. The sound of clinking glass rings throughout the dining room. The cafe also offers pastries and decent breakfasts, but some of the main courses are disappointments.

Av. Gómez Farías 34. ℂ **229/932-2584**. Breakfast $2–$5; coffee $1–$2; main courses $4–$10. No credit cards. Daily 6am–1am.

Samborcito ☆ *Finds* REGIONAL No need to say the name twice to any cab driver in town; everybody knows this place. Samborcito is simple eating at its best for either breakfast or lunch. The name pokes fun at Sanborn's, the oldest, best-known chain of restaurants in Mexico (never mind the difference in spelling). Classic dishes include *picadas* (thick *masa* pancake with cheese and sauce—a Veracruz tradition), and puffy *gordita negra* (*masa* cooked with black-bean paste and flavored with the toasted leaf of the aguacatillo—not spicy). Tamales are available on weekends. All the breakfasts are great. Samborcito is near downtown; a cab will run about $1.50.

16 de Septiembre 727. **℃ 229/931-4388.** Main courses $7–$12; breakfast $2.50–$5; *antojitos* $1–$5. No credit cards. Daily 6am–6pm.

2 Exploring North of Veracruz: Ruins, More Ruins & a Great Museum

THE RUINS OF ZEMPOALA

On Highway 180, about 22km (14 miles) north of Veracruz, is the village of Antigua (on the river of the same name). It's not very well known today, but for 75 years beginning in 1525, it was a seat of Spanish power. The village is known locally for its seafood restaurants and is especially popular on weekends.

About 40km (25 miles) north of Veracruz, a little past Antigua, are the ruins of **Zempoala** (or Cempoala), surrounded by lush foliage and rich agricultural land. Though not as large as the site of El Tajín, they're still noteworthy. Zempoala was the principal city of the Totonac at the time of the Spanish Conquest. The name means "place of the 20 waters," for the several creeks that converge near the site. When the conquerors saw Zempoala, the whitewashed stucco walls glimmered like silver in the tropical sun, which of course brought the Spaniards running. Disappointed at seeing little in the way of precious metals, the Spaniards made allies of the Totonac Indians, who were resentful of Aztec domination.

Most buildings at Zempoala date from the 14th and 15th centuries—late post-Classic. The area was populated at least 1,500 years earlier. The Great Temple is constructed in the Aztec style. The Temple of the Little Faces is decorated with stucco faces in the walls and hieroglyphs painted on the lower sections. The Temple of Quetzalcoatl, the feathered serpent god, is a square platform, and the Temple of Ehecatl, god of the wind, is (as usual) round. On weekends and during vacation months, you're likely to find a group of the famous *voladores* (flyers) from Papantla performing their acrobatic ritual (see the "The Ruins of El Tajín" on p. 499).

Admission to the archaeological site is $4; it's open daily from 9am to 6pm. A video camera permit costs $4. If you're going by car, driving time is 40 minutes north on Highway 180 through Cardel; the ruins of Zempoala are just north of Cardel. Transportes Regionales Veracruzanas (TRV) buses run hourly from Veracruz; the trip takes 1½ hours.

XALAPA: MUSEUMS & WHITE WATER

Xalapa (104km/65 miles northwest of Veracruz; pronounced "hah-*lah*-pa" and sometimes spelled "Jalapa") is a highland city in the middle of Mexico's prime coffee-growing area and the capital of the state of Veracruz. Less than 2 hours from the port of Veracruz, it offers an easy escape from the high temperatures there. It's a hilly city, crisscrossed by narrow, winding streets and alleys. A fine, misty rain known as *chipi chipi* often floats in the air, cloaking the views in a vaporous shroud. When the sky is clear, you can sometimes make out in the distance the snow-capped

> **Tasty Fun Fact**
> Xalapa, or "Jalapa," lent its name to the famed jalapeño pepper.

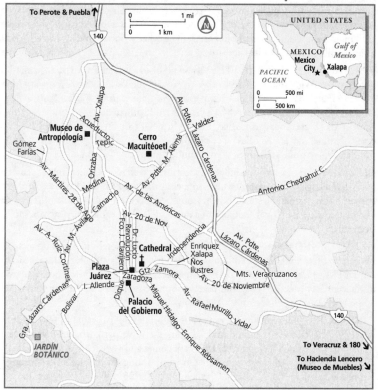

peak of Pico de Orizaba (also known as Citlaltépetl), an extinct volcano that is Mexico's tallest peak at 5,747m (18,850 ft.).

Xalapa is a university town and has the best music school in the country, which is part of the University of Veracruz. Xalapa is also known for its outstanding symphony orchestra. If your interests are more archaeological, Xalapa's anthropology museum is second only to Mexico City's monster of a museum. For active sorts, there's excellent white-water rafting nearby. Finally, Xalapa is known as the hometown of Antonio López de Santa Anna, whose 11 terms as president of Mexico spanned 22 years.

ESSENTIALS

GETTING THERE   Veracruz, less than 2 hours away, has the closest major airport, although some charter flights use the small Xalapa airport. If you're driving from Veracruz, take Highway 180 to Cardel, then turn left (west) onto Highway 140 past the coffee plantations. From Papantla, you can avoid the mountains by taking Highway 180 south to Cardel. From Mexico City and Puebla, there's a turn-off for Highway 140 on the toll highway to Veracruz (150D). Fog is common and dangerous between Perote and Xalapa. The trip by bus to or from Papantla takes 4 hours.

The **bus station** (CAXA) is 2.5km (1½ miles) east of the town center just off Calle 20 de Noviembre. Taxis are downstairs, and prices are controlled. Tickets to the center of town cost around $2. Buses run to Veracruz every 20 to 30 minutes and to Puebla 9 or 10 times a day. You can buy tickets downtown at the **Ticket Bus** agency, Av. Enríquez 13, a block east of the cathedral (no phone). The office is open Monday through Friday from 10am to 2pm and 4 to 7pm.

VISITOR INFORMATION The easiest place to go is the **tourist information booth** at the Ayuntamiento (city hall), across from the Plaza Juárez. Hours are Monday through Friday from 9am to 2pm and 4 to 6pm, Saturday from 9am to 1pm. Occasionally it closes for a week. Much more difficult to reach and not worth the effort is the **State Tourism Office,** on the first floor of Bulevar Cristóbal Colón 5 Fracc. Jardines de las Animas (© **228/812-8500,** ext. 133). Hours are Monday through Friday from 8:30am to 9pm, Saturday from 9am to 1pm.

CITY LAYOUT Xalapa is a hilly town with streets that defy order. In the center of town is the large **Plaza Juárez,** where on a clear day the Pico de Orizaba is visible to the southwest. Across the street (north) from the plaza is the Ayuntamiento (city hall); just east is the Palacio del Gobierno (state capitol). The cathedral is across (north) from this.

GETTING AROUND Most of the recommended hotels and restaurants (see "Where to Stay" and "Where to Dine," below) are within easy walking distance of the central Plaza Juárez. Taxis in Xalapa are inexpensive, as are city buses. Because streets in the center of town are busy and narrow, cabs aren't allowed to stop just anywhere. Sometimes you have to look for a TAXI sign.

FAST FACTS The telephone **area code** is 228. The city is 1,430m (4,690 ft.) above sea level. The **climate** is humid and cool for the most part. It can be warm from March to early May. The light *chipi chipi* rain comes and goes at any time of year. The rainy season is May through July and can bring strong downpours. The **American Express** office is in Viajes Xalapa, Clavijero 311 (© **228/840-6971**). Hours for traveler services are weekdays from 9am to 2pm and 4 to 7:30pm.

EXPLORING XALAPA

For information on cultural events, go to the **Agora,** a cultural center with a coffee shop beneath the Plaza Juárez (reached by steps on the south side of the plaza). Look for posters announcing upcoming concerts. There's usually something going on. Also, look in the local paper, *Diario de Xalapa.*

Hacienda El Lencero Occasionally called the Museo de Muebles (Furniture Museum), this country estate 14km (9 miles) southeast of the town center was for 14 years (1842–56) the home of Antonio López de Santa Anna, the 11-time president of Mexico. Here, he retreated from the world, though on occasion he opened his doors to receive notable visitors.

Furniture from Mexico, Europe, and Asia fills the rooms, illustrating the cosmopolitan tastes of Mexico's upper classes during the 19th century. Among the notable pieces is the leader's bed, embellished with the national emblem (an eagle holding a serpent in its beak). The grounds are lovely and shaded by ancient trees. The grand house overlooks a spring-fed pond.

Carretera Xalapa-Veracruz Km 10. No phone. Admission $3.50; free guided tours (in Spanish only) on request. Tues–Sun 10am–5pm. Bus: Banderilla–P. Crystal–Lencero from Av. Lázaro Cárdenas to village of Lencero or nearby spot along the highway. Drive or take a taxi ($10 round-trip) about 10km (6 miles) south of town on Hwy. 140 toward Veracruz, past the country club; watch for the signs on the right.

Museo Antropología de Xalapa ★★★ This museum exhibits excellent examples of the megalithic heads and other monumental sculptures made by the Olmec—better than those in Mexico City or at the museum in Villahermosa. The collection of Totonac pieces, from the highly stylized smiling faces to the unadorned, realistic sculptures of faces and heads, is the best anywhere. The museum is laid out in order from earliest to latest cultures, from the Olmec—the mother culture of Mesoamerican civilization—to the post-Classic civilizations of Veracruz. Explanatory text is in Spanish. Bilingual guides are available.

Av. Xalapa s/n. ✆ **228/815-0920** or 228/815-0708. Admission $4. Tues–Sat 9am–5pm.

OTHER ATTRACTIONS

RIVER RAFTING Close by Xalapa are three popular rivers for rafting and a number of rafting companies that can accommodate you. No experience is necessary. If you're planning ahead, contact **Far Flung Adventures** at www.farflung.com. Another outfit that I can recommend is **México Verde** (✆ **01-800/362-8800** in Mexico, or 228/812-0134). Either company can do day trips from Xalapa (about $60).

WHERE TO STAY

Mesón del Alférez ★★ In most other parts of Mexico, rooms such as these, in a beautiful colonial house, would go for much more money. The owners have thoroughly renovated the old house and retained its residential feel. Rooms are spacious and beautifully decorated. Standard rooms and junior suites come with one double bed, suites with a choice of two doubles or one king. Rooms are colonial in style, accented by bright colors and stone. In some, a loft creates extra space. There are two smaller rooms in front that get noise from the street. Additional rooms are around the corner in a modern house, Balcones del Alférez. They are comfortable, modern, and a little quieter. The hotel faces the back of the Palacio del Gobierno.

Sebastián Camacho 2, corner of Zaragoza, 91000 Xalapa, Ver. ✆/fax **228/818-0113**. www.pradodelrio.com. 28 units. $59 double; $68 junior suite; $82 suite. Rates include continental breakfast. AE, MC, V. Free secure parking 2 blocks away. **Amenities:** Restaurant; tour desk; car rental; room service until 4pm; laundry service. *In room:* TV, coffeemaker, hair dryer.

Posada del Cafeto ★ This colorful, comfortable hotel has three stories of rooms surrounding a tidy garden. Furnishings and decor are simple and attractive, with handsome wood furniture and cheerful colors. Each room is slightly different. Some are small, but all have ample bathrooms. Bed choices include one double, two twins, a twin and a double, or two doubles. Lower rates are for one double.

Canovas 8 and 12, 91000 Xalapa, Ver. ✆ **228/817-0023**. www.pradodelrio.com. 29 units. $33–$40 double. Rates include continental breakfast. AE, MC, V. No parking available. From Plaza Juárez, walk 4 blocks east on Zaragoza, then 1 block south where it bends. Canovas is the 1st street on the right; the posada is farther down on the right. **Amenities:** Cafe (breakfast and supper); tour info; limited room service; laundry service. *In room:* TV, coffeemaker, hair dryer.

WHERE TO DINE

Because Xalapa is a student town, you can eat well for little money. **Callejón del Diamante** is an alley near the cathedral, with a half-dozen inexpensive restaurants that cater to office workers and students. One, **La Sopa,** offers a daily blue plate special for $3. Most of these restaurants are open Monday through Saturday from 8am to 10pm. To find them, turn your back to the cathedral and walk left on Enríquez across Lucio 1 block; the Callejón will be on the left.

Churrería del Recuerdo ★ MEXICAN For breakfast or supper, this is my favorite place in town. It serves the traditional supper fare of *antojitos*—enchiladas, *gorditas,* and tamales, which you can wash down with a good *horchata de coco* (coconut) or *tepache* (pineapple). The other specialty is *churros,* best described perhaps as the Spanish equivalent of doughnuts, but crispy and usually eaten with hot chocolate. All the breakfasts are good, and the food is safe: The restaurant has won awards for cleanliness. It's across from the Hotel Finca Real de Xalapa; take a cab ($2 from downtown).

Victoria 158. ℭ **228/818-1678.** *Antojitos* $3–$5. No credit cards. Daily 8am–1pm and 5pm–midnight.

Restaurant la Casona del Beaterio MEXICAN   This place near the *zócalo* offers good food and service and has a charming atmosphere. Dine on an outdoor patio with a tile roof and a fountain, or indoors under high, beamed ceilings. Specialties include *pastel azteca* (a casserole of chicken and tortilla) and a platter of traditional dishes called *cazuelitas mexicanas.* You can find La Casona 2 blocks east of Parque Juárez on the south side of the street. Live music begins at 9pm from Thursday to Sunday.

Zaragoza 20. ℭ **228/818-2119.** Breakfast $3–$4; main courses $5–$10; *comida corrida* $5. AE, MC, V. Mon–Sat 8am–11pm; Sun 8:30am–10pm.

EL TAJIN & THE CITY OF PAPANTLA

El Tajín (ehl tah-*heen*) is among the most important archaeological sites in Mexico. It has a large ceremonial center with several pyramids, platforms, and ball courts, some in the architectural styles of other cultures (Olmec, Teotihuacán, Maya) and some in the city's own unique style. It was probably built and inhabited (at least in its last stages) by the Totonac Indians who still live in this region. The Totonac culture is most famous for the "dance" of the *voladores,* a pre-Columbian religious ritual in which four men are suspended from the top of a tall pole while another beats a drum and plays a flute while balancing himself at the top.

The major stopover for seeing these ruins is **Papantla,** a hilly city of 165,000 in the coastal lowlands 225km (140 miles) north of Veracruz. In many respects, it's a typical Mexican town with lots of clay tile roofs, a jumble of small shops, and a lively street scene. One of the major products of Papantla, since the time of the Aztec, is vanilla beans. Vanilla is native to Mexico and was used principally to flavor chocolate, also indigenous to Mexico.

ESSENTIALS

GETTING THERE   By Car   If you're driving from the south, follow the coastal road, Highway 180, from Veracruz. From Xalapa, it's best to do the same: drive down to the coast and then north.

By Bus   The quaint ADO station (ℭ **784/842-0218**) is at the corner of Venustiano Carranza and Benito Juárez, 4 blocks below the main square. Almost all buses are *de paso* (originating elsewhere), so departure times can be a little earlier or later than the schedule says. Taxis pass in front of the station frequently.

CITY LAYOUT   Easily visible from many parts of town, the parish church and the Hotel El Tajín are at the top of a hill. This is where you'll find the *zócalo.*

GETTING AROUND   Taxis are available around the central plaza, and city buses go to the ruins of El Tajín (see below). Almost everything worth seeing is within easy walking distance of the central plaza.

FAST FACTS   The telephone **area code** is **784.** The **climate** is steamy for most of the year except for a few occasions in winter when a north wind blows.

SPECIAL EVENTS   The **Feast of Corpus Christi,** the ninth Sunday after Easter, is part of a very special week in Papantla. Well-known Mexican entertainers perform, and the native *voladores* (see "The Ruins of El Tajín," below) make special appearances. Lodging is scarce during this week, so be sure to book ahead.

EXPLORING PAPANTLA & EL TAJIN

In Papantla, the shady *zócalo* built of ceramic tile is where couples and families come in the evenings to sit or stroll. The large wall below the church facing the *zócalo* is covered with the image of El Tajín and a modern depiction of Totonac carved reliefs.

THE RUINS OF EL TAJIN   The ruined city sits among some low hills clothed in thick tropical forest. The views are lovely, but climbing on any of the pyramids is forbidden; your best view is from a high, man-made terrace that supports the Tajín Chico buildings towards the back. The city is divided into **Tajín Viejo** and **Tajín Chico**—the old and new sections. Of the 150 buildings identified at the site, 20 have been excavated and conserved, resurrecting their forms from what were grass-covered mounds. At least 12 ball courts have been found, of which 6 have been excavated. The most impressive structure, in the old section, is the **Pyramid of the Niches,** which is a unique stone-and-adobe pyramid with 365 recesses extending to all four sides of the building. The pyramid was formerly covered in red-painted stucco, and the niches were painted black. Try to imagine how that must have looked. Near the Pyramid of the Niches is a restored **ball court** with beautiful carved reliefs depicting gods and kings.

The most important building in the Tajín Chico section is the **Temple of the Columns.** A stairway divides the columns, three on either side, each decorated with reliefs of priests and warriors and hieroglyphic dates. Many mounds remain unexcavated, but with the reconstruction that has been done so far, it's increasingly easier to visualize the ruins as a city.

In a clearing near the museum, a group of local Totonac Indians called *voladores* **(flyers)** performs their acrobatic and symbolic ritual. This is a traditional, solemn ceremony that dates back centuries. The Totonac perform the unusual ritual in honor of the four directions of the earth. There's no set schedule for performances; the sound of a slow-beating drum and flute signals that the *voladores* are preparing to perform. Five flyers, dressed in brightly colored ceremonial garments and cone-shaped hats with ribbons and small round mirrors, climb to a square revolving platform at the top of a 25m (80-ft.) pole. While four flyers perch on the sides of the platform and attach themselves by the waist to a rope, the fifth stands and plays an instrument called a *chirimía,* used in rituals by the Toltec and Olmec. The instrument is a small bamboo flute with a deerskin drum attached. The performer plays the three-holed flute with his left hand and beats the drum with his right hand.

When the time is right, the four fall backward, suspended by the rope, and descend as they revolve around the post.

The small but impressive **museum** is worth seeing as well. A small snack and gift shop and small restaurant are across from the museum. Admission to the site and museum is $5. The fee to use a personal video camera is $3.50. If you look like a professional photographer, the authorities will ask you to get a permit from the **Instituto Nacional de Antropología e Historia** in Mexico City. If you watch a performance of the *voladores,* one of them will collect an additional $2 from each spectator. The site is open daily from 9am to 5pm.

To El Tajín from Papantla, taxis charge about $20, but it's easy to take a local bus for 75¢. Look for buses marked CHOTE/TAJIN, which run beside the town church (on the uphill side) every 15 minutes beginning at 7am. Buses marked CHOTE pass more frequently and leave you at the Chote crossroads; from there, take a taxi for around $5. From Veracruz, take Highway 180 to Papantla, then Route 127, a back road to Poza Rica that runs through El Tajín.

SHOPPING   There are two markets in Papantla, both near the central plaza. **Mercado Juárez** is opposite the front door of the church. **Mercado Hidalgo** is 1 block downhill on the same street. The former has more food stalls, where you can order a bowl of *zacahuil,* a typical dish of the region. The latter has locally made baskets, vanilla extract, *Xanath,* a locally produced vanilla liqueur, and whole vanilla beans. You'll also find vanilla beans worked into different shapes, such as a crucifix, for putting in closets and drawers.

WHERE TO STAY

Hotel Provincia Express   Opened in 1990, this hotel is a good choice in a place with meager selections. Rooms are nicely furnished, with tile floors, and hold a king-size or two double beds. The medium-to-small bathrooms have showers. On occasion it takes a while for water to heat up, but it will. Nos. 1 to 6 have small balconies overlooking the *zócalo.* Others, toward the back, are windowless and quiet, and are reached through a tunnel-like hallway.

Enríquez 103, 93400 Papantla, Ver. ② 784/842-1645. Fax 784/842-4213. hotprovi@prodigy.net.mx. 20 units. $45–$60 double. No credit cards. Free secure parking ½ block away. **Amenities:** Cafe; room service until 3pm; laundry service. *In room:* A/C, TV.

Hotel Tajín   At the top of the hill toward the back of the church sits this large, easily visible hotel. Rooms are small and tidy. Bed choices include one or two doubles or one king. Thirty-one rooms have air-conditioning, the rest have fans, and some have a view.

Núñez 104, 93400 Papantla, Ver. ② 784/842-0121 or 784/842-1623. Fax 784/842-1062. hoteltajin@hotmail.com. 73 units. $32–$55 double. MC, V. Free secure parking ½ block away. **Amenities:** Laundry service. *In room:* TV.

WHERE TO DINE

In the morning, numerous stands at the Mercado Juárez offer the local specialty, *zacahuil* (a huge tamal cooked in a banana leaf). In Papantla, the *zacahuil* is cooked in enough liquid to be served in a bowl. Look around until you see a cook with a line of patrons—that's where you'll get the best *zacahuil.*

Plaza Pardo   MEXICAN   This upstairs restaurant facing the main plaza serves plenty of Mexican standards and a couple of regional dishes. A few tables are on a balcony looking out over the *zócalo,* church, and giant statue of the *volador.* Specialties include *bocales* (small *gorditas* with different fillings), enchiladas, and *mole.*

Enríquez 105-altos. ② 784/842-0059. Breakfast $2–$4; sandwiches $2–$3; main courses $3–$7. No credit cards. Daily 7:30am–11pm.

3 Colonial Puebla ★★

128km (80 miles) E of Mexico City; 285km (178 miles) W of Veracruz

At an elevation of over 2,120m (7,000 ft.) in a broad plane between mountain ranges and snow-capped volcanoes, Puebla is blessed with the year-round spring-like climate of the highlands. It's considered the cradle of Mexican cuisine, having produced some of the country's classic dishes—the intricate *mole poblano* and *chiles en nogada,* as well

Puebla

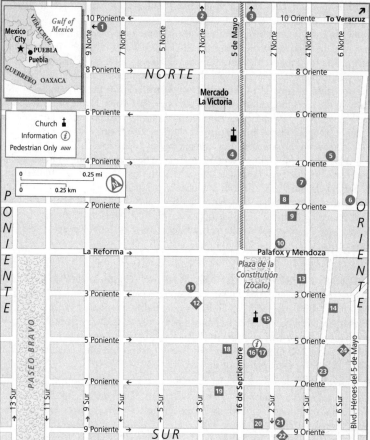

ACCOMMODATIONS ■
Hotel Camino Real Puebla **19**
Hotel Colonial **13**
Hotel Holiday Inn Puebla **9**
Hotel Posada San Pedro **8**
Hotel Puebla Plaza **18**
Mesón Sacristía de la Compañía **14**
Mesón Sacristía de las Capuchinas **20**

DINING ◆
Fonda de Santa Clara **12**
La Conjura **22**
La Guadalupana **24**

ATTRACTIONS ●
Biblioteca Palafoxiana **17**
Callejón de los Sapos **23**
Casa de la Cultura **16**
Casa de los Muñecos **10**
Cathedral **15**
Exconvento de Santa Mónica **3**
Exconvento de Santa Rosa **2**
Iglesia de Santo Domingo **4**
Mercado de Artesanías (El Parián) **6**
Museo Amparo **21**
Museo Bello y González **11**
Museo Casa del Alfeñique **5**
Museo Nacional del Ferrocarril **1**
Museo Poblano de Arte Virreinal **7**

as *tinga* (pork or chicken stewed in chiles) and *mixiotes* (spiced rabbit, lamb, or chicken wrapped and steamed in a sauce).

Puebla has a large colonial center, which is home to so many mansions, convents, and churches that it has been named a UNESCO World Heritage Site. Its architecture differs from that of the rest of Mexico in the extensive use of painted tiles, gold leaf, and molded plaster. Facades and walls are commonly surfaced with clay and Talavera tiles to cover the unattractive gray-black color of the local building stone. Early in the city's history, artisans from the Spanish town of Talavera settled here and established their craft of making hand-painted tiles—a tradition the Moors originally brought to Spain in the 8th century. These tiles, along with dishes, pots, and other objects made in the same tradition, are referred to as Talavera.

Puebla is a very Catholic city, even for Mexico; there are so many churches and former convents that even most Poblanos can't keep them all straight. Churches not to be missed include the **cathedral,** one of the largest in Mexico, and the **Capilla del Rosario,** with its overpowering baroque design and lavish use of gold leaf. Modern Puebla surrounds the historic district. The principal industry of the city is a large Volkswagen plant on the outskirts. It produces most of the Volkswagens sold in the United States.

ESSENTIALS

GETTING THERE & DEPARTING **By Plane** **Continental** (℃ **800/231-0856** in the U.S., or 01-800/900-5000 in Mexico) has a new direct flight to/from Houston. This is the third attempt by an airline to offer a direct connection to a U.S. airport. The others failed because they had to compete with Mexico City flights. Most travelers fly into Mexico City and take the bus directly from the airport to Puebla. Exit the door opposite Sala D (Gate D), and you'll see a ticket booth and buses lined up at the curb. They leave every half-hour; the cost is $17.

By Car There are two roads to Puebla from the capital: Highway 150, an old, winding two-lane scenic road with limited passing capabilities and the likelihood of slow traffic; and Highway 150D, a four- or six-lane toll road that's faster. From Veracruz, take Highway 150D west. From Xalapa, take Highway 140 west to the intersection with 150, then turn right. Tolls from Mexico City run $12; from Veracruz, $20.

By Bus The ride from **Veracruz** to Puebla takes 3½ hours and costs $18. From **Mexico City,** it takes 2 hours and costs $15. Several bus lines have regular departures from Mexico City's TAPO bus station, as frequently as every 15 minutes. Also keep in mind that you can catch a bus to Puebla directly from the **Mexico City airport** (see "By Plane," above).

You'll probably arrive at a large **bus station,** known by its acronym, CAPU. To get to downtown Puebla, look for one of several booths marked TAXI AUTORIZADO or a city bus marked CAPU CENTRAL CAMIONERA–CENTRO. Many buses to and from the Mexico City airport use the Estrella Roja station, 4 Poniente 2110, which is closer to downtown. The **Ticket Bus** agency (℃ **222/232-1952**), downtown, sells bus tickets. Look for a small counter inside the lobby of the office building at the corner of Palafox y Mendoza and 6 Norte. Hours are Monday through Saturday from 9am to 7pm.

VISITOR INFORMATION The **State Tourism Office** (℃ **222/246-2044,** ext. 8) is your best bet. It's at 5 Oriente 3, across the street from the south side of the cathedral. The office is open Monday through Saturday from 9am to 8pm, Sunday from

9am to noon. The staff can answer questions, provide a map, and set you up with a guide if you want a private tour of the city.

CITY LAYOUT   Puebla's streets are laid out on a Cartesian quadrant, with the two main avenues as the x and y axes. Instead of positive and negative numbers, you have even and odd. Streets north of the **horizontal axis** (Reforma/Palafox y Mendoza) are numbered 2, 4, 6, and so on. Streets to the south are 3, 5, 7, and so on. The **north-south axis** (5 de Mayo/16 de Septiembre) does the same thing. East of it are even-numbered streets, and west are odd-numbered. Street names also include a direction—*norte, sur, oriente, poniente* (north, south, east, west). So if someone tells you that a church is on 7 Oriente, then you know what part of town it's in: "Oriente" tells you that it's the eastern portion of an east-west street, and the odd number indicates that it's south of Palafox y Mendoza.

Don't count on taxi drivers to know where certain restaurants, hotels, or attractions are located; keep addresses handy.

FAST FACTS: **Puebla**

American Express   The office is at Plaza Dorado 2, local 21, Col. Ansures (© **222/ 229-1500**). Hours are Monday through Friday from 9am to 6pm, Saturday 9am to 1pm.

Area Code   The telephone area code is **222**.

Emergency   The emergency number is © **066**.

Hospital   **Beneficiencia Española** is at 19 Norte 1001 (© **222/232-0500**).

Internet Access   There are plenty of shops downtown. The going rate is $1.50 per hour. Try to check your mail in the morning, when connections are quicker; by 2pm there's a noticeable drop in speed.

Pharmacy   Drugstores are almost as common as churches. They usually close around 9pm but take turns staying open late *(de turno)*. Should you need something overnight, **Farmatodo** (© **222/237-7133**) delivers around the clock.

Population   Puebla has 1.8 million residents.

Post Office   The *correo* is around the corner from the State Tourism office, on 16 de Septiembre, the third door down from the corner (at 5 Oriente). Hours are Monday through Friday from 9am to 3pm, and Saturday mornings.

EXPLORING PUEBLA

Puebla is a city full of stories and anecdotes that color the colonial houses and convents of the historic district. To hear some of them, you can hire a guide from the State Tourism office, who can also provide historical context. For a quick (1-hr.) tour of the city, you can hop on one of the little buses that park on the street between the *zócalo* and the cathedral (3 Oriente). Tours are in Spanish, depart every half-hour, and cost $4. They include a quick view of the site where the Battle of 5 de Mayo was fought. Your ticket is valid for the entire day and allows you to get off at any location and board the next bus that comes along.

CHURCHES

If you were to stop to examine every church you pass, you would be in for a long stay. Still, it is something I enjoy doing, even with the smaller churches. Many have simple, austere interiors that express a sweetness and humility that I like. Three churches in the historic district require specific mention.

The **cathedral** ✶✶✶, completed in 1649, has the tallest bell towers in Mexico. Its dark stone exterior and severe *Herrerian* design lend it a lugubrious appearance that perhaps befits a cathedral but takes a little while to warm up to. In the country, only Mexico City's cathedral has a more interesting interior. In front, you can usually find guides (or they'll find you) who offer a short tour.

The **Iglesia de Santo Domingo** ✶✶✶, on the corner of Cinco de Mayo and 4 Poniente, was originally part of a Dominican monastery completed in 1611. Lining the walls of the nave are some exquisite baroque altars. In the left transept you'll find the **Capilla del Rosario,** built in 1690. It is a masterpiece of gold leaf and plaster convolutes dedicated to the Virgin of the Rosary. Some point to it as the epitome of Mexican baroque architecture. Note, too, the intricate Talavera wainscoting.

Last, there is the massive **church of the Compañía,** built by the Jesuits, where "La China Poblana" worshipped and was briefly entombed. Look to the right of the church doorway and you'll see a curious bit of text in Talavera. It marks the date of the execution of a con man. He arrived in Mexico on a boat from Spain carrying papers identifying him as a *visitador* (papal emissary and inspector). He was wined and dined by the bishops and lived the good life for several weeks before being found out and executed. As the text notes, his head was then hung from the front of this church.

Cinco de Mayo & the Battle of Puebla

In the United States, the Mexican holiday Cinco de Mayo is often compared to the Fourth of July, but it's not Mexican Independence Day. The date commemorates the Battle of Puebla, on May 5, 1862, which resulted in a memorable victory against foreign invaders.

At the time, Napoleon III of France was scheming to occupy Mexico. A well-trained and handsomely uniformed army of 6,000, under the command of General Laurencez, landed in Veracruz with the objective of occupying Mexico City. In its path were 4,000 ill-equipped Mexicans under General Ignacio Zaragoza. Despite the odds, the Mexicans won a resounding victory. The French were humiliated and suffered their first defeat in nearly a half-century at the hands of the penniless, war-torn republic of Mexico.

For Mexico, it marked the nation's first victory against foreign attack, and the battle remains a matter of national pride. Never mind that by the following year the French were in possession of both Puebla and Mexico City. Today, the Cinco de Mayo holiday is an enduring symbol of Mexico's sense of patriotism.

On a trip to Puebla, you can visit the forts of Guadalupe and Loreto, where the battle took place, just north of the old part of the city.

If you're in Puebla for any length of time, you will notice the iconic figure of "La China Poblana" virtually everywhere. A real person, she was originally a princess from India (not China) and was captured by a Portuguese raiding party, sold into slavery, and shipped to Mexico on a Philippine galleon in the 17th century. Somehow, she became the property of a rich family of Puebla. This family, impressed with the woman's simplicity and spirituality, eventually adopted her. Thus freed from domestic chores, she delved into a life of religious devotions, mixing elements of her native beliefs with Catholicism. She became a mystic who led an austere life of prayer, and in time became revered by the population of the city. At her death, she was interred in the church of the Compañía, but church authorities later moved her remains when a cult began to form around them. Her form of dress has become the standard folkloric outfit of the city.

MUSEUMS

In addition to those listed below, there are a couple of smaller attractions worth visiting: The **Biblioteca Palafoxiana** is an impressive colonial library, the collection of the famous 17th-century bishop who went on to become viceroy, Juan Palafox y Mendoza. The library is on the second floor of the Casa de Cultura, next to the state tourism office. It is closed at present for remodeling. The **Casa de Alfeñique** is a colonial mansion and a landmark for its exterior plaster decoration, which reminds one of cake icing; the museum collection, a hodgepodge of things Poblano, is fun if you have time. It's at the intersection of 4 Oriente and 6 Norte. The **Casa de los Muñecos,** 2 Norte 4, is more important for its exterior than for the museum collection inside. Large grotesques said to be caricatures of the town council adorn the late-18th-century facade, though this story is apocryphal.

Exconvento de Santa Mónica   After independence, a long political struggle arose between the national government and the Church. It climaxed in the Reform Wars of the 1850s, when the government instituted several anticlerical measures, including the closing of convents. The nuns here discreetly walled up their doors and kept functioning as a religious community with the aid of their neighbors and the blind eye of local officials. They survived with little assistance from the outside as over the years the convent slowly crumbled around them. Then, in 1934 (during another time of crisis between the government and the church), a local official "discovered" them. This history makes for an interesting visit: displays include the contents of this and two other clandestine convents confiscated at the same time. These nuns weren't sitting on great treasures—most of the paintings are poor examples of their era—but you will find a rare set of paintings on velvet that predate Elvis. Things not to miss are the crypt, the chapel, and the upper and lower *coros* (choirs). While you're there, visit the church next door and pay your respects to the much-revered image of Nuestro Señor de las Maravillas, alongside the back of the nave, to the left as you enter.

Av. 18 Poniente 103. © 222/232-0178. Admission $3. Tues–Sun 9am–6pm.

Exconvento de Santa Rosa   Unlike its neighbor, this former convent near Santa Mónica was unable to postpone confiscation and served variously as barracks, hospital, and public housing. It is now the home of the **Museo de Arte Popular.** Here you can see the kitchen where *mole* was invented (for this alone it is worth the pilgrimage), and afterward the museum guide will take you upstairs to see displays of the crafts practiced in the state of Puebla. If you enjoy handicrafts, don't miss this place; it has some rare and beautiful examples of artisanship. The main door is usually closed; enter through the public parking lot at 14 Poniente 305.

Calle 3 Norte (at 14 Poniente). ℂ 222/232-9240. Admission $2. Tues–Sun 10am–4:30pm.

Museo Amparo ✦✦✦   The finest museum in the city, the Museo Amparo (named for the deceased wife of the founder) has a stunning collection of pre-Columbian pieces from across Mexico, beautifully displayed and intelligently organized. Its collections of colonial and modern art are quite good, and the museum frequently gets important traveling exhibitions, which usually don't require an additional admission charge. The collection of *arte virreinal* (colonial art) is on the second floor and includes decorative objects and furniture. It is exhibited in the restored living quarters of the original mansion. The interiors are all from the Porfiriato (1870s), with the elaborate decoration that the period is known for. Audio tours of the pre-Columbian collection are for rent ($1, plus $1 deposit). You can hire an English-speaking guide for the entire museum ($20). Signs are in Spanish and English; no cameras are permitted.

Calle 2 Sur 708. ℂ 222/246-4210. Admission $3 adults; $2 children 3–12 and students; free Mon. Wed–Mon 10am–6pm.

Museo Bello y González ✦✦   Located near the corner of Calle 3 Sur and Avenida 3 Poniente, a block west of the *zócalo,* this museum houses a collection of fine 17th-, 18th-, and 19th-century art, furniture, and antiques from all over the world. Many of the oriental objects in the museum were brought over in colonial times on the Philippine galleon. The rooms of the house are richly decorated with wood paneling, painted finishes, molded plaster, carved molding, velvet curtains, French porcelain, and the rest. The museum is named for José Luis Bello y González, who made his fortune in tobacco and began to collect artifacts soon thereafter. He was a fine artist in his own right and an accomplished organist. He willed his collection and his house to the state. A guided tour (in English or Spanish) is included in the price of admission.

Av. 3 Poniente 302. ℂ 222/232-9475. Admission $4; Tues–Sun 10am–5pm.

Museo Nacional del Ferrocarril   This is a treat for railroad buffs. It consists of a large open area with several train engines (both steam and diesel), baggage cars, passenger cars, a presidential car, a dining car, Pullman coaches, and a caboose. You can board and inspect the cars. Even those not interested in railroads might enjoy seeing the design and details of some of these—they sketch in microcosm a bygone era. A small gallery exhibits railway landscapes.

11 Norte and 12 Poniente. ℂ 222/232-4988. Free admission. Tues–Sun 10am–5pm.

SHOPPING

Puebla is the home of the famous **Talavera dinnerware** ✦. Numerous workshops produce this expensive pottery. Operating since 1824, **Uriarte Talavera,** Calle 4 Poniente 911 (ℂ **222/232-1598**), is one of the city's established potters. Behind an unprepossessing doorway, the factory produces exquisite pieces, many examples of which are on display in its showrooms. Some are for sale, while others are samples. Tours of the factory start at 10am, 11am, noon, and 1pm from Monday to Saturday.

The factory is open Monday through Saturday from 9am to 6:30pm, Sunday from 11am to 6pm. The factory can ship your purchases; it accepts American Express, MasterCard, and Visa. The **Centro Talavera Poblana,** Calle 6 Oriente 11, between Calle 2 Norte and Avenida 5 de Mayo (© **222/242-0848**), offers a wide range of Talavera from producers in Puebla as well as Tlaxcala. The huge showroom stocks sets of 6 to 12 place settings. It's open Monday through Saturday from 9:30am to 8pm, Sunday from 10am to 7pm. You can ship your purchases; American Express, Diners Club, MasterCard, and Visa are accepted.

The **Mercado de Artesanías (El Parián),** is a pedestrians-only, open-air shopping area just east of Calle 6 Norte between avenidas 2 and 6 Oriente. You'll see rows of neat brick shops selling inexpensive crafts and souvenirs. Don't judge all Talavera pottery by what you see here, though; the style in many cases is overblown. The shops are open daily from 10am to 8pm. Bargain to get a good price. While you're in this area, you can take a look at the **Teatro Principal.**

For antiques browsing, go to **Callejón de los Sapos (Alley of the Frogs),** about 3 blocks southeast of the *zócalo* near Calle 4 Sur and Avenida 7 Oriente. Wander in and out; there's good stuff large and small. Shops are generally open daily from 10am to 2pm and 4 to 6pm. On Saturday mornings there's a flea market in the little square. If you're there between 2:30 and 5:30pm, stop by **La Pasita,** across Calle 5 from the Plaza de los Sapos, to taste homemade cordials and browse through the owner's humorous collection of Mexicana. Start with a *pasita,* then work your way up to a *china poblana*—a layered cordial of red, white, and green liqueurs. The owner is an inveterate leg-puller.

WHERE TO STAY

Prices quoted include the 17% tax. All hotels listed here are in the historic district. Puebla's comfortable **Crowne Plaza Hotel** (© **800/HOLIDAY** in the U.S. and Canada) is a short taxi ride from the center of town. Room rates are about $200 for a standard double. From late March to May, Puebla can experience heat waves. Consider getting a room with air-conditioning at this time of year.

VERY EXPENSIVE

Hotel Camino Real Puebla ✿✿✿   This hotel, in the 16th-century former convent of the Immaculate Conception, is a nicely restored colonial gem. Courtyards spill into more courtyards, and remnants of polychromed colonial-era frescos are everywhere, even in the rooms. Rooms are decorated in handsome blue-and-yellow schemes inspired by Talavera colors. All have tile floors and original paintings, and some contain antiques. The hotel is 2½ blocks south of the *zócalo.*

Av. 7 Poniente 105 (between Calle 3 Sur and Av. 16 de Septiembre), Centro Histórico, 72000 Puebla, Pue. © **800/ 722-6466** in the U.S., 222/229-0909, or -0910. Fax 222/232-9251. www.caminoreal.com/puebla. 84 units. $212 double; $320 junior suite. AE, DC, MC, V. **Amenities:** 2 restaurants; bar; whirlpool; tour desk; car rental; business center; room service until 11pm; babysitting; laundry service; dry cleaning. *In room:* A/C, TV, dataport, minibar, coffeemaker, hair dryer.

Mesones Sacristia ✿✿✿   Two small hotels offer different ways to delve into Puebla's colonial past. If you're looking for modern convenience rather than atmosphere, stay at the Holiday Inn or the Crowne Plaza. If you want some colonial flavor mixed with sophistication or gaiety, try one of these unique hotels. Both are elegant adaptations of colonial houses, excellently located, but otherwise very different. The **Capuchinas** offers quiet rooms, lots of privacy, and a smart blend of colonial and modern architecture. The small restaurant has won praise for its modern international cooking. The sister hotel, **Mesón de la Sacristía de la Compañía,** is less quiet and more fun. It offers an experience of the old city in all its antiquity and even quirkiness. For starters, you receive a massive colonial skeleton key to your room. And the rooms feel as colonial as the hotel could get away with. In the courtyard, a great restaurant and popular nightspot serves Poblano specialties. A guitarist performs romantic songs and ballads until about 11pm. Sometimes the entertainment is a guitar trio or some members of a *tuna* (traditional Spanish music sung to the accompaniment of string instruments)—not for those who like to retire early. The hotels offer packages for those interested in cooking lessons or Talavera.

Calle 6 Sur 304, Callejón de los Sapos, 72000 Puebla, Pue. ℂ/fax **222/232-4513** or 222/242-3554. www.mesones-sacristia.com. 8 units at Capuchinas; 7 units at Mesón de la Sacristía de la Compañía. $150 junior suite; $190 suite. Rates include full breakfast. AE, MC, V. Free secure parking. **Amenities:** Restaurant; bar; access to local health club; tour and activities desk; car rental; room service until 10pm; in-room massage; laundry service; dry cleaning. *In room:* TV, coffeemaker, hair dryer.

EXPENSIVE

Hotel Holiday Inn Puebla ⭐   The lobby here is more fun than that of any Holiday Inn I've ever visited, but the rooms are very much in character with the rest, especially the properties in the Midwest. The resemblance is so strong that it's a little unnerving. Still, the rooms are comfortable and have the best heat and air-conditioning in the downtown area. Rooms are midsize and carpeted. Bathrooms come with showers, good lighting, and good counter space. Avoid the lower rooms near the kitchen, which makes an unbelievable amount of noise.

Av. 2 Oriente 211, 72000 Puebla, Pue. ℂ **800/HOLIDAY** in the U.S. and Canada, or 222/223-6600. www.holiday-inn.com. 79 units. $130 double. AE, DC, MC, V. Free covered parking. **Amenities:** Restaurant; bar; heated pool; room service until 11pm; babysitting; laundry service; dry cleaning; nonsmoking rooms. *In room:* A/C, TV, coffeemaker, hair dryer, iron.

Hotel Posada San Pedro ⭐ *Kids*   A better bargain than most downtown hotels offering the same level of amenities, especially for families, this place is convenient and comfortable. Spacious rooms come with plain wooden furniture, carpeting, and midsize bathrooms. One section of the hotel has air-conditioning. There is a well-manicured courtyard with a small pool, surrounded by four stories of rooms. It's a family hotel, with afternoon videos for the kids and child care by prior arrangement.

Av. 2 Oriente 202, 72000 Puebla, Pue. ℂ **222/246-5077.** Fax 222/246-5376. www.hotelposadassanpedro.com.mx. 80 units. $105 double. Low-season rates available. AE, MC, V. Free covered parking. **Amenities:** Restaurant; bar; outdoor heated pool; Jacuzzi; children's activities; travel agency; car rental; business center; room service until 10:30pm; babysitting; laundry service; dry cleaning. *In room:* TV, hair dryer.

MODERATE

Hotel Colonial *Value*   This four-story hotel (with elevator) offers a great location at a good price. The rooms are ample and attractive, but avoid units along Calle 3. The furnishings are simple; standard rooms usually contain twin beds with thin pillows. Bathrooms are basic but sufficient. The hotel's restaurant is good. The Colonial is 1 block east of the *zócalo,* on a pedestrian way. One problem with this hotel is that it requires a credit card number to reserve a room.

Calle 4 Sur 105 (between Palafox y Mendoza and 3 Oriente), 72000 Puebla, Pue. ℂ **222/246-4199.** Fax 222/246-0818. www.colonial.com.mx. 70 units. $59 double. MC, V. **Amenities:** Restaurant; tour info; room service until 10pm; laundry service; dry cleaning. *In room:* TV, safe.

INEXPENSIVE

Hotel Puebla Plaza *Value* The most attractive and comfortable of the budget hotels in the historic district, the Puebla Plaza is almost in the shadow of the cathedral. Rooms are small to midsize, with small bathrooms equipped with showers. Get a room in back to avoid the commotion in the front courtyard and at the restaurant next door. Lower prices are for rooms with one double bed.

Calle 5 Poniente 111, 72000 Puebla, Pue. ℂ **222/246-3175.** Fax 222/242-5792. www.hotelpueblaplaza.com. 48 units. $36–$47 double. MC, V. Secure parking $4. **Amenities:** Restaurant; tour info. *In room:* TV.

WHERE TO DINE

Puebla is known throughout Mexico for *mole poblano,* a spicy sauce with more than 20 ingredients (including chocolate), as well as *mixiotes* (mee-*shoh*-tehs), a dish of beef, pork, or lamb in a spicy red sauce baked in maguey paper. Another regional specialty, *pipián,* is somewhat like *mole* but based on ground toasted squash seeds. *Dulces* (sweets) shops are scattered about, with display windows brim-full of marzipan crafted into various shapes and designs, candied figs, and guava paste. If you're in the city during the season for *chiles en nogada* (July–Sept), make a point of trying one. It's a dish of elegant contrasts involving a poblano chile, a spicy-sweet filling made of pork, chicken, and sweetmeats, and a walnut cream sauce. The city goes crazy for this dish, and you'll see it everywhere. Besides the restaurants listed below, try those in the **Mesones Sacristía** (see above). I love the *mole* and traditional *chalupas* at the **Compañía** hotel restaurant.

VERY EXPENSIVE

La Conjura ★★★ SPANISH It seems strange to eat Spanish food in this city known for its Mexican cuisine, but this restaurant is special. It plays with combinations of Old and New World ingredients, like tapas of *chistorra* (Spanish sausage) cooked with a small amount of *guajillo* peppers, or a shrimp dish with locally made goat cheese and passionfruit sauce. The ambitious menu changes daily, with offerings of seafood, lamb, and beef. On my last visit, I was especially impressed by the *arroz negro con calamares* (rice with squid cooked in the squid's ink), the *huachinango en alberino* (snapper in a scented wine sauce topped with mussels, clams, and shrimp), and a cream soup of sweet peppers and clams. The small, attractive dining room with its low, vaulted ceiling was formerly a bodega.

9 Oriente 201. ℂ **222/232-9693.** Reservations recommended. Main courses $14–$36; tapas $3–$10. AE, DC, MC, V. Sun–Tues 2–6pm; Wed–Sat 2–11pm.

MODERATE

Fonda de Santa Clara *Overrated* REGIONAL This is one of those restaurants invariably associated with a particular city. For many people, it is the automatic choice in Puebla, and unfortunately, this has caused a decline in quality. Still, many visitors love it, and the main restaurant is a pretty place. The *mole* is worth trying. It's 1½ blocks west of the *zócalo.*

Av. 3 Poniente 307. ℂ **222/242-2659.** Lunch $7–$14; dinner $5–$10. AE, DC, MC, V. Daily 9am–10pm.

La Guadalupana REGIONAL/MEXICAN This restaurant off the Callejón de Los Sapos serves good regional specialties, including *mole, mole verde,* and *pipián.* The restaurant has two dining areas—the central front courtyard of a colonial house and the narrow patio of a former working-class *vecindad* (an enclosed grouping of simple apartments that share kitchen and bathroom areas).

5 Oriente 605. ℂ **222/242-4886.** Main courses $6–$12. AE, MC, V. Daily 8am–9pm.

Mi Ciudad ★★ MEXICAN   For an excellent *mole* or *pipián,* take a cab to this restaurant, in the middle of Puebla's restaurant and club district along Avenida Juárez. The dining room is large, with lots of references to Puebla in the decoration. The menu is large as well. The *chileatole* and *sopa poblana,* both cream soups, are excellent choices. For a main course, try the above-mentioned dishes, especially the *pipián verde.* Not on the menu, but you can ask for it anyway, is a half-and-half combination of either *mole* and *pipián* or *pipián rojo* and *pipián verde.* I like these dishes better here than at La Guadalupana. Also on the menu are several dishes from other parts of Mexico, including grilled meats, enchiladas, and so on.

Av. Juárez 2507. (*C*) **222/231-5326.** Reservations recommended. Main courses $7–$14. AE, DC, MC, V. Tues–Sat 1:30pm–midnight; Sun 1:30–6:30pm.

PUEBLA AFTER DARK

Mariachis play daily, beginning at 6pm, on **Plaza de Santa Inés,** Avenida 11 Poniente and Calle 3 Sur. They stroll through the crowds that gather at the sidewalk cafes. Another square where you can hear live music is **Plaza de los Sapos,** Avenida 7 Oriente near Calle 6 Sur. To get there, walk 2 blocks south from the *zócalo* and take a left onto Avenida 7 Oriente, toward the river. The plaza will be on your left, spreading out between Avenida 7 and Avenida 5 Oriente just past Calle 4 Sur. If you take Avenida 5 Oriente from the cathedral to reach the Plaza de los Sapos, you'll pass several local hangouts where students, artists, and others gather for conversation, coffee, drinks, snacks, and live music.

Another place to hear live music is down the block from los Sapos at **Mesón Sacristía de la Compañía,** Calle 6 Sur 304. A singer-guitarist entertains with popular ballads from 9pm to midnight. The moderately priced restaurant serves a complete selection of Puebla specialties.

Teorema, Reforma 540 near Calle 7 Norte ((*C*) **222/242-1014**), is a good coffee shop and bookstore that features guitarists and folksingers every evening. It's open daily from 9:30am to 2:30pm and 4:30pm to midnight, and accepts MasterCard and Visa.

SIDE TRIPS FROM PUEBLA
CHOLULA, TONANTZINTLA & SAN FRANCISCO ACATEPEC

Ten minutes outside of Puebla on the old highway to Mexico City is the small town of **Cholula.** In pre-Columbian times, this was a large city—the religious capital of highland Mexico. The Spanish razed the hundreds of temples that stood here, and we know little about them. But the **Great Pyramid** still sits there, the largest pyramid in the New World. At first glimpse, it looks more like a hill crowned by a church (Nuestra Señora de los Remedios). But if you climb the unreconstructed pyramid beside it, you will see plainly the geometric outline of the original structure, which rises from the ground in four levels. From this viewpoint, you also get a good look at El Popocatépetl, the majestic snow-capped volcano that separates this valley from the valley of Mexico. The entrance fee for the Cholula pyramid is $2; the site is open Tuesday through Sunday from 9am to 5pm. Archaeologists have reconstructed one side of one of the lower segments of the pyramid and have dug tunnels into the pyramid, which visitors are free to explore.

A perfect complement to this trip is a visit to the church of **Tonantzintla** ★★★, just to the south. Leave the town on Bulevar Miguel Alemán, which becomes the road to Tonantzintla. Less than 1.5km (1 mile) ahead, it's within plain sight of the road.

This church is justly famous for its jewel-box interior, executed in an endearing style that people have come to call Indian baroque. It has mesmerized many visitors, including R. Gordon Wasson, who saw in its manifold imagery allusions to a secret mushroom cult. If this visit hasn't quenched your appetite for visiting churches, proceed a bit farther down the road, and you will imperceptibly cross into the neighboring community of **San Francisco Acatepec** ⭐⭐. Its church is also along the road and cannot be missed; it has a stunning tile facade.

COLONIAL TLAXCALA & THE CACAXTLA & XOCHITECATL RUINS

Tlaxcala, 40km (25 miles) north of Puebla and 120km (75 miles) east of Mexico City, is the capital of Mexico's smallest state (also named Tlaxcala) and a colonial-era city with several claims to fame. Tlaxcalan warriors allied with Cortez against the Aztec played an essential role in the conquest. Tlaxcalan chiefs were the first to be baptized by the Spaniards; the baptismal font is in the **Templo de San Francisco** (2 blocks from the main plaza, just above the bullring). The church is noted for the elaborately inlaid Moorish ceiling below the choir loft. A painting inside the Chapel of the Third Order shows the baptism of the chiefs.

To the right of the Templo is the **Exconvento,** now a museum containing early paintings and artifacts from nearby archaeological sites. The **Government Palace** ⭐⭐, on the handsome, tree-shaped central *zócalo,* contains vivid murals by a local artist, Desiderio Hernández Xochitiotzin, that illustrate the city's history. The expanded **Museo de Artesanías,** on Sanchez Piedras between Lardizabal and 1 de Mayo, showcases the state's wide-ranging crafts and customs. Here, local artisans give visitors demonstrations in such crafts as embroidery, weaving, and *pulque*-making (juice of fermented *agaves*). Don't plan to breeze through; tours are mandatory and rather structured, and take an hour or more—but are very interesting. The museum is open Tuesday through Sunday from 10am to 6pm; admission (including tour) is $1.

Tlaxcala's **tourist information office** is at the intersection of avenidas Juárez and Lardizábal (© **246/465-0961,** or 01-800/509-6557 in Mexico). Office hours are Monday through Friday from 9am to 7pm, Saturday and Sunday from 10am to 2pm.

Tlaxcala's main attractions are **Cacaxtla-Xochitécatl** ⭐⭐⭐ (pronounced "kah-*kahsh*-tlah soh-shee-*teh*-kahtl"), unique pre-Hispanic hilltop sites 19km (12 miles) southwest of the city. Tlaxcala attracts few tourists and retains its small-town atmosphere and overall low prices. If you are there on a weekend, the State Tourism Office sponsors a Saturday tour of the city and a Sunday tour of the Cacaxtla-Xochitécatl sites (both in Spanish). Tours leave from the front of the Museo de Arte at 10am. Board the bus; the guide will collect the $2 fee. The city also offers a tour of the city in an old trolley bus Friday, Saturday, and Sunday. Ask at the information office.

Less than 1km (just over ½ mile) from the town center is the famed **Ocotlán Sanctuary** ⭐, constructed after Juan Diego Bernardino claimed to have seen an apparition of the Virgin Mary on that site in 1541. Baroque inside and out, it has elaborate interior decorations of carved figures and curling gilded wood that date from the 1700s. The carvings are attributed to Francisco Miguel Tlayotehuanitzin, an Indian sculptor who labored for more than 20 years to create them.

Santa Ana, a wool-weaving village, is 2.5km (1½ miles) east of Tlaxcala. Shops selling large rugs, *sarapes,* and locally woven sweaters line the main street. Huamantla, 48km (30 miles) southeast of Tlaxcala, is a small village noted for its commemoration of the Assumption of the Virgin on August 14 and 15.

WHERE TO STAY & DINE IN TLAXCALA

Tlaxcala has several good restaurants beneath the portal on the east side of the *zócalo,* and some schedule live music in the evening. Budget hotels are nearby and along the road to Apizaco.

Hotel Alifer   The Alifer's rooms, with black-and-red Spanish colonial decor, are carpeted and have tile-and-marble bathrooms with showers. To get there from the Plaza Constitución, with your back to the Posada San Francisco, walk to the right 2 blocks (you'll reach the hotel entrance just before the street turns to the right). The parking lot is next to the lobby entrance. The restaurant is open daily from 7am to 10pm.

Morelos 11, 90000 Tlaxcala, Tlax. ℂ 246/462-5678. www.hotelalifer.com. 40 units. $30–$45 double. MC, V. Free parking. **Amenities:** Restaurant; room service until 10pm; laundry service. *In room:* TV.

Hotel Posada San Francisco   This *posada* (inn) opened in 1992 on Tlaxcala's *zócalo* in a 19th-century mansion known as the Casa de las Piedras (House of Stones) for its gray stone facade. Rooms are in two-story, colonial-style wings that face either the pool or small courtyards. The hotel is attractive because of its modern comforts and its ideal location on the town's central square. Even if you don't stay, stop in for a look around (there is some interesting art on display and for sale in the lobby) or for a meal at **La Trasquila,** a Mexican restaurant on the second story overlooking the plaza and lobby; it's open daily from 2 to 11pm. There's also a first-floor cafeteria and bar with evening entertainment.

Plaza de la Constitución 17, 90000 Tlaxcala, Tlax. ℂ 246/462-6022. Fax 246/462-6818. www.posadasanfrancisco. com. 68 units. $99 double; $143 suite. AE, MC, V. Free parking. **Amenities:** Restaurant; bar; tennis court; game room; room service; massage; laundry service; dry cleaning. *In room:* A/C, TV.

EXPLORING THE CACAXTLA-XOCHITÉCATL ARCHAEOLOGICAL SITE

Scholars were startled by the discovery in 1975 of vivid murals in red, blue, black, yellow, and white, showing Maya warriors (from the Yucatán Peninsula). Since then, more murals, more history, and at least eight construction phases have been uncovered.

Scholars attribute the influence of the site to a little-known tri-ethnic group (Náhuatl, Mixtec, and Chocho-popoloca) known as Olmec-Xicalanca, from Mexico's Gulf Coast. Among the translations of its name, "merchant's trade pack" seems most revealing. Like Casas Grandes north of Chihuahua City and Xochicalco between Cuernavaca and Taxco, Cacaxtla appears to have been an important crossroads for merchants, astronomers, and others in the Mesoamerican world. Its apogee, between A.D. 650 and 900, corresponds with the abandonment of Teotihuacán (near Mexico City), the decline of the classic Maya civilization, and the emergence of the Toltec culture at Tula.

How—or even if—those events affected Cacaxtla isn't known. The principal **mural** apparently is a vividly detailed victory scene, with triumphant dark-skinned warriors wearing jaguar skins, and the vanquished dressed in feathers and having their intestines extracted. Numerous symbols of Venus (a half-star with five points) found painted at the site have led archaeoastronomy scholar John Carlson to link historical events such as wars, captive-taking, and ritual sacrifice with the appearance of Venus; all of this was likely undertaken in hopes of assuring the continued fertility of crops.

The latest mural discoveries show a wall of corn plants from which human heads sprout, next to a merchant whose pack is laden with goods. The murals flank a grand

Tlaxcala

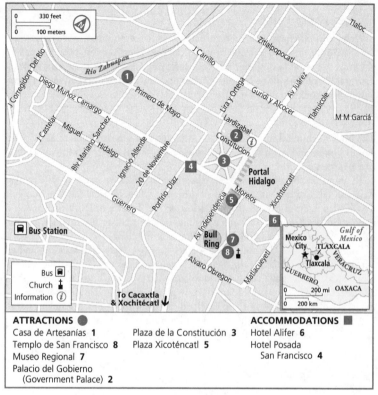

acropolis with unusual architectural motifs. A giant steel roof protects the grand plaza and murals.

Xochitécatl is a small ceremonial center located on a hilltop overlooking Cacaxtla, about 1km (½ mile) to the east and in plain sight of Cacaxtla. It was probably inhabited, at least in the Classical period, by the same people living in Cacaxtla. A curious **circular pyramid** stands atop this hill, 180km (600 ft.) above the surrounding countryside. Beside it are two other **pyramids** and three massive **boulders** (one about 3m/10 ft. in diameter), which were hollowed out for some reason. Hollowed boulders appear to have been restricted to the Puebla-Tlaxcala valley. Excavation of the Edificio de la Espiral (circular pyramid), dated between 1000 and 800 B.C. (middle formative period), encountered no stairways. Access is thought to have been by its spiral walkway. Rounded boulders from the nearby Zahuapan and Atoyac rivers were used in its construction. Rounded pyramids in this part of Mexico are thought to have been dedicated to Ehécatl, god of the wind. The base diameter exceeds 55m (180 ft.); it rises to a height of 15m (50 ft.).

The stepped and terraced **Pyramid of the Flowers,** made of rounded boulders, was started during the middle formative period. Modifications continued into colonial times, as exemplified by faced-stone and stucco-covered adobe. Of the 30 bodies found during excavations, all but one were children. Little is known about the people

---

Tips **Photo Pointer**

When you purchase admission to Cacaxtla-Xochitécatl, you'll have to pay an extra $6 for bringing in a still or video camera. Keep in mind, though, that at Cacaxtla, neither a flash nor a tripod is allowed, so the site is difficult to photograph from the inside because of dust and low light caused by shading from the giant roof.

---

who built Xochitécatl. Evidence suggests that the area was dedicated to Xochitl, goddess of flowers and fertility. The small **museum** contains pottery and small sculpture, and a **garden** holds larger sculpture.

To get to Cacaxtla from Tlaxcala, take a *combi* (collective minivan) or city bus to Nativitas (also called San Miguel Milagro), the village nearest the Cacaxtla ruins. *Combis* depart from behind the Hotel Posada San Francisco. From there, walk the paved road less than 1km (about a half-mile) or take a taxi to the entrance. From the parking lot, the archaeological site is a 90m (300-ft.) climb.

From Puebla, take Highway 119 north to the crossroads near Zacualpan and turn left, passing Tetlatlahuaca; turn right when you see signs to Nativitas and Cacaxtla. From Mexico City, take Highway 190 to San Martín Texmelucan, where you should ask directions for the road leading directly to the ruins, which are about 10km (6 miles) ahead. (This is the southern road you can use without going through Tlaxcala.)

Admission is $4 (a single ticket is good for both sites), plus $6 for a video or still camera. Both sites are open Tuesday through Sunday from 10am to 5pm.

13

Cancún

by Lynne Bairstow

Mexico's calling card to the world, Cancún perfectly showcases both the country's breathtaking natural beauty and the depth of its 1,000-year history. Simply stated, Cancún is the reason most people travel to Mexico. The sheer number of travelers underscores Cancún's magnetic appeal, with almost three million people visiting this enticing beach resort annually—most of them on their first trip to the country. The reasons for this are both numerous and obvious.

Cancún offers an unrivaled combination of high-quality accommodations, dreamy beaches, easy air access, and a wide diversity of shopping, dining, nightlife, and nearby activities—most of them exceptional values. There is also the lure of ancient cultures evident in all directions and a number of ecologically oriented theme parks.

No doubt about it—Cancún embodies Caribbean splendor, with translucent turquoise waters and powdery white-sand beaches, coupled with coastal areas of great natural beauty. But Cancún is also a modern megaresort. Even a traveler feeling apprehensive about visiting foreign soil will feel completely at ease here. English is spoken, dollars are accepted, roads are well paved, and lawns are manicured. Malls are the mode for shopping and dining, and you could swear that some hotels are larger than a small town. Travelers feel comfortable in Cancún. You do not need to spend a day getting your bearings,

because you immediately see familiar names for dining, shopping, nightclubbing, and sleeping.

You may have heard that in 1974 a team of Mexican government computer analysts picked Cancún for tourism development for its ideal mix of elements to attract travelers—and they were right on. It's actually an island, a 24km (14-mile) sliver of land connected to the mainland by two bridges and separated from it by the expansive Nichupté lagoon. (*Cancún* means "golden snake" in Mayan.)

In addition to attractions of its own, Cancún is a convenient distance from the more traditional resorts of Isla Mujeres and from the coastal zone now known as the Riviera Maya—extending down from Cancún, through Playa del Carmen, to the Maya ruins at Tulum, Cozumel, Chichén Itzá, and Cobá. All are within day-trip distance.

You will run out of vacation days before you run out of things to do in Cancún. Snorkeling, jet-skiing, jungle tours, and visits to ancient Maya ruins and modern ecological theme parks are among the most popular diversions. There are a dozen malls with name-brand and duty-free shops (with European goods at prices better than in the U.S.), and more than 350 restaurants and nightclubs. The 24,000-plus hotel rooms in the area offer something for every taste and every budget.

Cancún's luxury hotels have pools so spectacular that you may find it tempting to remain poolside, but don't. Set aside some time to simply gaze into the ocean and wriggle your toes in the fine, brilliantly white sand. It is, after all, what put Cancún on the map.

1 Orientation

GETTING THERE

BY PLANE If this is not your first trip to Cancún, you'll notice that the airport's facilities and services continue to expand. **Aeromexico** (© **800/237-6639** in the U.S., or 01/800-021-4000 in Mexico; www.aeromexico.com) offers direct service from Atlanta, Houston, Miami, and New York, plus connecting service via Mexico City from Dallas, Los Angeles, and San Diego. **Mexicana** (© **800/531-7921** in the U.S., or 01/800-502-2000 or 998/881-9090 in Mexico; www.mexicana.com.mx) flies from Chicago, Denver, Los Angeles, Oakland, San Antonio, San Francisco, and San Jose via Mexico City, with nonstop service from Miami and New York. In addition to these carriers, many **charter** companies—such as Apple Vacations, Funjet, and Friendly Holidays—travel to Cancún; these package tours make up as much as 60% of arrivals by U.S. visitors (see "Packages for the Independent Traveler," in chapter 2).

Regional carrier **AeroCaribe,** a Mexicana affiliate (© **998/884-2000**) flies from Cozumel, Havana, Mexico City, Mérida, Chetumal, and other points within Mexico. You'll want to confirm departure times for flights to the U.S.; here are the Cancún airport numbers of major international carriers: **American** (© **998/883-4461;** www.aa.com), **Continental** (© **998/886-0006;** www.continental.com), and **Northwest** (© **998/886-0044** or 998/886-0046; www.nwa.com).

Most major car-rental firms have outlets at the airport, so if you're renting a car, consider picking it up and dropping it off at the airport to save on airport-transportation costs. Another way to save money is to arrange for the rental before you leave home. If you wait until you arrive, the daily cost will be around $50 to $75 for a Chevrolet Atos. Major agencies include **Avis** (© **800/331-1212** in the U.S., or 998/886-0221; www.avis.com); **Budget** (© **800/527-0700** in the U.S., or 998/886-0417; fax 998/884-4812; www.budget.com); **Dollar** (© **800/800-4000** in the U.S., or 998/886-2300; www.dollar.com); **National** (© **800/328-4567** in the U.S., or 998/886-0655; www.nationalcar.com); and **Hertz** (© **800/654-3131** in the U.S. and Canada, or 998/884-1326; www.hertz.com). The Zona Hotelera (Hotel Zone) is 10km (6½ miles), or about a 20-minute drive, from the airport along wide, well-paved roads.

Rates for a private taxi from the airport are around $20 to downtown Cancún, or $28 to $40 to the Hotel Zone, depending on your destination. *Colectivos* (vans) run from the airport into town. Buy tickets, which cost about $9, from the booth to the far right as you exit the airport terminal. There's minibus transportation ($9.50) from the airport to the Puerto Juárez passenger ferry to Isla Mujeres, or you can hire a private taxi for about $40. There is no *colectivo* service returning to the airport from Ciudad Cancún or the Hotel Zone, so you'll have to take a taxi, but the rate will be much less than for the trip from the airport. (Only federally chartered taxis may take fares *from* the airport, but any taxi may bring passengers *to* the airport.) Ask at your hotel what the fare should be, but expect to pay about half what you paid from the airport to your hotel.

BY CAR From Mérida or Campeche, take Highway 180 east to Cancún. This is mostly a winding, two-lane road that branches off into the express toll road 180D

Downtown Cancún

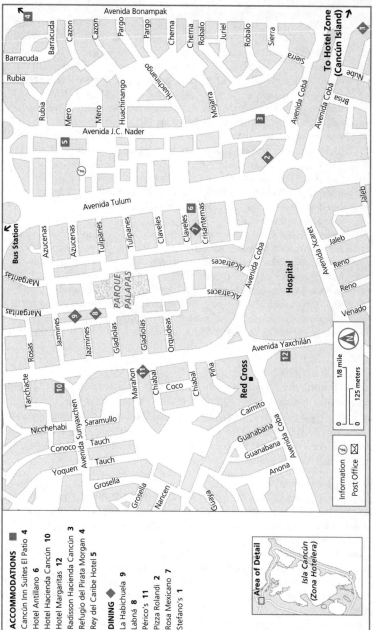

Avenida Bonampak

Barracuda
Barracuda
Cazon
Cazon
Pargo
Pargo
Cherna
Cherna
Robalo
Juriel
Robalo
Sierra
Sierra

Rubia
Rubia
Mero
Mero
Huachinango
Huachinango
Mojarra

To Hotel Zone (Cancún Island)
Nube
Brisa
Avenida Cobá
Avenida Cobá

Avenida J.C. Nader

Avenida Tulum

Bus Station

Azucenas
Azucenas
Tulipanes
Tulipanes
Claveles
Claveles
Crisántemas

Avenida Cobá
Avenida Xcaret
Jaleb
Jaleb
Reno
Reno
Venado

Margaritas
Margaritas

PARQUE PALAPAS

Alcatraces
Alcatraces

Hospital

Rosas
Jazmines
Jazmines
Gladiolas
Gladiolas
Orquideas

Tanchacte
Marañon
Chiabal
Coco
Chiabal
Piña

Avenida Yaxchilán

Red Cross

Nicchehabi
Saramullo
Conoco
Tauch
Tauch
Yoquen

Avenida Sunyaxchen

Caimito
Guanabana
Guanabana
Anona
Avenida Cobá

Grosella
Grosella
Nancen
Guaya

Information
Post Office

0   1/8 mile
0   125 meters

Area of Detail
Isla Cancún (Zona Hotelera)

ACCOMMODATIONS ■
Cancún Inn Suites El Patio **4**
Hotel Antillano **6**
Hotel Hacienda Cancún **10**
Hotel Margaritas **12**
Radisson Hacienda Cancún **3**
Refugio del Pirata Morgan **4**
Rey del Caribe Hotel **5**

DINING ◆
La Habichuela **9**
Labná **8**
Périco's **11**
Pizza Rolandi **2**
Rosa Mexicano **7**
Stefano's **1**

> ## *Tips* The Best Websites for Cancún
>
> - **All About Cancún: www.cancunmx.com** This site is a good place to start planning. There's a database of answers to the most common questions, called "The Online Experts." It's slow, but it has input from lots of recent travelers to the region.
> - **Cancún Convention & Visitors Bureau: www.cancun.info** The official site of the Cancún Convention & Visitors Bureau lists excellent information on events and attractions. Its hotel guide is one of the most complete available, and it has an active message board of recent visitors to Cancún.
> - **Cancún Online: www.cancun.com** This comprehensive guide has lots of information about things to do and see in Cancún, with most details provided by paying advertisers. You can even reserve a tee time or conduct wedding planning online.
> - **Cancún Travel Guide: www.go2cancun.com** This group specializing in online information about Mexico has put together an excellent resource for Cancún rentals, hotels, and attractions. Note that it lists only paying advertisers, but you'll find most of the major players.
> - **Mexico Web Cancún Chat: www.mexicoweb.com/chats/Cancún** This is one of the more active chats online specifically about Cancún. The users share inside information on everything from the cheapest beer to the quality of food at various all-inclusive resorts.

between Izamal and Nuevo Xcan. Nuevo Xcan is approximately 42km (26 miles) from Cancún. Mérida is about 83km (52 miles) away, a 3½-hour drive.

BY BUS Cancún's **ADO bus terminal** (© 998/884-4352 or 998/884-4804) is in downtown Ciudad Cancún at the intersection of avenidas Tulum and Uxmal. All out-of-town buses arrive here. Buses run to Playa del Carmen, Tulum, Chichén Itzá, other nearby beach and archaeological zones, and other points within Mexico.

VISITOR INFORMATION
The **State Tourism Office,** Av. Tulum 26 (© **998/881-9000** or 998/884-8073), is centrally located downtown next to Banco Bancomer, immediately left of the Ayuntamiento Benito Juárez building, between avenidas Cobá and Uxmal. It's open Monday to Friday from 9am to 5pm. The Convention & Visitors Bureau tourist information office, Avenida Cobá at Avenida Tulum (© **998/884-6531** or 998/884-3438), next to Pizza Rolandi, is open Monday through Friday from 9am to 7pm. Each office lists hotels and their rates, and ferry schedules. For information prior to your arrival in Cancún, visit the Convention Bureau's website, **www.cancun.info**.

Pick up copies of the free monthly *Cancún Tips* booklet and a seasonal tabloid of the same name. The publications are owned by the same people who own the Captain's Cove restaurants, a couple of sightseeing boats, and time-share hotels, so the information, though good, is not completely unbiased.

CITY LAYOUT

There are really two Cancúns: **Isla Cancún (Cancún Island)** and **Ciudad Cancún (Cancún City)**. The latter, on the mainland, has restaurants, shops, and less-expensive hotels, as well as pharmacies, dentists, automotive shops, banks, travel and airline agencies, and car-rental firms—all within an area about 9 blocks square. The city's main thoroughfare is **Avenida Tulum**. Heading south, Avenida Tulum becomes the highway to the airport and to Tulum and Chetumal; heading north, it intersects the highway to Mérida and the road to Puerto Juárez and the Isla Mujeres ferries.

The famed **Zona Hotelera,** or Hotel Zone (also called the Zona Turística, or Tourist Zone), stretches out along Isla Cancún, which is a sandy strip 22km (14 miles) long, shaped like a "7." It connects to the mainland by the Playa Linda Bridge at the north end and the Punta Nizuc Bridge at the southern end. Between the two areas lies Laguna Nichupté. Avenida Cobá from Cancún City becomes Bulevar Kukulkán, the island's main traffic artery. Cancún's international airport is just inland from the south end of the island.

FINDING AN ADDRESS   Cancún's street-numbering system is a holdover from its early days. Addresses are still given by the number of the building lot and by the *manzana* (block) or *supermanzana* (group of blocks). The city is relatively compact, and the downtown commercial section is easy to cover on foot.

On the island, addresses are given by kilometer number on Bulevar Kukulkán or by reference to some well-known location. In Cancún, streets are named after famous Maya cities. Chichén Itzá, Tulum, and Uxmal are the names of the boulevards in Cancún, as well as nearby archaeological sites.

GETTING AROUND

BY TAXI   Taxi prices in Cancún are clearly set by zone, although keeping track of what's in which zone can take some doing. The minimum fare within the Hotel Zone is $5 per ride, making it one of the most expensive taxi areas in Mexico. In addition, taxis operating in the Hotel Zone feel perfectly justified in having a discriminatory pricing structure: Local residents pay about half of what tourists pay, and prices for guests at higher-priced hotels are about double those for budget hotel guests—these are all established by the taxi union. Rates should be posted outside your hotel; if you have a question, all drivers are required to have an official rate card in their taxis, though it's generally in Spanish.

Within the downtown area, the cost is about $1.50 per cab ride (not per person); within any other zone, it's $5. Traveling between two zones will also cost $5, and if you cross two zones, that'll cost $7.50. Settle on a price in advance, or check at your hotel. Trips to the airport from most zones cost $14. Taxis can also be rented for $18 per hour for travel around the city and Hotel Zone, but this rate can generally be negotiated down to $12 or less. If you want to hire a taxi to take you to Chichén Itzá or along the Riviera Maya, expect to pay about $30 per hour—many taxi drivers feel that they are also providing guide services.

BY BUS   Bus travel within Cancún continues to improve and is increasingly popular. In town, almost everything is within walking distance. Ruta 1 and Ruta 2 (HOTELES) city buses travel frequently from the mainland to the beaches along Avenida Tulum (the main street) and all the way to Punta Nizuc at the far end of the Hotel Zone on Isla Cancún. Ruta 8 buses go to Puerto Juárez/Punta Sam for ferries to Isla Mujeres. They stop on the east side of Avenida Tulum. All these city buses operate between 6am and 10pm daily. Beware of private buses along the same route; they charge far more than the public ones. Public buses have the fare painted on the front; at press time, the fare was 60¢.

BY MOPED Mopeds are a convenient but dangerous way to cruise around through the very congested traffic. Rentals start at $25 for a day, and a credit card voucher is required as security. You should receive a crash helmet (it's the law) and instructions on how to lock the wheels when you park. Read the fine print on the back of the rental agreement regarding liability for repairs or replacement in case of accident, theft, or vandalism.

FAST FACTS: Cancún

American Express The local office is at Av. Tulum 208 and Agua (© **998/881-4000** or 998/881-4055; www.americanexpress.com/mexico), 1 block past the Plaza México. It's open Monday through Friday from 9am to 6pm, Saturday from 9am to 1pm. Another branch of American Express is located in the hotel zone, in the La Isla Shopping Center (© **998/885-3905**).

Area Code The telephone area code is **998**.

Climate It's hot but not overwhelmingly humid. The rainy season is May through October. August through October is hurricane season, which brings erratic weather. November through February is generally sunny but can also be cloudy, windy, somewhat rainy, and even cool.

Consulates The **U.S. Consular Agent** is in the Plaza Caracol 2, Bulevar Kukulkán Km 8.5, third level, 320–323 (© **998/883-0272**). The office is open Monday through Friday from 9am to 1pm. The **Canadian Consulate** is in the Plaza México 312 (© **998/883-3360**). The office is open Monday through Friday from 9am to 5pm. The **United Kingdom** has a consular office in Cancún (© **998/881-0100**, ext. 65898; fax 998/848-8662; information@britishconsulatecancun.com). Irish, Australian, and New Zealand citizens should contact their embassies in Mexico City.

Crime Car break-ins are just about the only crime here. They happen frequently, especially around the shopping centers in the Hotel Zone. VW Beetles and Golfs are frequent targets.

Currency Exchange Most banks are downtown along Avenida Tulum and are usually open Monday through Friday from 9:30am to 5pm. Many have automated teller machines for after-hours cash withdrawals. In the Hotel Zone, you'll find banks in the Kukulcan Plaza and next to the convention center. There are also many *casas de cambio* (exchange houses). Downtown merchants are eager to change cash dollars, but island stores don't offer very good exchange rates. Avoid changing money at the airport as you arrive, especially at the first exchange booth you see—its rates are less favorable than those of any in town or others farther inside the airport concourse.

Drugstores With locations in both Flamingo Plaza (© **998/885-1351**) and Kukulkan Plaza (© **998/885-0860**), **Farmacia Roxanna** offers delivery service within the Hotel Zone. Plenty of drugstores are in the major shopping malls in the Hotel Zone, and are open until 10pm. In downtown Cancún, **Farmacia Cancún** is located at Av. Tulum (© **998/884-1283**). You can stock up on Retin-A, Viagra, and many other prescription drugs without a prescription.

Emergencies To report an emergency, dial © **060,** which is supposed to be similar to 911 emergency service in the United States. For first aid, the **Cruz Roja,** or Red Cross (© **065** or **998/884-1616;** fax 998/883-9218), is open 24 hours on Avenida Yaxchilán between avenidas Xcaret and Labná, next to the Telmex building. **Total Assist,** Claveles 5, SM 22, at Avenida Tulum (© **998/884-1058** or 998/884-1092; totalassist@prodigy.net.mx), is a small (nine-room) emergency hospital with English-speaking doctors. It's open 24 hours and accepts American Express, MasterCard, and Visa. Desk staff may have limited command of English. Another facility that caters to English-speaking visitors is **Ameri-Med,** Plaza Las Américas, in downtown Cancún (© **998/881-3434**) with 24-hour emergency service. Air Ambulance service is available by calling © **01-800/305-9400** in Mexico.

Internet Access **C@ncunet,** in a kiosk on the second floor of Kukulcan Plaza, Bulevar Kukulkán Km 13 (© **998/885-0880**), offers Internet access at $2 for 10 minutes, or $7 per hour. It's open daily from 10am to 10pm.

Luggage Storage & Lockers Hotels will generally tag and store luggage while you travel elsewhere.

Newspapers & Magazines Most hotel gift shops and newsstands carry English-language magazines and English-language Mexican newspapers.

Police Cancún has a fleet of English-speaking tourist police to help travelers. Dial © **998/884-1913** or 998/884-2342. The **Procuraduría Federal del Consumidor (consumer protection agency),** Av. Cobá 9–11 (© **998/884-2634** or 998/884-2701), is opposite the Social Security Hospital and upstairs from the Fenix drugstore. It's open Monday through Saturday from 9am to 3pm.

Post Office The main *correo* is at the intersection of avenidas Sunyaxchen and Xel-Ha (© **998/884-1418**). It's open Monday through Friday from 9am to 4pm, and Saturday from 9am to noon just for the purchase of stamps.

Safety Aside from car break-ins, there is very little crime in Cancún. People are generally safe late at night in tourist areas; just use ordinary common sense. As at any other beach resort, don't take money or valuables to the beach. See "Crime," above.

Swimming on the Caribbean side presents a danger because of the undertow. See the information on beaches in "Beaches, Watersports & Boat Tours," later in this chapter, for information about flag warnings.

Seasons Technically, high season is from December 15 to April; low season is from May to December 15, when prices drop 10% to 30%. Some hotels are starting to charge high-season rates during June and July, when Mexican, European, and school-holiday visitors often travel, although rates may still be lower than in winter months.

Special Events The annual **Mexico-Caribbean Food Festival,** featuring special menus of culinary creations throughout town, is held each year over the first 2 weeks of November. Additional information is available through the Convention and Visitors Bureau.

2 Where to Stay

Island hotels—almost all of them offering clean, modern facilities—line the beach like dominoes. Extravagance is the byword in the newer hotels. Some hotels, while exclusive, affect a more relaxed attitude. The water on the upper end of the island facing Bahía de Mujeres is placid, while beaches lining the long side of the island facing the Caribbean are subject to choppier water and crashing waves on windy days. (For more information on swimming safety, see "Beaches, Watersports & Boat Tours," later in this chapter.) Be aware that the farther south you go on the island, the longer it takes (20–30 min. in traffic) to get back to the "action spots," which are primarily between the Plaza Flamingo and Punta Cancún on the island and along Avenida Tulum on the mainland.

Almost all major hotel chains are represented on Cancún Island, so this list can be viewed as a representative summary, with a select number of notable places. The reality is that Cancún is so popular as a package destination from the U.S. that prices and special deals are often the deciding factor for those traveling here (see "Packages for the Independent Traveler," in chapter 2). Ciudad Cancún offers independently owned, smaller, less expensive lodging; prices are lower here off season (May to early Dec). For condo, home, and villa rentals, check with **Cancún Hideaways** (www.cancun-hideaways.com), a company specializing in luxury properties, downtown apartments, and condos—many at prices much lower than comparable hotel stays. Owner Maggie Rodriguez, a former resident of Cancún, has made this niche market her specialty.

The hotel listings in this chapter begin on Cancún Island and finish in Cancún City, where bargain lodgings are available. Parking is free at all island hotels.

CANCUN ISLAND
VERY EXPENSIVE

Aqua 🏵🏵🏵   Stunning, stylish, and sensual, Aqua is certain to emerge as Cancún's most coveted place to stay. A new member of the Fiesta Americana chain, the resort was on the brink of opening at press time, so I can't comment on service or the actual details of a stay, but I was so enthused at its opening, I couldn't wait to share the news. The entire hotel seems to mirror the predominant colors of Cancún—turquoise and white—in a sublimely chic manner. This hotel was built for sophisticated travelers who appreciate hip style and look for the cutting edge in places to stay. Aqua aims to stimulate your five senses, and upon arrival—under a crystal cube fountain—you're offered a fusion tea, and a blend of relaxing and stimulating aromatherapy. The oasis of eight oceanfront pools is surrounded by chaises, queen-size recliners, and private cabanas. All rooms and common areas emphasize the views to the pool and ocean beyond. Rooms are generous in size, and all face the ocean and have balconies. Very large bathrooms feature a large soaking tub and organic bath products. Guests can tailor their turndown service by selecting from a pillow menu and choice of aromatherapy oils and candles. Miniature Zen gardens or a fishbowl add unique touches to room decor. Suites offer extras like Boise surround-sound systems. Twenty-nine rooms are "Grand Club," which include continental breakfast and a club room with butler service, snacks, bar service, and private check-in. The 1,500-sq.-m (500-sq.-ft.) spa is among the hotel's most notable attractions, with 12 treatment rooms offering a blend of Eastern, pre-Hispanic, and Western treatments. Outdoor pilates, Tai Chi, and yoga classes are offered daily, and massage cabanas are also available on the beach. Another hallmark of this hotel is certain to be its collection of restaurants, chief among them

Isla Cancún (Zona Hotelera)

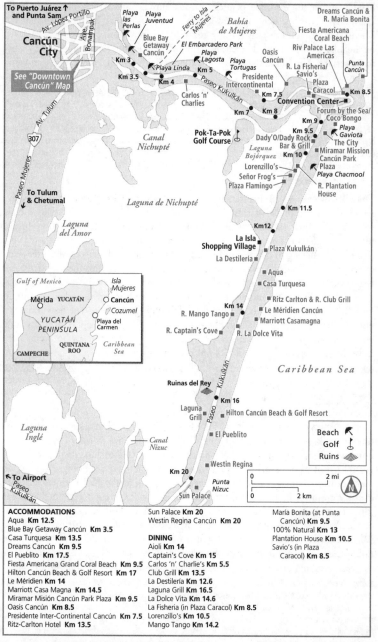

ACCOMMODATIONS
Aqua **Km 12.5**
Blue Bay Getaway Cancún **Km 3.5**
Casa Turquesa **Km 13.5**
Dreams Cancún **Km 9.5**
El Pueblito **Km 17.5**
Fiesta Americana Grand Coral Beach **Km 9.5**
Hilton Cancún Beach & Golf Resort **Km 17**
Le Méridien **Km 14**
Marriott Casa Magna **Km 14.5**
Miramar Misión Cancún Park Plaza **Km 9.5**
Oasis Cancún **Km 8.5**
Presidente Inter-Continental Cancún **Km 7.5**
Ritz-Carlton Hotel **Km 13.5**

Sun Palace **Km 20**
Westin Regina Cancún **Km 20**

DINING
Aioli **Km 14**
Captain's Cove **Km 15**
Carlos 'n' Charlie's **Km 5.5**
Club Grill **Km 13.5**
La Destilería **Km 12.6**
Laguna Grill **Km 16.5**
La Dolce Vita **Km 14.6**
La Fisheria (in Plaza Caracol) **Km 8.5**
Lorenzillo's **Km 10.5**
Mango Tango **Km 14.2**

María Bonita (at Punta
Cancún) **Km 9.5**
100% Natural **Km 13**
Plantation House **Km 10.5**
Savio's (in Plaza
Caracol) **Km 8.5**

SIETE, under the direction of premier Mexican chef and cookbook author Patricia Quintana, featuring her sophisticated take on traditional Mexican cuisine. Chef Michelle Bernstein, formerly a rising culinary star in Miami, presides over **MB,** serving healthy comfort food. There's also an Italian restaurant, deli, lounge, and 24-hour room service. After dark, the hotel shifts moods, with fire pits, torch lights, and ambient music.

Bulevar Kukulkán Km 12.5, 77500 Cancún, Q. Roo. Ⓒ **800/343-7821** or 800-FIESTA-1 in the U.S., or 998/881-7600. Fax 998/881-7601. www.fiestaamericana.com. 371 units. High season $393–$466 double, $516 Grand Club double, $750 suite; low season $215–$313 double, $363 Grand Club double, $600 suite. Ask about Fiesta Break packages. AE, DC, MC, V. Small pets allowed with prior reservation. **Amenities:** 4 restaurants; poolside snack bar; lounge and bar; 8 swimming pools; tennis court; fitness center and spa with 12 treatment rooms; watersports on the beach; concierge; travel agency; business center; salon; room service; babysitting; laundry service; Club floors with special amenities and complimentary cocktails. *In room:* A/C, flatscreen TV and DVD, minibar, hair dryer, iron, safe, high-speed Internet access, CD player.

Casa Turquesa ✶ Romantic, tranquil, and elegant, Casa Turquesa is an oasis of relaxation in the midst of this playful island. If the Mediterranean-style ambience weren't appealing enough, their exceptional stretch of beach (fronting brilliant turquoise waters) is sure to inspire a positive attitude adjustment. This is a true boutique hotel catering to couples and noted for its exceptional service. All suites feature queen- or king-size beds, plus balconies with Jacuzzis. Bathrooms themselves are extra large, with double sinks and a separate tub and shower. Blue-and-white canopy shade tents dot the area surrounding the attractive pool and beach; the adjacent Turquesa Pool Bar is open from 10am to 5pm daily. For dining, the Belle-Vue restaurant, serving international gourmet fare, is open 24 hours, and the formal Celebrity restaurant serves seafood and angus beef from 6pm to midnight. For those who prefer not to leave the comfort of their room, 24-hour room service is also available.

Bulevar Kukulkán, Km 13.5, 77500 Cancún, Q. Roo. Ⓒ **888/528-8300** in the U.S., or 998/885-2925. Fax 998/885-2922. www.casaturquesa.com. 33 suites. High season $204–$231; low season $136–$145. AE, DC, MC, V. **Amenities:** 2 restaurants; 2 bars; pool; concierge; travel agency; 24-hr. room service. *In room:* A/C, TV, minibar, hair dryer, iron, safe, CD player, bathrobes.

Fiesta Americana Grand Coral Beach ✶ This is an ideal choice for any type of traveler looking to be at the heart of all that Cancún has to offer. The spectacular hotel, which opened in 1991, has one of the best locations in Cancún, with 300m (1,000 ft.) of prime beachfront and proximity to the main shopping and entertainment centers. The key word here is *big*—everything at the Fiesta Americana seems oversize, from the lobby to the suites. Service is gracious, if cool: The hotel aims for a sophisticated ambience. It's embellished with elegant dark-green granite and an abundance of marble. The large guest rooms are also decorated with marble, and all have balconies facing the ocean, most of which were remodeled in 2004. The hotel's great Punta Cancún location (opposite the convention center) has the advantage of facing the beach to the north, meaning that the surf is calm and perfect for swimming.

Bulevar Kukulkán Km 9.5, 77500 Cancún, Q. Roo. Ⓒ **800/343-7821** in the U.S., or 998/881-3200. Fax 998/881-3273. www.fiestaamericana.com. 602 units. High season $328–$555 double, $529–$650 Club Floor double, $875 Caribbean suite; low season $222–$424 double, $381–$504 Club Floor double, $695 Caribbean suite. AE, MC, V. **Amenities:** 3 restaurants including the gourmet *Basilique;* poolside snack bar; 5 bars; swimming pool w/swim-up bars; 3 indoor tennis courts w/stadium seating; fitness center w/weights, sauna, and massage; watersports rentals on the beach; concierge; travel agency; car rental; business center; salon; room service; babysitting; laundry service; 2 concierge floors w/complimentary cocktails; 2 junior suites for travelers w/disabilities are available. *In room:* A/C, TV, minibar, hair dryer, iron, safe.

Hilton Cancún Beach & Golf Resort ⋆ *Kids*   Grand, expansive, and fully equipped, this is a true resort in every sense of the word and is especially perfect for anyone whose motto is "the bigger the better." The Hilton Cancún, sits on 100 hectares (250 acres) of prime beachside property, a location that gives every room a sea view (some have both sea and lagoon views), with an 18-hole par-72 golf course across the street. Like the sprawling resort, rooms are grandly spacious and immaculately decorated in minimalist style, all of which were renovated in 2004. Area rugs and pale furnishings soften marble floors and bathrooms throughout. It's a very "kid-friendly" hotel, with one of the island's best children's activity programs, special children's pool, and babysitting available. The hotel is especially appealing to golfers because it's one of only two in Cancún with an on-site course (the other is the Meliá). Greens fees for guests are $77 for 9 holes, $99 for 18 holes, and include the use of a cart. Just opened is the new Wellness Spa, highlights of which are oceanfront massage cabanas, yoga, and aromatherapy.

Bulevar Kukulkán Km 17, Retorno Lacandones, 77500 Cancún, Q. Roo. ℂ 800/228-3000 in the U.S., or 998/881-8000. Fax 998/881-8080. www.hiltoncancun.com.mx. 426 units. High season $269–$415 double, $440–$585 Beach Club double, $555–$779 suite; low season $119–$300 double, $350–$550 Beach Club double, $395–$500 suite. AE, DC, MC, V. **Amenities:** 2 restaurants; 7 interconnected pools w/swim-up bar; golf course across the street; 2 lighted tennis courts; Wellness Spa w/spa services and fully equipped gym; 2 whirlpools; watersports center; Kids Club; concierge; tour desk; car rental; salon; room service; babysitting; laundry service; golf clinic. *In room:* A/C, TV, minibar, coffeemaker, hair dryer, iron, safe, bathrobes, house shoes.

Le Méridien Cancún Resort & Spa ⋆⋆⋆   Of all the luxury properties in Cancún, Le Méridien is the most inviting, with a refined yet welcoming sense of personal service. From the intimate lobby and reception area to the best concierge service in Cancún, guests feel immediately pampered. The relatively small establishment is more elegant boutique hotel than immense resort—a welcome relief. The decor throughout the rooms and common areas is classy and comforting, not overdone. Rooms are generous in size, and most have small balconies overlooking the pool, with a view to the ocean. Each has a very large marble bathroom with a separate tub and glassed-in shower. The hotel attracts many Europeans as well as younger, sophisticated travelers, and is ideal for a second honeymoon or romantic break.

A highlight of—or even a reason for—staying here is the **Spa del Mar,** one of Mexico's most complete European spa facilities, with more than 4,570 sq. m (15,000 sq. ft.) of services dedicated to your body and soul. A complete fitness center with extensive cardio and weight machines is on the upper level. The spa consists of a health

---

⊝ *Tips* Important Note on Hotel Prices

Cancún's hotels, in all price categories, generally set their rates in dollars, so they are immune to swings in the peso. Travel agents and wholesalers always have air/hotel packages available, and Sunday papers often advertise inventory-clearing packages at prices much lower than the rates listed here. Cancún also has numerous all-inclusive properties, which allow you to take a fixed-cost vacation. Note that the price quoted when you call a hotel's reservation number from the United States may not include Cancún's 12% tax. Prices can vary considerably throughout the year, so it pays to consult a travel agent or shop around.

snack bar, a full-service salon, and 14 treatment rooms, as well as men's and women's steam rooms, saunas, whirlpools, cold plunge pool, inhalation rooms, tranquillity rooms, lockers, and changing areas.

Retorno del Rey Km 14, Zona Hotelera, 77500, Cancún, Q. Roo. ℂ 800/543-4300 in the U.S., or 998/881-2200. Fax 998/881-2201. www.lemeridien.com. 213 units. High season $290 double, $450 suite; low season $220 double, $350 suite. Ask about special spa packages. Additional $10 per day resort fee enables access to Spa de Mar, kids' club, and other extra services. AE, DC, MC, V. Small pets accepted with prior reservation. **Amenities:** 2 restaurants (including Aioli; see "Where to Dine," later in this chapter); lobby bar; 3 cascading swimming pools; 2 lighted championship tennis courts; whirlpool; watersports equipment and massage *palapa* on the beach; supervised children's program w/clubhouse, play equipment, wading pool; concierge; tour desk; car rental; business center w/Internet access; small shopping arcade; 24-hr. room service; babysitting; laundry service. *In room:* A/C, TV, dataport, minibar, hair dryer, iron, safe.

Ritz-Carlton Hotel 🏆🏆🏆   For those who want to feel indulged, this is the place to stay. On 3 hectares (7½ acres), the nine-story Ritz-Carlton sets the standard for elegance in Cancún. The hotel fronts a 370m (1,200-ft.) white-sand beach, and all rooms overlook the ocean, pool, and tropical gardens. The style—in both public areas and guest rooms—is sumptuous and formal, with thick carpets, elaborate chandeliers, and fresh flowers throughout. In all rooms, marble bathrooms have telephones, separate tubs and showers, and lighted makeup mirrors. The recently opened Kayantá Spa offers an excellent selection of Mayan and Mexican-inspired treatments and massages. The hotel has won countless accolades for service.

Retorno del Rey 36, off Bulevar Kukulkán Km 13.5, 77500 Cancún, Q. Roo. ℂ 800/241-3333 in the U.S. and Canada, or 998/881-0808. Fax 998/881-0815. www.ritzcarlton.com. 365 units. High season $369–$475 double, $389–$850 Club floor and suites; low season $189–$279 double, $295–$429 Club floor and suites. Ask about golf, spa, and weekend packages. AE, MC, V. **Amenities:** 5 restaurants (including the Club Grill, one of the best restaurants in the city; see "Where to Dine," later in this chapter); Lobby Lounge (see "Cancún After Dark," later in this chapter); 2 connecting swimming pools (heated in winter); 3 lighted tennis courts; fully equipped fitness center and Kayantá Spa; Ritz Kids program w/supervised activities; concierge; travel agency; business center; shopping arcade; salon; 24-hr. room service; babysitting; laundry service; dry cleaning; Club floors; deluxe beach cabañas for 2. *In room:* A/C, TV, dataport, minibar, hair dryer, iron, safe, bathrobes.

Riu Palace Las Américas 🏆🏆   The all-inclusive Riu Palace is part of a family of Riu resorts in Cancún known for their grand, opulent style. This one is the smallest of the three in Cancún, and the most elegant, steeped in pearl-white Greco style, and my choice for a high-end all-inclusive vacation in Cancún. The location is prime—near the central shopping, dining, and nightlife centers, just 5 minutes walking to the Convention Center. All rooms are spacious junior suites with ocean or lagoon views, a separate seating area, and a balcony or terrace. Eight also feature a Jacuzzi. Two central pools overlook the ocean and a wide stretch of beach, with one heated during winter months. The hotel offers guests virtually 24 hours of all-inclusive snacks, meals, and beverages. And, if that's not enough, guests have exchange privileges at the Riu Cancún, next door.

Bulevar Kukulkán, Lote 4, 77500 Cancún, Q. Roo. ℂ 888/666-8816 in the U.S., or 998/891-4300. www.riu.com. 368 units. High season $413–$627 double; low season $287–$464 double. Rates are all-inclusive. AE, MC, V. **Amenities:** 6 restaurants; 5 bars; 2 pools; tennis; fitness center; spa (extra charges apply); room service; solarium; sports program; windsurfing. *In room:* A/C, TV, hair dryer, iron, safe, bathrobes.

Sun Palace 🏆   If you're looking for an all-inclusive resort on a great stretch of Caribbean beach, this member of the popular Palace Resorts chain is a prime pick—and the most elegant of the Palace properties in Cancún. The fantastic beach is one of the widest on the island. Located toward the southern end of the island, next to the Westin Regina, this all-suite resort is farther away from the action of the hotel zone—

which may be what you want, considering all of the goodies that go with staying here. One of the best perks is that the activities program includes excursions to Tulum, Chichén Itzá, or Isla Mujeres. Suites feature modern Mexican decor, and all have marble floors and a combination bath with whirlpool tub. All units have oceanview balconies or terraces. In addition to the beachside pool, there's an indoor pool, plus a large Jacuzzi with a waterfall. A nicely equipped health club and tennis court complement the ample activities program. When you stay at a Palace resort, you have the option of playing at any of the other members of the chain—there are two in Cancún and three others farther south along the Riviera Maya.

Bulevar Kukulkán Km 20, 77500 Cancún, Q. Roo. ℭ **800/346-8225** in the U.S., or 998/85-0533. Fax 998/885-1593. www.palaceresorts.com. 237 suites. High season $310–$398 suite; low season $270–$350 suite. Rates are all-inclusive. AE, DC, MC, V. **Amenities:** 3 restaurants; 2 pools (1 indoor); tennis court; health club; Jacuzzi; 24-hr. room service. *In room:* A/C, TV, hair dryer, iron, safe, bathrobes.

EXPENSIVE

Dreams Cancún Resort & Spa 🜛🜛 *Kids* Formerly the Camino Real Cancún, the all-inclusive Dreams Resort is among the island's most appealing places to stay, located on 1.5 hectares (4 acres) at the tip of Punta Cancún. The setting is sophisticated, but the hotel is very welcoming to children. The architecture of the hotel is contemporary and sleek, with bright colors and strategic angles. Rooms in the newer 18-story Club section have extra services and amenities; rates here include full breakfast. The lower-priced rooms have lagoon views. Dreams all-inclusive concept is more oriented to quality experiences than unlimited buffets—your room price here includes gourmet meals, 24-hour room service, premium brand drinks, as well as the use of all resort amenities, watersports, evening entertainment, airport transfers, and tips. The fitness center and spa are the focal points of the resort's amenities.

Bulevar Kukulkán, 77500 Punta Cancún (Apdo. Postal 14), Cancún, Q. Roo. ℭ **866/237-3267** in the U.S., or 998/848-7000. Fax 998/848-7001. www.dreamscancun.com. 381 units. High season $275 double, $320 Club double; low season $195 double, $230 Club double. AE, DC, MC, V. **Amenities:** 3 restaurants; nightclub; pool; private saltwater lagoon w/sea turtles and tropical fish; 3 lighted tennis courts; fitness center w/steam bath; watersports center; travel agency; car rental; 24-hour business center with Internet access; salon; 24-hr. room service; massage; babysitting (w/advance notice); sailing pier; Jet Skis; beach volleyball. *In room:* A/C, TV, minibar, hair dryer, iron, safe.

Marriott Casa Magna 🜛🜛 *Kids* This is quintessential Marriott—those who are familiar with the chain's standards will feel at home here and appreciate the hotel's attention to detailed service. Entering through a half-circle of Roman columns, you pass through a domed foyer to a wide, lavishly marbled 14m-high (44-ft.) lobby filled with plants and shallow pools. Guest rooms hold contemporary furnishings, tiled floors, and ceiling fans; most have balconies. The hotel caters to family travelers with specially priced packages (up to two children stay free with parent) and the Club Amigos supervised children's program. In 2001 Marriott opened the 450-room luxury **JW Marriott Cancún,** Bulevar Kukulkán Km 14.5, 77500 Cancún, Q. Roo (ℭ **998/848-9600;** www. marriott.com), on the beach next to the Casa Magna.

Bulevar Kukulkán Km 14.5, 77500 Cancún, Q. Roo ℭ **800/228-9290** in the U.S., or 998/881-2000. Fax 998/881-2085. www.marriott.com. 452 units. High season $225–$254 double; $350 suite; low season $139–$160 double, $300 suite. Ask about packages. AE, MC, V. **Amenities:** 5 restaurants; lobby bar w/live music; swimming pool; 2 lighted tennis courts; health club w/saunas, whirlpool, aerobics, and juice bar; concierge; travel agency; car rental; salon w/massage and facials; room service; babysitting; laundry service. *In room:* A/C, TV, dataport, minibar, coffeemaker, hair dryer, iron, safe.

Presidente Inter-Continental Cancún 🜛 On the island's best beach, facing the placid Bahía de Mujeres, the Presidente's location is reason enough to stay here, and it's just a 2-minute walk to Cancún's public Pok-Ta-Pok Golf Club (Club de Golf Cancún). For its ambience, I consider it an ideal choice for a romantic getaway or for couples who enjoy indulging in the sports of golf, tennis, or even shopping. Cool and spacious, the Presidente sports a postmodern design with lavish marble and wicker accents and a strong use of color. Guests have a choice of two double beds or one king. All rooms have tastefully simple unfinished pine furniture. Sixteen units on the first floor have patios with outdoor whirlpool tubs. The expansive pool has a pyramid-shaped waterfall. Coming from Cancún City, you'll reach the Presidente on the left side of the street before you get to Punta Cancún.

Bulevar Kukulkán Km 7.5, 77500 Cancún, Q. Roo. ⓒ 800/327-0200 in the U.S., or 998/848-8700. Fax 998/883-2602. www.interconti.com. 299 units. High season $240–$300 double; low season $150–$230 double. Rates include unlimited golf at Pok-Ta-Pok. AE, MC, V. Ask about special packages. **Amenities:** 3 restaurants; 2 swimming pools; lighted tennis courts; fitness center; whirlpool; watersports equipment rental; travel agency; car rental; shopping arcade; 24-hr. room service; babysitting; laundry service; nonsmoking floors; Club floors; 2 rooms for travelers w/disabilities are available; marina. *In room:* A/C, TV, dataport, minibar, hair dryer, safe.

Westin Regina Cancún 🌟🌟 The strikingly austere architecture of the Westin Regina, impressive with its elegant use of stone and marble, is the stamp of leading Latin American architect Ricardo Legorreta. The hotel consists of two sections, the main building and the more exclusive six-story hot-pink tower. Standard rooms are unusually large and beautifully furnished with cool, contemporary furniture. Those on the sixth floor have balconies, and first-floor rooms have terraces. Rooms in the tower all have ocean or lagoon views, furniture with Olinalá lacquer accents, Berber area rugs, oak tables and chairs, and terraces with lounge chairs. It's important to note that this hotel is a 15- to 20-minute ride from the lively strip that lies between the Plaza Flamingo and Punta Cancún, so it's a good choice for those who want a little more seclusion than Cancún typically offers. However, it is easy to join the action—buses stop in front, and taxis are readily available.

Bulevar Kukulkán Km 20, 77500 Cancún, Q. Roo. ⓒ 800/228-3000 in the U.S., 01-800/215-7000 in Mexico, or 998/848-7400. Fax 998/885-0666. www.westin.com. 293 units. High season $285–$450 double; low season $160–$299 double. AE, DC, MC, V. **Amenities:** 2 restaurants; 2 bars; 5 swimming pools; 2 lighted tennis courts; gym w/Stairmaster, bicycle, weights, aerobics, sauna, steam, massage; *temazcal* (sweat lodge); 3 whirlpools; concierge; travel agency; car rental; salon; room service; babysitting; laundry service; pharmacy/gift shop. *In room:* A/C, TV, dataport, minibar, coffeemaker, hair dryer, iron, safe.

MODERATE

Blue Bay Getaway Cancún 🌟 The adults-only Blue Bay Getaway Cancún is a spirited yet relaxing all-inclusive resort favored by young adults. Surrounded by acres of tropical gardens, it's ideally located at the northern end of the Hotel Zone, close to the major shopping plazas, restaurants, and nightlife. It has a terrific beach with calm waters for swimming. The comfortable, modern rooms are in two sections. The central building features 72 rooms decorated in rustic wood, the main lobby, administrative offices, restaurants, and Las Margaritas bar. The remaining nine buildings feature colorful Mexican decor; rooms have lagoon, garden, and ocean views. Safes are available for an extra charge. During the evenings, guests may enjoy a variety of theme-night dinners, nightly shows, and live entertainment in an outdoor theater. Note that clothing is optional on the beaches of this Blue Bay resort.

Bulevar Kukulkán Km 3.5, 77500 Cancún, Q. Roo. ⓒ 800/211-1000 in the U.S., or 998/848-7900. Fax 998/848-7994. www.bluebayresorts.com. 385 units. High season $280 double; low season $180 double. Rates include food, beverages, and activities. AE, MC, V. **Amenities:** 4 restaurants; 4 bars; 3 swimming pools; tennis court; exercise room w/daily aerobics classes; 4 whirlpools; watersports equipment; bicycles; game room w/pool and Ping-Pong tables; rooms for those w/limited mobility; snorkeling and scuba lessons; marina. *In room:* A/C, TV, dataport, hair dryer.

El Pueblito 🌟 *Kids*   This hotel offers perhaps the top all-inclusive value in Cancún. Dwarfed by its ostentatious neighbors, the El Pueblito lobby resembles a traditional Mexican hacienda, with several three-story buildings (no elevators) terraced in a V-shape down a gentle hillside toward the sea. A meandering swimming pool with waterfalls runs between the two series of buildings. Rooms are very large, with modern rattan furnishings, travertine marble floors, and large bathrooms. Each has either a balcony or a terrace. In addition to a constant flow of buffet-style meals and snacks, there's also the choice of a nightly theme party, complete with entertainment. Minigolf and a water slide, plus a full program of kids' activities, make this an ideal place for families with children. The hotel is located toward the southern end of the island past the Hilton Resort.

Bulevar Kukulkán Km 17.5, 77500 Cancún, Q. Roo. ✆ **998/885-0422** or 998/881-8814. Fax 998/885-0731. www.pueblitohotels.com. 349 units. High season $300 double; low season $240 double. Rates are all-inclusive. Ask about specials. AE, MC, V. **Amenities:** 3 restaurants; 2 bars; lobby cafe; large pool; tennis courts; nonmotorized watersports; babysitting ($10 per hr.); aerobics; volleyball; cooking classes. *In room:* A/C, TV.

Miramar Misión Cancún Park Plaza   Each of the ingeniously designed rooms here has a partial view of both the lagoon and the ocean. Public spaces throughout the hotel have lots of dark wood accents, but the most notable feature is the large, rectangular swimming pool that extends through the hotel and down to the beach, with built-in, submerged sun chairs. There's also an oversize whirlpool (the largest in Cancún), a sun deck, and a snack bar on the seventh-floor roof. Rooms are on the small side but are bright and comfortable, with small balconies and bamboo furniture; bathrooms have polished limestone vanities. A popular nightclub, **Batacha,** has live music for dancing from 9pm to 4am Tuesday through Sunday.

Bulevar Kukulkán Km 9.5, 77500 Zona Hotelera Cancún, Q. Roo. ✆ **800/215-1333** in the U.S., or 998/883-1755. Fax 998/883-1136. www.hotelesmision.com. 266 units. High season $220 double; low season $160 double. AE, MC, V. **Amenities:** 3 restaurants; 2 bars; rooftop snack bar; pool; whirlpool. *In room:* A/C, TV, minibar, hair dryer, safe.

Oasis Cancún   From the street, this hotel may not be much to look at, but on the ocean side you'll find a small but pretty patio garden and Cancún's best beach for safe swimming. The location is ideal, close to all the shops and restaurants near Punta Cancún and the Convention Center. Rooms overlook the lagoon or the ocean, and all were remodeled in 2004. They are large, with pleasing, comfortable decor, marble floors, and either two double beds or a king-size bed. Several studios have kitchenettes.

Bulevar Kukulkán Km 8.5, 77500 Cancún, Q. Roo. ✆ **800/221-2222** in the U.S., or 998/883-0800. Fax 998/883-2087 units. High season $145–$250 double; low season $138–$158 double. Rates include buffet breakfast. Children under 12 stay free in parent's room. AE, MC, V. **Amenities:** Restaurant; 2 snack bars; 3 bars; 2 swimming pools (1 for adults, 1 for children); 2 lighted tennis courts; watersports equipment rental; nonsmoking areas; wheelchair access; marina. *In room:* A/C, TV.

CANCUN CITY
MODERATE
Radisson Hacienda Cancún 🌟🌟 *Value*   This is the nicest hotel in downtown Cancún, and one of the best values in the area. The Radisson offers all the expected comforts of a chain, yet in an atmosphere of Mexican hospitality. Resembling a hacienda, rooms are set off from a large rotunda-style lobby, lush gardens, and a pleasant pool area. All have brightly colored fabric accents; views of the garden, the pool, or the

street; and a small sitting area and balcony. Bathrooms have a combination tub and shower. Guests have access to a shuttle service to Isla Cancún's beaches, or to the Pok-Ta-Pok Golf course. The hotel is behind the state government building, within walking distance of downtown Cancún dining and shopping.

Av. Náder 1, SM2, Centro, 77500 Cancún, Q. Roo. ✆ **800/333-3333** in the U.S., or 998/887-4455. Fax 998/884-7954. www.radissoncancun.com. 248 units. High season $100 double, $125 junior suite; low season $90 double, $115 junior suite. Ask about special all-inclusive rates. AE, MC, V. **Amenities:** 2 restaurants; lively lobby bar; pool w/adjoining bar and separate wading area for children; tennis courts; small gym w/sauna; travel agency; car rental; salon. *In room:* A/C, TV, coffeemaker, hair dryer, iron, safe.

Rey del Caribe Hotel ★★ (Value)

This hotel, located in the center of downtown, is a unique oasis—a 100% ecological hotel, where every detail has been thought out to achieve the goal of living in an organic and environmentally friendly manner. The whole atmosphere of the place is one of warmth, which derives from the on-site owners, who, caring as much as they do for Mother Earth, extend this sentiment to guests as well. You easily forget you're in the midst of downtown Cancún in the tropical jungle setting, with blooming orchids and other flowering plants. Surrounding gardens are populated with statues of Maya deities—it's a lovely, tranquil setting. There's a daily-changing schedule of yoga, Tai Chi, and meditation sessions, as well as special classes on astrology, tarot, and other subjects. Rooms are large and sunny, with your choice of one king or two full-size beds, a kitchenette, and terrace. The detail of ecological sensitivity is truly impressive, ranging from the use of collected rain water to waste composting. Recycling is encouraged and solar power used wherever possible.

Av. Uxmal, corner with Nadar, SM 2A. ✆ 998/884-2028. Fax 998/884-9857. www.reycaribe.com. 24 units. High season $63–$100 double; low season $40–$80 double. Rates include breakfast. MC, V. **Amenities:** Restaurant; outdoor pool; hot tub; classes. *In room:* A/C, kitchenette.

INEXPENSIVE

Cancún INN Suites El Patio ★ (Finds)

Many guests at this small hotel stay for up to a month, drawn by its combination of excellent value and warm hospitality. The European-style guesthouse caters to travelers looking for more of the area's culture. You won't find bars, pools, or loud parties; you will find excellent service and impeccable accommodations. Rooms face the plant-filled interior courtyard, dotted with groupings of wrought-iron chairs and tables. Each room has slightly different appointments and amenities, but all have white tile floors and rustic wood furnishings. Some rooms have kitchenettes, and there's a common kitchen area with purified water and a cooler for stocking your own supplies. There is a public phone in the entranceway, and the staff can arrange for a cellular phone in your room on request. A game and TV room has a large-screen cable TV, a library stocked with books on Mexican culture, backgammon, cards, and board games. While smoking is not allowed in the rooms, it is allowed on the premises.

Av. Bonampak 51 and Cereza, SM2A, Centro, 77500 Cancún, Q. Roo. ✆ **998/884-3500.** Fax 998/884-3540. www.cancun-suites.com. 12 units. $40–$56 double. Spanish-lesson packages available. Ask about discounts for longer stays. AE, MC, V. **Amenities:** Small restaurant (breakfast and dinner). *In room:* A/C, kitchenette, safe.

Hotel Antillano

A quiet and very clean choice, the Antillano is close to the Ciudad Cancún bus terminal. Rooms overlook Avenida Tulum, the side streets, or the interior lawn and pool. Pool-view rooms are most desirable because they are quietest. Rooms feature coordinated furnishings, one or two double beds, a sink area separate from the bathroom, and red-tile floors. Guests have the use of the hotel's beach club on the island.

Av. Claveles 1 (corner of Av. Tulum, opposite Restaurant Rosa Mexicana), 77500 Cancún, Q. Roo. ☏ 998/884-1532. Fax 998/884-1878. www.hotelantillano.com. 48 units. High season $75 double; low season $60 double. AE, MC, V. Street parking. **Amenities:** Small bar; travel agency; babysitting. *In room:* A/C, TV.

Hotel Hacienda Cancún *Value*

This extremely pleasing little hotel is a great value. The facade has been remodeled to look like a hacienda. The guest rooms are very comfortable; all have rustic Mexican furnishings and two double beds, but no views. There's a nice small pool and cafe under a shaded *palapa* in the back.

Sunyaxchen 39–40, 77500 Cancún, Q. Roo. ☏ 998/884-3672. Fax 998/884-1208. hhda@cancun.com.mx. 35 units. High season $45 double; low season $38 double. MC, V. Street parking. From Av. Yaxchilán, turn west on Sunyaxchen; it's on the right next to the Hotel Caribe International, opposite 100% Natural. **Amenities:** Restaurant; pool. *In room:* A/C, TV, safe.

Hotel Margaritas *Value*

Located in downtown Cancún, this four-story hotel (with elevator) is comfortable and unpretentious, offering one of the best values in Cancún. The pleasantly decorated rooms, with white tile floors and small balconies, are exceptionally clean and bright. Lounge chairs surround the attractive pool, which has a wading section for children. The hotel offers complimentary safes at the front desk.

Av. Yaxchilán 41, SM22, Centro, 77500 Cancún, Q. Roo. ☏ 01-800/711-1531 in Mexico, or 998/884-9333. Fax 998/884-1324. www.margaritascancun.com. 100 units. High season $85 double; low season $78 double. AE, MC, V. **Amenities:** Restaurant; pool; travel agency; room service; babysitting; medical service; money exchange. *In room:* A/C, TV.

Refugio del Pirata Morgan

Although not actually in the town of Cancún, but on the highway leading north from Cancún to Punta Sam, this is the place for those who want a true encounter with nature. Located on a wide, virgin stretch of beach, away from the crowd of hotels and nightlife, this "refuge" is exactly that: no phones, no television, just blissful peace and quiet. There are 10 simple cabañas, with both beds and hammocks, each named for the predominate color of the decor. A small restaurant offers a basic selection of dining choices featuring fresh fish—otherwise, the nearest restaurant is 2km (1¼ miles) away.

Carretera Punta Sam, Isla Blanca, Km 9 77500 Cancún, Q. Roo. ☏ 998/860-3386 (within Mexico dial 044 first, as this is a cellphone). 10 units. $40 room; $5 hammock. **Amenities:** Restaurant. *In room:* Fan.

3 Where to Dine

U.S.-based franchise chains, which really need no introduction, dominate the Cancún restaurant scene. These include Hard Rock Cafe, Rainforest Cafe, Tony Roma's, TGI Friday's, Ruth's Chris Steak House, and the gamut of fast-food burger places. The establishments listed here are locally owned, one-of-a-kind restaurants or exceptional selections at area hotels. Many schedule live music. Unless otherwise indicated, parking is free.

One unique way to combine dinner with sightseeing is aboard the **Lobster Dinner Cruise** (☏ 998/849-4748). Cruising around the tranquil, turquoise waters of the lagoon, passengers feast on lobster dinners accompanied by wine. Cost is $49 per person. There are two daily departures from the Royal Mayan Marina. A sunset cruise leaves at 4:30pm during the winter and 5:30pm during the summer; a moonlight cruise leaves at 7:30pm winter, 8:30pm summer. Another—albeit livelier—option is the **Captain Hook Lobster Dinner Cruise** (☏ 998/849-4451), which is similar, but with the added attraction of a pirate show, making this the choice for families. It costs $58 and departs at 7pm from El Embarcadero.

The restaurants of the new Aqua Fiesta Americana (not yet opened at press time) promise to be exceptional, including "7," under the direction of renowned Mexican Chef Patricia Quintana.

CANCUN ISLAND
VERY EXPENSIVE

Aioli ★★★ FRENCH   For the quality and originality of the cuisine, coupled with excellent service, this is my top pick for the best fine-dining value in Cancún. The Provençal—but definitely not provincial—Aioli offers exquisite French and Mediterranean gourmet specialties in a warm and cozy country French setting. Though it serves perhaps the best breakfast buffet in Cancún (for $20), most diners from outside the hotel come here in the evening, when low lighting and superb service make it a top choice for a romantic dinner. Starters include traditional pâtés and a delightful escargot served in the shell with white wine and herbed butter sauce. A specialty is duck breast in honey and lavender sauce. Equally scrumptious is rack of lamb, prepared in Moroccan style and served with couscous. Pan-seared grouper is topped with a paste of black olives, crushed potato, and tomato, and bouillabaisse contains an exceptional array of seafood. Desserts are decadent; the signature "Fifth Element" is a sinfully delicious temptation rich with chocolate.

In Le Méridien Cancún Resort & Spa, Retorno del Rey Km 14. ℭ 998/881-2200. Reservations required. Main courses $14–$30. AE, DC, MC, V. Daily 6:30am–11pm.

Club Grill ★★★ INTERNATIONAL   This is the place for that special night out. Cancún's most elegant and stylish restaurant is also among its most delicious. Even rival restaurateurs give it an envious thumbs up. The gracious service starts as you enter the anteroom, with its comfortable seating and selection of fine tequilas and Cuban cigars. It continues in a candlelit dining room with shimmering silver and crystal. Elegant plates of peppered scallops, truffles, and potatoes in tequila sauce; grilled lamb; or mixed grill arrive at a leisurely pace. The restaurant has smoking and nonsmoking sections. A band plays romantic music for dancing from 8pm on.

In the Ritz-Carlton Hotel, Bulevar Kukulkán Km 13.5. ℭ 998/881-0808. Reservations required. No sandals or tennis shoes; men must wear long pants. Main courses $11–$40. AE, DC, MC, V. Tues–Sun 7–11pm.

The Plantation House ★ *Overrated* CARIBBEAN/FRENCH   This casually elegant, pale-yellow-and-blue clapboard restaurant overlooking Nichupté lagoon takes you back to the time when the Caribbean first experienced European tastes and culinary talents. The decor combines island-style colonial charm with elegant touches. The service is excellent, but the food is only mediocre, especially considering the price. For starters, try the signature poached shrimp with lemon juice and olive oil, or creamy crabmeat soup. Move on to the main event, which may consist of classic veal Wellington in puff pastry with duck pâté, fish filet crusted in spices and herbs and topped with vanilla sauce, or lobster medallions in mango sauce. Flambéed desserts are a specialty, and the Plantation House has one of the most extensive wine lists in town. It's generally quite crowded, which makes it a bit loud for a romantic evening.

Bulevar Kukulkán Km 10.5. ℭ 998/883-1433. Reservations recommended. Main courses $13–$35. AE, MC, V. Daily 5pm–midnight.

EXPENSIVE

Captain's Cove ⚓ INTERNATIONAL/SEAFOOD   Though it sits almost at the end of Bulevar Kukulkán, far from everything, the Captain's Cove continues to pack in customers with its consistent value. Diners sit on several levels, facing big open windows overlooking the lagoon and Royal Yacht Club Marina. For breakfast there's an all-you-can-eat buffet. Main courses of USDA Angus steak and seafood are the norm at lunch and dinner, and there's a children's menu. For dessert there are flaming coffees, crepes, and Key lime pie. The restaurant is on the lagoon side, opposite the Omni Hotel.

Bulevar Kukulkán Km 15. ✆ **998/885-0016**. Main courses $12–$40; breakfast buffet $10. AE, MC, V. Daily 7am–11pm.

La Dolce Vita ⚓⚓⚓ ITALIAN/SEAFOOD   Casually elegant La Dolce Vita is Cancún's favorite Italian restaurant. Appetizers include pâté of quail liver and carpaccio in vinaigrette, and mushrooms Provençal. The chef specializes in homemade pastas combined with fresh seafood. You can order green tagliolini with lobster medallions, linguine with clams or seafood, or rigatoni Mexican-style (with *chorizo*, mushrooms, and jalapeños) as a main course, or as an appetizer for half price. Other main courses include veal with morels, fresh salmon with cream sauce, and fresh fish in a variety of sauces. Recently added choices include vegetarian lasagna and grilled whole lobster. You have a choice of dining in air-conditioned comfort or on an open-air terrace with a view of the lagoon. Live jazz plays from 7 to 11:30pm Monday through Saturday.

Bulevar Kukulkán Km 14.6, on the lagoon, opposite the Marriott Casa Magna. ✆ **998/885-0150** or 998/885-0161. Fax 998/885-0590. www.cancun.com/dining/dolce. Reservations required for dinner. Main courses $9–$29. AE, MC, V. Daily noon–midnight.

Laguna Grill ⚓⚓ FUSION   Laguna Grill offers diners a contemporary culinary experience in a lush, tropical setting overlooking the lagoon. A tropical garden welcomes you at the entrance, while a small creek traverses through the restaurant set with tables made from the trunks of regional, tropical trees. As magical as the decor is, the real star here is the kitchen, with its offering of Pacific-rim cuisine fused with regional flavors. Starters include martini *gyoza* (steamed dumplings) and shrimp tempura served on a mango mint salad, or ahi tuna and shrimp *ceviche* in a spicy Oriental sauce. Fish and seafood dominate the menu of entrees, in a variety of preparations that combine Asian and Mexican flavors such as ginger, cilantro, garlic, and *hoisin* sauce. Grilled shrimp are served over a cilantro and *guajillo* chile risotto. For beef-lovers, the rib-eye served over a garlic, spinach, and sweet potato mash is sublime. Deserts are as creative as the main dishes; the pineapple-papaya strudel in Malibu rum sauce is a standout. If you're an early diner, request a table on the outside deck for a spectacular sunset view. An impressive selection of wines is available.

Bulevar Kukulkán Km 16.5. ✆ **998/885-0267**. www.lagunagrill.com.mx. Reservations recommended. Main courses $15–$45. AE, MC, V. Daily 2pm–midnight.

Lorenzillo's ⚓⚓⚓ *Kids* SEAFOOD   This festive, friendly restaurant is a personal favorite—I never miss a lobster stop here when I'm in Cancún. Live lobster is the overwhelming favorite, and part of the appeal is selecting your dinner out of the giant lobster tank. Lorenzillo's sits on the lagoon under a giant *palapa* roof. A dock leads down to the main dining area, and when that's packed (which is often), a wharf-side bar handles the overflow. In addition to lobster—which comes grilled, steamed, or stuffed—

good bets are shrimp stuffed with cheese and wrapped in bacon, the Admiral's filet coated in toasted almonds and light mustard sauce, and seafood-stuffed squid. Desserts include the tempting "Martinique": Belgian chocolate with hazelnuts, almonds, and pecans, served with vanilla ice cream. The sunset pier offers a lighter menu of cold seafood, sandwiches, and salads. Children are very welcome.

Bulevar Kukulkán Km 10.5. © 998/883-1254. www.lorenzillos.com.mx. Reservations recommended. Main courses $12–$50. AE, MC, V. Daily noon–midnight. Valet parking available.

Mango Tango 🎭🎭 INTERNATIONAL   The beauty of dining here is that you can stay and enjoy a hot nightspot—Mango Tango has made a name for itself with sizzling floor shows (featuring salsa, tango, and other Latin dancing) and live reggae music (see "Cancún After Dark," later in this chapter)—but its kitchen deserves attention as well. Try the peel-your-own shrimp, Argentine-style grilled meat with *chimichurri* sauce, and other grilled specialties. Mango Tango salad is shrimp, chicken, avocado, red onion, tomato, and mushrooms served on mango slices. Entrees include rice with seafood and fried bananas. Creole gumbo comes with lobster, shrimp, and squid, and coconut-and-mango cake is a suitable finish to the meal.

Bulevar Kukulkán Km 14.2, opposite the Ritz-Carlton Hotel. © 998/885-0303. Reservations recommended. Main courses $12–$57; 3-course dinner show $40. AE, MC, V. Daily 2pm–2am.

María Bonita 🎭 *Kids* REGIONAL/MEXICAN/NOUVELLE MEXICAN   In a stylish setting overlooking the water, María Bonita captures the essence of the country through its music and food. Prices are higher and the flavors more institutionalized than at traditional Mexican restaurants in Ciudad Cancún, but this is a good choice for the Hotel Zone. There are three sections: La Cantina Jalisco, with an open kitchen and tequila bar; the Salón Michoacán, which features that state's cuisine; and the Patio Oaxaca. The menu encompasses the best of Mexico's other cuisines, with a few international dishes. Prix-fixe dinners include appetizer, main course, and dessert. Jazz trios, *marimba* and *jarocho* music, and mariachis serenade you while you dine. A nice starter is Mitla salad, with slices of the renowned Oaxaca cheese dribbled with olive oil and coriander dressing. Wonderful stuffed chile La Doña—a mildly hot poblano pepper filled with lobster and *huitlacoche* (a type of mushroom that grows on corn) in a cream sauce—comes as an appetizer or a main course.

In the Hotel Dreams, Punta Cancún (enter from the street). © 998/848-7000, ext. 8060 or 8061. Reservations recommended. Prix-fixe dinner $30–$45; main courses $17–$31. AE, DC, MC, V. Daily 6:30–11:45pm.

MODERATE

La Destilería MEXICAN   If you want to experience tequila in its native habitat, you won't want to miss this place—even though it's across the country from the region that produces the beverage. La Destilería is more than a tequila-inspired restaurant; it's a minimuseum honoring the "spirit" of Mexico. It serves over 150 brands of tequila, including some treasures that never find their way across the country's northern border, so be adventurous! The margaritas are among the best on the island. When you decide to have some food with your tequila, the menu is refined Mexican, with everything from quesadillas with squash blossom flowers, to shrimp in a delicate tequila-lime sauce. They even serve *escamoles* (crisp-fried ant eggs) as an appetizer for the adventurous—or for those whose squeamishness has been diminished by the tequila!

Bulevar Kukulkán Km 12.65, across from Kukulcan Plaza. © 998/885-1086 or -1087. Main courses $8–30. AE, MC, V. Daily 1pm–midnight.

La Fisheria ⍟ *Kids* SEAFOOD If you're at the mall shopping, this is your best bet. Patrons find a lot to choose from at this restaurant overlooking Bulevar Kukulkán and the lagoon. The expansive menu includes shark fingers with jalapeño dip, grouper filet stuffed with seafood in lobster sauce, Acapulco-style *ceviche* in tomato sauce, New England clam chowder, steamed mussels, grilled red snapper with pasta—you get the idea. The menu changes daily, but there's always *tikin xik,* that great Yucatecan grilled fish marinated in *achiote* (a spice) sauce. For those not inclined toward seafood, a pizza from the wood-burning oven, or perhaps a grilled chicken or beef dish, might do. La Fisheria has a nonsmoking section.

Plaza Caracol shopping center, Bulevar Kukulkán Km 8.5, 2nd floor. ℂ 998/883-1395. Main courses $7–$21. AE, MC, V. Daily 11am–11pm.

Savio's ⍟ ITALIAN Centrally located at the heart of the Hotel Zone, Savio's is a great place to stop for a quick meal or coffee. Its bar is always crowded with patrons sipping everything from cappuccino to imported beer. Repeat diners look forward to large fresh salads and rich, subtly herb-flavored Italian dishes. Ravioli stuffed with ricotta and spinach comes in delicious tomato sauce. Stylish, with black-and-white decor and tile floors, it has two levels and faces Bulevar Kukulkán through two stories of awning-shaded windows.

Plaza Caracol shopping center, Bulevar Kukulkán Km 8.5. ℂ/fax 998/883-2085. Main courses $9–$30. AE, MC, V. Daily 10am–midnight.

INEXPENSIVE
100% Natural ⍟⍟ VEGETARIAN/MEXICAN If you want a healthy reprieve from an overindulgent night—or just like your meals as fresh and natural as possible— this is your oasis. No matter what your dining preference, you owe it to yourself to try a Mexican tradition, the fresh-fruit *licuado.* The blended drink combines fresh fruit, ice, and either water or milk. More creative combinations may mix in yogurt, granola, or other goodies. And 100% Natural serves more than just meal-quality drinks—there's a bountiful selection of basic Mexican fare and terrific sandwiches served on whole-grain bread, both with options for vegetarians. Breakfast is a delight as well as a good value. The space abounds with plants and cheery colors. There are several locations in town; another is located on Bulevar Kukulkán Km 13 (ℂ 998/885-2904) and is open 8am to 11pm.

Plaza Comercial Suite Terramar, next to Plaza Caracol, Local 40–41. ℂ 998/883-3636. Main courses $2.80–$13. MC, V. Daily 24 hr.

CANCUN CITY
EXPENSIVE
La Habichuela ⍟ GOURMET SEAFOOD/CARIBBEAN/MEXICAN In a garden setting with soft music playing in the background, this restaurant is ideal for a romantic evening. For an all-out culinary adventure, try *habichuela* (string bean) soup; shrimp in any number of sauces, including Jamaican tamarind, tequila, or ginger-and-mushroom; and Maya coffee with *xtabentun* (a strong, sweet, anise-based liqueur). Grilled seafood and steaks are excellent, but this is a good place to try a Mexican specialty such as *chicken mole* or *tampiqueña*-style beef (thinly sliced, marinated, and grilled). For something totally divine, try *cocobichuela,* which is lobster and shrimp in curry sauce served in a coconut shell and topped with fruit.

Margaritas 25. ℂ 998/884-3158. habichuela@infosel.net.mx. Reservations recommended in high season. Main courses $10–$32. AE, MC, V. Daily noon–midnight.

Périco's ☺☺☺ MEXICAN/SEAFOOD/STEAKS Périco's has colorful murals that almost dance off the walls, a bar area with saddles for barstools, colorful leather tables and chairs, and accommodating waiters; it's always booming and festive. The extensive menu offers well-prepared steak, seafood, and traditional Mexican dishes for reasonable rates (except for lobster). This is a place not only to eat and drink, but also to let loose and join in the fun, so don't be surprised if everybody drops their forks and dons huge sombreros to shimmy and shake in a conga dance around the dining room. It's fun whether or not you join in, but it's definitely not the place for a romantic evening alone. There's *marimba* music from 7:30 to 9:30pm, and mariachis from 9:30pm to midnight.

Yaxchilán 61. ⓒ **998/884-3152.** Reservations recommended. Main courses $9–$39. AE, MC, V. Daily 1pm–1am.

MODERATE

Labná ☺ YUCATECAN To steep yourself in Yucatecan cuisine and music, head directly to this showcase of Mayan moods and regional foods. Specialties served here include a sublime lime soup, *poc chuc* (marinated, barbecue-style pork), chicken or pork *pibil* (sweet and spicy barbecue sauce served over shredded meat), and appetizers such as *papadzules* (tortillas stuffed with boiled eggs in a green pumpkin sauce). The Labná Special is a sampler of four typically Yucatecan main courses, including *poc chuc*, while another specialty of the house is baked suckling pig, served with guacamole. The refreshing Yucatecan beverage, *agua de chaya*—a blend of sweetened water and the leaf of the chaya plant, abundant in the area, to which D'aristi liquor can be added for an extra kick—is also served here. The large, informal dining room is decorated with fascinating black and white photographs of the region, dating from the 1900s.

Margaritas 29, next to City hall and the Habicula restaurant. ⓒ **998/892-3056.** Main courses $5–$18. AE, MC, V. Daily noon–10pm.

Rosa Mexicano ☺☺ MEXICAN HAUTE CUISINE This beautiful little place has candlelit tables and a plant-filled patio in back, and is almost always packed. Colorful paper banners and piñatas hang from the ceiling, efficient waiters wear bow ties and cummerbunds that match the Mexican flag, and a trio plays romantic Mexican music nightly. The menu features "refined" Mexican specialties. Try *pollo almendro* (chicken covered in cream sauce and sprinkled with ground almonds), or pork baked in a banana leaf with a sauce of oranges, lime, *ancho* chile, and garlic. Steak *tampiqueño* is a huge platter that comes with guacamole salad, quesadillas, beans, salad, and rice.

Claveles 4. ⓒ **998/884-6313.** Fax 998/884-2371. Reservations recommended for parties of 6 or more. Main courses $9–$17; lobster $30. AE, MC, V. Daily 5–11pm.

Stefano's ITALIAN/PIZZA Call the food Mexitalian if you will, but it seems to be a winning combination. Stefano's began primarily as a local restaurant, serving Italian food with a few Mexican accents, and is now equally popular with tourists. Among the menu items are ravioli stuffed with *huitlacoche* (a type of mushroom that grows on corn); rigatoni in tequila sauce; and seafood with chile peppers, nestled proudly alongside the Stefano special pizza, made with fresh tomato, cheese, and pesto. For dessert, ricotta strudel is something out of the ordinary. Stefano's offers lots of different coffees and mixed drinks, plus an expanded wine list.

Bonampak 177. ⓒ **998/887-9964.** Main courses $7–$17; pizza $6–$17. AE, MC, V. Daily 1pm–midnight.

INEXPENSIVE

Pizza Rolandi _Kids_ ITALIAN   This is an institution in Cancún, and the Rolandi name is synonymous with dining in both Cancún and neighboring Isla Mujeres. Pizza Rolandi and its branch in Isla Mujeres (see chapter 14) have become standards for dependably good casual fare. At this shaded outdoor patio restaurant, you can choose from almost two dozen wood-oven pizzas and a full selection of spaghetti, calzones, Italian-style chicken and beef, and desserts. There's a full bar as well.

Cobá 12. © 998/884-4047. Fax 998/884-3994. www.rolandi.com. Pasta $5–$8; pizza and main courses $7–$14. AE, MC, V. Daily noon–11 pm.

4 Beaches, Watersports & Boat Tours

THE BEACHES   Big hotels dominate the best stretches of beach. All of Mexico's beaches are public property, so you can use the beach of any hotel by walking through the lobby or directly onto the sand. Be especially careful on beaches fronting the open Caribbean, where the undertow can be quite strong. By contrast, the waters of Mujeres Bay (Bahía de Mujeres), at the north end of the island, are usually calm and ideal for swimming. Get to know Cancún's water-safety pennant system, and make sure to check the flag at any beach or hotel before entering the water. Here's how it goes:

- **White**   Excellent
- **Green**   Normal conditions (safe)
- **Yellow**   Changeable, uncertain (use caution)
- **Black** or **red**   Unsafe; use the swimming pool instead!

In the Caribbean, storms can arrive and conditions can change from safe to unsafe in a matter of minutes, so be alert: If you see dark clouds heading your way, make for the shore and wait until the storm passes.

Playa Tortuga (Turtle Beach), Playa Langosta (Lobster Beach), Playa Linda (Pretty Beach), and **Playa Las Perlas (Beach of the Pearls)** are some of the public beaches. At most beaches, you can rent a sailboard and take lessons, ride a parasail, or partake in a variety of watersports. There's a small but beautiful portion of public beach on **Playa Caracol,** by the Xcaret Terminal. It faces the calm waters of Bahía de Mujeres and, for that reason, is preferable to those facing the Caribbean.

WATERSPORTS   Many beachside hotels offer watersports concessions that rent rubber rafts, kayaks, and snorkeling equipment. On the calm Nichupté lagoon are outlets for renting **sailboats, jet skis, windsurfers,** and **water skis.** Prices vary and are often negotiable, so check around.

DEEP-SEA FISHING   You can arrange a day of **deep-sea fishing** at one of the numerous piers or travel agencies for around $220 to $360 for 4 hours, $420 for 6 hours, and $520 for 8 hours for up to four people. Marinas will sometimes assist in putting together a group. Charters include a captain, a first mate, bait, gear, and beverages. Rates are lower if you depart from Isla Mujeres or from Cozumel—and frankly, the fishing is better closer to those departure points.

SCUBA & SNORKELING   Known for its shallow reefs, dazzling color, and diversity of life, Cancún is one of the best places in the world for beginning **scuba diving.** Punta Nizuc is the northern tip of the **Gran Arrecife Maya (Great Mesoamerican Reef),** the largest reef in the Western Hemisphere and one of the largest in the world.

In addition to the sea life along this reef system, several sunken boats add a variety of dive options. Inland, a series of caverns and *cenotes* (wellsprings) are fascinating venues for the more experienced diver. Drift diving is the norm here, with popular dives going to the reefs at **El Garrafón** and the **Cave of the Sleeping Sharks**—although be aware that the famed "sleeping sharks" have departed, driven off by too many people watching them snooze.

A variety of hotels offer resort courses that teach the basics of diving—enough to make shallow dives and slowly ease your way into this underwater world of unimaginable beauty. Scuba trips run around $64 for two-tank dives at nearby reefs, and $100 and up for locations farther out. **Scuba Cancún,** Bulevar Kukulkán Km 5 (© **998/849-7508** or 998/849-4736; www.scubacancun.com.mx), on the lagoon side, offers a 4-hour resort course for $84. Phone reservations (© **998/849-4736**) are available from 7:30 to 10:30pm. Full certification takes 4 to 5 days and costs around $368. Scuba Cancún is open daily from 9am to 6pm, and accepts major credit cards. The largest operator is **Aquaworld,** across from the Meliá Cancún at Bulevar Kukulkán Km 15.2 (© **998/848-8300** or 998/848-8327; www.aquaworld.com.mx). It offers resort courses and diving from a man-made anchored dive platform, Paradise Island. Aquaworld has the **Sub See Explorer,** a boat with picture windows that hang beneath the surface. The boat doesn't submerge—it's an updated version of a glass-bottom boat—but it does provide nondivers with a look at life beneath the sea. This outfit is open 24 hours a day and accepts all major credit cards.

Scuba Cancún also offers diving trips, in good weather only, to 20 nearby reefs, including Cuevones (9m/30 ft.) and the open ocean (9–18m/30–60 ft.). The average dive is around 11m (35 ft.). One-tank dives cost $55, and two-tank dives cost $65. Discounts apply if you bring your own equipment. Dives usually start around 10am and return by 2:15pm. Snorkeling trips cost $27 and leave every afternoon after 1:30pm for shallow reefs about a 20-minute boat ride away.

Besides snorkeling at **El Garrafón Natural Park** (see "Boating Excursions," below), travel agencies offer an all-day excursion to the natural wildlife habitat of **Isla Contoy,** which usually includes time for snorkeling. The island, 90 minutes past Isla Mujeres, is a major nesting area for birds and a treat for nature lovers. You can call any travel agent or see any hotel tour desk to get a selection of boat tours to Isla Contoy. Prices range from $44 to $65, depending on the length of the trip, and generally include drinks and snorkeling equipment.

The Great Mesoamerican Reef also offers exceptional snorkeling opportunities. In Puerto Morelos, 37km (23 miles) south of Cancún, the reef hugs the coastline for 15km (9 miles). The reef is so close to the shore (about 460m/1,500 ft.) that it forms a natural barrier for the village and keeps the waters calm on the inside of the reef. The water here is shallow, from 1.5 to 9m (5–30 ft.), resulting in ideal conditions for snorkeling. Stringent environmental regulations implemented by the local community have kept the reef here unspoiled. Only a select few companies are allowed to offer snorkel trips, and they must adhere to guidelines that will ensure the reef's preservation. **Cancún Mermaid** (© **998/843-6517;** www.cancunmermaid.com) is considered the best—it's a family-run ecotour company that has operated in the area since the 1970s. It's known for highly personalized service. The tour typically takes snorkelers to two sections of the reef, spending about an hour in each area. When conditions allow, the boat drops off snorkelers and then follows them along with the current—an activity known as "drift snorkeling," which enables snorkelers to see as much of the reef as possible. The trip costs $50 for adults, $35 for children, which includes boat, snorkeling gear, life jackets, a light lunch, bottled water, sodas, and beer, plus round-trip transportation to and from Puerto Morelos from Cancún hotels. Departures are Monday through Saturday at 9am or noon, a minimum of four snorkelers is required for a trip, and reservations are required.

JET SKI TOURS Several companies offer the popular **Jungle Cruise,** which takes you by jet ski or WaveRunner (you drive your own watercraft) through Cancún's lagoon and mangrove estuaries out into the Caribbean Sea and a shallow reef. The excursion runs about 2½ hours and costs $35 to $45, including snorkeling and beverages. Some of the motorized miniboats seat one person behind the other—meaning that the person in back gets a great view of the driver's head; others seat you side by side.

The operators and names of boats offering excursions change often. To find out what's available, check with a local travel agent or hotel tour desk. The popular **Aquaworld,** Bulevar Kukulkán Km 15.2 (© **998/848-8300,** or 998/885-2288), calls its trip the Jungle Tour and charges $45 for the 2½-hour excursion, which includes 45 minutes of snorkeling time. It even gives you a free snorkel, but has the less-desirable one-behind-the-other seating configuration. Departures are 8, 8:30, 9, 10:30, and 11:30am, noon, and 1, 2, 2:30, 3:30, and 4:30pm daily.

BOATING EXCURSIONS

ISLA MUJERES The island of **Isla Mujeres,** just 13km (8 miles) offshore, is one of the most pleasant day trips from Cancún. At one end is **El Garrafón Natural Park,** which is excellent for snorkeling. At the other end is a captivating village with small shops, restaurants, and hotels, and **Playa Norte,** the island's best beach. If you're looking for relaxation and can spare the time, it's worth several days. For complete information about the island, see chapter 14.

There are four ways to get there: **public ferry** from Puerto Juárez, which takes between 15 and 45 minutes; **shuttle boat** from Playa Linda or Playa Tortuga—an hour-long ride, with irregular service; **Watertaxi** (more expensive, but faster), next to the Xcaret Terminal; and daylong **pleasure-boat trips,** most of which leave from the Playa Linda pier.

The inexpensive Puerto Juárez **public ferries** ⚓ are just a few kilometers from downtown Cancún. From Cancún City, take the Ruta 8 bus on Avenida Tulum to Puerto Juárez. The air-conditioned *Caribbean Express* (20 min.) costs $4 per person. Departures are every half-hour from 6 to 8:30am and then every 15 minutes until 8:30pm. The slower *Caribbean Savage* (45–60 min.) is a bargain at about $2. It departs every 2 hours, or less frequently depending on demand. Upon arrival, the ferry docks in downtown Isla Mujeres near all the shops, restaurants, hotels, and Norte beach. You'll need a taxi to get to El Garrafón park, at the other end of the island. You can stay as long as you like on the island (even overnight) and return by ferry, but be sure to double-check the time of the last returning ferry.

Pleasure-boat cruises to Isla Mujeres are a favorite pastime. Modern motor yachts, catamarans, trimarans, and even old-time sloops—more than 25 boats a day—take swimmers, sun lovers, snorkelers, and shoppers out on the translucent waters. Some tours include a snorkeling stop at El Garrafón, lunch on the beach, and a short time for shopping in downtown Isla Mujeres. Most leave at 9:30 or 10am, last about 5 or 6 hours, and include continental breakfast, lunch, and rental of snorkel gear. Others,

---

> ## *Tips* An All-Terrain Tour
>
> Cancún Mermaid (© **998/843-6517** or 998/886-4117; www.cancunmermaid.com), in Cancún, offers all-terrain-vehicle (ATV) jungle tours for $49 per person. The ATV tours travel through the jungles of Cancún and emerge on the beaches of the Riviera Maya. The 2½-hour tour includes equipment, instruction, the services of a tour guide, and bottled water; it departs daily at 8am and 1:30pm. The company picks you up at your hotel. Another ATV option is Rancho Loma Bonita; see "Horseback Riding," below

---

particularly sunset and night cruises, go to beaches away from town for pseudo-pirate shows and include a lobster dinner or Mexican buffet. If you want to actually see Isla Mujeres, go on a morning cruise, or travel on your own using the public ferry from Puerto Juárez. Prices for the day cruises run around $45 per person.

El Garrafón Natural Park ✦✦ is under the same management as Xcaret (© **998/884-9422**). The basic entrance fee of $29 includes access to the reef and a museum, as well as use of kayaks, inner tubes, life vests, the pool, hammocks, and public facilities and showers. Snorkel gear and lockers can be rented for an extra charge. There are also nature trails as well as several restaurants on-site. An all-inclusive option is available for $59, which includes dining on whatever you choose at any of the restaurants, plus unlimited domestic drinks and use of snorkel gear, locker, and towel. El Garrafón also has full dive facilities and gear rentals, plus an expansive gift shop.

Other excursions go to the **reefs** in glass-bottom boats, so you can have a near-scuba-diving experience and see many colorful fish. However, the reefs are some distance from the shore and are impossible to reach on windy days with choppy seas. They've also suffered from over-visitation, and their condition is far from pristine. Nautibus's **Atlantis Submarine** (© **987/872-5671**) takes you close to the aquatic action. Departures vary, depending on weather conditions. Prices are $81 for adults, $48 for children ages 4 to 12. The submarine descends to a depth of 30m (100 ft.). Atlantis Submarine departs Monday to Saturday every hour from 8am until 2pm; the tour lasts about an hour. The submarine departs from Cozumel, so you either need to take a ferry to get there or purchase the package that includes round-trip ground and water transportation from your hotel in Cancún ($103 adults, $76 children 4–12). Reservations are recommended.

5 Outdoor Activities & Attractions

OUTDOOR ACTIVITIES

DOLPHIN SWIMS On Isla Mujeres, you have the opportunity to swim with dolphins at **Dolphin Discovery** ✦ (© **998/849-4757**; fax 998/849-4758; www.dolphindiscovery.com). There are several options for dolphin interaction, but my choice is the Royal Swim, which includes an educational introduction followed by 30 minutes of swim time. The price is $125 (MasterCard and Visa are accepted), with transportation to Isla Mujeres an additional $5 for program participants. Advance reservations are required. Assigned swimming times are 10am, noon, 2, or 3:30pm, and you must arrive 1½ hour before your scheduled swim time. In Cancún, the **Parque Nizuc** (© **998/881-3030**) marine park offers guests a chance to swim with dolphins and view them in their dolphin aquarium, Atlántida. The price of the dolphin swim ($135) includes admission to the park. It's a fun place for a family to spend the day, with its numerous pools, waterslides, and rides. Visitors can also snorkel with manta rays, tropical fish, and tame sharks. It's at the southern end of Cancún, between the airport and the Hotel Zone. Admission is $27 for adults, $23 for children 3 to 11 (American Express, MasterCard, and Visa are accepted). Open daily from 10am to 5:30pm.

La Isla Shopping Center, Bulevar Kukulkán Km 12.5, has an impressive **Interactive Aquarium** (© **998/883-0411,** 998/883-0436, or 998/883-0413; www.aquariumcancun. com.mx), with dolphin swims and the chance to feed a shark while immersed in the water in an acrylic cage. Guides inside the main tank use underwater microphones to point out the sea life, and even answer your questions. Open exhibition tanks enable visitors to touch a variety of marine life, including sea stars and manta rays. The educational dolphin program is $55, while the dolphin swim is $115. The entrance fee to the aquarium is $6 for adults, $4 for children, and it's open from 9am to 7pm, daily.

GOLF & TENNIS The 18-hole **Pok-Ta-Pok Club,** or Club de Golf Cancún (© **998/883-0871**), is a Robert Trent Jones, Sr., design on the northern leg of the island. Greens fees run $100 per 18 holes, with clubs renting for $26 and shoes for $15. Hiring a caddy costs $20. The club is open daily, accepts American Express, MasterCard, and Visa, and has tennis courts.

The **Hilton Cancún Golf & Beach Resort** (© **998/881-8016;** fax 998/881-8084) has a championship 18-hole, par-72 course designed around the Ruinas Del Rey. Greens fees for the public are $125 for 18 holes and $99 for 9 holes; Hilton Cancún guests receive a 20% discount off these rates, which includes a golf cart. Golf clubs and shoes are available for rent. The club is open daily from 6am to 6pm and accepts American Express, MasterCard, and Visa.

The **Meliá Cancún** (© **998/881-1100,** ext. 193) has a 9-hole executive course; the fee is $43. The club is open daily from 7am to 4:30pm and accepts American Express, MasterCard, and Visa.

The first Jack Nicklaus Signature Golf Course in the Cancún area has opened at the **Moon Palace Golf Resort,** along the Riviera Maya (www.palaceresorts.com). Two additional PGA courses are planned for the area just north of Cancún, Puerto Cancún, in 2007 and 2008.

HORSEBACK RIDING **Rancho Loma Bonita** (© **998/887-5465** or 998/887-5423; www.lomabonitamex.com), about 30 minutes south of town, is Cancún's most popular option for horseback riding. Five-hour packages include 2 hours of riding through the mangrove swamp to the beach, where you have time to swim and relax. The tour costs $72 for adults, $65 for children 6 to 12. The ranch also offers a four-wheel ATV ride on the same route as the horseback tour. It costs $72 per person if you want to ride on your own, $55 if you double up. Prices for both tours include transportation to the ranch, riding, soft drinks, and lunch, plus a guide and insurance. Visa is accepted, but cash is preferred.

ATTRACTIONS

A MUSEUM To the right side of the entrance to the Cancún Convention Center is the **Museo Arqueológico de Cancún** (© **998/883-0305**), a small but interesting museum with relics from archaeological sites around the state. Admission is $3; free on Sunday and holidays. It's open Tuesday through Friday from 9am to 8pm, Saturday and Sunday from 10am to 7pm.

Another cultural enclave is the **Museo de Arte Popular Mexicano** (© **998/849-4848**), located at on the second floor of the El Embarcadero Marina, Bulevar

Kukulkán Km 4. It displays a representative collection of masks, regional folkloric costumes, nativity scenes, religious artifacts, musical instruments, Mexican toys, and gourd art, spread over 1,370 sq. m (4,500 sq. ft.) of exhibition space. Admission is $10, with kids under 12 paying half price. The museum is open daily from 11am to 11 pm.

BULLFIGHTS   Cancún has a small bullring, **Plaza de Toros** (© **998/884-8372;** bull@prodigy.net.mx), near the northern (town) end of Bulevar Kukulkán opposite the Restaurant Los Almendros. Bullfights take place every Wednesday at 3:30pm during the winter tourist season. A sport introduced to Mexico by the Spanish viceroys, bullfighting is now as much a part of Mexican culture as tequila. The bullfights usually include four bulls, and the spectacle begins with a folkloric dance exhibition, followed by a performance by the *charros* (Mexico's sombrero-wearing cowboys). You're not likely to see Mexico's best bullfights in Cancún—the real stars are in Mexico City. Keep in mind that if you go to a bullfight, *you're going to see a bullfight,* so stay away if you're an animal lover or you can't bear the sight of blood. Travel agencies in Cancún sell tickets, which cost $35 for adults, free for children under 6; seating is by general admission. American Express, MasterCard, and Visa are accepted.

SIGHTSEEING   Get the best possible view of Cancún atop the **La Torre Cancún,** Bulevar Kukulkán Km 4 (© **998/849-4848**), a rotating tower at the El Embarcadero park and entertainment complex. One ride costs $9; a day and night pass goes for $14. Open daily from 9am to 11pm.

6 Shopping

Despite the surrounding natural splendor, shopping has become a favorite activity. Cancún is known throughout Mexico for its diverse shops and festive malls catering to a large number of international tourists. Visitors from the United States may find apparel more expensive in Cancún, but the selection is much broader than at other Mexican resorts. Numerous duty-free shops offer excellent value on European goods. The largest is **Ultrafemme,** Avenida Tulum, Supermanzana 25 (© **998/884-1402** or 998/885-0804), specializing in imported cosmetics, perfumes, and fine jewelry and watches. The downtown Cancún location offers slightly lower prices than branches in Plaza Caracol, Kukulcan Plaza, Plaza Mayafair, Flamingo Plaza, and the international airport.

Handicrafts are more limited and more expensive in Cancún than in other regions of Mexico because they are not produced here. They are available, though; several **open-air crafts markets** are on Avenida Tulum in Cancún City and near the convention center in the Hotel Zone. One of the biggest is **Coral Negro,** Bulevar Kukulkán Km 9.5 (© **998/883-0758;** fax 998/883-0758), open daily from 7am to 11pm. A small restaurant inside, Xtabentun, serves Yucatecan food and pizza slices, and metamorphoses into a dance club around 9 or 10pm.

Cancún's main venues are the **malls**—not quite as grand as their U.S. counterparts, but close. All are air-conditioned, sleek, and sophisticated. Most are on Bulevar Kukulkán between Km 7 and Km 12. They offer everything from fine crystal and silver to designer clothing and decorative objects, along with numerous restaurants and clubs. Stores are generally open daily from 10am to 10pm.

The **Kukulcan Plaza** (© **998/885-2200;** www.kukulcanplaza.com) offers a large selection—more than 300—of shops, restaurants, and entertainment. There's a branch of Banco Serfin; OK Maguey Cantina Grill; a theater with U.S. movies; an

Internet access kiosk; Tikal, which sells Guatemalan textile clothing; several crafts stores; a liquor store; several bathing-suit specialty stores; record and tape outlets; a leather goods store (including shoes and sandals); and a store specializing in silver from Taxco. The Fashion Gallery features designer clothing. In the food court are a number of U.S. franchise restaurants, including Ruth's Chris Steak House, plus one featuring specialty coffee. There's also a large indoor parking garage. The mall is open daily from 10am to 10pm, until 11pm during high season. Assistance for those with disabilities is available upon request, and wheelchairs, strollers, and lockers are available at the information desk.

Planet Hollywood anchors the **Plaza Flamingo** (© 998/883-2945), which has branches of Bancrecer, Subway, and La Casa del Habano (Cuban cigars).

The long-standing **Plaza Caracol** (© 998/883-1038) holds Cartier jewelry, Guess, Waterford Crystal, Señor Frog clothing, Samsonite luggage, and La Fisheria restaurant. It's just before you reach the convention center as you come from downtown Cancún.

Maya Fair Plaza/Centro Comercial Maya Fair, frequently called "Mayfair" (© 998/883-2801), is the oldest mall. The lively center holds open-air restaurants and bars, including the Outback Steakhouse and Sanborn's Café, and several stores sell silver, leather, and crafts.

The entertainment-oriented **Forum by the Sea,** Bulevar Kukulkán Km 9 (© 998/883-4425), has shops including Tommy Hilfiger, Levi's, Diesel, Swatch, and Harley Davidson. Most people come here for the food and fun, choosing from Hard Rock Cafe, Coco Bongo, Rainforest Cafe, Sushi-ito, and Santa Fe Beer Factory, plus an extensive food court. It's open daily from 10am to midnight (bars remain open later).

The newest and most intriguing mall is the **La Isla Shopping Village,** Bulevar Kukulkán Km 12.5 (© 998/883-5025; www.laislacancun.com.mx), an open-air festival mall that looks like a small village. Walkways lined with shops and restaurants cross little canals. It also has a "riverwalk" alongside the Nichupté lagoon, and an interactive aquarium and dolphin swim facility, as well as the Spacerocker and River Ride Tour—great for kid-friendly fun. Shops include Guess, Diesel, DKNY, Guess, Bulgari, and Ultrafemme. Dining choices include Johnny Rockets, Come and Eat, Häagen-Dazs, and the beautiful Mexican restaurant La Casa de las Margaritas. You also can find a movie theater, a video arcade, and several nightclubs, including Glazz. It's across from the Sheraton, on the lagoon side of the street.

7 Cancún After Dark

One of Cancún's main draws is its active nightlife. The hottest centers of action are the **Centro Comercial Maya Fair, Forum by the Sea,** and **La Isla Shopping Village.** Hotels also compete, with happy-hour entertainment and special drink prices to entice visitors and guests from other resorts. (Lobby bar–hopping at sunset is one great way to plan next year's vacation.)

THE CLUB & MUSIC SCENE

Clubbing in Cancún is a favorite part of the vacation experience and can go on each night until the sun rises over that incredibly blue sea. Several big hotels have nightclubs or schedule live music in their lobby bars. At the clubs, expect to stand in long lines on weekends, pay a cover charge of $15 to $25 per person, and pay $5 to $8 for a drink. Some of the higher-priced clubs include an open bar or live entertainment. The places listed in this section are air-conditioned and accept American Express, MasterCard, and Visa.

A great idea to get you started is the **Bar Leaping Tour** ★★ (© **998/883-5402**). For $49, it takes you by way of the *Froguibus* from bar to club—the list currently includes Sr. Frog's, Glazz, and Coco Bongo—where you'll bypass any lines and spend about two hours in each place. The price includes entry to the clubs, one welcome drink at each, and transportation by air-conditioned bus, allowing you to get a great sampling of the best of Cancún's nightlife. The tour runs from 8 pm to 3:30 am, with the meeting point at Come and Eat restaurant in the La Isla Hopping Village. American Express, Visa, and MasterCard, are accepted.

Numerous restaurants, such as **Carlos 'n' Charlie's, Hard Rock Cafe, Señor Frog's, TGI Friday's,** and **Iguana Wana,** double as nighttime party spots, offering wild-ish fun at a fraction of the price of more costly clubs.

Bulldog Café (formerly the opulent dance club Christine in the Hotel Krystal), Bulevar Kukulkán Km 7.5 (© **998/848-9800**), is an impressive space with room for over 2,000 revelers and features signature laser-light shows, infused oxygen, large video screens, and even a VIP Jacuzzi for some truly interesting nocturnal fun. The overall ambience is casual and funky. The music ranges from hip-hop to Latino rock, with a heavy emphasis on infectious dance tunes. Bulldog opens at 10 p.m. nightly and stays open until the party winds down. The cover charge is $12 per person or pay $25 for open bar all night long (domestic drinks only).

The City ★★★, Bulevar Kukulkán, Km 9.5 (© **998/848-8380**; www.thecity cancun.com), is currently Cancún's hottest club, featuring progressive electronic music spun by some of the world's top DJs. With visiting DJs from New York, L.A., and Mexico City—Moby even played here—the music is sizzling. You actually need never leave, as The City is a day-and-night club. The City Beach Club opens at 8am, and features a pool with a wave machine for surfing and boogie-boarding, a tower-high waterslide, food and bar service, plus beach cabañas. The Terrace Bar, overlooking the action on Bulevar Kukulkán, serves food and drinks all day long. For a relaxing evening vibe, the Lounge features comfy couches, chill music, and an extensive menu of martinis, snacks, and deserts. Open at 10pm, the 7,600-sq.-m (25,000-sq.-ft.) nightclub has nine bars, stunning light shows, and several VIP areas. Located in front of Coco Bongo, The City also has a second location in Playa del Carmen.

Carlos 'n' Charlie's, Bulevar Kukulkán Km 4.5 (© **998/883-1862**), is a reliable place to find both good food and packed-frat-house entertainment in the evening. There's a dance floor; live music starts nightly around 8:30pm. A cover charge kicks in if you're not planning to eat. It's open daily from 11am to 2am.

With recorded music, **Carlos O'Brian's,** Tulum 107, SM22 (© **998/883-1092**), is only slightly tamer than other Carlos Anderson restaurants and nightspots in town (Señor Frog and Carlos 'n' Charlie's). It's open daily from 9am to midnight.

Continuing its reputation as one of the hottest spots in town is **Coco Bongo** ★★ in Forum by the Sea, Bulevar Kukulkán Km 9.5 (© **998/883-5061**; www.cocobongo. com.mx). Its main appeal is that it has no formal dance floor, so you can dance anywhere—and that includes on the tables, on the bar, or even on the stage with the live band! This place can—and regularly does—pack in up to 3,000 people. You have to experience it to believe it. Despite its capacity, lines are long on weekends and in high season. The music alternates between Caribbean, salsa, house, hip-hop, techno, and classics from the 1970s and 1980s. It draws a mixed crowd, but the young and hip dominate. Choose between a $15 cover or $25 with an open bar.

Dady'O, Bulevar Kukulkán Km 9.5 (© **998/883-3333**), is a highly favored rave with frequent long lines. It opens nightly at 10pm and generally charges a cover of $15.

Dady Rock Bar and Grill, Bulevar Kukulkán Km 9.5 (© **998/883-1626**), the off-spring of Dady'O, opens at 6pm and goes as long as any other nightspot, offering a combination of live bands and DJs spinning music, along with an open bar, full meals, a buffet, and dancing.

Glazz, in the La Isla Shopping Village, Bulevar Kukulkán Km 12.5, Local B-7 (© **998/883-1881;** www.glazz.com/mx), is Cancún's newest nocturnal offering, combining a restaurant with a sleek lounge and sophisticated nightclub for a complete evening of entertainment. Geared for those over 30, music is mostly lounge and house, and there are live entertainment acts (anything from drummers to sultry dancers) periodically through the evening. The staff is known as being among the top in town. The China Bistro is already earning rave reviews, while the Lounge's vast selection of martinis and tequilitinis is dangerously tempting. The Club is pure Miami-style, with plenty of neon and a very hot DJ. It's open nightly from 7pm to 5am. Cover is $10, and a dress code prohibits sandals or shorts.

Hard Rock Cafe, in Plaza Lagunas Mall and Forum by the Sea (© **998/881-8120** or 998/883-2024; www.hardrock.com), schedules a live band at 10:30pm Thursday through Tuesday night. At other times you get lively recorded music to munch by—the menu combines the most popular foods from American and Mexican cultures. It's open daily from 11am to 2am.

La Boom, Bulevar Kukulkán Km 3.5 (© **998/883-1152;** fax 998/883-1458; www.laboom.com.mx), has two sections: one side is a video bar, the other a bi-level dance club with cranking music. Each night there's a special deal: no cover, free bar, ladies' night, bikini night, and others. Popular with early-20-somethings, it's open nightly from 10pm to 6am. A sound-and-light show begins at 11:30pm in the dance club. The cover varies depending on the night—most nights women enter free, and men pay $15 to $30, which includes an open bar.

The most refined and upscale of Cancún's nightly gathering spots is the **Lobby Lounge** at the **Ritz-Carlton Hotel** ✦ (© **998/885-0808**), with live dance music and a list of more than 120 premium tequilas for tasting or sipping.

THE PERFORMING ARTS

Several hotels host **Mexican fiesta nights,** including a buffet dinner and a folkloric dance show; admission, including dinner, ranges from $35 to $50.

You can also get in the party mood at **Mango Tango** ✦, Bulevar Kukulkán Km 14.2 (© **998/885-0303**), a lagoon-side restaurant and dinner-show establishment opposite the Ritz-Carlton Hotel. Diners can choose from two levels, one nearer the music and the other overlooking it all. Music is loud and varied but mainly features reggae or salsa. A 45-minute floor show starts nightly at 8:30pm. A variety of packages are available—starting at $40 per person—depending on whether you want dinner and the show, open bar and the show, or the show alone. For dancing, which starts at 9:30pm, there's a $10 cover charge. See "Where to Dine," earlier in this chapter, for a restaurant review.

Tourists mingle with locals at the downtown **Parque de las Palapas** (the main park) for Noches Caribeñas, which involves free live tropical music for anyone who wants to listen and dance. Performances begin at 7:30pm on Sunday, and sometimes there are performances on Friday and Saturday.

Isla Mujeres & Cozumel

by David Baird & Lynne Bairstow

Mexico's two main Caribbean islands are idyllic places to get away from the hustle and bustle of Cancún and the Riviera Maya. Neither Isla Mujeres nor Cozumel is particularly large, and they have that island feel—small roads that don't go very far, lots of mopeds, few (or no) buses and trucks, and a sense of being set apart from the rest of the world. Yet they're just a short ferry ride from the mainland. Both offer a variety of lodging choices, ample outdoor activities, and a laid-back atmosphere that makes a delightful contrast with the mainland experience.

EXPLORING MEXICO'S CARIBBEAN ISLANDS

ISLA MUJERES   A day trip to Isla Mujeres on a party boat is one of the most popular excursions from Cancún. This fish-shaped island is just 13km (8 miles) northeast of Cancún, a quick boat ride away, allowing ample time to get a taste of the peaceful pace of life. To fully explore the village and its shops and cafes, relax at the broad, tranquil Playa Norte, or snorkel or dive El Garrafón Reef (an underwater park), you'll need more time. Overnight accommodations range from rustic to offbeat chic.

Passenger ferries go to Isla Mujeres from Puerto Juárez, and car ferries leave from Punta Sam, both near Cancún. More expensive passenger ferries, with less frequent departures, leave from the Playa Linda pier on Cancún Island.

COZUMEL   Cozumel is larger than Isla Mujeres and farther from the mainland (19km/12 miles off the coast from Playa del Carmen). It has its own international airport. Life here turns around two major activities: scuba diving and being a port of call for cruise ships. It is far and away the most popular destination along this coast for both. Despite the cruise ship traffic and all the stores that it has spawned, life on the island moves at a relaxed and comfortable pace. There is just one town, San Miguel de Cozumel. North and south of town are resorts; the rest of the shore is deserted and predominantly rocky, with a scattering of small sandy coves that you can have practically all to yourself.

1 Isla Mujeres ★★★

16km (10 miles) N of Cancún

Isla Mujeres (Island of Women) is a casual, laid-back refuge from the conspicuously commercialized action of Cancún, visible across a narrow channel. It's known as the best value in the Caribbean, assuming that you favor an easy-going vacation pace and prefer simplicity to pretense. This is an island of white-sand beaches and turquoise waters, complemented by a town filled with Caribbean-colored clapboard houses and rustic, open-air restaurants. Hotels are clean and comfortable, but if you're looking for

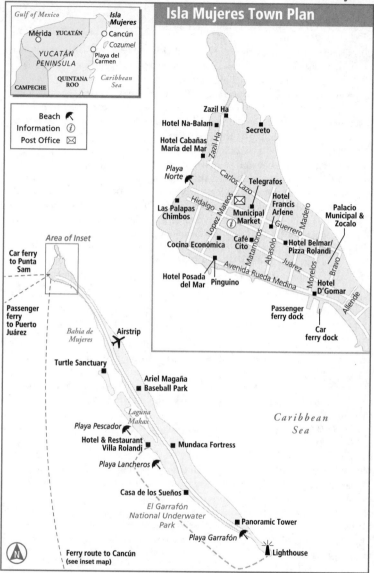

Isla Mujeres Town Plan

Gulf of Mexico

Isla Mujeres

Mérida YUCATÁN

Cancún

Cozumel

YUCATÁN PENINSULA

Playa del Carmen

CAMPECHE

QUINTANA ROO

Caribbean Sea

Beach

Information ⓘ

Post Office ⊠

Zazil Ha

Hotel Na-Balam

Secreto

Hotel Cabañas María del Mar

Zazil Ha

Playa Norte

Carlos Lazo

Telegrafos

Hidalgo

Las Palapas Chimbos

Lopez Mateos

Municipal Market

Hotel Francis Arlene

Guerrero

Madero

Palacio Municipal & Zocalo

Cocina Económica

Café Cito

Matamoros

Abasolo

Hotel Belmar/ Pizza Rolandi

Juárez

Morelos

Bravo

Allende

Hotel Posada del Mar   Pinguino

Avenida Rueda Medina

Hotel D'Gomar

Passenger ferry dock

Car ferry dock

Area of Inset

Car ferry to Punta Sam

Passenger ferry to Puerto Juárez

Bahia de Mujeres

Airstrip

Turtle Sanctuary

Ariel Magaña Baseball Park

Laguna Makax

Caribbean Sea

Playa Pescador

Hotel & Restaurant Villa Rolandi

Mundaca Fortress

Playa Lancheros

Casa de los Sueños

El Garrafón National Underwater Park

Panoramic Tower

Playa Garrafón

Lighthouse

N

Ferry route to Cancún (see inset map)

lots of action or opulence, you'll be happier in Cancún. A few recent additions provide more luxurious lodging, but they still maintain a decidedly casual atmosphere.

Francisco Hernández de Córdoba, seeing figurines of partially clad females along the shore, gave the island its name when he landed in 1517. These are now believed to have been offerings to the Maya goddess of fertility and the moon, Ixchel. Their presence indicates that the island was probably sacred to the Maya.

> ### (Tips) The Best Websites for Isla Mujeres & Cozumel
>
> - **Isla Mujeres Tourist Information: www.isla-mujeres.net**   The official site of the Isla Mujeres Tourism Board provides complete information on Isla, from getting there to where to stay.
> - **Cozumel.net: www.cozumel.net**   This site is a cut above the typical dining/lodging/activities sites. Click on "About Cozumel" to find schedules for ferries and island-hop flights, and to check the latest news. There's also a comprehensive listing of B&Bs and vacation home rentals, plus great info on diving, maps, and a chat room.
> - **Cozumel Travel Planner: www.go2cozumel.com**   This is a well-done guide to area businesses and attractions, by an online Mexico specialist.
> - **Travel Notes: www.travelnotes.cc**   This site boasts more than 1,000 pages of information on and photos of Cozumel island—with an emphasis on diving, deep sea fishing, and other ocean activities.
> - **Cozumel Hotel Association: www.islacozumel.com.mx**   Operated by the tourism-promotion arm of the hotel association, this site gives more than just listings of the member hotels. There's info on packages and specials, plus brief descriptions of most of the island's attractions, restaurants, and recreational activities.

At midday, suntanned visitors hang out in open-air cafes and stroll streets lined with frantic souvenir vendors. Calling attention to their bargain-priced wares, they give a carnival atmosphere to the hours when tour-boat traffic is at its peak. Befitting the size of the island, most of the traffic consists of golf carts, *motos* (mopeds), and bicycles. Once the tour boats leave, however, Isla Mujeres reverts to its more typical, tranquil way of life.

Days in "Isla"—as the locals call it—can alternate between adventurous activity and absolute repose. Trips to the Isla Contoy bird sanctuary are popular, as are the excellent diving, fishing, and snorkeling—in 1998, the island's coral coast became part of Mexico's Marine National Park. The island and several of its traditional hotels attract regular gatherings of yoga practitioners. In the evening, most people find the slow, casual pace one of the island's biggest draws. The cool night breeze is a perfect accompaniment to casual open-air dining and drinking in small street-side restaurants. Many people pack it in as early as 9 or 10pm, when most of the businesses close. Those in search of a party, however, will find kindred souls at the bars on Playa Norte that stay open late.

ESSENTIALS

GETTING THERE & DEPARTING   Puerto Juárez (© **998/877-0618**), just north of Cancún, is the dock for passenger ferries to Isla Mujeres, the least expensive way to travel to Isla. The air-conditioned *Caribbean Express* leaves every half-hour, makes the trip in 20 minutes, has storage space for luggage, and costs about $4. These boats operate daily, starting at 6:30am and ending at 8:30pm. They might leave early if they're full, so arrive ahead of schedule. Pay at the ticket office—or, if the ferry is about to leave, aboard.

Note: Upon arrival by taxi or bus in Puerto Juárez, be wary of pirate "guides" who tell you either that the ferry is canceled or that it's several hours until the next ferry. They'll offer the services of a private *lancha* (small boat) for about $40—and it's nothing but a scam. Small boats are available and, on a co-op basis, charge $15 to $25 one-way, based on the number of passengers. They take about 50 minutes and are not recommended on days with rough seas. Check with the clearly visible ticket office—the only accurate source—for information.

Taxi fares are posted by the street where the taxis park, so be sure to check the rate before agreeing to a taxi for the ride back to Cancún. Rates generally run $12 to $15, depending upon your destination. Moped and bicycle rentals are also readily available as you depart the ferry. This small complex also has public bathrooms, luggage storage, a snack bar, and souvenir shops.

Isla Mujeres is so small that a vehicle isn't necessary, but if you're taking one, you'll use the **Punta Sam** port a little beyond Puerto Juárez. The ferry (40 min.) runs five or six times daily between 8am and 8pm, year-round except in bad weather. Times are generally as follows: Cancún to Isla 8, 11am, 2:45, 5:30, and 8:15pm; Isla to Cancún 6:30, 9:30am, 12:45, 4:15, and 7:15pm. Always check with the tourist office in Cancún to verify this schedule. Cars should arrive an hour before the ferry departure to register for a place in line and pay the posted fee, which varies depending on the weight and type of vehicle. The sole gas pump in Isla is at the intersection of Avenida Rueda Medina and Calle Abasolo, just northwest of the ferry docks.

There are also ferries to Isla Mujeres from the **Playa Linda,** known as the Embarcadero pier in Cancún, but they're less frequent and more expensive than those from Puerto Juárez. A **Water Taxi** (© **998/886-4270** or 998/886-4847; asterix@cablered.net.mx) to Isla Mujeres operates from **Playa Caracol,** between the Fiesta Americana Coral Beach Hotel and the Xcaret terminal on the island, with prices about the same as those from Playa Linda and about four times the cost of the public ferries from Puerto Juárez. Scheduled departures are at 9am, 11am, and 1pm, with returns from Isla Mujeres at noon and 5pm. Adult round-trip fares are $15; kids 3 to 12 pay $7.50; free for children under 3.

To get to Puerto Juárez or Punta Sam from **Cancún,** take any Ruta 8 city bus from Avenida Tulum. If you're coming from **Mérida,** you can fly to Cancún and proceed to Puerto Juárez or take a bus directly to Puerto Juárez. From **Cozumel,** you can fly to Cancún (there are daily flights) or take a ferry to Playa del Carmen (see "Cozumel," later in this chapter), then travel to Puerto Juárez.

Arriving   Ferries arrive at the ferry docks (© **998/877-0065**) in the center of town. The main road that passes in front is Avenida Rueda Medina. Most hotels are close by. Tricycle taxis are the least expensive and most fun way to get to your hotel; you and your luggage pile in the open carriage compartment, and the driver pedals through the streets. Regular taxis are always lined up in a parking lot to the right of the pier, with their rates posted. If someone on the ferry offers to arrange a taxi for you, politely decline, unless you'd like some help with your luggage down the short pier—it just means an extra, unnecessary tip for your helper.

VISITOR INFORMATION   The **City Tourist Office** (©/fax **998/877-0767** or 998/877-0307) is at Av. Rueda Medina 130, on your left as you reach the end of the pier. It's open Monday through Friday from 8am to 8pm, Saturday from 8am to 2pm. Also look for *Islander,* a free publication with local information, advertisements, and event listings.

ISLAND LAYOUT Isla Mujeres is about 8km (5 miles) long and 4km (2½ miles) wide, with the town at the northern tip. "Downtown" is a compact 4 blocks by 6 blocks, so it's very easy to get around. The **ferry docks** are at the center of town, within walking distance of most hotels, restaurants, and shops. The street running along the waterfront is **Avenida Rueda Medina,** commonly called the *malecón* **(boardwalk).** The **Mercado Municipal (town market)** is by the post office on **Calle Guerrero,** an inland street at the north edge of town, which, like most streets in the town, is unmarked.

GETTING AROUND A popular form of transportation on Isla Mujeres is the electric **golf cart,** available for rent at many hotels for $15 per hour or $45 per day. **El Sol Golf Cart Rental,** Av. Francisco I. Madero 5 (*C* **998/877-0791** or 998/877-0068), will deliver, or you can pick one up. The golf carts don't go more than 32kmph (20 mph), but they're fun. Anyway, you aren't on Isla Mujeres to hurry. Many people enjoy touring the island by *moto* **(motorized bike or scooter).** Fully automatic versions are available for around $25 per day or $7 per hour. They come with seats for one person, but some are large enough for two. There's only one main road with a couple of offshoots, so you won't get lost. Be aware that the rental price does not include insurance, and any injury to yourself or the vehicle will come out of your pocket. **Bicycles** are also available for rent at some hotels for $3 per hour or $7 per day, including a basket and a lock.

If you prefer to use a taxi, rates are about $2.50 for trips within the downtown area, or $4.50 for a trip to the southern end of Isla. You can also hire them for about $10 per hour. The number to call for taxis is *C* **998/877-0066.**

FAST FACTS: Isla Mujeres

Area Code The telephone area code is **998.**

Consumer Protection You can reach the local branch of **Profeco** consumer protection agency at *C* **998/877-0106.**

Currency Exchange Isla Mujeres has numerous *casas de cambio,* or money exchanges, that you can easily spot along the main streets. Most of the hotels listed here change money for their guests, although often at less favorable rates than the commercial enterprises. There is only one bank in Isla, HSBC Bank, across from the ferry docks *C* **998/877-0104.** It's open Monday through Friday from 8:30am to 6pm, and Saturdays from 9am to 2pm.

Hospital The **Hospital de la Armada** is on Avenida Rueda Medina at Ojón P. Blanco (*C* **998/877-0001**). It's less than a kilometer (½ mile) south of the town center. It will only treat you in an emergency. Otherwise, you're referred to the **Centro de Salud** on Avenida Guerrero, a block before the beginning of the Malecón (*C* **998/877-0117**).

Internet Access Owned by a lifelong resident of Isla, **Cyber Isla Mujres.com,** Av. Francisco y Madero 17, between Hidalgo and Juaréz streets (*C* **998/877-0272**), offers Internet access for $1.50 per hour from Monday to Sunday 8am to 10pm, and serves complimentary coffee from Veracruz all day.

Pharmacy **Isla Mujeres Farmacia** (© **998/877-0178**) has the best selection of prescription and over-the-counter medicines. It's on Calle Benito Juárez, between Morelos and Bravo, across from Rachet & Rome jewelry store.

Post & Telegraph Office The *correo* is at Calle Guerrero 12 (© **998/877-0085**), at the corner of López Mateos, near the market. It's open Monday through Friday from 9am to 4pm.

Taxis To call for a taxi, dial © **998/877-0066**.

Telephone Ladatel phones accepting coins and prepaid phone cards are at the plaza and throughout town. **DigaMe,** Av. Guerrero between Matamoros and Abasolo (© **608/467-4202**; info@digame.com), has mobile phone rentals, private voicemail service, and long-distance phone services available.

Tourist Seasons Isla Mujeres's tourist season (when hotel rates are higher) is a bit different from that of other places in Mexico. High season runs December through May, a month longer than in Cancún. Some hotels raise their rates in August, and some raise their rates beginning in mid-November. Low season is from June to mid-November.

BEACHES & OUTDOOR ACTIVITIES

THE BEACHES   The most popular beach in town is alternately referred to as Playa Cocoteros ("Cocos," for short), or **Playa Norte** ⊕. The long stretch of beach extends around the northern tip of the island, to your left as you get off the boat. This is a truly splendid beach—a wide stretch of fine white sand and calm, translucent, turquoise-blue water. Topless sunbathing is permitted. The beach is easily reached on foot from the ferry and from all downtown hotels. Watersports equipment, beach umbrellas, and lounge chairs are available for rent. Those in front of restaurants usually cost nothing if you use the restaurant as your headquarters for drinks and food.

El Garrafón Natural Park ⊕⊕ (see "Snorkeling," below) is best known as a snorkeling area, but there is a nice stretch of beach on either side of the park. **Playa Lancheros** is on the Caribbean side of Laguna Makax. Local buses go to Lancheros, then turn inland and return downtown. The beach at Playa Lancheros is nice, but the few restaurants there are expensive.

SWIMMING   Wide Playa Norte is the best swimming beach, with Playa Lancheros second. There are no lifeguards on duty on Isla Mujeres, which does not use the system of water-safety flags employed in Cancún and Cozumel.

SNORKELING   By far the most popular place to snorkel is **El Garrafón Natural Park** ⊕⊕. It is at the southern end of the island, where you'll see numerous schools of colorful fish. The well-equipped park has two restaurant-bars, beach chairs, a swimming pool, kayaks, changing rooms, rental lockers, showers, a gift shop, and snack bars. Once a public national underwater park, Garrafón, since late 1999, has been operated by the same people who manage Xcaret, south of Cancún. Public facilities have been vastly improved, with new attractions and facilities added each year. Activities at the park include snorkeling and "Snuba" (a tankless version of scuba diving, when you descend while breathing through a long air tube), crystal-clear canoes for viewing underwater life, and a zip-line that takes you over the water. The underwater minisub **Sea Trek** provides a great view of the submarine landscape, and you can keep dry, if that's your preference. On land, they have tanning decks, shaded hammocks, a 12m (40-ft.) climbing tower, and—of course!—a souvenir superstore. Several restaurants and snack bars are available. Admission is $29 for adults, $15 for children (American Express, MasterCard, and Visa are accepted). You can also choose a package ($59) that includes food, beverages, locker rental, and snorkeling gear rental. Daytrip packages from Cancún (© **998/884-9422** or 984/875-6000) are also available. Prices start at $22 and include round-trip transportation from the pier on Km 4 outside Cancún. The park is open daily from 9am to 5pm.

Also good for snorkeling is the **Manchones Reef,** off the southeastern coast. The reef is just offshore and accessible by boat.

Another excellent location is around *el faro* (the lighthouse) in the **Bahía de Mujeres** at the southern tip of the island, where the water is about 2m (6 ft.) deep. Boatmen will take you for around $25 per person if you have your own snorkeling equipment or $30 if you use theirs.

DIVING   Most of the dive shops on the island offer the same trips for the same prices: one-tank dives cost $55, two-tank dives $70. **Bahía Dive Shop,** Rueda Medina 166, across from the car-ferry dock (© **998/877-0340**), is a full-service shop that offers resort and certification classes as well as dive equipment for sale or rent. The shop is open daily from 10am to 7pm, and accepts MasterCard and Visa. Another respected dive shop is **Coral Scuba Center,** at Matamoros 13A and Rueda Medina (© **998/877-0061** or 998/877-0763). It's open daily from 8am to 12:30pm and 4 to 10pm.

PADI-certified dive guides and dive instruction is available at **El Garrafón** (© **984/ 875-6000**). Discover Scuba classed are available for $65, with one-tank dives to the Garrafón reef priced at $45, or two-tank dives for $60. Open Water, Advanced, and Rescue PADI certification is also available.

Cuevas de los Tiburones (Caves of the Sleeping Sharks) is Isla's most renowned dive site—but the name is slightly misleading, as shark sightings are rare these days. Two sites where you could traditionally see the sleeping shark are the Cuevas de Tiburones and **La Punta,** but be forewarned—the sharks have mostly been driven off, and a storm collapsed the arch featured in a Jacques Cousteau film showing them, but the caves survive. Other dive sites include a **wreck** 15km (9 miles) offshore; **Banderas** reef, between Isla Mujeres and Cancún, where there's always a strong current; **Tabos** reef on the eastern shore; and **Manchones** reef, 1km (½ mile) off the southeastern tip of the island, where the water is 4.5 to 11m (15–35 ft.) deep. **The Cross of the Bay** is close to Manchones reef. A bronze cross, weighing 1 ton and standing 12m (40 ft.) high, was placed in the water between Manchones and Isla in 1994, as a memorial to those who have lost their lives at sea.

FISHING   To arrange a day of fishing, ask at the **Sociedad Cooperativa Turística** (the boatmen's cooperative), on Avenida Rueda Medina (no phone), next to Mexico Divers and Las Brisas restaurant, or the travel agency mentioned in "A Visit to Isla Contoy," below. Four to six others can share the cost, which includes lunch and drinks. Captain Tony Martínez (© **998/877-0274**) also arranges fishing trips aboard the *Marinonis,* with advanced reservations recommended. Year-round you'll find bonito, mackerel, kingfish, and amberjack. Sailfish and sharks (hammerhead, bull, nurse, lemon, and tiger) are in good supply in April and May. In winter, larger grouper and jewfish are prevalent. Four hours of fishing close to shore costs around $110;

8 hours farther out goes for $250. The cooperative is open Monday through Saturday from 8am to 1pm and 5 to 8pm, and Sunday from 7:30 to 10am and 6 to 8pm.

YOGA   Increasingly, Isla is becoming known as a great place to combine a relaxing beach vacation with yoga practice and instruction. The trend began at **Hotel Na Balam** ★★ (© **998/877-0279** or 998/877-0058; www.nabalam.com), which offers yoga classes under its large poolside *palapa,* complete with yoga mats and props. The classes, which begin at 9am Monday through Friday, are free to guests, $10 per class to visitors. Na Balam is also the site of frequent yoga instruction vacations featuring respected teachers and a more extensive practice schedule; the current schedule of yoga retreats is posted on their website. Local yoga culture extends down the island to Casa de los Sueños Resort and Zenter (© **998/877-0651;** www.casadelossuenosresort. com), where yoga classes, as well as chi gong and Pilates, are regularly held.

MORE ATTRACTIONS

DOLPHIN DISCOVERY ★★   You can swim with live dolphins (© **998/877-0207,** or 998/849-4757 in Cancún; fax 998/849-4751; www.dolphindiscovery.com) in an enclosure at Treasure Island, on the side of Isla Mujeres that faces Cancún. Groups of six people swim with two dolphins and one trainer. Swimmers view an educational video and spend time in the water with the trainer and the dolphins before enjoying 15 minutes of free swimming time with them. Reservations are recommended, and you must arrive an hour before your assigned swimming time, at 9am, 11am, 1pm, or 3pm. The cost is $125 per person, plus $10 if you need round-trip transportation from Cancún.

A TURTLE SANCTUARY ★★   As recently as 20 years ago, fishermen converged on the island nightly from May to September, waiting for the monster-size turtles to lumber ashore to deposit their Ping-Pong-ball-shaped eggs. Totally vulnerable once they begin laying their eggs, and exhausted when they have finished, the turtles were easily captured and slaughtered for their highly prized meat, shell, and eggs. Then a concerned fisherman, Gonzalez Cahle Maldonado, began convincing others to spare at least the eggs, which he protected. It was a start. Following his lead, the fishing secretariat founded the **Centro de Investigaciones** 11 years ago; although the local government provided assistance in the past, now the center relies solely on private donations. Since opening, at least 28,000 turtles have been released, and every year local schoolchildren participate in the event, thus planting the notion of protecting the turtles for a new generation of islanders.

Six species of sea turtles nest on Isla Mujeres. An adult green turtle, the most abundant species, measures 1 to 1.5m (4–5 ft.) in length and can weigh as much as 450 pounds. At the center, visitors walk through the indoor and outdoor turtle pool areas, where the creatures paddle around. The turtles are separated by age, from newly hatched up to 1 year. People who come here usually end up staying at least an hour, especially if they opt for the guided tour, which I recommend. They also have a small gift shop and snack bar. The sanctuary is on a piece of land separated from the island by Bahía de Mujeres and Laguna Makax, at Carr. Sac Bajo 5; you'll need a taxi to get there. Admission is $3; the shelter is open daily from 9am to 5pm. For more information, call © **998/877-0595.**

SIGHTS OF PUNTA SUR ★★   Also at Punta Sur (the southern point of the island, just inland from **Garrafón National Park** (© **998/877-1100;** www.garrafon.com) and part of the Park, is Isla's newest attraction, the **Panoramic Tower.** At 50m (225 ft.)

high, the tower offers visitors a birds' eye view of the entire island. The tower holds 20 visitors at a time, and rotates for ten minutes while you can snap photos or simply enjoy the scenery. Entry fee is $5, a professional photo of you at the tower (touch-ups are included!) is $10, and package prices are available.

Next to the tower you'll find **Sculptured Spaces,** an impressive and extensive garden of large sculptures donated to Isla Mujeres by internationally renowned sculptors as part of the 2001 First International Sculpture Exhibition. Among Mexican sculptors represented are works by Jose Luis Cuevas and Vlaadimir Cora.

Nearby is the **Caribbean Village,** with narrow lanes of colorful clapboard buildings that house cafes and shops displaying folkloric art. Plan to have lunch or a snack here at the kiosk and stroll around, before heading on to the lighthouse and Mayan ruins.

Also at this southern point of the island, and part of the ruins is **Cliff of the Dawn,** the southeastern-most point of Mexico. Services are available from 7am to 8pm, but you can enter at any time; if you make it there early enough to see the sun rise, you can claim you were the first person in Mexico that day to be touched by the sun!

A MAYA RUIN 🏛🏛 Just beyond the lighthouse, at the southern end of the island, are the strikingly beautiful remains of a small Maya temple, believed to have been built to pay homage to the moon and fertility goddess Ixchel. The location, on a lofty bluff overlooking the sea, is worth seeing and makes a great place for photos. It is believed that Maya women traveled here on annual pilgrimages to seek Ixchel's blessings of fertility. If you're at El Garrafón park and want to walk, it's not too far. Turn right from El Garrafón. When you see the lighthouse, turn toward it down the rocky path.

A PIRATE'S FORTRESS The Fortress of Mundaca is about 4km (2½ miles) in the same direction as El Garrafón, less than a kilometer (about ½ mile) to the left. A slave trader who claimed to have been the pirate Mundaca Marecheaga built the fortress. In the early 19th century, he arrived at Isla Mujeres and set up a blissful paradise, while making money selling slaves to Cuba and Belize. According to island lore, he decided to settle down and build this hacienda after being captivated by the charms of an island girl. However, she reputedly spurned his affections and married another islander, leaving him heartbroken and alone on Isla Mujeres. Admission is $2; the fortress is open daily from 10am to 6pm.

A VISIT TO ISLA CONTOY 🏛 If possible, plan to visit this pristine uninhabited island, 30km (20 miles) by boat from Isla Mujeres, that became a national wildlife reserve in 1981. Lush vegetation covers the oddly shaped island, which is 6km (3¾ miles) long and harbors 70 species of birds as well as a host of marine and animal life. Bird species that nest on the island include pelicans, brown boobies, frigates, egrets, terns, and cormorants. Flocks of flamingos arrive in April. June, July, and August are good months to spot turtles burying their eggs in the sand at night. Most excursions troll for fish (which will be your lunch), anchor en route for a snorkeling expedition, skirt the island at a leisurely pace for close viewing of the birds without disturbing the habitat, and then pull ashore. While the captain prepares lunch, visitors can swim, sun, follow the nature trails, and visit the fine nature museum, which has bathroom facilities. The trip from Isla Mujeres takes about 45 minutes each way and can be longer if the waves are choppy. Because of the tight-knit boatmen's cooperative, prices for this excursion are the same everywhere: $40. You can buy a ticket at the **Sociedad Cooperativa Turística** on Avenida Rueda Medina, next to Mexico Divers and Las Brisas restaurant (no phone), or at one of several **travel agencies,** such as **La Isleña,**

on Morelos between Medina and Juárez (© **998/877-0578**). La Isleña is open daily from 7:30am to 9:30pm and is a good source for tourist information. Isla Contoy trips leave at 8:30am and return around 4pm. The price (cash only) is $37 for adults, $18 for children. Boat captains should respect the cooperative's regulations regarding ecological sensitivity, and boat safety, including the availability of life jackets for everyone on board. Snorkeling equipment is usually included in the price, but double-check that before heading out. On the island, there is a small government museum with bathroom facilities.

SHOPPING

Shopping is a casual activity here. There are only a few shops of any sophistication. Shop owners will bombard you, especially on Avenida Hidalgo, selling Saltillo rugs, onyx, silver, Guatemalan clothing, blown glassware, masks, folk art, beach paraphernalia, and T-shirts in abundance. Prices are lower than in Cancún or Cozumel, but with such overeager sellers, bargaining is necessary.

The one treasure you're likely to take back is a piece of fine jewelry—Isla is known for its excellent, duty-free prices on gemstones and handcrafted work made to order. Diamonds, emeralds, sapphires, and rubies can be purchased as loose stones and then mounted while you're off exploring. The superbly crafted gold, silver, and gems are available at very competitive prices in the workshops near the central plaza. The stones are also available in the rough. **Rachet & Rome** (© **998/877-0331**) located at the corner of Morelos and Juárez streets, is the grandest store, with a broad selection of jewelry at competitive prices. It's open daily from 9:30am to 5pm and accepts all major credit cards.

WHERE TO STAY

You'll find plenty of hotels in all price ranges on Isla Mujeres. Rates peak during high season, which is the most expensive and most crowded time to go. Elizabeth Wenger of **Four Seasons Travel** in Montello, Wisconsin (© **800/552-4550**), specializes in Mexico travel and books a lot of hotels in Isla Mujeres. Her service is invaluable in the high season. Those interested in private home rentals or longer-term stays can contact **Mundaca Travel and Real Estate** in Isla Mujeres (© **998/877-0025;** fax 998/877-0076; www.mundacartravel.com).

VERY EXPENSIVE

Casa de los Sueños Resort & Spa Zenter ★★★   This "house of dreams" is easily Isla Mujeres's most intimate, sophisticated, and relaxing property. Though it was originally built as a private residence, luckily it became an upscale, adults-only B&B in early 1998 (it has since changed ownership), and now caters to guests looking for a rejuvenating experience, with its adjoining "Zenter" offering spa services and yoga classes. Its location on the southern end of the island, adjacent to El Garrafón National Park, also makes it ideal for snorkeling and diving enthusiasts. The captivating design features vivid sherbet-colored walls—think watermelon, mango, and blueberry—and a sculpted architecture. There's a large, open interior courtyard; tropical gardens; a sunken living area (with wireless Internet access); and an Infinity pool that melts into the cool Caribbean waters. All rooms have balconies or terraces and face west, offering stunning views of the sunset over the sea, as well as the night lights of Cancún. In addition, the rooms—which have names such as "Serenity," "Passion," and "Love"—also have large, marble bathrooms, Frette bedding, and L'Occitane bath amenities, and are decorated in a serene style that blends Asian simplicity with Mexican details. One master suite ideal for honeymooners has an exceptionally spacious bathroom area, complete with whirlpool and steam room shower, plus other deluxe amenities. Complementary continental breakfast is served in your room, and a restaurant adjacent to their private pier serves healthful, fusion cuisine—it's open to nonguests as well. The Zenter offers a very complete menu of massages and holistic spa treatments, as well as yoga classes, held either outdoors or in a serene indoor space.

Carretera Garrafón s/n, 77400 Isla Mujeres, Q. Roo. ⓒ **998/877-0651** or 998/877-0369. Fax 998/877-0708. www.casadelossuenosresort.com. 7 units. High season $300–$450 double; low season $240–$360 double. Rates include continental breakfast. MC, V. No children. **Amenities:** Restaurant; Infinity pool; spa, yoga center, and open-air massage area; 24-hr. room service; breakfast delivery. *In room:* TV/VCR, hair dryer, iron, safe.

Hotel Villa Rolandi Gourmet & Beach Club ★★★ This hotel has become a great addition to Isla's options for guests who enjoy its tranquillity—but also like being pampered. Villa Rolandi is a great value for a luxury stay, with Mediterranean-style rooms that offer every conceivable amenity, as well as its own small, private beach in a sheltered cove. Each of the oversize suites has an ocean view and a large terrace or balcony with a full-size private whirlpool. TVs offer satellite music and movies, and rooms all have a sophisticated in-room sound system. A recessed seating area extends out to the balcony or terrace. Bathrooms are large and tastefully decorated in deep-hued Tikal marble. The stained-glass shower has dual showerheads, stereo speakers, and jet options, and converts into a steam room.

Dining is an integral part of a stay at Villa Rolandi. Its owner is a Swiss-born restaurateur who made a name for himself with his restaurants on Isla Mujeres and in Cancún (see Casa Rolandi and Pizza Rolandi under "Where to Dine," below). This intimate hideaway with personalized service is ideal for honeymooners, who receive a complimentary bottle of domestic champagne upon arrival (when the hotel is notified in advance).

Fracc. Lagunamar SM 7 Mza. 75 L 15 and 16, 77400 Isla Mujeres, Q. Roo. ⓒ **998/877-0700.** Fax 998/877-0100. www.villarolandi.com. 20 units. High season $350–$420 double; low season $290–$350 double. Rates include round-trip transportation from Playa Linda in Cancún aboard private catamaran yacht; continental breakfast; and a la carte lunch or dinner in the on-site restaurant. AE, MC, V. Children under 14 not accepted. **Amenities:** Restaurant (see "Where to Dine," below); infinity pool w/waterfall; small fitness room w/basic equipment and open-air massage area; concierge; tour desk; 24-hr. room service; breakfast delivery. *In room:* TV/VCR, dataport, minibar, hair dryer, iron, safe.

EXPENSIVE

Hotel Na Balam ★★ *Finds* Na Balam is known as a haven for yoga students and those interested in an introspective vacation. This popular, two-story hotel near the end of Playa Norte has comfortable rooms on a quiet, ideally located portion of the beach. Rooms are in three sections; some face the beach, and others are across the street in a garden setting with a swimming pool. All rooms have a terrace or balcony with hammocks. Each spacious suite contains a king or two double beds, a seating area, and folk-art decorations. Two were redecorated in 2004 in a more sophisticated style, and with small pools with hydromassage situated under coconut trees—ask if these are available for the best of Na Balam. Though other rooms are newer, the older section is well kept, with a bottom-floor patio facing the peaceful, palm-filled, sandy inner yard and Playa Norte. Yoga classes (free for guests; $10 per class for nonguests) start at 9am Monday through Friday. The restaurant, **Zazil Ha,** is one of the island's most popular (see "Where to Dine," below). A beachside bar serves a selection of natural juices and is one of the most popular spots for sunset watching.

Zazil Ha 118, 77400 Isla Mujeres, Q. Roo. ✆ **998/877-0279.** Fax 998/877-0446. www.nabalam.com. 31 units. High season $162–$270 suite; low season $121–$200 suite. Ask about weekly and monthly rates. AE, MC, V. **Amenities:** Restaurant; 2 bars; swimming pool; mopeds, golf carts, and bikes for rent; game room w/TV, VCR, and Ping-Pong tables; salon; in-room massage; babysitting; laundry service; library; Internet access; yoga classes; diving and snorkeling trips available. *In room:* A/C, fan.

Secreto ★★ *Finds* This new boutique hotel looks like a Hamptons beach house, but it is one of the best B&B values in the Caribbean. What sets Secreto apart—aside from the stunning setting and outstanding value—is the exemplary service. The sophisticated, romantic property has nine suites that overlook a central pool area to the private beach beyond. Located on the northern end of the island, Secreto is within walking distance of town, yet feels removed enough to make for an idyllic, peaceful retreat. The captivating contemporary design features clean, white spaces and sculpted architecture in a Mediterranean style. Tropical gardens surround the pool area, and an outdoor living area offers comfy couches and places to dine. All rooms have private verandas with comfortable seating, ideal for ocean-gazing beyond Halfmoon Beach, and are accented with original artwork. Three suites have king-size beds, draped in mosquito netting, while the remaining six have two double beds; all rooms are non-smoking. Transportation from Cancún airport can be arranged on request, for an additional $50 per van (not per person).

Sección Rocas, Lote 1, 77400 Isla Mujeres, Q. Roo. ✆ **877/278-8018** in the U.S., or 998/877-1039. Fax 998/877-1048. www.hotelsecreto.com. 9 units. High season $183–$250 double; low season $167–$230 double. Extra person $15. 1 child under 5 stays free in parent's room. Rates include continental breakfast. MC, V. **Amenities:** Pool; private cove beach; tours, diving and snorkeling available; dinner delivery from Rolandi's restaurant available. *In room:* A/C, TV, fridge, safe, bathrobes, CD player.

MODERATE

Hotel Cabañas María del Mar ★ A good choice for simple beach accommodations, the Cabañas María del Mar is on the popular Playa Norte. The older two-story section behind the reception area and beyond the garden offers nicely outfitted rooms facing the beach. All have two single or double beds, refrigerators, and oceanview balconies strung with hammocks. Eleven single-story cabañas closer to the reception area are decorated in a rustic Mexican style. The third section, **El Castillo** is located across the street, over and beside Buho's restaurant. It contains all "deluxe" rooms, but some are larger than others; the five rooms on the ground floor have large patios. Upstairs rooms have small balconies. All have ocean views, and a predominately white decor. Rooms were remodeled in 2004. There's a small pool in the garden.

Av. Arq. Carlos Lazo 1 (on Playa Norte, ½ block from the Hotel Na Balam), 77400 Isla Mujeres, Q. Roo. ✆ **800/223-5695** in the U.S., or 998/877-0179. Fax 998/877-0213. 73 units. High season $109–$123 double; low season $70–$111 double. MC, V. From the pier, walk left 1 block and turn right on Matamoros. After 4 blocks, turn left on Lazo (the last street); hotel is at end of block. **Amenities:** Pool; bus for tours and boat for rent; golf cart and *moto* rentals. *In room:* Fridge in cabañas.

INEXPENSIVE

Hotel Belmar ★★ Situated in the center of Isla's small-town activity, this hotel sits above Pizza Rolandi (consider the restaurant noise) and is run by the same people. Each of the simple but stylish tile-accented rooms comes with two twin or double beds. Prices are high considering the lack of views, but the rooms are pleasant. This is one of the few island hotels that have televisions (with U.S. channels) in the room. It has one large colonial-decorated suite with a whirlpool and a patio.

Av. Hidalgo 110 (between Madero and Abasolo, 3½ blocks from the passenger-ferry pier), 77400 Isla Mujeres, Q. Roo. ©️ **998/877-0430.** Fax 998/877-0429. www.rolandi.com. 11 units. High season $56–$95 double; low season $28–$90 double. AE, MC, V. **Amenities:** Restaurant/bar (see "Where to Dine," below); room service until 11:30pm; laundry service. *In room:* A/C, TV, fan.

Hotel D'Gomar (Value)

This hotel is known for comfort at reasonable prices. You can hardly beat the value for basic accommodations, which are regularly updated. Rooms have two double beds and a wall of windows offers great breezes and views. The higher prices are for air-conditioning, which is hardly needed with the breezes and ceiling fans. The only drawback is that there are five stories and no elevator. But it's conveniently located cater-cornered (look right) from the ferry pier, with exceptional rooftop views. The name of the hotel is the most visible sign on the "skyline."

Rueda Medina 150, 77400 Isla Mujeres, Q. Roo. ©️ **998/877-0541.** 16 units. High season $35–$40 double; low season $30–$35 double. No credit cards. *In room:* Fan.

Hotel Francis Arlene (Finds)

The Magaña family operates this neat little two-story inn built around a small, shady courtyard. This hotel is very popular with families and seniors, and it welcomes many repeat guests. You'll notice the tidy cream-and-white facade from the street. Some rooms have ocean views, and all are remodeled or updated each year. They are comfortable, with tile floors, tiled bathrooms, and a very homey feel. Each downstairs room has a coffeemaker, refrigerator, and stove; each upstairs room comes with a refrigerator and toaster. Some have either a balcony or a patio. Higher prices are for the 14 rooms with air-conditioning; other units have fans. Rates are substantially better if quoted in pesos; in dollars they are 15% to 20% higher.

Guerrero 7 (5½ blocks inland from the ferry pier, between Abasolo and Matamoros), 77400 Isla Mujeres, Q. Roo. ©️/fax **998/877-0310** or 998/877-0861. 26 units. High season $50–$60 double; low season $40–$50 double. No credit cards. **Amenities:** In-room massage; safe; money exchange. *In room:* A/C in some, kitchenettes in some, fridge, no phone.

Hotel Posada del Mar (Kids)

Simply furnished, quiet, and comfortable, this long-established hotel faces the water and a wide beach 3 blocks north of the ferry pier. It has one of the few swimming pools on the island. This is probably the best choice in Isla for families. The ample rooms are in a three-story building or one-story bungalow units. For the spaciousness of the rooms and the location, this is among the best values on the island and is very popular with readers, though I consistently find the staff to be the least gracious on the island. A wide, seldom-used but appealing stretch of Playa Norte is across the street, where watersports equipment is available for rent. A great, casual *palapa*-style bar and a lovely pool are on the back lawn along with hammocks, and the restaurant **Pinguino** (see "Where to Dine," below) is by the sidewalk at the front of the property, and also provides room service to hotel guests.

Av. Rueda Medina 15 A, 77400 Isla Mujeres, Q. Roo. ©️ **800/544-3005** in the U.S., or 998/877-0044. Fax 998/877-0266. www.posadadelmar.com. 62 units. High season $67–$77 double; low season $40–$45 double. Children under 12 stay free in parent's room. AE, MC, V. From the pier, go left for 4 blocks; hotel is on the right. **Amenities:** Restaurant/bar; pool. *In room:* A/C, TV, fan.

WHERE TO DINE

At the **Municipal Market,** next to the telegraph office and post office on Avenida Guerrero, obliging, hardworking women operate several little food stands. At the **Panadería La Reyna** (no phone), at Madero and Juárez, you can pick up inexpensive sweet bread, muffins, cookies, and yogurt. It's open Monday through Saturday from 7am to 9:30pm.

Cocina económica (literally, "economical cuisine") restaurants usually aim at the local population. These are great places to find good food at rock-bottom prices, and especially so on Isla Mujeres, where you'll find several, most of which feature delicious regional specialties. But be aware that the hygiene is not what you'll find at more established restaurants, so you're dining at your own risk.

EXPENSIVE

Casa Rolandi ⚜ ITALIAN/SEAFOOD   The gourmet Casa Rolandi restaurant and bar has become Isla's favored fine-dining experience. It boasts a view of the Caribbean and the most sophisticated menu in the area. There's a colorful main dining area as well as more casual, open-air terrace seating for drinks or light snacks. The food is the most notable on the island, but the overall experience falls short—the lights are a bit too bright and the music a bit too close to what you'd hear on an elevator. Along with seafood and northern Italian specialties, the famed wood-burning-oven pizzas are a good bet. Careful—the wood-oven-baked bread, which arrives looking like a puffer fish, is so divine that you're likely to fill up on it. This is a great place to enjoy the sunset, and it offers a selection of more than 80 premium tequilas.

On the pier of Villa Rolandi, Lagunamar SM 7. © **998/877-0700.** Main courses $8–$35. AE, MC, V. Daily 11am–11pm.

MODERATE

Las Palapas Chimbo's ⚜ SEAFOOD   If you're looking for a beachside *palapa*-covered restaurant where you can wiggle your toes in the sand while relishing fresh seafood, this is the best of them. It's the locals' favorite on Playa Norte. Try the delicious fried whole fish, which comes with rice, beans, and tortillas. You'll notice a bandstand and dance floor in the middle of the restaurant, and sex-hunk posters all over the ceiling—that is, when you aren't gazing at the beach and the Caribbean. Chimbo's becomes a lively bar and dance club at night, drawing a crowd of drinkers and dancers (see "Isla Mujeres After Dark," below).

Norte Beach. No phone. Sandwiches and fruit $2.50–$4.50; seafood $6–$9. No credit cards. Daily 8am–midnight. From the pier, walk left to the end of the *malecón,* then right onto the Playa Norte; it's about ½ block on the right.

Pinguino MEXICAN/SEAFOOD   The best seats on the waterfront are on the deck of this restaurant and bar, especially in late evening, when islanders and tourists arrive to dance and party. This is the place to feast on sublimely fresh lobster—you'll get a large, beautifully presented lobster tail with a choice of butter, garlic, and secret sauces. The grilled seafood platter is spectacular, and fajitas and barbecued ribs are also popular. Breakfasts include fresh fruit, yogurt, and granola, or sizable platters of eggs, served with homemade wheat bread. Pinguino also has nonsmoking areas.

In front of the Hotel Posada del Mar (3 blocks west of the ferry pier), Av. Rueda Medina 15. © **998/877-0044,** ext. 157. Main courses $4–$7; daily special $7. AE, MC, V. Daily 7am–11pm; bar closes at midnight.

Pizza Rolandi ⚜⚜ ITALIAN/SEAFOOD   You're bound to dine at least once at Rolandi's, which is practically an Isla institution. The plate-size pizzas and calzones feature exotic ingredients—including lobster, black mushrooms, pineapple, and Roquefort cheese—as well as more traditional tomatoes, olives, basil, and salami. A wood-burning oven provides the signature flavor of the pizzas, as well as baked chicken, roast beef, and mixed seafood casserole with lobster. The extensive menu also offers a selection of salads and light appetizers, as well as an ample array of pasta dishes, steaks, fish, and scrumptious desserts. The setting is the open courtyard of the Hotel Belmar, with a porch overlooking the action on Avenida Hidalgo.

Av. Hidalgo 10 (3½ blocks inland from the pier, between Madero and Abasolo). ✆ **998/877-0430**, ext. 18. Main courses $3.70–$13. AE, MC, V. Daily 11am–11:30pm.

Zazil Ha ✿✿ CARIBBEAN/INTERNATIONAL   Here you can enjoy some of the island's best food while sitting at tables on the sand among palms and gardens. The food—terrific pasta with garlic, shrimp in tequila sauce, fajitas, seafood pasta, and delicious *mole* enchiladas—enhances the serene environment. Caribbean specialties include cracked conch, coconut sailfish, jerk chicken, and stuffed squid. A selection of fresh juices complements the vegetarian menu, and there's even a special menu for those participating in yoga retreats. Between the set meal times, you can order all sorts of enticing food, such as vegetable and fruit drinks, tacos and sandwiches, *ceviche,* and terrific nachos. It's likely you'll stake this place out for several meals.

At the Hotel Na Balam (at the end of Playa Norte, almost at the end of Calle Zazil Ha). ✆ **998/877-0279**. Fax 998/877-0446. Main courses $8.50–$16. AE, MC, V. Daily 7:30–10:30am, 12:30–3:30pm, and 6:30–11pm.

INEXPENSIVE

Café Cito ✿ CREPES/ICE CREAM/COFFEE/FRUIT DRINKS   Sabina and Luis Rivera own this cute, Caribbean-blue corner restaurant where you can begin the day with flavorful coffee and a croissant and cream cheese, or end it with a hot-fudge sundae. Terrific crepes come with yogurt, ice cream, fresh fruit, or chocolate sauce, as well as ham and cheese. The two-page ice cream menu satisfies almost any craving, even one for waffles with ice cream and fruit. The three-course fixed-price dinner includes soup, a main course (such as fish or curried shrimp with rice and salad), and dessert.

Calle Matamoros 42, at Juárez (4 blocks from the pier). ✆ **998/877-1470**. Crepes $2–$4.50; breakfast $2.50–$4.50; sandwiches $2.80–$2.90. No credit cards. Year-round daily 8am–2pm; high season Fri–Wed 5:30–10:30 or 11:30pm.

Cocina Económica Carmelita MEXICAN/HOME COOKING   Few tourists find their way to this tiny restaurant, but locals know they can get a filling, inexpensive, home-cooked meal. Carmelita prepares food in the back kitchen, and her husband serves it at the three cloth-covered tables in the front room of their home. Two or three *comida corridas* are available each day until they run out. They begin with the soup of the day and include *agua fresca* (a fruit water drink). Common selections include *paella, cochinita pibil,* and fish-stuffed chiles. Menu specialties include chicken in *mole* sauce, pork cutlet in a spicy sauce, and breaded shrimp. For fancier tastes, the least expensive lobster in town—served grilled or in a garlic sauce—costs $13 for an ample portion.

Calle Juárez 14 (2 blocks from the pier, between Bravo and Allende). No phone. Main dishes $4–$6; daily lunch special $4. No credit cards. Year-round Mon–Sat 12:30–3pm; Dec–Mar Mon–Sat 4–8pm.

ISLA MUJERES AFTER DARK

Those in a party mood by day's end may want to start out at the beach bar of the **Na Balam** hotel on Playa Norte, which hosts a crowd until around midnight. On Saturday and Sunday, live music plays between 4 and 7pm. **Las Palapas Chimbo's** restaurant on the beach becomes a jammin' dance joint with a live band from 9pm until whenever. Farther along the same stretch of beach, **Buho's,** the restaurant/beach bar of the Cabañas María del Mar, has its moments as a popular, low-key hangout, complete with swinging seats! **Pinguino** in the Hotel Posada del Mar offers a convivial late-night hangout, where a band plays nightly during high season from 9pm to midnight. Near Matéos and Hidalgo, **KoKo Nuts** caters to a younger crowd, with alternative music for late-night dancing. The **Om Bar and Chill Lounge,** on Calle

Matamoros, serves beer on tab at each table, in a jazzy atmosphere. For a late night dance club, **Club Nitrox,** on Avenida Guererro, is open Wednesday to Sunday from 9pm to 3am.

2 Cozumel ⭐⭐⭐

70km (44 miles) S of Cancún; 19km (12 miles) SE of Playa del Carmen

Cozumel has ranked for years among the top five dive destinations in the world. Tall reefs line the southwest coast, creating towering walls that offer divers a fairy-tale landscape to explore. For nondivers, it has the beautiful water of the Caribbean with all the accompanying watersports and seaside activities. The island gets a lot more visitors from North America than Europe for reasons that probably have to do with the limited flights. It is in many ways more "cozy and mellow" than the mainland—no big highways, no big construction projects. It's dependable. And one of my favorite things about this island is that the water on the protected side (western shore) is as calm as an aquarium, unless a norther is blowing. The island is 45km (28 miles) long and 18km (11 miles) wide, and lies 19km (12 miles) from the mainland. Most of the terrain is flat and clothed in a low tropical forest.

The only town on the island is San Miguel, which, despite the growth of the last 20 years, can't be called anything more than a small town. It's not a stunningly beautiful place, but it and its inhabitants are agreeable—on Sunday evenings, everybody congregates around the plaza to be sociable and have a good time. Staying in town can be fun and convenient. You get a choice of a number of restaurants and nightspots. Because Cozumel enjoys such popularity with the cruise ships, the waterfront section of town holds wall-to-wall jewelry stores and souvenir shops. This and the area around the town's main square are about as far as most cruise ship passengers venture into town.

Should you come down with a case of island fever, **Playa del Carmen** and the mainland are a 40-minute ferry ride away. Some travel agencies on the island can set you up with a tour of the major ruins on the mainland, such as **Tulum** or **Chichén Itzá,** or a visit to a nature park such as **Xel-Ha** or **Xcaret** (see "Trips to the Mainland," later in this chapter).

The island has its own ruins, but they cannot compare with the major sites of the mainland. During pre-Hispanic times, Maya women would cross over to the island to make offerings to the goddess of fertility, Ixchel. More than 40 sites containing shrines remain around the island, and archaeologists still uncover the small dolls that were customarily part of those offerings.

ESSENTIALS

GETTING THERE & DEPARTING

BY PLANE   There are fewer international commercial flights in and out of Cozumel than charter flights. You might inquire about buying a ticket on one of these charters. Some packagers, such as **FunJet** (www.funjet.com), will sell you just a ticket. But look into packages, too. Several of the island's independent hotels work with packagers. Flight availability changes between high season and low season. **Continental** (© **800/ 231-0856** in the U.S., or 987/872-0487 in Cozumel) flies to and from Houston and Newark. **US Airways** (© **800/428-4322** in the U.S., or 987/872-2824 in Cozumel [only on days when the flight is operating], or 998/886-0549 in Cancún) flies to and from Charlotte. **American Airlines** (© **800/433-7300** in the U.S., or 01-800/904-6000 in Cozumel) offers nonstop service to/from Dallas. **Aerocaribe** (© **987/872-0877**), an affiliate of Mexicana, has flights to and from Cancún and Mérida. **Mexicana** (© **800/531-7921** in the U.S.; 987/872-0157 or 987/872-2945 at the airport) and **Aeromexico** (© **800/237-6639** in the U.S., or 01-800/021-4000 in Cozumel) fly from Mexico City.

BY FERRY   Passenger ferries run to and from Playa del Carmen. **Barcos México** (© **987/872-1508** or 987/872-1588) and **Ultramar** (© **987/869-2775**) offer departures almost every hour on the hour between 5am and midnight. It is rather curious that the two companies have arranged their service to coincide instead of spacing them so as to offer the consumer more choices. The trip takes 30 to 45 minutes, depending on conditions, and costs $9 one-way. The boats are air-conditioned. In Playa del Carmen, the ferry dock is 1½ blocks from the main square. In Cozumel, the ferries use Muelle Fiscal, the town pier, a block from the main square. Luggage storage at the Cozumel dock costs $2 per day.

The car ferry that used to operate from Puerto Morelos now uses the Calica pier just south of Playa del Carmen. The fare for a standard car is $80. **Marítima Chancanaab** (© **987/872-0916**) has four departures daily from Calica at 7am, 1pm, 5pm, and 9pm. Arrive one hour before departure. The schedule is subject to change, so double-check it. The ferry docks in Cozumel at the **Muelle Internacional (International Pier),** which is south of town near La Ceiba Hotel.

BY BUS   If you plan to travel on the mainland by bus, there is a ticket office for **ADO buses** where you can purchase tickets in advance. It's on Calle 2 Norte and Avenida 10 (© **987/872-1706**). Hours are from 8am to 9:30pm daily.

ORIENTATION

ARRIVING   Cozumel's **airport** is inland from downtown. **Transportes Terrestres** provides hotel transportation in air-conditioned Suburbans. Buy your ticket as you exit the terminal. To hotels downtown, the fare is $4 per person; to hotels along the north shore, $7, and to hotels along the south shore, $8 to $12. Passenger ferries arrive at the Muelle Fiscal, the dock by the town's main square. Cruise ships dock at the **Punta Langosta** pier, a few blocks south of the Muelle Fiscal; at the **International Pier,** near La Ceiba hotel; and at the **Puerta Maya** pier, further south.

VISITOR INFORMATION   The **Municipal Tourism Office** (©/fax **987/869-0212**) is on the second floor of the Plaza del Sol commercial building facing the town's main square. Hours are Monday through Friday from 9am to 4pm. The office operates an information booth at the ferry pier, open Monday through Friday from 8:30am to 4pm.

CITY LAYOUT   San Miguel's main waterfront street is **Avenida Rafael Melgar.** Running parallel to Rafael Melgar are other *avenidas* numbered in multiples of five—5, 10, 15. **Avenida Juárez** runs perpendicular to these, heading inland from the ferry dock. Avenida Juárez divides the town into northern and southern halves. The *calles* (streets)

Tips **Be Streetwise**

North-south streets—the avenidas—have the right of way, and traffic doesn't slow down or stop.

Cozumel

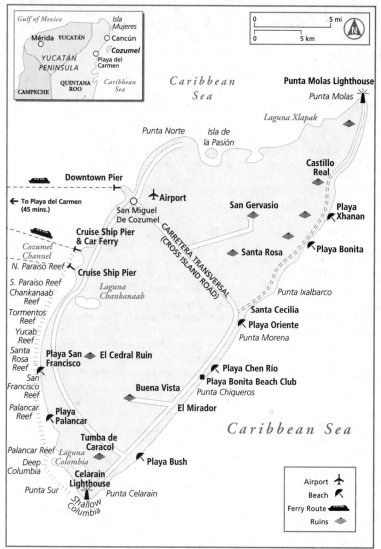

that run parallel Juárez to the north have even numbers. The ones to the south have odd numbers, with the exception of Calle Rosado Salas, which runs between calles 1 and 3.

ISLAND LAYOUT   One road runs along the western coast of the island, which faces the Yucatán mainland. It has different names. North of town it's **Santa Pilar** or **San Juan;** in the city it is **Avenida Rafael Melgar;** south of town it's **Costera Sur.** Hotels stretch along this road north and south of town. The road runs to the southern tip of the island (Punta Sur), passing **Chankanaab National Park. Avenida**

An All-Inclusive Vacation in Cozumel

Booking a room at an all-inclusive should be done through a vacation package. Booking only lodging, even with frequent-flyer mileage to burn, doesn't make economic sense—the discounts offered by most packagers are so deep. I include websites for you to find out more info about the properties, but don't expect to find clear info on rates. The game of setting rates with these hotels is complicated and always in flux.

There are seven all-inclusives on the island. Two are north of town: **El Cozumeleño** (www.elcozumeleno.com) and the **Meliá Cozumel** (www.melia cozumel.com). Both occupy multistory modern buildings. Both have attractive rooms. El Cozumeleño is the larger of the two resorts and has the nicest hotel pool on the island. It's best suited for active types. The Meliá is quieter and offers golf discounts for the nearby golf course. The Cozumeleño has a small beach that's made a comeback from the hurricane that swept by a couple of years ago. The Meliá's beach is long and narrow and pretty, but occasionally seaweed washes up, which doesn't happen on the rest of the island's coast. The advantages of staying in these two are the proximity to town, with its restaurants, clubs, movie theaters, and so on, and the fact that most rooms at these hotels come with lovely views of the ocean.

Of the all-inclusives to the south, my favorites are the two **Occidental** properties (**Allegro Cozumel** and **Grand Cozumel**; www.occidentalhotels.com) and the **Iberostar Cozumel** (www.iberostar.com). These are "village" style resorts with two- and three-story buildings, often with thatched roofs, spread over a large area at the center of which is the pool and activities area. The Allegro is older than the other two and has the plainest rooms, but these are being remodeled this year. It does, however, have the nicest beach. The Grand Cozumel, next door to the Allegro, is the newest. The rooms are the most attractive, and staying here gives you access to both resorts. Like the Occidental chain, Iberostar has several properties in the Mexican Caribbean. This one is the smallest. I like its food and service and the beauty of the grounds. The rooms are attractive and well maintained. The beach is wide and sandy, but has a rocky floor under the water. The advantage to staying in these places is that you're close to a lot of dive sites; the disadvantage is that you're somewhat isolated from town.

Of the other two all-inclusives, I've heard several complaints about the service at the **Reef Club** (unless you stay in the VIP section), and I think the rooms are too closely set together. The **Costa Club** is on the inland side of the road in a crowded section of the island.

Juárez (and its extension, the **Carretera Transversal**) runs east from the town across the island. It passes the airport and the turnoff to the ruins of San Gervasio before reaching the undeveloped ocean side of the island. It then turns south and follows the coast to the southern tip of the island, where it meets the Costera Sur.

GETTING AROUND   You can walk to most destinations in town. Getting to out-lying hotels and beaches requires a taxi or rental car or a moped.

Car rentals are roughly the same price as on the mainland, depending on demand. **Avis** (© 987/872-0099) and **Executive** (© 987/872-1308) have counters in the air-port. Other major rental companies have offices in town. Rentals are easy to arrange through your hotel or at any of the many local rental offices.

Moped rentals are readily available and cost $15 to $30 for 24 hours, depending upon the season. If you rent a moped, be careful. Riding a moped made a lot more sense when Cozumel had less traffic; now it involves a certain amount of risk as taxi drivers and other motorists have become more numerous and pushier. Moped acci-dents easily rank as the greatest cause of injury in Cozumel. Before renting one, inspect it carefully to see that all the gizmos—horn, light, starter, seat, mirror—are in good shape. I've been offered mopeds with unbalanced wheels, which made them unsteady at higher speeds, but the renter quickly exchanged them for another upon my request. You are required to stay on paved roads. It's illegal to ride a moped without a helmet outside of town (subject to a $25 fine).

Cozumel has lots of **taxis** and a strong drivers' union. Fares have been standardized—there's no bargaining. Here are a few sample fares for two people (there is an additional charge for extra passengers to most destinations): island tour, $60; town to southern hotel zone, $5 to $18; town to northern hotels, $5 to $6; town to Chankanaab, $9 (for up to four people); in and around town, $3 to $4.

FAST FACTS: Cozumel

Area Code   The telephone area code is **987**.

Climate   From October to December there can be strong winds all over the Yucatán, as well as some rain. June through October is the rainy season.

Diving   Bring proof of your diver's certification and your log. Underwater cur-rents can be strong, and many of the reef drops are quite steep, so dive oper-ators want to make sure divers are experienced.

Internet Access   Several cybercafes are in and about the main square. If you go just a bit off Avenida Rafael Melgar and the main square, prices drop. **Modu-tel,** Av. Juárez 15 (at Av. 10) offers good rates. Hours are Monday through Sat-urday from 10am to 8pm.

Money Exchange   The island has several banks and *casas de cambio,* as well as ATMs. Most places accept dollars, but you usually get a better deal paying in pesos.

Post Office   The *correo* is on Avenida Rafael Melgar at Calle 7 Sur (© 987/872-0106), at the southern edge of town. It's open Monday through Friday from 9am to 3pm, Saturday from 9am to noon.

Recompression Chamber   There are four *cámaras de recompresión* (recompres-sion chambers). The best are **Buceo Médico Mexicano,** Calle 5 Sur 21-B, between Avenida Rafael Melgar and Avenida 5 Sur (© 987/872-2387 or -1430), which is staffed 24 hours; and the **Hyperbaric Center of Cozumel,** Calle 4 Norte, between avenidas 5 and 10 (© 987/872-3070).

Seasons   High season is August and from Christmas to Easter.

Moments Carnaval

Carnaval (similar to Mardi Gras) is Cozumel's most colorful fiesta. It begins the Thursday before Ash Wednesday, with daytime street dancing and nighttime parades on Thursday, Saturday, and Monday (the best).

EXPLORING THE ISLAND

For **diving** and **snorkeling,** there are plenty of dive shops to choose from, including those recommended below. For **island tours, ruins tours** on and off the island, evening cruises, and other activities, go to a travel agency. I recommend **InterMar Cozumel Viajes,** Calle 2 Norte 101-B, between avenidas 5 and 10 (© **987/872-1535** or 987/872-2022; fax 987/872-0895; cozumel@travel2mexico.com). Office hours are Monday through Saturday from 8am to 8pm, Sunday from 9am to 5pm.

WATERSPORTS

SCUBA DIVING Cozumel is the number one dive destination in the Western Hemisphere. Don't forget your dive card and dive log. Dive shops will rent you scuba gear, but won't take you out on a boat until you show some documentation. If you have a medical condition, bring a letter signed by a doctor stating that you've been cleared to dive. A two-tank morning dive costs around $55; some shops offer an additional afternoon one-tank dive for $9 for those who took the morning dives. A lot of divers save some money by buying a dive package with a hotel. These usually include two dives a day.

Diving in Cozumel is drift diving, which can be a little disconcerting for novices. The current that sweeps along Cozumel's reefs, pulling nutrients into them and making them as large as they are, also dictates how you dive here. The problem is that it pulls at different speeds at different depths and in different places. When it's pulling strong, it can quickly scatter a dive group. The role of the dive master becomes more important, especially with choosing the dive location. Cozumel has a lot of dive locations. To mention but a few: the famous **Palancar Reef,** with its caves and canyons, plentiful fish, and a wide variety of sea coral; the monstrous **Santa Rosa Wall,** famous for its depth, sea life, coral, and sponges; the **San Francisco Reef,** which has a shallower drop-off wall and fascinating sea life; and the **Yucab Reef,** with its beautiful coral.

Finding a dive shop in town is even easier than finding a jewelry store. Cozumel has more than 50 dive operators. I know and can recommend Bill Horn's **Aqua Safari,** which has a location on Avenida Rafael Melgar at Calle 5 (© **987/872-0101;** fax 987/ 872-0661; www.aquasafari.com) and a PADI five-star instructor center with full equipment and parts in the Hotel Plaza Las Glorias (© **987/872-3362** or 987/872-2422). I also know Roberto Castillo at **Liquid Blue Divers** (© **987/869-0593;** www. liquidbluedivers.com), on Avenida 5 between Rosado Salas and Calle 3 Sur. He does a good tour, has a fast boat, and keeps the number of divers to 12 or fewer. His wife, Michelle, handles the Internet inquiries and reservations and is quick to respond to questions.

A popular activity in the Yucatán is *cenote* diving. The peninsula's underground *cenotes* (seh-*noh*-tehs)—sinkholes or wellsprings—lead to a vast system of underground caverns. The gently flowing water is so clear that divers seem to float on air

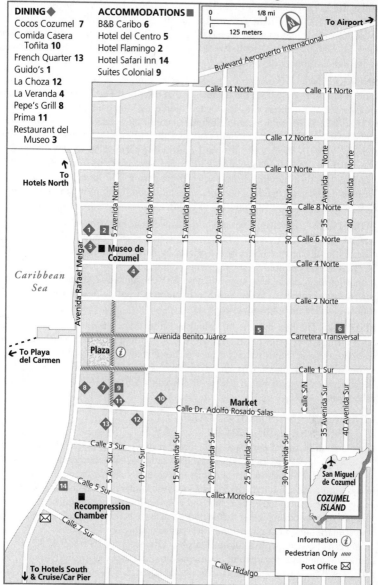

San Miguel de Cozumel

DINING ◆
Cocos Cozumel **7**
Comida Casera
Toñita **10**
French Quarter **13**
Guido's **1**
La Choza **12**
La Veranda **4**
Pepe's Grill **8**
Prima **11**
Restaurant del
Museo **3**

ACCOMMODATIONS ■
B&B Caribo **6**
Hotel del Centro **5**
Hotel Flamingo **2**
Hotel Safari Inn **14**
Suites Colonial **9**

0 _____ 1/8 mi
0 _____ 125 meters

To Airport →

Bulevard Aeropuerto Internacional

Calle 14 Norte   Calle 14 Norte

Calle 12 Norte

↑ To Hotels North

Calle 10 Norte

5 Avenida Norte · 10 Avenida Norte · 15 Avenida Norte · 20 Avenida Norte · 25 Avenida Norte · 30 Avenida Norte · 35 Avenida Norte · 40 Avenida Norte

Calle 8 Norte

Calle 6 Norte

Avenida Rafael Melgar

■ Museo de Cozumel

Caribbean Sea

Calle 4 Norte

Calle 2 Norte

5   **6**

Avenida Benito Juárez   Carretera Transversal

← To Playa del Carmen

Plaza ⓘ

Calle 1 Sur

8 7 9
11   **10**

Market
Calle Dr. Adolfo Rosado Salas

Calle S/N · 35 Avenida Sur · 40 Avenida Sur

13   **12**

Calle 3 Sur

5 Av. Sur · 10 Av. Sur · 15 Avenida Sur · 20 Avenida Sur · 25 Avenida Sur · 30 Avenida Sur

San Miguel de Cozumel

COZUMEL ISLAND

14

Calle 5 Sur

Calles Morelos

■ Recompression Chamber

✉

Calle 7 Sur

Information ⓘ
Pedestrian Only ////
Post Office ✉

↓ To Hotels South & Cruise/Car Pier

Calle Hidalgo

through caves complete with stalactites and stalagmites. If you want to try this but didn't plan a trip to the mainland, contact **Yucatech Expeditions,** Av. 15 no. 144, between Calle 1 and Rosado Salas (ⓒ/fax **987/872-5659;** http://yucatech.net), which offers a trip five times a week. *Cenotes* are 30 to 45 minutes from Playa del Carmen, and a dive in each *cenote* lasts around 45 minutes. Dives are within the daylight zone, about 40m (130 ft.) into the caverns, and no more than 18m (60 ft.) deep. Company owner Germán Yañez Mendoza inspects diving credentials carefully, and divers must meet his list of requirements before cave diving is permitted. For information and prices, call or drop by the office.

SNORKELING Anyone who can swim can snorkel. When contracting for a snorkel tour, stay away from the companies that cater to the cruise ships. Those tours are crowded and not very fun. For a good snorkeling tour, contact **Víctor Casanova** (© 987/872-1028; wildcatcozumel@hotmail.com). He speaks English, owns a couple of boats, and does a good 5-hour tour. He takes his time and doesn't rush through the trip. You can also try the **Kuzamil Snorkeling Center,** 50 Av. bis 565 Int. 1, between 5 Sur and Hidalgo, Col. Adolfo López Mateos (© 987/872-4637 or 987/872-0539). A full-day snorkel trip costs $65 per person, $50 for children under 8. It includes the boat, the guide, a buffet lunch, and snorkel equipment, and it visits four reefs. Half-day trips are $40 adults, $30 children.

BOAT TRIPS Travel agencies and hotels can arrange boat trips, a popular pastime on Cozumel. There are evening cruises, cocktail cruises, glass-bottom boat cruises, and other options. One novel boat ride is offered by **Atlantis Submarines** (© 987/872-5671). The sub can hold 48 people. It operates almost 3km (2 miles) south of town in front of the Casa del Mar hotel and costs $81 per adult, $42 for kids 4 to 12. This is a superior experience to the **Sub See Explorer** offered by **Aqua World,** which is really a glorified glass-bottom boat.

FISHING The best months for fishing are from March through June, when the catch includes blue and white marlin, sailfish, tarpon, and swordfish. The least expensive option would be to contact a boat owner directly. Try Victor Casanova, listed above under snorkeling. Or try an agency such as **Aquarius Travel Fishing,** Calle 3 Sur 2 between Avenida Rafael Melgar and Avenida 5 (© 987/872-1092; gabdiaz@yahoo.com).

CHANKANAAB NATIONAL PARK & PUNTA SUR ECOLOGICAL RESERVE

Chankanaab National Park ★★ is the pride of many islanders. Chankanaab means "little sea," which refers to a beautiful land-locked pool connected to the sea through an underground tunnel—a sort of miniature ocean. Snorkeling in this natural aquarium is not permitted, but the park has a lovely ocean beach for sunbathing and snorkeling. Arrive early to stake out a chair and *palapa* before the cruise-ship crowd arrives. Likewise, the snorkeling is best before noon. There are bathrooms, lockers, a gift shop, several snack huts, a restaurant, and a *palapa* for renting snorkeling gear.

You can also swim with dolphins. **Dolphin Discovery** (© 998/849-4757 in Cancún; www.dolphindiscovery.com) has several programs for experiencing these sea creatures. You'll need to make reservations well in advance. The surest way is by e-mail (salesinternet@dolphindiscovery.com.mx) or through the website. The dolphin swim and other programs are very popular, so your best bet is to plan ahead. Still, if you're already in Cozumel, you can try by calling © 987/872-9702. The dolphin swim costs $125 and features close interaction with the beautiful swimmers. There's also a swim and snorkel program for $99 that gets you in the water with them but offers less interaction. Dolphin Discovery also offers a program only in Cozumel where you can swim with sea lions ($59); make reservations for this. There is also a sea lion show, which doesn't require reservations. The show includes some scarlet macaws, which, like the sea lions, were rescued from illegal captivity. It costs $5 per adult, $3.50 per child. Tickets are available through any travel agency in town (and remember that you also have to pay for admission to the park).

Surrounding the land-locked pool is a botanical garden with shady paths and 351 species of tropical and subtropical plants from 22 countries, as well as 451 species from Cozumel. Several Maya structures have been re-created within the gardens to give visitors an idea of Maya life in a jungle setting. There's a small natural history museum as well. Admission to the park costs $10; it's open daily from 8am to 5pm. The park is south of town, just past the Fiesta Americana Hotel. Taxis run constantly between the park, the hotels, and town ($9 from town for up to four people).

Punta Sur Ecological Reserve (admission $10) is a large area that encompasses the southern tip of the island, including the Columbia Lagoon. The only practical way of going there is to rent a car or scooter; there is no taxi stand, and, usually, few people. This is an ecological reserve, not a park, so don't expect much infrastructure. The reserve has an information center, several observation towers, and a snack bar. In addition, there are four boat rides per day around the Colombia Lagoon, where guides point out things of interest about the habitat (bring bug spray). Punta Sur has some interesting snorkeling (bring your own gear), and lovely beaches kept as natural as possible. Regular hours are from 9am to 5pm. A special program (© 987/872-2940 for info) allows visitors to observe turtle nests in season, and you can participate as a volunteer in the evenings during the nesting season.

THE BEACHES

Along both the west and east sides of the island you'll see signs advertising beach clubs. A "beach club" in Cozumel can mean just a *palapa* hut that's open to the public and serves soft drinks, beer, and fried fish. It can also mean a recreational beach with the full gamut of offerings from banana boats to parasailing. They also usually have locker rooms and a pool, and food. The two biggest of these are **Mr. Sancho's** (© 987/879-0021; www.mrsanchos.com) and **Playa Mia** (© 987/872-9030; www.playamia.com.mx). Quieter versions are **Nachi Cocom** (no phone), **Playa San Francisco** (no phone), and **Playa Palancar** (no phone). All of these beaches are south of Chankanaab Park, and easily visible from the road. The last three have a swimming pool with beach furniture, a restaurant, and snorkel rental. The quality of the beaches is excellent, especially the last three. Admission for Mr. Sancho's is free (it does a lot of business with the cruise ships); Playa Mia is $12 for the basic package, $42 for the all-inclusive package; Nachi Cocom is $10; the other two cost around $5.

Once you get to the end of the island the beach clubs become simple places where you can eat and drink and lay out on the beach. **Paradise Cafe** is on the southern tip of the island across from Punta Sur nature park, and as you go up the eastern side of the island you pass **Playa Bonita, Chen Río,** and **Punta Morena.** Except on Sundays, when the locals head for the beaches, these places are practically deserted. Most of the east coast is unsafe for swimming because of the surf. The beaches tend to be small and occupy gaps in the rocky coast.

TOURS OF THE ISLAND

Travel agencies can arrange a variety of tours, including horseback, jeep, and ATV tours. Taxi drivers charge $60 for a 4-hour tour of the island, which most people would consider only mildly amusing, depending on the driver's personality. The best horseback tours are offered at **Rancho Palmitas** (no phone) on the Costera Sur highway, across from the Occidental Cozumel resort. Unless you're staying in one of the resorts on the south end, the easiest way to arrange a tour is probably to talk to the owners of Cocos Cozumel restaurant (see the listing later in this chapter, making sure to note the limited hours). Rides can be from 1 to 2½ hours long and cost $20 to $30.

OTHER ATTRACTIONS

MAYA RUINS One of the most popular island excursions is to **San Gervasio** (100 B.C.–A.D. 1600). Follow the paved transversal road. You'll see the well-marked turnoff about halfway between town and the eastern coast. Stop at the entrance gate and pay the $1 road-use fee. About 3km (2 miles) farther, pay the $5 fee to enter; still and video camera permits cost $5 each. A small tourist center at the entrance sells cold drinks and snacks.

When it comes to Cozumel's Maya ruins, getting there is most of the fun—do it for the mystique and for the trip, not for the size or scale of the ruins. The buildings, though preserved, are crudely made and would not be much of a tourist attraction if they were not the island's principal ruins. More significant than beautiful, this site was once an important ceremonial center where the Maya gathered, coming even from the mainland. The important deity was Ixchel, the goddess of weaving, women, childbirth, pilgrims, the moon, and medicine. Although you won't see any representations of Ixchel at San Gervasio today, Bruce Hunter, in his *Guide to Ancient Maya Ruins,* writes that priests hid behind a large pottery statue of her and became the voice of the goddess, speaking to pilgrims and answering their petitions. Ixchel was the wife of Itzamná, the sun god.

Guides charge $10 for a tour for one to six people. A better option is to find a copy of the green booklet *San Gervasio,* sold at local checkout counters and bookstores, and tour the site on your own. Seeing it takes 30 minutes. Taxi drivers offer a tour to the ruins for about $30; the driver will wait for you outside the ruins.

A HISTORY MUSEUM The **Museo de la Isla de Cozumel** ⭐, Avenida Rafael Melgar between calles 4 and 6 Norte (© **987/872-1475**), is more than just a nice place to spend a rainy hour. On the first floor an exhibit illustrates endangered species, the origin of the island, and its present-day topography and plant and animal life, including an explanation of coral formation. The second-floor galleries feature the history of the town, artifacts from the island's pre-Hispanic sites, and colonial-era cannons, swords, and ship paraphernalia. It's open daily from 9am to 5pm. Admission is $3. A good rooftop restaurant serves breakfast and lunch.

GOLF Cozumel has a new 18-hole course designed by Jack Nicklaus. It's at the **Cozumel Country Club** (© **987/872-9570**), just north of San Miguel. Greens fees are $149, including cart rental and tax. Tee times can be made 3 days in advance. A few hotels have special memberships with discounts for guests and advance tee times; guests at Playa Azul Golf and Beach Club pay no greens fees, just the cart cost ($20).

TRIPS TO THE MAINLAND

PLAYA DEL CARMEN & XCARET Going on your own to the nearby seaside village of **Playa del Carmen** and the **Xcaret** nature park is as easy as a quick ferry ride from Cozumel (for ferry information, see "Getting There & Departing," earlier in this chapter). For information on Playa, see chapter 15; Xcaret is covered in chapter 13.

Cozumel travel agencies offer an Xcaret tour that includes the ferry ride, transportation to the park, and the admission fee. The price is $90 for adults, $48 for kids. Available Monday through Saturday.

CHICHEN ITZA, TULUM & COBA   Travel agencies can arrange day trips to the ruins of **Chichén Itzá** 🏆🏆🏆 by air or bus. The ruins of **Tulum** 🏆, overlooking the Caribbean, and **Cobá** 🏆, in a dense jungle setting, are closer and cost less to visit. These cities are quite a contrast to Chichén Itzá. Cobá is a large, mostly unrestored city beside a lake in a remote jungle setting, while Tulum is smaller, more compact, and right on the beach. It's more intact than Cobá. A trip to both Cobá and Tulum begins at 8am and returns around 6pm. A shorter, more relaxing excursion goes to Tulum and the nearby nature park of Xel-Ha.

SHOPPING

If you like shopping for silver jewelry, you can spend a great deal of time examining the wares of all the jewelers along Avenida Rafael Melgar. Some duty-free stores sell items such as perfumes and designer wares. If you're interested in Mexican folk art, there are three stores on Avenida Rafael Melgar that have merchandise better than what most stores offer: **Los Cinco Soles** (✆ **987/872-2040**), **Indigo** (✆ **987/872-1076**), and **Viva México** (✆ **987/872-5466**). There are also some import/export stores in the new Punta Langosta Shopping Center in the southern part of town in front of the Punta Langosta Pier. Prices for serapes, T-shirts, and the like are lower on the side streets off Avenida Melgar. At the corner of Avenida 5 and Calle 5 is a small gallery called **Casa Chaak** (no phone), which is the joint effort of eight island artists.

WHERE TO STAY

I've grouped Cozumel's hotels by location—**north** of town, **in town,** and **south** of town—and I describe them in that order. The prices I've quoted are rack rates and include the 12% tax. High season is from December to Easter. Expect rates from Christmas to New Year's to be still higher than the regular high-season rates quoted here. Low season is the rest of the year, though a few hotels raise their rates in August when Mexican families go on vacations.

All of the beach hotels in Cozumel, even the small ones, have deals with vacation packagers. Keep in mind that some packagers will offer last-minute deals to Cozumel with hefty discounts; if you're the flexible sort, keep an eye open for these.

Most hotels have an arrangement with a dive shop and offer dive packages. These can be good deals, but if you don't buy a dive package, it's quite okay to stay at one hotel and dive with a third-party operator—any dive boat can pull up to any hotel pier to pick up customers. Most dive shops won't pick up from the hotels north of town. In these cases, it's easiest to make arrangements through the hotel.

As an alternative to a hotel, you can try **Cozumel Vacation Villas and Condos,** Av. Rafael Melgar 685, between calles 3 and 5 Sur (✆ **800/224-5551** in the U.S., or 987/872-0729; www.cvvmexico.com), which offers accommodations by the week.

NORTH OF TOWN

Carretera Santa Pilar, or San Juan, is the name of Avenida Rafael Melgar's northern extension. All the hotels lie close to each other on the beach side of the road a short distance from town and the airport.

Expensive

Playa Azul Golf and Beach Hotel ★★★ This quiet hotel is perhaps the most relaxing of the island's beachside properties. It is an excellent choice for golfers; guests pay no greens fees, only cart rental. It has a small, sandy beach—with shade *palapas*—that is one of the best on the north coast. Service is attentive and personal. Almost all the rooms have balconies and ocean views. The units in the original section are all suites—very large, with oversize bathrooms with showers. The new wing has mostly standard rooms that are comfortable and large, decorated with light tropical colors and rattan furniture. The corner rooms are master suites and have large balconies with Jacuzzis overlooking the sea. If you prefer lots of space over having a Jacuzzi, opt for a suite in the original building. Rooms contain a king-size bed or two double beds; suites offer two convertible single sofas in the separate living room. The hotel also offers deep-sea- and fly-fishing trips. For a family or group, the hotel rents a garden house with lovely rooms.

Carretera San Juan Km 4, 77600 Cozumel, Q. Roo. ⓒ **987/872-0199** or 987/872-0043. Fax 987/872-0110. www. playa-azul.com. 50 units. High season $185 double, $220–$300 suite; low season $135 double, $165–$260 suite. Discounts and packages sometimes available. AE, MC, V. **Amenities:** Restaurant; 2 bars; medium-size pool; unlimited golf privileges at Cozumel Country Club; watersports equipment rental; game room; tour info; room service until 11pm; in-room massage; babysitting; laundry service. *In room:* A/C, TV, fridge, coffeemaker, hair dryer, safe.

Moderate

Condumel Condobeach Apartments If you want some distance from the crowds, consider lodging here. It's not a full-service hotel, but in some ways it's more convenient. The one-bedroom apartments are designed and furnished in practical fashion—large and airy, with glass sliding doors that face the sea and allow for good cross-ventilation (especially in the upper units). They also have ceiling fans, air-conditioning, and two twin beds or one king-size. Each apartment has a separate living room and a full kitchen with a partially stocked fridge, so you don't have to run to the store on the first day. There's a small, well-tended beach area (with shade *palapas* and a grill for guests' use) that leads to a low, rocky fall-off into the sea.

Carretera Hotelera Norte s/n, 77600 Cozumel, Q. Roo. ⓒ **987/872-0892.** Fax 987/872-0661. www.aquasafari.com. 10 units. High season $160 double; low season $135 double. No credit cards. *In room:* A/C, kitchen, no phone.

Sol Cabañas del Caribe This hotel offers good rates for oceanfront lodging. It's quaint and a little worn. There's a small beach on one side and a nice snorkeling area by the rocky section in front of the restaurant (which is at the water's edge). You have a choice of two types of rooms for the same price. Medium-size standard rooms in the two-story main section face the water and are comfortable but a little dark. These units have one double and one twin bed, a small sitting area, and a porch or a balcony. I prefer them to the one-story cabañas, which are smaller and have just one double bed, but do have patios near the pool. Bathrooms are small. Service is friendly. The owners also run the Sol Meliá, an all-inclusive hotel a little way up the coast.

Carretera Santa Pilar Km 4.5 (Apdo. Postal 9), 77600 Cozumel, Q. Roo. ⓒ **800/33-MELIA** in the U.S. and Canada, or 987/872-0017. Fax 987/872-1599. www.solmelia.com. 48 units. High season $120–$132 double; low season $95–$104 double. Honeymoon packages available. AE, MC, V. Free secured parking. **Amenities:** Restaurant; bar; small pool; wading pool; membership in local golf club; watersports equipment; tour desk; car rental; room service until 10:30pm; babysitting; laundry service. *In room:* A/C, no phone.

IN TOWN

Staying in town is not like staying in Playa del Carmen, where you can walk to the beach. The oceanfront in town is too busy for swimming, and there's no beach, only the *malecón*. Consequently, there's no real premium for staying close to the water. You'll have to drive or take a cab to the beach; it's pretty easy. The hotels in town are the most economical on the island (except for Hotel Plaza Las Glorias, which is an oceanfront hotel away from the harbor). The staff at almost all of them speaks English.

Moderate

Hotel del Centro
Five blocks from the waterfront, this stylish two-story hotel is a bargain for those wanting a pool. The rooms are small to medium in size but modern and attractive. They come with two double beds or one king-size (costing $10 less). Bathrooms are medium-size. The rooms surround a garden courtyard with an oval pool framed by comfortable lounge chairs.

Av. Juárez 501, 77600 Cozumel, Q. Roo. © 987/872-5471. Fax 987/872-0299. hcentro@cozumel.com.mx. 14 units. High season $60–$85 double; low season $45–$60 double. Special discounts available. No credit cards. **Amenities:** Medium-size pool. *In room:* A/C, TV.

Hotel Flamingo ★
A small hotel just off Avenida Rafael Melgar, the Flamingo offers three stories of attractive, comfortable rooms around a small, plant-filled inner courtyard. Highlights include an inviting rooftop terrace and a comfortable bar and coffee bar that serves breakfast. Second- and third-story rooms, which have air-conditioning and TV, cost more. Rooms are large, with two double beds, white-tile floors, medium-size bathrooms, and ceiling fans. A penthouse suite comes with a full kitchen and sleeps up to six. The English-speaking staff is helpful and friendly.

Calle 6 Norte 81, 77600 Cozumel, Q. Roo. © 800/806-1601 in the U.S., or 987/872-1264. Fax 987/872-1264. www.hotelflamingo.com. 22 units. High season $77–$100 double; low season $66–$85 double. Discounts sometimes available. AE, MC, V. From the plaza, walk 3 blocks north on Av. Rafael Melgar and turn right on Calle 6; hotel is on the left. **Amenities:** Cafe; bar; scuba rental; tour info; car rental; laundry service. *In room:* A/C, TV, no phone.

Suites Colonial
Around the corner from the main square, on a pedestrian-only street, you'll find this pleasant four-story hotel. Standard rooms, called "studios," have large bathrooms and attractive red-tile floors, but they could be better lit. These units have one double and one twin bed and are trimmed in yellow pine, which seems oddly out of place here. The suites hold two double beds, a kitchenette, and a sitting and dining area. There's free coffee and sweet bread in the morning. When making a reservation, specify the Suites Colonial.

Av. 5 Sur 9 (Apdo. Postal 286), 77600 Cozumel, Q. Roo. © 987/872-9080. Fax 987/872-9073. www.suitescolonial. com. 28 units. High season $60–$69 studio, $81 suite; low season $50 studio, $58–$68 suite. Rates include continental breakfast. Extra person $20. AE, MC, V. From the plaza, walk ½ block south on Av. 5 Sur; the hotel is on the left. *In room:* A/C, TV, fridge.

Inexpensive

B&B Caribo ★ (Value
Cindy Cooper, the American owner of this B&B, goes out of her way to make guests feel at home. The rates are a good deal and include air-conditioning, breakfast, and several little extras. Six neatly decorated rooms come with cool tile floors, white furniture, and big bottles of purified drinking water; these units share a guest kitchen. The six apartments (three have 1-month minimums) have small kitchens. Rooms have a double bed and a twin bed. There are a number of common rooms and a rooftop terrace. Breakfasts are good.

Av. Juárez 799, 77600 Cozumel, Q. Roo. © 987/872-3195. www.visit-caribo.com. 12 units. High season $50 double, $60 apt; low season $35 double, $40 apt. Rates include breakfast. Long-term discounts available. Ask about yoga vacations. AE, MC, V. From the plaza, walk 6½ blocks inland on Juárez; Caribo is on the left. **Amenities:** Massage. *In room:* A/C.

Hotel Safari Inn This budget hotel offers a convenient location for divers: directly above the Aqua Safari Dive Shop and across the street from the shop's pier, which means that you don't have to lug your gear very far. The large rooms have little in the way of furniture aside from beds. They have small bathrooms with good hot showers. Some rooms could use better lighting, and in some the air-conditioning is noisy. The hotel becomes a real bargain when four or five people are willing to share a room (some units hold a king-size and two or three twin beds).

Av. Rafael Melgar, between calles 5 and 7 Sur (Apdo. Postal 41), 77600. Cozumel, Q. Roo. ℂ **987/872-0101.** Fax 987/872-0661. dive@aquasafari.com. 12 units. $45 double. MC, V. From the pier, turn right (south) and walk 4½ blocks on Melgar. *In room:* A/C, no phone.

SOUTH OF TOWN

The hotels in this area tend to be more spread out and farther from town than hotels to the north. Some are on the inland side of the road; some are on the beach side, which means a difference in price. Those farthest from town are all-inclusive properties. The beaches tend to be slightly better than those to the north, but all the hotels have swimming pools and piers from which you can snorkel, and all of them accommodate divers. Head south on Avenida Rafael Melgar, which becomes the coastal road **Costera Sur** (also called Carretera a Chankanaab).

Very Expensive

Presidente InterContinental Cozumel 🌟🌟🌟 This is Cozumel's finest hotel in terms of location, on-site amenities, and service. Palatial in scale and modern in style, the Presidente spreads out across a long stretch of coast with only distant hotels for neighbors. Rooms come in four categories distributed throughout four buildings (two to five stories tall). The "superior" or "garden-view" rooms are large and comfortable. Most are in the five-story building. The deluxe rooms are in a long two-story building facing the water. They are described as "oceanfront" (second floor) and "beachfront" rooms (ground floor, with direct access to the beach). These two are pretty much the same except that one comes with a patio, the other with a balcony. They are oversize and have large, well-lit bathrooms. Guests in beachfront rooms can request in-room dining on the patio with a serenading trio. Most rooms come with a choice of one king-size or two double beds and are furnished in understated modern style. The 17 suites and reef rooms are extremely large and well furnished. A long stretch of sandy beach area dotted with *palapas* and palm trees fronts the entire hotel.

Costera Sur Km 6.5, 77600 Cozumel, Q. Roo. ℂ **800/327-0200** in the U.S., or 987/872-9500. Fax 987/872-9528. www.cozumel.intercontinental.com. 253 units. High season $358 garden-view, $460–$730 oceanfront/beachfront, from $851 reef rooms and suites; low season $276 garden-view, $391–$675 oceanfront/beachfront, from $788 reef rooms and suites. Discounts and packages available. AE, DC, MC, V. **Amenities:** 2 restaurants (international, Mexican); snack bar; 2 bars; large pool; wading pool; access to golf club; 2 lighted tennis courts; fully equipped gym; whirlpool; watersports equipment rental; children's activities center; concierge; tour desk; car rental; business center; shopping arcade; 24-hr. room service; in-room massage; babysitting; laundry service; dry cleaning; nonsmoking rooms; dive shop. *In room:* A/C, TV w/pay movies, dataport, minibar, hair dryer.

Expensive

El Cid La Ceiba 🌟🌟 On the beach side of the road, La Ceiba is a fun place to stay. It has snorkeling and shore diving to a submerged airplane (the hotel provides unlimited tanks) in front of the hotel. Lots of divers come here: it is the Mares Hub system center for Cozumel and was voted one of the world's top 15 dive resorts in

Rodale's Scuba Diving magazine. All rooms have ocean views, balconies, and two doubles or one king-size bed. Bathrooms are roomy and well lit, with granite countertops and strong water pressure. Superior rooms are larger than standard and have
more furniture. Some suites are available for limited periods and only to guests who
make direct reservations, not to groups. The emphasis here is on watersports, particularly scuba diving, but nondivers can enjoy the large pool area, tennis court, and
seaside restaurant.

Costera Sur Km 4.5 (Apdo. Postal 284), 77600 Cozumel, Q. Roo. © **800/435-3240** in the U.S., or 987/872-0844. Fax
987/872-0065. www.elcid.com. 98 units. High season $250 double, $533 suite; low season $126 double, $164 suite.
Ask for the Frommer's discount. AE, MC, V. **Amenities:** 2 restaurants; 2 bars; 2 large pools; access to golf club; lighted
tennis court; small exercise room w/sauna; whirlpool; watersports equipment rental; tour desk; car rental, room service until 10:30pm; in-room massage; babysitting; laundry service; dive shop. *In room:* A/C, TV, fridge, coffeemaker.

WHERE TO DINE

The island offers a number of good restaurants. Taxi drivers will often steer you
toward restaurants that pay them commissions; don't heed their advice.

   Zermatt (© **987/872-1384**), a nice little bakery, is on Avenida 5 at Calle 4 Norte.
For inexpensive local fare during the day, I like **Comida Casera Toñita,** listed below,
and a small hole in the wall on Calle 6 Norte between Rafael Melgar and Av. 5 called
El Morrito III (no phone). In the evenings, my favorite place to eat tacos is at the corner of Avenida 30 and Calle Morelos. It's called **Los Seras** (no phone). It's next to a
car wash of the same name.

VERY EXPENSIVE

Cabaña del Pescador (Lobster House) ★★★ LOBSTER   The thought I often
have when I eat a prepared lobster dish is that the cook could have simply boiled the
lobster to better effect. The owner of this restaurant seems to agree. The only item on
the menu is lobster boiled with a hint of spices and served with melted butter, accompanied by sides of rice, vegetables, and bread. The weight of the lobster you select
determines the price, with side dishes included. Candles and soft lights illuminate the
inviting dining rooms set amid gardens, fountains, and a small duck pond—*muy
romántico.* The owner, Fernando, welcomes you warmly and will even send you next
door to his brother's excellent Mexican seafood restaurant, El Guacamayo, if you must
have something other than lobster.

Carretera Santa Pilar Km 4 (across from Playa Azul Hotel). No phone. Lobster (by weight) $19–$30. No credit cards.
Daily 6–10:30pm.

Pepe's Grill ★★ STEAKS/SEAFOOD   The chefs at Pepe's seem fascinated with
fire; what they don't grill in the kitchen, they flambé at your table. The most popular
grilled items are the good-quality beef (prime rib or filet mignon) and the lobster. For
something out of the ordinary, try shrimp Bahamas, flambéed with a little banana and
pineapple in a curry sauce. Pepe's is a second-story restaurant with one large air-conditioned dining room under a massive beamed ceiling. The lighting is soft, and a guitar trio plays background music. Large windows look out over the harbor. The
children's menu offers breaded shrimp and broiled chicken. For dessert there are more
incendiary specialties: bananas Foster, crêpes Suzettes, and *café* Maya (coffee, vanilla
ice cream, and three liqueurs).

Av. Rafael Melgar (at Salas). © **987/872-0213.** Reservations recommended. Main courses $18–$35; children's
menu $7. AE, MC, V. Daily 5–11:30pm.

EXPENSIVE

French Quarter ✸✸ LOUISIANA/SOUTHERN   In a pleasant upstairs open-air setting, French Quarter serves Southern and Creole classics. I found the jambalaya and étouffée delicious. You also have the choice of dining indoors or having a cocktail in the downstairs bar. The menu lists blackened fish (very good) and fresh lump crabmeat. Filet mignon with red-onion marmalade is a specialty of the house.

Av. 5 Sur 18. ℂ **987/872-6321**. Reservations recommended during Carnaval. Main courses $10–$27. AE, MC, V. Daily 5–10:30pm.

La Veranda ✸✸✸ SEAFOOD/INTERNATIONAL   This is the perfect place to go if you're getting tired of fried fish or fish with *achiote* sauce, or if you just want something different. The inventive menu emphasizes tropical ingredients and fuses West Indian with European cooking. What I tried was delicious and artfully presented. The spiced mussel soup had a broth scented with white wine. Veranda mango fish had a sauce that was both light and satisfying. And Palancar coconut shrimp consisted of shrimp boiled in a coconut sauce. The indoor and outdoor dining areas are airy and quite pleasant. You can hear soft jazz and the whirring of ceiling fans in the background. The tables are well separated and attractively set.

Calle 4 Norte (between avs. 5 and 10). ℂ **987/872-4132**. Reservations recommended during high season. Main courses $14–$20. MC, V. Daily 4:30pm–midnight.

Prima ✸✸✸ NORTHERN ITALIAN   Everything at this ever-popular hangout is fresh—pastas, vegetables, and seafood. Owner Albert Domínguez grows most of the vegetables in his local hydroponic garden. The menu changes daily and concentrates on seafood. It might include shrimp scampi, fettuccine with pesto, and lobster and crab ravioli with cream sauce. The fettuccine Alfredo is wonderful, the salads crisp, and the steaks USDA choice. Pizzas are cooked in a wood-burning oven. Desserts include Key lime pie and tiramisu. Dining is upstairs on the breezy terrace.

Calle Rosado Salas 109A (corner of Av. 5) ℂ **987/872-4242**. Reservations recommended during high season. Pizzas and pastas $6–$14; seafood $10–$20; steaks $15–$20. AE, MC, V. Daily 5–11pm.

MODERATE

El Moro ✸ *Value* REGIONAL   El Moro is an out-of-the-way place that has been around for a long time and has always been popular with the locals, who come for the food, the service, and the prices—but not the decor, which is orange, orange, orange, and Formica. Get there by taxi, which will cost a couple of bucks. Portions are generous. Any of the shrimp dishes use the real jumbo variety when available. For something different, try the *pollo ticuleño*, a specialty from the town of Ticul, a layered dish of tomato sauce, mashed potatoes, crispy baked corn tortilla, and fried chicken breast, topped with shredded cheese and green peas. Other specialties include enchiladas and seafood prepared many ways, plus grilled steaks and sandwiches.

75 bis Norte 124 (between calles 2 and 4 Norte). ℂ **987/872-3029**. Reservations not accepted. Main courses $5–$15. MC, V. Fri–Wed 1–11pm.

Guido's ✸✸ MEDITERRANEAN   The inviting interior, with sling chairs and rustic wood tables, makes this a restful place in daytime and a romantic spot at night. The specialty is oven-baked pizzas. Also keep an eye out for the daily specials, which may include an appetizer of sea bass carpaccio, a couple of meat dishes, and usually a fish dish. The other thing that people love here is *pan de ajo*—a house creation of bread made with olive oil, garlic, and rosemary. There's a good, well-priced wine list.

Av. Rafael Melgar, between calles 6 and 8 Norte. © 987/872-0946. Main courses $8–$13; daily specials $10–$14. AE. Mon–Sat 11am–11pm.

La Choza ⭐ YUCATECAN/MEXICAN   Local residents consider this one of the best Mexican restaurants in town. Platters of poblano chiles stuffed with shrimp, *arrachera* (skirt steak), and *pollo en relleno negro* (chicken in a sauce of blackened chiles) are among the specialties. The table sauces and guacamole are great, and the daily specials can be good, too. This is an open-air restaurant with well-spaced tables under a tall thatched roof.

Rosado Salas 198 (at Av. 10 Sur). © 987/872-0958. Reservations accepted for groups of 6 or more. Breakfast $4; main courses $9–$15. AE, MC, V. Daily 7am–11pm.

INEXPENSIVE

Cocos Cozumel MEXICAN/AMERICAN   Cocos offers the largest breakfast menu on the island, including all the American and Mexican classics, from *huevos divorciados* (fried eggs on corn tortillas) to ham and eggs. Indulge in stateside favorites like hash browns, corn flakes and bananas, gigantic blueberry muffins, cinnamon rolls, and bagels, or go for something with tropical ingredients, like a blended fruit drink. The service and the food are excellent. The American and Mexican owners, Terri and Daniel Ocejo, are good folk and can set you up with a horseback ride or a fishing or snorkeling trip.

Av. 5 Sur 180 (1 block south of the main plaza). © 987/872-0241. Breakfast $3–$6. No credit cards. Tues–Sun 6am–noon. Closed Sept–Oct.

Comida Casera Toñita HOME-STYLE YUCATECAN   The owners have made the living room of their home into a comfortable dining room, complete with filled bookshelves and classical music playing in the background. Whole fried fish, fish filet, and fried chicken are on the regular menu. Daily specials give you a chance to taste authentic regional food, including *pollo a la naranja* (chicken in bitter-orange sauce), chicken *mole* (in a vinegar-based sauce), *pollo en escabeche* (chicken stewed in a lightly pickled sauce), and pork chops with *achiote* seasoning.

Calle Rosado Salas 265 (between avs. 10 and 15). © 987/872-0401. Breakfast $1.75–$3; main courses $4–$7; daily specials $3; fruit drinks $2. No credit cards. Mon–Sat 8am–6pm.

Restaurant del Museo BREAKFAST/MEXICAN   The most pleasant place in San Miguel to have breakfast or lunch (weather permitting) is at this rooftop cafe above the island's museum. It offers a serene view of the water, removed from the traffic noise below and sheltered from the sun above. The tables and chairs are comfortable and the food reliable. Choices are limited to the mainstays of American and Mexican breakfasts, and lunch dishes such as enchiladas and guacamole.

Av. Rafael Melgar (corner of Calle 6 Norte). © 987/872-0838. Reservations not accepted. Breakfast $4–$5; lunch main courses $5–$9. No credit cards. Daily 7am–2pm.

COZUMEL AFTER DARK

Most of the music and dance venues are in two areas: one is just north of the main plaza on Rafael Melgar, and includes the **Hard Rock Cafe** (© 987/872-5271); the other is in the Punta Langosta shopping center, in front of the pier of the same name, not far from Hotel Plaza Las Glorias. Here you'll find **Carlos 'n' Charlie's**

(© 987/869-1646) and **Señor Frog's** (© 987/869-1651). At the corner of Rosado Salas and Avenida 5 Sur (across from Prima) is a new nightclub called **La Pura Vida** (© 987/878-7831) that offers live salsa music (from a good Cuban band) Wednesday to Sunday with no cover and no minimum. It also offers free salsa dance lessons early in the evening. On Sunday evenings the place to be is the main square, which usually has a free concert and lots of people strolling about and visiting with friends. People sit in outdoor cafes enjoying the cool night breezes until the restaurants close.

The town of San Miguel has three **movie theaters.** Your best option is **Cinépolis,** the modern multicinema in the Chedraui Plaza Shopping Center, across Avenida Melgar from the Plaza Las Glorias Hotel. It mainly shows Hollywood movies. Most of these are in English with Spanish subtitles *(película subtitulada),* but before buying your tickets, make sure the movie hasn't been dubbed *(doblada).*

15

The Caribbean Coast: The Riviera Maya, Including Playa del Carmen & the Costa Maya

by David Baird

Perhaps it's worth reiterating that the Riviera Maya has "endless stretches of pristine beaches of soft white sand gently caressed by the turquoise-blue waters of the Caribbean," yadda, yadda, yadda . . . but my bet is that you've already heard it all. You've seen the ads, the brochures, and the articles in the Sunday travel sections. So I'll spare you the purple prose and get right to the things you'll need to know.

The Yucatán's Caribbean coast is 380km (240 miles) long, stretching from Cancún all the way to Chetumal, at the border with Belize. The northern half of the coast has been dubbed the "Riviera Maya"; the southern half, the "Costa Maya." In between is the large Sian Ka'an Biopreserve.

A long reef system, the second longest in the world, protects most of the shore. Where there are gaps in the reef—Playa del Carmen, Xpu-Ha, and Tulum—you find good beaches. The action of the surf

washes away silt and seagrass and erodes rocks, leaving a sandy bottom. Where the reef is prominent, you get good snorkeling and diving with lots of fish and other sea creatures. Here mangrove often occupies the shoreline; the beaches are usually sandy up to the water's edge, but shallow, with a silty or rocky floor.

Inland you'll find jungle, caverns, the famous *cenotes* (natural wells leading to underwater rivers), and the even more famous ruins of the Maya. Activities abound.

So do lodging options. On this coast you can stay in a variety of communities or distance yourself from all of them. There's just about every choice you can think of: rustic cabins, secluded spa resorts, boutique hotels, B&Bs, all-inclusive megaresorts, whatever you want. With so many options, you need to make some decisions. I hope that what follows will help.

EXPLORING MEXICO'S CARIBBEAN COAST

A single road, Highway 307, runs down the coast from Cancún to Chetumal. The section between Cancún's airport and Playa del Carmen (51km/32 miles) is a four-lane divided highway with speed limits up to 110kmph (70 mph). There are a couple of traffic lights and several reduced-speed zones around the major turnoffs. From Playa to Tulum (80km/50 miles), the road becomes a smooth two-lane highway with wide shoulders. Speed limits are the same, but more places require you to slow down. It takes 1½ hours to drive from the Cancún airport to Tulum.

The Yucatán Peninsula

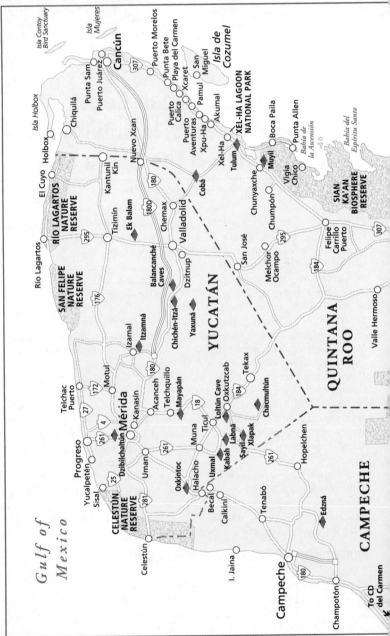

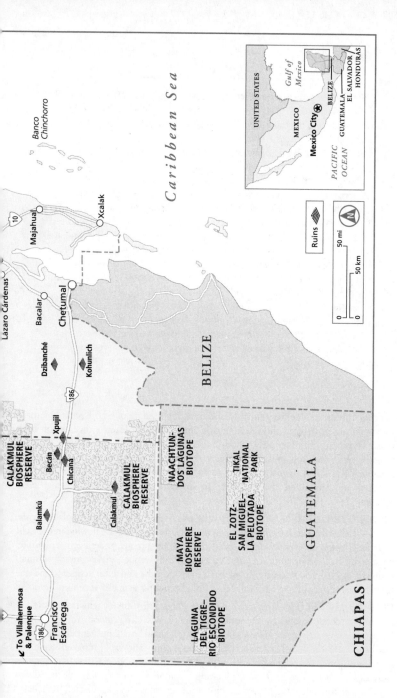

> **Tips   The Best Websites for Playa del Carmen & the Caribbean Coast**
>
> - **Tourism Board: www.rivieramaya.com**   Good general info that's kept up to date. You'll find a comprehensive list of accommodations and service providers for this coast as well as special deals that some hotels occasionally offer through this website.
> - **Ecotravels in Mexico: www.planeta.com/mexico.html**   This site covers the whole country and has a nice section on the Yucatán (about halfway down the page).
> - **Kuartos.com: www.kuartos.com**   Here's a well-designed and easy-to-use site for finding hotels and making reservations throughout Cancún and the Riviera Maya. Each hotel listing has a photo and detailed description (plus lowest rates) and allows you to check availability and make reservations. It also features super specials for selected properties.
> - ***Playa* Magazine Online: www.playadelcarmen.com**   This online version of the popular guide offers plenty of tips, news, and tourist information for those bound for Playa del Carmen.
> - **The Net Traveler: www.thenettraveler.com**   This site specializes in information about the Yucatán, Quintana Roo (home state of Cancún), and Chiapas, as well as other areas in the old Maya empire. Its information on archaeological sites, as well as on diving in the region's caves and *cenotes,* is especially good.

From Tulum, the highway turns inland to skirt the edges of Sian Ka'an. The roadway is narrower, without shoulders, and in some areas the forest crowds in on both sides. The speed limit is mostly 90kmph (60 mph), but you'll need to slow down in several places, and you must watch for *topes* (speed bumps) where the road passes through villages and towns. After the town of Limones, new road construction has widened and smoothed the highway. To drive from Tulum to Chetumal takes 3 hours.

PLAYA DEL CARMEN   Playa, as it is called, is the most happening place on the coast—a delightful beach (especially when the wind and currents are flowing in the right direction), hotels for every budget, a good choice of restaurants, and an active nightlife, most of which is on or around Quinta Avenida (Fifth Avenue), Playa's popular promenade. In the last few years the town has grown quickly, and local residents and the tourism board are working hard to keep it from becoming a smaller version of Cancún.

PUERTO MORELOS   This town between Playa and Cancún remains a little village affectionately known by the locals as "Muerto Morelos" (*muerto* means "dead") for it's phenomenally quiet low season. It has a few small hotels and rental houses, and nearby are a few secluded spa resorts. The coast is sandy and well protected by an offshore reef, which means good snorkeling and diving nearby, but the lack of surf means seagrass and shallow water. If you're looking for good swimming, head farther down the coast. If you're looking for a relaxing seaside retreat with a clean beach in an easygoing community, this will work for you.

PUERTO AVENTURAS The first major town south of Playa, it is a modern condo-marina development with a nine-hole golf course, several restaurants, and a few hotels. I don't think it's a fun place to stay, but you might come here to go deep-sea fishing or swim with dolphins.

AKUMAL A bit further south is Akumal and Half Moon Bay. The community is relatively old for this shore, which means that it's already built up and doesn't have the boomtown feel of Playa and Tulum. Akumal has a strong ecological orientation and is a prominent scuba and snorkeling center. The locals are a mix of Americans and Mexicans, who enjoy the unhurried lifestyle of the tropics, making this a good place to relax and work on your hammock technique. There are a few hotels; most of the lodging is rental houses and condos. Consequently, the town is a favorite with families who enjoy the calmness of the place and can save money by buying groceries and cooking for themselves.

TULUM The town of Tulum (near the ruins of the same name) has a hotel district of about 30 *palapa* hotels, which stretch down the coast of the Punta Allen peninsula. A few years ago it was mainly a destination for backpacker types, but with some of the most beautiful beaches on this coast and many improvements in hotel amenities, it now attracts people with bigger budgets. Construction is booming, both in the town and along the coast. Here you can enjoy the beach in relative solitude and quiet (unless your hotel is busy building additional rooms). The flip side of this is that Tulum doesn't have the variety of restaurants that Playa and Cancún do, but you can still eat well.

COSTA MAYA South of Tulum lies the large Sian Ka'an Biosphere Preserve and, beyond that, what is known as the Costa Maya, which designates the rest of the coast all the way down to Belize. The Costa Maya doesn't have beaches as good as those of the Riviera Maya. Most of the coast is along the Majahual Peninsula, which is very attractive for scuba divers and fly fishermen. Farther south is Lake Bacalar, a large, clear freshwater lake fed by *cenotes*. Inland from here are the many fascinating ruins of the Río Bec area.

1 Playa del Carmen ★★★

32km (20 miles) S of Puerto Morelos; 70km (44 miles) S of Cancún; 10km (6½ miles) N of Xcaret; 13km (8 miles) N of Puerto Calica

Though it no longer has the feel of a village, Playa still provides that rare combination of simplicity (a small town that can be traversed on foot) and variety (many unique hotels, restaurants, and stores). There is a comfortable feel to the town. The local architecture has adopted elements of native building—rustic clapboard walls, stucco, thatched roofs, rough-hewn wood, and a ramshackle, unplanned look to many structures—that reflect the town's taste for third-world chic. Slicker architecture has appeared, with chain restaurants and stores, detracting from Playa's individuality, but Playa retains the feel of a cosmopolitan getaway still with a counterculture ethos.

Playa is perfect for enjoying the simple (and perhaps the best) pleasures of a seaside vacation—taking in the sun and the sea air while working your toes into the sand; cooling down with a swim in clear water; and strolling aimlessly down the beach, listening to the wash of waves, and feeling the light touch of tropical breezes. A strong European influence has made topless sunbathing (nominally against the law in Mexico) a nonchalantly accepted practice anywhere there's a beach. The beach grows and shrinks, from broad and sandy to narrower with rocks, depending on the currents and wind. When this happens, head to the beaches in north Playa.

From Playa it's easy to shoot out to Cozumel on the ferry, drive south to the nature parks and the ruins at Tulum and Cobá, or drive north to Cancún. Directly south of town is the Playacar development, which has a golf course, several large all-inclusive resorts, and a residential section.

ESSENTIALS

GETTING THERE & DEPARTING **By Air** You can fly into Cancún and take a bus directly from the airport (see "By Bus," below), or fly into Cozumel and take the passenger ferry.

By Car **Highway 307** is the only highway that passes through Playa. As you approach Playa from Cancún, the highway divides. Stay in the inside lanes; you'll be able to make a left turn at either of two traffic lights. The first is Avenida Constituyentes, which works well for destinations in northern Playa. The second is Avenida Juárez, which leads to the town's main square and the ferry pier. If you stay in the outside lanes, you will need to continue past Playa until you get to the turnaround, then double back, this time staying to your right.

By the Playa del Carmen–Cozumel Passenger Ferry Air-conditioned passenger ferries to Cozumel leave every hour on the hour from the town's pier one block from the main square. Construction of a second pier at the end of Avenida Constituyentes proceeds in fits and starts. There is also a car ferry to Cozumel from the Calica pier just south of the Playacar development. For more information about both ferries, see "Getting There & Departing" in the Cozumel section of chapter 14.

By Taxi Taxi fares from the Cancún airport are about $50 to $60 one-way.

By Bus **Autobuses Riviera** offers service from the Cancún airport about 12 times a day. Cost is $8 one-way. You'll see a ticket counter in the corridor leading out of the airport. From the Cancún bus station there are frequent departures—almost every 30 minutes.

ORIENTATION

ARRIVING The **ferry** dock in Playa is 1 block from the main square and within walking distance of hotels. Playa has two **bus** stations. Buses coming from Cancún and places along the coast, such as Tulum, arrive at the Riviera bus station, at the corner of Juárez and Quinta Avenida, by the town square. Buses coming from destinations in the interior of the peninsula arrive at the new ADO station, on Avenida 20 between calles 12 and 14.

CITY LAYOUT The main street, **Avenida Juárez,** leads to the *zócalo* (town square) from Highway 307. As it does so, it crosses several numbered avenues that run parallel to the beach, all of which are multiples of 5. **Quinta Avenida (Fifth Avenue)** is

---

Tips **Speed Zone**

On Highway 307 lots of cars travel faster than the posted speed limits, and ticketing for speeding is seldom seen. But the police in Playa have been ticketing zealously on the section of highway that passes through town. Maximum speed for the center lanes is 60kmph (40 mph), and for the outside lanes 40kmph (25 mph). Careful.

Playa del Carmen

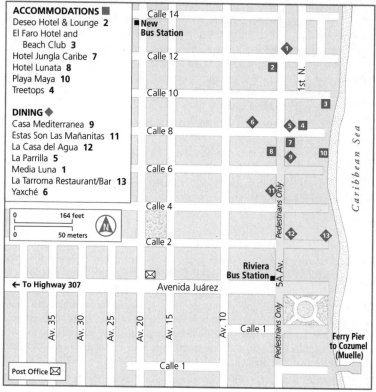

ACCOMMODATIONS ■
Deseo Hotel & Lounge **2**
El Faro Hotel and
  Beach Club **3**
Hotel Jungla Caribe **7**
Hotel Lunata **8**
Playa Maya **10**
Treetops **4**

DINING ◆
Casa Mediterranea **9**
Estas Son Las Mañanitas **11**
La Casa del Agua **12**
La Parrilla **5**
Media Luna **1**
La Tarroma Restaurant/Bar **13**
Yaxché **6**

0   164 feet
0   50 meters

← To Highway 307

Post Office ⊠

Calle 14
■ New
Bus Station
Calle 12
Calle 10
Calle 8
Calle 6
Calle 4
Calle 2

Riviera
Bus Station ■

Avenida Juárez

Av. 35
Av. 30
Av. 25
Av. 20
Av. 15
Av. 10
Calle 1

1st N.

Caribbean Sea

Pedestrians Only

5A Av.

Pedestrians Only

Calle 1

Ferry Pier
to Cozumel
(Muelle)

closest to the beach; it's closed to traffic from the *zócalo* to Calle 6 (and some blocks beyond, in the evening). On this avenue are many hotels, restaurants, and shops. Almost all of the town is north and west of the *zócalo*. Immediately south are the ferry pier and the Continental Plaza Playacar Hotel. This is the southern edge of town. Beyond it are the airstrip and the golf course development called Playacar, with lots of private residences and a dozen resort hotels.

FAST FACTS: Playa del Carmen

Area Code The telephone area code is **984**.

Doctor For serious medical attention, go to Hospiten in Cancún. In Playa, Dr. Jorge Mercado is a capable general practitioner who speaks English. His office is at the corner of avenidas 10 and Constituyentes (© **984/873-3908**); after hours he can be reached at his cellphone (© **984/877-7400**).

Internet Access Internet cafes are all over town; most have speedy connection speeds.

Money Exchange Playa has several banks and ATMs. Many currency-exchange houses are close to the pier or along Quinta Avenida at Calle 8.

Parking Most parking in Playa is on the street. Spots can be hard to come by. The most accessible parking lot is the Estacionamiento México, at avenidas Juárez and 10 (where the entrance is located). It's open daily 24 hours and charges $1.25 per hour, $8 per day. There's also a 24-hour lot a block from the pier, where you can leave your car while you visit Cozumel.

Pharmacy The **Farmacia del Carmen,** Avenida Juárez between avenidas 5 and 10 (✆ **984/873-2330**), is open 24 hours.

Post Office The *correo,* on Avenida Juárez, 3 blocks from the plaza, is on the right past the Hotel Playa del Carmen and the launderette.

Seasons The main high season is from mid-December to Easter. There is a mini high season in August. Low season is all other months.

EXPLORING PLAYA & THE RIVIERA MAYA

The main activity in Playa is hanging out on the beach and enjoying the Quinta Avenida nightlife. But there are actually plenty of activities to do up and down this coast. The following is a brief list to help you consider your options.

GOLF & TENNIS If golf is your bag, an 18-hole championship **golf course** (✆ **984/873-0624**), designed by Robert Von Hagge, is adjacent to the Continental Plaza Playacar. Greens fees are $160 in the morning (including tax and cart) and $100 after 2pm; caddies cost $20, and club rental costs $20. The club also has two **tennis** courts, which cost $10 per hour.

HORSEBACK RIDING There are several places along the highway that offer horseback rides. The best of these is just south of Playa near the Calica Pier. It's called **Rancho Punta Venado** (✆ **984/877-9701**). You'll see a clearly marked sign. This place is less touristy than the others and less noisy (no ATVs), and the owner, a rancher, takes good care of his horses.

DAY SPA To relax after all that exertion, try **Itzá Spa** (yes, it's a spa—and a good one, right in the heart of Playa) between calles 12 and 14 in a retail area called Calle Corazón. The phone is ✆ **984/803-2588.**

VISITING THE RUINED CITIES OF THE MAYA There are four cities within easy reach of Playa and most of the coast. The easiest to reach is **Tulum** (see the box on Tulum later in this chapter where my co-author and I air our different views of the city). A half-hour inland from Tulum on a pock-marked road is **Cobá,** rising up from a jungle setting. This city has not been reconstructed to the same degree as the other three and doesn't have the rich imagery or clearly delineated architecture. Its description is also in the Tulum section. The other two cites, **Chichén Itzá** and **Ek Balam,** are 2½ hours distant in the interior of the peninsula. My favorite way of seeing them is to rent a car and drive to Chichén in the afternoon, check into a hotel (perhaps one with a pool), see the sound-and-light show that evening, and then tour the ruins in the cool of the morning before the big bus tours arrive. Then drive back via Valladolid and **Ek Balam.** See chapter 16 for a description of these places.

TOURS From Playa and the rest of the coast there are tours to these ruins. As yet I haven't seen any to Ek Balam, but it's just a question of time. The tour buses usually stop at a few places along the way for refreshments and souvenirs, which is why I prefer the small tours. Some combine the ruins of Tulum with a visit to a nature park. There is a tour agency in Playa called **Alltournative** (© **984/873-2036;** www. alltournative.com), which offers small tours that combine a little of everything: culture (visit a contemporary Maya village); adventure (kayaking, rappelling, snorkeling, *cenote* diving); natural history; and ruins. It offers these tours daily using vans for transportation. The tours are fun. You can call the agency directly or arrange a tour through your hotel; they pick up at most of the large resorts that are along the coast. Another interesting option is an ecological tour of the **Sian Ka'an Biopreserve.** To do this, however, you have to get to Tulum. See the Tulum section, later in this chapter.

DEEP-SEA FISHING The largest marina on the coast is at **Puerto Aventuras,** not far south of Playa. Here's where you'll find most of your options for boating and fishing. See p. 603.

SCUBA/SNORKELING In Playa, **Tank-Ha Dive Center** (© **984/873-0302;** fax 984/873-1355; www.tankha.com) arranges reef and cavern diving. The owner, Alberto Leonard, came to Playa by way of Madrid and offers reef and *cenote* diving excursions. He and his staff speak English. Snorkeling trips cost around $30 and include soft drinks and equipment. Two-tank dive trips are $55; resort courses with SSI and PADI instructors cost $75. I also recommend a good dive shop in Puerto Morelos, north of Playa, and a couple in Akumal, south of Playa. The area around Akumal has a number of underwater caverns and *cenotes* that have become popular scuba and snorkeling destinations. The **Akumal Dive Shop** specializes in cavern diving and offers a variety of dives. But the easiest way to try Cavern diving or snorkeling is through **Hidden Worlds Cenotes,** which is right on the highway 15km (9 miles) south of Akumal. They provide everything, including wet suit. See "South of Playa del Carmen," later in this chapter.

SWIMMING WITH DOLPHINS In the two nature parks south of Playa, Xcaret and Xel-Ha, you can have the opportunity of interacting with these intelligent creatures. Also, there's an outfit in Puerto Aventuras called Dolphin Discovery that is quite good. See "South of Playa del Carmen," later in this chapter.

THE NATURE PARKS: XCARET, XEL-HA & TRES RIOS These parks make full-day excursions, offering opportunities for swimming, snorkeling and other seaside activities, educational tours about the region's natural history as well as the local Maya culture, and entertainment. They are completely self-contained and offer food, drink, watersports equipment, and various kinds of merchandise. Tres Ríos isn't far north of Playa. Xcaret is just south of Playa, while Xel-Ha is further south, almost to Tulum. (See sections 2 and 3, later in this chapter.)

   Cozumel is a half-hour away by ferry; in my opinion, it makes for a poor day trip unless you simply want to shop. You'll see exactly what the cruise-ship passengers see—lots of duty-free, souvenir, and jewelry stores. To enjoy Cozumel best, you have to spend at least a couple of nights there to explore the island. See chapter 14.

WHERE TO STAY

Playa has a lot of small hotels with affordable prices that give you a better feel for the town than staying in one of the resorts in Playacar. Don't hesitate to book a place that's not on the beach. Town life here is much of the fun, and staying on the beach in Playa has its disadvantages—in particular, the noise of a couple of beachside bars. Beaches are public property in Mexico, and you can lay out your towel anywhere you like. There are some beach clubs in north Playa where for a small sum you can have the use of lounge chairs, towels, and food and drink.

High season is from mid-December to Easter. July and August is also high season for some hotels but not others. During other parts of the year you can come to Playa and look for walk-in offers. The rates listed below include the 12% hotel tax. I don't include the rates for Christmas to New Year's, which are still higher than the standard high-season rates.

VERY EXPENSIVE

Deseo Hotel + Lounge ✶✶✶ In a town where being hip is a raison d'être, there is no hotel hipper than this one. Its creators, the owners of **Habita** in Mexico City, seek to redefine our notions of a hotel by designing an environment that fosters social interaction. The lounge plays the central role, appropriating all the functions of lobby, restaurant, bar, and pool area. It's a raised open-air platform with bar, pool, and self-serve kitchen furnished with large daybeds for sunning or for enjoying an evening drink when the bar is in full swing. The rooms face two sides of the lounge. The clientele is predominantly 25- to 45-year-olds, and the music, too, seems by design to provide an artsy background that's sufficiently monotonous not to compete with the setting or the conversation.

The guest rooms play their part. They are comfortable, original, and visually striking, but, unlike the usual plush hotel room, they don't tempt one to isolation amidst an array of amenities—no TV, no minibar, no cushy armchair. There is a simplicity that gives them an almost Asian feel, heightened by nice touches such as sliding doors of wood and frosted glass. The mattresses, however, are thick and luxurious. All rooms have king-size beds. From the bottom of each bed, a little drawer slides out with a night kit containing three things: incense, earplugs, and condoms.

Av. 5 (at Calle 12), 77710 Playa del Carmen, Q. Roo. ✆ **984/879-3620.** Fax 984/879-3621. www.hoteldeseo.com. 15 units. $180 lounge view; $199 balcony; $244 suite. Rates include continental breakfast. AE, MC, V. No parking. Children not accepted. **Amenities:** Bar; small rooftop pool; Jacuzzi; tour info; ground transfer; room service until 11pm; in-room massage; laundry service. *In room:* A/C, minibar, hair dryer on request, safe.

El Faro Hotel and Beach Club ✶✶ Rooms encircle a lawn graced by palm trees and gardens fronting 75m (250 ft.) of sandy beachfront. A stunning pool (heated in winter) has islands of palms and a *palapa* bar. The rooms, most of which are in a long three-story building running perpendicular to the beach, are attractive, with clay-tile and marble floors, ceiling fans, and rattan furniture. The bathrooms are large and smart looking, with lots of marble countertop. Bed choices include one king-size, one queen-size, or two double beds. Most rooms have a balcony or terrace. Rates for deluxe rooms vary according to location—oceanfront, oceanview, or garden view. Oceanfront rooms are right on the beach and are larger than the others, but occasionally the music from the beach bars can drift in. The rates below are for all year, except December, when they run 50% higher.

Calle 10 Norte, 77710 Playa del Carmen, Q. Roo. ✆ **888/243-7413** in the U.S., or 984/873-0970. Fax 984/873-0968. www.hotelelfaro.com. 28 units. $190–$240 double. Rates include full breakfast. Look for Internet specials. AE, MC, V. Limited free guarded parking. **Amenities:** Restaurant; bar; pool; tour info; ground transfer; limited room service; massage; babysitting. *In room:* Hair dryer in room or available on request.

Shangri-La Caribe ★★★   This hotel—a loose grouping of cabañas on one of the best beaches in Playa—is hard to beat for sheer fun and leisure. And it's far enough from the center of town to be quiet. The older, south side of the hotel (the "Caribe" section) consists of one- and two-story cabañas. The north side ("Playa" section) has a few larger buildings, holding four to six rooms. A preference for one or the other section is a matter of taste; the units in both are similar in amenities, privacy, and price. All rooms have a patio or porch complete with hammock. Most come with two double beds, but a few have a king-size bed. Windows are screened, and ceiling fans circulate the breeze. The real difference in price depends on the proximity to the water—oceanfront, oceanview, or garden view. Garden view is the best bargain, being only a few steps farther from the water. Many garden view rooms (mostly in a third section called "Pueblo") have air-conditioning, which adds $6 to the price. Book well in advance during high season.

Calle 38 (Apdo. Postal 253), 77710 Playa del Carmen, Q. Roo. ✆ **800/538-6802** in the U.S. and Canada, or 984/ 873-0611. Fax 984/873-0500. www.shangrilacaribe.net. 107 units. High season $155–$190 garden view, $210 ocean-view, $285 oceanfront; low season $95–$155 garden view, $150–$175 oceanview, $220–$240 oceanfront. Rates include breakfast and dinner. AE, MC, V. Free guarded parking. From Hwy. 307 from Cancún, U-turn at the light for Av. Constituyentes, making sure to get into the far right lane. Backtrack to the Volkswagen dealership, turn right, and head for the beach. This will be Calle 38. **Amenities:** 2 restaurants; poolside grill; 3 bars; 2 large pools; whirlpool; watersports equipment; game room; tour desk; ground transfer; car rental; in-room massage; babysitting; laundry service; dive shop. *In room:* Hair dryer, no phone.

EXPENSIVE

Hotel Lunata ★★   In the middle of Playa there isn't a more comfortable or more attractive place to stay than this small hotel on Quinta Avenida. The rooms offer character, good looks, and polish. There are a few standard rooms, which are midsize and come with a queen-size or a double bed. Deluxe rooms are large and come with a king-size bed and small fridge. Junior suites come with two doubles. Bathrooms are well designed and have good showers. Light sleepers should opt for a room facing the garden. On my last stay, I took a room facing the street with double-glazed glass doors that opened to a balcony. I enjoyed looking out over Quinta Avenida, and, with the doors shut, the noise was not particularly bothersome.

Av. 5 (between calles 6 and 8), 77710 Playa del Carmen, Q. Roo. ✆ **984/873-0884.** Fax 984/873-1240. www. lunata.com. 10 units. High season $110 standard, $140–$155 deluxe and junior suite; low season $100 standard, $120–$135 deluxe and junior suite. Rates include continental breakfast. Promotional rates available. AE, MC, V. No children under 13. **Amenities:** Free use of bike and watersports equipment; tour desk; in-room massage; laundry service; nonsmoking rooms. *In room:* A/C, TV, fridge in some, hair dryer on request, safe, no phone.

Hotel Quinto Sol ★   This three-story hotel in north Playa wraps around an ancient-looking tree laden with orchids. The building's design has an Italian touch, with a lot of curves and rounded corners in the stuccowork. Highlights include a rooftop Jacuzzi, and proximity to the beaches on Playa's north side. The rooms are large and attractive, with good air-conditioning; bathrooms come with showers and could use a little more light. "Studios" are comparable to "standards" but come with kitchenettes. Minisuites are larger than either, have a few extra details plus balconies. This part of Quinta Avenida is usually quiet.

Av. 5 Norte 330 (at Calle 28), 77710 Playa del Carmen, Q. Roo. ✆ **984/873-3292** or -3293. Fax 984/873-3294. www. hotelquintosol.com. 20 units. High season $100–$125 standard or studio, $140–$165 suite; low season $80–$95 standard or studio, $100–$120 suite. Rates include continental breakfast. Ask for Frommer's discount. MC, V. Street parking. **Amenities:** Restaurant; bar; free access to Playa Mamita's beach club; Jacuzzi; tour info; room service until 11pm; laundry service; nonsmoking rooms. *In room:* A/C, TV, kitchenette in some, minibar, coffeemaker on request, hair dryer, safe.

MODERATE

Hotel Jungla Caribe ⭐ Located right in the heart of the action, "La Jungla" is an imaginative piece of work—a colorful execution of neoclassical *a la tropical*. It's the right place for those who enjoy original lodging and seek out the commotion that comes with the location, which quiets down around 11pm. All but the eight *sencilla* (standard) rooms are large, with gray-and-black marble floors, air-conditioning, large bathrooms and the occasional Roman column. Doubles and junior suites face Quinta Avenida and come with two double beds. Catwalks lead from the main building to the "tower" section of suites in back (the quietest). The *sencilla* rooms face Calle 8, are small with ample bathrooms, and have no air-conditioning. They come with one double bed and a balcony. It is best for people who go to bed late because of the mariachis who play across the street. There's an attractive pool in the courtyard surrounded by vegetation and shaded by a giant *ramón* tree.

Av. 5 Norte (at Calle 8), 77710 Playa del Carmen, Q. Roo. ℂ/fax **984/873-0650**. www.junglacaribe.com. 25 units. High season $70 *sencilla*, $90 double, $120–$130 suite; low season $50 *sencilla*, $65 double, $90–$100 suite. AE, MC, V. **Amenities:** Restaurant; 2 bars; pool; tour info; room service until 11pm. *In room:* A/C, TV, no phone.

Playa Maya ⭐ *Value* Of the beach hotels in downtown Playa, this one would be my first choice. There are a lot of reasons to like it (good location, good price, attractive, comfortable rooms, and friendly and helpful management), but one thing that really strikes my fancy is that you enter this hotel from the beach. This little, seemingly inconsequential detail shouldn't be any reason for picking a hotel, but it just sets the mood of the place and creates a little separation from the busy street scene. To get back to more practical matters, the design and location make it a quiet hotel, too, as it is a couple of blocks away from the nearest beach bar and it's sheltered by the neighboring hotels. The pool and sunning terrace are attractive and nicely set apart. Rooms are large with midsize bathrooms. A couple come with private garden terraces with Jacuzzis, others have balconies facing the beach.

Zona FMT between calles 6 and 8 Norte, 77710 Playa del Carmen, Q. Roo. ℂ **984/803-2022**. www.playa-maya.com. 20 units. High season $112 standard, $129 superior, $145 deluxe; low season $90 standard, $100 superior, $112 deluxe. Rates include continental breakfast. MC, V. **Amenities:** Restaurant; bar; outdoor pool; fitness room; Jacuzzi; room service until 6pm; massage, laundry service. *In room:* A/C, TV, fridge, hair dryer, safe, high-speed wireless Internet.

INEXPENSIVE

Treetops ⭐ *Value* The rooms at Treetops encircle a patch of preserved jungle (and a small *cenote*) that shades the hotel and lends it the proper tropical feel. Rooms are large and comfortable and have balconies or patios that overlook the "jungle." Some of the upper rooms have the feel of a treehouse, especially the "treehouse" suite. The two other suites are large, with fully loaded kitchenettes—good for groups of four. The location is excellent: a half-block from the beach, a half-block from Quinta Avenida. The American owners are helpful, attentive hosts.

Calle 8 s/n, 77710 Playa del Carmen, Q. Roo. ℂ/fax **984/873-0351**. www.treetopshotel.com. 18 units. High season $45–$83 double, $121–$146 suite; low season $35–$72 double, $99–$123 suite. MC, V. **Amenities:** Restaurant; bar; small pool. *In room:* A/C, kitchenette in some, fridge, no phone.

WHERE TO DINE

Ahhhh, so many restaurants, so little time. Aside from those listed below, I would point you in the direction of a few that don't need a full review. For a quick bite in the afternoon or evening, try the *taquería* **Los 3 Carboncitos** on Calle 12 between avenidas 10 and 15 (no phone; closed Mon). It is the only *taquería* I know of that is run by a trained biologist—a telling difference because the usual problem with *taque-rías* is cleanliness. The danger lies not with the meat or cooked fillings but with the cilantro and salsas. Here you can eat without fear; Sonia runs a tight operation. Try the *tacos al pastor* with cilantro and *cebolla* (onion) and douse them with one of several salsas—I can't decide which I like best: the *verde* (green), the *chile de árbol,* or the *tres-chiles* (three chiles).

For fish tacos and inexpensive seafood, try **El Oasis,** also on Calle 12, between avenidas 5 and 10 (no phone). For something Mexican farther off the beaten path, try **Pozolería Mi Abuelita** (no phone) on Avenida 30, between calles 20 and 22. This is a restaurant of the people and should be considered only by adventurous diners. It's open in the evenings and serves good *pozole rojo* and *enchiladas verdes.* The best steak in town is served at **Carmencita** (© **984/803-3649**) at Quinta Avenida and Calle 20. It also serves Argentine-style *empanadas.* For pizza, the consensus favorite is **La Siesta,** where you can order to go (© **984/879-3982**). It's at Avenida 1 Norte 238, between calles 12 and 16. (Av. 1 is in north Playa between Quinta Avenida and the ocean). La Siesta is aptly named: Service is on the sleepy side.

EXPENSIVE

La Casa del Agua ★★ EUROPEAN/MEXICAN   Excellent food in inviting surroundings. Instead of obtrusive background music, you hear the sound of falling water. The Swiss owners work at presenting what they like best about Old and New Worlds. For starters they offer mushrooms flavored with white wine, garlic, and *epazote* (a Mexican herb). For a mild dish, try chicken in a wonderfully scented sauce of fine herbs accompanied by fettuccine; for something heartier, there's the tortilla soup listed as "Mexican soup." The restaurant offers a number of cool and light dishes that would be appetizing for lunch or an afternoon meal, for example, an avocado stuffed with shrimp and flavored with a subtle horseradish sauce on a bed of alfalfa sprouts and julienne carrots—a good mix of tastes and textures. For dessert, try the chocolate mousse. This is an upstairs restaurant under a large and airy *palapa* roof. A bit of advice: *ixnay* on the *mole.*

Av. 5 (at Calle 2). © **984/803-0232**. Main courses $9–$22. AE, MC, V. Daily noon–midnight.

La Parrilla MEXICAN/GRILL   Still a fun place, but it's having problems handling its success. Prices have gone up, and service is slower. But the fajitas remain good as well as many of the Mexican standards such as tortilla soup, enchiladas, and quesadillas. Mariachis show up around 8pm; plan accordingly. If you want cheaper (and, in my opinion, a more authoritative rendition of Mexican food), try **Casa Mestiza** on Avenida Constituyentes (on the right, two doors down from Quinta Avenida—good food, but the restaurant is a bit cramped). It's operated by a woman from Mexico City who has the gift. For grilled steaks I like **Carmencita**—see the description in the dining intro, above.

Av. 5 (at Calle 8). © **984/873-0687**. Reservations recommended in high season. Main courses $8–$22. AE, MC, V. Daily noon–1am.

Yaxché ★★★ REGIONAL   The menu here makes use of many native foods and spices to present a more elaborate regional cooking than the usual offerings at Yucatecan restaurants. And it was about time for someone to show a little creativity with such an interesting palette of tastes. Excellent examples are a cream of *chaya* (a native leafy vegetable), and an *xcatic* chile stuffed with *cochinita pibil.* I also like the classic

Mexican-style fruit salad with lime juice and dried powdered chile. There are several seafood dishes; the ones I had were fresh and well prepared.

Calle 8 (between avs. 5 and 10). ② 984/873-2502. Reservations recommended in high season. Main courses $9–$25. AE, MC, V. Daily noon–midnight.

MODERATE

Casa Mediterránea ★★★ ITALIAN   Tucked away on a quiet little patio off Quinta Avenida, this small, homey restaurant serves excellent food. Maurizio Gabrielli and Mary Michelon are usually there to attend the customers and make recommendations. Maurizio came to Mexico to enjoy the simple life, and this inclination shows in the restaurant's welcoming, unhurried atmosphere. The menu is mostly northern Italian, with several dishes from other parts of Italy. There are daily specials, too. Pastas (except penne and spaghetti) are made in-house, and none is precooked. Try fish and shrimp ravioli or penne alla Veneta. There are several wines, mostly Italian, to choose from. The salads are good and carefully prepared—dig in without hesitation.

Av. 5 (between calles 6 and 8; look for a sign for Hotel Marieta). ② 984/876-3926. Reservations recommended in high season. Main courses $8–$15. No credit cards. Daily 1–11pm.

Estas Son Las Mañanitas MEXICAN/ITALIAN   For dependable food in an advantageous spot for people-watching try this restaurant. It's simple outdoor dining on "la Quinta"—comfortable chairs and tables under *palapa* umbrellas. The Italian owner is vigilant about maintaining quality and consistency. He offers an excellent *sopa de lima,* a large seafood pasta, grilled shrimp with herbs, and Tex-Mex specialties such as chili and fajitas. The hot sauces are good.

Av. 5 (between calles 4 and 6). ② 984/873-0114. Main courses $7–$14. AE, MC, V. Daily 7am–11:30pm.

La Cueva del Chango ★ HIPPIE MEXICAN   Good food for breakfast or lunch in original surroundings with a relaxed "mañana" attitude. True to its name, the place suggests a cave and has these nifty little waterways meandering through it. But, take away the water and the jungle vegetation, and, oddly enough, it brings to mind the Flintstones. Great coffee, juices, blended fruit drinks, salads, soups, Mexican specialties with a natural twist, and handmade tortillas. The food is fresh and delicious.

Calle 38 between Av. 5 and the beach (near the Shangri-la Caribe). ② 984/873-2137. Main courses $5–$10. No credit cards. Daily 8am–5pm.

La Vagabunda ITALIAN/MEXICAN   This place is old-style Playa in its simplicity and charm. A large *palapa* shelters several simple wood tables sitting on a gravel floor. It's low-key and quiet—a good place for breakfast, with many options, including delicious blended fruit drinks, waffles, and omelets. The specials are a good value. In the afternoon and evening you can order light fare such as panini, pastas, and *ceviche.*

Av. 5 (between calles 24 and 26). ② 984/873-3753. Breakfast $3–$5; main courses $6–$14. MC, V. High season daily 7am–11:30pm; low season daily 7am–3:30pm.

Media Luna ★★★ FUSION   The owner-chef has come up with an outstanding menu that favors grilled seafood, sautés, and pasta dishes. Everything is fresh and prepared beautifully. Try the pan-fried fish cakes with mango and honeyed *hoisin* sauce— very good. Another choice is the black pepper–crusted fish. Be sure to eye the daily specials. For lunch you can get sandwiches and salads, as well as black-bean quesadillas and crepes. The decor is primitive-tropical chic.

Av. 5 (between calles 12 and 14). © 984/873-0526. Breakfast $4–$6; main courses $8–$15; sandwich with salad $5–$7. No credit cards. Daily 8am–11:30pm.

INEXPENSIVE

La Tarraya Restaurant/Bar *Value* SEAFOOD   THE RESTAURANT THAT WAS BORN WITH THE TOWN, proclaims the sign. It's right on the beach, with the water practically lapping at the foundations. Because the owners are fishermen, the fish is so fresh it's practically still wiggling. The wood hut doesn't look like much, but you can have your fish prepared in several ways. If you haven't tried the Yucatecan specialty *tik-n-xic* fish (with *achiote* and bitter-orange sauce, cooked in a banana leaf), this is a good place to do so.

Calle 2 Norte. © 984/873-2040. Main courses $4–$7; whole fish $8 per kilo. No credit cards. Daily 7am–9pm.

PLAYA DEL CARMEN AFTER DARK

It seems as if everyone in town is out strolling along "la quinta" until 10 or 11pm; there's pleasant browsing, dining, and drinking available at the many establishments on the street, such as **Apasionado** (© **984/803-1101**) at the corner of Calle 14 with live jazz Wednesday to Saturday. Here's a quick rundown of the bars that you won't find on Quinta Avenida. The beach bar that is an institution in Playa is the **Blue Parrot** (© **984/873-0083**). It gets live acts, mostly rock, and attracts a mixed crowd. It's between calles 12 and 14. Just to the south is **Om** (no phone), which gets a younger crowd with louder musical acts. Farther south along the beach is **Captain Tutix** (no phone). It's designed like a pirate ship and has a large bar area, dance floor, and live entertainment nightly. Each time I go, the live bands are worse than the ones before. Down by the ferry dock is a **Señor Frog's** (© **984/873-0930**), which dishes out its patented mix of thumping dance music, Jell-O shots, and frat-house antics. For salsa, go to **Mambo Café**, on Calle 6 between avenidas 5 and 10 (© **984/803/2656**).

Alux (© **984/803-0713**) is a one-of-a-kind club occupying a large cave with two dramatically lit chambers and several nooks and sitting areas. It's worth going to, if only for the novelty. The local conservancy group approved all the work, and great care was taken not to contaminate the water, which is part of a larger underground river system. The club books a variety of music acts, usually with no cover. Often there's belly dancing, which is quite in keeping with the surroundings, and I couldn't help but think that I had stepped into a scene from a James Bond film. The bar is cash only and is open Tuesday to Sunday from 7pm to 2am. Take Avenida Juárez across to the other side of the highway—2 blocks down on your left.

For movie going, **Cine Hollywood,** Avenida 10 and Calle 8, in the Plaza Pelícanos shopping center, shows a lot of films in English with Spanish subtitles *(subtitulada)*. Before you buy your ticket, make sure the film is subtitled and not dubbed *(doblada)*.

A word of caution: Approach any time-share salesperson as you would a wounded rhino. And remember that whatever free trinket is offered for simply viewing apartments, it either won't materialize or won't be worth the time you invest in your dealings with these people. I've heard reports here that take the chicanery of these operators to whole new depths, especially the selling of the Mayan Palace resort. You have been warned.

Choosing an All-Inclusive in the Riviera Maya

There are more than 40 all-inclusive resorts on this coast. Most people are familiar with the concept—large hotels that work with economies of scale to offer lodging, food, and drink all for a single, low rate. All-inclusives offer convenience and economy, especially for families with many mouths to feed. And, because they are enclosed areas, they make it easy for parents to keep an eye on their children.

There is a certain sameness about these hotels so that a lot can be said that applies to all. They're usually built around a large pool with activities and an activities organizer. There is often a quiet pool, too. One large buffet restaurant and a snack bar serve the needs of most guests, but there will be a couple of specialty restaurants at no extra charge but to which the guest has to make reservations. Colored bracelets serve to identify who are guests. In the evenings a show is presented at the hotel's theater.

These hotels work best for those who are looking for a beach vacation to get away from the cold weather. It's not a getaway from people—these hotels are large and work with a high occupancy rate. Yes, staying at these all-inclusives is relaxing, convenient, and hassle-free. They make everything easy, including taking tours and day trips. All the organizing is done for you. On the downside, you don't often get the spontaneity or the sense of adventure that comes with other styles of travel. The question you have to ask yourself is what kind of vacation are you looking for?

The best way to get a room at an all-inclusive is through a vacation packager or one of its travel agents. You get a better deal than by contacting the hotel directly. Even if you have frequent-flyer miles to burn, you will still find it difficult to match the rates of a full package offered by one of the biggies like FunJet.

2 North of Playa del Carmen
EN ROUTE TO PUERTO MORELOS

As you drive north from Playa del Carmen, you'll pass a number of roadside attractions, all-inclusive hotels, small cabaña hotels, secluded resorts, and the nature park of Tres Ríos. The turnoff for Puerto Morelos is only 32km (20 miles) from Playa.

Tres Ríos is halfway between Playa and Puerto Morelos. It's the simplest of the nature parks and, indeed, might better be thought of as an elaborate beach club with organized activities such as beach volleyball and soccer, snorkel and scuba tours, watersports equipment rental, horseback riding, and food and beverage service. Yes, there are three little rivers that give the name to this place and add considerably to the charms of spot (except in the rainy season of late summer/early fall when the water is brackish), and there are a few environmental activities, but the main draw is the beach and the sea (3km/2 miles of coastline).

The park is open daily 9am to 5pm. For basic entrance, which gives you access to the park's main features and use of beach chairs, admission is $34 adults, $20 children 5 to 11. There is an array of inclusive packages that include food and drink and tours.

Of the many all-inclusives in the Riviera Maya, there are a few that are my favorites and might bear looking into:

Iberostar Quetzal or **Tucan** (two names for different halves of the same hotel; www.iberostar.com). Of the several all-inclusives that are in Playa del Carmen/Playacar, I like this one. The food is better than at most, and the central part of the hotel is made of raised walkways and terraces over the natural mangrove habitat. Its neighbor the **Gala** (www.galaresorts.com.mx) is also a good choice.

The **Copacabana** resort in Xpu-Ha (www.hotelcopacabana.com), also has raised walkways preserving much of the flora and making it visually interesting. And Xpu-Ha is blessed with a stunning beach.

Also in Xpu-Ha is the **Xpu-Ha Palace** (www.palaceresorts.com), built on the grounds of a failed nature park. It has some keen features including lagoons and jungle and offers several facilities for kids, including a small crocodile hatchery. The hotel is spread out over a large area and necessarily involves a good bit of walking, but this also makes it feel like more of a getaway.

Aventura Spa Palace (www.palaceresorts.com) is another hotel in the Palace chain—this one just for grown ups. It has a large spa and gym and attractive common areas and guest rooms. There is a large pool but no beach; guests can take a shuttle to the Xpu-Ha property if they want.

Freedom Paradise (www.freedomparadise.com) is billed as the first size-friendly vacation resort. The management has worked hard to create an environment that large people will find comfortable. I like it because it doesn't have all the froufrou of so many other resorts—it's friendly and unpretentious.

Prices run $61 to $116 for adults and $36 to $58 for children. For more information try ℂ **998/887-8077** or www.tres-rios.com.

Just before you get to the Puerto Morelos turnoff, you'll pass **Rancho Loma Bonita,** which has all the markings of a tourist trap and offers horseback riding and ATV tours. You'll also come across **Jardín Botánico Dr. Alfredo Barrera** (no phone). Opened in 1990 and named after a biologist who studied tropical forests, the botanical garden is open Monday to Saturday from 9am to 5pm. Admission is $7. It will be of most interest to gardeners and plant enthusiasts, but I'm afraid it will bore children. They are much more likely to enjoy the interactive zoo at Croco Cun (see "Exploring in & around Puerto Morelos," below).

BEACH CABAÑAS   Five kilometers (3 miles) north of Playa are some economical lodgings on a mostly rocky beach. A sign that says PUNTA BETE marks the access road to Xcalacoco. The last time I visited, there was a large warehouse-like structure and a sign advertising a subdivision somewhere that read ARBOLEDAS. The road is rough in places, but in a short time you arrive at the water. Before you do, the road forks off in a few places, and you'll see signs for different cabañas. The word conjures up visions of idyllic native-style dwellings with thatched roofs, but as often as not on the Yucatecan coast, it means simple lodging. This is mostly the case here, with rates running $45 to $60 a night for two people. Of the four groupings of cabañas in Xcalacoco, the one I like best is **Coco's Cabañas** (© 998/874-7056; www.travel-center.com), which has electricity and ceiling fans; a good, inexpensive little restaurant; and a small pool. It shares a wall with Ikal del Mar, a spa resort (see "Spa Resorts Near Puerto Morelos," below). In the future, one or two of the rooms might have air-conditioning.

A few minutes after passing Xcalacoco/Punta Bete, you'll see a large sign on the right side of the road marking the entrance to La Posada del Capitán Lafitte.

La Posada del Capitán Lafitte ⭐ Two kilometers (1¼ miles) from the highway, down a dirt road, this lovely seaside retreat sits on a solitary stretch of sandy beach. Here you can enjoy being isolated while still having all the amenities of a relaxing vacation. The beach is powdery white sand, but with a rocky bottom below the water. The one- and two-story white-stucco bungalows hold one to four rooms each. They are small to medium in size but comfortable, with tile floors and bathrooms, either two double beds or one king-size bed, and an oceanfront porch. Twenty-nine bungalows have air-conditioning; the rest have fans. Coffee can be served as early as 6:30am in the game room.

Carretera Cancún–Tulum Km 62, 77710 Playa del Carmen, Q. Roo. © 800/538-6802 in the U.S. and Canada, or 984/873-0214. Fax 984/873-0212. www.mexicoholiday.com. 62 units. High season $220–$270 double; low season $140–$170 double. Christmas and New Year's rates are higher. Minimum 2–4 nights. Rates include breakfast and dinner. MC, V. Free guarded parking. **Amenities:** Restaurant; poolside grill; bar; midsize pool; watersports equipment; game/TV room; activities desk; car rental; limited room service; laundry service; dive shop. *In room:* A/C in some, minibar.

PUERTO MORELOS

Puerto Morelos remains a quiet place—perfect for a relaxed vacation of lying on the white-sand beach and reading, with perhaps the occasional foray into watersports, especially snorkeling, diving, windsurfing, and kayaking. Offshore is a prominent reef, which has been declared a national park for its protection. Because of the reef, the beaches in Puerto Morelos have a lot of sea grass growing on the bottom. But the water is as clear as anywhere along the coast, and if a little sea grass doesn't bother you, you'll find this a cozy spot. The beaches in town are cleaned daily. Another attraction of the town is a large English-language new and used bookstore that stocks 20,000 titles. The ferry that used to depart from here for Cozumel has moved down the coast to the Calica pier just south of Playa del Carmen.

ESSENTIALS

GETTING THERE **By Car** At Km 31 there's a traffic light at the intersection, and a large sign pointing to Puerto Morelos.

By Bus Buses from Cancún to Tulum and Playa del Carmen usually stop here, but be sure to ask in Cancún if your bus makes the Puerto Morelos stop.

EXPLORING IN & AROUND PUERTO MORELOS

Puerto Morelos attracts visitors who seek seaside relaxation without crowds and high prices. The town has several hotels, a few restaurants, and an English-language bookstore. For outdoor recreation, there are two dive shops and plenty of recreational boats for fishing or snorkeling. On the main square, you'll find the bookstore, **Alma Libre** (© 998/871-0713; www.almalibrebooks.com). It has more English-language books than any other in the Yucatán, and not just whodunits, sci-fi, and spy novels. The owners, Rob and Joanne Birce, stock everything from volumes on Maya culture to

The Yucatán's Upper Caribbean Coast

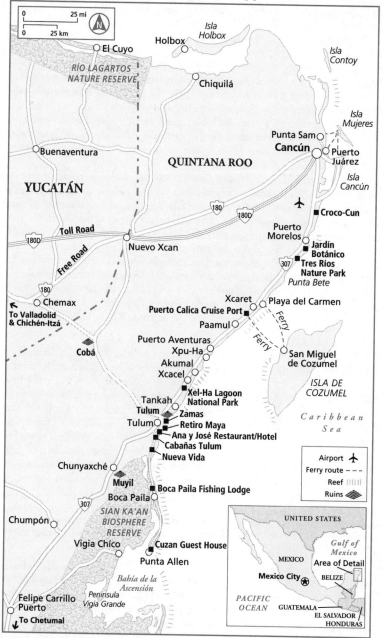

English classics to maps of the region. The store is open from October through the first week in June. Hours are Tuesday to Sunday from 10am to 3pm and 6 to 9pm.

On the ocean side of the main square is **Mystic Divers** (℗/fax **998/871-0634;** www.mysticdiving.com). It's well recommended, not only for diving but for fishing trips, too. The owner, Victor Reyes, speaks English and takes small groups. He is a PADI and NAUI instructor and gives his customers a lot of personal attention. The shop is open all year. A two-tank dive costs $45. The reef directly offshore is very shallow and is protected by law. Snorkelers are required to wear a life vest to prevent them from damaging the reef. I snorkeled for a bit and wasn't bothered by the vest. Much of the reef is within a foot or two of the water's surface and, at its deepest, is only about 3m (10 ft.). There was abundant life, and in a short time I spotted four different eels and sea snakes, lots of fish, and a ray.

North of Puerto Morelos is **Croco Cun** (℗ **998/884-4782**), a zoological park that raises crocodiles. It's a lot more than just your average roadside attraction. There's an interactive zoo with crocodiles in all stages of development, as well as animals of nearly all the species that once roamed the Yucatán Peninsula. A visit to the new reptile house is fascinating, though it may make you think twice about venturing into the jungle. The rattlesnakes and boa constrictors are particularly intimidating, and the tarantulas are downright enormous. The guided tour lasts 1½ hours. Children enjoy the guides' enthusiasm and are entranced by the spider monkeys and wild pigs. Wear plenty of bug repellent. The restaurant sells refreshments. Croco Cun is open daily from 8:30am to 5:30pm. As with other attractions along this coast, entrance fees are high: $15 adults, $9 children 6 to 12, free for children under 6. The park is at Km 31 on Highway 307.

WHERE TO STAY

Amar Inn   Simple, rustic rooms on the beach, in a home-style setting, make this small inn a good place for those wanting a quiet seaside retreat. The cordial hostess, Ana Luisa Aguilar, is the daughter of Luis Aguilar, a Mexican singer and movie star of the 1940s and 1950s. She keeps busy promoting environmental and equitable-development causes. She can line up snorkeling and fishing trips and jungle tours for guests with small operators. There are three cabañas in back, opposite the main house, and five upstairs rooms with views of the beach. The best is a third-story room with a great view of the ocean. The cabañas get less of a cross-breeze than the rooms in the main house but still have plenty of ventilation. They are large and come with kitchenettes. Rooms in the main building are medium to large. Bedding choices include one or two doubles, one king-size, or five twin beds. A full Mexican breakfast is served in the garden.

Av. Javier Rojo Gómez (at Lázaro Cárdenas), 77580 Puerto Morelos, Q. Roo. ℗ 998/871-0026. amar_inn@hotmail. com. 7 units. High season $55–$65 double; low season $45–$55 double. Rates include full breakfast. No credit cards. From the plaza, turn left; it's 1km (½ mile) down, immediately after the Hotel Ojo de Agua. **Amenities:** Tour and rental info. *In room:* Fridge, fan, no phone.

Casita del Mar ⟡   An attractive hotel on the beach, Casita del Mar offers pleasant rooms and good prices. Rooms come with either two full beds or one king-size. The standard units are midsize and well furnished. The beds I tried had soft mattresses. Oceanview rooms are larger, with larger bathrooms; three have tubs. There's a pretty terrace overlooking the beach. The hotel reception offers Internet access.

Calle Roberto Frías, SMZA 2, MZA 14, Lote 6, 77580 Puerto Morelos, Q. Roo. ℗/fax 998/871-0301. www.hotel casitadelmar.com. 19 units. High season $70 standard double, $84 oceanview double; low season $56 standard double, $64 oceanview double. Rates include full breakfast. AE, MC, V. Street parking. **Amenities:** Restaurant; bar; pool; tour info; massage; laundry service; dive shop. *In room:* A/C, no phone.

Hotel Ojo de Agua ⭐ (*Value*)   What I like best about this hotel is that it offers the convenience and service of a higher-priced hotel, including a good dive shop and watersports equipment rental service. Two three-story buildings stand on the beach at a right angle to each other. The simply furnished rooms have balconies or terraces; most have a view of the ocean. Standard rooms have one double bed. Deluxe rooms are large and have two doubles. Studios have a double and a twin and a small kitchenette but no air-conditioning (the rest of the rooms do have air-conditioning). Some rooms come with TV and phone. A highly respected instructor heads the dive shop. If you've wanted to try windsurfing, this is the place: The American who rents the boards takes his time with customers and is quite helpful.

Av. Javier Rojo Gómez. Supermanzana 2, Lote 16, 77580 Puerto Morelos, Q. Roo. ℂ 998/871-0027 or 998/871-0507. Fax 998/871-0202. www.ojo_de_agua.com. 36 units. High season $60 double, $65–$75 studio or deluxe; low season $50 double, $55–$60 studio or deluxe. Weekly and monthly rates available. AE, MC, V. **Amenities:** Restaurant; bar; pool; watersports equipment; tour info; room service until 10pm; scuba shop. *In room:* A/C in some, TV in some, kitchenette in some, no phone in some.

WHERE TO DINE

Puerto Morelos has a few restaurants. Most are on or around the main square and include **Caffe del Puerto** for salads, sandwiches, and the like; **Los Pelícanos** for seafood (overpriced); **Hola Asia** for Asian food; and **Le Café d'Amancia** for coffee and pastries. The most expensive restaurant in town is **John Grey's,** which is a couple of blocks north of the plaza and about 3 blocks inland. It's open for dinner except on Sundays. The owner is a former chef for the Ritz-Carlton, and I've enjoyed his cooking.

SPA RESORTS NEAR PUERTO MORELOS ⭐⭐⭐

In the area around Puerto Morelos, four spa resorts offer different versions of the hedonistic resort experience. Only 20 to 30 minutes from the Cancún airport, they are well situated for a quick weekend escape from the daily grind. You can jet down to Cancún, get whisked away by the hotel car, and be on the beach with a cocktail in hand before you can figure out whether you crossed a time zone. All four resorts pride themselves on their service, amenities, and spa and salon treatments. Being in the Yucatán, they like to add the healing practices of the Maya, especially the use of the native steam bath called *temazcal.* Rates quoted below include taxes but not the 5% to 10% service charge.

Ceiba del Mar   Eight three-story buildings make up this resort, the largest of the four. Each building has a rooftop terrace with Jacuzzi and service area with a concierge. The carefully tended white sand beach adjoins a seaside pool with Jacuzzi and bar. I like it a tad less than Maroma's and Paraíso de la Bonita's. Rooms are large and have a terrace or balcony. The bathtub area can be opened up to the entire room. Service is attentive and unobtrusive, as exemplified by the delivery of coffee and juice each morning, accomplished without disturbing the guests through the use of a blind pass-through. Check the website for rates that include meals.

Av. Niños Héroes s/n, 77580 Puerto Morelos, Q. Roo. ℂ 877/545-6221 in the U.S., or 998/872-8060. Fax 998/872-8061. www.ceibadelmar.com. 126 units. High season $410–$450 deluxe double, from $470 suite; low season $370–$410 deluxe double, from $430 suite. Rates include continental breakfast and ground transfer. Spa packages available. AE, MC, V. Free parking. **Amenities:** 2 restaurants; 2 bars; 2 pools; lighted tennis court; complete state-of-the-art gym w/sauna, steam room, whirlpool, and Swiss showers; spa offering a wide variety of treatments; 8 rooftop Jacuzzis; dive shop w/watersports equipment; bikes for guests' use; concierge; tour info; car rental; salon; 24-hr. room service; babysitting; laundry service; nonsmoking rooms. *In room:* A/C, TV/VCR, minibar, hair dryer, safe, CD player.

Ikal del Mar   The smallest and most private of the four resorts in this section, Ikal has 30 well-separated bungalows, each with its own piece of jungle, a little pool, and an outdoor shower. The bungalows are large, filled with amenities, and decorated in a modern, simple style. The bathrooms have only a shower. Service here is the most personal of the four—the numerous staff will get you just about anything you need. A bar and restaurant (with excellent food) overlooking an inviting pool make for an attractive common area. If there's a drawback, it's the beach, which is rockier than the beaches of the other three.

Playa Xcalacoco, Carretera Cancún–Tulum, 77710 Q. Roo. ℂ **888/230-7330** in the U.S. and Canada, or 984/877-3000. Fax 713/528-3697 in the U.S. www.ikaldelmar.com. 30 units. High season $700–$750 double; low season $588 double. Rates include breakfast. AE, MC, V. Free secure parking. Children not accepted. **Amenities:** Restaurant; 2 bars; large pool; spa; 2 Jacuzzis; steam bath; watersports equipment; concierge; tour info; car rental; courtesy shuttle to Playa; salon; 24-hr. room service; in-room massage; laundry service. *In room:* A/C, TV/DVD, fridge, hair dryer, safe.

Maroma   My personal favorite, this resort has been around the longest, owns a large parcel of land inland that it protects from development, and has a gorgeous beach and beautifully manicured grounds. Two- and three-story buildings contain the large guest rooms; most have king-size beds and rattan furniture. While it is not the retreat into the jungle that Ikal is, my two most vivid memories of the place are the sound of the sea breeze rustling the lush palm trees, and the sight of a pair of toucans—most uncommon on this coast. I also have a fond memory of the beach bar, which is my ideal for the genre—quiet, simple, surrounded by natural beauty. I could do without the staff dressing in native peasant garb, but they don't seem to mind. As at Ikal, the smaller size makes for more personal service and a deeper sense of escape.

Carretera 307 Km 51, 77710 Q. Roo. ℂ **866/454-9351** in the U.S., or 998/872-8200. Fax 998/872-8220. www.maromahotel.com. 61 units. $440–$520 garden-view double; $565–$660 premium double; $770–$850 oceanfront double; from $880 suite. Rates include ground transfer, full breakfast, 1 snorkeling tour. AE, MC, V. Free valet parking. No children under 16. **Amenities:** Restaurant; 3 bars; 3 outdoor spring-fed pools; fitness center; spa; Jacuzzi; steam bath; watersports equipment rental; game room; concierge; tours; car rental; salon; room service until 11pm; in-room massage; laundry service; dry cleaning. *In room:* A/C, hair dryer.

Paraíso de la Bonita   This recently opened resort has the most elaborate spa of all. I'm not a spa-goer and cannot discuss the relative merits of different treatments, but my work takes me to plenty of spas, and this one, which operates under the French system of thalassotherapy, is beyond anything in my experience. It uses seawater, sea salts, and sea algae in its treatments. I was impressed just in viewing the different apparatuses. InterContinental manages the hotel part of the resort and handles the hospitality smoothly. The beach is lovely and open, but without the mature palms and vegetation that grace Maroma and Ikal. The pool area and the common areas of the spa are uncommonly attractive. The rooms occupy some unremarkable three-story buildings. They are, in decor and furnishings, more impressive than the rooms of the other three. The ground-floor rooms have a plunge pool; upstairs rooms come with a balcony.

Carretera Cancún–Chetumal Km 328, Bahía Petempich, 77710 Q. Roo. ℂ **800/327-0200** in the U.S., or 998/873-8300. Fax 998/872-8301. www.paraisodelabonitaresort.com. 90 units. $705–$790 suite; $1,200 2-bedroom master suite. Rates include ground transfer. AE, MC, V. Free valet parking. No children under 12. **Amenities:** 2 restaurants; 2 bars; 4 pools; 1 lighted tennis court; spa; 2 Jacuzzis; watersports equipment rental; concierge; tour info; rental cars; salon; 24-hr. room service; in-room massage; laundry service; dry cleaning; nonsmoking rooms. *In room:* A/C, TV/DVD, dataport, minibar, hair dryer, safe.

3 South of Playa del Carmen

South of Playa del Carmen you'll find a succession of nature parks, resort communities, and beaches. From north to south, this section covers them in the following order: Xcaret, Paamul, Puerto Aventuras, Xpu-Ha, Akumal, Xel-Ha, Punta Solimán, and Tankah. The distance from Playa del Carmen to Xel-Ha is 54km (33 miles).

HEADING SOUTH FROM PLAYA DEL CARMEN The best way to travel this coast is in a rental car; Playa has many rental agencies. The wide, well-paved highway to Tulum makes for a 1-hour drive.

It's custom for drivers here to pretend that there's a center passing lane. Oncoming traffic moves to the right to make room for the passing vehicle. You do the same. When making a left turn where there is no left-turn lane, you are supposed to move to the shoulder and wait to cross the road until you have the opportunity. Do not stop in the middle of the lane. It's best not to drive at night. (And it gets dark early on this coast.) *Note:* Be sure to pay attention when buying gas—short-changing is a common practice of attendants when they think they are dealing with a distracted customer.

Southbound buses depart regularly from Playa. Most stop several times along the highway; however, from the highway it can be a hot walk to the coast and to your final destination. There's also bus service to and from Cobá three times a day. Another option is to hire a car and driver.

Beyond Paamul, you'll see signs for this or that *cenote* (well) or cave. There are thousands of *cenotes* in the Yucatán, and each is slightly different. These turnoffs are less visited than the major attractions and can make for a pleasant visit. Two major attractions bear specific mention: **Hidden Worlds,** offering remarkable snorkeling and diving tours of a couple of *cenotes,* and **Aktun Chen** cavern with a small nature park. Both are south of Akumal and described later in this chapter.

XCARET: A PARK CELEBRATING THE YUCATAN

A billboard in the airport of faraway Guadalajara reads in Spanish "And when visiting Xcaret, don't forget to enjoy the pleasures of the Riviera Maya, too." An exaggeration, but its point is well taken: Xcaret (pronounced "eesh-ca-*ret*") is the biggest attraction in these parts and is practically a destination unto itself. It even has its own all-inclusive resort (I don't recommend it). If you're coming to these shores to avoid crowds, avoid this place. If you're here for entertainment and activities, you should consider visiting Xcaret. What Xcaret does, it does very well, and that is to present in one package a little bit of everything that the Yucatán (and the rest of Mexico for that matter) has to offer.

Think of the activities that people come to the Yucatán for: hanging out on the beach, scuba and snorkeling, cavern diving, visiting ruins, taking a siesta in a hammock under a grove of palm trees, hiking through tropical forest, meeting native Maya peoples—Xcaret has all that plus handicraft exhibitions, a bat cave, a butterfly pavilion, mushroom and orchid nurseries, and lots of wildlife on display (the park has several conservation programs for endangered species), native jaguars, manatees, sea turtles, monkeys, macaws, flamingos, and a petting aquarium. Children love it. What probably receives most of the comments is the underground river (a natural feature of the park and common in much of the Yucatán) that's been opened in places to allow snorkelers to paddle along with the current. What else? A number of tours and shows, including *charros* (Mexican cowboys) from the state of Jalisco, and the Totonac Indian *voladores* ("flyers" who do a daring pole dance high above the ground) from the state of Veracruz.

The park is famous for its evening spectacle that is a celebration of the Mexican nation. I've seen it and have to say that it is some show, with a large cast and lots of props. It starts with the Maya and an interpretation of how they may have played the pre-Hispanic game/ritual known as *pok-ta-pok,* and then to another version of a ball game still practiced in the western state of Michoacán. From there it moves on to the arrival of the Spanish and eventually to the forging of the new nation, its customs, its dress, and its music and dance.

Xcaret is 10km (6½ miles) south of Playa del Carmen (you'll know when you get to the turnoff). It's open daily from 8:30am to 9pm. Admission prices are $54 for adults, $28 for children 5 to 12. Certain activities cost extra: horseback ride $30, snuba/sea trek/snorkel tour $45, scuba $50 to $75, swimming with dolphins $85 to $115. Other costs: lockers $2 per day, snorkel equipment $10 per day, food and drink variable. The park is an all-day affair; it's best to arrive early and register for tours and activities as soon as you can. For more info call ℂ **998/883-3143** or visit www.xcaret.net.

Four kilometers (2½ miles) south of the entrance to Xcaret is the turnoff for **Puerto Calica,** the cruise-ship pier. Passengers disembark here for tours of Playa, Xcaret, the ruins, and other attractions on the coast.

Here's a tip: Fewer ships arrive on weekends than on weekdays, which makes the weekend a good time for visiting the major attractions on this coast.

PAAMUL: SEASIDE GETAWAY

About 15km (10 miles) beyond Xcaret and 25km (15 miles) from Playa del Carmen is Paamul, which in Mayan means "a destroyed ruin." The exit is clearly marked. At Paamul (also written Pamul), you can enjoy the Caribbean with relative quiet; the water at the out-of-the-way beach is wonderful, but the shoreline is rocky. There are 18 rooms for rent, a restaurant, and many trailer and RV lots with hookups.

There's also a dive shop. **Scubamex** (ℂ **984/873-0667;** fax 984/874-1729; www.scubamex.com) is a fully equipped PADI-, NAUI-, and SSI-certified dive shop next to the cabañas. Using two boats, the staff takes guests on dives 8km (5 miles) in either direction. If it's too choppy, the reefs in front of the hotel are also good. The cost for a two-tank dive is $45, plus $25 to rent gear. Snorkeling is also excellent in this protected bay and the one next to it. The shop offers a great 3-hour snorkeling trip ($25).

WHERE TO STAY & DINE

Cabañas Paamul ⊛ Lodging options include eight rooms in a couple of long one-story concrete buildings and 10 freestanding wood cabañas, all just a few steps from the water. The rooms are large and clean, with ample bathrooms. Each comes with two double beds, tile floors, rattan furniture, air-conditioning, and a ceiling fan. In front of each is a porch with hammocks. Remodeling has made them much more attractive. The cabañas are also attractive, with a more native feel. They have wooden floors, stucco walls, *palapa* roofs, two double beds with comfortable mattresses, and a private porch. The trailer park isn't what you might expect—some trailers have decks or patios and thatched *palapa* shade covers. Trailer guests have access to 12 showers and separate bathrooms for men and women. Laundry service is available nearby. Turtles nest here from June to September. The large, breezy *palapa* restaurant is a Brazilian-style grill under the management of Kalú da Silva, a retired Brazilian soccer player, who closed his restaurant in León, Guanajuato, to live on the coast. Restaurant customers are welcome to use the beach.

Carretera Cancún–Tulum Km 85. © **984/875-1053**. paamulmx@yahoo.com. 18 units; 190 trailer spaces (all with full hookups). July–Aug and Dec–Feb $75–$85 double; Mar–June and Sept–Nov $50–$65 double. Ask about discount for stays longer than 1 week. RV space with hookups $25 per day, $500 per month. No credit cards. **Amenities:** Restaurant; bar.

PUERTO AVENTURAS: A RESORT COMMUNITY

Five kilometers (3 miles) south of Paamul and 104km (65 miles) from Cancún is the glitzy development of Puerto Aventuras, on Chakalal Bay. It's a condo-marina community with a nine-hole golf course. At the center of the development is a collection of restaurants bordering a dolphin pool. They offer a variety of food—Mexican, Italian, steaks, even a popular pub. The major attraction is the dolphins. To swim with them in a highly interactive program, you must make reservations by contacting **Dolphin Discovery** (© **998/849-4757** in Cancún; www.dolphindiscovery.com). Make reservations well in advance. The surest way is by e-mail to salesinternet@dolphindiscovery.com.mx or through the link on the website. A 1-hour session costs $119.

This is also the place to come for boating and deep-sea fishing. I recommend **Captain Rick's Sportfishing Center** (© **984/873-5195** or 984/873-5387; www.fishyucatan.com). The best fishing on this coast is from March to August. The captain will be happy to combine a fishing trip with some snorkeling, which makes for a leisurely day.

I don't find Puerto Aventuras to be an interesting place for lodging and prefer to stay elsewhere on the coast. It's like a mini Cancún, but lacking Cancún's vibrancy. There are a couple of fancy hotels. The main one is the **Omni Puerto Aventuras** (© **800/THE-OMNI** in the U.S., or 984/873-5101). It looks larger than its 30 rooms would indicate and was probably intended to be bigger but didn't get the expected traffic.

XPU-HA: BEAUTIFUL BEACH

Three kilometers (2 miles) beyond Puerto Aventuras is **Xpu-Ha** ★★★ (eesh-poo-*hah*), a wide bay lined by a broad, beautiful sandy beach, perhaps the best beach on the entire coast. All-inclusive resorts sit at each end of the bay (Xpu-Ha Palace and Robinson Club) and in the middle (Hotel Copacabana). The beach is big enough to accommodate the hotel crowds (who usually stay on the beach in front of their lodgings) as well as the people trucked in on weekdays from the cruise ships that dock at Calica. The cruise-ship vans usually pull in to the beach entrance called La Playa, on the far side (south) of the Copacabana, which means that you'll want to take one of the entrances before the hotel.

There are some restaurants and small hotels at Xpu-Ha. The rooms in these hotels are simple: two twin or full beds, private bathroom, cement floor. Most are rented on a first-come, first-served basis. Rates vary from $40 to $60 a night, depending upon how busy they are. The nicest establishment is **Villas del Caribe Xpu-Ha** (© **984/ 873-2194;** cafedelmarxpuha@yahoo.com.mx), run by a personable Mexican named León who speaks English. Rooms are on the beach and have private bathrooms with hot water and 24-hour electricity, but no ceiling fans. León also runs a little beach restaurant next to the hotel. It serves seafood and is a pleasant place to have lunch. If you find a good lodging deal in nearby Akumal or Paamul, you might consider staying there and driving here for the day. That's what a lot of locals do.

In the sidebar on all-inclusives (earlier in this chapter) I include information on two of the resorts on this beach. The third, the **Robinson Club** (© **984/871-3000**), has small rooms that tend to be rather plain. The hotel markets 80% of its rooms to Germans, making it an excellent choice if you've taken German lessons and are looking for an opportunity for cultural immersion without actually having to go to Germany. Otherwise, consider one of the other two.

AKUMAL: BEAUTIFUL BAYS & CAVERN DIVING

Continuing south on Highway 307 for 2km (1¼ miles), you'll come to the turnoff for Akumal, a small, modern, ecologically oriented community built on the shores of two beautiful bays. This community has been around long enough that it feels more relaxed than developing places such as Playa and Tulum. It draws a lot of families. You'll see a turtle icon everywhere you go because the name Akumal means "place of the turtles." From the highway, turn off at the sign that reads PLAYA AKUMAL. (Don't be confused by other signs reading VILLAS AKUMAL, AKUMAL AVENTURAS, or AKUMAL BEACH RESORT.) Instead of making a left, you'll exit to the right and then turn left, and cross the highway. Less than 1km (½ mile) down the road is a white arch. Just before it are a couple of convenience stores (the one named Super Chomak has an ATM) and a laundry service. Just after it (to the right) is the Club Akumal Caribe/Hotel Villas Maya. If you follow the road to the left and keep to the left, you'll come to Half Moon Bay, lined with two- and three-story condos, and eventually to Yal-ku Lagoon, which is a snorkeling park. Families can rent most of these condos for a week at a time. Contact **Info-Akumal** (© **800/381-7048** in the U.S.; www.info-akumal.com), **Akumal Vacations** (© **800/448-7137** in the U.S.; www.akumalvacations.com), or **Caribbean Fantasy** (© **800/523-6618** in the U.S.; www.caribbfan.com).

You don't have to be a guest to enjoy the beach, swim, snorkel, or eat at one of the restaurants. This is a comfortable place to spend a day on a trip down the coast. There are three dive shops in town and at least 30 dive sites offshore. The **Akumal Dive Shop** (© **984/875-9032;** www.akumal.com), one of the oldest and best dive shops on the coast, offers courses in technical diving and cavern diving trips. It and **Akumal Dive Adventures** (© **984/875-9157**), at the Vista del Mar hotel on Half Moon Bay, offer resort courses as well as complete certification. The operator of Akumal Dive Adventures is an American who is competent and personable. He took me to one of his favorite dive sites, where we had some close encounters with a couple of nursing sharks, a ray, and a turtle.

Yal-ku Lagoon is a park that is like a miniature and more primitive Xel-Ha. It's open daily from 8am to 5:30pm. Admission is $6 for adults, $3 for children 3 to 14. The lagoon is about 700m (2,300 ft.) long and about 200m (660 ft.) at its widest. You can paddle around comfortably in sheltered water with little current and see fish and a few other creatures. It makes for a relaxing outing, but for sheer variety, I prefer snorkeling along the reefs.

WHERE TO STAY

Rates below are for two people and include taxes. Most hotels and condo rentals charge higher rates for the holidays than those listed here.

Club Akumal Caribe/Hotel Villas Maya Club ★★ (Kids)

The hotel rooms and garden bungalows of this hotel sit along Akumal Bay. Both are large and comfortable, with tile floors and good-size bathrooms. The 40 **Villas Maya Bungalows** are simply and comfortably furnished and have kitchenettes. The 21 rooms in the three-story beachside **hotel** are more elaborately furnished and come with refrigerators. They have a king-size bed or two queen-size beds, tile floors, and Mexican accents. There is a large pool on the grounds. Other rooms belonging to the hotel are condos and the lovely **Villas Flamingo** on Half Moon Bay. The villas have two or three bedrooms and large living, dining, and kitchen areas, as well as lovely furnished patios just steps from the beach. The four villas share a pool.

Carretera Cancún–Tulum (Hwy. 307) Km 104. © **984/875-9010.** (Reservations: P.O. Box 13326, El Paso, TX 79913. © **800/351-1626** in the U.S., 800/343-1440 in Canada, or 915/584-3552.) www.hotelakumalcaribe.com. 70 units. High season $110 bungalow, $140 hotel room, $200–$500 villa or condo; low season $66 bungalow, $84 hotel room, $130–$245 villa or condo. Reservations with prepayment by check only. AE, MC, V. Cash only at restaurants. Low-season packages available. **Amenities:** 2 restaurants; bar; large pool; children's activities (seasonal); tour desk; in-room massage; babysitting; dive shop. *In room:* A/C, kitchenette in some, fridge, coffeemaker, no phone.

Vista del Mar Hotel and Condos ★ (Value)

This beachside property is a great place to stay for several reasons. It offers hotel rooms at good prices, and large, fully equipped condos that you don't have to rent by the week. The lovely, well-tended beach in front of the hotel has chairs and umbrellas. There's an on-site dive shop with an experienced staff, which eliminates the hassle of organizing dive trips. Hotel rooms are small and contain either a queen-size bed or a double and a twin bed; all have air conditioning. The 12 condos are large and have ceiling fans and good cross ventilation; some come with air-conditioning for $22 above the prices quoted below. They consist of a well-equipped kitchen, a living area, two or three bedrooms, and one or two bathrooms. All have balconies or terraces facing the sea and are furnished with hammocks. Several rooms come with whirlpool tubs.

Half Moon Bay, 77760 Akumal, Q Roo. © **877/425-8625** in the U.S. Fax 505/988-3882 in the U.S. www.akumal info.com. 27 units. High season $90 double, $185–$280 condo; low season $73 double, $106–$162 condo. MC, V. **Amenities:** Restaurant; bar; small pool; watersports equipment rental; dive shop. *In room:* A/C, TV, fridge, coffeemaker, CD player, no phone.

WHERE TO DINE

There are about 10 places to eat in Akumal, and a convenient grocery store, **Super Chomak,** by the archway. The **Turtle Bay Café and Bakery** is good for breakfast or a light lunch. A good dining spot for lunch or dinner is **La Buena Vida,** on Half Moon Bay.

XEL-HA: SNORKELING & SWIMMING ★★

Thirteen kilometers (8 miles) south of Akumal is a nature park called **Xel-Ha** (© **998/884-9422** in Cancún, 984/873-3588 in Playa, or 984/875-6000 at the park; www.xelha.com.mx). But before you get there you'll pass the turnoff for **Aktun Chen** ★ cavern (a bit beyond Akumal). Of the several caverns that I've toured in the Yucatán, this is one of the best—lots of geological features, good lighting, several underground pools, and large chambers, all carefully preserved. The tour takes about an hour and requires a good amount of walking. The footing is good. You exit not far from where you enter. There is also a zoo with specimens of the local fauna. Some of the critters are allowed to run about freely. In my opinion, the cost of admission is high—$17 for adults, $9 for children—but this is true of several attractions on this coast. The cavern is open 9am to 5pm daily. The turnoff is to the right, and the cave is about 4km (2½ miles) from the road.

The centerpiece of Xel-Ha (shell-*hah*) is a large, beautiful lagoon where freshwater and saltwater meet. You can swim, float, and snorkel in beautifully clear water surrounded by jungle. A small train takes guests upriver to a drop-off point. There, you can store all your clothes and gear in a locked sack that is taken down to the locker rooms in the main part of the building. The water moves calmly toward the sea, and you can float along with it. Snorkeling here offers a higher comfort level than the open sea—there are no waves and currents to pull you about, but there are a lot of fish of several species, including rays.

Inside the park, you can rent snorkeling equipment and an underwater camera. Platforms allow nonsnorkelers to view the fish. Another way to view fish is to use the park's "snuba" gear—a contraption that allows you to breathe air through 6m (20-ft.) tubes connected to scuba tanks floating on the surface. It frees you of the cumbersome tank while allowing you to stay down without having to hold your breath. Rental costs $42 for approximately an hour. Like snuba but more involved is "sea-trek," a device consisting of an elaborate plastic helmet with air hoses. It allows you to walk around on the bottom breathing normally and perhaps participate in feeding the park's stingrays. Another attraction is swimming with dolphins. A 1-hour swim costs $115; a 15-minute program costs $40. Make reservations (© **998/887-6840**) at least 24 hours in advance for one of the four daily sessions.

Other attractions include a plant nursery, an apiary for the local, stingless Maya bees, and a lovely path through the tropical forest bordering the lagoon. Xel-Ha is open daily from 8:30am to 5pm. Parking is free. For the basic package, adult admission is $36 on weekdays, $28 on weekends; admission for children ages 5 to 11 is $18 on weekdays, $13 on weekends; children under 5 enter free. Admission includes use of inner tubes, life vest, and shuttle train to the river, and the use of changing rooms and showers. An all-inclusive option includes snorkeling equipment rental, locker rental, towels, food, and beverages. Adults can visit all week long for $67, and children visit for $33. The park has five restaurants, two ice cream shops, and a store. It accepts American Express, MasterCard, and Visa, and has an ATM.

Signs clearly mark the turnoff to Xel-Ha. Xel-Ha is close to the ruins of Tulum. A popular day tour from Cancún or Playa combines the two. If you're traveling on your own, the best time to enjoy Xel-Ha without the crowds is during the weekend from 9am to 2 pm.

About 2km (1 mile) south of Xel-Ha is the **Hidden Worlds Cenotes** 🐟🐟🐟 (© **984/877-8535;** www.hiddenworlds.com.mx), which offers an excellent opportunity to snorkel or dive in a couple of nearby caverns. The caverns are part of a vast network that makes up a single underground river system. The water is crystalline (and a bit cold) and the rock formations impressive. These caverns were filmed for the IMAX production *Journey into Amazing Caves.* The people running the show are resourceful. When I was last there, they were putting together a new way to view the caverns using 90 to 120m (300–400 ft.) of submerged half-sections of tubes that will create a long air pocket for viewing the cavern. This is their own invention (which they've dubbed "tube-a-scuba"), and I'm curious to see how it will work. The snorkel tour costs $40 and takes you to different caverns. The main form of transportation is "jungle mobile," with a guide who throws in tidbits of information and lore about the jungle plant life that you see. There is some walking involved, so take shoes or sandals. I've toured several caverns, but floating through one gave me an entirely different perspective.

PUNTA SOLIMAN & TANKAH BAYS

The next couple of turnoffs to the left lead to Punta Solimán and Tankah bays. On Punta Solimán Bay is a good beach restaurant called **Oscar y Lalo's.** Here you can rent kayaks and snorkel equipment and paddle out to the reefs for some snorkeling. Three kilometers (2 miles) farther is the turnoff for Tankah, where there are a handful of lodgings. The most interesting is **Casa Cenote** (© **998/874-5170;** www.casacenote. com). It has an underground river that surfaces at a *cenote* in the back of the property then goes underground and bubbles up into the sea just a few feet offshore. Casa Cenote has seven rooms, all on the beach. The double rate, including breakfast and dinner at the restaurant, is $185. The owner, an American, provides kayaks and snorkeling gear and can arrange dives, fishing trips, and sailing charters.

A beach road connects the two bays. I found the snorkeling in Tankah better than in Punta Solimán. Snorkeling in the latter was both interesting and frustrating. I've never before experienced so many thermoclines, which are produced by freshwater seeping from the floors of the bay and coming in contact with the warmer saltwater. Light passing through the water is refracted in funny ways. At first I found the effect interesting—it lent an ethereal shininess to everything I was seeing—but then it just got annoying as it cut down sharply on visibility. At one point I was floating through some of the worst of it, trying not to stir up the water, when a giant silvery barracuda came ghostlike through the shimmering water and crossed my field of vision about 2m (6 ft.) away. As he passed slowly by me I was astonished at how beautiful and luminescent he looked. Still, I will take clear water over shimmering water every time.

4 Tulum, Punta Allen & Sian Ka'an

Tulum (130km/80 miles from Cancún) and the Punta Allen Peninsula border the northern edge of the Sian Ka'an biopreserve. The walled Maya city of Tulum is a large post-Classic site overlooking the Caribbean in dramatic fashion. Tour companies and public buses make the trip regularly from Cancún and Playa del Carmen; get there early to avoid the crowds. Tulum also has wonderful, sandy beaches and no large resort hotels. It's a perfect spot for those who like to splash around in the water and lie on the beach away from the resort scene. The town has a dozen restaurants, five pharmacies, three cybercafes, a bank, two cash machines, and several stores.

For those who really want to leave the modern world behind, there's the Punta Allen Peninsula. Getting to the end of the peninsula from Tulum can take 1½ to 3 hours, depending on the condition of the road. It's a place without crowds, frenetic action, or creature comforts; the generator (if there is one) shuts down at 10pm. You'll find great fishing and snorkeling, the natural riches of the Sian Ka'an Biosphere Reserve, and a chance to rest up at what truly feels like the end of the road. A few beach cabañas offer reliable power, telephones, and hot showers.

ORIENTATION   Highway 307 passes the entrance to the ruins (on your left) before running through town. After the entrance to the ruins but before entering the town you'll come to a highway intersection with a traffic light. The light wasn't functioning the last time I was there. To the right is the highway leading to the ruins of Cobá (see "Cobá Ruins," later in this chapter); to the left is the Tulum hotel zone, which begins about 2km (1½ miles) away. The road sign reads BOCA PAILA, which is a place halfway down the **Punta Allen Peninsula.** This road eventually goes all the way to the tip of the peninsula and the town of Punta Allen, a lobstering and fishing village. It is a rough road that is slow going for most of the way. A few kilometers down the road, you will enter the **Sian Ka'an Biosphere Reserve.**

EXPLORING THE TULUM ARCHAEOLOGICAL SITE

Thirteen kilometers (8 miles) south of Xel-Ha are the ruins of Tulum, a Maya fortress-city overlooking the Caribbean. The ruins are open to visitors daily from 7am to 5pm in the winter, 8am to 6pm in the summer. It's always best to go early, before the crowds start showing up (around 9:30am). The entrance to the ruins is about a 5-minute walk from the archaeological site. There are artisans' stands, a bookstore, a museum, a restaurant, several large bathrooms, and a ticket booth. Admission fee to the ruins is $4. If you want to ride the shuttle from the visitor center to the ruins, it's another $1.50. Parking is $3. A video camera permit costs $4. Licensed guides have a stand next to the path to the ruins and charge $20 for a 45-minute tour in English, French, or Spanish for up to four persons. In some ways, they are like performers and will tailor their presentation to the responses they receive from you. Some will try to draw connections between the Maya and Western theology. But they will point out architectural details that you might otherwise miss.

Fun Fact **Tulum: A Friendly Difference of Opinion**

Two of us cover the entirety of Mexico for Frommer's, and almost without exception we agree on the country's top destinations. However, we have an ongoing dialogue regarding the relative merits and beauty of the ruins at Tulum. Herewith we present our respective cases, and leave it for you to decide with whom you agree.

    Lynne says: Ancient Tulum is my favorite of all the ruins, poised as it is on a rocky hill overlooking the transparent, turquoise Caribbean. It's not the largest or most important of the Maya ruins in this area, but it's the only one by the sea, which makes it the most visually impressive. Intriguing carvings and reliefs decorate the well-preserved structures, which date from the 12th to 16th centuries A.D., in the post-Classic period.

    David says: Aside from the spectacular setting, Tulum is not as impressive a city as Chichén Itzá, Uxmal, or Ek Balam (discussed in chapter 16). The stonework is cruder than that at these other sites, as if construction of the platforms and temples had been hurried. The city's builders were concerned foremost with security and defense. They chose the most rugged section on this coast and then built stout walls on the other three sides. This must have absorbed a tremendous amount of energy that might otherwise have been used to build the large ceremonial centers and more varied architecture that we see in other sites in the Yucatán.

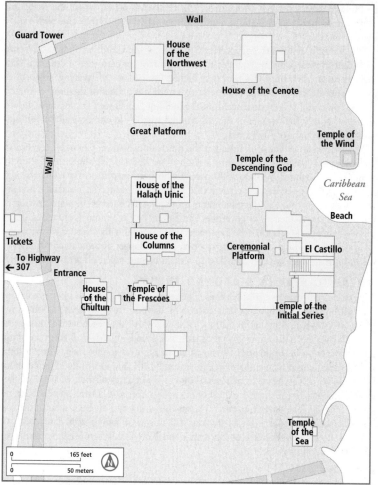

By A.D. 900, the end of the Classic period, Maya civilization had begun its decline, and the large cities to the south were abandoned. Tulum is one of the small city-states that rose to fill the void. It came to prominence in the 13th century as a seaport, controlling maritime commerce along this section of the coast, and remained inhabited well after the arrival of the Spanish. The primary god here was the diving god, depicted on several buildings as an upside-down figure above doorways. Seen at the Palace at Sayil and Cobá, this curious, almost comical figure is also known as the bee god.

The most imposing building in Tulum is a large stone structure above the cliff called the **Castillo (castle).** Actually a temple as well as a fortress, it was once covered with stucco and painted. In front of the Castillo are several unrestored palace-like buildings partially covered with stucco. On the **beach** below, where the Maya once came ashore, tourists swim and sunbathe, combining a visit to the ruins with a dip in the Caribbean.

The **Temple of the Frescoes,** directly in front of the Castillo, contains interesting 13th-century wall paintings, though entrance is no longer permitted. Distinctly Maya, they represent the rain god Chaac and Ixchel, the goddess of weaving, women, the moon, and medicine. On the cornice of this temple is a relief of the head of the rain god. If you pause a slight distance from the building, you'll see the eyes, nose, mouth, and chin. Notice the remains of the red-painted stucco—at one time all the buildings at Tulum were painted bright red.

Much of what we know of Tulum at the time of the Spanish Conquest comes from the writings of Diego de Landa, third bishop of the Yucatán. He wrote that Tulum was a small city inhabited by about 600 people who lived in platform dwellings along a street and who supervised the trade traffic from Honduras to the Yucatán. Though it was a walled city, most of the inhabitants probably lived outside the walls, leaving the interior for the residences of governors and priests and ceremonial structures. Tulum survived about 70 years after the Conquest, when it was finally abandoned. Because of the great number of visitors this site receives, it is no longer possible to climb all of the ruins. In many cases, visitors are asked to remain behind roped-off areas to view them.

WHERE TO STAY IN & AROUND TULUM

This stretch of coast has great beaches. The seven or eight hotels in town are cheaper than all but the most basic of beach accommodations, but they aren't as much fun. They offer no-frills lodging for $20 to $50 a night. All the beach hotels must generate their own electricity, and this raises the price of lodging. Most of them are simple affairs without a lot of luxuries. Turn east at the highway intersection. Three kilometers (2 miles) ahead, you come to a T junction. North are most of the cheap cabañas. Over the years, I've heard from several sources about cases of theft at a few of these establishments. To the south are most of the *palapa* hotels, including some moderately priced lodging. The pavement quickly turns into sand, and on both sides of the road you start seeing cabañas. You can try your luck at one of many places. The rates listed below don't include the week of Christmas and New Year, when prices go above regular high season rates.

Expensive

Hotel Nueva Vida ⭐   I like this place because it's so different, with few rooms, much space, and an ecological orientation. It has 150m (500 ft.) of beautiful beachfront, but the cabañas are built behind the beach, in the jungle, which has been preserved as much as possible. Most of the rooms are in freestanding thatched cabañas 4m (12 ft.) off the ground. Each is midsize with a private bathroom, a double and a twin bed with mosquito netting, and a ceiling fan (solar cells and wind generators provide energy around the clock; there are no electrical outlets in the units). There are also some junior suites housed in a two-story building, which are larger and come with a few more amenities, also there are some two-bedroom units, which go for a bit more than the junior suites. The owners are from South America and operate a family-style restaurant.

Carretera Punta Allen Km 8.5, 77780 Tulum, Q. Roo. ⓒ **984/877-8512.** Fax 984/871-2092. www.tulumnv.com. 9 units. High season $132 double, $181 suite; low season $83 double, $122 suite. Rates include continental breakfast. MC, V. **Amenities:** Restaurant; tour information; limited room service; massage; laundry service; nonsmoking rooms. *In room:* No phone.

Restaurant y Cabañas Ana y José ★★   This comfortable hotel sits on a great beach with a good beach restaurant. The rock-walled cabañas in front (called "oceanfront"), closest to the water, are a little larger than the others and come with two double beds. I also like the attractive second-floor oceanview rooms, which have tall *palapa* roofs. The garden-view rooms are much like the others but don't face the sea. Newer construction has crowded them in back, making them much less desirable. There is 24-hour electricity for lights and ceiling fans. Sometimes you can book a package deal that includes hotel and a rental car waiting for you at the Cancún airport. Ana y José is 6.5km (4 miles) south of the Tulum ruins.

Carretera Punta Allen Km 7 (Apdo. Postal 15), 77780 Tulum, Q. Roo. ℂ **998/887-5470** in Cancún. Fax 998/887-5469. www.anayjose.com. 21 units. High season $112–$153 double, $225–$260 suite; low season $97–$139 double, $168–$230 suite. AE, MC, V. Free parking. **Amenities:** Restaurant; small pool; spa; tour info; car rental. *In room:* No phone.

Moderate

Cabañas Tulum   Next to Ana y José is a row of cinderblock facing the same beautiful ocean and beach. These accommodations are basic. Rooms are simple, not unattractive, though poorly lit. The bathrooms are ample. All rooms have two double beds (most with new mattresses), screens on the windows, a table, one electric light, and a porch facing the beach. Electricity is available from 7 to 11am and 6 to 11pm.

Carretera Punta Allen Km 7 (Apdo. Postal 63), 77780 Tulum, Q. Roo. ℂ **984/879-7395**. Fax 984/871-2092. www. hotelstulum.com. 32 units. $70–$100 double. No credit cards. **Amenities:** Restaurant; game room.

Retiro Maya   *Retiro* is Spanish for retreat, and the word is used aptly here. I suspect that the English-speaking owner, Lu Montiel, was looking for something that would be the exact opposite of her native Mexico City. This place is it—supremely quiet and lit only by candles. The 12 attractive Maya-style cottages are arranged for privacy on 50m (165 ft.) of immaculate beachfront. Each has a king-size bed draped in mosquito netting. There is no electricity, just candles. There is no floor, only swept sand. The units share a common bathroom area. A restaurant has reasonable prices and good food.

Carretera Punta Allen Km 6.5 (Apdo. Postal 166), 77780 Tulum, Q. Roo. ℂ **998/101-1154**. www.retiromaya.com. 12 units. $90–$115 double with shared bathroom. No credit cards. No children. **Amenities:** Restaurant. *In room:* No phone.

Zamas ★★   The owners of these cabañas, a couple from San Francisco, have made their rustic getaway most enjoyable by concentrating on the essentials: comfort, privacy, and good food. The cabañas are simple, attractive, well situated for catching the breeze, and not too close together. Most rooms are in individual structures; the suites and oversize rooms are in modest two-story buildings. For the money, I like the six individual garden *palapas,* which are attractive and comfortable, with either two double beds or a double and a twin. Two small beachfront cabañas with one double bed go for a little less. The most expensive rooms are the upstairs oceanview units, which enjoy a large terrace and lots of sea breezes. I like these especially. They come with a king-size and a queen-size bed or a double and a queen-size bed. The restaurant serves the freshest seafood—I've seen the owner actually flag down passing fishermen to buy their catch. A white-sand beach stretches between large rocky areas.

Carretera Punta Allen Km 5, 77780 Tulum, Q. Roo. ℂ **415/387-9806** in the U.S. www.zamas.com. 20 units. High season $90–$130 beachfront double, $100 garden double, $120–$155 oceanview double; low season $65–$95 beachfront double, $65 garden double, $85–$110 oceanview double. No credit cards. **Amenities:** Restaurant.

The Sian Ka'an Biosphere Reserve

Down the peninsula a few miles south of the Tulum ruins, you'll pass the guardhouse of the Sian Ka'an Biosphere Reserve. The reserve is a tract of 500,000 hectares (1.3 million acres) set aside in 1986 to preserve tropical forests, savannas, mangroves, coastal and marine habitats, and 110km (70 miles) of coastal reefs. The area is home to jaguars, pumas, ocelots, margays, jaguarundis, spider and howler monkeys, tapirs, white-lipped and collared peccaries, manatees, brocket and white-tailed deer, crocodiles, and green, loggerhead, hawksbill, and leatherback sea turtles. It also protects 366 species of birds—you might catch a glimpse of an ocellated turkey, a great curassow, a brilliantly colored parrot, a toucan or trogon, a white ibis, a roseate spoonbill, a jabiru (wood stork), a flamingo, or one of 15 species of herons, egrets, and bitterns.

The park has three parts: a "core zone" restricted to research; a "buffer zone," to which visitors and families already living there have restricted use; and a "cooperation zone," which is outside the reserve but vital to its preservation. Driving south from Tulum on Highway 307, everything on the left side of the highway is part of the reserve. Most tours enter the biopreserve on this side at the community of Muyil where there are canals built by the Maya that lead to a lagoon. At least 22 archaeological sites have been charted within Sian Ka'an.

Visitors can arrange day trips in Tulum at **Sian Ka'an Tours** (© **984/871-2363**; siankaan_tours@hotmail.com), on the east side of the road, .3km (less than ¼ mile) south of the highway intersection, next to Los Tucanes restaurant.

WHERE TO DINE

There are several restaurants in the town of Tulum. They are reasonably priced and do an okay job. On the main street are **Charlie's** (© **984/871-2136**), my favorite for Mexican food, and **Don Cafeto's** (© **984/871-2207**). A good Italian-owned Italian restaurant, **Il Giardino di Toni e Simone** (© **984/804-1316;** closed Wed), is 1 block off the highway—you'll see a large building-supply store called ROCA. It's on the opposite side of the road, 1 block away. Also in town are a couple of roadside places that grill chicken and serve it with rice and beans. Out on the coast, you can eat at **Zamas** or at **Ana y José** (see above).

EXPLORING THE PUNTA ALLEN PENINSULA

If you've been captured by an adventurous spirit and have an excessively sanguine opinion of your rental car, you might want to take a trip down the Punta Allen Peninsula, especially if your interests lie in fly-fishing, birding, or simply exploring new country. The far end of the peninsula is only 50km (30 miles) away, but it can be a very slow trip (up to 3 hr., depending on the condition of the road). Not far from the last cabaña hotel is the entrance to the 500,000-hectare (1.3-million-acre) **Sian Ka'an Biosphere Reserve** (see below). Halfway down the peninsula, at Boca Paila, a bridge crosses to the lower peninsula, where the Boca Paila Fishing Lodge is. On your right is a large lagoon. Another 25km (15 miles) gets you to the village of **Punta Allen,** where you can arrange a birding expedition (available June–Aug, with July being best) or a boat trip (see the entry for Cuzan Guest House in "Where to Stay," below).

WHERE TO STAY

The peninsula offers simple but comfortable lodgings. One or two have electricity for a few hours in the evening, but it goes off around 10pm. Halfway down the peninsula, the **Boca Paila Fishing Lodge** (© **800/245-1950,** or 412/935-1577 in the U.S.) specializes in hosting fly-fishers. Its weeklong packages include everything, even the boat and guide.

Between Boca Paila and Punta Allen are a couple of small, comfortable hotels run by Americans, perfect for getting away from it all. One is **Rancho Sol Caribe** (no phone; www.cancun.com), which has only two or three rooms on a private beach. Punta Allen is a lobstering and fishing village on a palm-studded beach. Isolated and rustic, it's the most laid-back end of the line you'll find for a long time. The small town has a lobster cooperative, a few streets with modest homes, and a lighthouse at the very end of the peninsula.

Cuzan Guest House 🅐 *Finds*   This place has a rustic charm perfectly in character with its location at the end of the road, plus the great benefits of hot water, 24-hour solar electricity, comfortable beds, and private bathrooms. You have a choice of Maya-style stucco buildings with thatched roofs, concrete floors, and a combination of twin and king-size beds with mosquito netting, or raised wooden cabins with thatched roofs and little porches that overlook the water. These have two double beds each. The hotel's restaurant, a large *palapa* with a sand floor, serves three meals a day. Full breakfast and lunch run about $5 each, and dinner costs $12 to $15. The menu sometimes includes lobster in season (July–Apr). The food is good, and, of course, the seafood is fresh. Payment for meals must be in cash or traveler's checks.

Co-owner Sonja Lilvik, a Californian, offers fly-fishing trips for bone, permit, snook, and tarpon to the nearby saltwater flats and lagoons of Ascension Bay. One-week packages (priced per person, double occupancy) include lodging, three meals a day, a boat, and a guide. She also offers a fascinating 3-hour boat tour of the coastline that includes snorkeling, slipping in and out of mangrove-filled canals for birding, and skirting the edge of an island rookery loaded with frigate birds. November to March is frigate mating season, when the male shows off his big, billowy red breast pouch to impress potential mates. You can also go kayaking along the coast or relax in a hammock on the beach.

Punta Allen. (Reservations: Apdo. Postal 24, 77200 Felipe Carrillo Puerto, Q. Roo.) © 983/834-0358. Fax 983/834-0292. www.flyfishmx.com. 12 units. High season $40–$80 double. Low-season discounts available. All-inclusive fly-fishing packages $1,999 per week. No credit cards. **Amenities:** Restaurant; tours and activities desk. *In room:* No phone.

5 Cobá Ruins

168km (105 miles) SW of Cancún

Older than most of Chichén Itzá and much larger than Tulum, Cobá was the dominant city of the eastern Yucatán before A.D. 1000. The site is large and spread out, with thick forest growing between the temple groups. Rising high above the forest canopy are tall, steep classic Maya pyramids. Of the major sites, this one is the least reconstructed and so disappoints those who expect another Chichén Itzá. Appreciating it requires a greater exercise of the imagination. Bordering the ruins are two lakes, an uncommon feature in the Yucatán, where surface water is rare.

ESSENTIALS

GETTING THERE & DEPARTING **By Car** The road to Cobá begins in Tulum, across Highway 307 from the turnoff to the Punta Allen Peninsula. Turn right when you see signs for Cobá, and continue on that road for 65km (40 miles). Watch out for both *topes* (speed bumps) and potholes. Enter the village, proceed straight until you see the lake, then turn left. The entrance to the ruins is a short distance down the road past some small restaurants. There's a large parking area.

By Bus Several buses a day leave Tulum and Playa del Carmen for Cobá. Several companies offer bus tours.

EXPLORING THE COBA RUINS

The Maya built many intriguing cities in the Yucatán, but few grander than Cobá ("water stirred by wind"). Much of the 67-sq.-km (26-sq.-mile) site remains unexcavated. A 100km (60-mile) *sacbé* (a pre-Hispanic raised road or causeway) through the jungle linked Cobá to Yaxuná, once a large, important Maya center 50km (30 miles) south of Chichén Itzá. It's the Maya's longest known *sacbé,* and at least 50 shorter ones lead from here. An important city-state, Cobá flourished from A.D. 632 (the oldest carved date found here) until after the rise of Chichén Itzá, around 800. Then Cobá slowly faded in importance and population until it was finally abandoned. Scholars believe Cobá was an important trade link between the Yucatán Caribbean coast and inland cities.

Once at the site, keep your bearings—you can get turned around in the maze of dirt roads in the jungle. And bring bug spray. As spread out as this city is, renting a bike (which you can do at the entrance for $2.50) is a good option. Branching off from every labeled path, you'll notice unofficial narrow paths into the jungle, used by locals as shortcuts through the ruins. These are good for birding, but be careful to remember the way back.

The **Grupo Cobá** boasts an impressive pyramid, **La Iglesia (The Church),** which you'll find if you take the path bearing right after the entrance. As you approach, notice the unexcavated mounds on the left. Though the urge to climb the temple is great, the view is better from El Castillo in the Nohoch Mul group farther back.

From here, return to the main path and turn right. You'll pass a sign pointing right to the ruined *juego de pelota* (**ball court**), but the path is obscure.

Continuing straight ahead on this path for 5 to 10 minutes, you'll come to a fork in the road. To the left and right you'll notice jungle-covered, unexcavated pyramids, and at one point, you'll see a raised portion crossing the pathway—this is the visible remains of the *sacbé* to Yaxuná. Throughout the area, intricately carved stelae stand by pathways or lie forlornly in the jungle underbrush. Although protected by crude thatched roofs, most are weatherworn enough that they're indiscernible.

The left fork leads to the **Nohoch Mul Group,** which contains **El Castillo.** With the exception of Structure 2 in Calakmul, this is the tallest pyramid in the Yucatán

---

For Your Comfort at Cobá

Visit Cobá in the morning or after the heat of the day has passed. Mosquito repellent, drinking water, and comfortable shoes are imperative.

(rising even higher than the great El Castillo at Chichén Itzá and the Pyramid of the Magician at Uxmal). So far, visitors are still permitted to climb to the top. From this magnificent lofty perch, you can see unexcavated jungle-covered pyramidal structures poking up through the forest all around.

The right fork (more or less straight on) goes to the **Conjunto Las Pinturas.** Here, the main attraction is the **Pyramid of the Painted Lintel,** a small structure with traces of its original bright colors above the door. You can climb up to get a close look. Though maps of Cobá show ruins around two lakes, there are really only two excavated groups.

Admission is $4, free for children under age 12. Parking is $1. A video camera permit costs $4. The site is open daily from 8am to 5pm, sometimes longer.

WHERE TO STAY & DINE

El Bocadito   El Bocadito, on the right as you enter town (next to the hotel's restaurant of the same name), offers rooms arranged in two rows facing an open patio. They're simple, with tile floors, two double beds, no bedspreads, a ceiling fan, and a washbasin separate from the toilet and cold-water shower cubicle. The open-air restaurant offers good meals at reasonable prices, served by a friendly, efficient staff.

Calle Principal, Cobá, Q. Roo. (Reservations: Apdo. Postal 56, 97780 Valladolid, Yuc.) No phone. 8 units. $18–$25 double. No credit cards. Free unguarded parking. **Amenities:** Restaurant. *In room:* No phone.

Villas Arqueológicas Cobá   This lovely lakeside hotel is a 5-minute walk from the ruins. It is laid out like its Club Med counterparts in Chichén Itzá and Uxmal. The beautiful grounds hold a pool and tennis court. The restaurant is top-notch, though expensive, and the rooms are stylish and modern, but small. Beds occupy niches that surround the mattress on three sides and can be somewhat uncomfortable for those taller than about 2m (6 ft.). The hotel also has a library on Mesoamerican archaeology (with books in French, English, and Spanish). Make reservations—this hotel fills with touring groups.

Cobá, Q. Roo. © 800/258-2633 in the U.S., or 55/5203-3086 in Mexico City. 41 units. $105 double. Rates include continental breakfast. Half-board (breakfast plus lunch or dinner) $15 per person; full board (3 meals) $30 per person. AE, MC, V. Free guarded parking. Drive through town and turn right at lake; hotel is straight ahead on the right. **Amenities:** Restaurant; bar; midsize pool. *In room:* No phone.

EN ROUTE TO THE LOWER CARIBBEAN COAST: FELIPE CARRILLO PUERTO

Mexico's lower Caribbean coast is often called the Costa Maya. This area attracts fishermen, divers, and travelers looking to get away from the crowds. For divers it's especially interesting for the highly regarded Chinchorro reefs, which lie 32km (20 miles) offshore (see below). You'll find sandy beaches good for sunbathing—but not for swimming, because the shore usually has a muddy bottom. For swimming, the beaches around Tulum and Playa del Carmen are better. But if you want to snorkel or dive among pristine reefs, kayak in calm turquoise water, or perhaps do some fly-fishing away from the crowds, this area is a good option. And there's fine swimming in Lake Bacalar.

You also might enjoy the astounding Maya ruins in the Río Bec area, west of Bacalar. I prefer them over Tulum or Cobá. Here, too, you'll find a richer ecosystem than the northern part of the peninsula. The forest canopy is higher, and the wildlife is more abundant. If you're interested in exploring this territory, see "The Río Bec Ruin Route," later in this chapter.

Tips Last Gas

Felipe Carrillo Puerto is the only place to buy **gasoline** between Tulum and Chetumal. If you're desperate, there is a guy who sells gas in Bacalar; just ask when you get there.

Continue south on Highway 307 from Tulum. The road narrows, the speed limit drops, and you begin to see *topes* (speed bumps). Down the road some 25km (15 miles), a sign points to the small but interesting ruins of **Muyil.** Take bug spray. The principal ruins are a small group of buildings and a plaza dominated by the Castillo, a pyramid of medium height but unusual construction. From here, a canal dug by the Maya enters what is now the Sian Ka'an preserve and empties into a lake, with other canals going from there to the saltwater estuary of Boca Paila. The local community offers a boat ride ($35) through these canals and lakes. The 3½-hour tour includes snorkeling the canal and letting the current carry you along. Soft drinks are also included. A few travel agencies in Tulum offer this tour among their Sian Ka'an trips. The agencies charge more but provide transportation, better interpretation, and lunches.

Felipe Carrillo Puerto (pop. 60,000) is the first large town you pass on the road to Ciudad Chetumal. It has two gas stations, a market, a bus terminal, and a few modest hotels and restaurants. Next to the gas station in the center of town is a bank with an ATM. Highway 184 goes from here into the interior of the peninsula, leading eventually to Mérida, which makes Carrillo Puerto a turning point for those making the "short circuit" of the Yucatán Peninsula.

The town is of interest for having been a rebel stronghold during the War of the Castes and the center of the intriguing millenarian cult of the "Talking Cross." The town is still home to a strong community of believers in the cult who practice their own brand of religion and are respected by the whole town. Every month a synod of sorts is held here for the church leaders in 12 neighboring towns.

6 Majahual, Xcalak & the Chinchorro Reef

South of Felipe Carrillo Puerto, the speed bumps begin in earnest. In 45 minutes you reach the turnoff for Majahual and Xcalak, which is at the town of Limones. From here the highway has recently been widened and repaved. The roadwork is being done to facilitate bus tours from the new cruise-ship pier in **Majahual** (mah-hah-*wahl*) to some of the Maya ruins close by, especially Chacchoben. Many passengers elect to enjoy some beach time in Majahual instead. Even before the cruise-ship pier came to Majahual, I saw little that was attractive about the town. The best option is to keep your distance and stay farther down the peninsula in the area of Xcalak. You'll come to the turnoff for Xcalak before you get to Majahual. Xcalak has better lodging than Majahual, a decent dive shop, and more interesting coastal features. It used to take about 1½ hours to get there from Highway 307, but it will be quicker when the new road is finished.

Xcalak (eesh-kah-*lahk*) is a depopulated, weather-beaten fishing village with a few comfortable places to stay and a couple of restaurants. It once had a population as large as 1,200 before the 1958 hurricane washed most of the town away; now it has

The Yucatán's Lower Caribbean Coast

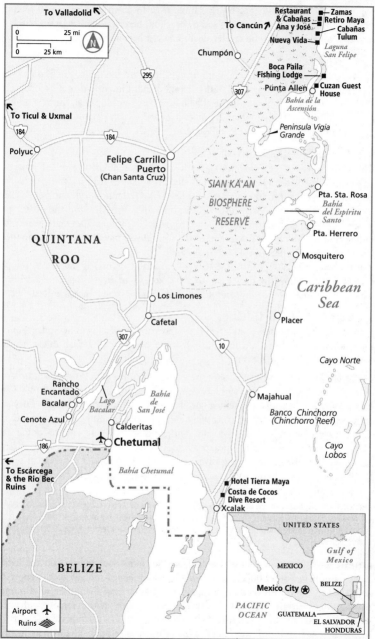

To Valladolid

0 — 25 mi
0 — 25 km

To Cancún

Restaurant & Cabañas Ana y José
Zamas
Retiro Maya
Cabañas Tulum
Nueva Vida

Laguna San Felipe

Chumpón

295

307

Boca Paila Fishing Lodge
Punta Allen
Cuzan Guest House

Bahía de la Ascensión

To Ticul & Uxmal

184

184

Peninsula Vigia Grande

Polyuc

SIAN KA'AN BIOSPHERE RESERVE

Felipe Carrillo Puerto (Chan Santa Cruz)

Pta. Sta. Rosa

Bahía del Espíritu Santo

Pta. Herrero

QUINTANA ROO

Mosquitero

Caribbean Sea

Los Limones

Cafetal

Placer

307

10

Cayo Norte

Rancho Encantado
Bacalar

Lago Bacalar

Bahía de San José

Majahual

Banco Chinchorro (Chinchorro Reef)

Cenote Azul

Calderitas

Chetumal

186

Cayo Lobos

To Escárcega & the Rio Bec Ruins

Bahía Chetumal

Hotel Tierra Maya
Costa de Cocos Dive Resort
Xcalak

UNITED STATES

Gulf of Mexico

MEXICO

BELIZE

Mexico City

BELIZE

PACIFIC OCEAN

GUATEMALA

EL SALVADOR
HONDURAS

Airport
Ruins

617

only 300 permanent residents. It's charming in a run-down way, and you'll certainly feel miles away from the crush of the crowds. From here you work your way back up the coast to get to one of the several small inns just beyond the town.

ORIENTATION

ARRIVING By Car Driving south from Felipe Carrillo Puerto, you'll come to the turnoff (left) onto Highway 10, 2.5km (1½ miles) after Limones; then it's a 50km (30-mile) drive to the coastal settlement of **Majahual.** Before Majahual, there's a military guard station. Tell the guard your destination and turn right to continue to **Xcalak** on the paved highway for 55km (35 miles) more.

DIVING THE CHINCHORRO REEF

The **Chinchorro Reef Underwater National Park** is 38km (24 miles) long and 13km (8 miles) wide. The oval reef is as shallow as 1m (3 ft.) on its interior and as deep as 900m (3,000 ft.) on its exterior. It lies 32km (20 miles) offshore. Locals claim it's the last virgin reef system in the Caribbean. It's invisible from the ocean side; hence, one of its diving attractions is the **shipwrecks**—at least 30—that decorate the underwater landscape. One is on top of the reef. Divers have counted 40 cannons at one wreck site. On the west side are walls and coral gardens.

Aventuras XTC (© **983/831-0461;** www.xcalak.com.mx) is the fully equipped dive shop for the hotels in the Xcalak area. It does a lot of dives around the local reefs, which offer some good diving, and it also does tours to the Chinchorro Reef.

WHERE TO STAY & DINE

Aside from the two places mentioned here, there are six small inns in Xcalak. Americans run most of them, including a four-room property in Xcalak called **Marina Mike's Hotel** (www.xcalak.com).

Costa de Cocos Dive Resort 🏨🏨   Several freestanding cabañas sit around a large, attractive sandy beach graced with coconut palms. The cabañas are comfortable and have a lot of cross-ventilation, ceiling fans, hot water, and comfortable beds. They also come with 24-hour electricity using wind and solar power and purified tap water.

Activities for guests include kayaking, snorkeling, scuba diving, and fly-fishing. The resort has experienced English-speaking fishing guides and a dive instructor. It has a large dive boat capable of taking divers to the Chinchorro reef. The casual restaurant/bar offers good home-style cooking, usually with a choice of one or two main courses at dinner and sandwiches at lunch.

Carretera Majahual–Xcalak Km 52, Q. Roo. © 983/831-0110. www.costadecocos.com. 16 cabañas. High season $90 double; low season $75 double. Dive and fly-fishing packages available by e-mail request. Rates include breakfast buffet. No credit cards. **Amenities:** Restaurant; bar; watersports equipment; airport transportation; dive shop. *In room:* No phone.

Hotel Tierra Maya 🏨   This is a comfortable, modern-style hotel on the beach. Rooms in the two-story building are spacious and designed to have good cross ventilation. They come with ceiling fans, and some rooms have the option of air-conditioning for an extra charge. All have private balconies or terraces looking out to the sea, hammocks, and bottled purified water. Solar generators provide electricity. Bathrooms are large, and beds are either twins or queen-size beds. The owners recently opened a restaurant and can arrange diving, fishing, and snorkeling trips for guests. Guests have Internet access and the use of kayaks and bikes.

Carretera Majahual–Xcalak Km 54, Q. Roo. ℂ 800/480-4505 in the U.S., or 983/831-0404. www.tierramaya.net. 6 units. High season $90–$100 double; low season $75–$85 double. Rates include continental breakfast. MC, V for advance payments. **Amenities:** Restaurant; Internet access. *In room:* A/C in some, no phone.

7 Lago Bacalar ★★★

104km (65 miles) SW of Felipe Carrillo Puerto; 37km (23 miles) NW of Chetumal

Bacalar Lake is an elaborate trick played upon the senses. I remember once standing on a pier on the lake and gazing down into perfectly clear water. As I lifted my eyes I could see the blue tint of the Caribbean. Beyond lay a dense tropical forest. A breeze blowing in from the sea smelled of the salt air, and though I knew it to be untrue, I couldn't help but believe that the water I was gazing on was, in fact, an inlet of the sea and not a lake at all—perhaps a well-sheltered lagoon like Xel-Ha. Lakes in tropical lowlands, especially those surrounded by tropical jungle, are always turbid and muddy. How could this one be so clear? The answer is that Bacalar is not fed by surface runoff, but by several *cenotes* that lie beneath its surface. Only in the Yucatán is such a thing possible. It's enchanting.

This is the perfect spot for being bone idle. But there's plenty to do, too. You can explore the jungle, visit some particularly elegant Maya ruins in the nearby Río Bec area, or take in a wonderful museum about the Maya in Chetumal. Given the choice, I would rather stay in Bacalar and visit Chetumal than the reverse. The town of Bacalar is quiet and quaint. There are a few stores and a couple of restaurants. An 18th-century fort with a moat and stout bastions is by the lake. Inside the fort is a small museum (admission is 50¢) that has several artifacts on display. All text is in Spanish.

ORIENTATION Driving south on Highway 307, the town of Bacalar is 1½ hours beyond Felipe Carrillo Puerto, clearly marked by signs. If you're driving north from Chetumal, it takes about a half-hour. Buses going south from Cancún and Playa del Carmen stop here, and there are frequent buses from Chetumal.

WHERE TO STAY

Hotel Laguna The Laguna overlooks the lake from a lovely vantage point. All the rooms share the view and have little terraces that make enjoyable sitting areas. The midsize rooms have ceiling fans, and most come with two double beds. The mattresses in the bungalows aren't good. The bathrooms are simple but have no problem delivering hot water. A restaurant that shares the same view is open from 7am to 9pm. The bar makes a credible margarita. The highest occupancy rates are from July to August and December to January, when you should make a reservation. The hotel is easy to spot from the road; look for the sign about 1km (½ mile) after you pass through the town of Bacalar.

Bulevar Costera de Bacalar 479, 77010 Lago Bacalar, Q. Roo. ℂ 983/834-2206. Fax 983/834-2205. 34 units. $50 double; $80–$95 bungalow for 5–8 persons. MC, V. **Amenities:** Restaurant; bar; small pool. *In room:* No phone.

Rancho Encantado Cottage Resort ★★ This beautiful, serene lakeside retreat consists of 12 immaculate white-stucco cottages scattered over a shady lawn beside the smooth Lago Bacalar. Each is large and has mahogany louvered windows, a red-tile floor, a dining table and chairs, a living room or sitting area, a porch with chairs, and hammocks strung between trees. Some rooms have cedar ceilings and red-tiled roofs, and others have thatched roofs. All are decorated with folk art and murals inspired by Maya ruins. The newest units are the four waterfront cottages (nos. 9–12). Beds come in different combinations of doubles and twins. Orange, lime, mango, sapote, ceiba, banana, palm, and oak trees; wild orchids; and bromeliads on the grounds make great bird shelters, attracting flocks of chattering parrots, turquoise-browed motmots, toucans, and at least 100 more species, many of which are easy to spot outside your room.

The hotel offers almost a dozen excursions. Among them are day trips to the **Río Bec** ruin route, an extended visit to **Calakmul,** outings to the **Majahual Peninsula,** and a riverboat trip to the Maya ruins of **Lamanai,** deep in a Belizian forest. Excursions cost $55 to $115 per person, depending on the length and difficulty of the trip, and several have a three-person minimum. To find the Rancho, look for the hotel's sign on the left about 1.5km (1 mile) before Bacalar.

Carretera Felipe Carrillo Puerto–Chetumal Km 3, 77000 Chetumal, Q. Roo. ©/fax **983/831-0037.** (Reservations: P.O. Box 1256, Taos, NM 87571. © **800/505-MAYA** in the U.S. Fax 505/751-0972.) www.encantado.com. 13 units. Dec–Apr $150–$180 double; May–Nov $100–$120 double. Rates include continental breakfast and dinner. MC, V. **Amenities:** Restaurant; bar; large outdoor whirlpool; watersports equipment; tour desk; massage service. *In room:* Fridge, coffeemaker.

WHERE TO DINE

Besides the restaurants at the hotels discussed above, you may enjoy the **Restaurante Cenote Azul,** a comfortable open-air thatched-roof restaurant on the edge of the beautiful Cenote Azul. Main courses cost $5 to $12. To get to Restaurant Cenote Azul, follow the highway to the south edge of town and turn left at the restaurant's sign; follow the road around to the restaurant. At Rancho Encantado you can swim in Lago Bacalar, and at the Restaurant Cenote you can take a dip in placid Cenote Azul—but without skin lotion of any kind, because it collects in the *cenote.*

8 Chetumal

251km (156 miles) S of Tulum; 37km (23 miles) S of Lago Bacalar

Capital of the state, and the second-largest city (after Cancún), Chetumal (pop. 210,000) is not a tourist destination. The old part of town, down by the river (Río Hondo), has a Caribbean feel, but the rest is unremarkable. Chetumal is the gateway to Belize, to Tikal, and to the Río Bec ruins. If you're going to spend the night here, visit the **Museo de la Cultura Maya** (© **983/832-6838**), especially if you plan to follow the Río Bec ruin route (see below).

ESSENTIALS
GETTING THERE & DEPARTING
BY PLANE   Aviacsa (© **983/872-7698**) has a direct flight to and from Mexico City. The airport is west of town, just north of the entrance from the highway.

BY CAR   It's a little more than 3 hours from Tulum. If you're heading to Belize, you won't be able to take your rental car because the rental companies won't allow it. To get to the ruins of Tikal in Guatemala, you must go through Belize to the border crossing at Ciudad Melchor de Mencos.

BY BUS   The main bus station (© **983/832-5110**) is 20 blocks from the town center on Insurgentes at Niños Héroes. Buses go to Cancún, Tulum, Playa del Carmen, Puerto Morelos, Mérida, Campeche, Villahermosa, and Tikal, Guatemala.

To Belize: Buses depart from the Lázaro Cárdenas market (most often called *el mercado nuevo*). Ask for Autobuses Novelo. The company has local service every 45 minutes ($10) and four express buses per day ($14).

VISITOR INFORMATION

The **State Tourism Office** (© **983/835-0860,** ext. 1811) is at Calzada del Centenario 622, between Comonfort and Ciricote. Office hours are Monday to Friday from 9am to 6pm.

ORIENTATION

The telephone **area code** is **983.**

All traffic enters the city from the west and feeds onto Avenida Obregón into town. Avenida Héroes is the main north-south street.

A MUSEUM NOT TO MISS

Museo de la Cultura Maya ★★★ This modern museum unlocks the complex world of the Maya through interactive exhibits and genuine artifacts. Push a button, and an illustrated description appears, explaining the medicinal and domestic uses of plants with their Maya and scientific names; another exhibit describes the social classes of the Maya by their manners of dress. One of the most fascinating exhibits describes the Maya's ideal of personal beauty and the subsequent need to deform craniums, scar the face and body, and induce cross-eyed vision. An enormous screen flashes images taken from an airplane flying over more than a dozen Maya sites from Mexico to Honduras. Another large television shows the architectural variety of Maya pyramids and how they were probably built. Then a walk on a glass floor takes you over representative ruins in the Maya world. In the center of the museum is the three-story, stylized, sacred ceiba tree, which the Maya believed connected Xibalba (the underworld), Earth, and the heavens. If you can arrange it, see the museum before you tour the Río Bec ruins.

Av. Héroes s/n. © 983/832-6838. Admission $5. Tues–Thurs 9am–7pm; Fri–Sat 9am–8pm. Between Colón and Gandhi, 8 blocks from Av. Obregón, just past the Holiday Inn.

WHERE TO STAY

Hotel Holiday Inn Puerta Maya This modern hotel (formerly the Hotel Continental) has the best air-conditioning in town and is only a block from the Museo de la Cultura Maya. Most rooms are midsize and come with two double beds or one king-size bed. Bathrooms are roomy and well lit.

Av. Héroes 171, 77000 Chetumal, Q. Roo. © 800/465-4329 in the U.S., or 983/835-0400. Fax 983/832-1676. 85 units. $125 double. AE, MC, V. Free secure parking. From Av. Obregón, turn left on Av. Héroes, go 6 blocks, and look for the hotel on the right. **Amenities:** Restaurant; bar; midsize pool; room service; laundry service. *In room:* A/C, TV.

Hotel Nachancán One block from *el mercado nuevo* (the new market) and buses to Belize, this hotel offers plain but comfortable rooms, with one or two double beds. Also a block away is El Buen Gusto, which serves some of the best Yucatecan food in Chetumal. Bathrooms are small, with no counter space, but they offer plenty of hot water (once it finally arrives). A cab to the Museo de la Cultura Maya costs $1.

Calzada Veracruz 379, 77000 Chetumal, Q. Roo. © 983/832-3232. 20 units. $33 double; $45 suite. No credit cards. Drive the length of Av. Obregón to where it stops at Calzada Veracruz, turn left, and drive 2km (1¼ miles); the hotel will be on the right. **Amenities:** Restaurant; bar. *In room:* A/C, TV, no phone.

WHERE TO DINE

I can recommend just a few restaurants in Chetumal. If you want to eat in air-conditioned surroundings in a modern, comfortable setting, try **Espress Café & Restaurant,** Calle 22 de Enero 141, corner of Boulevard Bahía (© **983/833-3013**). It serves well-prepared Mexican food, light fare such as sandwiches, and good breakfasts. Open daily from 8am to midnight. For an economical meal with some local atmosphere, try **Restaurante Pantoja,** on the corner of calles Ghandi and 16 de Septiembre (no phone), 2 blocks east of the Museum of Maya Culture. It offers a cheap daily special, good green enchiladas, and such local specialties as *poc chuc.* It's open Monday to Saturday from 7am to 9pm. To sample excellent *antojitos,* the local supper food, go to **El Buen Gusto,** on Calzada Veracruz across from the market (no phone). A Chetumal institution, it serves excellent *salbutes* and *panuchos* (both dishes are similar to *gorditas*). Doors open around 7pm and close around midnight every night.

ONWARD FROM CHETUMAL
From Chetumal you have several choices. The Maya ruins of Lamanai, in Belize, are an easy day trip if you have transportation (not a rental car). You can explore the Río Bec ruin route directly west of the city (see below) by taking Highway 186.

9 The Río Bec Ruin Route
A few miles west of Bacalar and Chetumal begins an area of Maya settlement known to archaeologists as the Río Bec region. A number of ruins stretch from close to Bacalar well into the state of Campeche. These ruins are numerous, intriguing, and dramatic. Their architecture is heavily stylized, with lots of decoration. In recent years, excavation has led to many discoveries. With excavation has come restoration, but the ruins here have not been rebuilt to the same degree as those at Uxmal and Chichén Itzá. But, in some cases, the archaeologists found buildings so well preserved that they needed little restoration.

Nor have these sites been cleared of jungle growth in the same manner as the marquee ruins mentioned above. Trees and vines grow in profusion around the buildings, giving the sites the feel of lost cities. Keep the mosquito repellent handy. In visiting them, you can imagine what John Lloyd Stephens and Catherwood must have felt when they traipsed through the Yucatán in the 19th century. And watch for wildlife; on my last visit I saw several denizens of the tropical forest. The fauna along the entire route is especially rich. You might see a toucan, a grand curassow, or a macaw hanging about the ruins, and orioles, egrets, and several birds of prey are extremely common. Gray fox, wild turkey, tesquintle (a bushy-tailed, plant-eating rodent), the raccoon relative coatimundi (with its long tapered snout and tail), and armadillos inhabit the area in abundance. At Calakmul, a family of howler monkeys resides in the trees overlooking the parking area.

THE ROUTE'S STARTING POINT Halfway between Bacalar and Chetumal is the turnoff for Highway 186 to Escárcega (about 20km/12 miles from either town). It's a major highway and is well marked. This is the same road that leads to Campeche, Palenque, and Villahermosa. There are a couple of gas stations on the route. One is at

---

Tips **In Case of Emergency**

The Riviera Maya south of Puerto Aventuras is susceptible to power failures that can last for hours. Gas pumps and cash machines shut down when this happens, and once the power returns, they attract long lines. It's a good idea to keep a reserve of gas and cash.

the town of Xpujil. The Río Bec sites are at varying distances off this highway. You pass through a guard station at the border with Campeche state. The guards might ask you to present your travel papers, or they might just wave you on. Either way, it's no big deal. You can divide your sightseeing into several day trips from Bacalar or Chetumal, or you can spend the night in this area and see more the next day. If you get an early start, you can easily visit a few of the sites mentioned here in a day.

Evidence shows that these ruins, especially Becán, were part of the **trade route** linking the Caribbean coast at Cobá to Edzná and the Gulf coast, and to Lamanai in Belize and beyond. At one time, a great number of cities thrived in this region, and much of the land was dedicated to the intensive cultivation of maize. Today all of this lies hidden under a dense jungle, which blankets the land from horizon to horizon.

I have listed the following sites in east-to-west order, the way you would see them driving from the Caribbean coast. If you decide to tour these ruins, take the time to visit the Museo de la Cultura Maya in Chetumal first. It will lend context to what you see. If you want a guide to show you the area, contact **Luis Téllez (✆ 983/832-3496;** www.sacbetravel.com), who lives in Chetumal. The best way to reach him is through the e-mail link on his website. Luis is the best guide for this region; he is knowledgeable, speaks English, is a good driver, and is acquainted with most of the archaeologists working in this area and stays current with their findings. He also knows a lot about local wildlife and guides many tours for birders. Entry to each site is $2 to $4. Informational signs at each building are in Mayan, Spanish, and English. There are few if any refreshments at the ruins, so bring your own water and food. All the principal sites have toilets.

Food & Lodging   Your lodging choices are growing. On the upscale side are the Explorean hotel near Kohunlich and the ecovillage in Chicanná. Food and lodging of the no-frills sort can be found in the town of Xpujil and near Calakmul.

The **Explorean (✆ 888/679-3748** in the U.S.; www.theexplorean.com) is an ecolodge for adventure travelers who like their comfort. It sits all alone on the crest of a small hill not far from the ruins of Kohunlich. It has a small pool and spa and lovely rooms, and offers guide services and adventure tours (mountain biking, rappelling, kayaking) all as part of an all-inclusive package. The cost is over $500 for two people and, in addition to the tours, includes food and drink. The hotel is a member of the Fiesta Americana chain.

The **Chicanná Eco Village,** Km 144 Carretera Escárcega (✆ **981/816-2233** in Campeche for reservations), is just beyond the town of Xpujil. It offers 28 nicely furnished rooms distributed among several two-story thatched bungalows. The comfortable rooms have two doubles or a king-size bed, ceiling fans, a large bathroom, and screened windows. The manicured lawns and flowerbeds are lovely, with pathways linking the bungalows to each other and to the restaurant and swimming pool. Double rooms go for $113.

In the village of Xpujil (just before the ruins of Xpujil) are three modest hotels and a couple of restaurants. The best food and lodging are at **Restaurant y Hotel Calakmul (✆ 983/871-6029),** run by Doña María Cabrera. The hotel has 12 comfortable rooms that go for $40. They have tile floors, private bathrooms with hot water, and good beds. The restaurant is open daily from 6am to midnight. Main courses cost $4 to $8. The chicken cooked in herbs is worth ordering. Near the turnoff to Calakmul are three new hotels. Two are simple, one was made with bus tours in mind. I think that **Rio Bec Dreams (✆ 983/871-6057;** www.riobecdreams.com) is the best choice

---

> **Tips** **Recommended Reading**
>
> For a bit of background reading to help you make the most of your visit, I rec-
> ommend *A Forest of Kings: The Untold Story of the Ancient Maya,* by Linda
> Schele and David Freidel (William Morrow, 1990); *The Blood of Kings: Dynasty
> and Ritual in Maya Art,* by Linda Schele and Mary Ellen Miller (George Braziller,
> 1968); and *The Maya Cosmos,* by David Freidel and Linda Schele (William Mor-
> row, 1993). *Arqueología Mexicana* magazine devoted its July/August 1995 issue
> to the Quintana Roo portion of the Río Bec ruin route. Last, though it lacks his-
> toric and cultural information and many sites have expanded since it was written,
> Joyce Kelly's *An Archaeological Guide to Mexico's Yucatán Peninsula* (University
> of Oklahoma, 1993), is the best companion book to have. For a crash course,
> focus on the meaning of the jaguar, Xibalba (the underworld), and the earth
> monster.

---

because the owners are present and hence the service is better. It's 12km (7½ miles) west of Xpujil. The rooms have shared bathrooms, but everything is comfortable and you get a feel for the jungle.

DZIBANCHE & KINICHNA

The turnoff for this site is 37km (23 miles) from the highway intersection and is well marked. From the turnoff it's another 23km (14 miles) to the ruins. The road has recently been repaired and is in good condition. Dzibanché (or Tzibanché) means "place where they write on wood"—obviously not the original name, which remains unknown. Exploration began here in 1993, and the site opened to the public in late 1994. Scattered over 42 sq. km (16 sq. miles) are several groupings of buildings and plazas; only a small portion is excavated. It dates from the Classic period (A.D. 300–900) and was occupied for around 700 years.

TEMPLES & PLAZAS Two large adjoining plazas have been cleared. The most important structure yet excavated is called the Temple of the Owl, which is in the main plaza, Plaza Xibalba. Archaeologists found a stairway that descends from the top of the structure deep into the pyramid, ending in a burial chamber. It is closed to vis-itors. There they uncovered a number of beautiful polychromatic lidded vessels, one of which has an owl painted on the top handle with its wings spreading onto the lid. White owls were messengers of the gods of the underworld in the Maya religion. Also found here were the remains of a sacrificial victim and what appear to be the remains of a Maya queen, which is unique in the archaeology of the Maya.

Opposite the Temple of the Owl is the **Temple of the Cormorant,** named after a polychromed drinking vessel found here depicting the bird. Here, too, archaeologists have found evidence of an interior tomb similar to the one in the Temple of the Owl, but excavations of it have not yet begun. Other magnificently preserved pottery pieces found during excavations include an incense burner with an almost three-dimensional figure of the diving god attached to the outside, and another incense burner with an elaborately dressed representation of the god Itzamná attached.

Situated all by itself is **Structure 6,** a miniature rendition of Teotihuacán's style of *tablero* and *talud* architecture. Each step of the pyramid is made of a *talud* (sloping surface) crowned by a *tablero* (vertical stone facing). Teotihuacán was near present-day

Mexico City, but its influence stretched as far as Guatemala. At the top of the pyramid is a doorway, its wooden lintel still intact after centuries of weathering. This detail gave the site its name. Carved into the wood are date glyphs for the year A.D. 733.

Near the site is another city, **Kinichná** (kee-neech-*nah*). About 2.5km (1½ miles) north, it is reachable only by a rutted road that's impassable during the rainy season. An Olmec-style jade figure was found there. It has a large acropolis with five buildings on three levels, which have been restored and are in good condition, with fragments of the remaining stucco still visible.

KOHUNLICH

Kohunlich (koh-*hoon*-leech), 42km (26 miles) from the turnoff for Highway 186, dates from around A.D. 100 to 900. Turn left off the road, and the entrance is 9km (5½ miles) ahead. From the parking area, you enter the grand, parklike site, crossing a large and shady ceremonial area flanked by four large, conserved pyramidal edifices. Continue walking, and just beyond this grouping you'll come to Kohunlich's famous **Pyramid of the Masks** under a thatched covering. The masks, actually enormous plaster faces, date from around A.D. 500 and are on the facade of the building. Each mask has an elongated face and wears a headdress with a mask on its crest and a mask on the chin piece, essentially masks within masks. The top one is thought to represent the astral world, while the lower one represents the underworld, suggesting that the wearer of this headdress is among the living and not in either of the other worlds. Note the carving on the pupils, which suggests a solar connection, possibly with the night sun that illuminated the underworld. This may mean that the person had shamanic vision.

It's speculated that masks covered much of the facade of this building, which is built in the Río Bec style, with rounded corners, a false stairway, and a false temple on the top. At least one theory holds that the masks are a composite of several rulers at Kohunlich. Recent excavations of buildings immediately to the left after you enter uncovered two intact pre-Hispanic skeletons and five decapitated heads that were probably used in a ceremonial ritual. To the right after you enter (follow a shady path through the jungle) is another recently excavated plaza. It's thought to have housed priests or rulers, due to the high quality of pottery found there and the fine architecture of the rooms. Scholars believe that Kohunlich became overpopulated, leading to its decline.

XPUJIL

Xpujil (eesh-poo-*heel*; also spelled Xpuhil), meaning either "cattail" or "forest of kapok trees," flourished between A.D. 400 and 900. This is a small site that's easy to get to. Look for a blue sign on the highway pointing to the right. The entrance is just off the highway. After buying a ticket ($3), you have to walk 180m (600 ft.) to the main structure. Along the path are some *chechén* trees. Don't touch; they are poisonous and will provoke blisters. You can recognize them by their blotchy bark. On the right, you'll see a platform supporting a restored two-story building with a central staircase on the eastern side. Decorating the first floor are the remnants of a decorative molding and two galleries connected by a doorway. About 90m (300 ft.) farther you come to the site's main structure—a rectangular ceremonial platform 2m (6 ft.) high and 50m (170 ft.) long supporting the palace, decorated with three tall towers shaped like miniature versions of the pyramids in Tikal, Guatemala. These towers are purely decorative, with false stairways and temples, too small to serve as such. The effect is beautiful. The main body of the building holds 12 rooms, which are now in ruins.

BECAN ★★★

Becán (beh-*kahn*) is about 7km (4½ miles) beyond Xpujil and is visible on the right side of the highway. Becán means "moat filled by water," and, in fact, it was protected by a moat spanned by seven bridges. The extensive site dates from the early Classic to the late post-Classic (600 B.C.–A.D. 1200) period. Although it was abandoned by A.D. 850, ceramic remains indicate that there may have been a population resurgence between 900 and 1000, and it was still used as a ceremonial site as late as 1200. Becán was an administrative and ceremonial center with political sway over at least seven other cities in the area, including Chicanná, Hormiguero, and Payán.

The first plaza group you see after you enter was the center for grand ceremonies. From the highway, you can see the back of a pyramid (Structure 1) with two temples on top. Beyond and in between the two temples you can see the Temple atop Structure 4, which is opposite Temple 1. When the high priest appeared through the mouth of the earth monster in the center of this temple (which he reached by way of a hidden side stairway that's now partly exposed), he was visible from what is now the highway. It's thought that commoners had to watch ceremonies from outside the ceremonial plaza—thus the site's position was for good viewing purposes. The back of Structure 4 is believed to have been a civic plaza where rulers sat on stone benches while pronouncing judgments. The second plaza group dates from around A.D. 850 and has perfect twin towers on top, where there's a big platform. Under the platform are 10 rooms that are thought to be related to Xibalba (shee-*bahl*-bah), the underworld. Hurricane Isidore damaged them, and they are closed until they can be repaired. Earth monster faces probably covered this building (and appeared on other buildings as well). Remains of at least one ball court have been unearthed. Next to the ball court is a well-preserved figure in an elaborate headdress behind glass. He was excavated not far from where he is now displayed. The markings are well defined, displaying a host of details.

CHICANNA

Slightly over 1.5km (1 mile) beyond Becán, on the left side of the highway, is Chicanná, which means "house of the mouth of snakes." Trees loaded with bromeliads shade the central square surrounded by five buildings. The most outstanding edifice features a monster-mouth doorway and an ornate stone facade with more superimposed masks. As you enter the mouth of the earth monster, note that you are walking on a platform configured as the open jaw of the monster with stone teeth on both sides. Again you find a lovely example of an elongated building with ornamental miniature pyramids on each end.

CALAKMUL ★★★

This area is both a massive Maya archaeological zone, with at least 60 sites, and a 70,000-hectare (180,000-acre) rainforest designated in 1989 as the Calakmul Biosphere Reserve, which includes territory in both Mexico and Guatemala. The best way to see Calakmul is to spend the night at Xpujil or Chicanná and leave early in the morning for Calakmul. If you're the first one to drive down the narrow access road to the ruins (1½ hr. from the highway), you'll see plenty of wildlife.

THE ARCHAEOLOGICAL ZONE Since 1982, archaeologists have been excavating the ruins of Calakmul, which dates from 100 B.C. to A.D. 900. It's the largest of the area's 60 known sites. Nearly 7,000 buildings have been discovered and mapped.

At its zenith, at least 60,000 people may have lived around the site, but by the time of the Spanish Conquest in 1519, there were fewer than 1,000 inhabitants. Visitors arrive at a large plaza filled with a forest of trees. You immediately see several stelae; Calakmul contains more of these than any other site, but they are much more weathered and indistinguishable than the stelae of Palenque or Copán in Honduras. On one of them you can clearly see the work of looters who carefully used some sort of stone-cutting saw to slice off the face of the monument. By Structure 13 is a stele of a woman dating from A.D. 652. She is thought to have been a ruler, which would be exceedingly unusual.

Several structures here are worth checking out; some are built in the Petén style, some in the Río Bec style. Structure 3 must have been the residence of a noble family. Its design is unique and quite lovely; it managed to retain its original form and was never remodeled the way so many other structures were. Offerings of shells, beads, and polychromed tripod pottery were found inside. Structure 2 is the tallest pyramid in the Yucatán, at 54m (178 ft.). From the top of it you can see the outline of the ruins of El Mirador, 50km (30 miles) across the forest in Guatemala. Notice the two stairways that ascend along the sides of the principal face of the pyramid in the upper levels. This has no equivalent in Maya architecture, and when appreciated in conjunction with how the masks break up the space of the front face, you can see just how complex the design was.

Temple 4 charts the line of the sun from June 21, when it falls on the left (north) corner; to September 21 and March 21, when it lines up in the east behind the middle temple on the top of the building; to December 21, when it falls on the right (south) corner. Numerous jade pieces, including spectacular masks, were uncovered here, most of which are on display in the Museo Regional in Campeche. Temple 7 is largely unexcavated except for the top, where in 1984 the most outstanding jade mask yet to be found at Calakmul was uncovered. In *A Forest of Kings,* Linda Schele and David Freidel tell of wars between the Calakmul, Tikal, and Naranjo (the latter two in Guatemala), and how Ah-Cacaw, king of Tikal (120km/75 miles south of Calakmul), captured King Jaguar-Paw in A.D. 695 and later Lord Ox-Ha-Te Ixil Ahau, both of Calakmul. The site is open Tuesday to Sunday from 7am to 5pm, but it gets so wet during the rainy season from June to October that it's best not to go.

CALAKMUL BIOSPHERE RESERVE Set aside in 1989, this is the peninsula's only high-forest *selva*, a rainforest that annually records as much as 5m (16 ft.) of rain. Notice that the canopy of the trees is higher here than in the forest of Quintana Roo. It lies very close to the border with Guatemala, but, of course, there is no way to get there. Among the plants are cactus, epiphytes, and orchids. Endangered animals include the white-lipped peccary, jaguar, and puma. So far, more than 250 species of birds have been recorded. At present, no overnight stay or camping is permitted. If you want a tour of a small part of the forest and you speak Spanish, you can inquire for a guide at one of the two nearby *ejidos* (cooperatives). Some old *chicleros* (the men who tap sapodilla trees for their gum) living there can take you on a couple of trails.

The turnoff on the left for Calakmul is located approximately 230km (145 miles) from the intersection of highways 186 and 307, just before the village of Conhuas. There's a guard station there where you pay $3 to enter. From the turnoff, it's a 1½-hour drive on a paved, but very narrow and somewhat rutted, road that may be difficult during the rainy season, from May to October.

A Driving Caution

Numerous curves in the road make seeing oncoming traffic (what little there is) difficult, and there have been head-on collisions.

BALAMKU ★★

Balamkú (bah-lahm-*koo*) is a site that should not be missed. A couple of buildings in it were so well preserved that they required almost no reconstruction, just uncovering. Inside one you will find three impressive figures of men sitting in the gaping maws of crocodiles and toads as they descend into the underworld. The whole concept of this building, with its molded stucco facade, is life and death. On the head of each almost-three-dimensional figure are the eyes, nose, and mouth of a jaguar figure, followed by the full face of the human figure, then a neck formed by the eyes and nose of another jaguar, and an Olmec-like face on the stomach, with its neck decorated by a necklace. These figures were saved in dramatic fashion from looters who managed to get away with a fourth one. Now they are under the protection of a caretaker, who keeps the room under lock and key, but he can be persuaded to open it for visitors. (A tip is appreciated.) If you speak Spanish, you can get the caretaker to explain something of the figures and their complex symbolism. There is also a beautiful courtyard and another set of buildings adjacent to the main group.

16

Mérida, Chichén Itzá & the Maya Interior

by David Baird

Ask most people about the Yucatán, and they think of Cancún, the Caribbean coast, and Chichén Itzá. But there's much more to visit in the Yucatán than just those places. With a little exploring, you'll find a variety of things to do. You might spend a morning scrambling over Maya ruins and in the afternoon take a dip in the cool, clear water of a *cenote* (natural well). The next day may find you strolling along a lonely beach or riding in a skiff through mangroves to visit a colony of pink flamingos, and by the evening you might be dancing in the streets of **Mérida.** This chapter covers the interior of the Yucatán peninsula, including the famous Maya ruins at **Chichén Itzá** and **Uxmal,** the flamingo sanctuaries at **Celestún** and **Río Lagartos,** as well as many other spots that might find special favor with you.

EXPLORING THE YUCATAN'S MAYA HEARTLAND

The best way to see the Yucatán is by car. The terrain is flat, there is little traffic, and the main highways are in good shape. If you do drive around the area, you will add one Spanish word to your vocabulary, which through much repetition will stick with you: *topes* (*toh*-pehs), or "speed bumps." *Topes* come in varying shapes and sizes and with varying degrees of warning. Don't let them catch you by surprise. Off the beaten path, the roads are narrow and rough, but hey—we're talking rental cars. Rentals are, in fact, a little pricey compared with those in the U.S. (due perhaps to wear and tear?), but some promotional deals are available, especially in the low season. For more on renting a car, see "By Car," in "Mérida: Gateway to the Maya Heartland," below.

Plenty of buses ply the roads between the major towns and ruins. And plenty of tour buses circulate, too. But buses to the smaller towns and ruins and the haciendas are infrequent or nonexistent. One bus company, Autobuses del Oriente (ADO), controls most of the first-class bus service and does a good job with the major destinations. Second-class buses go to some out-of-the-way places, but they can be slow, stop a lot, and aren't air-conditioned. I will take them when I'm going only a short distance, say around 25km (40 miles). If you don't want to rent a car, a few tour operators take small groups to more remote attractions such as ruins, *cenotes,* and villages.

The Yucatán is *tierra caliente* (the hotlands). Don't travel in this region without a hat, sunblock, mosquito repellent, and water. The coolest weather is from November to February; the hottest is from April to June. From July to October, thundershowers moderate temperatures. More tourists come to the interior during the winter months, but not to the same extent as on the Caribbean coast. The high-season/low-season distinction is less pronounced here.

Should you decide to travel into this part of the world, don't miss **Mérida.** It is, and has been for centuries, the cultural and commercial center of the Yucatán. You won't find a more vibrant tropical city anywhere. Every time I visit, there is some festival or celebration to attend, on top of the nightly performances that the city offers its citizens and visitors. It's also the Yucatán's shopping center, where you can buy the area's specialty items, such as hammocks, Panama hats, and the embroidered native blouses known as *huipiles*. And Mérida makes the perfect base from which to launch a variety of side trips. Here are some of the essential places to visit:

Tips Mapping the Region

To check out the region surrounding Mérida, see "The Yucatán Peninsula" map on p. 580.

CHICHEN ITZA & VALLADOLID

These destinations are almost midway between Mérida and Cancún. From Mérida it's 2½ hours by car to Chichén on the new *autopista* (toll road). You can spend a day at the ruins and then stay at one of the nearby hotels—or drive 40km (25 miles) to Valladolid, a quiet, charming colonial town with a pleasant central square. Valladolid features two eerie *cenotes*. The spectacular ruins at Ek Balam are only 40km (25 miles) to the north. Also in the area is the Río Lagartos Nature Reserve, teeming with flamingos and other native birds.

CELESTUN NATIONAL WILDLIFE REFUGE These flamingo-sanctuary wetlands along the Gulf coast contain a unique shallow-water estuary where freshwater from *cenotes* mixes with saltwater, creating the perfect feeding grounds for flamingos. Touring this area by launch is relaxing and rewarding. Only 1½ hours from Mérida, Celestún makes for an easy day trip.

DZIBILCHALTUN This Maya site, now a national park, is 14km (9 miles) north of Mérida along the road to Progreso. Here you'll find pre-Hispanic ruins, nature trails, a *cenote*, and the Museum of the Maya. You can make this the first stop in a day trip to Progreso and other attractions north of Mérida.

PROGRESO A modern city and Gulf coast beach escape 34km (21 miles) north of Mérida, Progreso has a wide beach and oceanfront drive that's popular on the weekends and during the summer. The recent arrival of cruise ships might make Progreso even more popular, but with so much beach, you'll easily have a place to yourself. From Progreso you can drive down the coast to **Uaymitún** to see some flamingos and visit the recently excavated ruins of **Xcambó.**

UXMAL Smaller than Chichén, but architecturally more striking and mysterious, Uxmal is about 80km (50 miles) south of Mérida. You can see it in a day, though it's a good idea to extend that somewhat to see the sound-and-light show and spend the night at one of the hotels by the ruins. Several other nearby sites make up the Puuc route and can be explored the following day. It's also possible, though a bit rushed, to see Uxmal and the other ruins on a 1-day trip by special excursion bus from Mérida.

---

1 Mérida: Gateway to the Maya Heartland ★ ★

1,440km (900 miles) E of Mexico City; 320km (200 miles) W of Cancún

Mérida is the capital of the state of Yucatán and has been the dominant city in the region since the Spanish Conquest. It is a busy city and suffers from the same problems that plague other colonial cities in Mexico—traffic and noise, especially the noisy and

> (Tips) **The Best Websites for Mérida, Chichén Itzá &**
> **the Maya Interior**
>
> • **Maya: Portraits of a People: www.nationalgeographic.com/explorer/maya/**
>   **more.html** A fascinating collection of articles from *National Geographic*
>   and other sources.
> • **Yucatán Travel Guide: www.mayayucatan.com** Yucatán's newly formed
>   Ministry of Tourism maintains this site. It has an update section and good
>   general info on different destinations in the state.
> • **Mexico's Yucatán Directory: www.mexonline.com/yucatan.htm** A nice
>   roundup of vacation rentals, tour operators, and information on the
>   Maya sites. For more information on Mexico's indigenous history, see the
>   links on the pre-Columbian page (www.mexonline.com/precolum.htm).

smoky urban buses. Still, it is a fun city and has many admirers. I get comments from people all the time about how much they enjoyed Mérida. People here know how to have a good time, and they seem driven to organize concerts, theater productions, art exhibits, and such. In recent years the city has been in the midst of a cultural explosion.

ESSENTIALS

GETTING THERE & DEPARTING   By Plane   Aeromexico (℗ **999/927-9277** or 999/927-9433; www.aeromexico.com) and **Mexicana** (℗ **999/924-6633** or 999/924-6910; www.mexicana.com.mx) have nonstop flights to and from Miami. **Continental** (℗ **999/946-1888** or 999/946-1900; www.continental.com) has nonstop service to and from Houston. Otherwise, you will most likely have to fly through Cancún, Cozumel, or Mexico City. **Mexicana** flies to and from Mexico City. **Aeromexico** flies to and from Cancún and Mexico City. **Aerocaribe** (℗ **999/928-6786**), a Mexicana affiliate, provides service to and from Cozumel, Cancún, Veracruz, Villahermosa, and points in Central America. **Aviacsa** (℗ **999/926-9087**) provides service to and from Cancún, Monterrey, Villahermosa, Tuxtla Gutiérrez, Tapachula, Oaxaca, and Mexico City. Taxis from the airport to the city run $11.

By Car   Highway 180 is the old *carretera federal* (federal highway) between Mérida and Cancún. The trip takes 6 hours, and the road is in good shape; you will pass through many Maya villages. A four-lane divided *cuota*, or *autopista* (toll road) parallels Highway 180 and begins at the town of Kantunil, 56km (35 miles) east of Mérida. By avoiding the tiny villages and their not-so-tiny speed bumps, the autopista cuts 2 hours from the journey between Mérida and Cancún; one-way tolls cost $28. Coming from Cancún (or, for that matter, Valladolid or Chichén Itzá, both of which are en route), Highway 180 enters Mérida by feeding into Calle 65, which passes 1 block south of the main square.

Coming from the south (Campeche or Uxmal), you will enter the city on Avenida Itzáes. To get to the town center, turn right on Calle 59 (the first street after the zoo).

A *periférico* (traffic loop) encircles Mérida, making it possible to skirt the city. Directional signs into the city are generally good, but going around the city on the loop requires vigilance.

By Bus There are five bus stations in Mérida, two of which offer first-class buses; the other three provide local service to nearby destinations. The larger of the first-class stations, **CAME,** is on Calle 70, between calles 69 and 71 (see "City Layout," below). The ADO bus line and its affiliates operate the station. When you get there, you'll see a row of ticket windows. All but the last couple to the right sell first-class tickets. The last two windows sell tickets for ADO's deluxe services, ADO-GL and UNO. The former is only slightly better than first class; the latter has superwide roomy seats. Unless it's a long trip, I generally choose the bus that has the most convenient departure time. Tickets can be purchased in advance; just ask the ticket agent for the different options and departure times for the route you need.

The other first-class station is the small **Maya K'iin** used by the bus company **Elite.** It's at Calle 65 no. 548, between calles 68 and 70.

To and from Cancún: You can pick up a bus at the CAME (almost every hour) or through Elite (five per day). Both bus lines also pick up passengers at the Fiesta Americana Hotel, across from the Hyatt (12 per day). You can buy a ticket there at the **Ticket Bus** agency or at the Elite ticket agency. Cancún is 4 hours away; a few buses stop in **Valladolid.**

To and from Chichén Itzá: Three buses per day (2½-hr. trip) depart from the CAME. Also, check out tours operating from the hotels in Mérida if you want to visit for the day.

To and from Playa del Carmen, Tulum, and Chetumal: From the CAME, there are 10 departures per day for Playa del Carmen (5-hr. trip), six for Tulum (6-hr. trip), and eight for Chetumal (7-hr. trip). From Maya K'iin there are three per day to Playa, which stop at the Fiesta Americana.

To and from Campeche: From the CAME station, there are 36 departures per day. Elite has four departures per day. It's a 2½-hour trip.

To and from Palenque and San Cristóbal de las Casas: There is service to San Cristóbal twice daily from the CAME, and once daily on Elite. To Palenque there are three and one, respectively. There have been reports of minor theft on buses to Palenque. You should do three things: Don't take second-class buses to this destination; check your luggage so that it's stowed in the cargo bay; and put your carry-on in the overhead rack, not on the floor.

The main **second-class bus station** is around the corner from the CAME on Calle 69, between calles 68 and 70.

To and from Uxmal: There are four buses per day. (You can also hook up with a tour to Uxmal through most hotels or any travel agent or tour operator in town.) One bus per day combines Uxmal with the other sites to the south (Kabah, Sayil, Labná, and Xlapak—known as the Puuc route) and does the whole round-trip in a day. It stops for 2 hours at Uxmal and 30 minutes at each of the other sites.

To and from Progreso and Dzibilchaltún: The bus station that serves these destinations is the **Estación Progreso,** Calle 62 no. 524, between calles 65 and 67. The trip to Progreso takes an hour by second-class bus. *Colectivos* (Volkswagen vans) to Dzibilchaltún stop beside the San Juan church, south of the main plaza off of Calle 62.

To and from Celestún: The Celestún station is at Calle 71 no. 585 between calles 64 and 66. The trip takes 1½ to 2 hours, depending on how often the bus stops. There are 10 buses per day.

ORIENTATION   Arriving by Plane   Mérida's airport is 13km (8 miles) from the city center on the southwestern outskirts of town, near the entrance to Highway 180.

The airport has desks for renting a car, reserving a hotel room, and getting tourist information. Taxi tickets to town ($11) are sold outside the airport doors, under the covered walkway.

VISITOR INFORMATION   There are city tourism offices and state tourism offices, which have different resources; if you can't get the info you're looking for at one, go to the other. The state operates two downtown tourism offices: One is in the **Teatro Peón Contreras,** facing Parque de la Madre (© **999/924-9290**); and the other is on the main plaza, in the **Palacio de Gobierno,** immediately to the left as you enter. These offices are open daily from 8am to 9pm. There are also information booths at the airport and the CAME bus station. The city's **visitor information offices** (© **999/942-0000,** ext. 133) are on the ground floor of the Ayuntamiento building facing the main square on Calle 62. Look for a glass door under the arcade. Hours are Monday to Saturday from 8am to 8pm and Sunday from 8am to 2pm. At 9:30am every day it offers visitors a free tour of the area around the main square.

Also keep your eye out for the free monthly magazine *Yucatán Today;* it's a good source of info for Mérida and the rest of the region.

CITY LAYOUT   Downtown Mérida has the standard layout of towns in the Yucatán: Streets running north-south are even numbers; those running east-west are odd numbers. The numbering begins on the north and the east sides of town, so if you're walking on an odd-numbered street and the even numbers of the cross streets are increasing, then you are heading west; likewise, if you are on an even-numbered street and the odd numbers of the cross streets are increasing, you are going south.

Address numbers don't tell you anything about what cross street to look for. This is why addresses almost always list cross streets, usually like this: "Calle 60 no. 549 × 71 y 73." The "×" is a multiplication sign—shorthand for the word *por* (meaning "by")—and *y* means "and." So this place would be on Calle 60 between calles 71 and 73. Outside of the downtown area, the numbering of streets gets a little crazy, so it's important to know the name of the neighborhood where you're going. This is the first thing taxi drivers will ask you.

The town's main square is the busy **Plaza Mayor,** referred to simply as **El Centro.** It's bordered by calles 60, 62, 61, and 63. Calle 60, which runs in front of the cathedral, is an important street to remember; it connects the main square with several smaller plazas, some theaters and churches, and the University of Yucatán, just to the north. Here, too, you'll find a concentration of handicraft shops, restaurants, and hotels. Around Plaza Mayor are the cathedral, the Palacio de Gobierno (state government building), the Ayuntamiento (town hall), and the Palacio Montejo. The plaza always has a crowd, and it's full on Sunday, when it holds a large street fair. (See "Festivals & Special Events in Mérida," below.) Within a few blocks are several smaller plazas and the bustling market district.

Mérida's most fashionable district is the broad, tree-lined boulevard **Paseo de Montejo** and its surrounding neighborhood. The Paseo de Montejo parallels Calle 60 and begins 7 blocks north and a little east of the main square. There are a number of trendy restaurants, modern hotels, offices of various banks and airlines, and a few clubs here, but the boulevard is mostly known for its stately mansions built during the boom times of the henequén industry. Near where the Paseo intersects Avenida Colón, you'll find the two fanciest hotels in town: the Hyatt and the Fiesta Americana.

GETTING AROUND   By Car   In general, reserve your car in advance from the U.S. to get the best weekly rates during high season (Nov–Feb); in low season, I usually do better renting a car once I get to Mérida. The local rental companies are competitive and have promotional deals that you can get only if you are there. When comparing, make sure that it's apples to apples; ask if the price quote includes the IVA tax and insurance coverage. (Practically everybody offers free mileage.) For tips on saving money on

---

Moments **Festivals & Special Events in Mérida**

Many Mexican cities offer weekend concerts in the park and such, but Mérida surpasses them all with performances every day of the week. Unless otherwise indicated, admission to the following is free.

Sunday Each Sunday from 9am to 9pm, there's a fair called Mérida en Domingo (Mérida on Sunday). The main plaza and a section of Calle 60 from El Centro to Parque Santa Lucía close to traffic. Parents come with their children to stroll around and take in the scene. There are booths selling food and drink, along with a lively little flea market and used-book fair, children's art classes, and educational booths. At 11am in front of the Palacio del Gobierno, musicians play everything from jazz to classical and folk music. Also at 11am, the police orchestra performs Yucatecan tunes at the Santa Lucía park. At 11:30am, you'll find bawdy comedy acts at the Parque Hidalgo, on Calle 60 at Calle 59. There's a lull in the midafternoon, and then the plaza fills up again as people walk around and visit with friends. Around 7pm in front of the Ayuntamiento, a large band starts playing mambos, rumbas, and cha-cha-chas with great enthusiasm; you may see 1,000 people dancing in the street. Afterward, folk ballet dancers reenact a typical Yucatecan wedding inside.

Monday *Vaquería regional,* traditional music and dancing to celebrate the Vaquerías feast, was associated originally with the branding of cattle on Yucatecan haciendas. Among the featured performers are dancers with trays of bottles or filled glasses on their heads—a sight to see.

Tuesday At 9pm in Parque Santiago, Calle 59 at Calle 72, the Municipal Orchestra plays Latin and American big-band music from the 1940s.

Wednesday At 9pm in the Teatro Peón Contreras, Calle 60 at Calle 57, the University of Yucatán Ballet Folklórico presents "Yucatán and Its Roots." Admission is $5.

Thursday Yucatecan *trova* music (boleros, ballads) and dance are presented at the Serenata (serenade) in Parque Santa Lucía at 9pm.

Friday At 9pm in the courtyard of the University of Yucatán, Calle 60 at Calle 57, the University of Yucatán Ballet Folklórico performs typical regional dances from the Yucatán.

Saturday Noche Mexicana at the park at the beginning of Paseo de Montejo begins at 9pm. It features several performances of traditional Mexican music and dance. Some of the performers are amateurs who acquit themselves reasonably well; others are professional musicians and dancers who thoroughly know their craft. Food stands sell very good *antojitos* (finger foods), as well as drinks and ice cream.

car rentals, see "Getting Around," in chapter 2. Rental cars are generally a little more expensive (unless you find a promotional rate) than in the U.S. By renting for only a day or two, you can avoid the high cost of parking lots in Mérida. These *estacionamentos* charge one price for the night and double that if you leave your car for the following day. Many hotels offer free parking, but make sure they include daytime parking in the price.

By Taxi   Taxis are easy to come by and much cheaper than in Cancún.

By Bus   City buses are a little tricky to figure out but aren't needed very often because almost everything of interest is within walking distance of the main plaza. Still, it's a bit of a walk from the plaza to the Paseo de Montejo, and you can save yourself some work by taking a bus, minibus, or *colectivo* (Volkswagen minivan) that is heading north on Calle 60. Most of these will take you to Paseo de Montejo or drop you off at Plaza Santa Ana, right by the Paseo. The *colectivos* or *combis* (usually painted white) run out in several directions from the main plaza along simple routes. They usually line up along the side streets next to the plaza.

FAST FACTS: Mérida

American Express   The office is at Paseo de Montejo 492 (© **999/942-8200**). It's open for travelers' services weekdays from 9am to 2pm and 4 to 6pm.

Area Code   The telephone area code is **999**.

Bookstore   The Librería Dante, Calle 59 between calles 60 and 62 (© **999/928-3674**), has a small selection of English-language cultural-history books on Mexico. It's open Monday to Saturday from 8am to 9:30pm, Sunday from 10am to 6pm. There is another Librería Dante on the main plaza in the Nuevo Olimpo.

Business Hours   Generally, businesses are open Monday to Saturday from 10am to 2pm and 4 to 8pm.

Climate   From November to February, the weather can be pleasantly cool and windy. In other months, it's just hot, especially during the day. Rain can occur any time of year, especially during the rainy season (July–Oct), and usually comes in the form of afternoon tropical showers.

Consulates   The **American Consulate** is at Paseo de Montejo 453, at Avenida Colón (© **999/925-6219** or 999/925-5011). Office hours are Monday to Friday from 9am to 1pm.

Currency Exchange   I prefer *casas de cambio* (currency exchange offices) over banks. There are many of these; one called **Cambios Portales,** Calle 61 no. 500 (© **999/923-8709**), is on the north side of the main plaza in the middle of the block. It's open daily from 8:30am to 8:30pm. There are also many ATMs; one is on the south side of the same plaza.

Hospitals   The best hospital is **Centro Médico de las Américas,** Calle 54 no. 365 between 33-A and Avenida Pérez Ponce. The main phone number is © **999/926-2619;** for emergencies, call © **999/927-3199.** You can also call the Cruz Roja (Red Cross) at © **999/924-9813.**

Internet Access   There are so many Internet access providers in town that you hardly have to walk more than a couple of blocks to find one.

Pharmacy **Farmacia Yza,** Calle 63 no. 502, between calles 60 and 62 ((℃) **999/ 924-9510**), on the south side of the plaza, is open 24 hours.

Police Mérida has a special body of police to assist tourists. They patrol the downtown area and the Paseo de Montejo. They wear white shirts bearing the words POLICIA TURISTICA. Their phone number is (℃) **999/925-2555.**

Post Office The *correo* is near the market at the corner of calles 65 and 56. A branch office is at the airport. Both are open Monday to Friday from 8am to 7pm, Saturday from 9am to noon.

Seasons There are two high seasons for tourism, but they aren't as pronounced as on the coast. One is in July and August, when Mexicans take their vacations, and the other is between November 15 and Easter Sunday, when Canadians and Americans flock to the Yucatán to escape winter weather.

Spanish Classes Maya scholars, Spanish teachers, and archaeologists from the United States are among the students at the **Centro de Idiomas del Sureste,** Calle 14 no. 106 at Calle 25, Col. México, 97000 Mérida, Yuc. ((℃) **999/926-1155;** fax 999/926-9020). The school has two locations: in the Colonia México, a northern residential district, and on Calle 66 at Calle 57, downtown. Students live with local families or in hotels; sessions running 2 weeks or longer are available for all levels of proficiency and areas of interest. For brochures and applications, contact Chloe Conaway de Pacheco, Directora.

Telephones There are long-distance phone service centers at the airport and the bus station. In the downtown area is **TelWorld,** Calle 59 no. 495-4 between calles 56 and 58. To use the public phones, buy a **Ladatel** card from just about any newsstand or store. The cards come in a variety of denominations and work for long distance within Mexico and even abroad. Also see "Telephone & Fax" in "Fast Facts: Mexico," in chapter 2.

EXPLORING MERIDA

Most of Mérida's attractions are within walking distance from the downtown area. To see a larger area of the city, a popular **bus tour** is worth taking. The man who operates these tours has bought a few buses and given them a fancy paint job, pulled out all the windows, raised the roof several inches, and installed wooden benches so that the buses remind you of the folksy buses of coastal Latin America, known as *chivas* in Colombia and Venezuela or as *guaguas* in other places. You can find these buses on the corner of calles 60 and 55 (next to the church of Santa Lucía) at 10am, 1pm, 4pm, and 7pm. The tour costs $9 per person and lasts 2 hours. Another option for seeing the city is a **horse-drawn carriage.** A 45-minute ride around central Mérida costs $17. You can usually find the carriages beside the cathedral on Calle 61.

EXPLORING PLAZA MAYOR Downtown Mérida is a great example of a lowland colonial city. The town has a casual, relaxed feel. Buildings lack the severe baroque and neoclassical features that characterize central Mexico; most are finished in stucco and painted light colors. Mérida's gardens add to this relaxed, tropical atmosphere. Gardeners do not strive for control over nature. Here, natural exuberance is the ideal, with plants growing in a wild profusion that disguises human intervention. Mérida's plazas

Where to Stay & Dine in Mérida

UNITED STATES

Gulf of Mexico

MEXICO

Mexico City ★

Mérida ●

PACIFIC OCEAN

0   500 mi
0   500 km

† Church
ⓘ Information
///// Pedestrian Only
✉ Post Office

0   0.25 mi
0   0.25 km

Av. Colon
Av. Perez
Calle 35
Paseo de Montejo
Calle 37
Calle 39
Calle 41
Calle 43
Calle 45
Calle 47
Calle 49
Calle 51
Calle 53
Calle 55
Calle 57
Calle 59
Calle 61
Calle 63
Calle 65
Calle 67
Calle 69

Parque Santa Ana
Parque Santa Lucía
Parque Santiago
Parque de la Madre
Parque Cepeda Peraza
Plaza Mayor
Parque San Juan

Calle 72
Calle 70
Calle 68
Calle 66
Calle 64
Calle 62
Calle 60
Calle 58
Calle 56
Calle 54

To Train Station →

Bus Station

Portal de Granos
Mercado Lucas de Gálvez
Bazaar de Artesanías

■ACCOMMODATIONS

Casa Mexilio Guest House **7**
Casa San Juan **20**
Fiesta Americana Mérida **1**
Hotel Caribe **16**
Hotel Dolores Alba **19**
Hotel Maison Lafitte **10**
Hotel Medio Mundo **5**
Hotel Mucuy **13**
Hyatt Regency Mérida **2**
Posada Toledo **11**

◆ DINING

Alberto's Continental **8**
Café Alameda **12**
Eladio's **18**
El Pórtico del Peregrino **9**
La Casa del Paseo **3**
La Flor de Santiago **6**
Restaurante Amaro **14**
Restaurante Kantún **4**
Restaurant Los Almendros **17**
Vito Corleone **15**

are a slightly different version of this aesthetic: Unlike the highland plazas, with their carefully sculpted trees, Mérida's squares are typically built around large trees that are left to grow as tall as possible. Hurricane Isidore blew down several of these, and has changed the appearance of these plazas as well as the Paseo de Montejo.

Plaza Mayor has this sort of informality. Even when there's no orchestrated event in progress, the park is full of people sitting on the benches, talking with friends, or taking a casual stroll. A plaza like this is a great advantage for a big city such as Mérida, giving it a personal feel and a sense of community. Notice the beautiful scale and composition of the major buildings surrounding it. The most prominent of these is the cathedral.

The oldest **cathedral** on the continent, it was built between 1561 and 1598. Much of the stone in the cathedral's walls came from the ruined buildings of Tihó, the former Maya city. The original finish was stucco, and you can see some remnants still clinging to the bare rock. However, people like the way the unfinished walls show the cathedral's age. Notice how the two top levels of the bell towers are built off-center from their bases—an uncommon feature. Inside, decoration is sparse, with altars draped in fabric colorfully embroidered like a Maya woman's shift. The most notable item is a picture of Ah Kukum Tutul Xiú, chief of the Xiú people, visiting the Montejo camp to make peace; it's hanging over the side door on the right.

To the left of the main altar is a small shrine with a curious figure of Christ that is a replica of one recovered from a burned-out church in the town of Ichmul. In the 1500s a local artist carved the original figure from a miraculous tree that was hit by lightning and burst into flames—but did not char. The statue later became blistered in the church fire at Ichmul, but it survived. In 1645 it was moved to the cathedral in Mérida, where the locals attached great powers to the figure, naming it *Cristo de las Ampollas (Christ of the Blisters)*. It did not, however, survive the sacking of the cathedral in 1915 by revolutionary forces, so another figure, modeled after the original, was made. Take a look in the side chapel (daily 8–11am and 4:30–7pm), which contains a life-size diorama of the Last Supper. The Mexican Jesus is covered with prayer crosses brought by supplicants asking for intercession.

Next door to the cathedral is the old bishop's palace, now converted into the city's contemporary art museum, **Museo de Arte Contemporáneo Ateneo de Yucatán** (© **999/928-3236**). The palace was confiscated and rebuilt during the Mexican Revolution in 1915. The museum's entrance faces the cathedral from the recently constructed walkway between the two buildings called the Pasaje de la Revolución. The 17 exhibition rooms display work by contemporary artists, mostly from the Yucatán. (The best known are Fernando García Ponce and Fernando Castro Pacheco, whose works also hang in the government palace described below.) Nine of the rooms hold the museum's permanent collection; the rest are for temporary exhibits. It's open Wednesday to Monday from 10am to 6pm. Admission is $2.50.

Moving clockwise around the plaza, on the south side is the **Palacio Montejo.** Its facade, with heavy decoration around the doorway and windows, is a good example of the Spanish architectural style known as plateresque. But the content of the decoration is very much a New World creation. Conquering the Yucatán was the Montejo family business, begun by the original Francisco Montejo and continued by his son and nephew, both named Francisco Montejo. Construction of the house started in 1542 under the son, Francisco Montejo El Mozo ("The Younger"). Bordering the entrance are politically incorrect figures of conquistadors standing on the heads of vanquished

Indians—borrowed, perhaps, from the pre-Hispanic custom of portraying victorious Maya kings treading on their defeated foes. The posture of the conquistadors and their facial expression of wide-eyed dismay make them less imposing than the Montejos might have wished. A bank now occupies the building, but you can enter the courtyard, view the garden, and see for yourself what a charming residence it must have been for the descendants of the Montejos, who lived here as recently as the 1970s. (Curiously enough, not only does Mérida society keep track of who is descended from the Montejos, but it also keeps track of who is descended from the last Maya king, Tutul Xiú.)

In stark contrast to the severity of the cathedral and Casa Montejo is the light, unimposing **Ayuntamiento** or **Palacio Municipal (town hall).** The exterior dates from the mid–19th century, an era when a tropicalist aesthetic tinged with romanticism began asserting itself across coastal Latin America. On the second floor, you can see the meeting hall of the city council and enjoy a view of the plaza from the balcony. Next door to the Ayuntamiento is a recently completed building called **El Nuevo Olimpo (The New Olympus).** It took the place of the old Olimpo, which a misguided town council demolished in the 1970s, to the regret of many older Meridanos. The new building tries to incorporate elements of the original while presenting something new. It holds concert and gallery space, a bookstore, and a lovely courtyard. There is a comfortable cafe under the arches, and a bulletin board at the entrance to the courtyard with postings of upcoming performances.

Cater-cornered from the Nuevo Olimpo is the old **Casa del Alguacil (Magistrate's House).** Under its arcades is something of an institution in Mérida: the **Dulcería y Sorbetería Colón,** an ice cream and sweet shop that will appeal to those who prefer less-rich ice creams. A spectacular side doorway on Calle 62 bears viewing, and across the street is the new **Cine Mérida,** with two movie screens showing art films and one stage for live performances. Returning to the main plaza, down a bit from the ice cream store is a **shopping center** of boutiques and convenience food vendors called Pasaje Picheta. At the end of the arcade is the **Palacio de Gobierno (state government building),** dating from 1892. Large murals by the Yucatecan artist Fernando Castro Pacheco, executed between 1971 and 1973, decorate the walls of the courtyard. Scenes from Maya and Mexican history abound, and the painting over the stairway depicts the Maya spirit with ears of sacred corn, the "sunbeams of the gods." Nearby is a painting of mustachioed Lázaro Cárdenas, who as president in 1938 expropriated 17 foreign oil companies and was hailed as a Mexican liberator. Upstairs is a long, wide gallery with more of Pacheco's paintings, which achieve their effect by localizing color and imitating the photographic technique of double exposure. The palace is open Monday to Saturday from 8am to 8pm, Sunday from 9am to 5pm. There is a small tourism office to the left as you enter.

Further down Calle 61 is the **Museo de la Ciudad (City Museum).** It faces the side of the cathedral and occupies the former church of San Juan de Dios. An exhibit outlining the history of Mérida will be of interest to those curious about the city; there is explanatory text in English. Hours are Monday to Friday from 10am to 2pm and 4 to 8pm, Saturday and Sunday from 10am to 2pm. Admission is free.

EXPLORING CALLE 60   Heading north from Plaza Mayor up Calle 60, you'll see many of Mérida's old churches and squares. Several stores along Calle 60 sell gold-filigree jewelry, pottery, clothing, and folk art. A stroll along this street leads to the Parque Santa Ana and continues to the fashionable boulevard Paseo de Montejo and its **Museo Regional de Antropología (Anthropology Museum).**

The first place of interest is the **Teatro Daniel de Ayala,** only because it sometimes schedules interesting performances. On the right side of Calle 60 will be a small park called **Parque Cepeda Peraza** (or Parque Hidalgo). Named for 19th-century General Manuel Cepeda Peraza, the *parque* was part of Montejo's original city plan. Small outdoor restaurants front hotels on the park, making it a popular stopping place at any time of day. Across Calle 59 is the **Iglesia de Jesús,** or El Tercer Orden (The Third Order). Built by the Jesuit order in 1618, it has the richest interior of any church in Mérida, making it a favorite spot for weddings. The entire block on which the church stands belonged to the Jesuits, who are known as great educators. The school they left behind after their expulsion became the Universidad de Yucatán.

On the other side of the church is the **Parque de la Madre.** The park contains a modern statue of the Madonna and Child, a copy of the work by Renoir. Beyond the Parque de la Madre and across the pedestrian-only street is the **Teatro Peón Contreras,** an opulent theater designed by Italian architect Enrico Deserti a century ago. The theater is noted for its Carrara marble staircase and frescoed dome. Try to get a peek at it, and look at the performance schedule to see if anything of interest will take place during your stay. National and international performers appear here frequently. In the southwest corner of the theater, facing the Parque de la Madre, is a **tourist information office.** Across Calle 60 is the main building of the **Universidad de Yucatán.** Inside is a flagstone courtyard where the *ballet folklórico* performs on Friday nights.

A block farther north is **Parque Santa Lucía.** Bordered by an arcade on the north and west sides, this park was where visitors first alighted from the stagecoach. On Sunday, Parque Santa Lucía holds a used-book market, and several evenings a week it hosts popular entertainment. On Thursday nights, performers present Yucatecan songs and poems. Facing the park is the **Iglesia de Santa Lucía** (1575).

Four blocks farther up Calle 60 is **Parque Santa Ana;** if you turn right, you'll come to the beginning of the Paseo de Montejo in 2 blocks.

EXPLORING THE PASEO DE MONTEJO The Paseo de Montejo is a broad, tree-lined boulevard that runs north-south starting at Calle 47, 7 blocks north and 2 blocks east of the main square. In the late 19th century, stalwarts of Mérida's upper crust (mostly plantation owners) decided that the city needed something grander than its traditional narrow streets lined by wall-to-wall town houses. They built this monumentally proportioned boulevard and lined it with mansions. Things went sour with the henequén bust, but several of these mansions survive—some in private hands, others as offices, restaurants, or consulates. Today, this is the fashionable part of town, with many fine restaurants, trendy dance clubs, and expensive hotels.

Of the mansions that survived, the most notable is the Palacio Cantón, which houses the **Museo Regional de Antropología (Anthropology Museum)** 🕭🕭 (ⓒ **999/923-0557).** Designed and built by Enrico Deserti, the architect of the Teatro Peón Contreras, it was constructed between 1909 and 1911, during the last years of the Porfiriato. It was the residence of General Francisco Cantón Rosado, who enjoyed his palace for only 6 years before dying in 1917. For a time the mansion served as the official residence of the state's governor.

Viewing the museum also affords you an opportunity to see some of the surviving interior architecture. The museum's main focus is the pre-Columbian cultures of the peninsula, especially the Maya. Topics include cosmology, history, and culture. Captions for the permanent displays are mostly in Spanish. Starting with fossil mastodon teeth, the exhibits take you through the Yucatán's history, paying special attention to the daily life of its inhabitants.

Exhibits illustrate such strange Maya customs as tying boards to babies' heads to create the oblong shape that they considered beautiful, and filing teeth or perforating them to inset jewels. There are enlarged photos of several archaeological sites and drawings that illustrate the various styles of Maya dwellings. Even if you know only a little Spanish, this is a worthwhile stop, and it provides good background for explorations of Maya sites. The museum is open Tuesday to Saturday from 8am to 8pm, Sunday from 8am to 2pm. Admission is $3.50.

SHOPPING

Mérida is known for **hammocks, guayaberas** (lightweight men's shirts worn untucked), and **Panama hats. Baskets** and **pottery** made in the Yucatán and crafts from all over Mexico are sold cheaply in the **central market.** Mérida is also the place to pick up prepared *achiote,* a pastelike mixture of ground *achiote* seeds (annatto), oregano, garlic, masa, and other spices used in Yucatecan cuisine. Mixed with sour orange to a soupy consistency, it makes a great marinade, especially for grilled meat and fish. It can be found bottled in this form. It's also the sauce for baked chicken and *cochinita pibil.*

EXPLORING THE MARKET Mérida's bustling **market district** is a few blocks southeast of the Plaza Mayor. The market and surrounding few blocks make up the commercial center of the city. Hordes of people come here to shop and work. It is by far the most crowded part of town, and the city government is refurbishing the whole area to relieve the traffic congestion, modernize the market building, and add green space. Behind the post office (at calles 65 and 56) is the oldest part of the market, the **Portal de Granos (Grains Arcade),** a row of maroon arches where the grain merchants used to sell their goods. Just east, between calles 56 and 54, is the market building, Mercado Lucas de Gálvez. Inside, chaos seems to reign, but after a short while a certain order emerges. Here you can find anything from fresh fish to flowers to leather goods. In the building directly south of the market, you can find more locally manufactured goods; on the second floor is the **Bazaar de Artesanías (crafts market).** Another crafts market, **Bazaar García Rejón,** lies a block west of the market on Calle 65 between calles 58 and 60.

CRAFTS

Casa de las Artesanías This store occupies the front rooms of a restored monastery. Here you can find a wide selection of crafts, 90% of which come from the Yucatán. For the most part, the quality of work is higher than elsewhere, but so are the prices. The monastery's back courtyard is used as a gallery, with rotating exhibits on folk and fine arts. It's open Monday to Saturday from 9am to 8pm, Sunday from 9am to 1pm. Calle 63 no. 513 (between calles 64 and 66). © 999/928-6676.

Miniaturas This fun little store is packed to the rafters with miniatures, a traditional Mexican folk art form that has been evolving in a number of directions, including social and political satire, pop art, and bawdy humor. Alicia Rivero, the owner, collects them from several parts of Mexico and offers plenty of variety, from traditional miniatures, such as dollhouse furniture, to popular cartoon characters and celebrities. The store also sells other forms of folk art such as masks, games, and traditional crafts. Hours are Monday to Saturday from 10am to 8pm. Calle 59 no. 507A-4 (between calles 60 and 62). © 999/928-6503.

GUAYABERAS

Business suits are hot and uncomfortable in Mérida's soaking humidity, so business-men, politicians, bankers, and bus drivers alike wear the guayabera, a loose-fitting shirt decorated with narrow tucks, pockets, and sometimes embroidery, worn over the pants rather than tucked in. Mérida is famous as the best place to buy guayaberas, which can go for less than $15 at the market or for more than $50 custom-made by a tailor. A guayabera made of linen can cost about $80. Most are made of cotton, although other materials are available. The traditional color is white.

Most shops display ready-to-wear shirts in several price ranges. Guayabera makers pride themselves on being innovators. I have yet to enter a shirt-maker's shop in Mérida that did not present its own version of the guayabera. When looking at guayaberas, here are a few things to keep in mind: When Yucatecans say *seda,* they mean polyester; *lino* is linen or a linen/polyester combination. Take a close look at the stitching and such details as the way the tucks line up over the pockets; with guayaberas, the details are everything.

Guayaberas Jack The craftsmanship here is good, the place has a reputation to maintain, and some of the salespeople speak English. Prices are as marked. This will give you a good basis of comparison if you want to hunt for a bargain elsewhere. If the staff does not have the style and color of shirt you want, they will make it for you in about 3 hours. This shop also sells regular shirts and women's blouses. Hours are Monday to Saturday from 10am to 8pm, Sunday from 10am to 2pm. Calle 59 no. 507A (between calles 60 and 62). ✆ 999/928-6002.

HAMMOCKS

Natives across tropical America used hammocks long before the Europeans arrived in the New World. The word comes from the Spanish *hamaca,* which is a borrowing from Taino, a Caribbean Indian language. Hammocks are still in use throughout Latin America and come in a wide variety of forms, but none is so comfortable as the Yucatecan hammock, which is woven with cotton string in a fine mesh. For most of us, of course, the hammock is lawn furniture, something to relax in for an hour or so on a lazy afternoon. But for the vast majority of Yucatecans, hammocks are the equiv-alent of beds, and they greatly prefer hammocks to mattresses. I know a hotel owner who has 150 beds in his establishment but won't sleep on any of them. When he does, he complains of waking up unrested and sore. Many well-to-do Meridanos keep a bed just for show. In hotels that cater to Yucatecans, you will always find hammock hooks in the walls because many Yucatecans travel with their own hammock.

My advice to the hammock buyer: The woven part should be cotton, it should be made with fine string, and the strings should be so numerous that when you get in it and stretch out diagonally (the way you're supposed to sleep in these hammocks), the gaps between the strings remain small. Don't pay attention to the words used to describe the size of a hammock; they have become practically meaningless. Good ham-mocks don't cost a lot of money ($20–$35). If you want a superior hammock, ask for one made with fine crochet thread (*hilo de crochet;* the word *crochet* is also sometimes bandied about, but you can readily see the difference). This should run about $100.

Nothing beats a tryout; the shops mentioned here will gladly hang a hammock for you to test-drive. When it's up, look to see that there are no untied strings. You can also see what street vendors are offering, but you have to know what to look for, or they are likely to take advantage of you.

Hamacas El Aguacate   El Aguacate sells hammocks wholesale and retail. It has the greatest variety and is the place to go for a really fancy or extra-large hammock. A good hammock is the no. 6 in cotton; it runs $33. The store is open Monday to Friday from 8:30am to 7:30pm, Saturday from 8am to 5pm. It's 6 blocks south of the main square. Calle 58 no. 604 (at Calle 73). ✆ **999/928-6429.**

Tejidos y Cordeles Nacionales   This place near the municipal market sells only cotton hammocks, priced by weight—a pretty good practice because hammock lengths are standard here. The prices are better than at El Aguacate, but quality control isn't as good. My idea of a good hammock weighs about 1½ kilograms (3½ lb.) and runs about $25. Calle 56 no. 516-B (between calles 63 and 65). ✆ **999/928-5561.**

PANAMA HATS

Another useful and popular item is this soft, pliable hat made from the fibers of the *jipijapa* palm in several towns south of Mérida along Highway 180, especially Becal, in the neighboring state of Campeche. The hat makers in these towns work inside caves so that the moist air keeps the palm fibers pliant.

Jipi hats come in various grades determined by the quality (pliability, softness, and fineness) of the fibers and closeness of the weave. The difference in weave is easy to see, as a fine weave improves the shape of a hat. It has more body and regains its shape better. I like two places in particular for Panama hats; if you speak Spanish, you can hear two different takes on buying a hat. Expect to pay between $15 and $80. One store is **El Becaleño,** Calle 65 no. 483, across from the post office. The owner can show you differences in quality and has some very expensive hats. The other store is a short distance away in one of the market buildings: Walk south down Calle 56 past the post office; right before the street ends in the market place, turn left into a passage with hardware stores at the entrance. The fourth or fifth shop is the **Casa de los Jipis.** You can always ask people in the area to point it out to you.

WHERE TO STAY

Mérida is easier on the budget than the resort cities. The stream of visitors is steadier than on the coast, so most hotels no longer use a high-season/low-season rate structure. Still, you are more likely to find promotional rates during low season. Mérida has a convention center, which attracts large trade shows that can fill the city's hotels, so it's a good idea to make reservations. The rates quoted here include the 17% tax. When inquiring about prices, always ask if the price quoted includes tax. Most hotels in Mérida offer at least a few air-conditioned rooms, and some also have pools. But many hotels, especially in the inexpensive range, haven't figured out how to provide a comfortable bed. Either the mattresses are bad, or the bottom sheet is too small to tuck in properly. Some hotels here would offer a really good deal if only they would improve their beds. One last thing to note: In Mérida, free parking is a relative concept—for many hotels, free parking means only at night; during the day there may be a charge.

VERY EXPENSIVE

Fiesta Americana Mérida ★★   This six-story hotel on the Paseo de Montejo is built in the grand fin-de-siècle style of the old mansions along the Paseo. Guest rooms are off the cavernous lobby, so all face outward and have views of one or another of the avenues. The rooms are comfortable and large, with furnishings and decorations striving for, and achieving, innocuousness in light, tropical colors. The floors are tile

Hacienda Hotels

Haciendas in the Yucatán have had a bumpy history. In the colonial period they were isolated, almost-autonomous fiefdoms. While the owners were absolute masters over their domains, they did not get rich from the inefficient production of mostly cattle, corn, beans, and other foodstuffs.

Then in the second half of the 19th century, growing demand for the natural fiber *henequén,* or sisal, made haciendas profitable operations. Their owners used the cash to make improvements to their estates in keeping with their growing wealth. But demand for the fiber fell throughout the 1920s and put an end to the high life. There was no other commodity that could replace sisal, and the owners eventually abandoned their haciendas to ruin.

Now another boom of sorts has brought the haciendas back; this time as retreats, country residences, and hotels. The hotels convey an air of the past—elegant gateways, thick walls, open arches, and high ceilings—you get the feel of an era gone by. And in keeping with the romantic notion of the haciendas, there are a few features that make a guest feel like a lord and master, especially the extravagant suites and personal service. But what strikes us the most was that each hacienda seems a little island of order and tranquillity in the sea of chaos that is the Yucatán. I love Mérida and its energy; I like small-town Yucatán and its rough edges; but sometimes it's good to retire from all the commotion.

There are five luxury hacienda hotels. The most opulent of these is **Xcanatún** (© 888/883-3633 in the U.S.; www.xcanatun.com). It's on the outskirts of Mérida, off the highway to Progreso. The suites are large and have extravagant bathrooms. The decor is in muted colors with rich materials and modern pieces that evoke the simplicity of an earlier age. It has the best restaurant in the Mérida area and a complete spa. The owners personally manage their hotel and keep the service sharp.

and the bathrooms large and well equipped. Service is very attentive, better than at the Hyatt. There is a shopping center on the ground floor, below the lobby.

Av. Colón 451, corner of Paseo Montejo, 92127 Mérida, Yuc. © 800/343-7821 in the U.S. and Canada, or 999/942-1111. Fax 999/942-1112. www.fiestaamericana.com.mx. 350 units. $195 double; $220 executive level; $230 junior suite. AE, DC, MC, V. Free secure parking. **Amenities:** 2 restaurants; bar; midsize pool; tennis court; health club w/saunas, men's steam room, unisex whirlpool, and massage; children's programs; concierge; tour desk; small business center; shopping arcade; 24-hr. room service; babysitting; laundry service; dry cleaning; executive-level rooms. *In room:* A/C, TV w/pay movies, minibar, coffeemaker, hair dryer, safe, Internet connection.

Hyatt Regency Mérida ★★ This Hyatt is much like Hyatts elsewhere, wherein lies this hotel's chief asset. The rooms are dependably comfortable and quiet, the quietest in a noisy city. They're carpeted and well furnished, with great bathrooms. In decoration and comfort, I find them superior to those of the Fiesta Americana, but they certainly don't have any local flavor. The Hyatt's facilities, especially its tennis courts and health club, also rank above the Fiesta Americana's. The pool is more attractive and larger, but its location keeps it in the shade for most of the day, and the

The other four luxury hotels are all owned by Roberto Hernández, one of the richest men in Mexico. The hospitality and reservation system are handled by **Starwood Hotels** (© 800/325-3589 in the U.S. and Canada; www.luxurycollection.com). Hernández has taken great pains to restore all four haciendas to original condition, and all are beautiful. **Temozón,** off the highway to Uxmal, is the most magnificent. **Uayamón,** located between the ruins of Edzná and the colonial city of Campeche, is perhaps the most romantic. **San José Cholul,** located east of Mérida towards Izamal, is my personal favorite. And the fourth, **Santa Rosa,** lies southwest of Mérida, near the town of Maxcanú. Packages are available for staying at two or more of these haciendas.

Two haciendas offer economical lodging. On the western outskirts of Mérida by the highway to Chichén Itzá and Cancún is **San Pedro Noh Pat** (© 999/988-0542; www.haciendaholidays.com). It retains only the land that immediately surrounds the residence, but it offers a great bargain in lodging—large comfortable rooms and an attractive garden area and pool. The other is **Blanca Flor** (© 999/925-8042; www.mexonline.com/blancaflor_htm), which lies between Mérida and Campeche just off the highway. It's the only hacienda that actually operates like one, producing most of the food served there. The owners work with bus tours but also welcome couples and individuals. Rooms are in a modern building and are large and simply furnished.

Two other haciendas can be leased by small groups for retreats and group vacations: **Hacienda Petac** (© 999/910-4334; www.haciendapetac.com) and **San Antonio Millet** (© 999/910-6144; www.haciendasanantonio.com.mx). Both have beautiful rooms, common areas, and grounds.

water never gets a chance to heat up. Rising 17 stories, the Hyatt is not hard to find in Mérida's skyline; it's near the Paseo de Montejo and across Avenida Colón from the Fiesta Americana.

Calle 60 no. 344 (at Av. Colón), 97000 Mérida, Yuc. © 800/223-1234 in the U.S. and Canada, or 999/942-1234. Fax 999/925-7002. www.merida.regency.hyatt.com. 299 units. $155 standard double; $190 Regency club double. Ask about promotional rates. AE, DC, MC, V. Free guarded parking. **Amenities:** 2 restaurants; 2 bars (1 swim-up, open seasonally); large pool; 2 lighted tennis courts; state-of-the-art health club w/men's and women's steam rooms, whirlpool, sauna, and massage; children's activities (seasonal); concierge; tour desk; car rental; business center; shopping arcade; 24-hr. room service; babysitting; laundry service; dry cleaning; nonsmoking rooms; executive-level rooms. *In room:* A/C, TV, dataport, minibar, hair dryer.

MODERATE

Casa Mexilio Guest House ★★ *Finds* This bed-and-breakfast is unlike any other I know. The owners are geniuses at playing with space in an unexpected and delightful manner. Rooms are at different levels, creating private spaces joined to each other and to rooftop terraces by stairs and catwalks. Most are spacious and airy, furnished and decorated in an engaging mix of new and old, polished and primitive. Five come with air-conditioning. A small pool with a whirlpool and profuse tropical vegetation take up most of the central patio. Breakfasts are great. It's 4 blocks west of the plaza. A small bar serves drinks during happy hour, and, weather permitting, you can have your cocktail on one of the rooftop terraces.

Calle 68 no. 495 (between calles 57 and 59), 97000 Mérida, Yuc. ℂ **800/538-6802** in the U.S., or 999/928-2505. Fax 999/928-2505. www.mexicoholiday.com. 9 units. $55–$75 double; $120 penthouse. Rates include full breakfast. MC, V. **Amenities:** Bar; small pool; whirlpool. *In room:* No phone.

Hotel Caribe   This three-story colonial-style hotel (no elevator) is great for a couple of reasons: Its location at the back of Plaza Hidalgo is both central and quiet, and it has a nice little pool and sun deck on the rooftop with a view of the cathedral. The rooms are moderately comfortable, though they aren't well lit, and have only small windows facing the central courtyard. Thirteen *clase económica* rooms don't have air-conditioning; standard rooms do; and superior rooms (on the top floor) have been remodeled and have safes, hair dryers, larger windows, and quieter air-conditioning. Avoid the rooms on the ground floor. The hotel offers a lot of variety in bedding arrangements, mostly combinations of twins and doubles. Mattresses are often softer than standard. The TVs add little value to the rooms. Nearby parking is free at night but costs extra during the day beginning at 7am. The restaurant serves good Mexican food.

Calle 59 no. 500 (at Calle 60), 97000 Mérida, Yuc. ℂ **888/822-6431** in the U.S. and Canada, or 999/924-9022. Fax 999/924-8733. www.hotelcaribe.com.mx. 53 units. $48 *clase económica* double; $54–$60 standard or superior double. AE, MC, V. **Amenities:** Restaurant; bar; small pool; tour desk; room service until 10pm; laundry service. *In room:* A/C in some, TV, hair dryer in some, safe in some.

Hotel Maison Lafitte 👍 *Value*   This new three-story hotel offers modern, attractive rooms with good air-conditioning as well as tropical touches such as wooden louvers over the windows, and light furniture with caned backs and seats. Rooms are medium to large, with midsize bathrooms that have great showers and good lighting. Most rooms come with either two doubles or a king-size bed. Rooms are quiet and look out over a pretty little garden with a fountain. A couple of rooms don't have windows. The location is excellent.

Calle 60 no. 472 (between calles 53 and 55), 97000 Mérida, Yuc. ℂ **800/538-6802** in the U.S. and Canada, or 999/928-1243. Fax 999/923-9159. www.maisonlafitte.com.mx. 30 units. $80 double. Rates include full breakfast. AE, MC, V. Free limited secure parking for compact cars. **Amenities:** Restaurant; bar; small outdoor pool; tour desk; car rental; limited room service; in-room massage; laundry service; dry cleaning. *In room:* A/C, TV, minibar, hair dryer, safe.

Hotel Medio Mundo 👍 *Finds*   This is a quiet courtyard hotel with beautiful rooms and a good location 3 blocks north of the main plaza. The English-speaking owners have invested their money in the right places, going for high-quality mattresses, good lighting, quiet air-conditioning units, lots of space, and good bathrooms with strong showers. What they didn't invest in were TVs, which adds to the serenity of the place. Higher prices are for the seven rooms with air-conditioning, but all units have windows with good screens and get ample ventilation. Breakfast is served in one of the two attractive courtyards.

Calle 55 no. 533 (between calles 64 and 66), 97000 Mérida, Yuc. ℂ/fax **999/924-5472**. www.hotelmediomundo.com. 10 units. $55–$75 double. Internet specials sometimes available. MC, V. **Amenities:** Small outdoor pool; tour info; in-room massage; laundry service; nonsmoking rooms. *In room:* A/C in some.

INEXPENSIVE

Casa San Juan ✿ *Value*   This B&B, in a colonial house, is loaded with character and provides a good glimpse of the old Mérida that lies behind the colonial facades in the historic district. Guest rooms are beautifully decorated, large, and comfortable. Those in the original house have been modernized but maintain a colonial feel, with 7m (20-ft.) ceilings and 45cm-thick (18-in.) walls. The modern rooms in back look out over the rear patio. The lower rate is for the three rooms without air-conditioning (they have ceiling and floor fans). Choice of beds includes one queen-size, one double, or two twins, all with good mattresses and sheets. Breakfast includes fruit or juice, coffee, bread, and homemade preserves. Casa San Juan is 4 blocks south of the main square.

Calle 62 no. 545a (between calles 69 and 71), 97000 Mérida, Yuc. ℂ/fax **999/986-2937.** www.casasanjuan.com. 8 units (7 with private bathroom). $30–$60 double. No credit cards. Rates include continental breakfast. Parking nearby $2. *In room:* A/C in some, no phone.

Hotel Dolores Alba ✿ *Value*   The Dolores Alba offers attractive, comfortable rooms, air-conditioning, an inviting swimming pool, and free parking, all for a great price. The three-story section (with elevator) surrounding the back courtyard offers large rooms with good-size bathrooms. Beds (either two doubles or one double and one twin) have supportive foam-core mattresses, usually in a combination of one medium firm and one medium soft. All rooms have windows or balconies looking out over the pool. An old mango tree shades the front courtyard. The older rooms in this section are decorated with local crafts and have small bathrooms. The family that owns the Hotel Dolores Alba outside Chichén Itzá manages this hotel; you can make reservations at one hotel for the other. This hotel is 3½ blocks from the main square.

Calle 63 no. 464 (between calles 52 and 54), 97000 Mérida, Yuc. ℂ **999/928-5650.** Fax 999/928-3163. www.dolores alba.com. 100 units. $50–$60 double. No credit cards. Free guarded sheltered parking. **Amenities:** Restaurant; pool; tour desk; room service until 10pm; laundry service. *In room:* A/C, TV.

Hotel Mucuy   The Mucuy is a simple, quiet, pleasant hotel in a great location. The gracious owners strive to make guests feel welcome, with conveniences such as a communal refrigerator in the lobby and, for a small extra charge, the use of a washer and dryer. Guest rooms are basic; most contain two twin beds (with comfortable mattresses) and some simple furniture. A neat garden patio with comfortable chairs is the perfect place for sitting and reading. The Mucuy is named for a small dove said to bring good luck to places where it alights. The hotel has a few rooms with A/C, which cost $5 more.

Calle 57 no. 481 (between calles 56 and 58), 97000 Mérida, Yuc. ℂ **999/928-5193.** Fax 999/923-7801. E-mail: cofelia@ yahoo.com.mx 24 units. $22 double. No credit cards. **Amenities:** Laundry service. *In room:* A/C in some.

Posada Toledo   This hotel's charm lies in the fact that so much of the original domestic architecture survived the conversion from mansion to hotel. Furniture, decoration, paintings, details of design—from all this, you glean an uncontrived view of the past. As is typical in such old *casonas* (mansions), some guest rooms were meant to impress, while others were an expression of simple domesticity—make sure you get one you like. Rooms along the street can be noisy. Two of the grandest rooms, with ornate cornices and woodwork, have been converted into a large suite. Those on the third floor (not originally part of the house) are comfortable and have a rooftop terrace. The hotel has a couple of common rooms and a beautiful courtyard lobby. The location is exceptional.

Calle 58 no. 487 (at Calle 57), 97000 Mérida, Yuc. © 999/923-1690. Fax 999/923-2256. hptoledo@finred.com.mx. 23 units. $35–$45 double. MC, V. Free parking next door. **Amenities:** Restaurant (breakfast only); tour info. *In room:* A/C, TV.

WHERE TO DINE

The people of Mérida have strong ideas and traditions about food. Certain dishes are always associated with a particular day of the week. In households across the city, Sunday would feel incomplete without *puchero* (a kind of stew). On Monday, at any restaurant that caters to locals, you are sure to find *frijol con puerco* (pork and beans). Likewise, you'll find *potaje* (potage) on Thursday; fish, of course, on Friday; and *chocolomo* (a beef dish) on Saturday. These dishes are heavy and slow to digest; they are for the midday meal, and not suitable for supper. What's more, Meridanos don't believe that seafood is a healthy supper food. All seafood restaurants in Mérida close by 6pm unless they cater to tourists.

The preferred supper food is turkey (which, by the way, is said to be high in tryptophan, a soporific), and it's best served in the traditional *antojitos—salbutes* and *panuchos.* The best I've eaten were at a well-known restaurant in the village of Kanasín, on the outskirts of Mérida, **La Susana Internacional.** Practically the entire menu is based on turkey, including a delicious soup. The only way to get there is by taxi, but if you are with a fairly large party, it's worth organizing the expedition.

Another thing you may notice about Mérida is the surprising number of Middle Eastern restaurants. The city received a large influx of Lebanese immigrants around 1900. This population has had a strong influence on local society, to the point where Meridanos think of *kibbe* the way Americans think of pizza. Speaking of pizza, if you want to get some to take back to your hotel room, try **Vito Corleone,** on Calle 59 between calles 60 and 62. Its pizzas have a thin crust with a slightly smoky taste from the wood-burning oven.

EXPENSIVE

Alberto's Continental ⊛ LEBANESE/YUCATECAN/ITALIAN   There's nothing quite like dining here at night in a softly lit room or on the wonderful old patio framed in Moorish arches. Nothing glitzy—just elegant *mudejar*-patterned tile floors, simple furniture, decoration that's just so, and the gurgling of a fountain creating a romantic mood. I find the prices on the expensive side. For supper, you can choose a sampler plate of four Lebanese favorites, or traditional Yucatecan specialties, such as *pollo pibil* or fish Celestún (bass stuffed with shrimp). You can finish with Turkish coffee.

Calle 64 no. 482 (at Calle 57). © 999/928-5367. Reservations recommended. Main courses $8–$20. AE, MC, V. Daily 1–11pm.

El Pórtico del Peregrino ⊛ REGIONAL/INTERNATIONAL   El Pórtico is a favorite among visitors, who enjoy its charm, comfort, and distinctive Mérida flavor. The interior is a lovely garden with three dining areas—two air-conditioned rooms and a patio. One room is nonsmoking, a rarity in Mexico. The menu offers soups (*sopa de tortilla* and *sopa de lima* are both good), seafood (a platter, or grilled Gulf shrimp), and Yucatecan specialties *(pollo pibil).* Other favorites include baked eggplant with chicken and cheese, and coconut ice cream topped with Kahlúa. The restaurant is 2 blocks north of the main square.

Calle 57 no. 501 (between calles 60 and 62). © 999/928-6163. Reservations recommended. Main courses $6–$15. AE, MC, V. Daily noon–11pm.

La Casa del Paseo ★★ INTERNATIONAL   Set in one of the mansions on the Paseo de Montejo, this restaurant offers excellent food and service. You can dine inside or out on a small patio along the Paseo. The cooking is wonderful. Where to begin? Perhaps with *sopa de lima* or artichoke mousse. For main dishes, consider the daily specials. If you want something light, stuffed chicken breast, *pechuga suiza*, is good; for something meatier, try *medallones paseo*, three grilled beef filets, each with a different sauce. Or sample a local specialty, *queso relleno*.

Paseo de Montejo 465 (between Calle 35 and Av. Colón, 2 doors down from the American consulate). ✆ 999/920-0528. Reservations recommended on weekends. Main courses $9–$14. AE, MC, V. Daily 1pm–midnight.

MODERATE

Restaurant Amaro REGIONAL/VEGETARIAN   The menu in this courtyard restaurant offers some interesting vegetarian dishes, such as *crema de calabacitas* (cream of squash soup), apple salad, and avocado pizza. There is also a limited menu of fish and chicken dishes; you might want to try the Yucatecan chicken. The *agua de chaya* (*chaya* is a leafy vegetable prominent in the Maya diet) is refreshing on a hot afternoon. All desserts are made in-house. The restaurant is a little north of Plaza Mayor.

Calle 59 no. 507 interior 6 (between calles 60 and 62). ✆ 999/928-2451. Main courses $5–$9. MC, V. Mon–Sat 11am–2am.

Restaurante Kantún ★ *Value* SEAFOOD   This modest little restaurant serves up the freshest seafood for a good price. The owner-chef, a son of a cook, is always on the premises taking care of details. He tells me that he will open late by special arrangement for parties as small as four people. The menu includes excellent ceviches and seafood cocktails, and fish cooked in a number of ways. I had the *especial Kantún*, which was lightly battered and stuffed with lobster, crab, and shrimp. The dining room is air-conditioned, the furniture comfortable, and the service attentive.

Calle 45 no. 525-G (between calles 64 and 66). ✆ 999/923-4493. Reservations recommended on Good Friday. Main courses $4–$10. MC, V. Daily noon–6pm.

Restaurant Los Almendros *Overrated* YUCATECAN   Ask where to eat Yucatecan food, and locals will inevitably suggest this place because of its reputation. After all, this was the first place to offer tourists such Yucatecan specialties as *salbutes, panuchos papadzules* (both similar to *gorditas*), *cochinita pibil,* and *poc chuc.* The menu even comes with color photographs to facilitate acquaintance with these strange-sounding dishes. The food is okay and not much of a risk, but you can find better elsewhere. Still, it's a safe place to try Yucatecan food for the first time, and it's such a fixture that the idea of a guidebook that doesn't mention this restaurant is unthinkable. It's 5 blocks east of Calle 60, facing the Parque de la Mejorada.

Calle 50A no. 493. ✆ 999/928-5459. Main courses $4–$9; daily special $5–$9. AE, MC, V. Daily 10am–11pm.

INEXPENSIVE

Café Alameda ★ MIDDLE EASTERN/VEGETARIAN   The trappings here are simple and informal (metal tables, plastic chairs), and it's a good place for catching a light meal. The trick is figuring out the Spanish names for popular Middle Eastern dishes. Kibbe is *quebbe bola* (not *quebbe cruda*), hummus is *garbanza*, and shish kebab is *alambre*. I leave it to you to figure out what a spinach pie is called (and it's excellent). Café Alameda is a treat for vegetarians, and the umbrella-shaded tables on the patio are perfect for morning coffee and *mamules* (walnut-filled pastries).

Calle 58 no. 474 (between calles 55 and 57). © **999/928-3635.** Main courses $2–$5. No credit cards. Daily 7:30am–5:30pm.

Eladio's ☆ YUCATECAN This is where locals come to relax in their off hours, drink very cold beer, and snack or dine on Yucatecan specialties. You have two choices: order a beer and enjoy *una botana* (a small portion that accompanies a drink, in this case usually a Yucatecan dish), or order from the menu. *Cochinita, poc chuc,* and *longaniza asada* (a local variety of sausage) are all good. Or try a *panucho* or *salbute* if you're there in the evening. Often there is live music in this open-air restaurant, which is around the corner from Los Almendros, by Parque la Mejorada.

Calle 59 (at Calle 44). © **999/923-1087.** Main courses $4–$5. MC, V. Daily noon–8pm.

La Flor de Santiago REGIONAL This is a good place for breakfast, lunch, or supper—particularly supper, because the cooks do a good job with *antojitos* (*panuchos, salbutes,* and *vaporcitos*). They even offer *mucbil pollo;* a traditional food for Day of the Dead, it's much like a *tamal* on the outside, with chicken and a soft center on the inside. The menu includes several sandwiches, *comida corrida,* and a large choice of beverages. Service is excellent, and the dining area is classic, with its high ceiling, plain furniture, and clientele.

Calle 70 no. 478 (between calles 57 and 59). © **999/928-5591.** Main courses $3–$6; *comida corrida* $3.50. No credit cards. Daily 7am–11pm.

MERIDA AFTER DARK

For nighttime entertainment, see "Festivals & Special Events in Mérida," earlier in this chapter, or check out the theaters noted here.

Teatro Peón Contreras, calles 60 and 57, and **Teatro Ayala,** Calle 60 at Calle 61, feature a wide range of performing artists from Mexico and around the world. **El Nuevo Olimpo,** on the main square, schedules frequent concerts; and **Cine Mérida,** a half-block north of the Nuevo Olimpo, has two screens for showing classic and art films, and one live stage.

Mérida's club scene offers everything from ubiquitous rock/dance to some one-of-a-kind spots that are nothing like what you find back home. Most of the dance clubs are in the big hotels or on Paseo de Montejo. For dancing, a small cluster of clubs on Calle 60, around the corner from Santa Lucía, offer live rock and salsa music.

El Trovador Bohemio *Finds* It's hard to overstate the importance of *música de trío* and *trova* in Mexican popular culture. This music, mainly in the form of songs called *boleros,* may have been at its most popular in the 1940s and 1950s, but every new Mexican pop music heartthrob feels compelled to release a new version of the classics. I like the originals best, and so do most Mexicans. If you know something of this music and are curious about it, El Trovador gives you a chance to hear how it should be played. And if you understand colloquial Spanish, all the better; the language of boleros is vivid, passionate, and quite Mexican. The club is small and dark, and everything is red. It can be smoky. The best days to go are Thursday, Friday, and Saturday. The club faces the Santa Lucía park. El Trovador is open daily from 9pm to 3am. Calle 55 no. 504. © **999/923-0385.** Cover $4.

Pancho's If you take this place seriously, you won't like it. Pancho's, which serves Tex-Mex and international food, is a parody of a tourist attraction, a place for drinking beer and relaxing. Waiters wear bandoliers and oversize sombreros. Assorted emblems of Mexican identity adorn the walls. Live music in the courtyard begins at

9pm on most nights, 10:30pm on Saturday. The five-piece band, with its large reper-toire of cover tunes, is quite good; it cranks out salsa, rock, and jazz. Pancho's is open daily from 6pm to 3am. Calle 59 no. 509. ℂ **999/923-0942.** 2-drink minimum on weekends if you do not order food.

ECOTOURS & ADVENTURE TRIPS

The Yucatán Peninsula has seen a recent explosion of companies that organize nature and adventure tours. One well-established outfit with a great track record is **Ecoturismo Yucatán,** Calle 3 no. 235, Col. Pensiones, 97219 Mérida (ℂ **999/920-2772;** fax 999/925-9047; www.ecoyuc.com). Alfonso and Roberta Escobedo create itineraries to meet just about any special or general interest you may have for going to the Yucatán or southern Mexico. Alfonso has been creating adventure and nature tours for more than a dozen years. Specialties include archaeology, birding, natural history, and kayaking. The company also offers day trips that explore contemporary Maya culture and life in villages in the Yucatán. Package and customized tours are available.

SIDE TRIPS FROM MERIDA
IZAMAL

Izamal is a sleepy town some 80km (50 miles) east of Mérida, an easy day trip by car. You can visit the famous Franciscan convent of San Antonio de Padua and the ruins of four large pyramids that overlook the center of town. One pyramid is partially reconstructed. Life in Izamal is easygoing in the extreme, as evidenced by the *victorias,* the horse-drawn buggies that serve as taxis here. Even if you come by car, you should make a point of touring the town in one of these.

CELESTUN NATIONAL WILDLIFE REFUGE: FLAMINGOS & OTHER WATERFOWL

On the coast west of Mérida is a large wetlands area that has been declared a biopreserve. It is a long, shallow estuary where freshwater mixes with Gulf saltwater, creating a habitat perfect for flamingos and many other species of waterfowl. This *ría* (estuary), unlike others that are fed by rivers or streams, receives fresh water through about 80 *cenotes,* most of which are underwater. It is very shallow (.3–1m/1–4 ft. deep) and thickly grown with mangrove, with an open channel .5km (¼ mile) wide and 50km (30 miles) long, sheltered from the open sea by a narrow strip of land. Along this corridor, you can take a launch to see flamingos as they dredge the bottom of the shallows for a species of small crustacean and a particular insect that make up the bulk of their diet.

You can get here by car or bus; it's an easy 90-minute drive. (For information on buses, see "Getting There & Departing: By Bus," earlier in this chapter.) To drive, leave downtown Mérida on Calle 57. Shortly after Santiago Church, Calle 57 ends and there's a dogleg onto Calle 59-A. This crosses Avenida Itzáes, and its name changes to Jacinto Canek; continue until you see signs for Celestún Highway 178. This will take you through Hunucmá, where the road joins Highway 281, which takes you to Celestún. You'll know you have arrived when you get to the bridge.

In the last few years, the state agency CULTUR has come into Celestún and established order where once there was chaos. Immediately to your left after the bridge, you'll find modern facilities with a snack bar, clean bathrooms, and a ticket window. Prices for tours are fixed. A 75-minute tour costs about $45 and can accommodate up to six people. You can join others or hire a boat by yourself. On the tour you'll definitely see some flamingos; you'll also get to see some mangrove close up, and one of the many underwater springs. Please do not urge the boatmen to get any closer to the flamingos than they are allowed to; if pestered too much, the birds will abandon the area for other, less fitting habitat. The ride is quite pleasant—the water is calm, and CULTUR has supplied the boatmen with wide, flat-bottom skiffs that have canopies for shade.

In addition to flamingos, you will probably see frigate birds, pelicans, spoonbills, egrets, sandpipers, and other waterfowl feeding on shallow sandbars at any time of year. At least 15 duck species have been counted, and there are several species of birds of prey. Of the 175 bird species that are here, some 99 are permanent residents. Nonbreeding flamingos remain here year-round; the larger group of breeding flamingos takes off around April to nest on the upper Yucatán Peninsula east of Río Lagartos, returning to Celestún in October.

Hotel Eco Paraíso Xixim 🌟🌟   Eco Paraíso is meant to be a refuge from the modern world. It sits on a deserted 4km (3-mile) stretch of beach that was once part of a coconut plantation. It attracts much the same clientele as the former-haciendas-turned-luxury-hotels, but in some ways it has more going for it (like the beach). Some guests come here for a week of idleness; others use this as a base of operations for visiting the biopreserve and making trips to the Maya ruins in the interior. The hotel offers its own tours to various places. Rooms are quite private; each is a separate bungalow with *palapa* roof. Each comes with two comfortable queen-size beds, a sitting area, ceiling fans, and a private porch with hammocks. On my last visit, the food was very good, and the service was great. What's more, the concept is ecologically friendly in more than name only. The hotel composts waste, and treats and uses wastewater.

Antigua Carretera a Sisal Km 10, 97367 Celestún, Yuc. ⓒ **988/916-2100.** Fax 988/916-2111. www.ecoparaiso.com. 15 units. High season $198 double; low season $172 double. Rates include 2 meals per person. AE, MC, V. Free parking. **Amenities:** Restaurant; bar; midsize pool; tour desk. *In room:* Coffeemaker, hair dryer, safe.

DZIBILCHALTUN: MAYA RUINS & MUSEUM

This destination makes for a quick morning trip that will get you back to Mérida in time for a siesta, or it could be part of a longer trip to Progreso, Uaymitún, and Xcambó. It's located 14km (9 miles) north of Mérida along the Progreso road and 4km (3 miles) east of the highway. To get there, take Calle 60 all the way out of town and follow signs for Progreso and Highway 261. Look for the sign for Dzibilchaltún, which also reads UNIVERSIDAD DEL MAYAB; it will point you right. After a few miles you'll see a sign for the entrance to the ruins and the museum. If you don't want to drive, take one of the *colectivos* that line up along Parque San Juan.

Dzibilchaltún was founded about 500 B.C., flourished around A.D. 750, and was in decline long before the coming of the conquistadors. It may have been occupied for almost 100 years after their arrival. Since the ruins were discovered in 1941, more than 8,000 buildings have been mapped. The site covers an area of almost 15 sq. km (6 sq. miles) with a central core of almost 25 hectares (65 acres), but the area of prime interest is limited to the buildings surrounding two plazas next to the *cenote*, and another building, the Temple of the Seven Dolls, connected to these by a *sacbé* (causeway). Dzibilchaltún means "place of the stone writing," and at least 25 stelae have been found, many of them reused in buildings constructed after the original ones were covered or destroyed.

Start at the **Museo del Pueblo Maya,** which is worth seeing. It's open Tuesday to Sunday from 8am to 4pm. Admission is $6. The museum's collection includes artifacts from various sites in the Yucatán. Explanations are printed in bilingual format and are fairly thorough. Objects include a beautiful example of a plumed serpent from Chichén Itzá and a finely designed incense vessel from Palenque. From this general view of the Maya civilization, the museum moves on to exhibit specific artifacts found at the site of Dzibilchaltún, including the rather curious dolls that have given one structure its name. Then there's an exhibit on Maya culture in historical and present times, including a collection of *huipiles,* the woven blouses that Indian women wear. From here a door leads out to the site.

The first thing you come to is the *sacbé* that connects the two areas of interest. To the left is the **Temple of the Seven Dolls.** The temple's doorways line up with the *sacbé* to catch the rising sun at the spring and autumnal equinoxes. To the right are the buildings grouped around the Cenote Xlacah, the sacred well, and a complex of buildings around **Structure 38,** the **Central Group** of temples. The Yucatán State Department of Ecology has added nature trails and published a booklet (in Spanish) of birds and plants seen along the mapped trail.

PROGRESO, UAYMITUN & XCAMBO: GULF COAST CITY, FLAMINGO LOOKOUT & MORE MAYA RUINS

For a beach escape, go to the port of Progreso, Mérida's weekend beach resort. This is where Meridanos have their vacation houses and where they come in large numbers in July and August. It is also the part-time home of some Americans and Canadians escaping northern winters. Except for July and August, it is a quiet place where you can enjoy the Gulf waters without fuss. Along the *malecón,* the wide oceanfront drive that extends the length of a sandy beach, you can pull over and enjoy a swim anywhere you like. The water here isn't the blue of the Caribbean, but it is clean. A long pier extends several kilometers into the gulf to load and unload large ships. Cruise ships dock here twice a week. Along or near the *malecón* are several hotels and a number of restaurants where you can get good fresh seafood.

From Mérida, buses to **Progreso** leave from the bus station at Calle 62 no. 524, between calles 65 and 67, every 15 minutes, starting at 5am. The trip takes almost an hour and costs $2.50.

If you have a car, you might want to drive down the coastal road east toward Telchac Puerto. After about 20 minutes, at the right side of the road you'll see a large, solid-looking wooden observation tower for viewing flamingos. A sign reads UAYMITUN. The state agency CULTUR constructed the tower, operates it, and provides binoculars free of charge. A few years ago, flamingos from Celestún migrated here and established a colony. Your chances of spotting them are good, and you don't have to pay for a boat.

Twenty minutes farther down this road, there's a turnoff for the road to Dzemul. On my last trip I didn't see any flamingos at Uaymitún but just after turning here I found a flock of 500 only 30m (90 ft.) from the highway. After a few minutes, you'll see a sign for **Xcambó** that points to the right. This Maya city is thought to have prospered as a production center for salt, a valuable commodity. Archaeologists have reconstructed the small ceremonial center, which has several platforms and temples. Admission is free. After viewing these ruins, you can continue on the same road through the small towns of Dzemul and Baca. At Baca, take Highway 176 back to Mérida.

EN ROUTE TO UXMAL

Two routes go to Uxmal, about 80km (50 miles) south of Mérida. The most direct is Highway 261 via Uman and Muna. On the way, you can stop to see Hacienda Yaxcopoil, which is 30km (20 miles) from Mérida. From downtown, take Calle 65 or 69 to Avenida Itzáes and turn left; this feeds onto the highway.

If you have the time and want a more scenic route, try the meandering State Highway 18. This is sometimes known as the Convent Route, but all tourism hype aside, it makes for a pleasant drive with several interesting stops. You could make your trip to Uxmal into a loop by going one way and coming back the other with an overnight stay at Uxmal or in Ticul. One way to do this would be to take the long route on Highway 18, arriving in Uxmal in time to see the sound-and-light show. Stay overnight in Uxmal or Santa Elena and see the ruins early in the morning before returning to Mérida. All the attractions on these routes have the same hours: Churches are open from 10am to 1pm and 4 to 6pm; ruins are open from 8am to 5pm.

HIGHWAY 261: YAXCOPOIL & MUNA   After passing through Uman, you'll drive 15km (10 miles) to **Yaxcopoil** (yash-koh-*poyl*), a ruined 19th-century hacienda on the right side of the road. I've found that it is often closed, but when it's open, you can take a half-hour tour of the place, including the manor, and the henequén factory. Officially it's open from Monday to Saturday from 8am to 6pm, Sunday from 9am to 1pm. Admission is $3.50.

After Yaxcopoil comes the busy little market town of **Muna** (65km/40 miles from Mérida) where you might run into a traffic slowdown. The typical Yucatecan tricycle taxis are everywhere. Muna offers little for sightseers but may interest those curious about contemporary Maya life. Be sure to stay on Highway 261 as you leave; 15km (10 miles) beyond Muna is Uxmal.

HIGHWAY 18 (THE CONVENT ROUTE): KANASIN, ACANCEH, MAYAPAN & TICUL   From downtown take Calle 63 east to Circuito Colonias and turn right; look for a traffic circle with a small fountain and turn left. This feeds onto Highway 18 to Kanasín (kah-nah-*seen*) and then Acanceh (ah-kahn-*keh*). In **Kanasín,** the highway divides into two roads and a sign will tell you that you can't go straight, instead, you go to the right, which will curve around and flow into the next parallel street. Go past the market, church, and the main square on your left, stay to the right when you get to a fork.

Shortly after Kanasín the highway has been upgraded and now by-passes a lot of villages. After a few of these turnoffs you'll see a sign pointing left to Acanceh. Across the street from and overlooking Acanceh's church is a restored pyramid. On top of this pyramid under a makeshift roof are some recently discovered large stucco figures of Maya deities. The caretaker, Mario Uicab, will guide you up to see the fascinating figures and give you a little explanation (in Spanish). Admission is $2.50. There are some other ruins a couple of blocks away called **El Palacio de los Estucos.** In 1908, a stucco mural was found here in mint condition. It was left exposed and has deteriorated somewhat. Now it is sheltered, and you can still easily distinguish the painted figures in their original colors. To leave Acanceh head back to the highway on the street that passes between the church and the plaza. On this route you'll be passing through a lot of small villages without directional signs, so get used to poking your head out the window and saying *"Buenos días, ¿dónde está el camino para . . . ?"* which translates as "Good day, where is the road to . . . ?" This is what I do, and I ask more than one person. The streets in these villages are full of children, bicycles, and livestock, so drive carefully and, as always, keep an eye out for unmarked *topes.*

The next turnoff will be for **Tecoh** on the right side. Tecoh's parish church sits on a massive pre-Columbian raised platform—the remains of a ceremonial complex that was sacrificed to build the church. With its rough stone and simple twin towers that are crumbling around the edges, the church looks ancient. Inside are three carved *retablos* (altarpieces) covered in gold leaf and unmistakably Indian in style. In 1998 they were refurbished and are well worth seeing.

Also in Tecoh are some caverns, shown by a local. The bad news is that the owner doesn't have a very good flashlight, and I found myself groping around in the dark. You'll find them as you leave town heading back to the highway. Then it's on to the ruins of Mayapán.

MAYAPAN ✦

Founded, according to Maya lore, by the man-god Kukulkán (Quetzalcoatl in central Mexico) in about A.D. 1007, Mayapán ranked in importance with Chichén Itzá and Uxmal. It covered at least 4 sq. km (2½ sq. miles). For more than 2 centuries it was the capital of a Maya confederation of city-states that included Chichén and Uxmal. But before 1200, the rulers of Mayapán ended the confederation by attacking and conquering Chichén and forcing the rulers of Uxmal to live as vassals in Mayapán. Eventually, a successful revolt by the other cities brought down Mayapán, which was abandoned during the mid-1400s.

In the last few years, archaeologists have been busy excavating and rebuilding the city, and work continues. Several buildings bordering the principal plaza have been reconstructed, including one that is similar to El Castillo in Chichén Itzá. The scientists have discovered murals and stucco figures that provide more grist for the mill of conjecture: *atlantes,* skeletal soldiers, macaws, entwined snakes, and a stucco jaguar. This place is definitely worth stopping to see.

The site is open daily from 8am to 5pm. Admission is $3. Use of a personal video camera is $4.

FROM MAYAPAN TO TICUL   About 20km (12 miles) after Mayapán, you'll see the highway for **Mama** on your right. This will put you on a narrow road that quickly enters the town. For some reason I really like this village; some parts of it are quite pretty. It's often called Mamita by the locals, using the affectionate diminutive suffix. The main attraction is the church and former convent. Inside are several fascinating *retablos* sculpted in a native form of baroque. During the restoration of these buildings, colonial-age murals and designs were uncovered and restored. Be sure to get a peek at them in the sacristy. From Mama continue on for about 20km (12 miles) to Ticul, a large (for this area) market town with a couple of simple hotels.

TICUL

Best known for the cottage industry of *huipil* (native blouse) embroidery and for the manufacture of women's dress shoes, Ticul isn't the most exciting stop on the Puuc route, but it's a convenient place to wash up and spend the night. It's also a center for large commercially produced pottery; most of the widely sold sienna-colored pottery painted with Maya designs comes from here. If it's a cloudy, humid day, the potters may not be working (part of the process requires sun drying), but they still welcome visitors to purchase finished pieces.

One place worth a visit is **Arte Maya,** Calle 23 no. 301, Carretera Ticul-Muna (© **997/972-1669;** lumayaart@hotmail.com), owned and operated by Luis Echeverría and Lourdes Castillo. This shop and gallery produces museum-quality art in alabaster, stone, jade, and ceramics. Much of the work is done as it was in Maya times;

soft stone or ceramic is smoothed with the leaf of the siricote tree, and colors are derived from plant sources. The shop is open Monday to Saturday from 10am to 8pm.

Ticul is only 20km (12 miles) northeast of Uxmal, so thrifty tourists stay either here or in Santa Elena instead of at the more expensive hotels at the ruins. In Ticul I recommend the **Hotel Plaza,** Calle 23 no. 202, on the town square near the intersection with Calle 26 (© **997/972-0484**). It's a modest hotel, as you would expect in a town of this sort, but it's comfortable and recently remodeled. A double room with air-conditioning costs $30; without air-conditioning, $25. In both cases, there's a 5% charge if you want to pay with a credit card (MasterCard and Visa accepted). Get an interior room if you're looking for quiet, because Ticul has quite a lively plaza. From Ticul, you can do one of two things: head straight for Uxmal via Santa Elena, or loop around the Puuc Route, the long way to Santa Elena. For information on the Puuc route, see "The Puuc Maya Route & Village of Oxkutzcab," below.

FROM TICUL TO UXMAL   Follow the main street (Calle 23) west through town. Turn left on Calle 34. It's 15km (10 miles) to Santa Elena; and from there another 15km (10 miles) to Uxmal. In Santa Elena, by the side of Highway 261, is a clean restaurant with good food, **El Chac Mool** and on the opposite side of the road is the **Flycatcher Inn B&B** (see listing, below).

2 The Ruins of Uxmal ★★★

80km (50 miles) SW of Mérida; 19km (12 miles) W of Ticul; 19km (12 miles) S of Muna

One of the highlights of a Yucatán vacation, the ruins of Uxmal (pronounced "oosh-*mahl*")—noted for their rich geometric stone facades—are perhaps the most beautiful on the peninsula. Remains of an agricultural society indicate that the area was occupied possibly as early as 800 B.C. The great building period took place between A.D. 700 and 1000, when the population probably reached 25,000. After 1000, Uxmal fell under the sway of the Xiú princes (who may have come from central Mexico). In the 1440s, the Xiú conquered Mayapán, and not long afterward the age of the Maya ended with the arrival of the Spanish conquistadors.

Close to Uxmal, four other sites—**Sayil, Kabah, Xlapak,** and **Labná**—are worth visiting. With Uxmal, these ruins are collectively known as the **Puuc route,** for the Puuc hills of this part of the Yucatán. See "Seeing Puuc Maya Sites," below, if you want to explore these sites.

ESSENTIALS

GETTING THERE & DEPARTING   By Car   Two routes to Uxmal from Mérida, Highway 261 and State Highway 18, are described in "En Route to Uxmal," above. *Note:* There's no gasoline at Uxmal.

By Bus   See "Getting There & Departing" in "Mérida: Gateway to the Maya Heartland," earlier in this chapter, for information about bus service between Mérida and Uxmal. To return, wait for the bus on the highway at the entrance to the ruins. To see the sound-and-light show, don't bother with regular buses; sign up with a tour operator in Mérida.

ORIENTATION   Uxmal consists of the archaeological site and its visitor center, five hotels, and a highway restaurant. The visitor center, open daily from 8am to 9pm, has a restaurant (with good coffee); toilets; a first-aid station; shops selling soft drinks, ice cream, film, batteries, and books; and a state-run Casa de Artesanía (crafts house).

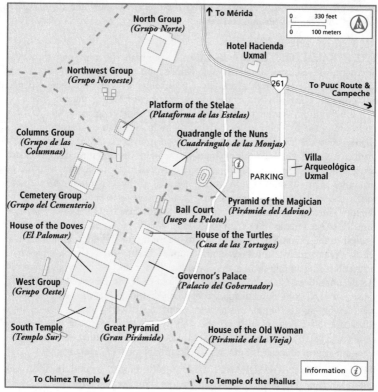

There are no phones except at the hotels. Most public buses pick up and let off passengers on the highway at the entrance to the ruins. The site is open daily from 8am to 5pm. Admission to the archaeological site is around $10, which includes admission to the nightly sound-and-light show. Bringing in a video camera costs $4. Parking costs $1. If you're staying the night in Uxmal, it is possible (and I think preferable) to get to the site late in the day and buy a ticket that allows you to see the sound-and-light show that evening and lets you enter the ruins the next morning to explore them before it gets hot. Just make sure that the ticket vendor knows what you intend to do and keep the ticket.

Guides at the entrance of Uxmal give tours in a variety of languages and charge $20 for a single person or a group. The guides frown on unrelated individuals joining a group. They'd rather charge you as a solo visitor, but you can ask other English speakers if they'd like to join you in a tour and split the cost. As at other sites, the guides vary in quality but will point out areas and architectural details that you might otherwise miss. You should think of these guided tours as performances—the guides try to be as entertaining as possible and adjust their presentations according to the interests of the visitors.

Included in the price of admission is a 45-minute **sound-and-light show,** staged each evening at 8pm. It's in Spanish, but headsets are available for rent ($2.50) for listening to the program in several languages. After the impressive show, the chant *"Chaaac, Chaaac"* will echo in your mind for weeks.

A TOUR OF THE RUINS

THE PYRAMID OF THE MAGICIAN   As you enter the ruins, note the *chultún,* or cistern, where Uxmal stored its water. Unlike most of the major Maya sites, Uxmal has no *cenote* to supply fresh water. The city's inhabitants were much more dependent on rainwater, which is why they seem so infatuated with Chaac, the rain god.

Just beyond the *chultún,* the remarkable Pyramid of the Magician (also called Pyramid of the Dwarf) looms majestically on the right. The name comes from a legend about a mystical dwarf who reached adulthood in a single day after being hatched from an egg, and who built this pyramid in one night. Beneath it are five earlier structures, which is a common feature of Maya pyramids; the practice was to build new structures atop old ones at regular intervals. The pyramid is unique because of its rounded sides, height, and steepness, and the doorway on the opposite (west) side near the top. The doorway's heavy ornamentation, a characteristic of the Chenes style, features 12 stylized masks of the rain god Chaac.

Next to the Pyramid of the Magician, to the west, is the Nunnery Quadrangle, and left of it is a partially restored ball court. South of that are several large complexes. The biggest building among them is the Governor's Palace, and behind it lies the massive, largely unrestored Great Pyramid. In the distance is the Dovecote (House of the Doves), a small building with a lacy roof comb that looks like the perfect apartment complex for pigeons. From this vantage point, note how Uxmal is unique among Maya sites for its use of huge terraces constructed to support the buildings; look closely and you'll see that the Governor's Palace is not on a natural hill, but rather on a giant platform of packed earth, as is the nearby Nunnery Quadrangle.

THE NUNNERY QUADRANGLE   The 16th-century Spanish historian Fray Diego López de Cogullado gave the building its name because it resembled a Spanish convent. Possibly it was a military academy or a training school for princes, who may have lived in the 70-odd rooms. The buildings were constructed at different times: The northern one was first; then the southern, eastern, and western buildings. The western building has the most richly decorated facade, composed of intertwined stone snakes and numerous masks of the hook-nosed rain god Chaac.

The corbeled archway to the south was once the main entrance to the Nunnery complex; as you head toward it out of the quadrangle, look above each doorway in that section for the motif of a Maya cottage, or *nah,* still seen throughout the Yucatán today.

THE BALL COURT   A small ball court is conserved to prevent further decay, but compare it later in your trip to the giant, magnificently restored court at Chichén Itzá.

THE TURTLE HOUSE   Up on the terrace south of the ball court is a little temple decorated with colonnade motif on the facade and a border of turtles. Though it's small and simple, its harmony makes it one of the gems of Uxmal.

THE GOVERNOR'S PALACE   In its size and intricate stonework, this rivals the Temple of the Magician as Uxmal's masterwork—an imposing three-level edifice with a 95m-long (320-ft.) mosaic facade done in the Puuc style. Puuc means "hilly country," the name given to the hills nearby and thus to the predominant style of pre-Hispanic architecture found here. Uxmal has many examples of Puuc decoration, characterized by elaborate stonework from door tops to the roofline. Fray Cogullado also gave this building its name. The Governor's Palace may have been just that—the administrative center of the Xiú principality, which included the region around Uxmal. It probably had astrological significance as well. For years, scholars pondered why this building was constructed slightly turned from adjacent buildings. Originally they thought the strange alignment was because of the *sacbé* (ceremonial road) that starts at this building and ends 18km (11 miles) away at the ancient city of Kabah. But recently scholars of archaeoastronomy (a relatively new science that studies the placement of archaeological sites in relation to the stars) discovered that the central doorway, which is larger than the others, is in perfect alignment with Venus.

Before you leave the Governor's Palace, note the elaborately stylized headdress patterned in stone over the central doorway. As you stand back from the building on the east side, note how the 103 stone masks of Chaac undulate across the facade like a serpent and end at the corners, where there are columns of masks.

THE GREAT PYRAMID   A massive, partially restored nine-level structure, it has interesting motifs of birds, probably macaws, on its facade, as well as a huge mask. The view from the top is wonderful.

THE DOVECOTE   This building is remarkable in that roof combs weren't a common feature of temples in the Puuc hills, although you'll see one (of a very different style) on El Mirador at Sayil.

WHERE TO STAY

There are some attractive hotels in Uxmal. If occupancy is low, you might bargain for a room.

Flycatcher Inn B&B   This pleasant little bed-and-breakfast is in the neighboring village of Santa Elena, just off Highway 261. The rooms are quiet, attractive, and spacious and come with queen-size beds and lots of decorative ironwork made by one of the owners, Santiago Domínguez. The other owner is Christine Ellingson, an American from the Northwest who has lived in Santa Elena for years and is happy to help her guests with their travels.

Carretera Uxmal–Kabah, 97840 Santa Elena, Yuc. No phone. www.mexonline.com/flycatcherinn.htm. 4 units. $30–$40 double; $50 suite. No credit cards. Free parking.

Hotel Hacienda Uxmal ★★   One of my favorites, this is also the oldest hotel in Uxmal. Located just up the highway from the ruins, it was built as the archaeology staff headquarters. Rooms are large and airy, exuding an impression of a well-kept building from yesteryear, with patterned tile floors, heavy furniture, and well-screened windows. Room nos. 202 through 214 and 302 through 305 are the nicest of the superiors. Corner rooms are labeled A through F and are even larger. A handsome garden courtyard with towering royal palms, a bar, and a pool adds the air of tranquillity. A guitar trio usually plays on the open patio in the evenings.

Mayaland Resorts, owner of the hotel, also runs the striking **Hotel Lodge at Uxmal,** next door. It has lovely rooms, but I like the stately feel of the older hotel better. Mayaland operates transfer service between the hotel and Mérida for about $30 one-way.

Carretera Mérida–Uxmal Km 80, 97840 Uxmal, Yuc. ✆ 997/976-2011. (Reservations: Mayaland Resorts, Robalo 30 SM3, 77500 Cancún, Q. Roo. ✆ 800/235-4079 in the U.S., or 997/887-0870. Fax 997/884-4510.) www.mayaland. com. 73 units. High season $148 double, $218 junior suite, $345 master suite; low season $88 double, $144 junior suite, $255 master suite. AE, MC, V. Free guarded parking. **Amenities:** Restaurant (see "Where to Dine," below); bar; 2 pools; tour info; room service until 10pm; laundry service. *In room:* A/C, TV, minibar, coffeemaker, no phone.

Villas Arqueológicas Uxmal ⚡ This hotel is associated with Club Med, but it is just a hotel, not a self-contained vacation village. A two-story layout surrounds a garden patio and a pool. At guests' disposal are a tennis court, a library, and an audiovisual show on the ruins in English, French, and Spanish. Each of the modern, smallish rooms has two oversize single beds that fit into spaces that are walled on three sides. Very tall people should stay elsewhere. You can also ask for rates that include half- or full board.

Ruinas Uxmal, 97844 Uxmal, Yuc. © 800/258-2633 in the U.S., or 997/976-2018. 43 units. $90 double. Rates include continental breakfast. Half-board (breakfast plus lunch or dinner) $15 per person; full board (3 meals) $30 per person. AE, MC, V. Free guarded parking. **Amenities:** Restaurant; bar; pool; tennis court. *In room:* A/C.

WHERE TO DINE

Besides the restaurants at the Villa Arqueológicas and the visitor center, there are a few other dining choices.

Café-Bar Nicte-Ha MEXICAN This small restaurant attached to the Hotel Hacienda Uxmal is a delightful place to eat. The food is decent, though prices tend to be high. If you eat here, take full advantage of the experience and spend a few hours by the pool near the cafe: Its use is free to customers. This is a favorite spot for bus tours that fill the place to overcrowding, so come early.

In the Hotel Hacienda Uxmal, Carretera Mérida–Uxmal Km 80. © 997/976-2011. Main courses $5–$8; fixed-price lunch $9. AE, MC, V. Daily 1–8pm.

Las Palapas MEXICAN/YUCATECAN Five kilometers (3 miles) north of the ruins on the road to Mérida, you'll find this pleasant open-air restaurant with a large *palapa* roof. The amiable owner, María Cristina Choy, charges the lowest prices around. Individual diners can sometimes become lost in the crowd if a busload of tourists arrives, but otherwise the service is fine and the food quite good. There's also a small gift shop with regional crafts and a few books.

Hwy. 261. No phone. Breakfast $3; *comida corrida* (served 1–4pm) $3.75. No credit cards. Daily 9am–6pm.

THE PUUC MAYA ROUTE & VILLAGE OF OXKUTZCAB

South and east of Uxmal are several other Maya cities worth visiting. Though smaller in scale than Uxmal or Chichén Itzá, each contains gems of Maya architecture. The Palace of Masks at **Kabah,** the palace at **Sayil,** and the fantastic caverns of **Loltún** are well worth viewing.

Kabah is 28km (17 miles) southeast of Uxmal via Highway 261 through Santa Elena. From there it's only a couple kilometers to Sayil. Xlapak is almost walking distance

---

⟮*Tips*⟯ Seeing Puuc Maya Sites

All of these sites are currently undergoing excavation and reconstruction, and some buildings may be roped off when you visit. Photographers, take note: You'll find afternoon light the best. The sites are open daily from 8am to 5pm. Admission is $2 to $3 for each site, and $5 for Loltún. Loltún has specific hours for tours—9:30 and 11am, and 12:30, 2, 3, and 4pm—but if the tour guide is there, a generous tip might persuade him to do a tour and not wait for a tour bus. Use of a video camera at any time costs $4; if you're visiting Uxmal in the same day, you pay only once for video permission and present your receipt as proof at each ruin.

(through the jungle) from Sayil, and Labná is just a bit farther east. A short drive beyond Labná brings you to the caves of Loltún. Oxkutzcab is at the road's intersection with Highway 184, which you can follow west to Ticul or east all the way to Felipe Carrillo Puerto. If you aren't driving, a daily bus from Mérida goes to all these sites, with the exception of Loltún. (See "By Bus" in "Getting There & Departing," earlier in this chapter.)

PUUC MAYA SITES

KABAH To reach Kabah from Uxmal, head southwest on Highway 261 to Santa Elena (1km/½ mile), then south to Kabah (13km/8 miles). The ancient city of Kabah lies along both sides of the highway. Turn right into the parking lot.

The most outstanding building at Kabah is the **Palace of Masks,** or Codz Poop ("rolled-up mat"), named for its decorative motif. You'll notice it to the right as you enter. Its outstanding feature is the Chenes-style facade, completely covered in a repeated pattern of 250 masks of the rain god Chaac, each one with curling remnants of Chaac's elephant-trunk-like nose. There's nothing else like this facade in all of Maya architecture. For years, stone-carved parts of this building lay lined up in the weeds like pieces of a puzzle awaiting the master puzzle-solver to put them into place. Sculptures from this building are in the anthropology museums in Mérida and Mexico City.

Just behind and to the left of the Codz Poop is the **Palace Group** (also called the East Group), with a fine Puuc-style colonnaded facade. Originally it had 32 rooms. On the front are seven doors, two divided by columns, a common feature of Puuc architecture. Across the highway is what was once the **Great Temple.** Past it is a **great arch,** which was much wider at one time and may have been a monumental gate into the city. A *sacbé* linked this arch to a point at Uxmal. Compare this corbeled arch to the one at Labná (see below), which is in much better shape.

SAYIL About 4km (3 miles) south of Kabah is the turnoff (left, or east) to Sayil, Xlapak, Labná, Loltún, and Oxkutzcab. The ruins of **Sayil** ("place of the ants") are 4km (2½ miles) along this road.

Sayil is famous for **El Palacio**. This palace of more than 90 rooms is impressive for its size alone. At present it is roped off because of some damage suffered in the last hurricane. Climbing is not permitted. But this is unimportant because what makes it a masterpiece of Maya architecture is the facade, which is best appreciated from the ground. It stretches across three terraced levels, and its rows of columns give it a Minoan appearance. On the second level, notice the upside-down stone figure known to archaeologists as the Diving God, or Descending God, over the doorway; the same motif was used at Tulum several centuries later. The large circular basin on the ground below the palace is an artificial catch basin for a *chultún* (cistern); this region has no natural *cenotes* (wells) to catch rainwater.

In the jungle past El Palacio is **El Mirador,** a small temple with an oddly slotted roof comb. Beyond El Mirador, a crude stele (tall, carved stone) has a phallic idol carved on it in greatly exaggerated proportions. Another cluster of buildings, the Southern Group, is a short distance down a trail that branches off from the one heading to El Mirador.

XLAPAK Xlapak (*shla*-pahk) is a small site with one building; it's 5.5km (3½ miles) down the road from Sayil. The Palace at Xlapak bears the masks of the rain god Chaac. You won't miss much if you skip this place.

LABNA Labná, which dates from between A.D. 600 and 900, is 30km (18 miles) from Uxmal and only 3km (2 miles) past Xlapak. Descriptive placards fronting the main buildings are in Spanish, English, and German. The first thing you see on the left as you enter is **El Palacio,** a magnificent Puuc-style building much like the one at Sayil, but in poorer condition. Over a doorway is a large, well-conserved mask of Chaac with eyes, a huge snout nose, and jagged teeth around a small mouth that seems on the verge of speaking. Jutting out on one corner is a highly stylized serpent's mouth from which pops a human head with an unexpectedly serene expression. From the front, you can gaze out to the enormous grassy interior grounds flanked by vestiges of unrestored buildings and jungle.

From El Palacio, you can walk across the interior grounds on a reconstructed *sacbé* leading to Labná's **corbeled arch,** famed for its beauty and for its representation of what many such arches must have looked like at other sites. This one has been extensively restored, although only remnants of the roof comb can be seen. It was once part of a more elaborate structure that is completely gone. Chaac's face is on the corners of one facade, and stylized Maya huts are fashioned in stone above the two small doorways.

You pass through the arch to **El Mirador,** or El Castillo, as the rubble-formed, pyramid-shaped structure is called. Towering on top is a singular room crowned with a roof comb etched against the sky.

There's a snack stand with toilets at the entrance.

LOLTUN   The caverns of Loltún are 31km (19 miles) past Labná on the way to Oxkutzcab, on the left side of the road. These fascinating caves, home of ancient Maya, were also used as a refuge during the War of the Castes (1847–1901). Inside are statuary, wall carvings and paintings, *chultúns* (cisterns), and other signs of Maya habitation. Guides will explain much of what you see. When I was there, the guide spoke English but was a little difficult to understand.

The admission price includes a 90-minute **tour;** they begin daily at 9:30 and 11am and 12:30, 2, 3 and 4pm. The floor of the cavern can be slippery in places; if you have a flashlight, take it with you. Admission is $5. What you see is quite interesting.

To return to Mérida from Loltún, drive the 7km (4½ miles) to Oxkutzcab. From there, head northwest on Highway 184. It's 19km (12 miles) to Ticul and (turning north onto Hwy. 261 at Muna) 105km (65 miles) to Mérida.

OXKUTZCAB

Oxkutzcab (ohsh-kootz-*kahb*), 11km (7 miles) from Loltún, is the center of the Yucatán's fruit-growing region. Oranges abound. The tidy village of 21,000 centers on a beautiful 16th-century church and the market. **Su Cabaña Suiza** (no phone) is a good restaurant in town. The last week of October and first week of November is the **Orange Festival,** when the village turns exuberant, with a carnival and orange displays in and around the central plaza.

EN ROUTE TO CAMPECHE

From Oxkutzcab, head back 43km (27 miles) to Sayil, and then drive south on Highway 261 to Campeche (126km/78 miles). After crossing the state line you'll pass through the towns of Bolonchén and Hopelchén. The drive is pleasant, and there's little traffic. Both towns have gas stations. From Hopelchén, Highway 261 heads west. After 42km (26 miles), you'll find yourself at Cayal and the well-marked turnoff for the ruins of the city of Edzná, 19km (12 miles) farther south.

EDZNA 🐾   This city is interesting for several reasons. The area was probably populated as early as 600 B.C., with urban formation by 300 B.C. From that point onward,

Edzná grew impressively in a manner that suggests considerable urban planning skills. An ambitious and elaborate canal system was dug, which must have taken decades to complete, but would have allowed for a great expansion in agricultural production and hence concentration of population. This made Edzná the preeminent city for a wide territory.

Another boom in construction begins around A.D. 500, during the middle of the Classic period. This would have been when the city's most prominent feature, the **Great Acropolis** was started.

Sitting on top of this raised platform are five main pyramids, the largest being the much-photographed **Pyramid of Five Stories.** This pyramid combines the features of platform and palace. In Maya architecture you have palace buildings with many vaulted chambers and you have solid pyramidal platforms—two mutually exclusive categories. But not here. Such a mix is found only in the Puuc and Rio Bec areas, and only in a few examples, and none similar to this, which makes this pyramid a bold architectural statement. Now, the four lesser pyramids on the Acropolis are each constructed in a different style, and each is a pure example of that style. It's as if the rulers of this city were flaunting their cosmopolitanism, showing that they could build in any style they chose, but preferred creating their own, superior architecture.

West of the Acropolis, across a large open plaza, is a long raised building whose purpose isn't quite clear. But its size as well as that of the plaza make you wonder just how many people this city actually held to necessitate such a large public space.

The site takes an hour to see, and is open daily from 8am to 5pm. Admission is $4, plus $4 to use your video camera.

Back on Highway 261, it's 19km (12 miles) to the intersection with Highway 180 and then another 42km (26 miles) to the center of Campeche.

3 Campeche 🗶🗶

251km (157 miles) SW of Mérida; 376km (235 miles) NE of Villahermosa

Campeche, the capital of the state of the same name, is the most thoroughly restored colonial city in Mexico. It's so well restored that, in some places, you can imagine that you've traveled back in time. The facades of all the houses in the old part of town have been repaired and painted, all electrical and telephone cables have been routed underground, and the streets have been paved to look cobbled. Several Mexican movie companies have taken advantage of the restoration to shoot period films here.

Despite its beauty, not many tourists come to Campeche. Those who do tend to be either on their way to the ruins at Palenque (see chapter 11) or the Río Bec region (see chapter 15), or the kind of travelers who are accidental wanderers rather than purposeful sightseers. A couple of things do need to be said: Campeche is not geared to foreign tourism the way Mérida is, so expect less in the way of English translations and such at museums and other sights. Campeche also is a sleepy town with little nightlife.

If you're interested in seeing the ruins and biosphere reserve at Calakmul and the rest of the ruins along the Río Bec route, see the section "The Río Bec Ruin Route," in chapter 15. Calakmul is a large and important site, with the tallest pyramid in the Yucatán peninsula, and if you're going that far, you must stop at Balamkú. From the Campeche side you can get information and contract a tour with one of several tour operators. You might talk with the travel agency at the Hotel Del Mar and arrange an overnight trip with accommodations at its eco-village at Chicanná.

The federal highway that leads to these sights crosses through the Río Bec region and eventually arrives at Chetumal, on Yucatán's southern Caribbean coast. From there you can head up the coast and complete a loop of the peninsula.

Campeche has an interesting history. The first contact between white men and natives occurred in 1517, when Francisco de Córdoba landed here while exploring the coast. Supposedly, it was the first place on the mainland where a Mass was celebrated. Francisco de Montejo the Elder established a settlement here in 1531, but the Indians soon expelled the Spaniards. Finally, Montejo the Younger refounded it in 1540.

For the next century, pirates repeatedly harassed the city. The list of pirates who have attacked Campeche reads like a who's who of pirating. On one occasion, several outfits joined forces under the famous Dutch pirate Peg Leg (who most likely was the inspiration for the many fictional one-legged sailors) and managed to capture the city. The Campechanos grew tired of playing host to pirate parties and erected walls around the city, showing as much industry then as they now show in renovating their historic district. The walls had a number of *baluartes* (bastions) at critical locations. For added security, they constructed two forts, complete with moats and drawbridges, on the hills flanking the city. There were four gates to the city, and the two main ones are still intact: the Puerta de Mar (Sea Gate) and the Puerta de Tierra (Land Gate). The pirates never cared to return, but, in Mexico's stormy political history, the city did withstand a couple of sieges by different armies. Eventually, in the early 1900s, the wall around the city was razed, but the bastions and main gates were left intact, as were the two hilltop fortresses. Most of the bastions and both forts now house museums.

ESSENTIALS

GETTING THERE & DEPARTING **By Plane** Aeromexico (© **981/816-6656** at the airport) flies once daily to and from Mexico City. The **airport** is several kilometers northeast of the town center, and you'll have to take a taxi into town (about $4).

BY CAR Highway 180 goes south from Mérida, passing near the basket-making village of Halacho and near Becal, known for its Panama-hat weavers. At Tenabo, take the shortcut (right) to Campeche rather than going farther to the crossroads near Chencoyí. The longer way from Mérida is along Highway 261 past Uxmal.

When driving in the other direction, toward Mérida via Highway 180, go north on Avenida Ruiz Cortines, bearing left to follow the water (this becomes Av. Pedro Sainz de Baranda, but there's no sign). Follow the road as it turns inland to Highway 180, where you turn left (there's a gas station at the intersection).

If you're leaving Campeche for Edzná and Uxmal, go north on either Ruiz Cortines or Gobernadores and turn right on Madero, which feeds onto **Highway 281.** To go south to Villahermosa, take Ruiz Cortines south.

BY BUS ADO (© **981/816-2802**) offers a first-class *de paso* (passing through) bus to Palenque (6 hr.; $15) four times a day and buses to Mérida (2½ hr.; $7) every hour from 5:30am to midnight. The ADO **bus station** is currently on Avenida Gobernadores, 9 blocks from Plaza Principal, but will be moved this year to Avenida Patricio Trueba, a kilometer (½ mile) from the Puerta de Tierra.

INFORMATION The **State of Campeche Office of Tourism** (©/fax **981/816-6767**) is in Plaza Moch-Couoh, Av. Ruiz Cortines s/n, 24000 Campeche. This is in one of the state buildings between the historic center and the shore. There are also information offices in the bastions of Santa Rosa, San Carlos, and Santiago. The tourism office here is better prepared and more helpful than in most other cities, and

Campeche

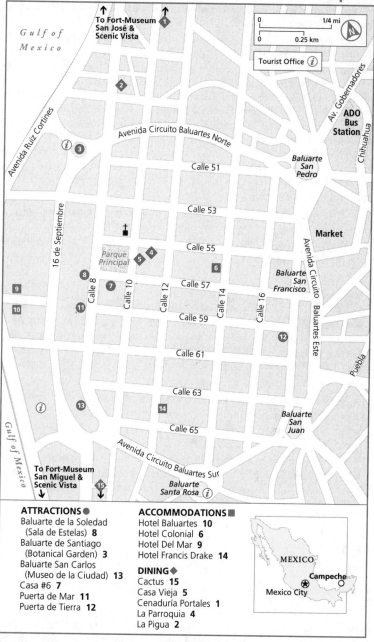

Gulf of Mexico

To Fort-Museum San José & Scenic Vista ↑ ↑ **1**

| 0 | | 1/4 mi |
| 0 | 0.25 km | |

Tourist Office *(i)*

2

Av. Gobernadores

Chihuahua

ADO Bus Station

Avenida Ruiz Cortines

(i) **3**

Avenida Circuito Baluartes Norte

Calle 51

Baluarte San Pedro

16 de Septiembre

Calle 53

Market

†
■

Calle 55

Parque Principal **5** **4**

6

Avenida Circuito

Baluarte San Francisco

8
9
7
Calle 8
Calle 10
Calle 12
Calle 57
Calle 14
Calle 16

10
11

Calle 59

Baluartes Este

12

Calle 61

Puebla

Calle 63

(i) **13**

14

Calle 65

Baluarte San Juan

Gulf of Mexico

To Fort-Museum San Miguel & Scenic Vista ↓

15

Avenida Circuito Baluartes Sur

Baluarte Santa Rosa *(i)*

ATTRACTIONS ●
Baluarte de la Soledad
(Sala de Estelas) **8**
Baluarte de Santiago
(Botanical Garden) **3**
Baluarte San Carlos
(Museo de la Ciudad) **13**
Casa #6 **7**
Puerta de Mar **11**
Puerta de Tierra **12**

ACCOMMODATIONS ■
Hotel Baluartes **10**
Hotel Colonial **6**
Hotel Del Mar **9**
Hotel Francis Drake **14**

DINING ◆
Cactus **15**
Casa Vieja **5**
Cenaduría Portales **1**
La Parroquia **4**
La Pigua **2**

MEXICO

Campeche

Mexico City

it hands out good maps. It keeps regular office hours: Monday to Friday from 9am to 2pm and 4 to 7pm.

CITY LAYOUT The most interesting part of the city is the restored old part, most of which once lay within the walls. Originally, the seaward wall was at the water's edge, but now land has been gained from the sea between the old walls and the coastline. This is where you'll find most of the state government buildings, which were built in a glaringly modernist style around **Plaza Moch-Couoh:** buildings such as the office tower **Edificio de los Poderes (Judicial Building)** or **Palacio de Gobierno** (headquarters for the state of Campeche), and the futuristic **Cámara de Diputados (Chamber of Deputies),** which looks like a cubist clam.

Campeche's system of street numbering is much like that of other cities in the Yucatán, except that the numbers of the north-south streets increase as you go east instead of the reverse. (See "City Layout" in "Mérida: Gateway to the Maya Heartland," earlier in this chapter.)

GETTING AROUND Most of the recommended sights, restaurants, and hotels are within walking distance of the old city, except for the two fort-museums. Campeche isn't easy to negotiate by bus; I recommend taxis for anything beyond walking distance. Taxis are inexpensive.

FAST FACTS: Campeche

American Express Local offices are at Calle 59 no. 4 and 5 (© 981/811-1010), in the Edificio Del Mar, a half-block toward town from the Hotel Del Mar. Open Monday to Friday from 9am to 2pm and 5 to 7pm, and Saturday from 9am to 1pm. This office does not cash traveler's checks.

Area Code The telephone area code is **981.**

ATMs There are more than 10 cash machines in and around the downtown area.

Internet Access There are plenty of places to check e-mail, too—just look for signs with the words INTERNET or CYBERCAFE.

Post Office The *correo* is in the Edificio Federal at the corner of Avenida 16 de Septiembre and Calle 53 (© 981/816-2134), near the Baluarte de Santiago; it's open Monday to Saturday from 7:30am to 8pm. The telegraph office is here as well.

EXPLORING CAMPECHE

With beautiful surroundings, friendly people, an easy pace of living, and orderly traffic, Campeche is worthy of at least a day on your itinerary. It has some interesting museums, one outstanding restaurant, and several shops worth investigating.

INSIDE THE CITY WALLS

A good place to begin is the pretty *zócalo,* or **Parque Principal,** bounded by calles 55 and 57 running east and west and calles 8 and 10 running north and south. Construction of the church on the north side of the square began in 1650 and was finally completed 1½ centuries later. A pleasant way to see the city is to take the *tranvía* (trolley) tour that leaves three or four times a day from the main plaza; check with one of the tourist information offices for the schedule. The cost is $7 for a 45-minute tour.

Baluarte de la Soledad   This bastion next to the sea gate houses Maya stelae recovered from around the state. Many are badly worn, but the line drawings beside the stones allow you to appreciate their former design.

Calle 57 and Calle 8, opposite Plaza Principal. No phone. Admission $2.50. Tues–Sat 9am–8pm; Sun 9am–1pm.

Baluarte de San Carlos/Museo de la Ciudad   The city museum deals primarily with the design and construction of the fortifications. A model of the city shows how it looked in its glory days and provides a good overview for touring within the city walls. There are several excellent ship models as well. All text is in Spanish.

Circuito Baluartes and Av. Justo Sierra. No phone. Admission $2.50. Tues–Sat 9am–8pm; Sun 9am–1pm.

Baluarte de Santiago   The Jardín Botánico Xmuch'haltun is a jumble of exotic and common plants within the stone walls of this bastion. More than 250 species of plants and trees share a small courtyard.

Av. 16 de Septiembre and Calle 49. No phone. Free admission. Mon–Fri 9am–8pm; Sat–Sun 9am–1pm.

Casa no. 6 Centro Cultural   In this remodeled colonial house, you'll see some rooms decorated with period furniture and accessories. The patio of mixtilinear arches supported by simple Doric columns is striking. Exhibited in the patio are photos of examples of the city's fine colonial architecture. Several of the photographed buildings have recently been renovated. There is also a small bookstore in back, as well as temporary exhibition space.

Calle 57 no. 6. No phone. Free admission. Daily 9am–9pm.

Puerta de Tierra   At the Land Gate is a small museum displaying portraits of pirates and the city founders. The 1732 French 5-ton cannon in the entryway was found in 1990. On Tuesday, Friday, and Saturday at 8pm, there's a light-and-sound show, as long as 15 or more people have bought tickets. Some shows are in English and some are in Spanish; it depends on the audience. The show is amusing.

Calle 59 at Circuito Baluartes/Av. Gobernadores. No phone. Free admission to museum. Show $2.50 adults, 50¢ children under 11. Daily 9am–9pm.

OUTSIDE THE WALLS: SCENIC VISTAS

Fuerte–Museo San José el Alto   This fort is higher and has a more sweeping view of Campeche and the coast than Fuerte San Miguel, but it holds only a small exhibit of 16th- and 17th-century weapons and scale miniatures of sailing vessels. This is a nice place for a picnic. Take a cab. On the way, you will pass by an impressive statue of Juárez.

Av. Morazán s/n. No phone. Admission $2.50. Tues–Sun 8am–8pm.

Fuerte–Museo San Miguel ★★   For a good view of the city and a great little museum, take a cab ($2–$3) up to Fuerte–Museo San Miguel. San Miguel is a small fort with a moat and a drawbridge. Built in 1771, it was the most important of the city's defenses. General Santa Anna captured it when he attacked the city in 1842. The museum of the Maya world was renovated in 2000 and is well worth seeing. It groups the artifacts around central issues in Maya culture. In a room devoted to Maya concepts of the afterlife, there's a great burial scene of "Jaguar Claw" with jade masks and jewelry from Maya tombs at Calakmul. Another room explains Maya cosmology, another depicts war, and another explains the gods. There are also exhibits on the history of the fort.

Ruta Escénica s/n. No phone. Admission $2.50. Tues–Sat 9am–8pm; Sun 8am–noon.

SHOPPING

Casa de Artesanías Tukulná   This store run by DIF (a government family-assistance agency) occupies a restored mansion. There is an elaborate display of regional arts and crafts in the back. The wares in the showrooms represent everything that is produced in the state. There are quality textiles, clothing, and locally made furniture. Open Monday to Saturday from 9am to 8pm. Calle 10 no. 333 (between calles 59 and 61). © 981/816-9088.

WHERE TO STAY

Rates quoted include the 17% tax. While I was here, I heard that Starwood Hotels was building a small luxury hotel in the downtown area (a first for Campeche), but it wasn't yet open, and I was unable to see what was being done.

Hotel Baluartes ⭐   Between the Sea Gate and the Gulf of Mexico, this was the city's original luxury hotel. All the rooms have been completely refurbished with new tile floors, new furniture, and new mattresses—one king-size bed or two doubles. They are cheerful and have good lighting but the bathrooms are small. Half of the rooms have a Gulf view, and half look toward the city.

Av. 16 de Septiembre no. 128, 24000 Campeche, Camp. © 981/816-3911. Fax 981/816-2410. baluarte@ campeche.sureste.com. 102 units. $82 double; $115 suite. AE, MC, V. Free guarded parking. **Amenities:** Restaurant; bar; large pool; travel agency, car rental; room service until 11pm; laundry service. *In room:* A/C, TV, hair dryer, safe.

Hotel Colonial *Moments*   What, you may ask, in a cheap hotel could possibly qualify for a Frommer's Mexican Moment? Well, first of all is the fact that the hotel hasn't changed in 50 years; it exudes an air of the past long since disappeared with the coming of globalization. The rooms have the original tiles—once made in Mérida, but alas, no longer—beautiful things with lovely colors in swirls and geometrics; each room has a different pattern. And then there's the plumbing, which, in my room was so bodacious in design and execution that to hide it within the walls would have been Philistinism. Remarkable, too, are the bathroom fixtures, the four-color paint job, and the '40s-style furniture. Sure, you have to make sacrifices for such character—the rooms and bathrooms are small, and the mattresses aren't the best—but even character aside, this hotel is cleaner and more cheerful than any in its class.

Calle 14 no. 122, 24000 Campeche, Camp. © 981/816-2222. 30 units. $22 double; $30 double with A/C. No credit cards.

Hotel Del Mar ⭐   Rooms in this four-story hotel are large, bright, and comfortably furnished. All have balconies that face the Gulf of Mexico. The beds (two doubles or one king-size) are comfortable. The Del Mar is on the main oceanfront boulevard, between the coast and the city walls. It offers many more services than the Baluartes (see above), but it costs considerably more. You can make a reservation here to stay at the Chicanná ecovillage hotel near Calakmul, or you can buy a package that includes guide and transportation. The hotel also offers a tour to Edzná.

Av. Ruiz Cortines 51, 24000 Campeche, Camp. © 981/811-9192 or -9193. Fax 981/811-1618. www.delmarhotel. com.mx. 145 units. $125 double; $140 executive level double. AE, MC, V. Free parking. **Amenities:** 2 restaurants; bar; large pool; gym w/sauna; children's center; tour desk; car rental; business center; room service until 10pm; babysitting; laundry service; executive level. *In room:* A/C, TV.

Hotel Francis Drake ⭐ *(Value)* A new three-story hotel in the *centro histórico* (historical district) with comfortable, attractive rooms at good prices. Rooms are midsize and come with tile floors and one king-size bed, two doubles, or two twins. They could use more light. The bathrooms are midsize with large showers. Suites are larger and better furnished.

Calle 12 no. 206 (between calles 63 and 65), 24000 Campeche, Camp. ℂ 981/811-5626 or -5627. www.hotelfrancis drake.com 24 units. $60 double; $75 junior suite; $85 suite. AE, MC, V. Limited free parking. **Amenities:** Restaurant; tour info; rental car; room service until midnight; laundry service. *In room:* A/C, TV, minibar, hair dryer on request.

WHERE TO EAT

Campeche is a fishing town, so seafood predominates. The outstanding restaurant is La Pigua, where I would eat all my afternoon meals. For breakfast, I like one of the traditional eateries such as **La Parroquia.** For a light supper, either get some *antojitos* (small dishes) in the old *barrio* of San Francisco, or have supper above the main plaza at **La Casa Vieja.** If you want a steak, your best bet is **Cactus.**

MODERATE

Cactus STEAKS/MEXICAN If seafood isn't to your taste, try this steakhouse; it's a favorite with the locals. The rib-eyes are good, as is everything but the *arrachera,* which is the same cut of meat used for fajitas and is very tough.

Av. Malecón Justo Sierra. ℂ 981/811-1453. Main courses $9–$15. No credit cards. Daily 7am–2am.

Casa Vieja MEXICAN/INTERNATIONAL I'm afraid that Casa Vieja has gotten old. There's been a drop in effort here, but it still has the prettiest dining space in the city—an upstairs arcade overlooking the main square. Your best option is to order something simple, and it just might be your luck that changes have been made in the kitchen.

Calle 10 no. 319. ℂ 981/811-1311. Reservations not accepted. Main courses $6–$16. No credit cards. Tues–Sun 9am–2am; Mon 5:30pm–2am.

La Pigua ⭐⭐⭐ SEAFOOD The dining area is an air-conditioned version of a traditional Yucatecan cabin, but with walls of glass looking out on green vegetation. There are not many tables, so by all means, make a reservation. Spanish nautical terms pepper the large menu as the headings for different courses. Sure to be on the menu is fish stuffed with shellfish, which I wholeheartedly recommend. If you're lucky, you might find pompano in a green herb sauce seasoned with a peppery herb known as *hierba santa.* Other dishes that are sure to please are coconut-battered shrimp with applesauce and chiles rellenos with shark. Service is excellent, and the accommodating owner can have your favorite seafood prepared in any style you want.

Av. Miguel Alemán no. 179A. ℂ 981/811-3365. Reservations recommended. Main courses $9–$17. AE, MC, V. Daily noon–6pm. From Plaza Principal, walk north on Calle 8 for 3 blocks. Cross Av. Circuito by the botanical garden where Calle 8 becomes Miguel Alemán. The restaurant is 1½ blocks farther up, on the right side of the street.

INEXPENSIVE

Cenaduría Portales ⭐ ANTOJITOS This is the most traditional of supper places for Campechanos. It's a small restaurant under the stone arches that face the Plaza San Francisco in the *barrio* (neighborhood) of San Francisco. This is the oldest part of town, but it lies outside the walls just to the north. Don't leave without ordering the *horchata* (a sweet drink milky white and made of a variety of things, in this case coconut). For food, try the turkey soup, which is wonderful, and the *sincronizadas* (tostadas) and *panuchos.*

Calle 10 no. 86, Portales San Francisco. (*C*) 981/811-1491. Reservations not accepted. *Antojitos* 40¢–$1.50. No credit cards. Daily 6pm–midnight.

La Parroquia MEXICAN   This local hangout offers good, inexpensive fare. Best for breakfasts and the afternoon *comida corrida*. Selections on the *comida corrida* might include pot roast, meatballs, pork, or fish, with rice or squash, beans, tortillas, and fresh-fruit-flavored water.

Calle 55 no. 9. (*C*) 981/816-8086. Breakfast $3–$4; main courses $3–$10; *comida corrida* (served 1–4pm) $3–$4. No credit cards. Daily 24 hr.

4 The Ruins of Chichén Itzá ★★★

179km (112 miles) W of Cancún; 120km (75 miles) E of Mérida

The fabled pyramids and temples of Chichén Itzá (no, it doesn't rhyme with "chicken pizza"; the accents are on the last syllables: chee-*chen* eet-*zah*) are the Yucatán's best-known ancient monuments. The ruins are plenty hyped, but Chichén is truly worth seeing. Walking among these stone platforms, pyramids, and ball courts gives you an appreciation for this ancient civilization that books cannot convey. The city is built on a scale that evokes a sense of wonder: To fill the plazas during one of the mass rituals that occurred here a millennium ago would have required an enormous number of celebrants. Even today, with the mass flow of tourists through these plazas, the ruins feel empty.

When visiting this old city, remember that much of what is said about the Maya (especially by tour guides, who speak in tones of utter certainty) is merely educated guessing—or just plain guessing. Itzáes established this post-Classic Maya city perhaps sometime during the 9th century A.D. Linda Schele and David Freidel, in *A Forest of Kings* (Morrow, 1990), have cast doubt on the legend of its founding. It says that the Toltec, led by Kukulkán (Quetzalcoatl), came here from the Toltec capital of Tula, in north-central Mexico. Along with Putún Maya coastal traders, they built a magnificent metropolis that combined the Maya Puuc style with Toltec motifs (the feathered serpent, warriors, eagles, and jaguars). Not so, say Schele and Freidel. According to them, readings of Chichén's bas-reliefs and hieroglyphs fail to support that legend and, instead, show that Chichén Itzá was a continuous Maya site influenced by association with the Toltec but not by an invasion. Not all scholars embrace this thinking, so the idea of a Toltec invasion still holds sway.

Though it's possible to make a round-trip from Mérida to Chichén Itzá in a day, it will be a long, tiring, very rushed day. Try to spend at least a night at Chichén Itzá (you will already have paid for the sound-and-light show) or the nearby town of Valladolid. Then you can see the ruins early the next morning when it is cool and before the tour buses arrive.

ESSENTIALS

GETTING THERE & DEPARTING   By Plane   Travel agents in the United States, Cancún, and Cozumel can arrange day trips from Cancún and Cozumel.

By Car   Chichén Itzá is on old Highway 180 between Mérida and Cancún. The fastest way to get there from either city is to take the *autopista* (or *cuota*). The toll is $8 from Mérida, $20 from Cancún. Once you have exited the *autopista,* you will turn onto the road leading to the village of Pisté. After you enter the village, you'll come to Highway 180, where you turn left. Signs point the way. Chichén is 1½ hours from Mérida and 2½ hours from Cancún.

Chichén Itzá Ruins

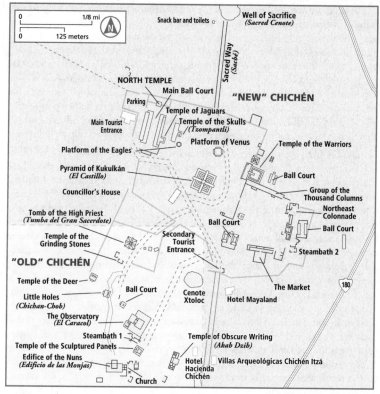

The village of **Pisté**, where most hotels and restaurants are located, is about 2.5km (1½ miles) from the ruins of Chichén Itzá. The following places are labeled on the map:

Snack bar and toilets; Well of Sacrifice (*Sacred Cenote*); Sacred Way (*Sacbé*); NORTH TEMPLE; Main Ball Court; "NEW" CHICHÉN; Parking; Temple of Jaguars; Main Tourist Entrance; Temple of the Skulls (*Tzompantli*); Temple of the Warriors; Platform of the Eagles; Platform of Venus; Pyramid of Kukulkán (*El Castillo*); Ball Court; Councillor's House; Group of the Thousand Columns; Tomb of the High Priest (*Tumba del Gran Sacerdote*); Northeast Colonnade; Temple of the Grinding Stones; Secondary Tourist Entrance; Ball Court; Ball Court; "OLD" CHICHÉN; Steambath 2; Temple of the Deer; The Market; Little Holes (*Chichan-Chob*); Ball Court; Cenote Xtoloc; Hotel Mayaland; The Observatory (*El Caracol*); Steambath 1; Temple of Obscure Writing (*Akab Dzib*); Temple of the Sculptured Panels; Edifice of the Nuns (*Edificio de las Monjas*); Hotel Hacienda Chichén; Villas Arqueológicas Chichén Itzá; Church

By Bus From Mérida, there are three first-class ADO buses per day, and a couple that go to Valladolid stop here. Also, there are several second-class buses per day. If you want to take a day trip from Mérida, go with a tour company. From Cancún, there are any number of tourist buses, and regular first-class buses leave for Chichén every hour.

AREA LAYOUT The village of **Pisté,** where most hotels and restaurants are located, is about 2.5km (1½ miles) from the ruins of Chichén Itzá. Public buses from Mérida, Cancún, Valladolid, and elsewhere discharge passengers here. A few hotels are at the edge of the ruins, and one, the Hotel Dolores Alba (see "Where to Stay," below), is out of town about 2.5km (1½ miles) from the ruins on the road to Valladolid.

EXPLORING THE RUINS

The site occupies 6.5 sq. km (2½ sq. miles), and it takes most of a day to see all the ruins, which are open daily from 8am to 5pm. Service areas are open from 8am to 10pm. Admission is $10, free for children under age 12. A video camera permit costs $4. Parking is extra. *You can use your ticket to reenter on the same day, but you'll have to pay again for an additional day.* The cost of admission includes the **sound-and-light show,** which is worth seeing. The show, held at 7 or 8pm depending on the season, is in Spanish, but headsets are available for rent ($4.50) in several languages.

The large, modern visitor center, at the main entrance where you pay the admission charge, is beside the parking lot and consists of a museum, an auditorium, a restaurant, a bookstore, and bathrooms. You can see the site on your own or with a licensed guide who speaks English or Spanish. Guides usually wait at the entrance and charge around $40 for one to six people. Although the guides frown on it, there's nothing wrong with approaching a group of people who speak the same language and asking if they want to share a guide. Be wary of the history-spouting guides—some of their information is just plain out-of-date—but the architectural details they point out are enlightening. Chichén Itzá has two parts: the northern (new) zone, which shows distinct Toltec influence, and the southern (old) zone, with mostly Puuc architecture.

EL CASTILLO   As you enter from the tourist center, the magnificent 25m (75-ft.) El Castillo pyramid (also called the Pyramid of Kukulkán) will be straight ahead across a large open area. It was built with the Maya calendar in mind. The four stairways leading up to the central platform each have 91 steps, making a total of 364, which when you add the central platform equals the 365 days of the solar year. On either side of each stairway are nine terraces, which makes 18 on each face of the pyramid, equaling the number of months in the Maya solar calendar. On the facing of these terraces are 52 panels (we don't know how they were decorated), which represent the 52-year cycle when both the solar and religious calendars would become realigned. The pyramid's alignment is such that on the **spring** or **fall equinox** (Mar 21 or Sept 21) a curious event occurs. The setting sun casts the shadow of the terraces onto the ramp of the northern stairway. A diamond pattern is formed, suggestive of the geometric designs on some snakes. Slowly it descends into the earth. The effect is more conceptual than visual, and to view it requires being with a large crowd. It's much better to see the ruins on other days when it's less crowded.

El Castillo was built over an earlier structure. A narrow stairway at the western edge of the north staircase leads inside that structure, where there is a sacrificial altar-throne—a red jaguar encrusted with jade. The stairway is open from 11am to 3pm and is cramped, usually crowded, humid, and uncomfortable. A visit early in the day is best. Photos of the jaguar figure are not allowed.

JUEGO DE PELOTA (MAIN BALL COURT)   Northwest of El Castillo is Chichén's main ball court, the largest and best preserved anywhere, and only one of nine ball courts built in this city. Carved on both walls of the ball court are scenes showing Maya figures dressed as ball players and decked out in heavy protective padding. The carved scene also shows a headless player kneeling with blood shooting from his neck; another player holding the head looks on.

Players on two teams tried to knock a hard rubber ball through one of the two stone rings placed high on either wall, using only their elbows, knees, and hips (no hands). According to legend, the losing players paid for defeat with their lives. However, some experts say the victors were the only appropriate sacrifices for the gods. One can only guess what the incentive for winning might be in that case. Either way, the game must have been riveting, heightened by the wonderful acoustics of the ball court.

THE NORTH TEMPLE   Temples are at both ends of the ball court. The North Temple has sculptured pillars and more sculptures inside, as well as badly ruined murals. The acoustics of the ball court are so good that from the North Temple, a person speaking can be heard clearly at the opposite end, about 135m (450 ft.) away.

TEMPLE OF JAGUARS Near the southeastern corner of the main ball court is a small temple with serpent columns and carved panels showing warriors and jaguars. Up the steps and inside the temple, a mural was found that chronicles a battle in a Maya village.

TZOMPANTLI (TEMPLE OF THE SKULLS) To the right of the ball court is the Temple of the Skulls, an obvious borrowing from the post-Classic cities of central Mexico. Notice the rows of skulls carved into the stone platform. When a sacrificial victim's head was cut off, it was impaled on a pole and displayed in a tidy row with others. Also carved into the stone are pictures of eagles tearing hearts from human victims. The word *Tzompantli* is not Mayan but comes from central Mexico. Reconstruction using scattered fragments may add a level to this platform and change the look of this structure by the time you visit.

PLATFORM OF THE EAGLES Next to the Tzompantli, this small platform has reliefs showing eagles and jaguars clutching human hearts in their talons and claws, as well as a human head emerging from the mouth of a serpent.

PLATFORM OF VENUS East of the Tzompantli and north of El Castillo, near the road to the Sacred Cenote, is the Platform of Venus. In Maya and Toltec lore, a feathered monster or a feathered serpent with a human head in its mouth represented Venus. This is also called the tomb of Chaac-Mool because a Chaac-Mool figure was discovered "buried" within the structure.

SACRED CENOTE Follow the dirt road (actually an ancient *sacbé,* or causeway) that heads north from the Platform of Venus; after 5 minutes you'll come to the great natural well that may have given Chichén Itzá (the Well of the Itzáes) its name. This well was used for ceremonial purposes, not for drinking water—according to legend, sacrificial victims were drowned in this pool to honor the rain god Chaac. Anatomical research done early in the 20th century by Ernest A. Hooten showed that bones of both children and adults were found in the well. Judging from Hooten's evidence, they may have been outcasts or diseased or feeble-minded persons.

Edward Thompson, who was the American consul in Mérida and a Harvard professor, purchased the ruins of Chichén early in the 20th century and explored the *cenote* with dredges and divers. His explorations exposed a fortune in gold and jade. Most of the riches wound up in Harvard's Peabody Museum of Archaeology and Ethnology—a matter that continues to disconcert Mexican classicists today. Excavations in the 1960s unearthed more treasure, and studies of the recovered objects detail offerings from throughout the Yucatán and even farther away.

TEMPLO DE LOS GUERREROS (TEMPLE OF THE WARRIORS) Due east of El Castillo is one of the most impressive structures at Chichén: the Temple of the Warriors, named for the carvings of warriors marching along its walls. It's also called the Group of the Thousand Columns for the rows of broken pillars that flank it. During the recent restoration, hundreds more of the columns were rescued from the rubble and put in place, setting off the temple more magnificently than ever. A figure of Chaac-Mool sits at the top of the temple, surrounded by impressive columns carved in relief to look like enormous feathered serpents. South of the temple was a square building that archaeologists called **El Mercado (The Market);** a colonnade surrounds its central court. Beyond the temple and the market in the jungle are mounds of rubble, parts of which are being reconstructed.

The main Mérida-Cancún highway once ran straight through the ruins of Chichén, and though it has been diverted, you can still see the great swath it cut. South and west of the old highway's path are more impressive ruined buildings.

TUMBA DEL GRAN SACERDOTE (TOMB OF THE HIGH PRIEST)   Past the refreshment stand to the right of the path is the Tomb of the High Priest, which stood atop a natural limestone cave in which skeletons and offerings were found, giving the temple its name.

CASA DE LOS METATES (TEMPLE OF THE GRINDING STONES)   This building, the next one on your right, is named after the concave corn-grinding stones the Maya used.

TEMPLOD DEL VENADO (TEMPLE OF THE DEER)   Past Casa de los Metates is this fairly tall though ruined building. The relief of a stag that gave the temple its name is long gone.

CHICHAN-CHOB (LITTLE HOLES)   This next temple has a roof comb with little holes, three masks of the rain god Chaac, three rooms, and a good view of the surrounding structures. It's one of the oldest buildings at Chichén, built in the Puuc style during the late Classic period.

EL CARACOL (OBSERVATORY)   Construction of the Observatory, a complex building with a circular tower, was carried out over centuries; the additions and modifications reflected the Maya's careful observation of celestial movements and their need for increasingly exact measurements. Through slits in the tower's walls, astronomers could observe the cardinal directions and the approach of the all-important spring and autumn equinoxes, as well as the summer solstice. The temple's name, which means "snail," comes from a spiral staircase within the structure.

On the east side of El Caracol, a path leads north into the bush to the **Cenote Xtoloc,** a natural limestone well that provided the city's daily water supply. If you see any lizards sunning there, they may well be *xtoloc,* the species for which this *cenote* is named.

TEMPLO DE LOS TABLEROS (TEMPLE OF PANELS)   Just south of El Caracol are the ruins of *temazcalli* (a steam bath) and the Temple of Panels, named for the carved panels on top. This temple was once covered by a much larger structure, only traces of which remain.

EDIFICIO DE LAS MONJAS (EDIFICE OF THE NUNS)   If you've visited the Puuc sites of Kabah, Sayil, Labná, or Xlapak, the enormous nunnery here will remind you of the palaces at those sites. Built in the Late Classic period, the new edifice was constructed over an older one. Suspecting that this was so, Le Plongeon, an archaeologist working early in the 20th century, put dynamite between the two and blew away part of the exterior, revealing the older structures within. You can still see the results of Le Plongeon's indelicate exploratory methods.

On the east side of the Edifice of the Nuns is **Anexo Este (annex)** constructed in highly ornate Chenes style with Chaac masks and serpents.

LA IGLESIA (THE CHURCH)   Next to the annex is one of the oldest buildings at Chichén, the Church. Masks of Chaac decorate two upper stories. Look closely, and you'll see other pagan symbols among the crowd of Chaacs: an armadillo, a crab, a snail, and a tortoise. These represent the Maya gods, called *bacah,* whose job it was to hold up the sky.

AKAB DZIB (TEMPLE OF OBSCURE WRITING)   Beloved of travel writers, this temple lies east of the Edifice of the Nuns. Above a door in one of the rooms are some Maya glyphs, which gave the temple its name because the writings have yet to be deciphered. In other rooms, traces of red handprints are still visible. Reconstructed and expanded over the centuries, Akab Dzib may be the oldest building at Chichén.

CHICHEN VIEJO (OLD CHICHEN)   For a look at more of Chichén's oldest buildings, constructed well before the time of Toltec influence, follow signs from the Edifice of the Nuns southwest into the bush to Old Chichén, about 1km (½ mile) away. Be prepared for this trek with long trousers, insect repellent, and a local guide. The attractions here are the **Templo de los Inscripciones Iniciales (Temple of the First Inscriptions),** with the oldest inscriptions discovered at Chichén, and the restored **Templo de los Dinteles (Temple of the Lintels),** a fine Puuc building.

WHERE TO STAY

The expensive hotels in Chichén all occupy beautiful grounds, are close to the ruins, and serve good food. All have toll-free reservations numbers. Some of these hotels do a lot of business with tour operators—they can be empty one day and full the next. The inexpensive hotels are in the village of Pisté, 2.5km (1½ miles) away. There is little to do in Pisté at night. Another option is to go on to the colonial town of Valladolid, 30 minutes away, but you'll want reservations because a lot of tour-bus companies use the hotels there (see below).

EXPENSIVE

Hacienda Chichén 🐝🐝   This is the smallest and most private of the hotels at the ruins. It is also the quietest. This former hacienda served as the headquarters for the Carnegie Institute's excavations in 1923. Several bungalows were built to house the staff; these have been modernized and are now the guest rooms. Each is simply and comfortably furnished (with a dehumidifier and ceiling fan in addition to air-conditioning) and is a short distance from the others. Each bungalow has a private porch from which you can enjoy the beautiful grounds. Standard rooms come with two twin or two double beds. Suites are bigger and have larger bathrooms and double or queen-size beds. The main building belonged to the hacienda; it houses the terrace restaurant, with dining outside by the pool or inside.

Zona Arqueológica, 97751 Chichén Itzá, Yuc. ✆/fax 985/851-0045. www.yucatanadventure.com.mx. (Reservations: Casa del Balam, Calle 60 no. 488, 97000 Mérida, Yuc. ✆ 800/624-8451 in the U.S., or 999/924-2150. Fax 999/924-5011.) 28 units. $150 double; $165 suite. AE, DC, MC, V. Free guarded parking. **Amenities:** Restaurant; bar; large pool. *In room:* A/C, minibar, hair dryer.

Hotel Mayaland 🐝🐝   The main doorway frames El Caracol (the observatory) in a stunning view—that's how close this hotel is to the ruins. The long main building is three stories high. The rooms are large, with comfortable beds and large tiled bathrooms. Bungalows, scattered about the rest of the grounds, are built native style, with thatched roofs and stucco walls; they're a good deal larger than the rooms. The grounds are gorgeous, with huge trees and lush foliage—the hotel has had 75 years to get them in shape. The suites are on the top floor of the main building and come with terraces and two-person Jacuzzis. The "lodge section" consists of two groupings of larger bungalows in the back of the property surrounded by a lovely garden and pool area—they are separate from the main hotel and offer greater privacy and quiet.

Zona Arqueológica, 97751 Chichén Itzá, Yuc. ✆ 985/851-0127. (Reservations: Mayaland Resorts, Robalo 30 SM3, 77500 Cancún, Q. Roo. ✆ 800/235-4079 in the U.S., or 998/887-0870. Fax 998/884-4510.) www.mayaland.com.

97 units. High season $190 double, $240–$290 bungalow, $290–$350 suite, $268–$330 lodge section; low season $88 double, $144–$196 bungalow, $196–$235 suite, $144–$264 lodge section. AE, MC, V. Free guarded parking. **Amenities:** 2 restaurants; bar; 3 pools; tour desk; room service until 10pm; babysitting; laundry service. *In room:* A/C, TV, minibar, coffeemaker.

Villas Arqueológicas Chichén Itzá 🛫

This hotel is built around a courtyard and a pool. Two massive royal poinciana trees tower above the grounds, and bougainvillea drapes the walls. This chain has similar hotels at Cobá and Uxmal, and is connected with Club Med. The rooms are modern and small but comfortable, unless you're 1.9m (6 ft., 2 in.) or taller—each bed is in a niche, with walls at the head and foot. Most rooms have one double bed and an oversize single bed. You can also book a half- or full-board plan.

Zona Arqueológica, 97751 Chichén Itzá, Yuc. ℂ **800/258-2633** in the U.S., or 985/851-0034 or 985/856-2830. 40 units. $90 double. Rates include continental breakfast. Half-board (breakfast plus lunch or dinner) $15 per person; full board (3 meals) $29 per person. AE, MC, V. Free parking. **Amenities:** Restaurant; bar; large pool; tennis court; tour desk. *In room:* A/C.

MODERATE

Hotel Dolores Alba 🛫 *Value*

This place is of the motel variety, perfect if you come by car. It is a bargain for what you get: two pools (one really special), *palapas* and hammocks around the place, and large, comfortable rooms. The restaurant serves good meals at moderate prices. The hotel provides free transportation to the ruins and the Caves of Balankanché during visiting hours, though you will have to take a taxi back. The hotel is on the highway 2.5km (1½ miles) east of the ruins (toward Valladolid). You can make reservations here for the Dolores Alba in Mérida.

Carretera Mérida–Valladolid Km 122, Yuc. ℂ **985/858-1555.** (Reservations: Hotel Dolores Alba, Calle 63 no. 464, 97000 Mérida, Yuc. ℂ **999/928-5650.** Fax 999/928-3163.) www.doloresalba.com. 40 units. $50 double. No credit cards. Free parking. **Amenities:** Restaurant; bar; 2 pools; room service until midnight; laundry service. *In room:* A/C.

Pirámide Inn

Less than 1.5km (1 mile) from the ruins, at the edge of Pisté, this hotel has simple rooms. Most hold two double beds, some three twins or one king-size. The bathrooms are nice, with counter space and tub/shower combinations. The air-conditioning is quiet and effective. Hot water comes on between 5 and 10am and 5 and 10pm. A well-kept pool and a *temazcal* (a native form of steam bath) occupy a small part of the landscaped grounds, which include the remains of a Maya wall. Try to get a room in the back—the hotel is right on the highway. There's a discount for those paying in cash.

Calle 15 no. 30, 97751 Pisté, Yuc. ℂ **985/851-0115.** Fax 985/851-0114. www.piramideinn.com. 44 units. $55 double. MC, V. **Amenities:** Restaurant; bar; midsize pool; steam room; room service. *In room:* A/C.

WHERE TO DINE

The restaurant in the visitor center at the ruins and the hotel restaurants in Pisté serve reasonably priced meals. Many places cater to large groups, which descend on them after 1pm.

Cafetería Ruinas INTERNATIONAL

Though it has the monopoly on food at the ruins, this cafeteria does a good job with such basic meals as enchiladas, pizza, and baked chicken. It even offers some Yucatecan dishes. Eggs and burgers are cooked to order, and the coffee is good. You can also get fruit smoothies and vegetarian dishes.

In the Chichén Itzá visitor center. ℂ **985/851-0111.** Breakfast $5; sandwiches $6–$7; main courses $5–$10. AE, MC, V. Daily 9am–6pm.

Fiesta YUCATECAN/MEXICAN   Though relatively expensive, the food here is dependable and good. You can dine inside or out, but make a point of going for supper or early lunch when the tour buses are gone. There is a full buffet, and the a la carte menu has many Yucatecan classics. Fiesta is on the west end of town.

Carretera Mérida–Valladolid, Pisté. ✆ **985/851-0038**. Main courses $4–$6; buffet (12:30–5pm) $8.50. No credit cards. Daily 7am–9pm.

Restaurant Bar "Poxil" YUCATECAN   A *poxil* is a Maya fruit somewhat akin to a *guanábana*. Although this place doesn't serve them, what is on the simple menu is good, though not gourmet, and the price is right. You will find the Poxil near the west entrance to town on the south side of the street.

Calle 15 no. 52, Pisté. ✆ **985/851-0123**. Main courses $4–$5; breakfast $3. No credit cards. Daily 8am–9pm.

A SIDE TRIP TO THE GRUTA (CAVE) DE BALANKANCHE

The Gruta de Balankanché is 5.5km (3½ miles) from Chichén Itzá on the road to Valladolid and Cancún. Taxis will make the trip and wait. The entire excursion takes about a half-hour, but the walk inside is hot and humid. Of the cave tours in the Yucatán, this is the tamest, having good footing and requiring the least amount of walking and climbing. It includes a cheesy and uninformative recorded tour. The highlight is a round chamber with a central column that gives the impression of being a large tree. You come up the same way you go down. The cave became a hideaway during the War of the Castes. You can still see traces of carving and incense burning, as well as an underground stream that served as the sanctuary's water supply. Outside, take time to meander through the botanical gardens, where most of the plants and trees are labeled with their common and scientific names.

The caves are open daily. Admission is $5, free for children 6 to 12. Children under age 6 are not admitted. Use of a video camera costs $4 (free if you've already bought a video permit in Chichén the same day). Tours in English are at 11am and 1 and 3pm, and, in Spanish, at 9am, noon, and 2 and 4pm. Double-check these hours at the main entrance to the Chichén ruins.

5 Valladolid

40km (25 miles) E of Chichén Itzá; 160km (100 miles) SW of Cancún

Valladolid (pronounced "bah-yah-doh-*leed*") is a small, pleasant colonial city halfway between Mérida and Cancún. The people are friendly and informal, and, except for the heat, life is easy. The city's economy is based on commerce and small-scale manufacturing. There is a large *cenote* in the center of town and a couple more 4km (3 miles) down the road to Chichén. A restoration project has reconstructed several rows of colonial housing in the neighborhood surrounding the convent of San Bernardino de Siena. Valladolid can also be the starting point for several interesting side trips (see below).

ESSENTIALS

GETTING THERE & DEPARTING   By Car   From Mérida or Cancún, you have two choices: the *cuota* (toll road) or Highway 180. The toll from Cancún is $18, from Mérida $10. The *cuota* passes 2km (1¼ miles) north of the city; the exit is at the crossing of Highway 295 to Tizimín. **Highway 180** takes significantly longer because it passes through a number of villages (with their requisite speed bumps). Both 180 and 295 lead directly to downtown. Leaving is just as easy: from the main square,

Calle 41 turns into 180 east to Cancún; Calle 39 heads to 180 west to Chichén Itzá and Mérida. To take the *cuota* to Mérida or Cancún, take Calle 40 (see "City Layout," below).

By Bus   There are plenty of buses to Mérida or Cancún. There are fewer to Playa and Tulum. To get to Chichén Itzá, you must take a second-class bus, which leaves every hour and sometimes on the half-hour. The recently remodeled bus station is at the corner of calles 39 and 46. Passengers going first-class to Mérida or Cancún are shuttled to a station called Isleta on the *autopista*. Tulum/Playa buses take a different road that passes close to Cobá.

VISITOR INFORMATION   At the small **tourism office** in the Palacio Municipal, you can get a map but little else. It's open daily from 9 to 8pm, Sunday 9am to 1pm.

CITY LAYOUT   Valladolid has the standard layout for towns in the Yucatán: Streets running north-south are even numbers; those running east-west are odd numbers. The main plaza is bordered by Calle 39 on the north, 41 on the south, 40 on the east, and 42 on the west. The plaza is named Parque Francisco Cantón Rosado, but everyone calls it **El Centro.** Taxis are easy to come by.

EXPLORING VALLADOLID

Before it became Valladolid, the city was a Maya settlement called Zací (zah-*kee*), which means "white hawk." There are two *cenotes* in the area. **Cenote Zací** is at the intersection of calles 39 and 36, in a small park in the middle of town. A trail leads down close to the water. Caves, stalactites, and hanging vines contribute to a wild, prehistoric atmosphere. The park has a large *palapa* restaurant. Admission is $2.

Ten blocks to the southwest of the main square is the Franciscan monastery of **San Bernardino de Siena** (1552). Most of the compound was built in the early 1600s; a large underground river is believed to pass under the convent and surrounding neighborhood, which is called Barrio Sisal. "Sisal" is, in this case, a corruption of the Mayan phrase *sis-ha,* meaning "cold water." The *barrio* has undergone extensive restoration and is a delight to behold.

Valladolid's main square is the social center of town and a thriving market for Yucatecan dresses. On its south side is the principal church, **La Parroquia de San Servacio.** Vallesoletanos, as the locals call themselves, believe that almost all cathedrals in Mexico point east, and they cherish a local legend to explain why theirs points north—but don't believe a word of it. On the east side of the plaza is the municipal building, **El Ayuntamiento.** Get a look at the highly dramatic paintings outlining the history of the peninsula. My personal favorite depicts a horrified Maya priest foreseeing the arrival of Spanish galleons. On Sunday nights, beneath the stone arches of the Ayuntamiento, the municipal band plays *jaranas* and other traditional music of the region.

SHOPPING

The **Mercado de Artesanías de Valladolid (crafts market),** at the corner of calles 39 and 44, gives you a good idea of the local merchandise. Perhaps the main handicraft of the town is embroidered Maya dresses, which can be purchased here or from women around the main square. The area around Valladolid is cattle country; locally made leather goods such as *huaraches* (sandals) and bags are inexpensive and plentiful. On the main plaza is a small shop above the municipal bazaar. A good sandal maker has a shop called **Elios,** Calle 37 no. 202, between calles 42 and 44 (no phone). An Indian named **Juan Mac** makes *alpargatas,* the traditional sandals of the Maya, in his

---

Sweet as Honey

Valladolid also produces a highly prized honey made from the *tzi-tzi-ché* flower. You can find it and other goods at the **town market,** Calle 32 between calles 35 and 37. The best time to see the market is Sunday morning.

---

shop on Calle 39, near the intersection with Calle 38, 1 block from the main plaza, before the store Cielito Lindo. Most of his output is for locals, but he's happy to knock out a pair for visitors.

WHERE TO STAY

Aside from the hotels listed below, your next best bet is **Hotel Zací,** Calle 44 between calles 37 and 39 (✆ **985/856-2167**); doubles are $34 with air-conditioning, and $30 without. Another option is the **Ecotel Quinta Regia** (✆ **985/856-3472;** www.ecotelquintaregia.com.mx) a few blocks farther from the main square on Calle 48 between calles 27 and 29. Doubles run $65; suites start at $100. The hotel is comfortable but with a phony Mexican decor that would be more appropriate in some place like Tijuana.

Hotel El Mesón del Marqués ✪   This was originally a small colonial hotel that has grown large and modern. The first courtyard surrounds a fountain and abounds with hanging plants and bougainvillea. This was the original house, now occupied mostly by the restaurant (see "Where to Dine," below). In back are the new construction and the pool. Rooms are medium to large and are attractive. Most come with two double beds. The hotel is on the north side of El Centro, opposite the church.

Calle 39 no. 203, 97780 Valladolid, Yuc. ✆ **985/856-3042** or 985/856-2073. Fax 985/856-2280. www.meson delmarques.com. 90 units. $45 double; $55 junior suite. AE. Free secure parking. **Amenities:** Restaurant; bar; pool; room service until 11pm; laundry service. *In room:* A/C, TV.

Hotel María de la Luz   The three-story María de la Luz is on the west side of the main square. The guest rooms have tile floors and bathrooms; three have balconies overlooking the main square. The wide interior space holds a restaurant that is comfortable and airy for most of the day—it's popular in the morning for the breakfast buffet.

Calle 42 no. 193, 97780 Valladolid, Yuc. ✆/fax **985/856-2071** or -1181. www.travel-rivieramaya.com/maria delaluz. 70 units. $35 double. MC, V. Free secure parking. **Amenities:** Restaurant; bar; midsize pool; tour desk. *In room:* A/C, TV.

WHERE TO DINE

Valladolid is not a center for haute cuisine, but you can try some of the regional specialties. The lowest prices are in the **Bazar Municipal,** a little arcade of shops beside the Hotel El Mesón del Marqués right on the main square.

Hostería del Marqués MEXICAN/YUCATECAN   This is part of the Hotel El Mesón del Marqués, facing the main square. The patio is calm and cool for most of the day. The extensive menu features local specialties. If you are hungry, try the Yucatecan sampler. Any of the enchiladas are good.

Calle 39 no. 203. ✆ **985/856-2073**. Breakfast $3–$5; main courses $4–$7. AE. Daily 7am–11:30pm.

SIDE TRIPS FROM VALLADOLID
CENOTES DZITNUP & SAMMULA

The **Cenote Dzitnup** (also known as Cenote Xkekén) 🐟, 4km (2½ miles) west of Valladolid off Highway 180, is worth a side trip, especially if you have time for a dip. You can take the bike trail there. Antonio Aguilar, who owns a sporting goods store at Calle 41 no. 225, between calles 48 and 50, rents bikes. Once you get there, you descend a short flight of rather perilous stone steps, and at the bottom, inside a beautiful cavern, is a natural pool of water so clear and blue that it seems plucked from a dream. If you decide to swim, be sure that you don't have creams or other chemicals on your skin—they damage the habitat of the small fish and other organisms living there. Also, no alcohol, food, or smoking is allowed in the cavern. Admission is $2. The *cenote* is open daily from 7am to 7pm. About 90m (300 ft.) down the road on the opposite side is another recently discovered *cenote,* **Sammulá,** where you can also swim. Admission is $2.

EK BALAM: DARK JAGUAR 🐟🐟🐟

About 18km (11 miles) north of Valladolid, off the highway to Río Lagartos, are the spectacular ruins of **Ek Balam,** which, owing to a certain ambiguity in Mayan, means either "dark jaguar" or "star jaguar." Relatively unvisited by tourists, the Ek Balam ruins are about to hit it big. On my last trip a brand new road was built from Highway 295 straight to the ruins. This can mean only one thing: tour buses. See these ruins as soon as possible.

In the last few years a team of archaeologists have been doing extensive excavation and renovation. What they have found has the Mayanist world of scholars all aquiver. Take Calle 40 north out of Valladolid to Highway 295; go 20km (12 miles) to a large marked turnoff. Ek Balam is 13km (8 miles) from the highway; the entrance fee is $3, plus $4 for each video camera. The site is open daily from 8am to 5pm.

Built between 100 B.C. and A.D. 1200, the smaller buildings are architecturally unique—especially the large, perfectly restored **Caracol.** Flanked by two smaller pyramids, the imposing central pyramid is about 160m (520 ft.) long and 60m (200 ft.) wide. At more than 30m (100 ft.) high, it is easily taller than the highest pyramids in Chichén Itzá and Uxmal. On the left side of the main stairway, archaeologists have uncovered a large ceremonial doorway of perfectly preserved stucco work. It is an astonishingly elaborate representation of the gaping mouth of the underworld god. Around it are several beautifully detailed human figures. Excavation inside revealed a long chamber filled with Mayan hieroglyphic writing. From the style, it appears that the scribes probably came from Guatemala. So far this chamber is closed to the public. From this script, an epigrapher, Alfonso Lacadena, has found the name of one of the principal kings of the city—Ukit Kan Le'k. He is still working on deciphering the full meaning of the text. If you climb to the top of the pyramid, in the middle distance you can see untouched ruins looming to the north. To the southeast, you can spot the tallest structures at **Cobá,** 50km (30 miles) away.

Also plainly visible are the **raised causeways** of the Maya—the *sacbé* appear as raised lines in the forest vegetation. More than any of the better-known sites, Ek Balam inspires a sense of mystery and awe at the scale of Maya civilization and the utter ruin to which it came.

RIO LAGARTOS NATURE RESERVE 🐟

Some 80km (50 miles) north of Valladolid (40km/25 miles north of Tizimín) on Highway 295 is Río Lagartos, a 50,000-hectare (120,000-acre) refuge established in

1979 to protect the largest nesting population of flamingos in North America. The nesting area is off limits, but you can see plenty of flamingos as well as many other species of fowl and take an enjoyable boat ride around the estuary here.

To get to Río Lagartos, you pass through Tizimín, which is about 30 minutes away. The best place to stay there is **Hotel 49,** Calle 49 373-A (© **986/863-2136**), by the main square. There is not much to do in Tizimín unless you are there during the first 2 weeks of January, when it holds the largest fair in the Yucatán. The prime fiesta day is January 6.

SEEING THE RIO LAGARTOS REFUGE   Río Lagartos is a small fishing village of around 3,000 people who make their living from the sea and from the occasional tourist who shows up to see the flamingos. Colorfully painted houses face the *malecón* (the oceanfront street), and brightly painted boats dock here and there.

When you drive into town keep going straight until you get to the shore. Look for where Calle 10 intersects with the *malecón;* it's near a modern church. There, in a little kiosk, you'll find the best-trained guides, members of a fishermen's co-op called Sindicato Unico de Lancheros. There you can make arrangements for a 2-hour tour, which will cost $45 to $50 for two to three people. The best time to go is in the early morning, so it's best to overnight here at one of the cheap hotels along the *malecón.* I looked at a few and liked **Posada Lucy** (no phone; $23 for two).

I had a very pleasant ride the next morning, and saw several species of ducks, hawks, cranes, cormorants, and osprey, and, of course, lots of flamingos. The guide also wanted to show me how easy it was to float in some evaporation pools used by the local salt producer at Las Coloradas (a good source of employment for the locals until it was mechanized) and a place where fresh water bubbles out from below the saltwater estuary.

ISLA HOLBOX

A remote island off the farthest eastern point of the Yucatán Peninsula, Holbox (pronounced "hohl-*bosh*") is a half-deserted fishing village, a modest wildlife refuge, and a desert-island getaway for travelers seeking solitude. From Valladolid, take Highway 180 east for about 90km (60 miles) toward Cancún; turn north after Nuevo Xcan at the tiny crossroads of El Ideal. Drive nearly 100km (60 miles) north on a poorly maintained state highway to the tiny port of Chiquilá, where you can park your car in a secure parking lot; walk 180m (600 ft.) to the pier, and haggle over the $20 boat ride 3km (2 miles) to the island. There is a ferry, but it runs only five times per day.

In the late 1840s, Holbox was a refuge for European landowners fleeing Indian mobs during the Caste Wars. Nowadays the village of Holbox is empty when the fishing fleet is out, and only half populated in the best of times. On the beach just beyond the village are a few comfortable *palapa* hotels, which charge $80 to $130 per night and have all the amenities, including a restaurant and a swimming pool. **Villas Delfines** (© **998/884-8606** or 998/874-4014; fax 998/884-6342) is one; **Villas Flamingos** (© **800/538-6802** in the U.S. and Canada) is another. Both of these places offer peace and quiet on a broad, sandy beach. Besides swimming in the Gulf waters, which are a dull green instead of the blue of the Caribbean, you can visit the nearby bird sanctuary that's on the island. Several of the town's residents will be happy to take you on a tour, but this place is more for people who simply want to relax by the seashore.

17

The Copper Canyon

by David Baird

The first time I went to the Copper Canyon I had a vision of the Grand Canyon because I had read many remarks comparing the two. This turned out to be misleading. Comparing the two does neither place justice. The canyons are not alike; they have different topography, geology, climate, flora, and fauna, and a different local culture, too.

If you are interested in viewing a rugged and beautiful land; if you're interested in taking one of the most remarkable train trips in the world; if you're interested in hiking or riding horseback through remote areas to see an astonishing variety of plants and animals; or if you're curious about a land still populated by indigenous people living pretty much the way they have for centuries, the Copper Canyon is the place to go.

Most often, when people say **Copper Canyon,** they are referring to a section of the Sierra Madre of northwestern Mexico,

known as the **Sierra Tarahumara** (after the Indians who live there). The area was formed through violent volcanic uplifting followed by the gradual process of erosion that carved a vast network of canyons into the soft volcanic stone. In geological terms, it's much newer than the Grand Canyon.

Crossing the Sierra Tarahumara is the famed **Chihuahua al Pacífico (Chihuahua to the Pacific)** railway. Acclaimed as an engineering marvel, the 624km (390-mile) railroad has 39 bridges—the highest is more than 300m (1,000 ft.) above the Chinipas River and the longest is about .5km (⅓ mile) long—and 86 tunnels, including one more than 1.5km (1 mile) long. It climbs from **Los Mochis,** at sea level, up nearly 2,425m (8,000 ft.) through some of Mexico's most magnificent scenery—thick pine forests, jagged peaks, and shadowy canyons—before descending to the city of **Chihuahua.**

EXPLORING THE COPPER CANYON

The principal airports for the region are Los Mochis and Chihuahua, the two terminal points of the railroad. This chapter covers these cities and how to get to them.

It's easier now than ever before to get to the region thanks to improved connecting flights out of Chihuahua and Los Mochis. But moving through the canyon still requires planning. Train tickets and hotel rooms are limited, and in high season (Mar–Apr and Oct–Nov) tour companies buy up large blocks of both. You should work your trip around an itinerary, and have train tickets and hotel reservations *in hand* when you arrive in the region. You can make arrangements on your own or go through a travel agent or tour operator. (For tips, see "Choosing a Package or Tour Operator," below.) During the rest of the year it's possible to buy train tickets as you need them and make last-minute reservations or no reservations at all. There is a little risk that you might run into a large group that has taken all the hotel rooms, but

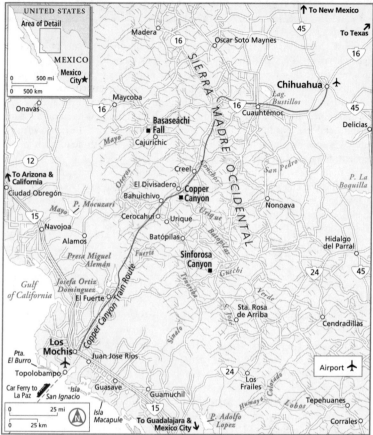

in most locations now, somebody usually has an inexpensive cabin for rent. The most plentiful lodging is to be found in Creel, and it would make a good base of operations for a minimally planned trip.

WHEN TO GO   There are two high seasons for the Sierra: from mid-October to mid-November, and March through April. These months are the most popular (and the most crowded) because of the likelihood of moderate temperatures—but even in these months, temperatures in the bottom of the canyon will be warm. Most canyon visitors stay up in the rim country. To avoid the crowds and get cheaper prices, I suggest **going in August or September** (the rainy season). During that time, barring drought, you'll find occasional afternoon thundershowers (very pretty in the canyon land), green vegetation, flowing water, and comfortable temperatures up along the rim. If you plan to do some serious hikes into the canyon, consider going in the winter, when temperatures will be the least tropical inside the canyons. **Avoid the Sierra from late April through June.** This is the driest part of the year, with chronic water shortages in many of the towns and hotels; the vegetation is brown, and the canyons can be hazy.

1 The Copper Canyon Train & Stops along the Way

TRAIN ESSENTIALS

First-class service between Chihuahua and Los Mochis operates daily in both directions. Departure times are listed below. Second-class trains also run daily. They stop more frequently than the first-class trains and are slower. First-class service has undergone major improvements. The passenger cars have been revamped, with clean bathrooms that work and improved seating and windows. (They already were air-conditioned in summer and heated in winter.) The train now hauls both a dining car and a club car. In addition, it makes fewer stops than before. The new owner, Ferromex, invested heavily in improving the tracks, making delays due to landslides less frequent. It has also spruced up some of the local stations.

The train makes seven stops; the five of principal interest to travelers are described in detail below. The schedule is a word problem that would gratify any high school algebra teacher: two trains depart from opposite ends of the line (Chihuahua and Los Mochis) at the same time (6am) to meet at point x (El Divisadero). So that you don't have to solve for y, I've included the "official" schedule below.

Train Departure Times

From Los Mochis		From Chihuahua	
Los Mochis	6am	Chihuahua	6am
El Fuerte	7:25am	Creel	11:25am
Bahuichivo/Cerocahui	11:15am	El Divisadero	12:45pm
Barrancas	11:25am	Barrancas	1:05pm
El Divisadero	12:35pm	Bahuichivo/Cerocahui	2:30pm
Creel	2:15pm	El Fuerte	6:15pm
Chihuahua (arrives)	7:50pm	Los Mochis (arrives)	7:50pm

Actual times vary; usually they are about an hour later than the official times. The local people at each stop are well attuned to train times, so it's good to ask them. The stops are short except at **El Divisadero,** where you have 20 minutes to get out and walk down the steps to the overlook for a spectacular panorama of the canyon, and perhaps time to buy a trinket or a taco from one of the many vendors.

DELAYS Travelers may have to contend with delays because of landslides, derailments, or maintenance projects. Traveling in this region requires some flexibility and patience. In case of a major service interruption, you can travel on a highway that parallels the railway from Chihuahua as far as Cerocahui, but the final stretch from Cerocahui to El Fuerte is not much of an option because it requires four-wheel-drive.

Tips **In Which Direction Should I Travel?**

For sightseeing, **Los Mochis,** the western terminus, is the better starting place: The most scenic part of the 12- to 15-hour journey comes between **El Fuerte** and **Bahuichivo/Cerocahui,** which you are guaranteed to see in daylight if you come from Los Mochis. The train that starts in Chihuahua often gets to this area in darkness. This chapter lists the stops in order from Los Mochis to Chihuahua.

Tips Choosing a Package or Tour Operator

A number of tour operators and packagers offer trips to the Copper Canyon. You can purchase your package through a travel agency; those that do frequent business with Copper Canyon trips have better knowledge of what's out there. Keep in mind that the travel agent may try to steer you toward one package over another because it pays a higher commission.

The industry breaks down into the following categories:

BUS TOURS Some outfits run buses from El Paso to Chihuahua or Tucson to Los Mochis, then put their customers on the train. The usual length of stay in the Sierra is 2 nights before returning by bus to the U.S. These tours involve a lot of sitting on a bus or train, but they are the least expensive.

TRAIN TOURS **Sierra Madre Express,** P.O. Box 26381, Tucson, AZ 85726 (© **800/666-0346**), runs its own deluxe trains, complete with dining and Pullman cars, through the canyon. The trip takes a week, with 2 nights in the canyon. **Tauck Tours** (© **800/468-2825**) uses this train.

STANDARD PACKAGES This option merely bundles airfare, train tickets, and lodging. Hotels in the canyon send drivers to meet the train, so getting to your hotel is not hard once you're in the canyon. With these tours, you can have more time in the canyon, but once you're there, it's up to you to line up activities.

CUSTOM TOUR OPERATORS These outfits sell fixed package tours through travel agents only because it simplifies the agent's job. If you eliminate the middle person and call any of the outfits directly, you might be able to arrange a custom trip. Travel through these companies generally allows you more time in the canyon and a better experience. Some assemble small groups with a guide; some allow you to travel by yourself and supply you with contacts in different locations. As the number of people visiting the Sierra increases, these companies are taking people deeper into the mountains to get away from the effects of mass tourism. The best of the bunch is **Canyon Travel** (formerly Columbus), 900 Ridge Creek Lane, Bulverde, TX 78163-2872 (© **800/843-1060;** www.canyontravel.com). Canyon Travel is pretty much in a class by itself. It has lined up some beautiful small lodges in the canyons and in El Fuerte and staffed them with talented local guides. It also offers a lot of flexibility, and it responds quickly to problems.

Other operators that provide good service are **The California Native,** 6701 W. 87th Place, Los Angeles, CA 90045 (© **800/926-1140;** www.calnative.com), and **Native Trails,** 613 Queretaro, El Paso, TX 79912-2210 (© **800/884-3107;** www.nativetrails.com).

BUYING A TICKET   The train offers no rail pass; you must buy a ticket for a particular day, point of departure, and destination. This is not usually a problem during the off season. You can buy a ticket for the first leg of your trip when you get to Los Mochis or Chihuahua, and then buy the rest each time you board the train. You're not going to have a guaranteed seat, but there's usually abundant seating during this part of the year. If you have an itinerary, you'll have guaranteed seating throughout the trip. You may not get to choose which seat, but that's a minor issue. Should you deviate from your itinerary, you can buy a new ticket at the local station or aboard the train. The cost of a ticket for the entire trip one-way is $110.

To buy train tickets by themselves, not as part of a package, call a specialized travel agency in Chihuahua or Los Mochis. It's easy; you can order over the phone and pay when you get there. To start out in Chihuahua, contact **Turismo al Mar** (© 614/410-9232 or 614/416-5950; www.copper-canyon.net); from Los Mochis, contact **Viajes Araceli** (© 668/815-5780; fax 668/815-8787; ventasaracely@viajearacely.com) or **Viajes Flamingo** (© 668/812-1613; fax 668/812-0046; www.mexicoscopper canyon.com). Travel agencies outside of Mexico sell tickets only as part of a package that includes transportation to the region and hotel accommodations. A wide variety of packages and custom trips are available. Look into these carefully before you book (see "Choosing a Package or Tour Operator," below).

LODGING   If you spend a night at any spot en route, you'll have roughly 24 hours to explore, unless you're heading back in the direction you came. Drivers from all canyon hotels pick up guests from the train station; if you don't have a reservation, ask a driver about room availability. Standard accommodations in the canyon are getting more expensive, especially in El Divisadero and Cerocahui. In high season, I wouldn't arrive at either place without reservations. Rates for hotels in both of these towns usually include meals. The number of rooms is limited, and with groups of 40 or 50 people going through the Sierra, a hotel can be empty one day and full the next. When hotels are full, you'll notice a decline in service in the dining room, or you'll have to wait in line at the buffet even if you're not part of the group. Overbooking rooms also seems to be a problem with some of the large hotels, though it's not common enough that you should worry about it. In Creel, you find the greatest variety of accommodations and restaurants. This is where most of the economical hotels are.

CLIMATE   Los Mochis and El Fuerte are warm year-round. Chihuahua can be warm in summer, windy at almost any time, and freezing in winter. The canyon rim may experience freezes from November through March; the bottom of the canyon may get cool enough for a sweater. In the other half of the year, it's hot below and cool above.

STOP 1: EL FUERTE ★
El Fuerte is on the coastal plain before the foothills of the Sierra Madre. It has charming cobblestone streets and handsome colonial mansions and is the prettiest town along the train route. At only 80m (260 ft.) above sea level, it is most comfortable in winter. The town owes its origin to silver mining, and its existence in recent times to booming agriculture. From the late 18th century onward, the town has been under

---

Tips   Going Solo: Not a Good Idea

If you're planning to do any hiking in the Copper Canyon, it's a good idea to have company, especially someone who knows the area. Guides tell me that they come across lost hikers all the time. Also, ankles can get sprained, knees can give out—it helps to have someone who knows where to get the nearest horse and such.

Tips Money Changing: Be Prepared

Be sure to start the journey with adequate funds, because exchanging money outside of Creel is almost impossible; even credit cards are only good at the expensive hotels. (I won't use a credit card at some of the hotels listed in this chapter because they use radio communication to the main office to confirm a card—hardly a secure system.)

---

the control of a few families, and to this day, much of the real estate in and about the center of town remains in their hands. The town's plaza is quaint and handsome, with a 19th-century bandstand surrounded by graceful palms. One way to see the town is to take a taxi from Los Mochis and pick up the train the next day. An added advantage to this plan is that it allows you an extra hour in bed. The train station is a few kilometers from town.

EXPLORING THE TOWN   Possible activities include visiting nearby villages, birding, fishing for black bass and trout, and hunting for duck and dove. Hotels can arrange guides and all equipment if notified in advance.

WHERE TO STAY & DINE

Besides the restaurants at the hotels mentioned here, there are inexpensive restaurants on and near the central plaza.

Hotel El Fuerte ⭐   This is a charming inn loaded with character. Rooms have double or king-size beds, tiled bathrooms, and colonial furnishings. The courtyard and common areas are shady and cool. The lodge usually books up with large tour groups for much of the high season, but for the rest of the year is a good option.

Montesclaro 37, 81820 El Fuerte, Sin. ℭ **698/893-0226.** Fax 698/893-1246. www.hotelelfuerte.com.mx. 32 units. $110 double. MC, V. **Amenities:** Restaurant; bar; Jacuzzi; tour info; laundry service. *In room:* A/C, no phone.

Hotel La Choza   Two stories of rooms are arranged around a modern courtyard/parking lot. The upstairs rooms are nicer as they come with a boveda ceiling, but all are comfortable and colorfully decorated and have nice, midsize bathrooms. Most have two double beds.

Cinco de Mayo 101, 81820 El Fuerte, Sin. ℭ **698/893-1274.** hotellachoza@prodigy.net.mx. 24 units. $75–$100 double. MC, V. Free secure parking. **Amenities:** Restaurant; bar/dance club; room service until 10pm. *In room:* A/C, TV, no phone.

Hotel Posada del Hidalgo ⭐⭐   This handsome hotel is one of the Balderrama properties and can be booked through the central reservations office in Los Mochis. It, too, gets several tour groups. The mansion section, with open arcades around a central patio, belonged to silver barons in the 18th century; there's even a steep carriage ramp from its days as a stagecoach stop. There are three courtyards, each in a different style, with bougainvillea and tall palm trees. The guest rooms are nicely finished with lovely tile or hardwood floors, attractive furniture, and good bathrooms. All have two double beds.

Hidalgo 101, 81820 El Fuerte, Sin. ℭ **800/896-8196** in the U.S. (to the Hotel Santa Anita in Los Mochis) or 698/893-1194 in El Fuerte. Fax 698/893-1194. www.mexicoscoppercanyon.com. 58 units. $120 double. AE, DC, DISC, MC, V. **Amenities:** Restaurant; bar; pool; Jacuzzi. *In room:* A/C, no phone.

Río Vista Lodge *Finds* Free-spirited owner Chal Gámez has done it his way in this small hotel on a hill atop the town. The common areas and rooms hold fanciful murals, artifacts of Yaqui and Maya Indians, decorations from northern Mexico, and a few things reminiscent of the Old West. The outdoor dining area is a lovely place to gaze out over the river or watch the swarms of hummingbirds that feast at Chal's feeders. These birds seem little bothered by the proximity of humans—you can even put your hand under the feeder and be fanned by their wings. Meals are simple but good.

Cerro de la Pilas s/n, 81820 El Fuerte, Sin. ℂ/fax **698/893-0413**. 13 units. $55 double. No credit cards. **Amenities:** Restaurant. *In room:* A/C, hair dryer, no phone.

STOP 2: BAHUICHIVO & CEROCAHUI ⭑⭑⭑

This is the first train stop in canyon country. **Bahuichivo** is merely the train depot and didn't exist before the train's construction. The village of **Cerocahui** (elevation 1,670m/5,550 ft.) dates from before the colonial era. It's home to 600 people and is in a valley about 10km (6 miles) from the train stop. The road is unpaved, so the trip takes about 30 minutes. The most dramatic part of the train ride is the section between El Fuerte and Bahuichivo.

EXPLORING CEROCAHUI Built around a sweet-looking mission church, Cerocahui consists of little more than rambling unpaved streets and 100 or so houses. It enjoys a wonderful view of the mountains, but you have to take an excursion to get real canyon vistas. All hotels can arrange horseback rides to the falls and other spots, as well as trips to **Cerro Gallego,** a famous lookout point with a beautiful vista of Urique canyon. It's possible to see the waterfall on arrival, schedule the Gallego trip for the next morning, have lunch, and still make the train, but I like the quiet of Cerocahui and recommend staying here as long as you can, provided you like hiking or horseback riding. There are a number of secluded places, both near and far, to visit. One possible trip is a hike down to the mining town of **Urique** at the bottom of the Urique Canyon (one of several canyons that make up the Copper Canyon), then a car ride back up. There are a few simple, but comfortable hotels where you can stay for between $30 and $40 a night. The nicest is **Hotel Barrancas Urique** (ℂ **635/456-6076**). It can provide you with a guide if you feel like doing some more hiking. The rooms come with fans, but the hotel might install air-conditioning units in a couple of the rooms.

WHERE TO STAY & DINE

Rates for doubles in the two hotels listed below include all meals for two people and transportation to and from the train station. The Paraíso del Oso is less than a kilometer (about a mile) short of the village. The Misión is in Cerocahui proper. In the town, you can find simple lodging for a fraction of the cost of the other places. There are also some cabins for rent up above town. They go for $60 for two people and include transportation from the train station. You can reserve a cabin through Rio Vista Lodge (see above) or by calling ℂ **635/456-5257** and saying you want a cabin in Cerocahui (the staff speaks English).

Hotel Misión Cerocahui ⭑ Established years ago, the Hotel Misión is right on the town's little plaza. Guest rooms have hot water and electricity. The lobby and restaurant area surrounds a large rock fireplace where a local guitarist and singer sometimes entertain in the evenings. The food is usually good, and the ranch-style rooms (with tile floors, wood-burning stoves, and kerosene lanterns) are comfortable. The hotel offers several tours, including rides to Cerro Gallego, Urique, and the local waterfalls. There are also hiking, mountain biking, and horseback riding trips.

Domicilio conocido, Cerocahui. No phone. www.mexicoscoppercanyon.com. (Reservations: Hotel Santa Anita, Apdo. Postal 159, 81200 Los Mochis, Sin. ℭ **800/896-8196** in the U.S.) 38 units. $250 double. Rates include meals. AE, MC, V. **Amenities:** Restaurant; transportation to and from train station.

Paraíso del Oso ⚑ *Moments*   Opened in 1990, Paraíso del Oso sits in a sheltered hollow with a backdrop of impressive stone palisades less than a kilometer (about a half-mile) from the town. Owner Doug Rhodes is an avid horseman and takes guests for rides that can last anywhere from 3 hours to more than a week. Rooms come with two double beds and ranch furniture. They are comfortable, with wood-burning stoves; there's plenty of hot water. Solar-generated electricity fuels such vital services as refrigeration, while lanterns provide light. This and the utter solitude of the area are charming traits that make you feel more in touch with the Sierra than the big canyon hotels along the railroad tracks do. There is a cash bar, a small but good library (with both novels and books on Mexican history), and topographical maps of the area.

Cerocahui. ℭ **800/884-3107** or 915/833-3107 in the U.S., or 614/421-3372 in Chihuahua. Fax 614/421-3372. www. mexicohorse.com. (Reservations: Paraíso del Oso, P.O. Box 31089, El Paso, TX 79931.) 21 units. $155 double. Rates include meals. MC, V. **Amenities:** Bar; transportation to and from train station.

STOPS 3 & 4: BARRANCAS/EL DIVISADERO ⚑⚑

Between Bahuichivo and here, the train stops at San Rafael to change crews. By the time it arrives in this area, it is at the highest part of its journey. Almost all packages include at least a night here for soaking up the great views of the canyons. Two nights would be better if you want to do some hiking or horseback riding.

Barrancas and El Divisadero are less than 3km (2 miles) apart. Coming from Los Mochis, you'll arrive at Barrancas first. At this stop, drivers from the **Posada Barrancas Mirador,** the **Posada Barrancas Rancho,** and the **Mansión Tarahumara** meet passengers. Then the train takes you to El Divisadero (elevation 2,240m/7,400 ft.), where you'll find the **Hotel Cabañas Divisadero-Barrancas,** taco stands (at train time), and the most **spectacular view of the canyon** that you'll get if you are making no overnight stops. The train stops for 20 minutes—time enough to walk down the steps to the lookout to enjoy the view and purchase one or two mementos from the Tarahumara Indians who sell sweet-smelling pine-needle baskets, homemade violins, and wood and cloth dolls. Hotels arrange various excursions, including a visit to a cave-dwelling Tarahumara family, hiking, and horseback riding.

WHERE TO STAY & DINE

Hotel Divisadero-Barrancas ⚑⚑   This location, on the edge of the canyon overlook, provides the most spectacular view of any hotel in the canyon. The restaurant has a large picture window, perfect for hours of sitting and gazing at the canyon. The rooms are in four sections. The newest section (nos. 35–48) is a two-story building perched on the edge of the canyon. These rooms have sliding glass doors that open on to balconies with a view. The bathrooms are midsize and modern. These are also probably the quietest rooms. I also like the original section with rooms 1 through 10. These are made of logs and stones and are more rustic, which for me is a good part of their appeal. They face the canyon.

El Divisadero. ℭ **635/578-3060.** www.hoteldivisadero.com. (Reservations: Av. Mirador 4516, Apdo. Postal 661, Col. Residencial Campestre, 31238 Chihuahua, Chih. ℭ **614/415-1199.** Fax 614/415-6575.) 48 units. High season $210 double; low season $140 double. Rates include meals. AE, MC, V. **Amenities:** Restaurant; bar; tours; transportation to and from train station. *In room:* Coffeemaker.

Hotel Posada Barrancas Mirador ⭐⭐ *Moments*   The Mirador sits on the edge of the canyon 5 minutes up the mountain from its sister hotel, the Rancho (see below). Every room has a dramatic balcony that seems to hang right over the cliff's edge. The views are beautiful. Rooms have attractive decorations and furniture, with bold Mexican color combinations; most hold two double beds. Each room has its own heater. The common areas are also comfortable and attractive.

El Divisadero. © 635/578-3020. www.mexicoscoppercanyon.com. (Reservations: Hotel Santa Anita, Apdo. Postal 159, 81200 Los Mochis, Sin. © 800/896-8196 in the U.S.) 50 units. $250 double. Rates include meals. AE, MC, V. **Amenities:** Restaurant; bar; tour info; transportation to and from train station.

Hotel Posada Barrancas Rancho   The train stops right in front of this inn. Rooms are comfortable, with two double beds and a wood-burning iron stove. Like those in other lodges, meals are a communal affair in the cozy living and restaurant area, and the food is good. You can rent horses or hike to the Tarahumara caves and to the rim of the canyon, where a more expensive sister hotel, the Barrancas Mirador (see above), has a beautiful restaurant and bar with a magnificent view. This hotel sometimes accommodates overbooking at its sister hotel.

El Divisadero. © 635/578-3020. (Reservations: Hotel Santa Anita, Apdo. Postal 159, 81200 Los Mochis, Sin. © 800/896-8196 in the U.S.) 33 units. $220 double. Rates include meals. AE, MC, V. **Amenities:** Restaurant; bar; transportation to and from train station.

Mansión Tarahumara ⭐   The Mansión Tarahumara spreads across a mountainside above the train stop at Posada Barrancas. The setting is lovely. The cabin rooms offer more privacy and space than the hotel rooms, but not direct views of the canyon. Made of stone and wood, each room has a big fireplace, a wall heater, and two double beds. The castlelike structure, which is the first thing that catches the guest's eye, houses the restaurant and bar. It offers lovely views from its big windows and good food from its kitchen.

El Divisadero. © 635/578-3030. (Reservations: Mansión Tarahumara, Calle Juárez 1602-A, Col. Centro, 31000 Chihuahua, Chih. © 614/415-4721. Fax 614/416-5444. www.mansiontarahumara.com.mx. 59 units. $170 double. Rates include meals. MC, V. **Amenities:** Restaurant; bar; heated pool; Jacuzzi; tours; transportation to and from train station.

STOP 5: CREEL ⭐

This rustic logging town with a handful of paved streets offers the most economical lodgings in the canyon. Creel (rhymes with "feel") is also the starting point for some of the best side trips, especially hiking and overnight camping.

ESSENTIALS

GETTING THERE & DEPARTING   By Train   See the chart on p. 684 for "official" arrival and departure times.

By Car   From Chihuahua, follow the signs to La Junta until you see signs for Hermosillo. Follow those signs until you see signs to Creel (left). The trip takes about 4 hours on a paved road.

By Bus   Estrella Blanca (© 635/456-0073), next to the Hotel Korachi, has six trips to Chihuahua per day. The trip takes 4 hours and costs $17. This is a lot cheaper and faster than the train.

ORIENTATION   The train station, around the corner from the Mission Store and the main plaza, is in the heart of the village and within walking distance of all lodgings except the Copper Canyon Sierra Lodge. Look for your hotel's van waiting at the station (unless you're staying at the Casa de Huéspedes Margarita, which is only 2 blocks away). There's one main street, **López Mateos,** and almost everything is within a couple of blocks.

FAST FACTS   The telephone **area code** is **635.** Electricity is available 24 hours daily in all Creel hotels. Creel has one ATM, one bank, and one *casa de cambio.* The best sources of **information** are the Mission Store and the hotels. Several businesses and many of the hotels offer long-distance **telephone** service; look for LARGA DISTANCIA signs or ask at your hotel. Creel sits at an **elevation** of 2,210m (7,300 ft.) and has a **population** of around 6,000. It's the largest town in the canyon area.

EXPLORING CREEL

You'll occasionally see the Tarahumara as you walk around town, but mostly, you'll see rugged logging types and tourists from around the world.

Several stores around Creel sell Tarahumara arts and crafts. The best is **Artesanías Misión (Mission Crafts),** which sells quality merchandise at reasonable prices; all profits go to the Mission Hospital run by Father Verplancken, a Jesuit, and benefit the Tarahumara. Here you'll find dolls, pottery, woven purses and belts, drums, violins (an instrument borrowed from the Spanish), bamboo flutes, bead necklaces, bows and arrows, cassettes of Tarahumara music, woodcarvings, baskets, and heavy wool rugs, as well as an excellent supply of books and maps relating to the Tarahumara and the region. Open daily from 9:30am to 1pm, and Monday through Saturday from 3 to 6pm. It's beside the railroad tracks on the main plaza.

NEARBY EXCURSIONS

Close by are several canyons, waterfalls, a lake, hot springs, Tarahumara villages and cave dwellings, and an old Jesuit mission. Ten kilometers (6 miles) north of town is an ecotourism complex, **San Ignacio de Arareko** (© **635/456-0126**). It has a lake, hiking and biking trails, horses, cabins, and a crafts shop, all run by indigenous peoples of the *ejido* (cooperative)—a change from the *mestizo* population's almost total control of tourism in Mexico. **Batopilas,** an 18th-century silver-mining town at the bottom of the canyon, requires an overnight excursion. You can ask for information about these and other things to do at your hotel.

From Creel, you can drive to **El Divisadero** (see "Stops 3 & 4: Barrancas/El Divisadero," above, for details) on a recently paved road. The trip takes about an hour.

ORGANIZED TOURS   Hotels offer 2- to 10-hour organized tours that cost $15 to $90 per person (four people minimum). The **Hotel Nuevo** and **Casa de Huéspedes Margarita** offer the most economical tours in town but not always the most available. All tour availability depends on whether a group can be assembled; your best chance is at the **Plaza Mexicana** or the **Parador de la Montaña.**

BASASEACHIC FALLS   This is an exhausting day tour to what is billed as the tallest single cascade in North America. The best time to go is during the rainy season, from July to September. The tour costs around $45 per person and takes about 11 hours. Driving time is 4 hours one-way, and the strenuous hike to the bottom and back up takes 3 hours—not a lot of time to be by the falls. Another option is to stay in one of the simple accommodations that have opened near the falls, if you can get transportation back the next day. Ask around Creel.

BATOPILAS   You can make an overnight side trip from Creel to the old silver-mining town of Batopilas, founded in 1708. It's 7 to 9 hours from Creel by town bus, 5 hours by

> **_Tips_ Caution: Don't Be a Dope**
>
> It's no secret that marijuana farmers use clandestine farmlands in the Copper Canyon, and that prominent names in the state are rumored to be linked to their activities. This has never affected any of my trips to the region. If you are hiking the backwoods and happen upon a field of marijuana, simply leave the area.

sport utility vehicle, along a narrow, winding dirt road through some of the most spectacular scenery in the Copper Canyon. In Batopilas, which lies beside a river at the bottom of a deep canyon, the weather is tropical, though it can get cool in the evenings. You can visit a beautiful little church and do several walks, including one to **Misión Satevó,** a ruined mission church that dates from the early 18th century. The place has many colorful little details: The dry-goods store has the original shelving and cash register, cobblestone streets twist past whitewashed homes, miners and ranchers come and go on horseback, and the Tarahumara frequently visit. A considerable number of pigs, dogs, and flocks of goats roam at will—this is, after all, Chihuahua's goat-raising capital.

Getting There   From Creel, take the **bus** from the Restaurant Herradero, López Mateos s/n, three doors past the turnoff to Hotel Plaza Mexicana. It goes to Batopilas on Tuesday, Thursday, and Saturday, leaving Creel at 7am and arriving midafternoon. Tickets are sold at the restaurant. Several Suburban-type **vans** offer transportation. One leaves on Monday, Wednesday, and Friday at 10:30am and arrives midafternoon. Both bus and van return the following day. There are no bathrooms, restaurants, or other conveniences of civilization along the way, but the bus may stop to allow passengers to stretch and find a bush.

Where to Stay & Dine   Batopilas has a few little restaurants and inns. There are no telephones, though, so don't expect to make reservations. One night probably isn't enough for a stay here, since you arrive midafternoon and must leave at 7am or 10:30am the next day.

The staff at the Parador de la Montaña in Creel provides information about vacancies at the basic, comfortable, 10-room **Hotel Mary** (formerly Parador Batopilas). All rooms have private bathrooms and cost around $20 double per night. There are also the rustic **Hotel Batopilas** and **Hotel Las Palmeras,** with five or six rooms each; if all else fails, you can probably find a family willing to let you stay in an extra room.

Restaurants in Batopilas are informal, so bring along some snacks and bottled water to tide you over; snacks are available at the general store. The place to eat in Batopilas is **Doña Mica's,** facing a little plaza tucked behind the main square. Ask anyone for directions (everyone knows her). She serves meals on her front porch surrounded by plants, but it's best to let her know in advance when to expect you. On short notice, she can probably rustle up some scrambled eggs.

WHERE TO STAY

Though a small town, Creel has several places to stay. A lot of these cater to backpackers. It's advisable to make reservations during high season.

Expensive

Best Western The Lodge at Creel   Each of the hotel's cheerfully decorated cabins holds four units, built completely of pine, including the furniture. Most have two double beds, and some have their own porches. Their construction, decor, and layout remind me of old-style motels that you find next to U.S. national parks. The lobby, next to the dining area, has a phone for guests' use and a small gift shop. The hotel offers 3-night backpacking trips to the bottom of the canyon, among other tours, for 4 to 10 people. The on-site restaurant serves all three meals. The van meets all trains.

Av. López Mateos 61, 33200 Creel, Chih. ☎ **888/879-4071** in the U.S., or 635/456-0071. Fax 635/456-0082. www. thelodgeatcreel.com. 30 units. $120 double. AE, MC, V. **Amenities:** Restaurant; bar; room service; laundry service; tours to various sites. *In room:* TV, coffeemaker.

Moderate

Copper Canyon Sierra Lodge ★★ *Finds* About 20 minutes (22km/14 miles) southwest of Creel, the Sierra Lodge has everything you hope for in a mountain lodge—rock walls, beamed ceilings, lantern lights, and wood-burning stoves; in other words, rustic charm and no electricity. Its out-of-town location is a great starting point for self-guided hikes and walks in the mountains to the Cusárare Waterfalls.

Apdo. Postal 3, 33200 Creel, Chih. ☎ **800/776-3942** in the U.S. Fax 635/456-0036 (in Creel). www.sierratrail.com. 18 units. $100 double. Rates include meals. No credit cards.

Inexpensive

Hotel Nuevo The Nuevo has two sections: the older one, across the tracks from the train station and next to the restaurant and variety store, and newer log cabañas in back. Rooms are small to midsize and not as attractive as the higher-priced (and carpeted) cabañas. Half the rooms have TVs. The nice hotel restaurant is open from 8:30am to 8pm, and the small general store carries local crafts as well as basic supplies. Ask at the store about rooms.

Francisco Villa 121, 33200 Creel, Chih. ☎ **635/456-0022.** Fax 635/456-0043. 27 units. $40–$85 double. MC, V. Free parking. **Amenities:** Restaurant; general store. *In room:* Heater or fireplace.

Motel Parador de la Montaña This is the largest hotel in town, located 4 blocks west of the plaza. The comfortable rooms have two double beds, high wood-beamed ceilings, central heating, tiled bathrooms, and thin walls. Guests congregate in the restaurant, bar, and lobby, which has a roaring fireplace. The hotel caters to groups and offers some 10 overland tours, priced from $10 to $60.

Av. López Mateos s/n, 33200 Creel, Chih. ☎ **635/456-0023.** Fax 635/456-0085. (Reservations: Calle Allende 1414, 31300 Chihuahua, Chih. ☎ **614/410-4580.** Fax 635/415-3468.) www.hotelparadorcreel.com. 50 units. $65 double. AE, MC, V. Free secure parking. **Amenities:** Restaurant; bar; tours. *In room:* TV.

WHERE TO DINE

There are several places to eat in Creel, but no standouts. Aside from the restaurants at the hotels, you might want to try one of the establishments on López Mateos, such as the **Caballo Bayo, Tío Molcas,** or **Verónica's.**

2 Los Mochis: The Western Terminus

202km (126 miles) SW of Alamos; 80km (50 miles) SW of El Fuerte; 309km (193 miles) SE of Guaymas; 416km (260 miles) NW of Mazatlán

Los Mochis, in Sinaloa State, is a coastal city of 350,000 founded in 1893 by Benjamin Johnson of Pennsylvania. It is a wealthy city in a fertile agricultural area but holds little of interest for the visitor. The most important aspects of the city are that it is a boarding point for the train, it has an airport, and it is connected to La Paz, Baja California, by ferry, and to the U.S. border by highway.

ESSENTIALS

GETTING THERE & DEPARTING **By Plane** Aeromexico/Aerolitoral (© 800/ 237-6639 in the U.S., or 668/815-2570 for reservations) has direct service from Phoenix, Chihuahua, Hermosillo, Mazatlán, and La Paz. **Aero California** (© 800/237-6225 in the U.S., or 668/815-2250) flies to and from Tucson, Los Angeles, La Paz, Guadalajara, Mexico City, Culiacán, and Tijuana.

Arriving: The airport is 21km (13 miles) north of town; transportation is by *combi* (collective minivan) or airport taxi ($10).

By Train The **Chihuahua al Pacífico (Copper Canyon train)** runs between Los Mochis and Chihuahua once daily, departing at 6am. First-class fare is $115.

By Car **Coastal Highway 15** is well maintained in both directions leading into Los Mochis.

By Ferry A ferry plies the waters between La Paz and Topolobampo, the port for Los Mochis carrying passengers, vehicles, and cargo. The company, **Baja Ferries** (© 668/ 817-3752; www.bajaferries.com), uses a larger and more dependable ship than the company that used to operate this ferry route. There's one departure per day leaving at 11pm.

By Bus Buses serve Los Mochis, however marginally. Most are *de paso*—passing through. All bus stations are downtown, within walking distance of the hotels. The **first-class station** is near Juárez at Degollado 200. From here, Elite buses go to and from Tijuana, Monterrey, Nogales, and Ciudad Juárez. Auto-transportes Transpacíficos, in the same station, serves Nogales, Tijuana, Mazatlán, Guadalajara, Querétaro, and Mexico City. A lot of travelers who arrive in Los Mochis prefer to go directly to El Fuerte, spend the night there, then catch the train. There are two places to catch the bus to El Fuerte (1½–2 hr.). The first is at the **Mercado Independencia;** the bus stops at the corner of Independencia and Degollado. The other is at the **corner of Cuauhtémoc and Prieto,** near the Hotel América. Ask hotel desk clerks or the tourism office for a schedule. These are second-class buses, which stop frequently, prolonging the trip well beyond the normal 1-hour travel time.

CITY LAYOUT Los Mochis contains no central plaza, and streets run northwest to southeast and southwest to northeast. The **Hotel Santa Anita** (Av. Leyva at Av. Obregón) is the reference point for giving directions to restaurants and hotels, which are all within a few blocks.

FAST FACTS The local **American Express** representative is **Viajes Araceli,** Av. Alvaro Obregón 471-A Poniente (© 668/815-5780; fax 668/815-8787). *Note:* Changing money outside of Los Mochis is difficult, so stock up on pesos before boarding the train. Most places in the canyons do not accept credit cards. The telephone **area code** for Los Mochis is **668.**

EXPLORING LOS MOCHIS

For most travelers, Los Mochis is a stopover en route to somewhere else. There isn't much here, but the town is pleasant, and you can enjoy some excellent seafood. The **Viajes Flamingo** travel agency, on the ground floor of the Hotel Santa Anita (© 668/ 812-1613 or 668/812-1929), arranges a city tour, hunting and fishing trips, and boat rides around **Topolobampo Bay.** It's open Monday through Saturday from 8:30am to 1pm and 3 to 6:30pm. The boat ride is really just a spin in the bay and not especially noteworthy, although the bay is pretty and dolphins often show up.

WHERE TO STAY

Hotel Corintios Behind a campy entrance with Greek columns and mirrored glass are two stories of rooms with ample light, carpeted floors, and adequate space for two comfortable double beds and luggage. The bathrooms are midsize and have marble tub/showers but poor lighting. The junior suites come with a king-size bed.

Obregón 580 Poniente, 81200 Los Mochis, Sin. © **668/818-2300** or 01-800/690-3000 in Mexico. Fax 668/818-2277. 59 units. $71 double; $78 junior suite. AE, MC, V. Rates include continental breakfast. Free parking. **Amenities:** Restaurant; Jacuzzi; room service until 11pm; laundry service. *In room:* A/C, TV.

Hotel Las Fuentes Of the inexpensive hotels in town, I like this one the best. The rooms are cheerful and clean and the staff is helpful. Each room comes with two double beds. Bathrooms are midsize with shower. They could use more light. The hotel is 5 minutes from downtown on one of the main arteries.

Bulevar Adolfo López Mateos 1251-A Norte, 81220 Los Mochis, Sin. © **668/818-8871** or 668/818-8172. Fax 668/812-5983. lasfuenteshotel@lmm.megared.net.mx 38 units. $50 double. AE, MC, V. Free secure parking. **Amenities:** Restaurant; bar; pool; Jacuzzi; room service until 11pm; laundry service. *In room:* A/C, TV.

Hotel Santa Anita The Santa Anita is the choice of most going to the canyon; not only is it a comfortable, quiet hotel, but it offers reliable transportation to and from the train station, so you don't have to bother with taxis. The rooms are modern and well furnished but vary a good deal in size. All are carpeted and have comfortable beds, color TVs with U.S. channels, and tap water purified for drinking. The hotel's popular restaurant is just off the lobby. There are two bars, one with live music at least 1 day a week.

Leyva, at the corner of Hidalgo (Apdo. Postal 159), 81200 Los Mochis, Sin. © **800/896-8196** in the U.S., or 668/818-7046. Fax 668/812-0046 116 units. $140 double. AE, MC, V. Free parking. **Amenities:** Restaurant; bar; transportation to and from the train station; business center; room service until 11pm; laundry service; nonsmoking rooms. *In room:* A/C, TV, hair dryer.

WHERE TO DINE

El Farallón ★★ SEAFOOD If you like seafood, there's no reason to eat anywhere else in Los Mochis. Don't be put off by the menu, which is confusing—to put it simply, you can order seafood cooked any way you want. Try a Mexican style such as *al ajillo,* with toasted *guajillo* chiles. If you're hungry, I recommend the *mariscada* for two or more, which comes with a cold and a hot platter of a variety of fish and shellfish. Try *calamares* (squid), the cheapest thing on the platter. Forget about those rubbery rings fried up in other restaurants; because the squid get to be giant-size in this region's waters, so the meat comes in big, tender chunks. One of my favorites is *machaca,* made with either shrimp or smoked marlin (cooked in a reduced fish stock, which is mild and satisfying). The atmosphere is casual, the air-conditioning functions with gusto, and the white-tiled dining area is simply furnished.

Obregón, at Angel Flores. © **668/812-1428.** Main courses $8–$12. AE, MC, V. Daily 8am–11pm. From the Hotel Santa Anita, turn right on Leyva and right again for 1 block on Obregón. It's on your left.

El Taquito *Value* MEXICAN Any time of the day or night, El Taquito serves standard Mexican fare at a good price. With orange booths and Formica tables, the cafe looks like an American fast-food place. Tortilla soup comes in a large bowl, and both breakfast and main-course portions are quite generous.

Leyva at Barrera. © **668/812-8119.** Breakfast $3–$5; main courses $4–$8. AE, DC, MC, V. Daily 24 hr. From the Hotel Santa Anita, turn left on Leyva, cross Hidalgo and go 1 block. It's on your right.

Restaurante España STEAK/SEAFOOD This Spanish-style restaurant is a favorite among downtown professionals, who feast on large plates of paella (available Thurs and Sun after 1pm; at other times it's made to order, taking 45 min.). The decor is upscale for Los Mochis, with a splashing fountain in the dining room and heavy, carved-wood tables and chairs.

Obregón 525 Pte. © **668/812-2221.** Breakfast $4–$6; main courses $9–$13. AE, MC, V. Daily 7am–11pm. From the Hotel Santa Anita, turn right out the front door to Obregón, then right on Obregón for 1½ blocks. It's on your right.

3 Chihuahua: The Eastern Terminus ⊛

341km (213 miles) S of El Paso; 440km (275 miles) NW of Torreón

Chihuahua, a city of wide boulevards and handsome buildings, is the capital of the state of Chihuahua, the largest and richest in Mexico. The wealth comes from mining, timber, cattle raising, *maquiladoras* (assembly plants for export goods), and tourism. The city has grown a lot in the last 30 years, thanks mainly to an increase in manufacturing plants, and has lost its frontier feeling. But the historic center of Chihuahua retains much of its character and holds a few museums and buildings worth visiting, including the house where Pancho Villa once lived.

ESSENTIALS

GETTING THERE & DEPARTING **By Plane** **Continental** (© **800/525-0280** in the U.S., or 01-800/900-5000 in Mexico) has nonstop service to and from Houston on a 50-seat jet. **Aeromexico/Aerolitoral** (© **614/415-6303**) fly direct from El Paso, Phoenix, Guadalajara, Hermosillo, Mexico City, Monterrey, Torreón, Tijuana, Culiacán, La Paz, and Los Mochis, with connecting flights from Los Angeles and San Antonio. **Transportes Terrestre** (© **614/420-3366**) controls minivan service from the airport ($6 per person, $10 if it's an early flight). Taxis from town charge $15 for up to four people.

By Train The **Chihuahua al Pacífico** (© **614/439-7212;** fax 614/439-7208) leaves Chihuahua daily for Los Mochis by way of the Copper Canyon country. The complete train schedule and the train route appear in "The Copper Canyon Train & Stops along the Way," earlier in this chapter. In that section you'll find information on purchasing tickets. It is easier to go through a travel agency than to deal directly with the company. The train is scheduled to leave at 6am daily. To get to the station in time, it's best to arrange transportation through one of the travel agencies recommended under "Canyon Arrangements" in "Fast Facts: Chihuahua," below. They pick up clients taking the train each morning.

By Car **Highway 45** leads south from Ciudad Juárez; **Highway 16** south from Ojinaga; and **Highway 49** north from Torreón. For the drive to Creel, see "Getting There & Departing" under "Stop 5: Creel," earlier in this chapter.

By Bus The Central Camionera **Terminal de Autobuses (bus station)** is on Avenida Juan Pablo II, 8km (5 miles) northeast of town en route to the airport. Buses leave hourly for major points inland and north and south on the coast. Transportes Chihuahuenses, the big local line, offers first-class service to Ciudad Juárez every half-hour; the trip takes 4 hours. Transportes del Norte and Autobuses Estrella Blanca also run buses hourly from the border through Chihuahua to points south. Omnibus de México has *servicio ejecutivo* (deluxe service) from Juárez, Mexico City, and Monterrey. Futura/Turistar also has deluxe service to Monterrey and Durango.

Chihuahua

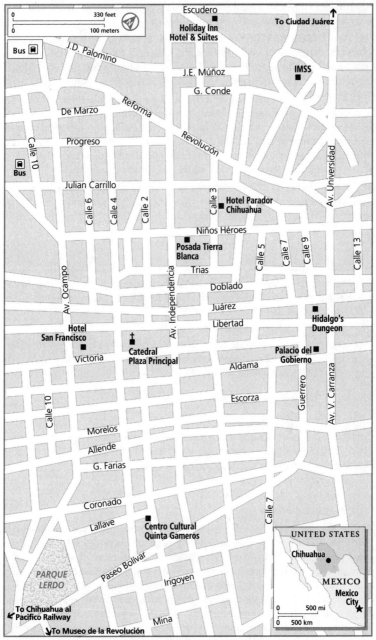

0 330 feet
0 100 meters

Bus 🚌

J.D. Palomino

To Ciudad Juárez

Escudero

Holiday Inn
Hotel & Suites

J.E. Múñoz

G. Conde

IMSS

De Marzo

Reforma

Revolución

Progreso

Calle 10

Bus 🚌

Julian Carrillo

Calle 6

Calle 4

Calle 2

Calle 3

Av. Universidad

Hotel Parador
Chihuahua

Niños Héroes

Av. Ocampo

Av. Independencia

Posada Tierra
Blanca

Calle 5

Calle 7

Calle 9

Calle 13

Trias

Doblado

Juárez

Libertad

Hotel
San Francisco

† Catedral
Plaza Principal

Victoria

Hidalgo's
Dungeon

Palacio del
Gobierno

Aldama

Guerrero

Av. V. Carranza

Escorza

Calle 10

Morelos

Allende

G. Farias

Coronado

Lallave

Centro Cultural
Quinta Gameros

Calle 7

Paseo Bolívar

Irigoyen

PARQUE
LERDO

To Chihuahua al
Pacífico Railway

Mina

To Museo de la Revolución

UNITED STATES

Chihuahua

MEXICO

Mexico
City

0 500 mi
0 500 km

697

For travel to Creel, look for the Estrella Blanca line. Buses leave every 2 hours from 6am to 6pm. Direct buses make the trip in 4 hours.

VISITOR INFORMATION For basic info, visit the **tourist information center** ((C) **614/410-1077** or 614/429-3596), Calle Aldama at Carranza in the Government Palace, just left of the altar and murals dedicated to Father Hidalgo. It's open Monday through Friday from 9am to 6pm, Saturday and Sunday from 10am to 5pm.

CITY LAYOUT The town center is laid out around the **Plaza Principal,** bounded by avenidas Libertad and Victoria (which run northeast-southwest) and Avenida Independencia and Calle 4 (which run northwest-southeast). The **cathedral** is at the southwest end of the plaza, and the city offices are on the northeast end. Standing on Independencia with the cathedral on your left, odd-numbered streets and blocks will be to your right, and even-numbered streets and blocks to your left.

GETTING AROUND Local buses run along main arteries beginning at the central plaza. Taxis are readily available. If you want to see the sights and have only 1 day, take a tour (see "Exploring Chihuahua," below).

FAST FACTS: **Chihuahua**

American Express The local representative is **Viajes Rojo y Casavantes,** with one agent in the Hotel San Francisco and a full office at Vicente Guerrero 1207 ((C) **614/415-4636;** fax 614/415-5384).

Area Code The telephone area code is **614.**

Canyon Arrangements If you have waited to purchase train tickets and make canyon hotel reservations, contact **Turismo al Mar,** Calle Berna 2202, Colonia Mirador, 31270 Chihuahua, Chih. ((C) **614/410-9232** or 614/416-5950; fax 614/416-6589).

Elevation Chihuahua sits at 1,425m (4,700 ft.).

Emergencies Call (C) **060.**

Hospital **Clínica del Parque** is at Pedro Leal del Rosal and de la Llave ((C) **614/415-7411**). For medical emergencies, call (C) **614/411-8141.**

Population Chihuahua has some 670,000 residents.

EXPLORING CHIHUAHUA

To see Chihuahua's sights in 1 day, consider taking a 3-hour city tour; English-speaking guides are available. Three recommended agencies are **Torre del Sol,** Independencia 116-2 ((C) **614/415-7380**), in the Hotel Palacio del Sol; **Turismo al Mar** (see "Canyon Arrangements" in "Fast Facts," above); and **Viajes Rojo y Casavantes** (see "American Express" in "Fast Facts," above). Any of these will pick you up at your hotel. A half-day city tour includes visits to the museums, the churches, the colonial aqueduct, the state capital building, the state penitentiary, and more. A 7-hour trip to the Mennonite village near Cuauhtémoc costs about $35 per person, with a minimum of four people. Unless you have a particular interest in cheese making or the Mennonites, it's not worth your time.

SIGHTS IN TOWN

Centro Cultural Universitaria ⚲   Quinta Gameros is a neoclassical, French Second Empire–style mansion with a beautiful Art Nouveau interior. Built in 1910 for Manuel Gameros, the mansion became a museum in 1961. Pancho Villa used it briefly as a headquarters. The interior walls, floors, and ceilings are lavishly decorated, which inspired the transfer of a beautiful collection of fine Mexican Art Nouveau furnishings from Mexico City to this museum. If you like design and beautiful antiques, especially Art Nouveau, don't miss this place.

Quinta Gameros, Paseo Bolívar 401. ℂ **614/416-6684**. Admission $2. Tues–Sun 11am–2pm and 4–7pm. Heading away from the Plaza Principal with the cathedral on your right, walk 7 blocks on Independencia to Bolívar, turn right, and walk 1 block; museum is on the right.

Hidalgo's Dungeon   Father Miguel Hidalgo y Costilla was a priest in Dolores, Guanajuato, when he started the War of Independence on September 15, 1810. Six months later, he was captured by the Spanish, brought to Chihuahua, and thrown in a dungeon for 98 days. He was then shot along with his lieutenants, Allende, Aldama, and Jiménez. The four were beheaded, and their heads hung in iron cages for 9½ years on the four corners of the Alhóndiga granary in Guanajuato (see chapter 6) as examples of the fate revolutionaries would meet. In this cell, Hidalgo lived on bread and water before his execution. The night before his death, he wrote a few words on the wall with a piece of charcoal to thank his guard and the warden for the good treatment they gave him. A bronze plaque commemorates his final message.

In the Palacio Federal, Av. Juárez at Guerrero. No phone. Admission 50¢. Tues–Sun 10am–6pm. From Plaza Principal, walk on pedestrian-only Calle Libertad for 3 long blocks to Guerrero, turn left, and walk to corner of Juárez. Turn right and go ½ block; museum entrance is on the right, below the post office.

Museo de la Revolución ⚲⚲ *Finds*   The Revolution Museum is Pancho Villa's house, where Luz Corral de Villa, Pancho Villa's widow, lived until her death in 1981. Exhibits include Villa's weapons, some personal effects, lots of period photos, and the 1922 Dodge in which he was shot in 1923 (you'll see the bullet holes). I found it interesting and recommend seeing the place with a guide, who can add lots of biographical details about this larger-than-life character. Be sure to ask about Villa's opinions on marriage and about the total number of his offspring and grandchildren.

Calle 10 no. 3014 (at Méndez). ℂ **614/416-2958**. Admission $1. Tues–Sat 9am–1pm and 3–7pm. Bus: Colonia Dale (runs west on Juárez, then south on Ocampo); exit at corner of Ocampo and Méndez.

Palacio del Gobierno   The Palacio del Gobierno is a magnificent, ornate structure dating in part from 1890; the original building, the Jesuit College, was built in 1718. A colorful, expressive mural encompasses the first floor of the large central courtyard and tells the history of the area around Chihuahua from the time of the first European visitation through the Revolution. In the far right corner, note the scene depicting Benito Juárez flanked by Abraham Lincoln and Simón Bolívar, liberator of South America. In the far left rear courtyard are a plaque and altar commemorating the execution in 1811 of Miguel Hidalgo, the father of Mexican independence; the plaque marks the spot where the hero was executed in the old building, and the mural portrays the scene.

Av. Aldama (between Guerrero and Carranza). ℂ **614/410-6324**. Free admission. Daily 8am–10pm. With the cathedral on your right, walk along Independencia 1 block, turn left on Aldama, continue 2 long blocks, and cross Guerrero; entrance is on the left.

WHERE TO STAY

EXPENSIVE

Holiday Inn Hotel and Suites ⭐ This Holiday Inn offers the most comfortable rooms in the downtown area. All units are suites, with kitchenettes that include stove, refrigerator, and coffeemaker. There's a sitting area, large writing table, and a choice of one king-size bed or two doubles. Guests have the use of a video library. The hotel staff is helpful and efficient. They can provide a continental breakfast for people heading off on the train, as well as a box lunch. The hotel is a 5-minute walk from downtown.

Escudero 702 (between Av. Universidad and Av. de Montes), 31240 Chihuahua, Chih. ⓒ **800/465-4329** in the U.S., or 614/439-0000. Fax 614/414-3313. 74 units. $140 double. Rates include breakfast buffet. AE, DC, MC, V. Free secure parking. **Amenities:** Restaurant; bar; 2 pools (1 indoor); fitness room; Jacuzzi; steam room; game room; business center; room service until 10:30pm; babysitting; laundry service; coin-op laundry; nonsmoking rooms. *In room:* A/C, TV, dataport, kitchenette, fridge, coffeemaker, hair dryer, iron, safe.

Hotel San Francisco The good location and comfortable midsize rooms are the main attractions here. Rooms are well furnished but could use a little more light. The bathrooms are well equipped and have ample counter space. Bed choices include two doubles, a queen or a king. Mattresses are firm. Don't worry about getting a view, ask for something quiet.

Victoria 409, 31000 Chihuahua, Chih. ⓒ **800/847-2546** in the U.S., or 614/439-9000. Fax 614/415-3538. www.hotelsanfrancisco.com.mx. 131 units. $125 double. AE, MC, V. Free covered parking. From the cathedral, walk to Victoria and turn right; the hotel is 1½ blocks down on your right, before Av. Ocampo. **Amenities:** Restaurant; bar; fitness room; travel agency; car rental; business center; room service until 10pm; babysitting; laundry service. *In room:* A/C, TV, coffeemaker, hair dryer, iron.

MODERATE

Posada Tierra Blanca A downtown hotel with an attractive large pool area shaded by trees. Rooms are in two- and three-story buildings. They are large and quiet (none have windows facing the street). Bathrooms are midsize with good counter space and better lighting than most of the hotels in Chihuahua.

Niños Héroes 102, 31000 Chihuahua, Chih. ⓒ 614/415-0000. www.posadatierrablanca.com.mx. 90 units. $70 double. AE, MC, V. Free secure parking. **Amenities:** Restaurant; bar; large pool; fitness room; room service until 11pm; laundry service. *In room:* A/C, TV.

INEXPENSIVE

Hotel Parador Chihuahua I like this motel for the price, the downtown location, and the well-maintained rooms. It occupies the interior of a small city block, with the rooms built around the pool and the garden area. The midsize rooms are carpeted and furnished rather plainly. Choice of one king-size bed or two doubles. Bathrooms are midsize.

Calle 3 no. 304 (between Julian Carrillo and Niños Héroes), 31000 Chihuahua, Chih. ⓒ 614/415-0827. hotel paradorchihuahua@terra.com.mx. 34 units. $52 double. AE, MC, V. Free secure parking. **Amenities:** Restaurant; bar; small pool; limited room service; laundry service. *In room:* A/C, TV.

WHERE TO DINE

Dining in Chihuahua is fine so long as you don't rely too heavily on the city's sophistication. Stick with steaks and Mexican food.

Degá MEXICAN/INTERNATIONAL This restaurant bar at the San Francisco hotel draws both downtown workers and travelers. The breakfast buffet features made-to-order omelets. The steaks and Mexican dishes are well priced; try the *plato mexicano,* a popular dish that comes with a *tamal,* chile relleno, beans, chips, and guacamole.

In the Hotel San Francisco, Calle Victoria 409. ⓒ 614/416-7550. Breakfast $4–$7; breakfast buffet $8; main courses $5–$17; Sun buffet $10. AE, MC, V. Daily 7am–11pm.

La Calesa STEAKS/MEXICAN   The dining room with its heavy furniture, wood paneling, and bound menus gets the message across that this is Chihuahua's establishment restaurant. Some of the steaks go by different names here, but the waiters are familiar with all the cuts. A piano serenades diners from 2:30 to 5pm and 9pm to midnight.

Av. Colón 3300, corner of Av. Juárez. ⓒ 614/410-1038. Reservations accepted. Steaks $11–$21. Mexican dishes $7–$10. AE, MC, V. Daily 12:30pm–midnight.

Restaurante Todo de Maíz ⭐ MEXICAN   To eat cheaply and eat well in Chihuahua is a bit of a trick—unless you go here. Señora María Matilde Salazar is a great cook and an unabashed leftist. She keeps quality and freshness up by keeping the menu simple. Between 1 and 2:30pm she offers a *comida corrida* that's a bargain. And the rest of the time she makes tacos, quesadillas, tostadas, and *peneques* (a local form of *antojito* that's like a *gordita*) all made with corn masa, as the restaurant's name suggests. This place is down the street from the Holiday Inn.

Calle Escudero 2103 (between calles 21 and 23). ⓒ 614/4145778. *Comida corrida* $3; *antojitos* $1–$2. No credit cards. Mon–Fri 9am–5pm; Sat 11am–5pm.

CHIHUAHUA AFTER DARK

Most nighttime action takes place in hotel lobby bars (see "Where to Stay," above). At the **Hotel San Francisco,** there's live music Monday through Saturday, with happy hour from 5 to 8pm. The lobby bar at the **Hotel Palacio del Sol** schedules live entertainment nightly.

Los Cabos & Baja California

by Lynne Bairstow

Baja California is a place of complementary contrasts: hot desert and cool ocean, manicured golf greens and craggy mountains. Baja lays claim to a striking and peculiar blend of Mexican and American cultures.

The Baja Peninsula is and is not part of Mexico. Attached mostly to the United States and separated from all but a sliver of Mexico by the Sea of Cortez (Gulf of California), the peninsula consists of one long granite ridge extending about 1,500km (1,000 miles)—longer than Italy—from Mexico's northernmost city of **Tijuana** to **Cabo San Lucas** at its southern tip. Desert terrain rises from both coasts; forests of cardon cactus, spiky Joshua trees, and spindly ocotillo bushes populate the raw landscape.

Baja is also legendary as a haven for sportfishing and rugged adventure activities.

For more in-depth coverage of this region, consult *Frommer's Los Cabos & Baja.*

EXPLORING THE REGION

The weather in this land of extremes can be sizzling hot in summer and cold and windy in winter. Though winter is often warm enough for watersports, bring a wetsuit if you're a serious diver or snorkeler, as well as warmer clothes for chilly weather. Though Baja's weather varies greatly by season, it is predictable—an important quality for the increasing number of golfers looking for sunny skies. Rainy days are few and far between, with most showers concentrated in September.

THE TWO CABOS The majority of visitors are lured by the popularity of the twin towns at the peninsula's tip—**Cabo San Lucas** and **San José del Cabo**—and the stretch of coastline that connects them, known as **the Corridor.** Collectively, they are known as Los Cabos (The Capes). "The end of the line," "the last resort," and "no man's land" are all terms used in the past to describe remote Baja Sur (*sur* means "south").

Cabo San Lucas and the Corridor are an extension of Southern California, with luxury accommodations, golf courses, shopping, franchise restaurants, and spirited nightlife. San José del Cabo, however, remains rooted in the traditions of a quaint Mexican town, though it, too, is becoming gentrified.

Thirty-three kilometers (21 miles) of smooth highway (the Corridor) lie between the two Cabos. The major new resorts and residential communities, including some of the world's finest golf courses, have been developed along this stretch.

Baja can seem like one of the least crowded corners of Mexico. **Todos Santos,** an artistic community on the Pacific side of the coastal curve (just north of the tip), draws travelers who find that Cabo San Lucas has outgrown them. **La Paz,** capital of Baja Sur, remains an easygoing maritime port.

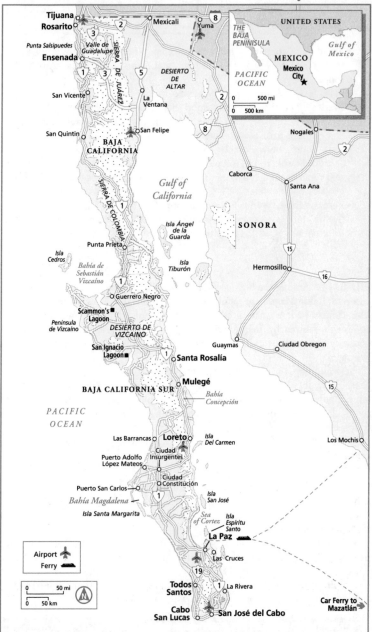

The Baja Peninsula

UNITED STATES

THE
BAJA
PENINSULA

MEXICO

PACIFIC
OCEAN

Gulf of
Mexico

Mexico City ★

0 ___ 500 mi
0 ___ 500 km

Tijuana
Rosarito
Mexicali
Yuma
8

Punta Salsipuedes
Valle de
Guadalupe
2
3
SIERRA DE JUAREZ

Ensenada
1
3
5
DESIERTO
DE
ALTAR

San Vicente
La
Ventana
2

San Quintín
San Felipe
8

BAJA
CALIFORNIA
Nogales
2

Caborca

Santa Ana

Gulf of
California

SIERRA DE COLOMBIA

1

Isla Ángel
de la
Guarda

SONORA

Punta Prieta

Isla
Cedros

Bahía de
Sebastián
Vizcaíno

Isla
Tiburón

15

1

Guerrero Negro

Hermosillo

16

Scammon's
Lagoon

Península
de Vizcaíno

DESIERTO DE
VIZCAÍNO

San Ignacio
Lagoon
1
Santa Rosalía

Guaymas

Ciudad Obregon

Mulegé

BAJA CALIFORNIA SUR
Bahía
Concepción

PACIFIC
OCEAN

15

Las Barrancas
Loreto
Isla
Del Carmen

Los Mochis

Ciudad
Insurgentes

Puerto Adolfo
López Mateos

Ciudad
Constitución

Puerto San Carlos
1

Isla
San José

Bahía Magdalena

Isla Santa Margarita

Sea
of Cortez

Isla
Espíritu
Santo

La Paz

Airport ✈
Ferry ⛴

Las Cruces

0 ___ 50 mi
0 ___ 50 km
N

19

Todos
Santos
1
La Rivera

Cabo
San Lucas
San José del Cabo

Car Ferry to
Mazatlán

> **Tips** **The Best Websites for Los Cabos & Baja**
>
> - **All About Cabo: www.allaboutcabo.com** This site features a weekly fishing report, live golf cam, and information on hotels, restaurants, golf courses, and more.
> - **Baja Travel Guide: www.bajatravel.com** Here you'll find a good overview of activities and transportation, but the extensive Yellow Pages are most useful. They can help you arrange tours, ground transportation, and outdoor excursions before you go.
> - **Visit Cabo: www.visitcabo.com** The official site of the Los Cabos Tourism Board. You'll find plenty of details about things to do and current news, as well as a lodging and dining guide. For selected hotels, you can also book online.
> - **Visit Los Cabos: www.visitloscabos.org** Another "official" site, this one by the state government tourism board. Also has hotel and restaurant information, as well as activities and general travel tips.

MID-BAJA Among the highlights of the mid-Baja region are the east coast towns of **Loreto, Bahía Magdalena, Mulegé,** and **Santa Rosalía.** These towns have a much richer cultural heritage than those located in Baja Sur. Although Loreto is experiencing growth—driven by an aggressive real estate project just outside of town—the remaining east coast towns have all but escaped the tourism boom experienced by the two Cabos.

These mid-Baja towns were the center of the 18th-century Jesuit mission movement. Today, they attract travelers who are drawn to Baja's wild natural beauty but find the popularity of Los Cabos a bit overwhelming. This area's natural attractions have made it a center for sea kayaking, sportfishing, and hiking—including excursions to view indigenous cave paintings.

This is the area to visit if you're interested in whale-watching; many tour companies operate out of Loreto and the smaller neighboring towns (see "Whale-Watching in Baja," later in this chapter).

BAJA NORTE **Tijuana** has the dubious distinction of being the most visited and perhaps most misunderstood town in all of Mexico. New cultural and sporting attractions, extensive shopping, and strong business growth—of the reputable kind—are brightening Tijuana's image.

Tranquil **Rosarito Beach** has also reemerged as a resort town; it got a boost after the movie *Titanic* was filmed there, and Fox Studios converted the former set into a film-themed amusement park. Farther south on the Pacific Coast is the lovely port town of **Ensenada,** also known for its surfing and sportfishing. Tours of nearby inland vineyards (Mexico's wine country) are growing in popularity.

1 Los Cabos: Resorts, Watersports & Golf ★★

The two towns at the tip of the rugged Baja Peninsula are commonly grouped together and referred to as Los Cabos, although they couldn't be more different. San José del Cabo and Cabo San Lucas are separated not just by 33km (21 miles), but also by distinct attitudes and ways of life. Where Cabo San Lucas mirrors a spirited version of Los Angeles lifestyle, San José del Cabo remains a traditional, tranquil Mexican small town, although recent gentrification is turning it into the more sophisticated of the two resorts.

Great sportfishing originally brought attention to Los Cabos, which were once accessible only by water. It remains a lure today, although golf has overtaken it as the principal attraction. As early as the 1940s, the area attracted a hearty community of cruisers, fishermen, divers, and adventurers. By the early 1980s, the Mexican government realized the growth potential of Los Cabos and invested in new highways, airport facilities, golf courses, and modern marine facilities. The increase in air access and the opening of Transpeninsular Highway 1 (in 1973) paved the way for spectacular growth.

The road that connects Cabo San Lucas and San José del Cabo is the centerpiece of resort growth. Known as "the Corridor," this well-paved four-lane stretch offers cliff-top vistas but still has no nighttime lighting. The area's deluxe resorts and renowned golf courses are here, along with a collection of dramatic beaches and coves. The view is especially outstanding in January and February, when gray whales often spout close to shore.

The Los Cabos area is more expensive than other Mexican resorts, because the boom in new hotel construction has been limited to luxury resorts. Unfortunately, prices have not adjusted downward with the added supply of rooms.

You should consider renting a car, even if only for a day. There are numerous attractions between the two Cabos, and taxis are expensive. If you are at all interested in exploring, a rental car is your most economical option.

Because of the distinctive character and attractions of each of the Cabos and the Corridor, they are treated separately here. It is common to stay in one and make day trips to the other two.

SAN JOSE DEL CABO

180km (113 miles) SE of La Paz; 33km (21 miles) NE of Cabo San Lucas; 1,760km (1,100 miles) SE of Tijuana

San José del Cabo, with its pastel cottages and narrow streets lined with flowering trees, retains the air of a provincial Mexican town. The main square, adorned with a wrought-iron bandstand and shaded benches, faces the cathedral, which was built on the site of an early mission. San José is becoming increasingly sophisticated, with a collection of noteworthy cafes, art galleries, interesting shops, and intriguing small inns adding a newly refined flavor to the central downtown area.

ESSENTIALS
Getting There & Departing
By Plane **Aeromexico** (© **800/237-6639** in the U.S., 01-800/021-4000 in Mexico, 624/146-5098, or -5097; www.aeromexico.com), flies nonstop from San Diego, Ontario, and Los Angeles, and has connecting flights from other cities; **Aero California** (© **800/237-6225** in the U.S., or 624/143-3700) offers flights from Los Angeles; **American Airlines** (© **800/433-7300** in the U.S., 624/146-5300, or 624/146-5309; www.aa.com) flies from Dallas/Ft. Worth, Los Angeles, and Chicago; **America West** (© **800/235-9292** in the U.S., or 624/146-5380; www.americawest.com) operates connecting flights through Phoenix; **Alaska Airlines** (© **800/426-0333** in the U.S., or 624/146-5210, 624/146-5212; www.alaskaair.com) flies from Los Angeles, San Diego, Seattle, and San Francisco; **Continental** (© **800/525-0280** in the U.S., or

San José del Cabo

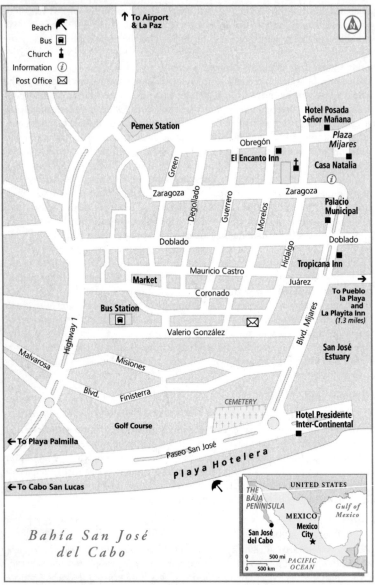

624/146-5040; www.continental.com) flies from Houston and Newark; **Delta** (© **800/221-1212** in the U.S., www.delta.com) has flights from Atlanta; **Frontier** (© **800/432-1359** in the U.S., www.frontierairlines.com) has direct service from Denver; **Mexicana** (© **800/531-7921** in the U.S., or 624/146-5001, 624/143-5352;

www.mexicana.com), has direct or connecting flights from Denver, Guadalajara, Los Angeles, and Mexico City; **United Airlines** (© **800/864-8331** in the U.S.; www.united.com) flies direct from both San Francisco and Denver; **AeroCalafia** (© **624/143-4302;** www.aereocalafia.com) offers regular flights from Mazatlán and Puerto Vallarta.

By Car   From La Paz, take Highway 1 south; the drive takes 3 to 4 hours. Or take Highway 1 south just past the village of San Pedro, then take Highway 19 south (a less winding road) through Todos Santos to Cabo San Lucas, where you pick up Highway 1 east to San José del Cabo. The latter route seems longer, but it is in better condition and takes only 2 to 3 hours. From Cabo San Lucas, it's a half-hour drive to San José.

By Bus   The **Terminal de Autobuses (bus station),** on Valerio González, a block east of Highway 1 (© **624/142-1100**), is open daily from 5:30am to 8pm.

Orientation

ARRIVING   The **airport** (© **624/146-5111**) that serves both Cabos and the connecting Corridor is 13km (8 miles) northwest of San José del Cabo and 48km (29 miles) northeast of Cabo San Lucas. It was expanded in 1999, and now has separate terminals for national and international flights—be sure to request the correct terminal when you return. Upon arrival at the airport, buy a ticket inside the building for a *colectivo* (minibus) or a taxi, which up to four passengers may share. *Colectivo* fares run about $9 for up to 8 passengers and are only available from the airport. A private van for up to 5 passengers is $70. Taxis charge about $15 to San José.

The major car-rental agencies all have counters at the airport, open during flight arrivals: **Avis** (© **800/331-1212** in the U.S., or 624/146-0201; avissjd@avis.com.mx; open Mon–Sat 7am–9pm, Sun 6am–9pm); **Budget** (© **800/527-0700** in the U.S., 624/146-5333 at the airport, or 624/143-4190 in Cabo San Lucas; daily 8am–6pm); **Hertz** (© **800/654-3131** in the U.S., 624/146-5088, or 624/142-0375 in San José del Cabo; daily 8am–8pm); and **National** (© **800/328-4567** in the U.S., 624/146-5022 at the airport, or 624/142-2424 in San José; daily 8am–8pm). Advance reservations are not always necessary.

VISITOR INFORMATION   The city tourist information office (© **624/142-3310** or 624/142-0465; fax 624/142-9628) is in the old post office building on Zaragoza at Mijares. It offers maps, free local publications, and other basic information about the area. It's open Monday through Friday from 8am to 2pm. Prior to arrival, contact the **Los Cabos Tourism Board** (© **866/567-2226**).

CITY LAYOUT   San José del Cabo consists of two zones: **downtown,** with sophisticated inns and traditional budget hotels, and the **hotel zone** along the beach. **Zaragoza** is the main street leading from the highway into town; **Paseo San José** runs parallel to the beach and is the principal boulevard of the hotel zone. The mile-long **Bulevar Mijares** connects the two areas, and is the center of most tourist activity in San Jose.

GETTING AROUND   There is no local bus service between downtown and the beach; **taxis** (© **624/142-0910** or 624/142-0580) connect the two. For day trips to **Cabo San Lucas,** catch a **bus** (see "Getting There & Departing," above) or a cab.

FAST FACTS: **San José del Cabo**

Area Code The local telephone area code is **624**.

Banks Banks exchange currency during business hours, which are generally Monday through Friday from 8:30am to 6pm, Saturday from 10am to 2pm. There are several major banks on Zaragoza between Morelos and Degollado.

Emergencies The local police number at City Hall is ☎ **624/142-0361**, or dial **066**.

Hospital **Hospital General** is at Retorno Atunero s/n, Col. Chamizal (☎ **624/142-0013**).

Internet Access **CaboOnline**, at Malvarosa and Gobernadora (☎ **624/142-2905**), is open Monday through Saturday from 10am to 8pm and charges $7.50 per hour. **Trazzo Internet**, on the corner of Zaragoza and Morelos, 1 block from the central plaza (no phone) is open Monday through Saturday from 10am to 8pm and charges $2.50 for 30 minutes or less of high-speed access.

Pharmacy **Farmacia ISSSTE**, Carretera Transpeninsular Km 34, Plaza California Local 7, San José del Cabo (☎ **624/142-2645**), is open daily from 8am to 8pm.

Post Office The *correo*, Bulevar Mijares 1924, at Valerio González (☎ **624/142-0911**), is open Monday through Friday from 8am to 6pm, Saturday from 9am to noon.

BEACHES & SPORTS OUTINGS

The relaxed pace of San José del Cabo makes it an ideal place to unwind and absorb authentic Mexican flavor. Beach aficionados who want to explore the beautiful coves and beaches along the 35km (22-mile) coast between the two Cabos should consider renting a car for a day or so. Expect to pay at least $50 per day.

BEACHES The nearest beach safe for swimming is **Pueblo la Playa** (also called La Playita), about 3km (2 miles) east of town. From Bulevar Mijares, turn east at the small PUEBLO LA PLAYA sign and follow the dusty dirt road through the cane fields and palms. You'll arrive at a small village and beautiful beach where a number of *pangas* (skiffs) that belong to local fishermen are pulled ashore. There are no shade *palapas*.

Estero San José, a nature reserve with at least 270 species of birds, is between Pueblo la Playa and the Hotel Presidente Inter-Continental. The estuary is a protected ecological reserve.

A beach with beautiful rock formations, **Playa Palmilla,** 8km (5 miles) west of San José, is near the One&Only Palmilla (see "Where to Stay", below). To reach Playa Palmilla, take a taxi to the road that leads to the Hotel Palmilla grounds, then take the fork to the left (without entering the hotel grounds) and follow signs to Pepe's restaurant on the beach.

For a list of other nearby beaches worth exploring if you have a rental car, see "Outdoor Activities: Fishing, Golf & More," under "Cabo San Lucas," later in this chapter.

LAND SPORTS **Golf** Los Cabos has become one of the world's leading golf destinations, with a collection of top courses and others under construction. The lowest greens fees in the area are at the 9-hole **Club Campo de Golf San José** (☎ **624/142-0901** or 624/142-0905), Paseo Finisterra 1, across from the Howard Johnson Hotel. The course doesn't take reservations for tee times. It is open daily from 6:30am to 4pm (to 4:30pm in summer). See p. 723 for fees.

Adventure Tours   Tío Sports (© 624/143-3399; www.tiosports.com) arranges a variety of land- and water-based adventure and nature tours, including popular ATV tours to Candelaria, parasailing, kayak, catamaran, snorkeling, and diving trips. The website gives current prices. **Gray Line Tours** (© 624/146-9410) is another great contact for a complete rundown of what's available. They offer all the tours from all the local companies rather than working with only a select few.

Horseback Riding   Horses can be rented near the Presidente Inter-Continental, Fiesta Inn, and Palmilla hotels for $15 to $20 per hour. Most people choose to ride on the beach. For a more organized riding experience, I highly recommend **Cuadra San Francisco Equestrian Center,** Km 19.5 along the Corridor, in front of the Casa del Mar resort (© **624/144-0160;** www.loscaboshorses.com). Owned by master horseman Francisco Barrena, he has over 30 years of experience in training horses and operating equestrian schools, and will assist any level rider in selecting and fitting a horse to their skill level. Your choice of English or Western saddles are available, on well-trained, exceptional horses. A 2-hour canyon ride in and around Arroyo San Carlos or Venado Blanco costs $70; a 1-hour ride to the beach or desert is $35.

Tennis   The two courts at the **Club Campo de Golf Los Cabos** (© **624/142-0905**), Paseo Finisterra 1, across from the Howard Johnson Hotel, rent for $13 an hour during the day, $22 an hour at night. Call the club to reserve. Club guests can also use the swimming pool. Tennis is also available at the **Presidente Inter-Continental** (two lighted courts).

WATERSPORTS   Fishing   The least expensive way to enjoy deep-sea fishing is to pair up with another angler and charter a *panga,* a 7m (22-ft.) skiff used by local fishermen, from Pueblo la Playa. Several *panga* fleets offer 6-hour sportfishing trips, usually from 6am to noon, for $25 per hour (3-hr. minimum). Two or three people can split the cost. For information, visit the fishermen's cooperative in Pueblo la Playa (no phone). For larger charter boats, you'll depart from the marina in Cabo San Lucas (below).

Sea Kayaking   Fully guided, ecologically oriented **Ocean Kayak Tours** are available through **Baja's Moto Rent** (© **624/143-2050**), **Cabo Expeditions** (© **624/143-2700**), and **Aqua Deportes** (© **624/143-0117**). Most ocean kayaking tours depart from Cabo San Lucas.

Snorkeling & Diving   Gray Line Los Cabos (© **624/146-9410;** www.grayline loscabos.com.) and **Amigos del Mar** in Cabo San Lucas (© **800/344-3349** in the U.S., or 624/143-0505; www.amigosdelmar.com) arrange trips. Prices start at $50 per person. Among the area's best dive sites are **Cabo Pulmo** and **Gordo Banks.** Cabo

---

(Tips Swimming Safety

Although this area is ideal for watersports, occasional strong currents and undertows can make swimming dangerous at **Playa Hotelera,** the town beach—check conditions before entering the surf. Swimming is generally safe at **Pueblo la Playa** (see "Beaches," above), though it, too, occasionally experiences a strong undertow. The safest area beach for swimming is **Medano Beach** in Cabo San Lucas.

Pulmo has seven sites geared for divers of all experience levels, so it never feels crowded. It also offers the possibility to snorkel with sea lions, depending on the currents and the animals' behavior. Gordo Banks is an advanced dive site where you can see whale sharks and hammerhead sharks. It's a deep dive—27 to 30m (90–110 ft.)—with limited visibility (9–12m/30–40 ft.). Most dives are drift dives, and wetsuits are highly recommended.

Surfing **Playa Costa Azul,** at Km 29 on Highway 1 just south of San José, is the most popular surfing beach in the area. A few bungalows are available for rent, or surfers can camp on the beach. The **Costa Azul Surf Shop,** Km 28, Playa Costa Azul (© 624/142-2771; www.costa-azul.com.mx), rents surfboards by the day. It charges $20 per day for a short or long board, leash, and rack for your rental car. Spectators can watch from the highway lookout point at the top of the hill south of Costa Azul. **Baja Wild** (© 624/142-5300; www.bajasalvaje.com) offers both surf lessons as well as surf tours, so you can get right to the best waves in the briefest amount of time. Trips take you to any of 15 breaks within the Sea of Cortez, to the big breaks on the Pacific Ocean, or even combine surfing and kayaking.

You can find good surfing from March through November all along the beaches west of Cabo, and **Playa Chileno,** near the Cabo San Lucas Hotel east of town, has a famous right break. Other good surfing beaches along the corridor are **Acapulquito, El Tule,** and **La Bocana.** *Warning:* Several accidents have involved visiting surfers who are not familiar with the rocky break, so surf with care!

Whale-Watching From January through March, migrating gray whales congregate offshore. Fishermen at Pueblo la Playa take small groups out to see them; a 4-hour trip runs about $45 per person. Organized half-day tours on sportfishing boats, glass-bottom boats, and cruise catamarans depart from Plaza las Glorias in Cabo San Lucas and cost $35 to $50, depending on the type of boat. The price includes snacks and beverages. The ultimate whale excursion is a trip to **Magdalena Bay.** Tours from San José take you by plane—a 75-minute flight—to Magdalena, where you board a *panga* and spend 3 hours watching gray whales and humpbacks loll around the coastal lagoons. This tour is $385, including air transportation, and can be arranged through **Xplora Adventours** (© 624/142-9135). It's truly an amazing experience, and a personal favorite of mine. You can also spot the whales from shore; good spots include the beach by the Solmar Suites hotel on the Pacific and the beaches and cliffs along the Corridor.

SHOPPING

The town has a growing selection of unique design shops, hip boutiques, and collections of fine Mexican *artesanía* (crafts). They cluster around **Bulevar Mijares** and **Zaragoza,** the main street. A municipal **market** on Mauricio Castro and Green sells edibles and utilitarian wares. The following businesses accept credit cards (American Express, MasterCard, and Visa are accepted).

ADD (Arte, Diseño y Decoración) This shop sells creative home accessories, fine arts and crafts, pewter, and authentic Talavera ceramics. Shipping is available. Open weekdays from 9am to 8pm, Saturday from 10am to 6pm. Zaragoza at Hidalgo. © 624/142-2777.

Copal Traditional and contemporary Mexican *artesanía* and silver jewelry are the specialties in this former residence, tastefully converted into a contemporary shop. Open Monday through Friday from 8am to 9:30pm, Saturday and Sunday from 10am to 2pm and 4 to 10:30pm. Plaza Mijares 10. © 624/142-3070.

Escape   This shop sells designer and casual sportswear and accessories, including designer jeans, leather bags, belts, and a trendy selection of sunglasses. An interior decor shop of the same name is next door. A small cafe and espresso bar, **Café Florentina** (daily 11am–11pm), is in the connecting courtyard. Open daily from 9am to 9pm. Plaza Florentine, Zaragoza 20, across from the cathedral. *©* **624/142-2799.**

Los Amigos Smokeshop and Cigar Bar   For fine Cuban cigars and cigarettes, as well as Veracruz cigars, a visit here is a must. They sell not only high quality cigars, but also a whole range of smoking accessories, including humidors and cutters, with friendly assistance from their knowledgeable staff. Also available are private lockers, a bar with an excellent selection of single malts, Wednesday evening cigar tastings, and a VIP club for frequent visitors. M. Doblado and Morelos, across from the French Riviera bakery. Open Monday through Wednesday 9am to 8pm; Thursday through Saturday from 9am to 1pm. Calle Manuel Doblado and Morelos. *©* **624/142-1138.**

SAX   For unusual and well-priced jewelry, visit this small shop where two local designers create one-of-a-kind pieces using silver, coral, and semi-precious stones. They'll even create a special request design for you, and have it ready in 24 hours. Open Monday through Saturday from 10am to 9pm, closed Sundays. Mijares 2. *©* **624/142-6053.** www.allaboutcabo.com/sax/index.htm.

WHERE TO STAY

There's more demand than supply in Baja Sur, so prices tend to be higher than those for equivalent accommodations in other parts of Mexico. San José has only a handful of budget hotels. It's best to call ahead for reservations. A new trend is toward smaller inns or bed-and-breakfasts, which offer stylish accommodations in town. Properties in the beachside hotel zone often offer package deals that bring room rates down to the moderate range, especially during summer months. Check with your travel agent.

Expensive

Casa Natalia ⭐⭐⭐ *Finds*   This exquisite boutique hotel is a real novelty in San José. Owners Nathalie and Loic have transformed a former residence into a beautiful amalgam of palms, waterfalls, and flowers. The inn is a completely renovated historic home that combines modern architecture with traditional Mexican touches. Each of the rooms has a name that reflects the decor, such as Conchas (seashells), Azul (blue), or Talavera (ceramics); all have sliding glass doors that open onto small private terraces or balconies with hammocks and chairs, shaded by bougainvillea and bamboo. The two spa suites each have a private terrace with a whirlpool and hammock. Tall California palms surround a small courtyard pool, and the terraces face onto it. Casa Natalia is in the heart of the Bulevar Mijares action, just off the central plaza.

Bulevar Mijares 4, 23400 San José del Cabo, B.C.S. *©* **888/277-3814** in the U.S., 866/826-1170 in Canada, or 624/142-5100. Fax 624/142-5110. www.casanatalia.com 16 units. High season $295 double, $475 spa suite; low season $180 double, $305 spa suite. AE, MC, V. Children under 14 not accepted. **Amenities:** Gourmet restaurant (see "Where to Dine," below); bar; heated swimming pool w/waterfall and swim-up bar; concierge; room service; massage; laundry service. *In room:* A/C, TV, hair dryer, safe-deposit box, bathrobes, fan.

Hotel Presidente InterContinental ⭐   Serenity, seclusion, and luxury are the hallmarks of the Presidente, set on a long stretch of beach next to the Estero San José. Lowrise, Mediterranean-style buildings frame the beach and San José's largest swimming pool, which has a swim-up bar. If possible, select a ground-floor oceanfront room; the lower level offers spacious terraces, while upper-level units have tiny balconies. The rooms have light-wood furnishings and brightly colored accents, with satellite TV and large bathrooms; suites include a separate sitting area. The all-inclusive resort is a good choice for those who primarily want to stay in one place and enjoy it; it's also popular with families.

Bulevar Mijares s/n, 23400 San José del Cabo, B.C.S. ℂ 800/327-0200 in the U.S., or 624/142-0211. Fax 624/142-0232. www.loscabos.interconti.com. 395 units. High season $285 standard double, $315 oceanfront double, $511–$693 double suite; low season rates from $250 double. Rates include all meals, beverages, and many sports. AE, DC, MC, V. **Amenities:** 5 restaurants; garden cafe; 4 swimming pools (2 heated, w/swim-up bars); children's pool; golf clinics; tennis; gym; bicycles; tour desk; twice-daily shuttle to Cabo San Lucas (fee); room service; laundry service; safe-deposit box (in reception area); horseback riding. *In room:* A/C, TV, hair dryer, makeup mirrors.

Moderate

El Encanto Inn ★ *Value* Located on a quiet street in the historic downtown district, this charming inn borders a grassy courtyard with a fountain and small pool. It offers a relaxing alternative to busy hotels, as well as excellent value. Rooms are decorated with rustic wood and contemporary iron furniture. Nice-size bathrooms have colorful tile accents. Rooms have two double beds, while suites have king-size beds and a sitting room. A pool area with *palapa* bar, and 14 poolside suites were recently added. These new suites have minibars and other extras, while all rooms offer satellite Direct TV. The owners, Cliff and Blanca (a lifelong resident of San José), can help arrange fishing packages and golf and diving outings. Jazmin's restaurant, a half-block away, serves the continental breakfast included in the room rate. The inn is a half-block from the church.

Morelos 133 (between Obregón and Comonfort), 23400 San José del Cabo, B.C.S. ℂ 624/142-0388. www.elencanto inn.com. 19 units. $75 double; $89–$169 suite. MC, V. Limited street parking available. **Amenities:** Small outdoor pool; *palapa* bar. *In room:* A/C, TV, coffeemaker, fan.

La Playita Inn Removed from even the slow pace of San José, this courtyard hotel is older yet impeccably clean and friendly. It's ideal for fishermen and those looking for something different from a traditional vacation. At the edge of the tiny village of Pueblo la Playa, it's the only hotel on the only beach in San José that's considered safe for swimming. Just steps from the water and the lineup of fishing *pangas*, the two stories of sunlit rooms frame a patio with a pool just large enough to allow you to swim laps. Each room is spacious, with high-quality basic furnishings, screened windows, a nicely tiled bathroom, and cable TV. Two large suites on the second floor have full kitchens. There's a golf-cart shuttle to the beach. Next door, the hotel's La Playita Restaurant (daily 11am–10pm) offers a great mix of seafood and standard favorites, plus occasional live jazz or tropical music.

Pueblo la Playa, Apdo. Postal 437, 23400 San José del Cabo, B.C.S. ℂ/fax 624/142-4166. www.laplayitahotel.com. 24 units. $60-$75 double. Rate includes continental breakfast. MC, V. Free parking. From Bulevar Mijares, follow sign pointing to Pueblo la Playa (dirt road) for about 3km (2 miles). Hotel is on the left. **Amenities:** Restaurant; outdoor pool. *In room:* A/C, TV.

Inexpensive

Hotel Posada Señor Mañana This comfortable two-story guesthouse, set in a grove of tropical fruit trees, offers basic rooms with tile floors and funky furniture. An abundance of hammocks are strewn about the property. Guests have cooking privileges in a large, fully equipped common kitchen. Upstairs rooms have two full-size beds, plus room for an extra single bed; downstairs rooms were remodeled in late 2004, and have one queen bed, plus either one or two single beds. The hotel is next to the Casa de la Cultura, behind the main square.

Alvaro Obregón 1, 23400 San José del Cabo, B.C.S. ℂ **624/142-1372**. Fax 624/142-5761. www.srmanana.com. 8 units. $38–$58 double. No credit cards. **Amenities:** Kitchen; pool table; half-court basketball; Ping-Pong. *In room:* Fan.

WHERE TO DINE
Expensive
Damiana ✿ SEAFOOD/MEXICAN   This casually elegant restaurant in an 18th-century hacienda is decorated in the colors of a Mexican sunset: deep-orange walls, and tables and chairs clad in bright rose, lavender, and orange cloth. The favored tables are in the tropical courtyard, where candles flicker under trees and bougainvillea. For an appetizer, try zesty mushrooms *diablo*. Grilled lobster tail and *ranchero* shrimp in cactus sauce are flavorful main-course choices. You can also enjoy brunch almost until the dinner hour. There is an interior dining room, but the courtyard is the most romantic dining spot in San José. It's on the east side of the town plaza.

San José town plaza. ℂ **624/142-0499** or 624/142-2899. Fax 624/142-5603. damiana@1cabonet.com.mx. Reservations recommended during Christmas and Easter. Lunch $8–$20; main courses $10–$50. AE, MC, V. Daily 11am–10:30pm.

El Chilar ✿✿ MEXICAN   In this rustically casual restaurant, you may feel like you're dining at a friend's home, as welcoming as chef Armando Montano is. His passion for Mexican cuisine is evident, as he blends the traditional flavors of this country—including an array of chiles—into imaginative and heavenly offerings. Among the most popular dinner options are shrimp in a roasted garlic and *guajillo* chile sauce, or the creative grilled tortilla and salmon Napoleon, accompanied by a mango pico de gallo. These choices may not be offered when you arrive, however, as chef Armando is known to frequently change his menu. At night, candlelight adds a sparkle of romance to the setting. El Chilar also offers a full bar, and an ample selection of wines, with suggestions for pairings with your meal. Air-conditioned indoor dining is available.

Benito Juárez 1497, corner with Morelos, near the Telmex tower. ℂ **624/142-2544** or 624/146-9798. Main courses $5–$29. No credit cards. Mon–Sat 3–10pm.

Mi Cocina ✿✿✿ *Finds* NOUVELLE MEXICAN-EURO   Without a doubt, this is the best dining choice in the entire Los Cabos area. This restaurant doesn't rely solely on the romance of its setting—the food is superb, creative, and consistently flavorful. Notable starters include steamed baby clams topped with a creamy cilantro sauce and served with garlic croutons, or a healthy slice of Camembert cheese, fried and served with homemade toast and grapes. Among the favorite main courses are the baked baby rack of lamb served with grilled vegetables, and the Provençal-style shrimp served with risotto, roasted tomato, basil, and cilantro-fish consommé. Save room for dessert; choices include their famous chocolate-chocolate cake and a perfect crème brûlée. The full-service *palapa* bar offers an excellent selection of wines, premium tequilas, and single-malt scotches. Be adventurous, and try one of their special martinis—like the Flor de México, an adaptation of the Cosmo, using Jamaica (hibiscus flower infusion) rather than cranberry juice.

In the Casa Natalia hotel, Bulevar Mijares. ℂ **624/142-5100**. www.casanatalia.com/dining.cfm. Main courses $15–$32. AE, MC, V. Daily 6:30–10pm (to hotel guests only 6:30am–6pm).

Tequila ✿ MEDITERRANEAN/ASIAN   Contemporary Mexican cuisine with a light and flavorful touch is the star attraction here, although the garden setting is lovely, with rustic *equipal* furniture and lanterns scattered among palms and giant mango trees. Try the specialty, shrimp in tequila sauce. Other enjoyable options include perfectly seared tuna with cilantro and ginger, ribs topped with tamarind sauce, and baked lobster with tequila sauce. Vegetarians can enjoy bell peppers stuffed with ricotta in tomato sauce, or one of several pasta dishes. The accompanying whole-grain bread arrives fresh and hot, and attentive service complements the fine meal. Cuban cigars and an excellent selection of tequilas are available, as is an extensive wine list emphasizing California vintages.

Manuel Doblado s/n, near Hidalgo. © 624/142-1155. Lunch $9–$22; main courses $10–$45. AE. Daily 5:30–10:30pm.

Moderate

French Riviera ★★ FRENCH/PASTRIES/COFFEE   What a great place to start the day . . . or end it! This casual restaurant, located in a classic historic building in San Jose, not only serves tempting French fare, but absolutely irresistible sweets. Its on-site bakery, with an exhibition window for watching the pastry chefs at work, results in smells so delectable I dare you to leave without a sweet something. Start the day with a croissant and cappuccino, or any number of coffee and pastry choices, or end it with a full meal of delectable French fare. A second location in Cabo San Lucas offers a more traditional restaurant setting, with a great selection of wines. It's found in Plaza del Rey, next to the Misiones del Cabo entrance on the highway, Km 6, and it's open from noon until 11pm (© **624/104-3125**).

Corner of Hidalgo and Manuel Doblado s/n. © 624/142-3350. www.frenchrivieraloscabos.com. Breakfast $1.50–$4; dinner $2.50–$6.50. No credit cards. Daily 7:30am–11pm.

Tropicana Bar and Grill SEAFOOD/MEAT   The Tropicana remains a popular mainstay, especially for tourists. The recently remodeled restaurant bar retains its steady clientele day and night, as well as its offerings of live music and special sporting events on satellite TV. The dining area is in a garden (candlelit in the evening) with a tiled mural at one end. Cafe-style sidewalk dining is also available. The menu is too extensive to lay claim to any specialty; it aims to please everyone. All meats and cheeses are imported; dinners include thick steaks and shrimp fajitas. *Paella* is the Sunday special.

Bulevar Mijares 30, 1 block south of the Plaza Mijares. © 624/142-1580. Breakfast $4–$6; main courses $10–$25. AE, MC, V. Daily 6am–11pm.

Zipper's BURGERS/MEXICAN/SEAFOOD   At the far south end of the beach heading toward Cabo San Lucas and fronting the best surfing waters, this casual hangout owned by Mike Posey and Tony Magdaleno has become popular with gringos in search of American food and TV sports. Burgers have that back-home flavor—order one with a side of spicy curly fries. Steaks, lobster, beer-battered shrimp, deli sandwiches, and Mexican combination plates round out the menu, which is printed with dollar prices.

Playa Costa Azul just south of San José (Km 28.5 on Transpeninsular Hwy.). No phone. Burgers and sandwiches $7–$10; main courses $7–$18. MC, V. Daily 11am–11pm.

SAN JOSE AFTER DARK

San José has no nightlife outside of the restaurant and hotel bars. Those intent on real action will find it in Cabo San Lucas. Of particular note here are the bars at **Casa Natalia** and **Tropicana**—the former caters to sophisticated romantics, the latter to those in search of livelier good times. This longstanding bar recently completed an extensive renovation, and now offers a more elegant ambience—rather than simply rustic, it is now "rustic chic." Don't worry though, the Tropicana still features all types of American sports events, however now they're on plasma TV screens, and a new area segregates drinkers from diners. Live mariachi music plays nightly from 6 to 9pm, with live Mexican and Cuban dance music playing from 9:30pm until about 1am. Truly, this is your sole nightlife option in tranquil San Jose. The Tropicana is open daily from 7am to 1am, and drinks are priced from $4 up.

Several of the larger hotels along the beach have Mexican fiestas and other weekly theme nights that include a buffet (usually all-you-can-eat), drinks, live music, and entertainment for $25 to $35 per person. There's also a large dance club on Mijares that seems to be under different ownership each year—it was closed at press time, undergoing yet another renovation.

THE CORRIDOR: BETWEEN THE TWO CABOS

The Corridor between the towns of San José del Cabo and Cabo San Lucas contains some of Mexico's most lavish resorts. Most growth at the tip of the peninsula is occurring along the Corridor, which has already become a major locale for championship golf. The five major resort areas are **Palmilla, Querencia, Cabo Real, Cabo del Sol,** and **Punta Ballena,** each an enclosed community with golf courses, elegant hotels, and million-dollar homes (or the promise of them). If you plan to explore the region while staying at a Corridor hotel, you'll need a rental car (available at the hotels) for at least 1 or 2 days. Even if you're not staying here, the beaches and dining options are worth investigating. All hotels listed here qualify as very expensive. Most resorts offer golf and fishing packages.

WHERE TO STAY

Casa del Mar 🌴 *Finds*   A little-known treasure, this intimate resort is one of the best values along the Corridor. The hacienda-style building offers luxury accommodations in an intimate setting, as well as an on-site spa and nearby golf facilities. It's convenient to the 18-hole championship Cabo Real golf course. Guest rooms have a bright feel, with white marble floors, light wicker furnishings, a separate sitting area, and a large whirlpool tub plus separate shower. Balconies have oversize chairs with a view of the ocean beyond the pool. It's a romantic hotel for couples and honeymooners; it's known for welcoming, personalized service.

Km 19.5 on Hwy. 1, 23410 Cabo San Lucas, B.C.S. ℂ 800/221-8808 in the U.S., or 624/144-0030. Fax 624/144-0034. www.casadelmarmexico.com. 56 units. High season $430 double, $480 suite; low season $290 double, $340 suite. AE, MC, V. **Amenities:** Restaurant; lobby bar; beach club (adults only) w/pool, hot tub, pool bar, open-air restaurant; 6 other pools (2 w/whirlpools and swim-up bars); privileges at Cabo Real and El Dorado golf clubs; 2 lighted tennis courts; small workout room; full-service spa; tour desk; room service; in-room massage; babysitting; laundry service; dry cleaning. *In room:* A/C, TV, minibar, dataport, hair dryer, safe-deposit box, bathrobes, Jacuzzi.

Esperanza 🌴🌴🌴   Although this new luxury resort along Cabo's over-the-tip Corridor sits on a bluff overlooking two small, rocky coves, the absence of a real beach doesn't seem to matter much to its guests—the hotel more than makes up for it in terms of pampering services and stylish details. Created by the famed Auberge Resorts group, the architecture of this hotel is similar in style to that of Careyes, on Mexico's Pacific coast, meaning it's dramatic, elegant, and comfortable. The casitas and villas are spread across 6.8 hectares (17 acres), designed to resemble a Mexican village, and are connected to the resort facilities by stone footpaths. The top-floor suites have handmade *palapa* ceilings and a private outdoor whirlpool spa. All rooms are exceptionally spacious, with woven wicker and tropical wood furnishings, original art, rugs and fabrics in muted colors with jewel-tone color accents, and Frette linens gracing the extra-comfortable feather beds. Terraces are large, extending the living area to the

The Two Cabos & The Corridor

outdoors, and all have hammocks and views of the Sea of Cortez. The oversize bathrooms have separate tub and showers with dual showerheads.

Carretera Transpeninsular Km 7 on Hwy. 1, at Punta Ballena 23140 Cabo San Lucas, B.C.S. ℂ **866/311-2226** in the U.S., or 624/145-6400. Fax 624/145-6403. www.esperanzaresort.com. 50 suites, 6 villas. High season $575–$925 suite, $775–$1,050 beachfront suite, $3,500–$5,000 villa; low season $375–$650 suite, $500–$775 beachfront suite, $2,000–$3,000 villa. AE, MC, V. Valet parking. **Amenities:** Oceanfront restaurant; bar; infinity swimming pool; golf privileges; fitness center; deluxe European full-service spa; concierge w/tour services; 24-hr. room service; in-room massage; babysitting; laundry service; dry cleaning; private beach w/club; gourmet market. *In room:* A/C, plasma TV w/DVD, in-suite bar, hair dryer, safe-deposit box, high-speed Internet access, stereo, bathrobes.

Las Ventanas al Paraíso ★★★ Las Ventanas is known for its luxury accommodations and attention to detail. The architecture, with adobe structures and rough-hewn wood accents, provides a soothing complement to the desert landscape. The only color comes from the dazzling *ventanas* (windows) of pebbled rainbow glass handmade by regional artisans. Richly furnished, Mediterranean-style rooms are large (starting at 300 sq. m/1,000 sq. ft.) and appointed with every conceivable amenity, from wood-burning fireplaces to computerized telescopes for star- or whale-gazing. Rooms contain satellite TV with VCRs, stereos with CD players, and dual-line cordless phones. Sizable whirlpool tubs overlook the room and may be closed off for privacy. Larger suites offer extras like rooftop terraces, sunken whirlpools on a private patio, or a personal pool. The spa is among the best in Mexico. With a staff that outnumbers guests by four to one, this is the place for those who want (and can afford) to be seriously spoiled. They even have special packages for pampered pets that can't be left behind. The 15% service charge is not included in the prices below, which do include taxes.

Km 19.5 on Hwy. 1, 23410 San José del Cabo, B.C.S. ℂ **888/525-0483** in the U.S., or 624/144-0300. Fax 624/144-0301. www.lasventanas.com. 61 suites. High season $600 garden-view double, $800 oceanview double, $950 split-level oceanview suite with rooftop terrace, $1,150 split-level oceanfront suite with rooftop terrace, luxury suites (1 and 3 bedrooms) $2,600–$4,500; low season $450 gardenview double, $550 oceanview double, $675 split-level oceanview suite with rooftop terrace, $900 split-level oceanfront suite with rooftop terrace, luxury suites $1,800–$3,800. Spa and golf packages and inclusive meal plans available. AE, DC, MC, V. Free valet parking. **Amenities:** Oceanview restaurant; terrace bar w/live music; seaside grill; fresh-juice bar; access to adjoining championship Cabo Real golf course; deluxe European spa w/complete treatment and exercise facilities; watersports; tour services; car rental; shuttle services; 24-hr. room service; laundry service; sportfishing and luxury yachts available; pet packages, including treats and massages. *In room:* A/C, TV, dataport, minibar, hair dryer, iron, safe-deposit box, bathrobes.

One&Only Palmilla ★★★ One of the most comfortably luxurious hotels in Mexico, the One&Only Palmilla is the grand dame of Los Cabos resorts, and it completed

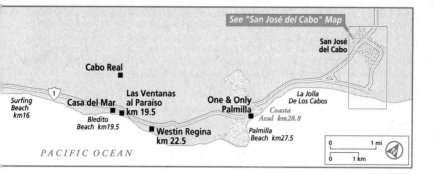

See "San José del Cabo" Map

San José del Cabo

Cabo Real

Las Ventanas
al Paraíso
km 19.5

One & Only
Palmilla

La Jolla
De Los Cabos

Surfing
Beach
km16

Casa del Mar

*Coasta
Azul km28.8*

Bledito
Beach km19.5

Westin Regina
km 22.5

Palmilla
Beach km27.5

PACIFIC OCEAN

0 ————— 1 mi
0 ————— 1 km

a complete renovation in late 2003, making it among the most spectacular resort hotels anywhere. Perched on a cliff top above the sea (with beach access), the resort is a series of white buildings with red-tile roofs, towering palms, and flowering bougainvillea. The feeling here remains one of classic resort-style comfort, but the new sophisticated details bring it up to date with the most modern of resorts. The new decor features muted desert colors and luxury fabrics, with special extras such as flatscreen TVs with DVD/CD players, and Bose surround-sound systems. Bathrooms feature inlaid stone rain showers and sculpted tubs. Ample, private balconies or terraces have extra comfortable, overstuffed chairs, and each room also has a separate sitting area. Guests receive twice-daily maid service, a personal butler, and an aromatherapy menu—to ensure you leave completely relaxed or rejuvenated. Their new "C" restaurant is under the direction of the renowned chef Charlie Trotter of Chicago, and it also offers 24-hour in-room dining. A second, more casual dining choice is the *palapa*-topped Agua restaurant, with "Mexiterranean" cuisine. The Palmilla has become renowned as a location for destination weddings and anniversary celebrations with a renewal of vows; ceremonies take place in its small, signature chapel that graces a sloped hillside. Across the highway, the resort's own championship golf course, designed by Jack Nicklaus, is available for guests, and the Palmilla also has two lighted tennis courts, a 600 sq. m (2,000 sq. ft.) state-of-the-art fitness center, and yoga garden. Also among the new additions is an exceptional spa, with 13 private treatment villas for one or two people.

Carretera Transpeninsular Km 7.5, 23400 San José Del Cabo, B.C.S. Ⓒ 800/637-2226 or 866/829-2977 in the U.S., or 624/146-7000, 624/144-5000. Fax 624/144-5100. www.oneandonlypalmilla.com. 114 units. High season $475 double, from $775–$1,600 suite and villa; low season $325 double, from $575–$1,300 suite and villa. AE, MC, V. **Amenities:** 2 restaurants; terrace bar; pool bar; championship Palmilla golf course; deluxe European spa w/complete treatment and exercise facilities; watersports; tour services; car rental; shuttle services; 24-hr. room service; laundry service; yoga garden; sportfishing. *In room:* A/C, TV, dataport, minibar, hair dryer, iron, safe-deposit box, bathrobes.

Westin Regina ★★ *Kids*   The architecturally dramatic Westin Regina sits at the end of a long paved road atop a seaside cliff. Vivid terra cotta, yellow, and pink walls rise against a landscape of sandstone, cacti, and palms, with fountains and gardens lining the long pathways from the lobby to the rooms. Electric carts carry guests and their luggage through the vast property. The rooms are lovely, with both air-conditioning and ceiling fans, private balconies, satellite TV, and walk-in showers separate from the bathtubs. This is probably the best choice among our selections for families vacationing along the corridor; it offers a wealth of activities for children.

Hwy. 1 Km 22.5, Apdo. Postal 145, 23400 San José del Cabo, B.C.S. ⓒ **800/228-3000** in the U.S., or 624/142-9000. Fax 624/142-9010. www.westin.com. 295 units. $308 partial oceanview double; $347 full oceanview double; $436–$705 suite. 20% low-season discount. AE, DC, MC, V. **Amenities:** 6 restaurants; 2 bars; 3 swimming pools; nearby Palmilla and Cabo Real golf courses; 18-hole putting course; 2 tennis courts; full fitness center and spa; children's activities; concierge; Xplora Adventour services; car-rental desk; business services; salon; 24-hr. room service; babysitting; laundry service; beach club. *In room:* A/C, TV, minibar, hair dryer, safe.

WHERE TO DINE

Pitahayas ⭐ PACIFIC RIM   In a beachside setting in the Hacienda del Mar resort, Pitahayas offers gourmet dining under a grand *palapa* or on open-air terraces under a starlit sky. Master chef Volker Romeike has assembled a creative menu that blends Pacific Rim cuisine with Mexican herbs and seasonings. Notable sauces include mango, black bean, and curry. Rotisserie barbecued duck is a house specialty, as are mesquite grill and wok cooking. A dessert pizza with fresh fruit, chocolate, and marzipan makes a fitting finish to a stunning meal. Formal resort attire is requested.

At Hacienda del Mar, Km 10 on Hwy. 1, Cabo del Sol. ⓒ **624/145-8010.** Reservations required during high season. Main courses $20–$60. AE, MC, V. Daily 5–10:30pm.

The Restaurant (Las Ventanas al Paraíso) ⭐⭐⭐ INTERNATIONAL   It may just be called "The Restaurant," but there's where simplicity ends, and the extraordinary begins. Where Los Cabos is known for its pricy dining, this is one Restaurant that is worth the price. Start off with a cocktail before dinner in The Lounge, the casually elegant bar area bordering Las Ventanas' stunning pool, lit from above with a constellation of tin stars illuminated by candles. When you move into the dining area, you'll get a sense of the Las Ventanas signature service—such as, should you be wearing black, you'll be given a black napkin. As remarkable as the service is, the dining itself is even better. First courses may include Ensenada steamed mussels, served in coconut milk with a hint of *chile árbol* and a dash of tequila, or a stone crab salad with baby watercress, mango, phillo, and sweet mustard sauce. The constantly changing menu of main courses generally includes an ample selection of seafood, including lobster, done in creative presentations, but their grilled rack of lamb with garlic potatoes, or prime filet mignon in a cabernet sauce, is as good as you'll find anywhere. A stellar selection of premium wines is served, and dress is resort attire. You have your choice of alfresco dining on the patio, or in indoor, air-conditioned comfort. Reserve early, as dinner at The Restaurant is quite popular in Cabo at any time during the year.

At Las Ventanas al Paraíso, Km 19.5 on Hwy. 1. ⓒ **624/144-0300.** Reservations required. Main courses $35–$50. AE, MC, V. Daily 5–11pm

CABO SAN LUCAS

183km (114 miles) S of La Paz; 33km (21 miles) W of San José del Cabo; 1,792km (1,120 miles) SE of Tijuana

The hundreds of luxury hotel rooms along the Corridor north of Cabo San Lucas have transformed this formerly rustic and rowdy outpost. Although it retains boisterous nightlife, Cabo San Lucas is no longer the simple town Steinbeck wrote about. Once legendary for big-game fish, Cabo San Lucas now draws more people for its nearby world-class fairways and greens. This has become Mexico's most elite resort destination. Travelers enjoy a growing roster of adventure-oriented activities, and the nightlife is as hot as the desert in July. A collection of popular restaurants and bars along Cabo's main street stay open and active until the morning's first fishing charters head out to sea. Despite the growth in diversions, Cabo remains more or less a one-stoplight town, with almost everything along the main strip.

Cabo San Lucas

ESSENTIALS

GETTING THERE & DEPARTING   By Plane   For information, see "Getting There & Departing," earlier, under San José del Cabo. Local airline numbers are as follows: **Aero California** (© **624/143-3700**); **Alaska Airlines** (© **624/146-5166**); and **Mexicana** (© **624/143-5352,** -5353, or 624/146-5001 at the airport).

By Car From La Paz, the best route is Highway 1 south past the village of San Pedro, then Highway 19 south through Todos Santos to Cabo San Lucas, a 2-hour drive.

By Bus The **bus terminal** (© **624/143-5020**) is on Héroes at Morelos; it is open daily from 6am to 7pm. Buses go to La Paz every 90 minutes between 6am and 6pm. To and from San José, the more convenient and economical **Suburcabos** public bus service runs every 20 minutes and costs $2.50.

Arriving At the airport, either buy a ticket for a *colectivo* (minibus) from the authorized transportation booth inside the building (about $13) or arrange for a rental car, the most economical way to explore the area. Up to four people can share a private taxi, which costs about $60.

VISITOR INFORMATION The **Los Cabos Tourism Office** (© **624/146-9628**) is in San Jose, located in the Plaza San Jose, locals 3 and 4. The English-language *Los Cabos Guide, Los Cabos News, Cabo Life,* and *Baja Sun* and the irreverent and extremely entertaining *Gringo Gazette* are distributed free at most hotels and shops, and have up-to-date information on new restaurants and clubs.

> **Tips Information, Please**
>
> The many "visitor information" booths along the street in Cabo are actually timeshare sales booths, and their staffs will pitch a visit to their resort in exchange for discounted tours, rental cars, or other giveaways.

CITY LAYOUT The small town spreads out north and west of the harbor of **Cabo San Lucas Bay,** edged by foothills and desert mountains to the west and south. The main street leading into town from the airport and San José del Cabo is **Lázaro Cárdenas;** as it nears the harbor, **Bulevar Marina** branches off from it and becomes the main artery that curves around the waterfront.

GETTING AROUND Taxis are easy to find but expensive, in keeping with the high cost of everything else. Expect to pay about $15 to $25 for a taxi between Cabo and the Corridor hotels.

For day trips to San José del Cabo, take the Suburcabos (see "Getting There & Departing," above) or a cab. You'll see car-rental specials advertised in town, but before signing on, be sure you understand the total price after insurance and taxes are added. Rates can run between $40 and $75 per day, with insurance an extra $10 per day.

FAST FACTS: Cabo San Lucas

Area Code The telephone area code is **624.**

Beach Safety Before swimming in the open water, *check if conditions are safe.* Undertows and large waves are common. **Medano Beach,** close to the marina and town, is the principal beach that's safe for swimming. The Hotel Meliá Cabo San Lucas, on Medano Beach, has a roped-off swimming area to protect swimmers from personal watercraft and boats. Colored flags to signal swimming safety aren't generally found in Cabo, and neither are lifeguards.

Currency Exchange Banks exchange currency during normal business hours, generally Monday through Friday from 9am to 6pm, Saturday from 10am to

2pm. Currency-exchange booths, throughout Cabo's main tourist areas, aren't as competitive, but they're more convenient. ATMs are widely available and even more convenient, dispensing pesos—and in some cases dollars—at bank exchange rates.

Emergencies & Hospital In Cabo, **Baja Médico,** Camino de la Plaza s/n, on the corner with Pedegral (© **624/143-0127** or 624/143-7777) has a 24-hour walk-in clinic, and provides air ambulance services. **Amerimed** (© **624/143-9671**) is a 24-hour, American-standards clinic with bilingual physicians, and accepts major credit cards. Most of the larger hotels have a doctor on call.

Internet Access **Onda net Café & Bar,** Lázaro Cárdenas 7, Edificio Posada, across from the Pemex gas station (© **624/143-5390**), charges $5 for 15 minutes, $7 for 30 minutes, or $8.50 for an hour. It's open Monday through Saturday from 8am to 6pm.

Pharmacy A drugstore with a wide selection of toiletries as well as medicine is **Farmacia Aramburo,** in Plaza Aramburo, on Lázaro Cárdenas at Zaragoza (© **624/143-1489**). It's open Monday through Friday from 7am to 11pm, and accepts MasterCard and Visa.

Post Office The *correo* is at Lázaro Cárdenas between Medano and Gomez Farías (© **624/143-0048**), on the highway to San José del Cabo, east of the bar El Squid Roe. It's open Monday through Friday from 9am to 5pm, Saturday from 9am to 3pm.

OUTDOOR ACTIVITIES: FISHING, GOLF & MORE

Although superb sportfishing put Cabo San Lucas on the map, there's more to do than dropping your line and waiting for the Big One. For most cruises and excursions, try to make fishing reservations at least a day in advance; keep in mind that some trips require a minimum number of people. Most sports and outings can be arranged through a travel agency; fishing can also be arranged directly at one of the fishing-fleet offices at the marina. The marina is located on the south side of the harbor.

Besides fishing, there's kayaking ($65 for a sunset trip around the Arch rock formation; $40 for morning trips) and boat trips to Los Arcos or uninhabited beaches. All-inclusive daytime or sunset cruises are available on a variety of boats, including a restored pirate ship. Many of these trips include snorkeling; serious divers have great underwater venues to explore.

Between January and March, whale-watching is one of the most popular local activities. Guided ATV tours take you down dirt roads and through desert landscape to the old Cabo lighthouse or an ancient Indian village. And then there's the challenge of world-class golf, a major attraction of Los Cabos.

For a complete rundown of what's available, contact **Gray Line Los Cabos** (© **624/146-9410;** www.graylineloscabos.com). It offers tours from any local company, rather than working with only a select few. Most businesses in this section are open from 10am to 2pm and 4 to 7pm.

BEACHES   All along the curving sweep of sand known as Medano Beach, on the east side of the bay, you can rent snorkeling gear, boats, WaveRunners, kayaks, and windsurf boards. You can also take windsurfing lessons. This is the town's main beach and is a great place for safe swimming—as well as people-watching from one of the many outdoor restaurants along its shore.

Beach aficionados may want to rent a car (see "Getting Around," above) and explore the five more remote beaches and coves between the two Cabos: Playa Palmilla, Chileno, Santa María, Barco Varado, and Vista del Arco. Beaches other than Medano are not considered safe for swimming, though many people don't heed the warning. Experienced snorkelers may wish to check them out, but other visitors should go for the view only. Always check at a hotel or travel agency for directions and swimming conditions. Although a few travel agencies run snorkeling tours to some of these beaches, there's no public transportation: Your only option for beach exploring is to rent a car.

CRUISES Glass-bottom boats leave from the town marina daily every 45 minutes between 9am and 4pm. They cost $14 for a 1-hour tour, which passes sea lions and pelicans on its way to the famous **El Arco (Rock Arch)** at Land's End, where the Pacific and the Sea of Cortez meet. Boats drop you off at Playa de Amor; make sure you understand which boat will pick you up—it's usually a smaller one run by the same company that ferries people back at regular intervals. Check the timing to make sure you have the correct boat, or expect an additional $10 charge for boarding a competitor's boat.

A number of **daylong** and **sunset cruises** use a variety of boats and catamarans. They cost $30 to $45, depending on the boat, duration of cruise, and amenities. A sunset cruise on the 42-foot catamaran **Pez Gato** (© **624/143-3797** or 624/143-5297; pezgato@cabotel.com.mx) departs from the Plaza las Glorias Hotel dock at 5pm. A 2-hour cruise costs $35 and includes margaritas, beer, and sodas. The seasonal (winter) whale-watching tour leaves at 10:30am and returns at 1:30pm. It costs $35, and includes open bar and snacks. Similar boats leave from the marina and the Plaza las Glorias Hotel. Check with travel agencies or hotel tour desks.

GOLF Los Cabos has become the golf mecca of Mexico, and though most courses are along the Corridor, people look to Cabo San Lucas for information about this sport in Baja Sur. The master plan for Los Cabos golf calls for a future total of 207 holes. Fees listed below are for 18 holes, including golf cart, water, club service, and tax. Summer rates are about 25% lower, and many hotels offer golf packages. (For specifics on the various courses, see "The Lowdown on Golf in Cabo," below.)

Several specialty tour operators offer golf packages to Los Cabos, which include accommodations, greens fees, and other amenities. These include **Best Golf** (© **888/ 817-GOLF** in the U.S.); **Golf Adventures** (© **800/841-6570** in the U.S.; www.golf adventures.com); and **Sportours** (© **888/GOLF-MEX** in the U.S.; www.sportours. com).

The 27-hole course at the **Palmilla Golf Club,** at the One&Only Palmilla resort (© **800/386-2465** in the U.S., or 624/144-5250; daily 7am–7pm) was the first Jack Nicklaus Signature layout in Mexico, on 360 hectares (900 acres) of dramatic oceanfront desert. The course offers your choice of two back-nine options, with high-season greens fees of $215 (lower after 1pm), and low-season greens fees running between $130 and $210. Guests at some hotels pay discounted rates.

Just a few kilometers away is another Jack Nicklaus Signature course, the 18-hole Ocean Course at **Cabo del Sol,** at the Cabo del Sol resort development in the Corridor (© **624/145-8200**). The 7,100-yard Ocean Course is known for its challenging three finishing holes. Tom Weiskopf designed the new 18-hole Desert Course. Greens fees for both are $220 to $275.

The 18-hole, 6,945-yard course at **Cabo Real,** by the Meliá Cabo Real Hotel in the Corridor (© **624/144-0232;** caborealgolf@1cabonet.com.mx; daily 6:30am–6pm), was designed by Robert Trent Jones, Jr., and features holes that sit high on mesas overlooking the Sea of Cortez. Fees run $220 for 18 holes. After 3pm rates drop to $150.

El Dorado Golf Course (© **624/144-5451;** www.caboreal.com) is a Jack Nicklaus Signature course next to the Westin Regina hotel at Cabo Real. The course is open daily 7am to dusk. Greens fees are $256 (after 2pm, $178). Carts are included; caddies are $100.

An 18-hole course designed by Roy Dye is at the **Raven Club,** formerly the Cabo San Lucas Country Club (© **800/854-2314** in the U.S., or 624/143-4653; fax 624/143-5809). The entire course overlooks the juncture of the Pacific Ocean and Sea of Cortez, including the famous Land's End rocks. It includes the 607-yard, par-5 seventh hole—the longest hole in Mexico. Greens fees are $176 for 18 holes, $130 after 2:30pm. The course was redone after a 2001 hurricane added substantial water features. It is still a Dye-design course, with the layout changing slightly, and regular players say it's a much-improved experience.

The lowest greens fees in the area are at the public 9-hole **Club Campo de Golf San José** (© **624/142-0900** or 624/142-0905) in San José del Cabo (see earlier in this chapter). Early morning greens fees are just $60 for 9 holes, and $109 for 18 holes; from 11am to 3pm, rates drop to $80 for 18 holes; after 3pm, rates are just $40 for 18 holes. All greens fees include use of cart.

HORSEBACK RIDING   You can rent **horses** through **Rancho Colin** (© **624/143-3652**) for around $25 per hour. Tours to the Pacific for sunset riding on the beach cost $35 per person per hour. It's open daily from 8am to noon, and 2–5pm. They're located in front of the parking lot of the Hotel Meliá Los Cabos. For information on the highly recommended **Cuadra San Francisco Equestrian Center,** see p. 709.

SNORKELING & DIVING   Several companies offer snorkeling; a 2-hour cruise to sites around El Arco costs $30, and a 4-hour trip to Santa María costs $55, including gear rental. Among the beaches visited on different trips are Playa de Amor, Santa María, Chileno, and Barco Varado. Snorkeling gear rents for $10 to $15. Contact **Gray Line** (© **624/146-9410**). For scuba diving, contact **Amigos del Mar** (© **800/344-3349** or 310/459-9861 in the U.S., or 624/143-0505 in Mexico; fax 310/454-1686 in the U.S., or 624/143-0887 in Mexico; www.amigosdelmar.com; daily 8am–4:30pm) at the marina, near the Solmar hotel. Dives are along the wall of a canyon in San Lucas Bay, where you can see the "sandfalls" that even Jacques Cousteau couldn't figure out—no one knows their source or cause. There are also scuba trips to Santa María Beach and more distant places, including the Gordo Banks and Cabo Pulmo. Prices start at $45 for a one-tank dive, $66 for two tanks; trips to the coral outcropping at Cabo Pulmo start at $125. You'll need a wetsuit for winter dives. A 5-hour resort course is available for $100, and open-water certification costs around $450.

SPORTFISHING   Many larger hotels, like the Solmar, have their own fleets. To make your own arrangements, go to the town marina on the south side of the harbor, where you'll find several fleet operators with offices near the docks. *Panga* fleets offer the best deals; 5 hours of fishing for two or three people costs $200 to $450. But stroll around

The Lowdown on Golf in Cabo

Los Cabos, one of the world's finest golf destinations, offers an ample and intriguing variety of courses to challenge golfers of all levels.

The reason so many choose to play here is not just the selection, quality, and beauty of the courses, but the very reliable weather. The courses highlighted below compare to the great ones in Palm Springs and Scottsdale, with the added beauty of ocean views and a wider variety of desert cacti and flowering plants.

Course fees are high in Cabo—generally over $200 per round. But these are world-class courses, worth the world-class price. Courses generally offer 20% to 30% off rates if you play after 2 or 2:30pm. This is actually a great time to play, because the temperature is cooler and play is generally faster. The golf offerings in Los Cabos will only continue to expand; four courses are in various phases of construction.

PALMILLA GOLF CLUB The original Cabo course is now a 27-hole layout. The original 18 holes are known as the Arroyo; the new holes are the Ocean 9. It's a bit of a misnomer—although the newer holes lie closer to the water, only one has a true ocean view, with a spectacular play directly down to the beach. You must play the Arroyo for your first nine holes, then you choose between Mountain and Ocean for your back nine. If you play this course only once, choose the Mountain, which offers better ocean views. The signature hole is the Mountain 5; you hit over a canyon, then down to the green below over a forced carry. This is target golf, on a Jack Nicklaus course that was constructed with strategy in mind. A mountaintop clubhouse provides spectacular views. Although it is currently a semiprivate club, most Corridor hotels have membership benefits. The eventual plan is for guests of the Palmilla Hotel and residents of the adjacent real estate development to have exclusive use of this course.

CABO DEL SOL The Ocean Course was the second Jack Nicklaus course constructed in Los Cabos. Its dramatic finishing oceanside holes make it the "Pebble Beach of Baja." It is much more difficult than the Palmilla course, with less room for error.

Don't be fooled by the wide, welcoming 1st hole. This is challenging target golf, with numerous forced carries—even from the red tees. Seven holes

the marina and talk with the captains—you may make a better deal. Try **ABY Charters** (© 624/144-4203; www.abycharters.com; daily 10am–4pm; Visa and MasterCard are accepted), or the **Picante/Blue Water Sportfishing Fleet** (© 624/143-2474; www.picantesportfishing.com; daily 6am–8pm; American Express, MasterCard, and Visa are accepted). Both have booths (with bathrooms) at the sportfishing dock at the far south end of the marina. A day on a fully equipped cruiser with captain and guide starts at around $1,070 for up to four people. For deluxe trips with everything included aboard a 12m (40-ft.) boat, you'll have to budget $1,455. (See also "The Active Traveler" in chapter 2 for companies that arrange fishing in advance.) If you're traveling in your own are along the water. The signature hole is 17, which runs by the water with a forced carry. Cabo del Sol offers another option, the Desert Course.

CABO REAL   This Robert Trent Jones, Jr., design is known for its holes along the Sea of Cortez, which sit high on mesas overlooking the sea; exceptional among these is the frequently photographed 12th. Jones designed the course to test low handicappers, but multiple tees make it enjoyable for average players as well. The par-72 layout is 6,945 yards long and was designed with professional tournament play in mind. The most famous hole is the 14th, right on the beach near the Meliá resort.

THE RAVEN CLUB   The front and back nines are the work of members of the Dye family, so the course plays like two different courses. Characteristic of Dye designs, it has deep waste bunkers, subtle terracing up hillsides, and holes built into the natural desert terrain. The most challenging hole is the 607-yard, par-5 7th hole, around a lake; it's the longest hole in Mexico. The course is designed to offer a variety of play options, from a short course played on front tees to a super-long course with numerous bunkers and hazards. The whole course was redone in 2002 by the Dye family, Although the layout is essentially the same, some greens have moved slightly and some holes are a little shorter than before, but all of the bunkers and hazards have remained, and the course is now considered even better.

EL DORADO GOLF COURSE   A Jack Nicklaus Signature course at Cabo Real, El Dorado is a links-style course in the Scottish tradition. The layout is challenging—7 holes border the Sea of Cortez, and 12 are carved out of two pristine canyons. The oceanview holes are not the only water; manmade lakes are also a part of the scenery. El Dorado bills itself as the "Pebble Beach of Baja"—but then again, so does Cabo del Sol. You decide.

   Note: Cabo's newest course, **Querencia** (© **624/145-6670;** www.bajagolf. com/querencia.html) is a Tom Fazio design. Originally a private club, with play limited to property owners and members, it now accepts guests of both Las Ventanas and Casa del Mar. Greens fees are $275.

vessel, you'll need a fishing permit. Depending on the size of the boat, it will cost $15 to $45 per month. Daily permits ($4–$10) and annual permits are also available.

   The fishing here lives up to its reputation: Bringing in a 100-pound marlin is routine. Angling is good all year, though the catch varies with the season. Sailfish and wahoo are best from June through November; yellowfin tuna, May through December; yellowtail, January through April; black and blue marlin, July through December. Striped marlin are prevalent year-round.

SURFING   Good surfing can be found March through November all along the beaches west of town, and there's a famous right break at **Chileno Beach,** near the

Cabo San Lucas Hotel east of town. (See "Surfing," in "San José del Cabo," earlier in this chapter.

WHALE-WATCHING   Whale-watching cruises are not to be missed. See "Whale-Watching in Baja," on p. 746, for information on the excursions, which operate between January and March.

A BREAK FROM SPORTS: EXPLORING CABO SAN LUCAS

FESTIVALS & EVENTS   October 12 is the festival of the patron saint of Todos Santos, a town about 105km (65 miles) north. **October 18** is the feast of the patron saint of Cabo San Lucas, celebrated with a fair, feasting, music, dancing, and other special events.

HISTORIC CABO SAN LUCAS   Sports and partying are Cabo's main attractions, but there are also a few cultural and historical points of interest. The Spanish missionary Nicolás Tamaral established the stone **Iglesia de San Lucas (Church of San Lucas)** on Calle Cabo San Lucas, close to the main plaza, in 1730. A large bell in a stone archway commemorates the completion of the church in 1746. The Pericúe Indians, who resisted Tamaral's demands that they practice monogamy, eventually killed him. Buildings on the streets facing the main plaza are gradually being renovated to house restaurants and shops, and the picturesque neighborhood has the most Mexican ambience in town.

DAY TRIPS   Most local and hotel travel agencies book day trips to the city of **La Paz;** they cost around $60, including beverages and a tour of the countryside along the way. Usually there's a stop at the weaving shop of Fortunato Silva, who spins his own cotton and weaves it into wonderfully textured rugs and textiles. Day trips are also available to **Todos Santos** ($60), with a guided walking tour of the Cathedral Mission, museum, Hotel California, and various artists' homes. (For more information, see "La Paz" and "Todos Santos," later in this chapter.)

SHOPPING

San José has the better shopping of the two towns when it comes to higher quality items, but if you're after a beer-themed T-shirt, Cabo San Lucas can't be topped. In Cabo San Lucas, the most notable shops are now concentrated in the **Puerto Paraíso Entertainment Plaza** (© 624/144-3000; www.puertoparaiso.com). Opened in 2002, this is now the focal point for shopping for tourists. It's a truly world-class mall, complete with parking, a food court, movie theaters, and a video arcade. With over 50,000 sq. m (538,000 sq. ft.) of air-conditioned space on three levels, it's too bad that the shops don't live up to the promise of this attractive mall. Although it bills itself as having an array of designer shops, this is a bit misleading; there may be one or two name-brand items within any store, and many of the stores are vacant. It is a good place to shop for swimwear or resort wear, and there are plenty of gift items to choose from, but don't expect the equivalent of a U.S. shopping mall experience. However, it does have some choice dining options, the best being the local branch of **Ruth's Chris Steak House,** adjacent to the marina (© 624/144-3232; daily 1–11:30pm). The plaza is located marina-side between the Plaza Bonita Mall and Marina Fiesta Resort—you can't miss it if you tried. Most other shops in Cabo are on or within a block or two of Boulevard Marina and the plaza.

   The Plaza Bonita Shopping Center (Cabo San Lucas, Bulevar Marina at Cárdenas) is an older shopping center that is still worth a visit. This large terra cotta-colored plaza on the edge of the Cabo San Lucas marina has been around since 1990, and it finally has a group of successful businesses. A branch of **Dos Lunas** (𝄐 **624/143-1969**) sells colorful casual sportswear. **Cartes** (𝄐 **624/143-1770**) is filled with hand-painted ceramic vases and dishes, pewter frames, carved furniture, and hand-woven textiles. Most shops in the plaza are open daily from 9am to 9pm.

In addition to the malls, I recommend the following specialty stores:

El Callejón   Cabo's best selection of fine Mexican furniture and decor items, plus gifts, accessories, tableware, fabrics, and lamps. Open Monday through Saturday 9:30am to 7:30pm. Guerrero between Cárdenas & Madero (across from Cabo Wabo). 𝄐 **624/143-3188**.

H2O   Here you'll find a tempting selection of women's swimwear, casual wear, dresses and evening wear, as well as casual resort wear for men. Open Monday through Saturday 9am to 8pm, and Sunday 11am to 5pm. Vicente Guerrero & Madero. 𝄐 **624/143-1219**.

J & J Habanos   Cabo's largest cigar shop, selling premium Cuban and fine Mexican cigars—it even has a walk-in humidor. Open Monday through Sat 9am to 10 pm, Sunday 9am to 9pm. Madero between Bulevar Marina and Guerrero. 𝄐 **624/143-6160** or 624/143-3839.

Necri   Fine home accessories and Mexican handicrafts, with an extensive selection of pewter and Talavera. Open Monday through Saturday 9am to 9pm. Bulevar Marina (across from Subway). 𝄐 **624/143-0283**.

Tequila's House   A large selection of fine tequilas and other liquors, as well as cigars. There are two locations. Open Monday through Saturday 8am to 11pm. 624 Bulevar Marina, in front of Caliente (𝄐 **624/143-5666**), and Morelos at Lázaro Cárdenas (𝄐 **624/143-9070**).

Ultrafemme   Mexico's largest duty-free shop, with an excellent selection of fine jewelry and watches, including Rolex, Cartier, Omega, TAG Heuer, and Tissot; perfumes, including Lancôme, Chanel, Armani, Carolina Herrera; and other gift items, all at duty free prices. Open daily 10am to 10pm. Plaza Ultrafemme, Bulevar Marina, across from Carlos & Charlies. 𝄐 **624/145-6090** or 624/145-6099. www.ultrafemme.com.mx.

WHERE TO STAY

High season prices are in effect from November to Easter. Several hotels offer package deals that significantly lower the nightly rate; ask your travel agent for information. Budget accommodations are scarce, but the number of small inns and B&Bs is growing. Several notable ones have opened in recent years. Because most of the larger hotels are well maintained and offer packages through travel agents, I will focus on smaller, unique accommodations.

Expensive

Solmar Suites ★   Set against sandstone cliffs at the very tip of the Baja Peninsula, the Solmar is beloved by those seeking seclusion, comfort, and easy access to Cabo's diversions. The suites are in two-story white stucco buildings along the edge of a broad beach. They have either a king or two double beds, satellite TV, separate seating areas, and private balconies or patios on the sand. Guests gather by the pool and on the beach at sunset and all day long during the winter whale migration. The Solmar has one of the best sportfishing fleets in Los Cabos, including the deluxe *Solmar V,* for long-range diving, fishing, and whale-watching expeditions. A small timeshare complex adjoins the Solmar; some units are available for nightly stays. Rates below include the hotel's mandatory 10% service charge.

Av. Solmar 1, 23410 Cabo San Lucas, B.C.S. 𝄐 **624/143-3535**. Fax 624/143-0410. www.solmar.com. (Reservations: Box 383, Pacific Palisades, CA 90272. 𝄐 **800/344-3349** in the U.S., or 310/459-9861. Fax 310/454-1686.) 194 units.

High season $170–$330 double; low season $145–$300 double. AE, MC, V. **Amenities:** Restaurant (w/Sat Mexican fiesta); 2 bars (1 beach, 1 swim-up); 3 pools; Jacuzzi; concierge; tour desk; car-rental desk; salon; room service; laundry service; dry cleaning; sportfishing. *In room:* A/C, TV, dataport, minibar, coffeemaker, hair dryer, safe-deposit box.

Moderate

The Bungalows ★ *Finds*   This is one of the most special places to stay in Los Cabos. Each "bungalow" is a charming retreat decorated with authentic Mexican furnishings. Terra cotta tiles, hand-painted sinks, wooded chests, blown glass, and other creative touches make you feel as if you're a guest at a friend's home rather than at a hotel. Each room has a mini-kitchenette, purified water, VCR, and designer bedding. Rooms surround a lovely heated pool with cushioned lounges and tropical gardens. A brick-paved breakfast nook serves a gourmet breakfast with fresh-ground coffee and fresh juices. Under the owner's warm and welcoming management, this is Cabo's most spacious, comfortable, full-service inn. A 100% smoke-free environment, it is 5 blocks from downtown Cabo.

Miguel A. Herrera s/n, in front of Lienzo Charro, 23410 Cabo San Lucas, B.C.S. ⓒ/fax **624/143-5035** or 624/143-0585. www.cabobungalows.com. 16 units. High season $115–$165 suite; low season $105–$165 suite; extra person $20. Rates include full breakfast. AE. Street parking available. **Amenities:** Breakfast room; pool; concierge; tour desk. *In room:* A/C, TV/VCR, dataport, kitchenette, fridge, coffeemaker.

Los Milagros   The elegant white two-level buildings containing the 11 suites and rooms of Los Milagros (the Miracles) border either a grassy garden area or the small pool. Rooms contain contemporary iron beds with straw headboards, buff-colored tile floors, and artistic details. Some units have kitchenettes, and the master suite has a sunken tub. E-mail, fax, and telephone service are available through the office, and there's coffee service in the mornings on the patio. Evenings are romantic: Candles light the garden, and classical music plays. Request a room in one of the back buildings, where noise from conversations is less intrusive. It's located just 1½ blocks from the Giggling Marlin and Cabo Wabo.

Matamoros 116, 23410 Cabo San Lucas, B.C.S. ⓒ/fax **624/143-4566**. www.losmilagros.com.mx. 11 units. $84 double. Ask about summer discounts, group rates, long-term discounts. No credit cards. Limited street parking. **Amenities:** Small pool. *In room:* A/C.

Inexpensive

Club Cabo Inn ★★ *Finds*   This three-story hotel on a quiet street is a real find, and it keeps getting better. It offers a rare combination of low rates, extra-friendly management, and great, funky style. Rooms are basic and very small, with either two twin beds or one queen; although this was a bordello in a prior incarnation, everything is kept new and updated, from the mattresses to the mini-refrigerators. Muted desert colors add a spark of personality. The rooms surround a courtyard where you can enjoy satellite TV, a barbecue grill, and free coffee. The third floor has a rooftop terrace with *palapa* and a small swimming pool. Also on this floor is "Juan's Love Palace," aka the honeymoon suite. It's a colorful, *palapa*-topped, open-air room with hanging *tapetes* (woven palm mats) for additional privacy. A large fish freezer is available, and most rooms have kitchenettes. The hotel's just 2 blocks from downtown and the marina. A lively restaurant next door will even deliver pitchers of margaritas and dinner to your room.

20 de Noviembre and Leona Vicario, 23410 Cabo San Lucas, B.C.S. ⓒ/fax **624/143-3348**. www.mexonline.com/clubcabo.htm. 23 units. $55–$85 double; $330 double weekly (low season only). No credit cards. Street parking. **Amenities:** Small rooftop pool and sunning area; communal TV and barbecue. *In room:* A/C, fridge.

Siesta Suites 🐾   Reservations are a must at this immaculate, small inn popular with return visitors to Cabo. (It's especially popular with fishermen.) The very basic rooms have white tile floors and white walls, kitchenettes with seating areas, refrigerators, and sinks. The mattresses are firm, and the bathrooms are large and sparkling clean. Rooms on the fourth floor have two queen-size beds each. The accommodating proprietors offer free movies and VCRs, a barbecue pit and outdoor patio table on the second floor, and a comfortable lobby with TV. They can also arrange fishing trips. Weekly and monthly rates are available. The hotel is 1½ blocks from the marina, where parking is available.

Calle Emiliano Zapata between Guerrero and Hidalgo, 23410 Cabo San Lucas, B.C.S. ℂ **866/271-0952** in the U.S., or 624/143-2773. www.cabosiestasuites.com. 20 suites (15 w/kitchenette). $55 double. AE, MC, V. **Amenities:** Pool; barbecue pit. *In room:* VCR, kitchenette (in some), fridges, fan.

WHERE TO DINE

It's not uncommon to pay a lot for mediocre food in Cabo, so try to get a couple of unbiased recommendations. If people are only drinking and not dining, take that as a clue—many seemingly popular places are long on party atmosphere but short on food. Prices decrease the farther you walk inland. The absolute local favorite is **Manuel's Tamales,** a street stand selling traditional treats of cornmeal stuffed with meat or cheese, then steamed in a cornhusk. Look for him on weekend nights on the corner of Lázaro Cárdenas and Zaragoza. Streets to explore for other good restaurants include Hidalgo and Lázaro Cárdenas, plus the Marina at the Plaza Bonita. Note that many restaurants automatically add the tip (15%) to the bill.

Very Expensive

Casa Rafael's 🐾 INTERNATIONAL   Looking for a little romance? Casa Rafael's, though overpriced, is among the most romantic places in Cabo. Dine in one of the large house's candlelit rooms and alcoves (which are air-conditioned), or outside beside the small swimming pool. Piano music plays in the background while you enjoy a leisurely meal. To start, try sublime smoked dorado pâté, or perhaps hearts of palm with raspberry vinaigrette. House specialties—a tasty combination of selections from the meat, seafood, and pasta menus—include Cornish game hen in champagne sauce. Black Angus steaks are imported from the United States; the lamb comes from New Zealand.

Calle Medano and Camino el Pescador. ℂ **624/143-0739.** Fax 624/143-1679. www.allaboutcabo.com. Reservations strongly recommended. Main courses $20–$58. AE, MC, V. Daily 7–10pm. Follow the Hacienda Rd. toward the ocean; when you top the hill, turn left and drive to the rosy-pink château with an arched front and a patio with caged birds and fountain.

Expensive

Nick-San 🐾🐾 JAPANESE/SUSHI   Exceptional Japanese cuisine and sushi are the specialties at this air-conditioned restaurant with minimalist decor. A rosewood sushi bar with royal blue tile accents allows diners to watch the master sushi chef at work. An exhibition kitchen behind him demonstrates why this place has been honored with a special award for cleanliness. It's a personal favorite of mine—as well as of many local residents.

Bulevar Marina, Plaza de la Danza, Local 2. ℂ **624/143-4484.** Reservations recommended. Main courses $12–$30; sushi from $3.50. MC, V. Tues–Sun 11:30am–10:30pm.

Moderate

La Dolce ITALIAN   This restaurant is the offspring of Puerto Vallarta's La Dolce Vita, with authentic Italian thin-crust, brick-oven pizzas and other specialties. It seems about 80% of the business is from local customers, underscoring the attention to detail and reasonable prices. The simple menu also features sumptuous pastas and calzones, plus great salads. This is the best late-night dining option.

M. Hidalgo and Zapata s/n. $\textcircled{C}$ 624/143-4122. Main courses $8–$19. MC, V. Mon–Sat 8pm–midnight. Closed Sept.

Mi Casa $\mathcal{R}$ MEXICAN   The building's vivid cobalt-blue facade is your first clue that this place celebrates Mexico, and the menu confirms that impression. This is one of Cabo's most renowned gourmet Mexican restaurants. Traditional specialties such as *manchamanteles* (literally, "tablecloth stainers"), *cochinita pibil,* and *chiles en nogada* are menu staples. Fresh fish is prepared with delicious seasonings from throughout Mexico. Especially pleasant at night, the restaurant's tables, scattered around a large patio, are set with colorful cloths, traditional pottery, and glassware. It's across from the main plaza.

Calle Cabo San Lucas (at Madero). $\textcircled{C}$ 624/143-1933. Reservations recommended. Main courses $15–$25. AE, MC, V. Daily 5:30–10pm.

Inexpensive

Cafe Cane $\mathcal{R}$ COFFEE/PASTRY/LIGHT MEALS   This cozy, tasty cafe and bistro is a welcome addition to the Cabo Marina boardwalk. Espresso drinks or fruit smoothies and muffins are good eye-openers for early risers. Enjoy a light meal or a tropical drink either inside or on the bustling waterfront terrace. The appealing menu also offers breakfast egg wraps, salads (for example, curried chicken salad with fresh fruit), sandwiches (such as blue-cheese quesadillas with smoked tuna and mango), and pastas—all reasonably priced. Full bar service is also available.

Marina boardwalk, below Plaza Las Glorias hotel. $\textcircled{C}$ 624/143-3435. Main courses: $4–$9; coffee $1.75–$3.50. AE, MC, V. Daily 6am–5pm.

Mocambo's $\mathcal{R}$ SEAFOOD   The location of this longstanding Cabo favorite is not inspiring—it's basically a large cement building—but the food obviously is. The place is always packed, generally with locals tired of high prices and small portions. Ocean-fresh seafood is the order of the day, and the specialty platter can easily serve four people. The restaurant is 1½ blocks inland from Lázaro Cárdenas.

Av. Leona Vicario and 20 de Noviembre. $\textcircled{C}$ 624/143-6070. Main courses $5–$23. MC, V. Daily noon–10pm.

CABO SAN LUCAS AFTER DARK

Cabo San Lucas is the nightlife capital of Baja. After-dark fun centers on the casual bars and restaurants on Bulevar Marina or facing the marina, rather than a flashy dance club scene. You can easily find a happy hour with live music and a place to dance, or a Mexican fiesta with mariachis.

MEXICAN FIESTAS & THEME NIGHTS   Some larger hotels have weekly fiesta nights, Italian nights, and other buffet-plus-entertainment theme nights that can be fun as well as a good buy. Check travel agencies and the following hotels: the **Solmar** (*$\textcircled{C}$ 624/143-3535*), the **Finisterra** (*$\textcircled{C}$ 624/143-3333*), and the **Meliá San Lucas** (*$\textcircled{C}$ 624/143-4444*). Prices range from $22 (not including drinks, tax, and tips) to $35 (which covers everything, including an open bar with national drinks).

SUNSET WATCHING   Come twilight, check out Land's End, where the two seas meet. At **Whale Watcher's Bar,** in the Hotel Finisterra (*$\textcircled{C}$ 624/143-3333*), you'll get a world-class view of the sun sinking into the Pacific. The high terrace offers vistas of both sea and beach, as well as magical glimpses of whales from January to March. Mariachis play on Friday from 6:30 to 9pm. The bar is open daily from 10am to 11pm.

HAPPY HOURS, CLUBS & HANGOUTS   If you shop around, you can usually find an *hora alegre* (happy hour) somewhere in town between noon and 7pm. The most popular places to drink and carouse until all hours are longstanding favorites like the Giggling Marlin, El Squid Roe, and the Cabo Wabo Cantina.

Two places to enjoy live music in a more adult setting are the **Sancho Panza Wine Bar and Bistro** (see below) and the **El Bistro** restaurant and live jazz bar, on Zaragoza at Niños Héroes (© **624/143-8999** or 624/143-3212). Both offer classic jazz in more of a club-style atmosphere, accommodating conversation.

Cabo Wabo Cantina   Owned by Sammy Hagar (formerly of Van Halen) and his Mexican and American partners, this "cantina" packs in youthful crowds, especially when rumors (frequent, and frequently false, just to draw a crowd) fly that a surprise appearance by a vacationing musician is imminent. Live rock bands from the United States, Mexico, Europe, and Australia perform. One of Cabo's few air-continued dance venues, it's especially popular in the summer months. When there isn't a band, a dance club-type sound system plays mostly rock and some alternative and techno. Overstuffed furniture frames the dance floor. Beer goes for $3, margaritas for $5. For snacks, the "Taco-Wabo," just outside the club's entrance, stays up late, too. The cantina is open from 11am to 4am. Vicente Guerrero at Lázaro Cárdenas. © **624/143-1188.**

El Squid Roe   El Squid Roe is one of the late Carlos Anderson's inspirations, and it still attracts wild, fun-loving crowds of all ages with its two stories of nostalgic decor. The eclectic food is far better than you'd expect from such a party place. As fashionable as blue jeans, this is a place to see—women's tops are known to be discarded with regularity, as the dancing on tables moves into high gear. There's also a patio out back for dancing when the tables, chairs, and bar spots are taken. It's open daily from noon to 3am. Bulevar Marina, opposite Plaza Bonita. © **624/143-0655.** www.elsquidroe.com.

Latitude 22+   This raffish restaurant and bar never closes. License plates, signs, sports caps, and a 959-pound blue marlin are the backdrop for U.S. sports events that play on six TVs scattered among pool tables, dart boards, and assorted games. You can order dishes from hamburgers to chicken-fried steak, or breakfast anytime. Happy hour is from 4 to 6pm. Lázaro Cárdenas s/n, 1 block north of the town's only traffic light. © **624/143-1516.** www.la22nobaddays.

Mambo Café   This latest addition to the Cabo nightlife scene, opened in December 2004, is part of a chain of bars around Mexico. It features a Caribbean concept club with a marine tropical ambience, playing contemporary Latin music. Live music is also featured. It's open Tuesday through Sunday from 9pm. Bulevar Marina Local 9–10, next to the Costa Real Cabo Resort. © **624/143-1484.** www.mambocafe.com.mx. Cover varies with the night.

Sancho Panza Wine Bar and Bistro   Finally, an alternative to beer bars. Sancho Panza combines a gourmet food market with a wine bar that features live jazz music plus an intriguing menu of Nuevo Latino cuisine (Mediterranean food with Latin flair). The place has a cozy neighborhood feeling, with tourists and locals sampling the selection of more than 150 wines, plus espresso drinks. During high season, make reservations. It's open Monday through Saturday from 3pm to midnight. Plaza Las Glorias boardwalk, next to the Lighthouse. © **624/143-3212.** www.sanchopanza.com.

2 Todos Santos: A Creative Oasis ⭐⭐⭐

68km (42 miles) N of Cabo San Lucas

On Highway 19, Todos Santos is known as "Bohemian Baja" among those looking for the latest, the trendiest, and the hippest of artist outposts—and among those simply weary of the L.A.-ization of Cabo San Lucas.

The art and artistry created here—from the kitchen to the canvas—is of an evolved type that seems to care less about commercial appeal than quality. In doing so, it becomes more of a draw. Not to be overlooked are the arts of agriculture, masonry, and weaving created by some of the town's original residents. From superb meals at **Café Santa Fe** to an afternoon browsing at **El Tecolote Libros,** the best bookstore I've come across in Mexico, Todos Santos is intriguing to its core.

Not only is the town a cultural oasis in Baja, it's an oasis in the true sense of the word—in this desert landscape, Todos Santos enjoys an almost continuous water supply from the peaks of the Sierra de la Laguna mountains. It's just over an hour's drive up the Pacific coast from Cabo San Lucas; you'll know you've arrived when the arid coastal scenery suddenly gives way to verdant groves of palms, mangos, avocados, and papayas.

During the Mission Period of Baja, this oasis valley was deemed the only area south and west of La Paz worth settling—it had the only reliable water supply. In 1723, an outpost mission was established, followed by the full-fledged Misión Santa Rosa de Las Palmas in 1733. At the time, the town was known as Santa Rosa de Todos Santos, eventually shortened to its current name, which translates as "All Saints."

Over the next 200 years, the town alternated between prosperity and difficulty. Its most recent boom lasted from the mid–19th century until the 1950s, when the town flourished as a sugar-cane production center and began to develop a strong cultural core. Many of the buildings now being restored and converted into galleries, studios, shops, and restaurants were built during this era. It wasn't until the 1980s that a paved road connected Todos Santos with La Paz, and tourism began to draw new attention to this tranquil town.

The demand for the town's older colonial-style structures by artists, entrepreneurs, and foreign residents has resulted in a real-estate boom. New shops, galleries, and cafes crop up continuously. The coastal strip south of Todos Santos has plans for development, so visit soon, before this perfect stretch of beach and desert changes. For the casual visitor, Todos Santos is easy to explore in a day, but a few tranquil inns welcome guests who want to stay a little longer.

WHAT TO SEE & DO

During the **Festival Fundador** (Oct 10–14), which celebrates the founding of the town in 1723, streets around the main plaza fill with food, games, and wandering troubadours. Many of the shops and the Café Santa Fe close from the end of September through the festival. A new **Arts Festival,** in February, seems to be gaining importance. It includes film festivals, dance and music performances, and more.

Todos Santos has at least half a dozen galleries, including the noted **Galería de Todos Santos,** corner of Topete and Legaspi (© **612/145-0500**), which features a changing collection of works by regional artists. It's open daily from 11am to 4pm (closed Sun May–Nov) and doesn't accept credit cards. The **Galería Santa Fe,** Centenario, across from the plaza (© **612/145-0340**), is an eclectic collection of original and creative Mexican folk art and *artesanía* (crafts) treasures that include Frida-adorned frames as well as "shrines"—kid-size chairs decorated in bottle caps, Virgin of Guadalupe images, *milagros* (depictions of miracles experienced by the artist), and more. It's open Wednesday through Monday from 12am to 9pm.

WHERE TO STAY & DINE

Consider the **Todos Santos Inn,** Calle Legaspi 33, between Topete and Obregón (𝄐 **612/145-0040**). An elegant place to stay, it is in a historic house that has served as a general store, cantina, school, and private residence. Now under new ownership, it retains its air of casual elegance, with luxurious white bed linens, netting draped romantically over the beds, Talavera tile bathrooms, antique furniture, and high, wood-beamed ceilings. Two rooms and four suites border a courtyard terrace, pool, and garden. Rates run $95 to $135 per night. The suites are air-conditioned, but have neither television nor telephone. A new wine bar, open to the public, serves libations Tuesdays through Saturdays from 5 to 9pm, and has possibly the town's best margaritas, in addition to an excellent selection of California and other imported wines. Currently, no credit cards are accepted. Seasonal discounts are available, but the inn closes for the month of September.

Hotel California, Calle Juarez, corner of Morelos (𝄐 **612/145-0525** or 612/145-0522), has been the stuff of legends—and claims to be the source of inspiration for the Eagles' song of the same name. A few years back it was a dilapidated guesthouse; however, after an extensive renovation, it's now the hippest place to stay in the area. Think Philippe Stark in the desert—the decor here is a fusion of jewel-tone colors with eclectic Mexican and Moroccan accents. Each room features a different decor, but all of it is high style, with rich hues and captivating details. Most rooms also offer an outdoor terrace or seating area. Rates for the eleven rooms range from $140 to $195 in high season, or $75 to $125 in low season. It's so stylishly accommodating that although you can check out anytime you want—you may not want to! On the ground floor, you'll find the Lobby, the low-lit Library—with deep blue walls, a profusion of candles, and tin stars, as well as a small outdoor pool with sun chairs. Also at ground level is the **Emporio Hotel California boutique** and the **La Coronela Restaurant and Bar,** the current nocturnal hot spot with live guitar, jazz, and blues on Saturday evenings. On Sundays, the restaurant serves a mixed grill of steak, fish, chicken breast, and sausage for $13 per person.

For myself—and I would suspect many others—a meal at the **Café Santa Fe** ✪, Calle Centenario 4 (𝄐 **612/145-0340**), is reason enough to visit Todos Santos. Much of the attention the town has received in recent years can be directly attributed to this outstanding cafe, and it continues to live up to its lofty reputation. Owners Ezio and Paula Colombo refurbished a large stucco house across from the plaza, creating an exhibition kitchen, several dining rooms, and a lovely courtyard adjacent to a garden of hibiscus, bougainvillea, papaya trees, and herbs. My favorite room is the one in homage to Frida Kahlo, with reproductions of her work on grand canvases that flatter her more than her originals.

The excellent northern Italian cuisine emphasizes local produce and seafood; try ravioli stuffed with spinach and ricotta in a Gorgonzola sauce, or ravioli with lobster and shrimp, accompanied by an organic salad. In high season, the wait for a table at lunch can be long. Everything is prepared to order, and reservations are recommended. Main courses run $10 to $20. It's open Wednesday through Monday from noon to 9pm, closed September and October, and accepts MasterCard and Visa.

A more casual option, and a magical place to start the day, is the garden setting of the **Café Todos Santos,** Centenario 33, across from the Todos Santos Inn (© **612/ 145-0300**). Among the espresso drinks is the bowl-size caffe latte, accompanied by a freshly baked croissant or one of the signature cinnamon buns. Lunch or a light meal may include a *frittata* (an egg-based dish similar to quiche), a filling sandwich on home-baked bread, or fish filet wrapped in banana leaves with coconut milk. Main courses average $3 to $6. The cafe is open Tuesday through Sunday from 7am to 9pm, and Monday from 7am to 2pm; credit cards are not accepted.

3 La Paz: Peaceful Port Town ★★

176km (110 miles) N of Cabo San Lucas; 195km (122 miles) NW of San José del Cabo; 1,544km (968 miles) SE of Tijuana

La Paz means "peace," and the feeling seems to float on the ocean breezes of this provincial town. Despite being an important port, home to almost 200,000 inhabitants, and the capital of the state of Baja California Sur, it remains slow-paced and relaxed. The easygoing yet sophisticated city is the guardian of "old Baja" atmosphere. Beautiful deserted beaches just minutes away complement the lively beach and palm-fringed *malecón* (seaside boulevard) that front the town center.

The presence of the University of South Baja California adds a unique cultural presence that includes museums and a theater and arts center. The surrounding tropical desert diversity and uncommon wildlife are also compelling reasons to visit. Adventurous travelers enjoy countless options, including hiking, rock climbing, diving, fishing, and sea kayaking. Islands and islets sit just offshore, once hiding places for looting pirates but now magnets for kayakers and beachcombers. At Espíritu Santo and Los Islotes, it's possible to swim with sea lions.

Despite its name, La Paz has historically been a place of conflict between explorers and indigenous populations. Beginning in 1535, Spanish conquistadors and Jesuit missionaries arrived and exerted their influence on the town's architecture and traditions. This was the center of pearl harvesting from the time conquistadors saw local Indians wearing pearl ornaments through the late 1930s, when an unknown disease killed off the oysters in the Bay of La Paz. John Steinbeck immortalized a local legend in his novella *The Pearl.*

La Paz is ideal for anyone nostalgic for Los Cabos the way it used to be. From accommodations to taxis, it's also one of Mexico's most outstanding beach vacation values and a great place for family travelers.

ESSENTIALS

GETTING THERE & DEPARTING   By Plane   Aero California (© **800/237-6225** in the U.S., or 612/125-1023) has flights from Los Angeles, Tijuana, and Mexico City; **Aeromexico** (© **800/237-6639** in the U.S., 612/122-0091, 612/122-0093, or 612/122-1636) connects through Tucson and Los Angeles in the United States, and flies from Mexico City and other points within Mexico. The airport is 18km (11 miles) northwest of town along the highway to Ciudad Constitución and Tijuana. Airport *colectivos* (around $11) run only from the airport to town, not vice versa. **Taxi** service (around $17) is available as well. Most major rental car agencies have booths inside the airport. **Budget**'s local number is © **612/124-6433** or 612/122-7655; you can contact **Avis** at © **612/122-6262** or -1813.

By Car   From San José del Cabo, Highway 1 north is the longer, more scenic route; a flatter and faster route is heading south and east along Highway 1 to Cabo San Lucas, then Highway 19 north through Todos Santos. A little before San Pedro,

Highway 19 rejoins Highway 1 and runs north into La Paz; the trip takes 2 to 3 hours. From the north, Highway 1 south is the only choice.

By Bus   The **Central Camionera (main bus station)** is at Jalisco and Héroes de la Independencia, about 25 blocks southwest of the center of town. It's open daily from 6am to 10pm. Local buses arrive at the **beach station,** along the *malecón.* Taxis line up out front of both.

By Ferry   A ferry plies the waters between La Paz and Topolobampo, the port for Los Mochis, carrying passengers, vehicles, and cargo. The company, **Baja Ferries** (*©* **668/ 817-3752;** www.bajaferries.com) has one departure per day at 11pm. **Buses** ($1.80 one-way) to Pichilingue depart from the beach bus terminal (*©* **612/122-7898**), on the *malecón* at Independencia, 10 times a day from 7am to 6pm. **Taxis** meet each ferry as well, and cost about $8 to downtown La Paz.

VISITOR INFORMATION   The most accessible visitor information office is on Alvaro Obregón across from the intersection of Calle 16 de Septiembre (*©* **612/122-5939;** turismo@correo.gbcs.gob.mx or turismo@lapaz.cromwell.com.mx). It's open Monday through Friday 8am to 10pm, Saturday and Sunday noon to midnight. The extremely helpful staff speaks English and can supply information on La Paz, Los Cabos, and the rest of the region. The official website of the La Paz Tourism Board is **www.vivalapaz.com**.

CITY LAYOUT   Although La Paz sprawls well inland from the *malecón* (Paseo Alvaro Obregón), you'll probably spend most of your time in the older, more congenial downtown section within a few blocks of the waterfront. The main plaza, **Plaza Pública,** or Jardín Velasco, is bounded by Madero, Independencia, Revolución, and Cinco de Mayo.

GETTING AROUND   Because most of what you'll need in town is on the *malecón* between the tourist information office and the Hotel Los Arcos, or a few blocks inland from the waterfront, it's easy to get around La Paz on foot. Public buses go to some of the beaches north of town (see "Beaches & Sports," below). To explore the many beaches within 80km (50 miles) of La Paz, your best bet is to rent a car or hire a taxi. There are several car-rental agencies on the *malecón.*

FESTIVALS & EVENTS   February features the biggest and best **Carnaval/Mardi Gras** in Baja, as well as a 4- to 5-week **Festival of the Gray Whale** (starting in late Jan or early Feb, sometimes extending through early Mar). On **May 3,** a festival celebrates the city's founding by Cortez in 1535, and features *artesanía* (crafts) exhibitions from throughout southern Baja. An annual marlin-fishing tournament is in **August,** with other fishing tournaments scheduled in **September** and **November.** On **November 1 and 2,** the Days of the Dead, altars are on display at the Anthropology Museum.

FAST FACTS: La Paz

Area Code   The telephone area code is **612.**

Banks   Banks generally exchange currency during normal business hours: Monday through Friday from 9am to 6pm, Saturday from 10am to 2pm. ATMs are readily available and offer bank exchange rates on withdrawals.

Emergencies Dial © **060.**

Hospitals **Hospital Especialidades Médicas,** in Fidepaz (© **612/124-0400**). Hospital **Juan María de Salvatierra** (© **612/122-1497**), Nicolás Bravo 1010, Col. Centro.

Internet Access **BajaNet,** Madero 430 (© **612/125-9380**), charges $1 for each 10 minutes. It's open Monday through Saturday from 8am to 10pm, Sunday from 9am to 9pm. Internet access is also available at the **Omni Services Internet Café,** located on the *malecón,* Alvaro Obregón 460-C, close to Burger King (© **612/ 123-4888**). They also offer hookups for laptops, color printers, copy, fax, and voice-over-Internet phone services to U.S. and Canada for 30¢ per minute.

Pharmacy One of the largest pharmacies is **Farmacia Baja California,** corner of Independencia and Madero (© **612/122-0240** or 612/123-4408).

Post Office The *correo,* 3 blocks inland at Constitución and Revolución de 1910 (© **612/122-0388**), is open Monday through Friday from 8am to 3pm, Saturday from 9am to 1pm.

Tourism Office The office is at Carretera al Norte Km 5.5, Edificio Fidepaz, Col. Fidepaz, 23090 La Paz, B.C.S. (© **612/124-0100**). It's open daily from 8am to 3pm. A tourist information module is located on the *malecón,* open from 8am to 8pm.

BEACHES & SPORTS

La Paz combines the unselfconscious bustle of a small capital port city with beautiful, isolated beaches not far from town. Well on its way to becoming the undisputed adventure-tourism capital of Baja, it's the starting point for whale-watching, diving, sea kayaking, climbing, and hiking tours throughout the peninsula. For those interested in day adventures, travel agencies in major hotels or along the *malecón* can usually arrange all of the above, plus beach tours, sunset cruises, and visits to the sea-lion colony. Agencies in the United States that specialize in Baja's natural history also book excursions (see "The Active Traveler," in chapter 2).

BEACHES Within a 10- to 45-minute drive from La Paz lie some of the loveliest beaches in Baja. Many rival those of the Caribbean with their clear, turquoise water. The beach bordering the *malecón* is the most convenient in town. Although the sand is soft and white and the water appears crystal clear and gentle, locals don't generally swim there. Because of the commercial port, the water is not considered as clean as that at the very accessible outlying beaches. With colorful playgrounds dotting the central beachfront and numerous open-air restaurants that front the water, it's best for a casual afternoon of postsightseeing lunch and play.

The best beach in town is immediately north of town at **La Concha Beach Resort;** nonguests may use the hotel restaurant and bar and rent equipment for snorkeling, diving, skiing, and sailing. It's 10km (6 miles) north of town on the Pichilingue Highway at Km 5.5. The other beaches are all farther north of town, but midweek you may have these distant beaches to yourself.

For more information about beaches and maps, check at the tourist information office on the *malecón.* For an overview of the beaches before deciding where to spend your precious vacation days, **Viajes Lybs,** 16 de Septiembre 408, between Revolución and Serdán (© **612/122-4680;** fax 612/125-9600), offers a 4-hour beach tour for $22 per person, with stops at Balandra and El Tecolote beaches.

CRUISES   A popular and very worthwhile cruise is to **Isla Espíritu Santo** and **Los Islotes.** You visit the largest sea-lion colony in Baja, stunning rock formations, and remote beaches, with stops for snorkeling, swimming, and lunch. If conditions permit, you may even be able to snorkel beside the sea lions. Both boat and bus tours are available to **Puerto Balandra,** where bold rock formations rising up like humpback whales frame pristine coves of crystal-blue water and ivory sand. **Viajes Lybs** (see above) and other travel agencies can arrange these all-day trips, weather permitting. Price is $67 per person.

SCUBA DIVING   Scuba-diving trips are best June through September. **Fernando Aguilar's Baja Diving and Services,** Obregón 1665-2 (© **612/122-1826;** fax 612/122-8644; info@clubcantamar.com), arranges them. Rates start at $92 per person for an all-day outing and two-tank dive. Other excellent dive operators include **Baja Quest** (© **612/123-5320;** www.bajaquest.com.mx), located at Navarro 55, between Abosolo and Topete, and **Sea & Scuba** (© **612/123-5233**) on the *malecón* at Ocampo. Day boat trips runs approximately $77 for two tank dives.

SEA KAYAKING   Kayaking in the many bays and coves near La Paz has become extremely popular. Many enthusiasts bring their own equipment. Several companies in the United States (see "The Active Traveler," in chapter 2) can book trips in advance. Locally, **Baja Quest** (see above) and **Mar y Aventuras** (© **612/122-7039;** fax 612/122-3559; www.kayakbaja.com) arranges trips.

SPORTFISHING   La Paz, justly famous for its sportfishing, attracts anglers from all over the world. Its waters are home to more than 850 species of fish. The most economical approach is to rent a *panga* boat with guide and equipment. It costs $125 for 3 hours, but you don't go very far out. Super *pangas,* which have a shade cover and comfortable seats, start at around $180 for two persons. Larger cruisers with bathrooms start at $240. Local hotels and tour agencies arrange sportfishing trips.

WHALE-WATCHING   Between January and March, and sometimes as early as December, 3,000 to 5,000 gray whales migrate from the Bering Strait to the Pacific coast of Baja. The main whale-watching spots are **Laguna San Ignacio** (on the Pacific near San Ignacio), **Magdalena Bay** (on the Pacific near Puerto López Mateos—about a 2-hr. drive from La Paz), and **Scammon's Lagoon** (near Guerrero Negro).

Most tours originating in La Paz go to Magdalena Bay, where the whales give birth to their calves in calm waters. Several companies arrange whale-watching tours that originate in La Paz or other Baja towns or in the United States; 12-hour tours from La Paz start at around $106 per person, including breakfast, lunch, transportation, and an English-speaking guide. Make reservations at **Viajes Lybs** (see above).

A BREAK FROM THE BEACHES: EXPLORING LA PAZ
Most tour agencies offer city tours of all the major sights. Tours last 2 to 3 hours, include time for shopping, and cost around $15 per person.

HISTORIC LA PAZ   When Cortez landed here on May 3, 1535, he named it Bahía Santa Cruz. It didn't stick. In April 1683, Eusebio Kino, a Spanish Jesuit, arrived and dubbed the place Nuestra Señora de la Paz (Our Lady of Peace). It wasn't until November 1, 1720, however, that Jaime Bravo, another Jesuit, set up a permanent mission. He used the same name as his predecessor, calling it the Misión de Nuestra Señora de la Paz. The mission church stands on La Paz's main square, on Revolución between Cinco de Mayo and Independencia.

The Anthropology Museum   The museum features large, though faded, color photos of Baja's prehistoric cave paintings. There are also exhibits on various topics, including the geological history of the peninsula, fossils, missions, colonial history, and daily life. All information is in Spanish.

Altamirano and Cinco de Mayo. ©/fax **612/122-0162** or 612/125-6424. Free admission (donations encouraged). Daily 9am–6pm.

El Teatro de la Ciudad   The city theater is the cultural center, with performances by visiting and local artists. Bookings include small ballet companies, experimental and popular theater, popular music, and an occasional classical concert or symphony.

Av. Navarro 700. © **612/125-0486.**

SHOPPING

La Paz has little in the way of folk art or other treasures from mainland Mexico. The dense cluster of streets behind the **Hotel Perla,** between 16 de Septiembre and Degollado, is full of small shops, some tacky, others quite upscale. In this area, there is also a very small but authentic **Chinatown,** dating from the time when Chinese laborers were brought to settle in Baja. Serdán from Degollado south is home to dozens of sellers of dried spices, piñatas, and candy. Stores carrying crafts, folk art, clothing, and handmade furniture and accessories lie mostly along the *malecón* (Paseo Obregón) or within 1 or 2 blocks.

WHERE TO STAY

Hotel Los Arcos   This three-story neocolonial-style hotel at the west end of the *malecón* is the best place for downtown accommodations with a touch of tranquillity. Los Arcos has functional furnishings and amenities, and the hotel is filled with fountains, plants, and even rocking chairs. Most of the rooms and suites come with two double beds. Each has a balcony overlooking the pool in the inner courtyard or the waterfront, plus a whirlpool tub. I prefer the South Pacific–style bungalows with thatched roofs and fireplaces located in the back part of the property. Satellite TVs carry U.S. channels.

Av. Alvaro Obregón 498, between Rosales and Allende (Apdo. Postal 112), 23000 La Paz, B.C.S. © **800/347-2252** or 714/450-9000 in the U.S., or 612/122-2744. Fax 612/125-4313. www.losarcos.com. 130 units; 52 bungalows. $95 double; $105 suite; $75–$95 bungalow. AE, MC, V. Free guarded parking. **Amenities:** Cafeteria; restaurant; bar w/live music; 2 pools (1 heated); sauna; travel agency; room service; laundry service; desk for fishing information; Ping-Pong. *In room:* A/C, TV, minibar.

Hotel Mediterrane ⭐   Simple yet stylish, this unique inn mixes Mediterranean with Mexican, creating a cozy place for couples or friends to share. All rooms face an interior courtyard and are decorated with white tile floors and *equipal* furniture, with colorful Mexican *sarapes* draped over the beds. Some rooms have minifridges. All have VCRs. Its location is great—just a block from the *malecón.* The adjacent La Pazta restaurant (see "Where to Dine," below) is one of La Paz's best. Rates include use of kayaks, and bicycles for exploring the town. This is a gay-friendly hotel.

Allende 36, 23000 La Paz, B.C.S. ©/fax **612/125-1195.** www.hotelmed.com. 8 units. $60–$75 double; $80 suite. AE, MC, V. Weekly discounts available. Street parking. *In room:* A/C, TV/VCR.

La Concha Beach Resort ⓖ   Ten kilometers (6 miles) north of downtown La Paz, this resort's setting is perfect: on a curved beach ideal for swimming and watersports. All rooms face the water and have double beds, balconies or patios, and small tables and chairs. Condos with full kitchens and one or three bedrooms are available on a nightly basis in the high-rise complex next door. If available, they're worth the extra price for a perfect family vacation stay. The hotel offers scuba, fishing, and whale-watching packages.

Carretera Pichilingue Km 5, 23000 La Paz, B.C.S. Ⓒ 800/999-2252 in the U.S., or 612/121-6161. www.laconcha.com. 113 units. $95 double; $125 junior suite; $126–$241 condo. AE, DC, MC, V. Free guarded parking. **Amenities:** Restaurant (w/theme nights); 2 bars; beachside pool; Jacuzzi; complete watersports center w/WaveRunners, kayaks, and paddleboats; tour desk; free twice-daily shuttle to town; room service; laundry service; beach club w/scuba program. *In room:* A/C, TV.

Posada Las Flores ⓖ   New owner Giussepe Marceletti has continued the tradition of hospitality in this elegant B&B (formerly Posada Santa Fe), the best bet for travelers looking for a more refined place to stay in La Paz. Each room is individually decorated with high-quality Mexican furniture and antiques, hand-loomed fabrics, and exquisite artisan details. Bathrooms are especially welcoming, with marble tubs and thick towels. Breakfast is served from 8 to 11am daily. Telephone, fax, and Internet service are available through the office. It's at the northern end of the *malecón.*

Alvaro Obregón 440, 23000 La Paz, B.C.S. Ⓒ 877/245-2860 in the U.S., or 612/125-5871. www.posadadelasflores. com. 8 units. $140 double; $199 suite; $450 master suite. Rates include full breakfast. MC, V. Street parking. **Amenities:** Small pool; Internet access; hospitality desk. *In room:* A/C, minibar.

WHERE TO DINE

Although La Paz is not known for culinary achievements, it has a growing assortment of small, pleasant restaurants that are good and reasonably priced. In addition to the usual seafood and Mexican dishes, you can find Italian, French, Spanish, Chinese, and vegetarian offerings. Restaurants along the *malecón* tend to be more expensive than those a few blocks inland.

MODERATE

Trattoria La Pazta ⓖ ITALIAN/SWISS   The trendiest restaurant in town, La Pazta gleams with black lacquered tables and white tile; the aromas of garlic and espresso float in the air. The menu features local fresh seafood in items such as pasta with squid in wine and cream sauce, and crispy fried calamari. There's also homemade lasagna, baked in a wood-fired oven. La Pazta is appealing for breakfast, too. The restaurant is in front of the Hotel Mediterrane, 1 block inland from the *malecón.*

Allende 36. Ⓒ 612/125-1195. Breakfast $2–$4; main courses $8–$11. AE, MC, V. Wed–Mon 7am–11pm.

INEXPENSIVE

Café Expresso FRENCH/CAFE   You'll feel as if you've suddenly been transported across the Atlantic in this incongruous but welcoming spot. Indulge in any number of espresso coffee drinks, plus French and Austrian pastries, while sitting at marble-topped bistro tables. Jazz music plays in the background.

Av. Obregón and 16 de Septiembre. Ⓒ 612/123-4373. Coffees and pastries $1–$3. No credit cards. Mon–Sat 7am–8pm; Sun 9am–3pm.

El Quinto Sol VEGETARIAN   Not only is this La Paz's principal health food market, it's a cheerful, excellent cafe for fresh fruit *licuados* (shakes), *tortas,* and vegetarian dishes. Tables sit beside oversize wood-framed windows with flowering planters in the sills. Sandwiches are served on whole-grain bread—also available for sale—and the potato tacos are an excellent way for vegetarians to indulge in a Mexican staple.

Av. Independencia and B. Domínguez. (✆ **612/122-1692**. Main courses $1.50–$6.50. No credit cards. Mon–Sat 7:30am–10pm; Sun 10am–4pm

LA PAZ AFTER DARK

A night in La Paz logically begins at a cafe along the *malecón* as the sun sinks into the sea—have your camera ready. A favorite ringside seat at dusk is a table at **La Terraza,** next to the Hotel Perla (✆ **612/122-0777**). La Terraza makes good schooner-size margaritas. **Pelícanos Bar,** on the second story of the Hotel Los Arcos (✆ **612/122-2744**), has a good view of the waterfront and a clubby, cozy feel. **Carlos 'n' Charlie's La Paz–Lapa** (✆ **612/122-9290**) has live music on weekends. **La Cabaña** nightclub in the Hotel Perla (✆ **612/122-0777**) features Latin rhythms. It opens at 9pm, and there's a $4 cover on weekends. **Las Varitas,** Independencia and Domínguez (✆ **612/125-2025**), is where you'll hear Latin rock, ranchero, and salsa. It's open from 9pm to 3 or 4am, with cover charges around $5.50. Note that covers may rise or fall depending on the crowd.

4 Mid-Baja: Loreto, Mulegé & Santa Rosalía

Halfway between the resort sophistication of Los Cabos and the frontier exuberance of Tijuana lies Baja's midsection, an area rich in history and culture. The indigenous cave paintings here are a UNESCO World Heritage Site, and the area was home to numerous Jesuit missions in the 1700s. These days, mid-Baja is known for its excellent sea kayaking, sportfishing, and hiking.

Overlooked by many travelers (except avid sportfishermen), **Loreto** is a rare gem that sparkles under the desert sky. The purple hues of the Giganta Mountains meet the indigo waters of the Sea of Cortez, providing a spectacular backdrop of natural contrasts for the historic town. **Mulegé** is, literally, an oasis in the Baja desert. The only freshwater river (Río Mulegé) in the peninsula flows through town. And the port town of **Santa Rosalía,** while slightly past its prime, makes a worthy detour, with its pastel clapboard houses and unusual steel-and-stained-glass church, designed by Gustave Eiffel (of Eiffel Tower fame).

The region is also a popular jumping-off point for whale-watching tours. To find out when, where, and how to view the gentle giants, consult "Whale-Watching in Baja," later in this chapter.

LORETO & THE OFFSHORE ISLANDS

389km (243 miles) NW of La Paz; 533km (333 miles) N of Cabo San Lucas; 1,125km (703 miles) SE of Tijuana

The center of the Spanish mission effort during colonial times, Loreto was the first capital of the Californias and the first European settlement in the peninsula. Founded on October 25, 1697, it was selected by Father Juan María Salvatierra as the site of the first mission in the Californias. (California, at the time, extended from Cabo San Lucas to the Oregon border.) He held Mass beneath a figure of the Virgin of Loreto, brought from a town in Italy bearing the same name. For 132 years, Loreto served as the state capital, until an 1829 hurricane destroyed most of the town. The capital moved to La Paz the following year.

The Lower Baja Peninsula

Bahía de Sebastián Viscaíno

Playa San Rafael

B. San Rafael

Bahía Tortugas

Guerrero Negro

18

Pto. Nuevo

Scammon's Lagoon

B. San Carlos

La Trinidad

Bahía Asuncion

B. La Asunción

Guadalupe

B. Santa Ana

Gulf of California

San Ignacio

Bahía San Hipólito

DESIERTO DE

VIZCAINO

1

Santa Rosalía

Laguna de San Ignacio

SE. COYOTE

Mulegé

Bahía Concepción

La Purisima

B. San Basílio

San Isidro

PACIFIC OCEAN

Loreto

Isla Del Carmen

Boca La Soledad

Va. Ignacio Zaragoza

Pto. Adolfo Lopez Mateos

Ciudad Insurgentes

Sea of Cortez

Puerto San Carlos

B. Santa María

Ciudad Constitución

Bahía Magdalena

1

El Ciruelo

Isla San José

San Ignacio

B. Coyote

Isla La Partida

Isla Espíritu Santo

Isla Cerralvo

Pichilingue

La Paz

Las Cruces

San Pedro

La Ventana

B. de los Muertos

Buena Vista

19

Los Barriles

B. de Palmas

SIERRA DE LA LAGUNA

Todos Santos

1

La Rivera

Santiago

Miraflores

Cabo Pulmo

Cabo San Lucas

San José del Cabo

Scale:
0 — 50 mi
0 — 50 km

Airport ✈
Beach ↗

UNITED STATES

MEXICO

Gulf of Mexico

Mexico City ★

Area of Detail

0 — 500 mi
0 — 500 km

PACIFIC OCEAN

During the late 1970s and early 1980s, the Mexican government saw in Loreto the possibility for another mega-development along the lines of Cancún, Ixtapa, or Huatulco. It invested in a golf course and championship tennis facility, modernized the infrastructure, and built an international airport and marina facilities at Puerto Loreto, several kilometers south of town. The economics, however, didn't make sense, and few hotel investors and even fewer tourists came. Today, Loreto remains the wonderfully funky fishing village and well-kept secret that it has been for decades. The celebration of its 300th anniversary had the added benefit of updating the streets, plaza, and mission. A new real estate development, Loreto Bay, is promising to bring an expanse of growth to the area. Already, new flights to this lovely town have been added, making it more accessible for visitors.

ESSENTIALS

The **Loreto International Airport** (© 613/135-0499) is 6km (4 miles) southwest of town. **Taxis** (© 613/135-1255) are readily available and charge about $16 for the 10-minute ride to Loreto. Loreto's Terminal de Autobuses, or **bus station** (© 613/135-0767) is on Salvatierra and Paseo Tamaral, a 10-minute walk from downtown. It's open 24 hours. The trip from La Paz takes 5 hours and costs $25.

The city **tourist information office** (© 613/135-0036 or 613/135-0411) is in the southeast corner of the Palacio de Gobierno building, across from the town square. It offers maps, local free publications, and other basic information about the area. It's open Monday through Friday from 8am to 3pm.

Salvatierra is the main street that runs northeast, merging into Paseo Hidalgo, which runs toward the beach. Calle Playa parallels the water; along this road you'll find many hotels, seafood restaurants, fishing charters, and the marina. Most of the town's social life revolves around the central square and the old mission.

The local telephone **area code** is **613.**

WHAT TO SEE & DO

The main reasons to come to Loreto are the Sea of Cortez and the five islands just offshore; they offer exceptional kayaking, sailing, diving, and fishing. **Isla del Carmen** and **Isla Danzante** are wonderful overnight sailing destinations. Kayakers launch here for trips to the offshore islands or down the remote coast of the Sierra la Giganta to La Paz. Loreto is the nearest major airport and city to **Bahía de Magdalena (Magdalena Bay),** the southernmost of the major gray whale calving lagoons on the Pacific coast of Baja. For more information on popular whale-watching spots and tour operators, see "Whale-Watching in Baja," below.

Misión Nuestra Señora de Loreto was the first mission in the Californias, started in 1699. The original Virgen de Loreto, brought to shore by Padre Kino in 1697, is on display in the church's 18th-century gilded altar. The mission is on Salvatierra, across from the central square. Adjacent to the mission church and of equal or greater interest is the **Museo de las Misiones,** Salvatierra 16 (© 613/135-0441). It has a small but complete collection of historical and anthropological exhibits. The museum is open Tuesday through Sunday from 9am to 1pm and 1:45 to 6pm. Admission is $3.

WHERE TO STAY

In general, accommodations in Loreto are the kind travelers to Mexico used to find all over: inexpensive and unique, with genuine, friendly owner-operators. You can choose between a secluded resort, more casual beachside inns, or even greater values in town.

Plaza Loreto   The location of the well-established Plaza Loreto, just 1 block from the mission church, makes it easy to find and a perennial favorite. The well-maintained two-story motel frames a courtyard with shady seating areas. Each of the basic rooms comes with one or two double beds, a table and two chairs, and a bathroom with a shower. It's a short walk from the mission, the museum, several favorite restaurants, and all the notable nightlife.

Hidalgo 2, Centro, 23880 Loreto, B.C.S. ⓒ 613/135-0280. Fax 613/135-0855. www.baja-web.com/loreto/loplaza.htm. 25 units. $62 double; $73 triple. AE, MC, V. **Amenities:** Restaurant; tour desk; laundry service. *In room:* A/C, TV.

Posada Las Flores ⭐⭐⭐   The most luxurious place to stay in Loreto conveniently sits adjacent to the main square, in the heart of historic Loreto. Every room is beautifully decorated with fine Mexican arts and crafts, including heavy wood doors, Talavera pottery, painted tiles, candles, and Mexican scenic paintings. The colors and decor of the hotel are nouveau-colonial Mexico, with wood and tin accents. Large bathrooms have thick white towels and bamboo doors. Every detail has been carefully selected, including the numerous antiques tucked into corners. This hotel exudes class and refinement, from the general ambience to the wake-up service of coffee and pastries. Italian-owned and operated, the sophisticated service has a European style to it. Only children over 12 are welcome.

Salvatierra and Francisco I. Madera, Centro, 23880 Loreto, B.C.S. ⓒ **877/245-2860** in the U.S., or 613/135-1162. Fax 613/135-1099. www.posadadelasflores.com. 15 units. $140–$170 double; $199–$230 suite. Rates include full breakfast. MC, V. Street parking. **Amenities:** Restaurant; rooftop glass-bottom swimming pool; hospitality desk; Internet access. *In room:* A/C, TV, minibar.

WHERE TO DINE

Dining in Loreto affords surprising variety, given the small size and simple nature of the town. The dominant menu features some combination of seafood and Mexican cuisine. Although selection is limited, Loreto after dark seems to offer a place for almost every nightlife preference, from rowdy beach pubs to **Jarros y Tarros,** an elegant billiard bar on Salvatierra, next to Deportes Blazer. Generally, though, closing time is around midnight. In addition, as is the tradition throughout Mexico, Loreto's central plaza offers a **free concert** in the bandstand every Sunday evening.

Café Olé LIGHT FARE   Along with specialty coffees, this breezy cafe is a good option for breakfast; try eggs with *nopal* cactus, hotcakes, or a not-so-light lunch of a burger and fries. Tacos and some Mexican standards are also on the menu, as are the fresh-fruit shakes, *licuados.*

Madero 14. ⓒ **613/135-0496.** Breakfast $2–$5; sandwiches $2–$3.50. No credit cards. Mon–Sat 7am–10pm; Sun 7am–2pm.

El Chile Willie ⭐ SEAFOOD/MEXICAN   Chile Willie serves a seafood menu in an attractive and appropriate setting—right at the water's edge. The extensive menu features Choco Clams (a local type of clam, not as bizarre as it sounds), clams Rockefeller, lobster served many different ways, and a succulent fish filet baked in foil with tamarind herb sauce. There is also chicken breast stuffed with *nopal* cactus, beef burger in barbecue sauce, and (the restaurant claims) the largest Mexican combo for two. The place is lively, and its location on the main beach in town makes it great for people-watching, especially during weekend breakfast and lunch. From 4 to 6pm, it features a two-for-one happy hour with free appetizers.

López Mateos s/n. ⓒ **613/135-0677.** Main courses $4–$16. AE, MC, V. Daily noon–11pm.

MULEGE: OASIS IN THE DESERT

989km (618 miles) SE of Tijuana; 136km (85 miles) N of Loreto; 493km (308 miles) NW of La Paz; 706km (441 miles) NW of Cabo San Lucas

Verdant Mulegé offers shady coolness in an otherwise scorching part of the world. Founded in 1705, it is home to one of the best preserved and most beautifully situated Jesuit missions in Baja.

Mulegé (pronounced "moo-leh-*heh*"), at the mouth of beautiful Bahía de Concepción, has great diving, kayaking, and fishing. Guided hikes into the mountains visit several well-preserved Indian caves with stunning paintings. Accommodations are limited and basic. Good beach camping is available just south of town along the Bahía de Concepción.

ESSENTIALS

The closest international airport is in Loreto, 136km (85 miles) south. From Loreto, 90 minutes away, you'll need to rent a car or hire a taxi; taxis average $75 each way. There is no formal **bus station** in Mulegé; buses pick up and drop passengers on the main highway at the fork in the road that marks the entrance leading into town (at La Cabaña restaurant).

Essentially, Mulegé has an east-west orientation, running from the Transpeninsular Highway in the west to the Sea of Cortez. The Mulegé River (also known as Río Santa Rosalía) borders the town to the south, with a few hotels and RV parks along its southern shore. It's easy to find the principal sights downtown; two main streets take you either east or west, and both border the town's central plaza. There is no local bus service in town or to the beach, but you can easily walk or take a **taxi.** Taxis line up around the central plaza, or you can call the taxi dispatch at © **615/153-0420.** They usually charge about $2.50 to $5 for a trip anywhere in town.

Tourist information is available at the office of the centrally located **Hotel Las Casitas,** Madero 50 (© **615/153-0019**).

WHAT TO SEE & DO

Mulegé has long been a favorite destination for adventurous travelers looking for a place to relax and enjoy the diversity of nature. Divers, sportfishermen, kayakers, history buffs, and admirers of beautiful beaches all find reasons to linger.

To the north are the mostly secluded beaches of **Bahía Santa Inés** and **Punta Chivato,** both known for their beauty and tranquillity. You can reach Santa Inez by way of a long dirt road that turns off from Highway 1 at Km 151. A few kilometers south is the majestic **Bahía Concepción,** a 48km-long (30-mile) body of water that's dotted with islands and protected on three sides by over 80km (50 miles) of beach. Along with fantastic landscapes, the bay has numerous soft, white-sand beaches, such as **Santispac, Concepción, Los Cocos, El Burro, El Coyote, Buenaventura, El Requesón,** and **Armenta.** You can enjoy swimming, diving, windsurfing, kayaking, and other watersports; local equipment rentals are available.

One of the big attractions in this region is the large **cave paintings** in the Sierra de Guadalupe. UNESCO has declared the cave paintings a World Heritage Site, and the locals take great pride in protecting them. Unlike many typical cave paintings, these are huge, complex murals. Legally, you are only allowed to visit the caves with a licensed guide. For a recommended guide check at the **Hotel Las Casitas** (© **615/153-0019**), or call **Salvador Castro** (© **615/153-0232**). Although **scuba diving** is very popular, be aware that Mulegé is not an ideal destination. Fresh water and the not-so-fresh water that flows into the sea from the numerous septic tanks in the area mar visibility. But as you head south into Bahía de Concepción, there is excellent snorkeling at the numerous shallow coves and tiny offshore islands. For information and tours, contact Claudia Quintana at **Mulege Divers,** General Martínez s/n (© **615/153-0059**).

Bahía de Concepción is also a **kayaker's** dream—clear, calm waters, fascinating shorelines, and lots of tempting coves with white sandy beaches. Rent a kayak at El Candil restaurant for $29 per day and explore on your own. **EcoMundo** (located at Playa Escondida; no phone) Mulegé's undisputed kayak expert, rents kayaks and offers fully guided tours.

Misión Santa Rosalía de Mulegé, founded in 1706 by Father Juan de Ugarte and Juan María Basaldúa, is just upstream from the bridge where Highway 1 crosses the Mulegé River. The original mission building was completed in 1766, to serve a local Indian population of about 2,000. In 1770, a flood destroyed nearly all of the common buildings, and the mission was rebuilt on the site it occupies today, on a bluff overlooking the river.

WHERE TO STAY & DINE

Accommodations in Mulegé are basic but clean and comfortable. The must-have meal is the traditional **pig roast.** It's an event—the pig is roasted Polynesian-style in a palm-lined open pit for hours, while guests enjoy a few beers or other beverages. When it's done, homemade tortillas, salsas, an assortment of toppings, and the ubiquitous rice and beans accompany the succulent pork. The perennially popular pig roast happens each Saturday night at both **Las Casitas Restaurant** and the **Hotel Serenidad,** and costs about $15.

Mulegé's nightlife pretty much centers on the **bars of the Hacienda Hotel and Las Casitas,** in town. In addition, **La Jungla Bambú,** corner of General Martínez and Zaragoza (no phone) is an American-style sports bar gone tropical. For dancing **Plaza Jose San Antonio** (located directly behind Las Casitas) serves up a fresh selection of dance music several nights a week in their garden-setting palapa. Also, the **Pick Up Bar** on the corner by the town square seems to generally have a lively group of English-speaking revelers, and the staff is generally helpful and fun.

Las Casitas Hotel *(Value)*   This longtime favorite welcomes many repeat visitors, along with the local literati—it was the birthplace of Mexican poet Alan Gorosave. Rooms are in a courtyard just behind (and adjacent to) Las Casitas Restaurant, one of Mulegé's most popular. The basic accommodations all have tile bathrooms and rustic decor. You can dine in the stone-walled dining area or on the adjoining plant-filled patio. Live music plays from 6pm on, and the place really livens up during the Saturday night pig roast. Friday features a Mexican fiesta and buffet with mariachi. If you're dining off the menu, how can you resist fresh lobster for $12? Menu offerings are standard fare with an emphasis on fresh seafood, but the quality is good. Expect to pay about $2 to $4 for breakfast, with main courses priced from $3.50 to $11. The inn and restaurant are on the main east-west street in Mulegé, 1 block from the central plaza.

Madero 50, Col. Centro 23900 Mulegé, B.C.S. © **615/153-0019**. 8 units. $30 double; $38 triple. MC, V. Limited street parking. *In room:* A/C.

SANTA ROSALIA

61km (38 miles) N of Mulegé

Located in an *arroyo* (dry streambed) north of Mulegé, Santa Rosalía is a mining town that dates to 1855. Founded by the French, the town has a European ambience and a distinctly Mexican culture. Pastel clapboard houses surrounded by picket fences line the streets, giving the town its nickname—*ciudad de madera* (city of wood). The large harbor and rusted ghost of a copper smelting facility dominate the central part of town bordering the waterfront.

The town was a copper-mining center for years. A French outfit operated here from 1885 until 1954, when the Mexicans regained the use of the land. But problems plagued the facility, which closed permanently in 1985.

Today, Santa Rosalía (pop. 14,000) is known for its manmade harbor—the recently constructed Marina Santa Rosalía, complete with concrete piers, floating docks, and full docking accommodations for up to a dozen ocean liners. Because this is the prime entry point of manufactured goods into Baja, the town abounds with auto-parts and electronics stores, along with shops selling Nikes and sunglasses.

The town has no real beach to speak of and few recreational attractions.

EXPLORING SANTA ROSALIA

The principal attraction in Santa Rosalía is the **Iglesia de Santa Bárbara,** a structure of galvanized steel designed by Gustave Eiffel (of Eiffel Tower fame) in 1884. It was

---

⟨*Moments* **Whale-Watching in Baja**

Few sights inspire as much reverence as close contact with a whale in its natural habitat. The various protected bays and lagoons on Baja's Pacific coast are the preferred winter waters for migrating gray whales as they journey south to mate and give birth to their calves. These whales are known to be so friendly and curious that they frequently come up to the boats and stay close by, and sometimes even allow people to pet them.

The experience is particularly rewarding in the protected areas of the **El Vizcaino Biosphere Reserve,** where you can easily see many whales. This area encompasses the famous **Laguna Ojo de Liebre**—also known as **Scammon's Lagoon**—close to Guerrero Negro, Laguna San Ignacio, and Bahía Magdalena.

Because these protected waters offer ideal conditions for gray whales during the winter, the neighboring towns have developed the infrastructure and services to accommodate whale-watchers. Whale-watching season generally runs from January to March. But remember that the colder the water, the farther south the whales migrate, so check on water temperatures and whale sightings before you plan your expedition. The temperature on the boat can be quite cool; bring a light jacket.

Loreto is the best place to launch a whale-watching journey; it has a well-developed tourist infrastructure and a number of lovely resort hotels. Trips take you by road to Bahía Magdalena, where you board a skiff to get up close to the gentle giants. Locally based **Loreto Center** (© **613/135-0798;** www.loretocenter.com) and **Las Parras Tours** (© **613/135-1010**) offer excellent tours. Among the many groups that run expeditions is U.S.-based **Baja Expeditions,** 2625 Garnet Ave., San Diego, CA 92109 (© **800/843-6967** in the U.S., or 612/125-3828 in La Paz). Prices for package trips from Loreto run around $90 to $100 per person for a daylong trip.

created for the 1889 Paris World Expo, then transported here section-by-section and reassembled in 1897. Its somber gray exterior belies the beauty of the intricate stained-glass windows as viewed from inside.

The other obligatory sight to see is the former Fundacíon del Pacifico, or **Museo Histórico Minero de Santa Rosalía.** Located in a landmark wooden building, it houses a permanent display of artifacts from the days of Santa Rosalía's mining operations. It's open Monday through Saturday from 8:30am to 2pm and 5 to 7pm. Admission is $1.50.

Bordering the museum are the most attractive of the **clapboard houses,** painted in a rainbow of colors—mango, lemon, blueberry, and cherry. The wood used to construct these houses was the return cargo on ships that transported copper to refineries in Oregon and British Columbia during the 1800s.

The **Plaza Benito Juárez,** or *zócalo* (town square), which fronts the **Palacio Municipal (City Hall),** is an intriguing structure of French Colonial architecture.

WHERE TO STAY & DINE

Santa Rosalía claims to have the best bakery in all of Baja—**El Boleo,** Avenida Obregón at Calle 4 (© 615/152-0310), which has been baking French baguettes since the late 1800s. It's 3 blocks west of the church, and is open from 8am to 9pm.

Hotel Francés   Founded in 1886, the Hotel Francés once set the standard of hospitality in Baja Sur, welcoming European dignitaries and hosting the French administrators and businessmen of the mining operations. Today it has a worn air of elegance but retains its position as the most welcoming accommodation in Santa Rosalía. Rooms are in the back, with wooden porches and balconies overlooking a small courtyard pool. Each room has individually controlled air-conditioning, plus windows that open for ventilation. Floors are wood-planked, and the small baths are beautifully tiled. You have a choice of two double beds or one king. Telephone service is available in the lobby. The popular restaurant serves Mexican cuisine and seafood from 6am to 10pm.

Calle Jean Michel Cousteau s/n, 23920 Santa Rosalía B.C.S. ©/fax 615/152-2052. 17 units. $32 single or double. MC, V. Free parking. **Amenities:** Restaurant and bar; small courtyard pool; tour desk. *In room:* A/C, TV.

5 Tijuana & Rosarito Beach

Northern Baja California is not only Mexico's most infamous border crossing, it also claims to be the birthplace of the original Caesar salad and the margarita. Along the Pacific coastline south of the border, the towns of Tijuana and Rosarito Beach combine to make one of the country's most important entry points.

Long notorious as a hard-partying 10-block border town, **Tijuana** has cleaned up its act a bit on its way to becoming a full-scale city. A growing number of sports and cultural attractions now augment the legendary shopping experience and wild nightlife. **Rosarito Beach,** of *Titanic* fame, remains a more tranquil resort town; the decidedly laid-back atmosphere makes enjoying its miles of beachfront easy.

TIJUANA: BAWDY BORDER TOWN

In northern Baja, 26km (16 miles) south of San Diego, the first point of entry from the West Coast of the U.S. is infamous Tijuana—a town that continues to delude travelers into thinking that a visit there means they've been to Mexico.

Tijuana's "sin city" image is gradually morphing into that of a shopper's mecca and a nocturnal playground. Vineyards associated with the expanding wine industry are nearby, and an increasing number of cultural offerings have joined the traditional sporting attractions of greyhound racing, jai alai, and bullfights.

You are less likely to find the Mexico you may be expecting here—no charming town squares and churches, no women in colorful embroidered skirts and blouses, no bougainvillea spilling out of every crevice. Tijuana has an urban culture, a profusion of U.S.-inspired goods and services, and relentless hawkers plying to the thousands of tourists.

ESSENTIALS

A visit to Tijuana requires little in the way of formalities—people who stay less than 72 hours in the border zone do not need a passport or tourist card. If you plan to stay longer, a tourist card is required. They're available free of charge from the border crossing station, or from any immigration office.

From downtown San Diego, you also have the option of taking the **bright-red trolley** headed for San Ysidro and getting off at the last, or San Ysidro, stop (it's nicknamed the Tijuana Trolley for good reason). From here, follow the signs to walk across the border. It's simple, quick, and inexpensive; the one-way fare is $2. The last trolley leaving for San Ysidro departs downtown around midnight; the last returning trolley from San Ysidro is at 1am. On Saturday, the trolley runs 24 hours.

Once you're in Tijuana, it's easy to get around by taxi. Cab fares from the border to downtown average $5. You can also hire a taxi to Rosarito for about $20 one-way.

The Tijuana airport is about 8km (5 miles) east of the city. To drive to Tijuana from the U.S., take I-5 south to the Mexican border at San Ysidro. The drive from downtown San Diego takes about a half-hour.

For **tourist information,** visit the Centro Cultural Tijuana, Paseo de los Héroes and Mina (© 664/687-9600). It's in the Zona Río, the principal shopping and dining district, adjacent to the Tijuana River.

There are major banks with ATMs and *casas de cambio* (money-exchange houses) all over Tijuana, but you can easily come here—or to Rosarito and Ensenada, for that matter—without changing money, because dollars are accepted everywhere.

EXPLORING TIJUANA

For many visitors, Tijuana's main event is the bustling **Avenida Revolución.** Beginning in the 1920s, American college students, servicemen, and hedonistic tourists discovered this street as a bawdy center for illicit fun. Some of the original attractions—gambling, back-alley cockfights (now illegal), and girlie shows—have fallen by the wayside, with drinking and shopping the main order of business these days. You'll find the action between calles 1 and 9; the landmark jai alai palace anchors the southern portion.

If you're looking to see a different side of Tijuana, the best place to start is the **Centro Cultural Tijuana,** Paseo de los Héroes and Mina Rio Zone (© **664/687-9600,** ext. 9650). You'll easily spot the ultramodern Tijuana Cultural Center complex, which houses an Omnimax theater, the museum's permanent collection of Mexican artifacts, and a gallery of visiting exhibits. The center is open daily from 9am to 9pm. Admission to the permanent exhibits is free, there's a $2 charge for the special event gallery, and tickets for Omnimax films are $2 to $4 for adults, depending on the film; children pay half-price.

You'll find some classier shopping and a colorful local marketplace, plus the ultimate kid destination at **Plaza Mundo Divertido,** Via Rapida Poniente 15035 (© **664/701-7133**). The park is open daily from noon to 8:30pm. Admission is free, and several booths inside sell tickets for the various rides; most rides cost $1 to $4.

Tijuana

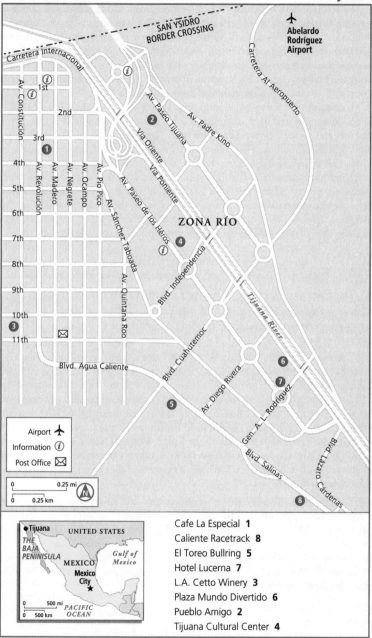

Cafe La Especial **1**

Caliente Racetrack **8**

El Toreo Bullring **5**

Hotel Lucerna **7**

L.A. Cetto Winery **3**

Plaza Mundo Divertido **6**

Pueblo Amigo **2**

Tijuana Cultural Center **4**

The fertile valleys of Northern Baja produce most of Mexico's finest wines and export many high-quality vintages to Europe. For an introduction to Mexican wines, stop into **Cava de Vinos L. A. Cetto (L. A. Cetto Winery),** Av. Cañón Johnson 2108, at Av. Constitución Sur (© **664/685-3031,** ext. 128, or 664/638-5848; lacetto@compuserve.com). Shaped like a wine barrel, this building's striking facade is made from old oak aging barrels—call it inspired recycling. It's open Monday through Friday from 9am to 6pm and Saturday from 10:30am to 5pm.

Tijuana's biggest attraction is **shopping.** People come to take advantage of low prices on a variety of merchandise(terra cotta and colorfully glazed pottery, woven blankets and serapes, embroidered dresses and sequined sombreros, onyx chess sets, beaded necklaces and bracelets, silver jewelry, leather bags and *huarache* sandals, rain sticks, Cuban cigars, and Mexican liquors. You're permitted to bring $400 worth of purchases back across the border (sorry, no Cuban cigars allowed), including 1 liter of alcohol per person. Many Americans have taken to Tijuana as a way to purchase inexpensive prescription drugs, and bring them back across the border. Be aware—authorities have cracked down on this practice, and are now making surprise arrests of foreigners purchasing drugs without valid prescriptions from a Mexican doctor.

If a marketplace atmosphere and spirited bargaining are what you're looking for, head to **Mercado de Artesanías (crafts market),** Calle 2 and Avenida Negrete. Here, vendors of pottery, clayware, clothing, and other crafts fill an entire city block.

OUTDOOR ACTIVITIES & SPECTATOR SPORTS
Tijuana is a spectator's (and gambler's) paradise.

BULLFIGHTING Whatever your opinion, bullfighting has a prominent place in Mexican heritage, and is even considered an essential element of the culture. The skill and bravery of matadors is closely linked with cultural ideals regarding *machismo,* and some of the world's best perform at Tijuana's two stadiums. The season runs May through September, with events held on Sunday at 4:30pm. Ticket prices range from $10 to $42 (the premium seats are on the shaded side of the arena) and can be purchased at the bullring or in advance from San Diego's **Five Star Tours** (© **619/232-5049,** or 664/622-2203). **El Toreo** (© **664/686-1510**) is 3km (2 miles) east of downtown on Bulevar Agua Caliente at Avenida Diego Rivera. **Plaza de Toros Monumental,** also called Bullring-by-the-Sea (© **664/680-1808**), is 10km (6 miles) west of downtown on Highway 1-D (before the first toll station); it's perched at the edge of both the ocean and the California border.

DOG RACING There's satellite wagering on U.S. horse races at the majestic **Caliente Racetrack,** off Bulevar Agua Caliente, 5km (3 miles) east of downtown (© **619/231-1910** in the U.S., or 664/681-7811), but only greyhounds actually kick up dust at the track. Races are held daily at 7:45pm, with Tuesday, Saturday, and Sunday matinees at 2pm. General admission is free, but bettors in the know congregate in the comfortable Turf Club; admission is free, and you pay $10 for your drinks, but that's refundable with a wagering voucher.

A PLACE TO STAY
Hotel Lucerna   Once the most chic hotel in Tijuana, Lucerna now feels slightly worn, though it still has personality. The flavor is Mexican Colonial—wrought-iron railings and chandeliers, rough-hewn heavy wood furniture, brocade wallpaper, and traditional tiles. The hotel is in the Zona Río, away from the noise and congestion of

downtown, so a quiet night's sleep is easily attainable. All of the rooms in the five-story hotel have balconies or patios. Hotel rates in Tijuana are subject to a 12% tax.

Av. Paseo de los Héroes, 10902 Zona Río, Tijuana. ⓒ 664/633-3900. 167 units. $172 double; $185 suite. AE, DC, MC, V. **Amenities:** Coffee shop; pool; room service. *In room:* A/C, TV, coffeemaker, hair dryer, iron.

WHERE TO DINE

Cafe La Especial MEXICAN   Tucked away in a shopping *pasaje* (pedestrian boulevard) at the bottom of some stairs (turn in at the taco stand of the same name), this restaurant is a well-known purveyor of home-style Mexican cooking at reasonable prices. The gruff, efficient waitstaff carry out platter after platter of *carne asada* (grilled marinated beef served with fresh tortillas, beans, and rice). Traditional dishes like tacos, enchiladas, and burritos round out the menu, augmented by frosty cold Mexican beers.

Av. Revolución 718 (between calles 3 and 4), Zona Centro. ⓒ 664/685-6654. Menu items $3–$12. MC, V. Daily 9am–10pm.

Cien Años MEXICAN   This elegant and gracious Zona Río restaurant offers artfully blended Mexican flavors (tamarind, poblano chile, mango) in stylish presentations. If you're interested in haute cuisine, the buzz around Tijuana is all about this place.

José María Velazco 1407. ⓒ **664/634-3039** or 664/634-7262. Main courses $10–$15. AE, MC, V. Mon–Thurs 7am–10:30pm; Fri–Sat 7am–2am; Sun 7am–8pm.

TIJUANA AFTER DARK

Avenida Revolución is the center of the city's nightlife; many compare it with Bourbon Street in New Orleans during Mardi Gras—except here it's a regular occurrence, not a once-a-year blowout.

A recent nightlife trend has been the proliferation of sports bars. The most popular cluster is in **Pueblo Amigo,** Via Oriente and Paseo Tijuana, in the Zona Río. Two of the town's hottest dance clubs, **Rodeo de Media Noche** (ⓒ **664/682-4967**) and **Señor Frog's** (ⓒ **664/682-4962**), are also in Pueblo Amigo. Pueblo Amigo is less than 3km (2 miles) from the border, a short taxi ride or—during daylight hours—a pleasant walk away.

ROSARITO BEACH: BAJA'S FIRST BEACH RESORT

Just 29km (18 miles) south of Tijuana and a complete departure in ambience, Rosarito Beach is a tranquil, friendly beach town. Hollywood has played a major part in Rosarito's recent renaissance—it was the location for the sound stage and filming of the Academy Award–winning *Titanic.* The former *Titanic* Museum—now called **Foxploration**—continues to draw the fans of this film, and movie-making in general. The beaches between Tijuana and Rosarito are also known for excellent surf breaks.

GETTING THERE   Two roads run between Tijuana and Ensenada (the largest and third-largest cities in Baja)—the scenic, coast-hugging toll road (Hwy. 1-D, marked *cuota*), and the free but slower public road (Hwy. 1, marked *libre*).

WHAT TO SEE & DO

A few kilometers south of Rosarito proper lies the **seaside production site** of 1997's mega-blockbuster *Titanic,* and more recently, *Master and Commander.* On 16 otherwise dry hectares (40 acres) along the Pacific Coast, the studio has several huge tanks that fill with water to reproduce seafaring conditions. Filled with *Titanic* memorabilia, it has now become the moviemaking theme park, **Foxploration,** devoted to the art of

The Upper Baja Peninsula

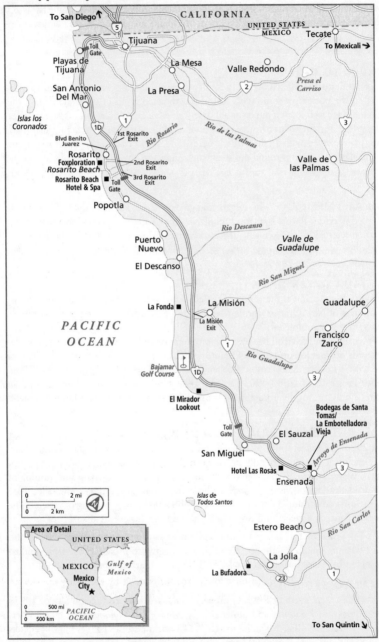

CALIFORNIA

UNITED STATES
MEXICO

To San Diego↑

Tijuana

Toll Gate

Tecate

To Mexicali →

Playas de Tijuana

La Mesa

Valle Redondo

Presa el Carrizo

San Antonio Del Mar

La Presa

Islas los Coronados

Rio Rosario

Rio de las Palmas

1D

1st Rosarito Exit

Valle de las Palmas

Blvd Benito Juarez

Rosarito
Foxploration ■
Rosarito Beach

2nd Rosarito Exit

Rosarito Beach ■
Hotel & Spa

Toll Gate

3rd Rosarito Exit

Popotla

Rio Descanso

Valle de Guadalupe

Puerto Nuevo

El Descanso

Rio San Miguel

La Fonda ■

La Misión

Guadalupe

La Misión Exit

PACIFIC OCEAN

1

Francisco Zarco

Rio Guadalupe

Bajamar Golf Course

1D

3

El Mirador Lookout

Bodegas de Santa Tomas/
La Embotelladora Vieja

Toll Gate

El Sauzal

Arroyo de Ensenada

San Miguel

3

Hotel Las Rosas ■

Ensenada

0   2 mi
0   2 km

Islas de Todos Santos

Estero Beach

Rio San Carlos

Area of Detail

UNITED STATES

La Jolla

MEXICO

Gulf of Mexico

La Bufadora ■

23

1

Mexico City ★

0   500 mi
0   500 km

PACIFIC OCEAN

To San Quintin ↘

752

moviemaking. The Cinemagico area has interactive displays about filmmaking and special effects, and guided tours are available in English and Spanish. There is also a play center for kids, plus a gift shop. Admission is a hefty $12 for adults, $9 for children 3 to 11. Foxploration (© **866/369-2252** in the U.S., or 661/614-9444; www.foxploration.com) is open Wednesday through Friday from 9am to 5:30pm, and Saturday and Sunday from 10am to 6:30pm.

If you have only a few hours to spend in Rosarito Beach, that's still enough time to have a swim or a horseback ride at the beach, shop for souvenirs, and dine on fish tacos or tamales from one of the family-run stands along **Bulevar Benito Juárez,** the town's main (and only) drag. The dozen or so blocks of Rosarito north of the Rosarito Beach Hotel are packed with stores typical of Mexican border towns: curio shops, cigar and *licores* (liquor) stores, and *farmacias* (where drugs like Viagra, Retin-A, Prozac, and many more are available at low cost).

Because the legal drinking age in Baja is 18, the under-21 crowd from Southern California tends to flock across the border on Friday and Saturday nights. The most popular spot in town is **Papas & Beer** (© **661/612-0444**). It's a relaxed come-as-you-are-type club on the beach, just a block north of the hotel. Even for those young in spirit only, it's great fun, with outdoor tables and a bar surrounding a sand volleyball court. The **Salón Mexicano** (© **661/612-0144**), in the Rosarito Beach Hotel, attracts a slightly more mature evening crowd, with live music on Friday and Saturday.

WHERE TO STAY & DINE

Rosarito Beach Hotel & Spa   Although this once-glamorous resort has been holding steady since its heyday, it's currently defined by glaring nighttime neon and party-mania. Despite the resort's changed personality, its unique artistic construction and lavish decoration remain. It has a wide, family-friendly stretch of beach. The stately home of the original owners has been transformed into the full-service **Casa Playa Spa,** where massages and other treatments are only slightly less costly than in the U.S. You'll pay more for a room with an ocean view, and more for the newer, air-conditioned units in the tower; the older rooms in the poolside building have only ceiling fans, but they prevail in the character department, with hand-painted trim and original tile. The mansion's dining room (Chabert's Steakhouse) charges top dollar for Continental cuisine; Azteca is a casual Mexican restaurant in the main building.

Bulevar Benito Juárez, Zona Centro, 22710 Rosarito, B.C. Mexico. (Mailing address: P.O. Box 430145, San Diego, CA 92143.) © **800/343-8582** in the U.S., or 661/612-0144. Fax 661/612-1125. www.rosaritobeachhotel.com. 278 units. $70–$140 double; $111–$175 suites. 2 children under 12 stay free in parent's room. Packages available. MC, V. Free parking. **Amenities:** 2 restaurants; bar; 2 swimming pools; wading pool; spa; playground; racquetball court. *In room:* A/C, TV.

6 Ensenada: Port of Call

134km (84 miles) S of San Diego; 109km (68 miles) S of Tijuana

Ensenada is an attractive town on a lovely bay, surrounded by sheltering mountains. Located about 40 minutes from Rosarito, it's the kind of place that loves a celebration—be it for a bicycle race or a seafood festival.

GETTING THERE & INFORMATION   After passing through the final tollgate, Highway 1-D curves sharply toward downtown Ensenada.

The **Tourist and Convention Bureau booth** (© **646/178-2411**) is at the western entrance to town, where the waterfront-hugging Bulevar Lázaro Cárdenas—also known as Bulevar Costero—curves away to the right. It's open Monday through Friday from 9am to 7pm. and Saturday and Sunday from 9am to 5pm. Taxis park along López Mateos.

EXPLORING ENSENADA

While Ensenada is technically a border town, one of its appeals is its multilayered vitality. The bustling port consumes the entire waterfront—beach access can be found only north or south of town—and the Pacific fishing trade and agriculture in the fertile valleys surrounding the city dominate the economy.

Even part-time oenophiles should pay a visit to the **Bodegas de Santo Tomás Winery** 🎯🎯, Av. Miramar 666, at Calle 7 (© **646/178-2509;** www.santotomas.com.mx), the oldest winery in Mexico, and the largest in Baja. It uses old-fashioned methods of processing grapes, first cultivated by Dominican monks in 1791 in the lush Santo Tomás Valley. Tours in English start daily at 10 and 11am, and 1 and 3pm. Admission is $5 (including tastings), $10 more gets you a souvenir wineglass, and wines for sale range from $3.50 to $10 a bottle.

Ensenada's equivalent of Tijuana's Avenida Revolución is crowded **Avenida López Mateos,** roughly parallel to Bulevar Lázaro Cárdenas (Bulevar Costero); the highest concentration of shops and restaurants is between avenidas Ruiz and Castillo. Compared to Tijuana, there is more authentic Mexican art- and craftwork in Ensenada.

South of the city, 45 minutes by car along the rural Punta Banda peninsula, is one of Ensenada's major attractions: **La Bufadora,** a natural sea spout in the rocks. With each incoming wave, water is forced upward through the rock, creating a geyser whose loud grunt gave the phenomenon its name (it means "buffalo snort"). From downtown Ensenada, take Avenida Reforma (Hwy. 1) south to Highway 23 west. La Bufadora is at the end of the road. Once parked ($1 per car in crude dirt lots), you must walk downhill to the viewing platform, at the end of a 270m (900-ft.) pathway lined with souvenir stands.

WHERE TO STAY

Hotel Las Rosas   Modern and comfortable, this pink oceanfront hotel 3km (2 miles) outside of Ensenada is the favorite of many Baja aficionados. It offers all the comforts of an American hotel. The atrium lobby is awash with pale pink and sea-foam green (including a back-lit, green-glass ceiling), a color scheme that pervades the hotel— including the guest rooms, which are sparsely appointed with quasi-tropical furniture. Some rooms have fireplaces, in-room whirlpools, or both. One of the resort's main photo ops is the spectacular swimming pool—it overlooks the Pacific and features a vanishing edge that appears to merge with the ocean beyond. If you're looking to maintain the highest comfort level possible in Ensenada, this is the hotel of choice.

Hwy. 1, 3km (2 miles) north of Ensenada. (Mailing address: Apdo. Postal 316, 22800 Ensenada, B.C., Mexico.) © 646/174-4310. www.lasrosas.com. 48 units. $145–$208 double. Children under 12 $16; extra adult $22. MC, V. **Amenities:** Restaurant; cocktail lounge; swimming pool; tennis and racquetball courts; small workout room; cliff-top hot tub. *In room:* TV.

WHERE TO DINE

La Embotelladora Vieja 🎯   FRENCH/MEXICAN/MEDITERRANEAN   Hidden on an industrial side street, and attached to the Bodegas de Santo Tomás winery, this looks more like a chapel than the elegant restaurant it is. Sophisticated diners will feel right at home in this stylish setting, a former aging room for the winery. It's now resplendent with red oak furniture (constructed from old wine casks), high brick walls, and crystal goblets and candlesticks on linen tablecloths. It goes without saying that the wine list is exemplary, featuring bottles from Santo Tomás and other Baja vintners. Look for appetizers like abalone ceviche or cream of garlic soup, followed by grilled swordfish in cilantro sauce, filet mignon in port wine–Gorgonzola sauce, or quail with a tart sauvignon blanc sauce.

Av. Miramar 666 (at Calle 7). © **646/174-0807.** Reservations recommended on weekends. Main courses $9–$25. MC, V. Lunch and dinner; call for seasonal hours. Closed Sun.

ENSENADA AFTER DARK

Just like in *Casablanca,* where "everyone goes to Rick's," everyone's been going to **Hussong's Cantina,** Av. Ruiz 113, near Avenida López Mateos (© **646/178-3210**), since the bar opened in 1892. Nothing much has changed—the place still sports Wild West–style swinging saloon doors, a long bar to slide beers along, and strolling mariachis bellowing above the din. Be aware that hygiene and privacy are low priorities in the restrooms. While the crowd (a pleasant mix of tourists and locals) at Hussong's can really whoop it up, they're amateurs compared to those who frequent **Papas & Beer,** Avenida Ruiz near Avenida López Mateos (© **646/174-0145;** www.papasandbeer.com), across the street. A tiny entrance leads to the upstairs bar and dance club. The music is loud and the hip young crowd is definitely here to party. Papas & Beer has quite a reputation with the Southern California college crowd, and has opened a branch in Rosarito Beach (see above).

Appendix A:
Mexico in Depth

by David Baird

Mexico stretches nearly 3,220km (2,000 miles) from east to west and more than 1,600km (1,000 miles) north to south. Only one-fifth the size of the United States, its territory includes trackless deserts in the north, dense jungles in the south, thousands of miles of lush seacoast and beaches along the Pacific and Caribbean, and the central highlands, crisscrossed by mountain ranges.

1 The Land & Its People

THE MEXICAN PEOPLE

Mexico has close to 100 million inhabitants, and 22 million of them live in the capital, Mexico City. Over the last few decades, the rate of population growth has been steadily declining, from 3.2% per year in the 1970s to 1.6% at present. Mexico City has the slowest growth rate, at less than 1% per year.

Today, close to almost 5 centuries after the Conquest, five million Mexicans speak a native language; of these, 800,000 do not speak Spanish at all. The states with the highest populations of Indians are Oaxaca, Chiapas, Yucatán, Michoacán, and Puebla.

By most measurements, the disparity between rich and poor has increased in the last 30 to 40 years. Cycles of boom and bust weigh heavier on the poor than on the rich. But in the face of all of this, Mexican society shows great resilience, due in part to the values Mexicans live by. For them, family and friends, social gatherings, and living in the present remain eminently important. In Mexico, there is always time to meet relatives or friends for a drink, a cup of coffee, or a special occasion.

SOCIAL MORES American and English travelers have often observed that Mexicans have a different conception of time, that life in Mexico obeys slower rhythms. This is true, and yet few observers go on to explain what the consequences of this are for the visitor to Mexico. This is a shame, because an imperfect appreciation of the difference causes a good deal of misunderstanding between tourists and locals.

On several occasions, Mexican acquaintances have asked me why Americans grin all the time. At first, I wasn't sure what to make of the question, and only gradually came to appreciate what was at issue. As the pace of life for Americans, Canadians, and others has quickened, they have come to skip some of the niceties of social interaction. When walking into a store, many Americans simply smile at a clerk and launch right into a question or request. The smile, in effect, replaces the greeting. In Mexico, it doesn't work that way. Mexicans misinterpret this American manner of greeting. After all, a smile when there is no context can be ambiguous; it can convey amusement, smugness, or superiority.

One of the most important pieces of advice I can offer travelers is this: Always give a proper greeting when addressing Mexicans. Don't try to abbreviate social intercourse. Mexican culture places a higher value on proper social form than on saving time. A Mexican must at least say *"¡Buenos días!"* or a quick *"¿Qué pasó?"*

(or its equivalent) to show proper respect. When an individual meets up with a group, he will greet each person separately, which can take quite a while. For us, the polite thing would be to keep our interruption to a minimum and give a general greeting to all.

Mexicans, like most people, will consciously or subconsciously make quick judgments about individuals they meet. Most divide the world into the *bien*

educado (well raised and cultured), and the *mal educado* (poorly raised). Unfortunately, many visitors are reluctant to try out their Spanish, preferring to keep exchanges to a minimum. Don't do this. To be categorized as a foreigner isn't a big deal. What's important in Mexico is to be categorized as one of the cultured foreigners and not one of the barbarians. This makes it easier to get the attention of waiters, hotel desk clerks, and people on the street.

2 A Look at the Past

PRE-HISPANIC CIVILIZATIONS

The earliest "Mexicans" were Stone Age hunter-gatherers from the north, descendants of a race that had probably crossed the Bering Strait and reached North America around 12,000 B.C. They arrived in what is now Mexico by 10,000 B.C. Sometime between 5200 and 1500 B.C., in what is known as the **Archaic period,** they began practicing agriculture and domesticating animals.

THE PRE-CLASSIC PERIOD (1500 B.C.–A.D. 300) Eventually, agriculture improved to the point that it could support large communities and free some of the population from agricultural work. A civilization emerged that we call the **Olmec**—an enigmatic people who settled the lower Gulf Coast in what is now Tabasco and Veracruz. Anthropologists regard them as the mother culture of Mesoamerica because they established a pattern for later civilizations in a wide area stretching from northern Mexico into Central America. The Olmec developed the basic calendar used throughout the region, established a 52-year cycle (which they used to schedule the construction of pyramids), established principles of urban layout and architecture, and originated the cult of the jaguar and the sanctity of jade.

The Maya civilization began developing in the late pre-Classic period, around

500 B.C. Our understanding of this period is sketchy, but Olmec influences are apparent everywhere. The Maya perfected the Olmec calendar and, somewhere along the way, developed an ornate system of hieroglyphic writing and early architectural concepts. Two other civilizations began the rise to prominence around this time: the people of Teotihuacán, just north of present-day Mexico City, and the Zapotec of Monte Albán in the valley of Oaxaca.

THE CLASSIC PERIOD (A.D. 300–900) The flourishing of these three civilizations marks the boundaries of this period—the heyday of pre-Columbian Mesoamerican artistic and cultural achievements. These include the pyramids and palaces in Teotihuacán; the ceremonial center of Monte Albán; and the stelae and temples of Palenque, Bonampak, and the Tikal site in Guatemala

The inhabitants of **Teotihuacán** (100 B.C.–A.D. 700), near present-day Mexico City, built a city that, at its zenith, is thought to have had 100,000 or more inhabitants. It was a well-organized city, covering 23 sq. km (9 sq. miles), and built on a grid with streams channeled to follow the city's plan.

Farther south, the **Zapotec,** influenced by the Olmec, raised an impressive civilization in the region of Oaxaca. Their two principal cities were **Monte Albán,** inhabited by an elite of merchants and artisans, and **Mitla,** reserved for the high priests.

THE POST-CLASSIC PERIOD (A.D. 900–1521)

Warfare was a more conspicuous activity of the civilizations that flourished in this period. Social development was impressive but not as cosmopolitan as the Maya, Teotihuacán, and Zapotec societies. In central Mexico, a people known as the **Toltec** established their capital at Tula in the 10th century. They revered a god known as **Tezcatlipoca,** or "smoking mirror," who later became an Aztec god. The Toltec maintained a large military class divided into orders symbolized by animals. At its height, Tula may have had 40,000 people, and its influence spread across Mesoamerica. By the 13th century, however, the Toltec had exhausted themselves, probably in civil wars and in battles with the invaders from the north.

Of those northern invaders, the **Aztec** were the most warlike. At first they served as mercenaries for established cities in the valley of Mexico—one of which allotted them an unwanted, marshy piece of land in the middle of Lake Texcoco for their settlement. It eventually grew into the island city of Tenochtitlán. Through aggressive diplomacy and military action, the Aztec soon conquered central Mexico and extended their rule east to the Gulf Coast and south to the valley of Oaxaca.

During this period, the Maya built beautiful cities near the Yucatán's Puuc hills. The regional architecture, called **Puuc style,** is characterized by elaborate exterior stonework appearing above doorframes and extending to the roofline. Examples of this architecture, such as the Codz Poop at Kabah and the palaces at Uxmal, Sayil, and Labná, are beautiful and quite impressive.

THE CONQUEST

In 1517, the first Spaniards arrived in what is today known as Mexico and skirmished with Maya Indians off the coast of the Yucatán Peninsula. One of the fledgling expeditions ended in shipwreck, leaving several Spaniards stranded as prisoners of the Maya. The Spanish sent out another expedition, under the command of **Hernán Cortez,** which landed on Cozumel in February 1519. Cortez inquired about the gold and riches of the interior, and the coastal Maya were happy to describe the wealth and splendor of the Aztec empire in central Mexico. Cortez promptly disobeyed all orders of his superior, the governor of Cuba, and sailed to the mainland.

Cortez arrived when the Aztec empire was at the height of its wealth and power. **Moctezuma II** ruled over the central and southern highlands and extracted tribute from lowland peoples. His greatest temples were literally plated with gold and encrusted with the blood of sacrificial captives. Moctezuma was a fool, a mystic, and something of a coward. Despite his wealth and military power, he dithered in his capital at Tenochtitlán, sending messengers with gifts and suggestions that Cortez leave. Meanwhile, Cortez blustered and negotiated his way into the highlands, always cloaking his real intentions. Moctezuma, terrified by the military tactics and technology of the Spaniard, convinced himself that Cortez was in fact the god Quetzalcoatl making his long-awaited return. By the time the Spaniards arrived in the Aztec capital, Cortez had gained some ascendancy over the lesser Indian states that were resentful tributaries to the Aztec. In November 1519, Cortez confronted Moctezuma and took him hostage in an effort to leverage control of the empire.

In the middle of Cortez's dangerous game of manipulation, another Spanish expedition arrived with orders to end Cortez's authority over the mission. Cortez hastened to meet the rival's force and persuade them to join his own. In the meantime, the Aztec chased the garrison out of Tenochtitlán, and either they or the Spaniards killed Moctezuma. For the next year and a half, Cortez laid siege to Tenochtitlán, with the help of rival Indians and a decimating epidemic of smallpox, to which the Indians had no resistance. In the end, the Aztec capital fell, and when it did, all of central Mexico lay at the feet of the conquistadors.

The Spanish Conquest started as a pirate expedition by Cortez and his men, unauthorized by the Spanish crown or its governor in Cuba. The Spanish king legitimized Cortez following his victory over the Aztec and ordered the forced conversion to Christianity of this new colony, to be called **New Spain.** Guatemala and Honduras were explored and conquered, and by 1540, the territory of New Spain included possessions from Vancouver to Panama. In the 2 centuries that followed, Franciscan and Augustinian friars converted millions of Indians to Christianity, and the Spanish lords built huge feudal estates on which the Indian farmers were little more than serfs. The silver and gold that Cortez looted made Spain the richest country in Europe.

THE COLONIAL PERIOD

Hernán Cortez set about building a new city upon the ruins of the old Aztec capital. To do this he collected from the Indians the tributes once paid to the Aztec emperor, many of these rendered in labor. This arrangement, in one form or another, became the basis for the construction of the new colony. But diseases brought by the Spaniards decimated the native population over the next century and drastically reduced the pool of labor.

Cortez soon returned to Spain and was replaced by a governing council, and, later, the office of viceroy. Over the 3 centuries of the colonial period, 61 viceroys governed Mexico. Spain became rich from New World gold and silver, chiseled out by Indian labor. The colonial elite built lavish homes in Mexico City and in the countryside. They filled their homes with ornate furniture, had many servants, and adorned themselves in imported velvets, satins, and jewels.

A new class system developed. Those born in Spain considered themselves superior to the *criollos* (Spaniards born in Mexico). Those of other races and the *castas* (mixtures of Spanish and Indian, Spanish and African, or Indian and African) occupied the bottom rungs of society. It took great cunning to stay a step ahead of the avaricious Crown, which demanded increasing taxes and contributions from its fabled foreign conquests. Still, wealthy colonists prospered enough to develop an extravagant society.

However, discontent with the mother country simmered for years over social and political issues: taxes, royal monopolies, the bureaucracy, Spanish-born citizens' advantages over Mexican-born subjects, and restrictions on commerce with Spain and other countries. In 1808, Napoleon invaded Spain and crowned his brother Joseph king in place of Charles IV. To many in Mexico, allegiance to France was out of the question; discontent reached the level of revolt.

INDEPENDENCE

The rebellion began in 1810, when **Father Miguel Hidalgo** gave the *grito,* a cry for independence, from his church in the town of Dolores, Guanajuato. The uprising soon became a full-fledged revolution, as Hidalgo and Ignacio Allende gathered an "army" of citizens and threatened Mexico City. Although Hidalgo ultimately failed and was executed, he is honored as "the Father of Mexican Independence." Another priest, José María Morelos, kept the revolt alive with several successful campaigns through 1815, when he, too, was captured and executed.

After the death of Morelos, prospects for independence were rather dim until the Spanish king who replaced Joseph Bonaparte decided to make social reforms in the colonies. This convinced the conservative powers in Mexico that they didn't need Spain after all. With their tacit approval, Agustín de Iturbide, then commander of royalist forces, changed sides and declared Mexico independent and himself emperor. Before long, however, internal dissension brought about the fall of the emperor, and Mexico was proclaimed a republic.

Political instability engulfed the young republic and Mexico waged a disastrous war with the United States and lost half its territory. A central figure was **Antonio López de Santa Anna,** who assumed the leadership of his country no fewer than 11 times and was flexible enough in those volatile days to portray himself variously as a liberal, a conservative, a federalist, and a centralist. He probably holds the record for frequency of exile; by 1855 he was finally left without a political comeback and ended his days in Venezuela.

Political instability persisted, and the conservative forces, with some encouragement from Napoleon III, hit upon the idea of inviting in a Hapsburg to regain control (as if that strategy had ever worked for Spain). They found a willing volunteer in Archduke Maximilian of Austria, who accepted the position of Mexican emperor with the support of French troops. The ragtag Mexican forces defeated the French force—a modern, well-equipped army—in a battle near Puebla (now celebrated annually as **Cinco de Mayo**). A second attempt was more successful, and Ferdinand Maximilian Joseph of Hapsburg became emperor. After 3 years of civil war, the French were finally induced to abandon the emperor's cause; Maximilian was captured and executed by a firing squad near Querétaro in 1867. His adversary and successor (as president of Mexico) was **Benito Juárez,** a Zapotec Indian lawyer and one of the great heroes of Mexican history. Juárez did his best to unify and strengthen his country before dying of a heart attack in 1872; his impact on Mexico's future was profound, and his plans and visions bore fruit for decades.

THE PORFIRIATO & THE REVOLUTION

A few years after Juárez's death, one of his generals, **Porfirio Díaz,** assumed power in a coup. He ruled Mexico from 1877 to 1911, a period now called the "Porfiriato." He stayed in power by imposing repressive measures and courting the favor of powerful nations. Generous in his dealings with foreign investors, Díaz became, in the eyes of most Mexicans, the archetypal *entreguista* (one who sells out his country for private gain). With foreign investment came the concentration of great wealth in few hands, and social conditions worsened.

In 1910, Francisco Madero called for an armed rebellion that became the **Mexican Revolution** (La Revolución in Mexico; the revolution against Spain is the Guerra de Independencia). Díaz was sent into exile; while in London, he became a celebrity at the age of 81, when he jumped into the Thames to save a drowning boy. He is buried in Paris. Madero became president but was promptly betrayed and executed by **Victoriano Huerta.** Those who had answered Madero's call responded again—to the great peasant hero **Emiliano Zapata** in the south, and to the seemingly invincible **Pancho Villa** in the central north, flanked by Alvaro Obregón and Venustiano Carranza. They eventually put Huerta to flight and began hashing out a new constitution.

For the next few years, the revolutionaries Carranza, Obregón, and Villa fought among themselves; Zapata did not seek national power, though he fought tenaciously for land for the peasants. Carranza, who was president at the time, betrayed and assassinated Zapata. Obregón finally consolidated power and probably had Carranza assassinated. He, in turn, was assassinated when he tried to break one of the tenets of the Revolution—no reelection. His successor, Plutarco Elias Calles, learned this lesson well, installing one puppet president after another, until **Lázaro Cárdenas** severed the puppeteer's strings and banished him to exile.

Until Cárdenas's election in 1934, the outcome of the revolution remained in doubt. There had been some land redistribution, but other measures took a back seat to political expediency. Cárdenas changed all that. He implemented massive redistribution of land and nationalized the oil industry. He instituted many reforms and gave shape to the ruling political party (now the **Partido Revolucionario Institucional,** or PRI) by bringing a broad representation of Mexican society under its banner and establishing mechanisms for consensus building. Most Mexicans practically canonize Cárdenas.

MODERN MEXICO

The presidents who followed were noted more for graft than for leadership. The party's base narrowed as many of the reform-minded elements were marginalized. Economic progress, a lot of it in the form of large development projects, became the PRI's main basis for legitimacy. In 1968, the government violently repressed a democratic student movement. Police forces shot and killed an unknown number of civilians in the Tlatelolco section of Mexico City. Though the PRI maintained its grip on power, it lost all semblance of being a progressive party. In 1985, a devastating **earthquake in Mexico City** brought down many of the government's new, supposedly earthquake-proof buildings, exposing shoddy construction and the widespread government corruption that fostered it. The government's handling of the relief efforts also drew heavy criticism. In 1994, a political and military **uprising in Chiapas** focused world attention on Mexico's great social problems. A new political force, the Ejército Zapatista de Liberación Nacional or EZLN (Zapatista National Liberation Army), has skillfully publicized the plight of the peasant.

In the years that followed, opposition political parties grew in power and legitimacy. Facing pressure and scrutiny from national and international organizations, and widespread public discontent, the PRI had to concede defeat in state and congressional elections throughout the '90s. The party began choosing its candidates through primaries, instead of through appointment. But in the presidential elections of 2000, Vicente Fox, candidate for the opposition party PAN, won by a landslide. In hindsight, there was no way that the PRI could have won in a fair election. For most Mexicans, a government under the PRI was all that they had ever known.

Since then, Mexico has been sailing into the uncharted waters of coalition politics. The three main parties, PRI, PAN, and PRD, have grown into their new roles within a more open, more transparent political system. To their credit, the sailing has been much smoother than many observers predicted. But the real test will be weathering the economic slowdown that accompanied the downturn in the U.S. economy, and in carrying out the next presidential elections, in 2006.

Appendix B:
Useful Terms & Phrases

1 Telephones & Mail

USING THE TELEPHONES

All phone numbers listed in this book have a total of 10 digits—a two- or three-digit area code plus the telephone number. Local numbers in Mexico City, Guadalajara, and Monterrey are eight digits; everywhere else, local numbers have seven digits.

To call long distance within Mexico, dial the national long-distance code **01** before dialing the area code and then the number. Mexico's *claves* (area codes) are listed in the front of telephone directories. Area codes are listed before all phone numbers in this book. For long-distance dialing, you will often see the term "LADA," which is the automatic long-distance service offered by Telmex, Mexico's former telephone monopoly and its largest phone company. To make a person-to-person or collect call inside Mexico, dial ℂ **020.** You can also call 020 to request the correct area codes for the number and place you are calling.

To make a long-distance call to the United States or Canada, dial **001,** then the area code and seven-digit number. For international long-distance numbers in Europe, Africa, and Asia, dial **00,** then the country code, the city code, and the number. To make a person-to-person or collect call to outside Mexico, to obtain other international dialing codes, or for further assistance, dial ℂ **090.**

For additional details on making calls within and to Mexico, see chapter 2 and the inside front cover of this book.

POSTAL GLOSSARY

Airmail   **Correo aéreo**

Customs   **Aduana**

General delivery   **Lista de correos**

Insurance (insured mail)   **Seguro (correo asegurado)**

Mailbox   **Buzón**

Money order   **Giro postal**

Parcel   **Paquete**

Post office   **Oficina de correos**

Post office box (abbreviation)   **Apdo. Postal**

Postal service   **Correos**

Registered mail   **Registrado**

Rubber stamp   **Sello**

Special delivery, express   **Entrega inmediata**

Stamp   **Estampilla** or **timbre**

2 Basic Vocabulary

Most Mexicans are very patient with foreigners who try to speak their language; it helps a lot to know a few basic phrases. I've included simple phrases for expressing basic needs, followed by some common menu items.

ENGLISH-SPANISH PHRASES

English	Spanish	Pronunciation
Good day	**Buen día**	bwehn *dee*-ah
Good morning	**Buenos días**	*bweh*-nohss *dee*-ahss
How are you?	**¿Cómo está?**	*koh*-moh ehss-*tah?*
Very well	**Muy bien**	mwee byehn
Thank you	**Gracias**	*grah*-syahss
You're welcome	**De nada**	deh *nah*-dah
Good-bye	**Adiós**	ah-*dyohss*
Please	**Por favor**	pohr fah-*vohr*
Yes	**Sí**	see
No	**No**	noh
Excuse me	**Perdóneme**	pehr-*doh*-neh-meh
Give me	**Déme**	*deh*-meh
Where is . . . ?	**¿Dónde está . . . ?**	*dohn*-deh ehss-*tah?*
the station	**la estación**	lah ehss-tah-*syohn*
a hotel	**un hotel**	oon oh-*tehl*
a gas station	**una gasolinera**	*oo*-nah gah-soh-lee-*neh*-rah
a restaurant	**un restaurante**	oon res-tow-*rahn*-teh
the toilet	**el baño**	el *bah*-nyoh
a good doctor	**un buen médico**	oon bwehn *meh*-dee-coh
the road to . . .	**el camino a/hacia . . .**	el cah-*mee*-noh ah/*ah*-syah
To the right	**A la derecha**	ah lah deh-*reh*-chah
To the left	**A la izquierda**	ah lah ees-*kyehr*-dah
Straight ahead	**Derecho**	deh-*reh*-choh
I would like	**Quisiera**	key-*syeh*-rah
I want	**Quiero**	*kyeh*-roh
to eat	**comer**	koh-*mehr*
a room	**una habitación**	*oo*-nah ah-bee-tah-*syohn*
Do you have . . . ?	**¿Tiene usted . . . ?**	tyeh-neh oo-*sted?*
a book	**un libro**	oon *lee*-broh
a dictionary	**un diccionario**	oon deek-syow-*nah*-ryo
How much is it?	**¿Cuánto cuesta?**	*kwahn*-toh *kwehss*-tah?
When?	**¿Cuándo?**	*kwahn*-doh?
What	**¿Qué?**	keh?

English	Spanish	Pronunciation
There is (Is there . . . ?)	(¿)Hay (. . . ?)	eye?
What is there?	¿Qué hay?	keh eye?
Yesterday	Ayer	ah-*yer*
Today	Hoy	oy
Tomorrow	Mañana	mah-*nyah*-nah
Good	Bueno	*bweh*-noh
Bad	Malo	*mah*-loh
Better (best)	(Lo) Mejor	(loh) meh-*hohr*
More	Más	mahs
Less	Menos	*meh*-nohss
No smoking	Se prohibe fumar	seh proh-*ee*-beh foo-*mahr*
Postcard	Tarjeta postal	tar-*heh*-ta pohs-*tahl*
Insect repellent	Repelente contra insectos	reh-peh-*lehn*-te *cohn*-trah een-*sehk*-tos

MORE USEFUL PHRASES

English	Spanish	Pronunciation
Do you speak English?	¿Habla usted inglés?	*ah*-blah oo-*sted* een-*glehs*?
Is there anyone here who speaks English?	¿Hay alguien aquí que hable inglés?	eye *ahl*-gyehn ah-*kee* keh *ah*-bleh een-*glehs*?
I speak a little Spanish.	Hablo un poco de español.	*ah*-bloh oon *poh*-koh deh ehss-pah-*nyohl*
I don't understand Spanish very well.	No (lo) entiendo muy bien el español.	noh (loh) ehn-*tyehn*-doh mwee byehn el ehss-pah-*nyohl*
The meal is good.	Me gusta la comida.	meh *goo*-stah lah koh-*mee*-dah
What time is it?	¿Qué hora es?	keh *oh*-rah ehss?
May I see your menu?	¿Puedo ver el menú (la carta)?	*pueh*-do vehr el meh-*noo* (lah *car*-tah)?
The check, please.	La cuenta, por favor.	lah *quehn*-tah pohr fa-*vorh*
What do I owe you?	¿Cuánto le debo?	*kwahn*-toh leh *deh*-boh?
What did you say?	¿Mande? (formal)	*mahn*-deh?
	¿Cómo? (informal)	*koh*-moh?

English	Spanish	Pronunciation
I want (to see) . . .	**Quiero (ver)** . . .	*kyeh*-roh (vehr)
a room	**un cuarto** or	oon *kwar*-toh,
	una habitación	*oo*-nah ah-bee-tah-*syohn*
for two persons	**para dos personas.**	*pah*-rah dohss pehr-soh-nahs
with (without) bathroom	**con (sin) baño**	kohn (seen) *bah*-nyoh
We are staying here only . . .	**Nos quedamos aquí solamente** . . .	nohs keh-*dah*-mohss ah-*kee* soh-lah-*mehn*-teh
one night.	**una noche.**	*oo*-nah *noh*-cheh
one week.	**una semana.**	*oo*-nah seh-*mah*-nah
We are leaving . . .	**Partimos (Salimos)** . . .	pahr-*tee*-mohss (sah-*lee*-mohss)
tomorrow.	**mañana.**	mah-*nya*-nah
Do you accept . . . ?	**¿Acepta usted . . . ?**	ah-*sehp*-tah oo-*sted*
traveler's checks?	**cheques de viajero?**	*cheh*-kehss deh byah-*heh*-roh?
Is there a laundromat . . . ?	**¿Hay una lavandería . . . ?**	eye *oo*-nah lah-*vahn*-deh-*ree*-ah
near here?	**cerca de aquí?**	*sehr*-kah deh ah-*kee*
Please send these clothes to the laundry.	**Hágame el favor de mandar esta ropa a la lavandería.**	*ah*-gah-meh el fah-*vohr* deh mahn-*dahr* ehss-tah roh-pah a lah lah-*vahn*-deh-*ree*-ah

NUMBERS

1	**uno** (*ooh*-noh)		17	**diecisiete** (dyess-ee-*syeh*-teh)
2	**dos** (dohss)		18	**dieciocho** (dyess-ee-*oh*-choh)
3	**tres** (trehss)		19	**diecinueve** (dyess-ee-*nweh*-beh)
4	**cuatro** (*kwah*-troh)		20	**veinte** (*bayn*-teh)
5	**cinco** (*seen*-koh)		30	**treinta** (*trayn*-tah)
6	**seis** (sayss)		40	**cuarenta** (kwah-*ren*-tah)
7	**siete** (*syeh*-teh)		50	**cincuenta** (seen-*kwen*-tah)
8	**ocho** (*oh*-choh)		60	**sesenta** (seh-*sehn*-tah)
9	**nueve** (*nweh*-beh)		70	**setenta** (seh-*tehn*-tah)
10	**diez** (dyess)		80	**ochenta** (oh-*chehn*-tah)
11	**once** (*ohn*-seh)		90	**noventa** (noh-*behn*-tah)
12	**doce** (*doh*-seh)		100	**cien** (syehn)
13	**trece** (*treh*-seh)		200	**doscientos** (do-*syehn*-tohs)
14	**catorce** (kah-*tohr*-seh)		500	**quinientos** (kee-*nyehn*-tohs)
15	**quince** (*keen*-seh)		1,000	**mil** (meel)
16	**dieciseis** (dyess-ee-*sayss*)			

TRANSPORTATION TERMS

English	Spanish	Pronunciation
Airport	**Aeropuerto**	ah-eh-roh-*pwehr*-toh
Flight	**Vuelo**	*bweh*-loh
Rental car	**Arrendadora de autos**	ah-rehn-da-doh-rah deh ow-tohs
Bus	**Autobús**	ow-toh-*boos*
Bus or truck	**Camión**	ka-*myohn*
Lane	**Carril**	kah-*reel*
Nonstop (bus)	**Directo**	dee-*rehk*-toh
Baggage (claim area)	**Equipajes**	eh-kee-*pah*-hehss
Intercity	**Foraneo**	foh-rah-*neh*-oh
Luggage storage area	**Guarda equipaje**	gwar-dah eh-kee-*pah*-heh
Arrival gates	**Llegadas**	yeh-*gah*-dahss
Originates at this station	**Local**	loh-*kahl*
Originates elsewhere	**De paso**	deh *pah*-soh
Stops if seats available	**Para si hay lugares**	*pah*-rah see eye loo-*gah*-rehs
First class	**Primera**	pree-*meh*-rah
Second class	**Segunda**	seh-*goon*-dah
Nonstop (flight)	**Sin escala**	seen ess-*kah*-lah
Baggage claim area	**Recibo de equipajes**	reh-see-boh deh eh-kee-*pah*-hehss
Waiting room	**Sala de espera**	*sah*-lah deh ehss-*peh*-rah
Toilets	**Sanitarios**	sah-nee-*tah*-ryohss
Ticket window	**Taquilla**	tah-*kee*-yah

3 Menu Glossary

Achiote   Small red seed of the *annatto* tree.

Achiote preparado   A Yucatecan prepared paste made of ground *achiote*, wheat and corn flour, cumin, cinnamon, salt, onion, garlic, and oregano.

Agua fresca   Fruit-flavored water, usually watermelon, cantaloupe, chia seed with lemon, hibiscus flour, rice, or ground melon-seed mixture.

Antojito   Typical Mexican supper foods, usually made with *masa* or tortillas and having a filling or topping such as sausage, cheese, beans, and onions; includes such things as *tacos, tostadas, sopes,* and *garnachas.*

Atole   A thick, lightly sweet, hot drink made with finely ground corn and usually flavored with vanilla, pecan, strawberry, pineapple, or chocolate.

Botana   An appetizer.

Buñuelos   Round, thin, deep-fried crispy fritters dipped in sugar.

Carnitas   Pork deep-cooked (not fried) in lard, and then simmered and served with corn tortillas for tacos.

Ceviche   Fresh raw seafood marinated in fresh lime juice and garnished with chopped tomatoes, onions, chiles, and sometimes cilantro.

Chayote A vegetable pear or mirliton, a type of spiny squash boiled and served as an accompaniment to meat dishes.

Chiles en nogada Poblano peppers stuffed with a mixture of ground pork and beef, spices, fruits, raisins, and almonds. Can be served either warm—fried in a light batter—or cold, sans the batter. Either way it is then covered in walnut-and-cream sauce.

Chiles rellenos Usually poblano peppers stuffed with cheese or spicy ground meat with raisins, rolled in a batter, and fried.

Churro Tube-shaped, breadlike fritter, dipped in sugar and sometimes filled with *cajeta* (milk-based caramel) or chocolate.

Cochinita pibil Pork wrapped in banana leaves, pit-baked in a *pibil* sauce of *achiote,* sour orange, and spices; common in the Yucatán.

Enchilada A tortilla dipped in sauce, usually filled with chicken or white cheese, and sometimes topped with *mole* (*enchiladas rojas* or *de mole*), or with tomato sauce and sour cream (*enchiladas suizas*—Swiss enchiladas), or covered in a green sauce (*enchiladas verdes),* or topped with onions, sour cream, and guacamole *(enchiladas potosinas).*

Escabeche A lightly pickled sauce used in Yucatecan chicken stew.

Frijoles refritos Pinto beans mashed and cooked with lard.

Garnachas A thickish small circle of fried *masa* with pinched sides, topped with pork or chicken, onions, and avocado, or sometimes chopped potatoes and tomatoes, typical as a *botana* in Veracruz and Yucatán.

Gorditas Thick, fried corn tortillas, slit and stuffed with choice of cheese, beans, beef, chicken, with or without lettuce, tomato, and onion garnish.

Horchata Refreshing drink made of ground rice or melon seeds, ground almonds, cinnamon, and lightly sweetened.

Huevos mexicanos Scrambled eggs with chopped onions, hot green peppers, and tomatoes.

Huitlacoche Sometimes spelled "cuitlacoche." A mushroom-flavored black fungus that appears on corn in the rainy season; considered a delicacy.

Manchamantel Translated, means "tablecloth stainer." A stew of chicken or pork with chiles, tomatoes, pineapple, bananas, and jicama.

Masa Ground corn soaked in lime; the basis for tamales, corn tortillas, and soups.

Mixiote Rabbit, lamb, or chicken cooked in a mild chile sauce (usually chile *ancho* or *pasilla*), and then wrapped like a tamal and steamed. It is generally served with tortillas for tacos, with traditional garnishes of pickled onions, hot sauce, chopped cilantro, and lime wedges.

Pan de muerto Sweet bread made around the Days of the Dead (Nov 1–2), in the form of mummies or dolls, or round with bone designs.

Pan dulce Lightly sweetened bread in many configurations, usually served at breakfast or bought in any bakery.

Papadzules Tortillas stuffed with hard-boiled eggs and seeds (pumpkin or sunflower) in a tomato sauce.

Pibil Pit-baked pork or chicken in a sauce of tomato, onion, mild red pepper, cilantro, and vinegar.

Pipián A sauce made with ground pumpkin seeds, nuts, and mild peppers.

Poc chuc   Slices of pork with onion marinated in a tangy sour orange sauce and charcoal-broiled; a Yucatecan specialty.

Pozole   A soup made with hominy in either chicken or pork broth.

Pulque   A drink made of fermented juice of the maguey plant; best in the state of Hidalgo and around Mexico City.

Quesadilla   Corn or flour tortillas stuffed with melted white cheese and lightly fried.

Queso relleno   "Stuffed cheese," a mild yellow cheese stuffed with minced meat and spices; a Yucatecan specialty.

Rompope   Delicious Mexican eggnog, invented in Puebla, made with eggs, vanilla, sugar, and rum.

Salsa verde   An uncooked sauce using the green tomatillo and puréed with spicy or mild hot peppers, onions, garlic, and cilantro; on tables countrywide.

Sopa de flor de calabaza   A soup made of chopped squash or pumpkin blossoms.

Sopa de lima   A tangy soup made with chicken broth and accented with fresh lime; popular in Yucatán.

Sopa de tortilla   A traditional chicken broth–based soup, seasoned with chiles, tomatoes, onion, and garlic, served with crispy fried strips of corn tortillas.

Sopa tlalpeña (or *caldo tlalpeño*)   A hearty soup made with chunks of chicken, chopped carrots, zucchini, corn, onions, garlic, and cilantro.

Sopa tlaxcalteca   A hearty tomato-based soup filled with cooked nopal cactus, cheese, cream, and avocado, with crispy tortilla strips floating on top.

Sope   Pronounced "*soh*-peh." An *antojito* similar to a *garnacha*, except spread with refried beans and topped with crumbled cheese and onions.

Tacos al pastor   Thin slices of flavored pork roasted on a revolving cylinder dripping with onion slices and juice of fresh pineapple slices. Served in small corn tortillas, topped with chopped onion and cilantro.

Tamal   Incorrectly called a tamale (*tamal* singular, *tamales* plural). A meat or sweet filling rolled with fresh *masa*, wrapped in a corn husk or banana leaf, and steamed.

Tikin xic   Also seen on menus as "tik-n-xic" and "tikik chick." Charbroiled fish brushed with *achiote* sauce.

Torta   A sandwich, usually on *bolillo* bread, typically with sliced avocado, onions, tomatoes, with a choice of meat and often cheese.

Xtabentun   Pronounced "shtah-behn-*toon*." A Yucatecan liquor made of fermented honey and flavored with anise. It comes *seco* (dry) or *crema* (sweet).

Zacahuil   Pork leg tamal, packed in thick *masa*, wrapped in banana leaves, and pit-baked, sometimes pot-made with tomato and *masa*; a specialty of mid- to upper Veracruz.

Index